GREEK LITERATURE
IN TRANSLATION

THE SPIRIT OF THE CLASSICS

GREEK LITERATURE IN TRANSLATION

ROMAN LITERATURE IN TRANSLATION

SELECTED AND EDITED BY
GEORGE HOWE, Ph.D.
University of North Carolina

AND

GUSTAVE ADOLPHUS HARRER, Ph.D.
University of North Carolina

HARPER & BROTHERS PUBLISHERS

The Spirit of the Classics

GREEK LITERATURE
IN TRANSLATION

Selected and Edited by

GEORGE HOWE, Ph.D.
UNIVERSITY OF NORTH CAROLINA

AND

GUSTAVE ADOLPHUS HARRER, Ph.D.
UNIVERSITY OF NORTH CAROLINA

HARPER & BROTHERS PUBLISHERS
NEW YORK AND LONDON
MCMXXIV

GREEK LITERATURE
IN TRANSLATION

I-Z

CONTENTS

PATRIARCHAL SOCIETY: THE EPIC

Tenth to Seventh Centuries B. C.

ARISTOCRATIC SOCIETY: THE LYRIC
Seventh to Fifth Centuries B. C.

CONTENTS

DEMOCRATIC SOCIETY: PROSE AND DRAMA

Fifth and Fourth Centuries B. C.

CONTENTS

COSMOPOLITAN SOCIETY

Fourth and Third Centuries B. C.

UNDER ROMAN SWAY

From Second Century B. C. to Second Century A. D.

CONTENTS

PREFACE

NOT very many years ago the only generally recognized approach to the literatures of ancient Greece and Rome was by way of the classical languages, and the majority of those who sought acquaintance with those great heritages equipped themselves to travel by that highway. But whether through changes that in recent times have been introduced into the curricula of our schools, or through the very general extension of a liberal education to those who might, even in the earlier time, have been completely shut out from the benefits and pleasures of the best in literature, or through a present-day alteration in the point of view as to what constitutes an adequate approach,— whatever the cause, it is now a fact that an ever increasing number of readers is seeking a passage through the gateway of translation. The movement betokens a continuance of the esteem in which the classical literatures have ever been held; it betokens further a widening of the general interest in the great literatures of the past, if more and more who would never, even in the good old days, have thought it lay within their possibilities to know Homer and Sophocles, Virgil and Horace, now demand such knowledge, whether at first hand or second. Regrettable in many respects though the change may be, still the ancient literatures have far too much of universal value to offer to remain longer the property of the restricted few who have trained themselves to read them in the original. Indeed they are necessary to all who would know the best things of the art of letters even of the present, for it is no exaggeration to say that modern literature cannot be fully understood and appreciated without a knowledge of the foundations upon which it is built. Quite apart from the much debated question of the amount of loss suffered by reading in translation, the books of the ancients are the property of all, and it is folly on account of certain losses to throw away the important and delightful remainder of profit.

It was because of such considerations as these that The Spirit of the Classics was undertaken. It is true of course that the great body of the Greek and Roman literatures has been available in English for a long time, and much of it in most excellent translation; it is true also that from time to time have appeared anthologies presenting in brief compass illustrative readings from the two literatures. But the difficulty heretofore has been either that the material has been spread over so many separate volumes that it has not been easy of access, or that the material has been reproduced in such fragmentary form that it did not give an adequate picture of the whole. The excuse for the present book is to be found partly in its effort to strike a happy medium between these two extremes, but mainly in its organization of the material in such a way as to give a somewhat more complete conception of the development and of the sweep of the literary product.

The Spirit of the Classics is designed, then, not merely as an anthology of the masterpieces of the Greek and Roman literatures. Its purpose is to reproduce through translation as fully as possible the life and thought of the ancient peoples as they expressed them in their literatures, in brief enough form to be accessible to all. It seeks to make plain what things they thought about, what they thought about them, and in what forms they gave their thinking expression. Since their experience of life was of course a development in time, the chronological order has been followed in the main. While, as a result of the principle of selection, the emphasis has been placed upon masterpieces of thinking, yet masterpieces of form too are as fully illustrated as can be done in translation, since it is eminently true of the classics that the criteria of clear thinking and of form coincide. Every effort has been made to present complete units; when such a course could not be followed because of the necessary limitations of space, it has been thought better to give a few extended passages carefully chosen rather than a large number of short fragments. With a few exceptions the work of the poets has been reproduced in verse translations.

One volume has been devoted to the Greek literature and one to the Roman. In each the accompanying apparatus has been reduced to a minimum. The table of contents has been so constructed as to provide a sort of syllabus, indicating by headings the course of development, interpreting the main currents of thought, and pointing out the forms used for the several sorts of material. The explanatory notes are of two sorts. At the beginning of each main division have been inserted short essays with the purpose of giving the social and political background against which the literature is to be viewed. In such brief compass it was of course impossible to sketch even in outline the political or literary history of the various periods; but the attempt has been made to supply at least the most important facts and to suggest the relation of the literature at any given moment to the broader currents of life. The second sort of notes is concerned with the identification and significance of individual authors and selections. These seek merely to point out the historical and literary position of each writer and of each passage quoted, in order that the main thought may be followed the more easily, and in order that that lack of an explanation of the relations existing between passages which is characteristic of any book of selections may be somewhat reduced.

The editors are indebted to many colleagues for valuable suggestions as to the selection of passages and the choice of translators. To every selection the translator's name has been appended. Grateful acknowledgment is made to Mr. James Loeb for permission to make wide use of The Loeb Classical Library for both volumes, and for the present volume to the following for permission to reprint copyrighted material: Houghton Mifflin Company, Boston, for translations from Homer by W. C. Bryant; Dodd Mead & Company, New York, for translations from Sappho in Wharton's *Sappho;* Henry Holt & Company, New York, for the translation from Alcman in *A History of Greek Literature* by T. S. Perry; Oxford University Press, London, for translations from Plato, Thucydides, and Aristotle by Benjamin Jowett; Macmillan & Company, London, for the translation of Aristotle's Poetics by S. H. Butcher, translations from Theophrastus' Characters by R. C. Jebb, and translations from Xenophon's Hellenica by H. G. Dakyns; Longmans Green & Company, New York, for the translation of Sophocles' Œdipus Rex by Robert Whitelaw; Parke Austin and Lipscomb, New York, for the translation from Isocrates by J. H. Freese in *The Greek and Latin Classics;* Cambridge University Press, London, for the translation from Archimedes by Thomas L. Heath; Nicholas L. Brown, New York, for translations from Herondas by M. S. Buck; Mr. J. S. Easby-Smith for translations from Alcaeus in his *Songs of Alcaeus.* The translation from Mimnermus by the late Professor Kirby Flower Smith on page 119 is printed now for the first time.

GREEK LITERATURE
IN TRANSLATION

PATRIARCHAL SOCIETY: THE EPIC

TENTH TO SEVENTH CENTURIES B.C.

It is practically impossible to distinguish between the historical and the mythological in the period that preceded the Homeric poems. We have a vast number of tales about the ancient heroes of the race, which no doubt had some foundation in fact, but which in the main were created out of the imagination of the poets of later days. The Trojan legend as set forth in the Homeric poems comes at the end of such an era, and though it shares with the other tales the traits of the myth as contrasted with history, it at least presents a fairly complete picture of Greek life before the historic period.

The Greeks, spread over the mainland, the islands, and the coast of Asia Minor, were split up into many small principalities. Although they knew no national unity, still in times of emergency they recognized a racial community of interest and banded together against a common foe. Over each separate state was a king, who was at once military chieftain, dispenser of justice, and high priest—a shepherd of his people. Associated with him was a council of nobles in the capacity of advisers, but all political power was in the hands of the king. There was further a crude sort of assembly of freemen below the rank of nobles, but it was practically without political significance. The wealth of the state was almost exclusively in the keeping of king and nobles, who also bore the brunt of all state burdens. The fighting was the business of the nobles too, for seldom do we hear of the common man actually taking part in battle.

The social unit was the family. The father of the family bore much the same relation to his household as the king did to the whole community. The matron was held in high esteem and seems to have had a greater degree of independence than in the later days. The home life and a generous hospitality to strangers were sacred obligations. Life was simple. There were few complexities of commerce. Agriculture, manufacture of the necessary articles of use, and war were the chief pursuits. In spite of the class distinctions, king and nobles and commons mingled freely together.

Even in that remote period the Greek gift for beauty as expressed in the arts was at work, crude though the products may have been. Their literature—if it may be called that before it received the permanence of the written word—they practised in hymns to the gods and in the tales of heroes. Minstrels attached to the court or wandering from court to court, receiving everywhere a cordial welcome, preserved and elaborated in song and story the traditions of the race. It is probable that in such ballads the origin of the epic is to be found. We may imagine that the story of a particular hero was at first a single deed of daring or adventure, that then other stories about the same personage were gradually added, that further elaboration branched off from the central figure to others associated with him in the stories, until finally quite a body of material was formed out of a multitude of various tales. It would be then but an easy step to fuse together into a single narrative all the stories that had so grown up about a hero or an event or a place. It is not unlikely that such epics, perhaps in shorter form, existed before Homer, and that the Homeric poems are the final culmination of a long period of growth and experimentation.

The epic was written in continuous long lines of six feet (hexameter) admirably suited to narration. It is simple and straightforward, possessing a dignity peculiarly its own.

1

I. THE EPIC OF MARTIAL ADVENTURE: HOMER'S ILIAD

Greek, indeed European, literature begins with the poems of Homer. Nothing definite is known about the time they were written or about the poet who wrote them. Ionia was the home of epic and its *floruit* probably the tenth and ninth centuries B.C. Seven cities claimed the honor of having given birth to Homer. Legend tells of a blind bard who wandered about from place to place earning his living by his minstrelsy. The poems themselves argue a poet of consummate skill, who must have come at the end rather than at the beginning of a long development.

The *Iliad* narrates only the events of some fifty days in the tenth, the last, year of the Trojan War. It is not concerned with the war as history, but with the action of certain heroes, particularly Achilles, ‿ played a leading part in it. The subject announced in the opening line is "the wrath of Achilles." Knowledge of what preceded its action is assumed—of how Paris, a Trojan prince, had awarded the prize of beauty to Aphrodite and had received as his reward Helen, wife of the Greek king Menelaus; of how the Greek chieftains had conspired together against Troy to avenge this wrong; of the expedition to Asia Minor, and of the prolonged struggle about the walls of the city.

THE WRATH OF ACHILLES [1]

[From Book I]

After the invocation and announcement of theme, the narrative begins with a quarrel over a maiden who had been captured by Achilles and was claimed by him as just spoils of war, but who is taken away from him by King Agamemnon. The hero, angered, withdraws from battle and sulks by the sea.

[1] Used by arrangement with Houghton Mifflin Company, the authorized publishers.

O Goddess! sing the wrath of Peleus'
　　son,
Achilles; sing the deadly wrath that
　　brought
Woes numberless upon the Greeks, and
　　swept
To Hades many a valiant soul, and gave
Their limbs a prey to dogs and birds of
　　air,—
For so had Jove appointed,—from the
　　time
When the two chiefs, Atrides, king of
　　men,
And great Achilles, parted first as foes.
　　Which of the gods put strife between
　　the chiefs,
That they should thus contend? Latona's
　　son
And Jove's. Incensed against the king,
　　he bade
A deadly pestilence appear among
The army, and the men were perishing.
For Atreus' son with insult had received
Chryses the priest, who to the Grecian
　　fleet
Came to redeem his daughter, offering
Uncounted ransom. In his hand he bore
The fillets of Apollo, archer-god,
Upon the golden sceptre, and he sued
To all the Greeks, but chiefly to the sons
Of Atreus, the two leaders of the host:—
"Ye sons of Atreus, and ye other
　　chiefs,
Well-greaved Achaians, may the gods
　　who dwell
Upon Olympus give you to o'erthrow
The city of Priam, and in safety reach
Your homes; but give me my beloved
　　child,
And take her ransom, honoring him who
　　sends
His arrows far, Apollo, son of Jove."
　　Then all the other Greeks, applauding,
　　bade
Revere the priest and take the liberal
　　gifts

He offered, but the counsel did not please
Atrides Agamemnon; he dismissed
The priest with scorn, and added threat-
ening words:—
"Old man, let me not find thee loiter-
ing here,
Beside the roomy ships, or coming back
Hereafter, lest the fillet thou dost bear
And sceptre of thy god protect thee not.
This maiden I release not till old age
Shall overtake her in my Argive home,
Far from her native country, where her
hand
Shall throw the shuttle and shall dress
my couch.
Go, chafe me not, if thou wouldst safely
go."
He spake; the aged man in fear obeyed
The mandate, and in silence walked
apart,
Along the many-sounding ocean-side,
And fervently he prayed the monarch-
god,
Apollo, golden-haired Latona's son:—
"Hear me, thou bearer of the silver
bow,
Who guardest Chrysa, and the holy isle
Of Cilla, and art lord in Tenedos,
O Smintheus! if I ever helped to deck
Thy glorious temple, if I ever burned
Upon thy altar the fat thighs of goats
And bullocks, grant my prayer, and let
thy shafts
Avenge upon the Greeks the tears I
shed."
So spake he supplicating, and to him
Phœbus Apollo hearkened. Down he
came,
Down from the summit of the Olympian
mount,
Wrathful in heart; his shoulders bore the
bow
And hollow quiver; there the arrows rang
Upon the shoulders of the angry god,
As on he moved. He came as comes the
night,
And, seated from the ships aloof, sent
forth
An arrow; terrible was heard the clang

Of that resplendent bow. At first he
smote
The mules and the swift dogs, and then
on man
He turned the deadly arrow. All around
Glared evermore the frequent funeral
piles.
Nine days already had his shafts been
showered
Among the host, and now, upon the
tenth,
Achilles called the people of the camp
To council. Juno, of the snow-white
arms,
Had moved his mind to this, for she
beheld
With sorrow that the men were perishing.
And when the assembly met and now was
full,
Stood swift Achilles in the midst and
said:—
"To me it seems, Atrides, that 't were
well,
Since now our aim is baffled, to return
Homeward, if death o'ertake us not; for
war
And pestilence at once destroy the
Greeks.
But let us first consult some seer or
priest,
Or dream-interpreter,—for even dreams
Are sent by Jove,—and ask him by what
cause
Phœbus Apollo has been angered thus;
If by neglected vows or hecatombs,
And whether savor of fat bulls and
goats
May move the god to stay the pestilence."
He spake, and took again his seat; and
next
Rose Calchas, son of Thestor, and the
chief
Of augurs, one to whom were known
things past
And present and to come. He, through
the art
Of divination, which Apollo gave,
Had guided Iliumward the ships of
Greece.

With words well ordered courteously he
  spake:—
"Achilles, loved of Jove, thou biddest
  me
Explain the wrath of Phœbus, monarch-
  god,
Who sends afar his arrows. Willingly
Will I make known the cause; but cove-
  nant thou,
And swear to stand prepared, by word
  and hand,
To bring me succor. For my mind
  misgives
That he who rules the Argives, and to
  whom
The Achaian race are subject, will be
  wroth.
A sovereign is too strong for humbler
  men,
And though he keep his choler down
  awhile,
It rankles, till he sate it, in his heart.
And now consider: wilt thou hold me
  safe?"
  Achilles, the swift-footed, answered
  thus:—
"Fear nothing, but speak boldly out
  whate'er
Thou knowest, and declare the will of
  Heaven.
For by Apollo, dear to Jove, whom thou,
Calchas, dost pray to, when thou givest
  forth
The sacred oracles to men of Greece,
No man, while yet I live, and see the
  light
Of day, shall lay a violent hand on thee
Among our roomy ships; no man of
  all
The Grecian armies, though thou name
  the name
Of Agamemnon, whose high boast it is
To stand in power and rank above them
  all."
  Encouraged thus, the blameless seer
  went on:—
" 'Tis not neglected vows or hecatombs
That move him, but the insult shown his
  priest,

Whom Agamemnon spurned, when he
  refused
To set his daughter free, and to receive
Her ransom. Therefore sends the archer-
  god
These woes, and still will send them on
  the Greeks,
Nor ever will withdraw his heavy hand
From our destruction, till the dark-eyed
  maid
Freely, and without ransom, be restored
To her beloved father, and with her
A sacred hecatomb to Chrysa sent.
So haply may we pacify the god."
  Thus having said, the augur took his
  seat.
And then the hero-son of Atreus rose,
Wide-ruling Agamemnon, greatly chafed.
His gloomy heart was full of wrath, his
  eyes
Sparkled like fire; he fixed a menacing
  look
Full on the augur Calchas, and began:—
  "Prophet of evil! never hadst thou yet
A cheerful word for me. To mark the
  signs
Of coming mischief is thy great delight.
Good dost thou ne'er foretell nor bring
  to pass.
And now thou pratest in thine auguries,
Before the Greeks, how that the archer-
  god
Afflicts us thus, because I would not take
The costly ransom offered to redeem
The virgin child of Chryses. 'T was my
  choice
To keep her with me, for I prize her
  more
Than Clytemnestra, bride of my young
  years,
And deem her not less nobly graced than
  she,
In form and feature, mind and pleasing
  arts.
Yet will I give her back, if that be best;
For gladly would I see my people saved
From this destruction. Let meet rec-
  ompense,
Meantime, be ready, that I be not left,

Alone of all the Greeks, without my
    prize.
That were not seemly. All of you
    perceive
That now my share of spoil has passed
    from me."
    To him the great Achilles, swift of
    foot,
Replied: "Renowned Atrides, greediest
Of men, where wilt thou that our noble
    Greeks
Find other spoil for thee, since none is
    set
Apart, a common store? The trophies
    brought
From towns which we have sacked have
    all been shared
Among us, and we could not without
    shame
Bid every warrior bring his portion back.
Yield, then, the maiden to the god, and
    we,
The Achaians, freely will appoint for
    thee
Threefold and fourfold recompense,
    should Jove
Give us to sack this well-defended Troy."
    Then the king Agamemnon answered
    thus:—
"Nay, use no craft, all valiant as thou
    art,
Godlike Achilles; thou hast not the power
To circumvent nor to persuade me thus.
Think'st thou that, while thou keepest
    safe thy prize,
I shall sit idly down, deprived of mine?
Thou bid'st me give the maiden back.
    'T is well,
If to my hands the noble Greeks shall
    bring
The worth of what I lose, and in a shape
That pleases me. Else will I come
    myself,
And seize and bear away thy prize, or
    that
Of Ajax or Ulysses, leaving him
From whom I take his share with cause
    for rage.
Another time we will confer on this.

Now come, and forth into the great salt
    sea
Launch a black ship, and muster on the
    deck
Men skilled to row, and put a hecatomb
On board, and let the fair-cheeked maid
    embark,
Chryseis. Send a prince to bear
    command,—
Ajax, Idomeneus, or the divine
Ulysses;—or thyself, Pelides, thou
Most terrible of men, that with due rites
Thou soothe the anger of the archer-
    god."
    Achilles the swift-footed, with stern
    look,
Thus answered: "Ha, thou mailed in
    impudence
And bent on lucre! Who of all the
    Greeks
Can willingly obey thee, on the march,
Or bravely battling with the enemy?
I came not to this war because of wrong
Done to me by the valiant sons of
    Troy.
No feud had I with them; they never
    took
My beeves or horses, nor, in Phthia's
    realm,
Deep-soiled and populous, spoiled my
    harvest fields.
For many a shadowy mount between us
    lies,
And waters of the wide-resounding sea.
Man unabashed! we follow thee that
    thou
Mayst glory in avenging upon Troy
The grudge of Menelaus and thy own,
Thou shameless one! and yet thou hast
    for this
Nor thanks nor care. Thou threatenest
    now to take
From me the prize for which I bore long
    toils
In battle; and the Greeks decreed it
    mine.
I never take an equal share with thee
Of booty when the Grecian host has
    sacked

Some populous Trojan town. My hands
    perform
The harder labors of the field in all
The tumult of the fight; but when the
    spoil
Is shared, the largest share of all is thine,
While I, content with little, seek my
    ships,
Weary with combat. I shall now go
    home
To Phthia; better were it to return
With my beaked ships; but here where
    I am held
In little honor, thou wilt fail, I think,
To gather, in large measure, spoil and
    wealth."

    Him answered Agamemnon, king of
    men:—
"Desert, then, if thou wilt; I ask thee
    not
To stay with me; there will be others
    left
To do me honor yet, and, best of all,
The all-providing Jove is with me still.
Thee I detest the most of all the men
Ordained by him to govern; thy delight
Is in contention, war, and bloody frays.
If thou art brave, some deity, no doubt,
Hath thus endowed thee. Hence, then,
    to thy home,
With all thy ships and men! there
    domineer
Over thy Myrmidons; I heed thee not,
Nor care I for thy fury. Thus, in turn,
I threaten thee; since Phœbus takes away
Chryseis, I will send her in my ship
And with my friends, and, coming to thy
    tent,
Will bear away the fair-cheeked maid,
    thy prize,
Briseis, that thou learn how far I stand
Above thee, and that other chiefs may
    fear
To measure strength with me, and brave
    my power."

    The rage of Peleus' son, as thus he
    spake,
Grew fiercer; in that shaggy breast his
    heart

Took counsel, whether from his thigh to
    draw
The trenchant sword, and, thrusting
    back the rest,
Smite down Atrides, or subdue his wrath
And master his own spirit. While he
    thus
Debated with himself, and half un-
    sheathed
The ponderous blade, Pallas Athene
    came,
Sent from on high by Juno, the white-
    armed,
Who loved both warriors and made both
    her care.
She came behind him, seen by him alone,
And plucked his yellow hair. The hero
    turned
In wonder, and at once he knew the look
Of Pallas, and the awful-gleaming eye,
And thus accosted her with winged
    words:—
"Why com'st thou hither, daughter of
    the god
Who bears the ægis? Art thou here to
    see
The insolence of Agamemnon, son
Of Atreus? Let me tell thee what I
    deem
Will be the event. That man may lose
    his life,
And quickly too, for arrogance like this."
Then thus the goddess, blue-eyed Pallas,
    spake:—
"I came from heaven to pacify thy wrath,
If thou wilt hear my counsel. I am sent
By Juno the white-armed, to whom ye
    both
Are dear, who ever watches o'er you both.
Refrain from violence; let not thy hand
Unsheathe the sword, but utter with thy
    tongue
Reproaches, as occasion may arise,
For I declare what time shall bring to
    pass;
Threefold amends shall yet be offered
    thee,
In gifts of princely cost, for this day's
    wrong.

Now calm thy angry spirit, and obey."
   Achilles, the swift-footed, answered
    thus:—
"O goddess, be the word thou bring'st
   obeyed,
However fierce my anger; for to him
Who hearkens to the gods, the gods give
   ear."
   So speaking, on the silver hilt he
    stayed
His strong right hand, and back into its
   sheath
Thrust his good sword, obeying. She,
   meantime,
Returned to heaven, where ægis-bearing
   Jove
Dwells with the other gods. And now
   again
Pelides, with opprobrious words, bespake
The son of Atreus, venting thus his
   wrath:—
   "Wine-bibber, with the forehead of a
    dog
And a deer's heart! Thou never yet
   hast dared
To arm thyself for battle with the rest,
Nor join the other chiefs prepared to lie
In ambush,—such thy craven fear of
   death.
Better it suits thee, midst the mighty
   host
Of Greeks, to rob some warrior of his
   prize
Who dares withstand thee. King thou
   art, and yet
Devourer of thy people. Thou dost rule
A spiritless race, else this day's insolence,
Atrides, were thy last. And now I say,
And bind my saying with a mighty oath:
By this my sceptre, which can never bear
A leaf or twig, since first it left its stem
Among the mountains,—for the steel has
   pared
Its bows and bark away, to sprout no
   more,—
And now the Achaian judges bear it,—
   they
Who guard the laws received from
   Jupiter,—

Such is my oath,—the time shall come
   when all
The Greeks shall long to see Achilles
   back,
While multitudes are perishing by the
   hand
Of Hector, the man-queller; thou,
   meanwhile,
Though thou lament, shalt have no power
   to help,
And thou shalt rage against thyself to
   think
That thou hast scorned the bravest of
   the Greeks."
   As thus he spake, Pelides to the
   ground
Flung the gold-studded wand, and took
   his seat.
Fiercely Atrides raged; but now uprose
Nestor, the master of persuasive speech,
The clear-toned Pylian orator, whose
   tongue
Dropped words more sweet than honey.
   He had seen
Two generations that grew up and lived
With him on sacred Pylos pass away,
And now he ruled the third. With pru-
   dent words
He thus addressed the assembly of the
   chiefs:—
   "Ye gods! what new misfortunes
    threaten Greece!
How Priam would exult and Priam's
   sons,
And how would all the Trojan race
   rejoice,
Were they to know how furiously ye
   strive,—
Ye who in council and in fight surpass
The other Greeks. Now hearken to my
   words,—
Ye who are younger than myself,—for I
Have lived with braver men than you,
   and yet
They held me not in light esteem. Such
   men
I never saw, nor shall I see again,—
Men like Pirithoüs and like Druas, lord
Of nations, Cæneus and Exadius,

And the great Polypheme, and Theseus, son
Of Ægeus, likest to the immortal gods,
Strongest of all the earth-born race they fought—
The strongest with the strongest of their time—
With Centaurs, the wild dwellers of the hills,
And fearfully destroyed them. With these men
Did I hold converse, coming to their camp
From Pylos in a distant land. They sent
To bid me join the war, and by their side
I fought my best, but no man living now
On the wide earth would dare to fight with them.
Great as they were, they listened to my words
And took my counsel. Heaken also ye,
And let my words persuade you for the best.
Thou, powerful as thou art, take not from him
The maiden; suffer him to keep the prize
Decreed him by the sons of Greece; and thou,
Pelides, strive no longer with the king,
Since never Jove on sceptred prince bestowed
Like eminence to his. Though braver thou,
And goddess-born, yet hath he greater power
And wider sway. Atrides, calm thy wrath—
'T is I who ask—against the chief who stands
The bulwark of the Greeks in this fierce war."
To him the sovereign Agamemnon said:—
"The things which thou hast uttered, aged chief,
Are fitly spoken; but this man would stand

Above all others; he aspires to be
The master, over all to domineer,
And to direct in all things; yet, I think,
There may be one who will not suffer this.
For if by favor of the immortal gods
He was made brave, have they for such a cause
Given him the liberty of insolent speech?"
Hereat the great Achilles, breaking in,
Answered: "Yea, well might I deserve the name
Of coward and of wretch, should I submit
In all things to thy bidding. Such commands
Lay thou on others, not on me; nor think
I shall obey thee longer. This I say,—
And bear it well in mind,—I shall not lift
My hand to keep the maiden whom ye gave
And now take from me; but whatever else
May be on board that swift black ship of mine,
Beware thou carry not away the least
Without my leave. Come, make the trial now,
That these may see thy black blood bathe my spear."
Then, rising from that strife of words, the twain
Dissolved the assembly at the Grecian fleet.
Pelides to his tents and well-manned ships
Went with Patroclus and his warrior friends,
While Agamemnon bade upon the sea
Launch a swift bark with twenty chosen men
To ply the oar, and put a hecatomb
Upon it for the god. He thither led
The fair-cheeked maid Chryseis; the command
He gave to wise Ulysses; forth they went,

Leader and crew, upon their watery
 path.
Meanwhile, he bade the camp be
 purified;
And, casting the pollutions to the waves,
They burned to Phœbus chosen
 hecatombs
Of bulls and goats beside the barren
 main,
From which the savor rose in smoke to
 heaven.
 So was the host employed. But not
 the less
Did Agamemnon persevere to urge
His quarrel with Pelides; and he thus
Addressed Talthybius and Eurybates,
His heralds and his faithful ministers:—
 "Go ye to where Achilles holds his
 tent,
And take the fair Briseis by the hand,
And bring her hither. If he yield her
 not,
I shall come forth to claim her with a
 band
Of warriors, and it shall be worse for
 him."
 He spake, and sent them forth with
 added words
Of menace. With unwilling steps they
 went
Beside the barren deep, until they
 reached
The tents and vessels of the Myrmidons,
And found Achilles seated by his tent
And his black ship; their coming pleased
 him not.
They, moved by fear and reverence of
 the king,
Stopped, and bespake him not, nor
 signified
Their errand; he perceived their thought
 and said:—
 "Hail, heralds, messengers of Jove and
 men!
Draw near; I blame you not, I only
 blame
Atrides, who hath sent you for the maid.
Noble Patroclus! bring the damsel
 forth,

And let them lead her hence. My
 witnesses
Are ye, before the blessed deities,
And mortal men, and this remorseless
 king,
If ever he shall need me to avert
The doom of utter ruin from his host.
Most sure it is, he madly yields himself
To fatal counsels, thoughtless of the past
And of the future, nor forecasting how
The Greeks may fight, unvanquished, by
 their fleet."
 He spake. Meantime Patroclus had
 obeyed
The word of his beloved friend. He
 brought
The fair-cheeked maid Briseis from her
 tent,
And she was led away. The messengers
Returned to where their barks were
 moored, and she
Unwillingly went with them. Then in
 tears
Achilles, from his friends withdrawing,
 sat
Beside the hoary ocean-marge, and gazed
And prayed to his dear mother,
 earnestly:—
 —WILLIAM CULLEN BRYANT.

HELEN AT THE WALL [1]

[From Book III]

The stealing of Helen was the immediate cause of the war. When the Trojans
see her on the wall they are not without
understanding of the motives which had
prompted Paris to the deed, or the Greeks
to cross the sea to compel her restoration.

Meanwhile to white-armed Helen Iris
 came
A messenger. She took a form that
 seemed
Laodice, the sister of Paris, whom

[1] Used by arrangement with Houghton Mifflin
Company, the authorized publishers.

Antenor's son, King Helicaon, wed,—
Fairest of Priam's daughters. She drew
  near
To Helen, in the palace, weaving there
An ample web, a shining double-robe,
Whereon were many conflicts fairly
  wrought,
Endured by the horse-taming sons of
  Troy
And brazen-mailed Achaians for her sake
Upon the field of Mars. Beside her
  stood
Swift-footed Iris, and addressed her
  thus:—
  "Dear lady, come and see the Trojan
    knights
And brazen-mailed Achaians doing things
To wonder at. They who, in this sad
  war,
Eager to slay each other, lately met
In murderous combat on the field, are
  now
Seated in silence, and the war hath
  ceased.
They lean upon their shields, their mas-
  sive spears
Are near them, planted in the ground
  upright.
Paris, and Menelaus, loved of Mars,
With their long lances will contend for
  thee,
And thou wilt be declared the victor's
  spouse."
  She said, and in the heart of Helen
    woke
Dear recollections of her former spouse
And of her home and kindred. Instantly
She left her chamber, robed and veiled
  in white,
And shedding tender tears; yet not alone,
For with her went two maidens,—Æthra,
  child
Of Pitheus, and the large-eyed Clymene.
Straight to the Scæan gates they walked,
  by which
Panthous, Priam, and Thymœtes sat,
Lampus and Clytius, Hicetaon sprung
From Mars, Antenor and Ucalegon,
Two sages,—elders of the people all.

Beside the gates they sat, unapt, through
  age,
For tasks of war, but men of fluent
  speech,
Like the cicadas that within the wood
Sit on the trees and utter delicate sounds.
Such were the nobles of the Trojan
  race
Who sat upon the tower. But when they
  marked
The approach of Helen, to each other
  thus
With winged words, but in low tones,
  they said:—
  "Small blame is theirs, if both the
    Trojan knights
And brazen-mailed Achaians have en-
  dured
So long so many evils for the sake
Of that one woman. She is wholly like
In feature to the deathless goddesses.
So be it: let her, peerless as she is,
Return on board the fleet, nor stay to
  bring
Disaster upon us and all our race."
  So spake the elders. Priam meantime
    called
To Helen: "Come, dear daughter, sit by
  me.
Thou canst behold thy former husband
  hence,
Thy kindred and thy friends. I blame
  thee not;
The blame is with the immortals who
  have sent
These pestilent Greeks against me. Sit
  and name
For me this mighty man, the Grecian
  chief,
Gallant and tall. True, there are taller
  men;
But of such noble form and dignity
I never saw: in truth, a kingly man."
  And Helen, fairest among women, thus
Answered: "Dear second father, whom
  at once
I fear and honor, would that cruel
  death
Had overtaken me before I left,

To wander with thy son, my marriage-
    bed,
And my dear daughter, and the company
Of friends I loved. But that was not
    to be;
And now I pine and weep. Yet will I
    tell
What thou dost ask. The hero whom
    thou seest
Is the wide-ruling Agamemnon, son
Of Atreus, and is both a gracious king
And a most dreaded warrior. He was
    once
Brother-in-law to me, if I may speak—
Lost as I am to shame—of such a tie."
    She said, the aged man admired, and
    then
He spake again: "O son of Atreus, born
Under the happy fate, and fortunate
Among the sons of men! A mighty
    host
Of Grecian youths obey thy rule. I
    went
To Phrygia once,—that land of vines,—
    and there
Saw many Phrygians, heroes on fleet
    steeds,
The troops of Otreus, and of Mygdon,
    shaped
Like one of the immortals. They
    encamped
By the Sangarius. I was an ally;
My troops were ranked with theirs upon
    the day
When came the unsexed Amazons to
    war.
Yet even there I saw not such a host
As this of black-eyed Greeks who muster
    here."
    Then Priam saw Ulysses, and in-
    quired:—
"Dear daughter, tell me also who is
    that,
Less tall than Agamemnon, yet more
    broad
In chest and shoulders. On the teeming
    earth
His armor lies, but he, from place to
    place,

Walks round among the ranks of sol-
    diery,
As when the thick-fleeced father of the
    flocks
Moves through the multitude of his
    white sheep."
    And Jove-descended Helen answered
    thus:—
"That is Ulysses, man of many arts,
Son of Laertes, reared in Ithaca,
That rugged isle, and skilled in every
    form
Of shrewd device and action wisely
    planned."
    Then spake the sage Antenor: "Thou
    hast said
The truth, O Lady. This Ulysses once
Came on an embassy, concerning thee,
To Troy with Menelaus, great in war;
And I received them as my guests, and
    they
Were lodged within my palace, and I
    learned
The temper and the qualities of both.
When both were standing 'mid the men
    of Troy,
I marked that Menelaus's broad chest
Made him the more conspicuous, but
    when both
Were seated, greater was the dignity
Seen in Ulysses. When they both
    addressed
The council, Menelaus briefly spake
In pleasing tones, though with few words,
    —as one
Not given to loose and wandering speech,
    —although
The younger. When the wise Ulysses
    rose,
He stood with eyes cast down, and fixed
    on earth
And neither swayed his sceptre to the
    right
Nor to the left, but held it motionless,
Like one unused to public speech. He
    seemed
An idiot out of humor. But when forth
He sent from his full lungs his mighty
    voice,

And words came like a fall of winter
snow,
No mortal then would dare to strive with
him
For mastery in speech. We less ad-
mired
The aspect of Ulysses than his words."
 Beholding Ajax then, the aged king
Asked yet again: "Who is that other
chief
Of the Achaians, tall, and large of
limb,—
Taller and broader-chested than the
rest?"
Helen, the beautiful and richly-robed,
Answered: "Thou seest the mighty Ajax
there,
The bulwark of the Greeks. On the
other side,
Among his Cretans, stands Idomeneus,
Of godlike aspect, near to whom are
grouped
The leaders of the Cretans. Oftentimes
The warlike Menelaus welcomed him
Within our palace, when he came from
Crete.
I could point out and name the other
chiefs
Of the dark-eyed Achaians. Two alone,
Princes among their people, are not
seen,—
Castor the fearless horseman, and the
skilled
In boxing, Pollux,—twins; one mother
bore
Both them and me. Came they not with
the rest
From pleasant Lacedæmon to the
war?
Or, having crossed the deep in their good
ships,
Shun they to fight among the valiant
ones
Of Greece, because of my reproach and
shame?"
 She spake; but they already lay in
earth
In Lacedæmon, their dear native land.
          —WILLIAM CULLEN BRYANT.

THE PARTING OF HECTOR AND ANDROMACHE [1]

[From Book VI]

Hector among the Trojans is what
Achilles is among the Greeks. Bidding
wife and son farewell, he goes forth to
battle, challenging the bravest and the
mightiest to meet him single-handed. The
Greeks draw lots and Ajax is chosen.

 Great Hector of the beamy helm
replied:—
"Nay, Helen, ask me not to sit; thy
speech
Is courteous, but persuades me not. My
mind
Is troubled for the Trojans, to whose aid
I hasten, for they miss me even now.
But thou exhort this man, and bid him
haste
To overtake me ere I leave the town.
I go to my own mansion first, to meet
My household,—my dear wife and little
child;
Nor know I whether I may come once
more
To them, or whether the great gods
ordain
That I must perish by the hands of
Greeks."
 So spake the plumèd Hector, and
withdrew,
And reached his pleasant palace, but
found not
White-armed Andromache within, for she
Was in the tower, beside her little son
And well-robed nurse, and sorrowed,
shedding tears.
And Hector, seeing that his blameless
wife
Was not within, came forth again, and
stood
Upon the threshold questioning the
maids.
 "I pray you, damsels, tell me whither
went

[1] Used by arrangement with Houghton Mifflin
Company, the authorized publishers.

White-armed Andromache? Has she
  gone forth
To seek my sisters, or those stately
  dames,
My brothers' wives? Or haply has she
  sought
The temple of Minerva, where are met
The other bright-haired matrons of the
  town
To supplicate the dreaded deity?"
  Then said the diligent housewife in
  reply:—
"Since thou wilt have the truth,—thy
  wife is gone
Not to thy sisters, nor those stately
  dames,
Thy brothers' wives; nor went she forth
  to join
The other bright-haired matrons of the
  town,
Where in Minerva's temple they are met
To supplicate the dreaded deity.
But to the lofty tower of Troy she went
When it was told her that the Trojan
  troops
Lost heart, and that the valor of the
  Greeks
Prevailed. She now is hurrying toward
  the walls,
Like one distracted, with her son and
  nurse."
  So spake the matron. Hector left in
  haste
The mansion, and retraced his way
  between
The rows of stately dwellings, traversing
The mighty city. When at length he
  reached
The Scæan gates, that issue on the field,
His spouse, the nobly-dowered Andro-
  mache,
Came forth to meet him,—daughter of
  the prince
Eetion, who, among the woody slopes
Of Placos, in the Hypoplacian town
Of Thebe, ruled Cilicia and her sons,
And gave his child to Hector great in
  arms.
She came attended by a maid, who bore

A tender child—a babe too young to
  speak—
Upon her bosom,—Hector's only son,
Beautiful as a star, whom Hector called
Scamandrius, but all else Astyanax,—
The city's lord,—since Hector stood the
  sole
Defence of Troy. The father on his child
Looked with a silent smile. Andromache
Pressed to his side meanwhile, and, all
  in tears,
Clung to his hand, and, thus beginning,
  said:—
  "Too brave! thy valor yet will cause
  thy death.
Thou hast no pity on thy tender child,
Nor me, unhappy one, who soon must be
Thy widow. All the Greeks will rush on
  thee
To take thy life. A happier lot were
  mine,
If I must lose thee, to go down to earth,
For I shall have no hope when thou art
  gone,—
Nothing but sorrow. Father have I
  none,
And no dear mother. Great Achilles
  slew
My father when he sacked the populous
  town
Of the Cilicians,—Thebe with high gates.
'Twas there he smote Eetion, yet forbore
To make his arms a spoil; he dared not
  that,
But burned the dead with his bright
  armor on,
And raised a mound above him. Moun-
  tain-nymphs,
Daughters of ægis-bearing Jupiter,
Came to the spot and planted it with
  elms.
Seven brothers had I in my father's
  house,
And all went down to Hades in one day.
Achilles the swift-footed slew them all
Among their slow-paced bullocks and
  white sheep.
My mother, princess on the woody slopes
Of Placos, with his spoils he bore away,

And only for large ransom gave her back.
But her Diana, archer-queen struck down
Within her father's palace. Hector, thou
Art father and dear mother now to me,
And brother and my youthful spouse
    besides.
In pity keep within the fortress here,
Nor make thy child an orphan nor thy
    wife
A widow. Post thine army near the
    place
Of the wild fig-tree, where the city-walls
Are low and may be scaled. Thrice in
    the war
The boldest of the foe have tried the
    spot,—
The Ajaxes and the famed Idomeneus,
The two chiefs born of Atreus, and the
    brave
Tydides, whether counselled by some
    seer
Or prompted to the attempt by their
    own minds."
    Then answered Hector, great in war:
    "All this
I bear in mind, dear wife; but I should
    stand
Ashamed before the men and long-robed
    dames
Of Troy, were I to keep aloof and shun
The conflict, coward-like. Not thus my
    heart
Prompts me, for greatly have I learned
    to dare
And strike among the foremost sons of
    Troy,
Upholding my great father's fame and
    mine;
Yet well in my undoubting mind I know
The day shall come in which our sacred
    Troy,
And Priam, and the people over whom
Spear-bearing Priam rules, shall perish
    all.
But not the sorrows of the Trojan race,
Nor those of Hecuba herself, nor those
Of royal Priam, nor the woes that wait
My brothers many and brave,—who all
    at last,

Slain by the pitiless foe, shall lie in
    dust,—
Grieve me so much as thine, when some
    mailed Greek
Shall lead thee weeping hence, and take
    from thee
Thy day of freedom. Thou in Argos
    then
Shalt, at another's bidding, ply the loom,
And from the fountain of Messeis draw
Water, or from the Hyperian spring,
Constrained unwilling by thy cruel lot.
And then shall some one say who sees
    thee weep,
'This was the wife of Hector, most
    renowned
Of the horse-taming Trojans, when they
    fought
Around their city.' So shall some one
    say,
And thou shalt grieve the more, lament-
    ing him
Who haply might have kept afar the day
Of thy captivity. O, let the earth
Be heaped above my head in death before
I hear thy cries as thou art borne
    away!"
    So speaking, mighty Hector stretched
    his arms
To take the boy; the boy shrank crying
    back
To his fair nurse's bosom, scared to see
His father helmeted in glittering brass,
And eyeing with affright the horse-hair
    plume
That grimly nodded from the lofty
    crest.
At this both parents in their fondness
    laughed;
And hastily the mighty Hector took
The helmet from his brow and laid it
    down
Gleaming upon the ground, and, having
    kissed
His darling son and tossed him up in
    play,
Prayed thus to Jove and all the gods of
    heaven:—
    "O Jupiter and all ye deities,

Vouchsafe that this my son may yet
become
Among the Trojans eminent like me,
And nobly rule in Ilium. May they say,
'This man is greater than his father
was!'
When they behold him from the battle-
field
Bring back the bloody spoil of the slain
foe,—
That so his mother may be glad at
heart."
　So speaking, to the arms of his dear
spouse
He gave the boy; she on her fragrant
breast
Received him, weeping as she smiled.
The chief
Beheld, and, moved with tender pity,
smoothed
Her forehead gently with his hand and
said:—
"Sorrow not thus, beloved one, for me.
No living man can send me to the
shades
Before my time; no man of woman born,
Coward or brave, can shun his destiny.
But go thou home, and tend thy labors
there,—
The web, the distaff,—and command thy
maids
To speed the work. The cares of war
pertain
To all men born in Troy, and most to
me."
　Thus speaking, mighty Hector took
again
His helmet, shadowed with the horse-
hair plume,
While homeward his beloved consort
went,
Oft looking back, and shedding many
tears.
Soon was she in the spacious palace-
halls
Of the man-queller Hector. There she
found
A troop of maidens,—with them all she
shared

Her grief; and all in his own house
bewailed
The living Hector, whom they thought
no more
To see returning from the battle-field,
Safe from the rage and weapons of the
Greeks.
　　　　　　—William Cullen Bryant.

The Battle over Patroclus [1]

[From Book XVIII]

　Achilles, moved at last by the defeat of
the Greeks, allows his friend Patroclus,
clad in the armor of Achilles, to go into
battle at the head of the Myrmidons. For
a while Patroclus is successful, but in the
end he is slain. His death is the incident
which brings Achilles back into action.

As thus they fought with all the rage
　of fire,
Antilochus, the nimble-footed, came
With tidings to Achilles. Him he found
Before his lofty galleys, deep in thought
Of what he knew had happened. With a
　sigh
The hero to his mighty spirit said:—
"Ah me! why should the Grecians thus
　be driven
In utter disarray across the plain?
I tremble lest the gods should bring to
　pass
What most I dread. My mother told me
　once
That the most valiant of the Myrmidons,
While yet I live, cut off by Trojan
　hands,
Shall see the sun no more. It must be
　so:
The brave son of Menœtius has been
　slain.
Unhappy! 'Twas my bidding that, when
　once
The enemy with his firebrands was re-
　pulsed,

[1] Used by arrangement with Houghton Mifflin
Company, the authorized publishers.

He should not think to combat gallantly
With Hector, but should hasten to the
fleet."
  As thus he mused, illustrious Nestor's
son
Drew near Achilles, and with eyes that
shed
Warm tears he gave his sorrowful mes-
sage thus:—
"Son of the warlike Peleus, woe is me!
For bitter are the tidings thou must hear
Of what should not have been. Patro-
clus lies
A naked corpse, and over it the hosts
Are fighting; crested Hector hath his
arms."
  He spake, and a black cloud of sor-
row came
Over the chieftain. Grasping in both
hands
The ashes of the hearth, he showered
them o'er
His head, and soiled with them his noble
face.
They clung in dark lumps to his comely
vest.
Prone in the dust of earth, at his full
length,
And tearing his disordered hair, he lay.
Then wailed aloud the maidens whom in
war
He and Patroclus captured. Forth they
came,
And, thronging round him, smote their
breasts and swooned.
Antilochus mourned also, and shed
tears,
Holding Achilles by the hand, for much
His generous nature dreaded that the
chief
Might aim at his own throat the sword he
wore.
  Loud were the hero's cries, and in the
deep
His gracious mother, where she sat be-
side
Her aged father, heard them. She too
raised
A wail of sorrow. All the goddesses,

Daughters of Nereus, dwelling in the
depths
Of ocean, gathered to her side. There
came
Glauce, Thaleia, and Cymodoce,
. . . .
And Orithya, and whoever else,
Children of Nereus, bide within the deep.
The concourse filled the glimmering cave;
they beat
Their bosoms, while the sorrowing Thetis
spake:—
  "Hear, sister Nereids, that ye all may
know
The sharpness of my sorrows. Woe is
me,
Unhappy! Woe is me! in evil hour
The mother of a hero,—me who gave
Birth to so noble and so brave a son,
The first among the warriors, saw him
grow
Like a green sapling, reared him like a
plant
Within a fruitful field, and sent him forth
With his beaked ships to Ilium and the
war
Against the Trojans. Never shall I see
That son returning to his home, the halls
Of Peleus. While he lives and sees the
light
Of day his lot is sorrow, nor can I
Help him in aught, though at his side;
and yet
I go to look on my beloved son,
And learn from him what grief, while he
remains
Aloof from war, o'ertakes him in his
tent."
  She spake, and left the cavern. All
the nymphs
Went with her weeping. Round their
way the waves
Of ocean parted. When they reached
the fields
Of fertile Troas, up the shore they went
In ordered files to where, a numerous
fleet,
Drawn from the water, round Achilles
lay

The swift ships of the Myrmidons. To
him
His goddess mother came, and with a cry
Of grief embraced the head of her dear
son,
And, mourning o'er him, spake these
winged words:—
"Why weepest thou, my son? What
sorrow now
O'ercomes thy spirit? Speak and hide it
not.
All thou didst pray for, with uplifted
hands,
Has been fulfilled by Jove; the sons of
Greece,
Driven to their galleys, and with thy good
help
Withdrawn from them, are routed and
disgraced."
The swift Achilles, sighing deeply,
made
This answer: "O my mother! true it is
Olympian Jove hath done all this for
me;
But how can that delight me, since my
friend
My well-beloved Patroclus, is no more?
He whom, of all my fellows in the war,
I prized the most, and loved as my own
self,
Is lost to me, and Hector, by whose hand
He was cut off, has spoiled him of his
arms,—
His dreaded arms, a wonder to the sight
And glorious, which the gods of heaven
bestowed
On Peleus, sumptuous bridal gifts, when
thou
Wert led by them to share a mortal's
bed.
Yet would that thou hadst evermore re-
mained
Among the immortal dwellers of the
deep,
And Peleus had espoused a mortal maid,
Since now thy heart must ache with in-
finite grief
For thy slain son, whom thou shalt never
more

Welcome returning to his home. No
wish
Have I to live or to concern myself
In men's affairs, save this: that Hector
first,
Pierced by my spear, shall yield his life,
and pay
The debt of vengeance for Patroclus
slain."
And Thetis, weeping, answered: "O
my son!
Soon must thou die; thou sayest true;
that fate
Hangs over thee as soon as Hector dies."
Again the swift Achilles, sighing, spake:
"Then quickly let me die, since fate
denied
That I should aid my friend against the
foes
That slew him. Far from his own land
he fell,
And longed for me to rescue him. And
now,
Since I am never more to see the land
I love, and since I went not to defend
Patroclus, nor the other Greeks, my
friends,
Of whom so many have fallen by the
hand
Of noble Hector, but beside the fleet
Am sitting here, a useless weight on
earth,
Mighty in battle as I am beyond
The other Grecian warriors, though ex-
celled
By other men in council,—would that
Strife
Might perish among gods and men, with
Wrath,
Which makes even wise men cruel, and,
though sweet
At first as dropping honey, growing, fills
The heart with its foul smoke. Such was
my rage,
Aroused by Agamemnon, king of men.
Yet now, though great my wrong, let
things like these
Rest with the past, and, as the time
requires,

Let us subdue the spirit in our breasts.
I go in quest of Hector, by whose hand
My friend was slain. My death will I
    accept
Whene'er to Jove and to the other gods
It shall seem good to send it. Hercules,
Though mighty and beloved of Jupiter,
The son of Saturn, could not shun his
    death,
For fate and Juno's cruel wrath prevailed
Against him. I shall lie in death like
    him,
If a like fate be measured out for me.
Yet now shall I have glory; I shall do
What many a Trojan and Dardanian
    dame,
Deep-bosomed, wiping with both hands
    the tears
From their fair cheeks, shall bitterly
    lament;
And well shall they perceive that, till
    this hour,
I paused from war. Thou lov'st me;
    but seek not
To keep me from the field, for that were
    vain."
    The silver-footed Thetis thus rejoined:
"Truly, my son, thy purpose is not ill,
To rescue thy endangered friends from
    death.
But with the Trojans are thy beautiful
    arms,
Brazen and dazzling bright; their crested
    chief,
Hector, exults to wear them: no long
    space,
I think, will he exult; his death is near.
Yet go not to the battle-field until
Thine eyes shall look upon me yet again.
I come to-morrow with the sun, and bring
Bright arms, the work of Vulcan's royal
    hand."
    So having said, and turning from her
    son,
She thus bespake her sisters of the sea:
"Return to the broad bosom of the deep,
To its gray Ancient and my father's
    halls,
And tell him all. I hasten to ascend

The summits of Olympus, there to ask
Of Vulcan, the renowned artificer,
Armor of glorious beauty for my son."
    She spake: at once they plunged into
    the deep,
While Thetis, silver-footed goddess,
    sought
Olympus, whence it was her hope to bring
New armor for her son. As thus her feet
Bore her toward heaven, the Achaians,
    fleeing fast,
With infinite clamor, driven before the
    arm
Of the man-queller Hector, reached the
    ships
And Hellespont. Nor could the well-
    armed Greeks
Bear off Patroclus from the shower of
    darts;
For rushing on them came both foot and
    horse,
And Hector, son of Priam, like a flame
In fury. Thrice illustrious Hector seized
The body by the heels to drag it off,
And called his Trojans with a mighty
    shout.
Thrice did the chieftain Ajax, terrible
In resolute valor, drive him from the
    dead.
Yet kept he to his purpose confident
In his own might, now charging through
    the crowd,
Now standing firm and shouting to his
    men,
And never losing ground. As when, at
    night,
Herdsmen that watch their cattle strive
    in vain
To drive a lion, fierce and famine-pinched,
From some slain beast, so the two Ajaxes,
With all their valor, vainly strove to keep
Hector, the son of Priam, from the corpse.
And now would he have dragged it thence,
    and won
Infinite glory, had not Iris come—
The goddess whose swift feet are like the
    wind—
To Peleus' son, a messenger from heaven,
In haste, unknown to Jupiter and all

The other gods,—for Juno sent her
  down,—
To bid the hero arm. She came and
  stood
Beside him, speaking thus with winged
  words:—
  "Pelides, rise, most terrible of men,
In rescue of Patroclus, over whom
They struggle fiercely at the fleet; for
  there
They slay each other,—these who fight to
  keep
The dead, and those, the men of Troy,
  who charge
To drag him off to Ilium's airy heights;
And chief, illustrious Hector longs to
  seize
The corpse, and from the delicate neck to
  hew
The head, and fix it on a stake. Arise,
Loiter no longer;—rise, ashamed to leave
Patroclus to be torn by Trojan dogs.
For thine will be the infamy, if yet
The corpse be brought dishonored to thy
  tent."
  The swift Achilles listened and in-
  quired:
"Which of the gods, O Iris, speaks by
  thee?"
And Iris, whose swift feet are like the
  wind,
Answered: "The glorious spouse of Jupi-
  ter,
Juno, hath sent me. Even Saturn's son,
On his high throne, knows not that I am
  sent,
Nor any of the other gods who dwell
Upon Olympus overspread with snow."
  "But how," the swift Achilles asked
  again,
"Shall I go forth to war? They have my
  arms,
And my beloved mother strictly bade
That I should put no armor on until
I saw her face again. She promised me
A suit of glorious mail from Vulcan's
  hand.
Nor know I any warrior here whose arms
Might serve me, save, perhaps, the shield

Of Telamonian Ajax, who, I hope,
Is in the van, and dealing death among
The foe, in vengeance for Patroclus slain."
  Then the swift-footed Iris spake again:
"They have thy glorious armor; that we
  know.
But go thou to the trench, and show thy-
  self
To them of Troy, that, haply smit with
  fear,
They may desist from battle, and the host
Of Grecian warriors, overtoiled, may
  breathe
In a brief respite from the stress of war."
  So the fleet Iris spake, and passed
  away,
And then arose Achilles, dear to Jove,
While o'er his ample shoulders Pallas held
Her fringed ægis. The great goddess
  caused
A golden cloud to gather round his head
And kindled in the cloud a dazzling flame.
And as when smoke, ascending to the
  sky,
Hangs o'er some city in a distant isle,
Which enemies beleaguer, swarming forth
From their own city, and in hateful strife
Contend all day, but when the sun goes
  down
Forthwith blaze many bale-fires, sending
  up
A brightness which the neighboring
  realms may see,
That haply they may send their ships
  and drive
The war away,—so from the hero's head
That flame streamed upward to the sky.
  He came
Without the wall and stood beside the
  trench,
Nor mingled with the Greeks, for he
  revered
His mother's words. He stood and called
  aloud,
And Pallas, from the host, returned his
  shout,—
A shout that carried infinite dismay
Into the Trojan squadrons. As the sound
Of trumpet rises clear when deadly foes

Lay siege to a walled city, such was
    heard
The clear shout uttered by Æacides.
The hearts of all who heard that brazen
    voice
Were troubled, and their steeds with flow-
    ing manes
Turned backward with the chariots,—
    such the dread
Of coming slaughter. When the chariot-
    eers
Beheld the terrible flame that played
    unquenched
Upon the brow of the magnanimous son
Of Peleus, lighted by the blue-eyed maid
Minerva, they were struck with panic
    fear.
Thrice o'er the trench Achilles shouted;
    thrice
The men of Troy and their renowned
    allies
Fell into wild disorder. Then there
    died,
Entangled midst their chariots, and trans-
    fixed
By their own spears, twelve of their
    bravest chiefs.
The Greeks bore off Patroclus from the
    field
With eager haste, and placed him on a
    bier,
And there the friends that loved him
    gathered round
Lamenting. With them swift Achilles
    came,
The hot tears on his cheek, as he beheld
His faithful comrade lying on his bier
Mangled with many wounds, whom he
    had sent
With steeds and car to battle, never more
To welcome him alive on his return.
    Now Juno, large-eyed and august, bade
    set
The never-wearied sun; unwillingly
He sank into the ocean streams. Then
    paused
The noble Greeks from that ferocious
    strife,
Deadly in equal measure to both hosts.

The Trojans also paused, and from their
    cars
Unharnessed the fleet steeds, and ere they
    took
Their evening meal assembled to consult.
        —WILLIAM CULLEN BRYANT.

THE SHIELD OF ACHILLES [1]

[From Book XVIII]

The shield is described in the making.
From no other single passage can so much
be learned of the civilization of Homeric
times.

So speaking he withdrew, and went
    where lay
The bellows, turned them toward the fire,
    and bade
The work begin. From twenty bellows
    came
Their breath into the furnaces,—a blast
Varied in strength as need might be; for
    now
They blew with violence for a hasty task,
And then with gentler breath, as Vulcan
    pleased
And as the work required. Upon the
    fire
He laid impenetrable brass, and tin,
And precious gold and silver; on its
    block
Placed the huge anvil, took the ponder-
    ous sledge,
And held the pincers in the other hand.
    And first he forged the huge and mas-
    sive shield,
Divinely wrought in every part,—its edge
Clasped with a triple border, white and
    bright.
A silver belt hung from it, and its folds
Were five; a crowd of figures on its disk
Were fashioned by the artist's passing
    skill.
For here he placed the earth and heaven,
    and here

[1] Used by arrangement with Houghton Mifflin
Company, the authorized publishers.

The great deep and the never-resting sun
And the full moon, and here he set the
    stars
That shine in the round heaven,—the
    Pleiades,
The Hyades, Orion in his strength,
And the Bear near him, called by some
    the Wain,
That, wheeling, keeps Orion still in sight,
Yet bathes not in the waters of the sea.
  There placed he two fair cities full of
    men.
In one were marriages and feasts; they
    led
The brides with flaming torches from
    their bowers,
Along the street, with many a nuptial
    song.
There the young dancers whirled, and
    flutes and lyres
Gave forth their sounds, and women at
    the doors
Stood and admired. Meanwhile a multi-
    tude
Was in the forum, where a strife went
    on,—
Two men contending for a fine, the price
Of one who had been slain. Before the
    crowd
One claimed that he had paid the fine,
    and one
Denied that aught had been received, and
    both
Called for the sentence which should end
    the strife.
The people clamored for both sides, for
    both
Had eager friends; the heralds held the
    crowd
In check; the elders, upon polished
    stones,
Sat in a sacred circle. Each one took,
In turn, a herald's sceptre in his hand
And, rising, gave his sentence. In the
    midst
Two talents lay in gold, to be the meed
Of him whose juster judgement should
    prevail.
  Around the other city sat two hosts

In shining armor, bent to lay it waste,
Unless the dwellers would divide their
    wealth,—
All that their pleasant homes contained,
    —and yield
The assailants half. As yet the citizens
Had not complied, but secretly had
    planned
An ambush. Their beloved wives mean-
    while,
And their young children, stood and
    watched the walls,
With aged men among them, while the
    youths
Marched on, with Mars and Pallas at
    their head,
Both wrought in gold, with golden gar-
    ments on,
Stately and large in form, and over all
Conspicuous, in bright armor, as be-
    came
The gods; the rest were of an humbler
    size.
And when they reached the spot where
    they should lie
In ambush, by a river's side, a place
For watering herds, they sat them down,
    all armed
In shining brass. Apart from all the
    rest
They placed two sentries, on the watch
    to spy
The approach of sheep and horned kine.
    Soon came
The herds in sight; two shepherds walked
    with them,
Who, all unweeting of the evil nigh,
Solaced their task with music from their
    reeds.
The warriors saw and rushed on them,
    and took
And drave away large prey of beeves,
    and flocks
Of fair white sheep, whose keepers they
    had slain.
When the besiegers in their council
    heard
The sound of tumult at the watering
    place,

They sprang upon their nimble-footed
   steeds,
And overtook the pillagers. Both bands
Arrayed their ranks and fought beside
   the stream,
And smote each other. There did Dis-
   cord rage,
And Tumult, and the great Destroyer,
   Fate.
One wounded warrior she had seized
   alive,
And one unwounded yet, and through the
   field
Dragged by the foot another, dead. Her
   robe
Was reddened o'er the shoulders with the
   blood
From human veins. Like living men
   they ranged
The battle field, and dragged by turns
   the slain.
   There too he sculptured a broad fallow
   field
Of soft rich mould, thrice ploughed, and
   over which
Walked many a ploughman, guiding to
   and fro
His steers, and when on their return they
   reached
The border of the field the master
   came
To meet them, placing in the hands of
   each
A goblet of rich wine. Then turned they
   back
Along the furrows, diligent to reach
Their distant end. All dark behind the
   plough
The ridges lay, a marvel to the sight,
Like real furrows, though engraved in
   gold.
   There, too, the artist placed a field
   which lay
Deep in ripe wheat. With sickles in their
   hands
The laborers reaped it. Here the hand-
   fuls fell
Upon the ground; there binders tied
   them fast

With bands, and made them sheaves.
   Three binders went
Close to the reapers, and behind them
   boys,
Bringing the gathered handfuls in their
   arms,
Ministered to the binders. Staff in
   hand,
The master stood among them by the
   side
Of the ranged sheaves and silently re-
   joiced.
Meanwhile the servants underneath an
   oak
Prepared a feast apart; they sacrificed
A fatling ox and dressed it, while the
   maids
Were kneading for the reapers the white
   meal.
   A vineyard also on the shield he
   graved,
Beautiful, all of gold, and heavily
Laden with grapes. Black were the clus-
   ters all;
The vines were stayed on rows of silver
   stakes.
He drew a blue trench round it, and a
   hedge
Of tin. One only path there was by
   which
The vintagers could go to gather grapes.
Young maids and striplings of a tender
   age
Bore the sweet fruit in baskets. Midst
   them all,
A youth from his shrill harp drew
   pleasant sounds,
And sang with soft voice to the murmur-
   ing strings.
They danced around him, beating with
   quick feet
The ground, and sang and shouted joyously.
   And there the artist wrought a herd of
   beeves,
High-horned, and sculptured all in gold
   and tin.
They issued lowing from their stalls to
   seek

Their pasture, by a murmuring stream,
   that ran
Rapidly through its reeds. Four herds-
   men, graved
In gold, were with the beeves, and nine
   fleet dogs
Followed. Two lions, seizing on a bull
Among the foremost cattle, dragged him
   off
Fearfully bellowing; hounds and herds-
   men rushed
To rescue him. The lions tore their prey,
And lapped the entrails and the crimson
   blood.
Vainly the shepherds pressed around and
   urged
Their dogs, that shrank from fastening
   with their teeth
Upon the lions, but stood near and bayed.
   There also did the illustrious Vulcan
      grave
A fair, broad pasture, in a pleasant glade,
Full of white sheep, and stalls, and cot-
   tages,
And many a shepherd's fold with shelter-
   ing roof.
   And there illustrious Vulcan also
      wrought
A dance,—a maze like that which
   Dædalus
In the broad realms of Gnossus once
   contrived
For fair-haired Ariadne. Blooming
   youths
And lovely virgins, tripping to light airs,
Held fast each other's wrists. The
   maidens wore
Fine linen robes; the youths had tunics
   on
Lustrous as oil, and woven daintily.
The maids wore wreaths of flowers; the
   young men swords
Of gold in silver belts. They bounded
   now
In a swift circle,—as a potter whirls
With both his hands a wheel to try its
   speed,
Sitting before it,—then again they crossed
Each other, darting to their former place.

A multitude around that joyous dance
Gathered, and were amused, while from
   the crowd
Two tumblers raised their song, and flung
   themselves
About among the band that trod the
   dance.
   Last on the border of that glorious
      shield
He graved in all its strength the ocean-
   stream.
   And when that huge and massive shield
      was done,
He forged a corselet brighter than the
   blaze
Of fire; he forged a solid helm to fit
The hero's temples, shapely and enchased
With rare designs, and with a crest of
   gold.
And last he forged him greaves of ductile
   tin.
   When the great artist Vulcan saw his
      task
Complete, he lifted all that armor up
And laid it at the feet of her who bore
Achilles. Like a falcon in her flight
Down plunging from Olympus capped
   with snow
She bore the shining armor Vulcan gave.
                    —WILLIAM CULLEN BRYANT.

THE SLAYING OF HECTOR [1]

[From Book XX]

Achilles, clad in the divine armor, succeeds in driving back the Trojans. Gods
as well as men become involved, taking
sides against each other. The battle
finally resolves itself into a duel between
the two leaders, and the death of Hector
foreshadows the downfall of Troy.

Thus were they driven within the city
   walls
Like frightened fawns, and there dispersing cooled

[1] Used by arrangement with Houghton Mifflin
Company, the authorized publishers.

Their sweaty limbs, and quenched their
    eager thirst,
And rested on the battlements. The
    Greeks,
Bearing their shields upon their shoul-
    ders, came
Close to the ramparts. Hector's adverse
    fate
Detained him still without the walls of
    Troy,
And near the Scæan gates. Meantime
    the god
Apollo to the son of Peleus said:—
    "O son of Peleus! why pursue me thus
With thy swift feet,—a mortal man in
    chase
Of an immortal? That I am a god
Thou seest not yet, but turnest all thy
    rage
On me, and, having put the host of Troy
To rout, dost think of them no more.
    They find
A refuge in their town, while far astray
Thou wanderest hither. Thou hast not
    the power
To slay me; I am not of mortal birth."
    The swift Achilles angrily replied:
"O archer-god, thou most unjust of all
The immortals! thou hast wronged me,
    luring me
Aside; since many a warrior I had forced
To bite the dust before they reached the
    gates
Of Ilium but for thee, who from my grasp
Hast snatched the glory and hast rescued
    them.
Thou didst not fear my vengeance; yet
    if power
Were given me, I would punish thee for
    this."
    He spake, and with heroic purpose
    turned
Toward Ilium. As a steed that wins the
    race
Flies at his utmost speed across the
    plain,
And whirls the chariot, with such speed
The son of Peleus moved his rapid feet.
    The aged monarch Priam was the first

To see him as he scoured the plain, and
    shone
Like to the star which in the autumn time
Rises and glows among the lights of
    heaven
With eminent lustre at the dead of
    night,—
Orion's Hound they call it, — bright
    indeed,
And yet of baleful omen, for it brings
Distressing heat to miserable men.
So shone the brass upon the warrior's
    breast
As on he flew. The aged Priam groaned,
And smote his head with lifted hands,
    and called
Aloud, imploring his beloved son,
Who eagerly before the city gate
Waited his foe Achilles. Priam thus,
With outstretched hands, besought him
    piteously:—
    "O wait not, Hector, my beloved son,
To combat with Pelides, thus alone
And far from succor, lest thou meet thy
    death,
Slain by his hand, for he is mightier
    far
Than thou art. Would that he, the cruel
    one,
Were but as much the favorite of the gods
As he is mine! then should the birds of
    prey
And the dogs devour his carcass, and the
    grief
That weighs upon my spirit would depart.
I have been robbed by him of many
    sons,—
Brave youths, whom he has slain or
    sold as slaves
In distant isles; and now I see no more
Among our host on whom the gates are
    closed
My Polydorus and Lycaon, whom
The peerless dame Laothoe bore to me.
If yet they are within the Grecian camp,
I will redeem their lives with brass and
    gold;
For I have store, which Altes, the re-
    nowned

And aged, gave his daughter. If they
  live
No longer, but have passed to the abode
Of Hades, bitter will our sorrow be,—
Mine and their mother's,—but the popu-
  lar grief
Will sooner be consoled if thou fall not,
Slain by Achilles. Come within the walls,
My son, that thou mayst still be the de-
  fence
Of Ilium's sons and daughters, nor in-
  crease
The glory of Pelides with the loss
Of thine own life. Have pity upon me,
Who only live to suffer,—whom the son
Of Saturn, on the threshold of my age,
Hath destined to endure a thousand
  griefs,
And then to be destroyed,—to see my
  sons
Slain by the sword, my daughters dragged
  away
Into captivity, their chambers made
A spoil, our infants dashed against the
  ground
By cruel hands, the consorts of my sons
Borne off by the ferocious Greeks; and
  last,
Perchance the very dogs which I have
  fed
Here in my palaces and at my board,
The guardians of my doors, when, by
  the spear
Or sword, some enemy shall take my
  life,
And at my threshold leave me stretched
  a corpse,
Will rend me, and, with savage greed-
  iness,
Will lap my blood, and in the porch lie
  down.
When one in prime of youth lies slain in
  war,
Gashed with the spear, his wounds be-
  come him well,
And honor him in all men's eyes; but
  when
An aged man is slain, and his white
  head

And his white beard and limbs are foully
  torn
By ravening dogs, there is no sadder
  sight."
  So the old monarch spake, and with
  his hands
Tore his gray hair, but moved not Hector
  thus.
Then came, with lamentations and in
  tears,
The warrior's mother forward. One hand
  held
Her bosom bare; she pressed the other
  hand
Beneath it, sobbed, and spake these
  winged words:—
"Revere this bosom, Hector, and on me
Have pity. If when thou wert but a babe
I ever on this bosom stilled thy cries,
Think of it now, beloved child; avoid
That dreadful chief; withdraw within the
  walls,
Nor madly think to encounter him alone,
Son of my love and of my womb! If he
Should slay thee, I shall not lament thy
  death
Above thy bier,—I, nor thy noble wife,—
But far from us the greedy dogs will
  throng
To mangle thee beside the Grecian fleet."
  Thus, weeping bitterly, the aged pair
Entreated their dear son, yet moved him
  not.
He stood and waited for his mighty foe
Achilles, as a serpent at his den,
Fed on the poisons of the wild, awaits
The traveller, and, fierce with hate of
  man,
And glaring fearfully, lies coiled within.
So waited Hector with a resolute heart,
And kept his ground, and, leaning his
  bright shield
Against a tower that jutted from the
  walls,
Conferred with his great soul im-
  patiently:—
"Ah me! if I should pass within the
  walls,
Then will Polydamus be first to cast

Reproach upon me; for he counselled me
To lead the Trojans back into the town
That fatal night which saw Achilles rise
To join the war again. I yielded not
To his advice; far better if I had.
Now, since my fatal stubbornness has
brought
This ruin on my people, I most dread
The censure of the men and long-robed
dames
Of Ilium. Men less brave than I will
say,
'Foolhardy Hector in his pride has
thrown
His people's lives away.' So will they
speak,
And better were it for me to return
Achilles slain, or, slain myself by him,
To perish for my country gloriously.
But should I lay aside this bossy shield
And this stout helm, and lean against the
wall
This spear, and go to meet the gallant son
Of Peleus, with a promise to restore
Helen and all the treasure brought with
her
To Troy by Paris, in his roomy ships,—
All that the war was waged for,—that the
sons
Of Atreus may convey it hence, besides
Wealth drawn from all the hoards within
the town,
And to be shared among the Greeks; for
I
Would bind the Trojans by a solemn oath
To keep back nothing, but divide the
whole—
Whate'er of riches this fair town con-
tains—
Into two parts—But why should I waste
thought
On plans like these? I must not act the
part
Of suppliant to a man who may not show
Regard or mercy, but may hew me
down
Defenceless, with my armor laid aside
As if I were a woman. Not with him
May I hold parley from a tree or rock,

As youths and maidens with each other
hold
Light converse. Better 't were to rush at
once
To combat, and the sooner learn to whom
Olympian Jove decrees the victory."
Such were his thoughts. Achilles now
drew near.
Like crested Mars, the warrior-god, he
came.
On his right shoulder quivered fearfully
The Pelian ash, and from his burnished
mail
There streamed a light as of a blazing
fire,
Or of the rising sun. When Hector saw,
He trembled, nor could venture to remain,
But left the gates and fled away in fear.
Pelides, trusting to his rapid feet,
Pursued him. As, among the mountain
wilds,
A falcon, fleetest of the birds of air,
Darts toward a timid dove that wheels
away
To shun him by a sidelong flight, while
he
Springs after her again and yet again,
And screaming follows, certain of his
prey,—
Thus onward flew Achilles, while as fast
Fled Hector in dismay, with hurrying
feet,
Beside the wall. They passed the Mount
of View,
And the wind-beaten fig-tree, and they
ran
Along the public way by which the wall
Was skirted, till they came where from
the ground
The two fair springs of eddying Xanthus
rise,—
One pouring a warm stream from which
ascends
And spreads a vapor like a smoke from
fire;
The other, even in summer, sending forth
A current cold as hail, or snow, or ice.
And there were broad stone basins, fairly
wrought,

At which, in time of peace, before the Greeks
Had landed on the plain, the Trojan dames
And their fair daughters washed their sumptuous robes.
Past these they swept; one fled, and one pursued,—
A brave man fled, a braver followed close,
And swiftly both. Not for a common prize,
A victim from the herd, a bullock's hide,
Such as reward the fleet of foot, they ran,—
The race was for the knightly Hector's life.
As firm-paced coursers, that are wont to win,
Fly toward the goal, when some magnificent prize,
A tripod or a damsel, is proposed
In honor of some hero's obsequies,
So these flew thrice on rapid feet around
The city of Priam. All the gods of heaven
Looked on, and thus the Almighty Father spake:—
"Alas! I see a hero dear to me
Pursued around the wall. My heart is grieved
For Hector, who has brought so many thighs
Of bullocks to my altar on the side
Of Ida ploughed with glens, or on the heights
Of Ilium. The renowned Achilles now
Is chasing him with rapid feet around
The city of Priam. Now bethink yourselves
And answer. Shall we rescue him from death?
Or shall we doom him, valiant as he is,
To perish by the hand of Peleus' son?"
Minerva, blue-eyed goddess, answered thus:
"O Father, who dost hurl the thunderbolt,
And hide the sky in clouds, what hast thou said?

Wouldst thou reprieve from death a mortal man,
Whose doom is fixed? Then do it; but know this,
That all the other gods will not approve."
Then spake again the cloud-compeller Jove:
"Tritonia, my dear child, be calm. I spake
Of no design. I would be kind to thee.
Do as thou wilt, and be there no delay."
He spake; and Pallas from the Olympian peaks,
Encouraged by his words in what her thought
Had planned already, downward shot to earth.
Still, with quick steps, the fleet Achilles pressed
On Hector's flight. As when a hound has roused
A fawn from its retreat among the hills,
And chases it through glen and forest ground,
And to close thickets, where it skulks in fear
Until he overtakes it, Hector thus
Sought vainly to elude the fleet pursuit
Of Peleus' son. As often as he thought
By springing toward the gates of Troy, to gain
Aid from the weapons of his friends who stood
On the tall towers, so often was the Greek
Before him, forcing him to turn away
From Ilium toward the plain. Achilles thus
Kept nearest to the city. As in dreams
The fleet pursuer cannot overtake,
Nor the pursued escape, so was it now;
One followed but in vain, the other fled
As fruitlessly. But how could Hector thus
Have put aside the imminent doom of death,
Had not Apollo met him once again,
For the last time, and given him strength and speed?
The great Achilles nodded to his host

A sign that no man should presume to strike
At Hector with his weapon, lest perchance
Another, wounding him, should bear away
The glory, and Pelides only wear
The second honors. When the twain had come
For the fourth time beside Scamander's springs,
The All-Father raised the golden balance high,
And, placing in the scales two lots which bring
Death's long dark sleep,—one lot for Peleus' son,
And one for knightly Hector,—by the midst
He poised the balance. Hector's fate sank down
To Hades, and Apollo left the field.
    The blue-eyed goddess Pallas then approached
The son of Peleus with these winged words:—
    "Renowned Achilles, dear to Jupiter!
Now may we, as I hope, at last return
To the Achaian army and the fleet
With glory, Hector slain, the terrible
In war. Escape he cannot, even though
The archer-god Apollo fling himself
With passionate entreaty at the feet
Of Jove the Ægis-bearer. Stay thou here
And breathe a moment, while I go to him
And lure him hither to encounter thee."
    She spake, and he obeyed, and gladly stood
Propped on the ashen stem of his keen spear;
While, passing on, Minerva overtook
The noble Hector. In the outward form,
And with the strong voice of Deiphobus,
She stood by him and spake these winged words:—
    "Hard pressed I find thee, brother, by the swift
Achilles, who, with feet that never rest,
Pursues thee round the walls of Priam's town.

But let us make a stand and beat him back."
    And then the crested Hector spake in turn:
"Deiphobus, thou ever hast been dear
To me beyond my other brethren, sons
Of Hecuba and Priam. Now still more
I honor thee, since thou hast seen my plight,
And for my sake hast ventured forth without
The gates, while all the rest remain within."
    And then the blue-eyed Pallas spake again:
"Brother! 't is true, my father, and the queen,
My mother, and my comrades, clasped my knees
In turn, and earnestly entreated me
That I would not go forth, such fear had fallen
On all of them; but I was grieved for thee.
Now let us combat valiantly, nor spare
The weapons that we bear, and we shall learn
Whether Achilles, having slain us both,
Will carry to the fleet our bloody spoil,
Or die himself, the victim of thy spear."
    The treacherous goddess spake, and led the way;
And when the advancing chiefs stood face to face,
The crested hero, Hector, thus began:—
    "No longer I avoid thee as of late,
O son of Peleus! Thrice around the walls
Of Priam's mighty city have I fled,
Nor dared to wait thy coming. Now my heart
Bids me encounter thee; my time is come
To slay or to be slain. Now let us call
The gods to witness, who attest and guard
The covenants of men. Should Jove bestow
On me the victory, and I take thy life,
Thou shalt meet no dishonor at my hands;

But, stripping off thy armor, I will send
The Greeks thy body. Do the like by
  me."
   The swift Achilles answered with a
    frown:
"Accursed Hector, never talk to me
Of covenants. Men and lions plight no
  faith,
Nor wolves agree with lambs, but each
  must plan
Evil against the other. So between
Thyself and me no compact can exist,
Or understood intent. First, one of us
Must fall and yield his life-blood to the
  god
Of battles. Summon all thy valor now.
A skillful spearman thou hast need to be,
And a bold warrior. There is no escape,
For now doth Pallas doom thee to be
  slain
By my good spear. Thou shalt repay to
  me
The evil thou hast done my country-
  men,—
My friends whom thou hast slaughtered
  in thy rage."
   He spake, and, brandishing his mas-
    sive spear,
Hurled it at Hector, who beheld its aim
From where he stood. He stooped, and
  over him
The brazen weapon passed, and plunged
  to earth.
Unseen by royal Hector, Pallas went
And plucked it from the ground, and
  brought it back
And gave it to the hands of Peleus'
  son,
While Hector said to his illustrious foe:—
   "Godlike Achilles, thou hast missed
    thy mark;
Nor hast thou learned my doom from
  Jupiter,
As thou pretendest. Thou art glib of
  tongue,
And cunningly thou orderest thy speech,
In hope that I who hear thee may forget
My might and valor. Think not I shall
  flee,

That thou mayst pierce my back; for
  thou shalt send
Thy spear, if God permit thee, through
  my breast
As I rush on thee. Now avoid in turn
My brazen weapon. Would that it might
  pass
Clean through thee, all its length! The
  tasks of war
For us of Troy were lighter for thy death,
Thou pest and deadly foe of all our race!"
He spake, and brandishing his massive
  spear,
Hurled it, nor missed, but in the centre
  smote
The buckler of Pelides. Far away
It bounded from the brass, and he was
  vexed
To see that the swift weapon from his
  hand
Had flown in vain. He stood perplexed
  and sad;
No second spear had he. He called aloud
On the white-bucklered chief, Deiphobus,
To bring another; but that chief was far,
And Hector saw that it was so, and
  said:—
   "Ah me! the gods have summoned me
    to die.
I thought my warrior friend, Deiphobus,
Was by my side; but he is still in Troy,
And Pallas has deceived me. Now my
  death
Cannot be far,—is near; there is no hope
Of my escape, for so it pleases Jove
And Jove's great archer-son, who have till
  now
Delivered me. My hour at last is come;
Yet not ingloriously or passively
I die, but first will do some valiant deed,
Of which mankind shall hear in after
  time."
   He spake, and drew the keen-edged
    sword that hung,
Massive and finely tempered, at his side,
And sprang—as when an eagle high in
  heaven,
Through the thick cloud, darts downward
  to the plain

To clutch some tender lamb or timid
hare,
So Hector, brandishing that keen-edged
sword,
Sprang forward, while Achilles opposite
Leaped toward him, all on fire with
savage hate,
And holding his bright buckler, nobly
wrought,
Before him.   On his shining helmet
waved
The fourfold crest; there tossed the
golden tufts
With which the hand of Vulcan lavishly
Had decked it.   As in the still hours of
night
Hesper goes forth among the host of
stars,
The fairest light of heaven, so brightly
shone,
Brandished in the right hand of Peleus'
son,
The spear's keen blade, as, confident to
slay
The noble Hector, o'er his glorious form
His quick eye ran, exploring where to
plant
The surest wound.   The glittering mail
of brass
Won from the slain Patroclus guarded
well
Each part, save only where the collar-
bones
Divide the shoulder from the neck, and
there
Appeared the throat, the spot where life
is most
In peril.   Through that part the noble son
Of Peleus drave his spear; it went quite
through
The tender neck, and yet the brazen
blade
Cleft not the windpipe, and the power to
speak
Remained.   The Trojan fell amid the
dust,
And thus Achilles boasted o'er his fall:—
"Hector, when from the slain Patro-
clus thou

Didst strip his armor, little didst thou
think
Of danger.   Thou hadst then no fear of
me,
Who was not near thee to avenge his
death.
Fool! there was left within the roomy
ships
A mightier one than he, who should come
forth,
The avenger of his blood, to take thy life.
Foul dogs and birds of prey shall tear
thy flesh;
The Greeks shall honor him with funeral
rites."
     And then the crested Hector faintly
said:
"I pray thee by thy life, and by thy
knees,
And by thy parents, suffer not the dogs
To tear me at the galleys of the Greeks.
Accept abundant store of brass and
gold,
Which gladly will my father and the
queen,
My mother, give in ransom.   Send to
them
My body, that the warriors and the
dames
Of Troy may light for me the funeral
pile."
     The swift Achilles answered with a
frown:
"Nay, by my knees entreat me not, thou
cur,
Nor by my parents.   I could even wish
My fury prompted me to cut thy flesh
In fragments, and devour it, such the
wrong
That I have had from thee.   There will
be none
To drive away the dogs about thy head,
Not though thy Trojan friends should
bring to me
Tenfold and twenty-fold the offered gifts,
And promise others,—not though Priam,
sprung
From Dardanus, should send thy weight
in gold.

Thy mother shall not lay thee on thy
bier,
To sorrow over thee whom she brought
forth;
But dogs and birds of prey shall mangle
thee."
    And then the crested Hector, dying
said:
"I know thee, and too clearly I foresaw
I should not move thee, for thou hast a
heart
Of iron. Yet reflect that for my sake
The anger of the gods may fall on
thee,
When Paris and Apollo strike thee down,
Strong as thou art, before the Scæan
gates."
    Thus Hector spake, and straightway
o'er him closed
The night of death; the soul forsook his
limbs,
And flew to Hades, grieving for its fate,—
So soon divorced from youth and youthful might.
Then said the great Achilles to the
dead:—
    "Die thou; and I, whenever it shall
please
Jove and the other gods, will meet my
fate."
    He spake, and, plucking forth his
brazen lance,
He laid it by, and from the body stripped
The bloody mail. The thronging Greeks
beheld
With wonder Hector's tall and stately
form,
And no one came who did not add a
wound;
And, looking to each other, thus they
said:—
    "How much more tamely Hector now
endures
Our touch than when he set the fleet on
fire!"
    Such were the words of those who
smote the dead;
But now, when swift Achilles from the
corpse

Had stripped the armor, he stood forth
among
The Achaian host, and spake these
winged words:—
    "Leaders and princes of the Grecian
host!
Since we, my friends, by favor of the
gods,
Have overcome the chief who wrought
more harm
To us than all the rest, let us assault
The town, and learn what they of Troy
intend,—
Whether their troops will leave the
citadel
Since he is slain, or hold it with strong
hand,
Though Hector is no more. But why give
thought
To plans like these while yet Patroclus
lies
A corpse, unwept, unburied at the fleet?
I never will forget him while I live
And while these limbs have motion.
Though below
In Hades they forget the dead, yet I
Will there remember my beloved friend.
Now then, ye youths of Greece, move on
and chant
A pæan, while, returning to the fleet
We bring great glory with us; we have
slain
The noble Hector, whom, throughout
their town,
The Trojans ever worshipped like a god."
    He spake, and, planning in his mind
to treat
The noble Hector shamefully, he bored
The sinews of his feet between the
heel
And ankle; drawing through them leath-
ern thongs
He bound them to the car, but left the
head
To trail in dust. And then he climbed
the car,
Took in the shining mail, and lashed to
speed
The coursers. Not unwillingly they flew.

Around the dead, as he was dragged along,
The dust arose; his dark locks swept the ground.
That head, of late so noble in men's eyes,
Lay deep amid the dust, for Jove that day
Suffered the foes of Hector to insult
His corpse in his own land. His mother saw,
And tore her hair, and flung her lustrous veil
Away, and uttered piercing shrieks. No less
His father, who so loved him, piteously
Bewailed him; and in all the streets of Troy
The people wept aloud, with such lament
As if the towery Ilium were in flames
Even to its loftiest roofs. They scarce could keep
The aged king within, who, wild with grief,
Struggled to rush through the Dardanian gates,
And, rolling in the dust, entreated all
Who stood around him, calling them by name:—
"Refrain, my friends, though kind be your intent.
Let me go forth alone, and at the fleet
Of Greece will I entreat this man of blood
And violence. He may perchance be moved
With reverence for my age and pity me
In my gray hairs; for such a one as I
Is Peleus, his own father, by whose care
This Greek was reared to be a scourge to Troy,
And, more than all, a cause of grief to me,
So many sons of mine in life's fresh prime
Have fallen by his hand. I mourn for them,
But not with such keen anguish as I mourn
For Hector. Sorrow for his death will bring
My soul to Hades. Would that he had died
Here in my arms! this solace had been ours,—
His most unhappy mother and myself
Had stooped to shed these tears upon his bier."
He spake, and wept, and all the citizens
Wept with him. Hecuba among the dames
Took up the lamentation, and began:—
"Why do I live, my son, when thou art dead,
And I so wretched?—thou who wert my boast
Ever, by night and day, where'er I went,
And whom the Trojan men and matrons called
Their bulwark, honoring thee as if thou wert
A god. They glory in thy might no more,
Since Fate and Death have overtaken thee."
Weeping she spake. Meantime Androm-ache
Had heard no tidings of her husband yet.
No messenger had even come to say
That he was still without the gates. She sat
In a recess of those magnificent halls,
And wove a twofold web of brilliant hues,
On which were scattered flowers of rare device;
And she had given her bright-haired maidens charge
To place an ample caldron on the fire,
That Hector, coming from the battle-field,
Might find the warm bath ready. Thoughtless one!
She knew not that the blue-eyed archer-queen,
Far from the bath prepared for him, had slain
Her husband by the hand of Peleus' son.
She heard the shrieks, the wail upon the tower,

Trembled in every limb, and quickly dropped
The shuttle, saying to her bright-haired maids:—
  "Come with me, two of you, that I may learn
What now has happened. 'T is my mother's voice
That I have heard. My heart leaps to my mouth;
My limbs fail under me. Some deadly harm
Hangs over Priam's sons; far be the hour
That I shall hear of it. And yet I fear
Lest that Achilles, having got between
The daring Hector and the city gates,
May drive him to the plain alone, and quell
The desperate valor that was ever his;
For never would he keep the ranks, but ranged
Beyond them, and gave way to no man's might."
  She spake, and from the royal mansion rushed
Distractedly, and with a beating heart.
Her maids went with her. When she reached the tower
And throng of men, and, standing on the wall,
Looked forth, she saw her husband dragged away
Before the city. Toward the Grecian fleet
The swift steeds drew him. Sudden darkness came
Over her eyes, and in a breathless swoon
She sank away and fell. The ornaments
Dropped from her brow,—the wreath, the woven band,
The net, the veil which golden Venus gave
That day when crested Hector wedded her,
Dowered with large gifts, and led her from her home,
Eetion's palace. Round her in a throng
Her sisters of the house of Priam pressed,

And gently raised her in that deathlike swoon.
But when she breathed again, and to its seat
The conscious mind returned, as in their arms
She lay, with sobs and broken speech she said:—
  "Hector,—O wretched me!—we both were born
To sorrow; thou at Troy, in Priam's house,
And I at Thebe in Eetion's halls,
By woody Placos. From a little child
He reared me there,—unhappy he, and I
Unhappy! O that I had ne'er been born!
Thou goest down to Hades and the depths
Of earth, and leavest me in thine abode,
Widowed, and never to be comforted.
Thy son, a speechless babe, to whom we two
Gave being,—hapless parents!—cannot have
Thy loving guardianship now thou art dead,
Nor be a joy to thee. Though he survive
The cruel warfare which the sons of Greece
Are waging, hard and evil yet will be
His lot hereafter; others will remove
His landmarks and will make his fields their own.
The day in which a boy is fatherless
Makes him companionless; with downcast eyes
He wanders, and his cheeks are stained with tears.
Unfed he goes where sit his father's friends,
And plucks one by the coat, and by the robe
Another. One who pities him shall give
A scanty draught, which only wets his lips,
But not his palate; while another boy,
Whose parents both are living, thrusts him hence

With blows and vulgar clamor: 'Get thee
        gone!
Thy father is not with us at the feast.'
Then to his widowed mother shall return
Astyanax in tears, who not long since
Was fed, while sitting in his father's
        lap,
On marrow and the delicate fat of lambs.
And ever when his childish sports had
        tired
The boy, and sleep came stealing over
        him,
He slumbered, softly cushioned, on a
        couch
And in his nurse's arms, his heart at ease
And satiate with delights. But now thy
        son
Astyanax,—whom so the Trojans name
Because thy valor guarded gate and
        tower,—
Thy care withdrawn, shall suffer many
        things.

While far from those who gave you birth,
        beside
The roomy ships of Greece, the restless
        worms
Shall make thy flesh their banquet when
        the dogs
Have gorged themselves. Thy garments
        yet remain
Within the palace, delicately wrought
And graceful, woven by the women's
        hands;
And these, since thou shalt put them on
        no more,
Nor wear them in thy death, I burn with
        fire
Before the Trojan men and dames; and
        all
Shall see how gloriously thou wert
        arrayed."
   Weeping she spake, and with her wept
        her maids.
                    —WILLIAM CULLEN BRYANT

II. THE EPIC OF ROMANTIC ADVENTURE: HOMER'S ODYSSEY

The *Odyssey* presents in epic form one
of a number of legends concerned with the
return of the heroes from captured Troy
to their homes in Greece. It is not centered, as is the *Iliad*, in one great event,
but in one individual, his home, his voy-
ages, mishaps, and adventures. The poem
represents interest in travel and discovery
and adventure over unknown seas and in
unknown lands. From this point of view
the hero, Odysseus, may stand as a glori-
fied representative of those sea-faring
Greeks,—a shrewd, daring, travel-loving
adventurer.

Instead of following the straightforward
march of events, as in the *Iliad*, the reader
is plunged *in medias res*. First a long account is given of conditions at Odysseus'
home during his absence. Then the hero
himself is introduced at a very advanced
stage in his wanderings, and is made to
tell the story of his earlier adventures.
Only after this narrative does he enter on
the final period of his journeyings, and

reach his home. By this novel method of
presentation the action of the poem is confined to some forty-two days.

NAUSICAA [1]

[From Book VI]

Odysseus has been detained on the island
of the goddess Calypso, whence he makes
his escape on a raft and comes to the
country of the Phæacians. Here he is
received by the princess Nausicaa.

Thus overcome with toil and weariness,
The noble sufferer Ulysses slept,
While Pallas hastened to the realm and
        town
Peopled by the Phæacians, who of yore
Abode in spacious Hypereia, near

[1] Used by arrangement with Houghton Mifflin
Company, the authorized publishers.

The insolent race of Cylops, and endured
Wrong from their mightier hands. A
    godlike chief,
Nausithous, led them to a new abode,
And planted them in Scheria, far away
From plotting neighbors. With a wall
    he fenced
Their city, built them dwellings there,
    and reared
Fanes to the gods, and changed the plain
    to fields.
But he had bowed to death, and had
    gone down
To Hades, and Alcinous, whom the gods
Endowed with wisdom, governed in his
    stead.
Now to his palace, planning the return
Of the magnanimous Ulysses, came
The blue-eyed goddess Pallas, entering
The gorgeous chamber where a damsel
    slept,
Nausicaa, daughter of the large-souled
    king
Alcinous, beautiful in form and face
As one of the immortals. Near her lay,
And by the portal, one on either side,
Fair as the graces, two attendant maids.
The shining doors were shut. But Pallas
    came
As comes a breath of air, and stood beside
The damsel's head and spake. In look
    she seemed
The daughter of the famous mariner
Dymas, a maiden whom Nausicaa loved,
The playmate of her girlhood. In her
    shape
The blue-eyed goddess stood, and thus
    she said:—
"Nausicaa, has thy mother then
    brought forth
A careless housewife? Thy magnificent
    robes
Lie still neglected, though thy marriage
    day
Is near, when thou art to array thyself
In seemly garments, and bestow the like
On those who lead thee to the bridal rite;
For thus the praise of men is won, and
    thus

Thy father and thy gracious mother both
Will be rejoiced. Now with the early
    dawn
Let us all hasten to the washing place.
I too would go with thee, and help thee
    there,
That thou mayest sooner end the task,
    for thou
Not long wilt be unwedded. Thou art
    wooed
Already by the noblest of the race
Of the Phæacians, for thy birth, like
    theirs,
Is of the noblest. Make thy suit at morn
To thy illustrious father, that he bid
His mules and car be harnessed to
    convey
Thy girdles, robes, and mantles mar-
    vellous
In beauty. That were seemlier than to
    walk,
Since distant from the town the lavers
    lie."
    Thus having said, the blue-eyed Pallas
        went
Back to Olympus, where the gods have
    made,
So saith tradition, their eternal seat.
The tempest shakes it not, nor is it
    drenched
By showers and there the snow doth
    never fall.
The calm clear ether is without a cloud;
And in the golden light, that lies on all,
Day after day the blessed gods rejoice.
Thither the blue-eyed goddess, having
    given
Her message to the sleeping maid,
    withdrew.
    Soon the bright morning came. Nausi-
        caa rose,
Clad royally, as marvelling at her dream
She hastened through the palace to
    declare
Her purpose to her father and the queen.
She found them both within. Her
    mother sat
Beside the hearth, with her attendant
    maids,

And turned the distaff loaded with a
fleece
Dyed in sea-purple. On the threshold
stood
Her father, going forth to meet the chiefs
Of the Phæacians in a council where
Their noblest asked his presence. Then
the maid,
Approaching her beloved father, spake:—
"I pray, dear father, give command to
make
A chariot ready for me, with high sides
And sturdy wheels, to bear to the river-
brink,
There to be cleansed, the costly robes
that now
Lie soiled. Thee likewise it doth well
beseem
At councils to appear in vestments fresh
And stainless. Thou hast also in these
halls
Five sons, two wedded, three in boy-
hood's bloom,
And ever in the dance they need attire
New from the wash. All this must I
provide."
She ended, for she shrank from saying
aught
Of her own hopeful marriage. He
perceived
Her thought and said: "Mules I deny
thee not,
My daughter, nor aught else. Go then;
my grooms
Shall make a carriage ready with high
sides
And sturdy wheels, and a broad rack
above."
He spake, and gave command. The
grooms obeyed,
And, making ready in the outer court
The strong-wheeled chariot, led the
harnessed mules
Under the yoke and made them fast; and
then
Appeared the maiden, bringing from her
bower
The shining garments. In the polished
car

She piled them, while with many pleas-
ant meats
And flavoring morsels for the day's
repast
Her mother filled a hamper, and poured
wine
Into a goatskin. As her daughter
climbed
The car, she gave into her hands a cruse
Of gold with smooth anointing oil for
her
And her attendant maids. Nausicaa
took
The scourge and snowy reins, and struck
the mules
To urge them onward. Onward with
loud noise
They went, and with a speed that slack-
ened not,
And bore the robes and her,—yet not
alone,
For with her went the maidens of her
train.
Now when they reached the river's
pleasant brink,
Where lavers had been hollowed out to
last
Perpetually, and freely through them
flowed
Pure water that might cleanse the foulest
stains,
They loosed the mules, and drove them
from the wain
To browse the sweet grass by the eddying
stream;
And took the garments out, and flung
them down
In the dark water, and with hasty feet
Trampled them there in frolic rivalry.
And when the task was done, and all the
stains
Were cleansed away, they spread the
garments out
Along the beach and where the stream
had washed
The gravel cleanest. Then they bathed,
and gave
Their limbs the delicate oil, and took
their meal

Upon the water's border,—while the
robes
Beneath the sun's warm rays were grow-
ing dry.
And now, when they were all refreshed
with food,
Mistress and maidens laid their veils
aside
And played at ball. Nausicaa the white-
armed
Began a song. As when the archer-
queen
Diana, going forth among the hills,—
The sides of high Taygetus or slopes
Of Erymanthus,—chases joyously
Boars and fleet stags, and round her in
a throng
Frolic the rural nymphs, Latona's heart
Is glad, for over all the rest are seen
Her daughter's head and brow, and she
at once
Is known among them, though they are
all fair:
Such was this spotless virgin midst her
maids.
  Now when they were about to move
for home
With harnessed mules and with the shin-
ing robes
Carefully folded, then the blue-eyed
maid,
Pallas, bethought herself of this,—to
rouse
Ulysses and to bring him to behold
The bright-eyed maiden, that she might
direct
The stranger's way to the Phæacian
town.
The royal damsel at a handmaid cast
The ball; it missed, and fell into the
stream
Where a deep eddy whirled. All shrieked
aloud.
The great Ulysses started from his sleep
And sat upright, discoursing to himself:—
"Ah me! upon what region am I
thrown?
What men are here,—wild, savage, and
unjust,

Or hospitable, and who hold the gods
In reverence? There are voices in the
air,
Womanly voices, as of nymphs that
haunt
The mountain summits, and the river-
founts,
And the moist grassy meadows. Or
perchance
Am I near men who have the power of
speech?
Nay, let me then go forth at once and
learn."
  Thus having said, the great Ulysses
left
The thicket. From the close-grown wood
he rent,
With his strong hand, a branch well set
with leaves,
And wound it as a covering round his
waist.
Then like a mountain lion he went forth,
That walks abroad, confiding in his
strength,
In rain and wind; his eyes shoot fire; he
falls
On oxen, or on sheep, or forest-deer,
For hunger prompts him even to attack
The flock within its closely guarded fold.
Such seemed Ulysses when about to
meet
Those fair-haired maidens, naked as he
was,
But forced by strong necessity. To them
His look was frightful, for his limbs were
foul
With sea-foam yet. To right and left
they fled
Along the jutting river-banks. Alone
The daughter of Alcinous kept her place,
For Pallas gave her courage and forbade
Her limbs to tremble. So she waited
there.
Ulysses pondered whether to approach
The bright-eyed damsel and embrace her
knees
And supplicate, or, keeping yet aloof,
Pray her with soothing words to show
the way

Townward and give him garments. Mus-
ing thus,
It seemed the best to keep at distance
still,
And use soft words, lest should he grasp
her knees,
The maid might be displeased. With
gentle words
Skillfully ordered thus Ulysses spake:—
"O queen, I am thy suppliant, whether
thou
Be mortal or a goddess. If perchance
Thou art of the immortal race who dwell
In the broad heaven, thou art, I deem,
most like
To Dian, daughter of imperial Jove,
In shape, in stature, and in noble air.
If mortal and a dweller of the earth,
Thrice happy are thy father and his
queen,
Thrice happy are thy brothers; and their
hearts
Must overflow with gladness for thy sake,
Beholding such a scion of their house
Enter the choral dance. But happiest he
Beyond them all, who, bringing princely
gifts,
Shall bear thee to his home a bride; for
sure
I never looked on one of mortal race,
Woman or man, like thee, and as I gaze
I wonder. Like to thee I saw of late,
In Delos, a young palm-tree growing up
Beside Apollo's altar; for I sailed
To Delos, with much people following
me,
On a disastrous voyage. Long I gazed
Upon it wonder-struck, as I am now,—
For never from the earth so fair a tree
Had sprung. So marvel I, and am
amazed
At thee, O lady, and in awe forbear
To clasp thy knees. Yet much have I
endured.
It was but yestereve that I escaped
From the black sea, upon the twentieth
day,
So long the billows and the rushing gales
Farther and farther from Ogygia's isle

Had borne me. Now upon this shore
some god
Casts me, perchance to meet new suffer-
ings here;
For yet the end is not, and many things
The gods must first accomplish. But do
thou,
O queen, have pity on me, since to thee
I come the first of all. I do not know
A single dweller of the land beside.
Show me, I pray, thy city; and bestow
Some poor old robe to wrap me,—if,
indeed,
In coming hither, thou hast brought with
thee
Aught poor and coarse. And may the
gods vouchsafe
To thee whatever blessing thou canst
wish,
Husband and home and wedded harmony.
There is no better, no more blessed state,
Than when the wife and husband in
accord
Order their household lovingly. Then
those
Repine who hate them, those who wish
them well
Rejoice, and they themselves the most
of all."
And then the white-armed maid Nausi-
caa said:
"Since then, O stranger, thou art not
malign
Of purpose nor weak-minded,—yet, in
truth,
Olympian Jupiter bestows the goods
Of fortune on the noble and the base
To each one at his pleasure; and thy
griefs
Are doubtless sent by him, and it is fit
That thou submit in patience,—now that
thou
Hast reached our lands, and art within
our realm,
Thou shalt not lack for garments nor for
aught
Due to a suppliant stranger in his need.
The city I will show thee, and will
name

Its dwellers, — the Phæacians, — they possess
The city; all the region lying round
Is theirs, and I am daughter of the prince
Alcinous, large of soul, to whom are given
The rule of the Phæacians and their power."

So spake the damsel, and commanded thus
Her fair-haired maids: "Stay! whither do ye flee,
My handmaids, when a man appears in sight?
Ye think, perhaps, he is some enemy.
Nay, there is no man living now, nor yet
Will live, to enter, bringing war, the land
Of the Phæacians. Very dear are they
To the great gods. We dwell apart, afar
Within the unmeasured deep, amid its waves
The most remote of men; no other race
Hath commerce with us. This man comes to us
A wanderer and unhappy, and to him
Our cares are due. The stranger and the poor
Are sent by Jove, and slight regards to them
Are grateful. Maidens, give the stranger food
And drink, and take him to the river-side
To bathe where there is shelter from the wind."

So spake the mistress; and they stayed their flight
And bade each other stand, and led the chief
Under a shelter as the royal maid,
Daughter of stout Alcinous, gave command,
And laid a cloak and tunic near the spot
To be his raiment, and a golden cruse
Of limpid oil. Then, as they bid him bathe
In the fresh stream, the noble chieftain said:—

"Withdraw, ye maidens, hence, while I prepare
To cleanse my shoulders from the bitter brine,
And to anoint them; long have these my limbs
Been unrefreshed by oil. I will not bathe
Before you. I should be ashamed to stand
Unclothed in presence of these bright-haired maids."

He spake; they hearkened and with-drew, and told
The damsel what he said. Ulysses then
Washed the salt spray of ocean from his back
And his broad shoulders in the flowing stream,
And wiped away the sea-froth from his brows.
And when the bath was over, and his limbs
Had been anointed, and he had put on
The garments sent him by the spotless maid,
Jove's daughter, Pallas, caused him to appear
Of statelier size and more majestic mien,
And bade the locks that crowned his head flow down,
Curling like blossoms of the hyacinth.
As when some skillful workman trained and taught
By Vulcan and Minerva in his art
Binds the bright silver with a verge of gold,
And graceful in his handiwork, such grace
Did Pallas shed upon the hero's brow
And shoulders, as he passed along the beach,
And, glorious in his beauty and the pride
Of noble bearing, sat aloof. The maid
Admired, and to her bright-haired women spake:—

"Listen to me, my maidens, while I speak.
This man comes not among the godlike sons

Of the Phæacian stock against the will
Of all the gods of heaven. I thought him
    late
Of an unseemly aspect; now he bears
A likeness to the immortal ones whose
    home
Is the broad heaven. I would that I
    might call
A man like him my husband, dwelling
    here,
And here content to dwell. Now hasten,
    maids,
And set before the stranger food and
    wine."
    She spake; they heard and cheerfully
        obeyed,
And set before Ulysses food and wine.
The patient chief Ulysses ate and drank
Full eagerly, for he had fasted long.
    White-armed Nausicaa then had other
        cares.
She placed the smoothly folded robes
    within
The sumptuous chariot, yoked the firm-
    hoofed mules,
And mounted to her place, and from the
    seat
Spake kindly, counselling Ulysses thus:—
    "Now, stranger, rise and follow to the
        town,
And to my royal father's palace I
Will be thy guide, where, doubt not, thou
    wilt meet
The noblest men of our Phæacian race.
But do as I advise,—for not inapt
I deem thee. While we traverse yet the
    fields
Among the tilth, keep thou among my
    train
Of maidens, following fast behind the
    mules
And chariot. I will lead thee in the
    way.
But when our train goes upward toward
    the town,
Fenced with its towery wall, and on each
    side
Embraced with a fair haven, with a
    strait

Of narrow entrance, where our well-
    oared barks
Have each a mooring-place along the
    road,
And there round Neptune's glorious fane
    extends
A market-place, surrounded by huge
    stones,
Dragged from the quarry hither, where
    is kept
The rigging of the barks,—sail-cloth and
    ropes,—
And oars are polished there,—for little
    reck
Phæacians of the quiver and the bow,
And give most heed to masts and shrouds
    and ships
Well poised, in which it is their pride to
    cross
The foamy deep,—when there I would
    not bring
Rude taunts upon myself, for in the
    crowd
Are brutal men. One of the baser sort
Perchance might say, on meeting us:
    'What man,
Handsome and lusty-limbed, is he who
    thus
Follows Nausicaa? where was it her luck
To find him? will he be her husband yet?
Perhaps she brings some wanderer from
    his ship,
A stranger from strange lands, for we
    have here
No neighbors; or, perhaps, it is a god
Called down by fervent prayer from
    heaven to dwell
Henceforth with her. 'Tis well if she
    have found
A husband elsewhere, since at home she
    meets
Her many noble wooers with disdain;
They are Phæacians.' Thus the crowd
    would say,
And it would bring reproach upon my
    name.
I too would blame another who should do
The like, and, while her parents were
    alive,

Without their knowledge should consort
    with men
Before her marriage. Stranger, now
    observe
My words, and thou shalt speedily obtain
Safe-conduct from my father, and be sent
Upon thy voyage homeward. We shall
    reach
A beautiful grove of poplars by the way,
Sacred to Pallas; from it flows a brook,
And round it lies a meadow. In this
    spot
My father has his country-grounds, and
    here
His garden flourishes, as far from town
As one could hear a shout. There sit
    thou down
And wait till we are in the city's streets
And at my father's house. When it shall
    seem
That we are there, arise and onward fare
To the Phæacian city, and inquire
Where dwells Alcinous the large-souled
    king,
My father; 'tis not hard to find; a child
Might lead thee thither. Of the houses
    reared
By the Phæacians there is none like that
In which Alcinous the hero dwells.
When thou art once within the court and
    hall,
Go quickly through the palace till thou
    find
My mother where she sits beside the
    hearth,
Leaning against a column in its blaze,
And twisting threads, a marvel to behold,
Of bright sea-purple, while her maidens
    sit
Behind her. Near her is my father's
    throne,
On which he sits at feasts, and drinks the
    wine
Like one of the immortals. Pass it by
And clasp my mother's knee; so mayst
    thou see
Soon and with joy the day of thy return,
Although thy home be far. For if her
    mood

Be kindly toward thee, thou mayst hope
    to greet
Thy friends once more, and enter yet
    again
Thy own fair palace in thy native land."
    Thus having said, she raised the shin-
    ing scourge
And struck the mules, that quickly left
    behind
The river. On they went with easy pace
And even steps. The damsel wielded
    well
The reins, and used the lash with gentle
    hand,
So that Ulysses and her train of maids
On foot could follow close. And now the
    sun
Was sinking when they came to that fair
    grove
Sacred to Pallas. There the noble chief
Ulysses sat him down, and instantly
Prayed to the daughter of imperial
    Jove:—
    "O thou unconquerable child of Jove
The Ægis-bearer! hearken to me now,
Since late thou wouldst not listen to my
    prayer,
What time the mighty shaker of the
    shores
Pursued and wrecked me! Grant me to
    receive
Pity and kindness from Phæacia's sons."
    So prayed he, supplicating. Pallas
    heard
The prayer, but came not to him openly.
Awe of her father's brother held her
    back;
For he would still pursue with violent
    hate
Ulysses, till he reached his native land.
           —WILLIAM CULLEN BRYANT.

THE CYCLOPS [1]

[From Book IX]

In the court of the king of the Phæacians Odysseus relates the wonderful ad-

[1] Used by arrangement with Houghton Mifflin Company, the authorized publishers.

ventures through which he has passed in his efforts to get back to Ithaca. Among them were his escape from the giant Cyclops and his detention by the magician Circe.

"Onward we sailed with sorrowing
    hearts, and reached
The country of the Cyclops, an untamed
And lawless race, who, trusting to the
    gods,
Plant not, nor plough the fields, but all
    things spring
For them untended,—barley, wheat, and
    vines
Yielding large clusters filled with wine,
    and nursed
By showers from Jove. No laws have
    they; they hold
No councils. On the mountain heights
    they dwell
In vaulted caves, where each one rules
    his wives
And children as he pleases; none give
    heed
To what the others do. Before the port
Of the Cyclopean land there is an isle,
Low-lying, neither near nor yet remote,—
A woodland region, where the wild goats
    breed
Innumerable; for the foot of man
Disturbs them not, and huntsmen toiling
    through
Thick woods, or wandering over moun-
    tain heights,
Enter not here. The fields are never
    grazed
By sheep, nor furrowed by the plough,
    but lie
Untilled, unsown, and uninhabited
By man, and only feed the bleating
    goats.
The Cyclops have no barks with crim-
    son prows,
Nor shipwrights skilled to frame a gal-
    ley's deck
With benches for the rowers, and
    equipped
For any service, voyaging by turns
To all the cities, as is often done

By men who cross the deep from place
    to place,
And make a prosperous region of an
    isle.
No meagre soil is there; it well might
    bear
All fruits in their due time. Along the
    shore
Of the gray deep are meadows smooth
    and moist.
The vine would flourish long; the plough-
    man's task
Is easy, and the husbandman would reap
Large harvests, for the mould is rich
    below.
And there is a safe haven, where no need
Of cable is; no anchor there is cast,
Nor hawsers fastened to the strand, but
    they
Who enter there remain until it please
The mariners, with favorable wind,
To put to sea again. A limpid stream
Flows from a fount beneath a hollow
    rock
Into that harbor at its further end,
And poplars grow around it. Thither
    went
Our fleet; some deity had guided us
Through the dark of night, for nothing
    had we seen.
Thick was the gloom around our barks;
    the moon
Shone not in heaven, the clouds had
    quenched her light.
No eye discerned the isle, nor the long
    waves
That rolled against the shore, till our
    good ships
Touched land, and, disembarking there,
    we gave
Ourselves to sleep upon the water-side
And waited for the holy morn to rise.
  "And when at length the daughter of
    the Dawn,
The rosy-fingered Morn, appeared, we
    walked
Around the isle, admiring as we went.
Meanwhile the nymphs, the daughters
    of the god

Who bears the ægis, roused the mountain
    goats,
That so our crews might make their
    morning meal.
And straightway from our ships we took
    in hand
Our crooked bows and our long-bladed
    spears.
" 'Let all the rest of my beloved friends
Remain while I, with my own bark and
    crew,
Go forth to learn what race of men are
    these,
Whether ill-mannered, savage, and
    unjust,
Or kind to guests and reverent toward
    the gods.'
"I spake, and, having ordered all my
    crew
To go on board and cast the hawsers
    loose,
Embarked on my own ship. They all
    obeyed,
And manned the benches, sitting there in
    rows,
And smote the hoary ocean with their
    oars.
But when we came upon that neighbor-
    ing coast,
We saw upon its verge beside the sea
A cave high vaulted, overbrowed with
    shrubs
Of laurel. There much cattle lay at
    rest,
Both sheep and goats. Around it was a
    court,
A high enclosure of hewn stone, and
    pines
Tall stemmed, and towering oaks. Here
    dwelt a man
Of giant bulk, who by himself alone,
Was wont to tend his flocks. He never
    held
Converse with others, but devised apart
His wicked deeds. A frightful prodigy
Was he, and like no man who lives by
    bread,
But more like a huge mountain summit,
    rough

With woods, that towers alone above the
    rest.
"Then, bidding all the others stay and
    guard
The ship, I chose among my bravest men
Twelve whom I took with me. I had
    on board
A goatskin of dark wine,—a pleasant
    sort,
Which Maron late, Evanthes' son, a
    priest
Of Phœbus, guardian god of Ismarus,
Gave me, when, moved with reverence,
    we saved
Him and his children and his wife from
    death.
For his abode was in the thick-grown
    grove
Of Phœbus. Costly were the gifts he
    gave,—
Seven talents of wrought gold; a chalice
    all
Of silver; and he drew for me, besides,
Into twelve jars, a choice rich wine,
    unspoiled
By mixtures, and a beverage for the
    gods.
No one within his dwellings, maids or
    men,
Knew of it, save the master and his wife,
And matron of the household. When-
    soe'er
They drank this rich red wine, he only
    filled
A single cup with wine, and tempered
    that
With twenty more of water. From the
    cup
Arose a fragrance that might please the
    gods,
And hard it was to put the draught aside.
Of this I took a skin well filled, besides
Food in a hamper,—for my thoughtful
    mind
Misgave me, lest I should encounter one
Of formidable strength and savage mood,
And with no sense of justice or of right.
"Soon were we at the cave, but found
    not him

Within it; he was in the fertile meads,
Tending his flocks. We entered, won-
    dering much
At all we saw. Around were baskets
    heaped
With cheeses; pens were thronged with
    lambs and kids,
Each in a separate fold; the elder ones,
The younger, and the newly yeaned, had
    each
Their place apart. The vessels swam
    with whey,—
Pails smoothly wrought, and buckets into
    which
He milked the cattle. My companions
    then
Begged me with pressing words to take
Part of the cheeses, and returning, drive
With speed to our good galley lambs and
    kids
From where they stabled, and set sail
    again
On the salt sea. I granted not their
    wish;
Far better if I had. 'Twas my intent
To see the owner of the flocks and prove
His hospitality. No pleasant sight
Was that to be for those with whom I
    came.
    "And then we lit a fire, and sacrificed,
And ate the cheeses, and within the
    cave
Sat waiting, till from pasturing his flocks
He came; a heavy load of well dried
    wood
He bore, to make a blaze at supper-time.
Without the den he flung his burden
    down
With such a crash that we in terror slunk
Into a corner of the cave. He drove
His well-fed flock, all those whose milk
    he drew,
Under that spacious vault of rock, but
    left
The males, both goats and rams, without
    the court.
And then he lifted a huge barrier up,
A mighty weight; not two-and-twenty
    wains,

Four-wheeled and strong, could move it
    from the ground:
Such was the enormous rock he raised,
    and placed
Against the entrance. Then he sat and
    milked
The ewes and bleating goats, each one
    in turn,
And gave to each its young. Next, half
    the milk
He caused to curdle, and disposed the
    curd
In woven baskets; and the other half
He kept in bowls to be his evening drink.
His tasks all ended thus, he lit a fire,
And saw us where we lurked, and ques-
    tioned us:—
    'Who are ye, strangers? Tell me
        whence ye came
Across the ocean. Are ye men of trade,
Or wanderers at will, like those who roam
The sea for plunder, and, with their own
    lives
In peril, carry death to distant shores?'
    "He spake, and we who heard with
        sinking heart
Trembled at that deep voice and fright-
    ful form,
And thus I answered: 'We are Greeks
    who come
From Ilium driven across the mighty
    deep
By changing winds, and while we sought
    our home
Have made a different voyage, and been
    forced
Upon another course: such was the will
Of Jupiter. We boast ourselves to be
Soldiers of Agamemnon, Atreus' son,
Whose fame is now the greatest under
    heaven,
So mighty was the city which he sacked,
So many were the warriors whom he
    slew;
And now we come as suppliants to thy
    knees,
And ask thee to receive us as thy guests,
Or else bestow the gifts which custom
    makes

The stranger's due. Great as thou art, revere
The gods; for suitors to thy grace are we,
And hospitable Jove, whose presence goes
With every worthy stranger, will avenge
Suppliants and strangers when they suffer wrong.'
  "I spake, and savagely he answered me:—
'Thou art a fool, O stranger, or art come
From some far country,—thou who biddest me
Fear or regard the gods. We little care—
We Cyclops—for the Ægis-bearer, Jove,
Or any other of the blessed gods;
We are their betters. Think not I would spare
Thee or thy comrades to avoid the wrath
Of Jupiter, unless it were my choice;
But say,—for I would know,—where hast thou left
Thy gallant bark in landing? was it near,
Or in some distant corner of the isle?'
  "He spake to tempt me, but I well perceived
His craft, and answered with dissembling words:—
" 'Neptune, who shakes the shores, hath wrecked my bark
On rocks that edge thine island, hurling it
Against the headland. From the open sea
The tempest swept it hitherward, and I,
With these, escaped the bitter doom of death.'
  "I spake; the savage answered not, but sprang,
And, laying hands on my companions, seized
Two, whom he dashed like whelps against the ground.
Their brains flowed out, and weltered where they fell.
He hewed them limb from limb for his repast,
And, like a lion of the mountain wilds,

Devoured them as they were, and left no part,—
Entrails nor flesh nor marrowy bones. We wept
To see his cruelties, and raised our hands
To Jove, and hopeless misery filled our hearts.
And when the Cyclops now had filled himself,
Devouring human flesh, and drinking milk
Unmingled, in his cave he laid him down,
Stretched out amid his flocks. The thought arose
In my courageous heart to go to him,
And draw the trenchant sword upon my thigh,
And where the midriff joins the liver deal
A stroke to pierce his breast. A second thought
Restrained me,—that a miserable death
Would overtake us, since we had no power
To move the mighty rock which he had laid
At the high opening. So all night we grieved,
Waiting the holy Morn; and when at length
That rosy fingered daughter of the Dawn
Appeared,—the Cyclops lit a fire, and milked
His fair flock one by one, and brought their young
Each to its mother's side. When he had thus
Performed his household tasks, he seized again
Two of our number for his morning meal.
These he devoured, and then he moved away
With ease the massive rock that closed the cave,
And, driving forth his well-fed flock, he laid
The massive barrier back, as one would fit
The lid upon a quiver. With loud noise

The Cyclops drove that well-fed flock
    afield,
While I was left to think of many a plan
To do him mischief and avenge our
    wrongs,
If haply Pallas should confer on me
That glory. To my mind, as I resolved
The plans, this seemed the wisest of them
    all.
    "Beside the stalls there lay a massive
        club
Of olive-wood, yet green, which from its
    stock
The Cyclops hewed, that he might carry
    it
When seasoned. As it lay it seemed to
    us
The mast of some black galley, broad of
    beam,
With twenty oarsmen, built to carry
    freight
Across the mighty deep,—such was its
    length
And thickness. Standing by it, I cut off
A fathom's length, and gave it to my
    men,
And bade them smooth its sides, and they
    obeyed
While I made sharp the smaller end, and
    brought
The point to hardness in the glowing fire;
And then I hid the weapon in a heap
Of litter, which lay thick about the cave.
I bade my comrades now decide by lot
Which of them all should dare, along
    with me,
To lift the stake, and with its point bore
    out
Our enemy's eye, when softly wrapped
    in sleep.
The lot was cast, and fell on those whom
    most
I wished with me,—four men, and I the
    fifth.
    "At eve the keeper of these fair-
        woolled flocks
Returned, and brought his well-fed sheep
    and goats
Into the spacious cavern, leaving none

Without it, whether through some doubt
    of us
Or through the ordering of some god.
    He raised
The massive rock again, and laid it close
Against the opening. Then he sat and
    milked
The ewes and bleating goats, each one
    in turn,
And gave to each her young. When he
    had thus
Performed his household tasks, he seized
    again
Two of our number for his evening
    meal.
Then I drew near, and bearing in my
    hand
A wooden cup of dark red wine I said:—
    "'Take this, O Cyclops, after thy
        repast
Of human flesh, and drink, that thou
    mayst know
What liquor was concealed within our
    ship.
I brought it as an offering to thee,
For I had hope that thou wouldst pity
    us,
And send us home. Yet are thy cruelties
Beyond all limit. Wicked as thou art,
Hereafter who, of all the human race,
Will dare approach thee, guilty of such
    wrong?'
    "As thus I spake, he took the cup and
        drank.
The luscious wine delighted mightily
His palate, and he asked a second
    draught.
    "'Give me to drink again, and gen-
        erously,
And tell thy name, that I might make a
    gift
Such as becomes a host. The fertile land
In which the Cyclops dwell yields wine,
    'tis true,
And the large grapes are nursed by rains
    from Jove,
But nectar and ambrosia are in this.'
    "He spake; I gave him of the gen-
        erous juice

Again, and thrice I filled and brought
the cup,
And thrice the Cyclops in his folly drank.
But when I saw the wine begin to cloud
His senses, I bespake him blandly
thus:—
 " 'Thou hast inquired, O Cyclops, by
what name
Men know me. I will tell thee, but do
thou
Bestow in turn some hospitable gift,
As thou hast promised. Noman is my
name,
My father and my mother gave it me,
And Noman am I called by all my
friends.'
 "I ended, and he answered savagely:—
'Noman shall be the last of all his band
Whom I will eat, the rest will I devour
Before him. Let that respite be my
gift.'
 "He spake, and, sinking backward at
full length,
Lay on the ground, with his huge neck
aside;
All-powerful sleep had overtaken him.
Then from his mouth came bits of human
flesh
Mingled with wine, and from his drunken
throat
Rejected noisily. I put the stake
Among the glowing coals to gather heat,
And uttered cheerful words, encouraging
My men, that none might fail me through
their fears.
And when the olive-wood began to
blaze,—
For though yet green it freely took the
fire,—
I drew it from the embers. Round me
stood
My comrades, whom some deity inspired
With calm, high courage. In their hands
they took
And thrust into his eye the pointed bar,
While perched upon a higher stand than
they
I twirled it round. As when a workman
bores

Some timber of a ship, the men who
stand
Below him with a strap, on either side
Twirl it, and round it spins unceasingly,
So, thrusting in his eye that pointed bar,
We made it turn. The blood came
streaming forth
On the hot wood; the eyelids and the
brow
Were scalded by the vapor, and the roots
Of the scorched eyeball crackled with the
fire.
As when a smith, in forging axe or adze,
Plunges, to temper it, the hissing blade
Into cold water, strengthening thus the
steel,
So hissed the eyeball of the Cyclops
round
That olive stake. He raised a fearful
howl;
The rocks rang with it, and we fled from
him
In terror. Plucking from his eye the
stake
All foul and dripping with the abundant
blood,
He flung it madly from him with both
hands.
Then called he to the Cyclops who in
grots
Dwelt on that breezy height. They
heard his voice
And came by various ways, and stood
beside
The cave, and asked the occasion of his
grief.
 " 'What hurts thee, Polyphemus, that
thou thus
Dost break our slumbers in the ambrosial
night
With cries? Hath any of the sons of
men
Driven off thy flocks in spite of thee, or
tried
By treachery or force to take thy life?'
 "Huge Polyphemus answered from his
den:—
'O friends! 'tis Noman who is killing
me;

By treachery Noman kills me; none by
force.'
"Then thus with winged words they
spake again:—
'If no man does thee violence, and thou
Art quite alone, reflect that none escape
Diseases; they are sent by Jove. But
make
Thy prayer to Father Neptune, ocean's
king.'
"So spake they and departed. In my
heart
I laughed to think that by the name I
took,
And by my shrewd device, I had deceived
The Cyclops. Meantime, groaning and
in pain,
And groping with his hands, he moved
away
The rock that barred the entrance.
There he sat,
With arms outstretched, to seize whoever
sought
To issue from the cavern with the flock,
So dull of thought he deemed me. Then
I planned
How best to save my comrades and
myself
From death. I framed a thousand
stratagems
And arts,—for here was life at stake,
and great
The danger was. At last I fixed on this.
"The rams were plump and beautiful,
and large
With thick, dark fleeces. These I silently
Bound to each other, three and three,
with twigs
Of which that prodigy of lawless guilt,
The Cyclops, made his bed. The middle
ram
Of every three conveyed a man; the two,
One on each side, were there to make
him safe.
Thus each of us was borne by three
but I
Chose for myself the finest one of all,
And seized him by the back, and slipping
down

Beneath his shaggy belly, stretched
myself
At length, and clung with resolute heart,
and hands
That firmly clenched the rich abundant
fleece.
Then sighed we for the holy Morn to
rise.
"And when again the daughter of the
Dawn,
The rosy-fingered Morn, looked forth,
the males
Went forth to pasture, while the ewes
remained
Within the stables, bleating, yet un-
milked,
For heavy were their udders. Carefully
The master handled, though in grievous
pain,
The back of every one that rose and
passed,
Yet, slow of thought, perceived not that
my men
Were clinging hid beneath their woolly
breasts.
As the last ram of all the flock went
out,
His thick fleece heavy with my weight,
and I
In agitated thought, he felt his back,
And thus the giant Polyphemus spake:—
" 'My favorite ram, how art thou now
the last
To leave the cave? It hath not been thy
wont
To let the sheep go first, but thou didst
come
Earliest to feed among the flowery grass,
Walking with stately strides, and thou
wert first
At the fresh stream, and first at eve to
seek
The stable; now thou art the last of all.
Grievest thou for thy master, who has
lost
His eye, put out by a deceitful wretch
And his vile crew, who stupefied me first
With wine,—this Noman, who, if I right
deem,

Has not escaped from death. O, didst
thou think
As I do, and hadst but the power of
speech
To tell me where he hides from my strong
arm,
Then should his brains, dashed out
against the ground,
Be scattered here and there; then should
my heart
Be somewhat lighter, even amid the woes
Which Noman, worthless wretch, has
brought on me!'
  "He spake, and sent him forth among
the rest;
And when we were a little way beyond
The cavern and the court, I loosed my
hold
Upon the animal and unbound my men.
Then quickly we surrounded and drove
off,
Fat sheep and stately paced, a numerous
flock,
And brought them to our ship, where
joyfully
Our friends received us, though with
grief and tears
For those who perished. Yet I suffered
not
That they should weep, but, frowning,
gave command
By signs to lift with speed the fair-
woolled sheep
On board, and launch our ship on the
salt sea.
They went on board, where each one
took his place
Upon the benches, and with diligent oars
Smote the gray deep; and when we
were as far
As one upon the shore could hear a shout,
Thus to the Cyclops tauntingly I
called:—
  "'Ha! Cyclops! those whom in thy
rocky cave
Thou, in thy brutal fury, hast devoured,
Were friends of one not unexpert in war;
Amply have thy own guilty deeds
returned

Upon thee. Cruel one! who didst not
fear
To eat the strangers sheltered by thy
roof,
Jove and the other gods avenge them
thus.'
  "I spake; the anger in his bosom raged
More fiercely. From a mountain peak
he wrenched
Its summit, hurling it to fall beside
Our galley, where it almost touched the
helm.
The rock dashed high the water where it
fell,
And the returning billow swept us back
And toward the shore. I seized a long-
stemmed pike
And pushed it from the shore, en-
couraging
The men to bend with vigor to their oars
And so escape. With nods I gave the
sign.
Forward to vigorous strokes the oarsmen
leaned
Till we were out at sea as far from land
As when I spake before, and then again
I shouted to the Cyclops, though my
crew
Strove to prevent it with beseeching
words,
And one man first and then another
said:—
  "'O most unwise! why chafe that savage
man
To fury,—him who just has cast his bolt
Into the sea, and forced us toward the
land
Where we had well-nigh perished?
Should he hear
A cry from us, or even a word of speech,
Then would he fling a rock to crush our
heads
And wreck our ship, so fatal is his cast.'
  "He spake, but moved not my cour-
ageous heart;
And then I spake again, and angrily:—
  "'Cyclops, if any man of mortal birth
Note thine unseemly blindness, and
inquire

The occasion, tell him that Laertes' son,
Ulysses, the destroyer of walled towns,
Whose home is Ithaca, put out thine eye!'
   "I spake; he answered with a wailing
      voice:—
'Now, woe is me! the ancient oracles
Concerning me have come to pass. Here
      dwelt
A seer named Telemus Eurymides,
Great, good, and eminent in prophecy,
And prophesying he grew old among
The Cyclops. He foretold my coming
      fate,—
That I should lose my sight, and by the
      hand
And cunning of Ulysses. Yet I looked
For one of noble presence, mighty
      strength,
And giant stature landing on our coast.
Now a mere weakling, insignificant
And small of stature, has put out my eye,
First stupefying me with wine. Yet
      come
Hither, I pray, Ulysses, and receive
The hospitable gifts which are thy due;
And I will pray to Neptune, and entreat
The mighty god to guide thee safely
      home.
His son am I, and he declares himself
My father. He can heal me if he will,
And no one else of all the immortal gods
Or mortal men can give me back my
      sight.'
   "He spake; I answered: 'Rather would
      I take
Thy life and breath, and send thee to the
      abode
Of Hades, where thou wouldst be past the
      power
Of even Neptune to restore thine eye.'
   "As thus I said, the Cyclops raised
      his hands,
And spread them toward the starry
      heaven, and thus
Prayed to the deity who rules the deep:—
   " 'Hear, dark-haired Neptune, who
      dost swathe the earth!
If I am thine, and thou dost own thyself
My father, grant that this ,Ulysses ne'er

May reach his native land! But if it be
The will of fate that he behold again
His friends, and enter his own palace-
      halls
In his own country, late and sorrowful
Be his return, and with his comrades lost,
And in a borrowed ship, and may he
      find
In his own home new griefs awaiting him.'
   "He prayed, and Neptune hearkened
      to his prayer.
And then the Cyclops seized another
      stone,
Far larger than the last, and swung it
      round,
And cast it with vast strength. It fell
      behind
Our black-prowed galley, where it almost
      struck
The rudder's end. The sea was dashed
      on high
Beneath the falling rock, and bore our
      ship
On toward the shore we sought. When
      we now reached
The island where together in a fleet
Our other galleys lay, we found our
      friends
Sitting where they had waited long in
      grief.
We touched the shore and drew our gal-
      ley up
On the smooth sand, and stepped upon
      the beach;
And taking from on board the sheep that
      formed
Part of the Cyclop's flock, divided them,
That none might be without an equal
      share.
When all the rest were shared, my warrior
      friends
Decreed the ram to me. Of him I made
Upon the beach a sacrifice to Jove
The Cloud-compeller, Saturn's son, whose
      rule
Is over all; to him I burned the thighs.
He heeded not the offering; even then
He planned the wreck of all my gallant
      ships,

And death of my dear comrades. All that
    day
Till set of sun we sat and feasted high
Upon the ·abundant meats and delicate
    wine.
But when the sun went down, and dark-
    ness crept
Over the earth, we slumbered on the
    shore;
And when again the daughter of the
    Dawn,
The rosy-fingered Morn, looked forth, I
    called
My men with cheerful words to climb
    the decks
And cast the hawsers loose. With speed
    they went
On board and manned the benches, took
    in hand
The oars and smote with them the hoary
    deep.
Onward with sadness, glad to have
    escaped,
We sailed, yet sorrowing for our com-
    rades lost."
    —WILLIAM CULLEN BRYANT.

CIRCE [1]

[From Books X and XI]

"Onward we sailed, with sorrow in our
    hearts
For our lost friends, though glad to be
    reprieved
From death. And now we landed at an
    isle,—
Ææa, where the fair-haired Circe dwelt,
A goddess high in rank and skilled in
    song,
Own sister of the wise Æætes. Both
Were children of the source of light, the
    Sun,
And Perse, Ocean's daughter, brought
    them forth.
We found a haven here, where ships
    might lie;

[1] Used by arrangement with Houghton Mifflin
Company, the authorized publishers.

And guided by some deity we brought
Our galley silently against the shore,
And disembarked, and gave two days
    and nights
To rest, unmanned with hardship and
    with grief.
"When bright-haired Morning brought
    the third day round,
I took my spear and my good sword, and
    left
The ship, and climbed a height, in hope
    to spy
Some trace of human toil, or hear some
    voice.
On a steep precipice I stood, and saw
From the broad earth below a rising
    smoke,
Where midst the thickets and the forest-
    ground
Stood Circe's palace. Seeing that dark
    smoke,
The thought arose within my mind that
    there
I should inquire. I pondered till at last
This seemed the wisest,—to return at
    once
To my good ship upon the ocean-side,
And give my crew their meal, and send
    them forth
To view the region. Coming to the spot
Where lay my well-oared bark, some pity-
    ing god
Beneath whose eye I wandered forth
    alone
Sent a huge stag into my very path,
High-horned, which from his pasture in
    the wood
Descended to the river-side to drink,
For grievously he felt the hot sun's
    power.
Him as he ran I smote; the weapon
    pierced,
Just at the spine, the middle of his back.
The brazen blade passed through, and
    with a moan
He fell amid the dust, and yielded up
His life. I went to him, and set my foot
Against him, and plucked forth the
    brazen spear,

And left it leaning there.   And then I broke
Lithe osiers from the shrubs, and twined of these
A rope, which, doubled, was an ell in length.
With that I tied the enormous creature's feet,
And slung him on my neck, and brought him thus
To my black ship.   I used the spear to prop
My steps, since he no longer could be borne
Upon the shoulder, aided by the hand,
Such was the animal's bulk.   I flung him down
Before the ship, encouraging my men
With cheerful words, and thus I said to each:—
   " 'My friends, we will not, wretched as we are,
Go down to Pluto's realm before our time.
While food and wine are yet within the hold
Of our good galley, let us not forget
Our daily meals, and famine-stricken pine.'
   "I spake; they all obeyed, and at my word
Came forth, and standing by the barren deep
Admired the stag, for he was huge of bulk;
And when their eyes were tired with wondering,
My people washed their hands, and soon had made
A noble banquet ready.   All that day
Till set of sun we sat and feasted there
Upon the abundant meat and delicate wine;
And when the sun went down, and darkness came,
We slept upon the shore.   But when the Morn,
The rosy-fingered child of Dawn, looked forth,

I called a council of my men and spake:—
   " 'Give ear, my friends, amid your sufferings,
To words that I shall say.   We cannot here
Know which way lies the west, nor where the east,
Nor where the sun, that shines for all mankind,
Descends below the earth, nor where again
He rises from it.   Yet will we consult,
If room there be for counsel,—which I doubt,
For when I climbed that height I overlooked
An isle surrounded by the boundless deep,—
An isle low lying.   In the midst I saw
Smoke rising from a thicket of the wood.'
   "I spake; their courage died within their hearts
As they remembered what Antiphates,
The Læstrigon, had done, and what foul deeds
The cannibal Cyclops, and they wept aloud.
Tears flowed abundantly, but tears were now
Of no avail to our unhappy band.
   "Numbering my well-armed men, I made of them
Two equal parties, giving each its chief.
Myself commanded one; Eurylochus,
The hero, took the other in his charge.
   "Then in a brazen helm we shook the lots;
The lot of brave Eurylochus leaped forth,
And he with two-and-twenty of our men
Went forward with quick steps, and yet in tears,
While we as sorrowful were left behind.
   "They found the fair abode where Circe dwelt,
A palace of hewn stone within the vale,
Yet nobly seated.   There were mountain wolves

And lions round it, which herself had
    tamed
With powerful drugs; yet these assaulted
    not
The visitors, but, wagging their long
    tails,
Stood on their hinder feet, and fawned
    on them,
Like mastiffs on their master when he
    comes
From banqueting and brings them food.
    So fawned
The strong-clawed wolves and lions on
    my men.
With fear my men beheld those beasts of
    prey,
Yet went, and, standing in the portico
Of the bright-haired divinity, they heard
Her sweet voice singing, as within she
    threw
The shuttle through the wide immortal
    web,
Such as is woven by the goddesses,—
Delicate, bright of hue, and beautiful.
    "Polites then, a chief the most beloved
And most discreet of all my comrades,
    spake:—
    " 'Some one is here, my friends, who
    sweetly sings,
Weaving an ample web, and all the floor
Rings to her voice. Whoever she may be,
Woman or goddess, let us call to her.'
    "He spake; aloud they called, and
    forth she came
And threw at once the shining doors
    apart,
And bade my comrades enter. Without
    thought
They followed her. Eurylochus alone
Remained without, for he suspected guile.
She led them in and seated them on
    thrones.
Then mingling for them Pramnian wine
    with cheese,
Meal, and fresh honey, and infusing drugs
Into the mixture,—drugs which made
    them lose
The memory of their home,—she handed
    them

The beverage and they drank. Then in-
    stantly
She touched them with a wand, and shut
    them up
In sties, transformed to swine in head
    and voice,
Bristles and shape, though still the hu-
    man mind
Remained to them. Thus sorrowing they
    were driven
Into their cells, where Circe flung to
    them
Acorns of oak and ilex, and the fruit
Of cornel, such as nourish wallowing
    swine.
    "Back came Eurylochus to our good
    ship
With news of our poor comrades and
    their fate;
He strove to speak, but could not; he was
    stunned
By that calamity; his eyes were filled
With tears, and his whole soul was given
    to grief.
We marvelled greatly; long we ques-
    tioned him,
And thus he spake of our lost friends at
    last:—
    " 'Through yonder thickets, as thou
    gav'st command,
Illustrious chief! we went, until we
    reached
A stately palace of hewn stones, within
A vale, yet nobly seated. Some one
    there,
Goddess or woman, weaving busily
An ample web, sang sweetly as she
    wrought.
My comrades called aloud, and forth
    she came,
And threw at once the shining doors
    apart,
And bade us enter. Without thought the
    rest
Followed, while I alone, suspecting guile,
Remained without. My comrades, from
    that hour,
Were seen no more; not one of them
    again

Came forth, though long I sat and
watched for them.'
"He spake; I slung my silver-studded
sword
Upon my shoulders,—a huge blade of
brass,—
And my bow with it, and commanded him
To lead the way. He seized and clasped
my knees
With both his hands in attitude of
prayer,
And sorrowfully said these winged
words:—
"'Take me not thither; force me not to
go,
O foster-child of Jove! but leave me here;
For thou wilt not return, I know, nor
yet
Deliver one of our lost friends. Our part
Is to betake ourselves to instant flight
With these who yet remain, and so es-
cape.'
"He spake, and I replied: 'Eurylochus,
Remain thou here, beside our roomy
ship,
Eating and drinking. I shall surely go.
A strong necessity is laid on me.'
"I spake, and from the ship and shore
went up
Into the isle; and when I found myself
Within that awful valley, and not far
From the great palace in which Circe
dwelt,
The sorceress, there met me on my way
A youth; he seemed in manhood's early
prime,
When youth has most of grace. He took
my hand
And held it, and, accosting me, began:—
"'Rash mortal! whither art thou wan-
dering thus
Alone among the hills, where every place
Is strange to thee? Thy comrades are
shut up
In Circe's palace in close cells like swine.
Com'st thou to set them free? Nay, thou
like them
Wilt rather find thyself constrained to
stay.

Let me bestow the means to make thee
safe
Against that mischief. Take this potent
herb,
And bear it with thee to the palace-halls
Of Circe, and it shall avert from thee
The threatened evil. I will now reveal
The treacherous arts of Circe. She will
bring
A mingled draught to thee, and drug the
bowl,
But will not harm thee thus; the virtu-
ous plant
I gave thee will prevent it. Hear yet
more:
When she shall smite thee with her wand,
draw forth
Thy good sword from thy thigh and rush
at her
As if to take her life, and she will crouch
In fear, and will solicit thine embrace.
Refuse her not, that so she may release
Thy comrades, and may send thee also
back
To thine own land; but first exact of
her
The solemn oath which binds the blessed
gods,
That she will meditate no other harm
To thee, nor strip thee of thy manly
strength.'
"The Argus-queller spake, and plucked
from earth
The potent plant and handed it to me,
And taught me all its powers. The root
is black,
The blossom white as milk. Among the
gods
Its name is Moly; hard it is for men
To dig it up; the gods find nothing hard.
"Back through the woody island
Hermes went
Toward high Olympus, while I took my
way
To Circe's halls, yet with a beating heart.
There, as I stood beneath the portico
Of that bright-haired divinity, I called
Aloud; the goddess heard my voice and
came,

And threw at once the shining doors apart,
And prayed me to come in. I followed her,
Yet grieving still. She led me in and gave
A seat upon a silver-studded throne,
Beautiful, nobly wrought, and placed beneath
A footstool, and prepared a mingled draught
Within a golden chalice, and infused
A drug with mischievous intent. She gave
The cup; I drank it off; the charm wrought not,
And then she smote me with her wand and said:—
'Go to the sty, and with thy fellows sprawl.'
    "She spake; but drawing forth the trusty sword
Upon my thigh, I rushed at her as if
To take her life. She shrieked and, stooping low,
Ran underneath my arm and clasped my knees,
And uttered piteously these winged words:—
    " 'Who art thou? of what race and of what land,
And who thy parents? I am wonder-struck
To see that thou couldst drink that magic juice
And yield not to its power. No living man
Whoever he might be, that tasted once
Those drugs, or passed them o'er his lips, has yet
Withstood them. In thy breast a spirit dwells
Not to be thus subdued. Art thou not then
Ulysses, master of wise stratagems,
Whose coming hither, on his way from Troy,
In his black galley, oft has been foretold
By Hermes of the golden wand? But sheathe

Thy sword and share my couch, that, joined in love,
Each may hereafter trust the other's faith.'
    "She spake, and I replied: 'How canst thou ask,
O Circe, that I gently deal with thee,
Since thou, in thine own palace, hast transformed
My friends to swine, and plottest even now
To keep me with thee, luring me to pass
Into thy chamber and to share thy couch,
That thou mayst strip me of my manly strength.
I come not to thy couch till thou engage,
O goddess, by a solemn oath, that thou
Wilt never seek to do me further harm.'
    "I spake; she straightway took the oath required,
And, after it was uttered and confirmed,
Up to her sumptuous couch I went. Meanwhile
Four diligent maidens ministered within
The palace,—servants of the household they,
Who had their birth from fountains and from groves,
And sacred rivers flowing to the sea.
One spread the thrones with gorgeous coverings;
Above was purple arras, and beneath
Were linen webs; another, setting forth
The silver tables just before the thrones,
Placed on them canisters of gold; a third
Mingled the rich wines in a silver bowl,
And placed the golden cups; and, last, a fourth
Brought water from the fountain, and beneath
A massive tripod kindled a great fire
And warmed the water. When it boiled within
The shining brass, she led me to the bath,
And washed me from the tripod. On my head
And shoulders pleasantly she shed the streams

That from my members took away the
  sense
Of weariness, unmanning body and mind.
And when she thus had bathed me and
  with oil
Anointed me, she put a princely cloak
And tunic on me, led me in; and showed
My seat,—a stately silver-studded throne,
High-wrought,—and placed a footstool
  for my feet.
Then came a handmaid with a golden
  ewer,
And from it poured pure water for my
  hands
Into a silver laver. Next she placed
A polished table near to me, on which
The matron of the palace laid the feast,
With many delicacies from her store,
And bade me eat. The banquet pleased
  me not.
My thoughts were elsewhere; dark
  imaginings
Were in my mind. When Circe marked
  my mood,
As in a gloomy revery I sat,
And put not forth my hands to touch the
  feast,
She came to me and spake these winged
  words:—
  " 'Why sittest thou like one who has no
  power
Of speech, Ulysses, wrapt in thoughts that
  gnaw
Thy heart, and tasting neither food nor
  wine?
Still dost thou dream of fraud? It is
  not well
That thou shouldst fear it longer, since I
  pledged
Myself against it with a mighty oath.'
  "She spake, and I replied: 'What man
  whose heart
Is faithful could endure to taste of food
Or wine till he could see his captive
  friends
Once more at large? If with a kind in-
  tent
Thou bidst me eat and drink, let me be-
  hold

With mine own eyes my dear companions
  free.'
  "I spake; and Circe took her wand and
  went
Forth from her halls, and, opening the
  gate
That closed the sty, drove forth what
  seemed a herd
Of swine in their ninth year. They
  ranged themselves
Before her, and she went from each to
  each
And shed on them another drug. Forth-
  with
Fell from their limbs the bristles which
  had grown
All over them, when mighty Circe gave
At first the baleful potion. Now again
My friends were men, and younger than
  before,
And of a nobler mien and statelier
  growth.
They knew me all; and each one pressed
  my hand
In his, and there were tears and sobs of
  joy
That sounded through the palace. Circe
  too
Was moved, the mighty goddess; she
  drew near
And stood by me, and spake these
  winged words:—
  " 'Son of Laertes, nobly born and wise,
Ulysses! go to thy good ship beside
The sea and draw it up the beach, and
  hide
The goods and weapons in the caverns
  there,
And come thou back and bring with thee
  thy friends.'
  "She spake, and easily my generous
  mind
Was moved by what she said. Forthwith
  I went
To my good ship beside the sea, and
  found
My friends in tears, lamenting bitterly.
As in some grange the calves come leaping
  round

A herd of kine returning to the stall
From grassy fields where they have grazed their fill,
Nor can the stall contain the young that spring
Around their mothers with continual bleat;
So when my comrades saw me through their tears
They sprang to meet me, and their joy was such
As if they were in their own native land
And their own city, on the rugged coast
Of Ithaca, where they were born and reared;
And as they wept they spake these winged words:—
"'O foster child of Jove! we welcome thee
On thy return with a delight as great
As if we all had reached again the land
That gave us birth, our Ithaca. And now
Tell by what death our other friends have died.'
"They spake; I answered with consoling words:—
'First draw our galley up the beach, and hide
Our goods and all our weapons in the caves,
And then let all make haste to follow me,
And see our friends in Circe's sacred halls,
Eating and drinking at the plenteous board.'
"I spake; and cheerfully my men obeyed,
Save that Eurylochus alone essayed
To hold them back, and spake these winged words:—
"'Ah, whither are we going, wretched ones?
Are ye so eager for an evil fate,
That ye must go where Circe dwells, who waits
To turn us into lions, swine, or wolves,
Forced to remain and guard her spacious house?

So was it with the Cyclops, when our friends
Went with this chief to his abode,
And perished there through his foolhardiness.'
"He spake; and then I thought to draw my sword
From my stout thigh, and with the trenchant blade
Strike off his head and let it fall to earth,
Though he were my near kinsman; yet the rest
Restrained me, each one speaking kindly words:—
"'Nay, foster-child of Jove! if thou consent,
This man shall stay behind and with the ship,
And he shall guard the ship, but lead us thou
To where the sacred halls of Circe stand.'
"They spake, and from the ship and shore went up
Into the land, nor was Eurylochus
Left with the ship; he followed, for he feared
My terrible threat. Meantime had Circe bathed
My comrades at the palace, and with oil
Anointed them, and robed them in fair cloaks
And tunics. There we found them banqueting.
When they and those who came with me beheld
Each other, and the memory of the past
Came back to them, they wept abundantly,
And all the palace echoed with their sobs.
And then the mighty goddess came and said:—
"'Son of Laertes, nobly born and wise,
Prolong thou not these sorrows. Well I know
What ye have suffered on the fishy deep,
And all the evil that malignant men
Have done to thee on land. Now take the food

Before you, drink the wine, till ye receive
Into your hearts the courage that was yours
When long ago ye left your fatherland,
The rugged Ithaca. Ye are unnerved
And spiritless with thinking constantly
On your long wanderings, and your minds allow
No space for mirth, for ye have suffered much.'
    "She spake; her words persuaded easily
Our generous minds, and there from day to day
We lingered a full year, and banqueted
Nobly on plenteous meats and delicate wines.
But when the year was ended, and the hours
Renewed their circle, my beloved friends
From Circe's palace called me forth and said:—
    " 'Good chief, do not forget thy native land,
If fate indeed permit that ever thou
Return in safety to that lofty pile
Thy palace in the country of thy birth.'
    "So spake they, and my generous mind was moved.
All that day long until the set of sun
We sat and feasted on the abundant meats
And delicate wines; and when the sun went down
They took their rest within the darkened halls,
While I to Circe's sumptuous couch went up,
A suppliant at her knees. The goddess heard
My prayer, as thus in winged words I said:—
    " 'O Circe! make, I pray, the promise good
Which thou hast given, to send me to my home.
My heart is pining for it, and the hearts
Of all my friends, who weary out my life

Lamenting round me when thou art not nigh.'
    "I spake; the mighty goddess thus replied:—
'Son of Laertes, nobly born and wise,
Ulysses! ye must not remain with me
Unwillingly; but ye have yet to make
Another voyage, and must visit first
The abode of Pluto, and of Proserpine
His dreaded queen, and there consult the soul
Of the blind seer Tiresias,—him of Thebes,—
Whose intellect was spared; for Proserpine
Gave back to him in death the power of mind,
That only he might know of things to come.
The rest are shades that flit from place to place.'
    "Thus spake the goddess; and my heart was wrung
With sorrow, and I sat upon the couch
And wept, nor could I longer wish to live
And see the light of day. But when my grief,
With shedding tears and tossing where I sat,
Was somewhat spent, I spake to Circe thus:—
    " 'O Circe, who will guide me when I make
This voyage? for no galley built by man
Has ever yet arrived at Pluto's realm.'
    "I spake; the mighty goddess answered me:—
'Son of Laertes, nobly born and wise,
Take thou no thought of who shall guide thy bark,
But raise the mast and spread the glimmering sail,
And seat thyself, and let the north-wind waft
Thy galley on. As soon as thou shalt cross
Oceanus, and come to the low shore
And groves of Proserpine, the lofty groups

Of poplars, and the willows that let fall
Their withered fruit, moor thou thy gal-
    ley there
In the deep eddies of Oceanus,
And pass to Pluto's comfortless abode.
There into Acheron are poured the
    streams
Of Pyriphlegethon, and of that arm
Of Styx, Cocytus. At the place where
    meet
The ever-roaring waters stands a rock;
Draw near to that, and there I bid thee
    scoop
In earth a trench, a cubit long and wide.
And round about it pour to all the dead
Libations,—milk and honey first, and
    next
Rich wine and lastly water, scattering
White meal upon them. Offer there thy
    prayer
Fervently to that troop of airy forms,
And make the vow that thou wilt sacri-
    fice,
When thou at last shalt come to Ithaca,
A heifer without blemish, barren yet,
In thine own courts, and heap the altar-
    pyre
With things of price; and to the seer
    alone,
Tiresias, by himself, a ram whose fleece
Is wholly black, the best of all thy flocks.
And after thou hast duly offered prayer
To all the illustrious nations of the dead,
Then sacrifice a ram and a black ewe,
Their faces turned toward Erebus, but
    thine
The other way and toward the river
    streams.
Thither the souls of those who died will
    flock
In multitudes. Then call thy friends, and
    give
Command to flay in haste the sheep that
    lie
Slain by the cruel brass, and, burning
    there
The carcasses, pay worship to the gods,—
The powerful Pluto, and dread Proser-
    pine.

Draw then the sword upon thy thigh, and
    sit,
And suffer none of all those airy forms
To touch the blood until thou first be-
    speak
Tiresias. He will come, and speedily,—
The leader of the people,—and will tell
What voyage thou must make, what
    length of way
Thou yet must measure, and will show
    thee how
Thou mayst return across the fishy deep.'
    "She spake; and while she spake the
        Morn looked forth
Upon her golden throne. The Nymph
    bestowed
On me a cloak and tunic, and arrayed
Herself in a white robe with ample
    folds,—
A delicate web and graceful. Round her
    loins
She clasped a shining zone of gold, and
    hung
A veil upon her forehead. Forth I went
Throughout the palace and aroused my
    friends,
And thus I said in cheerful tones to
    each:—
    " 'No longer give yourselves to idle
        rest
And pleasant slumber; we are to depart.
The gracious Circe counsels us to go.'
    "I spake, and easily their generous
        minds
Inclined to me. Yet brought I not away
All my companions safely from the isle.
Elpenor was the youngest of our band,
Not brave in war was he, nor wise in
    thought.
He, overcome with wine, and for the
    sake
Of coolness, had lain down to sleep, apart
From all the rest, in Circe's sacred House;
And as my friends bestirred themselves,
    the noise
And tumult roused him; he forgot to
    come
By the long staircase; headlong from the
    roof

He plunged; his neck was broken at the spine,
And his soul went to the abode of death.
"My friends came round me, and I said to them:—
'Haply your thought may be that you are bound
For the dear country of your birth; but know
That Circe sends us elsewhere, to consult
The Theban seer, Tiresias, in the abode
Of Pluto and the dreaded Proserpine.'
"I spake, and their hearts failed them as they heard;
They sat them down, and wept, and tore their hair,
But fruitless were their sorrow and their tears.
"Thus as we sadly moved to our good ship
Upon the sea-shore, weeping all the while,
Circe, meantime, had visited its deck,
And there had bound a ram and a black ewe
By means we saw not; for what eye discerns
The presence of a deity, who moves
From place to place, and wills not to be seen?
"Now when we reached our galley by the shore,
We drew it first into the mighty deep,
And set the mast and sails, and led on board
The sheep, and sorrowfully and in tears
Embarked ourselves. The fair-haired and august
Circe, expert in music, sent with us
A kindly fellow-voyager,—a wind
That breathed behind the dark-prowed bark, and swelled
The sails; and now, with all things in their place
Throughout the ship, we sat us down,— the breeze
And helmsman guiding us upon our way.
All day our sails were stretched, as o'er the deep

Our vessel ran; the sun went down; the paths
Of the great sea were darkened, and our bark
Reached the far confines of Oceanus."
—WILLIAM CULLEN BRYANT.

THE BOW OF ODYSSEUS [1]

[From Book XXI]

After the recital of his experiences, the hero is carried back to his native land by the Phæacians. He finds his home besieged by the suitors of Penelope, who in spite of every difficulty has kept alive her belief in his return and has remained faithful to him. He appears disguised as a beggar, and with his bow drives out the unwelcome suitors.

Pallas, the goddess of the azure eyes,
Woke in the mind of sage Penelope,
The daughter of Icarius, this design,—
To put into the suitors' hands the bow
And gray steel rings, and to propose a game
That in the palace was to usher in
The slaughter. So she climbed the lofty stair,
Up from the hall, and took in her plump hand
The fair carved key; its wards were wrought of brass,
And ivory was the handle. Soon she reached
The furthest room with her attendant maids.
There lay the treasures of Ulysses,— brass
And gold, and steel divinely wrought. There lay
His bow unstrung; there lay his quiver charged
With arrows; many were the deadly shafts

[1] Used by arrangement with Houghton Mifflin Company, the authorized publishers.

It held, a stranger's gift, who met him
  once
In Lacedæmon, Iphitus by name,
The son of Eurytus, and like the gods
In presence. In Messene met the twain,
And in the mansion of Orsilochus,
The warlike. Thither had Ulysses come
To claim a debt from all the region
  round;
For rovers from Messene to their ships
Had driven and carried off from Ithaca
Three hundred sheep and those who
  tended them.
For this Ulysses, though a stripling yet,
Came that long voyage, on an embassy,
Sent by his father and the other chiefs.
And Iphitus had come in search of steeds
Which he had lost,—twelve mares, and
  under them
Twelve hardy mules, their foals. That
  errand brought
The doom of death upon him. For he
  came,
In journeying, to the abode of Hercules,
The mighty hero-son of Jupiter,
Famed for his labors, who, in his own
  house,
Slew Iphitus, the stranger. Cruel wretch!
Who reverenced not the vengeance of the
  gods,
Nor what was due to his own board, at
  which
He placed his guest, and slew him after-
  ward,
And in his stables kept the goodly mares.
'Twas when this guest was seeking for
  his steeds
He met Ulysses, and bestowed on him
The bow, which mighty Eurytus once
  bore,
And dying in his lofty palace left
The weapon to his son. Ulysses gave
In turn a trenchant sword and massive
  lance,
A pledge of kindly hospitality,
Begun, but not continued till they sat
Each at the other's table; for the son
Of Jove first took the life of him who
  gave

The bow, the godlike son of Eurytus.
That bow Ulysses, when he went to
  war
In his black galleys, never took with him,
But left it in his palace, to be kept
In memory of a beloved friend,
And only bore it in his own domain.
  Now when the glorious lady reached
  the room,
And stood upon the threshold, wrought of
  oak
And polished by the workman's cunning
  hand,
Who stretched the line upon it, and set
  up
Its posts, and hung its shining doors, she
  loosed
With a quick touch the thong that held
  the ring,
Put in the key, and with a careful aim
Struck back the sounding bolts. As when
  a bull
Roars in the field, such sound the beau-
  tiful doors,
Struck with the key, gave forth, and
  instantly
They opened to her. Up the lofty floor
She stepped, where stood the coffer that
  contained
The perfumed garments. Reaching forth
  her hand,
The queen took down the bow, that hung
  within
Its shining case, and sat her down, and
  laid
The case upon her knees, and, drawing
  forth
The monarch's bow, she wept aloud. As
  soon
As the new gush of tears had ceased to
  fall,
Back to the hall she went, and that proud
  throng
Of suitors, bearing in her hand the bow
Unstrung, and quiver, where the arrows
  lay
Many and deadly. Her attendant maids
Brought also down a coffer, where were
  laid

Much brass and steel, provided by the
  king
For games like these. The glorious lady
  then,
In presence of the suitors, stood beside
The columns that upheld the stately roof.
She held a lustrous veil before her cheeks,
And, while on either side of her a maid
Stood modestly, bespake the suitors
  thus:—
  "Hear noble suitors! ye who throng
    these halls,
And eat and drink from day to day, while
  long
My husband has been gone; your sole
  excuse
For all this lawlessness the claim ye
  make
That I become a bride. Come then, for
  now
A contest is proposed. I bring to you
The mighty bow that great Ulysses bore.
Whoe'er among you he may be whose
  hand
Shall bend this bow, and send through
  these twelve rings
An arrow, him I follow hence, and leave
This beautiful abode of my young years,
With all its plenty,—though its memory,
I think, will haunt me even in my
  dreams."
  She spake, and bade the master of the
    swine,
The good Eumæus, place the bow and
  rings
Of hoary steel before the suitor-train.
In tears he bore the bow and laid it down.
The herdsman also wept to see again
His master's bow. Antinous called to
  both
With a loud voice, and chid them
  angrily:—
  "Ye silly rustics, who can never see
Beyond the hour, why trouble with your
  tears
The lady who had grief enough besides
For her lost husband? Sit and share the
  feast
In silence, or go forth and leave the bow;

A difficult contest it will be for us,
Nor, as I think, will this fair bow be
  bent
With ease, since surely there is no man
  here
Such as Ulysses was. I saw him once,
While but a child, and still remember
  him."
  He spake, yet in his secret heart be-
    lieved
That he should bend the bow, and send
  a shaft
Through all the rings. And yet he was
  the first
To taste the steel,—an arrow from the
  hand
Of the great chief Ulysses,—whom he
  wronged
In his own palace, and to equal wrong
Encouraged others. Then Telemachus
Rose in his sacred might, and thus be-
  gan:—
  "Alas! it must be that Saturnian Jove
Has made me lose my wits. Wise as she
  is,
My mother promises to leave her home
And follow some one else, and yet I
  laugh,
And am delighted in my foolish heart.
Come then, since such a contest is pro-
  posed,
Ye suitors! and for such a woman too.
The like is not in all the lands of Greece,
Argos, Mycenæ, or the hallowed shore
Of Pylos, or in Ithaca itself,
Or the dark mainland coast. Ye know it
  well;
Why should I praise my mother? Come
  then, all;
Let there be no excuses for delay,
Nor longer leave the bow untried, that we
May see the event. I too am moved to
  try;
And if I bend the bow, and send a shaft
Through all the rings, my gracious mother
  then
Will not to my great grief, renounce her
  home,
And, following another, leave me here,

Although my prowess even now might
 win
The glorious prizes that my father won."
 He spake and, rising, from his shoul-
 ders took
The purple cloak, and laid the trenchant
 sword
Aside; and first he placed the rings of
 steel
In order, opening for them in the ground
A long trench by a line, and stamping
 close
The earth around them. All admired the
 skill
With which he ranged them, never having
 seen
The game before. And then he took his
 place
Upon the threshold, and essayed the
 bow;
And thrice he made the attempt, and
 thrice gave o'er,
Yet hoping still to draw the cord, and
 send
An arrow through the rings. He would
 have drawn
The bow at the fourth trial, but a nod
Given by his father caused him to for-
 bear,
Though eager for the attempt. And then
 again
The princely youth bespake the suitors
 thus:—
 "Well, this is strange! I may here-
 after prove
A craven and a weakling, or perchance
Am too young yet, and cannot trust my
 arm
To do me right against the man who first
Assaults me. Come then, ye whose
 strength excels
My own, and try the bow, and end the
 strife."
 He spake, and setting down the bow
 to lean
Against the firm smooth panels of the
 wall,
And the swift shaft against the bow's
 fair curve,

He took again his seat upon the throne
From which he rose. And then
 Eupeithes' son,
Antinous, to the crowd of suitors said:—
 "Rise one by one, my friends, from
 right to left.
Begin where he begins who pours the
 wine."
 So spake Antinous, and the rest ap-
 proved.
Then rose Leiodes, son of Œnops, first.
He was their seer, and always had his
 seat
Beside the ample bowl. From deeds of
 wrong
He shrank with hatred, and was sore
 incensed
Against the suitors all. He took the bow
And shaft, and, going to the threshold,
 stood
And tried the bow, yet bent it not; it
 galled
His hands, for they were soft, and all
 unused
To such a task; and thus at length he
 spake:—
 "O friends, I bend it not; another hand
Must try. This bow, upon this very
 spot,
Will take from many a prince the breath
 of life.
And better were it thus to die, by far,
Than, living, fail of that intent for which
We haunt this place, and still from day
 to day
Assemble. There is many a one whose
 wish
And hope are strong to wed Penelope,
The consort of Ulysses; but so soon
As he shall see and try the hero's bow
Let him with marriage presents seek to
 gain
Some other bride among the long-robed
 dames,
Achaia's daughters. Let him leave the
 queen
To wed the suitor who shall bring to her
The richest gifts, and him whom fate
 appoints."

He spake, and setting down the bow to
lean
Against the firm smooth panels of the
wall,
And the swift shaft against the bow's
fair curve,
He took again his seat upon the throne
From which he rose. Antinous then took
up
The word and answered, and reproached
him thus:—
"What words are these, Leiodes, that
have passed
Thy lips? harsh words and fearful,—that
this bow
Shall take from many princes here the
breath
Of life, and all because thou hast no
power
To bend it? Thy good mother bore
thee not
To draw the bow and send the arrow
forth,
But others of the noble suitor-train
Are here, by whom this bow shall yet be
bent."
Then to Melanthius, keeper of the
goats,
Antinous gave this bidding. "Light a
fire
With speed, Melanthius, in the palace
here,
And place a seat before it. Lay a fleece
Upon the seat, and bring us from within
An ample roll of fat, that we young men
By warming and anointing may make soft
The bow, and draw the cord, and end the
strife."
He spake; Melanthius kindled in-
stantly
A glowing fire, and near it placed a seat,
And on the seat a fleece, and from within
Brought forth an ample roll of fat, with
which
The young men, having warmed it,
smeared the bow
And tried, but bent it not, too weak by
far
For such a feat. Antinous kept aloof,

He and the godlike youth Eurymachus,
Two princes who in might excelled the
rest.
The herdsman of Ulysses meantime left
The palace, and with him the swineherd
went,
And after them Ulysses. When they all
Were now without the gate and palace
court,
Ulysses spake to them, and blandly
said:—
"Herdsman and swineherd, shall I say
to you
Somewhat, or shall I keep it back? My
heart
Moves me to say it. Should Ulysses
come,
Led by some god, and suddenly, what aid
Would he receive from you? Would ye
take part
With him, or with the suitors? Frankly
speak;
And tell me what your hearts would bid
you do."
Then answered thus the keeper of the
herds:
"O Father Jove! wouldst thou but grant
my wish,
And let some god conduct him hither,
then
Shall it be seen what might is in these
hands!"
So also did Eumæus offer prayer
To all the deities, that speedily
The wise Ulysses might return; and when
The chief perceived in all its truth the
thought
And purpose of their hearts, he spake
and said:—
"Know, then, that I myself am he, at
home
Again, returning in the twentieth year,
And after many sufferings, to the land
That saw my birth. I know that I am
come
Welcome to you alone of all my train
Of servants, since I hear no others pray
For my return. Hear, then, what I
engage

Shall be hereafter. If some god o'ercome
For me these arrogant suitors, I will give
To each of you a wife and lands, and build
For each a house near mine, and ye shall be
The friends and brothers of Telemachus
Thenceforth. And now, that ye may surely know
And trust me, I will show a token here,—
A scar which once the white tooth of a boar
Made, when long since, on the Parnassian mount,
I hunted with Autolycus's sons."
  Thus having said, he drew from the broad scar
The covering rags; they looked and knew it well,
And wept, and round Ulysses threw their arms,
And kissed in that embrace the hero's head
And shoulders, while Ulysses also kissed
Their heads and hands. The sun would have gone down
Upon their weeping, but for him. He said:—
  "Cease now from tears, lest some one from the hall
Should see us, and report of us within.
Now let us enter, not in company,—
I first, and ye thereafter, one by one,
And let the sign be this: the others all—
The haughty suitors—will refuse to me
The bow and quiver. When thou bearest it,
My noble friend Eumæus, through the halls,
Bring it and place it in my hands, and charge
The women to make fast the solid doors;
And then if any one of them should hear
A groan or other noise of men within,
Let her not issue forth, but silently
Pursue her task. Meantime be it thy care,
My good Philœtius, with a key to lock

The portals of the court and fix the chain."
  Thus having said, into that noble pile
He passed again, and took the seat from which
He lately rose, and afterward, in turn
Entered the servants of the godlike chief.
  Eurymachus was busy with the bow,
Turning and warming it before the blaze
On both its sides. He could not bend it thus.
There came a deep sigh from his boastful heart,
And greatly was he vexed, and sadly said:—
  "Alas! great cause of grief indeed is here
For me and all. 'Tis not that I lament
So much the losing of the bride, although
That also vexes me,—there yet remain
Many fair ladies of the Achaian stock,
Both in the sea-girt lands of Ithaca
And other regions,—yet if we be found
To fall in strength of arm so far below
The great Ulysses that we cannot bend
His bow, our sons will hear of it with shame."
  Eupeithes' son, Antinous, answered thus:
"Not so, Eurymachus, as thou thyself
Shouldst know. This day is held a solemn feast
Of Phœbus by the people. Who would draw
The bow to-day? Nay, lay it by in peace,
And suffer all the rings to stand as now;
For no man, as I think, will dare to come
Into the palace of Laertes' son
And take them hence. Let him who bears the cup
Begin to serve the wine, that, having poured
Part to the gods, we may lay down the bow,
And with the morning let Melanthius come,—
The goatherd,—bringing with him from the flock

The choicest goats, that we may burn
the thighs,
An offering to the god of archery,
Apollo. Then will we again essay
The bow, and bring the contest to an
end."
  So spake Antinous, and they all ap-
proved.
Then heralds came, and on the suitors'
hands
Poured water; youths filled up the cups
with wine,
Beginning at the right, and gave to each
His share; and when they all had poured
a part,
And each had drunk, the shrewd Ulysses
thus
With artful speech bespake the suitor-
train:—
  "Hearken, ye suitors of the illustrious
queen,
To what my heart is prompting me to
say;
But chiefly to Eurymachus I make
My suit, and to Antinous, who so well
Hath counselled to lay by the bow and
trust
The gods. To-morrow Phœbus will be-
stow
The needed strength on whomsoe'er he
will;
But let me take that polished bow, and
try
Among you, whether still the power that
dwelt
In these once pliant limbs abides in them,
Or whether haply it has passed from me
Amid my wanderings and a life of want."
  He spake, and all were vehemently
moved
With anger, for they feared that he would
bend
The bow, and thus Antinous, railing,
spake:—
  "Thou worthless vagabond, without a
spark
Of reason, art thou not content to sit
And banquet with the proudest, where no
part

Of all the feast escapes thee, hearing all
That we are saying, which no other
man,
Stranger and beggar, is allowed to hear!
This good wine makes thee foolish, as
wine oft
Makes those who swallow it too greedily,
And drink not with due stint. It mad-
dened once
Eurytion, the famed Centaur, in the halls
Of the large-souled Pirithous. He had
come
Among the Lapithæ, and when inflamed
With wine to madness, in those very halls
Did lawless deeds. The heroes were in-
censed.
They rushed upon him, dragged him
through the porch
And out of doors, and there cut off his
nose
And ears, and he departed, frenzied still,
And bearing in bewilderment of mind
His punishment, whence war arose be-
tween
Centaurs and men; yet surely he had
brought
The evil on himself, when overcome
With wine. Such fearful mischief I
foretell
Will light on thee, if thou shouldst bend
this bow,
Nor canst thou hope for favour here
among
The people. We will send thee speedily,
In a black galley, to King Echetus,
The enemy of human kind, from whom
Thou shalt find no escape. Drink, then,
in peace
Thy wine, and seek no strife with younger
men."
  Then spake the sage Penelope again:
"Truly, Antinous, it becomes thee not,
Nor is it just, to vex the stranger guests
Who seek the palace of Telemachus.
Dost thou, then, think now, should this
stranger bend,
Proud as he is of his great strength of
arm,
The mighty bow that once Ulysses bore,

He leads me hence a bride? No hope of
   that
Is in his heart, and let no one of you
Who banquet here allow a thought like
   that
To vex him; 'tis a thing that cannot be."
   Then to the queen, Eurymachus, the
   son
Of Polybus, replied: "We do not fear,
Sage daughter of Icarius, that this man
Will lead thee hence a bride; it cannot
   be.
We fear the speech of men and women
   both.
The very meanest of the Achaian race
Will say: 'Degenerate men are these, who
   seek
To wed the consort of a glorious chief,
Not one of whom can draw the bow he
   bore;
And now there comes a wandering beg-
   gar-man,
Who draws the bow with ease, and sends
   a shaft
Through all the rings of steel.' Thus will
   they speak,
And this will be to us a cause of shame!"
   And then the sage Penelope rejoined:
"Eurymachus, it cannot be that those
Should earn the general praise who make
   the wealth
Of a most worthy man their spoil, and
   bring
Dishonor on his house. The stranger's
   frame
Is powerful and well knit; he claims to be
Of noble parentage. Now let him take
The bow, and we will see the event; but
   this
I promise, and will make my promise
   good,
If he should bend it,—if Apollo give
To him that glory,—he shall have from
   me
A tunic and a cloak, fair garments both,
And a keen javelin, his defence against
Both dogs and men, a two-edged sword
   besides,
And sandals for his feet, and I engage

To send him whither he desires to go."
   Then spake discreet Telemachus again:
"Mother, in all Achaia there is none
Who has more power than I can claim,
   to grant
Or to deny the bow to whom I will.
No one of those who rule the rugged coast
Of Ithaca, or isle where Elis breeds
Her mares, may interpose to thwart my
   will,
If on the stranger I bestow the bow
To be his own, and bid him take it hence.
Withdraw, O queen, into thy bower;
   direct
Thy household tasks, the distaff and the
   web,
And bid thy maidens speed the work.
   The bow
Belongs to men, and most to me; for
   here,
Within these walls, the authority is mine."
   The queen, astonished, heard him and
   withdrew,
But kept her son's wise sayings in her
   heart.
And then ascending to her bower, among
Her maids, she wept her well-beloved
   lord,
Ulysses, till the blue-eyed Pallas came,
And poured upon her lids the balm of
   sleep.
   Meantime the worthy swineherd bore
   the bow
In hand, and all along the palace-halls
The suitor-crew were chiding him aloud.
And thus an insolent youth among them
   spake:—
   "Thou awkward swineherd, whither
   goest thou
With the curved bow? Thy own fleet
   dogs which thou
Hast reared shall soon devour thee, far
   from men
And midst thy herds of swine, if we
   find grace
With Phœbus and the other deathless
   gods."
   Such were their words; the swineherd
   where he stood

Set down the bow in fear, for many a voice
Called to him in the hall. On the other side
Shouted Telemachus with threatening words:—
"Nay, father, carry on the bow, nor think
To stop at every man's command; lest I,
Though younger than thyself, cast stones at thee,
And chase thee to the fields, for I in strength
Excel thee. Would that I excelled as far
In strength of arm the suitors in these halls,
Then would I roughly through the palace-gates
Drive many who are plotting mischief now."
    He spake, and all with hearty laughter heard
His words, and for their sake allowed their wrath
Against the prince to cool. The swine-herd went
Forward, along the hall, and, drawing near
The wise Ulysses, gave into his hands
The bow; and then he called the nurse aside,
Dame Eurycleia, and bespake her thus:—
"Sage Eurycleia, from Telemachus
I charge thee to make fast the solid doors,
And then, if any of the maids should hear
A groan or other noise of men within,
Let her not issue forth, but silently
Pursue the task in hand, and keep her place."
    He spake, nor were his words in vain. The dame
Made fast the doors of that magnificent hall,
While silently Philœtius hastened forth
And locked the portals of the high-walled court.
A cable of the bark of Byblos lay
Beneath the portico,—it once had served

A galley,—and, with this the herdsman tied
The portals, and returning, took the seat
Whence he had risen, but ever kept his eye
Fixed on his lord. Ulysses, meantime, held
The bow, and, turning it, intently eyed
Side after side, and tried each part in turn,
For fear that worms, while he was far away,
Had pierced the horn. At this, a youth among
The suitors, turning to his neighbor, said:—
    "Lo an inspector and a judge of bows!
Perhaps he has a bow like that at home,
Or else would make one like it. How he shifts
The thing with busy hands from side to side,—
The vagabond, well trained in knavish tricks!"
    Then also said another insolent youth:
"May he in all things be as fortunate
As now, when he shall try to bend that bow!"
    Such was their talk; but when the wary chief
Had poised and shrewdly scanned the mighty bow,
Then, as a singer, skilled to play the harp,
Stretches with ease on its new fastenings
A string, the twisted entrails of a sheep,
Made fast at either end, so easily
Ulysses bent that mighty bow. He took
And drew the cord with his right hand; it twanged
With a clear sound as when a swallow screams.
The suitors were dismayed, and all grew pale.
Jove in loud thunder gave a sign from heaven.
The much-enduring chief, Ulysses, heard
With joy the friendly omen, which the son

Of crafty Saturn sent him. He took up
A winged arrow, that before him lay
Upon a table, drawn; the others still
Were in the quiver's womb; the Greeks
    were yet
To feel them. This he set with care
    against
The middle of the bow, and toward him
    drew
The cord and arrow-notch, just where he
    sat,
And, aiming opposite, let fly the shaft.
He missed no ring at all; from first to
    last
The brass-tipped arrow threaded every
    one.
Then to Telemachus Ulysses said:—
"Telemachus, the stranger sitting here
Hath not disgraced thee. I have neither
    missed
The rings, nor found it hard to bend the
    bow;
Nor has my manly strength decayed, as
    these
Who seek to bring me to contempt pre-
    tend;
And now the hour has come when we pre-
    pare
A supper for the Achaians, while the day
Yet lasts, and after supper the delights
Of song and harp, which nobly grace a
    feast."
    He spake, and nodded to Telemachus,
His well-beloved son, who girded on
His trenchant sword, and took in hand
    his spear,
And, armed with glittering brass for
    battle, came
And took his station by his father's seat.
    —WILLIAM CULLEN BRYANT.

ODYSSEUS AND PENELOPE [1]

[From Book XXIII]

Up to the royal bower the matron went
With an exulting heart, to tell the queen

[1] Used by arrangement with Houghton Mifflin
Company, the authorized publishers.

That her beloved husband was within.
With knees that faltered not, and quick
    light step
She went, and, standing by her mistress,
    said:—
"Awake, Penelope, dear child, and see
With thine own eyes what thou hast
    pined for long.
Ulysses has returned; thy lord is here,
Though late, and he has slain the arro-
    gant crew
Of suitors, who disgraced his house, and
    made
His wealth a spoil, and dared insult his
    son."
    And thus discreet Penelope replied:
"The gods, dear nurse, have made thee
    mad; for they
Have power to change the wisest men to
    fools,
And make the foolish wise, and they
    have warped
Thy mind once sound. How canst thou
    mock me thus,
Amidst my sorrows, with such idle tales?
Why wake me from the pleasant sleep
    that closed
My lids so softly? Never have I slept
So sweetly since Ulysses went from me
To that bad city, which no tongue should
    name.
Go, then; return into the lower rooms.
Had any of my women save thyself
Brought such a message to disturb my
    sleep,
I would have sent her back into the hall
With angry words; thy years are thy
    excuse."
    But Eurycleia, the dear nurse, re-
    joined:
"Nay, my dear child, I mock thee not.
    Most true
It is that thy Ulysses has returned,
And here he is at home, as I have said.
The stranger whom they scoffed at in the
    hall
Is he; and long Telemachus has known
That he was here, but wisely kept from
    all

His father's secret, till he should avenge
Upon those violent men their guilty
   deeds."
   She ended, and her mistress, overjoyed,
Sprang from her couch, embraced the
   aged dame,
And wept, and said to her in winged
   words:—
   "Tell me, dear nurse, and truly, if
   indeed
Ulysses have returned as thou hast said.
How smote he those proud suitors?—he
   alone,
And they so many gathered, in the hall."
   And thus the well-beloved nurse
   replied:
"I saw it not, nor knew of it. I heard
Only the moanings of the slain, while we
The maids, affrighted, sat in a recess
Of that well-vaulted chamber; the firm
   doors
Closed us all in, until at length thy son,
Sent by his father, called me forth. I
   found
Ulysses standing midst the dead that lay
Heaped on each other; everywhere along
The solid pavement. Thou wouldst have
   rejoiced
To see him like a lion with the stains
Of slaughter on him. Now the suitors
   lie
Before the portals of the palace-court,
And he has kindled a great fire, and
   steeps
In smoke the noble hall. He bade me
   come
To call thee. Follow me, that ye may
   give
Your hearts to gladness,—for ye have
   endured
Great sorrows both, and your long-
   cherished hope
Is now fulfilled. He hath returned alive
To his dear home, and finds thee and his
   son
Yet in his palace, and hath terribly
Avenged himself upon the guilty men
Who under his own roof have done him
   wrong."

   Then spake the sage Penelope again:
"Beloved nurse, exult not overmuch,
Nor rashly boast. Well is it known to
   thee,
Were he to come beneath this roof again,
How welcome he would be to all, but
   most
To me and to the son to whom we gave
His being. Yet thy tidings are not true.
Some one of the immortals must have
   slain
The arrogant suitors, angry to behold
Their foul injustice and their many
   crimes;
For no respect had they for mortal man,
Good he might be, or bad, whome'er they
   met;
And therefore have they made an evil
   end.
But my Ulysses must have perished far
From Ithaca, cut off from his return."
   Then Eurycleia, the dear nurse, re-
   joined:
"What words are these, my child, that
   pass thy lips?
Sayst thou, then, that thy husband, who
   now stands
Upon thy hearthstone, never will return?
O slow of faith! but thou wert ever
   thus.
Come, then, I give a certain proof. I
   saw
Myself, when he was at the bath, the
   scar
Left on him by the white tusk of a boar,
And would have told thee, but he laid
   his hands
Upon my mouth, and would not suffer
   me
To bear the tidings, such his forecast
   was.
Now follow me; I give my life in pledge.
If I deceive thee, slay me ruthlessly."
   Then spake discreet Penelope again:
"Dear nurse, though thou in many things
   art wise,
Think not to scan the counsels of the
   gods,
Who live forever. Yet will we descend,

And meet my son, and look upon the
   slain,
And see the avenger by whose hand they
   fell."
   She spake, and from the royal bower
      went down,
Uncertain whether she should stand aloof
And question there her lord, or haste to
   him
And clasp his hands in hers and kiss his
   brow.
But having passed the threshold of hewn
   stone,
Entering she took her seat right opposite
Ulysses, in the full glow of the fire,
Against the other wall. Ulysses sat
Beside a lofty column with his eyes
Cast down, and waiting for his high-born
   wife
To speak when she had seen him. Long
   she sat
In silence, for amazement overpowered
Her senses. Sometimes, looking in his
   eyes,
She saw her husband there, and then
   again
Clad in those sordid weeds, she knew
   him not.
Then spake Telemachus, and chid her
   thus:—
   "Mother, unfeeling mother! hard of
      heart
Art thou; how else couldst thou remain
   aloof?
How keep from taking, at my father's
   side,
Thy place, to talk with him, and question
   him?
No other wife could bring herself to bear
Such distance from a husband, just
   returned
After long hardships, in the twentieth
   year
Of absence, to his native land and her.
Mother! thy heart is harder than a
   stone."
   And thus the sage Penelope replied:
"Dear child, my faculties are over-
   powered

With wonder, and I cannot question him,
Nor even speak to him, nor fix my looks
Upon his face. But if it be indeed
Ulysses, and he have returned, we soon
Shall know each other; there are tokens
   known
To both of us, to none but him and me."
   She ended, and the much-enduring
      chief
Ulysses, smiling at her words, bespake
Telemachus at once, in winged words:—
   "Suffer thy mother, O Telemachus,
To prove me; she will know me better
   soon.
My looks are sordid, and my limbs are
   wrapped
In tattered raiment, therefore she does
   think
Meanly of me, and cannot willingly
Believe that I am he. But let us now
Consider what most wisely may be
   done.
He who hath slain, among a tribe of
   men,
A single one with few to avenge his
   death,
Flees from his kindred and his native
   land;
But we have slain the champions of the
   realm,
The flower of all the youth of Ithaca.
Therefore, I pray thee, think what shall
   be done."
   And then discreet Telemachus replied:
"Look thou to that, dear father; for
   they say
That thou of all mankind wert wont to
   give
The wisest counsels. None of mortal
   birth
In this was deemed thy peer. We follow
   thee
With cheerful hearts; nor will our cour-
   age fail,
I think, in aught that lies within our
   power."
   Ulysses, the sagacious, answered thus:
"Then will I tell thee what I deem most
   wise.

First take the bath, and then array
  yourselves
In tunics, bid the palace-maidens choose
Fresh garments; let the godlike bard,
  who bears
The clear-toned harp, be leader, and
  strike up
A melody to prompt the festive dance,
That all may say who hear it from
  without,—
Whether the passers by or dwellers
  near,—
'It is a wedding.' Else throughout the
  land
The rumor of the slaughter we have
  wrought
Among the suitors may have spread
  before
We reach our wooded farm, and there
  consult
Beneath the guidance of Olympian Jove."
  He spake; they hearkened and obeyed.
    They took
The bath, and then they put their gar-
  ments on.
The maids arrayed themselves; the god-
  like bard
Took the curved harp, and woke in all
  the love
Of melody, and of the graceful dance.
The spacious pile resounded to the steps
Of men and stately women in their mirth,
And one who stood without was heard to
  say:—
  "Some one, no doubt, has made the
    long-wooed queen
His bride at last; a worthless woman
  she,
Who could not, for the husband of her
  youth,
Keep his fair palace till he came again."
  Such words were said, but they who
    uttered them
Knew little what had passed. Eurynome,
The matron of the palace, meantime took
Magnanimous Ulysses to the bath
In his own dwelling, smoothed his limbs
  with oil,
And threw a gorgeous mantle over him

And tunic. Pallas on the hero's head
Shed grace and majesty; she made him
  seem
Taller and statelier, made his locks flow
  down
In curls like blossoms of the hyacinth,
As when a workman skilled in many arts,
And taught by Pallas and Minerva,
  twines
A golden border round the silver mass,
A glorious work; so did the goddess shed
Grace o'er his face and form. So from
  the bath
He stepped, like one of the immortals,
  took
The seat from which he rose, right
  opposite
Penelope, and thus addressed the
  queen:—
  "Lady, the dwellers of the Olympian
    heights
Have given thee an impenetrable heart
Beyond all other women. Sure I am,
No other wife could bring herself to
  bear
Such distance from a husband just re-
  turned
After long hardships, in the twentieth
  year
Of absence, to his native land and her.
Come, nurse, prepare a bed, where by
  myself
I may lie down; an iron heart is hers."
  To this the sage Penelope replied:
"Nay, sir, 'tis not through pride or
  disregard,
Or through excess of wonder, that I act
Thus toward thee. Well do I remember
  thee
As thou wert in the day when thy good
  ship
Bore thee from Ithaca. Bestir thyself,
Dame Eurycleia, and make up with care
A bed without the chamber, which he
  framed
With his own hands; bear out the mas-
  sive bed,
And lay upon it seemly coverings,
Fleeces and mantles for his nightly rest."

She spake to try her husband; but,
displeased,
Ulysses answered thus his virtuous
queen:—
"O woman, thou hast said unwelcome
words.
Who hath displaced my bed? That task
were hard
For long-experienced hands, unless some
god
Hath come to shift its place. No living
man,
Even in his prime of years, could easily
Have moved it, for in that elaborate
work
There was a mystery; it was I myself
Who shaped it, no one else. Within my
court
There grew an olive-tree with full-leaved
boughs,
A tall and flourishing tree; its massive
stem
Was like a column. Round it I built up
A chamber with cemented stones until
The walls were finished; then I framed
a roof
Above it, and put on the well-glued doors
Close fitting. Next I lopped the full-
leaved boughs,
And, cutting off the trunk above the
root,
Smoothed well the stump with tools, and
made of it
A post to bear the couch. I bored the
wood
With wimbles, placed it on the frame,
and carved
The work till it was done, inlaying it
With silver, gold, and ivory. I stretched
Upon it thongs of oxhide brightly dyed
In purple. Now, O wife, I cannot know
Whether my bed remains as then it was,
Or whether some one from the root has
hewn
The olive trunk, and moved it from its
place."
    He spake, and her knees faltered and
her heart
Was melted as she heard her lord recount

The tokens all so truly; and she wept,
And rose, and ran to him, and flung her
arms
About his neck, and kissed his brow, and
said:—
"Ulysses, look not on me angrily,
Thou who in other things art wise above
All other men. The gods have made our
lot
A hard one, jealous lest we should have
passed
Our youth together happily, and thus
Have reached old age. I pray, be not
incensed,
Nor take it ill that I embraced thee
not
As soon as I beheld thee, for my heart
Has ever trembled lest some one who
comes
Into this isle should cozen me with
words;
And they who practise fraud are num-
berless.
The Argive Helen, child of Jupiter,
Would ne'er have listened to a stranger's
suit
And loved him, had she known that in
the years
To come the warlike Greeks would bring
her back
To her own land. It was a deity
Who prompted her to that foul wrong.
Her thought
Was never of the great calamity
Which followed, and which brought such
woe on us.
But now, since thou, by tokens clear
and true,
Hast spoken of our bed, which human
eye
Has never seen save mine and thine, and
those
Of one handmaiden only, Actoris,—
Her whom my father gave me when I
came
To this thy palace, and who kept the
door
Of our close chamber,—thou hast won
my mind

To full belief, though hard it was to
   win."
  She spake, and he was moved to tears;
   he wept
As in his arms he held his dearly loved
And faithful wife. As welcome as the
   land
To those who swim the deep, of whose
   stout bark
Neptune has made a wreck amidst the
   waves,
Tossed by the billow and the blast, and
   few
Are those who from the hoary ocean
   reach
The shore, their limbs all crested with
   the brine,
These gladly climb the sea-beach, and
   are safe,—
So welcome was her husband to her eyes.
Nor would her fair white arms release his
   neck,
And there would rosy-fingered Morn
   have found
Both weeping, but the blue-eyed Pallas
   planned
That thus it should not be; she stayed
   the night
When near its close, and held the golden
   Morn
Long in the ocean deeps, nor suffered her
To yoke her steeds that bring the light
   to men,—
Lampas and Phaethon, swift steeds that
   bear
  The Morning on her way. Ulysses
   then,
The man of forecast, thus bespake his
   queen:—
  "Not yet, O wife, have we attained the
   close
Of all our labors. One remains which
   yet
I must achieve, toilsome, and measure-
   less
In difficulty; for so prophesied
The spirit of Tiresias, on the day
When to the abode of Pluto I went down
To ask the seer concerning the return

Of my companions, and my own. But
   now
Seek we our couch, dear wife, that, softly
   laid,
We may refresh ourselves with welcome
   sleep."
  Then spake in turn the sage Penelope:
"Whenever thou desirest it thy couch
Shall be made ready, since the gods
   vouchsafe
To bring thee back into thy pleasant
   home
And to thy native land. But now that
   thou
Hast spoken it, and that some deity
Is prompting thee, declare what this new
   task
May be. Hereafter I shall hear of it,
No doubt, nor were it worse to know it
   now."
Ulysses, the sagacious, answered thus:
"Dear wife, why wilt thou ask? why
   press me thus?
Yet will I tell thee truly, nor will keep
Aught from thee, though thou wilt not
   gladly hear,
Nor I relate. Tiresias bade me pass
Through city after city, till I found
A people who know not the sea, nor eat
Their food with salt, who never yet
   beheld
The red-prowed galley, nor the shapely
   oars,
Which are the wings of ships. And this
   plain sign
He gave, nor will I keep it back from
   thee,
That when another traveller whom I
   meet
Shall say it is a winnowing-fan I bear
On my stout shoulder, there he bade me
   plant
The oar upright in earth, and offer up
To monarch Neptune there a ram, a bull,
And sturdy boar, and then, returning
   home,
Burn hallowed hecatombs to all the gods
Who dwell in the broad heaven, each
   one in turn.

At last will death come over me, afar
From ocean, such a death as peacefully
Shall take me off in a serene old age,
Amid a people prosperous and content.
All this, the prophet said, will come to
    pass."
    And then the sage Penelope rejoined:
"If thus the immortals make thy later
    age
The happier, there is hope that thou
    wilt find
Escape from evil in the years to come."
    So talked they with each other. Mean-
time went
Eurynome, attended by the nurse,
And in the light of blazing torches
    dressed
With soft fresh drapery a bed; and when
Their busy hands had made it full and
    high,
The aged dame withdrew to take her
    rest
In her own chamber, while Eurynome,
Who kept the royal bower, upheld a
    torch
And thither led the pair, and, when they
    both
Were in the chamber, went her way.
    They took
Their place delighted in the ancient bed.
The prince, the herdsman, and the swine-
    herd ceased
Meantime to tread the dance, and bade
    the maids
Cease also, and within the palace-rooms
Dark with night's shadow, sought their
    place of rest.
Then came the time of pleasant mutual
    talk,
In which the noblest among women spake
Of wrongs endured beneath her roof from
    those
Who came to woo her,—an insatiate
    crew,—
Who made of beeves and fatlings of the
    flock
Large slaughter, and drained many a
    wine-cask dry.
Then nobly born Ulysses told what woes

His valor brought on other men; what
    toils
And suffering he had borne; he told her
    all,
And she, delighted, heard him, nor did
    sleep
Light on her eyelids till his tale was
    done.
    And first he told her how he overcame
The people of Ciconia; how he passed
Thence to the rich fields of the race who
    feed
Upon the lotus; what the Cyclops did,
And how upon the Cyclops he avenged
The death of his brave comrades, whom
    the wretch
Had piteously slaughtered and devoured.
And how he came to Æolus, and found
A friendly welcome, and was sent by him
Upon his voyage; yet 'twas not his fate
To reach his native land; a tempest
    caught
His fleet, and far across the fishy deep
Bore him away, lamenting bitterly.
And how he landed at Telepylus,
Among the Læstrigonians, who destroyed
His ships and warlike comrades, he alone
In his black ship escaping. Then he told
Of Circe, her deceit and many arts,
And how he went to Pluto's dismal realm
In his good galley, to consult the soul
Of him of Thebes, Tiresias, and beheld
All his lost comrades and his mother,—
    her
Who brought him forth, and trained him
    when a child.
And how he heard the Sirens afterward,
And how he came upon the wandering
    rocks,
The terrible Charybdis, and the crags
Of Scylla,—which no man had ever
    passed
In safety; how his comrades slew for
    food
The oxen of the Sun; how Jupiter,
The Thunderer, with a bolt of fire from
    heaven
Smote his swift bark; and how his gal-
    lant crew

All perished, he alone escaped with life.
And how he reached Ogygia's isle, he
 told,
And met the nymph Calypso, who de-
 sired
That he would be her husband, and long
 time
Detained and fed him in her vaulted
 grot,
And promised that he ne'er should die,
 nor know
Decay of age, through all the days to
 come;
Yet moved she not the purpose of his
 heart.
And how he next through many hard-
 ships came
To the Phæacians, and they welcomed
 him
And honored him as if he were a god,
And to his native country in a bark
Sent him with ample gifts of brass and
 gold
And raiment. As he uttered this last
 word,
Sleep softly overcame him; all his limbs
Lay loose in rest, and all his cares were
 calmed.
  The blue-eyed Pallas had yet new
 designs;
And when she deemed Ulysses was re-
 freshed
With rest and sleep, in that accustomed
 bed,
She called the Morning, daughter of the
 Dawn,
To rise from ocean in her car of gold,
And shed her light on men. Ulysses
 rose
From his soft couch, and thus enjoined
 his spouse:—
  "O wife! enough of misery have we
 borne
Already,—thou in weeping for my long
Unhappy absence,—I for years withheld
By Jupiter and all the other gods

From my return to this dear land,
 although
I pined for home. Now since upon this
 couch
We take the place so earnestly desired,
Take thou the charge of all that I possess
Here in the palace. For the herds and
 flocks
Which those high-handed suitors have
 devoured,
I shall seize many others as a spoil;
The rest the Greeks will bring me, till
 my stalls
Are filled again. I hasten to my farm
Embowered in trees, to greet the aged
 man
My excellent father, who continually
Grieves for me. Prudent as thou art, I
 give
This charge; a rumor, with the rising
 sun,
Will quickly go abroad that I have slain
The suitors in the palace. Now with-
 draw,
Thou and thy maidens, to the upper
 room,
And sit and look not forth, nor ask of
 aught."
  So spake the chief, and on his shoul-
 ders braced
His glorious armor. Then he called his
 son,
The herdsman, and the swineherd,
 bidding them
To take in hand their weapons. They
 obeyed,
And, having armed themselves in brass,
 they threw
The portals open. As they all went
 forth,
Ulysses led the way. The early light
Was on the earth, but Pallas, shrouding
 them
In darkness, led them quickly through
 the town.
                    —WILLIAM CULLEN BRYANT.

III. THE EPIC OF EVERYDAY LIFE: HESIOD'S WORKS AND DAYS

Hesiod, the Man of Ascra, a village in Bœotia, flourished about 800 B.C. He was the son of a small landholder, whose toil in the fields taught him the dignity of labor and filled him with a childlike love of the natural world about him. The loss of a suit against his brother concerning a division of inherited property, though it kindled in his heart a spirit of bitterness, was the impulse to an examination into the real values of life. His bitterness expressed itself in satiric attacks and in a general pessimism which pronounced the world a gloomy place and the gods hard masters. His reflection led to the glorification of the things of the spirit, to an abiding faith that good would ultimately prevail, and to the preaching of thrift, economy, labor, order, as the way to bring about this desired end.

He employed the epic form, but gave it a new direction. It was no longer merely a story of great deeds sung for purposes of entertainment, but was designed to instruct the common man in the ordinary pursuits of life. The two important books ascribed to him are the *Works and Days* and the *Theogony*. The theme of the former is the presence of evil in the world and the escape from it through industry and toil. The *Theogony*, a systematic summary of the stories about the gods current in Hesiod's time, groups the various divinities not according to their deeds and powers but according to their descent, so that the unifying principle is genealogy.

PANDORA'S BOX

The myth of Pandora is an allegory on the origin of evil.

"Oh, son of Japhet!" with indignant heart,
Spake the Cloud-gatherer: "Oh, unmatched in art!
Exultest thou in this the flame retrieved,
And dost thou triumph in the god deceived?

But thou, with the posterity of man,
Shalt rue the fraud whence mightier ills began:
I will send evil for thy stealthy fire,
An ill which all shall love, and all desire."
　The Sire who rules the earth and sways the pole
Had said, and laughter filled his secret soul:
He bade famed Vulcan with the speed of thought
Mould plastic clay with tempering waters wrought:
Inform with voice of man the murmuring tongue;
The limbs with man's elastic vigour strung;
The aspect fair as goddesses above,
A virgin's likeness with the brows of love.
He bade Minerva teach the skill, that sheds
A thousand colours in the gliding threads:
Bade lovely Venus breathe around her face
The charm of air, the witchery of grace:
Infuse corroding pangs of keen desire,
And cares that trick the form with pranked attire:
Bade Hermes last implant the craft refined
Of thievish manners and a shameless mind.
　He gives command; th' inferior powers obey:
The crippled artist moulds the tempered clay:
By Jove's design a maid's coy image rose:
The zone, the dress, Minerva's hands dispose:
Adored persuasion, and the Graces young,
With chains of gold her shapely person hung:

Round her smooth brow the beauteous-
  tressed Hours
A garland twined of spring's purpureal
  flowers:
The whole, Minerva with adjusting art
Forms to her shape and fits to every
  part.
Last by the counsels of deep-thundering
  Jove,
The Argicide, his herald from above,
Adds thievish manners, adds insidious
  lies,
And prattled speech of sprightly rail-
  leries:
Then by the wise interpreter of heaven
The name Pandora to the maid was
  given:
Since all in heaven conferred their gifts
  to charm,
For man's inventive race, this beauteous
  harm.
  When now the Sire had formed this
    mischief fair,
He bade heaven's messenger convey
  through air
To Epimetheus' hands th' inextricable
  snare:
Nor he recalled within his heedless
  thought
The warning lesson by Prometheus
  taught:
That he disclaim each present from the
  skies,
And straight restore, lest ill to man arise:
But he received; and conscious knew too
  late
Th' insidious gift, and felt the curse of
  fate.
  On earth of yore the sons of men
    abode,
From evil free and labour's galling load:
Free from diseases that with racking rage
Precipitate the pale decline of age.
Now swift the days of manhood haste
  away,
And misery's pressure turns the temples
  gray.
The woman's hands an ample casket
  bear;

She lifts the lid; she scatters ills in air.
Within th' unbroken vase Hope sole
  remained,
Beneath the vessel's rim from flight
  detained:
The maid, by counsels of cloud-gathering
  Jove,
The coffer sealed and dropped the lid
  above.
Issued the rest in quick dispersion hurled,
And woes innumerous roamed the breath-
  ing world:
With ills the land is rife, with ills the sea,
Diseases haunt our frail humanity:
Through noon, through night on casual
  wing they glide,
Silent, a voice the Power all-wise denied.
Thus mayst thou not elude th' omniscient
  mind.
                              —C. A. ELTON.

THE FIVE AGES OF MAN

Here is traced the gradual increase of
evil through the several successive stages
in the decline of man.

  Now if thy thoughts be to my speech
    inclined,
I in brief phrase would other law impart
Wisely and well: thou, grave it on thy
  heart.
  When gods alike and mortals rose to
    birth,
A golden race th' immortals formed on
  earth
Of many languaged men: they lived of
  old
When Saturn reigned in heaven, an age
  of gold.
Like gods they lived, with calm un-
  troubled mind;
Free from the toil and anguish of our
  kind:
Nor e'er decrepid age misshaped their
  frame,
The hand's, the foot's proportions still
  the same.

Strangers to ill, their lives in feasts
   flowed by:
Wealthy in flocks; dear to the blest on
   high:
Dying they sank in sleep, nor seemed to
   die.
Theirs was each good; the life-sustaining
   soil
Yielded its copious fruits, unbribed by
   toil:
They with abundant goods midst quiet
   lands
All willing shared the gatherings of their
   hands.
When earth's dark womb had closed this
   race around,
High Jove as dæmons raised them from
   the ground.
Earth-wandering spirits they their charge
   began,
The ministers of good, and guards of
   man.
Mantled with mist of darkling air they
   glide,
And compass earth, and pass on every
   side:
And mark with earnest vigilance of
   eyes
Where just deeds live, or crooked wrongs
   arise:
Their kingly state; and, delegate from
   heaven,
By their vicarious hands the wealth of
   fields is given.
   The gods then formed a second race
   of man,
Degenerate far; and silver years began.
Unlike the mortals of a golden kind:
Unlike in frame of limbs and mould of
   mind.
Yet still a hundred years beheld the boy
Beneath the mother's roof, her infant
   joy;
All tender and unformed: but when the
   flower
Of manhood bloomed, it withered in an
   hour.
Their frantic follies wrought them pain
   and woe:

Nor mutual outrage could their hands
   forego:
Nor would they serve the gods: nor altars
   raise
That in just cities shed their holy blaze.
Them angry Jove ingulfed; who dared
   refuse
The gods their glory and their sacred
   dues:
Yet named the second-blest in earth they
   lie,
And second honours grace their memory.
   The Sire of heaven and earth created
   then
A race, the third of many-languaged men.
Unlike the silver they: of brazen mould:
With ashen war-spears terrible and bold:
Their thoughts were bent on violence
   alone,
The deeds of battle and the dying groan.
Bloody their feasts, with wheaten food
   unblest:
Of adamant was each unyielding breast.
Huge, nerved with strength each hardy
   giant stands,
And mocks approach with unresisted
   hands:
Their mansions, implements, and armour
   shine
In brass; dark iron slept within the mine.
They by each other's hands inglorious
   fell,
In freezing darkness plunged, the house
   of hell:
Fierce though they were, their mortal
   course was run;
Death gloomy seized, and snatched them
   from the sun.
   Them when th' abyss had covered from
   the skies,
Lo! the fourth age on nurturing earth
   arise:
Jove formed the race a better, juster
   line;
A race of heroes and of stamp divine:
Lights of the age that rose before our
   own;
As demi-gods o'er earth's wide regions
   known.

Yet these dread battle hurried to their
end:
Some where the seven-fold gates of
Thebes ascend:
The Cadmian realm: where they with
fatal might
Strove for the flocks of Œdipus in fight.
Some war in navies led to Troy's far
shore;
O'er the great space of sea their course
they bore;
For sake of Helen with the beauteous
hair:
And death for Helen's sake o'erwhelmed
them there.
Them on earth's utmost verge the god
assigned
A life, a seat, distinct from human kind:
Beside the deepening whirlpools of the
main,
In those blest isles where Saturn holds
his reign,
Apart from Heaven's immortals: calm
they share
A rest unsullied by the clouds of care:
And yearly thrice with sweet luxuriance
crowned
Springs the ripe harvest from the teeming
ground.
    Oh would that nature had denied me
birth
Midst this fifth race; this iron age of
earth:
That long before within the grave I
lay,
Or long hereafter could behold the day!
Corrupt the race, with toils and griefs
opprest,
Nor day nor night can yield a pause of
rest.
Still do the gods a weight of care bestow,
Though still some good is mingled with
the woe.
Jove on this race of many-languaged
man,
Speeds the swift ruin which but slow
began·
For scarcely spring they to the light of
day

Ere age untimely strews their temples
gray.
No fathers in the sons their features
trace:
The sons reflect no more the father's
face:
The host with kindness greets his guest
no more,
And friends and brethren love not as of
yore.
Reckless of heaven's revenge, the sons
behold
The hoary parents wax too swiftly old:
And impious point the keen dishonouring
tongue
With hard reproofs and bitter mockeries
hung:
Nor grateful in declining age repay
The nurturing fondness of their better
day.
Now man's right hand is law: for spoil
they wait,
And lay their mutual cities desolate:
Unhonoured he, by whom his oath is
feared,
Nor are the good beloved, the just
revered.
With favour graced the evil-doer stands,
Nor curbs with shame nor equity his
hands:
With crooked slanders wounds the vir-
tuous man,
And stamps with perjury what hate
began.
Lo! ill-rejoicing Envy, winged with lies,
Scattering calumnious rumours as she
flies,
The steps of miserable men pursue
With haggard aspect, blasting to the
view,
Till those fair forms in snowy raiment
bright
Leave the broad earth and heaven-ward
soar from sight:
Justice and Modesty from mortals driven,
Rise to th' immortal family of heaven:
Dread sorrows to forsaken man remain;
No cure of ills: no remedy of pain.
                     —C. A. ELTON.

OF PLANTING

The lesson to be learned from the realization of evil is work. The latter part of the poem is concerned with advice and precepts on agriculture.

When, Atlas-born, the Pleiad stars arise
Before the sun above the dawning skies,
'Tis time to reap; and when they sink below
The morn-illumined west, 'tis time to sow.
Know too they set, immerged into the sun,
While forty days entire their circle run;
And with the lapse of the revolving year,
When sharpened is the sickle, re-appear.
Law of the fields, and known to every swain
Who turns the fallow soil beside the main;
Or who, remote from billowy ocean's gales,
Tills the rich glebe of inland-winding vales.
  Plough naked still, and naked sow the soil,
And naked reap; if kindly to thy toil
Thou hope to gather all that Ceres yields,
And view thy crops in season crown the fields;
Lest thou to strangers' gates penurious rove,
And every needy effort fruitless prove:
E'en as to me thou cam'st; but hope no more
That I shall give or lend thee of my store.
Oh foolish Perses! be the labours thine
Which the good gods to earthly man assign;
Lest with thy spouse, thy babes, thou vagrant ply,
And sorrowing crave those alms which all deny.
Twice may thy plaints benignant favour gain,
And haply thrice may not be poured in vain;
If still persisting plead thy wearying prayer,
Thy words are nought, thy eloquence is air.
Did exhortation move, the thought should be,
From debt releasement, days from hunger free.
  A house, a woman, and a steer provide,
Thy slave to tend the cows, but not thy bride.
Within let all fit implements abound,
Lest with refused entreaty wandering round,
Thy wants still press, the season glide away,
And thou with scanted labour mourn the day.
Thy task defer not till the morn arise,
Or the third sun th' unfinished work surprise.
The idler never shall his garners fill,
Nor he that still defers and lingers still.
Lo! diligence can prosper every toil;
The loiterer strives with loss and execrates the soil.
  When rests the keen strength of th' o'erpowering sun
From heat that made the pores in rivers run;
When rushes in fresh rains autumnal Jove,
And man's unburthened limbs now lighter move;
For now the star of day with transient light
Rolls o'er our heads and joys in longer night;
When from the worm the forest boles are sound,
Trees bud no more, but earthward cast around
Their withering foliage, then remember well
The timely labour, and thy timber fell.
Hew from the wood a timber of three feet;

Three cubits may the pestle's length complete;
Seven feet the fittest axle-tree extends;
If eight the log, the eighth a mallet lends.
Cleave many curved blocks thy wheel to round,
And let three spans its outmost orbit bound;
Whereon slow-rolling thy suspended wain,
Ten spans in breadth, may traverse firm the plain.
　If hill or field supply a holm-oak bough
Of bending figure like the downward plough,
Bear it away: this durable remains
While the strong steers in ridges cleave the plains:
If with fine nails thy artist join the whole,
Affix the share-beam, and adapt the pole.
　Two ploughs provide, on household works intent,
This art-compacted, that of native bent:
A prudent fore-thought: one may crashing fail,
The other instant yoked, shall prompt avail.
Of elm or bay the draught-pole firm endures,
The plough-tail holm, the share-beam oak secures.
　Two males procure: be nine their sum of years:
Then hale and strong for toil the sturdy steers:
Nor shall they head-strong-struggling spurn the soil,
And snap the plough and mar th' unfinished toil.
In forty's prime thy ploughman: one with bread
Of four-squared loaf in double portions fed.
He steadily shall cut the furrow true,
Nor towards his fellows glance a rambling view:
Still on his task intent: a stripling throws

Heedless the seed, and in one furrow strows
The lavish handful twice: while wistful stray
His longing thoughts to comrades far away.
　Mark yearly when among the clouds on high
Thou hear'st the shrill crane's migratory cry,
　Of ploughing-time the sign and wintry rains:
Care gnaws his heart who destitute remains
Of the fit yoke: for then the season falls
To feed thy horned steers within their stalls.
Easy to speak the word, "beseech thee friend!
Thy wagon and thy yoke of oxen lend:"
Easy the prompt refusal; "nay, but I
Have need of oxen, and their work is nigh."
Rich in his own conceit, he then too late
May think to rear the waggon's timbered weight:
Fool! nor yet knows the complicated frame
A hundred seasoned blocks may fitly claim:
These let thy timely care provide before,
And pile beneath thy roof the ready store.
　Improve the season: to the plough apply
Both thou and thine; and toil in wet and dry:
Haste to the field with break of glimmering morn,
That so thy grounds may wave with thickening corn.
　In spring upturn the glebe: and break again
With summer tilth the iterated plain,
It shall not mock thy hopes: be last thy toil,
Raised in light ridge, to sow the fallowed soil:

The fallowed soil bids execration fly,
And brightens with content the infant's eye.
   Jove subterrene, chaste Ceres claim thy vow,
When grasping first the handle of the plough,
O'er thy broad oxen's backs thy quickening hand
With lifted stroke lets fall the goading wand;
Whilst yoked and harnessed by the fastening thong,
They slowly drag the draught-pole's length along.
So shall the sacred gifts of earth appear,
And ripe luxuriance clothe the plenteous ear.
   A boy should tread thy steps: with rake o'erlay
The buried seed, and scare the birds away:
(Good is the apt economy of things,
While evil management its mischief brings:)
Thus, if aerial Jove thy cares befriend,
And crown thy tillage with a prosperous end,
Shall the rich ear in fulness of its grain
Nod on the stalk and bend it to the plain.
So shalt thou sweep the spider's films away,
That round thy hollow bins lie hid from day:
I ween, rejoicing in the foodful stores
Obtained at length, and laid within thy doors:
For plenteousness shall glad thee through the year
Till the white blossoms of the spring appear:
Nor thou on others' heaps a gazer be,
But others owe their borrowed store to thee.
   If, ill-advised, thou turn the genial plains
His wintry tropic when the sun attains;

Thou, then, may'st reap, and idle sit between:
Mocking thy gripe the meagre stalks are seen:
Whilst, little joyful, gather'st thou in bands
The corn whose chaffy dust bestrews thy hands.
In one scant basket shall thy harvest lie,
And few shall pass thee, then, with honouring eye.
Now thus, now otherwise is Jove's design;
To men inscrutable the ways divine:
But if thou late upturn the furrowed field,
One happy chance a remedy may yield.
O'er the wide earth when men the cuckoo hear
From spreading oak-leaves first delight their ear,
Three days and nights let heaven in ceaseless rains
Deep as thy ox's hoof o'erflow the plains;
So shall an equal crop thy time repair
With his who earlier launched the shining share.
Lay all to heart: nor let the blossomed hours
Of spring escape thee; nor the timely showers.
   Pass by the brazier's forge where loiterers meet,
Nor saunter in the portico's thronged heat;
When in the wintry season rigid cold
Invades the limbs and binds them in its hold,
Lo! then th' industrious man with thriving store
Improves his household management the more:
And this do thou: lest intricate distress
Of winter seize, and needy cares oppress:
Lest, famine-smitten, thou, at length, be seen
To gripe thy tumid foot with hand from hunger lean.
Pampering his empty hopes, yet needing food,

On ill designs behold the idler brood:
Sit in the crowded portico and feed
On that ill hope, while starving with his
　　need.

Thou in mid-summer to thy labourers cry,
"Make now your nests," for summer
　　hours will fly.
　　　　　　　　　　—C. A. ELTON.

IV. THE EPIC OF THE GODS: HESIOD'S THEOGONY

THE BATTLE OF THE TITANS

The battle of the Titans represents the
struggle for mastery between the generation that was born of Heaven and Earth
on the one hand and Zeus the son of
Cronos on the other.

When Heaven their sire 'gainst Cottus,
　　Briareus,
And Gyges, felt his moody anger chafe
Within him, sore amazed with that their
　　strength
Immeasurable, their aspect fierce, and
　　bulk
Gigantic, with a chain of iron force
He bound them down; and fixed their
　　dwelling-place
Beneath the spacious ground: beneath
　　the ground
They dwelt in pain and durance: in th'
　　abyss
There sitting, where earth's utmost
　　bound'ries end.
Full long oppressed with mighty grief of
　　heart
They brooded o'er their woes: but them
　　did Jove
Saturnian, and those other deathless gods
Whom fair-haired Rhea bare to Saturn's
　　love,
By policy of Earth, lead forth again
To light. For she successive all things
　　told:
How with the giant brethren they should
　　win
Conquest and splendid glory. Long they
　　fought
With toil soul-harrowing: they the deities
Titanic and Saturnian: each to each

Opposed, in valour of promiscuous war.
From Orthrys' lofty summit warred the
　　host
Of glorious Titans: from Olympus they,
The band of gift-dispensing deities
Whom fair-haired Rhea bore to Saturn's
　　love.
So waged they war soul-harrowing: each
　　with each
Ten years and more the furious battle
　　joined,
Unintermitted: nor to either host
Was issue of stern strife or end: alike
Did either stretch the limit of the war.
　　But now when Jove had set before his
　　powers
All things befitting; the repast of gods;
The nectar and ambrosia, in each breast
The heroic spirit kindled: and now all
With nectar and with sweet ambrosia
　　filled,
Thus spake the father of the gods and
　　men:
"Hear me! illustrious race of Earth and
　　Heaven!
That what the spirit in my bosom
　　prompts
I now may utter. Long, and day by day
Confronting each the other, we have
　　fought
For conquest and dominion: Titan gods,
And we the seed of Saturn. Still do ye,
Fronting the Titans in funereal war,
Show mighty strength: invulnerable
　　hands:
Remembering that mild friendship, and
　　those pangs
Remembering, when ye trod the upward
　　way

Back to the light: and by our counsels broke
The burthening chain, and left the murky gloom."
  He spake: and Cottus brave of soul replied:
"Oh Jove august! not darkly hast thou said:
Nor know we not how excellent thou art
In counsel and in knowledge: thou hast been
Deliverer of immortals from a curse
Of horror: by thy wisdom have we risen,
Oh kingly son of Saturn! from dark gloom
And bitter bonds, unhoping of relief.
Then with persisting spirit and device
Of prudent warfare, shall we still assert
Thy empire midst the fearful fray, and still
In hardy conflict brave the Titan foe."
  He said: the gods, the givers of all good,
Heard with acclaim: nor ever till that hour
So burned each breast with ardor to destroy.
All on that day stirred up the mighty strife,
Female and male: Titanic gods, and sons
And daughters of old Saturn; and that band
Of giant brethren, whom, from forth th' abyss
Of darkness under earth, deliverer Jove
Sent up to light: grim forms and strong, with force
Gigantic: arms of hundred-handed gripe
Burst from their shoulders: fifty heads upsprang,
Cresting their muscular limbs. They thus opposed
In dreadful conflict 'gainst the Titans stood,
In all their sinewy hands wielding aloft
Precipitous rocks. On th' other side, alert
The Titan phalanx closed: then hands of strength
Joined prowess, and showed forth the works of war.
Th' immeasurable sea tremendous dashed
With roaring; earth re-echoed; the broad heaven
Groaned shattering: vast Olympus reeled throughout
Down to its rooted base beneath the rush
Of those immortals: the dark chasm of hell
Was shaken with trembling, with the tramp
Of hollow footsteps and strong battle-strokes,
And measureless uproar of wild pursuit.
So they against each other through the air
Hurled intermixed their weapons, scattering groans
Where'er they fell. The voice of armies rose
With rallying shout through the starred firmament,
And with a mighty war-cry both the hosts
Encountering closed. Nor longer then did Jove
Curb down his force; but sudden in his soul
There grew dilated strength, and it was filled
With his omnipotence: his whole of might
Broke from him, and the godhead rushed abroad.
The vaulted sky, the mount Olympus, flashed
With his continual presence; for he passed
Incessant forth, and lightened where he trod.
Thrown from his nervous grasp the lightnings flew
Reiterated swift; the whirling flash
Cast sacred splendour, and the thunder-bolt
Fell. Then on every side the foodful earth
Roared in the burning flame, and far and near

The trackless depth of forests crashed
with fire.
Yea—the broad earth burned red, the
floods of Nile
Glowed, and the desert waters of the
sea.
Round and around the Titans' earthy
forms
Rolled the hot vapour, and on fiery surge
Streamed upward, swathing in one bound-
less blaze
The purer air of heaven. Keen rushed
the light
In quivering splendour from the writhen
flash:
Strong though they were, intolerable
smote
Their orbs of sight, and with bedimming
glare
Scorched up their blasted vision.
Through the void
Of Erebus, the preternatural flame
Spread, mingling fire with darkness. But
to see
With human eye and hear with ear of
man
Had been, as on a time the heaven and
earth
Met hurtling in mid-air: as nether earth
Crashed from the centre, and the wreck
of heaven
Fell ruining from high. Not less, when
gods
Grappled with gods, the shout and clang
of arms
Commingled, and the tumult roared from
heaven.
Shrill rushed the hollow winds, and
roused throughout
A shaking and a gathering dark of dust;
Crushing the thunders from the clouds of
air,
Hot thunderbolts and flames, the fiery
darts
Of Jove: and in the midst of either host
They bore upon their blast the cry con-
fused
Of battle, and the shouting. For the din
Tumultuous of that sight-appalling strife

Rose without bound. Stern strength of
hardy proof
Wreaked there its deeds, till weary sank
the fight.
But first, arrayed in battle, front to front,
Full long they stood, and bore the brunt
of war.

—C. A. ELTON.

TARTARUS

The struggle between the gods and the
giants resulted in the hurling of the giants
into Tartarus. The poet delights in the
awful and the horrible, and takes occasion
to enter into a description of the world of
torture.

Amid the foremost, towering in the
van,
The war-unsated Gyges, Briareus,
And Cottus, bitterest conflict waged: for
they
Successive thrice a hundred rocks in air
Hurled from their sinewy grasp: with
missile storm
The Titan host o'ershadowing, them they
drove,
Vain-glorious as they were, with hands
of strength
O'ercoming them, beneath th' expanse of
earth
And bound with galling chains: so far
beneath
This earth, as earth is distant from the
sky:
So deep the space to darksome Tartarus.
A brazen anvil rushing from the sky
Through thrice three days would toss in
airy whirl,
Nor touch this earth, till the tenth sun
arose:
Or down earth's chasm precipitate re-
volve,
Nor till the tenth sun rose attain the
verge
Of Tartarus. A fence of massive brass
Is forged around: around the pass is
rolled

A night of triple darkness; and above
Impend the roots of earth and barren
	sea.
There the Titanic gods in murkiest gloom
Lie hidden: such the cloud-assembler's
	will:
There in a place of darkness, where vast
	earth
Has end: from thence no egress open lies:
Neptune's huge hand has closed with
	brazen gates
The mouth: a wall environs every side.
There Gyges, Cottus, high-souled Bri-
	areus,
Dwell vigilant: the faithful sentinels
Of Ægis-bearer Jove. Successive there
The dusky Earth, and darksome Tartarus,
The sterile Ocean, and the starry Heaven,
Arise and end, their source and boundary.
A dread and ghastly wilderness, ab-
	horred
E'en by the gods; a vast vacuity:
Might none the space of one slow-circling
	year
Touch the firm soil, that portal entered
	once,
But him the whirls of vexing hurricanes
Toss to and fro. E'en by immortals
	loathed
This prodigy of horror. There too stand
The mansions drear of gloomy Night,
	o'erspread
With blackening vapours: and before the
	doors
Atlas upholding heaven his forehead
	rears,
And indefatigable hands. There Night
And Day, near passing, mutual greeting
	still
Exchange, alternate as they glide athwart
The brazen threshold vast. This enters,
	that
Forth issues; nor the two can one abode
At once constrain. This passes forth and
	roams
The round of earth; that in the mansion
	waits,
Till the due season of her travel come.
Lo! from the one the far-discerning light

Beams upon earthly dwellers; but a cloud
Of pitchy blackness veils the other
	round:
Pernicious Night: aye-leading in her hand
Sleep, Death's half-brother: sons of
	gloomy Night
There hold they habitation, Death and
	Sleep;
Dread deities: nor them the shining Sun
E'er with his beam contemplates, when
	he climbs
The cope of heaven, or when from heaven
	descends.
Of these the one glides gentle o'er the
	space
Of earth and broad expanse of ocean
	waves,
Placid to man. The other has a heart
Of iron; yea, the heart within his breast
Is brass, unpitying: whom of men he
	grasps
Stern he retains: e'en to immortal gods
A foe. The hollow-sounding palaces
Of Pluto strong the subterranean god,
And stern Proserpina, there full in front
Ascend: a grisly dog, implacable,
Holds watch before the gates: a stratagem
Is his, malicious: them who enter there,
With tail and bended ears he fawning
	soothes:
But suffers not that they with backward
	step
Repass: whoe'er would issue from the
	gates
Of Pluto strong and stern Proserpina,
For them with marking eye he lurks;
	on them
Springs from his couch, and pitiless de-
	vours.
	There, odious to immortals, dreadful
	Styx
Inhabits: refluent Ocean's eldest-born:
She from the gods apart forever dwells
In far-re-echoing mansions, with arched
	roofs
Of loftiest rock o'erhung: and all around
The silver columns lean upon the skies.
	Swift-footed Iris, nymph of Thaumas
	born,

Takes with no frequent embassy her way
O'er the broad main's expanse, when
    haply strife
Be risen, and midst the gods dissension
    sown:
And if there be among th' Olympian race
Who falsehood utters, Jove sends Iris
    down
To bring the great oath in a golden ewer:
The far-famed water, from steep, sky-
    capped rock
Distilling in cold stream. Beneath wide
    Earth
Abundant from the sacred river-head,
Through shades of blackest night, the
    Stygian horn
Of ocean flows: a tenth of all the streams
To the dread oath allotted. In nine
    streams
Circling the round of earth and the broad
    seas,
With silver whirlpools twined in many a
    maze,
It falls into the deep: one stream alone
Flows from the rock; a mighty bane to
    gods.
Who of immortals, that inhabit still
Olympus topped with snow, libation
    pours
And is forsworn, he one whole year entire
Lives reft of breath: nor yet approaches
    once
The nectared and ambrosial sweet repast:
But still reclines on the spread festive
    couch
Mute, breathless; and a mortal lethargy
O'erwhelms him: but, his malady ab-
    solved

With the great round of the revolving
    year,
More ills on ills afflictive seize: nine
    years
From ever-living deities remote
His lot is cast: in council nor in feast
Once joins he, till nine years entire are
    full:
The tenth again he mingles with the blest
Societies, who fill th' Olympian courts.
So great an oath the deities of heaven
Decreed the water of eternal Styx,
The ancient stream; that sweeps with
    wandering waves
A rugged region: where of dusky Earth,
And darksome Tartarus, and Ocean
    waste,
And starry Heaven, the source and
    boundary
Successive rise and end: a dreary wild
And ghastly: e'en by deities abhorred.
   There gates resplendent rise; the
    threshold brass;
Immovable; on deep foundations fixed;
Self-framed. Before them the Titanic
    gods
Abide, without the assembly of the Blest,
Beyond the gulf of darkness. There
    beneath
The ocean-roots, th' auxiliaries renowned
Of Jove who rolls the hollow-pealing
    thunder,
Cottus and Gyges in near mansions dwell:
But He that shakes the shores with dash-
    ing surge
Hailing him son, gave Briareus as bride
Cymopolia, prize of brave desert.
                 —C. A. Elton.

V. THE MOCK EPIC

The epics of Homer led to countless imitations, but they led also to burlesques. The Battle of the Frogs and Mice is an example of such satire on the martial epic.

THE BATTLE OF THE FROGS AND MICE

To fill my rising song with sacred fire,
Ye tuneful Nine, ye sweet celestial quire!
From Helicon's embowering height repair,
Attend my labours, and reward my
  prayer;
The dreadful toils of raging Mars I write,
The springs of contest, and the fields of
  fight;
How threatening mice advanc'd with war-
  like grace,
And wag'd dire combats with the croak-
  ing race.
Not louder tumults shook Olympus'
  towers,
When earth-born giants dar'd immortal
  powers.
These equal acts an equal glory claim,
And thus the Muse records the tale of
  Fame.
  Once on a time, fatigu'd and out of
    breath,
And just escap'd the stretching claws of
  Death,
A gentle mouse, whom cats pursued in
  vain,
Fled swift of foot across the neighbouring
  plain,
Hung o'er a brink, his eager thirst to
  cool,
And dipp'd his whiskers in the standing
  pool;
When near a courteous frog advanc'd
  his head,
And from the waters, hoarse-resounding,
  said,
  "What art thou, stranger? what the
    line you boast?
What chance has cast thee panting on
  our coast?

With strictest truth let all thy words
  agree.
Nor let me find a faithless mouse in thee.
If worthy, friendship, proffer'd friend-
  ship take,
And entering view the pleasurable lake;
Range o'er my palace, in my bounty
  share,
And glad return from hospitable fare:
This silver realm extends beneath my
  sway,
And me, their monarch, all its frogs obey.
Great Physignathus I, from Peleus' race,
Begot in fair Hydromede's embrace,
Where, by the nuptial bank that paints
  his side,
The swift Eridanus delights to glide.
Thee too, thy form, thy strength, and
  port, proclaim
A scepter'd king; a son of martial fame;
Then trace thy line, and aid my guessing
  eyes."
Thus ceas'd the frog, and thus the mouse
  replies.
  "Known to the gods, the men, the birds
    that fly
Through wild expanses of the midway
  sky,
My name resounds; and if unknown to
  thee,
The soul of great Psycarpax lives in me,
Of brave Troxartas' line, whose sleeky
  down
In love compress'd Lychomile the brown.
My mother she, and princess of the plains
Where'er her father Pternotractas reigns.
Born where a cabin lifts its airy shed,
With figs, with nuts, with vary'd dainties
  fed.
But, since our natures nought in common
  know,
From what foundation can a friendship
  grow?
These curling waters o'er thy palace roll:
But man's high food supports my princely
  soul:

In vain the circled loaves attempt to lie
Conceal'd in flaskets from my curious
  eye.
In vain the tripe that boasts the whitest
  hue,
In vain the gilded bacon shuns my view,
In vain the cheeses, offspring of the pail,
Or honey'd cakes, which gods themselves
  regale;
And as in arts I shine, in arms I fight,
Mix'd with the bravest, and unknown to
  flight;
Though large to mine the human form
  appear,
Not man himself can smite my soul with
  fear;
Sly to the bed with silent steps I go,
Attempt his finger, or attack his toe,
And six indented wounds with dextrous
  skill,
Sleeping he feels, and only seems to feel.
Yet have we foes which direful dangers
  cause,
Grim owls with talons arm'd, and cats
  with claws,
And that false trap, the den of silent
  Fate,
Where Death his ambush plants around
  the bait:
All dreaded these, and dreadful o'er the
  rest
The potent warriors of the tabby vest,
If to the dark we fly, the dark they trace,
And rend our heroes of the nibbling race.
But me, nor stalks nor waterish herbs
  delight,
Nor can the crimson radish charm my
  sight,
The lake-resounding frogs' selected fare,
Which not a mouse of any taste can
  bear."
  As thus the downy prince his mind
  exprest,
His answer thus the croaking king ad-
  drest:
  "Thy words luxuriant on thy dainties
  rove,
And, stranger, we can boast of bounteous
  Jove:

We sport in water, or we dance on land,
And born amphibious, food from both
  command.
But trust thyself where wonders ask thy
  view,
And safely tempt those seas, I'll bear thee
  through:
Ascend my shoulders, firmly keep thy
  seat,
And reach my marshy court, and feast
  in state."
He said, and bent his back; with nimble
  bound
Leaps the light mouse, and clasps his
  arms around,
Then wondering floats, and sees with glad
  survey
The winding banks resembling ports at
  sea.
But when aloft the curling water rides,
And wet with azure wave his downy
  sides,
His thoughts grow conscious of approach-
  ing woe,
His idle tears with vain repentance flow,
His locks he rends, his trembling feet he
  rears,
Thick beats his heart with unaccustomed
  fears;
He sighs, and, chill'd with danger, longs
  for shore:
His tail extended forms a fruitless oar,
Half drench'd in liquid death his prayers
  he spake,
And thus bemoan'd him from the dread-
  ful lake:
  "So pass'd Europa through the rapid
  sea,
Trembling and fainting all the venturous
  way;
With oary feet the bull triumphant rode,
And safe in Crete depos'd his lovely load.
Ah, safe at last, may thus the frog sup-
  port
My trembling limbs to reach his ample
  court!"
As thus he sorrows, death ambiguous
  grows,
Lo! from the deep a water-hydra rose;

He rolls his sanguin'd eyes, his bosom
  heaves,
And darts with active rage along the
  waves.
Confus'd the monarch sees his hissing
  foe,
And dives, to shun the sable fates below.
Forgetful frog! the friend thy shoulders
  bore,
Unskill'd in swimming, floats remote from
  shore.
He grasps with fruitless hands to find
  relief,
Supinely falls, and grinds his teeth with
  grief;
Plunging he sinks, and struggling mounts
  again,
And sinks, and strives, but strives with
  Fate in vain.
The weighty moisture clogs his hairy
  vest,
And thus the prince his dying rage ex-
  prest:
  "Nor thou, that fling'st me floundering
    from thy back,
As from hard rocks rebounds the shat-
  tering wrack,
Nor thou shalt 'scape thy due, perfidious
  king!
Pursued by vengeance on the swiftest
  wing!
At land thy strength could never equal
  mine,
At sea to conquer, and by craft, was
  thine.
But Heaven has gods, and gods have
  searching eyes:
Ye mice, ye mice, my great avengers
  rise!"
  This said, he sighing gasp'd, and gasp-
  ing dy'd.
His death the young Lychopynax espy'd,
As on the flowery brink he pass'd the day,
Bask'd in the beams, and loiter'd life
  away.
Loud shrieks the mouse, his shrieks the
  shore repeat,
The nibbling nation learn their hero's
  fate:

Grief, dismal grief ensues; deep murmurs
  sound,
And shriller fury fills the deafen'd ground.
From lodge to lodge, the sacred heralds
  run,
To fix their council with the rising Sun;
Where great Troxartas crown'd in glory
  reigns,
And winds his lengthening court beneath
  the plains.
Psycarpax' father, father now no more!
For poor Psycarpax lies remote from
  shore;
Supine he lies! the silent waters stand,
And no kind billow wafts the dead to
  land.
  When rosy-finger'd morn had ting'd the
    clouds,
Around their monarch-mouse the nation
  crowds,
Slow rose the sovereign, heav'd his
  anxious breast,
And thus the council, fill'd with rage,
  addrest:
  "For lost Psycarpax much my soul
    endures,
'Tis mine the private grief, the public
  yours.
Three warlike sons adorn'd my nuptial
  bed,
Three sons, alas! before their father
  dead!
Our oldest perish'd by the ravening cat,
As near my court the prince unheedful
  sat.
Our next, an engine fraught with danger
  drew,
The portal gap'd, the bait was hung in
  view,
Dire arts assist the trap, the Fates decoy,
And men unpitying kill'd my gallant boy!
The last, his country's hope, his parent's
  pride,
Plung'd in the lake by Physignathus
  dy'd;
Rouse all to war, my friends! avenge the
  deed;
And bleed that monarch, and his nation
  bleed."

His words in every breast inspir'd alarms,
And careful Mars supply'd their host with arms.
In verdant hulls despoil'd of all their beans,
The buskin'd warriors stalk'd along the plains:
Quills aptly bound their bracing corselet made,
Fac'd with the plunder of a cat they flay'd:
The lamp's round boss affords them ample shield;
Large shells of nuts their covering helmet yield,
And o'er the region, with reflected rays,
Tall groves of needles for their lances blaze:
Dreadful in arms the marching mice appear;
The wondering frogs perceive the tumult near,
Forsake the waters, thickening form a ring,
And ask, and hearken, whence the noises spring.
When near the crowd, disclos'd to public view,
The valiant chief Embasichytros drew:
The sacred herald's sceptre grac'd his hand,
And thus his word express'd his king's command:
"Ye frogs! the mice, with vengeance fir'd, advance,
And deck'd in armour shake the shining lance:
Their hapless prince by Physignathus slain,
Extends incumbent on the watery plain.
Then arm your host, the doubtful battle try;
Lead forth those frogs that have the soul to die."
The chief retires, the crowd the challenge hear,
And proudly swelling yet perplex'd appear:

Much they resent, yet much their monarch blame,
Who, rising, spoke to clear his tainted fame:
"O friends! I never forc'd the mouse to death,
Nor saw the gasping of his latest breath.
He, vain of youth, our art of swimming try'd,
And, venturous, in the lake the wanton dy'd.
To vengeance now by false appearance led,
They point their anger at my guiltless head;
But wage the rising war by deep device,
And turn its fury on the crafty mice.
Your king directs the way; my thoughts, elate
With hopes of conquest, form designs of fate.
Where high the banks their verdant surface heave,
And the steep sides confine the sleeping wave,
There, near the margin, clad in armour bright,
Sustain the first impetuous shocks of fight:
Then, where the dancing feather joins the crest,
Let each brave frog his obvious mouse arrest;
Each strongly grasping, headlong plunge a foe,
Till countless circles whirl the lake below;
Down sink the mice in yielding waters drown'd;
Loud flash the waters; and the shores resound:
The frogs triumphant tread the conquer'd plain,
And raise their glorious trophies of the slain."
He spake no more, his prudent scheme imparts
Redoubling ardour to the boldest hearts.
Green was the suit his arming heroes chose,

Around their legs the greaves of mallows close;
Green were the beets about their shoulders laid,
And green the colewort, which the target made.
Form'd of the vary'd shells the waters yield,
Their glossy helmets glisten'd o'er the field:
And tapering sea-reeds for the polish'd spear,
With upright order pierc'd the ambient air.
Thus dress'd for war, they take th' appointed height,
Poise the long arms, and urge the promis'd fight.
  But now, where Jove's irradiate spires arise,
With stars surrounded in ethereal skies,
(A solemn council call'd) the brazen gates
Unbar; the gods assume their golden seats:
The sire superior leans, and points to show
What wondrous combats mortals wage below:
How strong, how large, the numerous heroes stride,
What length of lance they shake with warlike pride!
What eager fire their rapid march reveals!
So the fierce Centaurs ravag'd o'er the dales;
And so confirm'd, the daring Titans rose,
Heap'd hills on hills, and bid the gods be foes.
  This seen, the Power his sacred visage rears,
He casts a pitying smile on worldly cares,
And asks what heavenly guardians take the list,
Or who the mice, or who the frogs assist?
  Then thus to Pallas: "If my daughter's mind

Have join'd the mice, why stays she still behind?
Drawn forth by savoury steams they wind their way,
And sure attendance round thine altar pay,
Where while the victims gratify their taste,
They sport to please the goddess of the feast."
  Thus spake the ruler of the spacious skies.
But thus, resolv'd, the blue-ey'd maid replies:
"In vain, my father! all their dangers plead,
To such thy Pallas never grants her aid.
My flowery wreaths they petulantly spoil,
And rob my crystal lamps of feeding oil.
(Ills following ills!) but what afflicts me more,
My veil that idle race profanely tore.
The web was curious, wrought with art divine;
Relentless wretches! all the work was mine!
Along the loom the purple warp I spread,
Cast the light shoot, and crost the silver thread;
In this their teeth a thousand breaches tear,
The thousand breaches skilful hands repair,
For which, vile earthly duns thy daughter grieve
(The gods, that use no coin, have none to give,
And learning's goddess never less can owe,
Neglected learning gains no wealth below).
Nor let the frogs to win my succour sue,
Those clamorous fools have lost my favour too.
For late, when all the conflict ceas'd at night,
When my stretch'd sinews work'd with eager fight,

When spent with glorious toil, I left the
field,
And sunk for slumber on my swelling
shield;
Lo, from the deep, repelling sweet repose
With noisy croakings half the nation
rose:
Devoid of rest, with aching brows I lay,
Till cocks proclaim'd the crimson dawn
of day.
Let all, like me, from either host forbear,
Nor tempt the flying furies of the spear;
Let heavenly blood (or what for blood
may flow)
Adorn the conquest of a meaner foe.
Some daring mouse may meet with won-
drous odds,
Though gods oppose, and brave the
wounded gods.
O'er gilded clouds reclin'd, the danger
view,
And be the wars of mortals scenes for
you."
  So mov'd the blue-ey'd queen; her
words persuade,
Great Jove assented, and the rest obey'd.
  Now front to front the marching armies
shine,
Halt ere they meet, and form the length-
ening line:
The chiefs conspicuous seen and heard
afar,
Give the loud signal to the rushing war;
Their dreadful trumpets deep-mouth'd
hornets sound,
The sounding charge remurmurs o'er the
ground,
E'en Jove proclaims a field of horrour
nigh,
And rolls his thunder through the
troubled sky.
  First to the fight large Hypsiboas flew,
And brave Lychenor with a javelin slew.
The luckless warrior, fill'd with generous
flame,
Stood foremost glittering in the post of
fame;
When, in his liver struck, the javelin
hung,

The mouse fell thundering, and the target
rung;
Prone to the ground, he sinks his closing
eye,
And soil'd in dust his lovely tresses lie.
  A spear at Pelion Troglodytes cast,
The missive spear within the bosom past;
Death's sable shades the fainting frog
surround,
And life's red tide runs ebbing from the
wound.
  Embasichytros felt Scutlæus' dart
Transfix and quiver in his panting heart;
But great Artophagus aveng'd the slain,
And big Scutlæus tumbling loads the
plain.
And Polyphonus dies, a frog renown'd
For boastful speech, and turbulence of
sound;
Deep through the belly pierc'd, supine
he lay,
And breath'd his soul against the face of
day.
  The strong Lymnocharis, who view'd
with ire
A victor triumph, and a friend expire;
With heaving arms a rocky fragment
caught,
And fiercely flung where Troglodytes
fought
(A warrior vers'd in arts, of sure retreat,
But arts in vain elude impending fate);
Full on his sinewy neck the fragment fell,
And o'er his eye-lids clouds eternal dwell.
Lychenor (second of the glorious name)
Striding advanc'd, and took no wandering
aim;
Through all the frogs the shining javelin
flies,
And near the vanquish'd mouse the victor
dies.
  The dreadful stroke Crambophagus
affrights,
Long bred to banquets, less inur'd to
fights,
Heedless he runs, and stumbles o'er the
steep,
And wildly foundering flashes up the
deep;

Lychenor, following with a downward blow,
Reach'd in the lake his unrecover'd foe;
Gasping he rolls, a purple stream of blood
Distains the surface of the silver flood;
Through the wide wound the rushing entrails throng,
And slow the breathless carcass floats along.
Lymnisius good Tyroglyphus assails,
Prince of the mice that haunt the flowery vales,
Lost to the milky fares and rural seat,
He came to perish on the bank of fate.
The dread Pternoglyphus demands the fight
Which tender Calaminthius shuns by flight,
Drops the green target, springing quits the foe,
Glides through the lake, and safely dives below.
But dire Pternophagus divides his way
Through breaking ranks, and leads the dreadful day.
No nibbling prince excell'd in fierceness more,
His parents fed him on the savage boar;
But where his lance the field with blood imbrued,
Swift as he mov'd Hydrocharis pursued,
Till fallen in death he lies, a shattering stone
Sounds on the neck, and crushes all the bone.
His blood pollutes the verdure of the plain,
And from his nostrils bursts the gushing brain.
Lychopinax with Borborocates fights,
A blameless frog, whom humbler life delights;
The fatal javelin unrelenting flies,
And darkness seals the gentle croaker's eyes.
Incens'd Prassophagus, with sprightly bound,
Bears Cuissodioctes off the rising ground,

Then drags him o'er the lake depriv'd of breath,
And, downward plunging, sinks his soul to death.
But now the great Psycarpax shines afar
(Scarce he so great whose loss provok'd the war);
Swift to revenge his fatal javelin fled,
And through the liver struck Pelusius dead;
His freckled corpse before the victor fell,
His soul indignant sought the shades of Hell.
This saw Pelobates, and from the flood
Heav'd with both hands a monstrous mass of mud;
The cloud obscene o'er all the hero flies,
Dishonours his brown face, and blots his eyes.
Enrag'd, and wildly sputtering, from the shore
A stone, immense of size, the warrior bore,
A load for labouring Earth, whose bulk to raise,
Asks ten degenerate mice of modern days.
Full on the leg arrives the crushing wound:
The frog, supportless, writhes upon the ground.
Thus flush'd, the victor wars with matchless force,
Till loud Craugasides arrests his course.
Hoarse croaking threats precede! with fatal speed
Deep through the belly ran the pointed reed,
Then, strongly tugg'd, return'd imbrued with gore,
And on the pile his reeking entrails bore.
The lame Sitophagus, oppress'd with pain,
Creeps from the desperate dangers of the plain:
And where the ditches rising weeds supply
To spread their lowly shades beneath the sky,

There lurks the silent mouse reliev'd from heat,
And, safe embower'd, avoids the chance of fate.
But here Troxartas, Physignathus there,
Whirl the dire furies of the pointed spear;
But where the foot around its ankle plies,
Troxartas wounds, and Physignathus flies,
Halts to the pool, a safe retreat to find,
And trails a dangling length of leg behind.
The mouse still urges, still the frog retires,
And half in anguish of the flight expires,
Then pious ardour young Pressæus brings
Betwixt the fortunes of contending kings:
Lank harmless frog! with forces hardly grown,
He darts the reed in combat not his own,
Which faintly tinkling on Troxartas' shield,
Hangs at the point, and drops upon the field.
Now nobly towering o'er the rest appears
A gallant prince that far transcends his years,
Pride of his sire, and glory of his house,
And more a Mars in combat than a mouse:
His action bold, robust his ample frame,
And Meridarpax his resounding name.
The warrior, singled from the fighting crowd,
Boasts the dire honours of his arms aloud;
Then strutting near the lake, with looks elate,
To all its nations threats approaching fate.
And such his strength, the silver lakes around
Might roll their waters o'er unpeopled ground,
But powerful Jove, who shows no less his grace
To frogs that perish, than to human race,
Felt soft compassion rising in his soul,

And shook his sacred head, then shook the pole.
Then thus to all the gazing powers began
The sire of gods, and frogs, and mice, and man:
"What seas of blood I view! what worlds of slain!
An Iliad rising from a day's campaign;
How fierce his javelin o'er the trembling lakes
The black-furr'd hero Meridarpax shakes!
Unless some favouring deity descend,
Soon will the frogs' loquacious empire end.
Let dreadful Pallas wing'd with pity fly,
And make her ægis blaze before his eye:
While Mars refulgent on his rattling car,
Arrests his raging rival of the war."
He ceas'd, reclining with attentive head,
When thus the glorious god of combats said:
"Nor Pallas, Jove! though Pallas take the field,
With all the terrours of her hissing shield;
Nor Mars himself, though Mars in armour bright
Ascend his car and wheel amidst the fight;
Not these can drive the desperate mouse afar,
Or change the fortunes of the bleeding war.
Let all go forth, all Heaven in arms arise,
Or launch thy own red thunder from the skies,
Such ardent bolts as flew that wondrous day,
When heaps of Titans mix'd with mountains lay;
When all the giant race enormous fell,
And huge Enceladus was hurl'd to Hell."
'Twas thus th' armipotent advis'd the gods,
When from his throne the cloud-compeller nods,
Deep-lengthening thunders run from pole to pole,
Olympus trembles as the thunders roll.

Then swift he whirls the brandish'd bolt
    around,
And headlong darts it at the distant
    ground;
The bolt discharg'd, inwrapp'd with light-
    ning flies,
And rends its flaming passage through
    the skies;
Then earth's inhabitants, the nibblers,
    shake,
And frogs, the dwellers in the waters,
    quake.
Yet still the mice advanc'd their dread
    design,
And the last danger threats the croaking
    line,
Till Jove, that inly mourn'd the loss they
    bore,
With strange assistants fill'd the frighted
    shore.
    Pour'd from the neighbouring strand,
      deform'd to view,
They march, a sudden unexpected crew!
Strong suits of armour round their bodies
    close,
Which, like thick anvils, blunt the force
    of blows;
In wheeling marches torn oblique they
    go;
With harpy claws they limbs divide
    below;
Fell sheers the passage to their mouth
    command;
From out the flesh their bones by nature
    stand;
Broad spread their backs, their shining
    shoulders rise;

Unnumber'd joints distort their length-
    en'd thighs;
With nervous cords their hands are firmly
    brac'd;
Their round black eye-balls in their
    bosom plac'd;
On eight long feet the wondrous warriors
    tread;
And either end alike supplies a head.
These, mortal wits to call the crabs agree,
The gods have other names for things
    than we.
    Now where the jointures from their
      loins depend,
The heroes' tails with severing grasps
    they rend.
Here, short of feet, depriv'd the power
    to fly,
There, without hands, upon the field they
    lie.
Wrench'd from their holds, and scatter'd
    all around,
The bended lances heap the cumber'd
    ground.
Helpless amazement, fear pursuing fear,
And mad confusion, through their host
    appear:
O'er the wild waste with headlong flight
    they go,
Or creep conceal'd in vaulted holes below.
    But down Olympus to the western seas
Far shooting Phœbus drove with fainter
    rays;
And a whole war (so Jove ordain'd) be-
    gun,
Was fought, and ceas'd, in one revolving
    sun.   —THOMAS PARNELL.

VI. HYMNS TO THE GODS

The *Homeric Hymns* are so called because they were once thought to be the
work of the great epic poet. They belong
rather to a later age, possibly the seventh
century B.C., and were the work of rhapsodists who used them as preludes to their
recitations of Homer. The extant collection contains thirty-four.

HYMN TO EARTH THE MOTHER OF ALL

O universal Mother, who dost keep
From everlasting thy foundations deep,
Eldest of things, Great Earth, I sing of
    thee!
All shapes that have their dwelling in
    the sea,

All things that fly, or on the ground divine
Live, move, and there are nourished—
these are thine;
These from thy wealth thou dost sustain;
from thee
Fair babes are born, and fruits on every tree
Hang ripe and large, revered Divinity!

The life of mortal men beneath thy sway
Is held; thy power both gives and takes away!
Happy are they whom thy mild favours nourish;
All things unstinted round them grow and flourish;
For them, endures the life-sustaining field
Its load of harvest, and their cattle yield
Large increase, and their house with wealth is filled.
Such honoured dwell in cities fair and free,
The homes of lovely women, prosperously;
Their sons exult in youth's new budding gladness,
And their fresh daughters free from care and sadness,
With bloom-inwoven dance and happy song,
On the soft flowers the meadow-grass among,
Leap round them sporting—such delights by thee
Are given, rich Power, revered Divinity.

Mother of gods, thou wife of starry Heaven,
Farewell! be thou propitious, and be given
A happy life for this brief melody,
Nor thou nor other songs shall unremembered be.
    —PERCY BYSSHE SHELLEY.

HYMN TO SELENE

Daughters of Jove, whose voice is melody,
Muses, who know and rule all minstrelsy,
Sing the wide-winged Moon!   Around the earth,
From her immortal head in Heaven shot forth,
Far light is scattered—boundless glory springs;
Where'er she spreads her many-beaming wings
The lampless air glows round her golden crown.

But when the Moon divine from Heaven is gone
Under the sea, her beams within abide,
Till, bathing her bright limbs in Ocean's tide,
Clothing her form in garments glittering far,
And having yoked to her immortal car
The beam-invested steeds whose necks on high
Curve back, she drives to a remoter sky
A western Crescent, borne impetuously.
Then is made full the circle of her light,
And as she grows, her beams more bright and bright
Are poured from Heaven, where she is hovering then,
A wonder and a sign to mortal men.

The Son of Saturn with this glorious Power
Mingled in love and sleep—to whom she bore
Pandeia, a bright maid of beauty rare
Among the Gods, whose lives eternal are.

Hail Queen, great Moon, white-armed Divinity,
Fair-haired and favourable! thus with thee
My song beginning, by its music sweet
Shall make immortal many a glorious feat

Of demigods, with lovely lips, so well
Which minstrels, servants of the Muses,
    tell.
—PERCY BYSSHE SHELLEY.

HYMN TO ATHENA

I sing the glorious Power with azure
    eyes,
Athenian Pallas! timeless, chaste, and
    wise,
Tritogenia, town-preserving Maid,
Revered and mighty; from his awful
    head
Whom Jove brought forth, in warlike
    armour dressed,
Golden, all radiant! wonder strange
    possessed
The everlasting Gods that Shape to see,
Shaking a javelin keen, impetuously
Rush from the crest of Ægis-bearing
    Jove;
Fearfully Heaven was shaken, and did
    move
Beneath the might of the Cerulean-eyed;
Earth dreadfully resounded, far and
    wide;
And, lifted from its depths, the sea
    swelled high
In purple billows, the tide suddenly
Stood still, and great Hyperion's son long
    time
Checked his swift steeds, till, where she
    stood sublime,
Pallas from her immortal shoulders threw
The arms divine; wise Jove rejoiced to
    view.
Child of the Ægis-bearer, hail to thee,
Nor thine nor others' praise shall unre-
    membered be.
—PERCY BYSSHE SHELLEY.

ARISTOCRATIC SOCIETY: THE LYRIC

SEVENTH TO FIFTH CENTURIES B. C.

LYRIC poetry was probably beginning to assume its definite forms in the epic period, but it did not reach its position of supremacy until the seventh century B.C. Its popularity continued through the sixth and fifth centuries, until it was largely absorbed by the drama.

The reason for the shift from epic to lyric is to be sought in the change that came over Greek society. In place of monarchies there arose oligarchies and tyrannies and the first struggles for democracies. Revolutions were frequent and political interest became more widespread. Partisanship and local patriotism were called more and more into play. It was also a period of widening experience in other lines. Commerce followed rapidly on the heels of exploration and colonization. Travel increased and knowledge deepened. Such circumstances stimulated the transfer of interest from the larger unit of life to the individual and the personal. More and more one examined oneself to find one's place among the changing governments and the broadening conditions of life. The epic form was too extended and cumbersome for the expression of single emotions or of personal experiences. New forms were invented.

The earliest types of lyric poetry were the elegy and the iambic, the former derived directly from epic, and the latter an attempt to reproduce more nearly the common speech. The elegy was found suitable for the expression of patriotism, grief, love, and political and moral instruction. The iambic was used mainly for satire and personal attack, but shared with elegy the field of moralizing on existing evils. Later developments were the Æolian lyric in shorter and more varied meters and more closely associated with the musical accompaniment than the others, and the Dorian choral celebrating public occasions.

Lyric poetry, as the name implies, was accompanied by music. In some cases the poem was intended to be sung, in others it was rather a recitation to the accompaniment of music, and in still others the musical feature was probably restricted to preludes and interludes. The art of music developed rapidly in this period.

I. THE MARTIAL SPIRIT

How Long Will Ye Slumber?

CALLINUS

Callinus of Ephesus (about 700 B.C.) is the earliest poet, so far as is known, to use the elegiac meter. The only extant piece by him is an appeal to his fellow-citizens to rouse themselves against the invaders of their country.

How long will ye slumber? when will ye
   take heart
And fear the reproach of your neighbors
   at hand?
Fie! comrades, to think ye have peace
   for your part
Whilst the sword and the arrow are wasting our land!
Shame! grasp the shield close! cover well
   the bold breast!
Aloft raise the spear as ye march on the
   foe!
With no thought of retreat, with no terror
   confessed,
Hurl your last dart in dying, or strike
   your last blow.
Oh, 'tis noble and glorious to fight for
   our all,—
For our country, our children, the wife
   of our love!
Death comes not the sooner; no soldier
   shall fall,
Ere his thread is spun out by the sisters
   above.
Once to die is man's doom; rush, rush to
   the fight!
He cannot escape though his blood were
   Jove's own.
For a while let him cheat the shrill arrow
   by flight;
Fate will catch him at last in his cham-
   ber alone.
Unlamented he dies;—unregretted. Not
   so,
When, the tower of his country, in death
   falls the brave;

Thrice hallowed his name amongst all,
   high or low,
As with blessings alive, so with tears in
   the grave.
      —HENRY NELSON COLERIDGE.

EXHORTATION TO BATTLE

TYRTÆUS

Tyrtæus, of the late seventh century B.C., is described in legend as a lame schoolmaster sent to Sparta by the Athenians in response to an appeal for a leader in time of war. Nothing is known of his origin, but he achieved great success with his martial songs in inspiring the Spartans to win the war against the Messenians.

Rouse, rouse, my youths! the chain of
   torpor break!
  Spurn idle rest, and couch the glitter-
    ing lance!
What! does not shame with blushes stain
   your cheek
  Quick-mantling, as ye catch the war-
    rior's glance?

Ignoble youths! say, when shall valour's
   flame
  Burn in each breast? here, here, while
    hosts invade,
And war's wild clangors all your courage
   claim,
  Ye sit, as if still peace embower'd the
    shade.

But, sure, fair honour crowns th' auspi-
   cious deed,
  When patriot love impels us to the
    field;
When, to defend a trembling wife, we
   bleed,
  And when our shelter'd offspring bless
    the shield.

What time the Fates ordain, pale death
    appears:
  Then with firm step and sword high
    drawn, depart;
And, marching through the first thick
    shower of spears
  Beneath thy buckler guard th' intrepid
    heart.

Each mortal, though he boast celestial
    sires,
  Slave to the sovereign destiny of death,
Or mid the carnage of the plain expires,
  Or yields unwept at home his coward
    breath.

Yet sympathy attends the brave man's
    bier;
  Sees on each wound the balmy grief
    bestow'd;
And, in his death the universal tear,
  Through life inspires the homage of a
    god.

For like a turret his proud glories rise,
  And stand, above the rival's reach,
    alone;
While millions hail, with fond adoring
    eyes,
  The deeds of many a hero meet in one!
                    —RICHARD POLWHELE.

THE RULES OF VALOUR

TYRTÆUS

Yet are ye Hercules' unconquer'd race—
  Remand, heroic tribe, your spirit lost!
Not yet all-seeing Jove averts his face;
  Then meet without a fear the throng-
    ing host.

Each to the foe his steady shield oppose,
  Accoutred to resign his hateful breath:
The friendly sun a mild effulgence throws
  On valour's grave, though dark the
    frown of death.

Yes! ye have known the ruthless work
    of war!
  Yes! ye have known its tears—its
    heavy woe;
When, scattering in pale flight, ye rush'd
    afar,
  Or chas'd the routed squadrons of the
    foe.

Of those who dare, a strong compacted
    band,
  Firm for the fight their warrior-spirits
    link,
And grapple with the foeman, hand to
    hand,
  How few, through deadly wounds ex-
    piring, sink.

They, foremost in the ranks of battle,
    guard
  Th' inglorious multitude that march
    behind;
While shrinking fears the coward's step
    retard,
  And dies each virtue in the feeble mind.

But 'tis not in the force of words to paint
  What varied ills attend th' ignoble
    troop,
Who trembling on the scene of glory faint,
  Or wound the fugitives that breathless
    droop.

Basely the soldier stabs, with hurried
    thrust,
  The unresisting wretch, that shieldless
    flies!
At his last gasp dishonour'd in the dust
  (His back transfix'd with spears) the
    dastard lies!

Thus then, bold youth, the rules of
    valour learn:
  Stand firm, and fix on earth thy rooted
    feet:
Bite with thy teeth thy eager lips; and
    stern
  In conscious strength, the rushing onset
    meet:

And shelter with thy broad and bossy
    shield
    Thy thighs and shins, thy shoulders
      and thy breast;
The long spear ponderous in thy right-
    hand wield,
    And on thy head high nod the dreadful
      crest.

Mark well the lessons of the warlike art,
    That teach thee, if the shield with
      ample round
Protect thy bosom, to approach the dart,
    Nor choose with timid care the distant
      ground.

But, for close combat with the fronting
    foe,
    Elate in valorous attitude draw near;
And aiming, hand to hand, the fateful
    blow,
    Brandish thy temper'd blade or massy
      spear.

Yes! for the rage of stubborn grapple
    steel'd,
    Grasp the sword's hilt, and couch the
      long-beat lance;
Foot to the foeman's foot, and shield to
    shield,
    Crest ev'n to crest, and helm to helm,
      advance.

But ye, light arm'd who, trembling in the
    rear,
    Bear smaller targets, at a distance,
      throw
The hissing stone, or hurl the polish'd
    spear,
    (Plac'd nigh your panoply) to mar the
      foe.
        —RICHARD POLWHELE.

A GLIMPSE OF BATTLE

ARCHILOCHUS

Archilochus, of the early seventh century B. C., was born at Paros of a noble
father and a slave mother. Story tells of
his love for Neobule and of how, when
the engagement was broken off, he delivered bitter attacks in verse on the girl's
family. He was an adventurous spirit—
loved, traveled, fought, and committed to
verse his varied experiences. His poetry
was intensely personal and passionate, perhaps the first of this type, and was much
more varied in form than that of other
lyric poets of the time. He wrote elegy,
and is credited with having invented the
iambic for purposes of satire and invec-
tive. By the ancients he was reckoned as
second to Homer.

Bows will not avail thee,
Darts and slings will fail thee,
    When Mars tumultuous rages
    On wide-embattled land:
Then with falchions clashing,
Eyes with fury flashing,
    Man with man engages
    In combat hand to hand.
But most Euboea's chiefs are known,
    Marshalled hosts of spearmen leading
    To conflict, whence is no receding,
To make this—war's best art—their own.
        —J. H. MERIVALE.

SPOILS OF WAR

ALCÆUS

Alcæus, of the late seventh century B.C.,
spent a great part of his life in civil strife
at Mytilene, a city of Lesbos, and in exile.
He was of the Æolian group of poets
who wrote in new forms mainly of
personal joys and sorrows, love, grief,
hymns, the cup. It is plain from his
political poems that, though he was patriotic, he was intensely and narrowly partisan. With so little of his poetry extant
on which to base a judgment, the fact that
Horace imitated him in so many odes is
the best proof we have of his high rank
as poet.

Glitters with brass my mansion wide,
The roof is decked on every side
    In martial pride;

With helmets ranged in order bright,
And plumes of horse-hair nodding
    white,
    A gallant sight—
Fit ornament for warrior's brow—
And 'round the walls in goodly row
    Refulgent glow
Stout greaves of brass like burnished
    gold,
And corselets there in many a fold
    Of linen rolled;
And shields that in the battle fray

The routed losers of the day
    Have cast away.
Eubœan falchions too are seen,
With rich embroidered belts between
    Of dazzling sheen;
And gaudy surcoats piled around,
And spoils of chiefs in war renowned
    May there be found.
These, and all else that here you see
Are fruits of glorious victory
    Achieved by me.
                —J. H. MERIVALE.

II. THE STATE

RICHES

SOLON

Solon of Athens, who lived from about 640 to about 558 B.C., was not only a poet, but also a statesman and lawgiver. When Archon, he revised the Athenian constitution so successfully that he was afterwards regarded as the founder of the democracy. His poetry reflects the events of his life and his character. His clarity and independence of thought, his balance and sanity, and his great achievements in politics won him rank as one of the Seven Wise Men of Greece. Solon employed mainly elegy, which before the invention of prose was the chief medium of literary expression for didactic and moralizing purposes.

The following selection is the longest extant fragment of his poetry. It sets forth his views on wealth and the relation between wealth and morals. Solon does not, like many other ancient poets, see only evil in great fortunes: the good or evil of riches depends upon how they were acquired. And since they are at best but a chance circumstance of life, they are not to be relied upon for happiness.

Fair offspring of Olympian Zeus and
    Memory,
    Pierian Muses, hear me as I pray.

Vouchsafe that I be blessed with true
    prosperity,
    And grant a good report be mine alway.
To trusting friends a welcome savor may
    I be,
    And bitter in the mouth of enemies.
Desire of honest wealth I have that
    leaveth me
    Unstained, and bringeth not late
    penalties.
Such riches as the Gods bestow upon a
    man remain
His own, from base to top a structure
    firm;
But riches sought in pride, which right
    and wrong disdain,
    Come not as nature's due, nor set a
    term
To impulse of dishonesty. There comes
    a burst
    Of folly blind which leads to ruin sure.
Like fire, it starts a single spark, and,
    small at first,
    It ends in downfall. Works cannot
    endure
Of wicked men. Zeus watcheth all things
    to the last.
    Oftimes in spring there starteth up a
    breeze,
Dispersing clouds, and stirring to its
    depths the vast

And surging sea, and laying waste the trees
And plantings fair of farmers in the fruitful fields;
Then coming to the home of Gods on high,
It bringeth once again the blue: the Sun-Lord yields
His beauty forth, nor clouds obscure the sky.
God's justice is like such a wind. Not quick to wrath
Is He, like man, for each offense. But he
Who hath an evil heart can never tread a path
That's hid from His all-waking eye; men see
His justice clearly at the last. One soon, one late,
Must pay the price of wrong. If guilty ones
Escape to-day and dodge a little while God's fate,
In after years it comes, when children's sons
And generations yet unborn, though innocent
Themselves, must pay for wrong of ancient sire.
All mortal men, the wicked and the good, intent
To win fair fame, possessed of their desire,
Strain every nerve, until a chance mishap befall
That, instant, bringeth pain. Like fools, till then
We take our joy of idle dreams. Thus do they call
Before their eyes a dream of health, what men
The dread diseases hold; the coward fain would think
That he is brave; the ugly, fair; who spends
His days in toil of poverty is on the brink
Of winning wealth before his life-span ends.

From different sources seek they wealth. Intent to get
A profit, one in ships on fishy seas
Sails far and near, and counts his life a slender bet,
And dares the chances of the fickle breeze.
A second, toiling with the plow, the soil upturns—
The whole year through he labors like a slave.
To learn Athena's useful arts another burns;
Hephæstus too may teach one how to save.
Another, by Olympic Muses taught, doth gain
An understanding sure of sweetest song.
Far-darting Lord Apollo doth a fifth maintain
With gift of prophecy: from distance long
He sees the evil coming on his fellow-man,
If Gods attend; yet neither bird averts,
Nor victim of the sacrifice, what Fate doth plan.
Another is physician and converts
To gain the arts of Pæon knowing many herbs:—
Success crowns not his work: from trivial pain
There grows great suffering, nor soothing potion curbs
And brings relief; while he who long has lain,
By cruel sickness overwhelmed, may even still
Be straightway rendered whole by touch of hand.
To mortal man brings Destiny both good and ill:
We must accept the gifts the Gods have planned.
And certain danger all the works of men attends:
None can foresee the issue of his deed.
One man, who, striving earnestly, but good intends,

Falls unaware upon the direst need;
Upon a second, working ill, the Gods be-
stow
  Great fortune and from folly sweet
    release.
Nor is there set a bound to wealth to
    check its flow:
  The richest strive the more for great
    increase.
What riches satisfy, though God give for-
    tunes vast?
  Wealth turns to madness, madness
    ruins all:
When Zeus sends madness as a punish-
    ment at last,
  On one and then another doth it fall.
          —George Howe.

Maxims

THEOGNIS

Theognis, of the late sixth century B.C.,
was a nobleman of Megara, who because
of his vigorous partisanship was forced
into exile when his party suffered defeat.
The experience colored his writings with
extreme bitterness and hatred towards the
common people. His verse, restricted to
elegy, was addressed to a young nobleman
by the name of Cyrnus as a pupil or as one
expected to become the leader of the
aristocratic party. The extant poems of
Theognis formed a collection of maxims
for the Athenian schools, and were carefully selected to teach old-time manners
and morals.

Lo, I have given thee plumes wherewith
    to skim
  The unfathomed deep, and lightly
    hover around
  Earth's huge circumference. Thou
    shalt be found
At banquets on the breath of pæan and
    hymn:
To shrill-voiced pipes with lips of
    seraphim,
  Lovely young men thy rapturous fame
    shall sound;

Yea, when thou liest lapped in noise-
    less ground,
Thy name shall live, nor shall oblivion
    dim
Thy dawn of splendour. For these lands,
    these isles,
  These multitudinous waves of refluent
    seas,
  Shall be thy pleasure ground where-
    through to roam,
Borne by no steed, but wafted by the
    smiles
  Of Muses violet-crowned, whose melo-
    dies,
  While earth endures, shall make all
    earth thy home.
          —John Addington Symonds.

To rear a child is easy, but to teach
Morals and manners is beyond our reach;
To make the foolish wise, the wicked
    good,
That science never yet was understood.
  The sons of Esculapius, if their art
Could remedy a perverse and wicked
    heart,
Might earn enormous wages! But, in
    fact,
The mind is not compounded and com-
    pact
Of precept and example; human art
In human nature has no share or part.
Hatred of vice, the fear of shame and
    sin,
Are things of native growth, not grafted
    in:
Else wise and worthy parents might cor-
    rect
In children's hearts each error and defect:
Whereas we see them disappointed still.
No scheme nor artifice of human skill
Can rectify the passions or the will.

Our commonwealth preserves its former
    frame,
Our common people are no more the
    same:
They that in skins and hides were rudely
    dress'd

Nor dreamt of law, nor sought to be re-
  dress'd
By rules of right, but in the days of old
Flock'd to the town, like cattle to the
  fold,
Are now the brave and wise; and we, the
  rest,
(Their betters nominally, once the best)
Degenerate, debas'd, timid, mean!
Who can endure to witness such a
  scene?
Their easy courtesies, the ready smile,
Prompt to deride, flatter, and beguile!
Their utter disregard of right or wrong,
Of truth or honour!—Out of such a
  throng
(For any difficulties, any need,
For any bold design or manly deed)
Never imagine you can choose a just
Or steady friend, or faithful in his trust.
  But change your habits! let them go
    their way!
Be condescending, affable, gay!

I walk by rule and measure, and incline
To neither side, but take an even line;
Fix'd in a single purpose and design.
With learning's happy gifts to celebrate,
To civilize and dignify the state:
Not leaguing with the discontented crew,
Nor with the proud and arbitrary few.

The generous and the brave, in common
  fame,
From time to time encounter praise or
  blame;
The vulgar pass unheeded; none escape
Scandal or insult in some form or shape.
Most fortunate are those, alive or dead,
Of whom the least is thought, the least
  is said.

Court not a tyrant's favour, nor combine
To further his iniquitous design;
But, if your faith is pledg'd, though late
  and loth,
If covenants have pass'd between you
  both,
Never assassinate him! keep your oath!

But should he still misuse his lawless
  power,
To trample on the people, and devour,
Depose or overturn him; anyhow!
Your oath permits it, and the gods allow.

The sovereign single person—what cares
  he
For love or hate, for friend or enemy?—
His single purpose is utility.

If popular distrust and hate prevail,
If saucy mutineers insult and rail,
Fret not your eager spirit,—take a line
Just, sober, and discreet, the same as
  mine.

Let no persuasive art tempt you to
  place
Your confidence in crafty minds and
  base;—
How can it answer? Will their help avail
When danger presses, and your foes
  assail?
The blessing which the gods in bounty
  send,
Will they consent to share it with a
  friend?
  No!—To bestrew the waves with scat-
    ter'd grain,
To cultivate the surface of the main,
Is not a task more absolutely vain
Than cultivating such allies as these,—
Fickle and unproductive as the seas.
  Such are all baser minds, never at
    rest,
With new demands importunately press'd,
A new pretension or a new request;
Till, foil'd with a refusal of the last,
They disavow their obligations past.
  But brave and gallant hearts are
    cheaply gain'd,
Faithful adherents, easily retain'd;
Men that will never disavow the debt
Of gratitude, or cancel or forget.

Waste not your efforts, struggle not, my
  friend,
Idle and old abuses to defend:

Take heed! the very measures that you
    press
May bring repentance with their own
    success.

Rash angry words, and spoken out of
    season,
When passion has usurp'd the throne of
    reason,
Have ruin'd many.—Passion is unjust,
And, for an idle transitory gust
Of gratified revenge, dooms us to pay
With a long repentance at a later day.

The gods send Insolence to lead astray
The man whom Fortune and the Fates
    betray;
Predestin'd to precipitate decay.
Wealth nurses Insolence, and wealth, we
    find,
When coupled with a poor and paltry
    mind,
Is evermore with insolence combin'd.
    Never in anger with the meaner sort
Be mov'd to a contemptuous retort,
Deriding their distresses; nor despise
In hasty speech their wants and miseries.
    Jove holds the balance, and the gods
    dispense
For all mankind riches and indigence.

Join with the world; adopt with every
    man
His party views, his temper, and his
    plan;
Strive to avoid offence, study to please,
Like the sagacious inmate of the seas,
That an accommodating colour brings,
Conforming to the rock to which he
    clings;
With every change of place changing his
    hue;
The model for a statesman such as you.

Let not a base calumnious pretence,
Exaggerating a minute offence,
Move you to wrong a friend; if, every
    time,
Faults in a friend were treated as a crime,

Here upon earth no friendship could have
    place.
But we, the creatures of a faulty race
Amongst ourselves, offend and are for-
    given:
Vengeance is the prerogative of heaven.

Schemes unadvisable and out of reason
Are best adjourn'd—wait for a proper
    season!
Time and a fair conjuncture govern all.
Hasty ambition hurries to a fall;
A fall predestin'd and ordain'd by
    heaven:
By a judicial madness madly driven,
Mistaking and confounding good and
    evil,
Men lose their senses, as they leave their
    level.

A trusty partisan, faithful and bold,
Is worth his weight in silver or in gold,
For times of trouble.—But the race is
    rare;
Steady determin'd men, ready to share
Good or ill fortune!—such, if such there
    are,
Could you survey the world, and search
    it round,
And bring together all that could be
    found;
The largest company you could enroll,
A single vessel could embark the
    whole!—
So few there are! the noble manly minds
Faithful and firm, the men that honour
    binds;
Impregnable to danger and to pain
And low seduction in the shape of gain.

From many a friend you must withhold
    your plans,
No man is safe with many partisans,
No secret!—With a party, sure but
    small,
Of bold adherents, trusty men withal,
You may succeed: else ruin must ensue,
Inevitable, for your friends and you.

An exile has no friends! no partisan
Is firm or faithful to the banish'd man;
A disappointment and a punishment,
Harder to bear, and worse than banish-
    ment.

Happy the man, with worldly wealth and
    ease,
Who, dying in good time, departs in
    peace.
Nor yet reduc'd to wander as a stranger
In exile and distress and daily danger;
To fawn upon his foes, to risk the trial
Of a friend's faith, and suffer a denial!

To mean or coward heart will I commend
In an old comrade or a past friend:
Nor with ungenerous, hasty zeal decry
A noble-minded gallant enemy.

Not to be born—never to see the sun—
No worldly blessing is a greater one!
And the next best is speedily to die,
And lapt beneath a load of earth to lie!

You, great Apollo, with its walls and
    towers
Fenc'd and adorn'd of old this town of
    ours!
Such favour in thy sight Alcathous won,
Of Pelops old the fair and manly son.
Now, therefore, in thy clemency divine,
Protect these very walls, our own and
    thine!
Guide and assist us, turn aside the boast
Of the destroying haughty Persian host!
  So shall thy people each returning
    spring
Lay fatted hecatombs, and gladly bring
Fair gifts, with chaunted hymns and
    lively song,
Dances and feasts, and happy shouts
    among:
Before thy altar, glorifying thee,
In peace and health and wealth, cheer-
    ful and free.
  Yet much I fear the faction and the
    strife,
Throughout our Grecian cities, raging
    rife;

And their wild councils. But do thou
    defend
This town of ours, our founder and our
    friend!
  Wide have I wander'd, far beyond the
    sea,
Even to the distant shores of Sicily,
To broad Euboea's plentiful domain,
With the rich vineyards in its planted
    plain;
And to the sunny wave and winding edge
Of fair Eurotas, with its reedy sedge;
Where Sparta stands in simple majesty,
Among her manly rulers, there was I!
Greeted and welcom'd (there and every-
    where)
With courteous entertainment, kind and
    fair;
Yet still my weary spirit would repine,
Longing again to view this land of mine.
  Henceforward no design nor interest
Shall ever move me, but the first and
    best,
With learning's happy gift to celebrate,
To adorn and dignify my native state.
  The song, the dance, music and verse
    agreeing,
Will occupy my life, and fill my being:
Pursuits of elegance and learned skill
(With good repute and kindness and
    good will,
Among the wiser sort) will pass my time
Without an enemy, without a crime;
Harmless and just with every rank of
    men,
Both the free native and the denizen.
                              —J. H. FRERE.

THE SHIP OF STATE

ALCÆUS

This poem is generally assumed to be an
allegory and the model which Horace imitated in his celebrated ode to the state
(I, 14). For Alcæus, see above, p. 103.

Now here, now there the wild waves
    sweep,
Whilst we, betwixt them o'er the deep

In shattered, tempest-beaten bark
With labouring ropes along are driven,
The billows dashing o'er our dark
Upheavèd deck—in tatters riven
Our sails—whose yawning rents be-
tween

The raging sea and sky are seen.
Loose from their hold our anchors burst
And then the third, the fatal wave,
Comes rolling onward like the first,
And doubles all our toil to save.

—J. H. MERIVALE.

III. THE INDIVIDUAL

ENDURE!

ARCHILOCHUS

For Archilochus, see above, p. 103.

Groans rise on griefs, O Pericles! nor
they
Who feed the woe, in wine or feast are
gay.
The billow of the many-roaring deep
Has borne these pleasures in its whelm-
ing sweep.
Our grief-swollen hearts, now, draw their
breath in pain;
Yet blessings, oh my friend! shall smile
again.
The gods reserve for seeming-cureless
woe
A balm, and antidotes on grief bestow.
In turn the cure and suffering take their
round,
And we now groaning feel the bleeding
wound:
Now other breasts the shifting tortures
know;
Endure, nor droop thus womanish in woe.

—C. A. ELTON.

SELF-CONTROL

ARCHILOCHUS

Tost on a sea of troubles, Soul, my Soul,
Thyself do thou control;
And to the weapons of advancing foes
A stubborn breast oppose:

Undaunted mid the hostile might
Of squadrons burning for the fight.
Thine be no boasting when the victor's
crown
Wins thee deserved renown;
Thine no dejected sorrow, when defeat
Would urge a base retreat:
Rejoice in joyous things—nor overmuch
Let grief thy bosom touch
Midst evil, and still bear in mind
How changeful are the ways of human-
kind.

—WILLIAM HAY.

INDEPENDENCE

ARCHILOCHUS

What's Gyges or his gold to me!
His royal state or rich array?
From envy's taint my breast is free,
I covet no proud tyrant's sway.
I envy not the gods in heaven!
The gods to me my lot have given.
That lot, for good or ill, I'll bear,
And for no other man's I care.

—WILLIAM MURE.

THE LOST SHIELD

ARCHILOCHUS

To the Greek it was a supreme disgrac
to lose one's shield and not one's life a
the same time. Archilochus, with a goo
deal of daring, makes light of the episode
and thereby sets a fashion for numerou
later poets.

The foeman glories in my shield;
 left it in the battle-field;
 threw it down beside the wood,
Unscathed by scars, unstained by blood;
And let him glory, since from death
Escaped, I keep my forfeit breath.
 soon may find, at little cost,
As good a shield as that I lost.
—J. H. MERIVALE.

A STORM AT SEA

ARCHILOCHUS

Behold, my Glaucus! how the deep
 Heaves, while the sweeping billows
 howl
And round the promontory steep
 The big black clouds portentous scowl,
With thunder fraught and lightning's
 glare,
While Terror rules and wild Despair.
—J. H. MERIVALE.

THE GODS DISPOSE

ARCHILOCHUS

Leave the gods to order all things;
 Often from the gulf of woe
They exalt the poor man, grovelling
 In the gloomy shades below;
Often turn again and prostrate
 Lay in dust the loftiest head,
Dooming him through life to wander,
 Reft of sense and wanting bread.
—J. H. MERIVALE.

HYMN TO APHRODITE [1]

SAPPHO

Sappho, of the late seventh century B.C.,
spent most of her life in Mytilene, where

[1] From Wharton's *Sappho*. Reprinted by
permission of Dodd Mead & Co., publishers.

she maintained a school of music and
poetry for the instruction of maidens. She
was of noble birth and as a consequence
suffered exile on some occasion of political
strife. The story is told that she rejected
the poet Alcæus, and that in consequence
of an unrequited love for a certain Phaon
she committed suicide, but nothing certain
is known of her life. She was the only
woman of Greece to win a place in the
front rank of poets. Like Alcæus, she was
the author of Æolian songs set to music,
and her main theme was love. Only
fragments of her work are extant.

Glittering-throned, undying Aphrodite,
Wile-weaving daughter of Zeus, I pray
 thee,
Tame not my soul with heavy woe, dread
 mistress,
 Nay, nor with anguish!

But hither come, if ever erst of old time
Thou didst incline, and listenedst to my
 crying,
And from thy father's palace down de-
 scending,
 Camest with golden

Chariot yoked: thee fair swift-flying
 sparrows
Over dark earth with multitudinous
 fluttering,
Pinion on pinion, through middle ether
 Down from heaven hurried.

Quickly they came like light, and thou,
 blest lady,
Smiling with clear undying eyes didst
 ask me
What was the woe that troubled me, and
 wherefore
 I had cried to thee:

What thing I longed for to appease my
 frantic
Soul: and Whom now must I persuade,
 thou askedst,
Whom must entangle to thy love, and
 who now,
 Sappho, hath wronged thee?

Yea, for if now he shun, he soon shall
    chase thee;
Yea, if he take not gifts, he soon shall
    give them;
Yea, if he love not, soon shall he begin to
    Love thee, unwilling.

Come to me now too, and from tyrannous
    sorrow
Free me, and all things that my soul
    desires to
Have done, do for me, queen, and let
    thyself too
    Be my great ally!
        —JOHN ADDINGTON SYMONDS.

A RIVAL OF THE GODS

SAPPHO

Blest as the immortal gods is he,
The youth whose eyes may look on thee,
Whose ears thy tongue's sweet melody
    May still devour.

Thou smilest too?—sweet smile, whose
    charm
Has struck my soul with wild alarm,
And, when I see thee, bids disarm
    Each vital power.

Speechless I gaze: the flame within
Runs swift o'er all my quivering skin;
My eyeballs swim; with dizzy din
    My brain reels round;

And cold drops fall; and tremblings frail
Seize every limb; and grassy pale
I grow; and then—together fail
    Both sight and sound.
        —J. H. MERIVALE.

THE MOON

SAPPHO

The stars around the lovely moon
Their radiant visage hide as soon

As she, full-orbed, appears to sight,
Flooding the earth with her silvery light.
        —FELTON.

SLUMBER

SAPPHO

Through orchard-plot with fragrance
    crowned
The clear cold fountain murmuring
    flows;
And forest leaves with rustling sound
    Invite to soft repose.
        —J. H. MERIVALE.

COME, VENUS!

SAPPHO

Come Venus, come
Hither with thy golden cup,
    Where nectar-floated flowerets swim.
Fill, fill the goblet up;
    These laughing lips shall kiss the
      brim,—
    Come, Venus, come!
        —ANON.

FOREVER DEAD [1]

SAPPHO

Thou liest dead, and there will be no
    memory left behind
Of thee or thine in all the earth, for
    never didst thou bind
The roses of Pierian streams upon thy
    brow; thy doom
Is writ to flit with unknown ghosts in
    cold and nameless gloom.
        —EDWIN ARNOLD.

[1] From Wharton's *Sappho.* Reprinted by
permission of Dodd Mead & Co., publishers.

GARLANDS [1]

SAPPHO

Of foliage and flowers love-laden
  Twine wreaths for thy flowing hair,
With thine own soft fingers, maiden,
  Weave garlands of parsley fair;
For flowers are sweet, and the Graces
  On suppliants wreathed with may
Look down from their heavenly places,
  But turn from the crownless away.
            —JOHN ADDINGTON SYMONDS.

THE DAUGHTER

SAPPHO

I have a child, a lovely one,
In beauty like the golden sun,
Or like sweet flowers of earliest bloom;
And Clais is her name, for whom
I Lydia's treasures, were they mine,
Would glad resign.
            —J. H. MERIVALE.

LOVE'S DISTRACTION

SAPPHO

Oh, my sweet mother, 'tis in vain,
  I cannot weave as once I wove,
So wildered is my heart and brain
  With thinking of that youth I love.
            —THOMAS MOORE.

LIKE THE SWEET APPLE

SAPPHO

Like the sweet apple which reddens upon
    the topmost bough,
A-top on the topmost twig,—which the
    pluckers forgot, somehow,—
Forgot it not, nay, but got it not, for
    none could get it till now.
            —D. G. ROSSETTI.

[1] From Wharton's *Sappho*. Reprinted by permission of Dodd Mead & Co., publishers.

EVENING [1]

SAPPHO

Hesperus brings all things back
Which the daylight made us lack,
Brings the sheep and goats to rest,
Brings the baby to the breast.
            —EDWIN ARNOLD.

SUMMER [2]

ALCÆUS

For Alcæus, see above, p. 103.

Come all and wet your throats with wine,
  The dog-star reigns on high,
The Summer parches tree and vine,
  And everything is dry.
Full cheerily the locust sings
  Within the leafy shade,
Rasping away beneath his wings
  A shrill-toned serenade.
Come all, and drink, the star is up!
Come all and drain the sparkling cup.

The artichokes are all ablow
  And all the fields ablaze,
Where Phœbus draws his dazzling bow
  And hurls his spreading rays.
The women burn with fierce desire,
  The men are dead with heat,
For Sirius sends a baleful fire
  And parches head and feet.
Come all, and drink, the star is up!
Come all and drain the sparkling cup.
            —J. S. EASBY-SMITH.

WINTER

ALCÆUS

Jove descends in sleet and snow,
  Howls the vexed and angry deep;

[2] Reprinted by permission of Mr. J. S. Easby-Smith.

Every stream forgets to flow,
Bound in winter's icy sleep.
Ocean wave and forest hoar
To the blast responsive roar.

Drive the tempest from your door,
  Blaze on blaze your hearthstone piling,
And unmeasured goblets pour
Brimful, high with nectar smiling.
Then beneath your poet's head
Be a downy pillow spread.
          —J. H. MERIVALE.

DRINKING SONG

ALCÆUS

Why wait we for the torches' lights?
Now let us drink while day invites.
In mighty flagons hither bring
The deep-red blood of many a vine,
That we may largely quaff, and sing
The praises of the god of wine,
The son of Jove and Semele
Who gave the jocund wine to be
A sweet oblivion to our woes.
Fill, fill the goblet, one and two;
Let every brimmer, as it flows,
In sportive chase the last pursue.
          —J. H. MERIVALE.

THE TYRANT'S DEATH [1]

ALCÆUS

Alcæus in an age of petty princes opposed the type of government that tended invariably towards tyranny. He is in this sense a forerunner of the coming age of democracy.

Now for wine and joy divine,
  Myrsilus is dead!
Now 'tis meet the earth to beat
With quick and happy tread.
  For Myrsilus is dead!
  Myrsilus is dead!
          —J. S. EASBY-SMITH.

[1] Reprinted by permission of Mr. J. S. Easby-Smith.

THE SEA-COCKLE [1]

ALCÆUS

Child of the aged rocks,
Child of the hoary sea,
  Thou fillest with joy
  The heart of the boy,
O cockle from the sea.
          —J. S. EASBY-SMITH.

OLD AGE

ANACREON

Like many other poets of the lyric period, Anacreon of Teos (late sixth century B.C.) moved about from place to place, sojourning now with one tyrant and now with another, welcome everywhere for his gifts of song. He is known to later times chiefly through skillful imitations which were long thought to be genuine and which are now called the *Anacreontics.*

Golden hues of youth are fled;
Hoary locks deform my head.
Bloomy graces, dalliance gay,
All the flowers of life decay.
Withering age begins to trace
Sad memorials o'er my face;
Time has shed its sweetest bloom,
All the future must be gloom!
This awakes my hourly sighing;
Dreary is the thought of dying!
Pluto's is a dark abode,
Sad the journey, sad the road:
And, the gloomy travel o'er,
Ah! we can return no more!
          —THOMAS MOORE.

YOUTH AND PLEASURE

ANACREON

Rich in bliss, I proudly scorn
The stream of Amalthea's horn!

Nor should I ask to call the throne
Of the Tartessian prince my own;
To totter through his train of years,
The victim of declining fears.
One little hour of joy for me
Is worth a dull eternity.
—THOMAS MOORE.

ANACREONTICS

BEAUTY

Horns to bulls wise Nature lends;
Horses she with hoofs defends;
Hares with nimble feet relieves;
Dreadful teeth to lions gives;
Fishes learn through streams to slide;
Birds through yielding air to glide;
Men with courage she supplies;
But to women these denies.
What then gives she? Beauty, this
Both their arms and armour is:
She, that can this weapon use,
Fire and sword with ease subdues.
—THOMAS STANLEY.

LOVE, THE CHEAT

Downward was the wheeling Bear
Driven by the Waggoner:
Men by powerful sleep opprest,
Gave their busy troubles rest;
Love, in this still depth of night,
Lately at my house did light;
Where, perceiving all fast lock'd,
At the door he boldly knock'd.
"Who's that," said I, "that does keep
Such a noise and breaks my sleep?"
"Ope," saith Love, "for pity hear;
'Tis a child, thou need'st not fear,
Wet and weary, from his way
Led by this dark night astray."
With compassion this I heard;
Light I struck, the door unbarr'd;
Where a little boy appears,
Who wings, bow, and quiver bears;
Near the fire I made him stand,
With my own I chaf'd his hand,
And with kindly busy care
Wrung the chill drops from his hair.

When well warm'd he was, and dry,
"Now," saith he, " 'tis time to try
If my bow no hurt did get,
For methinks the string is wet."
With that, drawing it, a dart
He let fly that pierc'd my heart;
Leaping then, and laughing said,
"Come, my friend, with me be glad;
For my bow thou seest is sound
Since thy heart has got a wound."
—THOMAS STANLEY.

ROSES

Roses (Love's delight) let's join
To the red-cheek'd God of Wine;
Roses crown us, while we laugh,
And the juice of Autumn quaff!
Roses of all flowers the king,
Roses the fresh pride o' th' Spring,
Joy of every deity.
Love, when with the Graces he
For the ball himself disposes,
Crowns his golden hair with roses.
Circling then with these our brow,
We'll to Bacchus' temple go:
There some willing beauty lead,
And a youthful measure tread.
—THOMAS STANLEY.

THE COMBAT

Now will I a lover be;
Love himself commanded me.
Full at first of stubborn pride,
To submit my soul denied;
He his quiver takes and bow,
Bids defiance, forth I go,
Arm'd with spear and shield, we meet;
On he charges, I retreat:
Till perceiving in the fight
He had wasted every flight,
Into me, with fury hot,
Like a dart himself he shot,
And my cold heart melts; my shield
Useless, no defence could yield;
For what boots an outward screen
When, alas, the fight's within!
—THOMAS STANLEY.

THE SWALLOW

Chattering swallow! what shall we,
Shall we do to punish thee?
Shall we clip thy wings, or cut
Tereus-like thy shrill tongue out?
Who Rhodantha driv'st away
From my dreams by break of day.
—THOMAS STANLEY.

CAREFREE

I not care for Gyges' sway,
Or the Lydian sceptre weigh;
Nor am covetous of gold,
Nor with envy kings behold;
All my care is to prepare
Fragrant unguents for my hair;
All my care is where to get
Roses for a coronet;
All my care is for to-day;
What's to-morrow who can say?
Come then, let us drink and dice,
And to Bacchus sacrifice,
Ere death come and take us off,
Crying, Hold! th' hast drunk enough.
—THOMAS STANLEY.

THE CUP

All thy skill if thou collect,
Make a cup as I direct:
Roses climbing o'er the brim,
Yet must seem in wine to swim;
Faces too there should be there,
None that frowns or wrinkles wear;
But the sprightly son of Jove,
With the beauteous Queen of Love;
There, beneath a pleasant shade,
By a vine's wide branches made,
Must the Loves, their arms laid by,
Keep the Graces company;
And the bright-hair'd god of day
With a youthful bevy play.
—THOMAS STANLEY.

ALL THINGS DRINK

Fruitful earth drinks up the rain;
Trees from earth drink that again;
The sea drinks the air, the sun
Drinks the sea, and him the moon.
Is it reason then, d'ye think,
I should thirst when all else drink?
—THOMAS STANLEY.

THE PICTURE

Painter, by unmatch'd desert
Master of the Rhodian art,
Come, my absent mistress take,
As I shall describe her: make
First her hair, as black as bright,
And if colours so much right
Can but do her, let it too
Smell of aromatic dew;
Underneath this shade, must thou
Draw her alabaster brow;
Her dark eye-brows so dispose
That they neither part nor close,
But by a divorce so slight
Be disjoin'd, may cheat the sight:
From her kindly killing eye
Make a flash of lightning fly,
Sparkling like Minerva's, yet
Like Cythera's mildly sweet:
Roses in milk swimming seek
For the pattern of her cheek:
In her lip such moving blisses,
As from all may challenge kisses;
Round about her neck (outvying
Parian stone) the Graces flying;
And o'er all her limbs at last
A loose purple mantle cast;
But so ordered that the eye
Some part naked may descry,
An essay by which the rest
That lies hidden, may be guess'd.
  So, to life th' hast come so near,
  All of her, but voice, is here.
—THOMAS STANLEY.

SPRING

See the Spring herself discloses,
And the Graces gather roses;
See how the becalmed seas
Now their swelling waves appease;

How the duck swims, how the crane
Comes from winter home again;
See how Titan's cheerful ray
Chaseth the dark clouds away;
Now in their new robes of green
Are the ploughman's labours seen:
Now the lusty teeming Earth
Springs each hour with a new birth;
Now the olive blooms: the vine
Now doth with plump pendants shine;
And with leaves and blossoms now
Freshly bourgeons every bough.

—THOMAS STANLEY.

OLD I AM

Old I am, yet can (I think)
Those that younger are out-drink;
When I dance no staff I take,
But a well-fill'd bottle shake:
He that doth in war delight,
Come, and with these arms let's fight;
Fill the cup, let loose a flood
Of the rich grape's luscious blood;
Old I am, and therefore may,
Like Silenus, drink and play.

—THOMAS STANLEY.

THE BEE

Love, a Bee that lurk'd among
Roses saw not, and was stung:
Who for his hurt finger crying,
Running sometimes, sometimes flying,
Doth to his fair mother hie,
And, "O help," cries he, "I die;
A winged snake hath bitten me,
Call'd by countrymen a Bee:"
At which Venus, "If such smart
A Bee's little sting impart,
How much greater is the pain,
They, whom thou hast hurt, sustain?"

—THOMAS STANLEY.

THE GRASSHOPPER

Grasshopper thrice-happy! who
Sipping the cool morning dew,
Queen-like chirpest all the day
Seated on some verdant spray;

Thine is all whate'er earth brings,
Or the hours with laden wings;
Thee, the ploughman calls his joy,
'Cause thou nothing dost destroy:
Thou by all art honour'd; all
Thee the spring's sweet prophet call;
By the Muses thou admired,
By Apollo art inspir'd,
Ageless, ever-singing, good,
Without passion, flesh or blood;
Oh how near thy happy state
Comes the gods to imitate!

—THOMAS STANLEY.

YOUTHFUL AGE

Young men dancing, and the old
Sporting I with joy behold;
But an old man gay and free
Dancing most I love to see;
Age and youth alike he shares,
For his heart belies his hairs.

—THOMAS STANLEY.

WINE AND SONG

Bring me hither Homer's lute,
Taught with mirth (not wars) to suit;
Reach a full cup, that I may
All the laws of wine obey,
Drink, and dance, and to the lyre
Sing what Bacchus shall inspire.

—THOMAS STANLEY.

NIGHT [1]

ALCMAN

Alcman (early seventh century B.C.) was born in Sardis in Lydia, but lived most of his life in Sparta whither he was brought as a slave. He employed his talents in various sorts of short lyric as well as in choral odes and hymns. Of the six books produced by him only very small fragments remain.

[1] From T. S. Perry, *A History of Greek Literature.* Copyright by Henry Holt & Co. Reprinted by permission.

Stillness upon the mountain-heads and
    deep abysses,
    The cliffs of ocean and each gloomy
    cave;
And quiet reigns throughout the craggy
    forests,
    Where fiercest, wildest beasts are wont
    to rave!
All living things upon this dark earth
    nourished,
    Even the swarms of busy bees, are
    still;
In purple depths of ocean sleep sea-
    monsters,
And merry wingèd birds forget to trill.
              —T. S. PERRY.

RETURN OF SPRING

IBYCUS

Ibycus (late sixth century B.C.), of
Rhegium in Italy, later moved to the court
of Polycrates. While still in Italy he
seems to have produced mainly hymns and
choral lyrics, but during his stay in Samos
he devoted himself to love poetry in the
manner of Sappho.

What time soft zephyrs fan the trees
In the blest gardens of th' Hesperides,
Where those bright golden apples
    glow,
Fed by the fruitful streams that round
    them flow,
And new-born clusters teem with wine
Beneath the shadowy foliage of the
    vine;
To me the joyous season brings
But added torture on his sunny wings.
Then Love, the tyrant of my breast,
Impetuous ravisher of joys and rest,
Bursts, furious, from his mother's
    arms,
And fills my trembling soul with new
    alarms;
Like Boreas from his Thracian plains,
Cloth'd in fierce lightnings, in my bosom
    reigns,

And rages still, the madd'ning power—
His parching flames my wither'd heart
    devour:
Wild Phrensy comes my senses o'er,
Sweet Peace is fled, and Reason rules
    no more.
              —J. H. MERIVALE.

THE LONG SLEEP

SIMONIDES

Simonides (about 556 to about 467
B.C.) was born on the island of Ceos, and
was finally attracted to the brilliant court
of Hiero of Syracuse, where he is thought
to have remained until his death. He was
a whole-hearted supporter of the Greek
struggle for freedom, and his brief epi-
taphs celebrating the victory over the
Persians are his most famous work.

Long, long and dreary is the night
    That waits us in the silent grave;
Few, and of rapid flight,
    The years from Death we save.
Short—ah, how short—that fleeting
    space;
And when man's little race
Is run, and Death's grim portals o'er him
    close,
How lasting his repose!
              —J. H. MERIVALE.

SHORTNESS OF LIFE

MIMNERMUS

Mimnermus (late sixth century B.C.),
flute player and elegist, was a native of
Colophon in Ionia. In his hands elegy
became a form of love poetry, meditative
and melancholy in character.

We, like the leaves of many blossomed
    Spring,
When the sun's rays their sudden
    radiance fling

In growing strength, on earth, a little
    while,
Delighted, see youth's blooming flow-
    erets smile.
Not with that wisdom of the Gods
    endued,
To judge aright of evil and of good.
Two Fates, dark-scowling, at our side
    attend;
Of youth, of life, each points the destined
    end,
Old age and death: the fruit of youth
    remains
Brief, as the sunshine scattered o'er the
    plains:
And when these fleeting hours have sped
    away,
To die were better than to breathe the
    day.
A load of grief the burdened spirit
    wears;
Domestic troubles rise; penurious cares;
One with an earnest love of children
    sighs;
The grave is opened and he childless
    dies:
Another drags in pain his lingering days,
While slow disease upon his vitals
    preys.
Nor lives there one, whom Jupiter on
    high
Exempts from years of mixt calamity.
          —C. A. ELTON.

THE SUN'S GOLDEN BOWL

MIMNERMUS

Toil is the Sun-god's portion, toil all
    the livelong day,
Day in, day out, forever; there is no
    stop, no stay—
So soon as Dawn leaves Ocean, and, rosy-
    fingered, speeds
Upon her journey skyward—for him, nor
    for his steeds.
For when his course is ended, back
    through the dusky deep
A hollow couch goes faring, wherein he
    lies asleep.
A mighty bowl this couch is, and lovely
    to behold,
The gift of wise Hephaistos, who wrought
    it all in gold,
And furnished it with pinions. It darts
    across the seas,
Skimming the crested waves from the
    far Hesperides
Back to the ruddy Sun-folk, where
    steeds and car remain
Till Morning's own dear daughter, the
    Dawn, comes up again.
The Sun then mounts his chariot, seeks
    that far western shore
And rushing, rushing onward, gives us
    the day once more.
          —KIRBY FLOWER SMITH.

IV. CEREMONIAL SONGS

CHILDREN'S SONG

THE SWALLOW

It was a custom in Rhodes for children to go about from house to house singing the coming of spring. The authorship of the following example of such a song is not known.

She is here, she is here, the swallow!
Fair seasons bringing, fair years to
    follow!
    Her belly is white,
    Her back black as night!
    From your rich house
    Roll forth to us
    Tarts, wine, and cheese:
    Or if not these,

Oatmeal and barley-cake
The swallow deigns to take.
What shall we have? or must we hence
    away?
Thanks, if you give; if not, we'll make
    you pay!
The house-door hence we'll carry;
Nor shall the lintel tarry;
From hearth and home your wife we'll
    rob;
She is so small,
To take her off will be an easy job!
Whate'er you give, give largess free!
Up! open, open to the swallow's call!
No grave old men, but merry children
    we!
—JOHN ADDINGTON SYMONDS.

BANQUET SONGS

HARMODIUS AND ARISTOGEITON

CALLISTRATUS

Nothing is known of Callistratus aside
from the fact that he was the author of
this banquet song. The two popular
heroes, Harmodius and Aristogeiton, were
long celebrated as the deliverers of Athens
from the power of the tyrants. They murdered Hipparchus on the occasion of a
festival in 514 B.C., and suffered death as
a consequence.

In a wreath of myrtle I'll wear my glaive,
Like Harmodius and Aristogeiton brave,
    Who, striking the tyrant down,
    Made Athens a freeman's town.

Harmodius, our darling, thou art not
    dead!
Thou liv'st in the isles of the blest, 'tis
    said,
    With Achilles first in speed,
    And Tydides Diomede.

In a wreath of myrtle I'll wear my glaive,
Like Harmodius and Aristogeiton brave,
    When the twain on Athena's day
    Did the tyrant Hipparchus slay.

For aye shall your fame in the land be
    told,
Harmodius and Aristogeiton bold,
    Who, striking the tyrant down,
    Made Athens a freeman's town.
        —JOHN CONINGTON.

THE WARRIOR

HYBRIAS

The name is all that is known of the
author of this banquet song.

My wealth's a burly spear and brand,
And a right good shield of hides un-
    tanned,
    Which on my arm I buckle:
With these I plough, I reap, I sow,
With these I make sweet vintage flow,
    And all around me truckle.
But your wights that take no pride to
    wield
A massy spear and well-made shield,
    Nor joy to draw the sword:
O, I bring those heartless, hapless drones,
Down in a trice on their marrow-bones,
To call me king and lord.
        —THOMAS CAMPBELL.

THEOXENOS

PINDAR

Pindar (522 to about 441 B.C.) was
born at Thebes of noble family. Little
more is known of his life than that he received a very careful training and that he
travelled extensively. He was the greatest
representative of the Doric, or choral,
lyric, as contrasted with the Æolic, or
personal, lyric, of Alcæus and Sappho.
Most of his odes were written in celebration of athletic victories at the great
national festivals of Elis, Delphi, and
Corinth. The origin and nature of these
games, as also the poet's own connection
with the worship of Apollo at Delphi,
account for the religious quality of the

odes. Pindar was a devout follower of the national faith, but he would take no part in promoting the fanciful stories that attributed faulty human conduct to the gods. Of seventeen books of odes known to antiquity only three and fragments of a fourth are now extant.

O soul, 'tis thine in season meet,
To pluck of love the blossom sweet,
　When hearts are young:
But he who sees the blazing beams,
The light that from that forehead
　streams,
　And is not stung;—
Who is not storm-tost with desire,—
Lo! he, I ween, with frozen fire,
Of adamant or stubborn steel,
Is forged in his cold heart that cannot
　feel.

Disowned, dishonoured, and denied
By Aphrodite glittering-eyed,
　He either toils
All day for gold, a sordid gain,
Or bent beneath a woman's reign,
　In petty broils,
Endures her insolence, a drudge,
Compelled the common path to trudge;
But I, apart from this disease,
Wasting away like wax of holy bees,

Which the sun's splendor wounds, do
　pine,
Whene'er I see the young-limbed bloom
　divine
Of boys. Lo! look you well; for here in
　Tenedos,
Grace and Persuasion dwell in young
　Theoxenos.
　　　—JOHN ADDINGTON SYMONDS.

PROCESSIONAL

RETURN OF DEMETRIUS

This is a late example of the processionals which in early times were addressed to the gods and sung by choruses of boys and girls on their way to the shrine. Here Demetrius Poliorcetes (end of the fourth century B.C.) is hailed as a god.

See how the mightiest gods, and best-
　beloved
　Towards our town are winging!
For lo, Demeter and Demetrius
　This glad day is bringing!
She to perform her daughter's solemn
　rites;
　Mystic pomps attend her:
He, joyous as a god should be, and blithe,
　Comes with laughing splendor.
Show forth your triumph! Friends all,
　troop around!
　Let him shine above you!
Be you the stars to circle him with
　love;
　He's the sun to love you.
Hail, offspring of Poseidon, powerful god,
　Child of Aphrodite!
The other gods keep far away from
　earth;
　Have no ears, though mighty;
They are not, or they will not hear us
　wail:
　Thee our eye beholdeth;
Not wood, not stone, but living, breath-
　ing, real,
　Thee our prayer enfoldeth.
First give us peace! Give, dearest, for
　thou canst:
　Thou art Lord and Master!
The Sphinx, who not on Thebes, but on
　all Greece
　Swoops to gloat and pasture;
The Ætolian, he who sits upon his
　rock,
　Like that old disaster;
He feeds upon our flesh and blood, and
　we
　Can no longer labor;
For it was ever thus the Ætolian thief
　Preyed upon his neighbor;
Him punish thou, or if not thou, then
　send
　Œdipus to harm him,

Who'll cast his Sphinx down from his
    cliff of pride,
Or to stone will charm him.
    —JOHN ADDINGTON SYMONDS.

DIRGES

DANAE ADRIFT

SIMONIDES

Danae and her son had been set adrift
for the purpose of defeating the fulfilment
of an oracle, which had predicted that the
king would be slain by his daughter's son.
For Simonides, see above, p. 118.

When, in the carven chest,
The winds that blew and waves in wild
    unrest
Smote her with fear, she, not with cheeks
    unwet,
Her arms of love round Perseus set,
    And said: "O child, what grief is mine!
But thou dost slumber, and thy baby
    breast
Is sunk in rest,
Here in the cheerless brass-bound bark,
Tossed amid starless night and pitchy
    dark.
Nor dost thou heed the scudding brine
Of waves that wash above the curls so
    deep,
Nor the shrill winds that sweep,—
Lapped in thy purple robe's embrace,
Fair little face!
But if this dread were dreadful too to
    thee,
Then wouldst thou lend thy listening ear
    to me;
Therefore I cry,—Sleep, babe, and sea be
    still,
And slumber our unmeasured ill!
    Oh, may some change of fate, sire
    Zeus, from thee
Descend, our woes to end!
But if this prayer, too overbold, offend
Thy justice, yet be merciful to me."
    —JOHN ADDINGTON SYMONDS.

ELYSIUM

PINDAR

For Pindar, see above, p. 120.

For them the night all through,
In that broad realm below,
The splendor of the sun spreads endless
    light;
'Mid rosy meadows bright,
Their city of the tombs with incense-
    trees,
    And golden chalices
Of flowers, and fruitage fair,
Scenting the breezy air,
Is laden. There with horses and with
    play,
With games and lyres, they while the
    hours away.

On every side around
Pure happiness is found,
With all the blooming beauty of the
    world;
There fragrant smoke, upcurled
From altars where the blazing fire is
    dense
    With perfumed frankincense,
    Burned unto gods in heaven,
    Through all the land is driven,
Making its pleasant places odorous
With scented gales and sweet airs
    amorous.
    —JOHN ADDINGTON SYMONDS.

EPITAPHS

THE HEROES OF THERMOPYLÆ

SIMONIDES

For Simonides, see above, p. 118.

Of those who at Thermopylæ were
    slain,
    Glorious the doom, and beautiful the
    lot;

Their tomb an altar: men from tears
     refrain
   To honor them, and praise, but mourn
     them not.
Such sepulchre, nor drear decay
Nor all-destroying time shall waste; this
   right have they.
Within their grave the home-bred glory
   Of Greece was laid: this witness gives
Leonidas the Spartan, in whose story
   A wreath of famous virtue ever lives.
                              —JOHN STIRLING.

SALAMIS

SIMONIDES

Well-watered Corinth was our home
   before;
We lie on Salamis' Aiantian shore.
The ships of Tyre, the Persian, and the
   Mede
We routed, and thus holy Greece we
   freed.
                              —LORD NEAVES.

HEROES OF THE PERSIAN INVASION

SIMONIDES

Noble to die! if that be virtue's crown,
Fortune to us her bounty well displayed.
Striving to make Greece free, we gained
   renown
That shrouds us where we lie, and ne'er
   can fade.
                              —LORD NEAVES.

ODES OF VICTORY

THE FIRST OLYMPIAN

PINDAR

This ode celebrates the victory won for
Hiero, king of Syracuse, by his horse
Pherenikos. Woven into the song of victory and praises of the king is the myth of
Pelops. This linking of a well known
myth with a theme of the moment is characteristic of Pindar's epinicia, or songs of
victory, and is one of the charms of his
poetry. For Pindar, see above, p. 120.

For Pindar, see above, p. 120.

(Strophe 1)

Chiefest is water of all things, for
   streaming
   Therefrom all life and existence came;
And all proud treasure of princes the
   gleaming
     Splendour of gold outshines, as the
       flame
Of a great fire flings through the night its
   rays.
But, heart of mine, if thou fain wouldst
   praise
   Triumphs in athlete-contests won,
Search not, when day with his glory is
   glowing,
For a radiant star more life-bestowing
   In the whole void sky, than the kingly
     sun.
Even so shall we find no brighter crown
   Than Olympia giveth whereof to sing;
For thence doth the chant of high
   renown
   O'er the spirits of bards its perfume
     fling,
When, the praise of Kronion in song
   resounding,
Unto Hiero's blest hearth wealth-
   abounding
   The hymn of his praise they bring.

(Antistrophe 1)

Hiero!—yea, for the rod of his power
   Is a sceptre of righteousness stretched
     o'er the land
Of the myriad flocks; and the choice of
   the flower
     Of chivalry ever is plucked by his
       hand.
Yea, and he also is garlanded.
With the blossom of song enstarring his
   head,
   The song that with gladsome voices
     now

We singers chant, at the banquet meeting
Of the Prince who giveth us friendship's
    greeting.
  Now, O my Muse, from its rest take
    thou
The lyre that is strung to the Dorian
    strain,
  If the glory of fleet Pherenikus, he
Who triumphed in Pisa's Olympian plain,
  Haply with rapture of song thrilled
    thee,
When flashed in the course of Alpheus'
    river
His body by lash or by goad touched
    never,
  And wedded to victory

                            (*Epode 1*)
His lord, the ruler of Syracuse-town,
  The king who joyeth in gallant steeds.
Flasheth afar his name's renown,
  Flasheth from Sicily far oversea
  Where Pelops, the exile from Lydia's
    meads,
  Founded a hero-colony—
Pelops, beloved of the Earth-enfolder,
  Poseidon the strong, when the Fate
    of the Thread
Drew him resplendent with ivory shoul-
    der
  From the undefiled laver, whom men
    deemed dead.
There be marvels full many; and fables
    hoary
  With inventions manifold broidered
    o'er
Falsify legend, I wot, with a story
  Wherein truth liveth no more.

                            (*Str. 2*)
But the Grace of Beauty, which aye is
    weaving
  All manner of charm round the souls
    of men,
Taketh these tales unworthy believing,
  And arrays them in honour: so cometh
    it then
That man with unwavering credence
    clings
To a false-feigned tale of impossible
    things.

But the after-days are the witnesses
That be wisest. Reverent speech be-
    seemeth
The mortal who uttereth that which he
    deemeth
  Of the Gods—so shall his reproach be
    less.
O Tantalus' son, I will speak not as
    they
Who told thy story in days of old!
But thy father bade thee a guest that
    day
  To a banquet arrayed by the righteous-
    souled
Upon Sipylus' loved height—so he
    tendered
To the Gods requital for boons they had
    rendered.
  On a sudden the chariot of gold
                            (*Ant. 2*)
Of the Lord of the Trident gleaming
    splendid,
  Whose soul was with love for thy
    youth overcome,
Bare thee, as up through the blue ye
    ascended,
  To imperial Zeus's glory-home,
Whither also came in the after-day
Ganymedes ravished from earth away
  In halls celestial the nectar to pour.
But when viewless thus from the earth
    they had caught thee,
Nor the questers that far and near had
    sought thee
  To the arms of thy mother could thee
    restore,
Then spake some neighbor in envious
    spite
  A whispered slander of sin and
    shame,
How that over the boiling water's
    might
  Which hissed in the bronze that be-
    strode the flame
Did they carve thy flesh with the knife,
    and seethe it,
And served at the feast, and—dare lips
    breathe it?—
  That the God-guests ate of the same!

(Ep. 2)

But impossible it is for me to call
  Any Blest One man-eater—with loath-
    ing and scorn
I recoil! O, the profit is passing small
  That the dealer in slander hath oft
    times found.
But if ever man on earth was born
Whom the Watchers from Heaven with
    honour crowned,
That man was Tantalus; yet of their
    favour
  No profit he had, nor of that high
    bliss.
But the man's proud stomach was drunk
    with its savour
  And gorged with pride; and by reason
    of this
He drew on him ruin utter-crushing;
  For Zeus hung o'er him a huge black
    scaur,
And he cowers from it aye on his head
    down-rushing
  From happiness exiled far.

(Str. 3)

And there unto torment fettered for ever
  Living on, living on in eternal despair
He abides with the Three on whom hope
    dawns never,
  He who from the feast of the Gods
    could dare
To steal the ambrosia and nectar whereby
They had given him immortality,
  That the guests of his wine-cup might
    revel thereon!
But who thinketh to hide his evil
    doing
From God, he errs to his bitter ruing!
  So then the Immortals sent back his
    son
Exiled to earth from the heavenly home,
  Thenceforth with the sons of a day
    to abide.
But in process of time, when Pelops was
    come
  To the flower-bright season of life's
    springtide,
When the soft rose-tint of his cheek 'gan
    darken,

To the whisper of love did his spirit
    hearken,
  And he dreamed of the world-famed
    bride

(Ant. 3)

Hippodameia, the glorious daughter
Of the Lord of Pisa, a prize for him
Who could win her. Alone by the surf-
    white water
  Of the sea he stood in the darkness
    dim.
To the Thunder-voiced he cried o'er
    the wave,
To the Lord of the Trident mighty to
    save:
  And lo, at his side did the God appear,
And 'O Poseidon,' he spake imploring,
'If the gifts of the Cyprian Queen's
    outpouring
  To thy spirit, O King, be in any wise
    dear,
His bronze lance let not Oenomaus lift
  To mine hurt, but cause me to Elis to
    ride
On a god-given chariot passing swift:
  There throne thou me by victory's
    side.
For lovers by that spear merciless-
    slaying
Have died thirteen, and he still is
    delaying
  To bestow his child as a bride.

(Ep. 3)

In the path doth a mighty peril lie;
  To the craven soul no welcome it
    gives.
But, seeing a man must needs once die,
  Wherefore should I unto old age screen
  From peril a life that only lives,
  Sitting nameless and fameless in dark-
    ness unseen,
In the deeds of the valiant never sharing?
  Nay, lies at my feet the challenge
    now:
I will accept it for doing and daring!
  Good speed to mine heart's desire
    grant thou!'
Not fruitless the cry of his heart's de-
    siring

Was uttered. The God heard gracious-
souled,
And crowned him with honour. Winged
steeds untiring
He gave, and a chariot of gold.
(Str. 4)
So he won for his bride that maiden
peerless;
For her terrible father he overcame.
And she bare to him six sons battle-
fearless,
Captains of war-hosts, thirsting for
fame.
And his portion assured hath Pelops
still
Where the priests the blood of the sacri-
fice spill;
And unto his tomb resorteth the throng
Of strangers from far who have heard
his story.
From his grave-mound his spirit behold-
eth the glory
Of the mighty Olympian strife of the
strong
In the course that from Pelops its name
hath ta'en,
Wherein be contending the swift to run
And the thews that be mighty in
wrestling-strain.
And whoso therein hath the victory
won,
Thereafter on through his life-days ever
Sweetly his peace shall flow as a river
Blissfully gliding on
(Ant. 4)
For those Games' sake. Yea, the good
that unceasing
On man's lot daily as dew droppeth
down
Is that which to each is most well-
pleasing.
Now is it my bounden duty to crown
With a strain wherein hoof-beats tri-
umphant ring
In Æolian moods Sicilia's King.
And hereof is my spirit assured past
doubt
That amidst all men on the wide earth
dwelling

There is found no host whom with
prouder-swelling
Notes in many a winding bout
Of noble song I may glorify,
Yea, none more learned in honour's
lore,
None who showeth therein more potency.
The God who guardeth thee watcheth
o'er
Thine hopes and thine aims, that no evil
assail thee;
And if—O nay, but he cannot fail thee!—
I trust ere long once more
(Ep. 4)
To chant a triumph than all more sweet,
Inspiration-wafted, as one that flies
In a chariot, on paths of utterance
meet,
Till I win unto Kronos' Hill sunbright,
O yea, in my Muses' quiver lies
A song-arrow winged for stronger
flight.
By diverse paths men upward aspire:
Earth's highest summit by kings is
attained.
Thou therefore look to attain no higher
Than earth. Be it thine on the height
thou hast gained
To pace mid splendour of royal achiev-
ing
Thy life through: mine be it no less
long
To consort with victors, from Hellas
receiving
The world o'er praise for my song.
—A. S. WAY.

THE THIRD OLYMPIAN

PINDAR

This ode celebrates a victory for Theron
of Akragas and is a banquet song sung in
the temple of Castor and Pollux. Combined with the praises of Theron is the
story of the olive, token of victory,
brought from Ister's springs by Hercules.

(*Str. 1*)

Oh Tyndarids, lords of all guest-welcom-
ing,
  Oh Helen of the tresses beauty-
    crowned,
Take pleasure in my praises, when I sing
  Akragas far-renowned,
Chanting her son's Olympian victory,
  The glory of his tireless-footed team.
The Muse hath thrilled me with new har-
mony
  Of wedded song and dance, in revelry
    Where Dorian sandals gleam.

(*Ant. 1*)

Garlands of victory twined in Theron's
hair
  Exact of me this debt that Heaven
    ordains
For Ainesidamus' son in order fair
  To blend the varying strains
Of lyres with voice of flutes and ordering
  Of chanted words; and Pisa bids pro-
    claim
His glory—Pisa, poesy's well-spring
Whence, by the Gods inspired, the great
  songs ring
    That give men deathless fame,

(*Ep. 1*)

Even they about whose hair the silvery-
gleaming
  Adorning of the olive-leaf is laid
By the Ætolian judge's righteous deem-
ing
  The victor's brows to shade,
According unto Herakles' ancient hest.
  From Ister's shadowy springs he
    brought this tree,
When fared Amphitryon's son on perilous
quest
And gave Olympia's games this fairest,
best
    Trophy of victory.

(*Str. 2*)

His courteous speech that Norland people
swayed—
  The folk who serve Apollo—to bestow

To his true-hearted prayer for Zeus's
glade,
  Whither all Hellenes go,
A shadowing tree, a universal boon,
  A wreath for prowess of the mighty
    given.
When hallowed were Zeus' altars, lo, the
Moon
Of midmonth flashed her splendour pleni-
lune
    Full in the face of Even.

(*Ant. 2*)

Then for those great Games he ordained
for ever
  Just judgment and a Five-year Festi-
    val
By the steep banks of Alpheus' hallowed
river.
  But of fair trees and tall
In Kronian Pelops' glen, that chosen
place,
  His garden-close, was as a desert bare.
Him-seemed it lay unscreened beneath
the blaze
Of scorching Helios' arrow-darting rays.
    Wherefore he yearned to fare

(*Ep. 2*)

To Ister's land, where She of the swift
horses,
  Queen Leto's Child, received him gra-
    ciously
When from the hills and winding water-
courses
  He came of Arcady,
Sped on Eurystheus' mission forth to
find—
  By his sire's doom, wherefrom is no
    appeal —
The Orthian Wood-queen's golden-
antlered hind,
Vowed to her by Taygete, and signed
    With consecration's seal.

(*Str. 3*)

And in that chase he looked upon the
land
  That sheltered lies behind the North-
    wind cold,

And saw its olive-trees. There did he
    stand
  And marvelled to behold,
And dearly yearned to enring with those
    same trees
  The goal round which twelve times
    swift horses strain.
Graciously still to these festivities
He comes: with him be godlike presences,
  Even Leda's scions twain.

                                    (*Ant. 3*)

These charged he with the Great Games'
    ordering
  Ere hence he passed to heavenly halls
    afar,
The struggle of strong men, the sweep
    and swing
  Of the swift-rushing car.
'The Emmenids and Theron Fame hath
    crowned
  This day!' my soul constraineth me to
    cry,
'Fame given by Tyndareus' Sons the
    steed-renowned,
Since unto these of all men most they
    abound
  In hospitality,

                                    (*Ep. 3*)

With hearts of reverence rendering due
    measure
  Of service to the Gods for ever blest.'
As water chiefest is, and of all treasure
  Gold is held goodliest,
So Glory's pinnacle doth Theron gain
  By his high prowess: yea, his fame
    hath won
To Herakles' pillars! Farther to attain
Wise and unwise all fruitlessly should
    strain,
  Nor press I vainly on.
                          —A. S. Way.

THE SECOND PYTHIAN

PINDAR

The subject celebrated is a victory in a
chariot race won for Hiero of Syracuse

at Thebes. The myth of Ixion and the
moral lessons to be derived from it are
interwoven with the praises of Hiero.

                                    (*Str. 1*)

O Syracuse, city in greatness excelling,
  Precinct of Ares through gulfs of war
Who plungeth, O nurse of the warrior
    and steed
That in clash of the steel of battle-weed
Exult, from radiant Thebes do I speed
Bearing a song of the great race, telling
  Of the swift earth-shaking four-horsed
    car,
The race wherein Hiero triumphward
    riding
  Flashed down the course with his
    glorious team,
And crowned with garlands that glowed
    far-seen
Ortygia, the haunt of the River-queen
Artemis—aided of her, I ween,
His hands as with spells of enchantment
    were guiding
  Those steeds with a bridle of rainbow-
    gleam;

                                    (*Ant. 1*)

For she, the arrow-triumphant Maiden,
  And Hermes the Ruler of Contests,
    bring—
Yea, the gifts of the Gods' linked hands
    they are—
These harness-adornings that glitter afar
When he yokes strong steeds to his
    shining car
And its wheels rein-piloted, victory-laden,
  Invoking the wide-ruling Trident-king.
The prowess-guerdon of song sweet-ring-
    ing
  From the lips of many a bard shall
    swell
To the feet of lords that o'er far lands
    reign;
As the Cyprian bards in triumphant
    strain
Chant Kinyras' praises once and again,
Aphrodite's priestly minion singing
  Whom Apollo the golden-haired loved
    well;

(Ep. 1)

For their gratitude's praise for his kind-
ness is gushing
From the hearts in loving reverence
bowed.
O Deinomenes' son, the Lokrian maid
In the far west sings at her door un-
afraid
The delivering might of thine arm, that
stayed
War's march of afflictions spirit-crushing,
That her eyes no longer are terror-
cowed.
In old-time legend it stands recorded
That Ixion, the while on the fire-
winged wheel
By the sentence of Gods he is endlessly
whirled,
Ever shrieketh his warning, a cry that is
hurled
Unto men's ears up from the under-
world—
'Be the kindness of thy benefactors re-
warded
With all the love that thine heart can
reveal!'

(Str. 2)

That lesson he learned in uttermost
measure;
For, though he received a life of bliss
Mid the Children of Kronos, the gracious-
souled,
He contented him not with its joys un-
told,
But for Hera he lusted frenzy-bold,
Of Zeus's couch the inviolate treasure;
For presumption drave him on into
this
His overweening infatuation.
But swiftly he reaped meet harvest of
sin
To suffer of all hell's torments the worst:
For his twofold transgression earned the
Accurst
That vengeance—the one, that he was the
first
Who stained mankind with contamination
Of the treacherous spilling of blood of
kin;

(Ant. 2)

The other, that in the recesses most holy
Of the bride-bower of Zeus did he make
essay
Of the Queen of Heaven! Meet is it to
know
Our mortality's limits, meet to forego
The lawless loves that their victim throw
Into gulfs of destruction. Such was his
folly;
For with nought but a cloud it was
that he lay,
Unknowing all, to his own confusion
Lured on by a sweetly-beckoning lie;
For the cloud-wrought image the sem-
blance bare
Of Kronos' Child, Heaven's fairest fair;
For the hands of Zeus had fashioned the
snare,
The beautiful bane, for his soul's de-
lusion.
So he compassed his own dire doom
thereby,

(Ep. 2)

Outstretched on the wheel's arms cruci-
fying,
Tangled in bonds whence escape is
none,
Shrieking that warning the whole world
o'er.
And his cloud-mate, unblessed of the
Graces, bore
A monstrous child—such dam never
more
Nor such offspring shall be, 'neath a
black curse lying
Of menfolk, of godfolk—a thing to
shun!
And the cloud-mother reared that evil
abortion
And named Kentaurus. By Pelion's
foot
In Magnesia he mated with many a
mare;
And a horde of monsters was born of
them there
Wondrous to see, for the likeness they
bare

Of either parent; the upper portion
　As man was shapen, the nether as
　brute.

(*Str. 3*)

What purpose soever God conceiveth
　He accomplisheth; none his intent may
　defy—
God, who o'ertaketh the eagle's wing,
Who outstrippeth the dolphin, o'er waves
　though it spring,
And the pride of man to the dust can
　bring,
While unto the lowly one glory he giveth
　That waxeth not old as the years fleet
　by.
But for me it is well that I lack not dis-
　cretion
　From slander's viper-fangs to refrain.
Ay, venomous-tongued Archilochus' fate
Have I known from of old, and his low
　estate
Who with rancorous speech fed fat his
　hate.
Of all things that Fortune can give in
　possession
　Riches with wisdom are best to attain.

(*Ant. 3*)

These blessings be thine, may all see
　plainly;
　And this thou showest, O liberal-
　souled,
O princely ruler of many a street
Fair-circled with towers where thy
　squadrons meet;
And such riches and honour thy weal
　complete
That in fantasy's folly he striveth
　vainly
　Who saith that any surpassed thee of
　old
Among Hellene lords that be famed in
　story.
　On the prow of my galley with flowers
　hung round
Will I take my stand as the praises I sing
Of thy prowess.　Young hearts win
　strengthening

From courage when trumpets for onset
　ring.
Yea, thou, I proclaim it, hast won thee
　glory
　Therefrom, a glory that knows no
　bound,

(*Ep. 3*)

Now warring mid horsemen battleward
　racing,
　And now mid warriors afoot that fight.
And thy wisdom now when thy locks be
　grey
Is of all gainsaying unperilled—O yea,
It giveth me fullest assurance aye
For extolling thy name with manifold
　praising.
　All hail!　This song o'er the sea-foam
　white
Like Tyrian merchandise lo, I have
　brought thee.
　Let thine eyes then smile on the
　Kastor-strain
That my fingers from chords Æolian
　drew:
O greet it thou with the honour due
To the seven-stringed lute.　To thyself
　be true,
To the royal wisdom the years have
　taught thee.
　'Tis from children alone that the ape
　doth gain

(*Str. 4*)

The praise of beauty, is beauteous ever!
　Rhadamanthus is homed in the Isles of
　the Blest,
For the fruit of his soul was uncankered
　of guile:
No pleasure he hath in the treacherous
　wile
Of the whisperer working by calumnies
　vile.
The secret speakings of slander never
　Can be openly fought and forever re-
　pressed.
There is nothing of man in them—nay,
　'tis the slinking
　Spirit of foxes they show; and yet

From his cunning what gain doth the sly
    fox reap?
As for me—while the rest of the net-
    tackle deep
In the briny darkness doth toilsomely
    sweep
The sea-floor—I, like the float unsinking
    Am riding the waves high over the net.

(*Ant. 4*)

In a city of honest men unavailing
    Is the trickster's babble, yet still he
    essays,
Fawning on all men, the toils to twine
Of his subtlety. Never his vaunt shall
    be mine—
'To a friend be I friend, to a foe
    malign!
As a wolf will I covertly track him, assail-
    ing
    This side and that side, by crooked
    ways.'
In what state soever a people be dwelling,
    'Tis the man of straightforward speech
    alway
That unto the foremost place attains;
Whether it be where a despot reigns,
Or where the rabble hot-headed strains
Against use and wont, or where sages
    excelling
    In wisdom the helm of the common-
    weal sway.

(*Ep. 4*)

Strive not against God, who exalts at his
    pleasure
Now one, now setteth another on high.
Yet doth not even His will seem right
Unto envious ones, but they strain over-
    tight
The line, and their own hearts so do they
    smite
With a wound whose bitterness none may
    measure,
    Ere the prize be gained for the which
    they sigh.
Nay, better it is that a man bear lightly
    The yoke of Fate on his neck that
    lies.

But he makes for his feet a perilous
    road
Who backward lashes against the goad.
But on me be this fair fortune bestowed,
To dwell among them which walk up-
    rightly,
    And to be well-pleasing in good men's
    eyes.

—A. S. Way.

PRAISE OF PEACE

BACCHYLIDES

Bacchylides (early fifth century B.C.)
of Ceos, nephew of Simonides of Ceos,
was reckoned by the ancients among the
foremost of poets. Recent discoveries
have restored his work to us in part. He
wrote dithyrambs, pæans, and odes of victory after the manner of Pindar. Like
Pindar, he visited the court of Hiero of
Syracuse and celebrated some of the same
victories recounted by Pindar.

To mortal men Peace giveth these good
    things:
Wealth, and the flowers of honey-
    throated song;
The flame that springs
On carven altars from fat sheep and
    kine,
Slain to the gods in heaven; and, all day
    long,
Games for glad youths, and flutes, and
    wreaths, and circling wine.
Then in the steely shield swart spiders
    weave
Their web and dusky woof:
Rust to the pointed spear and sword doth
    cleave;
The brazen trump sounds no alarms;
Nor is sleep harried from our eyes aloof,
But with sweet rest my bosom warms:
The streets are thronged with lovely men
    and young,
And hymns in praise of boys like flames
    to heaven are flung.

—JOHN ADDINGTON SYMONDS

DEMOCRATIC SOCIETY: PROSE AND DRAMA

FIFTH AND FOURTH CENTURIES B.C.

In the sixth century the conquering power of Persia had pushed forward through Asia Minor to the shores of the Ægean, subjecting all the Greek cities in her path. Two attempts the barbarian made then on Greece itself. The one failed at Marathon before the Athenian citizen-soldier; the other, at Thermopylæ, at Salamis, and at Platæa. Victory brought growth. Mingled feelings of relief at the repelling of the awful danger, of joy in so thorough a decision of the struggle, led to a quickening of the Greek spirit along many lines of endeavor.

To repel the invader the Greeks had then united. One might have imagined that the intense feelings of national consciousness aroused by the wars would have fostered a more permanent political union of all Greece. But union did not result, although combination of states were often arranged. Democratic forms of government however were certainly promoted. The people had won the wars; the people would run the government. But, as of old, each little city-state with its few thousand inhabitants and its few square miles of territory, would have its complete independence. Within such little political entities the growth of democracy took place. It is a phenomenon peculiarly Greek. Toward the end of this period Aristotle stated that a successful democracy should not contain over 10,000 citizens, that is, grown men with full political rights. His theory was that a larger number would prove unwieldy in a government in which the citizens met (somewhat as in New England town-meetings) to pass laws directly, and often to handle matters which today the executive would control. Athens developed an unlimited democracy, which, in foreign relations at any rate, worked very well when skilled leaders such as Pericles guided the state, and worked infinitely ill, when demagogues won control of the people.

Athens, because of her naval strength, had emerged from the Persian wars as the natural protector of the Greeks on the Ægean. Under her presidency a league, offensive and defensive, was formed, and for years expeditions in Asia Minor, and even in Egypt, were undertaken against Persia. During these years Athens promoted her own position so vigorously that she gradually transformed her leadership into supreme power over the league. She made herself also treasurer, and used the funds of the league to enlarge her own navy and to embellish her acropolis with wonderful buildings.

Jealousy of her commanding position in the Greek world finally brought about a coalition against her in which Sparta took the lead. For some twenty-five years (431-404 B.C.), with some interruptions, the struggle lasted, and ended with the fall of Athens. Supreme in folly, as in many a better quality, the democracy here needlessly exhausted its powers by a vain attempt to subdue Syracuse and Sicily in the far West. After disaster there the outcome of the war was never uncertain. Sparta then became the chief power of Greece for a time. Her power yielded to a revival of the strength of Thebes. Athens regained a modicum of her former power. Meantime in the North the half-Greek kingdom of Macedon was quietly extending its sway. Athens finally awoke to the threat of danger for all Greece; but too late. The battle of Chæronea (338 B.C.) put an end to real freedom in Greece forever.

Within the limits of a period beginning with the repulse of Persia (479 B.C.) and ending with the subjugation of Greece by Philip of Macedon (338 B.C.) the tide of

Greek civilization reached its height. In government democracies developed to their utmost possibilities direct rule by the people. In literature prose appeared as a highly perfected form. Oratory, always flourishing under democratic patronage, reached its culmination in the speeches of a Demosthenes. In the pages of a Thucydides and a Herodotus was pictured the history of the Greek. Philosophy, a development only of high culture, was marvelously expressed in the studies of a Plato. Drama, growing with the people from crude beginnings, in the plays of the great trio of tragedians presented profound studies of life and its problems. The comedies of Aristophanes mirror for modern readers aspects of civilization, political, social, literary, and prove, better than a historian could, how absolutely complete freedom of speech was allowed in fifth-century Athens even in time of war. Of the art of the period in various branches splendid remains still testify today to a beauty and perfection almost absolute. And in every department of civilization and culture it was Athens which took first place.

I. TALES OF A TRAVELER: HERODOTUS

Herodotus (about 484 to about 425 B.C.) the Father of History, was a native of Halicarnassus in Asia Minor. Political strife caused him to leave his native city and turn traveler, in which capacity he collected a mass of material at first hand for use in his great history. He was the first to give artistic form to what hitherto had been a mere jumble of unconnected stories, or a dry annalistic recital of events. He was quite childlike in his acceptance of hearsay evidence, indulged in delightful digressions which are more of the nature of gossip than of history, and colored all he wrote with the imagination of an epic poet. He was in fact strongly influenced by the great epics of Greece. Like Homer, to diversify his narrative, he uses not only digressions, but makes the chief characters speak in their own persons. The history, which is extant entire, tells of the affairs of Greek and of Persian, beginning with the time of Crœsus, king at Sardis, about the middle of the sixth century B.C. and extending through the period of the Persian wars to 478 B.C. Diffuse as it may seem, it is built upon an artistic plan. A first section, of three books, relates the rise of Persia to great power; the second section, of three books, pictures a struggle between Greeks and Persians marked by many successes and failures; the final section, also of three books, describes the utter defeat of Persia.

CRŒSUS OF LYDIA

[From Book I]

The author's prime interest in this story is clearly in the speculative question of what constitutes happiness. It has been suggested that Crœsus and Solon are brought into contrast as representatives of the conflict between the Oriental and the Greek points of view. Certainly political institutions and events are kept in the background as compared with the description of characters and the exposition of their ideas.

On the death of Alyattes, Crœsus, his son, who was in his thirty-fifth year, succeeded to the throne. Of the Greek cities, Ephesus was the first that he attacked. The Ephesians, when he laid siege to the place, made an offering of their city to Diana, by stretching a rope from the town wall to the temple of the Goddess, which was distant from the ancient city, then besieged by Crœsus, a space of seven furlongs. They were, as I said, the first Greeks whom he attacked. Afterwards, on some pretext or other, he made war in turn upon every Ionian and Æolian state, bringing forward, where he could, a substantial ground of complaint;

where such failed him, advancing some poor excuse.

In this way he made himself master of all the Greek cities in Asia, and forced them to become his tributaries; after which he began to think of building ships, and attacking the islanders. Everything had been got ready for this purpose, when Bias of Priene (or, as some say, Pittacus the Mytilenean) put a stop to the project. The king had made inquiry of this person, who was lately arrived at Sardis, if there were any news from Greece; to which he answered. "Yes, sire, the islanders are gathering ten thousand horse, designing an expedition against thee and against thy capital." Crœsus, thinking he spake seriously, broke out, "Ah, might the gods put such a thought into their minds as to attack the sons of the Lydians with cavalry!" "It seems, oh! king," rejoined the other, "that thou desirest earnestly to catch the islanders on horseback on the mainland, —thou knowest well what would come of it. But what thinkest thou the islanders desire better, now that they hear thou art about to build ships and sail against them, than to catch the Lydians at sea, and there revenge on them the wrongs of their brothers upon the mainland, whom thou holdest in slavery?" Crœsus was charmed with the turn of the speech; and thinking there was reason in what was said, gave up his shipbuilding and concluded a league of amity with the Ionians of the isles.

Crœsus afterwards, in the course of many years, brought under his sway almost all the nations to the west of the Halys. The Lycians and Cilicians alone continued free; all the other tribes he reduced and held in subjection. They were the following: the Lydians, Phrygians, Mysians, Mariandynians, Chalybians, Paphlagonians, Thynian and Bithynian Thracians, Carians, Ionians, Dorians, Æolians and Pamphylians.

When all these conquests had been added to the Lydian empire, and the prosperity of Sardis was now at its height, there came thither, one after another, all the sages of Greece living at the time, and among them Solon, the Athenian. He was on his travels, having left Athens to be absent ten years, under the pretense of wishing to see the world, but really to avoid being forced to repeal any of the laws which, at the request of the Athenians, he had made for them. Without his sanction the Athenians could not repeal them, as they had bound themselves under a heavy curse to be governed for ten years by the laws which should be imposed on them by Solon.

On this account, as well as to see the world, Solon set out upon his travels, in the course of which he went to Egypt to the court of Amasis, and also came on a visit to Crœsus at Sardis. Crœsus received him as his guest, and lodged him in the royal palace. On the third or fourth day after, he bade his servants conduct Solon over his treasuries, and show him all their greatness and magnificence. When he had seen them all, and, so far as time allowed, inspected them, Crœsus addressed this question to him: "Stranger of Athens, We have heard much of thy wisdom and of thy travels through many lands, from love of knowledge and a wish to see the world. I am curious therefore to inquire of thee, whom, of all the men that thou hast seen, thou deemest the most happy?" This he asked because he thought himself the happiest of mortals: but Solon answered him without flattery, according to his true sentiments, "Tellus of Athens, sire." Full of astonishment at what he heard, Crœsus demanded sharply, "And wherefore dost thou deem Tellus happiest?" To which the other replied, "First, because his country was flourishing in his days, and he himself had sons both beautiful and good, and he lived to see children born to each of them, and these children all grew up; and further

because, after a life spent in what our
people look upon as comfort, his end was
surpassingly glorious. In a battle between the Athenians and their neighbours
near Eleusis, he came to the assistance
of his countrymen, routed the foe, and
died upon the field most gallantly. The
Athenians gave him a public funeral on
the spot where he fell, and paid him the
highest honours."

Thus did Solon admonish Crœsus by
the example of Tellus, enumerating the
manifold particulars of his happiness.
When he had ended, Crœsus inquired a
second time, who after Tellus seemed
to him the happiest, expecting that, at
any rate, he would be given the second
place. "Cleobis and Bito," Solon answered; "they were of Argive race: their
fortune was enough for their wants, and
they were besides endowed with so much
bodily strength that they had both gained
prizes at the Games. Also this tale is
told of them:—There was a great festival
in honour of the goddess Juno at Argos,
to which their mother must needs be
taken in a car. Now the oxen did not
come home from the field in time: so
the youths, fearful of being too late, put
the yoke on their own necks, and themselves drew the car in which their mother
rode. Five and forty furlongs did they
draw her, and stopped before the temple.
This deed of theirs was witnessed by the
whole assembly of worshippers, and
then their life closed in the best possible
way. Herein, too, God showed forth
most evidently, how much better a thing
for man death is than life. For the
Argive men stood thick around the car
and extolled the vast strength of the
youths; and the Argive women extolled
the mother who was blessed with such a
pair of sons; and the mother herself,
overjoyed at the deed and at the praises
it won, standing straight before the
image, besought the goddess to bestow
on Cleobis and Bito, the sons who had
so mightily honoured her, the highest

blessing to which mortals can attain.
Her prayer ended, they offered sacrifice,
and partook of the holy banquet, after
which the two youths fell asleep in the
temple. They never woke more, but so
passed from the earth. The Argives,
looking on them as among the best of
men, caused statues of them to be made,
which they gave to the shrine at Delphi."

When Solon had thus assigned these
youths the second place, Crœsus broke
in angrily, "What, stranger of Athens, is
my happiness, then, so utterly set at
nought by thee, that thou dost not even
put me on a level with private men?"

"Oh! Crœsus," replied the other,
"thou askedst a question concerning the
condition of man, of one who knows that
the power above us is full of jealousy,
and fond of troubling our lot. A long life
gives one to witness much, and experience
much oneself, that one would not choose.
Seventy years I regard as the limit of the
life of man. In these seventy years are
contained, without reckoning intercalary
months, twenty-five thousand and two
hundred days. Add an intercalary month
to every other year, that the seasons may
come round at the right time, and there
will be, besides the seventy years, thirty-
five such months, making an addition of
one thousand and fifty days. The whole
number of the days contained in the
seventy years will thus be twenty-six
thousand two hundred and fifty, whereof
not one but will produce events unlike
the rest. Hence man is wholly accident.
For thyself, oh! Crœsus, I see that thou
art wonderfully rich, and art the lord of
many nations; but with respect to that
whereon thou questionest me, I have no
answer to give, until I hear that thou
hast closed thy life happily. For assuredly he who possesses great store of
riches is no nearer happiness than he who
has what suffices for his daily needs, unless it so hap that luck attend upon
him, and so he continue in the enjoyment
of all good things to the end of life. For

many of the wealthiest men have been unfavoured of fortune, and many whose means were moderate have had excellent luck. Men of the former class excel those of the latter but in two respects; these last excel the former in many. The wealthy man is better able to content his desires, and to bear up against a sudden buffet of calamity. The other has less ability to withstand these evils (from which, however, his good luck keeps him clear), but he enjoys all these following blessings: he is whole of limb, a stranger to disease, free from misfortune, happy in his children, and comely to look upon. If, in addition to all this, he end his life well, he is of a truth the man of whom thou art in search, the man who may rightly be termed happy. Call him, however, until he die, not happy but fortunate. Scarcely, indeed, can any man unite all these advantages: as there is no country which contains within it all that it needs, but each, while it possesses some things, lacks others, and the best country is that which contains most, so no single human being is complete in every respect—something is always lacking. He who unites the greatest number of advantages, and retaining them to the day of his death, then dies peaceably, that man alone, sire, is, in my judgment, entitled to bear the name of 'happy.' But in every matter it behoves us to mark well the end; for oftentimes God gives men a gleam of happiness and then plunges them into ruin."

Such was the speech which Solon addressed to Crœsus, a speech which brought him neither largess nor honour. The king saw him depart with much indifference, since he thought that a man must be an arrant fool who made no account of present good, but bade men always wait and mark the end. . . .

After this Crœsus, having resolved to propitiate the Delphic god with a magnificent sacrifice, offered up three thousand of every kind of sacrificial beast, and besides made a huge pile, and placed upon it couches coated with silver and with gold, and golden goblets, and robes and vests of purple; all which he burnt in the hope of thereby making himself more secure of the favour of the god. Further he issued orders to all the people of the land to offer a sacrifice according to their means. When the sacrifice was ended, the king melted down a vast quantity of gold, and ran it into ingots, making them six palms long, three palms broad, and one palm in thickness. The number of ingots was a hundred and seventeen, four being of refined gold, in weight two talents and a half; the others of pale gold, and in weight two talents. He also caused a statue of a lion to be made in refined gold, the weight of which was ten talents. At the time when the temple of Delphi was burnt to the ground, this lion fell from its place upon the ingots; it now stands in the Corinthian treasury, and weighs only six talents and a half, having lost three talents and a half by the fire.

On the completion of these works Crœsus sent them away to Delphi, and with them two bowls of an enormous size, one of gold, the other of silver, which used to stand, the latter upon the right, the former upon the left, as one entered the temple. They too were moved after the fire; and now the golden one is in the Clazomenian treasury, and weighs eight talents and forty-two minæ; the silver one stands in the corner of the antechapel, and holds six hundred amphoræ. This is known, because the Delphians fill it at the time of the Theophania. It is said by the Delphians to be a work of Theodore the Samian, and I think that they say true, for assuredly it is the work of no common artist. Crœsus sent also four silver casks, which are in the Corinthian treasury, and two lustral vases, a golden and a silver one. On the former is inscribed the name of the Lacedæmonians, and they claim it as a gift of theirs, but wrongly, since it was really given by Crœsus. The inscription upon it was cut by a Delphian, who wished to pleasure the Lacedæmonians. His name is known to me, but I forbear to mention it. The boy, through whose hand the water runs, is (I confess) a Lacedæmonian gift, but they did not give either of the lustral vases. Besides these various offerings, Crœsus sent to Delphi many others of less account, among the rest a number of round silver basins. Also he dedicated a female figure in gold, three cubits high, which is said by the Delphians to be the statue of his baking-woman; and further, he presented the necklace and the girdles of his wife.

These were the offerings sent by Crœsus to Delphi. To the shrine of Amphiaraus, with whose valour and misfortune he was acquainted, he sent a shield entirely of gold, and a spear, also of solid gold, both head and shaft. They were still existing in my day at Thebes, laid up in the temple of Ismenian Apollo.

The messengers who had the charge of conveying these treasures to the shrines, received instructions to ask the oracles whether Crœsus should go to war with the Persians, and if so, whether he should strengthen himself by the forces of an ally. Accordingly, when they had reached their destination and presented the gifts, they proceeded to consult the oracles in the following terms:—"Crœsus, king of Lydia and other countries, believing that these are the only real oracles in all the world, has sent you such presents as your discoveries deserved, and now inquires of you whether he shall go to war with the Persians, and if so, whether he shall strengthen himself by the forces of a confederate." Both the oracles agreed in the tenor of their reply, which was in each case a prophecy that if Crœsus attacked the Persians, he would destroy a mighty empire, and a recommendation to him to look and see who

were the most powerful of the Greeks, and to make alliance with them.

At the receipt of these oracular replies Crœsus was overjoyed, and feeling sure now that he would destroy the empire of the Persians, he sent once more to Pytho, and presented to the Delphians, the number of whom he had ascertained, two gold staters apiece. In return for this the Delphians granted to Crœsus and the Lydians the privilege of precedency in consulting the oracle, exemption from all charges, the most honourable seat at the festivals, and the perpetual right of becoming at pleasure citizens of their town.

After sending these presents to the Delphians, Crœsus a third time consulted the oracle, for having once proved its truthfulness, he wished to make constant use of it. The question whereto he now desired an answer was—"Whether his kingdom would be of long duration?" The following was the reply of the Pythoness:

"Wait till the time shall come when a
    mule is monarch of Media;
Then, thou delicate Lydian, away to the
    pebbles of Hermus;
Haste, oh! haste thee away, nor blush to
    behave like a coward."

Of all the answers that had reached him, this pleased him far the best, for it seemed incredible that a mule should ever come to be king of the Medes, and so he concluded that the sovereignty would never depart from himself or his seed after him. Afterwards he turned his thoughts to the alliance which he had been recommended to contract, and sought to ascertain by inquiry which was the most powerful of the Grecian states. His inquiries pointed out to him two states as pre-eminent above the rest. These were the Lacedæmonians and the Athenians, the former of Doric, the latter of Ionic blood. . . .

Cyrus had captured this Astyages, who was his mother's father, and kept him prisoner, for a reason which I shall bring forward in another part of my history. This capture formed the ground of quarrel between Cyrus and Crœsus, in consequence of which Crœsus sent his servants to ask the oracle if he should attack the Persians; and when an evasive answer came, fancying it to be in his favour, carried his arms into the Persian territory. When he reached the river Halys, he transported his army across it, as I maintain, by the bridges which exist there at the present day; but, according to the general belief of the Greeks, by the aid of Thales the Milesian. The tale is, that Crœsus was in doubt how he should get his army across, as the bridges were not made at that time, and that Thales, who happened to be in the camp, divided the stream and caused it to flow on both sides of the army instead of on the left only. This he effected thus:—Beginning some distance above the camp, he dug a deep channel, which he brought round in a semicircle, so that it might pass to rearward of the camp; and that thus the river, diverted from its natural course into the new channel at the point where this left the stream, might flow by the station of the army, and afterwards fall again into the ancient bed. In this way the river was split into two streams, which were both easily fordable. It is said by some that the water was entirely drained off from the natural bed of the river. But I am of a different opinion; for I do not see how, in that case, they could have crossed it on their return.

Having passed the Halys, with the forces under his command, Crœsus entered the district of Cappadocia which is called Pteria. It lies in the neighbourhood of the city of Sinope upon the Euxine, and is the strongest position in the whole country thereabouts. Here Crœsus pitched his camp, and began to ravage the fields of the Syrians. He besieged and took the chief city of the Pterians, and reduced the inhabitants to slavery: he likewise made himself master of the surrounding villages. Thus he brought ruin on the Syrians, who were guilty of no offence towards him. Meanwhile, Cyrus had levied an army and marched against Crœsus, increasing his numbers at every step by the forces of the nations that lay in his way. Before beginning his march he had sent heralds to the Ionians, with an invitation to them to revolt from the Lydian king: they, however, had refused compliance. Cyrus, notwithstanding, marched against the enemy, and encamped opposite them in the district of Pteria, where the trial of strength took place between the contending powers. The combat was hot and bloody, and upon both sides the number of the slain was great; nor had victory declared in favour of either party, when night came down upon the battle-field. Thus both armies fought valiantly.

Crœsus laid the blame of his ill success on the number of his troops, which fell very short of the enemy; and as on the next day Cyrus did not repeat the attack, he set off on his return to Sardis, intending to collect his allies and renew the contest in the spring. . . .

Cyrus, however, when Crœsus broke up so suddenly from his quarters after the battle at Pteria, conceiving that he had marched away with the intention of disbanding his army, considered a little, and soon saw that it was advisable for him to advance upon Sardis with all haste, before the Lydians could get their forces together a second time. Having thus determined, he lost no time in carrying out his plan. He marched forward with such speed that he was himself the first to announce his coming to the Lydian king. That monarch, placed in the utmost difficulty by the turn of events which had gone so entirely against all his calculations, nevertheless led out the Lydians to battle. In all Asia there was not at that time a braver or more warlike people. Their manner of fighting was on horseback; they carried long lances, and were clever in the management of their steeds.

The two armies met in the plain before Sardis. It is a vast flat, bare of trees, watered by the Hyllus and a number of other streams, which all flow into one larger than the rest, called the Hermus. This river rises in the sacred mountain of the Dindymenian Mother, and falls into the sea near the town of Phocæa.

When Cyrus beheld the Lydians arranging themselves in order of battle on this plain, fearful of the strength of their cavalry, he adopted a device which Harpagus, one of the Medes, suggested to him. He collected together all the camels that had come in the train of his army to carry the provisions and the baggage, and taking off their loads, he mounted riders upon them accoutred as horsemen. These he commanded to advance in front of his other troops against the Lydian horse; behind them were to follow the foot soldiers, and last of all the cavalry. When his arrangements were complete, he gave his troops orders to slay all the other Lydians who came in their way without mercy, but to spare Crœsus and not kill him, even if he should be seized and offer resistance. The reason why Cyrus opposed his camels to the enemy's horse was, because the horse has a natural dread of the camel, and cannot abide either the sight or the smell of that animal. By this stratagem he hoped to make Crœsus's horse useless to him, the horse being what he chiefly depended on for victory. The two armies then joined battle, and immediately the Lydian warhorses, seeing and smelling the camels, turned round and galloped off; and so it came to pass that all Crœsus's hopes withered away. The Lydians, however, behaved manfully. As soon as they understood what was happening, they leaped off their horses, and engaged with the Persians on foot. The combat was long; but at last, after a great slaughter on both sides, the Lydians turned and fled. They were driven within their walls, and the Persians laid siege to Sardis.

Thus the siege began. . . . The following is the way in which Sardis was taken. On the fourteenth day of the siege Cyrus bade some horsemen ride about his lines, and make proclamation to the whole army that he would give a reward to the man who should first mount the wall. After this he made an assault, but without success. His troops retired, but a certain Mardian, Hyrœades by name, resolved to approach the citadel and attempt it at a place where no guards were ever set. On this side the rock was so precipitous, and the citadel (as it seemed) so impregnable, that no fear was entertained of its being carried in this place. Here was the only portion of the circuit round which their old king Meles did not carry the lion which his leman bore to him. For when the Telmessians had declared that if the lion were taken round the defences, Sardis would be impregnable, and Meles, in consequence, carried it round the rest of the fortress where the citadel seemed open to attack, he scorned to take it round this side, which he looked on as a sheer precipice, and therefore absolutely secure. It is on that side of the city which faces Mount Tmolus. Hyrœades, however, having the day before observed a Lydian soldier descend the rock after a helmet that had rolled down from the top, and having seen him pick it up and carry it back, thought over what he had witnessed, and formed his plan. He climbed the rock himself, and other Persians followed in his track, until a large number had mounted to the top. Thus was Sardis taken, and given up entirely to pillage.

With respect to Crœsus himself, this is what befell him at the taking of the town. He had a son, of whom I made mention above, a worthy youth, whose only defect was that he was deaf and dumb. In the days of his prosperity Crœsus had done the utmost that he could for him, and among other plans which he had devised, had sent to Delphi to consult the oracle on his behalf. The answer which he had received from the Pythoness ran thus:—

"Lydian, wide-ruling monarch, thou wondrous simple Crœsus,
Wish not ever to hear in thy palace the voice thou hast prayed for,
Utt'ring intelligent sounds. Far better thy son should be silent!
Ah! woe worth the day when thine ear shall first list to his accents."

When the town was taken, one of the Persians was just going to kill Crœsus, not knowing who he was. Crœsus saw the man coming, but under the pressure of his affliction, did not care to avoid the blow, not minding whether or no he died beneath the stroke. Then this son of his, who was voiceless, beholding the Persian as he rushed towards Crœsus, in the agony of his fear and grief burst into speech, and said, "Man, do not kill Crœsus." This was the first time that he had ever spoken a word, but afterwards he retained the power of speech for the remainder of his life.

Thus was Sardis taken by the Persians, and Crœsus himself fell into their hands, after having reigned fourteen years, and been besieged in his capital fourteen days; thus too did Crœsus fulfil the oracle, which said that he should destroy a mighty empire,—by destroying his own. Then the Persians who had made Crœsus prisoner brought him before Cyrus. Now a vast pile had been raised by his orders, and Crœsus, laden with fetters, was placed upon it, and with him twice seven of the sons of the Lydians. . . . Crœsus was already on the pile, when it entered his mind in the depth of his woe that there was a divine warning in the words which had come to him from the lips of Solon, "No one while he lives is happy." When this thought smote him he fetched

a long breath, and breaking his deep silence, groaned out aloud, thrice uttering the name of Solon. Cyrus caught the sounds, and bade the interpreters inquire of Crœsus who it was he called on. They drew near and asked him, but he held his peace, and for a long time made no answer to their questionings, until at length, forced to say something, he exclaimed, "One I would give much to see converse with every monarch." Not knowing what he meant by this reply, the interpreters begged him to explain himself; and as they pressed for an answer, and grew to be troublesome, he told them how, a long time before, Solon, an Athenian, had come and seen all his splendour, and made light of it; and how whatever he had said to him had fallen out exactly as he foreshowed, although it was nothing that especially concerned him, but applied to all mankind alike, and most to those who seemed to themselves happy. Meanwhile, as he thus spoke, the pile was lighted, and the outer portion began to blaze. Then Cyrus, hearing from the interpreters what Crœsus had said, relented, bethinking himself that he too was a man, and that it was a fellow-man, and one who had once been as blessed by fortune as himself, that he was burning alive; afraid, moreover, of retribution, and full of the thought that whatever is human is insecure. So he bade them quench the blazing fire as quickly as they could, and take down Crœsus and the other Lydians, which they tried to do, but the flames were not to be mastered.

Then, the Lydians say that Crœsus, perceiving by the efforts made to quench the fire that Cyrus had relented, and seeing that all was in vain, and that the men could not get the fire under, called with a loud voice upon the god Apollo, and prayed him, if he had ever received at his hands any acceptable gift, to come to his aid, and deliver him from his present danger. As thus with tears he besought the god, suddenly, though up to that time the sky had been clear and the day without a breath of wind, dark clouds gathered, and the storm burst over their heads with rain of such violence, that the flames were speedily extinguished. Cyrus, convinced by this that Crœsus was a good man and a favourite of heaven, asked him after he was taken off the pile, "Who it was that had persuaded him to lead an army into his country, and so become his foe rather than continue his friend?" to which Crœsus made answer as follows: "What I did, oh! king, was to thy advantage and to my own loss. If there be blame, it rests with the god of the Greeks, who encouraged me to begin the war. No one is so foolish as to prefer to peace war, in which, instead of sons burying their fathers, fathers bury their sons. But the gods willed it so."

Thus did Crœsus speak. Cyrus then ordered his fetters to be taken off, and made him sit down near himself, and paid him much respect, looking upon him, as did also the courtiers, with a sort of wonder.

—GEORGE RAWLINSON.

BABYLON

[From Book I]

The Greeks were wide awake and intensely curious about how the rest of the world lived. Babylon was a land of romance and mystery to them.

Assyria possesses a vast number of great cities, whereof the most renowned and strongest at this time was Babylon, whither, after the fall of Nineveh, the seat of government had been removed. The following is a description of the place:—The city stands on a broad plain, and is an exact square, a hundred and twenty furlongs each way, so that the entire circuit is four hundred and eighty furlongs. While such is its size, in magnificence there is no other city that approaches to it. It is surrounded, in the first place, by a broad and deep moat, full of water, behind which rises a wall fifty royal cubits in width, and two hundred in height. (The royal cubit is longer by three fingers' breadth than the common cubit.)

And here I may not omit to tell the use to which the mould dug out of the great moat was turned, nor the manner wherein the wall was wrought. As fast as they dug the moat the soil which they got from the cutting was made into bricks, and when a sufficient number were completed they baked the bricks in kilns. Then they set to building, and began with bricking the borders of the moat, after which they proceeded to construct the wall itself, using throughout for their cement hot bitumen, and interposing a layer of wattled reeds at every thirtieth course of the bricks. On the top, along the edges of the wall, they constructed buildings of a single chamber facing one another, leaving between them room for a four-horse chariot to turn. In the circuit of the wall are a hundred gates, all of brass, with brazen lintels and sideposts. The bitumen used in the work was brought to Babylon from the Is, a small stream which flows into the Euphrates at the point where the city of the same name stands, eight days' journey from Babylon. Lumps of bitumen are found in great abundance in this river.

The city is divided into two portions by the river which runs through the midst of it. This river is the Euphrates, a broad, deep, swift stream, which rises in Armenia, and empties itself into the Erythræan sea. The city wall is brought down on both sides to the edge of the stream: thence from the corners of the wall, there is carried along each bank of the river a fence of burnt bricks. The houses are mostly three and four stories high; the streets all run in straight lines, not only those parallel to the river, but also the cross streets which lead down to the waterside. At the river end of these cross streets are low gates in the fence that skirts the stream, which are, like the great gates in the outer wall, of brass, and open on the water.

The outer wall is the main defence of the city. There is, however, a second inner wall, of less thickness than the first, but very little inferior to it in strength. The centre of each division of the town was occupied by a fortress. In the one stood the palace of the kings, surrounded by a wall of great strength and size: in the other was the sacred precinct of Jupiter Belus, a square enclosure two furlongs each way, with gates of solid brass; which was also remaining in my time. In the middle of the precinct there was a tower of solid masonry, a furlong in length and breadth, upon which was raised a second tower, and on that a third, and so on up to eight. The ascent to the top is on the outside, by a path which winds round all the towers. When one is about half way up, one finds a resting place and seats, where persons are wont to sit some time on their way to the summit. On the topmost tower there is a spacious temple and inside the temple stands a couch of unusual size, richly adorned, with a golden table by its side. There is no statue of any kind set up in the place, nor is the chamber occupied of nights by any one but a single native woman, who, as the Chaldæans, the priests of this god, affirm, is chosen for himself by the deity out of all the women of the land.

They also declare—but I for my part do not credit it—that the god comes down in person into this chamber, and sleeps upon the couch. This is like the story told by the Egyptians of what takes place in their city of Thebes, where a woman always passes the night in the temple of the Theban Jupiter. In each case the woman is said to be debarred all intercourse with men. It is also like the custom at Patara, in Lycia, where the priestess who delivers the oracles, during the time that she is so employed—for at Patara there is not always an oracle—is shut up in the temple every night.

Below, in the same precinct, there is a second temple, in which is a sitting figure of Jupiter, all of gold. Before the figure stands a large golden table, and the throne whereon it sits, and the base on which the throne is placed, are likewise of gold. The Chaldæans told me that all the gold together was eight hundred talents' weight. Outside the temple are two altars, one of solid gold, on which it is only lawful to offer sucklings; the other a common altar, but of great size, on which the full-grown animals are sacrificed. It is also on the great altar that the Chaldæans burn the frankincense, which is offered to the amount of a thousand talents' weight, every year, at the festival of the god. In the time of Cyrus there was likewise in this temple the figure of a man, twelve cubits high, entirely of solid gold. I myself did not see this figure, but I relate what the Chaldæans report concerning it. Darius, the son of Hystaspes, plotted to carry the statue off, but had not the hardihood to lay his hands upon it. Xerxes, however, the son of Darius, killed the priest who forbade him to move the statue, and took it away. Besides the ornaments which I have mentioned, there are a large number of private offerings in this holy precinct. . . .

But little rain falls in Assyria, enough, however, to make the corn begin to sprout, after which the plant is nourished and the ears formed by means of irrigation from the river. For the river does not, as in Egypt, overflow the corn-lands of its own accord, but is spread over them by the hand, or by the help of engines. The whole of Babylonia is, like Egypt, intersected with canals. The largest of them all, which runs towards the winter sun, and is impassable except in boats, is carried from the Euphrates into another stream, called the Tigris, the river upon which the town of Nineveh formerly stood. Of all the countries that we know there is none which is so fruitful in grain. It makes no pretension indeed of growing the fig, the olive, the vine, or any other tree of the kind; but in grain it is so fruitful as to yield commonly two-hundred-fold, and when the production is the greatest, even three-hundred-fold. The blade of the wheat-plant and barley-plant is often four fingers in breadth. As for the millet and the sesame, I shall not say to what height they grow, though within my own knowledge; for I am not ignorant that what I have already written concerning the fruitfulness of Babylonia must seem incredible to those who have never visited the country. The only oil they use is made from the sesame-plant. Palm-trees grow in great numbers over the whole of the flat country, mostly of the kind which bears fruit, and this fruit supplies them with bread, wine, and honey. They are cultivated like the fig-tree in all respects, among others in this. The natives tie the fruit of the male-palms, as they are called by the Greeks, to the branches of the date-bearing palm, to let the gall-fly enter the dates and ripen them, and to prevent the fruit from falling off. The male-palms, like the wild fig-trees, have usually the gall-fly in their fruit.

But the greatest wonder of all that I saw in the land, after the city itself, I will now proceed to mention. The boats which come down the river to Babylon are circular, and made of skins. The frames, which are of willow, are cut in the country of the Armenians above Assyria, and on these, which serve for hulls, a covering of skins is stretched outside, and thus the boats are made, without either stem or stern, quite round like a shield. They are then entirely filled with straw, and their cargo is put on board, after which they are suffered to float down the stream. Their chief freight is wine, stored in casks made of wood of the palm-tree. They are managed by two men who stand upright in them, each plying an oar, one pulling and the other pushing. The boats are of various sizes, some larger, some smaller; the biggest reach as high as five thousand talents' burthen. Each vessel has a live ass on board; those of larger size have more than one. When they reach Babylon, the cargo is landed and offered for sale; after which the men break up their boats, sell the straw and the frames, and loading their asses with the skins, set off on their way back to Armenia. The current is too strong to allow a boat to return up-stream, for which reason they make their boats of skins rather than wood. On their return to Armenia they build fresh boats for the next voyage.

—GEORGE RAWLINSON.

STORIES OF EGYPT

[From Books II and III]

Herodotus found that Egypt differed more widely from Greece in its people, its customs, its climate, its appearance than any other country visited in his wanderings. He was particularly interested in the religious foundations on which its whole civilization was reared.

Now the Nile, when it overflows, floods not only the Delta, but also the tracts of country on both sides the stream which are thought to belong to Libya and Arabia, in some places reaching to the extent of two days' journey from its banks, in some even exceeding that distance, but in others falling short of it.

Concerning the nature of the river, I was not able to gain any information either from the priests or from others. I was particularly anxious to learn from them why the Nile, at the commencement of the summer solstice, begins to rise, and continues to increase for a hundred days—and why, as soon as that number is past, it forthwith retires and contracts its stream, continuing low during the whole of the winter until the summer solstice comes round again. On none of these points could I obtain any explanation from the inhabitants, though I made every inquiry, wishing to know what was commonly reported—they could neither tell me what special virtue the Nile has which makes it so opposite in its nature to all other streams, nor why, unlike every other river, it gives forth no breezes from its surface.

Some of the Greeks, however, wishing to get a reputation for cleverness, have offered explanations of the phenomena of the river, for which they have accounted in three different ways. Two of these I do not think it worth while to speak of, further than simply to mention what they are. One pretends that the Etesian winds cause the rise of the river by preventing the Nile-water from running off into the sea. But in the first place it has often happened, when the Etesian winds did not blow, that the Nile has risen according to its usual wont; and further, if the Etesian winds produced the effect, the other rivers which flow in a direction opposite to those winds ought to present the same phenomena as the Nile, and the more so as they are all smaller streams, and have a weaker current. But these rivers, of which there are many both in Syria and Libya, are entirely unlike the Nile in this respect.

The second opinion is even more unscientific than the one just mentioned, and also, if I may say so, more marvellous. It is that the Nile acts so strangely, because it flows from the ocean, and that the ocean flows all round the earth.

The third explanation, which is very much more plausible than either of the others, is positively the furthest from the truth; for there is really nothing in what it says, any more than in the other theories. It is that the inundation of the Nile is caused by the melting of snows.

Now, as the Nile flows out of Libya, through Ethiopia, into Egypt, how is it possible that it can be formed of melted snow, running, as it does, from the hottest regions of the world into cooler countries? Many are the proofs whereby any one capable of reasoning on the subject may be convinced that it is most unlikely this should be the case. The first and strongest argument is furnished by the winds, which always blow hot from these regions. The second is, that rain and frost are unknown there. Now, whenever snow falls, it must of necessity rain within five days; so that, if there were snow, there must be rain also in those parts. Thirdly, it is certain that the natives of the country are black with the heat, that the kites and the swallows remain there the whole year, and that the cranes, when they fly from the rigours of a Scythian winter, flock thither to pass the cold season. If then, in the country where the Nile has its source, or in that through which it flows, there fell ever so little snow, it is absolutely impossible that any of these circumstances could take place.

As for the writer who attributes the phenomenon to the ocean, his account is involved in such obscurity, that it is impossible to disprove it by argument. For my part I know of no river called Ocean, and I think that Homer, or one of the earlier poets, invented the name, and introduced it into his poetry.

Perhaps, after censuring all the opinions that have been put forward on this obscure subject, one ought to propose some theory of one's own. I will therefore proceed to explain what I think to be the reason of the Nile's swelling in the summer time. During the winter, the sun is driven out of his usual course by the storms, and removes to the upper parts of Libya. This is the whole secret in the fewest possible words; for it stands to reason that the country to which the Sun-god approaches the nearest, and which he passes most directly over, will be scantest of water, and that there the streams which feed the rivers will shrink the most.

To explain, however, more at length, the case is this. The sun, in his passage across the upper parts of Libya, affects them in the following way. As the air in those regions is constantly clear, and the country warm through the absence of cold winds, the sun in his passage across them acts upon them exactly as he is wont to act elsewhere in summer, when his path is in the middle of heaven—that is, he attracts the water. After attracting it, he again repels it into the upper regions, where the winds lay hold of it, scatter it, and reduce it to a vapour, whence it naturally enough comes to pass that the winds which blow from this quarter—the south and south-west—are of all winds the most rainy. And my own opinion is that the sun does not get rid of all the water which he draws year by year from the Nile, but retains some about him. When the winter begins to soften, the sun goes back again to his old place in the middle of the heaven, and proceeds to attract water equally from all countries. Till then the other rivers run big, from the quantity of rain-water which they bring down from countries where so much moisture falls that all the land is cut into gullies; but in summer, when the showers fail, and the sun attracts their water, they become low. The Nile, on the contrary, not deriving any of its bulk from rains, and being in winter subject to the attraction of the sun, naturally runs at that season, unlike all other streams, with a less burthen of water than in the summer time. For in summer it is exposed to attraction equally with all other rivers, but in winter it suffers alone. The sun, therefore, I regard as the sole cause of the phenomenon. . . .

Concerning Egypt itself I shall extend my remarks to a great length, because there is no country that possesses so many wonders, nor any that has such a number of works which defy description. Not only is the climate different from that of the rest of the world, and the rivers unlike any other rivers, but the people also, in most of their manners and customs, exactly reverse the common practice of mankind. The women attend the markets and trade, while the men sit at home at the loom; and here, while the rest of the world works the woof up the warp, the Egyptians work it down; the women likewise carry burthens upon their shoulders, while the men carry them upon their heads. They eat their food out of doors in the streets, but retire for private purposes to their houses, giving as a reason that what is unseemly, but necessary, ought to be done in secret, but what has nothing unseemly about it should be done openly. A woman cannot serve the priestly office, either for god or goddess, but men are priests to both; sons need not support their parents unless they choose, but daughters must, whether they choose or no.

In other countries the priests have long hair, in Egypt their heads are shaven; elsewhere it is customary, in mourning, for near relations to cut their hair close; the Egyptians, who wear no hair at any other time, when they lose a relative, let their beards and the hair of their heads grow long. All other men pass their lives separate from animals, the Egyptians have animals always living with them; others make barley and wheat their food, it is a disgrace to do so in Egypt, where the grain they live on is spelt, which some call *zea*. Dough they knead with their feet, but they mix mud, and even take up dirt, with their hands. They are the only people in the world—they at least, and such as have learnt the practice from them—who use circumcision. Their men wear two garments apiece, their women but one. They put on the rings and fasten the ropes to sails inside, others put them outside. When they write or calculate, instead of going, like the Greeks, from left to right; they move their hand from right to left; and they insist, notwithstanding, that it is they who go to the right, and the Greeks who go to the left. They have two quite different kinds of writing, one of which is called sacred, the other common.

They are religious to excess, far beyond any other race of men, and use the following ceremonies:—They drink out of brazen cups, which they scour every day: there is no exception to this practice. They wear linen garments, which they are specially careful to have always fresh washed. They practice circumcision for the sake of cleanliness, considering it better to be cleanly than comely. The priests shave their whole body every other day, that no lice or other impure thing may adhere to them when they are engaged in the service of the gods. Their dress is entirely of linen, and their shoes of the papyrus plant: it is not lawful for them to wear either dress or shoes of any other material. They bathe twice every day in cold water, and twice each night. Besides which they observe, so to speak, thousands of ceremonies. They enjoy, however, not a few advantages. They consume none of their own property, and are at no expense for anything; but every day bread is baked for them of the sacred corn, and a plentiful supply of beef and of goose's flesh is assigned to each, and also a portion of wine made from the grape. Fish they are not allowed to eat; and beans—which none of the Egyptians ever sow, or eat, if they come up of their own accord, either raw or boiled—the priests will not even endure to look on, since they consider it an unclean kind of pulse. Instead of a single priest, each god has the attendance of a college, at the head of which is a chief priest; when one of these dies, his son is appointed in his room.

Male kine are reckoned to belong to Epaphus, and are therefore tested in the following manner:—One of the priests appointed for the purpose searches to see if there is a single black hair on the whole body, since in that case the beast is unclean. He examines him all over, standing on his legs, and again laid upon his back; after which he takes the tongue out of his mouth, to see if it be clean in respect of the prescribed marks (what they are I will mention elsewhere); he also inspects the hairs of the tail, to observe if they grow naturally. If the animal is pronounced clean in all these points, the priest marks him by twisting a piece of papyrus round his horns, and attaching thereto some sealing-clay, which he then stamps with his own signet-ring. After this the beast is led away; and it is forbidden, under the penalty of death, to sacrifice an animal which has not been marked in this way.

The following is their manner of sacrifice:—They lead the victim, marked with their signet, to the altar where they are about to offer it, and setting the wood alight, pour a libation of wine upon the altar in front of the victim, and at the same time invoke the god. Then they slay the animal, and cutting off his head, proceed to flay the body. Next they take the head, and heaping imprecations on it, if there is a market-place and a body of Greek traders in the city, they carry it there and sell it instantly; if, however, there are no Greeks among them, they throw the head into the river. The imprecation is to this effect:—They pray that if any evil is impending either over those who sacrifice, or over universal Egypt, it may be made to fall upon that head. These practices, the imprecations upon the heads, and the libations of wine, prevail all over Egypt, and extend to victims of all sorts; and hence the Egyptians will never eat the head of any animal. . . .

About the time when Cambyses arrived at Memphis, Apis appeared to the Egyptians. Now Apis is the god whom the

Greeks call Epaphus. As soon as he appeared, straightway all the Egyptians arrayed themselves in their gayest garments, and fell to feasting and jollity: which when Cambyses saw, making sure that these rejoicings were on account of his own ill success, he called before him the officers, who had charge of Memphis, and demanded of them,—"Why, when he was in Memphis before, the Egyptians had done nothing of this kind, but waited until now, when he had returned with the loss of so many of his troops?" The officers made answer, "That one of their gods had appeared to them, a god who at long intervals of time had been accustomed to show himself in Egypt—and that always on his appearance, the whole of Egypt feasted and kept jubilee." When Cambyses heard this, he told them that they lied, and as liars he condemned them all to suffer death.

When they were dead, he called the priests to his presence, and questioning them received the same answer; whereupon he observed, "That he would soon know whether a tame god had really come to dwell in Egypt"—and straightway, without another word, he bade them bring Apis to him. So they went out from his presence to fetch the god. Now this Apis, or Epaphus, is the calf of a cow which is never afterwards able to

bear young. The Egyptians say that fire comes down from heaven upon the cow, which thereupon conceives Apis. The calf which is so called has the following marks:—He is black, with a square spot of white upon his forehead, and on his back the figure of an eagle; the hairs in his tail are double, and there is a beetle upon his tongue.

When the priests returned bringing Apis with them, Cambyses, like the harebrained person that he was, drew his dagger, and aimed at the belly of the animal, but missed his mark, and stabbed him in the thigh. Then he laughed, and said to the priests:—"Oh! blockheads, and think ye that gods become like this, of flesh and blood, and sensible to steel? A fit god indeed for Egyptians, such an one! But it shall cost you dear that you have made me your laughing-stock." When he had so spoken, he ordered those whose business it was to scourge the priests, and if they found any of the Egyptians keeping festival to put them to death. Thus was the feast stopped throughout the land of Egypt. Apis, wounded in the thigh, lay some time pining in the temple; at last he died of his wound, and the priests buried him secretly without the knowledge of Cambyses.

—GEORGE RAWLINSON.

II. WAR AND POLITICS

THE PERSIAN INVASIONS: HERODOTUS

MARATHON

[From Book VI]

The battle of Marathon (490 B.C.) was the climax of the first Persian invasion. For Herodotus, see above, p. 133.

Thus did war rage between the Eginetans and Athenians. Meantime the Per-

sian pursued his own design, from day to day exhorted by his servant to "remember the Athenians," and likewise urged continually by the Pisistratidæ, who were ever accusing their countrymen. Moreover it pleased him well to have a pretext for carrying war into Greece, that so he might reduce all those who had refused to give him earth and water. As for Mardonius, since his expedition had succeeded so ill, Darius took the command of the troops from him, and appointed other generals in his stead, who were to lead the host against Eretria and Athens; to wit, Datis, who was by descent a Mede, and Artaphernes, the son of Artaphernes, his own nephew. These men received orders to carry Athens and Eretria away captive, and to bring the prisoners into his presence.

So the new commanders took their departure from the court and went down to Cilicia, to the Aleian plain, having with them a numerous and well-appointed land army. Encamping here, they were joined by the sea force which had been required of the several states, and at the same time by the horse-transports which Darius had, the year before, commanded his tributaries to make ready. Aboard these the horses were embarked, and the troops were received by the ships of war; after which the whole fleet, amounting in all to six hundred triremes, made sail for Ionia. Thence, instead of proceeding with a straight course along the shore to the Hellespont and to Thrace, they loosed from Samos and voyaged across the Icarian sea through the midst of the islands; mainly, as I believe, because they feared the danger of doubling Mount Athos, where the year before they had suffered so grievously on their passage; but a constraining cause also was their former failure to take Naxos.

When the Persians, therefore, approaching from the Icarian sea, cast anchor at Naxos, which, recollecting what there befell them formerly, they had determined to attack before any other state, the Naxians, instead of encountering them, took to flight, and hurried off to the hills. The Persians however succeeded in laying hands on some, and them they carried away captive, while at the same time they burnt all the temples together with the town. This done, they left Naxos, and sailed away to the other islands.

While the Persians were thus employed, the Delians likewise quitted Delos, and took refuge in Tenos. And now the expedition drew near, when Datis sailed forward in advance of the other ships; which he commanded, instead of anchoring at Delos, to rendezvous at Rhenea, over against Delos, while he himself proceeded to discover whither the Delians had fled, after which he sent a herald to them with this message:—

"Why are ye fled, O holy men? Why have ye judged me so harshly and so wrongfully? I have surely sense enough, even had not the king so ordered, to spare the country which gave birth to the two gods,—to spare, I say, both the country and its inhabitants. Come back therefore to your dwellings, and once more inhabit your island." Such was the message which Datis sent by his herald to the Delians. He likewise placed upon the altar three hundred talents' weight of frankincense, and offered it.

After this he sailed with his whole host against Eretria, taking with him both Ionians and Æolians. When he was departed, Delos (as the Delians told me) was shaken by an earthquake, the first and last shock that has been felt to this day. And truly this was a prodigy whereby the god warned men of the evils that were coming upon them. For in the three following generations of Darius the son of Hystaspes, Xerxes the son of Darius, and Artaxerxes the son of Xerxes, more woes befell Greece than in the twenty generations preceding Darius;— woes caused in part by the Persians, but in part arising from the contentions among their own chief men respecting the supreme power. Wherefore it is not surprising that Delos, though it had never before been shaken, should at that time have felt the shock of an earthquake. And indeed there was an oracle, which said of Delos—

"Delos self will I shake, which never yet
has been shaken."

Of the above names Darius may be
rendered "Worker," Xerxes "Warrior,"
and Artaxerxes "Great Warrior." And so
we might call these kings in our own
language with propriety.

The barbarians, after loosing from
Delos, proceeded to touch at the other
islands, and took troops from each, and
likewise carried off a number of the
children as hostages. Going thus from
one to another, they came at last to
Carystus; but here the hostages were
refused by the Carystians, who said they
would neither give any, nor consent to
bear arms against the cities of their
neighbours, meaning Athens and Eretria.
Hereupon the Persians laid siege to
Carystus, and wasted the country round,
until at last the inhabitants were brought
over and agreed to do what was required
of them.

Meanwhile the Eretrians, understanding that the Persian armament was coming against them, besought the Athenians
for assistance. Nor did the Athenians
refuse their aid, but assigned to them as
auxiliaries the four thousand landholders
to whom they had allotted the estates of
the Chalcidean Hippobatæ. At Eretria,
however, things were in no healthy state;
for though they had called in the aid of
the Athenians, yet they were not agreed
among themselves how they should act;
some of them being minded to leave the
city and to take refuge in the heights
of Eubœa, while others, who looked to
receiving a reward from the Persians,
were making ready to betray their country. So when these things came to the
ears of Æschines, the son of Nothon,
one of the first men in Eretria, he made
known the whole state of affairs to the
Athenians who were already arrived, and
besought them to return home to their
own land, and not perish with his countrymen. And the Athenians hearkened
to his counsel, and crossing over to
Oropus, in this way escaped the
danger.

The Persian fleet now drew near and
anchored at Tamynæ, Chœreæ, and
Ægilia, three places in the territory of
Eretria. Once masters of these posts,
they proceeded forthwith to disembark
their horses, and made ready to attack
the enemy. But the Eretrians were not
minded to sally forth and offer battle;
their only care, after it had been resolved not to quit the city, was, if possible, to defend their walls. And now
the fortress was assaulted in good
earnest, and for six days there fell on
both sides vast numbers, but on the
seventh day Euphorbus, the son of Alci-
machus, and Philagrus, the son of
Cyneas, who were both citizens of good
repute, betrayed the place to the
Persians. These were no sooner entered
within the walls than they plundered and
burnt all the temples that there were
in the town, in revenge for the burning
of their own temples at Sardis; moreover, they did according to the orders
of Darius, and carried away captive all
the inhabitants.

The Persians, having thus brought
Eretria into subjection, after waiting a
few days, made sail for Attica, greatly
straitening the Athenians as they approached, and thinking to deal with them
as they had dealt with the people of
Eretria. And because there was no place
in all Attica so convenient for their
horse as Marathon, and it lay moreover
quite close to Eretria, therefore Hippias,
the son of Pisistratus, conducted them
thither.

When intelligence of this reached the
Athenians, they likewise marched their
troops to Marathon, and there stood on
the defensive, having at their head ten
generals, of whom one was Miltiades.

Now this man's father, Cimon, the son
of Stesagoras, was banished from Athens
by Pisistratus, the son of Hippocrates.
. . . At the time of Cimon's death,

Stesagoras, the elder of his two sons, was in the Chersonese, where he lived with Miltiades his uncle; the younger, who was called Miltiades after the founder of the Chersonesite colony, was with his father in Athens.

It was this Miltiades who now commanded the Athenians, after escaping from the Chersonese, and twice nearly losing his life. First he was chased as far as Imbrus by the Phœnicians, who had a great desire to take him and carry him up to the king; and when he had avoided this danger, and, having reached his own country, thought himself to be altogether in safety, he found his enemies waiting for him, and was cited by them before a court and impeached for his tyranny in the Chersonese. But he came off victorious here likewise, and was thereupon made general of the Athenians by the free choice of the people.

And first, before they left the city, the generals sent off to Sparta a herald, one Pheidippides, who was by birth an Athenian, and by profession and practice a trained runner. This man, according to the account which he gave the Athenians on his return, when he was near Mount Parthenium, above Tegea, fell in with the god Pan, who called him by his name, and bade him ask the Athenians "wherefore they neglected him so entirely, when he was kindly disposed towards them, and had often helped them in times past, and would do so again in time to come?" The Athenians, entirely believing in the truth of this report, as soon as their affairs were once more in good order, set up a temple to Pan under the Acropolis, and, in return for the message which I have recorded, established in his honour yearly sacrifices and a torch-race.

On the occasion of which we speak, when Pheidippides was sent by the Athenian generals, and, according to his own account, saw Pan on his journey, he reached Sparta on the very next day

after quitting the city of Athens. Upon his arrival he went before the rulers, and said to them—

"Men of Lacedæmon, the Athenians beseech you to hasten to their aid, and not allow that state, which is the most ancient in all Greece, to be enslaved by the barbarians. Eretria, look you, is already carried away captive, and Greece weakened by the loss of no mean city."

Thus did Pheidippides deliver the message committed to him. And the Spartans wished to help the Athenians, but were unable to give them any present succour, as they did not like to break their established law. It was the ninth day of the first decade, and they could not march out of Sparta on the ninth, when the moon had not reached the full. So they waited for the full of the moon.

The barbarians were conducted to Marathon by Hippias, the son of Pisistratus, who the night before had seen a strange vision in his sleep. He dreamt of lying in his mother's arms, and conjectured the dream to mean that he would be restored to Athens, recover the power which he had lost, and afterwards live to a good old age in his native country. Such was the sense in which he interpreted the vision. He now proceeded to act as guide to the Persians, and in the first place he landed the prisoners taken from Eretria upon the island that is called Ægileia, belonging to the Styreans, after which he brought the fleet to anchor off Marathon, and marshalled the bands of the barbarians as they disembarked. As he was thus employed it chanced that he sneezed and at the same time coughed with more violence than was his wont. Now as he was a man advanced in years, and the greater number of his teeth were loose, it so happened that one of them was driven out with the force of the cough, and fell down into the sand. Hippias took all the pains he could to find it, but the tooth was nowhere to be seen; whereupon he fetched a deep sigh, and said to the bystanders—

"After all the land is not ours, and we shall never be able to bring it under. All my share in it is the portion of which my tooth has possession." So Hippias believed that in this way his dream was out.

The Athenians were drawn up in order of battle in a sacred close belonging to Hercules, when they were joined by the Platæans, who came in full force to their aid. Some time before, the Platæans had put themselves under the rule of the Athenians, and these last had already undertaken many labours in their behalf. . . . And now they were come to Marathon to bear the Athenians aid.

The Athenian generals were divided in their opinions; and some advised not to risk a battle, because they were too few to engage such a host as that of the Medes; while others were for fighting at once, and among these last was Miltiades. He therefore, seeing that opinions were thus divided, and that the less worthy counsel appeared likely to prevail, resolved to go to the polemarch, and have a conference with him. For the man on whom the lot fell to be polemarch at Athens was entitled to give his vote with the ten generals, since anciently the Athenians allowed him an equal right of voting with them. The polemarch at this juncture was Callimachus of Aphidnæ; to him therefore Miltiades went, and said:—

"With thee it rests, Callimachus, either to bring Athens to slavery, or, by securing her freedom, to leave behind thee to all future generations a memory beyond even Harmodius and Aristogeiton. For never since the time that the Athenians became a people were they in so great a danger as now. If they bow their necks beneath the yoke of the Medes, the woes which they will have to suffer when given into the power of Hippias are already determined on; if, on the other hand, they fight and overcome, Athens may rise to be the very first city in Greece. How it comes to pass that these things are likely to happen, and how the determining of them in some sort rests with thee, I will now proceed to make clear. We generals are ten in number, and our votes are divided; half of us wish to engage, half to avoid a combat. Now, if we do not fight, I look to see a great disturbance at Athens which will shake men's resolutions, and then I fear they will submit themselves; but if we fight the battle before any unsoundness show itself among our citizens, let the gods but give us fair play, and we are well able to overcome the enemy. On thee therefore we depend in this matter, which lies wholly in thine own power. Thou hast only to add thy vote to my side and thy country will be free, and not free only, but the first state in Greece. Or, if thou preferrest to give thy vote to them who would decline the combat, then the reverse will follow."

Miltiades by these words gained Callimachus; and the addition of the polemarch's vote caused the decision to be in favour of fighting. Hereupon all those generals who had been desirous of hazarding a battle, when their turn came to command the army, gave up their right to Miltiades. He however, though he accepted their offers, nevertheless waited, and would not fight, until his own day of command arrived in due course.

Then at length, when his own turn was come, the Athenian battle was set in array, and this was the order of it. Callimachus the polemarch led the right wing, for it was at that time a rule to give the right wing to the polemarch. After this followed the tribes, according as they were numbered, in an unbroken line; while last of all came the Platæans, forming the left wing. And ever since that day it has been a custom with the Athenians, in the sacrifices and assemblies held each fifth year at Athens, for the Athenian herald to implore the blessing of the gods on the Platæans conjointly with the Athenians. Now as they marshalled the host upon the field of Marathon, in order that the Athenian front might be of equal length with the Median, the ranks of the centre were diminished, and it became the weakest part of the line, while the wings were both made strong with a depth of many ranks.

So when the battle was set in array, and the victims showed themselves favourable, instantly the Athenians, so soon as they were let go, charged the barbarians at a run. Now the distance between the two armies was little short of eight furlongs. The Persians, therefore, when they saw the Greeks coming at speed, made ready to receive them, although it seemed to them that the Athenians were bereft of their senses, and bent upon their own destruction; for they saw a mere handful of men coming on at a run without either horsemen or archers. Such was the opinion of the barbarians; but the Athenians in close array fell upon them, and fought in a manner worthy of being recorded. They were the first of the Greeks, so far as I know, who introduced the custom of charging the enemy at a run, and they were likewise the first who dared to look upon the Median garb, and to face men clad in that fashion. Until this time the very name of the Medes had been a terror to the Greeks to hear.

The two armies fought together on the plain of Marathon for a length of time; and in the mid battle, where the Persians themselves and the Sacæ had their place, the barbarians were victorious, and broke and pursued the Greeks into the inner country; but on the two wings the Athenians and the Platæans defeated the enemy. Having so done, they suffered the routed barbarians to fly at their ease, and joining the two wings in one, fell upon those who had broken their own centre, and fought and conquered them. These likewise fled, and now the Athenians hung upon the runaways and cut them down, chasing them all the way to the shore, on reaching which they laid hold of the ships and called aloud for fire.

It was in the struggle here that Callimachus the polemarch, after greatly distinguishing himself, lost his life; Stesilaus too, the son of Thrasilaus, one of the generals, was slain; and Cynægirus, the son of Euphorion, having seized on a vessel of the enemy's by the ornament at the stern, had his hand cut off by the blow of an axe, and so perished; as likewise did many other Athenians of note and name.

Nevertheless the Athenians secured in this way seven of the vessels, while with the remainder the barbarians pushed off, and taking aboard their Eretrian prisoners from the island where they had left them, doubled Cape Sunium, hoping to reach Athens before the return of the Athenians. The Alcmæonidæ were accused by their countrymen of suggesting this course to them; they had, it was said, an understanding with the Persians, and made a signal to them, by raising a shield, after they were embarked in their ships.

The Persians accordingly sailed round Sunium. But the Athenians with all possible speed marched away to the defence of their city, and succeeded in reaching Athens before the appearance of the barbarians; and as their camp at Marathon had been pitched in a precinct of Hercules, so now they encamped in another precinct of the same god at Cynosarges. The barbarian fleet arrived, and lay to off Phalerum, which was at that time the haven of Athens; but after resting awhile upon their oars, they departed and sailed away to Asia.

There fell in this battle of Marathon, on the side of the barbarians, about six thousand and four hundred men; on that of the Athenians, one hundred and ninety-two. Such was the number of the slain on the one side and the other. A strange prodigy likewise happened at this fight. Epizelus, the son of Cyphagoras, an Athenian, was in the thick of the fray, behaving himself as a brave man should, when suddenly he was stricken with blindness, without blow of sword or dart, and this blindness continued thenceforth during the whole of his after life. The following is the account which he himself, as I have heard, gave of the matter: he said that a gigantic warrior, with a huge beard, which shaded all his shield, stood over against him, but the ghostly semblance passed by him, and slew the man at his side. Such, as I understand, was the tale which Epizelus told.

—George Rawlinson.

Bridging the Hellespont

[From Book VII]

The crossing of the Hellespont (480 B.C.) marks the beginning of the second invasion of Greece by the Persians.

Xerxes, after this, made preparations to advance to Abydos, where the bridge across the Hellespont from Asia to Europe was lately finished. Midway between Sestos and Madytus in the Hellespontine Chersonese, and right over against Abydos, there is a rocky tongue of land which runs out for some distance into the sea. This is the place where no long time afterwards The Greeks under Xanthippus, the son of Ariphron, took Artayctes the Persian, who was at that time governor of Sestos, and nailed him living to a plank. He was the Artayctes who brought women into the temple of Protesilaus at Elæus, and there was guilty of most unholy deeds.

Towards this tongue of land then, the men to whom the business was assigned, carried out a double bridge from Abydos; and while the Phœnicians constructed one line with cables of white flax, the Egyptians in the other used ropes made of papyrus. Now it is seven furlongs across from Abydos to the opposite coast. When, therefore, the channel had been bridged successfully, it happened that a great storm arising broke the whole work to pieces, and destroyed all that had been done.

So when Xerxes heard of it, he was full of wrath, and straightway gave orders that the Hellespont should receive three hundred lashes, and that a pair of fetters should be cast into it. Nay, I have even heard it said, that he bade the branders take their irons and therewith brand the Hellespont. It is certain that he commanded those who scourged the waters to utter, as they lashed them, these barbarian and wicked words: "Thou bitter water, thy lord lays on thee this punishment because thou hast wronged him without a cause, having suffered no evil at his hand. Verily, King Xerxes will cross thee, whether thou wilt or no. Well dost thou deserve that no man should honour thee with sacrifice; for thou art of a truth a treacherous and unsavoury river." While the sea was thus punished by his orders, he likewise commanded that the overseers of the work should lose their heads.

Then they, whose business it was, executed the unpleasing task laid upon them; and other master-builders were set over the work, who accomplished it in the way which I will now describe.

They joined together triremes and penteconters, 360 to support the bridge on the side of the Euxine Sea, and 314 to sustain the other; and these they placed at right-angles to the Sea, and in the direction of the current of the Hellespont, relieving by these means the tension of the shore cables. Having joined the vessels, they moored them with anchors of unusual size, that the vessels of the bridge towards the Euxine might resist the winds which blow from within the straits, and that those of the more western bridge facing the Ægean might withstand the wind which set in from the south and from the south-east. A gap was left in the penteconters in no fewer than three places, to afford a passage for such light craft as chose to enter or leave the Euxine. When all this was done, they made the cables taut from the shore by the help of wooden capstans. This time, moreover, instead of using the two materials separately, they assigned to each bridge six cables, two of which were of white flax, while four were of papyrus. Both cables were of the same size and quality; but the flaxen were the heavier, weighing not less than a talent the cubit. When the bridge across the channel was thus complete, trunks of trees were sawn into planks, which were cut to the width of the bridge, and these were laid side by side upon the tightened cables, and then fastened on the top. This done, brushwood was brought, and arranged upon the planks, after which earth was heaped upon the brushwood, and the whole trodden down into a solid mass. Lastly a bulwark was set up on either side of this causeway, of such a height as to prevent the sumpter-beasts and the horses from seeing over it and taking fright at the water.

—GEORGE RAWLINSON.

THE SPARTANS

[From Book VII]

In this and in the following passage the historian makes use of the dramatic poet's method of sketching in the general setting and the characters which are to play the leading rôles in the imminent conflict. The device of the report on the Spartans to the Persian king enables him inci-dentally to picture the Persian character while speaking of the Greek.

Now after Xerxes had sailed down the whole line and was gone ashore, he sent for Demaratus the son of Ariston, who had accompanied him in his march upon Greece, and bespake him thus:—

"Demaratus, it is my pleasure at this time to ask thee certain things which I wish to know. Thou art a Greek, and, as I hear from the other Greeks with whom I converse, no less than from thine own lips, thou art a native of a city which is not the meanest or the weakest in their native land. Tell me, therefore, what thinkest thou? Will the Greeks lift a hand against us? Mine own judgment is, that even if all the Greeks and all the barbarians of the west were gathered together in one place, they would not be able to abide my onset, not being really of one mind. But I would fain know what thou thinkest hereon."

Thus Xerxes questioned; and the other replied in his turn,—"O king, is it thy will that I give thee a true answer, or dost thou wish for a pleasant one?"

Then the king bade him speak the plain truth, and promised that he would not on that account hold him in less favour than heretofore.

So Demaratus, when he heard the promise, spake as follows:—

"O king, since thou biddest me at all risks speak the truth, and not say what will one day prove me to have lied to thee, thus I answer. Want has at all times been a fellow-dweller with us in our land, while Valour is an ally whom we have gained by dint of wisdom and strict laws. Her aid enables us to drive out want and escape thraldom. Brave are all the Greeks who dwell in any Dorian land, but what I am about to say does not concern all, but only the Lacedæmonians. First then, come what may, they will never accept thy terms, which would reduce Greece to slavery; and further, they are sure to join battle with thee, though all the rest of the Greeks should submit to thy will. As for their numbers, do not ask how many they are, that their resistance should be a possible thing; for if a thousand of them should take the field, they will meet thee in battle, and so will any number, be it less than this, or be it more."

When Xerxes heard this answer of Demaratus, he laughed and answered,—"What wild words, Demaratus! A thousand men join battle with such an army as this! Come then, wilt thou—who wert once, as thou sayest, their king—engage to fight this very day with ten men? I trow not. And yet, if all thy fellow citizens be indeed such as thou sayest they are, thou oughtest, as their king, by thine own country's usages, to be ready to fight with twice the number. If then each one of them be a match for ten of my soldiers, I may well call upon thee to be a match for twenty. So wouldst thou assure the truth of what thou hast now said. If, however, you Greeks, who vaunt yourselves so much, are of a truth men like those whom I have seen about my court, as thyself, Demaratus, and the others with whom I am wont to converse,—if, I say, you are really men of this sort and size, how is the speech which thou hast uttered more than a mere empty boast? For, to go to the very verge of likelihood,—how could a thousand men, or ten thousand, or even fifty thousand, particularly if they were all alike free, and not under one lord,—how could such a force, I say, stand against an army like mine? Let them be five thousand, and we shall have more than a thousand men to each one of theirs. If, indeed, like our troops, they had a single master, their fear of him might make them courageous beyond their natural bent, or they might be urged by lashes against an enemy which far outnumbered them. But left to their own free choice, assuredly they will act differently. For mine own part, I believe, that if the Greeks had to contend with the Persians only, and the numbers were equal on both sides, the Greeks would find it hard to stand their ground. We too have among us such men as those of whom thou spakest—not many indeed, but still we possess a few. For instance, some of my body-guard would be willing to engage singly with three Greeks. But this thou didst not know, and therefore it was thou talkedst so foolishly."

Demaratus answered him,—"I knew, O king, at the outset, that if I told thee the truth, my speech would displease thine ears. But as thou didst require me to answer thee with all possible truthfulness, I informed thee what the Spartans will do. And in this I speak not from any love that I bear them—for none knows better than thou what my love towards them is likely to be at the present time, when they have robbed me of my rank and my ancestral honours, and made me a homeless exile, whom thy father did receive, bestowing on me both shelter and sustenance. What likelihood is there that a man of understanding should be unthankful for kindness shown him, and not cherish it in his heart? For mine own self, I pretend not to cope with ten men, or with two,—nay, had I the choice, I would rather not fight even with one. But, if need appeared, or if there were any great cause urging me on, I would contend with right good-will against one of those persons who boast themselves a match for any three Greeks. So likewise the Lacedæmonians, when they fight singly, are as good men as any in the world, and when they fight in a body, are the bravest of all. For though they be free men, they are not in all respects free; Law is the master whom they own, and this master they fear more than any subjects fear thee. Whatever he commands they do; and his commandment is always the same: it forbids them to flee in battle, whatever the number of their foes, and requires them to stand firm, and either to conquer or die. If in these words, O king, I seem to thee to speak foolishly, I am content from this time forward evermore to hold my peace. I had not now spoken unless compelled by thee. Certes, I pray that all may turn out according to thy wishes."

Such was the answer of Demaratus, and Xerxes was not angry with him at all, but only laughed, and sent him away with words of kindness.

—George Rawlinson.

The Athenians

[From Book VII]

The sketch of the Spartans reads as if the author were repeating the estimate of them generally accepted by the Greeks. His account of the Athenians reveals his own opinion, to the effect that the salvation of Greece depended upon them rather than upon the Spartans. Some historians believe that Herodotus unduly magnified the relative importance of the Athenians in the great war.

The expedition of the Persian king, though it was in name directed against Athens, threatened really the whole of Greece. And of this the Greeks were aware some time before, but they did not all view the matter in the same light. Some of them had given the Persian earth and water, and were bold on this account, deeming themselves thereby secured against suffering hurt from the barbarian army; while others, who had refused compliance, were thrown into extreme alarm. For whereas they considered all the ships in Greece too few to engage the enemy, it was plain that the greater number of states would take no part in the war, but warmly favoured the Medes.

And here I feel constrained to deliver an opinion, which most men, I know, will mislike, but which, as it seems to me to be true, I am determined not to withhold. Had the Athenians from fear of the approaching danger, quitted their country, or had they without quitting it submitted to the power of Xerxes, there would certainly have been no attempt to resist the Persians by sea; in which case, the course of events by land would have been the following. Though the Peloponnesians might have carried ever so many breastworks across the Isthmus, yet their allies would have fallen off from the Lacedæmonians, not by voluntary desertion, but because town after town must have been taken by the fleet of the barbarians; and so the Lacedæmonians would at last have stood alone, and, standing alone, would have displayed prodigies of valour, and died nobly. Either they would have done thus, or else, before it came to that extremity, seeing one Greek state after another embrace the cause of the Medes, they would have come to terms with King Xerxes;—and thus, either way Greece would have been brought under Persia. For I cannot understand of what possible use the walls across the Isthmus could have been, if the king had had the mastery of the sea. If then a man should now say that the Athenians were the saviours of Greece, he would not exceed the truth. For they truly held the scales, and whichever side they espoused must have carried the day. They too it was who, when they had determined to maintain the freedom of Greece, roused up that portion of the Greek nation which had not gone over to the Medes, and so, next to the gods, *they* repulsed the invader. Even the terrible oracles which reached them from Delphi, and struck fear into their hearts, failed to persuade them to fly from Greece. They had the courage to remain faithful to their land, **and await the** coming of the foe.

When the Athenians, anxious to consult the oracle, sent their messengers to Delphi, hardly had the envoys completed the customary rites about the sacred precinct, and taken their seats inside the sanctuary of the god, when the Pythoness, Aristonice by name, thus prophesied—

"Wretches, why sit ye here? Fly, fly to
  the ends of creation,
Quitting your homes, and the crags which
  your city crowns with her circlet.
Neither the head, nor the body is firm in
  its place, nor at bottom
Firm the feet, nor the hands, nor resteth
  the middle uninjur'd.
All—all ruined and lost. Since fire, and
  impetuous Ares,
Speeding along in a Syrian chariot,
  haste to destroy her.
Not alone shalt thou suffer; full many the
  towers he will level,
Many the shrines of the gods he will give
  to a fiery destruction.
Even now they stand with dark sweat
  horribly dripping,
Trembling and quaking for fear, and lo!
  from the high roofs trickleth
Black blood, sign prophetic of hard distresses impending.
Get ye away from the temple, and brood
  on the ills that await ye!"

When the Athenian messengers heard this reply, they were filled with the deepest affliction: whereupon Timon, the son of Androbulus, one of the men of most mark among the Delphians, seeing how utterly cast down they were at the gloomy prophecy, advised them to take an olive-branch, and entering the sanctuary again, consult the oracle as suppliants. The Athenians followed this advice, and going in once more, said— "O King, we pray thee reverence these boughs of supplication which we bear in our hands, and deliver to us something more comforting concerning our country. Else we will not leave your sanctuary,

but will stay here till we die." Upon this the priestess gave them a second answer, which was the following:—

"Pallas has not been able to soften the
  lord of Olympus,
Though she has often prayed him, and
  urged him with excellent counsel,
Yet once more I address thee in words
  than adamant firmer.
When the foe shall have taken whatever
  the limit of Cecrops
Holds within it, and all which divine
  Cithæron shelters,
Then far-seeing Jove grants this to the
  prayers of Athene;
Safe shall the wooden wall continue for
  thee and thy children.
Wait not the tramp of the horse nor the
  footmen mightily moving
Over the land, but turn your back to the
  foe, and retire ye.
Yet shall a day arrive when ye shall meet
  him in battle.
Holy Salamis, thou shalt destroy the offspring of women
When men scatter the seed, or when they
  gather the harvest."

This answer seemed, as indeed it was, gentler than the former one; so the envoys wrote it down, and went back with it to Athens. When, however, upon their arrival, they produced it before the people, and inquiry began to be made into its true meaning, many and various were the interpretations which men put upon it; two, more especially, seemed to be directly opposed to one another. Certain of the old men were of opinion that the god meant to tell them that the citadel would escape; for this was anciently defended by a palisade; and they supposed that barrier to be the "wooden wall" of the oracle. Others maintained that the fleet was what the god pointed at; and their advice was that nothing should be thought of except the ships, which had best be at once got ready. Still such as said the "wooden wall" meant the fleet, were perplexed by the last two lines of the oracle—

"Holy Salamis, thou shalt destroy the offspring of women,
When men scatter the seed, or when they
gather the harvest."

These words caused great disturbance
among those who took the wooden wall
to be the ships; since the interpreters
understood them to mean, that, if they
made preparations for a sea-fight, they
would suffer a defeat off Salamis.

Now there was at Athens a man who
had lately made his way into the first
rank of citizens; his true name was
Themistocles, but he was known more
generally as the son of Neocles. This
man came forward and said, that the
interpreters had not explained the oracle
altogether aright—"for if," he argued,
"the clause in question had really respected the Athenians, it would not have,
been expressed so mildly; the phrase used
would have been 'Luckless Salamis,'
rather than 'Holy Salamis,' had those
to whom the island belonged been about
to perish in its neighbourhood. Rightly
taken, the response of the god threatened the enemy, much more than the
Athenians." He therefore counselled his
countrymen to make ready to fight on
board their ships, since *they* were the
wooden wall in which the god told them
to trust. When Themistocles had thus
cleared the matter, the Athenians embraced his view, preferring it to that of
the interpreters. The advice of these
last had been against engaging in a sea-
fight; "all the Athenians could do," they
said, "was, without lifting a hand in
their defence, to quit Attica, and make
a settlement in some other country."

Themistocles had before this given a
counsel which prevailed very seasonably.
The Athenians, having a large sum of
money in their treasury, the produce of
the mines at Laureium, were about to
share it among the full-grown citizens,
who would have received ten drachmas
apiece, when Themistocles persuaded

them to forbear the distribution, and
build with the money two hundred ships,
to help them in their war against the
Eginetans. It was the breaking out of
the Eginetan war which was at this time
the saving of Greece, for hereby were
the Athenians forced to become a maritime power. The new ships were not
used for the purpose for which they had
been built, but became a help to Greece
in her hour of need. And the Athenians
had not only these vessels ready before
the war, but they likewise set to work to
build more; while they determined, in a
council which was held after the debate
upon the oracle, that, according to the
advice of the god, they would embark
their whole force aboard the ships, and
with such Greeks as chose to join them,
give battle to the barbarian invader.
Such, then, were the oracles which had
been received by the Athenians.

—GEORGE RAWLINSON.

THE PERSIAN HOST

[From Book VII]

Number is added to number in thoroughly epic fashion. The greater the host
of the enemy, the greater the achievement
of the Greeks in the final issue of events.

As far as this point then, and on land,
as far as Thermopylæ, the armament of
Xerxes had been free from mischance;
and the numbers were still, according to
my reckoning, of the following amount.
First there was the ancient complement
of the twelve hundred and seven vessels
which came with the king from Asia—
the contingents of the nations severally
—amounting, if we allow to each ship a
crew of two hundred men, to 241,400.
Each of these vessels had on board, besides native soldiers, thirty fighting men,
who were either Persians, Medes, or
Sacans; which gives an addition of
36,210. To these two numbers I shall

further add the crews of the pentecon- ters; which may be reckoned, one with another, at fourscore each. Of such vessels there were (as I said before) three thousand; and the men on board them accordingly would be 240,000. This was the sea force brought by the king from Asia; and it amounted in all to 517,610 men. The number of the foot soldiers was 1,700,000; that of the horsemen 80,000; to which must be added the Arabs who rode on camels, and the Libyans who fought in chariots, whom I reckon at 20,000. The whole number, therefore, of the land and sea forces added together amounts to 2,317,- 610 men. Such was the force brought from Asia, without including the camp followers, or taking any account of the provision-ships and the men whom they had on board.

To the amount thus reached we have still to add the forces gathered in Europe, concerning which I can only speak from conjecture. The Greeks dwelling in Thrace, and in the islands off the coast of Thrace, furnished to the fleet one hundred and twenty ships; the crews of which would amount to 24,000 men. Besides these, footmen were furnished by the Thracians, the Pæonians, the Eor- dians, the Bottiæans, by the Chalcidean tribes, by the Brygians, the Pierians, the Macedonians, the Perrhæbians, the Enianians, the Dolopians, the Magnes- ians, the Achæans, and by all the dwell- ers upon the Thracian sea-board; and the forces of these nations amounted, I believe, to three hundred thousand men. These numbers, added to those of the force which came out of Asia, make the sum of the fighting men 2,641,610.

Such then being the number of the fighting men, it is my belief that the attendants who followed the camp, to- gether with the crews of the corn-barks, and of the other craft accompanying the army, made up an amount rather above than below that of the fighting men.

However I will not reckon them as either fewer or more, but take them at an equal number. We have therefore to add to the sum already reached an exactly equal amount. This will give 5,283,220 as the whole number of men brought by Xerxes, the son of Darius, as far as Sepias and Thermopylæ.

Such then was the amount of the entire host of Xerxes. As for the num- ber of the women who ground the corn, of the concubines, and the eunuchs, no one can give any sure account of it; nor can the baggage-horses and other sumpter-beasts, nor the Indian hounds which followed the army, be calculated, by reason of their multitude. Hence I am not at all surprised that the water of the rivers was found too scant for the army in some instances; rather it is a marvel to me how the provisions did not fail, when the numbers were so great. For I find on calculation that if each man consumed no more than a chœnix of corn a-day, there must have been used daily by the army 110,340 medimni, and this without counting what was eaten by the women, the eunuchs, the sumpter-beasts, and the hounds. Among all this multi- tude of men there was not one who, for beauty and stature, deserved more than Xerxes himself to wield so vast a power.

—GEORGE RAWLINSON.

THERMOPYLÆ

[From Book VII]

To the Greeks Thermopylæ (480 B.C.) was a material defeat but a spiritual victory.

King Xerxes pitched his camp in the region of Malis called Trachinia, while on their side the Greeks occupied the straits. These straits the Greeks in general call Thermopylæ (the Hot Gates); but the natives and those who dwell in the neighbourhood call them

Pylæ (the Gates). Here then the two armies took their stand; the one master of all the region lying north of Trachis, the other of the country extending southward of that place to the verge of the continent.

The Greeks who at this spot awaited the coming of Xerxes were the following:— From Sparta, three hundred men-at-arms: from Arcadia, a thousand Tegeans and Mantineans, five hundred of each people; a hundred and twenty Orchomenians, from the Arcadian Orchomenus; and a thousand from other cities; from Corinth, four hundred men: from Phlius, two hundred: and from Mycenæ, eighty. Such was the number from the Peloponnese. There were also present, from Bœotia, seven hundred Thespians and four hundred Thebans.

Besides these troops, the Locrians of Opus and the Phocians had obeyed the call of their countrymen, and sent, the former all the force they had, the latter a thousand men. For envoys had gone from the Greeks at Thermopylæ among the Locrians and Phocians, to call on them for assistance, and to say—"They were themselves but the vanguard of the host, sent to precede the main body, which might every day be expected to follow them. The sea was in good keeping, watched by the Athenians, the Eginetans, and the rest of the fleet. There was no cause why they should fear; for after all the invader was not a god but a man; and there never had been, and never would be, a man who was not liable to misfortunes from the very day of his birth, and those greater in proportion to his own greatness. The assailant, therefore, being only a mortal, must needs fall from his glory." Thus urged, the Locrians and the Phocians had come with their troops to Trachis.

The various nations had each captains of their own under whom they served; but the one to whom all especially looked up, and who had the command of the entire force, was the Lacedæmonian, Leonidas. Now Leonidas was the son of Anaxandridas, who was the son of Leo, who was the son of Eurycratidas, who was the son of Anaxander, who was the son of Eurycrates, who was the son of Polydorus, who was the son of Alcamenes, who was the son of Telecles, who was the son of Archelaus, who was the son of Agesilaus, who was the son of Doryssus, who was the son of Labotas, who was the son of Echestratus, who was the son of Agis, who was the son of Eurysthenes, who was the son of Aristodemus, who was the son of Aristomachus, who was the son of Cleodæus, who was the son of Hyllus, who was the son of Hercules.

Leonidas had come to be king of Sparta quite unexpectedly. Having two elder brothers, Cleomenes and Dorieus, he had no thought of ever mounting the throne. However when Cleomenes died without male offspring, as Dorieus was likewise deceased, having perished in Sicily, the crown fell to Leonidas, who was older than Cleombrotus, the youngest of the sons of Anaxandridas, and, moreover, was married to the daughter of Cleomenes. He had now come to Thermopylæ, accompanied by the three hundred men which the law assigned him, whom he had himself chosen from among the citizens, and who were all of them fathers with sons living. On his way he had taken the troops from Thebes, whose number I have already mentioned, and who were under the command of Leontiades the son of Eurymachus. The reason why he made a point of taking troops from Thebes and Thebes only was, that the Thebans were strongly suspected of being well inclined to the Medes. Leonidas therefore called on them to come with him to the war, wishing to see whether they would comply with his demand, or openly refuse, and disclaim the Greek alliance. They, however, though their wishes leant the other way, nevertheless sent the men.

The force with Leonidas was sent forward by the Spartans in advance of their main body, that the sight of them might encourage the allies to fight, and hinder them from going over to the Medes, as it was likely that they might have done had they seen Sparta backward. They intended presently, when they had celebrated the Carneian festival, which was what now kept them at home, to leave a garrison in Sparta, and hasten in full force to join the army. The rest of the allies also intended to act similarly; for it happened that the Olympic festival fell exactly at this same period. None of them looked to see the contest at Thermopylæ decided so speedily; wherefore they were content to send forward a mere advanced guard. Such accordingly were the intentions of the allies.

The Greek forces at Thermopylæ, when the Persian army drew near to the entrance of the pass, were seized with fear, and a council was held to consider about a retreat. It was the wish of the Peloponnesians generally that the army should fall back upon the Peloponnese, and there guard the Isthmus. But Leonidas, who saw with what indignation the Phocians and Locrians heard of this plan, gave his voice for remaining where they were, while they sent envoys to the several cities to ask for help, since they were too few to make a stand against an army like that of the Medes.

While this debate was going on, Xerxes sent a mounted spy to observe the Greeks, and note how many they were, and what they were doing. He had heard, before he came out of Thessaly, that a few men were assembled at this place, and that at their head were certain Lacedæmonians, under Leonidas, a descendant of Hercules. The horseman rode up to the camp, and looked about him, but did not see the whole army; for such as were on the further side of the wall (which had been rebuilt and now was carefully guarded) it was not possible for him to behold; but he observed those on the outside, who were encamped in front of the rampart. It chanced that at this time the Lacedæmonians held the outer guard, and were seen by the spy, some of them engaged in gymnastic exercises, others combing their long hair. At this the spy greatly marvelled, but he counted their number, and when he had taken accurate note of everything, he rode back quietly; for no one pursued after him, or paid any heed to his visit. So he returned and told Xerxes all that he had seen.

Upon this, Xerxes, who had no means of surmising the truth—namely, that the Spartans were preparing to do or die manfully—but thought it laughable that they should be engaged in such employments, sent and called to his presence Demaratus the son of Ariston, who still remained with the army. When he appeared, Xerxes told him all that he had heard, and questioned him concerning the news, since he was anxious to understand the meaning of such behaviour on the part of the Spartans. Then Demaratus said—

"I spake to thee, O king, concerning these men long since, when we had but just begun our march upon Greece; thou, however, didst only laugh at my words, when I told thee of all this, which I saw would come to pass. Earnestly do I struggle at all times to speak the truth to thee, sire; and now listen to it once more. These men have come to dispute the pass with us, and it is for this that they are now making ready. 'Tis their custom, when they are about to hazard their lives, to adorn their heads with care. Be assured, however, that if thou canst subdue the men who are here and the Lacedæmonians who remain in Sparta, there is no other nation in all the world which will venture to lift a hand in their defence. Thou hast now to deal with the first kingdom and town in Greece, and with the bravest men."

Then Xerxes, to whom what Demaratus said seemed altogether to surpass belief, asked further, "how it was possible for so small an army to contend with his?"

"O king," Demaratus answered, "let me be treated as a liar, if matters fall not out as I say."

But Xerxes was not persuaded any the more. Four whole days he suffered to go by, expecting that the Greeks would run away. When, however, he found on the fifth that they were not gone, thinking that their firm stand was mere imprudence and recklessness, he grew wroth, and sent against them the Medes and Cissians, with orders to take them alive and bring them into his presence. Then the Medes rushed forward and charged the Greeks, but fell in vast numbers: others however took the places of the slain, and would not be beaten off, though they suffered terrible losses. In this way it became clear to all, and especially to the king, that though he had plenty of combatants, he had but very few warriors. The struggle, however, continued during the whole day.

Then the Medes, having met so rough a reception, withdrew from the fight; and their place was taken by the band of Persians under Hydarnes, whom the king called his "Immortals": they, it was thought, would soon finish the business. But when they joined battle with the Greeks, 'twas with no better success than the Median detachment—things went much as before—the two armies fighting in a narrow space, and the barbarians using shorter spears than the Greeks, and having no advantage from their numbers. The Lacedæmonians fought in a way worthy of note, and showed themselves far more skillful in fight than their adversaries, often turning their backs, and making as though they were all flying away, on which the barbarians would rush after them with much noise and shouting, when the Spartans at their approach would wheel round and face their pursuers, in this way destroying vast numbers of the enemy. Some Spartans likewise fell in these encounters, but only a very few. At last the Persians, finding that all their efforts to gain the pass availed nothing, and that whether they attacked by divisions or in any other way, it was to no purpose, withdrew to their own quarters.

During these assaults, it is said that Xerxes, who was watching the battle, thrice leaped from the throne on which he sate, in terror for his army.

Next day the combat was renewed, but with no better success on the part of the barbarians. The Greeks were so few that the barbarians hoped to find them disabled, by reason of their wounds, from offering any further resistance; and so they once more attacked them. But the Greeks were drawn up in detachments according to their cities, and bore the brunt of the battle in turns,—all except the Phocians, who had been stationed on the mountain to guard the pathway. So when the Persians found no difference between that day and the preceding, they again retired to their quarters.

Now, as the king was in a great strait, and knew not how he should deal with the emergency, Ephialtes, the son of Eurydemus, a man of Malis, came to him and was admitted to a conference. Stirred by the hope of receiving a rich reward at the king's hands, he had come to tell him of the pathway which led across the mountain to Thermopylæ; by which disclosure he brought destruction on the band of Greeks who had there withstood the barbarians. This Ephialtes afterwards, from fear of the Lacedæmonians, fled into Thessaly; and during his exile, in an assembly of the Amphictyons held at Pylæ, a price was set upon his head by the Pylagoræ. When some time had gone by, he returned from exile, and went to Anticyra, where he was slain by Athenades, a native of Trachis. Athenades did not slay him for his treachery, but for another reason, which I shall mention in a later part of my history: yet still the Lacedæmonians honoured him none the less. Thus then did Ephialtes perish a long time afterwards.

Besides this there is another story told, which I do not at all believe—to wit, that Onetas the son of Phanagoras, a native of Carystus, and Corydallus, a man of Anticyra, were the persons who spoke on this matter to the king, and took the Persians across the mountain. One may guess which story is true, from the fact that the deputies from the Greeks, the Pylagoræ, who must have had the best means of ascertaining the truth, did not offer the reward for the heads of Onetas and Corydallus, but for that of Ephialtes of Trachis; and again from the flight of Ephialtes, which we know to have been on this account. Onetas, I allow, although he was not a Malian, might have been acquainted with the path, if he had lived much in that part of the country; but as Ephialtes was the person who actually led the Persians round the mountain by the pathway, I leave his name on record as that of the man who did the deed.

Great was the joy of Xerxes on this occasion; and as he approved highly of the enterprise which Ephialtes undertook to accomplish, he forthwith sent upon the errand Hydarnes, and the Persians under him. The troops left the camp about the time of the lighting of the lamps. The pathway along which they went was first discovered by the Malians of these parts, who soon afterwards led the Thessalians by it to attack the Phocians, at the time when the Phocians fortified the pass with a wall, and so put themselves under covert from danger. And ever since the path has always been put to an ill use by the Malians.

The course which it takes is the following:—Beginning at the Asopus, where that stream flows through the cleft in the hills, it runs along the ridge of the mountain (which is called, like the pathway over it, Anopæa), and ends at the city of Alpenus—the first Locrian town as you come from Malis—by the stone called Melampygus and the seats of the Cercopians. Here is it as narrow as at any other point.

The Persians took this path, and crossing the Asopus, continued their march through the whole of the night, having the mountains of Œta on their right hand, and on their left those of Trachis. At dawn of day they found themselves close to the summit. Now the hill was guarded, as I have already said, by a thousand Phocian men-at-arms, who were placed there to defend the pathway, and at the same time to secure their own country. They had been given the guard of the mountain path, while the other Greeks defended the pass below, because they had volunteered for the service, and had pledged themselves to Leonidas to maintain the post.

The ascent of the Persians became known to the Phocians in the following manner:—During all the time that they were making their way up, the Greeks remained unconscious of it, inasmuch as the whole mountain was covered with groves of oak; but it happened that the air was very still, and the leaves which the Persians stirred with their feet made, as it was likely they would, a loud rustling, whereupon the Phocians jumped up and flew to seize their arms. In a moment the barbarians came in sight, and perceiving men arming themselves, were greatly amazed; for they had fallen in with an enemy when they had expected no opposition. Hydarnes, alarmed at the sight, and fearing lest the Phocians might be Lacedæmonians, enquired of Ephialtes to what nation these troops belonged. Ephialtes told him the exact truth, whereupon he arrayed his Persians for battle. The Phocians, galled by the showers of arrows to which they were exposed, and imagining themselves the special object of the Persian attack, fled hastily to the crest of the mountain, and there made ready to meet death; but while their mistake continued, the Persians, with Ephialtes and Hydarnes, not thinking it worth their while to delay on account of Phocians, passed on and descended the mountain with all possible speed.

The Greeks at Thermopylæ received the first warning of the destruction which the dawn would bring on them from the seer Megistias, who read their fate in the victims as he was sacrificing. After this deserters came in, and brought the news that the Persians were marching round by the hills: it was still night when these men arrived. Last of all, the scouts came running down from the heights, and brought in the same accounts, when the day was just beginning to break. Then the Greeks held a council to consider what they should do, and here opinions were divided: some were strong against quitting their post, while others contended to the contrary. So when the council had broken up, part of the troops departed and went their ways homeward to their several states; part however resolved to remain, and to stand by Leonidas to the last.

It is said that Leonidas himself sent away the troops who departed, because he tendered their safety, but thought it unseemly that either he or his Spartans should quit the post which they had been especially sent to guard. For my own part, I incline to think that Leonidas gave the order, because he perceived the allies to be out of heart and unwilling to encounter the danger to which his own mind was made up. He therefore commanded them to retreat, but said that he himself could not draw

back with honour; knowing that, if he stayed, glory awaited him, and that Sparta in that case would not lose her prosperity. For when the Spartans, at the very beginning of the war sent to consult the oracle concerning it, the answer which they received from the Pythoness was, "that either Sparta must be overthrown by the barbarians, or one of her kings must perish." The prophecy was delivered in hexameter verse, and ran thus:—

"Oh! ye men who dwell in the streets of broad Lacedæmon,
Either your glorious town shall be sacked by the children of Perseus,
Or, in exchange, must all through the whole Laconian country
Mourn for the loss of a king, descendant of great Heracles.
He cannot be withstood by the courage of bulls or of lions,
Strive as they may; he is mighty as Jove; there is nought that shall stay him,
Till he have got for his prey your king, or your glorious city."

The remembrance of this answer, I think, and the wish to secure the whole glory for the Spartans, caused Leonidas to send the allies away. This is more likely than that they quarrelled with him, and took their departure in such unruly fashion.

To me it seems no small argument in favour of this view, that the seer also who accompanied the army, Megistias, the Acarnanian,—said to have been of the blood of Melampus, and the same who was led by the appearance of the victims to warn the Greeks of the danger which threatened them,—received orders to retire (as it is certain he did) from Leonidas, that he might escape the coming destruction. Megistias, however, though bidden to depart, refused, and stayed with the army; but he had an only son present with the expedition, whom he now sent away.

So the allies, when Leonidas ordered them to retire, obeyed him and forthwith departed. Only the Thespians and the Thebans remained with the Spartans; and of these the Thebans were kept back by Leonidas as hostages, very much against their will. The Thespians, on the contrary, stayed entirely on their own accord, refusing to retreat, and declaring that they would not forsake Leonidas and his followers. So they abode with the Spartans, and died with them. Their leader was Demophilus, the son of Diadromes.

At sunrise Xerxes made libations, after which he waited until the time when the forum is wont to fill, and then began his advance. Ephialtes had instructed him thus, as the descent of the mountain is much quicker, and the distance much shorter, than the way round the hills, and the ascent. So the barbarians under Xerxes began to draw nigh; and the Greeks under Leonidas, as they now went forth determined to die, advanced much further than on previous days, until they reached the more open portion of the pass. Hitherto they had held their station within the wall, and from this had gone forth to fight at the point where the pass was the narrowest. Now they joined battle beyond the defile, and carried slaughter among the barbarians, who fell in heaps. Behind them the captains of the squadrons, armed with whips, urged their men forward with continual blows. Many were thrust into the sea, and there perished; a still greater number were trampled to death by their own soldiers; no one heeded the dying. For the Greeks, reckless of their own safety and desperate, since they knew that, as the mountains had been crossed, their destruction was nigh at hand, exerted themselves with the most furious valour against the barbarians.

By this time the spears of the greater number were all shivered, and with their swords they hewed down the ranks of the Persians; and here, as they strove, Leonidas fell fighting bravely, together with many other famous Spartans, whose names I have taken care to learn on account of their great worthiness, as indeed I have those of all the three hundred. There fell too at the same time very many famous Persians: among them, two sons of Darius, Abrocomes and Hyperanthes, his children by Phratagune, the daughter of Artanes. Artanes was brother of King Darius, being a son of Hystaspes, the son of Arsames; and when he gave his daughter to the king, he made him heir likewise of all his substance; for she was his only child.

Thus two brothers of Xerxes here fought and fell. And now there arose a fierce struggle between the Persians and the Lacedæmonians over the body of Leonidas, in which the Greeks four times drove back the enemy, and at last by their great bravery succeeded in bearing off the body. This combat was scarcely ended when the Persians with Ephialtes approached; and the Greeks, informed that they drew nigh, made a change in the manner of their fighting. Drawing back into the narrowest part of the pass, and retreating even behind the cross wall, they posted themselves upon a hillock, where they stood all drawn up together in one close body, except only the Thebans. The hillock whereof I speak is at the entrance of the straits, where the stone lion stands which was set up in honour of Leonidas. Here they defended themselves to the last, such as still had swords using them, and the others resisting with their hands and teeth; till the barbarians who in part had pulled down the wall and attacked them in front, in part had gone round and now encircled them upon every side, overwhelmed them and buried the remnant left beneath showers of missile weapons.

Thus nobly did the whole body of Lacedæmonians and Thespians behave, but nevertheless one man is said to have distinguished himself above all the rest, to wit, Dieneces the Spartan. A speech which he made before the Greeks engaged the Medes, remains on record. One of the Trachinians told him, "such was the number of the barbarians, that when they shot forth their arrows the sun would be darkened by their multitude." Dieneces, not at all frightened at these words, but making light of the Median numbers, answered, "Our Trachinian friend brings us excellent tidings. If the Medes darken the sun, we shall have our fight in the shade." Other sayings too of a like nature are said to have been left on record by this same person.

Next to him two brothers, Lacedæmonians, are reputed to have made themselves conspicuous: they were named Alpheus and Maro, and were the sons of Orsiphantus. There was also a Thespian who gained greater glory than any of his countrymen: he was a man called Dithyrambus, the son of Harmatidas.

The slain were buried where they fell; and in their honour, nor less in honour of those who died before Leonidas sent the allies away, an inscription was set up, which said,—

"Here did four thousand men from Pelops'
    land
Against three hundred myriads bravely
    stand."

This was in honour of all. Another was for the Spartans alone:—

"Go, stranger, and to Lacedæmon tell
That here, obeying her behest, we fell."

This was for the Lacedæmonians. The seer had the following:—

"The great Megistias' tomb you here may
    view,
Whom slew the Medes, fresh from
    Spercheius' fords.

Well the wise seer the coming death
    foreknew,
Yet scorned he to forsake his Spartan
    lords."

These inscriptions, and the pillars likewise, were all set up by the Amphictyons, except that in honour of Megistias, which was inscribed to him (on account of their sworn friendship) by Simonides, the son of Leoprepes.

—GEORGE RAWLINSON.

SALAMIS

[From Book VIII]

Salamis (480 B.C.) was the denouement of the drama. Persia's naval power was crushed. Xerxes withdrew to Asia Minor, but left a large army in Greece. The next year witnessed the defeat of this force at the decisive battle of Platæa.

So the Greeks at the Isthmus toiled unceasingly as though in the greatest peril; since they never imagined that any great success would be gained by the fleet. The Greeks at Salamis, on the other hand, when they heard what the rest were about, felt greatly alarmed; but their fear was not so much for themselves as for the Peloponnese. At first they conversed together in low tones, each man with his fellow, secretly, and marvelled at the folly shown by Eurybiades; but presently the smothered feeling broke out, and another assembly was held; whereat the old subjects provoked much talk from the speakers, one side maintaining that it was best to sail to the Peloponnese and risk battle for that, instead of abiding at Salamis and fighting for a land already taken by the enemy; while the other, which consisted of the Athenians, Eginetans, and Megarians, was urgent to remain and have the battle fought where they were.

Then Themistocles, when he saw that

the Peloponnesians would carry the vote against him, went out secretly from the council, and instructing a certain man what he should say, sent him on board a merchant ship to the fleet of the Medes. The man's name was Sicinnus; he was one of Themistocles' household slaves, and acted as tutor to his sons; in after times, when the Thespians were admitting persons to citizenship, Themistocles made him a Thespian, and a rich man to boot. The ship brought Sicinnus to the Persian fleet, and there he delivered his message to the leaders in these words:—

"The Athenian commander has sent me to you privily, without the knowledge of the other Greeks. He is a well-wisher to the king's cause, and would rather success should attend on you than on his countrymen; wherefore he bids me tell you, that fear has seized the Greeks and they are meditating a hasty flight. Now then it is open to you to achieve the best work that ever ye wrought, if only ye will hinder their escaping. They no longer agree among themselves, so that they will not now make any resistance— nay, 'tis likely ye may see a fight already begun between such as favour and such as oppose your cause." The messenger, when he had thus expressed himself, departed and was seen no more.

Then the captains, believing all that the messenger had said, proceeded to land a large body of Persian troops on the islet of Psyttaleia, which lies between Salamis and the mainland; after which, about the hour of midnight, they advanced their western wing towards Salamis, so as to inclose the Greeks. At the same time the force stationed about Ceos and Cynosura moved forward, and filled the whole strait as far as Munychia with their ships. This advance was made to prevent the Greeks from escaping by flight, and to block them up in Salamis, where it was thought that vengeance might be taken upon them for the battles

fought near Artemisium. The Persian troops were landed on the islet of Psyttaleia, because as soon as the battle began, the men and wrecks were likely to be drifted thither, as the isle lay in the very path of the coming fight,—and they would thus be able to save their own men and destroy those of the enemy. All these movements were made in silence, that the Greeks might have no knowledge of them; and they occupied the whole night, so that the men had no time to get their sleep.

I cannot say that there is no truth in prophecies, or feel inclined to call in question those which speak with clearness, when I think of the following—

"When they shall bridge with their ships
    to the sacred strand of Diana
Girt with the golden falchion, and eke to
    marine Cynosura,
Mad hope swelling their hearts at the
    downfall of beautiful Athens—
Then shall godlike Right extinguish
    haughty Presumption,
Insult's furious offspring, who thinketh to
    overthrow all things.
Brass with brass shall mingle, and Mars
    shall with blood empurple
Ocean's waves. Then—then shall the day
    of Grecia's freedom
Come from Victory fair, and Saturn's son
    all-seeing."

When I look to this, and perceive how clearly Bacis spoke, I neither venture myself to say anything against prophecies, nor do I approve of others impugning them.

Meanwhile, among the captains at Salamis, the strife of words grew fierce. As yet they did not know that they were encompassed, but imagined that the barbarians remained in the same places where they had seen them before.

In the midst of their contention, Aristides, the son of Lysimachus, who had crossed from Egina, arrived in Salamis. He was an Athenian, and had been ostracised by the commonalty; yet I believe, from what I have heard concerning his character, that there was not in all Athens a man so worthy or so just as he. He now came to the council, and standing outside, called for Themistocles. Now Themistocles was not his friend, but his most determined enemy. However, under the pressure of the great dangers impending, Aristides forgot their feud, and called Themistocles out of the council, since he wished to confer with him. He had heard before his arrival of the impatience of the Peloponnesians to withdraw the fleet to the Isthmus. As soon therefore as Themistocles came forth, Aristides addressed him in these words:—

"Our rivalry at all times, and especially at the present season, ought to be a struggle, which of us shall most advantage our country. Let me then say to thee, that so far as regards the departure of the Peloponnesians from this place, much talk and little will be found precisely alike. I have seen with my own eyes that which I now report; that, however much the Corinthians or Eurybiades himself may wish it, they cannot now retreat; for we are enclosed on every side by the enemy. Go in to them and make this known."

"Thy advice is excellent," answered the other, "and thy tidings are also good. That which I earnestly desired to happen, thine eyes have beheld accomplished. Know that what the Medes have now done was at my instance; for it was necessary, as our men would not fight here at their own free will, to make them fight whether they would or no. But come now, as thou hast brought the good news, go in and tell it. For if I speak to them, they will think it a feigned tale, and will not believe that the barbarians have enclosed us around. Therefore do thou go to them, and inform them how matters stand. If they believe thee, 'twill be for the best; but if otherwise, it will not harm. For it is impossible that they

should now flee away, if indeed we are shut in on all sides, as thou sayest."

Then Aristides entered the assembly, and spoke to the captains: he had come, he told them, from Egina, and had but barely escaped the blockading vessels— the Greek fleet was entirely inclosed by the ships of Xerxes—and he advised them to get themselves in readiness to resist the foe. Having said so much, he withdrew. And now another contest arose, for the greater part of the captains would not believe the tidings.

But while they still doubted, a Tenian trireme, commanded by Panætius the son of Sosimenes, deserted from the Persians and joined the Greeks, bringing full intelligence. For this reason the Tenians were inscribed upon the tripod at Delphi among those who overthrew the barbarians. With this ship, which deserted to their side at Salamis, and the Lemnian vessel, which came over before at Artemisium, the Greek fleet was brought to the full number of 380 ships; otherwise it fell short by two of that amount.

The Greeks now, not doubting what the Tenians told them, made ready for the coming fight. At the dawn of day, all the men-at-arms were assembled together, and speeches were made to them, of which the best was that of Themistocles; who throughout contrasted what was noble with what was base, and bade them, in all that came within the range of man's nature and constitution, *always* to make choice of the nobler part. Having thus wound up his discourse, he told them to go at once on board their ships, which they accordingly did; and about this time the trireme, that had been sent to Egina for the Æacidæ, returned; whereupon the Greeks put to sea with all their fleet.

The fleet had scarce left the land when they were attacked by the barbarians. At once most of the Greeks began to back water, and were about touching the shore, when Ameinias of Pallene, one of the Athenian captains, darted forth in front of the line, and charged a ship of the enemy. The two vessels became entangled, and could not separate, whereupon the rest of the fleet came up to help Ameinias, and engaged with the Persians. Such is the account which the Athenians give of the way in which the battle began; but the Eginetans maintain that the vessel which had been to Egina for the Æacidæ, was the one that brought on the fight. It is also reported, that a phantom in the form of a woman appeared to the Greeks, and, in a voice that was heard from end to end of the fleet, cheered them on to the fight; first, however, rebuking them, and saying—"Strange men, how long are ye going to back water?"

Against the Athenians, who held the western extremity of the line towards Eleusis, were placed the Phœnicians; against the Lacedæmonians, whose station was eastwards towards the Piræus, the Ionians. Of these last a few only followed the advice of Themistocles, to fight backwardly; the greater number did far otherwise. I could mention here the names of many trierarchs who took vessels from the Greeks, but I shall pass over all excepting Theomestor the son of Androdamas, and Phylacus the son of Histiæus, both Samians. I show this preference to them, inasmuch as for this service Theomestor was made tyrant of Samos by the Persians, while Phylacus was enrolled among the king's benefactors, and presented with a large estate in land. In the Persian tongue the king's benefactors were called *Orosangs*.

Far the greater number of the Persian ships engaged in this battle were disabled —either by the Athenians or by the Eginetans. For as the Greeks fought in order and kept their line, while the barbarians were in confusion and had no plan in anything that they did, the issue of the battle could scarce be other than it was. Yet the Persians fought far more bravely here than at Eubœa, and indeed surpassed themselves; each did his utmost through fear of Xerxes, for each thought that the king's eye was upon himself.

What part the several nations, whether Greek or barbarian, took in the combat, I am not able to say for certain; Artemisia, however, I know, distinguished herself in such a way as raised her even higher than she stood before in the esteem of the king. For after confusion had spread throughout the whole of the king's fleet, and her ship was closely pursued by an Athenian trireme, she, having no way to fly, since in front of her were a number of friendly vessels, and she was nearest of all the Persians to the enemy, resolved on a measure which in fact proved her safety. Pressed by the Athenian pursuer, she bore straight against one of the ships of her own party, a Calyndian, which had Damasithymus, the Calyndian king, himself on board. I cannot say whether she had had any quarrel with the man while the fleet was at the Hellespont, or no—neither can I decide whether she of set purpose attacked his vessel, or whether it merely chanced that the Calyndian ship came in her way—but certain it is that she bore down on his vessel and sank it, and that thereby she had the good fortune to procure herself a double advantage. For the commander of the Athenian trireme, when he saw her bear down on one of the enemy's fleet, thought immediately that her vessel was a Greek, or else had deserted from the Persians, and was now fighting on the Greek side; he therefore gave up the chase, and turned away to attack others.

Thus in the first place she saved her life by the action, and was enabled to get clear off from the battle; while further, it fell out that in the very act of doing the king an injury she raised herself to a greater height than ever in his esteem. For as Xerxes beheld the fight, he remarked (it is said) the destruction of the vessel, whereupon the bystanders observed to him—"Seest thou, master, how well Artemisia fights, and how she has just sunk a ship of the enemy?" Then Xerxes asked if it were really Artemisia's doing; and they answered, "Certainly; for they knew her ensign:" while all made sure that the sunken vessel belonged to the opposite side. Every thing, it is said, conspired to prosper the queen—it was especially fortunate for her, that not one of those on board the Calyndian ship survived to become her accuser. Xerxes, they say, in reply to the remarks made to him, observed—"My men have behaved like women, and my women like men!"

There fell in this combat Ariabignes, one of the chief commanders of the fleet, who was son of Darius and brother of Xerxes, and with him perished a vast number of men of high repute, Persians, Medes, and allies. Of the Greeks there died only a few; for as they were able to swim, all those that were not slain outright by the enemy escaped from the sinking vessels and swam across to Salamis. But on the side of the barbarians more perished by drowning than in any other way, since they did not know how to swim. The great destruction took place when the ships which had been first engaged began to fly; for they who were stationed in the rear, anxious to display their valour before the eyes of the king, made every effort to force their way to the front, and thus became entangled with such of their own vessels as were retreating.

In this confusion the following event occurred: certain Phœnicians belonging to the ships which had thus perished made their appearance before the king, and laid the blame of their loss on the Ionians, declaring that they were traitors, and had wilfully destroyed the vessels. But the upshot of this complaint was, that the Ionian captains escaped the death which threatened them, while their Phœnician accusers received death as their reward. For it happened that, exactly as they spoke, a Samothracian vessel bore down on an Athenian and sank it, but was attacked and crippled immediately by one of the Eginetan squadron. Now the Samothracians were expert with the javelin, and aimed their weapons so well, that they cleared the deck of the vessel which had disabled their own, after which they sprang on board, and took it. This saved the Ionians. Xerxes, when he saw the exploit, turned fiercely on the Phœnicians —(he was ready, in his extreme vexation, to find fault with any one)—and ordered their heads to be cut off, to prevent them, he said, from casting the blame of their own misconduct upon braver men. During the whole time of the battle Xerxes sate at the base of the hill called Ægaleos, over against Salamis; and whenever he saw any of his own captains perform any worthy exploit he inquired concerning him; and the man's name was taken down by his scribes, together with the names of his father and his city. Ariaramnes too, a Persian, who was a friend of the Ionians, and present at the time whereof I speak, had a share in bringing about the punishment of the Phœnicians.

When the rout of the barbarians began, and they sought to make their escape to Phalerum, the Eginetans, awaiting them in the channel, performed exploits worthy to be recorded. Through the whole of the confused struggle the Athenians employed themselves in destroying such ships as either made resistance or fled to shore, while the Eginetans dealt with those which endeavoured to escape down the straits; so that the Persian vessels were no sooner clear of the Athenians than straightway they fell into the hands of the Eginetan squadron.

It chanced here that there was a meeting between the ship of Themistocles, which was hasting in pursuit of the enemy, and that of Polycritus, son of Crius the Eginetan, which had just charged a Sidonian trireme. The Sidonian vessel was the same that captured the Eginetan guard-ship off Sciathus, which had Pytheas, the son of Ischenous, on board—that Pytheas, I mean, who fell covered with wounds, and whom the Sidonians kept on board their ship, from admiration of his gallantry. This man afterwards returned in safety to Egina, for when the Sidonian vessel with its Persian crew fell into the hands of the Greeks, he was still found on board. Polycritus no sooner saw the Athenian trireme, than knowing at once whose vessel it was, as he observed that it bore the ensign of the admiral, he shouted to Themistocles jeeringly, and asked him, in a tone of reproach, if the Eginetans did not show themselves rare friends to the Medes. At the same time, while he thus reproached Themistocles, Polycritus bore straight down on the Sidonian. Such of the barbarian vessels as escaped from the battle fled to Phalerum, and there sheltered themselves under the protection of the land army.

The Greeks who gained the greatest glory of all in the sea-fight of Salamis were the Eginetans, and after them the Athenians. The individuals of most distinction were Polycritus the Eginetan, and two Athenians, Eumenes of Anagyrus, and Ameinias of Pallene; the latter of whom had pressed Artemisia so hard. And assuredly, if he had known that the vessel carried Artemisia on board, he would never have given over the chase till he had either succeeded in taking her, or else been taken himself. For the Athenian captains had received special orders touching the queen, and moreover a reward of ten thousand drachmas had been proclaimed for any one who should make her prisoner, since there was great indignation felt that a woman should appear in arms against Athens. However, as I said before, she escaped; and so did

some others whose ships survived the engagement; and these were all now assembled at the port of Phalerum.

The Athenians say that Adeimantus, the Corinthian commander, at the moment when the two fleets joined battle, was seized with fear, and being beyond measure alarmed, spread his sails, and hasted to fly away; on which the other Corinthians, seeing their leader's ship in full flight, sailed off likewise. They had reached in their flight that part of the coast of Salamis where stands the temple of Minerva Sciras, when they met a light bark, a very strange apparition: it was never discovered that any one sent it to them, and till it appeared they were altogether ignorant how the battle was going. That there was something beyond nature in the matter they judged from this—that when the men in the bark drew near to their ships they addressed them, saying—"Adeimantus, while thou playest the traitor's part, by withdrawing all these ships, and flying away from the fight, the Greeks whom thou hast deserted are defeating their foes as completely as they ever wished in their prayers." Adeimantus, however, would not believe what the men said; whereupon they told him, "he might take them with him as hostages, and put them to death if he did not find the Greeks winning." Then Adeimantus put about, both he and those who were with him; and they rejoined the fleet when the victory was already gained. Such is the tale which the Athenians tell concerning them of Corinth; these latter however do not allow its truth. On the contrary, they declare that they were among those who distinguished themselves most in the fight. And the rest of Greece bears witness in their favour.

In the midst of the confusion Aristides, the son of Lysimachus, the Athenian, of whom I lately spoke as a man of the greatest excellence, performed the following service. He took a number of the Athenian heavy-armed troops, who had previously been stationed along the shore of Salamis, and landing with them on the islet of Psyttaleia, slew all the Persians by whom it was occupied.

As soon as the sea-fight was ended, the Greeks drew together to Salamis all the wrecks that were to be found in that quarter, and prepared themselves for another engagement, supposing that the king would renew the fight with the vessels which still remained to him. Many of the wrecks had been carried away by a westerly wind to the coast of Attica, where they were thrown upon the strip of shore called Colias. Thus not only were the prophecies of Bacis and Musæus concerning this battle fulfilled completely, but likewise, by the place to which the wrecks were drifted, the prediction of Lysistratus, an Athenian soothsayer, uttered many years before these events, and quite forgotten at the time by all the Greeks, was fully accomplished. The words were:—

"Then shall the sight of the oars fill Colian dames with amazement."

Now this must have happened as soon as the king was departed.

Xerxes, when he saw the extent of his loss, began to be afraid lest the Greeks might be counselled by the Ionians, or without their advice might determine, to sail straight to the Hellespont and break down the bridges there; in which case he would be blocked up in Europe, and run great risk of perishing. He therefore made up his mind to fly; but as he wished to hide his purpose alike from the Greeks and from his own people, he set to work to carry a mound across the channel to Salamis, and at the same time began fastening a number of Phœnician merchant ships together, to serve at once for a bridge and a wall. He likewise made many warlike preparations, as if he were about to engage the Greeks once more at sea. Now, when these things were seen, all grew fully persuaded that the king was bent on remaining, and intended to push the war in good earnest. Mardonius, however, was in no respect deceived; for long acquaintance enabled him to read all the king's thoughts. Meanwhile, Xerxes, though engaged in this way, sent off a messenger to carry intelligence of his misfortune to Persia.

—GEORGE RAWLINSON.

THE DEFEAT OF THE PERSIANS

ÆSCHYLUS

[From *The Persians*]

Æschylus was born at Eleusis in Attica in 525 B. C. and possibly held some priestly office there. He took part in the Persian War and fought in the battles of Marathon and Salamis. The latter part of his life was spent in Sicily, where he died in 456 B.C. He is called the Father of Tragedy because of the innovations he introduced making possible that conflict of characters essential to all drama. He was the inventor of the trilogy—a series of three plays dealing with the successive parts of the same legend and together forming a complete unit. The central thought running through all his work is that of dependence of man upon the will of God. Æschylus is said to have produced about seventy plays, of which only seven have come down to us.

The play from which this passage is taken, produced in 472 B.C., is the only extant Greek historical tragedy. Remarkable as it is for its qualities of pageantry and its interpretation of the moral issues involved in the conduct of the chief characters, it is still more remarkable as a piece of contemporaneous history. For Æschylus' understanding of the meaning of the conflict with the Persians is practically identical with that generally accepted by the later historians who were entirely free from the patriotic motives and passions of the moment. By laying the scene

t the Persian court the poet secured to
imself the advantage of an objective
presentation of the Greek cause and of a
contrast with the Persian standpoint. The
rôle of messenger was designed, here and
in all Greek tragedy, to admit of narrative
passages more or less after the manner of
epic. The following description of the
Persian disaster at Salamis may be regarded as that of an eye-witness.

MESSENGER. O walls and towers of all
     the Asian realm,
O Persian land, O treasure-house of gold!
How, by one stroke, down to destruction,
     down,
Hath sunk our pride, and all the flower
     of war
That once was Persia's, lieth in the dust!
Woe on the man who first announceth
     war—
Yet must I all the tale of death unroll!
Hark to me, Persians! Persia's host lies
     low.
CHORUS. O ruin manifold, and woe, and
     fear!
Let the wild tears run down, for the
     great doom is here!
MESSENGER. This blow hath fallen, to
     the utterance,
And I, past hope, behold my safe return!
CHORUS. Too long, alack, too long this
     life of mine,
That in mine age I see this sudden woe
     condign!
MESSENGER. As one who saw, by no
     loose rumour led,
Lords, I would tell what doom was dealt
     to us.
CHORUS. Alack, how vainly have they
     striven!
Our myriad hordes with shaft and bow
Went from the Eastland, to lay low
     Hellas, beloved of Heaven!
MESSENGER. Piled with men dead, yea,
     miserably slain,
Is every beach, each reef of Salamis!
CHORUS. Thou sayest sooth—ah well-
     a-day!
Battered amid the waves, and torn,

On surges hither, thither, borne,
Dead bodies, bloodstained and forlorn,
In their long cloaks they toss and
     stray!
MESSENGER. Their bows availed not! all
     have perished, all,
By charging galleys crushed and whelmed
     in death.
CHORUS. Shriek out your sorrow's wist-
     ful wail!
To their untimely doom they went;
Ill strove they, and to no avail,
     And minished is their armament!
MESSENGER. Out on thee, hateful name
     of Salamis,
Out upon Athens, mournful memory!
CHORUS. Woe upon this day's evil fame!
Thou, Athens, art our murderess;
Alack, full many a Persian dame
Is left forlorn and husbandless!
ATOSSA. Mute have I been awhile, and
     overwrought
At this great sorrow, for it passeth speech,
And passeth all desire to ask of it.
Yet if the gods send evils, men must
     bear.
Unroll the record! stand composed and
     tell,
Although thy heart be groaning in-
     wardly,
Who hath escaped, and, of our leaders,
     whom
Have we to weep? what chieftains in the
     van
Stood, sank, and died and left us leader-
     less?
MESSENGER. Xerxes himself survives
     and sees the day.
ATOSSA. Then to my line thy word re-
     news the dawn
And golden dayspring after gloom of
     night!
MESSENGER. But the brave marshal of
     ten thousand horse,
Artembares, is tossed and flung in death
Along the rugged rocks Silenian.
And Dadaces no longer leads his troop,
But, smitten by the spear, from off the
     prow

Hath lightly leaped to death; and
    Tenagon,
In true descent a Bactrian nobly born,
Drifts by the sea-lashed reefs of Salamis,
The isle of Ajax. Gone Lilæus too,
Gone are Arsames and Argestes! all,
Around the islet where the sea-doves
    breed,
Dashed their defeated heads on iron
    rocks:
Arcteus, who dwelt beside the founts of
    Nile,
Adeues, Pheresseues, and with them
Pharnuchus, from one galley's deck went
    down.
Matallus, too, of Chrysa, lord and king
Of myriad hordes, who led unto the fight
Three times ten thousand swarthy
    cavaliers,
Fell, with his swarthy and abundant
    beard
Incarnadined to red, a crimson stain
Outrivalling the purple of the sea!
There Magian Arabus and Artames
Of Bactra perished—taking up, alike,
In yonder stony land their long sojourn.
Amistris too, and he whose strenuous
    spear
Was foremost in the fight, Amphistreus
    fell,
And gallant Ariomardus, by whose death
Broods sorrow upon Sardis: Mysia
    mourns
For Seisames, and Tharubis lies low—
Commander, he, of five times fifty ships,
Born in Lyrnessus: his heroic form
Is low in death, ungraced with sepulchre.
Dead too is he, the lord of courage high,
Cilicia's marshal, brave Syennesis,
Than whom none dealt more carnage on
    the foe,
Nor perished by a more heroic end.
So fell the brave: so speak I of their
    doom,
Summing in brief the fate of myriads!
ATOSSA. Ah well-a-day! these crowning
    woes I hear,
The shame of Persia and her shrieks of
    dole!

But yet renew the tale, repeat thy words
Tell o'er the count of those Hellenic ships
And how they ventured with their beaked
    prows
To charge upon the Persian armament.
MESSENGER. Know, if mere count o[f]
    ships could win the day,
The Persians had prevailed. The Greeks
    in sooth,
Had but three hundred galleys at the
    most,
And other ten, select and separate.
But—I am witness—Xerxes held com[
    mand
Of full a thousand keels, and, those apart
Two hundred more, and seven, for spee[d]
    renowned,—
So stands the reckoning, and who sha[ll]
    dare
To say we Persians had the lesser host?
ATOSSA. Nay, we were worsted by a[n]
    unseen power
Who swayed the balance downward t[o]
    our doom!
MESSENGER. In ward of heaven dot[h]
    Pallas' city stand.
ATOSSA. How then? Is Athens yet in
    violate?
MESSENGER. While her men live, he[r]
    bulwark standeth firm!
ATOSSA. Say, how began the struggle o[f]
    the ships?
Who first joined issue? did the Greek[s]
    attack,
Or Xerxes, in his numbers confident?
MESSENGER. O queen, our whole dis[
    aster thus befell,
Through intervention of some fiend o[r]
    fate—
I know not what—that had ill will to u[s]
From the Athenian host some Greek cam[e]
    o'er,
To thy son Xerxes whispering this tale—
Once let the gloom of night have gathere[d]
    in,
The Greeks will tarry not, but swiftl[y]
    spring
Each to his galley-bench, in furtive fligh[t]
Softly contriving safety for their life.

Thy son believed the word and missed the craft
Of that Greek foeman, and the spite of Heaven,
And straight to all his captains gave this charge—
As soon as sunlight warms the ground no more,
And gloom enwraps the sanctuary of sky,
Range we our fleet in triple serried lines
To bar the passage from the seething strait,
This way and that: let other ships surround
The isle of Ajax, with this warning word—
That if the Greeks their jeopardy should 'scape
By wary craft, and win their ships a road,
Each Persian captain shall his failure pay
By forfeit of his head. So spake the king,
Inspired at heart with over-confidence,
Unwitting of the gods' predestined will.
Thereon our crews, with no disordered haste,
Did service to his bidding and purveyed
The meal of afternoon: each rower then
Over the fitted rowlock looped his oar.
Then, when the splendour of the sun had set,
And night drew on, each master of the oar
And each armed warrior straightway went aboard.
Forward the long ships moved, rank cheering rank,
Each forward set upon its ordered course.
And all night long the captains of the fleet
Kept their crews moving up and down the strait.
So the night waned, and not one Grecian ship
Made effort to elude and slip away.
But as dawn came and with her coursers white
Shone in fair radiance over all the earth,

First from the Grecian fleet rang out a cry,
A song of onset! and the island crags
Re-echoed to the shrill exulting sound.
Then on us Eastern men amazement fell
And fear in place of hope; for what we heard
Was not a call to flight! the Greeks rang out
Their holy, resolute, exulting chant,
Like men come forth to dare and do and die!
Their trumpets pealed, and fire was in that sound,
And with the dash of simultaneous oars
Replying to the war-chant, on they came,
Smiting the swirling brine, and in a trice
They flashed upon the vision of the foe!
The right wing first in orderly advance
Came on, a steady column; following then,
The rest of their array moved out and on,
And to our ears there came a burst of sound,
A clamour manifold.—*On, sons of Greece!*
On, for your country's freedom! strike to save
Wives, children, temples of ancestral gods,
Graves of your fathers! now is all at stake.
Then from our side swelled up the mingled din
Of Persian tongues, and time brooked no delay—
Ship into ship drave hard its brazen beak
With speed of thought, a shattering blow! and first
One Grecian bark plunged straight, and sheared away
Bowsprit and stem of a Phœnician ship.
And then each galley on some other's prow
Came crashing in. Awhile our stream of ships
Held onward, till within the narrowing creek
Our jostling vessels were together driven,

And none could aid another: each on
each
Drave hard their brazen beaks, or brake
away
The oar-banks of each other, stem to
stern,
While the Greek galleys, with no lack of
skill,
Hemmed them and battered in their sides,
and soon
The hulls rolled over, and the sea was
hid,
Crowded with wrecks and butchery of
men.
No beach nor reef but was with corpses
strewn,
And every keel of our barbarian host
Hurried to flee, in utter disarray.
Thereon the foe closed in upon the
wrecks
And hacked and hewed, with oars and
splintered planks,
As fishermen hack tunnies or a cast
Of netted dolphins, and the briny sea
Rang with the screams and shrieks of
dying men,
Until the night's dark aspect hid the
scene.
Had I a ten days' time to sum that count
Of carnage, 'twere too little! know this
well—
One day ne'er saw such myriad forms of
death!
ATOSSA. Woe on us, woe! disaster's
mighty sea
Hath burst on us and all the Persian
realm!
MESSENGER. Be well assured, the tale is
but begun—
The further agony that on us fell
Doth twice outweigh the sufferings I have
told!
ATOSSA. Nay, what disaster could be
worse than this?
Say on! what woe upon the army came,
Swaying the scale to a yet further fall?
MESSENGER. The very flower and crown
of Persia's race,
Gallant of soul and glorious in descent,

And highest held in trust before the
king,
Lies shamefully and miserably slain.
ATOSSA. Alas for me and for this ruin,
friends!
Dead, sayest thou? by what fate over-
thrown?
MESSENGER. An islet is there, fronting
Salamis—
Strait, and with evil anchorage: thereon
Pan treads the measure of the dance he
loves
Along the sea-beach. Thither the king
sent
His noblest, that, whene'er the Grecian
foe
Should 'scape, with shattered ships, unto
the isle,
We might make easy prey of fugitives
And slay them there, and from the wash-
ing tides
Rescue our friends. It fell out other-
wise
Than he divined, for when, by aid of
Heaven,
The Hellenes held the victory on the sea,
Their sailors then and there begirt them-
selves
With brazen mail and bounded from their
ships,
And then enringed the islet, point by
point,
So that our Persians in bewilderment
Knew not which way to turn. On every
side,
Battered with stones, they fell, while
arrows flew
From many a string, and smote them to
the death.
Then, at the last, with simultaneous rush
The foe came bursting on us, hacked and
hewed
To fragments all that miserable band,
Till not a soul of them was left alive.
Then Xerxes saw disaster's depth, and
shrieked,
From where he sat on high, surveying
all—
A lofty eminence, beside the brine,

Whence all his armament lay clear in
view.
His robe he rent, with loud and bitter
wail,
And to his land-force swiftly gave com-
mand
And fled, with shame beside him! Now,
lament
That second woe, upon the first imposed!
ATOSSA. Out on thee, Fortune! thou hast
foiled the hope
And power of Persia: to this bitter end
My son went forth to wreak his great
revenge
On famous Athens! all too few they
seemed,
Our men who died upon the Fennel-field!
Vengeance for them my son had mind to
take,
And drew on his own head these whelm-
ing woes.
But thou, say on! the ships that 'scaped
from wreck—
Where didst thou leave them? make thy
story clear.
MESSENGER. The captains of the ships
that still survived
Fled in disorder, scudding down the
wind,
The while our land-force on Bœotian soil
Fell into ruin, some beside the springs
Dropping before they drank, and some
outworn,
Pursued, and panting all their life away.
The rest of us our way to Phocis won,
And thence to Doris and the Melian gulf,
Where with soft stream Spercheus laves
the soil.
Thence to the northward did Phthiotis'
plain,
And some Thessalian fortress, lend us aid,
For famine-pinched we were, and many
died
Of drought and hunger's twofold present
scourge.
Thence to Magnesia came we, and the
land
Where Macedonians dwell, and crossed
the ford

Of Axius, and Bolbe's reedy fen,
And mount Pangæus, in Edonian land.
There, in the very night we came, the god
Brought winter ere its time, from bank
to bank
Freezing the holy Strymon's tide. Each
man
Who heretofore held lightly of the gods,
Now crouched and proffered prayer to
Earth and Heaven!
Then, after many orisons performed,
The army ventured on the frozen ford:
Yet only those who crossed before the
sun
Shed its warm rays, won to the farther
side.
For soon the fervour of the glowing orb
Did with its keen rays pierce the ice-
bound stream,
And men sank through and thrust each
other down—
Best was his lot whose breath was stifled
first!
But all who struggled through and
gained the bank,
Toilfully wending through the land of
Thrace
Have made their way, a sorry, scanted
few,
Unto this homeland. Let the city now
Lament and yearn for all the loved and
lost.
My tale is truth, yet much untold re-
mains
Of ills that Heaven hath hurled upon our
land.
—E. D. A. MORSHEAD.

PRIMITIVE GREECE [1]

THUCYDIDES

[From Book I]

Thucydides, born an Athenian about
460 B.C., was the greatest of the ancient

[1] Reprinted by permission of Oxford University Press.

historians. He had served as a general in the early part of the Peloponnesian war which he described, had suffered banishment on some charge, possibly that of incompetency, and had used the long period of his exile in travel and in gathering information at first hand for his history. Thus he became the first writer of strictly contemporary history. He was enabled as a result of these experiences to view the conflict from the standpoint of the Spartans as well as that of the Athenians, and to treat his subject with a degree of impartiality very rare in ancient historians. He worked with the method and in the spirit of the scientific investigator, acquiring his materials from original sources, carefully and impartially weighing the evidence, avoiding the haphazard and the supernatural, and arranging his matter in logical sequence.

Like Herodotus, Thucydides introduced speeches into his narrative, but made them a great deal more than a dramatic embellishment. By this device he was able to present effectively the causes of events, the circumstances surrounding them, and the ideas, the prejudices, and the passions of the time. He tells us that when possible he gave in the speeches the substance of what was actually said, but when this was impossible, he gave what was suited to the occasion. The method enabled the historian like a dramatist to keep himself in the background, while the characters spoke for themselves. After Thucydides the use of speeches became a part of the historian's stock in trade.

Unlike Herodotus, Thucydides seldom made use of digression, and when he did, it was always with a definite, serious purpose. At the beginning of his history of the Sicilian expedition, for example, he pauses to introduce a very succinct account of the Greek settlements in the island, and of the rivalries which led Athens to see an opening for conquest.

Thucydides' plan was to write simply the history of the Peloponnesian war in chronological order, grouping the materials by campaigns year by year. He carried the narrative from the beginning of the war down into the year 411, but the last seven years of the war he did not relate. Probably he died while engaged on the work. Xenophon later in his *Hellenica* completed the account.

The author's purpose in this review of primitive times is to give the reader a right understanding of the importance and meaning of the Peloponnesian war in Greek history. Nothing reveals more clearly Thucydides' historical sense than his discriminating use of Homer as evidence. By the average Greek Homer was accepted as a final authority; Thucydides realized that allowance must be made for the poet's fancy and imagination.

Thucydides, an Athenian, wrote the history of the war in which the Peloponnesians and the Athenians fought against one another. He began to write when they first took up arms, believing that it would be great and memorable above any previous war. For he argued that both states were then at the full height of their military power, and he saw the rest of the Hellenes either siding or intending to side with one or other of them. No movement ever stirred Hellas more deeply than this; it was shared by many of the Barbarians, and might be said even to affect the world at large. The character of the events which preceded, whether immediately or in more remote antiquity, owing to the lapse of time cannot be made out with certainty. But, judging from the evidence which I am able to trust after most careful enquiry, I should imagine that former ages were not great either in their wars or in anything else.

The country which is now called Hellas was not regularly settled in ancient times. The people were migratory, and readily left their homes whenever they were overpowered by numbers. There was no commerce, and they could not safely hold intercourse with one another either by land or sea. The several tribes cultivated their own soil just enough to obtain a maintenance. But they had no accumulations of wealth, and did not plant the ground; for, being without walls, they were never sure that an invader might not come and despoil them. Living in this manner and knowing that they could anywhere obtain a bare subsistence, they were always ready to migrate; so that they had neither great cities nor any considerable resources. The richest districts were most constantly changing their inhabitants; for example, the countries which are now called Thessaly and Bœotia, the greater part of the Peloponnesus with the exception of Arcadia, and all the best parts of Hellas. For the productiveness of the land increased the power of individuals; this in turn was a source of quarrels by which communities were ruined, while at the same time they were more exposed to attacks from without. Certainly Attica, of which the soil was poor and thin, enjoyed a long freedom from civil strife, and therefore retained its original inhabitants. And a striking confirmation of my argument is afforded by the fact that Attica through immigration increased in population more than any other region. For the leading men of Hellas, when driven out of their own country by war or revolution, sought an asylum at Athens; and from the very earliest times, being admitted to rights of citizenship, so greatly increased the number of inhabitants that Attica became incapable of containing them, and was at last obliged to send out colonies to Ionia.

The feebleness of antiquity is further proved to me by the circumstance that there appears to have been no common action in Hellas before the Trojan War. And I am inclined to think that the very name was not as yet given to the whole country, and in fact did not exist at all before the time of Hellen, the son of Deucalion; the different tribes, of which the Pelasgian was the most widely spread, gave their own names to different districts. But when Hellen and his sons became powerful in Phthiotis, their aid was invoked by other cities, and those who associated with them gradually began to be called Hellenes, though a long time elapsed before the name prevailed over the whole country. Of this Homer affords the best evidence; for he, although he lived long after the Trojan War, nowhere uses this name collectively, but confines it to the followers of Achilles from Phthiotis, who were the original Hellenes; when speaking of the entire host he calls them Danaans, or Argives, or Achæans. Neither is there any mention of Barbarians in his poems, clearly because there were as yet no Hellenes opposed to them by a common distinctive name. Thus the several Hellenic tribes (and I mean by the term Hellenes those who, while forming separate communities, had a common language, and were afterwards called by a common name), owing to their weakness and isolation, were never united in any great enterprise before the Trojan War. And they only made the expedition against Troy after they had gained considerable experience of the sea.

Minos is the first to whom tradition ascribes the possession of a navy. He made himself master of a great part of what is now termed the Hellenic sea; he conquered the Cyclades, and was the first coloniser of most of them, expelling the Carians and appointing his own sons to govern in them. Lastly, it was he who, from a natural desire to protect his growing revenues, sought, as far as he was able, to clear the sea of pirates.

For in ancient times both Hellenes and Barbarians, as well the inhabitants of the coast as of the islands, when they began to find their way to one another by sea had recourse to piracy. They were commanded by powerful chiefs, who took this means of increasing their wealth and providing for their poorer followers. They would fall upon the unwalled and straggling towns, or rather villages, which they plundered, and maintained themselves by the plunder of them; for, as yet, such an occupation was held to be honourable and not disgraceful. This is proved by the practice of certain tribes on the mainland who, to the present day, glory in piratical exploits, and by the witness of the ancient poets, in whose verses the question is invariably asked of newly-arrived voyagers, whether they are pirates; which implies that neither those who are questioned disclaim, nor those who are interested in knowing censure the occupation. The land too was infested by robbers; and there are parts of Hellas in which the old practices still continue, as for example among the Ozolian Locrians, Ætolians, Acarnanians, and the adjacent regions of the continent. The fashion of wearing arms among these continental tribes is a relic of their old predatory habits. For in ancient times all Hellenes carried weapons because their homes were undefended and intercourse was unsafe; like the Barbarians they went armed in their every-day life. And the continuance of the custom in certain parts of the country proves that it once prevailed everywhere.

The Athenians were the first who laid aside arms and adopted an easier and more luxurious way of life. Quite recently the old-fashioned refinement of dress still lingered among the elder men of their richer class, who wore undergarments of linen, and bound back their hair in a knot with golden clasps in the form of grasshoppers; and the same customs long survived among the elders of Ionia, having been derived from their Athenian ancestors. On the other hand, the simple dress which is now common was first worn at Sparta; and there, more than anywhere else, the life of the rich was assimilated to that of the people. The Lacedæmonians too were the first who in their athletic exercises stripped naked and rubbed themselves over with oil. But this was not the ancient custom;

athletes formerly, even when they were contending at Olympia, wore girdles about their loins, a practice which lasted until quite lately, and still prevails among Barbarians, especially those of Asia, where the combatants at boxing and wrestling matches wear girdles. And many other customs which are now confined to the Barbarians might be shown to have existed formerly in Hellas.

In later times, when navigation had become general and wealth was beginning to accumulate, cities were built upon the sea-shore and fortified; peninsulas too were occupied and walled-off with a view to commerce and defence against the neighbouring tribes. But the older towns both in the islands and on the continent, in order to protect themselves against the piracy which so long prevailed, were built inland. For the piratical tribes plundered, not only one another, but all those who, without being sailors, lived on the sea-coast.

The islanders were even more addicted to piracy than the inhabitants of the mainland. They were mostly Carian or Phœnician settlers. This is proved by the fact that when the Athenians purified Delos during the Peloponnesian War and the tombs of the dead were opened, more than half of them were found to be Carians. They were known by the fashion of their arms which were buried with them, and by their mode of burial, the same which is still practised among them.

After Minos had established his navy, communication by sea became more general. For, he having expelled the pirates when he colonised the greater part of the islands, the dwellers on the sea-coast began to grow richer and to live in a more settled manner; and some of them finding their wealth increase beyond their expectations, surrounded their towns with walls. The love of gain made the weaker willing to serve the stronger, and the command of wealth enabled the more powerful to subjugate the lesser cities. This was the state of society which was beginning to prevail at the time of the Trojan War.

I am inclined to think that Agamemnon succeeded in collecting the expedition, not because the suitors of Helen had bound themselves by oath to Tyndareus, but because he was the most powerful king of his time. Those Peloponnesians who possess the most accurate traditions say that originally Pelops gained his power by the great wealth which he brought with him from Asia into a poor country, whereby he was enabled, although a stranger, to give his name to the Peloponnesus; and that still greater fortune attended his descendants after the death of Eurystheus, king of Mycenæ, who was slain in Attica by the Heraclidæ. For Atreus the son of Pelops was the maternal uncle of Eurystheus, who, when he went on the expedition, naturally committed to his charge the kingdom of Mycenæ. Now Atreus had been banished by his father on account of the murder of Chrysippus. But Eurystheus never returned; and the Mycenæans, dreading the Heraclidæ, were ready to welcome Atreus, who was considered a powerful man and had ingratiated himself with the multitude. So he succeeded to the throne of Mycenæ and the other dominions of Eurystheus. Thus the house of Pelops prevailed over that of Perseus.

And it was, as I believe, because Agamemnon inherited this power and also because he was the greatest naval potentate of his time that he was able to assemble the expedition; and the other princes followed him, not from good-will, but from fear. Of the chiefs who came to Troy, he, if the witness of Homer be accepted, brought the greatest number of ships himself, besides supplying the Arcadians with them. In the "Handing down of the Sceptre" he is described as "The king of many islands, and of all

Argos." But, living on the mainland, he could not have ruled over any except the adjacent islands (which would not be "many") unless he had possessed a considerable navy. From this expedition we must form our conjectures about the character of still earlier times.

When it is said that Mycenæ was but a small place, or that any other city which existed in those days is inconsiderable in our own, this argument will hardly prove that the expedition was not as great as the poets relate and as is commonly imagined. Suppose the city of Sparta to be deserted, and nothing left but the temples and the ground-plan, distant ages would be very unwilling to believe that the power of the Lacedæmonians was at all equal to their fame. And yet they own two-fifths of the Peloponnesus, and are acknowledged leaders of the whole, as well as of numerous allies in the rest of Hellas. But their city is not regularly built, and has no splendid temples or other edifices; it rather resembles a straggling village like the ancient towns of Hellas, and would therefore make a poor show. Whereas, if the same fate befell the Athenians, the ruins of Athens would strike the eye, and we should infer their power to have been twice as great as it really is. We ought not then to be unduly sceptical. The greatness of cities should be estimated by their real power and not by appearances. And we may fairly suppose the Trojan expedition to have been greater than any which preceded it, although according to Homer, if we may once more appeal to his testimony, not equal to those of our own day. He·was a poet, and may therefore be expected to exaggerate; yet, even upon his showing, the expedition was comparatively small. For it numbered, as he tells us, twelve hundred ships, those of the Bœotians carrying one hundred and twenty men each, those of Philoctetes fifty; and by these numbers he may be presumed to indicate the largest and the smallest ships; else why in the catalogue is nothing said about the size of any others? That the crews were all fighting men as well as rowers he clearly implies when speaking of the ships of Philoctetes; for he tells us that all the oarsmen were likewise archers. And it is not to be supposed that many who were not sailors would accompany the expedition, except the kings and principal officers; for the troops had to cross the sea, bringing with them the materials of war, in vessels without decks, built after the old piratical fashion. Now if we take a mean between the crews, the invading forces will appear not to have been very numerous when we remember that they were drawn from the whole of Hellas.

The cause of the inferiority was not so much the want of men as the want of money; the invading army was limited by the difficulty of obtaining supplies to such a number as might be expected to live on the country in which they were to fight. After their arrival at Troy, when they had won a battle (as they clearly did, for otherwise they could not have fortified their camp), even then they appear not to have used the whole of their force, but to have been driven by want of provisions to the cultivation of the Chersonese and to pillage. And in consequence of this dispersion of their forces, the Trojans were enabled to hold out against them during the whole ten years, being always a match for those who remained on the spot. Whereas if the besieging army had brought abundant supplies, and, instead of betaking themselves to agriculture or pillage, had carried on the war persistently with all their forces, they would easily have been masters of the field and have taken the city; since, even divided as they were, and with only a part of their army available at any one time, they held their ground. Or, again, they might have regularly invested Troy, and the place would have been captured in less time and with less trouble. Poverty was the real reason why the achievements of former ages were insignificant, and why the Trojan War, the most celebrated of them all, when brought to the test of facts, falls short of its fame and of the prevailing traditions to which the poets have given authority.

Even in the age which followed the Trojan War, Hellas was still in process of ferment and settlement, and had no time for peaceful growth. The return of the Hellenes from Troy after their long absence led to many changes: quarrels too arose in nearly every city, and those who were expelled by them went and founded other cities. Thus in the sixtieth year after the fall of Troy, the Bœotian people, having been expelled from Arne by the Thessalians, settled in the country formerly called Cadmeis, but now Bœotia: a portion of the tribe already dwelt there, and some of these had joined in the Trojan expedition. In the eightieth year after the war, the Dorians led by the Heraclidæ conquered the Peloponnesus. A considerable time elapsed before Hellas became finally settled; after a while, however, she recovered tranquillity and began to send out colonies. The Athenians colonised Ionia and most of the islands; the Peloponnesians the greater part of Italy and Sicily, and various places in Hellas. These colonies were all founded after the Trojan War.

As Hellas grew more powerful and the acquisition became more and more rapid, the revenues of her cities increased, and in most of them tyrannies were established; they had hitherto been ruled by hereditary kings, having fixed prerogatives. The Hellenes likewise began to build navies and to make the sea their element. The Corinthians are said to have first adopted something like the modern style of shipbuilding, and the oldest Hellenic triremes to have been constructed at Corinth. A Corinthian ship-builder, Ameinocles, appears to have built four ships for the Samians; he went to Samos about three hundred years before the end of the Peloponnesian War. And the earliest naval engagement on record is that between the Corinthians and Corcyræans which occurred about forty years later. Corinth, being seated on an isthmus, was naturally from the first a centre of commerce; for the Hellenes within and without the Peloponnese in the old days, when they communicated chiefly by land, had to pass through her territory in order to reach one another. Her wealth too was a source of power, as the ancient poets testify, who speak of "Corinth the rich." When navigation grew more common, the Corinthians, having already acquired a fleet, were able to put down piracy; they offered a market both by sea and land, and with the increase of riches the power of their city increased yet more. Later, in the time of Cyrus, the first Persian king, and of Cambyses his son, the Ionians had a large navy; they fought with Cyrus, and were for a time masters of the sea around their own coasts. Polycrates, too, who was tyrant of Samos in the reign of Cambyses, had a powerful navy and subdued several of the islands, among them Rhenea, which he dedicated to the Delian Apollo. And the Phocæans, when they were colonising Massalia, defeated the Carthaginians in a sea-fight.

These were the most powerful navies, and even these, which came into existence many generations after the Trojan War, appear to have consisted chiefly of fifty-oared vessels and galleys of war, as in the days of Troy; as yet triremes were not common. But a little before the Persian War and the death of Darius, who succeeded Cambyses, the Sicilian tyrants and the Corcyræans had them in considerable numbers. No other maritime powers of any consequence arose in Hellas before the expedition of Xerxes. The Æginetans, Athenians, and a few more had

small fleets, and these mostly consisted of fifty-oared galleys. Even the ships which the Athenians built quite recently at the instigation of Themistocles, when they were at war with the Æginetans and in expectation of the Barbarian, even these ships with which they fought at Salamis were not completely decked.

So inconsiderable were the Hellenic navies in recent as well as in more ancient times. And yet those who applied their energies to the sea obtained a great accession of strength by the increase of their revenues and the extension of their dominion. For they attacked and subjugated the islands, especially when the pressure of population was felt by them. Whereas by land, no conflict of any kind which brought increase of power ever occurred; what wars they had were mere border feuds. Foreign and distant expeditions of conquest the Hellenes never undertook; they were not as yet ranged under the command of the great states, nor did they form voluntary leagues or make expeditions on an equal footing. Their wars were only the wars of the several neighbouring tribes with one another. It was in the ancient conflict between the Chalcidians and the Eretrians that the rest of Hellas was most divided and took the greatest part.

There were different impediments to the progress of different states. The Ionians had attained great prosperity when Cyrus and the Persians, having overthrown Crœsus and subdued the countries between the river Halys and the sea, made war against them and enslaved the cities on the mainland. Some time afterwards, Darius, strong in the possession of the Phœnician fleet, conquered the islands also.

Nor again did the tyrants of the Hellenic cities extend their thoughts beyond their own interest, that is, the security of their persons, and the aggrandisement of themselves and their families. They were extremely cautious in the administration of their government, and nothing considerable was ever effected by them; they only fought with their neighbours, as in Sicily, where their power attained its greatest height. Thus for a long time everything conspired to prevent Hellas from uniting in any great action and to paralyse enterprise in the individual states.

At length the tyrants of Athens and of the rest of Hellas (which had been under their dominion long before Athens), at least the greater number of them, and with the exception of the Sicilian the last who ever ruled, were put down by the Lacedæmonians. For although Lacedæmon, after the conquest of the country by the Dorians who now inhabit it, remained long unsettled, and indeed longer than any country which we know, nevertheless she obtained good laws at an earlier period than any other, and has never been subject to tyrants; she has preserved the same form of government for rather more than four hundred years, reckoning to the end of the Peloponnesian War. It was the excellence of her constitution which gave her power, and thus enabled her to regulate the affairs of other states. Not long after the overthrow of the tyrants by the Lacedæmonians, the battle of Marathon was fought between the Athenians and the Persians; ten years later, the Barbarian returned with the vast armament which was to enslave Hellas. In the greatness of the impending danger, the Lacedæmonians, who were the most powerful state in Hellas, assumed the lead of the confederates. The Athenians, as the Persian host advanced, resolved to forsake their city, broke up their homes, and, taking to their ships, became sailors. The Barbarian was repelled by a common effort; but soon the Hellenes, as well those who had revolted from the king as those who formed the original confederacy, took different sides and became the allies, either of the Athenians or of the

Lacedæmonians; for these were now the two leading powers, the one strong by land and the other by sea. The league between them was of short duration; they speedily quarrelled and with their respective allies, went to war. Any of the other Hellenes who had differences of their own now resorted to one or other of them. So that from the Persian to the Peloponnesian War, the Lacedæmonians and the Athenians were perpetually fighting or making peace, either with one another or with their own revolted allies; thus they attained military efficiency, and learned experience in the school of danger.

The Lacedæmonians did not make tributaries of those who acknowledged their leadership, but took care that they should be governed by oligarchies in the exclusive interest of Sparta. The Athenians, on the other hand, after a time deprived the subject cities of their ships and made all of them pay a fixed tribute, except Chios and Lesbos. And the single power of Athens at the beginning of this war was greater than that of Athens and Sparta together at their greatest, while the confederacy remained intact.

Such are the results of my enquiry into the early state of Hellas. They will not readily be believed upon a bare recital of all the proofs of them. Men do not discriminate, and are too ready to receive ancient traditions about their own as well as about other countries. For example, most Athenians think that Hipparchus was actually tyrant when he was slain by Harmodius and Aristogeiton; they are not aware that Hippias was the eldest of the sons of Peisistratus, and succeeded him, and that Hipparchus and Thessalus were only his brothers. At the last moment, Harmodius and Aristogeiton suddenly suspected that Hippias had been forewarned by some of their accomplices. They therefore abstained from attacking him, but, wishing to do something before they were seized, and not to risk their lives in vain, they slew Hipparchus, with whom they fell in near the temple called Leocorium as he was marshalling the Panathenaic procession. There are many other matters, not obscured by time, but contemporary, about which the other Hellenes are equally mistaken. For example, they imagine that the kings of Lacedæmon in their council have not one but two votes each, and that in the army of the Lacedæmonians there is a division called the Pitanate division; whereas they never had anything of the sort. So little trouble do men take in the search after truth; so readily do they accept whatever comes first to hand.

Yet any one who upon the grounds which I have given arrives at the same conclusion as my own about those ancient times, would not be far wrong. He must not be misled by the exaggerated fancies of the poets, or by tales of chroniclers who seek to please the ear rather than to speak the truth. Their accounts cannot be tested by him; and most of the facts in the lapse of ages have passed into the region of romance. At such a distance of time he must make up his mind to be satisfied with conclusions resting upon the clearest evidence which can be had. And, though men will always judge any war in which they are actually fighting to be the greatest at the time, but, after it is over, revert to their admiration of some other which has preceded, still the Peloponnesian, if estimated by the actual facts, will certainly prove to have been the greatest ever known.

As to the speeches which were made either before or during the war, it was hard for me, and for others who reported them to me, to recollect the exact words. I have therefore put into the mouth of each speaker the sentiments proper to the occasion, expressed as I thought he would be likely to express them, while at the same time I endeavoured, as nearly as I could, to give the general purport of what was actually said. Of the events of the war I have not ventured to speak from any chance information, nor according to any notion of my own; I have described nothing but what I either saw myself, or learned from others of whom I made the most careful and particular enquiry. The task was a laborious one, because eye-witnesses of the same occurrences gave different accounts of them, as they remembered or were interested in the actions of one side or the other. And very likely the strictly historical character of my narrative may be disappointing to the ear. But if he who desires to have before his eyes a true picture of the events which have happened, and of the like events which may be expected to happen hereafter in the order of human things, shall pronounce what I have written to be useful, then I shall be satisfied. My history is an everlasting possession, not a prize composition which is heard and forgotten.

The greatest achievement of former times was the Persian War; yet even this was speedily decided in two battles by sea and two by land. But the Peloponnesian War was a protracted struggle, and attended by calamities such as Hellas had never known within a like period of time. Never were so many cities captured and depopulated—some by Barbarians, others by Hellenes themselves fighting against one another; and several of them after their capture were repeopled by strangers. Never were exile and slaughter more frequent, whether in the war or brought about by civil strife. And rumours, of which the like had often been current before, but rarely verified by fact, now appeared to be well grounded. There were earthquakes unparalleled in their extent and fury, and eclipses of the sun more numerous than are recorded to have happened in any former age; there were also in some places great droughts causing famines, and lastly the plague which did immense harm and destroyed numbers of the people. All these calamities fell upon Hellas simultaneously with the war, which began when the Athenians and Peloponnesians violated the thirty years' truce concluded by them after the recapture of Eubœa. Why they broke it and what were the grounds of quarrel I will first set forth, that in time to come no man may be at a loss to know what was the origin of this great war. The real though unavowed cause I believe to have been the growth of the Athenian power, which terrified the Lacedæmonians and forced them into war.

—BENJAMIN JOWETT.

THE ATHENIAN EMPIRE [1]

THUCYDIDES

[From Book I]

Thucydides was not content simply to explain that Athens held the leadership in Greek affairs at the outbreak of the war, but he desired to make clear how she had gradually grown into that position.

How the Athenians attained the position in which they rose to greatness I will now proceed to describe. When the Persians, defeated both by sea and land, had retreated from Europe, and the remnant of the fleet, which had escaped to Mycale, had there perished, Leotychides, the Lacedæmonian king, who had commanded the Hellenes in the battle, returned home with the allies from Peloponnesus. But the Athenians and their allies from Ionia and the Hellespont, who had recently revolted from the king, persevered and besieged Sestos, at that time still in the hands of the Persians. Remaining there through the winter they took the place, which the Barbarians deserted. The allies then sailed back from the Hellespont to their respective homes. Meanwhile the Athenian people, now quit of

[1] Reprinted by permission of Oxford University Press.

the Barbarians, fetched their wives, their children, and the remains of their property from the places in which they had been deposited, and set to work, rebuilding the city and the walls. Of the old line of wall but a small part was left standing. Most of the houses were in ruins, a few only remaining in which the chief men of the Persians had lodged.

The Lacedæmonians knew what would happen and sent an embassy to Athens. They would rather themselves have seen neither the Athenians nor any one else protected by a wall; but their main motive was the importunity of their allies, who dreaded not only the Athenian navy, which had until lately been quite small, but also the spirit which had animated them in the Persian War. So the Lacedæmonians requested them not to restore their walls, but on the contrary to join with them in razing the fortifications of other towns outside the Peloponnesus which had them standing. They did not reveal their real wishes or the suspicion which they entertained of the Athenians, but argued that the Barbarian, if he again attacked them, would then have no strong place which he could make his head-quarters as he had lately made Thebes. Peloponnesus would be a sufficient retreat for all Hellas and a good base of operations. To this the Athenians, by the advice of Themistocles, replied, that they would send an embassy of their own to discuss the matter, and so got rid of the Spartan envoys. He then proposed that he should himself start at once for Sparta, and that they should give him colleagues who were not to go immediately, but were to wait until the wall reached the lowest height which could possibly be defended. The whole people, men, women, and children, should join in the work, and they must spare no building, private or public, which could be of use, but demolish them all. Having given these instructions and intimated that he would manage affairs at Sparta, he departed. On his arrival he did not at once present himself officially to the magistrates, but delayed and made excuses; and when any of them asked him "why he did not appear before the assembly," he said "that he was waiting for his colleagues, who had been detained by some engagement; he was daily expecting them, and wondered that they had not appeared."

The friendship of the Lacedæmonian magistrates for Themistocles induced them to believe him; but when everybody who came from Athens declared positively that the wall was building and had already reached a considerable height, they did not know what to think. He, aware of their suspicions, desired them not to be misled by reports, but to send to Athens men whom they could trust out of their own number who would see for themselves and bring back word. They agreed; and he at the same time privately instructed the Athenians to detain the envoys as quietly as they could, and not let them go until he and his colleagues had got safely home. For by this time Habronicus the son of Lysicles, and Aristides the son of Lysimachus, who were joined with him in the embassy, had arrived, bringing the news that the wall was of sufficient height; and he was afraid that the Lacedæmonians, when they heard the truth, might not allow them to return. So the Athenians detained the envoys, and Themistocles, coming before the Lacedæmonians, at length declared in so many words that Athens was now provided with walls and could protect her citizens; henceforward, if the Lacedæmonians or their allies wished at any time to negotiate, they must deal with the Athenians as with men who knew quite well what was for their own and the common good. When they boldly resolved to leave their city and go on board ship, they did not first ask the advice of the Lacedæmonians, and, when the two states met in council,

their own judgment had been as good as that of any one. And now they had arrived at an independent opinion that it was better far, and would be more advantageous both for themselves and for the whole body of the allies, that the city should have a wall; when any member of a confederacy had not equal military advantages, his counsel could not be of equal weight or worth. Either all the allies should pull down their walls, or they should acknowledge that the Athenians were in the right.

On hearing these words the Lacedæmonians did not openly quarrel with the Athenians; for they professed that the embassy had been designed, not to interfere with them, but to offer a suggestion for the public good; besides at that time the patriotism which the Athenians had displayed in the Persian War had created a warm feeling of friendliness between the two cities. They were annoyed at the failure of their purpose, but they did not show it. And the envoys on either side returned home without any formal complaint.

In such hurried fashion did the Athenians rebuild the walls of their city. To this day the structure shows evidence of haste. The foundations are made up of all sorts of stones, in some places unwrought, and laid just as each worker brought them; there were many columns too, taken from sepulchres, and many old stones already cut, inserted in the work. The circuit of the city was extended in every direction, and the citizens, in their ardour to complete the design, spared nothing.

Themistocles also persuaded the Athenians to finish the Piræus, of which he had made a beginning in his year of office as Archon. The situation of the place, which had three natural havens, was excellent; and now that the Athenians had become sailors, he thought that a good harbour would greatly contribute to the extension of their power. For he first dared to say that "they must make the sea their domain," and he lost no time in laying the foundations of their empire. By his advice, they built the wall of such a width that two waggons carrying the stones could meet and pass on the top; this width may still be traced at the Piræus; inside there was no rubble or mortar, but the whole wall was made up of large stones hewn square, which were clamped on the outer face with iron and lead. The height was not more than half what he had originally intended; he had hoped by the very dimensions of the wall to paralyse the designs of an enemy, and he thought that a handful of the least efficient citizens would suffice for its defence, while the rest might man the fleet. His mind was turned in this direction, as I conceive, from observing that the Persians had met with fewer obstacles by sea than by land. The Piræus appeared to him to be of more real consequence than the upper city. He was fond of telling the Athenians that if they were hard pressed they should go down to the Piræus and fight the world at sea.

Thus the Athenians built their walls and restored their city immediately after the retreat of the Persians.

Pausanias the son of Cleombrotus was now sent from Peloponnesus with twenty ships in command of the Hellenic forces; thirty Athenian ships and a number of the allies sailed with him. They first made an expedition against Cyprus, of which they subdued the greater part; and afterwards against Byzantium, which was in the hands of the Persians, and was taken while he was still in command.

He had already begun to be oppressive, and the allies were offended with him, especially the Ionians and others who had been recently emancipated from the king. So they had recourse to their kinsmen the Athenians and begged them to be their leaders, and to protect them against Pausanias, if he attempted to oppress them. The Athenians took the matter up and prepared to interfere, being fully resolved to manage the confederacy in their own way. In the meantime the Lacedæmonians summoned Pausanias to Sparta, intending to investigate certain reports which had reached them; for he was accused of numerous crimes by Hellenes returning from the Hellespont, and appeared to exercise his command more after the fashion of a tyrant than of a general. His recall occurred at the very time when the hatred which he inspired had induced the allies, with the exception of the Peloponnesians, to transfer themselves to the Athenians. On arriving at Lacedæmon he was punished for the wrongs which he had done to particular persons, but he had also been accused of conspiring with the Persians, and of this, which was the principal charge and was generally believed to be proven, he was acquitted. The government however did not continue him in his command, but sent in his place Dorcis and certain others with a small force. To these the allies refused allegiance, and Dorcis, seeing the state of affairs, returned home. Henceforth the Lacedæmonians sent out no more commanders, for they were afraid that those whom thy appointed would be corrupted, as they had found to be the case with Pausanias; they had had enough of the Persian War; and they thought that the Athenians were fully able to lead, and at that time believed them to be their friends.

Thus the Athenians by the good-will of the allies, who detested Pausanias, obtained the leadership. They immediately fixed which of the cities should supply money and which of them ships for the war against the Barbarians, the avowed object being to compensate themselves and the allies for their losses by devastating the King's country. Then was first instituted at Athens the office of Hellenic treasurers, who received the tribute, for so the impost was termed. The amount was originally fixed at 460 talents. The island of Delos was the treasury, and the meetings of the allies were held in the temple.

At first the allies were independent and deliberated in a common assembly under the leadership of Athens. But in the interval between the Persian and the Peloponnesian Wars, by their military success and by policy in dealing with the Barbarian, with their own rebellious allies and with the Peloponnesians who came across their path from time to time, the Athenians made immense strides in power. I have gone out of my way to speak of this period because the writers who have preceded me treat either of Hellenic affairs previous to the Persian invasion or of that invasion itself; the intervening portion of history has been omitted by all of them, with the exception of Hellanicus; and he, where he has touched upon it in his Attic history, is very brief, and inaccurate in his chronology. The narrative will also serve to explain how the Athenian empire grew up.

First of all under the leadership of Cimon, the son of Miltiades, the Athenians besieged and took from the Persians Eion upon the Strymon, and sold the inhabitants into slavery. The same fate befell Scyros, an island in the Ægean inhabited by Dolopes; this they colonised themselves. They also carried on a war with the Carystians of Eubœa, who, after a time, capitulated; the other Eubœans took no part in the war. Then the Naxians revolted, and the Athenians made war against them and reduced them by blockade. This was the first of the allied cities which was enslaved contrary to Hellenic law; the turn of the others came later.

The causes which led to the defections of the allies were of different kinds, the principal being their neglect to pay the tribute or to furnish ships, and, in some cases, failure of military service. For the Athenians were exacting and oppressive, using coercive measures towards men who were neither willing nor accustomed to work hard. And for various reasons they soon began to prove less agreeable leaders than at first. They no longer fought upon an equality with the rest of the confederates, and they had no difficulty in reducing them when they revolted. Now the allies brought all this upon themselves; for the majority of them disliked military service and absence from home, and so they agreed to contribute a regular sum of money instead of ships. Whereby the Athenian navy was proportionally increased, while they themselves were always untrained and unprepared for war when they revolted.

A little later the Athenians and their allies fought two battles, one by land and the other by sea, against the Persians, at the river Eurymedon in Pamphylia. The Athenians, under the command of Cimon, the son of Miltiades, on the same day conquered in both, and took and destroyed Phœnician vessels, numbering in all two hundred. After a while the Thasians revolted; a quarrel had arisen between them and the Athenians about the Thracian market and the mine on the Thracian coast opposite, of which the Thasians received the profits. The Athenians sailed to Thasos and, gaining a victory at sea, landed upon the island. About the same time they sent ten thousand of their own people and of their allies to the Strymon, intending to colonise the place then called the Nine Ways and now Amphipolis. They gained possession of the Nine Ways, which were inhabited by the Edoni, but, advancing into the interior of Thrace, they were destroyed at Drabescus in Edonia by the united Thracians, whose country was threatened by the new settlement.

The Thasians, now defeated and blockaded, had recourse to the Lacedæmonians and entreated them to invade Attica. Unknown to the Athenians they agreed, and were on the point of setting out when the great earthquake occurred and was immediately followed by the revolt of the Helots and the Periœci of Thuria and Æthæa, who seized Ithome. These Helots were mostly descendants of the Messenians who had been enslaved in ancient times, and hence all the insurgents were called Messenians.

While the Lacedæmonians were thus engaged, the Thasians, who had now been blockaded for more than two years, came to terms with the Athenians; they pulled down their walls and surrendered their ships; they also agreed to pay what was required of them whether in the shape of immediate indemnity or of tribute for the future; and they gave up their claim to the mainland and to the mine.

The siege of Ithome proved tedious, and the Lacedæmonians called in, among other allies, the Athenians, who sent to their aid a considerable force under Cimon. The Athenians were specially invited because they were reported to be skillful in siege operations, and the length of the blockade proved to the Lacedæmonians their own deficiency in that sort of warfare; else why had they not taken the place by assault? This expedition of the Athenians led to the first open quarrel between them and the Lacedæmonians. For the Lacedæmonians, not succeeding in storming the place, took alarm at the bold and original spirit of the Athenians. They reflected that they were aliens in race, and fearing that, if they were allowed to remain, they might be tempted by the Helots in Ithome to change sides, they dismissed them, while they retained the other allies. But they concealed their mistrust, and merely said that they no longer needed their services. Now the Athenians saw that their dismissal was due to some suspicion which had arisen and not to the less offensive reason which was openly avowed; they felt keenly that such a slight ought not

to have been offered them by the Lacedæmonians; and so, on their return home, they forthwith abandoned the alliance which they had made with them against the Persians and went over to their Argive enemies. At the same time both Argos and Athens bound themselves to Thessaly by a common oath of alliance.

In the tenth year of the siege the defenders of Ithome were unable to hold out any longer, and capitulated to the Lacedæmonians. The terms were as follows: They were to leave Peloponnesus under a safe conduct, and were never again to return; if any of them were taken on Peloponnesian soil, he was to be the slave of his captor. Now an ancient oracle of Delphi was current among the Lacedæmonians, bidding them let the suppliant of Ithomæan Zeus go free. So the Messenians left Ithome with their wives and children; and the Athenians, who now were the avowed enemies of Sparta, gave them a home at Naupactus, a place which they had just taken from the Ozolian Locrians.

The Athenians obtained the alliance of the Megarians, who revolted from the Lacedæmonians because the Corinthians were pressing them hard in a war arising out of a question of frontiers. Thus they gained both Megara and Pegæ; and they built for the Megarians the long walls extending from the city to the port of Nisæa, which they garrisoned themselves. This was the original and the main cause of the intense hatred which the Corinthians entertained towards the Athenians.

Meanwhile Inaros the son of Psammetichus, king of the Libyans who border on Egypt, had induced the greater part of Egypt to revolt from Artaxerxes the King. He began the rebellion at Mareia, a city opposite the island of Pharos, and, having made himself ruler of the country, called in the Athenians. They were just then carrying on war against Cyprus with two hundred ships of their own and of the allies; and, quitting the island, they went to his aid. They sailed from the sea into the Nile, and, getting possession of two-thirds of Memphis, proceeded to attack the remaining part called the White Castle, in which the Persians and Medes had taken refuge, and with them such Egyptians as had not joined in the revolt.

An Athenian fleet made a descent upon Halieis, where a battle took place against some Corinthian and Epidaurian troops; the Athenians gained the victory. Soon afterwards the Athenians fought at sea off Cecryphaleia with a Peloponnesian fleet, which they defeated. A war next broke out between the Æginetans and the Athenians, and a great battle was fought off the coast of Ægina, in which the allies of both parties joined; the Athenians were victorious, and captured seventy of the enemy's ships; they then landed on Ægina and, under the command of Leocrates the son of Strœbus, besieged the town. Thereupon the Peloponnesians sent over to the assistance of the Æginetans three hundred hoplites who had previously been assisting the Corinthians and Epidaurians. The Corinthians seized on the heights of Geraneia, and thence made a descent with their allies into the Megarian territory, thinking that the Athenians, who had so large a force absent in Ægina and in Egypt, would be unable to assist the Megarians; or, if they did, would be obliged to raise the siege of Ægina. But the Athenians, without moving their army from Ægina, sent to Megara under the command of Myronides a force consisting of their oldest and youngest men, who had remained at home. A battle was fought, which hung equally in the balance; and when the two armies separated, they both thought that they had gained the victory. The Athenians, who did however get rather the better, on the departure of the Corinthians erected a trophy. And then the Corinthians, irritated by the reproaches of the aged men in the city, after twelve days' preparation came out again, and, claiming the victory, raised another trophy. Hereupon the Athenians sallied out of Megara, killed those who were erecting the trophy, and charged and defeated the rest of the army.

The Corinthians now retreated, but a considerable number of them were hard pressed, and missing their way got into an enclosure belonging to a private person, which was surrounded by a great ditch and had no exit. The Athenians, perceiving their situation, closed the entrance in front with heavy-armed troops, and, placing their light troops in a circle round, stoned all who had entered the enclosure. This was a great blow to the Corinthians; but still the main body of their army returned home.

About this time the Athenians began to build their long walls extending to the sea, one to the harbour of Phalerum, and the other to the Piræus. The Phocians made an expedition against the Dorians, who inhabit Bœum, Citinium, and Erineum, and are the mother people of the Lacedæmonians; one of these towns they took. Thereupon the Lacedæmonians under the command of Nicomedes the son of Cleombrotus, who was general in the place of the king Pleistoanax the son of Pausanias (he being at that time a minor), came to the assistance of the Dorians with fifteen hundred hoplites of their own, and, of their allies, ten thousand, and compelled the Phocians to make terms and to restore the town. They then thought of returning; but there were difficulties. Either they might go by sea across the Crisæan Gulf, in which case the Athenian fleet would be sure to sail round and intercept them, or they might march over Mount Geraneia; but this seemed dangerous when the Athenians were holding Megara and Pegæ. The pass was not easy, and was always guarded by the Athenians, who were obviously intending to stop them by that route also. So they determined to remain in Bœotia and consider how they could best get home. They had another motive:—Certain Athenians were privately making overtures to them, in the hope that they would put an end to the democracy and the building of the long walls. But the Athenians were aware of their embarrassment, and they also suspected their design against the democracy. So they went out to meet them with their whole force, including a thousand Argives and contingents from the other allies; they numbered in all fourteen thousand men. Among them were some Thessalian cavalry, who came to their aid in accordance with the treaty, but these deserted to the Lacedæmonians during the engagement.

The battle was fought at Tanagra in Bœotia, and the Lacedæmonians and their allies, after great slaughter on both sides, gained the victory. They then marched into the Megarian territory, and, cutting down the fruit-trees, returned home by way of Geraneia and the Isthmus. But on the sixty-second day after the battle, the Athenians made another expedition into Bœotia under the command of Myronides, and there was a battle at Œnophyta, in which they defeated the Bœotians and became masters of Bœotia and Phocis. They pulled down the walls of Tanagra and took as hostages from the Opuntian Locrians a hundred of their richest citizens. They then completed their own long walls. Soon afterwards the Æginetans came to terms with the Athenians, dismantling their walls, surrendering their ships, and agreeing to pay tribute for the future. The Athenians, under the command of Tolmides the son of Tolmæus, sailed round Peloponnesus and burnt the Lacedæmonian dock-yard. They also took the Corinthian town of Chalcis, and,

making a descent upon Sicyon, defeated a Sicyonian force.

The Athenians and their allies were still in Egypt, where they carried on the war with varying fortune. At first they were masters of the country. The King sent to Lacedæmon Megabazus a Persian, who was well supplied with money, in the hope that he might persuade the Peloponnesians to invade Attica, and so draw off the Athenians from Egypt. He had no success; the money was being spent and nothing done; so, with what remained of it, he found his way back to Asia. The King then sent into Egypt Megabyzus the son of Zopyrus, a Persian, who marched overland with a large army and defeated the Egyptians and their allies. He drove the Hellenes out of Memphis, and finally shut them up in the island of Prosopitis, where he blockaded them during eighteen months. At length he drained the canal and diverted the water, thus leaving their ships high and dry and joining nearly the whole island to the mainland. He then crossed over with a land force, and took the island.

Thus, after six years' fighting, the cause of the Hellenes in Egypt was lost. A few survivors of their great army found their way through Libya to Cyrene; by far the larger number perished. Egypt again submitted to the Persian yoke, although Amyrtæus, the king in the fens, still held out. He escaped capture owing to the extent of the fens and the bravery of their inhabitants, who are the most warlike of all the Egyptians. Inarus the king of Libya, the chief author of the revolt, was betrayed and impaled. Fifty additional triremes, which had been sent by the Athenians and their allies to relieve their other forces, in ignorance of what had happened, sailed into the Mendesian mouth of the Nile, but they were at once attacked both from the land and from the sea, and the greater part of them destroyed by the Phœnician fleet, a few ships only escaping. Thus ended the great Egyptian expedition of the Athenians and their allies.

About this time Orestes, the exiled son of the Thessalian king Echecratides, persuaded the Athenians to restore him. Taking with them a force of Bœotians and Phocians, who were now their allies, they marched against Pharsalus in Thessaly. They made themselves masters of the country in the neighbourhood of their camp, but the Thessalian cavalry stopped any further advance. They could not take the place, and none of their plans succeeded; so they returned and brought back Orestes.

A short time afterwards a thousand Athenians, under the command of Pericles the son of Xanthippus, embarking on board the fleet which they had at Pegæ, now in their possession, coasted along to Sicyon, and there landing, defeated the Sicyonians who came out to meet them. With the least possible delay taking on board Achæan troops and sailing to the opposite coast, they attacked and besieged Œniadæ, a town of Acarnania; but failing to reduce it, they returned home.

After an interval of three years a five years' truce was concluded between the Peloponnesians and the Athenians. The Athenians now abstained from war in Hellas itself, but made an expedition to Cyprus with two hundred ships of their own and of their allies, under the command of Cimon. Sixty ships were detached from the armament and sailed to Egypt, at the request of Amyrtæus the king in the fens; the remainder proceeded to blockade Citium. Here Cimon died, and a famine arose in the country; so the fleet quitted Citium. Arriving off Salamis in Cyprus they fought at sea and also on land with Phœnician and Cilician forces. Gaining a victory in both engagements, they returned home, accompanied by the ships which had

gone out with them and had now come back from Egypt. After this the Lacedæmonians engaged in the so-called Sacred War and took possession of the temple of Delphi, which they handed over to the Delphians. But no sooner had they retired than the Athenians sent an expedition and recovered the temple, which they handed over to the Phocians.

Some time afterwards the Athenians, under the command of Tolmides the son of Tolmæus, with a thousand hoplites of their own and contingents of their allies, made an expedition against Orchomenus, Chæronea, and certain other places in Bœotia which were in the hands of oligarchical exiles from different Bœotian towns, and still remained hostile to them. They took Chæronea, and leaving a garrison there, departed. But while they were on their march, the exiles who had occupied Orchomenus, some Locrians, some Eubœan exiles and others of the same party, set upon them at Coronea and defeated them, killing many and taking many prisoners. The Athenians then agreed to evacuate Bœotia upon condition that their prisoners should be restored. And so the Bœotian exiles returned to their homes, and all the Bœotians regained their independence.

Not long afterwards Eubœa revolted from Athens. Pericles had just arrived in the island with an Athenian army when the news came that Megara had likewise revolted, that the Peloponnesians were on the point of invading Attica, and that the Megarians had slaughtered the Athenian garrison, of whom a few only had escaped to Nisæa. The Megarians had introduced a force of Corinthians, Sicyonians, and Epidaurians into the city, and by their help had effected the revolt. Pericles in haste withdrew his army from Eubœa. The Peloponnesians then invaded Attica under the command of Pleistoanax son of Pausanias, the Lacedæmonian king. They advanced as far as Eleusis and Thria but no further, and after ravaging the country, returned home. Thereupon the Athenians under the command of Pericles again crossed over to Eubœa and reduced the whole country; the Hestiæans they ejected from their homes and appropriated their territory; the rest of the island they settled by agreement.

Soon after their return from Eubœa they made a truce for thirty years with the Lacedæmonians and their allies, restoring Nisæa, Pegæ, Troezen, and Achaia, which were the places held by them in Peloponnesus. Six years later the Samians and Milesians fell out about the possession of Priene, and the Milesians, who were getting worsted in the war, came to Athens and complained loudly of the Samians. Some private citizens of Samos, who wanted to overthrow the government, supported their complaint. Whereupon the Athenians, sailing to Samos with forty ships, established a democracy, and taking as hostages fifty boys and fifty men whom they deposited at Lemnos, they returned leaving a garrison. But certain of the Samians who had quitted the island and fled to the mainland entered into an alliance with the principal oligarchs who remained in the city, and with Pissuthnes the son of Hystaspes, then governor of Sardis, and collecting troops to the number of seven hundred they crossed over by night to Samos. First of all they attacked the victorious populace and got most of them into their power; then they stole away the hostages from Lemnos, and finally revolted from Athens. The officers and garrison of the Athenians whom they captured were delivered by them into the hands of Pissuthnes. They at once prepared to make an expedition against Miletus. The Byzantians joined in their revolt.

When the Athenians heard of the insurrection they sailed to Samos with sixty ships. But of this number they sent away sixteen, some towards Caria to keep a look out for the Phœnician fleet, others to summon aid from Chios and Lesbos. With the remaining forty-four ships they fought at sea under the command of Pericles and nine others, near the island of Tragia, against seventy Samian vessels, all sailing from Miletus, of which twenty were transports; the Athenians gained the victory. After receiving a reinforcement of forty ships from Athens and of twenty-five from Chios and Lesbos they disembarked, and having the superiority on shore, invested the city with three walls; they also blockaded it by sea. At the same time Pericles took sixty ships of the blockading force and sailed hastily towards Caunus in Caria, news having arrived that a Phœnician fleet was approaching; Stesagoras and others had already gone with five ships from Samos to fetch it.

Meanwhile the Samians made a sudden sally, and attacking the naval station of the Athenians which was unprotected, destroyed the guard-ships and engaged and defeated the other vessels which put out to meet them. During some fourteen days they were masters of the sea about their own coasts, and carried in and out whatever they pleased. But when Pericles returned, they were again closely blockaded; and there soon arrived from Athens forty additional ships under Thucydides, Hagnon, and Phormio, twenty more under Tlepolemus and Anticles, and thirty from Chios and Lesbos. The Samians made a feeble attempt at a sea-fight, but soon they were unable to resist, and after nine months were forced to surrender. The terms of capitulation were as follows:— They were to raze their walls, give hostages, surrender their ships, and pay a full indemnity by regular instalments. The Byzantians too agreed to return to their allegiance.

Not long afterwards occurred the

affairs of Corcyra and Potidæa, which have been already narrated, and the various other circumstances which led to the Peloponnesian War. Fifty years elapsed between the retreat of Xerxes and the beginning of the war; during these years took place all those operations of the Hellenes against one another and against the Barbarian which I have been describing. The Athenians acquired a firmer hold over their empire and the city itself became a great power. The Lacedæmonians saw what was going on, but during most of the time they remained inactive and hardly attempted to interfere. They had never been of a temper prompt to make war unless they were compelled; and they were in some degree embarrassed by enemies near home. But the Athenians were growing too great to be ignored and were laying hands on their allies. They could now bear it no longer: they made up their minds that they must put out all their strength and overthrow the Athenian power by force of arms. And therefore they commenced the Peloponnesian War. They had already voted in their own assembly that the treaty had been broken and that the Athenians were guilty; they now sent to Delphi and asked the god if it would be for their advantage to make war. He is reported to have answered that, if they did their best, they would be conquerors, and that he himself, invited or uninvited, would take their part.

—BENJAMIN JOWETT.

THE FUNERAL ORATION [1]

THUCYDIDES

[From Book II]

Whether this is the speech actually delivered by Pericles in 431 B.C. at the end

[1] Reprinted by permission of Oxford University Press.

of the first year of the war, or one written by the historian himself, in keeping with the general practice of presenting the views of statesmen by inserting orations manufactured for the occasion, it is a splendid estimate of Athens as the leader of the world not only in a political sense but also in a spiritual. It is the earliest recognition of her rôle as the school of Hellas, a view which was later universally accepted by Greek and Roman alike. It is unique in ancient literature as a summary of the function and services of a state.

During the same winter, in accordance with an old national custom, the funeral of those who first fell in this war was celebrated by the Athenians at the public charge. The ceremony is as follows: Three days before the celebration they erect a tent in which the bones of the dead are laid out, and every one brings to his dead any offering which he pleases. At the time of the funeral the bones are placed in chests of cypress wood, which are conveyed on hearses; there is one chest for each tribe. They also carry a single empty litter decked with a pall for all whose bodies are missing, and cannot be recovered after the battle. The procession is accompanied by any one who chooses, whether citizen or stranger, and the female relatives of the deceased are present at the place of interment and make lamentation. The public sepulchre is situated in the most beautiful spot outside the walls; there they always bury those who fall in war; only after the battle of Marathon the dead, in recognition of their pre-eminent valour, were interred on the field. When the remains have been laid in the earth, some man of known ability and high reputation, chosen by the city, delivers a suitable oration over them; after which the people depart. Such is the manner of interment; and the ceremony was repeated from time to time throughout the war. Over those who were the first buried Pericles was chosen to speak. At the fitting moment he advanced from the sepulchre to a lofty stage, which had been erected in order that he might be heard as far as possible by the multitude, and spoke as follows:—

"Most of those who have spoken here before me have commended the lawgiver who added this oration to our other funeral customs; it seemed to them a worthy thing that such an honour should be given at their burial to the dead who have fallen on the field of battle. But I should have preferred that, when men's deeds have been brave, they should be honoured in deed only, and with such an honour as this public funeral, which you are now witnessing. Then the reputation of many would not have been imperilled on the eloquence or want of eloquence of one, and their virtues believed or not as he spoke well or ill. For it is difficult to say neither too little nor too much; and even moderation is apt not to give the impression of truthfulness. The friend of the dead who knows the facts is likely to think that the words of the speaker fall short of his knowledge and of his wishes; another who is not so well informed, when he hears of anything which surpasses his own powers, will be envious and will suspect exaggeration. Mankind are tolerant of the praises of others so long as each hearer thinks that he can do as well or nearly as well himself, but, when the speaker rises above him, jealousy is aroused and he begins to be incredulous. However, since our ancestors have set the seal of their approval upon the practice, I must obey, and to the utmost of my power shall endeavour to satisfy the wishes and beliefs of all who hear me.

"I will speak first of our ancestors, for it is right and becoming that now, when we are lamenting the dead, a tribute should be paid to their memory. There has never been a time when they did not inhabit this land, which by their valour they have handed down from generation to generation, and we have received from them a free state. But if they were worthy of praise, still more were our fathers, who added to their inheritance, and after many a struggle transmitted to us their sons this great empire. And we ourselves assembled here to-day, who are still most of us in the vigour of life, have chiefly done the work of improvement, and have richly endowed our city with all things, so that she is sufficient for herself both in peace and war. Of the military exploits by which our various possessions were acquired, or of the energy with which we or our fathers drove back the tide of war, Hellenic or Barbarian, I will not speak; for the tale would be long and is familiar to you. But before I praise the dead, I should like to point out by what principles of action we rose to power, and under what institutions and through what manner of life our empire became great. For I conceive that such thoughts are not unsuited to the occasion, and that this numerous assembly of citizens and strangers may profitably listen to them.

"Our form of government does not enter into rivalry with the institutions of others. We do not copy our neighbours, but are an example to them. It is true that we are called a democracy, for the administration is in the hands of the many and not of the few. But while the law secures equal justice to all alike in their private disputes, the claim of excellence is also recognized; and when a citizen is in any way distinguished, he is preferred to the public service, not as a matter of privilege, but as the reward of merit. Neither is poverty a bar, but a man may benefit his country whatever be the obscurity of his condition. There is no exclusiveness in our public life, and in our private intercourse we are not suspicious of one another, nor angry with our neighbour if he does what he likes; we do not put on sour looks at him which, though harmless, are not pleasant. While we are thus unconstrained in our private intercourse, a spirit of reverence pervades our public acts; we are prevented from doing wrong by respect for authority and for the laws, having an especial regard to those which are ordained for the protection of the injured as well as to those unwritten laws which bring upon the transgressor of them the reprobation of the general sentiment.

"And we have not forgotten to provide for our weary spirits many relaxations from toil; we have regular games and sacrifices throughout the year; at home the style of our life is refined; and the delight which we daily feel in all these things helps to banish melancholy. Because of the greatness of our city the fruits of the whole earth flow in upon us; so that we enjoy the goods of other countries as freely as of our own.

"Then again, our military training is in many respects superior to that of our adversaries. Our city is thrown open to the world, and we never expel a foreigner or prevent him from seeing or learning anything of which the secret if revealed to an enemy might profit him. We rely not upon management or trickery, but upon our own hearts and hands. And in the matter of education, whereas they from early youth are always undergoing laborious exercises which are to make them brave, we live at ease, and yet are equally ready to face the perils which they face. And here is the proof. The Lacedæmonians come into Attica not by themselves, but with their whole confederacy following; we go alone into a neighbour's country; and although our opponents are fighting for their homes and we on a foreign soil, we have seldom any difficulty in overcoming them. Our enemies have never yet felt our united strength; the care of a navy divides our attention, and on land we are obliged to send our own citizens everywhere. But they, if they meet and defeat a part of our army, are as proud as if they had routed us all, and when defeated they pretend to have been vanquished by us all.

"If then we prefer to meet danger with a light heart but without laborious training, and with a courage which is gained by habit and not enforced by law, are we not greatly the gainers? Since we do not anticipate the pain, although, when the hour comes, we can be as brave as those who never allow themselves to rest; and thus too our city is equally admirable in peace and in war. For we are lovers of the beautiful, yet simple in our tastes, and we cultivate the mind without loss of manliness. Wealth we employ, not for talk and ostentation, but when there is a real use for it. To avow poverty with us is no disgrace; the true disgrace is in doing nothing to avoid it. An Athenian citizen does not neglect the state because he takes care of his own household; and even those of us who are engaged in business have a very fair idea of politics. We alone regard a man who takes no interest in public affairs, not as a harmless, but as a useless character; and if few of us are originators, we are all sound judges of a policy. The great impediment to action is, in our opinion, not discussion, but the want of that knowledge which is gained by discussion preparatory to action. For we have a peculiar power of thinking before we act and of acting too, whereas other men are courageous from ignorance but hesitate upon reflection. And they are surely to be esteemed the bravest spirits who, having the clearest sense both of the pains and pleasures of life, do not on that account shrink from danger. In doing good, again, we are unlike others; we make our friends by conferring, not by receiving favours. Now he who confers a favour is the firmer friend, because he would fain by kindness keep alive the memory of an obligation; but the recipient is colder in his feelings, because he knows that in requiting another's generosity he will not be winning gratitude but only paying a debt. We alone do good to our neighbours not upon a calculation of interest, but in the confidence of freedom and in a frank and fearless spirit. To sum up: I say that Athens is the school of Hellas, and that the individual Athenian in his own person seems to have the power of adapting himself to the most varied forms of action with the utmost versatility and grace. This is no passing and idle word, but truth and fact; and the assertion is verified by the position to which these qualities have raised the state. For in the hour of trial Athens alone among her contemporaries is superior to the report of her. No enemy who comes against her is indignant at the reverses which he sustains at the hands of such a city; no subject complains that his masters are unworthy of him. And we shall assuredly not be without witnesses; there are mighty monuments of our power which will make us the wonder of this and succeeding ages; we shall not need the praises of Homer or of any other panegyrist whose poetry may please for the moment, although his representation of the facts will not bear the light of day. For we have compelled every land and every sea to open a path for our valour, and have everywhere planted eternal memorials of our friendship and of our enmity. Such is the city for whose sake these men nobly fought and died; they could not bear the thought that she might be taken from them; and every one of us who survive should gladly toil on her behalf.

"I have dwelt upon the greatness of Athens because I want to show you that we are contending for a higher prize than those who enjoy none of these privileges, and to establish by manifest proof the merit of these men whom I am now commemorating. Their loftiest praise has been already spoken. For in magnifying the city I have magnified them, and men like them whose virtues made her glorious. And of how few Hellenes can it be said as of them, that their deeds when weighed in the balance have been found equal to their fame! Methinks that a death such as theirs has been gives the true measure of a man's worth; it may be the first revelation of his virtues, but is at any rate their final seal. For even those who come short in other ways may justly plead the valour with which they have fought for their country; they have blotted out the evil with the good, and have benefited the state more by their public services than they have injured her by their private actions. None of these men were enervated by wealth or hesitated to resign the pleasures of life; none of them put off the evil day in the hope, natural to poverty, that a man, though poor, may one day become rich. But, deeming that the punishment of their enemies was sweeter than any of these things, and that they could fall in no nobler cause, they determined at the hazard of their lives to be honourably avenged, and to leave the rest. They resigned to hope their unknown chance of happiness; but in the face of death they resolved to rely upon themselves alone. And when the moment came they were minded to resist and suffer, rather than to fly and save their lives; they ran away from the word of dishonour, but on the battle-field their feet stood fast, and in an instant, at the height of their fortune, they passed away from the scene, not of their fear, but of their glory.

"Such was the end of these men; they were worthy of Athens, and the living need not desire to have a more heroic spirit, although they may pray for a less fatal issue. The value of such a spirit is not to be expressed in words. Any one can discourse to you for ever about the advantages of a brave defence which you know already. But instead of listening to him I would have you day by day fix your eyes upon the greatness of Athens, until you become filled with the love of her; and when you are impressed by the spectacle of her glory, reflect that this empire has been acquired by men who knew their duty and had the courage to do it, who in the hour of conflict had the fear of dishonour always present to them, and who, if ever they failed in an enterprise, would not allow their virtues to be lost to their country, but freely gave their lives to her as the fairest offering which they could present at her feast. The sacrifice which they collectively made was individually repaid to them; for they received again each one for himself a praise which grows not old, and the noblest of all sepulchres—I speak not of that in which their remains are laid, but of that in which their glory survives, and is proclaimed always and on every fitting occasion both in word and deed. For the whole earth is the sepulchre of famous men; not only are they commemorated by columns and inscriptions in their own country, but in foreign lands also there dwells an unwritten memorial of them, graven not on stone but in the hearts of men. Make them your examples, and, esteeming courage to be freedom and freedom to be happiness, do not weigh too nicely the perils of war. The unfortunate who has no hope of a change for the better has less reason to throw away his life than the prosperous who, if he survive, is always liable to a change for the worse, and to whom any accidental fall makes the most serious difference. To a man of spirit, cowardice and disaster coming together are far more bitter than death striking him unperceived at a time when he is full of courage and animated by the general hope.

"Wherefore I do not now commiserate the parents of the dead who stand here; I would rather comfort them. You know that your life has been passed amid manifold vicissitudes; and that they may be deemed fortunate who have gained most honour, whether an honourable death like theirs, or an honourable sorrow like yours, and whose days have been so ordered that the term of their happiness is likewise the term of their life. I know how hard it is to make you feel this, when the good fortune of others will too often remind you of the gladness which once lightened your hearts. And sorrow is felt at the want of those blessings, not which a man never knew, but which were a part of his life before they were taken from him. Some of you are of an age at which they may hope to have other children, and they ought to bear their sorrow better; not only will the children who may hereafter be born make them forget their own lost ones, but the city will be doubly a gainer. She will not be left desolate, and she will be safer. For a man's counsel cannot have equal weight or worth, when he alone has no children to risk in the general danger. To those of you who have passed their prime, I say: 'Congratulate yourselves that you have been happy during the greater part of your days; remember that your life of sorrow will not last long, and be comforted by the glory of those who are gone. For the love of honour alone is ever young, and not riches, as some say, but honour is the delight of men when they are old and useless.'

"To you who are the sons and brothers of the departed, I see that the struggle to emulate them will be an arduous one. For all men praise the dead, and, however pre-eminent your virtue may be, hardly will you be thought, I do not say to equal, but even to approach them. The living have their rivals and detractors, but when a man is out of the way, the honour and good-will which he receives is unalloyed. And, if I am to speak of womanly virtues to those of you who will henceforth be widows, let me sum them up in one short admonition: To a woman not to show more weakness than is natural to her sex is a great glory, and not to be talked about for good or for evil among men.

"I have paid the required tribute, in obedience to the law, making use of such fitting words as I had. The tribute of deeds has been paid in part; for the dead have been honourably interred, and it remains only that their children should be maintained at the public charge until they are grown up: this is the solid prize with which, as with a garland, Athens crowns her sons living and dead, after a struggle like theirs. For where the rewards of virtue are greatest, there the noblest citizens are enlisted in the service of the state. And now, when you have duly lamented, every one his own dead, you may depart."

—BENJAMIN JOWETT.

THE GREAT PLAGUE [1]

THUCYDIDES

[From Book II]

To the Greeks plagues seemed the natural accompaniment of wars. They had no scientific explanation of them and no safeguards against them. Thucydides feels that the discussion of their geographical origin is irrelevant, and that there may be a possibility of discovering their secret, if as historian he records the actual facts, so as to provide means of comparison in case of recurrences.

As soon as summer returned, the Peloponnesian army, comprising as before two-thirds of the force of each confed-

[1] Reprinted by permission of Oxford University Press.

erate state, under the command of the Lacedæmonian king Archidamus, the son of Zeuxidamus, invaded Attica, where they established themselves and ravaged the country. They had not been there many days when the plague broke out at Athens for the first time. A similar disorder is said to have previously smitten many places, particularly Lemnos, but there is no record of such a pestilence occurring elsewhere, or of so great a destruction of human life. For a while physicians, in ignorance of the nature of the disease, sought to apply remedies; but it was in vain, and they themselves were among the first victims, because they oftenest came into contact with it. No human art was of any avail, and as to supplication in temples, enquiries of oracles, and the like, they were utterly useless, and at last men were overpowered by the calamity and gave them all up.

The disease is said to have begun south of Egyptian Æthiopia; thence it descended into Egypt and Libya, and after spreading over the greater part of the Persian empire, suddenly fell upon Athens. It first attacked the inhabitants of the Piræus, and it was supposed that the Peloponnesians had poisoned the cisterns, no conduits having as yet been made there. It afterwards reached the upper city, and then the mortality became far greater. As to its probable origin or the causes which might or could have produced such a disturbance of nature, every man, whether a physician or not, will give his own opinion. But I shall describe its actual course, and the symptoms by which any one who knows them beforehand may recognise the disorder should it ever reappear. For I was myself attacked, and witnessed the sufferings of others.

The season was admitted to have been remarkably free from ordinary sickness; and if anybody was already ill of any other disease, it was absorbed in this.

Many who were in perfect health, all in a moment, and without any apparent reason, were seized with violent heats in the head and with redness and inflammation of the eyes. Internally the throat and the tongue were quickly suffused with blood, and the breath became unnatural and fetid. There followed sneezing and hoarseness; in a short time the disorder, accompanied by a violent cough, reached the chest; then fastening lower down, it would move the stomach and bring on all the vomits of bile to which physicians have ever given names; and they were very distressing. An ineffectual retching producing violent convulsions attacked most of the sufferers; some as soon as the previous symptoms had abated, others not until long afterwards. The body externally was not so very hot to the touch, nor yet pale; it was of a livid colour inclining to red, and breaking out in pustules and ulcers. But the internal fever was intense; the sufferers could not bear to have on them even the finest linen garment; they insisted on being naked, and there was nothing which they longed for more eagerly than to throw themselves into cold water. And many of those who had no one to look after them actually plunged into the cisterns, for they were tormented by unceasing thirst, which was not in the least assuaged whether they drank little or much. They could not sleep; a restlessness which was intolerable never left them. While the disease was at its height the body, instead of wasting away, held out amid these sufferings in a marvellous manner, and either they died on the seventh or ninth day, not of weakness, for their strength was not exhausted, but of internal fever, which was the end of most; or, if they survived, then the disease descended into the bowels and there produced violent ulcerations; severe diarrhœa at the same time set in, and at a later stage caused exhaustion,

which finally with few exceptions carried them off. For the disorder which had originally settled in the head passed gradually through the whole body, and, if a person got over the worst, would often seize the extremities and leave its mark, attacking the privy parts and the fingers and the toes; and some escaped with the loss of these, some with the loss of their eyes. Some again had no sooner recovered than they were seized with a forgetfulness of all things and knew neither themselves nor their friends.

The malady took a form not to be described, and the fury with which it fastened upon each sufferer was too much for human nature to endure. There was one circumstance in particular which distinguished it from ordinary diseases. The birds and animals which feed on human flesh, although so many bodies were lying unburied, either never came near them, or died if they touched them. This was proved by a remarkable disappearance of the birds of prey, who were not to be seen either about the bodies or anywhere else; while in the case of the dogs the fact was even more obvious, because they live with man.

Such was the general nature of the disease: I omit many strange peculiarities which characterized individual cases. None of the ordinary sicknesses attacked any one while it lasted, or, if they did, they ended in the plague. Some of the sufferers died from want of care, others equally who were receiving the greatest attention. No single remedy could be deemed a specific; for that which did good to one did harm to another. No constitution was of itself strong enough to resist or weak enough to escape the attacks; the disease carried off all alike and defied every mode of treatment. Most appalling was the despondency which seized upon any one who felt himself sickening; for he instantly abandoned his mind to despair and, instead of holding out, absolutely threw away his chance of life. Appalling too was the rapidity with which men caught the infection; dying like sheep if they attended on one another; and this was the principal cause of mortality. When they were afraid to visit one another, the sufferers died in their solitude, so that many houses were empty because there had been no one left to take care of the sick; or if they ventured they perished, especially those who aspired to heroism. For they went to see their friends without thought of themselves and were ashamed to leave them, even at a time when the very relations of the dying were at last growing weary and ceased to make lamentations, overwhelmed by the vastness of the calamity. But whatever instances there may have been of such devotion, more often the sick and the dying were tended by the pitying care of those who had recovered, because they knew the course of the disease and were themselves free from apprehension. For no one was ever attacked a second time, or not with a fatal result. All men congratulated them, and they themselves, in the excess of their joy at the moment, had an innocent fancy that they could not die of any other sickness.

The crowding of the people out of the country into the city aggravated the misery; and the newly-arrived suffered most. For, having no houses of their own, but inhabiting in the height of summer stifling huts, the mortality among them was dreadful, and they perished in wild disorder. The dead lay as they had died, one upon another, while others hardly alive wallowed in the streets and crawled about every fountain craving for water. The temples in which they lodged were full of the corpses of those who died in them; for the violence of the calamity was such that men, not knowing where to turn, grew reckless of all law, human and divine. The customs which had hitherto been observed at funerals were universally violated, and they buried their dead each one as best he could. Many, having no proper appliances, because the deaths in their household had been so frequent, made no scruple of using the burial-place of others. When one man had raised a funeral pile, others would come, and throwing on their dead first, set fire to it; or when some other corpse was already burning, before they could be stopped would throw their own dead upon it and depart.

There were other and worse forms of lawlessness which the plague introduced at Athens. Men who had hitherto concealed their indulgence in pleasure now grew bolder. For seeing the sudden change,—how the rich died in a moment, and those who had nothing immediately inherited their property,—they reflected that life and riches were alike transitory, and they resolved to enjoy themselves while they could, and to think only of pleasure. Who would be willing to sacrifice himself to the law of honour when he knew not whether he would ever live to be held in honour? The pleasure of the moment and any sort of thing which conduced to it took the place both of honour and of expediency. No fear of God or law of man deterred a criminal. Those who saw all perishing alike, thought that the worship or neglect of the Gods made no difference. For offences against human law no punishment was to be feared; no one would live long enough to be called to account. Already a far heavier sentence had been passed and was hanging over a man's head; before that fell, why should he not take a little pleasure?

Such was the grievous calamity which now afflicted the Athenians; within the walls their people were dying, and without, their country was being ravaged. In their troubles they naturally called to mind a verse which the elder men among them declared to have been current long ago:—

"A Dorian war will come and a plague with it."

There was a dispute about the precise expression; some saying that *limos,* a famine, and not *loimos,* a plague, was the original word. Nevertheless, as might have been expected, for men's memories reflected their sufferings, the argument in favour of *loimos* prevailed at the time. But if ever in future years another Dorian war arises which happens to be accompanied by a famine, they will probably repeat the verse in the other form. The answer of the oracle to the Lacedæmonians when the God was asked "whether they should go to war or not," and he replied "that if they fought with all their might, they would conquer, and that he himself would take their part," was not forgotten by those who had heard of it, and they quite imagined that they were witnessing the fulfilment of his words. The disease certainly did set in immediately after the invasion of the Peloponnesians, and did not spread into Peloponnesus in any degree worth speaking of, while Athens felt its ravages most severely, and next to Athens the places which were most populous. Such was the history of the plague.

—BENJAMIN JOWETT.

PERICLES [1]

THUCYDIDES

[From Book II]

Thucydides presents Pericles only in his capacity as statesman; he has nothing to say about his private life. He would thus seem to draw a sharp line between the function of the historian and that of the biographer. Nevertheless, he makes the personality of a man like Pericles stand out in sharp relief against the background

[1] Reprinted by permission of Oxford University Press.

of the Athenian electorate by the very tone of the words which he attributes to him and by his estimate of his policies as compared with the policies of others.

After the second Peloponnesian invasion, now that Attica had been once more ravaged, and the war and the plague together lay heavy upon the Athenians, a change came over their spirit. They blamed Pericles because he had persuaded them to go to war, declaring that he was the author of their troubles; and they were anxious to come to terms with the Lacedæmonians. Accordingly envoys were despatched to Sparta, but they met with no success. And now, being completely at their wit's end, they turned upon Pericles. He saw that they were exasperated by their misery and were behaving just as he had always anticipated that they would. And so, being still general, he called an assembly, wanting to encourage them and to convert their angry feelings into a gentler and more hopeful mood. At this assembly he came forward and spoke as follows:—

"I was expecting this outburst of indignation; the causes of it are not unknown to me. And I have summoned an assembly that I may remind you of your resolutions and reprove you for your inconsiderate anger against me, and want of fortitude in misfortune. In my judgment it would be better for individuals themselves that the citizens should suffer and the state flourish than that the citizens should flourish and the state suffer. A private man, however successful in his own dealings, if his country perish is involved in her destruction; but if he be an unprosperous citizen of a prosperous city is much more likely to recover. Seeing then that states can bear the misfortunes of individuals, but individuals cannot bear the misfortunes of the state, let us all stand by our country and not do what you are doing now, who because you are stunned by your private calamities are letting go the common hope of safety, and condemning not only me who advised, but yourselves who consented to, the war. Yet I with whom you are so angry venture to say of myself, that I am as capable as any one of devising and explaining a sound policy; and that I am a lover of my country, and incorruptible. Now a man may have a policy which he cannot clearly expound, and then he might as well have none at all; or he may possess both ability and eloquence, but if he is disloyal to his country he cannot, like a true man, speak in her interest; or again he may be unable to resist a bribe, and then all his other good qualities will be sold for money. If, when you determined to go to war, you believed me to have somewhat more of the statesman in me than others, it is not fair that I should now be charged with anything like crime.

"I allow that for men who are in prosperity and free to choose it is great folly to make war. But when they must either submit and at once surrender independence, or strike and be free, then he who shuns and not he who meets the danger is deserving of blame. For my own part, I am the same man and stand where I did. But you are changed; for you have been driven by misfortune to recall the consent which you gave when you were yet unhurt, and to think that my advice was wrong because your own characters are weak. The pain is present and comes home to each of you, but the good is as yet unrealised by any one; and your minds have not the strength to persevere in your resolution, now that a great reverse has overtaken you unawares. Anything which is sudden and unexpected and utterly beyond calculation, such a disaster for instance as this plague coming upon other misfortunes, enthralls the spirit of a man. Nevertheless, being the citizens of a great city and educated in a temper of greatness, you should not succumb to calamities however overwhelming, or darken the lustre of your fame. For if men hate the presumption of those who claim a reputation to which they have no right, they equally condemn the faintheartedness of those who fall below the glory which is their own. You should lose the sense of your private sorrows and lay fast hold of the common good.

"As to your sufferings in the war, if you fear that they may be very great and after all fruitless, I have shown you already over and over again that such a fear is groundless. If you are still unsatisfied I will indicate one element of your superiority which appears to have escaped you, although it nearly touches your imperial greatness. I too have never mentioned it before, nor would I now, because the claim may seem too arrogant, if I did not see that you are unreasonably depressed. You think that your empire is confined to your allies, but I say that of the two divisions of the world accessible to man, the land and the sea, there is one of which you are absolute master, and have, or may have, the dominion to any extent which you please. Neither the great King nor any nation on earth can hinder a navy like yours from penetrating whithersoever you choose to sail. When we reflect on this great power, houses and lands, of which the loss seems so dreadful to you, are as nothing. We ought not to be troubled about them or to think much of them in comparison; they are only the garden of the house, the superfluous ornament of wealth; and you may be sure that if we cling to our freedom and preserve that, we shall soon enough recover all the rest. But, if we are the servants of others, we shall be sure to lose not only freedom, but all that freedom gives. And where your ancestors doubly succeeded, you will doubly fail. For their empire was not nherited by them from others but won by the labour of their hands, and by hem preserved and bequeathed to us. And surely to be robbed of what you have is a greater disgrace than to fail n obtaining more. Meet your enemies herefore not only with spirit but with disdain. Any coward or fortunate fool may brag or vaunt, but he only is capable of disdain whose conviction that he is stronger than his enemy rests, like our own, on grounds of reason. Courage ighting in a fair field is fortified by the intelligence which looks down upon an enemy; an intelligence relying, not on hope, which is the strength of helplessness, but on that surer foresight which is given by reason and observation of facts.

"Once more, you are bound to maintain the imperial dignity of your city in which you all take pride; for you should not covet the glory unless you will endure the toil. And do not imagine that you are fighting about a simple issue, freedom or slavery; you have an empire to lose, and there is the danger to which the hatred of your imperial rule has exposed you. Neither can you resign your power, if, at this crisis, any timorous or inactive spirit is for thus playing the honest man. For by this time your empire has become a tyranny which in the opinion of mankind may have been unjustly gained, but which cannot be safely surrendered. The men of whom I was speaking, if they could find followers, would soon ruin the city, and if they were to go and found a state of their own, would equally ruin that. For inaction is secure only when arrayed by the side of activity; nor is it expedient or safe for a sovereign, but only for a subject state, to be a servant.

"You must not be led away by the advice of such citizens as these, nor be angry with me; for the resolution in favour of war was your own as much as mine. What if the enemy has come and done what he was certain to do when you refused to yield? What too if the plague followed? That was an unexpected blow, but we might have foreseen all the rest. I am well aware that your hatred of me is aggravated by it. But how unjustly, unless to me you also ascribe the credit of any extraordinary success which may befall you! The visitations of heaven should be borne with resignation, the sufferings inflicted by an enemy with manliness. This has always been the spirit of Athens, and should not die out in you. Know that our city has the greatest name in all the world because she has never yielded to misfortunes, but has sacrificed more lives and endured severer hardships in war than any other; wherefore also she has the greatest power of any state up to this day; and the memory of her glory will always survive. Even if we should be compelled at last to abate somewhat of our greatness (for all things have their times of growth and decay), yet will the recollection live, that, of all Hellenes we ruled over the greatest number of Hellenic subjects; that we withstood our enemies, whether single or united, in the most terrible wars, and that we were the inhabitants of a city endowed with every sort of wealth and greatness. The indolent may indeed find fault, but the man of action will seek to rival us, and he who is less fortunate may envy us. To be hateful and offensive has ever been at the time the fate of those who have aspired to empire. But he judges well who accepts unpopularity in a great cause. Hatred does not last long, and, besides the immediate splendour of great actions, the renown of them endures for ever in men's memories. Looking forward to such future glory and present avoidance of dishonour, make an effort now and secure both. Let no herald be sent to the Lacedæmonians, and do not let them know that you are depressed by your sufferings. For the greatest states and the greatest men, when misfortunes come, are the least depressed in spirit and the most resolute in action."

By these and similar words Pericles endeavoured to appease the anger of the Athenians against himself, and to divert their minds from their terrible situation. In the conduct of public affairs, they took his advice, and sent no more embassies to Sparta; they were again eager to prosecute the war. Yet in private they felt their sufferings keenly; the common people had been deprived even of the little which they possessed, while the upper class had lost fair estates in the country with all their houses and rich furniture. Worst of all, instead of enjoying peace, they were now at war. The popular indignation was not pacified until they had fined Pericles; but, soon afterwards, with the usual fickleness of the multitude, they elected him general and committed all their affairs to his charge. Their private sorrows were beginning to be less acutely felt, and for a time of public need they thought that there was no man like him. During the peace while he was at the head of affairs he ruled with prudence; under his guidance Athens was safe, and reached the height of her greatness in his time. When the war began he showed that here too he had formed a true estimate of the Athenian power. He survived the commencement of hostilities two years and six months, and, after his death, his foresight was even better appreciated than during his life. For he had told the Athenians that if they would be patient and would attend to their navy, and not seek to enlarge their dominion while the war was going on, nor imperil the existence of the city, they would be victorious; but they did all that he told them not to do, and in matters which seemingly had nothing to do with the war, from motives of private ambition and private interest they adopted a policy which had disastrous effects in respect both of themselves and of their allies; their measures, had they been successful, would only have brought honour and profit to individuals, and, when unsuccessful, crippled the city in the conduct of the war. The reason of the difference was that he, deriving authority from his capacity and acknowledged worth, being also a man of transparent integrity, was able to control the multitude in a free spirit; he led them rather than was led by them; for, not seeking power by dishonest arts, he had no need to say pleasant things, but, on the strength of his own high character, could venture to oppose and even to anger them. When he saw them unseasonably elated and arrogant, his words humbled and awed them; and, when they were depressed by groundless fears, he sought to reanimate their confidence. Thus Athens, though still in name a democracy, was in fact ruled by her greatest citizen. But his successors were more on an equality with one another, and each one struggling to be first himself, they were ready to sacrifice the whole conduct of affairs to the whims of the people. Such weakness in a great and imperial city led to many errors, of which the greatest was the Sicilian expedition; not that the Athenians miscalculated their enemy's power, but they themselves, instead of consulting for the interests of the expedition which they had sent out, were occupied in intriguing against one another for the leadership of the democracy, and not only grew remiss in the management of the army, but became embroiled, for the first time, in civil strife. And yet after they had lost in the Sicilian expedition the greater part of their fleet and army, and were distracted by revolution at home, still they held out three years not only against their former enemies, but against the Sicilians who had combined with them, and against most of their own allies who

ad risen in revolt. Even when Cyrus
he son of the King joined in the war and
upplied the Peloponnesian fleet with
noney, they continued to resist, and
vere at last overthrown, not by their
·nemies, but by themselves and their
·wn internal dissensions. So that at the
ime Pericles was more than justified in
he conviction at which his foresight had
.rrived, that the Athenians would win
.n easy victory over the unaided forces
·f the Peloponnesians.
—BENJAMIN JOWETT.

FAILURE OF THE SICILIAN EXPEDITION [1]

THUCYDIDES

[From Book VII]

During a lull in hostilities, Athens un-
lertook, in the years 415 to 413 B.C., to
·ring Sicily under her dominion, instead
·f concentrating on preparations for the
·urther prosecution of the war with
Sparta. The expedition from beginning
o end was but a series of costly blunders,
.nd resulted finally in the downfall of
Athens. Thucydides believed in the
·arlier policy of Pericles, who had advo-
·ated the focusing of all efforts on bring-
ng the war to a successful conclusion
·efore undertaking any other enterprise.
Yet, when he narrates the story of the
·xpedition, he confines himself strictly and
·mpartially to the sequence of events, re-
·raining from all comment on a matter
.bout which he must have thought and
·elt very deeply.

The Athenians, seeing the closing of
he harbour and inferring the intentions
·f the enemy, proceeded to hold a coun-
·il. The generals and officers met and
·onsidered the difficulties of their posi-
ion. The most pressing was the want
·f food. For they had already sent to
Catana, when they intended to depart,

[1] Reprinted by permission of Oxford Univer-
.ity Press.

and stopped the supplies; and they could
get no more unless they recovered the
command of the sea. They resolved
therefore to quit their lines on the higher
ground and to cut off by a cross-wall a
space close to their ships, no greater than
was absolutely required for their baggage
and for their sick; after leaving a guard
there they meant to put on board every
other man, and to launch all their ships,
whether fit for service or not; they would
then fight a decisive battle, and, if they
conquered, go to Catana; but if not, they
would burn their ships, and retreat by
land in good order, taking the nearest
way to some friendly country, Barbarian
or Hellenic. This design they proceeded
to execute, and withdrawing quietly from
the upper walls, manned their whole fleet,
compelling every man of any age at all
suitable for service to embark. The
entire number of the ships which they
manned was about a hundred and ten.
They put on board numerous archers
and javelin-men, Acarnanians, and other
foreigners, and made such preparations for action as the nature of the plan
imposed upon them by their necessities
allowed. When all was nearly ready,
Nicias, perceiving that the soldiers were
depressed by their severe defeat at sea,
which was so new an experience to them,
while at the same time the want of provisions made them impatient to risk a
battle with the least possible delay, called
his men together, and before they engaged exhorted them as follows:
"Soldiers of Athens and of our allies,
we have all the same interest in the coming struggle; every one of us as well as
of our enemies will now have to fight for
his life and for his country, and if only
we can win in the impending sea-fight,
every man may see his native city and
his own home once more. But we must
not be faint-hearted, nor behave as if
we were mere novices in the art of war,
who when defeated in their first battle
are full of cowardly apprehensions and

continually retain the impress of their disaster. You, Athenians, have had great military experience; and you, allies, are always fighting at our side. Remember the sudden turns of war; let your hope be that fortune herself may yet come over to us; and prepare to retrieve your defeat in a manner worthy of the greatness of your own army which you see before you.

"We have consulted the pilots about any improvements which seemed likely to avail against the crowding of ships in the narrow harbour, as well as against the troops on the enemy's decks, which in previous engagements did us so much harm, and we have adopted them as far as we had the means. Many archers and javelin-men will embark, and a great number of other troops, whom if we were going to fight in the open sea we should not employ because they increase the weight of the ships, and therefore impede our skill; but here, where we are obliged to fight a land-battle on shipboard, they will be useful. We have thought of all the changes which are necessary in the construction of our ships, and in order to counteract the thickness of the beams on the enemy's prows, for this did us more mischief than anything else, we have provided iron grapnels, which will prevent the ship striking us from retreating if the marines are quick and do their duty. For, as I tell you, we are positively driven to fight a land-battle on ship-board, and our best plan is neither to back water ourselves nor to allow the enemy to back water after we have once closed with him. Recollect that the shore, except so far as our land-forces extend, is in their hands.

"Knowing all this, you must fight to the last with all your strength, and not be driven ashore. When ship strikes ship refuse to separate until you have swept the enemy's heavy-armed from their decks. I am speaking to the hop-lites rather than to the sailors; for this is the special duty of the men on deck. We may still reckon on the superiority of our infantry. The sailors I would exhort, nay I would implore them, not to be paralysed by their disasters; for they will find the arrangements on deck improved, and the numbers of the fleet increased. Some among you have long been deemed Athenians, though they are not; and to them I say, Consider how precious is that privilege, and how worthy to be defended. You were admired in Hellas because you spoke our language and adopted our manners, and you shared equally with ourselves in the substantial advantages of our empire, while you gained even more than we by the dread which you inspired in subject states and in your security against injustice. You alone have been free partners in that empire; you ought not to betray it now. And so, despising the Corinthians whom you have beaten again and again, and the Sicilians who never dared to withstand us when our fleet was in its prime, repel your enemies, and show that your skill even amid weakness and disaster is superior to the strength of another in the hour of his success.

"Let me appeal once more to you who are Athenians, and remind you that there are no more ships like these in the dockyards of the Piræus, and that you have no more recruits fit for service. In any event but victory your enemies will instantly sail against Athens, while our countrymen at home, who are but a remnant, will be unable to defend themselves against the attacks of their former foes reinforced by the new invaders. You who are in Sicily will instantly fall into the hands of the Syracusans (and you know how you meant to deal with them), and your friends at Athens into the hands of the Lacedæmonians. In this one struggle you have to fight for yourselves and them. Stand firm therefore now, if ever, and remember one and all of you who are embarking that you are both the fleet and army of your country, and that on you hangs the whole state and the great name of Athens: for her sake if any man exceed another in skill or courage let him display them now; he will never have a better opportunity of doing good to himself and saving his country."

Nicias, as soon as he had done speaking, gave orders to man the ships. Gylippus and the Syracusans could see clearly enough from the preparations which the Athenians were making that they were going to fight. But they had also previous notice, and had been told of the iron grapnels; and they took precautions against this as against all the other devices of the Athenians. They covered the prows of their vessels with hides, extending a good way along the upper part of their sides, so that the grapnels might slip and find no hold. When all was ready, Gylippus and the other generals exhorted their men in the following words:—

"That our recent actions have been glorious, and that in the coming conflict we shall be fighting for a glorious prize, most of you, Syracusans and allies, seem to be aware: what else would have inspired you with so much energy? But if any one is not so quick in apprehending these things as he ought to be, he shall hear of them from me. The Athenians came hither intending to enslave first of all Sicily, and then, if they succeeded, Peloponnesus and the rest of Hellas, they having already the largest dominion of any Hellenic power, past or present. But you set mankind the example of withstanding that invincible navy; which you have now defeated in several engagements at sea, and which you will probably defeat in this. For when men are crippled in what they assume to be their strength, any vestige of self-respect is more completely lost than if they had never believed in themselves at all. When once their pride has had a fall they throw away the power of resistance which they might still exert. And this we may assume to be the condition of the Athenians.

"Far otherwise is it with us. The natural courage, which even in the days of our inexperience dared to risk all, is now better assured, and when we go on to reflect that he is the strongest who has overcome the strongest, the hopes of every one are redoubled. And in all enterprises the highest hopes infuse the greatest courage. Their imitation of our modes of fighting will be useless to them. To us they come naturally, and we shall readily adapt ourselves to any arrangement of ours which they have borrowed. But to them the employment of troops on deck is a novelty; they will be encumbered with crowds of hoplites and of javelin-men, Acarnanians and others, who are mere awkward landsmen put into a ship, and will not even know how to discharge their darts when they are required to keep their places. Will they not imperil the ships? And their own movements will be so unnatural to them that they will all fall into utter confusion. The greater number of the enemy's ships will be the reverse of an advantage to him, should any of you fear your inequality in that respect; for a large fleet confined in a small space will be hampered in action and far more likely to suffer from our devices. And I would have you know what I believe on the best authority to be the simple truth. Their misfortunes paralyse them, and they are driven to despair at finding themselves helpless. They have grown reckless, and have no confidence in their own plans. They will take their chance as best they can, and either force a way out to sea, or in the last resort retreat by land; for they know that they cannot in any case be worse off than they are.

"Against such disorder, and against hateful enemies whose good-fortune has run away from them to us, let us advance with fury. We should remember in the first place that men are doing a most lawful act when they take vengeance upon an enemy and an aggressor, and that they have a right to satiate their heart's animosity; secondly, that this vengeance, which is proverbially the sweetest of all things, will soon be within our grasp. I need not tell you that they are our enemies, and our worst enemies. They came against our land that they might enslave us, and if they had succeeded they would have inflicted the greatest sufferings on our men, and the worst indignities upon our wives and children, and would have stamped a name of dishonour upon our whole city. Wherefore let no one's heart be softened towards them. Do not congratulate yourselves at the mere prospect of getting safely rid of them. Even if they conquer they can only depart. But supposing that we obtain, as we most likely shall, the fulness of our desires, in the punishment of the Athenians and in the confirmation to Sicily of the liberties which she now enjoys, how glorious will be our prize! Seldom are men exposed to hazards in which they lose little if they fail, and win all if they succeed."

When Gylippus and the other Syracusan generals had, like Nicias, encouraged their troops, perceiving the Athenians to be manning their ships, they presently did the same. Nicias, overwhelmed by the situation, and seeing how great and how near the peril was (for the ships were on the very point of rowing out), feeling too, as men do on the eve of a great struggle, that all which he had done was nothing, and that he had not said half enough, again addressed the trierarchs, and calling each of them by his father's name, and his own name, and the name of his tribe, he entreated those who had made any reputation for themselves not to be false to it, and those whose ancestors were eminent not to tarnish

their hereditary fame. He reminded them that they were the inhabitants of the freest country in the world, and how in Athens there was no interference with the daily life of any man. He spoke to them of their wives and children and their father's Gods, as men will at such a time; for then they do not care whether their commonplace phrases seem to be out of date or not, but loudly reiterate the old appeals, believing that they may be of some service at the awful moment. When he thought that he had exhorted them, not enough, but as much as the scanty time allowed, he retired, and led the land-forces to the shore, extending the line as far as he could, so that they might be of the greatest use in encouraging the combatants on board ship. Demosthenes, Menander, and Euthydemus, who had gone on board the Athenian fleet to take the command, now quitted their own station, and proceeded straight to the closed mouth of the harbour, intending to force their way to the open sea where a passage was still left.

The Syracusans and their allies had already put out with the same number of ships as before. A detachment of them guarded the entrance of the harbour; the remainder were disposed all round it in such a manner that they might fall on the Athenians from every side at once, and that their land-forces might at the same time be able to co-operate wherever the ships retreated to the shore. Sicanus and Agatharchus commanded the Syracusan fleet, each of them a wing; Pythen and the Corinthians occupied the centre. When the Athenians approached the closed mouth of the harbour the violence of their onset overpowered the ships which were stationed there; they then attempted to loosen the fastenings. Whereupon from all sides the Syracusans and their allies came bearing down upon them, and the conflict was no longer confined to the entrance, but extended throughout the harbour. No previous engagement had been so fierce and obstinate. Great was the eagerness with which the rowers on both sides rushed upon their enemies whenever the word of command was given; and keen was the contest between the pilots as they manœuvred one against another. The marines too were full of anxiety that, when ship struck ship, the service on deck should not fall short of the rest; every one in the place assigned to him was eager to be foremost among his fellows. Many vessels meeting— and never did so many fight in so small a space, for the two fleets together amounted to nearly two hundred—they were seldom able to strike in the regular manner, because they had no opportunity of first retiring or breaking the line; they generally fouled one another as ship dashed against ship in the hurry of flight or pursuit. All the time that another vessel was bearing down, the men on deck poured showers of javelins and arrows and stones upon the enemy; and when the two closed, the marines fought hand to hand, and endeavoured to board. In many places, owing to the want of room, they who had struck another found that they were struck themselves; often two or more vessels were unavoidably entangled about one, and the pilots had to make plans of attack and defence, not against one adversary only, but against several coming from different sides. The crash of so many ships dashing against one another took away the wits of the sailors, and made it impossible to hear the boatswains, whose voices in both fleets rose high, as they gave directions to the rowers, or cheered them on in the excitement of the struggle. On the Athenian side they were shouting to their men that they must force a passage and seize the opportunity now or never of returning in safety to their native land. To the Syracusans and their allies was represented the glory of preventing the escape of their enemies, and of a victory by which every man would exalt the honour of his own city. The commanders too, when they saw any ship backing water without necessity, would call the captain by his name, and ask, of the Athenians, whether they were retreating because they expected to be more at home upon the land of their bitterest foes than upon that sea which had been their own so long; on the Syracusan side whether, when they knew perfectly well that the Athenians were only eager to find some means of flight, they would themselves fly from the fugitives.

While the naval engagement hung in the balance the two armies on shore had great trial and conflict of soul. The Sicilian soldier was animated by the hope of increasing the glory which he had already won, while the invader was tormented by the fear that his fortunes might sink lower still. The last chance of the Athenians lay in their ships, and their anxiety was dreadful. The fortune of the battle varied; and it was not possible that the spectators on the shore should all receive the same impression of it. Being quite close and having different points of view, they would some of them see their own ships victorious; their courage would then revive, and they would earnestly call upon the Gods not to take from them their hope of deliverance. But others, who saw their ships worsted, cried and shrieked aloud, and were by the sight alone more utterly unnerved than the defeated combatants themselves. Others again, who had fixed their gaze on some part of the struggle which was undecided, were in a state of excitement still more terrible; they kept swaying their bodies to and fro in an agony of hope and fear as the stubborn conflict went on and on; for at every instant they were all but saved or all but lost. And while the strife hung in the balance you might hear in the Athenian army at once lamentation, shouting, cries of victory or defeat, and all the various sounds which are wrung from a great host in extremity of danger. Not less agonising were the feelings of those on board. At length the Syracusans and their allies, after a protracted struggle, put the Athenians to flight, and triumphantly bearing down upon them, and encouraging one another with loud cries and exhortations, drove them to land. Then that part of the navy which had not been taken in the deep water fell back in confusion to the shore, and the crews rushed out of the ships into the camp. And the land-forces, no longer now divided in feeling, but uttering one universal groan of intolerable anguish, ran, some of them to save the ships, others to defend what remained of the wall; but the greater number began to look to themselves and to their own safety. Never had there been a greater panic in an Athenian army than at that moment. They now suffered what they had done to others at Pylos. For at Pylos the Lacedæmonians, when they saw their ships destroyed, knew that their friends who had crossed over into the island of Sphacteria were lost with them. And so now the Athenians, after the rout of their fleet, knew that they had no hope of saving themselves by land unless events took some extraordinary turn.

Thus, after a fierce battle and a great destruction of ships and men on both sides, the Syracusans and their allies gained the victory. They gathered up the wrecks and bodies of the dead, and sailing back to the city, erected a trophy. The Athenians, overwhelmed by their misery, never so much as thought of recovering their wrecks or of asking leave to collect their dead. Their intention was to retreat that very night. Demosthenes came to Nicias and proposed that they should once more man their remaining vessels and endeavour to force the passage at daybreak, saying that they had more ships fit for service than the enemy. For the Athenian fleet still numbered

sixty, but the enemy had less than fifty. Nicias approved of his proposal, and they would have manned the ships, but the sailors refused to embark; for they were paralysed by their defeat, and had no longer any hope of succeeding. So the Athenians all made up their minds to escape by land. . . .

When the day dawned Nicias led forward his army, and the Syracusans and the allies again assailed them on every side, hurling javelins and other missiles at them. The Athenians hurried on to the river Assinarus. They hoped to gain a little relief if they forded the river, for the mass of horsemen and other troops overwhelmed and crushed them; and they were worn out by fatigue and thirst. But no sooner did they reach the water than they lost all order and rushed in; every man was trying to cross first, and, the enemy pressing upon them at the same time, the passage of the river became hopeless. Being compelled to keep close together they fell one upon another, and trampled each other under foot: some at once perished, pierced by their own spears; others got entangled in the baggage and were carried down the stream. The Syracusans stood upon the further bank of the river, which was steep, and hurled missiles from above on the Athenians, who were huddled together in the deep bed of the stream and for the most part were drinking greedily. The Peloponnesians came down the bank and slaughtered them, falling chiefly upon those who were in the river. Whereupon the water at once became foul, but was drunk all the same, although muddy and dyed with blood, and the crowd fought for it.

At last, when the dead bodies were lying in heaps upon one another in the water and the army was utterly undone, some perishing in the river, and any who escaped being cut off by the cavalry, Nicias surrendered to Gylippus, in whom he had more confidence than in the

Syracusans. He entreated him and the Lacedæmonians to do what they pleased with himself, but not to go on killing the men. So Gylippus gave the word to make prisoners. Thereupon the survivors, not including however a large number whom the soldiers concealed, were brought in alive. As for the three hundred who had broken through the guard in the night, the Syracusans sent in pursuit and seized them. The total of the public prisoners when collected was not great; for many were appropriated by the soldiers, and the whole of Sicily was full of them, they not having capitulated like the troops under Demosthenes. A large number also perished; the slaughter at the river being very great, quite as great as any which took place in the Sicilian war; and not a few had fallen in the frequent attacks which were made upon the Athenians during their march. Still many escaped, some at the time, others ran away after an interval of slavery, and all these found refuge at Catana.

The Syracusans and their allies collected their forces and returned with the spoil, and as many prisoners as they could take with them, into the city. The captive Athenians and allies they deposited in the quarries, which they thought would be the safest place of confinement. Nicias and Demosthenes they put to the sword, although against the will of Gylippus. For Gylippus thought that to carry home with him to Lacedæmon the generals of the enemy, over and above all his other successes, would be a brilliant triumph. One of them, Demosthenes, happened to be the greatest foe, and the other the greatest friend of the Lacedæmonians, both in the same matter of Pylos and Sphacteria. For Nicias had taken up their cause, and had persuaded the Athenians to make the peace which set at liberty the prisoners taken in the island. The Lacedæmonians were grateful to him for the service, and this was the main reason why he trusted Gylippus and surrendered himself to him. But certain Syracusans, who had been in communication with him, were afraid (such was the report) that on some suspicion of their guilt he might be put to the torture and bring trouble on them in the hour of their prosperity. Others, and especially the Corinthians, feared that, being rich, he might by bribery escape and do them further mischief. So the Syracusans gained the consent of the allies and had him executed. For these or the like reasons he suffered death. No one of the Hellenes in my time was less deserving of so miserable an end; for he lived in the practice of every virtue.

Those who were imprisoned in the quarries were at the beginning of their captivity harshly treated by the Syracusans. There were great numbers of them, and they were crowded in a deep and narrow place. At first the sun by day was still scorching and suffocating, for they had no roof over their heads, while the autumn nights were cold, and the extremes of temperature engendered violent disorders. Being cramped for room they had to do everything on the same spot. The corpses of those who died from their wounds, exposure to the weather, and the like, lay heaped one upon another. The smells were intolerable; and they were at the same time afflicted by hunger and thirst. During eight months they were allowed only about half a pint of water and a pint of food a day. Every kind of misery which could befall man in such a place befell them. This was the condition of all the captives for about ten weeks. At length the Syracusans sold them, with the exception of the Athenians and of any Sicilians or Italian Greeks who had sided with them in the war. The whole number of the public prisoners is not acurately known, but they were not less than seven thousand.

Of all the Hellenic actions which took

place in this war, or indeed of all Hellenic actions which are on record, this was the greatest—the most glorious to the victors, the most ruinous to the vanquished; for they were utterly and at all points defeated, and their sufferings were prodigious. Fleet and army perished from the face of the earth; nothing was saved, and of the many who went forth few returned home.

Thus ended the Sicilian expedition. . . .

The news was brought to Athens, but the Athenians could not believe that the armament had been so completely annihilated, although they had the positive assurances of the very soldiers who had escaped from the scene of action. At last they knew the truth; and then they were furious with the orators who had joined in promoting the expedition—as if they had not voted it themselves—and with the soothsayers, and prophets, and all who by the influence of religion had at the time inspired them with the belief that they would conquer Sicily. Whichever way they looked there was trouble; they were overwhelmed by their calamity, and were in fear and consternation unutterable. The citizens mourned and the city mourned; they had lost a host of cavalry and hoplites and the flower of their youth, and there were none to replace them. And when they saw an insufficient number of ships in their docks, and no crews to man them, nor money in the treasury, they despaired of deliverance. They had no doubt that their enemies in Sicily, after the great victory which they had already gained, would at once sail against the Piræus. Their enemies in Hellas, whose resources were now doubled, would likewise set upon them with all their might both by sea and land, and would be assisted by their own revolted allies. Still they determined under any circumstances not to give way. They would procure timber and money by whatever means they might,

and build a navy. They would make sure of their allies, and above all of Eubœa. Expenses in the city were to be economised, and they were to choose a council of the elder men, who should advise together, and lay before the people the measures which from time to time might be required. After the manner of a democracy, they were very amenable to discipline while their fright lasted. They proceeded to carry out these resolutions. And so the summer ended.

—BENJAMIN JOWETT.

THE BATTLE OF ARGINUSÆ [1]

XENOPHON

[From *Hellenica*, Book I]

Xenophon was born at Athens about 430 and died at Corinth about 355 B.C. After an adventurous life of soldiering he withdrew into the country to devote himself to writing. His experience as a pupil of Socrates led to his *Memorabilia* of the great master; his participation, with many other soldiers of fortune typical of the time, in the expedition of Cyrus the Younger resulted in an account of that adventure entitled *Anabasis,* in which he played a leading rôle, and in the *Cyropædia,* a kind of historical novel of Cyrus the Great; and his interest in history found expression in the *Hellenica,* a continuation of the work of Thucydides. He wrote also a number of essays on various subjects, the most important of which is the *Economics,* which deals with household management. Xenophon writes in a simple, graceful, straightforward style which won him many admirers in antiquity; but he can not be compared with Thucydides as a scientific historian, nor with Herodotus as an interesting narrator of events.

This passage throws strong light on the instability of the Athenian democracy,

[1] From *The Works of Xenophon,* by H. G. Dakyns. Copyright by Macmillan & Co., Ltd. Reprinted by permission.

which gave absolute power to the assembly of the people. While the constitution opened the way to positions of leadership for such statesmen as Themistocles and Pericles, at other times it was capable of becoming the tool of mere demagogues. The battle, which was fought in 406 B.C., was the last victory of Athens in the Peloponnesian war.

Now that the position of affairs, including the blockade, was fully known at Athens, a vote was passed to send out a reinforcement of one hundred and ten ships. Every man of ripe age, whether slave or free, was impressed for this service, so that within thirty days the whole one hundred and ten vessels were fully manned and weighed anchor. Amongst those who served in this fleet were also many of the knights. The fleet at once stood out across to Samos, and picked up the Samian vessels in that island. The muster-roll was swelled by the addition of more than thirty others from the rest of the allies, to whom the same principle of conscription was applied, as also it did to the ships already engaged on foreign service. The actual total, therefore, when all the contingents were collected, was over one hundred and fifty vessels.

Callicratidas, hearing that the relief squadron had already reached Samos, left fifty ships, under command of Eteonicus, in the harbour of Mitylene, and setting sail with the other one hundred and twenty, hove to for the evening meal off Cape Malea in Lesbos, opposite Mitylene. It so happened that the Athenians on this day were supping on the islands of Arginusæ, which lie opposite Lesbos. In the night the Spartan not only saw their watch-fires, but received positive information that "these were the Athenians," and about midnight he got under weigh, intending to fall upon them suddenly. But a violent downpour of rain with thunder and lightning prevented him putting out to sea. By daybreak it had

cleared, and he sailed towards Arginusæ. On their side, the Athenian squadron stood out to meet him, with their left wing facing towards the open sea, and drawn up in the following order:—Aristocrates, in command of the left wing, with fifteen ships, led the van; next came Diomedon with fifteen others, and immediately in the rear of Aristocrates and Diomedon respectively, as their supports, came Pericles and Erasinides. Parallel with Diomedon were the Samians, with their ten ships drawn up in single line, under the command of a Samian officer named Hippeus. Next to these came the ten vessels of the taxiarchs, also in single line, and supporting them, the three ships of the navarchs, with any other allied vessels in the squadron. The right wing was entrusted to Protomachus with fifteen ships, and next to him (on the extreme right) was Thrasylus with another division of fifteen. Protomachus was supported by Lysias with an equal number of ships, and Thrasylus by Aristogenes. The object of this formation was to prevent the enemy from manœuvring so as to break their line by striking them amidships, since they were inferior in sailing power.

The Lacedæmonians, on the contrary, trusting to their superior seamanship, were formed opposite with their ships all in single line, with the special object of manœuvring so as either to break the enemy's line or to wheel round them. Callicratidas commanded the right wing in person. Before the battle the officer who acted as his pilot, the Megarian Hermon, suggested that it might be well to withdraw the fleet as the Athenian ships were far more numerous. But Callicratidas replied that Sparta would be no worse off even if he personally should perish, but to flee would be disgraceful. And now the fleets approached, and for a long space the battle endured. At first the vessels were engaged in crowded masses, and later on in scattered groups. At length Callicratidas, as his vessel dashed her beak into her antagonist, was hurled off into the sea and disappeared. At the same instant Protomachus, with his division on the right, had defeated the enemy's left, and then the flight of the Peloponnesians began towards Chios, though a very considerable body of them made for Phocæa, whilst the Athenians sailed back again to Arginusæ. The losses on the side of the Athenians were twenty-five ships, crews and all, with the exception of the few who contrived to reach dry land. On the Peloponnesian side, nine out of the ten Lacedæmonian ships, and more than sixty belonging to the rest of the allied squadron, were lost.

After consultation the Athenian generals agreed that two captains of triremes, Theramenes and Thrasybulus, accompanied by some of the taxiarchs, should take forty-seven ships and sail to the assistance of the disabled fleet and of the men on board, while the rest of the squadron proceeded to attack the enemy's blockading squadron under Eteonicus at Mitylene. In spite of their desire to carry out this resolution, the wind and a violent storm which arose prevented them. So they set up a trophy, and took up their quarters for the night. As to Eteonicus, the details of the engagement were faithfully reported to him by the express despatch-boat in attendance. On receipt of the news, however, he sent the despatch-boat out again the way she came, with an injunction to those on board of her to sail off quickly without exchanging a word with anyone. Then on a sudden they were to return garlanded with wreaths of victory and shouting, "Callicratidas has won a great sea fight, and the whole Athenian squadron is destroyed." This they did, and Eteonicus, on his side, as soon as the despatch-boat came sailing in, proceeded to offer sacrifice of thanksgiving in honour of the good news. Meanwhile he gave orders that the troops were to take their evening meal, and that the masters of the trading ships were silently to stow away their goods on board the merchant ships and make sail as fast as the favourable breeze could speed them to Chios. The ships of war were to follow suit with what speed they might. This done, he set fire to his camp, and led off the land forces to Methymna. Conon, finding the enemy had made off, and the wind had grown comparatively mild, got his ships afloat, and so fell in with the Athenian squadron, which had by this time set out from Arginusæ. To these he explained the proceedings of Eteonicus. The squadron put into Mitylene, and from Mitylene stood across to Chios, and thence, without effecting anything further, sailed back to Samos.

All the above-named generals, with the exception of Conon, were presently deposed by the home authorities. In addition to Conon two new generals were chosen, Adeimantus and Philocles. Of those concerned in the late victory two never returned to Athens: these were Protomachus and Aristogenes. The other six sailed home. Their names were Pericles, Diomedon, Lysias, Aristocrates, Thrasylus, and Erasinides. On their arrival Archidemus, the leader of the democracy at that date, who had charge of the two obol fund, inflicted a fine on Erasinides, and accused him before the Dicastery of having appropriated money derived from the Hellespont, which belonged to the people. He brought a further charge against him of misconduct while acting as general, and the court sentenced him to imprisonment.

These proceedings in the law court were followed by the statement of the generals before the senate touching the late victory and the magnitude of the storm. Timocrates then proposed that the other five generals should be put in custody and handed over to the public assembly. Whereupon the senate committed them all to prison. Then came the meeting of the public assembly, in which others, and more particularly Theramenes, formally accused the generals. He insisted that they ought to show cause why they had not picked up the shipwrecked crews. To prove that there had been no attempt on their parts to attach blame to others, he might point, as conclusive testimony, to the despatch sent by the generals themselves to the senate and the people, in which they attributed the whole disaster to the storm, and nothing else. After this the generals each in turn made a defence, which was necessarily limited to a few words, since no right of addressing the assembly at length was allowed by law. Their explanation of the occurrences was that, in order to be free to sail against the enemy themselves, they had devolved the duty of picking up the shipwrecked crews upon certain competent captains of men-of-war, who had themselves been generals in their time, to wit Theramenes and Thrasybulus, and others of like stamp. If blame could attach to any one at all with regard to the duty in question, those to whom their orders had been given were the sole persons they could hold responsible. "But," they went on to say, "we will not, because these very persons have denounced us, invent a lie, and say that Theramenes and Thrasybulus are to blame, when the truth of the matter is that the magnitude of the storm alone prevented the burial of the dead and the rescue of the living." In proof of their contention, they produced the pilots and numerous other witnesses from among those present at the engagement. By these arguments they were in a fair way to persuade the people of their innocence. Indeed many private citizens rose wishing to become bail for the accused, but it was resolved to defer decision till another meeting of the assembly. It was indeed already so late that it would have been impossible to see to count the show of hands. It was further resolved that the senate meanwhile should prepare

a measure, to be introduced at the next assembly, as to the mode in which the accused should take their trial.

Then came the festival of the Apaturia, with its family gatherings of fathers and kinsfolk. Accordingly the party of Theramenes procured numbers of people clad in black apparel, and close-shaven, who were to go in and present themselves before the public assembly in the middle of the festival, as relatives, presumably, of the men who had perished; and they persuaded Callixenus to accuse the generals in the senate. The next step was to convoke the assembly, when the senate laid before it the proposal just passed by their body, at the instance of Callixenus, which ran as follows: "Seeing that both parties to this case, to wit, the prosecutors of the generals on the one hand, and the accused themselves in their defence on the other, have been heard in the late meeting of the assembly; we propose that the people of Athens now record their votes, one and all, by their tribes; that a couple of voting urns be placed for the convenience of each several tribe; and the public crier in the hearing of each several tribe proclaim the mode of voting as follows: 'Let every one who finds the generals guilty of not rescuing the heroes of the late sea fight deposit his vote in urn No. 1. Let him who is of the contrary opinion deposit his vote in urn No. 2. Further, in the event of the aforesaid generals being found guilty, let death be the penalty. Let the guilty persons be delivered over to the eleven. Let their property be confiscated to the State, with the exception of one tithe, which falls to the goddess.'"

Now there came forward in the assembly a man, who said that he had escaped drowning by clinging to a meal tub. The poor fellows perishing around him had commissioned him, if he succeeded in saving himself, to tell the people of Athens how bravely they had fought for their fatherland, and how the generals had left them there to drown.

Presently Euryptolemus, the son of Peisianax, and others served a notice of indictment on Callixenus, insisting that his proposal was unconstitutional, and this view of the case was applauded by some members of the assembly. But the majority kept crying out that it was monstrous if the people were to be hindered by any stray individual from doing what seemed to them right. And then Lyciscus, embodying the spirit of those cries, formally proposed that if these persons would not abandon their action, they should be tried by the same vote along with the generals: a proposition to which the mob gave vociferous assent; and so these were compelled to abandon their summonses. Again, when some of the Prytanes objected to put a resolution to the vote which was in itself unconstitutional, Callixenus again got up and accused them in the same terms, and the shouting began again. "Yes, summons all who refuse," until the Prytanes, in alarm, all agreed with one exception to permit the voting. This obstinate dissentient was Socrates, the son of Sophroniscus, who insisted that he would do nothing except in accordance with the law. After this Euryptolemus rose and spoke in behalf of the generals. He said:—

"I stand here, men of Athens, partly to accuse Pericles, though he is a close and intimate connection of my own, and Diomedon, who is my friend, and partly to urge certain considerations on their behalf, but chiefly to press upon you what seems to me the best course for the State collectively. I hold them to blame in that they dissuaded their colleagues from their intention to send a despatch to the senate and this assembly, which should have informed you of the orders given to Theramenes and Thrasybulus to take forty-seven ships of war and pick up the shipwrecked crews, and of the neglect of the two officers to carry out those orders. And it follows that though the offence was committed by one or two, the responsibility must be shared by all; and in return for kindness in the past, they are in danger at present of sacrificing their lives to the machinations of these very men, and others whom I could mention. In danger, do I say, of losing their lives? No, not so, if you will suffer me to persuade you to do what is just and right; if you will only adopt such a course as shall enable you best to discover the truth and shall save you from too late repentance, when you find you have transgressed irremediably against heaven and your own selves. In what I urge you there is no trap nor plot whereby you can be deceived by me or any other man; it is a straightforward course which will enable you to discover and punish the offender by whatever process you like, collectively or individually. Let them have, if not more, at any rate one whole day to make what defence they can for themselves; and trust to your own unbiassed judgment to guide you to a right conclusion.

"You know, men of Athens, the exceeding stringency of the decree of Cannonus, which orders that man, whosoever he be, who is guilty of treason against the people of Athens, to be put in irons, and so to meet the charge against him before the people. If he be convicted, he is to be thrown into the Barathron and perish, and the property of such an one is to be confiscated, with the exception of the tithe which falls to the goddess. I call upon you to try these generals in accordance with this decree. Yes, and so help me God—if it please you, begin with my own kinsman Pericles, for base would it be on my part to make him of more account than the whole of the State. Or, if you prefer, try them by that other law, which is directed against robbers of temples and betrayers of their country, which says: if a man betray his city or rob a sacred temple of the gods, he shall be tried before a law court, and if he be convicted, his body shall not be buried in Attica, and his goods shall be confiscated to the State. Take your choice as between these two laws, men of Athens, and let the prisoners be tried by one or other. Let three portions of a day be assigned to each respectively, one portion wherein they shall listen to their accusation, a second wherein they shall make their defence, and a third wherein you shall meet and give your votes in due order on the question of their guilt or innocence. By this procedure the malefactors will receive the desert of their misdeeds in full, and those who are innocent will owe to you, men of Athens, the recovery of their liberty, in place of unmerited destruction.

"On your side, in trying the accused by recognized legal procedure, you will show that you obey the dictates of pious feeling, and can regard the sanctity of an oath, instead of joining hands with our enemies the Lacedæmonians and fighting their battles. For is it not to fight their battles, if you take their conquerors, the men who deprived them of seventy vessels, and at the moment of victory send them to perdition untried and in the teeth of the law? What are you afraid of, that you press forward with such hot haste? Do you imagine that you may be robbed of the power of life and death over whom you please, should you condescend to a legal trial? but that you are safe if you take shelter behind an illegality, like the illegality of Callixenus, when he worked upon the senate to propose to this assembly to deal with the accused by a single vote? But consider, you may actually put to death an innocent man, and then repentance will one day visit you too late. Bethink you how painful and unavailing remorse will then be, and more particularly if your error has cost a fellow-creature his life. What a travesty on justice it would be if in the

case of a man like Aristarchus, who first tried to destroy the democracy and then betrayed Œnoe to our enemy the Thebans, you granted him a day for his defence, consulting his wishes, and conceded to him all the benefits of the law; whereas you are now proposing to deprive of these same privileges your own generals, who in every way conformed to your views and defeated your enemies. Do not you, of all men, I implore you, men of Athens, act thus. Why, these laws are your own, to them beyond all else you owe your greatness. Guard them jealously; in nothing, I implore you, act without their sanction.

"But now, turn for a moment and consider with me the actual occurrences which have created the suspicion of misconduct on the part of our late generals. The sea-fight had been fought and won, and the ships had returned to land, when Diomedon urged that the whole squadron should sail out in line and pick up the wrecks and floating crews. Erasinides was in favour of all the vessels sailing as fast as possible to deal with the enemy's forces at Mitylene. And Thrasylus represented that both objects could be effected, by leaving one division of the fleet there, and with the rest sailing against the enemy; and if this resolution were agreed to, he advised that each of the eight generals should leave three ships of his own division with the ten vessels of the taxiarchs, the ten Samian vessels, and the three belonging to the navarchs. These added together make forty-seven, four for each of the lost vessels, twelve in number. Among the taxiarchs left behind, two were Thrasybulus and Theramenes, the man who in the late meeting of this assembly undertook to accuse the generals. With the remainder of the fleet they were to sail to attack the enemy's fleet. Everything, you must admit, was duly and admirably planned. It is only common justice, therefore, that those whose duty it was to attack the enemy should render an account for all mis-carriage of operations against the enemy; while those who were commissioned to pick up the dead and dying should, if they failed to carry out the instructions of the generals, be put on trial to explain the reasons of the failure. This indeed I may say in behalf of both parties. It was really the storm which, in spite of what the generals had planned, prevented anything being done. There are witnesses to attest the truth of this: the men who escaped as by a miracle, and among these one of these very generals, who was on a sinking ship and was saved. And this man, who needed picking up as much as anybody at that moment, is, they in-sist, to be tried by one and the same vote as those who neglected to perform their orders! Once more, I beg you, men of Athens, to accept your victory and your good fortune, instead of behaving like the desperate victims of misfortune and defeat. Recognize the finger of divine necessity; do not incur the reproach of stony-heartedness by discovering treason where there was merely powerlessness, and condemning as guilty those who were prevented by the storm from carrying out their instructions. Nay! you will better satisfy the demands of justice by crowning these conquerors with wreaths of victory than by punishing them with death at the instigation of wicked men."

At the conclusion of his speech Eury-ptolemus proposed, as an amendment, that the prisoners should, in accordance with the decree of Cannonus, be tried each separately, as against the proposal of the senate to try them all by a single vote.

At the show of hands the tellers gave the majority in favour of Euryptolemus's amendment, but upon the application of Menecles, who took formal exception to this decision, the show of hands was gone through again, and now the verdict was in favour of the resolution of the senate. At a later date the balloting was made,

and by the votes recorded the eight generals were condemned, and the six who were in Athens were put to death.

Not long after, repentance seized the Athenians, and they passed a decree au-thorizing the public prosecution of those who had deceived the people, and the ap-pointment of proper securities for their persons until the trial was over. Cal-lixenus was one of these committed for trial. There were, besides Callixenus, four others against whom true bills were declared, and they were all five im-prisoned by their sureties. But all sub-sequently effected their escape before the trial, at the time of the sedition in which Cleophon was killed. Callixenus eventu-ally came back when the party in Piræus returned to the city, at the date of the amnesty, but only to die of hunger, an object of universal detestation.

—H. G. DAKYNS.

THE FALL OF ATHENS [1]

XENOPHON

[From *Hellenica*, Book II]

In the year after the battle of Arginusæ the Athenian fleet was completely defeated at Ægospotami (405 B.C.). The defeat was followed by the siege of Athens and the end of the war in 404 B.C. Although Athens was forced to give up her politi-cal supremacy, she retained and even strengthened her intellectual leadership.

But now Alcibiades, from one of his fortresses, could espy the position of his fellow-countrymen, moored on an open beach beyond reach of any city, and forced to send for supplies to Sestos, which was nearly two miles distant, while their enemies were safely lodged in a har-bour, with a city adjoining, and every-

[1] From *The Works of Xenophon*, by H. G. Dakyns. Copyright by Macmillan & Co., Ltd. Reprinted by permission.

thing within reach. The situation did not please him, and he advised them to shift their anchorage to Sestos, where they would have the advantage of a harbour and a city. "Once there," he concluded, "you can engage the enemy whenever it suits you." But the generals, and more particularly Tydeus and Menander, bade him go about his business. "We are generals now—not you," they said; and so he went away. And now for five days in succession the Athenians had sailed out to offer battle, and for the fifth time retired, followed by the same swift sailers of the enemy. But this time Lysander's orders to the vessels so sent in pursuit were, that as soon as they saw the enemy's crew fairly disembarked and dispersed along the shores of the Chersonesus (a practice, it should be mentioned, which had grown upon them from day to day owing to the distance at which eatables had to be purchased, and out of sheer contempt, no doubt, of Lysander, who refused to accept battle), they were to begin their return voyage, and when in mid-channel to hoist a shield. The orders were punctually carried out, and Lysander at once signalled to his whole squadron to put across with all speed, while Thorax, with the land forces, was to march parallel with the fleet along the coast. Aware of the enemy's fleet, which he could see bearing down upon him, Conon had only time to signal to the crews to join their ships and rally to the rescue with all their might. But the men were scattered far and wide, and some of the vessels had only two out of their three banks of rowers, some only a single one, while others again were completely empty. Conon's own ship, with seven others in attendance on him and the *Paralus*, put out to sea, a little cluster of nine vessels, with their full complement of men; but every one of the remaining one hundred and seventy-one vessels were captured by Lysander on the beach. As to the men themselves, the

large majority of them were easily made prisoners on the shore, a few only escaping to the small fortresses of the neighbourhood. Meanwhile Conon and his nine vessels made good their escape. For himself, knowing that the fortune of Athens was ruined, he put into Abarnis, the promontory of Lampsacus, and there picked up the great sails of Lysander's ships, and then with eight vessels set sail himself to seek refuge with Evagoras in Cyprus, while the *Paralus* started for Athens with tidings of what had taken place.

Lysander, on his side, conveyed the ships and prisoners and all other spoil back to Lampsacus, having on board some of the Athenian generals, notably Philocles and Adeimantus. On the very day of these achievements he despatched Theopompus, a Milesian privateersman, to Lacedæmon to report what had taken place. This envoy arrived within three days and delivered his message. Lysander's next step was to convene the allies and bid them deliberate as to the treatment of the prisoners. Many were the accusations here levied against the Athenians. There was talk of crimes committed against the law of Hellas, and of cruelties sanctioned by popular decrees; which, had they conquered in the late sea-fight, would have been carried out; such as the proposal to cut off the right hand of every prisoner taken alive, and lastly the ill-treatment of two captured men-of-war, a Corinthian and an Andrian vessel, when every man on board had been hurled headlong down the cliff. Philocles was the very general who had so ruthlessly destroyed those men. Many other tales were told; and at length a resolution was passed to put all the Athenian prisoners, with the exception of Adeimantus, to death. He alone, it was pleaded, had taken exception to the proposal to cut off the prisoners' hands. On the other hand, he was himself accused by some people of having betrayed the fleet.

As to Philocles, Lysander put to him one question, as the officer who had thrown the Corinthians and Andrians down the cliff: What fate did the man deserve to suffer who had embarked on so cruel a course of illegality against Hellenes? and so delivered him to the executioner.

When he had set the affairs of Lampsacus in order, Lysander sailed to Byzantium and Chalcedon, where the inhabitants, having first dismissed the Athenian garrison under a flag of truce, admitted him within their walls. Those citizens of Byzantium, who had betrayed Byzantium into the hands of Alcibiades, fled as exiles into Pontus, but subsequently betaking themselves to Athens, became Athenian citizens. In dealing with the Athenian garrisons, and indeed with all Athenians wheresoever found, Lysander made it a rule to give them safe conduct to Athens, and to Athens only, in the certainty that the larger the number collected within the city and Piræus, the more quickly the want of the necessaries of life would make itself felt. And now, leaving Sthenelaus, a Laconian, as governor-general of Byzantium and Chalcedon, he sailed back himself to Lampsacus and devoted himself to refitting his ships.

It was night when the *Paralus* reached Athens with her evil tidings, on receipt of which a bitter wail of woe broke forth. From Piræus, following the line of the long walls up to the heart of the city, it swept and swelled, as each man to his neighbour passed on the news. On that night no man slept. There was mourning and sorrow for those that were lost, but the lamentation for the dead was merged in even deeper sorrow for themselves, as they pictured the evils they were about to suffer, the like of which they had themselves inflicted upon the men of Melos, who were colonists of the Lacedæmonians, when they mastered them by siege. Or on the men of Histiæa; on Scione and Torone; on the Æginetans, and many

another Hellene city. On the following day the public assembly met, and, after debate, it was resolved to block up all the harbours save one, to put the walls in a state of defence, to post guards at various points, and to make all other necessary preparations for a siege. Such were the concerns of the men of Athens.

Lysander presently left the Hellespont with two hundred sail and arrived at Lesbos, where he established a new order of things in Mitylene and the other cities of the island. Meanwhile he despatched Eteonicus with a squadron of ten ships to the northern coasts, where that officer brought about a revolution of affairs which placed the whole region in the hands of Lacedæmon. Indeed, in a moment of time, after the sea-fight, the whole of Hellas had revolted from Athens, with the solitary exception of the men of Samos. These, having massacred the notables, held the state under their control. After a while Lysander sent messages to Agis at Deceleia, and to Lacedæmon, announcing his approach with a squadron of two hundred sail.

In obedience to a general order of Pausanias, the other king of Lacedæmon, a levy in force of the Lacedæmonians and all the rest of Peloponnesus, except the Argives, was set in motion for a campaign. As soon as the several contingents had arrived, the king put himself at their head and marched against Athens, encamping in the gymnasium of the Academy, as it is called. Lysander had now reached Ægina, where, having got together as many of the former inhabitants as possible, he formally reinstated them in their city; and what he did in behalf of the Æginetans, he did also in behalf of the Melians, and of the rest who had been deprived of their countries. He then pillaged the island of Salamis, and finally came to moorings off Piræus with one hundred and fifty ships of the line, and established a strict blockade against all merchant ships entering that harbour.

The Athenians, finding themselves besieged by land and sea, were in sore perplexity what to do. Without ships, without allies, without provisions, the belief gained hold upon them that there was no way of escape. They must now, in their turn, suffer what they had themselves inflicted upon others; not in retaliation, indeed, for ills received, but out of sheer insolence, overriding the citizens of petty states, and for no better reason than that these were allies of the very men now at their gates. In this frame of mind they enfranchised those who at any time had lost their civil rights, and schooled themselves to endurance; and, albeit many succumbed to starvation, no thought of truce or reconciliation with their foes was breathed. But when the stock of corn was absolutely insufficient, they sent an embassage to Agis, proposing to become allies of the Lacedæmonians on the sole condition of keeping their fortification walls and Piræus; and to draw up articles of treaty on these terms. Agis bade them betake themselves to Lacedæmon, seeing that he had no authority to act himself. With this answer the ambassadors returned to Athens, and were forthwith sent on to Lacedæmon. On reaching Sellasia, a town in Laconian territory, they waited till they got their answer from the ephors, who, having learnt their terms (which were identical with those already proposed to Agis), bade them instantly to be gone, and, if they really desired peace, to come with other proposals, the fruit of happier reflection. Thus the ambassadors returned home, and reported the result of their embassage, whereupon despondency fell upon all. It was a painful reflection that in the end they would be sold into slavery; and meanwhile, pending the return of a second embassy, many must needs fall victims to starvation. The razing of their fortifications was not a solution which any one cared to recommend. A senator, Archestratus, had indeed put the question in the senate, whether it were not best to make peace with the Lacedæmonians on such terms as they were willing to propose; but he was thrown into prison. The Laconian proposals referred to involved the destruction of both long walls for a space of more than a mile. And a decree had been passed making it illegal to submit any such proposition about the walls. Things having reached this pass, Theramenes made a proposal in the public assembly as follows: If they would choose to send him as ambassador to Lysander, he would go and find out why the Lacedæmonians were so unyielding about the walls; whether it was they really intended to enslave the city, or merely they wanted a guarantee of good faith. Despatched accordingly, he lingered on with Lysander for three whole months and more, watching for the time when the Athenians, at the last pinch of starvation, would be willing to accede to any terms that might be offered. At last, in the fourth month, he returned and reported to the public assembly that Lysander had detained him all this while, and had ended by bidding him betake himself to Lacedæmon, since he had no authority himself to answer his questions, which must be addressed directly to the ephors. After this Theramenes was chosen with nine others to go to Lacedæmon as ambassador with full powers. Meanwhile Lysander had sent an Athenian exile, named Aristoteles, in company of certain Lacedæmonians, to Sparta to report to the board of ephors how he had answered Theramenes, that they, and they alone, had supreme authority in matters of peace and war.

Theramenes and his companions presently reached Sellasia, and being questioned as to the reason of their visit, replied that they had full powers to treat of peace. After which the ephors ordered them to be summoned to their presence. On their arrival a general assembly was convened, in which the Corinthians and Thebans more particularly, though their views were shared by many other Hellenes also, urged the meeting not to come to terms with the Athenians, but to destroy them. The Lacedæmonians replied that they would never reduce to slavery a city which was itself an integral portion of Hellas, and had performed a great and noble service to Hellas in the most perilous of emergencies. On the contrary, they were willing to offer peace on the terms now specified—namely, "That the long walls and the fortifications of Piræus should be destroyed; that the Athenian fleet, with the exception of twelve vessels, should be surrendered; that the exiles should be restored; and lastly, that the Athenians should acknowledge the leadership of Sparta in peace and war, leaving to her the choice of friends and foes, and following her lead by land and sea." Such were the terms which Theramenes and the rest who acted with him were able to report on their return to Athens. As they entered the city, a vast crowd met them, trembling lest their mission should have proved fruitless. For indeed delay was no longer possible, so long already was the list of victims daily perishing from starvation. On the day following, the ambassadors delivered their report, stating the terms upon which the Lacedæmonians were willing to make peace. Theramenes acted as spokesman, insisting that they ought to obey the Lacedæmonians and pull down the walls. A small minority raised their voice in opposition, but the majority were strongly in favour of the proposition, and the resolution was passed to accept the peace. After that, Lysander sailed into the Piræus, and the exiles were readmitted. And so they fell to levelling the fortifications and walls with much enthusiasm, to the accompaniment of female flute-players, deeming that day the beginning of liberty to Greece.

—H. G. DAKYNS.

III. SPIRITUAL AND MORAL PROBLEMS

Tragedy was an outgrowth of the special form of choral lyric known as the dithyramb, a convivial song associated with the worship of Dionysus. The chorus producing a dithyramb was composed of satyrs, persons clad in goat costume—whence the name "tragedy," meaning "goat-song." The first step towards dramatic representation of the subject of the song was taken by Thespis in 534 B.C., when he appeared as a reciter of verses distinct from, but addressed to, the chorus of satyrs. He employed for his recitation the Ionic iambic verse, while the chorus still retained the Dorian choral lyric form. The later drama continued this use of the one form for the dialogue and the other for the choral lyrics. The introduction by Æschylus of a second actor distinct from the chorus was the development which brought about the essential change from song and narrative to drama, since it made possible dialogue and action. Gradually, but rapidly in point of time, the line of demarkation between the chorus on the one hand and the dialogue on the other became more and more pronounced. At first the chorus still carried the major part of the whole production, then it was subordinated to a position secondary to that of the actors, until finally it became little more than an interested hearer and onlooker interrupting the action to comment and interpret. The introduction of a third actor by Sophocles hastened this development, since it increased the opportunity for complex action and dramatic situation and quickened the interchange of dialogue.

Tragedy drew its subject matter from epic, dealing almost exclusively with the well known myths related in narrative poetry. Occasionally it treated of an historical and contemporary theme, but the dim past of legend and the heroic figures, gods and men, of ancient story were looked upon as the most appropriate material. Tragedy is thus a natural development, practically a welding together, into a new form, of the epic, the lyric and choral song of earlier days.

That the writers of tragedy gave it a moral and religious significance was due to the dramatic handling of their material rather than to an intention on the part of the poets to discuss and solve such problems. In the first instance the artist was concerned with making a thing of beauty. But as he unfolded his story, not through narration but through the action and speech of living characters, he was inevitably led into questions of the meaning of such action—the relation of man to the gods and to his environment and circumstances. What the Greeks of that era thought about such things can therefore be learned from their tragic poets as clearly as from their philosophers.

AGAMEMNON

ÆSCHYLUS

A Greek tragedy concentrates absolutely upon a single theme. It has but one plot to unfold, one issue to resolve, one climax to achieve. The *Agamemnon* (458 B.C.) is a perfect example. Not a word is spoken by any of the characters which does not bear more or less directly upon the murder of the king. The tragedy is the first of a trilogy known as the *Oresteia,* whose other two members are the *Choephoræ* (Libation-bearers) and the *Eumenides* (Furies). The whole represents Æschylus' interpretation of the meaning of sin. Sin is not a matter of chance, nor of the whims and jealousies of the gods; it is grounded in the logic of

life. Crime begets crime, sin is the child of sin, and the only escape from crime and sin is to be found in complete submission to the divine will. For Æschylus, see above, p. 172.

CHARACTERS

A WATCHMAN.	A HERALD.
CHORUS.	AGAMEMNON.
CLYTEMNESTRA.	CASSANDRA.
ÆGISTHUS.	

The Scene is the Palace of Atreus at Mycenæ. In front of the Palace stand statues of the gods, and altars prepared for sacrifices.

A WATCHMAN. I pray the gods to quit me of my toils,
To close the watch I keep, this livelong year;
For as a watch-dog lying, not at rest,
Propped on one arm, upon the palace roof
Of Atreus' race, too long, too well I know
The starry conclave of the midnight sky,
Too well, the splendors of the firmament,
The lords of light, whose kingly aspect shows—
What time they set or climb the sky in turn—
The year's divisions, bringing frost or fire.

And now, as ever, am I set to mark
When shall stream up the glow of signal-flame,
The bale-fire bright, and tell its Trojan tale—
Troy town is ta'en: such issue holds in hope
She in whose woman's breast beats heart of man.

Thus upon mine unrestful couch I lie,
Bathed with the dews of night, unvisited
By dreams—ah me!—for in the place of sleep

Stands Fear as my familiar, and repels
The soft repose that would mine eyelids
   seal.

And if at whiles, for the lost balm of
   sleep,
I medicine my soul with melody
Of trill or song—anon to tears I turn,
Wailing the woe that broods upon this
   home,
Not now by honor guided as of old.

But now at last fair fall the welcome
   hour
That sets me free, whene'er the thick
   night glow
With beacon-fire of hope deferred no
   more.
All hail!
    *(A beacon-light is seen reddening
     the distant sky.)*
Fire of the night, that brings my spirit
   day,
Shedding on Argos light, and dance, and
   song,
Greetings to fortune, hail!

Let my loud summons ring within the
   ears
Of Agamemnon's queen, that she anon
Start from her couch and with a shrill
   voice cry
A joyous welcome to the beacon-blaze,
For Ilion's fall; such fiery message
   gleams
From yon high flame; and I, before the
   rest,
Will foot the lightsome measure of our
   joy;
For I can say, *My master's dice fell
   fair—*
*Behold! the triple sice, the lucky
   flame!*
Now be my lot to clasp, in loyal love,
The hand of him restored, who rules our
   home:
Home—but I say no more: upon my
   tongue
Treads hard the ox o' the adage.

                 Had it voice,
The home itself might soothliest tell its
   tale;
I, of set will, speak words the wise may
   learn,
To others, nought remember nor discern.
    *(Exit. The chorus of old men of
     Mycenæ enter, each leaning on
     a staff. During their song* CLY-
     TEMNESTRA *appears in the back-
     ground, kindling the altars.)*
   CHORUS.   Ten livelong years have
     rolled away,
Since the twin lords of sceptered sway,
By Zeus endowed with pride of place,
The doughty chiefs of Atreus' race,
   Went forth of yore,
To plead with Priam, face to face,
   Before the judgment-seat of War!

A thousand ships from Argive land
Put forth to bear the martial band,
That with a spirit stern and strong
Went out to right the kingdom's
    wrong—
Pealed, as they went, the battle-song,
Wild as the vultures' cry;
When o'er the eyrie, soaring high,
In wild bereavèd agony,
Around, around, in airy rings,
They wheel with oarage of their wings,
But not the eyas-brood behold,
That called them to the nest of old;
But let Apollo from the sky,
Or Pan, or Zeus, but hear the cry,
The exile cry, the wail forlorn,
Of birds from whom their home is torn—
On those who wrought the rapine fell,
Heaven sends the vengeful fiends of hell.

Even so doth Zeus, the jealous lord
And guardian of the hearth and board,
Speed Atreus' sons, in vengeful ire,
'Gainst Paris—sends them forth on fire,
Her to buy back, in war and blood,
Whom one did wed but many woo'd!
And many, many, by his will,
The last embrace of foes shall feel,
And many a knee in dust be bowed,

And splintered spears on shields ring
  loud,
Of Trojan and of Greek, before
That iron bridal-feast be o'er!
But as he willed 't is ordered all,
And woes, by Heaven ordained, must
  fall—
Unsoothed by tears or spilth of wine
Poured forth too late, the wrath divine
Glares vengeance on the flameless shrine.

And we in gray dishonored eld,
Feeble of frame, unfit were held
To join the warrior array
That then went forth unto the fray:
And here at home we tarry, fain
Our feeble footsteps to sustain,
Each on his staff—so strength doth wane,
And turns to childishness again.
For while the sap of youth is green,
And, yet unripened, leaps within,
The young are weakly as the old,
And each alike unmeet to hold
The vantage post of war!
And ah! when flower and fruit are o'er,
And on life's tree the leaves are sere,
Age wendeth propped its journey drear,
As forceless as a child, as light
And fleeting as a dream of night
Lost in the garish day!

But thou, O child of Tyndareus,
Queen Clytemnestra, speak! and say
What messenger of joy to-day
Hath won thine ear? what welcome news,
That thus in sacrificial wise
E'en to the city's boundaries
Thou biddest altar-fires arise?
Each god who doth our city guard,
And keeps o'er Argos watch and ward
From heaven above, from earth below—
The mighty lords who rule the skies,
The market's lesser deities,
To each and all the altars glow,
Piled for the sacrifice!
And here and there, anear, afar,
Streams skyward many a beacon-star,
Conjur'd and charm'd and kindled well
By pure oil's soft and guileless spell,

Hid now no more
Within the palace' secret store.

O queen, we pray thee, whatsoe'er,
Known unto thee, were well revealed,
That thou wilt trust it to our ear,
And bid our anxious heart be healed!
That waneth now unto despair—
Now, waxing to a presage fair,
Dawns, from the altar, Hope—to scare
From our rent hearts the vulture Care.

List! for the power is mine, to chant on
  high
The chiefs' emprise, the strength that
  omens gave!
List! on my soul breathes yet a harmony,
From realms of ageless powers, and
  strong to save!

How brother kings, twin lords of one
  command,
Led forth the youth of Hellas in their
  flower,
Urged on their way, with vengeful spear
  and brand,
By warrior-birds, that watched the parting hour.

Go forth to Troy, the eagles seemed to
  cry—
And the sea-kings obeyed the sky-kings'
  word,
When on the right they soared across the
  sky,
And one was black, one bore a white tail
  barred.
High o'er the palace were they seen to
  soar,
Then lit in sight of all, and rent and tare,
Far from the fields that she should range
  no more,
Big with her unborn brood, a mother-
  hare.

And one beheld, the soldier-prophet true,
And the two chiefs, unlike of soul and
  will,

In the twy-colored eagles straight he
knew,
And spake the omen forth, for good and
ill.

(Ah, woe and well-a-day! but be the
issue fair!)

*Go forth, he cried, and Priam's town shall
fall.*
*Yet long the time shall be; and flock and
herd,*
*The people's wealth, that roam before
the wall,*
*Shall force hew down, when Fate shall
give the word.*

But O beware! lest wrath in heaven abide,
*To dim the glowing battle-forge once
more,*
*And mar the mighty curb of Trojan
pride,*
*The steel of vengeance, welded as for
war!*

For virgin Artemis bears jealous hate
Against the royal house, the eagle-pair,
Who rend the unborn brood, insatiate—
*Yea, loathes their banquet on the quiver-
ing hare.*

(Ah, woe and well-a-day! but be the
issue fair!)

*For well she loves—the goddess kind and
mild—*
*The tender new-born cubs of lions
bold,*
*Too weak to range—and well the sucking
child*
*Of every beast that roams by wood and
wold.*

*So to the Lord of Heaven she prayeth
still,*
"Nay, if it must be, be the omen true!
Yet do the visioned eagles presage ill;
*The end be well, but crossed with evil
too!"*

Healer Apollo! be her wrath controll'd,
*Nor weave the long delay of thwarting
gales,*
*To war against the Danaans and with-
hold*
*From the free ocean-waves their eager
sails!*

She craves, alas! to see a second life
Shed forth, a curst unhallowed sacrifice—
'Twixt wedded souls, artificer of strife,
*And hate that knows not fear, and fell
device.*

*At home there tarries like a lurking
snake,*
Biding its time, a wrath unreconciled,
A wily watcher, passionate to slake,
*In blood, resentment for a murdered
child.*

Such was the mighty warning, pealed of
yore—
Amid good tidings, such the word of
fear,
What time the fateful eagles hovered o'er
The kings, and Calchas read the omen
clear.

(In strains like his, once more,
Sing woe and well-a-day! but be the
issue fair)

Zeus—if to The Unknown
That name of many names seem good—
Zeus, upon Thee I call.
Thro' the mind's every road
I passed, but vain are all,
Save that which names thee Zeus, the
Highest One,
Were it but mine to cast away the load,
The weary load, that weighs my spirit
down.

He that was Lord of old,
In full-blown pride of place and valor
bold,
Hath fallen and is gone, even as an old
tale told!

And he that next held sway,
By stronger grasp o'erthrown
Hath pass'd away!
And whoso now shall bid the triumph-
chant arise
To Zeus, and Zeus alone,
He shall be found the truly wise.
'T is Zeus alone who shows the perfect
way
Of knowledge: He hath ruled,
Men shall learn wisdom, by affliction
schooled.

In visions of the night, like dropping
rain,
Descend the many memories of pain
Before the spirit's sight: through tears
and dole
Comes wisdom o'er the unwilling soul—
A boon, I wot, of all Divinity,
That holds its sacred throne in strength,
above the sky!

And then the elder chief, at whose com-
mand
The fleet of Greece was manned,
Cast on the seer no word of hate,
But veered before the sudden breath of
Fate—

Ah, weary while! for, ere they put forth
sail,
Did every store, each minish'd vessel,
fail,
While all the Achæan host
At Aulis anchored lay,
Looking across to Chalcis and the coast
Where refluent waters welter, rock, and
sway;
And rife with ill delay
From northern Strymon blew the thwart-
ing blast—
Mother of famine fell,
That holds men wand'ring still
Far from the haven where they fain
would be!—
And pitiless did waste
Each ship and cable, rotting on the sea,

And, doubling with delay each weary
hour,
Withered with hope deferred th'
Achæan's warlike flower.

But when, for bitter storm, a deadlier
relief,
And heavier with ill to either chief,
Pleading the ire of Artemis, the seer
avowed,
The two Atridæ smote their sceptres on
the plain,
And, striving hard, could not their tears
restrain!
And then the elder monarch spake
aloud—
Ill lot were mine, to disobey!
And ill, to smite my child, my house-
hold's love and pride!
To stain with virgin blood a father's
hands, and slay
My daughter, by the altar's side!
'Twixt woe and woe I dwell—
I dare not like a recreant fly,
And leave the league of ships, and fail
each true ally;
For rightfully they crave, with eager fiery
mind,
The virgin's blood, shed forth to lull the
adverse wind—
God send the deed be well!

Thus on his neck he took
Fate's hard compelling yoke;
Then, in the counter-gale of will abhorr'd,
accursed,
To recklessness his shifting spirit
veered—
Alas! that Frenzy, first of ills and worst,
With evil craft men's souls to sin hath
ever stirred!

And so he steeled his heart—ah, well-a-
day—
Aiding a war for one false woman's sake,
His child to slay,
And with her spilt blood make
An offering, to speed the ships upon their
way!

Lusting for war, the bloody arbiters
Closed heart and ears, and would not
    hear nor heed
The girl-voice plead,
Pity me, Father! nor her prayers,
Nor tender, virgin years.

So, when the chant of sacrifice was done,
Her father bade the youthful priestly
    train
Raise her, like some poor kid, above the
    altar-stone,
From where amid her robes she lay
Sunk all in swoon away—
Bade them, as with the bit that mutely
    tames the steed,
Her fair lips' speech refrain,
Lest she should speak a curse on Atreus'
    home and seed.

So, trailing on the earth her robe of
    saffron dye,
With one last piteous dart from her be-
    seeching eye
Those that should smite she smote—
Fair, silent, as a pictur'd form, but fain
To plead, *Is all forgot?*
How oft those halls of old,
Wherein my sire high feast did hold,
Rang to the virginal soft strain,
When I, a stainless child,
Sang from pure lips and undefiled,
Sang of my sire, and all
His honored life, and how on him should
    fall
Heaven's highest gift and gain!
And then—but I beheld not, nor can tell,
What further fate befell:
But this is sure, that Calchas' boding
    strain
Can ne'er be void or vain.
This wage from Justice' hand do sufferers
    earn,
The future to discern:
And yet—farewell, O secret of To-
    morrow!
Fore-knowledge is fore-sorrow.
Clear with the clear beams of the mor-
    row's sun,

The future presseth on.
Now, let the house's tale, how dark
    soe'er,
Find yet an issue fair!—
So prays the loyal, solitary band
That guards the Apian land.
        (*They turn to* CLYTEMNESTRA,
        who leaves the altars and comes
        forward.)
O queen, I come in reverence of thy
    sway—
For, while the ruler's kingly seat is void,
The loyal heart before his consort bends.
Now—be it sure and certain news of
    good,
Or the fair tidings of a flatt'ring hope,
That bids thee spread the light from
    shrine to shrine,
I, fain to hear, yet grudge not if thou
    hide.
    CLYTEMNESTRA. As saith the adage,
    From the womb of Night
Springs forth, with promise fair, the young
    child Light.
Aye—fairer even than all hope my
    news—
By Grecian hands is Priam's city ta'en!
    CHORUS. What say'st thou? doubtful
    heart makes treach'rous ear.
    CLYTEMNESTRA. Hear then again, and
    plainly—Troy is ours!
    CHORUS. Thrills thro' my heart such
    joy as wakens tears.
    CLYTEMNESTRA. Aye, thro' those
    tears thine eye looks loyalty.
    CHORUS. But hast thou proof, to
    make assurance sure?
    CLYTEMNESTRA. Go to; I have—un-
    less the god has lied.
    CHORUS. Hath some night-vision won
    thee to belief?
    CLYTEMNESTRA. Out on all presage of
    a slumb'rous soul!
    CHORUS. But wert thou cheered by
    Rumor's wingless word?
    CLYTEMNESTRA. Peace—thou dost
    chide me as a credulous girl.
    CHORUS. Say then, how long ago the
    city fell?

CLYTEMNESTRA.   Even in this night that now brings forth the dawn.

CHORUS.   Yet who so swift could speed the message here?

CLYTEMNESTRA.   From Ida's top Hephæstus, lord of fire,
Sent forth his sign; and on, and ever on,
Beacon to beacon sped the courier-flame.
From Ida to the crag, that Hermes loves,
Of Lemnos; thence unto the steep sublime
Of Athos, throne of Zeus, the broad blaze flared.
Thence, raised aloft to shoot across the sea,
The moving light, rejoicing in its strength,
Sped from the pyre of pine, and urged its way,
In golden glory, like some strange new sun,
Onward, and reached Macistus' watching heights.
There, with no dull delay nor heedless sleep,
The watcher sped the tidings on in turn,
Until the guard upon Messapius' peak
Saw the far flame gleam on Euripus' tide,
And from the high-piled heap of withered furze
Lit the new sign and bade the message on.
Then the strong light, far-flown and yet undimned,
Shot thro' the sky above Asopus' plain,
Bright as the moon, and on Cithæron's crag
Aroused another watch of flying fire.
And there the sentinels no whit disowned,
But sent redoubled on, the hest of flame—
Swift shot the light, above Gorgopis' bay,
To Ægiplanctus' mount, and bade the peak
Fail not the onward ordinance of fire.
And like a long beard streaming in the wind,
Full-fed with fuel, roared and rose the blaze,
And onward flaring, gleamed above the cape,
Beneath which shimmers the Saronic bay,
And thence leapt light unto Arachne's peak,
The mountain watch that looks upon our town.
Thence to th' Atrides' roof—in lineage fair,
A bright posterity of Ida's fire.
So sped from stage to stage, fulfilled in turn,
Flame after flame, along the course ordained,
And lo! the last to speed upon its way
Sights the end first, and glows unto the goal.
And Troy is ta'en, and by this sign my lord
Tells me the tale, and ye have learned my word.

CHORUS.   To heaven, O queen, will I upraise new song:
But, wouldst thou speak once more, I fain would hear
From first to last the marvel of the tale.

CLYTEMNESTRA.   Think you — this very morn—the Greeks in Troy,
And loud therein the voice of utter wail!
Within one cup pour vinegar and oil,
And look! unblent, unreconciled, they war.
So in the twofold issue of the strife
Mingle the victor's shout, the captives' moan.
For all the conquered whom the sword has spared
Cling weeping—some unto a brother slain,
Some childlike to a nursing father's form,
And wail the loved and lost, the while their neck
Bows down already 'neath the captive's chain.
And lo! the victors, now the fight is done,
Goaded by restless hunger, far and wide

Range all disordered thro' the town, to
 snatch
Such victual and such rest as chance
 may give
Within the captive halls that once were
 Troy—
Joyful to rid them of the frost and dew,
Wherein they couched upon the plain of
 old—
Joyful to sleep the gracious night all
 through,
Unsummoned of the watching sentinel.
Yet let them reverence well the city's
 gods,
The lords of Troy, tho' fallen, and her
 shrines;
So shall the spoilers not in turn be
 spoiled.
Yea, let no craving for forbidden gain
Bid conquerors yield before the darts of
 greed.
For we need yet, before the race be won,
Homewards, unharmed, to round the
 course once more.
For should the host wax wanton ere it
 come,
Then, tho' the sudden blow of fate be
 spared,
Yet in the sight of gods shall rise once
 more
The great wrong of the slain, to claim
 revenge.
Now, hearing from this woman's mouth
 of mine,
The tale and eke its warning, pray with
 me,
*Luck sway the scale, with no uncertain
 poise,*
*For my fair hopes are changed to fairer
 joys.*
CHORUS. A gracious word thy woman's
 lips have told,
Worthy a wise man's utterance, O my
 queen;
Now with clear trust in thy convincing
 tale
I set me to salute the gods with song,
Who bring us bliss to counterpoise our
 pain.   (*Exit* CLYTEMNESTRA.)

Zeus, Lord of heaven! and welcome night
Of victory, that hast our might
With all the glories crowned!
On towers of Ilion, free no more,
Hast flung the mighty mesh of war,
And closely girt them round,
Till neither warrior may 'scape,
Nor stripling lightly overleap
The trammels as they close, and close,
Till with the grip of doom our foes
In slavery's coil are bound!

Zeus, Lord of hospitality,
.In grateful awe I bend to thee—
'T is thou hast struck the blow!
At Alexander, long ago,
We marked thee bend thy vengeful bow,
But long and warily withhold
The eager shaft, which, uncontrolled
And loosed too soon or launched too high,
Had wandered bloodless through the sky.

Zeus, the high God!—whate'er be dim in
 doubt,
This can our thought track out—
The blow that fells the sinner is of God,
And as he wills, the rod
Of vengeance smiteth sore. One said of
 old,
The gods list not to hold
A reckoning with him whose feet oppress
The grace of holiness—
An impious word! for whensoe'er the sire
Breathed forth rebellious fire—
What time his household overflowed the
 measure
Of bliss and health and treasure—
His children's children read the reckon-
 ing plain,
At last, in tears and pain.

On me let weal that brings no woe be
 sent,
And therewithal, content!
Who spurns the shrine of Right, nor
 wealth nor power
Shall be to him a tower,
To guard him from the gulf: there lies
 his lot,

Where all things are forgot.
Lust drives him on—lust, desperate and
  wild,
Fate's sin-contriving child—
And cure is none; beyond concealment
  clear,
Kindles sin's baleful glare.
As an ill coin beneath the wearing touch
Betrays by stain and smutch
Its metal false—such is the sinful wight.
Before, on pinions light,
Fair Pleasure flits, and lures him child-
  like on,
While home and kin make moan
Beneath the grinding burden of his
  crime;
Till, in the end of time,
Cast down of heaven, he pours forth
  fruitless prayer
To powers that will not hear.

And such did Paris come
Unto Atrides' home,
And thence, with sin and shame his wel-
  come to repay,
Ravished the wife away—
And she, unto her country and her kin
Leaving the clash of shields and spears
  and arming ships,
And bearing unto Troy destruction for
  a dower,
And overbold in sin,
Went fleetly thro' the gates, at midnight
  hour.
Oft from the prophets' lips
Moaned out the warning and the wail—
  Ah, woe!
Woe for the home, the home! and for
  the chieftains, woe!
Woe for the bride-bed, warm
Yet from the lovely limbs, the impress
  of the form
Of her who loved her lord, awhile ago!
And woe! for him who stands
Shamed, silent, unreproachful, stretch-
  ing hands
That find her not, and sees, yet will not
  see,
That she is far away!

And his sad fancy, yearning o'er the sea,
Shall summon and recall
Her wraith, once more to queen it in his
  hall.
And sad with many memories,
The fair cold beauty of each sculptured
  face—
And all to hatefulness is turned their
  grace,
Seen blankly by forlorn and hungering
  eyes!
And when the night is deep,
Come visions, sweet and sad, and bearing
  pain
Of hopings vain—
Void, void and vain, for scarce the sleep-
  ing sight
Has seen its old delight,
When thro' the grasps of love that bid it
  stay
It vanishes away
On silent wings that roam adown the
  ways of sleep.

Such are the sights, the sorrows fell,
About our hearth—and worse, whereof I
  may not tell.
But, all the wide town o'er,
Each home that sent its master far away
From Hellas' shore,
Feels the keen thrill of heart, the pang
  of loss, to-day.
For, truth to say,
The touch of bitter death is manifold!
Familiar was each face, and dear as
  life,
That went unto the war,
But thither, whence a warrior went of
  old,
Doth nought return—
Only a spear and sword, and ashes in an
  urn!
For Ares, lord of strife,
Who doth the swaying scales of battle
  hold,
War's money-changer, giving dust for
  gold,
Sends back, to hearts that held them
  dear,

Scant ash of warriors, wept with many a
    tear,
Light to the hand, but heavy to the soul;
Yea, fills the light urn full
With what survived the flame—
Death's dusty measure of a hero's frame!

Alas! one cries, and yet alas again!
Our chief is gone, the hero of the spear,
And hath not left his peer!
Ah, woe! another moans—*my spouse is*
    slain,
The death of honor, rolled in dust and
    blood,
Slain for a woman's sin, a false wife's
    shame!
Such muttered words of bitter mood
Rise against those who went forth to
    reclaim;
Yea, jealous wrath creeps on against th'
    Atrides' name.

And others, far beneath the Ilian wall,
Sleep their last sleep—the goodly chiefs
    and tall,
Couched in the foeman's land, whereon
    they gave
Their breath, and lords of Troy, each in
    his Trojan grave.

Therefore for each and all the city's
    breast
Is heavy with a wrath supprest,
As deep and deadly as a curse more loud
Flung by the common crowd:
And, brooding deeply, doth my soul await
Tidings of coming fate,
Buried as yet in darkness' womb.
For not forgetful is the high god's
    doom
Against the sons of carnage: all too long
Seems the unjust to prosper and be
    strong,
Till the dark Furies come,
And smite with stern reversal all his
    home,
Down into dim obstruction—he is gone,
And help and hope, among the lost, is
    none!

O'er him who vaunteth an exceeding
    fame,
Impends a woe condign;
The vengeful bolt upon his eyes doth
    flame.
Sped from the hand divine.
This bliss be mine, ungrudged of God,
    to feel—
To tread no city to the dust,
Nor see my own life thrust
Down to a slave's estate beneath an-
    other's heel!

Behold, throughout the city wide
Have the swift feet of Rumor hied,
Roused by the joyful flame:
But is the news they scatter, sooth?
Or haply do they give for truth
Some cheat which heaven doth frame?
A child were he and all unwise,
Who let his heart with joy be stirred,
To see the beacon-fires arise,
And then, beneath some thwarting word,
Sicken anon with hope deferred.
The edge of woman's insight still
Good news from true divideth ill;
Light rumors leap within the bound
That fences female credence round,
But, lightly born, as lightly dies
The tale that springs of her surmise.

Soon shall we know whereof the bale-
    fires tell,
The beacons, kindled with transmitted
    flame;
Whether, as well I deem, their tale is
    true,
Or whether like some dream delusive
    came
The welcome blaze but to befool our soul.
For lo! I see a herald from the shore
Draw hither, shadowed with the olive-
    wreath—
And thirsty dust, twin-brother of the
    clay,
Speaks plain of travel far and truthful
    news—
No dumb surmise, nor tongue of flame
    in smoke,

Fitfully kindled from the mountain pyre;
But plainlier shall his voice say, *All is
well,*
Or—but away, forebodings adverse, now,
And on fair promise fair fulfillment
come!
And whoso for the state prays otherwise,
Himself reap harvest of his ill desire!

Enter HERALD

HERALD. O land of Argos, fatherland
of mine!
To thee at last, beneath the tenth year's
sun,
My feet return; the bark of my em-
prise,
Tho' one by one hope's anchors broke
away,
Held by the last, and now rides safely
here.
Long, long my soul despaired to win, in
death,
Its longed-for rest within our Argive
land:
And now all hail, O earth, and hail to
thee,
New-risen sun! and hail our country's
God,
High-ruling Zeus, and thou, the Pythian
lord,
Whose arrows smote us once—smite thou
no more!
Was not thy wrath wreaked full upon our
heads,
O king Apollo, by Scamander's side?
Turn thou, be turned, be savior, healer,
now!
And hail, all gods who rule the street
and mart,
And Hermes hail! my patron and my
pride,
Herald of heaven, and lord of heralds
here!
And Heroes, ye who sped us on our
way—
To one and all I cry, *Receive again
With grace such Argives as the spear has
spared.*

Ah, home of royalty, belovèd halls,
And solemn shrines, and gods that front
the morn!
Benign as erst, with sun-flushed aspect
greet
The king returning after many days.
For as from night flash out the beams of
day,
So out of darkness dawns a light, a king,
On you, on Argos—Agamemnon comes.
Then hail and greet him well! such need
befits
Him whose right hand hewed down the
towers of Troy
With the great axe of Zeus who righteth
wrong—
And smote the plain, smote down to
nothingness
Each altar, every shrine; and far and
wide
Dies from the whole land's face its off-
spring fair.
Such mighty yoke of fate he set on
Troy—
Our lord and monarch, Atreus' elder son,
And comes at last with blissful honor
home;
Highest of all who walk on earth to-
day—
Not Paris nor the city's self that paid
Sin's price with him, can boast, *Whate'er
befall,
The guerdon we have won outweighs it
all.*
But at Fate's judgment-seat the robber
stands
Condemned of rapine, and his prey is
torn
Forth from his hands, and by his deed is
reaped
A bloody harvest of his home and land
Gone down to death, and for his guilt
and lust
His father's race pays double in the
dust.
CHORUS. Hail, herald of the Greeks,
new-come from war.
HERALD. All hail! not death itself can
fright me now.

CHORUS. Was thine heart wrung with longing for thy land?

HERALD. So that this joy doth brim mine eyes with tears.

CHORUS. On you, too, then, this sweet distress did fall—

HERALD. How say'st thou? make me master of thy word.

CHORUS. You longed for us who pined for you again.

HERALD. Craved the land us who craved it, love for love?

CHORUS. Yea, till my brooding heart moaned out with pain.

HERALD. Whence thy despair, that mars the army's joy?

CHORUS. *Sole cure of wrong is silence,* saith the saw.

HERALD. Thy kings afar, couldst thou fear other men?

CHORUS. Death had been sweet, as thou didst say but now.

HERALD. 'T is true; Fate smiles at last. Throughout our toil,
These many years, some chances issued fair,
And some, I wot, were checkered with a curse.
But who, on earth, hath won the bliss of heaven,
Thro' time's whole tenor an unbroken weal?
I could a tale unfold of toiling oars,
Ill rest, scant landings on a shore rock-strewn,
All pains, all sorrows, for our daily doom.
And worse and hatefuller our woes on land;
For where we couched, close by the foe-man's wall,
The river-plain was ever dank with dews,
Dropped from the sky, exuded from the earth,
A curse that clung unto our sodden garb,
And hair as horrent as a wild beast's fell.
Why tell the woes of winter, when the birds

Lay stark and stiff, so stern was Ida's snow?
Or summer scorch, what time the stirless wave
Sank to its sleep beneath the noonday sun?
Why mourn old woes? their pain has passed away;
And passed away, from those who fell, all care,
Forevermore, to rise and live again.
Why sum the count of death, and render thanks
For life by moaning over fate malign?
Farewell, a long farewell to all our woes!
To us, the remnant of the host of Greece,
Comes weal beyond all counterpoise of woe;
Thus boast we rightfully to yonder sun,
Like him far-fleeted over sea and land.
The Argive host prevailed to conquer Troy,
And in the temples of the gods of Greece
Hung up these spoils, a shining sign to Time.
Let those who learn this legend bless aright
The city and its chieftains, and repay
The meed of gratitude to Zeus who willed
And wrought the deed. So stands the tale fulfilled.

CHORUS. Thy words o'erbear my doubt: for news of good,
The ear of age hath ever youth enow;
But those within and Clytemnestra's self
Would fain hear all; glad thou their ears and mine.

Re-enter CLYTEMNESTRA

CLYTEMNESTRA. Last night, when first the fiery courier came,
In sign that Troy is ta'en and razed to earth,
So wild a cry of joy my lips gave out,
That I was chidden—*Hath the beacon watch*
Made sure unto thy soul the sack of Troy?

A very woman thou, whose heart leaps light
At wandering rumors!—and with words like these
They showed me how I strayed, misled of hope.
Yet on each shrine I set the sacrifice,
And, in the strain they held for feminine,
Went heralds thro' the city, to and fro,
With voice of loud proclaim, announcing joy;
And in each fane they lit and quenched with wine
The spicy perfumes fading in the flame.
All is fulfilled: I spare your longer tale—
The king himself anon shall tell me all.

Remains to think what honor best may greet
My lord, the majesty of Argos, home.
What day beams fairer on a woman's eyes
Than this, whereon she flings the portal wide,
To hail her lord, heaven-shielded, home from war?
This to my husband, that he tarry not,
But turn the city's longing into joy!
Yea, let him come, and coming may he find
A wife no other than he left her, true
And faithful as a watch-dog to his home,
His foemen's foe, in all her duties leal,
Trusty to keep for ten long years unmarred
The store whereon he set his master-seal.
Be steel deep-dyed, before ye look to see
Ill joy, ill fame, from other wight, in me!

HERALD. 'T is fairly said: thus speaks a noble dame,
Nor speaks amiss, when truth informs the boast.

(*Exit* CLYTEMNESTRA.)

CHORUS. So has she spoken—be it yours to learn
By clear interpreters her specious word.
Turn to me, herald,—tell me if anon
The second well-loved lord of Argos comes?

Hath Menelaus safely sped with you?

HERALD. Alas—brief boon unto my friends it were,
To flatter them, for truth, with falsehoods fair!

CHORUS. Speak joy, if truth be joy, but truth, at worst—
Too plainly, truth and joy are here divorced.

HERALD. The hero and his bark were rapt away
Far from the Grecian fleet—'t is truth I say.

CHORUS. Whether in all men's sight from Ilion borne,
Or from the fleet by stress of weather torn?

HERALD. Full on the mark thy shaft of speech doth light,
And one short word hath told long woes aright.

CHORUS. But say, what now of him each comrade saith?
What their forebodings, of his life or death?

HERALD. Ask me no more: the truth is known to none,
Save the earth-fostering, all-surveying Sun.

CHORUS. Say, by what doom the fleet of Greece was driven?
How rose, how sank the storm, the wrath of Heaven?

HERALD. Nay, ill it were to mar with sorrow's tale
The day of blissful news. The gods demand
Thanksgiving sundered from solicitude.
If one as herald came with rueful face
To say, *The curse has fallen, and the host*
Gone down to death; and one wide wound has reached
The city's heart, and out of many homes
Many are cast and consecrate to death,
Beneath the double scourge, that Ares loves,
The bloody pair, the fire and sword of doom—

If such sore burden weighed upon my
tongue,
'T were fit to speak such words as glad-
den fiends.
But—coming as he comes who bringeth
news
Of safe return from toil, and issues fair,
To men rejoicing in a weal restored—
Dare I to dash good words with ill, and
say
How the gods' anger smote the Greeks in
storm?
For fire and sea, that erst held bitter
feud,
Now swore conspiracy and pledged their
faith,
Wasting the Argives worn with toil and
war.
Night and great horror of the rising wave
Came o'er us, and the blasts that blow
from Thrace
Clashed ship with ship, and some with
plunging prow
Thro' scudding drifts of spray and raving
storm
Vanished, as strays by some ill shepherd
driven.
And when at length the sun rose bright,
we saw
Th' Ægean sea-field flecked with flowers
of death,
Corpses of Grecian men and shattered
hulls.
For us, indeed, some god 'twas, well I
deem,
No human power, laid hand upon our
helm,
Snatched us or prayed us from the powers
of air,
And brought our bark thro' all, unharmed in hull:
And saving Fortune sat and steered us
fair,
So that no surge should gulf us deep in
brine,
Nor grind our keel upon a rocky shore.

So 'scaped we death that lurks beneath
the sea,
But, under day's white light, mistrustful
all
Of Fortune's smile, we sat and brooded
deep,
Shepherds forlorn of thoughts that wan-
dered wild,
O'er this new woe; for smitten was our
host,
And lost as ashes scattered from the
pyre.
Of whom if any draw his life-breath yet,
Be well assured, he deems of us as
dead,
As we of him no other fate forebode.
But Heaven save all! If Menelaus live,
He will not tarry, but will surely come:
Therefore if anywhere the high sun's ray
Descries him upon earth, preserved by
Zeus,
Who wills not yet to wipe his race away,
Hope still there is that homeward he may
wend.
Enough—thou hast the truth unto the
end.

(*Exit* HERALD)

CHORUS. Say, from whose lips the
presage fell?
Who read the future all too well,
And named her, in her natal hour,
Helen, the bride with war for dower?
'T was one of the Invisible,
Guiding his tongue with prescient power.
On fleet, and host, and citadel,
War, sprung from her, and death did
lour,
When from the bride-bed's fine-spun
veil
She to the Zephyr spread her sail.
Strong blew the breeze—the surge closed
o'er
The cloven track of keel and oar,
But while she fled, there drove along,
Fast in her wake, a mighty throng—
Athirst for blood, athirst for war,
Forward in fell pursuit they sprung,
Then leapt on Simois' bank ashore,
The leafy coppices among—
No rangers, they, of wood and field,
But huntsmen of the sword and shield.

Heaven's jealousy, that works its will,
Sped thus on Troy its destined ill,
Well named, at once, the Bride and
Bane;
And loud rang out the bridal strain;
But they to whom that song befell
Did turn anon to tears again;
Zeus tarries, but avenges still
The husband's wrong, the household's
stain!
He, the hearth's lord, brooks not to see
Its outraged hospitality.

Even now, and in far other tone,
Troy chants her dirge of mighty moan,
Woe upon Paris, woe and hate!
Who wooed his country's doom for
mate—
This is the burden of the groan,
Wherewith she wails disconsolate
The blood, so many of her own
Have poured in vain, to fend her fate;
Troy! thou hast fed and freed to roam
A lion-cub within thy home!

A suckling creature, newly ta'en
From mother's teat, still fully fain
Of nursing care; and oft caressed,
Within the arms, upon the breast,
Even as an infant, has it lain;
Or fawns and licks, by hunger pressed,
The hand that will assuage its pain;
In life's young dawn, a well-loved guest,
A fondling for the children's play,
A joy unto the old and gray.

But waxing time and growth betrays
The blood-thirst of the lion-race,
And, for the house's fostering care,
Unbidden all, it revels there,
And bloody recompense repays—
Rent flesh of kine, its talons tare:
A mighty beast, that slays, and slays,
And mars with blood the household fair,
A God-sent pest invincible,
A minister of fate and hell.

Even so to Ilion's city came by stealth
A spirit as of windless seas and skies,

A gentle phantom-form of joy and
wealth,
With love's soft arrows speeding from its
eyes—
Love's rose, whose thorn doth pierce the
soul in subtle wise.

Ah, well-a-day! the bitter bridal-bed,
When the fair mischief lay by Paris'
side!
What curse on palace and on people sped
With her, the Fury sent on Priam's
pride,
By angered Zeus! what tears of many a
widowed bride!

Long, long ago to mortals this was told,
How sweet security and blissful state
Have curses for their children—so men
hold—
And for the man of all-too prosperous
fate
Springs from a bitter seed some woe
insatiate.

Alone, alone, I deem far otherwise;
Not bliss nor wealth it is, but impious
deed,
From which that after-growth of ill doth
rise!
Woe springs from wrong, the plant is like
the seed—
While Right, in Honor's house, doth its
own likeness breed.
Some past impiety, some gray old crime,
Breeds the young curse, that wantons in
our ill,
Early or late, when haps th' appointed
time—
And out of light brings power of dark-
ness still,
A master-fiend, a foe, unseen, invincible;

A pride accursed, that broods upon the
race
And home in which dark Atè holds her
sway—
Sin's child and Woe's, that wears its
parents' face;

While Right in smoky cribs shines clear
    as day,
And decks with weal his life, who walks
    the righteous way.

From gilded halls, that hands polluted
    raise,
Right turns away with proud averted
    eyes,
And of the wealth, men stamp amiss with
    praise,
Heedless, to poorer, holier temples hies,
And to Fate's goal guides all, in its ap-
    pointed wise.

Hail to thee, chief of Atreus' race,
Returning proud from Troy subdued!
How shall I greet thy conquering face?
How nor a fulsome praise obtrude,
Nor stint the meed of gratitude?
For mortal men who fall to ill
Take little heed of open truth,
But seek unto its semblance still:
The show of weeping and of ruth
To the forlorn will all men pay,
But, of the grief their eyes display,
Nought to the heart doth pierce its
    way.
And, with the joyous, they beguile
Their lips unto a feignèd smile,
And force a joy, unfelt the while;
But he who as a shepherd wise
Doth know his flock, can ne'er misread
Truth in the falsehood of his eyes,
Who veils beneath a kindly guise
A lukewarm love in deed.
And thou, our leader—when of yore
Thou badest Greece go forth to war
For Helen's sake—I dare avow
That then I held thee not as now;
That to my vision thou didst seem
Dyed in the hues of disesteem.
I held thee for a pilot ill,
And reckless, of thy proper will,
Endowing others doomed to die
With vain and forced audacity!
Now from my heart, ungrudgingly,
To those that wrought, this word be
    said—

Well fall the labor ye have sped—
Let time and search, O king, declare
What men within thy city's bound
Were loyal to the kingdom's care,
And who were faithless found.

Enter AGAMEMNON *in a chariot,
    accompanied by* CASSANDRA.
    He speaks without descending

AGAMEMNON. First, as is meet, a
    king's All-hail be said
To Argos, and the gods that guard the
    land—
Gods who with me availed to speed us
    home,
With me availed to wring from Priam's
    town
The due of justice. In the court of
    heaven
The gods in conclave sat and judged the
    cause,
Not from a pleader's tongue, and at the
    close,
Unanimous into the urn of doom
This sentence gave, *On Ilion and her
    men,*
Death: and where hope drew nigh to
    pardon's urn
No hand there was to cast a vote therein.
And still the smoke of fallen Ilion
Rises in sight of all men, and the flame
Of Atè's hecatomb is living yet,
And where the towers in dusty ashes sink,
Rise the rich fumes of pomp and wealth
    consumed.
For this must all men pay unto the gods
The meed of mindful hearts and grati-
    tude:
For by our hands the meshes of revenge
Closed on the prey, and for one woman's
    sake
Troy trodden by the Argive monster
    lies—
The foal, the shielded band that leapt the
    wall,
What time with autumn sank the
    Pleiades.
Yea, o'er the fencing wall a lion sprang

Ravening, and lapped his fill of blood of
kings.
Such prelude spoken to the gods in full,
To you I turn, and to the hidden thing
Whereof ye spake but now: and in that
thought
I am as you, and what ye say, say I.
For few are they who have such inborn
grace,
As to look up with love, and envy not,
When stands another on the height of
weal.
Deep in his heart, whom jealousy hath
seized,
Her poison lurking doth enhance his
load;
For now beneath his proper woes he
chafes,
And sighs withal to see another's weal.

I speak not idly, but from knowledge
sure—
There be who vaunt an utter loyalty,
That is but as the ghost of friendship
dead,
A shadow in a glass, of faith gone by.
One only—he who went reluctant forth
Across the seas with me—Odysseus—he
Was loyal unto me with strength and will,
A trusty trace-horse bound unto my car.
Thus—be he yet beneath the light of day,
Or dead; as well I fear—I speak his
praise.

Lastly, whate'er be due to men or gods,
With joint debate, in public council held,
We will decide, and warily contrive
That all which now is well may so abide:
For that which haply needs the healer's
art,
That will we medicine, discerning well
If cautery or knife befit the time.

Now, to my palace and the shrines of
home,
I will pass in, and greet you first and fair,
Ye gods, who bade me forth, and home
again—
And long may Victory tarry in my train!

Enter CLYTEMNESTRA, *followed by maidens bearing purple robes*

CLYTEMNESTRA. Old men of Argos,
lieges of our realm,
Shame shall not bid me shrink lest ye
should see
The love I bear my lord. Such blushing fear
Dies at the last from hearts of human
kind.
From mine own soul and from no alien
lips,
I know and will reveal the life I bore,
Reluctant, through the lingering livelong
years,
The while my lord beleaguered Ilion's
wall.

First, that a wife sat sundered from her
lord,
In widowed solitude, was utter woe—
And woe, to hear how Rumor's many
tongues
All boded evil—woe, when he who came
And he who followed spake of ill on ill,
Keening *lost, lost, all lost!* thro' hall
and bower.
Had this my husband met so many
wounds,
As by a thousand channels Rumor told,
No network e'er was full of holes as he.
Had he been slain, as oft as tidings came
That he was dead, he well might boast
him now
A second Geryon of triple frame,
With triple robe of earth above him
laid—
For that below, no matter—triply dead,
Dead by one death for every form he
bore.
And thus distraught by news of wrath
and woe,
Oft for self-slaughter had I slung the
noose,
But others wrenched it from my neck
away.
Hence haps it that Orestes, thine and
mine,

The pledge and symbol of our wedded
troth,
Stands not beside us now, as he should
stand.
Nor marvel thou at this: he dwells with
one
Who guards him loyally; 't is Phocis'
king,
Strophius, who warned me erst, *Bethink
thee queen,*
*What woes of doubtful issue well may
fall!*
Thy lord in daily jeopardy at Troy,
While here a populace uncurbed may cry
*"Down with the council, down!" bethink
thee too,*
'T is the world's way to set a harder heel
On fallen power.
For thy child's absence, then,
Such mine excuse, no wily afterthought.
For me, long since the gushing fount of
tears
Is wept away; no drop is left to shed.
Dim are the eyes that ever watched till
dawn,
Weeping, the bale-fires, piled for thy
return,
Night after night unkindled. If I slept,
Each sound—the tiny humming of a
gnat
Roused me again, again, from fitful
dreams
Wherein I felt thee smitten, saw thee
slain,
Thrice for each moment of mine hour of
sleep.

All this I bore, and now, released from
woe,
I hail my lord as watch-dog of a fold,
As saving stay-rope of a storm-tossed
ship,
As column stout that holds the roof aloft,
As only child unto a sire bereaved,
As land beheld, past hope, by crews
forlorn,
As sunshine fair when tempest's wrath is
past,
As gushing spring to thirsty wayfarer.

So sweet it is to 'scape the press of pain.
With such salute I bid my husband hail!
Nor Heaven be wroth therewith! for long
and hard
I bore that ire of old.
Sweet lord, step forth,
Step from thy car, I pray—nay, not on
earth
Plant the proud foot, O king, that trod
down Troy!
Women! why tarry ye, whose task it is
To spread your monarch's path with tap-
estry?
Swift, swift, with purple strew his pas-
sage fair,
That justice lead him to a home, at last,
He scarcely looked to see.
For what remains,
Zeal unsubdued by sleep shall nerve my
hand
To work as right and as the gods com-
mand.
AGAMEMNON. Daughter of Leda,
watcher o'er my home,
Thy greeting well befits mine absence
long,
For late and hardly has it reached its
end.
Know, that the praise which honor bids
us crave,
Must come from others' lips, not from
our own:
See too that not in fashion feminine
Thou make a warrior's pathway delicate;
Not unto me, as to some Eastern lord,
Bowing thyself to earth, make homage
loud.
Strew not this purple that shall make
each step
An arrogance; such pomp beseems the
gods,
Not me. A mortal man to set his foot
On these rich dyes? I hold such pride
in fear,
And bid thee honor me as man, not god.
Fear not—such footcloths and all gauds
apart,
Loud from the trump of Fame my name
is blown.

cassandra

Best gift of Heaven it is, in glory's hour,
To think thereon with soberness: and
thou—
Bethink thee of the adage, *Call none
blest*
*Till peaceful death have crowned a life
of weal.*
'T is said: I fain would fare unvexed by
fear.

CLYTEMNESTRA. Nay, but unsay it—
thwart not thou my will!

AGAMEMNON. Know, I have said, and
will not mar my word.

CLYTEMNESTRA. Was it fear made
this meekness to the gods?

AGAMEMNON. If cause be cause, 't is
mine for this resolve.

CLYTEMNESTRA. What, think'st thou,
in thy place had Priam done?

AGAMEMNON. He surely would have
walked on broidered robes.

CLYTEMNESTRA. Then fear not thou
the voice of human blame.

AGAMEMNON. Yet mighty is the murmur of a crowd.

CLYTEMNESTRA. Shrink not from
envy, appanage of bliss.

AGAMEMNON. War is not woman's
part, nor war of words.

CLYTEMNESTRA. Yet happy victors
well may yield therein.

AGAMEMNON. Dost crave for triumph
in this petty strife?

CLYTEMNESTRA. Yield; of thy grace
permit me to prevail!

AGAMEMNON. Then, if thou wilt, let
some one stoop to loose
Swiftly these sandals, slaves beneath my
foot:
And stepping thus upon the sea's rich
dye,
I pray, *Let none among the gods look
down*
With jealous eye on me—reluctant all,
To trample thus and mar a thing of price,
Wasting the wealth of garments silver-
worth.
Enough hereof: and, for the stranger
maid,

Lead her within, but gently: God on
high
Looks graciously on him whom triumph's
hour
Has made not pitiless. None willingly
Wear the slave's yoke—and she, the
prize and flower
Of all we won, comes hither in my train,
Gift of the army to its chief and lord.
—Now, since in this my will bows down
to thine,
I will pass in on purples to my home.

CLYTEMNESTRA. A Sea there is—and
who shall stay its springs?
And deep within its breast, a mighty
store,
Precious as silver, of the purple dye,
Whereby the dipped robe doth its tint
renew.
Enough of such, O king, within thy halls
There lies, a store that cannot fail; but
I—
I would have gladly vowed unto the gods
Cost of a thousand garments trodden
thus
(Had once the oracle such gift required),
Contriving ransom for thy life preserved.
For while the stock is firm the foliage
climbs,
Spreading a shade, what time the dog-
star glows;
And thou, returning to thine hearth and
home,
Art as a genial warmth in winter hours,
Or as a coolness, when the lord of heaven
Mellows the juice within the bitter
grape.
Such boons and more doth bring into a
home
The present footstep of its proper lord.
Zeus, Zeus, Fulfillment's lord! my vows
fulfill,
And whatsoe'er it be, work forth thy will!
(*Exeunt all but* CASSANDRA *and
the* CHORUS.)

CHORUS. Wherefore forever on the
wings of fear
Hovers a vision drear
Before my boding heart? a strain,

Unbidden and unwelcome, thrills mine ear,
Oracular of pain.
Not as of old upon my bosom's throne
Sits Confidence, to spurn
Such fears, like dreams we know not to discern.
Old, old and gray long since the time has grown,
Which saw the linked cables moor
The fleet, when erst it came to Ilion's sandy shore;
And now mine eyes and not another's see
Their safe return.
Yet none the less in me
The inner spirit sings a boding song,
Self-prompted, sings the Furies' strain—
And seeks, and seeks in vain,
To hope and to be strong!

Ah! to some end of Fate, unseen, unguessed,
Are these wild throbbings of my heart and breast—
Yea, of some doom they tell—
Each pulse, a knell.
Lief, lief I were, that all
To unfulfillment's hidden realm might fall.

Too far, too far our mortal spirits strive,
Grasping at utter weal, unsatisfied—
Till the fell curse, that dwelleth hard beside,
Thrust down the sundering wall. Too fair they blow,
The gales that waft our bark on Fortune's tide!
Swiftly we sail, the sooner all to drive
Upon the hidden rock, the reef of woe.

Then if the hand of caution warily
Sling forth into the sea
Part of the freight, lest all should sink below,
From the deep death it saves the bark: even so,

Doom-laden though it be, once more may rise
His household, who is timely wise.

How oft the famine-stricken field
Is saved by God's large gift, the new year's yield!
But blood of man once spilled,
Once at his feet shed forth, and darkening the plain,—
Nor chant nor charm can call it back again.
So Zeus hath willed:
Else had he spared the leech Asclepius, skilled
To bring man from the dead: the hand divine
Did smite himself with death—a warning and a sign.

Ah me! if Fate, ordained of old,
Held not the will of gods constrained, controlled,
Helpless to us-ward, and apart—
Swifter than speech my heart
Had poured its presage out!
Now, fretting, chafing in the dark of doubt,
'T is hopeless to unfold
Truth, from fear's tangled skein; and, yearning to proclaim
Its thought, my soul is prophecy and flame.

Re-enter CLYTEMNESTRA

CLYTEMNESTRA. Get thee within thou too, Cassandra, go!
For Zeus to thee in gracious mercy grants
To share the sprinklings of the lustral bowl,
Beside the altar of his guardianship,
Slave among many slaves. What, haughty still?
Step from the car; Alcmena's son, 't is said,
Was sold perforce and bore the yoke of old.
Aye, hard it is, but if such fate befall,

'T is a fair chance to serve within a home
Of ancient wealth and power. An up-
start lord,
To whom wealth's harvest came beyond
his hope,
Is as a lion to his slaves, in all
Exceeding fierce, immoderate in sway.
Pass in: thou hearest what our ways will
be.
CHORUS. Clear unto thee, O maid, is
her command,
But thou—within the toils of Fate thou
art—
If such thy will, I urge thee to obey;
Yet I misdoubt thou dost nor hear nor
heed.
CLYTEMNESTRA. I wot—unless like
swallows she doth use
Some strange barbarian tongue from
oversea—
My words must speak persuasion to her
soul.
CHORUS. Obey: there is no gentler
way than this.
Step from the car's high seat and follow
her.
CLYTEMNESTRA. Truce to this boot-
less waiting here without!
I will not stay: beside the central shrine
The victims stand, prepared for knife and
fire—
Offerings from hearts beyond all hope
made glad.
Thou—if thou reckest aught of my com-
mand,
'T were well done soon: but if thy sense
be shut
From these my words, let thy barbarian
hand
Fulfill by gesture the default of speech.
CHORUS. No native is she, thus to
read thy words
Unaided: like some wild thing of the
wood,
New-trapped, behold! she shrinks and
glares on thee.
CLYTEMNESTRA. 'T is madness and
the rule of mind distraught,
Since she beheld her city sink in fire,

And hither comes, nor brooks the bit,
until
In foam and blood her wrath be champed
away.
See ye to her; unqueenly 't is for me,
Unheeded thus to cast away my words.
(*Exit* CLYTEMNESTRA.)
CHORUS. But with me pity sits in
anger's place.
Poor maiden, come thou from the car;
no way
There is but this—take up thy servitude.
CASSANDRA. Woe, woe, alas! Earth,
Mother Earth! and thou
Apollo, Apollo!
CHORUS. Peace! shriek not to the
bright prophetic god,
Who will not brook the suppliance of
woe.
CASSANDRA. Woe, woe, alas! Earth,
Mother Earth! and thou
Apollo, Apollo!
CHORUS. Hark, with wild curse she
calls anew on him,
Who stands far off and loathes the voice
of wail.
CASSANDRA. Apollo, Apollo!
God of all ways, but only Death's to me,
Once and again, O thou, Destroyer
named,
Thou hast destroyed me, thou, my love
of old!
CHORUS. She grows presageful of her
woes to come,
Slave tho' she be, instinct with prophecy.
CASSANDRA. Apollo, Apollo!
God of all ways, but only Death's to me,
O thou Apollo, thou Destroyer named!
What way hast led me, to what evil
home?
CHORUS. Know'st thou it not? The
home of Atreus' race:
Take these my words for sooth and ask
no more.
CASSANDRA. Home cursed of God!
Bear witness unto me,
Ye visioned woes within—
The blood-stained hands of them that
smite their kin—

The strangling noose, and, spattered o'er
With human blood, the reeking floor!
  CHORUS. How like a sleuth-hound
    questing on the track,
Keen-scented unto blood and death she
  hies!
  CASSANDRA. Ah! can the ghostly
    guidance fail,
Whereby my prophet-soul is onwards
  led?
Look! for their flesh the specter-children
  wail,
Their sodden limbs on which their father
  fed!
  CHORUS. Long since we knew of thy
    prophetic fame,—
But for those deeds we seek no prophet's
  tongue.
  CASSANDRA. God! 'tis another crime—
Worse than the storied woe of olden
  time,
Cureless, abhorred, that one is plotting
  here—
A shaming death, for those that should
  be dear!
Alas! and far away, in foreign land,
He that should help doth stand!
  CHORUS. I knew th' old tales, the city
    rings withal—
But now thy speech is dark, beyond my
  ken.
  CASSANDRA. O wretch, O purpose
    fell!
Thou for thy wedded lord
The cleansing wave hast poured—
A treacherous welcome!
              How the sequel tell?
Too soon 't will come, too soon, for now,
  even now,
She smites him, blow on blow!
  CHORUS. Riddles beyond my rede—I
    peer in vain
Thro' the dim films that screen the
  prophecy.
  CASSANDRA. God! a new sight! a net,
    a snare of hell,
Set by her hand—herself a snare more
  fell!
A wedded wife, she slays her lord,

Helped by another hand!
              Ye powers, whose hate
Of Atreus' home no blood can satiate,
Raise the wild cry above the sacrifice
  abhorred!
  CHORUS. Why biddest thou some
    fiend, I know not whom,
Shriek o'er the house? Thine is no
  cheering word.
Back to my heart in frozen fear I feel
My waning life-blood run—
The blood that round the wounding
  steel
Ebbs slow, as sinks life's parting sun—
Swift, swift and sure, some woe comes
  pressing on!
  CASSANDRA. Away, away—keep him
    away—
The monarch of the herd, the pasture's
  pride,
Far from his mate! In treach'rous
  wrath,
Muffling his swarthy horns, with secret
  scathe
She gores his fenceless side!
Hark! in the brimming bath,
The heavy plash—the dying cry—
Hark—in the laver—hark, he falls by
  treachery!
  CHORUS. I read amiss dark sayings
    such as thine,
Yet something warns me that they tell
  of ill.
O dark prophetic speech,
Ill tidings dost thou teach
Ever, to mortals here below!
Ever some tale of awe and woe
Thro' all thy windings manifold
Do we unriddle and unfold!
  CASSANDRA. Ah, well-a-day! the cup
    of agony,
Whereof I chant, foams with a draught
  for me.
Ah, lord, ah, leader, thou hast led me
  here—
Was 't but to die with thee whose doom
  is near?
  CHORUS. Distraught thou art, divinely
    stirred,

And wailest for thyself a tuneless lay,
As piteous as the ceaseless tale
Wherewith the brown melodious bird
Doth ever Itys! Itys! wail,
Deep-bowered in sorrow, all its little
life-time's day!
   CASSANDRA. Ah, for thy fate, O shrill-
voiced nightingale!
Some solace for thy woes did Heaven
afford,
Clothed thee with soft brown plumes, and
life apart from wail—
But for my death is edged the double-
biting sword!
   CHORUS. What pangs are these, what
fruitless pain,
Sent on thee from on high?
Thou chantest terror's frantic strain,
Yet in shrill measured melody.
How thus unerring canst thou sweep
along
The prophet's path of boding song?
   CASSANDRA. Woe, Paris, woe on thee! thy bridal joy
Was death and fire upon thy race and
Troy!
And woe for thee, Scamander's flood!
Beside thy banks, O river fair,
I grew in tender nursing care
From childhood unto maidenhood!
Now not by thine, but by Cocytus'
stream
And Acheron's banks shall ring my bod-
ing scream.
   CHORUS. Too plain is all, too plain!
A child might read aright thy fateful
strain.
Deep in my heart their piercing fang
Terror and sorrow set, the while I heard
That piteous, low, tender word,
Yet to mine ear and heart a crushing
pang.
   CASSANDRA. Woe for my city, woe for
Ilion's fall!
Father, how oft with sanguine stain
Streamed on thine altar-stone the blood
of cattle, slain
That Heaven might guard our wall!
But all was shed in vain.

Low lie the shattered towers whereas they
fell,
And I—ah burning heart!—shall soon
lie low as well.
   CHORUS. Of sorrow is thy song, of
sorrow still!
Alas, what power of ill
Sits heavy on thy heart and bids thee
tell
In tears of perfect moan thy deadly tale?
Some woe—I know not what—must
close thy piteous wail.
   CASSANDRA. List! for no more the
presage of my soul,
Bride-like, shall peer from its secluding
veil;
But as the morning wind blows clear the
east,
More bright shall blow the wind of
prophecy,
And as against the low bright line of
dawn
Heaves high and higher yet the rolling
wave,
So in the clearing skies of prescience
Dawns on my soul a further, deadlier
woe,
And I will speak, but in dark speech no
more.
Bear witness, ye, and follow at my side—
I scent the trail of blood, shed long
ago.
Within this house a choir abidingly
Chants in harsh unison the chant of ill;
Yea, and they drink, for more en-
hardened joy,
Man's blood for wine, and revel in the
halls,
Departing never, Furies of the home.
They sit within, they chant the primal
curse,
Each spitting hatred on that crime of
old,
The brother's couch, the love incestuous
That brought forth hatred to the ravisher.
Say, is my speech or wild and erring
now,
Or doth its arrow cleave the mark, in-
deed?

They called me once, *The prophetess of
lies,*
*The wandering hag, the pest of every
door*—
Attest ye now, *She knows in very sooth
The house's curse, the storied infamy.*

    CHORUS. Yet how should oath—how
    loyally soe'er
I swear it—aught avail thee? In good
    sooth,
My wonder meets thy claim: I stand
    amazed
That thou, a maiden born beyond the
    seas,
Dost as a native know and tell aright
Tales of a city of an alien tongue.

    CASSANDRA. That is my power—a
    boon Apollo gave.
    CHORUS. God though he were, yearn-
    ing for mortal maid?
    CASSANDRA. Aye! what seemed shame
    of old is shame no more.
    CHORUS. Such finer sense suits not
    with slavery.
    CASSANDRA. He strove to win me,
    panting for my love.
    CHORUS. Came ye by compact unto
    bridal joys?
    CASSANDRA. Nay—for I plighted troth,
    then foiled the god.
    CHORUS. Wert thou already dowered
    with prescience?
    CASSANDRA. Yea—prophetess to Troy
    of all her doom.
    CHORUS. How left thee, then, Apollo's
    wrath unscathed?
    CASSANDRA. I, false to him, seemed
    prophet false to all.
    CHORUS. Not so—to us at least thy
    words seem sooth.
    CASSANDRA. Woe for me, woe! Again
    the agony—
Dread pain that sees the future all too
    well
With ghastly preludes whirls and racks
    my soul.
Behold ye—yonder on the palace roof
The specter-children sitting—look, such
    things

As dreams are made on, phantoms as of
    babes,
Horrible shadows, that a kinsman's hand
Hath marked with murder, and their
    arms are full—
A rueful burden—see, they hold them up,
The entrails upon which their father fed!

For this, for this, I say there plots re-
    venge
A coward lion, couching in the lair—
Guarding the gate against my master's
    foot—
My master—mine—I bear the slave's
    yoke now.
And he, the lord of ships, who trod down
    Troy,
Knows not the fawning treachery of
    tongue
Of this thing false and dog-like—how
    her speech
Glozes and sleeks her purpose, till she
    win
By ill fate's favor the desirèd chance,
Moving like Atè to a secret end.
O aweless soul! the woman slays her
    lord—
Woman? what loathsome monster of the
    earth
Were fit comparison? The double
    snake—
Or Scylla, where she dwells, the seaman's
    bane,
Girt round about with rocks? some hag of
    hell,
Raving a truceless curse upon her kin?
Hark—even now she cries exultingly
The vengeful cry that tells of battle
    turned—
How fain, forsooth, to greet her chief
    restored!
Nay, then, believe me not: what skills
    belief
Or disbelief? Fate works its will—and
    thou
Wilt see and say in truth, *Her tale was
true.*

    CHORUS. Ah—'t is Thyestes' feast on
    kindred flesh—

I guess her meaning and with horror thrill,
Hearing no shadow'd hint of th' o'er-true tale,
But its full hatefulness: yet, for the rest,
Far from the track I roam, and know no more.

CASSANDRA. 'T is Agamemnon's doom thou shalt behold.

CHORUS. Peace, hapless woman, to thy boding words!

CASSANDRA. Far from my speech stands he who sains and saves.

CHORUS. Aye—were such doom at hand—which God forbid!

CASSANDRA. Thou prayest idly—these move swift to slay.

CHORUS. What man prepares a deed of such despite?

CASSANDRA. Fool! thus to read amiss mine oracles.

CHORUS. Deviser and device are dark to me.

CASSANDRA. Dark! all too well I speak the Grecian tongue.

CHORUS. Aye—but in thine, as in Apollo's strains,
Familiar is the tongue, but dark the thought.

CASSANDRA. Ah, ah, the fire! it waxes, nears me now—
Woe, woe for me, Apollo of the dawn!

Lo, how the woman-thing, the lioness
Couched with the wolf—her noble mate afar—
Will slay me, slave forlorn! Yea, like some witch,
She drugs the cup of wrath, that slays her lord,
With double death—his recompense for me!
Aye, 't is for me, the prey he bore from Troy,
That she hath sworn his death, and edged the steel!
Ye wands, ye wreaths that cling around my neck,
Ye showed me prophetess yet scorned of all—
I stamp you into death, or e'er I die—
Down, to destruction!
                        Thus I stand revenged—
Go, crown some other with a prophet's woe.
Look! it is he, it is Apollo's self
Rending from me the prophet-robe he gave.
God! while I wore it yet, thou saw'st me mocked
There at my home by each malicious mouth—
To all and each, an undivided scorn.
The name alike and fate of witch and cheat—
Woe, poverty, and famine—all I bore;
And at this last the god hath brought me here
Into death's toils, and what his love had made,
His hate unmakes me now: and I shall stand
Not now before the altar of my home,
But me a slaughter-house and block of blood
Shall see hewn down, a reeking sacrifice.
Yet shall the gods have heed of me who die,
For by their will shall one requite my doom.
He, to avenge his father's blood out-poured,
Shall smite and slay with matricidal hand.
Aye, he shall come—tho' far away he roam,
A banished wanderer in a stranger's land—
To crown his kindred's edifice of ill,
Called home to vengeance by his father's fall:
Thus have the high gods sworn, and shall fulfill.
And now why mourn I, tarrying on earth,
Since first mine Ilion has found its fate
And I beheld, and those who won the wall

Pass to such issue as the gods ordain?
I too will pass and like them dare to die!
(*Turns and looks upon the palace door.*)
Portal of Hades, thus I bid thee hail!
Grant me one boon—a swift and mortal stroke,
That all unwrung by pain, with ebbing blood
Shed forth in quiet death, I close mine eyes.

CHORUS. Maid of mysterious woes, mysterious lore,
Long was thy prophecy: but if aright
Thou readest all thy fate, how, thus unscared,
Dost thou approach the altar of thy doom,
As fronts the knife some victim, heaven-controlled?

CASSANDRA. Friends, there is no avoidance in delay.

CHORUS. Yet who delays the longest, his the gain.

CASSANDRA. The day is come—flight were small gain to me!

CHORUS. O brave endurance of a soul resolved!

CASSANDRA. That were ill praise, for those of happier doom.

CHORUS. All fame is happy, even famous death.

CASSANDRA. Ah sire, ah, brethren, famous once were ye!
(*She moves to enter the house, then starts back.*)

CHORUS. What fear is this that scares thee from the house?

CASSANDRA. Pah!

CHORUS. What is this cry? some dark despair of soul?

CASSANDRA. Pah! the house fumes with stench and spilth of blood.

CHORUS. How? 't is the smell of household offerings.

CASSANDRA. 'T is rank as charnel-scent from open graves.

CHORUS. Thou canst not mean this scented Syrian nard?

CASSANDRA. Nay, let me pass within to cry aloud
The monarch's fate and mine—enough of life.
Ah, friends!
Bear to me witness, since I fall in death,
That not as birds that shun the bush and scream
I moan in idle terror. This attest
When for my death's revenge another dies,
A woman for a woman, and a man
Falls, for a man ill-wedded to his curse.
Grant me this boon—the last before I die.

CHORUS. Brave to the last! I mourn thy doom foreseen.

CASSANDRA. Once more one utterance,
,   but not of wail,
Though for my death—and then I speak no more.

Sun! thou whose beam I shall not see again,
To thee I cry, Let those whom vengeance calls
To slay their kindred's slayers, quit withal
The death of me, the slave, the fenceless prey.

Ah, state of mortal man! in time of weal,
A line, a shadow! and if ill fate fall,
One wet sponge-sweep wipes all our trace away—
And this I deem less piteous, of the twain.
(*Exit into the palace.*)

CHORUS. Too true it is! our mortal state
With bliss is never satiate,
And none, before the palace high
And stately of prosperity,
Cries to us with a voice of fear,
Away! 't is ill to enter here!

Lo! this our lord hath trodden down,
By grace of Heaven, old Priam's town,
And praised as god he stands once more
On Argos' shore!

Yet now—if blood shed long ago
Cries out that other blood shall flow—
His life-blood, his, to pay again
The stern requital of the slain—
Peace to that braggart's vaunting vain,
Who, having heard the chieftain's tale,
Yet boasts of bliss untouched by bale!

       (A loud cry from within.)

VOICE OF AGAMEMNON. O I am sped
  —a deep, a mortal blow.

CHORUS. Listen, listen! who is screaming as in mortal agony?

VOICE OF AGAMEMNON. O! O! again,
  another, another blow!

CHORUS. The bloody act is over—I
  have heard the monarch's cry—
Let us swiftly take some counsel, lest we
  too be doomed to die.

ONE OF THE CHORUS. 'T is best, I
  judge, aloud for aid to call,
"Ho! loyal Argives! to the palace, all!"

ANOTHER. Better, I deem, ourselves
  to bear the aid,
And drag the deed to light, while drips
  the blade.

ANOTHER. Such will is mine, and what
  thou say'st I say:
Swiftly to act! the time brooks no delay.

ANOTHER. Aye, for 't is plain, this
  prelude of their song
Foretells its close in tyranny and wrong.

ANOTHER. Behold, we tarry—but thy
  name, Delay,
They spurn, and press with sleepless hand
  to slay.

ANOTHER. I know not what 't were
  well to counsel now—
Who wills to act, 't is his to counsel
  how.

ANOTHER. Thy doubt is mine: for
  when a man is slain,
I have no words to bring his life again.

ANOTHER. What? e'en for life's sake,
  bow us to obey
These house-defilers and their tyrant
  sway?

ANOTHER. Unmanly doom! 't were
  better far to die—
Death is a gentler lord than tyranny.

ANOTHER. Think well—must cry or
  sign of woe or pain
Fix our conclusion that the chief is
  slain?

ANOTHER. Such talk befits us when
  the deed we see—
Conjecture dwells afar from certainty.

LEADER OF THE CHORUS. I read one
  will from many a diverse word,
To know aright, how stands it with our
  lord!

      (The scene opens, disclosing CLY-
      TEMNESTRA, *who comes forward.*
      The body of AGAMEMNON *lies,*
      muffled in a long robe, within a
      silver-sided laver; the corpse of
      CASSANDRA *is laid beside him.)*

CLYTEMNESTRA. Ho, ye who heard
  me speak so long and oft
The glozing word that led me to my
  will—
Hear how I shrink not to unsay it all!
How else should one who willeth to re-
  quite
Evil for evil to an enemy
Disguised as friend, weave the mesh
  straitly round him,
Not to be overleaped, a net of doom?
This is the sum and issue of old strife,
Of the deep-pondered and at length ful-
  filled.
All is avowed, and as I smote I stand
With foot set firm upon a finished thing!
I turn not to denial: thus I wrought
So that he could nor flee nor ward his
  doom.
Even as the trammel hems the scaly
  shoal,
I trapped him with inextricable toils,
The ill abundance of a baffling robe;
Then smote him, once, again—and at
  each wound
He cried aloud, then as in death relaxed
Each limb and sank to earth; and as he
  lay,
Once more I smote him, with the last
  third blow,
Sacred to Hades, savior of the dead.
And thus he fell, and as he passed away,

Spirit with body chafed; each dying
 breath
Flung from his breast swift bubbling jets
 of gore,
And the dark sprinklings of the rain of
 blood
Fell upon me; and I was fain to feel
That dew—not sweeter is the rain of
 heaven
To cornland, when the green sheath
 teems with grain.

Elders of Argos—since the thing stands
 so,
I bid you to rejoice, if such your will:
Rejoice or not, I vaunt and praise the
 deed,
And well I ween, if seemly it could be,
'T were not ill done to pour libations
 here,
Justly—aye, more than justly—on his
 corpse
Who filled his home with curses as with
 wine,
And thus returned to drain the cup he
 filled.
  CHORUS. I marvel at thy tongue's
 audacity,
To vaunt thus loudly o'er a husband
 slain.
    CLYTEMNESTRA. Ye hold me as a
 woman, weak of will,
And strive to sway me: but my heart is
 stout,
Nor fears to speak its uttermost to you,
Albeit ye know its message. Praise or
 blame,
Even as ye list,—I reck not of your
 words.
Lo! at my feet lies Agamemnon slain,
My husband once—and him this hand of
 mine,
A right contriver, fashioned for his death.
Behold the deed!
  CHORUS. Woman, what deadly birth,
What venomed essence of the earth
Or dark distilment of the wave,
To thee such passion gave,
Nerving thine hand

To set upon thy brow this burning
 crown,
The curses of thy land?
Our king by thee cut off, hewn down!
Go forth—they cry—*accursèd and for-
 lorn,*
To hate and scorn!
  CLYTEMNESTRA. O ye just men, who
 speak my sentence now,
The city's hate, the ban of all my realm!
Ye had no voice of old to launch such
 doom
On him, my husband, when he held as
 light
My daughter's life as that of sheep or
 goat,
One victim from the thronging fleecy
 fold!
Yea, slew in sacrifice his child and
 mine,
The well-loved issue of my travail-pangs,
To lull and lay the gales that blew from
 Thrace.
That deed of his, I say, that stain and
 shame,
Had rightly been atoned by banishment;
But ye, who then were dumb, are stern
 to judge
This deed of mine that doth affront your
 ears.
Storm out your threats, yet knowing this
 for sooth,
That I am ready, if your hand prevail
As mine now doth, to bow beneath your
 sway:
If God say nay, it shall be yours to learn
By chastisement a late humility.
  CHORUS. Bold is thy craft, and proud
Thy confidence, thy vaunting loud;
Thy soul, that chose a murd'ress' fate,
Is all with blood elate—
Maddened to know
The blood not yet avenged, the damnèd
 spot
Crimson upon thy brow.
But Fate prepares for thee thy lot—
Smitten as thou didst smite, without a
 friend,
To meet thine end!

CLYTEMNESTRA. Hear then the sanction of the oath I swear—
By the great vengeance for my murdered child,
By Atè, by the Fury unto whom
This man lies sacrificed by hand of mine,
I do not look to tread the hall of Fear,
While in this hearth and home of mine there burns
The light of love—Ægisthus—as of old
Loyal, a stalwart shield of confidence—
As true to me as this slain man was false,
Wronging his wife with paramours at Troy,
Fresh from the kiss of each Chryseis there!
Behold him dead—behold his captive prize,
Seeress and harlot—comfort of his bed,
True prophetess, true paramour—I wot
The sea-bench was not closer to the flesh,
Full oft, of every rower, than was she.
See, ill they did, and ill requites them now.
His death ye know: she as a dying swan
Sang her last dirge, and lies, as erst she lay,
Close to his side, and to my couch has left
A sweet new taste of joys that know no fear.
    CHORUS. Ah, woe and well-a-day! I would that Fate—
Not bearing agony too great,
Nor stretching me too long on couch of pain—
Would bid mine eyelids keep
The morningless and unawakening sleep!
For life is weary, now my lord is slain,
The gracious among kings!
Hard fate of old he bore and many grievous things,
And for a woman's sake, on Ilian land—
Now is his life hewn down, and by a woman's hand.

O Helen, O infatuate soul,
Who bad'st the tides of battle roll,
O'erwhelming thousands, life on life,
'Neath Ilion's wall!
And now lies dead the lord of all.
The blossom of thy storied sin
Bears blood's inexpiable stain,
O thou that erst, these halls within,
Wert unto all a rock of strife,
A husband's bane!
    CLYTEMNESTRA. Peace! pray not thou for death as though
Thine heart was whelmed beneath this woe,
Nor turn thy wrath aside to ban
The name of Helen, nor recall
How she, one bane of many a man,
Sent down to death the Danaan lords,
To sleep at Troy the sleep of swords,
And wrought the woe that shattered all.
    CHORUS. Fiend of the race! that swoopest fell
Upon the double stock of Tantalus,
Lording it o'er me by a woman's will,
Stern, manful, and imperious—
A bitter sway to me!
Thy very form I see,
Like some grim raven, perched upon the slain,
Exulting o'er the crime, aloud, in tuneless strain!
    CLYTEMNESTRA. Right was that word —thou namest well
The brooding race-fiend, triply fell!
From him it is that murder's thirst,
Blood-lapping, inwardly is nursed—
Ere time the ancient scar can sain,
New blood comes welling forth again.
    CHORUS. Grim is his wrath and heavy on our home,
That fiend of whom thy voice has cried,
Alas, an omened cry of woe unsatisfied,
An all-devouring doom!

Ah, woe, ah, Zeus! from Zeus all things befall—
Zeus the high cause and finisher of all!—
Lord of our mortal state, by him are willed

All things, by him fulfilled!
Yet ah, my king, my king no more!
What words to say, what tears to pour
Can tell my love for thee?
The spider-web of treachery
She wove and wound, thy life around,
And lo! I see thee lie,
And thro' a coward, impious wound
Pant forth thy life and die!
A death of shame—ah, woe on woe!
A treach'rous hand, a cleaving blow!
    CLYTEMNESTRA. My guilt thou harp-
    est, o'er and o'er!
I bid thee reckon me no more
As Agamemnon's spouse.
The old Avenger, stern of mood
For Atreus and his feast of blood,
Hath struck the lord of Atreus' house,
And in the semblance of his wife
The king hath slain.—
Yea, for the murdered children's life,
A chieftain's in requital ta'en.
    CHORUS. Thou guiltless of this mur-
    der, thou!
Who dares such thought avow?
Yet it may be, wroth for the parent's
    deed,
The fiend hath holpen thee to slay the
    son.
Dark Ares, god of death, is pressing on
Thro' streams of blood by kindred shed,
Exacting the accompt for children dead,
For clotted blood, for flesh on which
    their sire did feed.

Yet, ah, my king, my king no more!
What words to say, what tears to pour
Can tell my love for thee?
The spider-web of treachery
She wove and wound, thy life around,
And lo! I see thee lie,
And thro' a coward, impious wound
Pant forth thy life and die!
A death of shame—ah, woe on woe!
A treach'rous hand, a cleaving blow!
    CLYTEMNESTRA. I deem not that the
    death he died
Had overmuch of shame:
For this was he who did provide

Foul wrong unto his house and name:
His daughter, blossom of my womb,
He gave unto a deadly doom,
Iphigenia, child of tears!
And as he wrought, even so he fares.
Nor be his vaunt too loud in hell;
For by the sword his sin he wrought,
And by the sword himself is brought
Among the dead to dwell.
    CHORUS. Ah, whither shall I fly?
For all in ruin sinks the kingly hall;
Nor swift device nor shift of thought
    have I,
To 'scape its fall.
A little while the gentler rain-drops fail;
I stand distraught—a ghastly interval,
Till on the roof-tree rings the bursting
    hail
Of blood and doom. Even now Fate
    whets the steel
On whetstones new and deadlier than of
    old,
The steel that smites, in Justice' hold,
Another death to deal.
O Earth! that I had lain at rest
And lapped forever in thy breast,
Ere I had seen my chieftain fall
Within the laver's silver wall,
Low-lying on dishonored bier!
And who shall give him sepulcher,
And who the wail of sorrow pour?
Woman, 't is thine no more!
A graceless gift unto his shade
Such tribute, by his murd'ress paid!
Strive not thus wrongly to atone
The impious deed thy hand hath done.
Ah who above the god-like chief
Shall weep the tears of loyal grief?
Who speak above his lowly grave
The last sad praises of the brave?
    CLYTEMNESTRA. Peace! for such task
    is none of thine.
By me he fell, by me he died,
And now his burial rites be mine!
Yet from these halls no mourners' train
Shall celebrate his obsequies;
Only by Acheron's rolling tide
His child shall spring unto his side,
And in a daughter's loving wise

Shall clasp and kiss him once again!
   CHORUS. Lo! sin by sin and sorrow
    dogg'd by sorrow—
And who the end can know?
The slayer of to-day shall die to-mor-
   row—
The wage of wrong is woe.
While Time shall be, while Zeus in
   heaven is lord,
His law is fixed and stern;
On him that wrought shall vengeance be
   outpoured—
The tides of doom return.
The children of the curse abide within
These halls of high estate—
And none can wrench from off the home
   of sin
The clinging grasp of Fate.
   CLYTEMNESTRA. Now walks thy word
   aright, to tell
This ancient truth of oracle;
But I with vows of sooth will pray
To him, the power that holdeth sway
O'er all the race of Pleisthenes—
Tho' dark the deed and deep the guilt,
With this last blood, my hands have spilt,
I pray thee let thine anger cease!
I pray thee pass from us away
To some new race in other lands,
There, if thou wilt, to wrong and slay
The lives of men by kindred hands.

For me 't is all sufficient meed,
Tho' little wealth or power were won,
So I can say, *'T is past and done.*
The bloody lust and murderous,
The inborn frenzy of our house,
Is ended, by my deed!

     Enter ÆGISTHUS.

ÆGISTHUS. Dawn of the day of right-
   ful vengeance, hail!
I dare at length aver that gods above
Have care of men and heed of earthly
   wrongs.
I, I who stand and thus exult to see
This man lie wound in robes the Furies
   wove,

Slain in requital of his father's craft.
Take ye the truth, that Atreus, this
   man's sire,
The lord and monarch of this land of old,
Held with my sire Thyestes deep dispute,
Brother with brother, for the prize of
   sway,
And drave him from his home to banish-
   ment.
Thereafter, the lorn exile homeward stole
And clung a suppliant to the hearth
   divine,
And for himself won this immunity—
Not with his own blood to defile the
   land
That gave him birth. But Atreus, god-
   less sire
Of him who here lies dead, this welcome
   planned—
With zeal that was not love he feigned to
   hold
In loyal joy a day of festal cheer,
And bade my father to his board, and set
Before him flesh that was his children
   once.
First, sitting at the upper board alone,
He hid the fingers and the feet, but gave
The rest—and readily Thyestes took
What to his ignorance no semblance wore
Of human flesh, and ate: behold what
   curse
That eating brought upon our race and
   name!
For when he knew what all unhallowed
   thing
He thus had wrought, with horror's bit-
   ter cry
Back-starting, spewing forth the frag-
   ments foul,
On Pelop's house a deadly curse he
   spake—
As darkly as I spurn this damnèd food,
So perish all the race of Pleisthenes!
Thus by that curse fell he whom here ye
   see,
And I—who else?—this murder moved
   and planned;
For me, an infant yet in swaddling
   bands,

Of the three children youngest, Atreus
sent
To banishment by my sad father's side:
But Justice brought me home once more,
grown now
To manhood's years; and stranger tho' I
was,
My right hand reached unto the chief-
tain's life,
Plotting and planning all that malice
bade.
And death itself were honor now to me,
Beholding him in Justice' ambush ta'en.
CHORUS. Ægisthus, for this insolence
of thine
That vaunts itself in evil, take my scorn.
Of thine own will, thou sayest, thou hast
slain
The chieftain, by thine own unaided plot
Devised the piteous death: I rede thee
well,
Think not thy head shall 'scape, when
right prevails,
The people's ban, the stones of death and
doom.
ÆGISTHUS. This word from thee, this
word from one who rows
Low at the oars beneath, what time we
rule,
We of the upper tier? Thou'lt know
anon,
'T is bitter to be taught again in age,
By one so young, submission at the word.
But iron of the chain and hunger's throes
Can minister unto an o'erswoln pride
Marvelous well, aye, even in the old.
Hast eyes, and seest not this? Peace—
kick not thus
Against the pricks, unto thy proper pain!
CHORUS. Thou womanish man, wait-
ing till war did cease,
Home-watcher and defiler of the couch,
And arch-deviser of the chieftain's doom!
ÆGISTHUS. Bold words again! but
they shall end in tears.
The very converse, thine, of Orpheus'
tongue:
He roused and led in ecstacy of joy
All things that heard his voice melodious;

But thou as with the futile cry of curs
Wilt draw men wrathfully upon thee.
Peace!
Or strong subjection soon shall tame thy
tongue.
CHORUS. Aye, thou art one to hold an
Argive down—
Thou, skilled to plan the murder of the
king,
But not with thine own hand to smite the
blow!
ÆGISTHUS. That fraudful force was
woman's very part,
Not mine, whom deep suspicion from of
old
Would have debarred. Now by his treas-
ure's aid
My purpose holds to rule the citizens.
But whoso will not bear my guiding
hand,
Him for his corn-fed mettle I will drive
Not as a trace-horse, light-caparisoned,
But to the shafts with heaviest harness
bound.
Famine, the grim mate of the dungeon
dark,
Shall look on him and shall behold him
tame.
CHORUS. Thou losel soul, was then
thy strength too slight
To deal in murder, while a woman's
hand,
Staining and shaming Argos and its gods,
Availed to slay him? Ho, if anywhere
The light of life smite on Orestes' eyes,
Let him, returning by some guardian fate,
Hew down with force her paramour and
her!
ÆGISTHUS. How thy word and act
shall issue, thou shalt shortly under-
stand.
CHORUS. Up to action, O my com-
rades! for the fight is hard at hand.
Swift, your right hands to the sword hilt!
bare the weapon as for strife—
ÆGISTHUS. Lo! I too am standing
ready, hand on hilt for death or
life.
CHORUS. 'T was thy word and we ac-

cept it: onward to the chance of
war!

CLYTEMNESTRA. Nay, enough, enough,
my champion! we will smite and
slay no more.

Already have we reaped enough the har-
vest-field of guilt:

Enough of wrong and murder, let no
other blood be spilt.

Peace, old men! and pass away unto the
homes by Fate decreed,

Lest ill valor meet our vengeance—'t was
a necessary deed.

But enough of toils and troubles—be the
end, if ever, now,

Ere thy talon, O Avenger, deal another
deadly blow.

'T is a woman's word of warning, and let
who will list thereto.

ÆGISTHUS. But that these should
loose and lavish reckless blossoms of
the tongue,

And in hazard of their fortune cast upon
me words of wrong,

And forget the law of subjects, and revile
their ruler's word—

CHORUS. Ruler? but 't is not for
Argives, thus to own a dastard
lord!

ÆGISTHUS. I will follow to chastise
thee in my coming days of sway.

CHORUS. Not if Fortune guide Orestes
safely on his homeward way.

ÆGISTHUS. Ah, well I know how
exiles feed on hopes of their return.

CHORUS. Fare and batten on pollution
of the right, while 't is thy turn.

ÆGISTHUS. Thou shalt pay, be well
assurèd, heavy quittance for thy
pride.

CHORUS. Crow and strut, with her to
watch thee, like a cock, his mate
beside!

CLYTEMNESTRA. Heed not thou too
highly of them—let the cur-pack
growl and yell:

I and thou will rule the palace and will
order all things well.   (*Exeunt.*)
    —E. D. A. MORSHEAD.

ŒDIPUS THE KING [1]

SOPHOCLES

Sophocles was born about 495 B.C. in
Colonus, near Athens, and died in 406
B.C. He was representative of the highly
cultured classes of the time, aristocratic
in feeling, possessed of great personal
beauty, and enjoying great popularity
throughout his life. The innovations in
dramatic art attributed to Sophocles are
the introduction of a third actor and the
use of painted scenery. He also restricted
the function of the chorus, without however depriving it of an integral relation
to the dialogue. Harmony, proportion,
and restraint are the characteristics of
his art. He was more interested in the
human motives to action than in the problem of divine law as a determining factor
in man's life, and the widening of the
scope of the dialogue afforded him greater
opportunity to reveal the interplay of
character. His material grows out of the
conflict of man with man's institutions,
rather than, as in Æschylus, out of the
conflict of man's will with the divine will.
Sophocles wrote more than a hundred
plays, but only seven have come down
to us.

Like the *Agamemnon,* the *Œdipus the
King* (about 430 B.C.) moves relentlessly
forward to the inevitable catastrophe, but
the action proceeds rather in successive
waves than in a single stream of even
current. It is the most perfect example
of dramatic irony—the very acts which
the king designs to save him from the
doom foretold lead surely and logically
to that very doom. It may be questioned
whether the poet intended the play as the
tragedy of an innocent man caught in the
toils of destiny, or of a great and good
man brought low through the defect of
arrogant self-sufficiency.

[1] From *Sophocles,* by Robert Whitelaw.
Copyright by Longmans Green & Co. Reprinted by permission.

PERSONS

ŒDIPUS.   MESSENGER.
PRIEST.   SHEPHERD, *of Laius*.
CREON.   SECOND MESSENGER.
TEIRESIAS.   JOCASTA.
  CHORUS *of Theban Elders*.

ŒD. Children—of ancient Cadmus
  latest birth—
Why in such eager session sit ye here,
With chaplets twined around your sup-
  pliant boughs?
And all the city is thick with incense-
  smoke
And loud with lamentation and with
  dirge:
Whereof, O children, choosing not to
  hear
From lips of others, hither I have come—
I, who am called all-famous Œdipus:
Now therefore tell me, thou, whose
  reverend mien
Proclaims thee spokesman, wherefore are
  ye come—
What fearing—craving what? In nought
  would I
Withhold my succour; fearing to be
  found
Heartless, your suppliant session pitying
  not.
  PRIEST. Prince of my people, Œdipus
  the king,
Thou seest us, what tale of years we tell,
Who at thine altars sit, some fledged as
  yet
For no far flight, and some oppressed
  with age,
Priests—I of Zeus: and lo, with us, of
  youths
Our chosen: and the general crowd, white-
  wreathed,
Sit in our squares, and at the temples
  twain
Of Pallas, and Ismenus' prescient hearth.
For Thebes, thyself art witness, sinks be-
  neath
The tempest's stress, and lifts no more
  her head

Out of the drenching of the deadly
  surge—
Blighted all fruitful blossoms of the land,
Blighted our grazing herds, and barren
  births
Of women: and withal the god, fire-
  fraught,
Grim pestilence, strikes with his scourge
  the city,
Whereby the house of Cadmus is made
  void,
And rich with sorrow and sighing Death's
  dark halls.
Thee therefore, not as equalled with the
  gods,
Suppliant with these children I entreat,
But chief of men, in casualties of life,
And Heaven's visitations, we esteem
  thee:
Who, at thy coming hither, didst rid the
  land
Of that fell songster's tribute which we
  paid,
Albeit of us no knowledge hadst thou
  gained,
No prompting, but by aidance of a god
We say and think thou didst redeem our
  life;
And now, revered of all men, Œdipus,
Behold us here thy suppliants: help for
  us,
Some help contrive, by oracle from
  heaven
Instructed, or wise counsel of a man:
For oft 'tis seen, that most abiding fruit
Experience bears, when counsellors con-
  fer.
O then, uplift our state, thou man of
  men!
Yea, and beware: for now indeed the
  land
Hails thee her saviour, for thy former
  help;
And of thy reign O never be it said,
That thou didst lift us up and cast us
  down;
But stablish thou our state's prosperity;
And, as before deliverance wrought by
  thee

Was blest by heaven, so help us now
  again.
For if thou wilt be king in Thebes, as
  now,
Better a peopled than a vacant realm:
Since neither tower nor ship avails to
  help,
Empty of men and tenantless within.
  ŒD. O woful children, longings known
    too well
To me you come outpouring. Well I
  know
Ye all are grieved, and yet, grieve as ye
  may,
There is not one of you hath grief like
  mine.
For yours is private sorrow, touching
  each
Himself and not another, but my heart
Aches all at once for Thebes and me and
  thee.
Ye do not wake me slumbering and
  asleep:
But many tears doubt not that I have
  shed,
And threaded many a labyrinth of the
  mind.
And the one cure that I by searching
  found
I put to proof: for Creon, Menœceus' son,
My own wife's brother, to the Delphic
  shrine
Of Phœbus I have sent, that he might
  ask
What act or speech of mine should save
  the state:
And counting o'er the days that he is
  gone
I marvel how he fares; for overlong
He tarries, past the time that should have
  served.
But when he comes, base should I be
  indeed,
Failing to do all that the god requires.
  PRIEST. 'Tis seasonably spoken, and
    ev'n now
I hear it said that Creon hither comes.
  ŒD. Brightly he looks: O King
    Apollo, grant

Bright fortune, fraught with safety, he
  may bring!
  PRIEST. Glad news, no doubt, he
    brings: else had he not
With wealth of fruitful laurel decked his
  brows.
  ŒD. Soon we shall know. 'Tis not
    too far to speak.
Son of Menœceus and my kinsman,
  prince,
What answer dost thou from the god
  report?
  CRE. Good: all our sufferings, if it
    chance aright,
May turn to our advantage, as I think.
  ŒD. What says the god? Hearing
    thy present speech,
I neither hope nor fear before the time.
  CRE. If thou wilt hear while these
    are standing by,
Thou shalt: I am ready, or else to go
  within.
  ŒD. Speak in the ears of all: since
    more for these
Than for my own life is the grief I bear.
  CRE. All that the god hath spoken
    thou shalt hear.
A plain command Apollo lays on us;
Pollution, harboured in the land, we
  must
Drive hence, nor harbour irremediably.
  ŒD. Yea, with what cleansing? How
    is our plight relieved?
  CRE. Some one's to banish, or for
    blood that's shed
Blood must atone: such guilt disturbs our
  state.
  ŒD. Of what man spake the god, so
    foully slain?
  CRE. Laius, O king, was ruler of the
    land
Aforetime, ere the sceptre fell to thee.
  ŒD. I know his fame: himself I
    never saw.
  CRE. His death requires our venge-
    ance, and to do
Swift execution on his murderers.
  ŒD. But where are they? Where
    shall we look to trace

The faded record of an ancient crime?

CRE. In this land, so he said. Who seek may find:
The careless searcher makes the baffled search.

ŒD. In city or in field—or was 't abroad
That Laius encountered with this death?

CRE. Bound, as he said, for Delphi, from his home
He fared, but to his home came not again.

ŒD. Was there no messenger—companion, none—
Who saw, and might have told, if one had asked?

CRE. All died save one, who, flying, crazed with fear,
Of all he saw knew but one thing to tell.

ŒD. Out then with that! One thing may find out many,
If but a little we take heart to hope.

CRE. Robbers, he said, met with the king and slew him,
Not single-handed, but a company.

ŒD. How had a robber so presumed, unless
Traitors from Thebes had lined him with their gold?

CRE. So we surmised: but, Laius being dead,
No one was there to help us in our grief.

ŒD. What grief withheld you, not to learn the truth—
The royal house struck down by such a blow?

CRE. The subtle-singing Sphinx compelled our thoughts
Back from the vague doubt to the instant need.

ŒD. I will begin again, and find out all.
Phœbus has well fulfilled his part, thou thine,
Spending this trouble for the dead man's sake:
Claim then and find in me no vain ally,
Helping at once this city and the god.
Not on behalf of friends of no account,

But for my own sake, shall I purge this guilt.
For who slew him, by such another blow
Belike may choose to be revenged on me.
So then in helping him I save myself.
But quickly, children, from this altar-foot
Rise ye, and take these suppliant boughs away:
And some one summon hither the Theban folk;
Nought will I leave undone. All hangs on this—
Weal, with the help of heaven, or woe to Thebes.

PRIEST. Children, let us be gone: for to obtain
Ev'n what this man announces, came we hither.
Come, who didst send these oracles, Apollo,
To save and heal us of our sickness, thou!

CHORUS. Sweet-sounding answer of Zeus, what art thou, that comest from Pytho,
To glorious Thebes from the golden shrine?
Low at thy feet I am laid, with my heart in a flutter of fear,
Delian, Healer Apollo!
Filled full of wonder and dread,
What stern requirement thou wilt enact for us,
What word of doom, or new or old,
Come with revolving seasons back—
O tell us, daughter of golden Hope.
Immortal Voice!
Daughter of Zeus, thee first I invoke, immortal Athene;
Our city's champion, thy sister, next,
Artemis high o'er the Agora's circle in glory enthroned,
Thee too, Far-shooter, Apollo!
Threefold averters of doom,
O now from heav'n come forth to deliver us,
If ever, when hung o'er our heads
Menace of woe, at your behest
The flaming ruin was rolled away,

Visit us now!
Unnumbered woes, alas, are mine to
    bear:
I see the sickness sweep our ranks along,
Nor weapon hath my thought,
That can its breath avert:
For neither of the goodly earth
Prosper the springing fruits,
Nor women from the lamentable pangs
Of childbirth rise again:
But one upon another shalt thou see
Like folks of feather'd birds,
Swifter than fire that no man tames,
Swept onward to the shore,
Far west, of Pluto and the night.
Unnumbered dead! a city perishing!
For children unregarded in the streets
Lie, tainting the air with death,
Unwept: and gentle wives,
And grey-haired mothers, pressing round,
Their sad petitions pour,
Where the great altar lifted o'er the
    crowd
Stands like a seaward cliff:
And high and clear with flutes in solemn
    dirge
The wailing voices blend:—
O golden goddess, child of Zeus,
Have pity and send us Help,
Fair-visaged Help, with eyes benign.
And this fierce Ares, who,
Not now with brazen shields,
But with the blasting of his fiery breath,
Wakes worse than din of battle in our
    midst,
I pray that he, far from my country's
    shores,
Backward at headlong speed may turn
    and flee,
Either to Amphitrite's western bower
Under the great salt sea,
Or those inhospitable tides that rave
On rock-bound shores of Thrace:
For, what the ravin'd night at last lets
    go,
Day makes of this his prey:
But, O our Father, Zeus,
Lord of the lightning's flaming might,
Slay with thy bolt the dreaded foe.

Lyceius, lord of light,
Showered from thy golden string
Fain would I see thy shafts invincible
Fly forth, each shaft a champion winged
    with help,
And see in either hand of Artemis
The splendour of a torch that flames afar,
Wherewith the Lycian hills she ranges
    o'er:
And, lustrous as the juice
Of thine own vines, named of this Theban
    land,
Bacchus, I cry to thee—
Crowned with a golden diadem, and girt
With shouting Mænads round,
Come to our rescue now,
With blazing pinebrand all aglow,
Against the god whom gods disown.

ŒD. Thou askest: as thou askest, if
    thou wilt
Be serviceable and hearken to my words,
Help thou shalt have and respite of thine
    ills—
Words I shall speak, a stranger to the
    tale,
A stranger to the deed: else had I tracked
    it,
And not gone far, ere I had found some
    clue.
But I was then no citizen of Thebes;
Now therefore, Thebans, hear me, all of
    you.
Whoever among you knows by what
    man's hand
Died Laius the son of Labdacus,
I bid him speak to me, and tell me all:
Speak tho he fears, and clear us of the
    guilt,
Yea, and accuse himself: for he shall
    suffer
Nought worse than to depart out of the
    land
Unscathed: or, if he knows the murderer
Some stranger come to Thebes, yet let
    him speak:
I will reward and give him thanks to
    boot.
But, if ye hide this thing, and one,
    afraid

For his own sake or friend's sake, slights my words,
How then concludes my purpose, ye shall hear.
I charge all dwellers in the land, whereof
Sceptre and sovereignty are mine, to yield
That man, whoe'er he be, nor speech nor shelter:
No man must pray or sacrifice with him,
Or of the lustral water let him share:
To him all doors be barred, whose presence breeds
In Thebes pollution: as the oracle,
From Delphi newly brought, reveals to me.
So stands my purpose: to the god such help
I dedicate and to the murdered man:
And for the murderer, whether alone
He hides his guilt or has accomplices,
May he unblest wear out his guilty life!
And for myself I pray, my hearth and home
With my consent if ever he should share,
This doom I doomed for others fall on me!
And all these things I charge you to perform,
For my sake, and the god, and for this land,
Blighted and banned and ruined as ye see.
For even if this thing were not from heaven,
Ye should not thus have left such guilt unpurged,
The murder of your noblest and a king,
But sought the slayer: and now, because on me
There hath devolved succession to his throne,
And to his couch withal and fruitful wife,
From whom had sprung, had not his offspring failed,
A common race of children, his and mine—
But on his head this sudden mischief leapt—
Therefore, as son for father, I will fight
For him, and nothing spare, and shrink from nought,
Seeking the murderer of your king, whose sire
Was Labdacus, as Polydorus his,
From Cadmus sprung, son of Agenor old:
And, who'll not help in this, I pray the gods
Neither to yield them harvest of their fields,
Nor children of their wives, but let them perish
Slain by this present plague or worse than this.
But you the rest, good Thebans all, who cleave
To my consent, be Justice your ally,
And all the gods befriend you evermore.

CHOR. King, as thy curse constrains me, I will speak—
I neither did the deed, nor can declare
The doer. Phœbus, he alone, who laid
This quest on us, could name the guilty one.

ŒD. True, but to wrest a secret from the gods,
Against their will, passes all power of men.

CHOR. Yet, if not this, there is a second-best.

ŒD. Second or third-best, speak: withhold it not.

CHOR. Teiresias with Phœbus, seer with seer,
I know more than all men like-gifted: ask
Of him, O king, and thou shalt learn the truth.

ŒD. This also, friends, I have not left undone.
I sent two messengers, when Creon spoke:
Long since I marvel that he is not here.

CHOR. Enough: mere dull stale talk, no doubt, all else.

ŒD. What talk mean you? I question every hint.

CHOR. By travellers we heard the king was slain.

ŒD. And I: but gone from sight is he who saw it.

CHOR. Yet, if he knows what fear is, rest assured
He'll not endure, hearing thy grievous curse.

ŒD. From deeds who shrinks not, him no words affright.

CHOR. There's one who shall convict him: hither led
Comes even now the seer, the man inspired,
Whose eyes, of all men's most, behold the truth.

ŒD. Teiresias, master-seer, who understandest
All mysteries and all knowledge, things in heaven
And things on earth, thou seest not but knowest
What plague afflicts our state: whereof we find
No champion and no saviour, sage, but thee.
For Phœbus, if indeed the messengers
Told thee not, to our sending sent reply,
No riddance of this sickness should we have,
Until the murderers of Laius
Were found and slain, or banished from the land.
Now therefore grudge neither thine auguries,
Nor any divinations that thou hast,
But save thyself and city, and save me,
And make us clean from all blood-guiltiness.
On thee we hang: and for a man to help
With all he has and can, is noblest toil.

TEIR. Alas, how sore a burden is the knowledge
That profits not the knower. This I knew,
But had forgotten: else had I not come hither.

ŒD. Why with thy looks so downcast art thou come?

TEIR. Let me go hence: most easily will be
Performed my part and thine, if thou consent.

ŒD. 'Twere treason and ingratitude to Thebes,
Thy mother, thus to lock from her thy counsel.

TEIR. Nay, for thy speech, I see, toward no good end
Is making; and I would not likewise err.

ŒD. By heaven, if aught thou knowest, all we here
Thy suppliants pray, turn not thy face from us.

TEIR. Ay, for ye all know nought: Urge me no more,
Lest my tale prove—an evil tale for thee.

ŒD. How? dost thou know and wilt not tell, but rather
Betray thy people and destroy thy town?

TEIR. I'll neither grieve myself nor thee. In vain
Thou dost importune me: my lips are sealed.

ŒD. What, miscreant—for the patience of a stone
Thou'dst anger—not a word thou'lt speak, but keep
Thy stubborn and impracticable mood?

TEIR. Thou dost reprove my temper, but thine own,
Lodged in thy breast, thou seest not, blaming me.

ŒD. Who could refrain his anger, hearing now
Such words, wherewith thou dost dishonour Thebes?

TEIR. Too soon the blow will fall, howe'er I hide it.

ŒD. What blow will fall, I should be warned by thee.

TEIR. I'll speak no more. Now bluster, if thou wilt:
The fiercest of thine anger let me feel.

ŒD. This shall my anger do: what I perceive,
I'll speak. For know that now I understand,
Thou didst contrive, nay thou hast done, this deed—

All save to deal the blow: and, couldst
   thou see,
Then surely I had said 'twas wholly
   thine.
   TEIR. Is't come to this? I charge thee
     to obey
Thine own commandment, and from this
   day forth
Speak neither to this people nor to me:
Thou art unclean: for thee we are
   accursed.
   ŒD. Such words, unblenching, blurtest
     thou at me?
How dost thou deem thou shalt escape
   for this?
   TEIR. Nay, I am safe. 'Tis true; and
     truth is strong.
   ŒD. Truth taught by whom? Not
     surely by thine art.
   TEIR. By thee: my lips, unwilling,
     thou hast opened.
   ŒD. What saidst thou? Speak
     again: I'll mark thee better.
   TEIR. Was my speech dark? or say'st
     thou this to prove me?
   ŒD. Perchance I understood not:
     speak again.
   TEIR. Him, of whose death thou ask-
     est, thou didst slay.
   ŒD. Not twice, unpunished, shall
     thy tongue offend.
   TEIR. More wilt thou hear, to be
     incensed the more?
   ŒD. Say what thou wilt: 'twill be
     but wasted breath.
   TEIR. Consorting with thy nearest,
     to thy shame,
Thou knowest not, nor seest what plight
   is thine.
   ŒD. Shalt thou say this, and triumph
     to the end?
   TEIR. If there is any potency in
     truth.
   ŒD. There is, except for thee. For
     thee there's none,
Blind as thou art, in ears and mind and
   eyes.
   TEIR. I pity thee, flinging the taunts,
     which soon

There's no one here will spare to fling at
   thee.
   ŒD. One lifelong night's thy portion;
     so that me
Thou canst not harm, nor any man who
   sees.
   TEIR. 'Tis not appointed thee by me
     to fall:
Sufficient is Apollo—he will do it.
   ŒD. By thee, or Creon, was this plot
     contrived?
   TEIR. Nay, Creon harms thee not:
     thou harm'st thyself.
   ŒD. O wealth and kingly state and
     sovereign art,
All art excelling, of our high-placed life—
What jealousy ye have in store for us;
When for this sceptre's sake, which
   Thebes to me
Intrusted—a free gift, by me unsought—
Creon from first to last the faithful friend,
Seeks to dethrone me, springing unawares,
And has suborned a cunning sorcerer,
A cheating juggler, one who for his gains
Has eyes to see, but in his art is blind.
For, tell me, sirrah, when wast thou true
   prophet?
Why, when the chanting hound was at
   your doors,
Didst thou not save thy people by a
   word?
And yet to read such riddle was no task
For common men, but asked a prophet's
   skill:
But thou wast found with no such lore
   by birds
Instructed or by gods inspired:—then
   came
I, who knew nothing, Œdipus, and freed
   you,
Taught not by birds, but by my mind's
   sure guess;
Whom now thou wouldst thrust out, in
   hope to stand
By the right hand of Creon on his throne.
Methinks ye both should rue your
   precious plot
Of cleansing thus the land: thou'rt old,
   I think—

Else hadst thou learnt—plagued with thine own inventions.

Chor. In anger spoken to our conjecture seems
Both this man's words, O Œdipus, and thine.
But other need is ours, to ponder well,
What heaven decrees, how best we may perform.

Teir. Though thou'rt a king, an equal right I claim
To give thee word for word: I too may speak—
No slave to thee—but slave to Loxias;
Not needing therefore, for a patron, Creon.
Blind thou didst call me, taunting me; I tell thee,
Thou seest and seest not what plight is thine,
Nor where thy home is, nor with whom 'tis shared.
Knowest thou whence thou art? and thou hast been
Foe to thy friends, unknowing, alive and dead;
And from this land of mother and of sire
The twofold curse shall drive thee with fierce feet,
Seeing with thine eyes, light now, but darkness then:
And then, responsive to thine outcries wild,
What haven, what Kithæron will not ring,
Those nuptials known, that fatal harbour-home,
Wherein thy bark was moored, fair winds to help?
And many another grief hast thou to learn,
Both to thyself made equal and thy children.
Now upon Creon and these words of mine
Heap insults if thou wilt. There waits for no man
More swift and sure perdition than for thee.

Œd. These things from him can I endure to hear?
Hence to destruction! hence and tarry not,
But void these doors, and from my sight be gone!

Teir. I had not come, but thou didst summon me.

Œd. I knew not that thou wouldst speak foolishness,
Else had I made small haste to bring thee hither.

Teir. Let it be so: I am a fool for thee—
Wise enough for the father who begat thee.

Œd. What father?—Stay: tell me, whose son am I?

Teir. This day shall both beget thee and destroy.

Œd. Thou dark'nest counsel still with riddling words.

Teir. In reading riddles famous is thy skill.

Œd. Ay—find what makes me great and sneer at that!

Teir. This same success however has undone thee.

Œd. But, if it saved the city, what care I?

Teir. 'Tis time that I were gone. Boy, lead me hence.

Œd. So let him lead. A hindrance and offence
Thou art, being present: gone, thou'lt plague no more.

Teir. But first I'll speak my errand, unafraid,
Out to thy face: thy frown can nowise slay.
Hear then: this man, whom thou with threats requirest,
And makest inquisition for the blood
Of Laius slain, he is amongst us here,
Lodged in our midst, an alien, as we deemed—
Now to be proved true Theban with the best—

No glad surprise: for blind, who now
 boasts sight,
Who now has wealth, a beggar, staff in
 hand,
To a strange land shall he grope forth
 his way.
Then shall he of the children round his
 hearth
Brother be proved and sire; both son and
 husband
Of her who bare him; having usurped
 the couch
O' the father whom he slew. Get thee
 within,
And meditate these things: if they prove
 false,
Say then my prophet's skill has taught
 me nothing.
CHOR. What man is he,
Whom the prophetic Delphian cliff de-
 nounces,
With blood-stained hands
Doer of deeds inexpiable, nameless?
Now, now let him flee with feet
Than storm-footed steeds more swift
Far, far from the sunlight.
For with the fire of his lightnings leaps
 on him,
Armed, the Avenger, the Son of the
 Highest:
And the Fates, the relentless,
Track him, not to be baffled.
For, late revealed,
Forth from the snow-capt summits of
 Parnassus
Flashed there a voice,
'Seek ye the sinner! from his hiding place
 drag him!'
For through the wild woodland ways,
O'er rocks, and in mountain caves,
He roams, as a bull might,
Restless, joyless, far from his fellows,
Shunning the oracles pealed from earth's
 centre,
But for ever he hears them,
Deathless, hovering round him.
Sorely, most sorely, is my mind perplexed,
By the wise augur's word:
I cannot yet believe, nor dare deny—

I know not what to say.
'Twixt hope and fear I hover doubtfully:
The present and the future—both are
 dark.
What quarrel had the son of Polybus
With Laius or his house,
I neither heard before, nor now have
 learnt
Aught that should make me challenge to
 the proof
The general praise of Œdipus the king,
For Laius moved with zeal,
And his mysterious end.
Wise are the gods: Apollo knows, and
 Zeus,
What things are done on earth:
But what know I? and prophets are but
 men,
And, if this seer's voice
Be more than mine there is no man who
 knows.
Yet one man's wit another's may sur-
 pass.
Still, let them talk, I will not say ' 'Tis
 so,'
Until I see the proof.
Once in our sight he met the winged Pest;
We saw him wise, we proved him sweet
 to Thebes:
And of this guilt my thoughts
Shall not condemn him now.
  CRE. Friends and my townsmen,
 hither, having heard
With what hard words King Œdipus as-
 sails me,
I come impatient. For, in this distress
If aught in word or deed importing harm
He thinks that he has suffered at my
 hand,
I have no pleasure to prolong my days,
Laden with this reproach. No single
 loss
The danger of such charge imports to me,
But loss of all, if base by Thebes, and
 base
By thee and by my friends, I shall be
 called.
  CHOR. Belike this accusation rather
 came,

Forced from his lips by anger, than believed.

CRE. What proof had he, that, what the prophet spoke,

He falsely spoke, induced by my suggestion?

CHOR. This charge was made: what prompted it, I know not.

CRE. With steadfast eyes and mind unfaltering

Against me was this accusation launched?

CHOR. I know not: what kings do, I do not see.

But from the palace look you where he comes.

ŒD. Sirrah, how cam'st thou hither? Hast thou such

A face of boldness, to confront me here,

Being, as well appears, my murderer,

And of my sovereign place convicted thief?

I prithee, say, what cowardice having seen

Or folly in me, hast thou devised this deed?

Its stealthy coming-on didst thou suppose

I should not mark, nor, if I marked, withstand?

Foolish I rather deem thy rash attempt,

Unhelped by numbers or by friends, to snatch

At power, that friends and wealth alone can win.

CRE. King, be advised. As thou hast said thy say,

Hear me say mine, and having heard consider.

ŒD. Thou hast more skill to speak than I to hear

Thee, having found thee bitter and unkind.

CRE. Even of this hear first what I shall say.

ŒD. This, that thou art no traitor, tell me not.

CRE. If mere self-will, divorced from reason, seems

A precious thing to thee, thou art deceived.

ŒD. If wronging thus a kinsman thou dost think

Thou'lt 'scape the reckoning, thou art deceived.

CRE. That this is justly said, I do confess:

But tell me what's the wrong that thou hast suffered?

ŒD. Didst thou advise or no, that I should send

Some one to bring this reverend man, the prophet?

CRE. The counsel that I gave, I'd give again.

ŒD. Say now what time has passed since Laius—

CRE. Since he did what? I know not what thou askest.

ŒD. Vanished from hence, slain by a murderous blow?

CRE. The time grows old: 'tis many years agone.

ŒD. And did this prophet then profess his art?

CRE. Wise was he then as now, honoured no less.

ŒD. And made he any mention then of me?

CRE. Whilst I was standing by to hear him, none.

ŒD. But did ye not inquire who slew your king?

CRE. We asked, as we were bound: but asked in vain.

ŒD. Why did not this wise prophet help you then?

CRE. I know not: things beyond me, I let be.

ŒD. But this thou knowest; and if thou'rt wise, wilt own.

CRE. What is it? what I know, I'll not deny.

ŒD. That had he not conspired with thee, the blood

Of Laius to my charge he had not laid.

CRE. What he hath said, thou knowest: but I claim

To question thee, as thou hast questioned me.

ŒD. Ask on: thou wilt not fix this guilt on me.

CRE. What then? Hast thou my sister to thy wife?

ŒD. What thou hast asked, I may not well deny.

CRE. Reigns she with thee, the partner of thy power?

ŒD. Her will is mine: nought is withheld from her.

CRE. Equalled with you twain am not I, the third?

ŒD. How false a friend thou art, appears in this.

CRE. Not so, if to thyself thou 'dst put my case.

Consider first—who, thinkest thou, would choose
To be a king with dreams of evil cheer,
When he might sleep secure, and reign no less?
Think not, I am so much ambition's fool,
I'd rather be a king than do like one—
So would not I, nor any prudent man.
Now without fear I have all things from thee;
But, were I king, I might not please myself.
How should I crave the name of king, who have
The power and kingliness without the pain?
I am not yet so senseless to misprise
An honourable lot that costs me nought.
Now all men greet me, I am friends to all,
And those who'd speak with thee, call me aside;
'Tis the sure way to prosper in their suit:
And dost thou think I'd change my place for thine?
I needs must be a fool to be a traitor.
But neither of such treachery am I fain,
Nor to another's plots would I consent.
For proof—get thee to Delphi first, and ask,
Did I report the oracle aright:
This too—if thou dost find that with the seer

In aught I have conspired, pronounce my death,
Not with one voice but two, both thine and mine.
But on mere vague surmise condemn me not.
Unjust alike are random trust and blame,
To reckon false men true, or true men false:
And one had better lose, what he loves best,
His life, than throw away a faithful friend.
In time this lesson thou shalt surely learn:
For time alone can show the honest man,
But in a single day a knave is known.

CHOR. One who walked warily, O king, might own,
He argued well: swift judgments are not sure.

ŒD. When secret foes are sudden in attack,
Swiftly to meet them must my plans be laid.
If I sit still and wait, the moment's gone—
His plans have prospered, mine are frustrated.

CRE. What wilt thou do then? Wilt thou banish me?

ŒD. Not banishment, but death, shall be thy doom.

CRE. When men have seen, and gauged, a tyrant's spite?

ŒD. Wilt thou defy me, and dispute my will?

CRE. I see thy judgment errs.

ŒD.   I guard my own.

CRE. Have I no rights as well?

ŒD.   Thou art a traitor.

CRE. If thou 'rt mistaken?

ŒD.   Yet I must be king.

CRE. Not if thou rul'st unjustly.

ŒD.   Hear him, Thebes!

CRE. I have a voice in Thebes, as well as thou.

CHOR. Princes, forbear: for hither in good time

Comes forth the queen, Jocasta, from the house:
The feud that is between you, she may heal.

Joc. What means this senseless din of warring tongues?
Unhappy men, have ye no shame, to voice
Your private wrongs, when Thebes is sick to death?
Go thou within, and, Creon, get thee home,
Make no more mountains of your mole-hill griefs.

Cre. Sister, this man, thy husband, Œdipus,
Claims to propound to me a bitter choice—
To be driv'n from my country, or to die.

Œd. 'Tis true: for I have found him, good my queen,
Contriving with base arts against my life.

Cre. May I not thrive, but be accurst, and perish,
If I have done aught that thou dost pretend!

Joc. O by the gods, believe him, Œdipus,
Revering both this oath which he has sworn,
And me, and all this friendly company.

Chor. Hear us, O king, we entreat,
With goodwill, and a prudent mind.

Œd. In what, then, shall I yield to you?

Chor. Have thou regard to this man,
Who never before was foolish, and now
In the strength of his oath is strong.

Œd. Know ye, for what ye ask?

Chor. I know.

Œd. Say, what?

Chor. The friend, who binds his conscience with an oath,
On bare suspicion tax not nor disgrace.

Œd. But, when ye ask me this, be well assured
That death or banishment ye ask for me.

Chor. By Helios, no—chief of the hosts of heaven!
Godless and friendless, if I wish thee ill,

To deepest depths of ruin let me fall!
But, seeing all the city perishing,
My spirit fails within me, if indeed
New ills to former ills your strife shall add.

Œd. Well—let him go: and let me die outright,
Or else be thrust dishonoured from the land.
Thy mournful pleading moves me: therefore thee,
Not him, I pity; him my hate shall follow.

Cre. Ungraciously thou yieldest: but for this
Thou wilt be sorry when the fit is past.
'Tis just, such tempers most should plague themselves.

Œd. Wilt thou not hold thy peace and go?

Cre. I go,
Stranger'd by thee, but friended by my friends.

Chor. Lady, why tarriest thou,
To shut the doors upon thy lord?

Joc. Not till ye tell me what has chanced.

Chor. Words have been angrily spoken,
Suspicious, impatient, ignorant words,
Unjust—but they carry a sting.

Joc. From both did they proceed?

Chor. Yes.

Joc. What was spoken?

Chor. Thebes has enough to bear: where the strife rests,
There let it end; and let no more be said.

Œd. See, with thy friendliness what thou hast done,
My will unbent, and blunted my resolve.

Chor. King, I have said it and will say it again—
Ill-counselling nor for wise counsels apt
Should I be proved, if thee I now renounce,
Who with a straight course home didst safely bring

The storm-tossed vessel of my people's
    hope —
And now again comfort us, if thou canst!
  Joc. I pray thee, king, hide not from
    me the cause,
That to such fierce displeasure thou art
    moved.
  Œd. Yea, for I honour thee, queen,
    more than these—
What Creon hath planned against me,
    thou shalt hear.
  Joc. Thy ground of quarrel let me
    clearly know.
  Œd. By me he says that Laius was
    slain.
  Joc. As knowing it of himself, or
    from another?
  Œd. A lying prophet he has set to
    say it;
Nor speaks one word that may commit
    himself.
  Joc. Why, think no more then of
    what troubles thee.
Listen to me; I tell thee, there is not
Any such thing as prophecy on earth.
And, what I speak, I'll shortly prove it
    true.
There came to Laius once an oracle,
I say not from the god, but from his ser-
    vants,
That fate would bring to pass that he
    should die
Slain by his son, whom I should bear to
    him.
But Laius, in a place where three roads
    meet,
As rumour went, robbers and strangers
    slew:
And from the child's birth ere three days
    had passed,
Binding his feet with cords, by hands of
    others
On the lone mountain-side his father
    flung him.
So failed Apollo's word that he should
    slay
His father, and that Laius (the fate
He feared so much) should by his son be
    slain.

So prophets order the affairs of men;
Whom heed not thou: for, knowledge
    that the god
Seeks to impart, he will himself reveal.
  Œd. Bewilderment, O lady, fills my
    soul,
Hearing thy word, and troubles all my
    thoughts.
  Joc. What sudden doubt hath so
    surprised thy mind?
  Œd. Methought I heard thee say
    that in a place
Where three roads met was Laius over-
    thrown.
  Joc. 'Twas rumoured so, and so is
    still believed.
  Œd. Where is the spot, where this
    disaster chanced?
  Joc. The land is Phocian, and the
    branching roads
From Delphi and from Daulis thither
    lead.
  Œd. And how long is it since these
    things were done?
  Joc. A little ere we hailed thee king
    of Thebes—
So long ago came tidings of the deed.
  Œd. O Zeus, what is thy will con-
    cerning me?
  Joc. What is it that so moves thee,
    Œdipus?
  Œd. Ask me not yet: but tell me
    first, how looked
This Laius—how far was his manhood
    spent?
  Joc. Tall, and his hair a little mixed
    with grey,
And in his looks not all unlike to thee.
  Œd. Ah me unhappy! a grievous
    curse, not knowing,
Upon myself it seems that I have laid.
  Joc. What dost thou say? O king, I
    fear thy face.
  Œd. I much misdoubt the seer in
    deed can see.
But tell me one thing more, and I shall
    know.
  Joc. I fear, but what thou askest I
    will tell.

Œd. How went he—with a slender company,
Or with a goodly following, like a king?
Joc. Five men were all that followed him, and one
A herald: and one chariot bore the king.
Œd. It is enough: there is no doubt. But, lady,
What man was he who told this tale in Thebes?
Joc. A servant, who alone escaped alive.
Œd. About the palace now may he be found?
Joc. Not so: for when, come hence, he saw thee throned
King in the room of Laius who was dead,
He touched my hand, and prayed that I would send him
Into the fields, that he might tend the flocks,
As far from sight of Thebes as he could go;
And so he went: he was an honest slave,
And greater boon than this had well deserved.
Œd. Let him come hither again without delay.
Joc. He can be called. But what wouldst thou with him?
Œd. More than I should, I fear that I myself
Have uttered, and would speak with him of this.
Joc. The man shall come. But have not I a right
To learn, O king, what so disquiets thee?
Œd. What dark forebodings weigh upon my soul,
I will not hide from thee. Who if not thou
Should share the knowledge of the path I tread?
Polybus, king of Corinth, was my father,
My mother Dorian Merope. No peer
Had I in Corinth, till upon a day
An incident befell, worthy indeed
Of wonder, but not worth the heed I paid it.

For at a feast a man, heated with wine,
Called me a foundling, not my father's son.
And I, indignant, till that day had passed
Hardly endured, and on the next I taxed
My parents face to face; and they, incensed
Against the slanderer, brooked not that reproach.
So was I satisfied by them, and yet
The rumour grew, and stung me night and day,
Till I without my parents' knowledge came
To Delphi. But in vain: Apollo deigned
No answer to the question that I asked:
But what a tale instead, as from his lips,
I heard—of woe and horror and despair!
That I was doomed to marry with my mother,
And show the world a sight intolerable,
The children of that union; and to be
The murderer of the father who begat me.
And hearing this I fled—fled through the night—
Away from Corinth, never to return—
Shaping my course by starlight—to a land
Where I should never see my life fulfil
The shameful presage of that dreaded doom.
So came I to the very place whereat
I hear thee say the king, thy lord, was slain.
Queen, I will tell thee all. When, journeying,
I drew near to the meeting of the ways,
There did a herald meet me, and a man
Rode in a colt-drawn chariot, as thou sayest.
They met me face to face: and from the path
Servant and master both essayed to force me.
Then I in wrath struck at the charioteer,
Who turned me back: but, when the old man saw it,

Waiting until I passed, with double goad
Full on the head he smote me from
 above.
Heavily he paid for it. For in a minute
The good staff in my hand dealt such a
 blow,
Backward from the mid-car he reeled and
 fell.
I slew them every one. But, if this
 stranger
Was any kinsman of the king that's dead,
Who is more miserable than I this day?
What man could be more hated by the
 gods?
Whom, citizen or stranger, no one must
Receive under his roof, or speak to me,
But thrust me from his doors. And it
 was I,
No other, who laid this curse upon
 myself.
And these foul hands, that did the mur-
 der, stain
The bed o' the murdered man. Am I
 not vile—
Unclean, from head to foot? who must
 pass hence
Exiled, and passing not reseek my home,
Not tread my native soil, or fear that
 curst
Incestuous marriage, and to slay my sire,
Polybus—from whom I sprang, who
 reared my youth.
Should not one justly tax the heavens
 with spite,
That rained down such afflictions on my
 head?
Let me not live, ye high and holy gods,
Not live to see that day, but pass away
From sight of all men first, and not
 behold
The blot of evil, blackening all my life!
 CHOR. O king, this troubles us in-
 deed: but, till
Thou hear'st from him who saw, hope
 for the best.
 ŒD. Why, so much hope in truth is
 mine, to wait
The shepherd's coming: this, and only
this.

JOC. And should he come—what
 makes thine eagerness?
 ŒD. I'll tell thee: if his tale agrees
 with thine,
Then I am free; there's nought for me
 to fear.
 JOC. What in my story squared not
 with thy deed?
 ŒD. Thou saidst he spake of robbers
 —of a band,
Who slew the king. If the same number
 still
He shall report, it is not I who slew him.
One man is not mistaken for a host.
But let him speak of one sole traveller—
That turns the scale: plainly the deed
 was mine.
 JOC. Doubt not, he told the tale as I
 have said,
And what he spoke he cannot now reject,
For all the city heard, not I alone.
But should he swerve aught from his
 former speech,
Yet nowise, king, the death of Laius
Shall he show true to promise, whom the
 god
Foredoomed to die, slain by his babe and
 mine.
Yet never did that child, the hapless
 boy,
Slay him—but died himself before his
 sire;
That never again should I take pains to
 look
This way or that, for fear of prophecy.
 ŒD. I hold with thee in that. But
 yet send one
To bid the hind come hither: omit not
 this.
 JOC. I'll send with speed. But go
 we now within:
For I will nothing do but what thou
 wouldst.
 CHOR. O may my constant feet not
 fail,
Walking in paths of righteousness,
Sinless in word and deed—
True to those eternal laws
That scale forever the high steep

Of heaven's pure ether, whence they sprang:
For only in Olympus is their home,
Nor mortal wisdom gave them birth,
And, howsoe'er men may forget,
They will not sleep;
For the might of the god within them grows not old.
Rooted in pride, the tyrant grows;
But pride that with its own too-much
Is rashly surfeited,
Heeding not the prudent mean,
Down the inevitable gulf
From its high pinnacle is hurled,
Where use of feet or foothold there is none.
But, O kind gods, the noble strength,
That struggles for the state's behoof,
Unbend not yet:
In the gods have I put my trust—I will not fear.
But whoso walks disdainfully,
In act or word,
And fears not justice, nor reveres
The throned gods, Him let misfortune slay
For his ill-starred wantoning,
Should he heap unrighteous gains,
Nor from unhallowed paths withhold his feet,
Or reach rash hands to pluck forbidden fruit.
Who shall do this, and boast
That yet his soul is proof
Against the arrows of offended Heaven?
If honour crowns such deeds as these,
Not song, but silence, then for me!
To Earth's dread centre, unprofaned
By mortal touch,
No more with awe will I repair,
Nor Abæ's shrine,
Nor the Olympian plain,
If the truth stands not confessed,
Pointed at by all the world.
O Zeus supreme, if rightly thou art called—
Lord over all—let not these things escape
Thee and thy timeless sway!

For now men set at nought
Apollo's word, and cry 'Behold, it fails!'
His praise is darkened with a doubt;
And faith is sapped, and Heaven defied.
  Joc. Elders of Thebes, 'twas borne upon my mind,
Shrines of the gods to visit, and to bring
These garlands and this incense in my hands.
The soul of Œdipus is idly stirred
With manifold misgivings; and, whereas
Wise men conclude things present from things past,
Him the last speaker sways—who speaks of fear.
Now therefore, since my counsel nought avails,
To thee, Lyceian Apollo, who art most nigh,
With these entreaties suppliant I am come,
That thou wouldst cleanse and make us free from guilt.
For now our hearts wax faint, beholding him,
The pilot of our ship, distraught with fear.
  Mess. Friends, might I of your courtesy inquire
Where is the house of Œdipus the king?
Or, better, where is he—if this ye know?
  Chor. These are his doors, O friend, and he within;
And this his wife, the mother of his children.
  Mess. Blessings on her, and blessings on her house
For ever—being a perfect wife to him!
  Joc. I wish thee back thy wishes: for no less
Deserves thy courteous speech. But wherefore, friend,
Art thou come hither—with what news to tell?
  Mess. Good news, queen, to thy house, and to thy lord.
  Joc. What news? And by whose sending art thou come?

MESS. I come from Corinth. Tidings I shall tell—
Joyful past doubt, yet haply sorrowful.
Joc. What tidings—sweet and bitter in a breath?
MESS. The people of the Isthmian land are purposed—
So there 'twas said—to have him for their king.
Joc. How? Doth not the aged Polybus still reign?
MESS. Not he: for death has laid him in the tomb.
Joc. What sayest thou? Polybus, old man, is dead?
MESS. Let me not live, if I have spoken falsely.
Joc. Lose not a moment, sirrah; to thy lord
Go, tell this news. O oracles of the gods,
Where are ye now? Fearing to slay this man
Did Œdipus flee from his home—who now
In nature's course, not by his act, is dead.
Œd. O dearest presence of my wife Jocasta,
Why hast thou called me hither from the house?
Joc. Hear this man's news; hear, and perceive, to what
The boasted oracles of the gods are come.
Œd. Who is this man? what tidings does he bring?
Joc. From Corinth he reports that Polybus,
Thy father, lives no longer, but is dead.
Œd. How, sirrah? From thine own lips let me hear it.
MESS. If first thou'dst have the certainty of this
Doubt not, but know, that Polybus is dead.
Œd. Visited by sickness, or by treason slain?
MESS. The lives of old men hang upon a thread.

Œd. Poor soul, 'twas sickness, then, that took him off?
MESS. That, and the length of years which weighed him down.
Œd. Alas, why then, O queen, should men regard
The Delphian hearth prophetic, or the birds
That scream i' the air; by whose direction I
Was to have slain my father—but he is dead
And in his grave, and I remain, whose hand
No sword came near; unless for love of me
He pined away—and so I caused his death:—
But certainly this prophecy at least
Is with the dead man buried, out of mind.
Joc. Said I not from the first this would be so?
Œd. Ay, so thou didst: but me my fears misled.
Joc. Bid now thy fears farewell: despond no more.
Œd. My mother's couch how can I cease to fear?
Joc. Why should men fear, who see that chance rules all,
And forecast of the future there is none?
Careless to live, as best one can, is best.
And this unnatural union fear not thou:
For many a man ere now, aghast, has dreamed
Of coupling with a mother. But who sets
At naught such fancies, bears life's burden best.
Œd. All this indeed were well and wisely spoken,
Did not my mother live: but, while she lives,
How true soe'er thy words, I needs must fear.
Joc. Is not thy father's death new sight to thee?

ŒD. Ay, there I see: yet dread the living mother.

MESS. What woman is it of whom ye are afraid?

ŒD. The wife of Polybus, Merope, old man.

MESS. And what see ye in her that tends to fear?

ŒD. A dreadful prophecy the god has uttered.

MESS. May it be spoken? Or must no man know it?

ŒD. Nay, thou shalt hear. To marry with my mother—

This doom hath Loxias pronounced for me,

And with these hands to shed my father's blood.

And therefore far from Corinth many a day

My life was passed; and this was well— and yet

Into their parents' eyes men love to look.

MESS. Was this the fear that banished thee from thence?

ŒD. This—and my father's murderer not to be.

MESS. What hinders then, that, as I came thy friend,

I from this fear, king, should deliver thee?

ŒD. I should not prove a niggard of my thanks.

MESS. Indeed to this end chiefly did I come,

That I might profit by thy coming home.

ŒD. Beneath my parents' roof I may not come.

MESS. 'Tis plain, my son, thou know'st not what thou dost.

ŒD. What meanest thou, old man? I prithee, speak.

MESS. If for this cause thou dost avoid thy home.

ŒD. Yea, for I fear lest the god's word come true.

MESS. Pollution from thy parents dost thou fear?

ŒD. This ever—this, old man, makes me afraid.

MESS. Then dost thou know thou startest at a shadow?

ŒD. How, if these were my parents, I their son?

MESS. Because no kin was Polybus to thee.

ŒD. What dost thou tell me? was he not my father?

MESS. As much—no more than I who speak to thee.

ŒD. Thou'rt nought to me—how then my father's equal?

MESS. Neither from his loins didst thou spring, nor mine.

ŒD. How did he let me then be called his son?

MESS. From my hands he received thee as a gift.

ŒD. And yet a foundling he so greatly loved?

MESS. Persuaded by his former childlessness.

ŒD. Bought by thy gold was I, or found by chance?

MESS. Among Kithæron's wooded folds I found thee.

ŒD. What errand led thee to the mountain ways?

MESS. The sheep upon the mountain were my charge.

ŒD. Wast thou a vagrant and a hireling shepherd?

MESS. But on that day, my son, I rescued thee.

ŒD. In what distress, forsaken, didst thou find me?

MESS. Thy bruised feet may testify of this.

ŒD. Ha, thou hast harped upon an ancient grief!

MESS. I loosed thy feet, pierced through and bound with cords.

ŒD. O dread memorial of my childhood's shame!

MESS. So that from this misfortune thou wast named.

ŒD. By father or mother was this done? O say!

MESS. Not I, but he who gave thee, should know this.

ŒD. Thou didst receive me, then, and didst not find me?

MESS. Nay, from another shepherd's hands I had thee.

ŒD. Who was he? Dost thou know how to describe him?

MESS. He fed the sheep of Laius as I heard.

ŒD. Of him who was aforetime king of Thebes?

MESS. Ay, that was he: his feeder this man was.

ŒD. Is that man still alive, that I may see him?

MESS. That should be best known to your Theban folk.

ŒD. Is any one among the standers-by
Who knows about this hind, of whom he speaks—
Has seen him, in the city or the fields?
Speak out: the time has come to find the truth.

CHOR. I think he is none other than the man
Whose presence from the fields thou didst desire:
But the queen best can tell if this be so.

ŒD. Lady, thou mindest him, whom we erewhile
Bade summon hither? Spake this man of him?

JOC. What skills of whom he spake? Heed not his talk:
Vainly it were remembered: let it pass.

ŒD. This cannot be, that having found this clue
I should not bring my parentage to light.

JOC. As thou dost love thy life, in-quire no more—
I charge thee by the gods: my grief's enough.

ŒD. Nay, never fear; for, though three mothers back

Should stamp me thrice a slave, thou shalt not blush.

JOC. Yet be advised, I pray thee, and forbear.

ŒD. I'll not consent not to learn all the truth.

JOC. Ah, yet in prudence I advise the best.

ŒD. Too long thou dost torment me with this best.

JOC. O may'st thou never know what man thou art!

ŒD. Will some one go and bring the shepherd hither?
And let this woman of rich kinsmen boast.

JOC. Woe to thee, miserable! no other word
Have I for thee—now or for evermore!
(She goes out.)

CHOR. What sudden frenzy, Œdipus, of grief
Swept hence the queen? To mischief, much I fear,
Her passion, from this silence, will break forth.

ŒD. Break forth to what it will—yet I will choose
To trace, though mean, the sources of my blood.
Perchance this woman, more than women proud,
Of my ignoble lineage is ashamed.
But I am not dishonoured, since I deem
Myself a child of Fortune, ever kind.
She truly is my mother, and the months,
Her children too, have made me small and great.
This, which I am, I cannot cease to be,
That I should fear the secret of my birth.

CHOR. If with my human wit
The future I can read—
Olympus, hear me swear,
That of Kithæron, all the moonlit night,
When next the moon's at full,
Our praises shall not fail—
Of Œdipus compatriot true,
And nurse, and mother proved:
Nor shall the mountain miss

Due meed of dance and song
For kindness rendered to our lord the
king.
O Phœbus, hear our cry,
And let our prayer with thee acceptance
find!
Thy mother, O fair son—
Some mountain nymph was she,
In fadeless beauty clad,
Whom Pan upon the mountain saw and
loved?
Or her to his embrace
Did Loxias woo and win?
For well our pastoral lawns he loves:
Or else Kyllene's lord,
Or Bacchus, who delights
The mountain-peaks to haunt—
Did some fair nymph o' the Heliconian
train
(His playmates best-beloved)
Leave on the hills his babe for him to
find?

ŒD. If I may make conjecture,
friends, of one
Whose face I never saw, here comes
methinks
The shepherd of our quest. For, full of
years,
Chimes with this man the measure of
his age:
Besides, my servants lead him, whom I
know—
My own: yet may my knowledge be surpassed
Perchance by thine, who hast this
shepherd seen.

CHOR. I know him, doubtless. No
more trusty fellow
Had Laius for a herdsman, sire, than
he.

ŒD. Thee, sir, who art from Corinth,
first I ask,
Is this the man?

MESS. This, whom thine eyes behold.

ŒD. Now, aged sir, for thee: look
hither and speak
To what I ask: Didst thou serve Laius?

SERV. Not bought, but of his household born and bred.

ŒD. Minding what task—to what
employment bound?

SERV. Most of my time I followed
with the flocks.

ŒD. And whereabouts didst thou thy
shepherding?

SERV. Now 'twas Kithæron, now
some neighbor hill.

ŒD. Hadst thou with this man any
dealings there?

SERV. What made he there? Of
what man dost thou ask?

ŒD. Who stands before thee: hast
thou met him ever?

SERV. I can not on this instant call
to mind.

MESS. No marvel, sire, if he forgets:
but soon
Clearly he shall remember. Well I
know
He knows the time when on Kithæron's
slopes
He fed two flocks together; while with
one
From springtime till Arcturus, year by
year,
Three times, each time six months, I
was his neighbour:
Then, for the winter, home we drove our
sheep,
He to the folds of Laius, I to mine:
Sounds this like truth, or have I dreamed
it all?

SERV. No dream, but truth, though
it is long since then.

MESS. A child thou gavest me—dost
thou remember?
A tender babe, to nurse him for my
own.

SERV. What wouldst thou have?
Why dost thou ask me this?

MESS. The child became a man: look
where he stands!

SERV. Hence to perdition—go; and
cease thy prate!

ŒD. Ah, do not chide, old man, his
speaking: thine
Of such reproof stands more in need than
his.

SERV. Most gracious sire, wherein do I offend?

ŒD. Not speaking of the child of whom he asks.

SERV. This trail is false: he speaks he knows not what.

ŒD. In kindness thou'lt not speak: perforce thou shalt.

SERV. Me, who am old, I pray thee, do not harm!

ŒD. Let some one bind me, quick, this fellow's arms.

SERV. Alas, for what? what more wouldst thou be told?

ŒD. Thou gavest him this child of whom he asks?

SERV. Would I had died that day! but so I did.

ŒD. Thou'lt come to this, not speaking all the truth.

SERV. Much more, if I shall speak, I am undone.

ŒD. This man, it seems, will palter with us yet.

SERV. What paltering? Said I not, I gave the child?

ŒD. Whose was the babe? another's or thine own?

SERV. Nay, none of mine: one gave him to my hands.

ŒD. Which of these Thebans gave— where dwelt the man?

SERV. No more: by heaven, O king, ask me no more.

ŒD. Thou art undone, if I must ask again.

SERV. Born in the house of Laius was the child.

ŒD. And of the king's blood was he, or a slave?

SERV. Now, now, ah me, the fatal words to speak.

ŒD. Fatal for me to hear: but I must hear it.

SERV. His child 'twas called indeed: but one within,

Thy queen, can best attest if this was so.

ŒD. She gave thee, then, the babe?

SERV. My lord, she did.

ŒD. And wherefore did she so?

SERV. That it might die.

ŒD. O cruel mother!

SERV. Dire prophecies she feared.

ŒD. What were they?

SERV. That the child should slay his sire.

ŒD. How then gav'st thou the child to this old man?

SERV. For pity, O master: to another land

Thinking that he would bear it, whence he came.

O woful life, ill-saved! For, if thou art

What this man says, thou art most miserable.

ŒD. Out and alas! so all at last comes true!

Here let me look my last upon the sun,

That sees me father'd, mother'd, wived amiss,

And, whom I should not, sees that I have slain.

CHOR. O generations of the race of men,

How all as if ye were not I account

This human life ye live.

For which, O which of you may hope to win

Of bliss a larger share,

Than just enough to seem,

Then from that seeming to decline?

I, with thy fate for proof,

Thine, thine, O hapless Œdipus,

May deem no mortal blest:

Who as a master-bowman cleft the mark,

And all-admired prosperity he won—

O Zeus, and is this he?—

Against that maiden with her vulture claws,

And subtle songs of doom,

He rose, a tower of strength,

And slew her, and our lives redeemed:

We hailed him then our king,

Our worship at his feet we laid:

This mighty Thebes he ruled.

Now what name sounds more lamentable than his?

Or who, in life's reverse,

With fierce calamity hath dwelt,
And anguish, like to this?
Where is his glory now,
Whom, entering rash that chamber, son
    with sire,
The same wide harbour hath received?
How could, how could, O hapless
    Œdipus,
The furrows of thy father's field
So long in silence bear with thee?
But now all-seeing Time hath found and
    doomed
This thine unconscious sin—
In guilty union linked with one,
Thy mother, and thy wife.
O son of Laius, thee
I would that never, never I had seen!
No measure of my grief I know,
Nor how my cries to stint. For, sooth
    to tell,
Thou didst my life renew, and now
Because of thee my days are dark.

MESS. O ye most honoured ever of
    this land,
What deeds your ears, your eyes, what
    grief your souls
Shall know, if for the race of Labdacus
Ye from your hearts are careful as of
    old.
Not Ister's flood, nor Phasis, as I think,
With pure ablution could make clean
    this house—
Such guilt it hides—and other guilt full
    soon,
Willing and not unwilling, shall disclose:
Worst grief of all, when men afflict
    themselves.

CHOR. That which we knew before
    lacked not to be
Most lamentable; what hast thou more
to tell?

MESS. Word soonest told and soonest
    heard is this—
The godlike presence of the queen is
dead.

CHOR. Unhappy lady, what cause
    had she to die?

MESS. Her own rash act: the worst
of what was done

Thou canst not know, not having it to
    see,
But yet, far as my memory may serve,
The tale of her undoing thou shalt
    hear.
Soon as in that fierce mood she came
    inside
The porch of the house, straight to her
    nuptial couch
She hied, with all the strength of both
    her hands
Rending her hair, and violently she made
The doors upon herself, and called aloud
On Laius, her dead lord, and made her
    moan
Of that her ancient childbed, whence
    he gat
A son that slew himself—and died and
    left
That mother to that son, quick-wombed
    to bear
Offspring accursed: O hateful marriage-
    bed,
Twice fruitful, whence to her, ill-starred,
    there sprang
Husband from husband, children from
    her child!
So much I know, but know not how she
    died:
For in there burst, with outcries loud,
    the king,
And filled my sight: her end I might
    not see.
But him my eyes still followed where
    he roamed,
Now here, now there, craving of us a
    sword,
And where to find that wife, no wife
    indeed,
Mother and wife in one, a field twice-
    tilled,
That bore himself for fruit, and fruit
    to him.
So as he raved, some god directed him—
No man at least, of us who watched him
    there:
And with a dreadful cry he leapt against
The folded doors, as one had led the
    way,

And from their sockets burst the bending bolts,
And entered. Hanging there—the queen
we saw
Tight in the death-grip of a pendent
cord.
With one dread voice of horror at that
sight
He loosed the hanging noose, and on the
ground
Laid down the piteous corse: and then
we saw
A dreadful sight: for, tearing from her
robe
The golden clasp that pinned its folds
aright,
He smote and stabbed the circles of his
eyes,
Exclaiming, that on him they should not
look,
What things he suffered and what things
he did;
Nor see henceforth whom not to see
behoved—
See and mistake those whom he craved
to know.
Such burden chanting, he full many a
time
With lifted hand struck at his eyes: and
both
Their bleeding orbs rained forth unceasingly
Great drops of oozing gore that drenched
his beard,
Two pelting showers together of dark
red hail.
Such sudden doom, not single, his and
hers,
On both, by act of both, hath broken
forth.
Gone is the former bliss, which, while
it was,
Was bliss indeed: a day, and all is
changed,
Wailing and woe are here, and death,
and shame,
And all are here, all evils that are named.

CHOR. From grief, poor soul, what
respite finds he now?

MESS. Loudly he bids unbolt the
doors, and let
All eyes in Thebes look on the parricide,
Who with his mother—unhallowed deeds
he names
Nameless for me!—then from the land
he will
Banish himself, nor here abide the curse
Himself invoked. But strength he lacks,
and one
To lead him: his affliction else is more
Than he can bear. Look for thyself. I
hear
The bolts undraw. A sight thou shalt
behold,
Should wring compassion even from his
foes.

CHOR. O woful plight for men to see,
Most woful sight that ever I have seen!
What madness, O unhappy king,
Possessed thee? On thine ill-starred life,
A leap beyond all measure of how far,
What god hath leapt?
I cannot bear to look on thee,
Albeit of many things I fain would ask,
Of many things my ears, my eyes inform:
Such shuddering takes hold of me.

ŒD. Alas, alas unhappy that I am!
Whither I wend, I know not; and my
voice
To the four winds of heaven is idly borne.
Whereunto hath this fierce fate leapt on
me?

CHOR. To horror, neither to be heard
nor seen.

ŒD. O thou thick cloud of darkness,
That on my life hast settled,
Abominable, unutterable,
Indomitable,
By pitiless winds swept hitherward on
me;
Alas!
And yet again, alas, and woe is me!
Such maddening pain
Of those sharp daggers at my eyes,
Blent with remembrance of my misery,
Pierces my inmost soul.

CHOR. No marvel if, in such extremity,

Thy grief is twofold, as thy suffering is.
ŒD. O my good friend,
I am not then forsaken yet by thee?
O constant friend, who of thy love for me
Yet weariest not though I am blind!—
    Ah me!
Ah woe is me!
Spite of this darkness, yet I know thee
    well,
Hearing thy voice: a friend hath no
    disguise.
CHOR. O rash and overbold, how
    didst thou dare
Mar thus thy sight? What god stirred
    thee to this?
ŒD. Apollo, O my friends,
Apollo on my life
This evil doom, this evil doom hath laid;
But no hand dealt,
No hand save mine alone, the grievous
    blow:
For what to me did eyes avail,
Who seeing had no pleasant sight to see?
CHOR. Even as thou sayest, so it was.
ŒD. What should my eyes behold,
Or heart desire, or ears
Take pleasure any more
Of human speech, O friends, to hear:
Convey me hence as quickly as ye may,
Hence, O my friends, from all men's
    sight,
Me, most pernicious—me,
Of mortals most accurst,
And hated by the gods of all men most.
CHOR. Would god that I had never
    seen thy face,
In wisdom as in fortune all unblest!
ŒD. Perish the man who found me
On the wild mountain-side,
And from the cruel cords that bound my
    feet
Loosed me, and rescued me, and saved
    from death,
A kindness most unkind:
For then should I have died,
Not lived, to grieve my friends and vex
    myself.
CHOR. My wish in this consents to
    thine.

ŒD. So had I not my father slain,
And not been called by all the world
Husband of her from whom I sprang:
Now I am godless—son of an impious
    race—
Wedded, O miserable, with her from
    whom I sprang.
All misery that misery exceeds
Hath Œdipus obtained.
CHOR. I know not how to say thou
    hast counselled well:
Better thou hadst not been than blind
    to live.
ŒD. That I have done what was not
    best to do,
Instruct me not, nor counsel any more.
I know not with what eyes I should have
    met
My father face to face in the halls of
    death,
Or that my wretched mother—having
    done
Wrongs worse than hanging both to him
    and her.
But was the sight of children then so
    dear,
For me to see them, born as they were
    born?
Nay, to my eyes no welcome sight were
    they,
Nor yet this city, not these towers of
    Thebes,
Nor sacred shrines o' the gods, where-
    from I wretched
Who once most nobly lived of all in
    Thebes
Debarred myself, myself charging all
    men
To drive me forth, the impious one, by
    heaven
Proclaimed unclean—and son of Laius.
How, having brought home to myself
    such guilt,
With steadfast eyes this people could I
    face?
Nay but, the fount of hearing in mine
    ears
Could I have choked withal, I had not
    spared

This miserable body to seal up,
That sight nor sound had reached me: could my soul
So dwell, fenced round from evil, that were bliss.
Why did Kithæron nurse me? Why not rather
Take me and slay me there, never to show
The shuddering world the secret of my birth?
O Polybus, O Corinth, and O home
That once I deemed my sire's, what festering sore
Lurked underneath your love that showed so fair!
Vile of a vile race I am found the son.
O triple ways, and dark mysterious dell,
Where 'neath the copse the three roads straitly met,
O ye that from my hands drank deep my blood,
My father's that I shed, do ye remember
What deed ye saw me do, ere hither I came,
And did what deeds again? O marriage-bed
My bed of birth, that bore me, and again
By that self seed requickened gave to view
The father, brother, son, one blood with her,
That bride, both wife and mother: O horrid sight
Of deeds most shameful that on earth are done!
But, since of things ill done 'tis ill to speak,
Now by the gods make haste and hale me forth
And hide me hence, or slay, or in the deep
Fling me where ye shall see me never more.
Shrink not to touch me, wretched that I am:
Fear nothing, but consent. For this my load
Of sorrow none may bear but I alone.

CHOR. Lo timely to thine asking, even now,
To do and to advise, comes Creon—he,
Who single in thy stead protects the land.
ŒD. Ah me, what speech to him shall I address?
What plea shall now suffice me? for to him
All that I said before is found unjust.
CRE. I am not come to mock thee, Œdipus,
Nor to reproach thee with the former wrong.
But ye—grown reckless that the sons of men
Should see such sight unblest, yet to the beam,
All-quickening, of the Sun-god fear to show,
Unveiled, a man impure, whom earth rejects,
And rain that drops from heaven, and holy light.
Into the house conduct him speedily.
Most right it is, the evils of their kin
Kinsmen should see and hear, and none but they.
ŒD. By heaven, for thou hast plucked my fears away,
With nobleness requiting me most vile,
Grant, for thy sake, not mine, the boon I crave.
CRE. With what request dost thou importune me?
ŒD. Make haste to banish me out of this land,
Where none shall see me, none shall speak to me.
CRE. Surely ere now I had done this, but first
I wished to learn the pleasure of the god.
ŒD. One voice we heard from him, to let me perish,
The parricide, the impious that I am.
CRE. It was reported so: but in this need
'Twere best we should learn further what to do.

Œd. Will ye inquire for one so miserable?

Cre. 'Tis time that even thou shouldst trust the gods.

Œd. Thou therefore do my bidding, and consent:—

Bury indeed the woman in the house
According to thy pleasure: 'tis thy right,
For she is thine: but doom not me alive
Here in my father's city to abide:
Out on the mountain yonder let me dwell,
Kithæron called, and mine, that living tomb
My parents gave me once to be my own:
So shall their murderous will at last be done.
And yet I know no sickness and no harm
Could touch me then: else had I not been saved
Out of that death, but to fulfil my doom.
So be that doom fulfilled, whate'er it be.
But for my children, Creon—for the boys
No need that thou shouldst care: for they are men,
And cannot starve, wherever they may be—
But of my daughters twain, poor helpless maids,
Whose place at board was ever at my side,
One board for me and them, one fare for both,
And nothing that I touched they might not share—
Care thou for them: and let me, if I may,
Touch them but once, and weep, and bid farewell.
Grant this, O prince,
Out of thy noble heart. For, might I touch them,
My own, as when I saw them, they would seem.—
What do I say?
O heaven, do I not hear my darlings somewhere
Weeping, and Creon has had pity on me,
And brought them here, my children, my beloved?
Is it not so?

Cre. I brought them here indeed, thee having seen
In former days delighted even as now.

Œd. O for this meeting be thou blest, and safe
In heaven's good keeping rest, more safe than I!
Children, where are ye? Come hither and draw near,
To these fraternal hands, my hands that have
A goodly sight provided you to see,
Your father's eyes, dark now, that once were bright,
Since you I gat whence I myself was born,
Seeing and knowing not what now appears.
Children, I see you not, but weep for you,
Of your sad life's remainder when I think,
What life abhorred by men ye both shall lead.
Into what concourse or what festival
Of Thebans shall ye come, nor thence go home
Blind with your tears, that festal sight unseen?
And, when at last for marriage ye are ripe,
Who will consent, O children, who will dare
Such scathing taunts to meet as then shall light
Both on my parents and on yours no less?
For what reproach is wanting? I, your father,
My father slew, and with the mother couched
From whom my life began; and, from the womb
That bare your sire, ye to your sire were born.
Such taunts shall ye endure. Who then will wed you?
No man, my daughters, none; but certainly
Unwedded and unfruitful ye shall pine.

Son of Menœceus, then—for thou art left
Sole father that they have—since parents both
They both have lost—O leave them not to wander
Begging their bread, unhusbanded, thy kin;
Let them not in misfortune rival me:
But pity them, seeing their tender years
Left destitute and friendless, but for thee.
Lay hand in mine; be noble, and consent.
And you, my children, could ye mark my words,
Much had I counselled: now, pray this for me,
To live where chance will have me—but that you
A better than your father's life may find.

CRE. Thou hast had enough of weeping: now within the house begone.

ŒD. I must do, though hard, thy bidding.

CRE. All things are, in season, best.

ŒD. On what terms I go, thou knowest?

CRE. Let me hear, then I shall know.

ŒD. From the land I must be banished.

CRE. With the god thy asking rests.

ŒD. Am I not of gods most hated?

CRE. Therefore thou shalt have thy wish.

ŒD. Is it promised?

CRE. I have said it: what I say shall be performed.

ŒD. 'Tis enough; now hence conduct me.

CRE. Loose thy daughters, then, and go.

ŒD. Do not take from me my children.

CRE. Something be content to yield: More thou hast obtained already than thy life had well deserved.

CHOR. Look and learn, all Theban people, and this Œdipus behold,
This, that read the famous riddle, and we hailed him chief of men,
And his glory and his fortune was no Theban but admired—
Now upon his head the billows of disaster dire are poured.
Therefore, waiting still and watching for that final day of all,
On no mortal man the verdict 'He is happy' we pronounce,
Till his goal of life he passes, clear of sorrow to the close.

—ROBERT WHITELAW

MEDEA [1]

EURIPIDES

Euripides was born on the island of Salamis in 480 B.C., the year—tradition says, on the very day—of the famous battle of Salamis against the Persians. He preferred the life of retirement and study to that of public affairs, and spent the closing years of his life in Macedonia, where he died in 406 B.C. The remark of Sophocles that he had painted men as they ought to be while Euripides painted them as they are indicates the most important change wrought by the last of the great tragedians in the Greek drama. It was at once a change to the romantic and to the realistic—romantic in its novelties, its surprises, its use of the pathetic; and realistic in bringing the characters of heroic legends down to earth to feel and act as ordinary mortals. Plot became more intricate, dialogue more subtle, and the chorus more of a conventional interlude. The new conception of tragedy was the natural result of the changed conditions in Athens after the fear of Persian conquest had been removed, when wealth and luxury had begun to undermine traditional morality, and when sophistry and dialectic had begun to subject all things to skeptical questioning. Eighteen of the ninety plays which Euripides wrote are extant.

Euripides characteristically prefers a story of human passion and its immediate

[1] From The Loeb Classical Library, reprinted by permission.

consequences to problems of hereditary sin or of destiny. Medea is the personification of jealousy, and our interest is centered solely on the manifestations of that passion. The tragedy of Medea's situation consists not only in Jason's treatment of her, but also in the conflict within her own heart between her maternal love and her hatred for Jason's offspring. The play was produced in 432 B.C.

DRAMATIS PERSONÆ

NURSE OF MEDEA'S CHILDREN.
CHILDREN'S GUARDIAN.
MEDEA.
CHORUS OF CORINTHIAN LADIES.
CREON, *King of Corinth.*
JASON.
ÆGEUS, *King of Athens.*
MESSENGER.
CHILDREN OF MEDEA.

The Scene is in front of JASON'S *house at Corinth.*

Enter NURSE OF MEDEA'S CHILDREN

NURSE. Would God that Argo's hull had never flown
Through those blue Clashing Rocks to Colchis-land,
Nor that the axe-hewn pine in Pelion's glens
Ever had fallen, nor filled with oars the hands
Of hero-princes, who at Pelias' hest
Quested the Golden Fleece! My mistress then,
Medea, ne'er had sailed to Iolcos' towers
With love for Jason thrilled through all her soul,
Nor had on Pelias' daughters wrought to slay
Their sire, nor now in this Corinthian land
Dwelt with her lord and children, gladdening
By this her exile them whose land received her,

Yea, and in all things serving Jason's weal,
Which is the chief salvation of the home,
When wife stands not at variance with her lord.
Now all is hatred: love is sickness-stricken.
For Jason, traitor to his babes and her,
My mistress, weddeth with a child of kings,
Daughter of Creon ruler of the land.
And, slighted thus, Medea, hapless wife,
Cries on the oaths, invokes that mightiest pledge
Of the right hand, and calls the Gods to witness
What recompense from Jason she receives.
Fasting, with limbs in grief's abandonment
Flung down, she weeps and wastes through all the days
Since first she knew her lord's wrong done to her,
Never uplifting eye, nor turning ever
From earth her face. No more than rock or sea-wave
Hearkeneth she to friends that counsel her;
Saving at whiles, when lifting her white neck,
To herself she wails her father once beloved,
Her land, her home, forsaking which she came
Hither with him who holds her now contemned.
Alas for her! she knows, by affliction taught,
How good is fatherland unforfeited.
She loathes her babes, joys not beholding them.
And what she may devise I dread to think.
Grim is her spirit, one that will not brook
Mishandling: yea, I know her, and I fear
Lest to her bridal bower she softly steal,

And through her own heart thrust the whetted knife,
Or slay the king and him that weds his child,
And get herself some doom yet worse thereby;
For dangerous is she: who begins a feud
With her, not soon shall sing the triumph-song.
But lo, her boys, their racing-sport put by,
Draw near, all careless of their mother's wrongs,
For the young heart loves not to brood in grief.

Enter CHILDREN'S GUARDIAN *with boys*

CHILDREN'S GUARDIAN. O ancient chattel of my mistress' home,
Why at the gates thus lonely standest thou,
Thyself unto thyself discoursing ills?
How wills Medea to be left of thee?
NURSE. O grey attendant thou of Jason's sons,
The hearts of faithful servants still are touched
By ill-betiding fortunes of their lords.
For I have sunk to such a depth of grief,
That yearning took me hitherward to come
And tell to earth and heaven my lady's plight.
CHILDREN'S GUARDIAN. Ceaseth not yet the hapless one from moan?
NURSE. Cease!—her pain scarce begun, far from its height!
CHILDREN'S GUARDIAN. Ah fool!—if one may say it of his lords—
Little she knoweth of the latest blow.
NURSE. What is it, ancient? Grudge not thou to tell me.
CHILDREN'S GUARDIAN. Naught: I repent me of the word that 'scaped me.
NURSE. Nay, by thy beard, hide not from fellow-thrall—

Silence, if need be, will I keep thereof.
CHILDREN'S GUARDIAN. I heard one saying—feigning not to hear,
As I drew near the old stone seats, where sit
The ancients round Peirene's hallowed fount,—
"Creon, this land's lord, is at point to banish
Mother and sons from soil Corinthian."
Howbeit, if the tale I heard be true
I know not: fain were I it were not so.
NURSE. Will Jason brook such dealing with his sons,
Though from their mother he be wholly estranged?
CHILDREN'S GUARDIAN. Old bonds of love are aye outrun by feet
Of new:—no friend is *he* unto this house.
NURSE. Ruined we are then, if we add fresh ill
To old, ere lightened be our ship of this.
CHILDREN'S GUARDIAN. But thou—for 'tis not season that thy lady
Should know—keep silence, and speak not the tale.
NURSE. Hear, babes, what father this is unto you!
I curse him—not: he is my master still:
But to his friends he stands convict of baseness.
CHILDREN'S GUARDIAN. What man is not? Hast learnt this only now,
That no man loves his neighbour as himself?
Good cause have some, with most 'tis greed of gain—
As here: their sire for a bride's sake loves not these.
NURSE. Pass in, dear children, for it shall be well.
But thou, keep these apart to the uttermost:
Bring them not nigh their mother angry-souled.
For late I saw her glare, as glares a bull,
On these, as 'twere for mischief; nor her wrath,

I know, shall cease, until its lightning
strike.
To foes may she work ill, and not to
friends!

MEDEA (*behind the scenes*).
O hapless I! O miseries heaped on
mine head!
Ah, me! ah me! would God I were
dead!
NURSE. Lo, darlings, the things that I
told you!
Lo the heart of your mother astir!
And astir is her anger: withhold you
From her sight, come not nigh
unto her.
Haste, get you within: O beware
ye
Of the thoughts as a wild-beast
brood,
Of the nature too ruthless to spare
ye
In its desperate mood.

Pass ye within now, departing
With all speed. It is plain to
discern
How a cloud of lamenting, upstart-
ing
From its viewless beginnings, shall
burn
In lightnings of fury yet fiercer.
What deeds shall be dared of that
soul,
So haughty, when wrong's goads
pierce her,
So hard to control?
(*Exeunt* CHILDREN *with* GUARDIAN.)

MEDEA (*behind the scenes*).
Woe! I have suffered, have suffered,
foul wrongs that may waken,
may waken
Mighty lamentings full well! O ye
children accursed from the
womb,
Hence to destruction, ye brood of a
loathed one forsaken, forsaken!
Hence with your father, and perish our
home in the blackness of doom!

NURSE. Ah me, in the father's offences
What part have the babes, that
thine hate
Should blast them?—forlorn inno-
cences,
How sorely I fear for your fate!
How terrible princes' moods are!—
Long ruling, unschooled to obey,—
Unforgiving, unsleeping their feuds
are:
Better life's level way.

Be it mine, if in greatness I may
not,
In quiet and peace to grow old.
Sweeter name than "The Mean"
shall ye say not,
And to taste it is sweetness
untold.
But to men never weal above
measure
Availed: on its perilous height
The Gods in their hour of displeas-
ure
The heavier smite.

Enter CHORUS OF CORINTHIAN LADIES

CHORUS. I have hearkened the voice
of the daughter of Colchis, the sound
of the crying
Of the misery-stricken; nor yet is she
stilled. Now the tale of her tell,
Grey woman; for moaned through the
porch from her chamber the wail of
her sighing;
And I cannot, I cannot be glad while the
home in affliction is lying,
The house I have loved so well.

NURSE. Home?—home there is none:
it hath vanished away:
For my lord to a bride of the princes
is thrall;
And my lady is pining the livelong day
In her bower, and for naught that her
friends' lips say
On her heart may the dews of comfort
fall.

MEDEA (*behind the scenes*)
Would God that the flame of the light-
    ning from heaven descending, de-
    scending,
    Might burn through mine head!—for
    in living wherein any more is my
    gain?
Alas, and alas! Would God I might
    bring to an ending, an ending,
    The life that I loathe, and behind me
    might cast all its burden of pain!

CHORUS. O Zeus, Earth, Light, did ye
         hear her, (*Str.*)
    How waileth the woe-laden breath
      Of the bride in unhappiest
      plight?
    What yearning for vanished de-
    light,
      O passion-distraught, should
      have might
    To cause thee to wish death nearer—
    The ending of all things, death?

Make thou not for this supplica-
    tion!
      If thine husband hath turned
      and adored
      New love, that estranged he
      is,
      O harrow thy soul for this:
      It is Zeus that shall right
      thee, I wis.
    Ah, pine not in over-vexation
    Of spirit, bewailing thy lord!

MEDEA (*behind the scenes*)
O Lady of Justice, O Artemis' Majesty,
    see it, O see it—
    Look on the wrongs that I suffer, by
    oaths everlasting who tied
The soul of mine husband, that ne'er
    from the curse he might free it, nor
    free it
    From your vengeance! O may I be-
    hold him at last, even him and his
    bride,
Them, and these halls therewithal, all
    shattered in ruin, in ruin!—

Wretches, who dare unprovoked to do
    to Medea despite!
O father, O city, whom erst I forsook
    for undoing, undoing,
    And for shame, when the blood of my
    brother I spilt on the path of my
    flight!

NURSE. Do ye hear what she saith, and
    uplifteth her cry
    Unto Themis and Zeus; to the Sup-
    pliant's King,
Oath-steward of men that be born but
    to die?
O my lady will lay not her anger by
    Soon, making her vengeance a little
    thing.

CHORUS. If she would but come forth
         where we wait her, (*Ant.*)
    If she would but give ear to the
    sound
      Of our speech, that her spirit
      would learn
      From its fierceness of anger to
      turn,
      And her lust for revenge not
      burn!
    O ne'er may my love prove traitor,
      Never false to my friends be it
      found!

But go thou, and forth of the
      dwelling
    Thy mistress hitherward lead:
      Say to her that friends be we
      all.
      O hasten, ere mischief befall
      The lords of the palace-hall;
    For her grief, like a tempest up-
      swelling,
    Resistless shall ruin-ward speed.

NURSE. I will do it: but almost my
    spirit despaireth
    To win her: yet labour of love shall it
    be.
But my queen on her thralls as a mad
    bull glareth,

Or a lioness couched mid her whelps, whoso dareth
With speech to draw near her, so tameless is she.

He should err not, who named the old singers in singing
Not cunning, but left-handed bards, for their lays
Did they frame for the mirth-tide, the festal inbringing
Of the wine, and the feast, when the harp-strings are ringing
To sweeten with melody life's sweet days.

But the dread doom of mortals, the anguish heart-rending—
Never minstrel by music hath breathed on them peace,
Nor by song with his harp-notes in harmony blending;
Albeit thereof cometh death's dark ending
Unto many a home that is wrecked by these.

And yet were it surely a boon to bring healing
Of sorrow to mortals with song; but in vain
Mid the fulness of feasting ring voices clear-pealing,
And the banquet itself hath a glamour, concealing
From mortals their doom, flinging spells over pain. (*Exit* NURSE)

CHORUS. I have heard it, the sigh-laden cry of the daughter
Of Colchis, the woe-thrilling anguish of wailing
For the traitor to love who with false vows caught her
Who in strength of her wrongs chideth Heaven, assailing
The Oath-queen of Zeus, who with cords all-prevailing

Forth haled her and brought her o'er star-litten water,
Where the brine-mists hover o'er Pontus' Key,
Unto Hellas far over the boundless sea.

Enter MEDEA

MEDEA. Corinthian dames, I have come forth my doors
Lest ye condemn me. Many I know are held
Mis-proud—some, since they shrink from public gaze;
Some, from their bearing to their fellow-men;
Some quiet lives for indolence are defamed;
For justice dwells not in the eyes of man,
Who, ere he hath discerned his neighbour's heart,
Hates him at sight, albeit nowise wronged.
A stranger must conform to the city's wont;
Nor citizens uncondemned may flout their fellows,
Like mannerless churls, a law unto themselves.
But me—the blow ye wot of suddenly fell
Soul-shattering. 'Tis my ruin: I have lost
All grace of life: I long to die, O friends.
He, to know whom well was mine all in all,
My lord, of all men basest hath become!
Surely, of creatures that have life and wit,
We women are of all unhappiest,
Who, first, must buy, as buys the highest bidder,
A husband—nay, we do but win for our lives
A master! Deeper depth of wrong is this.
Here too is dire risk—will the lord we gain

Be evil or good? Divorce?—'tis infamy
To us: we may not even reject a suitor!
Then, coming to new customs, habits new,
One need be a seer, to know the thing unlearnt
At home, what manner of man her mate shall be.
And *if* we learn our lesson, *if* our lord
Dwell with us, plunging not against the yoke,
Happy our lot is; else—no help but death.
For the man, when the home-yoke galls his neck,
Goes forth, to ease a weary sickened heart
By turning to some friend, some kindred soul:
We to one heart alone can look for comfort.
But we, say they, live an unperilled life
At home, while they do battle with the spear—
Unreasoning fools! Thrice would I under shield
Stand, rather than bear childbirth-peril once.
But ah, thy story is not one with mine!
Thine is this city, thine a father's home,
Thine bliss of life and fellowship of friends;
But I, lone, cityless, and outraged thus
Of him who kidnapped me from foreign shores,
Mother nor brother have I, kinsman none,
For port of refuge from calamity.
Wherefore I fain would win of thee this boon:—
If any path be found me, or device,
Whereby to avenge these wrongs upon mine husband,
On her who weds, on him who gives the bride,
Keep silence. Woman quails at every peril,
Faint-heart to face the fray and look on steel;

But when in wedlock-rights she suffers wrong,
No spirit more bloodthirsty shall be found.
CHORUS. This will I; for 'tis just that thou, Medea,
Requite thy lord: no marvel thou dost grieve.
But I see Creon, ruler of this land,
Advancing, herald of some new decree.

Enter CREON

CREON. Black-lowering woman, wroth against thy lord,
Medea, forth this land I bid thee fare
An exile, taking thy two sons with thee;
And make no tarrying: daysman of this cause
Am I, and homeward go I not again
Ere from the land's bounds I have cast thee forth.
MEDEA. Ah me! undone am I in utter ruin!
My foes crowd sail pursuing: landing-place
Is none from surges of calamity.
Yet, howso wronged, one question will I ask—
For what cause, Creon, dost thou banish me?
CREON. I fear thee—need is none to cloak my words—
Lest thou wreak cureless vengeance on my child.
And to this dread do many things conspire:
Wise art thou, cunning in much evil lore;
Chafed art thou, of thine husband's couch bereft:
I hear thou threatenest, so they bring me word,
To wreak on sire, on bridegroom, and on bride
Mischief. I guard mine head ere falls the blow.
Better be hated, woman, now of thee,
Than once relent, and sorely groan too late.

MEDEA. Not now first, Creon,—many a time ere now
Rumour hath wronged and wrought me grievous harm.
Ne'er should the man whose heart is sound of wit
Let teach his sons more wisdom than the herd.
They are burdened with unprofitable lore,
And spite and envy of other folk they earn.
For, if thou bring strange wisdom unto dullards,
Useless shalt thou be counted, and not wise:
And, if thy fame outshine those heretofore
Held wise, thou shalt be odious in men's eyes.
Myself too in this fortune am partaker.
Of some my wisdom wins me jealousy,
Some count me spiritless; outlandish some;
Unsocial some. Yet no deep lore is mine.
And thou, thou fear'st me, lest I work thee harm.
Not such am I—O Creon, dread not me—
That against princes I should dare transgress.
How hast thou wronged me? Thou hast given thy child
To whomso pleased thee. But—I hate mine husband;
So, doubtless, this in prudence hast thou done.
Nay, but I grudge not thy prosperity.
Wed ye, and prosper. But in this your land
Still let me dwell: for I, how wronged soe'er,
Will hold my peace, o'ermastered by the strong.

CREON. Soft words to hear!—but in thine inmost heart,
I fear, thou plottest mischief all the while;

And all the less I trust thee than before.
The vehement-hearted woman—yea, or man—
Is easier watched-for than the silent-cunning.
Nay, forth with all speed: plead me pleadings none;
For this is stablished: no device hast thou
To bide with us, who art a foe to me.

MEDEA (clasping his feet). Nay,—by thy knees, and by the bride, thy child!

CREON. Thou wastest words; thou never shalt prevail.

MEDEA. Wilt drive me forth, respecting naught my prayers?

CREON. Ay: more I love not thee than mine own house.

MEDEA. My country! O, I call thee now to mind!

CREON. Ay, next my children, dear to me is Corinth.

MEDEA. Alas! to mortals what a curse is love!

CREON. Blessing or curse, I trow, as fortune falls.

MEDEA. Zeus, Zeus, forget not him who is cause of this!

CREON. Hence, passionate fool, and rid me of my trouble.

MEDEA. Troubled am I; new troubles need I none.

CREON. Soon shalt thou be by servants' hands thrust out.

MEDEA. Nay — nay — not this, O Creon, I implore!

CREON. So, woman, thou, it seems, wilt make a coil.

MEDEA. I will flee forth:—not this the boon I crave.

CREON. Why restive then?—why rid not Corinth of thee?

MEDEA. Suffer me yet to tarry this one day,
And somewhat for our exile to take thought,
And find my babes a refuge, since their sire

Cares naught to make provision for his sons.
Compassionate these—a father too art thou
Of children—meet it is thou show them grace.
Not for myself I fret, if I be banished:
For them in their calamity I mourn.

CREON. My spirit least of all is tyrannous.
Many a plan have my relentings marred:
And, woman, now I know I err herein,
Yet shalt thou win this boon. But I forewarn thee,
If thee the approaching Sun-god's torch behold
Within this country's confines with thy sons,
Thou diest:—the word is said that shall not lie.
Now, if remain thou must, remain one day—
Too short for thee to do the deeds I dread.   (*Exit*.)

CHORUS. O hapless thou!
Woe's me for thy misery, woe for the trouble and anguish that meet thee!
Whitherward wilt thou turn thee?—what welcoming hand mid the strangers shall greet thee?
What home or what land to receive thee, deliverance from evils to give thee,
Wilt thou find for thee now?
How mid surge of despair to o'erwhelm thee in ruin God's hand on thine helm
Hath steered, O Medea, thy prow!

MEDEA. Wronged—wronged by God and man! Who shall gainsay?
But is it mere despair?—deem not so yet.
Bridegroom and bride grim wrestlings yet await;
Nor troubles light abide these marriage-makers.
Dost think that I had cringed to yon man ever,
Except to gain some gain, or work some wile?
Nor word nor touch of hand had I vouch-safed him!
But to such height of folly hath he come,
That, when he might forestall mine every plot
By banishment, this day of grace he grants me
To stay, wherein three foes will I lay dead,
The father, and the daughter, and mine husband.
And, having for them many paths of death,
Which first to take in hand I know not, friends—
To fire yon palace midst their marriage-feast,
Or to steal softly to their bridal-bower,
And through their two hearts thrust the whetted knife.
Yet one thing bars the way—if I be found
Crossing the threshold of the house and plotting,
Die shall I mid the mocking laughter of foes.
Best the sure path, wherein my nature's cunning
Excels, by poisons to destroy them—yea.
Now, grant them dead: what city will receive me,
What host vouchsafe a land of refuge, home
Secure, and from the avenger shield my life?
There is none. Tarrying then a little space,
If any tower of safety shall appear,
These deaths by guile and silence will I compass;
But if misfortune drive me desperate forth,
Myself will grip the sword,—yea, though I die,—
And slay, and dare the strong hand's reckless deed.

Ah, by the Queen of Night, whom I revere
Above all, and for fellow-worker chose,
Hecate, dweller by mine hearth's dark shrine,
None, none shall vex my soul, and rue it not.
Bitter and woeful bridal will I give them,
Bitter troth-plight and banishing of me.
Up then!—spare naught of all thy sorcery-lore,
Medea, of thy plotting and contriving;
On to the dread deed! Now is need of daring.
Look on thy wrongs: thou must not make derision
For sons of Sisyphus, for Jason's bride,—
Thou, sprung from royal father, from the Sun!
Thou know'st the means. I prove me woman indeed!
Men say we are most helpless for all good,
But of dark deeds most cunning fashioners.

CHORUS. (Str. 1.)
Upward and back to their fountains the sacred rivers are stealing;
Justice is turned to injustice, the order of old to confusion:
The thoughts of the hearts of men are treachery wholly, and, reeling
From its ancient foundations, the faith of the Gods is become a delusion.
Everywhere change!—even me men's voices henceforth shall honour;
My life shall be sunlit with glory; for woman the old-time story
Is ended, the slanders hoary no more shall as chains be upon her.

(Ant. 1.)
And the strains of the singers of old generations for shame shall falter,
Which sang evermore of the treason of woman, her faithlessness ever.
Alas, that our lips are not touched with the fire of song from the altar
Of Phœbus, the Harper-king, of the inspiration-giver!
Else had I lifted my voice in challenge of song high-ringing
Unto men: for the roll of the ages shall find for the poet-sages
Proud woman-themes for their pages, heroines worthy their singing.

(Str. 2.)
But thou from the ancient home didst sail over leagues of foam,
On-sped by a frenzied heart, and the sea-gates sawest dispart,
The Twin Rocks. Now, in the land
Of the stranger, thy doom is to waken
To a widowed couch, and forsaken
Of thy lord, and woe-overtaken,
To be cast forth shamed and banned.

(Ant. 2.)
Disannulled is the spell of the oath: no shame for the broken troth
In Hellas the wide doth remain, but heavenward its flight hath it ta'en.
No home of a father hast thou
For thine haven when trouble-storms lower.
Usurped is thy bridal bower
Of another, in pride of her power,
Ill-starred, overqueening thee now.

Enter JASON

JASON. Not now first, nay, but ofttimes have I marked
What desperate mischief is a froward spirit.
Thou mightest stay in Corinth, in these halls,
Bearing unfractiously thy rulers' pleasure,
Yet for wild whirling words banished thou art.

Me they vex not—cease never, an' thou
wilt,
Clamouring, "Jason is of men most
base!"
But, for thy railing on thy rulers, count
it
All gain, that only exile punisheth thee.
For me—I have striven long to appease
the wrath
Of kings incensed: fain would I thou
shouldst stay.
But thou rein'st not thy folly, speaking
still
Evil of dignities; art therefore banished.
Yet, for all this, not wearied of my
friends,
With so much forethought come I for
thee, lady,
That, banished with thy babes, thou lack
not gold,
Nor aught beside; for exile brings with it
Hardships full many. Though thou hat-
est me,
Never can I bear malice against thee.
  MEDEA. Caitiff of caitiffs!—blackest
of reproaches
My tongue for thine unmanliness can
frame—
Com'st thou to me—dost come, most
hateful proved
To heaven, to me, to all the race of men?
This is not daring, no, nor courage this,
To wrong thy friends, and blench not
from their eyes,
But, of all plagues infecting men, the
worst,
Even shamelessness. And yet 'tis well
thou cam'st,
For I shall ease the burden of mine heart
Reviling thee, and thou be galled to
hear.
And with the first things first will I
begin.
I saved thee: this knows every son of
Greece
That stepped with thee aboard thine
Argo's hull,
Thee, sent to quell the flame-outbreath-
ing bulls

With yoke-bands, and to sow the tilth
of death.
The dragon, warder of the Fleece of
Gold,
That sleepless kept it with his manifold
coils,
I slew, and raised deliverance-light for
thee.
Myself forsook my father and mine
home,
And I to Iolcos under Pelion came
With thee, more zealous in thy cause
than wise.
Pelias I slew by his own children's
hands—
Of all deaths worst,—and dashed their
house to ruin.
Thus dealt with, basest of all men, by
me,
For a new bride hast thou forsaken me,
Though I had borne thee children!
Wert thou childless,
Not past forgiving were this marriage-
craving.
But faith of oaths hath vanished. I
know not
Whether thou deem'st the olden Gods yet
rule,
Or that new laws are now ordained for
men;
For thine heart speaks thee unto me for-
sworn.
Out on this right hand, which thou oft
wouldst clasp,—
These knees!—I was polluted by the
touch
Of a base man, thus frustrate of mine
hopes!
Come, as a friend will I commune with
thee—
Yet what fair dealing should I hope from
thee?—
Yet will I: questioned, baser shalt thou
show.
Now, whither turn I?—to my father's
house,
My land?—which I betrayed, to flee with
thee!
To Pelias' hapless daughters? Graciously

Their father's slayer would they welcome
    home!
For thus it is—a foe am I become
To mine own house: no quarrel I had
    with those
With whom I have now a death-feud for
    thy sake.
For all this hast thou made me passing-
    blest
Midst Hellas' daughters! Oh, in thee
    have I—
O wretched I!—a wondrous spouse and
    leal,
Since from the land cast forth I pass to
    exile
Forlorn of friends, alone with children
    lone.
A proud reproach for our new bride-
    groom this—
"In poverty his babes, his saviour,
    wander!"
O Zeus, ah wherefore hast thou given to
    men
Plain signs for gold which is but counter-
    feit,
But no assay-mark nature-graven shows
On man's form, to discern the base
    withal?
    CHORUS. Awful and past all healing
    is that wrath
When they that once loved clash in feud
    of hate.
    JASON. Needs must I be not ill at
    speech, meseems,
But, like the careful helmsman of a ship,
With close-reefed canvas run before the
    gale,
Woman, of thy tempestuous-railing
    tongue.
I—for thy kindness tower-high thou
    pilest—
Deem Cypris saviour of my voyaging,
Her, and none other of Gods or men.
Thou art subtle of wit—nay, but
    ungenerous
It were to tell how Love, by strong
    compulsion
Of shafts unerring, made thee save my
    life.

Yet take I not account too strict thereof;
For, in that thou didst save me, thou
    didst well.
Howbeit, more hast thou received than
    given
From my deliverance, as my words shall
    prove:—
First, then, in Hellas dwell'st thou, in
    the stead
Of land barbaric, knowest justice,
    learnest
To live by law without respect of force;
And all the Greeks have heard thy wis-
    dom's fame.
Renown is thine; but if on earth's far
    bourn
Thou dwelledst yet, thou hadst not lived
    in story.
Now mine be neither gold mine halls
    within,
Nor sweeter song be mine than Orpheus
    sang,
If my fair fortune be to fame unknown.
Thus far of my great labours have I
    spoken,—
This challenge to debate didst thou fling
    down:—
But, for thy railings on my royal mar-
    riage,
Herein will I show, first, that wise I
    was;
Then, temperate; third, to thee the best
    of friends
And to my children—nay, but hear me
    out.
When I came hither from Iolcos-land
With many a desperate fortune in my
    train,
What happier treasure-trove could I have
    found
Than to wed—I, an exile—with a
    princess?
Not—where it galls thee—loathing couch
    of thine,
And for a new bride smitten with
    desire,
Nor eager I to multiply mine offspring:—
Suffice these born to me: no fault in
    them:

But that—this chiefly—we might live in honour,
And be not straitened,—for I know full well
How all friends from the poor man stand aloof,—
And I might nurture as beseems mine house
Our sons, and to these born of thee beget
Brethren, and, knitting in one family all,
Live happy days. Thou, what wouldst thou of children?
But me if profits, through sons to be born
To help the living. Have I planned so ill?
Not thou wouldst say it, save for jealousy's sting.
But ye—ye women—so unreasoning are
That, wedlock-rights untrespassed-on, all's well;
But, it once your sole tenure be infringed,
With the best, fairest lot are ye at feud
Most bitter. Would that mortals otherwise
Could get them babes, that womankind were not,
And so no curse had lighted upon men.

CHORUS. Words, Jason, words, tricked out full cunningly!
Yet to me—though I speak not to thy mind—
Unjust thou seem'st, betraying thus thy wife.

MEDEA. Not as the world thinks think I oftentimes;
Nay, to my thought, a villain's artful tongue
Doubles the hurt his villainy doth to him:
So sure his tongue can gloze the wrong, he grows
Reckless in sin—a mere fool's wisdom this.
Then be not thou, as touching me, fair-seeming

And crafty-tongued: one word shall overthrow thee:
Thou shouldst, wert thou not base, have wed this bride
With my consent, not hid it from thy friends.

JASON. Ay, this my purpose nobly hadst thou helped,
Had I a marriage named, who even now
Canst not refrain thy heart's exceeding wrath!

MEDEA. Not this thine hindrance, but the alien wife
No crown of honour was as eld drew on.

JASON. Now know this well—not for the woman's sake
I wed the royal bride whom I have won,
But, as I said, of my desire to save
Thee, and beget seed royal, to my sons
Brethren, and for mine house a tower of strength.

MEDEA. No prosperous life 'neath sorrow's cloud for me,
Nor weal, with thorns aye rankling in mine heart!

JASON. Know'st how to change thy prayer, and wiser show?
May thy good never seem to thee thy grief;
Nor in fair fortune deem thy lot misfortune.

MEDEA. O yea, insult! Thou hast a refuge, thou;
But desolate I am banished from this land.

JASON. Thyself hast chosen this: blame none beside.

MEDEA. I?—sooth, by wedding and betraying thee!

JASON. By cursing princes with an impious curse.

MEDEA. Ay—and to thine house hast thou found me a curse!

JASON. With thee no more I wrangle touching this.
But if, or for the children or thyself,
For help in exile thou wilt take my gold,
Speak: ready am I to give with hand ungrudging,

And send guest-tokens which shall find
    thee friends.
If this thou wilt not, foolish shalt thou
    be:
Refrain wrath, and advantaged shalt
    thou be.
    MEDEA. Thy friends!—nothing will I
    of friends of thine.
No whit will I receive, nor offer thou.
No profit is there in a villain's gifts.
    JASON. In any wise I call the Gods to
    witness
That all help would I give thee and thy
    sons;
But thy good likes thee not: thy stub-
    born pride
Spurns friends: the more thy grief shall
    therefore be.   (*Exit*.)
    MEDEA. Away!—impatience for the
    bride new-trapped
Consumes thee loitering from her bower
    afar!
Wed: for perchance—and God shall
    speed the word—
Thine shall be bridal thou wouldst fain
    renounce.
    CHORUS.   (*Str. 1*.)
Love bringeth nor honour nor profit to
    men when it cometh restraining
Not its unscanted excess: but if Cypris,
    in measure raining
    Her joy, cometh down, there is none
    other Goddess so winsome as she.
Not upon me, O Queen, do thou aim
    from thy bow all-golden
    The arrow desire-envenomed that none
    may avoid—not on me!

    (*Ant. 1*.)
But let Temperance shield me, the fairest
    of gifts of the Gods ever-living:
Nor ever with passion of jarring con-
    tention, nor feuds unforgiving,
    In her terrors may Love's Queen visit
    me, smiting with maddened unrest
For a couch mismated my soul; but the
    peace of the bride-bed be holden
    In honour of her, and her keen eyes
    choose for us bonds that be best.

    (*Str. 2*.)
O fatherland, O mine home,
Not mine be the exile's doom!
Into poverty's pathways hard to be trod
    may my feet not be guided!
Most piteous anguish were this.
By death—O by death ere then may the
    conflict of life be decided,
Ended be life's little day! To be thus
    from the home-land divided—
    No pang more bitter there is.

    (*Ant. 2*.)
We have seen, and it needeth naught
That of others herein we be taught:
For thee not a city, for thee not a friend
    hath compassionated
    When affliction most awful is thine.
But he, who regardeth not friends, ac-
    cursed may he perish, and hated,
Who opes not his heart with sincerity's
    key to the hapless-fated—
    Never such shall be friend of mine.

Enter ÆGEUS

    ÆGEUS. Medea, joy to thee!—for
    fairer greeting
None knoweth to accost his friends
    withal.
    MEDEA. Joy to thee also, wise Pan-
    dion's son.
Whence art thou journeying through this
    land?
    ÆGEUS. Leaving the ancient oracle of
    Phœbus.
    MEDEA. Why didst thou fare to
    earth's prophetic navel?
    ÆGEUS. To ask how seed of children
    might be mine.
    MEDEA. 'Fore Heaven!—aye child-
    less is thy life till now?
    ÆGEUS. Childless I am, by chance of
    some God's will.
    MEDEA. This, with a wife, or know-
    ing not the couch?
    ÆGEUS. Nay, not unyoked to wed-
    lock's bed am I.
    MEDEA. Now what to thee spake
    Phœbus touching issue?

ÆGEUS. Deep words of wisdom not for man to interpret.

MEDEA. Without sin might I know the God's reply?

ÆGEUS. O yea—good sooth, it asks a wise wit most.

MEDEA. What said he? Say, if sin be not to hear.

ÆGEUS. "Loose not the wine-skin's forward-jutting foot"—

MEDEA. Till thou shouldst do what thing, or reach what land?

ÆGEUS. "Till to the hearth ancestral back thou come."

MEDEA. And thou, what wouldst thou sailing to this shore?

ÆGEUS. There is one Pittheus, king of Troezen he,—

MEDEA. A man most pious, Pelops' son, they say.

ÆGEUS. To him the God's response I fain would tell.

MEDEA. Yea—a wise man, who hath much skill therein.

ÆGEUS. Yea, and my best beloved spear-ally.

MEDEA. Now prosper thou, and win thine heart's desire.

ÆGEUS. Why droops thine eye?—why this wan-wasted hue?

MEDEA. Ægeus, of all men basest is mine husband.

ÆGEUS. What say'st thou? Clearly tell me thine heart's pain.

MEDEA. He wrongs me—Jason, never wronged of me.

ÆGEUS. What hath he done? More plainly tell it out.

MEDEA. Another wife he takes, his household's queen.

ÆGEUS. Ha! hath he dared in truth this basest deed?

MEDEA. Yea: I am now dishonoured, once beloved.

ÆGEUS. Another love was this?—or hate of thee?

MEDEA. *Love?*—deep and high his love is!—traitor in love!

ÆGEUS. Away with him, if he be base as this!

MEDEA. His love was for affinity with princes.

ÆGEUS. Who giveth him his daughter? Tell me all.

MEDEA. Creon, who ruleth this Corinthian land.

ÆGEUS. Sooth, lady, reason was that thou shouldst grieve.

MEDEA. 'Tis death to me! Yea, also am I banished.

ÆGEUS. Of whom? A monstrous wrong thou namest now!

MEDEA. Creon from Corinth driveth me an exile.

ÆGEUS. Doth Jason suffer this?—I count it shame!

MEDEA. In pretence, no—yet O, he bears it well!

But I beseech thee, lo, thy beard I touch,—
I clasp thy knees, thy suppliant am I now:—
Pity, O pity me the evil-starred,
And see me not cast forth to homelessness:
Receive to a hearth-place in thy land, thine halls.
So by heaven's blessing fruitful be thy love
In children, and in death thyself be blest.
Thou know'st not what good fortune thou hast found;
For I will end thy childlessness, will cause
Thy seed to grow to sons; such charms I know.

ÆGEUS. For many causes am I minded, lady,
This grace to grant thee: for the God's sake first;
Then, for thy promise of a seed of sons;
For herein Ægeus' name is like to die.
But thus it is—if to my land thou come,
I will protect thee all I can: my right
Is this; but I forewarn thee of one thing—

Not from this land to lead thee I consent;
But, if thou reachest of thyself mine halls,
Safe shalt thou bide; to none will I yield thee.
But from this land thou must thyself escape;
For even to strangers blameless will I be.
  MEDEA. So be it. Yet, were oath-pledge given for this
To me, then had I all I would of thee.
  ÆGEUS. Ha, dost not trust me?—or at what dost stumble?
  MEDEA. I trust thee; but my foes are Pelias' house
And Creon. Oath-bound, thou couldst never yield me
To these, when they would drag me from the land.
Hadst thou but promised, to the Gods unpledged,
Thou mightest turn their friend, might'st lightly yield
To herald-summons. Strengthless is my cause:
Wealth is on their side, and a princely house.
  ÆGEUS. Foresight exceeding, lady, in thy words.
Yet, if this be thy will, I draw not back.
Yea, for myself is this the safest course,
To have a plea to show unto thy foes;
And firmer stands thy cause. The Oath-god's name.
  MEDEA. Swear by Earth's plain, and by my father's father,
The Sun, and join the Gods' whole race thereto.
  ÆGEUS. That I will do or not do—what? Say on.
  MEDEA. Never thyself to cast me forth thy land,
Nor, if a foe of mine would hale me thence,
To yield me willingly up, while thou dost live.
  ÆGEUS. By Earth, the Sun's pure majesty, and all

The Gods, I swear to abide by this thou hast said.
  MEDEA. Enough. For broken troth what penalty?
  ÆGEUS. The worst that scourgeth God-despairing men.
  MEDEA. Pass on thy way rejoicing: all is well.
I too will come with all speed to thy burg,
When mine intent is wrought, my wish attained. (*Exit* ÆGEUS.)

  CHORUS. Now the Scion of Maia, the Wayfarer's King,
Bring thee safe to thine home, and the dream of thine heart,
The sweet visions that wing thy feet, mayst thou bring
To accomplishment, Ægeus, for now this thing
Hath taught me how noble thou art.

  MEDEA. O Zeus, Zeus' daughter Justice, Light of the Sun!
Over my foes triumphant now, my friends,
Shall we become: our feet are on the path.
Now is there hope of vengeance on my foes.
For this man, there where my chief weakness lay,
Hath for my plots a haven in storm appeared.
To him my bark's stern-hawser make I fast,
To Pallas' burg and fortress when I go.
And all my plots to thee will I tell now;
Nor look I that my words should pleasure thee:—
One of mine household will I send to Jason,
And will entreat him to my sight to come;
And soft words, when he cometh, will I speak,
Saying, "Thy will is mine, and, "It is well";

Saying, his royal marriage, my betrayal,
Is our advantage, and right well devised.
I will petition that my sons may stay—
Not for that I would leave on hostile soil
Children of mine for foes to trample on,
But the king's daughter so by guile to
slay.
For I will send them bearing gifts in
hand
Unto the bride, that they may not be
banished,
A robe fine-spun, a golden diadem.
If she receive and don mine ornaments,
Die shall she wretchedly, and all who
touch her;
With drugs so dread will I anoint my
gifts.
Howbeit here I pass this story by,
And wail the deed that yet for me re-
mains
To bring to pass; for I will slay my
children,
Yea, mine; no man shall pluck them from
mine hand.
Then, having brought all Jason's house
to wrack,
I leave the land, fleeing my dear babes'
blood
And having dared a deed most impious.
For unendurable are mocks of foes.
Let all go; what is life to me? Nor
country
Nor home have I, nor refuge from mine
ills.
Then erred I, in the day when I forsook
My father's halls, by yon Greek's words
beguiled,
Who with God's help shall render me
requital.
For never living shall he see henceforth
The sons I bare him, nor shall he beget
A son of his new bride, that wretch fore-
doomed
In agony to die by drugs of mine.
Let none account me impotent, nor weak,
Nor spiritless!—O nay, of other sort,
Grim to my foes, and kindly to my
friends.
Most glorious is the life of such as I.

CHORUS. Since thou hast made me partner of this tale,—
Wishing to help thee, and yet cham-
pioning
The laws of men, I say, do thou not this!
MEDEA. It cannot be but so: yet
reason is
That thou say this, who art not wronged
as I.
CHORUS. Woman, wilt have the heart
to slay thy sons?
MEDEA. Yea: so mine husband's
heart shall most be wrung.
CHORUS. But thou of wives most
wretched shouldst become.
MEDEA. So be it: wasted are all
hindering words.
But ho! (*enter* NURSE) go thou and
Jason bring to me—
Thou whom I use for every deed of trust,
And look thou tell none aught of mine
intent,
If thine is loyal service, thou a woman.
(*Exeunt* MEDEA *and* NURSE)

(*Str. 1.*)
CHORUS. O happy the race in the ages
olden
Of Erechtheus, the seed of the blest
Gods' line,
In a land unravaged, peace-enfolden,
Aye quaffing of Wisdom's glorious
wine,
Ever through air clear-shining brightly
As on wings uplifted pacing lightly,
Where Harmonia, they tell, of the tresses
golden,
Bare the Pierid Muses, the stainless
Nine.

(*Ant. 1.*)
And the streams of Cephisus the lovely-
flowing
They tell how the Lady of Cyprus
drew,
And in Zephyr-wafts of the winds sweet-
blowing
Breathed far over the land their dew.
And she sendeth her Loves which,
throned in glory

By Wisdom, fashion all virtue's story;
And over her hair is she throwing, throwing,
    Roses in odorous wreathes aye new.

Re-enter MEDEA
(Str. 2.)
How then should the hallowed city,
  The city of sacred waters,
    Which shields with her guardian hand
    All friends that would fare through her land,
    Receive a murderess banned,
Who had slaughtered her babes without pity,
  A pollution amidst of her daughters?

In thine heart's thoughts set it before thee—
  To murder the fruit of thy womb!
    O think what it meaneth to slay
    Thy sons—what a deed this day
    Thou wouldst do! By thy knees we pray,
By heaven and earth we implore thee,
  Deal not to thy babes such a doom!

(Ant. 2.)
O whence, and O whence wilt thou gain thee
  Such desperate hardihood
    That for spirit so fiendish shall serve,
    That shall strengthen thine heart, that shall nerve
    Thine hand, that it shall not swerve
From the ruthless deed that shall stain thee
  With horror of children's blood?

O how, when thine eyes thou art turning
  On thy little ones, wilt thou refrain
    The motherhood in thee, to feel
    No upwelling of tears? Canst thou steel
    Thy breast when thy children kneel,
To crimson thine hand, with unyearning
  Heart for thy darlings slain?

Enter JASON

JASON. I at thy bidding come: albeit my foe,
This grace thou shalt not miss; but I will hear
What new thing, lady, thou dost wish of me.
MEDEA. Jason, I ask thee to forgive the words
Late-spoken. Well thou mayest gently bear
With my wild mood, for all the old love's sake.
Now have I called myself to account, and railed
Upon myself—"wretch, wherefore am I mad?
And wherefore rage against good counsellors,
And am at feud with rulers of the land,
And with my lord, who works my veriest good,
Wedding a royal house, to raise up brethren
Unto my sons? Shall I not cease from wrath?
What aileth me, when the Gods proffer boons?
Have I not children? Know I not that we
Are exiles from our own land, lacking friends?"
Thus musing, was I ware that I had nursed
Folly exceeding, anger without cause.
Now then I praise thee: wise thou seem'st to me
In gaining us this kinship, senseless I,
Who in these counsels should have been thine ally,
Have furthered all, have decked the bridal couch,
And joyed to minister unto the bride.
But we are—women: needs not harsher word.
Yet shouldst thou not for evil render evil,
Nor pit against my folly folly of thine.

I yield, confessing mine unwisdom then,
But unto better counsels now am come.
Children, my children, hither: leave the house;

Enter CHILDREN

Come forth, salute your father, and with me
Bid him farewell: be reconciled to friends
Ye, with your mother, from the hate o'erpast.
Truce is between us, rancour hath given place.
Clasp ye his right hand. Woe for ambushed ills!
I am haunted by the shadow of hidden things!
Ah children, will ye thus, through many a year
Living, still reach him loving arms? Ah me,
How swift to weep am I, how full of fear!
Feuds with your father ended—ah, so late!—
Have filled with tears these soft-relenting eyes.

CHORUS.   And from mine eyes start tears of pale dismay.
Ah, may no evil worse than this befall!

JASON.   Lady, I praise this mood, yet blame not that:
'Tis nothing strange that womanhood should rage
When the spouse trafficketh in alien marriage.
But now to better thoughts thine heart hath turned,
And thou, though late, hast seen which policy
Must win: a prudent woman's part is this.
And for you, children, not unheedfully
Your sire hath ta'en much forethought, so help heaven.
For ye, I ween, in this Corinthian land
Shall with your brethren stand the foremost yet.

Grow ye in strength: the rest shall by your sire,
And whatso God is gracious, be wrought out.
You may I see to goodly stature grown,
In manhood's prime, triumphant o'er my foes.
Thou, why with wan tears thus bedew thine eyes,
Turning away from them thy pallid cheek?
Why hear'st thou not with gladness this my speech?

MEDEA.   'Tis naught; but o'er these children broods mine heart.

JASON.   Fear not: all will I order well for them.

MEDEA.   I will be brave—will not mistrust thy words;
But woman is but woman—born for tears.

JASON.   Why, hapless one, dost thou sigh over these?

MEDEA.   I bare them. When thou prayedst life for them,
Pity stole o'er me, whispering, "Shall this be?"
But that for which thou cam'st to speech of me
In part is said; to speak the rest is mine:
Since the king pleaseth forth the land to send me,—
Yea, for me too 'tis best, I know it well,
That I bide not, a stumblingblock to thee
And the land's lord, whose house's foe I seem,—
Lo, from this land I fare to exile forth:
But, that my sons by thine hand may be reared,
Entreat thou Creon that they be not banished.

JASON.   Prevail I may not, yet must I essay.

MEDEA.   Nay then, thy bride bid thou to pray her sire
That thy sons be not banished from this land.

JASON.   Yea surely; and, I trow, her shall I win.

MEDEA. If of her sister women she is one.
I too will bear a part in thine endeavour;
For I will send her gifts outrivalling far
In beauty aught in these days seen, I know,
A robe fine-spun, a golden diadem;
Our sons to bear them. Now must an attendant
With all speed hither bring the ornaments. (HANDMAID goes.)
Blessings shall hers be, not one, but untold,
Who winneth thee for lord, a peerless spouse,
Who owneth ornaments which once the Sun,
My father's father, to his offspring gave!

Enter HANDMAID *with casket*

Take in your hands, my sons, these bridal gifts,
And to the happy princess-bride bear ye
And give—my gifts she shall not lightly esteem!
    JASON. But, fond one, why make void thine hands of these?
Deem'st thou a royal house hath lack of robes,
Or gold, deem'st thou? Keep these and give them not.
For, if my wife esteems me aught, my wish
Will she prefer to treasure, well I wot.
    MEDEA. Nay, speak not so: gifts sway the Gods, they say.
Gold weigheth more with men than countless words.
Hers fortune is; God favoureth now her cause—
Young, and a queen! Life would I give for ransom
Of my sons' banishment, not gold alone.
Now, children, enter ye the halls of wealth.
Unto your sire's new wife, my lady-queen,

Make supplication, pray ye be not exiled,
And give mine ornaments—most importeth this,
That she in her own hands receive my gifts.
Haste ye, and to your mother bring glad tidings
Of good success in that she longs to win.
    (*Exeunt* JASON *and* CHILDREN)

(*Str. 1.*)
    CHORUS. Now for the life of the children mine hope hath been turned to despairing.
No hope any more! On the slaughter-ward path even now are they faring!
The bride shall receive it, the diadem-garland that beareth enfolden
Doom for the hapless mid glittering sheen:
And to set the adorning of Hades about her tresses golden
She shall take it her hands between.

(*Ant. 1.*)
For its glamour of beauty, its splendour unearthly, shall swiftly persuade her
To bedeck her with robe and with gold-wrought crown; she shall soon have arrayed her
In attire as a bride in the presence of phantoms from Hades uprisen;
    In such dread shall the hapless be whelmed, and from Doom's dark prison
Shall she steal forth never again.

(*Str. 2.*)
And thou, wretch, bridegroom accurst, who art fain of a princely alliance,
    Blasting thou bringest—unknowing, unthinking!—
Of life on thy sons, and thy bride shall to foul death plight her affiance.
How far from thy fortune of old art thou sinking!

(Ant. 2.)
And amidst my lamenting I mourn for
  thine anguish,
O hapless mother
Of children, who makest thee ready to
  slaughter
Thy babes, to avenge thee on him who
  would lawlessly wed with another,
  Would forsake thee to dwell with a
  prince's daughter.

Enter CHILDREN'S GUARDIAN, *with*
  CHILDREN

CHILDREN'S GUARDIAN. Mistress, re-
  mission for thy sons of exile!
Thy gifts the princess-bride with joy
  received
In hand; and there is peace unto thy
  sons.
Ha!
Why dost thou stand confounded mid
  good hap?
Now wherefore turnest thou thy face
  away,
And dost not hear with gladness this my
  speech?
  MEDEA. Woe's me!
  CHILDREN'S GUARDIAN. This cry is
  to the tidings not attuned.
  MEDEA. Woe yet again!
  CHILDREN'S GUARDIAN. Can I have
  brought ill hap
Unwitting—erred in deeming these glad
  tidings?
  MEDEA. As they are, are thy tidings:
  thee I blame not.
  CHILDREN'S GUARDIAN. Why down-
  drooped is thine eye? Why flow
  thy tears?
  MEDEA. Needs must they, ancient;
  for these things the Gods
And I withal—O fool!—have ill contrived.
  CHILDREN'S GUARDIAN. Fear not:
  thy children yet shall bring thee
  home.
  MEDEA. Others ere then shall I send
  home—ah me!

  CHILDREN'S GUARDIAN. Not thou
  alone art severed from thy sons.
Submissively must mortals bear mis-
  chance.
  MEDEA. This will I: but within the
  house go thou,
And for my children's daily needs pre-
  pare.
  (Exit CHILDREN'S GUARDIAN.*)*
O children, children, yours a city is,
And yours a home, where, leaving
  wretched me,
Ye shall abide, for ever motherless!
I shall go exiled to another land,
Ere I have joyed in you, have seen your
  bliss,
Ere I have decked for you the couch, the
  bride,
The bridal bower, and held the torch on
  high.
O me accurst in this my desperate mood!
For naught, for naught, my babes, I
  nurtured you,
And all for naught I laboured, travail-
  worn,
Bearing sharp anguish in your hour of
  birth.
Ah for the hopes—unhappy!—all mine
  hopes
Of ministering hands about mine age,
Of dying folded round with loving arms,
All men's desire! But now—'tis past—
  'tis past,
That sweet imagining! Forlorn of you
A bitter life and woeful shall I waste.
Your mother never more with loving
  eyes
Shall ye behold, passed to another life.
Woe! woe! why gaze your eyes on me,
  my darlings?
Why smile to me the latest smile of all?
Alas! what shall I do? Mine heart is
  failing
As I behold the light in my sons' eyes!
Women, I cannot! farewell, purposes
O'erpast! I take my children from the
  land.
What need to wring their father's heart
  with ills

Of these, to gain myself ills twice so
  many?
Not I, not I! Ye purposes, farewell!
Yet—yet—what ails me? Would I earn
  derision,
Letting my foes slip from mine hand
  unpunished?
I must dare this. Out on my coward
  mood
That let words of relenting touch mine
  heart!
Children, pass ye within.
            (*Exeunt* CHILDREN.)
          Now, whoso may not
Sinless be present at my sacrifice,
On his head be it: mine hand faltereth
  not.
Oh! oh!
O heart, mine heart, do not—do not this
  deed!
Let them be, wretched heart, spare thou
  my babes!
There dwelling with me shall they glad-
  den thee.
No!—by the nether fiends that dwell
  with Hades,
Never shall this betide, that I will leave
My children for my foes to trample on!
They needs must die. And, since it needs
  must be,
Even I will slay them, I, who gave them
  life.
All this is utter doom:—she shall not
  'scape!
Yea, on her head the wreath is; in my
  robes
The princess-bride is perishing—I know
  it!
But—for I fare on journey most un-
  happy,
And shall speed these on yet unhappier—
I would speak to my sons.

Re-enter CHILDREN

          Give, O my babes,
Give to your mother the right hand to
  kiss.
O dearest hand, O lips most dear to me,

O form and noble feature of my children,
Blessings be on you—*there!*—for all
  things here
Your sire hath stolen. Sweet, O sweet
  embrace!
O children's roseleaf skin, O balmy
  breath!
Away, away! Strength faileth me to
  gaze
On you, but I am overcome of evil.
            (*Exeunt* CHILDREN.)
Now, now, I learn what horrors I intend:
But passion overmastereth sober thought;
And this is cause of direst ills to men.

CHORUS. Full oft ere this my soul hath
    scaled
  Lone heights of thought, empyreal
    steeps,
  Or plunged far down the darkling
    deeps,
Where woman's feebler heart hath
    failed:—

Yet wherefore failed? Should woman
    find
  No inspiration thrill her breast,
  Nor welcome ever that sweet guest
Of song, that uttereth Wisdom's mind?

Alas! not all! Few, few, are they,—
  Perchance amid a thousand one
  Thou shouldest find,—for whom the
    sun
Of poesy makes an inner day.

Now this I say—calm bliss, that ne'er
  Knew love's wild fever of the blood,
  The pains, the joys, of motherhood,
Passeth all parents' joy-blent care.

The childless, they that never prove
  If sunshine comes, or cloud, to men
  With babes—far lie beyond their ken
The toils, the griefs, of parent-love.

But they whose halls with flowerets
    sweet
  Of childhood bloom—I mark them aye

Care-fretted, travailing alway
To win their loved ones nurture meet.

One toils with love more strong than
  death:
  Yet—yet—who knoweth whether he
  A wise man or a fool shall be
To whom he shall his wealth bequeath?

But last, but worst, remains to tell:
  For though ye get you wealth enow,
  And though your sons to manhood
  grow,
Fair sons and good;—if Death the fell,

To Hades vanishing, bears down
  Your children's lives, what profit is
  That Heaven hath laid, with all else,
  this
Upon mankind, lone sorrow's crown?

MEDEA. Friends, long have I, abid-
  ing fortune's hap,
Expected what from yonder shall befall.
And lo, a man I see of Jason's train
Hitherward coming: his wild-fluttering
  breath
Proclaimeth him the herald of strange
  ills.

Enter MESSENGER

MESSENGER. O thou who hast wrought
  an awful deed and lawless,
Flee, O Medea, flee, nor once leave
  thou
The sea-wain, or the car that scours the
  plain.
  MEDEA. Now what has happed that
  calleth for such flight?
  MESSENGER. Dead is the princess
  even now, and dead
Creon her father, by thy poison-drugs.
MEDEA. A glorious tale thou tellest:
  thou henceforth
Art of my benefactors and my friends.
  MESSENGER. What say'st? Of sound
  mind art thou, and not mad,
Who, hearing of the havoc of the hearth

Of kings, art glad, and hast no fear for
  this?
  MEDEA. O yea: I too with words of
  controversy
Could answer thee:—yet be not hasty,
  friend,
But tell how died they: thou shouldst
  gladden me
Doubly, if these most horribly have per-
  ished.
  MESSENGER. When, with their father,
  came thy children twain,
And passed into the halls for marriage
  decked,
Glad were we thralls who sorrowed for
  thy woes;
And straightway buzzed from ear to ear
  the tale
Of truce to old feuds 'twixt thy lord and
  thee.
One kissed the hand, and one the golden
  head
Of those thy sons: myself by joy drawn
  on
Followed thy children to the women's
  bowers.
Now she which had our worship in thy
  stead,
Ere she beheld thy chariot-yoke of sons,
Aye upon Jason turned her yearning
  gaze.
But then before her eyes she cast her
  veil,
And swept aback the scorn of her white
  neck,
Loathing thy sons' approach; but now
  thy lord,
To turn the maiden's wrath and spite
  aside,
Thus spake: "Nay, be not hostile to thy
  friends:
Cease from thine anger, turn thine head
  again,
Accounting friends whomso thy spouse
  accounts.
Their gifts receive, and plead thou with
  thy sire
To pardon these their exile—for my
  sake."

She, when she saw the attire, could not
refrain,
But yielded her lord all. And ere their
father
Far from her bower with those thy sons
had gone,
She took the rich-wrought robes and clad
herself,
Circling her ringlets with the golden
crown,
And by a shining mirror ranged her
tresses,
Smiling at her own phantom image there.
Then, rising from her seat, adown the
halls
She paced with mincing tread of ivory
feet,
Exulting in the gifts, and oftentimes
Sweeping her glance from neck to ankle-
hem.
But then was there a fearful sight to see.
Suddenly changed her colour: reeling
back
With trembling limbs she goes; and
scarce in time
Drops on the couch to fall not on the
ground.
Then a grey handmaid, deeming perad-
venture
That frenzy was of Pan or some God sent,
Raised the prayer-cry, before she saw
the foam
White-frothing from her lips, or marked
how rolled
Her eyeballs, and her face's bloodless
hue;
Then a long cry of horror, not of prayer,
She shrilled forth. Straight to her
father's chambers one
Darted, and one unto her new-made
spouse,
To tell the bride's affliction: all the roof
Echoed with multitudinous-hurrying feet.
And a swift athlete's straining limbs had
paced
By this the full length of the furlong
course,
When she from trance all speechless of
closed eyes

In anguish woke with horrible-shrilling
shriek;
For like two charging hosts her torment
came:—
The golden coil about her head that
lay
'Gan spurt a marvellous stream of ravening fire:
The delicate robes, the gift thy children
brought,
Had fangs to gnaw her delicate tortured
flesh!
Upstarting from her seat she flees, all
flame,
Shaking her hair, her head, this way and
that,
To cast from her the crown; but firmly
fixed
The gold held fast its grip: the fire,
whene'er
She shook her locks, with doubled fury
blazed.
Then agony-vanquished falls she on the
floor,
Marred past all knowledge, save for a
father's eyes.
No more was seen her eyes' imperial
calm,
No more her comely features; but the
gore
Dripped from her head's crown flecked
with blended fire.
The flesh-flakes from her bones, like the
pine's tears,
'Neath that mysterious drug's devourings
melted,—
Dread sight! and came on all folk fear
to touch
The corpse: her hideous fate had we for
warning.
But, ignorant of all, her wretched sire,
Suddenly entering, falls upon her corpse,
And straightway wailed and clasped the
body round,
And kissed it, crying, "O my hapless
child,
What God thus horribly hath thee de-
stroyed?
Who maketh this old sepulchre bereft

Of thee? Ah, me, would I might die with
thee!"
But when from wailing and from groans
he ceased,
Fain would he have upraised his aged
frame,
Yet clave, as ivy clings to laurel boughs,
To the filmy robes: then was a ghastly
wrestling;
For, while he strained to upraise his
knee, she seemed
To upwrithe and grip him: if by force
he haled,
Torn from the very bones was his old
flesh.
Life's light at last quenched, he gave up
the ghost,
Ill-starred, down-sinking 'neath destruc-
tion's sea.
There lie the corpses, child by grey old
sire
Clasped;—such affliction tears, not
words, must mourn.
And of thy part no word be said by
me:—
Thyself from punishment wilt find es-
cape.
But man's lot now, as oft, I count a
shadow,
Nor fear to say that such as seem to be
In wit most keen of men, most subtle
of speech,
Even these pay heaviest penalty of all;
For among mortals happy man is none.
In fortune's flood-tide might a man
become
More prosperous than his neighbor:
happy?—no!   (*Exit*.)
CHORUS. Fortune, meseems, with
many an ill this day
Doth compass Jason,—yea, and right-
fully.
But O the pity of thy calamity,
Daughter of Creon, who to Hades'
halls
Hast passed because with thee would
Jason wed!
MEDEA.   Friends, my resolve is taken,
with all speed

To slay my children, and to flee this
land,
And not to linger and to yield my
sons
To death by other hands more merci-
less.
They needs must die: and, since it needs
must be,
Even I will give them death, who gave
them life.
Up, gird thee for the fray, mine heart!
Why loiter
To do the dread ill deeds that must be
done?
Come, wretched hand of mine, grasp
thou the sword;
Grasp!—on to the starting-point of a
blasted life!
Oh, turn not craven!—think not on thy
babes,
How dear they are, how thou didst bear
them: nay,
For this short day do thou forget thy
sons,
Thereafter mourn them. For, although
thou slay,
Yet dear they are, and I—am wretched,
wretched!   (*Exit* MEDEA.)

(*Str.*)
CHORUS. O Earth, O all-revealing splen-
dour
Of the Sun, look down on a woman
accurst,
Or ever she slake the murder-thirst
Of a mother whose hands would smite
the tender
Fruit of her womb.
Look down, for she sprang of thy lineage
golden:
Men's vengeance threatens—thy seed are
holden
'Neath the shadow of doom!
But thou, O heaven-begotten glory,
Restrain her, refrain her: the wretched,
the gory
Erinys by demons dogged, we implore
thee,
Snatch thou from yon home!

(Ant.)

For naught was the childbirth-travail
wasted;
For naught didst thou bear them, the
near and the dear,
O thou who hast fled through the Pass
of Fear,
From the dark-blue Clashing Crags who
hast hasted
Speeding thy flight!
Alas for her!—wherefore hath grim
wrath stirred her
Through depths of her soul, that ruth-
less murder
Her wrongs must requite?
For stern upon mortals the vengeance
falleth
For kin's blood spilt; from the earth it
calleth,
A voice from the Gods, and the slayers
appalleth
On whose homes it shall light.

(CHILDREN'S *cries behind the scenes*)

CHILD 1. What shall I do?—how flee
my mother's hands?
CHILD 2. I know not, dearest brother.
Death is here!
CHORUS. Ah the cry!—dost thou hear
it?—the children's cry!
Wretch!—woman of cursed destiny!
Shall I enter? My heart crieth, "Rescue
the children from murder nigh!"
(They beat at the barred doors.)

CHILD. 1. Help!—for the God's sake
help! Sore is our need!
CHILD 2. The sword's death-net is
closing round us now!

*(Silence within. Blood flows out
beneath the door. The women
shrink back.)*

CHORUS. Wretch! of what rock is thy
breast?—of what steel is the heart
of thee moulded,
That the babes thou hast borne, with the
selfsame hands that with love
have enfolded

These, thou hast set thee to slay?
Of one have I heard that laid hands on
her loved ones of old, one only,
Even Ino distraught of the Gods, when
Zeus' bride drave her, lonely
And lost, from her home to stray;
And she fell—ah wretch!—on the
brink as she stood
Of the sea-scaur: guilt of children's
blood
Dragged downwards her feet to the
salt sea-flood,
And she died with her children
twain.
What ghastlier horror remains to be
wrought?
O bride-bed of women, with anguish
fraught,
What scathe upon mortals ere now hast
thou brought,
What manifold bane!

Enter JASON, *with servants*

JASON. Women, which stand anear
unto this roof—
Is she within the halls, she who hath
wrought
Dread deeds, Medea, or in flight passed
thence?
For either must she hide her 'neath the
earth,
Or lift on wings her frame to heaven's
far depths,
Or taste the vengeance of a royal house.
How, trusts she, having murdered the
land's lords,
Scatheless herself from these halls forth
to flee?
Yet not for her care I, but for my sons,
Whom she hath wronged shall recom-
pense her wrong:
But I to save my children's life am come,
Lest to my grief the kinsmen of the
dead
Avenge on them their mother's impious
murder.
CHORUS. Wretch, thou know'st not
how deep thou art whelmed in woe,

Jason, or thou hadst uttered not such words.

JASON. What now?—and is she fain to slay me too?

CHORUS. Thy sons are dead, slain by the mother's hand.

JASON. Ah me!—what say'st thou?— thou hast killed me, woman!

CHORUS. Thy children are no more: so think of them.

JASON. How?—Slew them? Where? —within, without, the halls?

CHORUS (*pointing to pavement before doors*). Open, and thou shalt see thy children's corpses.

JASON. Burst in the bolts with all speed, serving-men—
Force hinges!—let me see this twofold horror,—
The dead, and her,—and in her blood avenge me!

MEDEA *appears above the palace roof in a chariot drawn by dragons*

MEDEA. Why shakest thou these doors and wouldst unbar,
Seeking thy dead and me who wrought the deed?
Cease this essay. If thou wouldst aught of me,
Say what thou wilt: thine hand shall touch me never.
Such chariot hath my father's sire, the Sun,
Given me, a defence from foeman's hand.

JASON. O thing abhorred! O woman hatefullest
To Gods, to me, to all the race of men,
Thou that couldst thrust the sword into the babes
Thou bar'st, and me hast made a childless ruin!
Thus hast thou wrought, yet look'st thou on the sun
And earth, who hast dared a deed most impious?
Now ruin seize thee!—clear I see, who saw not

Then, when from halls and land barbarian
To a Greek home I bare thee, utter bane,
Traitress to sire and land that nurtured thee!
Thy guilt's curse-bolt on me the Gods have launched;
For thine own brother by his hearth thou slewest
Ere thou didst enter fair-prowed Argo's hull.
With such deeds thou beganest. Wedded then
To this man, and the mother of my sons,
For wedlock-right's sake hast thou murdered them.
There is no Grecian woman that had dared
This:—yet I stooped to marry thee, good sooth,
Rather than these, a hateful bride and fell,
A tigress, not a woman, harbouring
A fiercer nature than Tyrrhenian Scylla.
But—for untold revilings would not sting
Thee, in thy nature is such hardihood:—
Avaunt, thou miscreant stained with thy babes' blood!
For me remains to wail my destiny,
Who of my new-wed bride shall have no joy,
And to the sons whom I begat and nurtured
Living I shall not speak—lost, lost to me!

MEDEA. I might have lengthened out long controversy
To these thy words, if Father Zeus knew not
How I have dealt with thee and thou with me.
'Twas not for thee to set my rights at naught,
And live a life of bliss, bemocking me,
Nor for thy princess, and thy marriage-kinsman,
Creon, unscathed to banish me this land!
Wherefore a tigress call me, an' thou wilt,

Or Scylla, haunter of Tyrrhenian shore;
For thine heart have I wrung, as well
  behoved.

JASON. Ha, but thou sorrowest too,
  dost share mine ills!

MEDEA. O yea: yet grief is gain, so
  thou laugh not.

JASON. O children mine, what miscreant mother had ye!

MEDEA. O sons, destroyed by your
  own father's lust!

JASON. Sooth, 'twas no hand of mine
  that murdered them.

MEDEA. Nay, but thine insolence and
  thy new-forged bonds.

JASON. How, claim the right for
  wedlock's sake to slay them!

MEDEA. A light affliction count'st
  thou this to a wife?

JASON. A virtuous wife:—in *thy* sight
  naught were good!

MEDEA. These live no more: this,
  this shall cut thine heart!

JASON. They live—ah me!—avengers on thine head.

MEDEA. The Gods know who began
  this misery.

JASON. Yea, verily, thy spirit abhorred they know.

MEDEA. Abhorred art thou: I loathe
  thy bitter tongue.

JASON. And I thine:—yet were
  mutual riddance easy.

MEDEA. How then?—what shall I
  do?—fain would I this.

JASON. Yield me my dead to bury
  and bewail.

MEDEA. Never: with this hand will
  I bury them,
To Mountain Hera's precinct bearing
  them,
That never foe may do despite to them,
Rifling their tomb. This land of Sisy-
  phus
Will I constrain with solemn festival
And rites to atone for this unhallowed
  murder.
But I—I go unto Erechtheus' land,
With Ægeus to abide, Pandion's son.

Thou, as is meet, foul wretch, shalt
  foully die,
By Argo's wreckage smitten on the skull;
Who hast seen this new bridal's bitter
  ending.

JASON. Now the Fury-avenger of
  children smite thee,
And Justice that looketh on murder
  requite thee!

MEDEA. What God or what spirit
  will heed thy request,
Caitiff forsworn, who betrayest the
  guest?

JASON. Avaunt, foul thing by whose
  deed thy children have died!

MEDEA. Go hence to thy halls, thence
  lead to the grave of thy bride!

JASON. I go, a father forlorn of the
  two sons reft from his home!

MEDEA. Not yet dost thou truly
  mourn: abide till thine old age come.

JASON. O children beloved above all!

MEDEA. O their mother beloved, not
  of thee.

JASON. Yet she slew them!

MEDEA. That thou mightest fall in
  the net that thou spreadest for me.

JASON. Woe's me! I yearn with my
  lips to press
My sons' dear lips in my wretchedness.

MEDEA. Ha, now art thou calling
  upon them, now wouldst thou kiss,
Who rejectedst them then?

JASON. For the God's sake grant me
  but this,
The sweet soft flesh of my children to
  feel!

MEDEA. No—wasted in air is all
  thine appeal.

JASON. O Zeus, dost thou hear it,
  how spurned I am?—
What outrage I suffer of yonder abhorred
Child-murderess, yonder tigress-dam?
Yet out of mine helplessness, out of my
  shame,
I bewail my beloved, I call to record
High heaven, I bid God witness the word,
  That my sons thou hast slain, and
    withholdest me,

That mine hands may not touch them,
   nor bury their clay!
Would God I had gotten them never, this
   day
To behold them destroyed of thee!

CHORUS. All dooms be of Zeus in
   Olympus; 'tis his to reveal them.
Manifold things unhoped-for the Gods
   to accomplishment bring.
And the things that we looked for, the
   Gods deign not to fulfil them;
And the path undiscerned of our eyes, the
   Gods unseal them.
So fell this marvelous thing.
            (*Exeunt omnes.*)
            —ARTHUR S. WAY.

ALCESTIS [1]

EURIPIDES

It was the early practice of the Greek
tragedians to follow a trilogy with a
fourth play lighter in character and concluding with a happy ending, designed to
relieve the gloom and depression consequent upon the witnessing of a series of
tragedies. The chorus of such an after-
piece represented the satyrs of the older
choral lyric—whence the name "satyr
play"—and its nature was usually that of
a burlesque. In place of a satyr play
Euripides substituted the *Alcestis* (produced in 438 B.C.), an interesting combination of the tragic and the comic. The
treatment of domestic life and the element
of the romantic in it hint at the later
dramatic development known as New
Comedy.

DRAMATIS PERSONÆ

APOLLO.
DEATH.
CHORUS, *composed of elders of Pheræ.*
HANDMAID.
ALCESTIS, *daughter of* PELIAS, *and wife
of* ADMETUS.

[1] From The Loeb Classical Library, reprinted
by permission.

ADMETUS, *King of Pheræ.*
EUMELUS, *son of* ADMETUS *and* ALCESTIS.
HERCULES.
PHERES, *father of* ADMETUS.
SERVANT, *steward of the palace.*
GUARDS, ATTENDANTS, HANDMAIDS, *and*
   MOURNERS.

*The scene throughout is in front of the
palace of* ADMETUS *at Pheræ.*

Enter APOLLO

APOLLO. Halls of Admetus, hail! I
   stooped my pride
Here to brook fare of serfs, yea, I, a God!
The fault was fault of Zeus: he slew my
   son
Asclepius—hurled the levin through his
   heart.
Wroth for the dead, his smiths of heav-
   enly fire,
The Cyclopes, I slew: for blood-atone-
   ment
Allfather made me serf to a mortal man.
To this land came I, tended mine host's
   kine,
And warded still his house unto this day.
Righteous myself, I found a righteous
   man,
The son of Pheres: him I snatched from
   death,
Cozening the Fates: the Sisters promised
   me—
"Admetus shall escape the imminent death
If he for ransom gives another life."
To all he went—all near and dear,—and
   asked
Father and grey-haired mother who gave
   him life;
But, save his wife, found none that would
   consent
For him to die and never more see light.
Now in his arms upborne within yon
   home
She gaspeth forth her life: for on this day
Her weird it is to die and fleet from life.
I, lest pollution taint me in their house,
Go forth of yonder hall's beloved roof.

Enter DEATH

Lo, yonder Death;—I see him nigh at hand,
Priest of the dead, who comes to hale her down
To Hades' halls—well hath he kept his time,
Watching this day, whereon she needs must die.

DEATH. Ha, thou at the palace! Wilt not make room,
Phœbus?—thou wrestest the right yet again:
Thou removest the landmarks of Gods of Gloom,
And thou makest their honours vain.
Did not this suffice thee, to thwart that doom
Of Admetus, when, all by thy cunning beguiled
Were the Fates, that thou now must be warding the wife
With thine hand made ready the bow-string to strain,
Though she pledged her from death, to redeem with her life
Her lord,—she, Pelias' child?

APOLLO. Fear not: fair words and justice are with me.

DEATH. Justice with thee! — what needeth then the bow?

APOLLO. This?—'tis my wont to bear it evermore.

DEATH. Yea, and to aid yon house in lawless wise.

APOLLO. Mine heart is heavy for my friend's mischance.

DEATH. What, wilt thou wrest from me this second corpse?

APOLLO. Nay, not that other did I take by force.

DEATH. Not?—why on earth then? —why not underground?

APOLLO. She was his ransom, she for whom thou comest.

DEATH. Yea, and will hale her deep beneath the earth.

APOLLO. Take her and go: I trow I shall not bend thee!

DEATH. To slay the victim due!—mine office this.

APOLLO. Nay, but to smite with death the ripe for death.

DEATH. I grasp thine argument—and thine earnestness!

APOLLO. And may Alcestis never see old age?

DEATH. Never:—should I not love mine honours too?

APOLLO. 'Tis soon or late,—thou canst but take one life.

DEATH. Yet mine the goodlier prize when die the young.

APOLLO. Though she die old, rich obsequies still are thine.

DEATH. Lo, Phœbus making laws to shield the rich!

APOLLO. How say'st thou?—thou a sophist unawares!

DEATH. Would wealth not buy the boon of dying old?

APOLLO. So then thou wilt not grant this grace to me?

DEATH. Nay surely—dost not know my wonted way?

APOLLO. Hateful to mortals this, and loathed of Gods.

DEATH. All things beyond thy rights thou canst not have.

APOLLO. Surely thou shalt forbear, though ruthless thou,
So mighty a man to Pheres' halls shall come,
Sent of Eurystheus forth, the courser-car
From winter-dreary lands of Thrace to bring.
Guest-welcomed in Admetus' palace here,
By force yon woman shall he wrest from thee.
Yea, thou of me shalt have no thank for this,
And yet shalt do it, and shalt have mine hate.   (*Exit* APOLLO.)

DEATH. Talk on, talk on; no profit shalt thou win.

This woman down to Hades' halls shall
    pass.
For her I go: my sword shall seal her
    ours:
For consecrated to the Nether Gods
Is every head whose hair this sword hath
    shorn.   (*Exit* DEATH.)

Enter CHORUS, *dividing to right and left,*
so that the sections answer one another
till they unite.
HALF-CHORUS 1. What meaneth this
    hush afront of the hall?
The home of Admetus, why voiceless
    all?
HALF-CHORUS 2. No friend of the house
    who should speak of its plight
Is nigh, who should bid that we raise
    the keen
For the dead, or should tell us that yet
    on the light
Alcestis looketh, and liveth the Queen,
The daughter of Pelias, noblest, I
    ween—
    Yea, in all men's sight
Most leal to her lord of all wives hath
    she been.

                    (*Str. 1.*)
HALF-CHORUS 1. Or hearest thou
    mourning of sighing
    Or beating of hands,
Or the wail of bereaved ones outcry-
    ing?
    No handmaid stands
    At the palace-gate.
O Healer, appear for the dying, appear
    as a bright bird flying
    'Twixt the surges of fate!
HALF-CHORUS 2. She lives!—were
    she dead, they had raised the
    keen.
HALF-CHORUS 1. Nay, a corpse is all
    that was once a queen.
HALF-CHORUS 2. But not forth of the
    doors is the death-train gone.
HALF-CHORUS 1. Whence cometh
    thine hope, which I boast not mine
    own?

HALF-CHORUS 2. Would the King
    without pomp of procession have
    yielded the grave the possession
Of so dear, of so faithful an one?

                    (*Ant. 1.*)
HALF-CHORUS 1. Nor the cup in the
    gateway appeareth,
From the spring that they bear
To the gate that pollution feareth,
    Nor the severed hair
    In the porch for the dead,—
Which the mourner in bitterness shear-
    eth, neither beating of hands
    one heareth
    On maiden's head.
HALF-CHORUS 2. Yet surely is this
    the appointed day—
HALF-CHORUS 1. Ah! what wilt thou
    say?
HALF-CHORUS 2. Whereon of her
    doom she must pass to the tomb.
HALF-CHORUS 1. With a keen pang's
    smart hast thou stabbed mine heart.
HALF-CHORUS 2. It is meet, when the
    good are as flowers plucked away,
    That in sorrow's gloom
Should the breast of the old tried friend
    have part.

                    (*Str. 2.*)
CHORUS. Though ye voyage all seas,
    Ye shall light on no lands,
    Nor on Lycia's leas,
    Nor Ammonian sands,
Whence redemption shall come for the
    wretched, or loosing of Death's
    dread bands.

Doom's chasm hard by
Yawns fathomless-deep.
What availeth to cry
    To the Gods, or to heap
Their altars with costly oblations, to
    plead with the slaughter of sheep?

                    (*Ant. 2.*)
Ah, once there was one!—
Were life's light in the eyes

Of Phœbus's son,
  Then our darling might rise
From the mansions of darkness, through
    portals of Hades return to our
    skies;

For he raised up the dead,
  Ere flashed from the heaven,
From Zeus' hand sped,
  That bolt of the levin.
But now what remaineth to wait for?—
    what hope of her life is given?

No sacrifice more
  Unrendered remaineth;
No God, but the gore
  From his altars down-raineth;
Yet healing is none for our ills, neither
    balm that the spirit sustaineth.

Enter HANDMAID

But hither cometh of the handmaids
    one,
Weeping the while. What tidings shall I
    hear?
For all afflictions that befall thy lords
Well mayst thou grieve; but if thy lady
    lives
Or even now hath passed, fain would we
    know.
  HANDMAID. She liveth, and is dead:
    both mayst thou say.
  CHORUS. Ay so!—how should the
    same be dead and live?
  HANDMAID. Even now she droopeth,
    gasping out her life.
  CHORUS. O stricken king—how noble
    a queen thou losest!
  HANDMAID. His depth of loss he
    knows not ere it come.
  CHORUS. And hope—is no hope left
    her life to save?
  HANDMAID. None—for the day fore-
    doomed constraineth her.
  CHORUS. Are all things meet, then,
    being done for her?
  HANDMAID. Yea, ready is her burial-
    attire.

  CHORUS. Let her be sure that glorious
    she dies
And noblest far of women 'neath the
    sun.
  HANDMAID. Noblest? — how not? —
    what tongue will dare gainsay?
What must the woman be who passeth
    her?
How could a wife give honour to her lord
More than by yielding her to die for him?
And this—yea, all the city knoweth this;
But what within she did, hear thou, and
    marvel.
For when she knew that the appointed
    day
Was come, in river-water her white skin
She bathed, and from the cedar-chests
    took forth
Vesture and jewels, and decked her
    gloriously,
And before Vesta's altar stood, and
    prayed:
"Queen, for I pass beneath the earth, I
    fall
Before thee now, and nevermore, and
    pray:—
Be mother to my orphans: mate with him
A loving wife, with her a noble husband.
Nor, as their mother dieth, so may they,
My children, die untimely, but with weal
In the home-land fill up a life of bliss."
To all the altars through Admetus' halls
She went, with wreaths she hung them,
    and she prayed,
Plucking the while the tresses of the
    myrtle,
Tearless, unsighing, and the imminent
    fate
Changed not the lovely rose-tint of her
    cheek.
Then to her bower she rushed, fell on the
    bed;
And there, O there she wept, and thus
    she speaks:
"O couch, whereon I loosed the maiden
    zone
For this man, for whose sake I die to-day,
Farewell: I hate thee not. Me hast
    thou slain,

Me only: loth to fail thee and my lord
I die; but thee another bride shall own,
Not more true-hearted; happier perchance."
Then falls thereon, and kisses: all the bed
Is watered with the flood of melting eyes.
But having wept her fill of many tears,
Drooping she goeth, reeling from the couch;
Yet oft, as forth the bower she passed, returned,
And flung herself again upon the bed.
And the babes, clinging to their mother's robes,
Were weeping; and she clasped them in her arms.
Fondling now this, now that, as one death-doomed.
And all the servants 'neath the roof were weeping,
Pitying their lady. But to each she stretched
Her right hand forth; and none there was so mean
To whom she spake not and received reply.
Such are the ills Admetus' home within.
Now, had he died, he had ended; but, in 'scaping,
He bears a pain that he shall ne'er forget.
CHORUS. Doth not Admetus groan for this affliction
Of such a noble wife to be bereft?
HANDMAID. Ay, weeps, and clasps his dear one in his arms,
And prays, "Forsake me not!"—asking the while
The impossible, for still she wanes and wastes,
Drooping her hand, a misery-burdened weight;
But yet, albeit hardly breathing still,
To the sun's rays fain would she lift her eyes,
As nevermore, but for the last time now
Destined to see the sun's beam and his orb.

But I will go and make thy presence known:
For 'tis not all that love so well their kings
As to stand by them, in afflictions loyal.
But from of old my lords were loved of thee. (*Exit.*)

(*Nine members of the* CHORUS *chant successively*)

CHORUS 1. O Zeus, for our lords is there naught but despair?
No path through the tangle of evils, no loosing of chains that have bound them?
CHORUS 2. No tidings? — remaineth but rending of hair,
And the stricken ones turned to the tomb with the garments of sorrow around them?

CHORUS 3. Even so—even so! yet uplift we in prayer
Our hands to the Gods, for that power from the days everlasting hath crowned them.
CHORUS 4. O Healer-king,
Find thou for Admetus the balm of relief, for the captive deliverance!
CHORUS 5. Vouchsafe it, vouchsafe it, for heretofore
Hast thou found out a way; even now once more
Pluck back our beloved from Hades' door,
Strike down Death's hand red-reeking with gore!
CHORUS 6. Woe's me! woe's me!— let the woe-dirge ring!
Ah, scion of Pheres, alas for thy lot, for love's long severance!
CHORUS 7. For such things on his sword might a man not fall,
Or knit up his throat in the noose 'twixt the heaven and the earth that quivereth?
CHORUS 8. For his dear one—nay, but his dearest of all

Shall he see on this day lying dead, while
  her spirit by Lethe shivereth.
  CHORUS 9. O look!—look yonder,
  where forth of the hall
She cometh, and he at her side whose life
  by her life she delivereth.

CHORUS (*united*). Cry, Land Pheræan,
  shrill the keen!
Lift up thy voice to wail thy best
There dying, and thy queenliest
Slow wasting to the Gates Unseen!

Tell me not this, that wedlock brings
  To them that wed more bliss than woe.
I look back to the long-ago:
I muse on these unhappiest things.

Lo, here a king—he forfeiteth
  The truest heart, the noblest wife;
And what shall be henceforth his life?
A darkened day, a living death.

Enter female attendants supporting AL-
CESTIS, *accompanied by* ADMETUS *and*
CHILDREN

(*Str. 1.*)
ALCESTIS. O Sun, and the day's dear
  light,
And ye clouds through the wheeling
  heaven in the race everlasting flying!
ADMETUS. He seeth thee and me, two
  stricken ones,
Which wrought the Gods no wrong, that
  thou shouldst die.

(*Ant. 1.*)
ALCESTIS. O Land, O stately height
Of mine halls, and my bridal couch in
  Iolcos my fatherland lying!
ADMETUS. Uplift thee, hapless love,
  forsake me not,
And pray the mighty Gods in ruth to
  turn.

(*Str. 2.*)
ALCESTIS. I see the boat with the
  oars twin-sweeping,
And, his hand on the pole as in haste
  aye keeping,

Charon the Ferryman calleth, "What ho,
  wilt thou linger and linger?
Hasten,—'tis thou dost delay me!" he
  crieth with beckoning finger.
ADMETUS. Ah me! a bitter ferrying this
  thou namest!
O evil-starred, what woes endure we now!

(*Ant. 2.*)
ALCESTIS. One haleth me—haleth me
  hence to the mansion
Of the dead!—dost thou mark not the
  darkling expansion
Of the pinions of Hades, the blaze of his
  eyes 'neath their caverns out-
  glaring?
What wouldst thou?—Unhand me!—In
  anguish and pain by what path am
  I faring!
ADMETUS. Woeful to them that love
  thee: most to me
And to thy babes, sad sharers in this
  grief.

(*Epode.*)
ALCESTIS. Let be—let me sink back to
  rest me:
  There is no strength left in my feet.
  Hades is near, and the night
  Is darkening down on my sight.
  Darlings, farewell: on the light
Long may ye look:—I have blessed ye
  Ere your mother to nothingness fleet.
ADMETUS. Ah me! for thy word rush-
  eth bitterness o'er me,
  Bitterness passing the anguish of
  death!
Forsake me not now, by the Gods I im-
  plore thee.
  By the babes thou wilt orphan, O yield
  not thy breath!
Look up, be of cheer: if thou diest, before
  me
  Is nothingness. Living, we aye live
  thine,
And we die in thy death; for our hearts
  are a shrine
Wherein for thy love passing word we
  adore thee!

ALCESTIS. Admetus,—for thou seest all my plight,—
Fain would I speak mine heart's wish ere I die.
I, honouring thee, and setting thee in place
Before mine own soul still to see this light,
Am dying, unconstrained to die for thee.
I might have wed what man Thessalian I would, have dwelt wealth-crowned in princely halls;
Yet would not live on, torn away from thee,
With orphaned children: wherefore spared I not
The gifts of youth still mine, wherein I joyed.
Yet she that bare, he that begat, forsook thee,
Though fair for death their time of life was come,
Yea, fair, to save their son and die renowned.
Their only one wert thou: no hope there was
To get them sons thereafter, hadst thou died.
So had I lived, and thou, to after days:
Thou wert not groaning, of thy wife bereaved,
Thy children motherless. Howbeit this
Some God hath brought to pass: it was to be.
So be it. Remember thou what thank is due
For this,—I never can ask full requital;
For naught there is more precious than the life,—
And justly due; for these thy babes thou lovest
No less than I, if that thine heart be right.
Suffer that they have lordship in mine home:
Wed not a stepdame to supplant our babes,
Whose heart shall tell her she is no Alcestis,
Whose jealous hand shall smite them, thine and mine.
Do not, ah, do not this—I pray thee, I!
For the new stepdame hateth still the babes
Of her that's gone with more than viper-venom.
The boy—his father is his tower of strength
To whom to speak, of whom to win reply;
But, O my child, what girlhood will be thine?
To thee what would she be, thy father's yoke-mate?
What if with ill report she smirched thy name,
And in thy youth's flower marred thy marriage-hopes?
For thee thy mother ne'er shall deck for bridal,
Nor hearten thee in travail, O my child,
There, where naught gentler than the mother is.
For I must die; nor shall it be to-morn,
Nor on the third day comes on me this doom:
Straightway of them that are not shall I be.
Farewell, be happy. Now for thee, my lord,
Abides the boast to have won the noblest wife,
For you, my babes, to have sprung from noblest mother.
CHORUS. Fear not; for I am bold to speak for him:
This will he do, an if he be not mad.
ADMETUS. It shall, it shall be, fear not: thou alone
Living wast mine; and dead, mine only wife
Shalt thou be called: nor ever in thy stead
Shall bride Thessalian hail me as her lord.
None is there of a father so high-born,
None so for beauty peerless among women.

Children enough have I: I pray the Gods
For joy in these—lost is our joy in thee!
Not for a year's space will I mourn for
thee,
But long as this my life shall last, dear
wife,
Loathing my mother, hating mine own
sire,
For in word only, not in deed, they loved
me.
Thou gav'st in ransom for my life thine
all
Of precious, and didst save. Do I not
well
To groan, who lose such yokefellow in
thee?
Revels shall cease, and gatherings at the
wine,
Garlands, and song, which wont to fill
mine house.
No, never more mine hand shall touch
the lyre:
Nor will I lift up heart to sing to flute
Of Libya: stolen is life's joy with thee.
Fashioned by craftsmen's cunning hands,
thy form
Imaged, shall lie as sleeping on a bed,
Falling whereon, and clasping with my
hands,
Calling thy name, in fancy shall mine
arms
Hold my beloved, though I hold her
not:—
A drear delight, I wot: yet shall I lift
The burden from my soul. In dreams
shalt thou
Haunt me and gladden: sweet to see the
loved,
Though but as fleeting phantoms of the
night.
But, were the tongue and strain of
Orpheus mine,
To witch Demeter's daughter and her
lord,
And out of Hades by my song to win
thee,
I had fared down; nor Pluto's Hound
had stayed me,
Nor Spirit-wafter Charon at the oar,

Or ever I restored thy life to light.
Yet there look thou for me, whenso I
die:
Prepare a home, as who shall dwell with
me.
For in the selfsame cedar chest, wherein
Thou liest, will I bid them lay my bones
At thy side: never, not in death, from
thee,
My one true loyal love, may I be sun-
dered!

CHORUS. Yea, I with all will mourn,
as friend with friend,
With thee for this thy wife, for she is
worthy.

ALCESTIS. My children, ye yourselves
have heard all this,
Have heard your father pledge him ne'er
to wed
For your oppression and for my dishonour.

ADMETUS. Yea, now I say it, and I
will perform.

ALCESTIS. On these terms take the
children from mine hand.

ADMETUS. I take them—precious gift
from precious hand.

ALCESTIS. Thou in my stead be a
mother now to these.

ADMETUS. I must, I must—they are
bereft of thee!

ALCESTIS. Darlings, when most I
need to live, I die.

ADMETUS. Ah me!—what shall I do,
forlorn of thee?

ALCESTIS. Thy wound shall time
heal:—nothingness are the dead.

ADMETUS. Take me, ah take me with
thee to the grave!

ALCESTIS. Suffice it that one dies—
she dies for thee.

ADMETUS. O Fate, of what a wife
dost thou bereave me!

ALCESTIS. Dark—dark mine eyes are
drooping, heavy-laden.

ADMETUS. Oh, I am lost if thou wilt
leave me, wife!

ALCESTIS. No more—I am no more:
as naught account me.

ADMETUS. Uplift thy face: forsake not thine own children!

ALCESTIS. Sore loth do I—yet O farewell, my babes!

ADMETUS. Look on them—look!

ALCESTIS. Nothing am I henceforth.

ADMETUS. Ah, leav'st thou us?

ALCESTIS. Farewell.   (*Dies*.)

ADMETUS. O wretch undone!

CHORUS. Gone, gone! No more she lives, Admetus' wife!

(*Str.*)

EUMELUS. Woe for my lot!—to the tomb hath my mother descended, descended!

Never again, O my father, she seeth the light of the sun.

In anguish she leaves us forsaken: the story is ended, is ended,

Of her sheltering love, and the tale of the motherless life is begun.

Look—look on her eyelids, her hands drooping nerveless! O hear me, O hear me!

It is I—I beseech thee, my mother!— thine own little, own little bird!

It is I—O, I cast me upon thee—thy lips are so near me, so near me;

Unto mine am I pressing them, mother!—I plead for a word—but a word!

ADMETUS. With her who heareth not, nor seeth: ye

And I are stricken with a heavy doom.

(*Ant.*)

EUMELUS. And I am but a little one, father—so young and forsaken, forsaken,

Forlorn of my mother—O hapless! a weariful lot shall be mine!

And thou, little maiden, my sister, the burden hast taken, hast taken,

Which thy brother may bear not alone, and a weariful lot shall be thine.

O father, of long-living love was thy marriage uncherished, uncherished:

Thou hast won not the goal of old age

with the love of thy youth at thy side;

For, or ever she came to the fulness of days, she hath perished, hath perished:

And the home is a wreck and a ruin, for thou, O my mother, hast died!

CHORUS. Admetus, this affliction must thou bear.

Not first of mortals thou, nor thou the last

Hast lost a noble wife; and, be thou sure,

From us, from all, this debt is due—to die.

ADMETUS. I know it: nowise unforeseen this ill

Hath swooped on me: long anguished I foreknew it.

But—for the burial must I bear my dead—

Stay ye, and, tarrying, echo back my wail

To that dark God whom no drink-offerings move.

And all Thessalians over whom I rule

I bid take part in mourning for this woman

With shaven head and sable-shrouding robe.

And ye which yoke the cars four-horsed, or steeds

Of single frontlet, sheer with steel their manes.

Music of flutes the city through, or lyres, Be none, while twelve moons round their circles out:

For dearer dead, or kinder unto me

I shall not bury: worthy of mine honour Is she, for she alone hath died for me.

(*Exit with attendants bearing in the corpse.*)

(*Str. 1.*)

CHORUS. O Pelias' daughter, I hail thee:

I wave thee eternal farewell

To thine home where the darkness must veil thee,

Where in Hades unsunned thou shalt
      dwell.
Know, Dark-haired, thy grey Spirit-
      wafter
Hath sped not with twy-plashing oar
Woman nobler, nor shall speed hereafter
      To Acheron's shore.

(Ant. 1.)

For the seven-stringed shell, or for
      pæan
Unharped, shall thy fame be a song,
When o'er Sparta the moon Carnean
      High rideth the whole night long.
And in Athens the wealthy and splendid
      Shall thy name on her bards' lips ring;
Such a theme hast thou left to be blended
      With the lays that they sing.

(Str. 2.)

O that the power were but in me,
      From the chambers of Hades, to light,
And from streams of Cocytus to win
      thee
      With the oar of the river of night!
O dear among women, strong-hearted
      From Hades to ransom thy lord!
Never spirit in such wise departed.
      Light lie on thee, lady, the sward!
And, if ever thine husband shall mate
      him
Again with a bride in thy stead,
I will loathe him, his children will hate
      him,
      The babes of the dead.

(Ant. 2.)

When his mother would not be con-
      tented
To hide her for him in the tomb,
Nor his grey-haired father consented,
      Unholpen he looked on his doom.
Whom they bare—the hard-hearted!—
      they cared not,
      Though hoary their locks were, to
      save!
Thou art gone, for thy great love spared
      not
Thy blossom of youth from the grave

Ah, may it be mine, such communion
      Of hearts!—'tis vouchsafed unto
      few:—
Then ours should be sorrowless union
      Our life-days through.

Enter HERCULES

HERCULES. Strangers, who dwell in
      this Pheræan land,
Say, do I find Admetus in his home?
CHORUS. Hercules, in his home is
      Pheres' son.
Yet say, what brings thee to Thessalian
      land,
That thou shouldst come to this Pheræan
      town?
HERCULES. A toil for King Eurys-
      theus, lord of Tiryns.
CHORUS. And whither journeyest?
      To what wanderings yoked?
HERCULES. For Thracian Diomedes'
      four-horsed car.
CHORUS. How canst thou? Sure he
      is unknown to thee!
HERCULES. Unknown: Bistonian land
      I never saw.
CHORUS. Not save by battle may
      those steeds be won.
HERCULES. Yet flinch I may not from
      the appointed toils.
CHORUS. Thy life or his—a triumph
      or a grave.
HERCULES. Not this the first time I
      have run such course.
CHORUS. What profit is it if thou
      slay their lord?
HERCULES. Those steeds shall I drive
      back to Tiryn's king.
CHORUS. Hard task, to set the bit
      betwixt their jaws.
HERCULES. That shall I, if their
      nostrils breathe not fire.
CHORUS. Yea, but with ravening jaws
      do they rend men.
HERCULES. Go to—thus mountain-
      wolves, not horses, feast.
CHORUS. Nay, thou canst see their
      cribs besprent with gore.

HERCULES. Whom boasteth he for father, he that reared them?

CHORUS. Ares, the lord of Thracia's golden shields.

HERCULES. Thou say'st: such toil my fate imposeth still,

Harsh evermore, uphillward straining aye,

If I must still in battle close with sons

Gotten of Ares; with Lycaon first,

And Cycnus then; and lo, I come to grapple—

The third strife this—with yon steeds and their lord.

But the man lives not who shall ever see

Alcmena's son flinch from a foeman's hand.

CHORUS. Lo, there himself, the ruler of the realm,

Admetus, cometh forth his palace-hall.

Enter ADMETUS

ADMETUS. Joy to thee, sprung from Zeus' and Perseus' blood!

HERCULES. Admetus, joy to thee, Thessalia's king!

ADMETUS (*aside*). *Joy?*—would 'twere mine! (*aloud*) Thanks!—thy good heart I know.

HERCULES. Wherefore for mourning shaven show'st thou thus?

ADMETUS. This day must I commit to earth a corpse.

HERCULES. Now heaven forfend thou mourn'st for children dead!

ADMETUS. In mine home live the babes whom I begat.

HERCULES. Sooth, death-ripe were thy sire, if he be gone.

ADMETUS. He liveth, and my mother, Hercules.

HERCULES. Surely, O surely, not thy wife, Admetus?

ADMETUS. Twofold must be mine answer touching her.

HERCULES. Or hath she died, say'st thou, or liveth yet?

ADMETUS. She is, and she is not: here lies my grief.

HERCULES. Nothing the more I know: dark sayings thine.

ADMETUS. Know'st not the fate to which she is foredoomed?

HERCULES. I know she pledged herself to die for thee.

ADMETUS. How lives she then, if she to this consented?

HERCULES. Mourn not thy wife ere dead: abide the hour.

ADMETUS. One doomed is dead; the dead hath ceased to be.

HERCULES. Diverse are these—to be and not to be.

ADMETUS. This, Hercules, thy sentence: that is mine.

HERCULES. But now, why weep'st thou? What dear friend is dead?

ADMETUS. A woman—hers the memory we mourn.

HERCULES. Some stranger born, or nigh of kin to thee?

ADMETUS. A stranger born: yet near and dear to us.

HERCULES. How died a stranger then in house of thine?

ADMETUS. An orphan here she dwelt, her father dead.

HERCULES. Would I had found thee mourning not, Admetus.

ADMETUS. Ay so?—what purpose lurketh 'neath thy word?

HERCULES. On will I to another host's hearth-welcome.

ADMETUS. It cannot be: may no such grief befall!

HERCULES. A burden unto mourners comes the guest.

ADMETUS. Dead are the dead:—but enter thou mine house.

HERCULES. 'Twere shame to banquet in the house of weeping.

ADMETUS. Aloof the guest-halls are where we will lodge thee.

HERCULES. Let me pass on: so earn my thanks untold.

ADMETUS. Unto another's hearth thou canst not go.

[*To an attendant*] Ho thou, lead on: open the guest halls looking
Away from these our chambers. Tell my stewards
To set on meat in plenty. Shut withal
The mid-court doors: it fits not that the guests,
The while they feast, hear wailings, and be vexed.   (*Exit* HERCULES.)

CHORUS. What dost thou? — such affliction at the door,
And guests for thee, Admetus? Art thou mad?

ADMETUS.   But had I driven him from my home and city
Who came my guest, then hadst thou praised me more?
Nay, verily: mine affliction so had grown
No less, and more inhospitable were I!
And to mine ills were added this beside,
That this my home were called "Guest-hating hall."
Yea, and myself have proved him kind-liest host
Whene'er to Argos' thirsty plain I fared.

CHORUS. Why hide then the dread Presence in the house,
When came a friend? Thyself hast named him friend.

ADMETUS.   Never had he been won to pass my doors,
Had he one whit of mine afflictions known.
To some, I wot, not wise herein I seem,
Nor will such praise: but mine halls have not learnt
To thrust away nor to dishonour guests.

(*Str. 1.*)
CHORUS. Halls thronged of the guests ever welcome, O dwelling
  Of a hero, forever the home of the free,
The Lord of the lyre-strings sweet be-yond telling,
  Apollo, hath deigned to sojourn in thee.

Amid thine habitations, a shepherd of sheep,
The flocks of Admetus he scorned not to keep,
While the shepherds' bridal-strains, soft-swelling
  From his pipe, pealed over the slant-sloped lea.

(*Ant. 1.*)
And the spotted lynxes for joy of thy singing
  Mixed with thy flocks; and from Othrys' dell
Trooped tawny lions: the witchery-winging
  Notes brought dancing around thy shell,
Phœbus, the dappled fawn from the shadow
Of the tall-tressed pines tripping forth to the meadow,
Beating time to the chime of the rapture-ringing
  Music, with light feet tranced by its spell.

(*Str. 2.*)
Wherefore the flocks of my lord unnum-bered
  By the Bœbian mere fair-rippling stray:
Where the steeds of the sun halt, dark-ness cumbered,
  By Molossian mountains, far away
The borders lie of his golden grain,
And his rolling stretches of pasture-plain;
And the havenless beach Ægean hath slumbered
  Under Pelion long 'neath the peace of his sway.

(*Ant. 2.*)
And now, with the tears from his eyes fast-raining,
  Wide hath he opened his doors to the guest,
While newly his heart 'neath its burden is straining,

For the wife that hath died in his halls
  distressed.
For to honour's heights are the high-
  born lifted,
And the good are with truest wisdom
  gifted;
And there broods on mine heart bright
  trust unwaning
  That the god-reverer shall yet be blest.

 ADMETUS. O kindly presence of
  Pheræan men,
This corpse even now, with all things
  meet, my servants
Bear on their shoulders to the tomb and
  pyre.
Wherefore, as custom is, hail ye the dead.
On the last journey as she goeth forth.
 CHORUS. Lo, I behold thy sire with
  aged foot
Advancing: his attendants in their hands
Bear ornaments to deck the dead withal.

Enter PHERES *with attendants bearing
gifts*

 PHERES. I come in thine afflictions
  sorrowing, son:
A noble wife and virtuous hast thou lost,
None will gainsay: yet these calamities
We needs must bear, how hard to bear
  soever.
Receive these ornaments, and let her pass
Beneath the earth: well may the corpse
  be honoured
Of her who for thy life's sake died, my
  son;
Who made me not unchilded, left me not
Forlorn of thee to pine in woeful eld.
In all her sisters' eyes she hath crowned
  her life
With glory, daring such a deed as this.
O saviour of my son, who hast raised us
  up
In act to fall, all hail! May bliss be
  thine
Even in Hades. Thus to wed, I say,
Profiteth men—or nothing-worth is mar-
  riage.

 ADMETUS. Not bidden of me to her
  burial comest thou,
Nor count I thine the presence of a
  friend.
Thine ornaments she never shall put on;
She shall be buried needing naught of
  thine.
Thou grieve!—thou shouldst have
  grieved in my death-hour!
Thou stood'st aloof—the old, didst leave
  the young
To die:—and wilt thou wail upon this
  corpse?
Wast thou not, then, true father of my
  body?
Did she that said she bare me, and was
  called
Mother, not give me birth? Of bondman
  blood
To thy wife's breast was I brought
  privily?
Put to the test, thou showedst who thou
  art,
And I account me not thy true-born son.
Peerless of men in soulless cowardice!
So old, and standing on the verge of life,
Thou hadst no will, no heart hadst thou
  to die
For thine own son! Ye let her die, a
  woman
Not of our house, whom I with righteous
  cause
Might count alone my mother and my
  father.
Yet here was honour, hadst thou dared
  the strife,
In dying for thy son. A paltry space
To cling to life in any wise was left.
Then had I lived, and she, through days
  to come,
Nor I, left lorn, should thus mine ills
  bemoan.
Yet all that may the fortunate betide
Fell to thy lot; in manhood's prime a
  king,
Me hadst thou son and heir unto thine
  house,
So that thou wast not, dying, like to
  leave

A childless home for stranger folk to
spoil.
Nor canst thou say that flouting thy grey
hairs
I had given thee up to death, whose
reverence
For thee was passing word:—and this the
thank
That thou and she that bare me render
me!
Wherefore, make haste: beget thee other
sons
To foster thy grey hairs, to compass thee
With death's observance, and lay out
thy corpse.
Not I with this mine hand will bury thee.
For thee dead am I. If I see the light,—
Another saviour found,—I call me son
To him, and loving fosterer of his age.
With false lips pray the old for death's
release,
Plaining of age and weary-wearing time.
Let death draw near—who hails his com-
ing? None:
No more is eld a burden unto them.

   CHORUS. O hush! Suffice the affliction at the doors.
O son, infuriate not thy father's soul.

   PHERES. Son, whom, think'st thou—
some Lydian slave or Phrygian
Bought with thy money?—thus beratest
thou?
What, know'st thou not that I Thessalian
am,
Sprung from Thessalian sire, free man
true-born?
This insolence passeth!—hurling mala-
pert words
On me, not lightly thus shalt thou come
off!
Thee I begat and nurtured, of mine house
The heir: no debt is mine to die for thee.
Not from my sires such custom I re-
ceived
That sires for sons should die: no Greek
law this.
Born for thyself wast thou, to fortune
good
Or evil: all thy dues from me thou hast.

O'er many folk thou rulest: wide de-
mesnes
Shall I leave thee: to me my father left
them.
What is my wrong, my robbery of thee?
For me die thou not, I die not for thee.
Thou joy'st to see light—shall thy father
joy not?
Sooth, I account our time beneath the
earth
Long, and our life-space short, yet is it
sweet.
Shamelessly hast thou fought against thy
death:
Thy life is but transgression of thy doom
And murder of thy wife! *My* coward-
ice!—
This from thee, dastard, by a woman
outdone
Who died for thee, the glorious-gallant
youth!
Cunning device hast thou devised to die
Never, cajoling still wife after wife
To die for thee!—and dost revile thy
friends
Who will not so—and thou the coward,
thou?
Peace! e'en bethink thee, if thou lov'st
thy life,
So all love theirs. Thou, if thou speakest
evil
Of us, shalt hear much evil, and that
true.

   CHORUS. Ye have said too much,
thou now, and he before.
Refrain, old sire, from railing on thy
son.

   ADMETUS. Say on, say on; I have
said: if hearing truth
Gall thee, thou shouldst not have done
me wrong.

   PHERES. I had done more wrong, had
I died for thee.

   ADMETUS. What, for the young and
old is death the same?

   PHERES. One life to live, not twain—
this is our due.

   ADMETUS. Have thy desire—one life
outlasting Zeus.

PHERES. Dost curse thy parents, who
hast had no wrong?

ADMETUS. Ay, whom I marked love-
sick for dateless life.

PHERES. What?—art not burying her
in thine own stead?

ADMETUS. A token, dastard, of thy
cowardice.

PHERES. *I* did her not to death: thou
canst not say it.

ADMETUS. Mayest thou feel thy need
of me some day!

PHERES. Woo many women, that the
more may die.

ADMETUS. This taunt strikes thee—
'tis thou wast loth to die.

PHERES. Sweet is yon sun-god's light,
yea, it is sweet.

ADMETUS. Base is thy spirit, and
unmeet for men.

PHERES. Not mine old corpse to the
grave thou bear'st with glee!

ADMETUS. Yet, when thou diest, in
ill fame shalt thou die.

PHERES. Ill fame is naught to me
when I have died.

ADMETUS. Hear him! how full of
shamelessness is eld!

PHERES. Not shameless she,—but
senseless hast thou found her.

ADMETUS. Begone: leave me to bury
this my dead.

PHERES. I go! her murderer will bury
her!
Thou shalt yet answer for it to her kin.
Surely Acastus is no more a man,
If he of thee claim not his sister's blood.
(*Exit.*)

CHORUS. Alas for the loving and
daring!
Farewell to the noblest and best!
May Hermes conduct thee down-faring
Kindly, and Hades to rest
Receive thee! If any atonement
For ills even there may betide
To the good, O thine be enthronement
By Hades' bride!
(*Exeunt omnes in funeral procession.*)

Enter SERVANT

SERVANT. Full many a guest, from
many a land which came
Unto Admetus' dwelling, have I known,
Have set before them meat: but never
guest
More pestilent received to this hearth:
Who first, albeit he saw my master
mourning,
Entered, and passed the threshold un-
ashamed;
Then, nowise courteously received the
fare
Found with us, though our woeful plight
he knew,
But, what we brought not, hectoring bade
us bring.
The ivy cup uplifts he in his hands,
And swills the darkling mother's fiery
blood,
Till the wine's flame enwrapped him,
heating him.
Then did he wreathe his head with myr-
tle sprays,
Dissonant-howling. Diverse strains were
heard:
For he sang on, regardless all of ills
Darkening Admetus' house; we servants
wept
Our mistress: yet we showed not to the
guest
Eyes tear-bedewed, for so Admetus bade.
And now within the house must I be
feasting
This guest,—a lawless thief, a bandit
rogue,
While forth the house she is borne! I
followed not,
Nor stretched the hand, nor wailed unto
my mistress
Farewell, who was to me and all the
household
A mother; for from ills untold she saved
us,
Assuaging her lord's wrath. Do I not
well
To loathe this guest, intruder on our
griefs?

Enter HERCULES

HERCULES. Ho, fellow, why this solemn brooding look?
The servant should not lower upon the guest,
But welcome him with kindly-beaming cheer.
Thou, seeing here in presence thy lord's friend,
With visage sour and cloud of knitted brows
Receiv'st him, fretting o'er an alien grief.
Hither to me, that wiser thou mayst grow.
The lot of man—its nature knowest thou?
I trow not: how shouldst thou? Give ear to me.
From all mankind the debt of death is due,
Nor of all mortals is there one that knows
If through the coming morrow he shall live:
For trackless is the way of fortune's feet,
Not to be taught, nor won by art of man.
This hearing then, and learning it from me,
Make merry, drink: the life from day to day
Account thine own, all else in fortune's power.
Honour withal the sweetest of the Gods
To men, the Cyprian Queen—a gracious Goddess!
Away with other thoughts, and heed my words,
If thou dost think I speak wise words and true:
So think I. Hence with sorrow over-wrought;
Rise above this affliction: drink with me,
Thy brows with garlands bound. Full well I wot,
From all this lowering spirit prison-pent
Thine anchor shall Sir Beaker's plash upheave.

What, man!—the mortal must be mortal-minded.
So, for your solemn wights of knitted brows,
For each and all,—if thou for judge wilt take me,—
Life is not truly life, but mere affliction.
SERVANT. All this we know: but now are we in plight
Not meet for laughter and for revelry.
HERCULES. The woman dead is alien-born: grieve not
Exceeding much. Yet live the house-hold's lords.
SERVANT. Live, quotha!—know'st thou not the house's ills?
HERCULES. Yea, if thy master lied not unto me.
SERVANT. Guest-fain he is—ah, guest-fain overmuch!
HERCULES. A stranger dead—and no guest-cheer for me?
SERVANT. O yea, an alien—overmuch an alien!
HERCULES. Ha! was he keeping some affliction back?
SERVANT. Go thou in peace: our lord's ills are for us.
(*Turns away; but* HERCULES *seizes him, and makes him face him.*)
HERCULES. Grief for a stranger—such words mean not that!
SERVANT. Else had I not sore vexed beheld thy revel.
HERCULES. How! have I sorry handling of mine hosts?
SERVANT. Thou cam'st in hour un-meet for welcoming,
For grief is on us; and thou see'st shorn hair
And vesture of black robes.
HERCULES. But who hath died?
Not of the children one, or grey-haired sire?
SERVANT. Nay, but Admetus' wife is dead, O guest.
HERCULES. How say'st thou?—Ha, even then ye gave me welcome?

SERVANT. For shame he could not thrust thee from these doors.

HERCULES. O hapless! what a helpmeet hast thou lost!

SERVANT. We have all perished, and not she alone.

HERCULES. I felt it, when I saw his tear-drowned eyes,

His shaven hair, his face: yet he prevailed,

Saying he bare a stranger-friend to burial.

I passed this threshold in mine heart's despite,

And drank in halls of him that loves the guest,

When thus his plight! And am I revelling

With wreathed head? O my friend, that thou shouldst say

Naught, when on thine home such affliction lay! . . .

Where doth he bury her? Where shall I find her?

SERVANT. By the straight path that leads Larissa-wards

Shalt see the hewn-stone tomb without the walls.

HERCULES. O much-enduring heart and hand of mine,

Now show what son the Lady of Tiryns bare,

Electryon's child Alcmena, unto Zeus.

For I must save the woman newly dead,

And set Alcestis in this house again,

And render to Admetus good for good.

I go. The sable-vestured King of Corpses,

Death, will I watch for, and shall find, I trow,

Drinking the death-draught hard beside the tomb.

And if I lie in wait, and dart from ambush,

And seize, and with mine arms' coil compass him,

None is there shall deliver from mine hands

His straining sides, ere he yield up his prey.

Yea, though I miss the quarry, and he come not

Unto the blood-clot, to the sunless homes

Down will I fare of Cora and her King,

And make demand. I doubt not I shall lead

Alcestis up, and give to mine host's hands,

Who to his halls received, nor drave me thence,

Albeit smitten with affliction sore,

But hid it, like a prince, respecting me.

Who is more guest-fain of Thessalians?

Who in all Hellas? O, he shall not say

That one so princely showed a base man kindness. (*Exit.*)

Enter ADMETUS, *with* CHORUS *and attendants, returning from the funeral*

ADMETUS. O hateful returning!
O hateful to see
Drear halls full of yearning
For the lost—ah me!
What aim or what rest have I?—silence or speech, of what help shall they be?
Would God I were dead!
O, I came from the womb
To a destiny dread!
Ah, those in the tomb—
How I envy them! How I desire them, and long to abide in their home!

To mine eyes nothing sweet
Is the light of the heaven,
Nor the earth to my feet;
Such a helpmeet is riven
By Death from my side, and my darling to Hades the spoiler hath given.

(*Str.*)
CHORUS. Pass on thou, and hide thee
In thy chambers.
ADMETUS. Ah woe!
CHORUS. Wail the griefs that betide thee:
How canst thou but so?
ADMETUS. O God!

CHORUS. Thou hast passed through deep waters of anguish—I know it, I know.

ADMETUS. Woe! darkest of days!
CHORUS. No help bringeth this
To thy love in that place.
ADMETUS. Woe!
CHORUS. Bitter it is
The face of a wife well beloved forever and ever to miss.
ADMETUS. Thou hast stricken mine heart
Where the wound will not heal.
What is worse than to part
From the loving and leal?
Would God I had wedded her not, home-bliss with Alcestis to feel!

O, I envy the lot
Of the man without wife,
Without child: single-wrought
Is the strand of his life:
No soul-crushing burden of sorrow, no strength-overmastering strife.
But that children should sicken,
That gloom of despair
Over bride-beds should thicken,
What spirit can bear,
When childless, unwedded, a man through life's calm journey might fare?

(Ant.)

CHORUS. Thee fortune hath met,
Strong wrestler, and thrown;
Yet no bounds hast thou set—
ADMETUS. Woe's me!—
CHORUS.   To thy moan.
O, thy burden is heavy!
ADMETUS. Alas!
CHORUS. Yet endure it: thou art not alone.
Not thou art the first
Of bereaved ones.
ADMETUS. Ah me!
CHORUS. Such tempest hath burst
Upon many ere thee
Unto each his mischance, when the surges roll up from Calamity's sea.

ADMETUS. O long grief and pain
For beloved ones passed!
Why didst thou restrain,
When myself I had cast
Down into her grave, with the noblest to lie peace-lulled at the last?
Not one soul, but two
Had been Hades' prey,
Souls utterly true
United for aye,
Which together o'er waves of the underworld-mere had passed this day.

(Str.)

CHORUS. Of my kin was there one,
And the life's light failed
In his halls of a son
One meet to be wailed,
His only beloved: howbeit the manhood within him prevailed;
And the ills heaven-sent
As a man did he bear,
Though by this was he bent
Unto silvered hair,
Far on in life's path, without son for his remnant of weakness to care.

ADMETUS. O, how can I tread
Thy threshold, fair home?
How shelter mine head
'Neath thy roof, now the doom
Of my fate's dice changeth?—ah me, what change upon all things is come!
For with torches aflame
Of the Pelian pine,
And with bride-song I came
In that hour divine,
Upbearing the hand of a wife—thine hand, O darling mine!

Followed revellers, raising
Acclaim: ever broke
From the lips of them praising,
Of the dead as they spoke,
And of me, how the noble, the children of kings, Love joined 'neath his yoke.

But for bridal song
  Is the wail for the dead,
And, for white-robed throng,
  Black vesture hath led
Me to halls where the ghost of delight
  lieth couched on a desolate bed.

(*Ant.*)

CHORUS. To the trance of thy bliss
  Sudden anguish was brought.
Never lesson like this
  To thine heart had been taught:
Yet thy life hast thou won, and thy soul
  hast delivered from death:—is it
  naught?
Thy wife hath departed:
  Love tender and true
Hath she left:—stricken-hearted,
  Wherein is this new?
Hath Death not unyoked from the
  chariot of Love full many ere you?

ADMETUS. Friends, I account the for-
  tune of my wife
Happier than mine, albeit it seem not
  so.
For naught of grief shall touch her any
  more,
And glorious rest she finds from many
  toils.
But I, unmeet to live, my doom outrun,
Shall drag out bitter days: I know it
  now.
How shall I bear to enter this mine
  home?
Speaking to whom, and having speech of
  whom,
Shall I find joy of entering?—whither
  turn me?
The solitude within shall drive me forth,
Whenso I see my wife's couch tenantless,
And seats whereon she sat, and, 'neath
  the roof,
All foul the floor; when on my knees my
  babes
Falling shall weep their mother, servants
  moan
The peerless mistress from the mansion
  lost.

All this within: but from the world
  without
Me shall Thessalian bridals chase, and
  throngs
Where women gossip—oh, I shall not
  bear
On these, young matrons like my wife, to
  look!
And whatsoever foe I have shall scoff:
"Lo there who basely liveth—dared not
  die,
But whom he wedded gave, a coward's
  ransom,
And 'scaped from Hades. Count ye him
  a man?
He hates his parents, though himself was
  loth
To die!" Such ill report, besides my
  griefs,
Shall mine be. Ah, what honour is mine
  to live,
O friends, in evil fame, in evil plight?

(*Str. 1.*)

CHORUS. I have mused on the words
  of the wise,
  Of the mighty in song;
I have lifted mine heart to the skies,
I have searched all truth with mine
  eyes;
  But naught more strong
Than Fate have I found: there is
  naught
In the tablets of Thrace,
Neither drugs whereof Orpheus taught,
Nor in all that Apollo brought
  To Asclepius' race,
When the herbs of healing he severed,
  and out of their anguish delivered
The pain-distraught.

(*Ant. 1.*)

There is none other Goddess beside
  To the altars of whom
No man draweth near, nor hath cried
To her image, nor victim hath died,
  Averting her doom.
O Goddess, more mighty for ill
  Come not upon me

Than in days overpast: for his will
Even Zeus may in no wise fulfil
  Unholden of thee.
Steel is molten as water before thee, but
    never relenting came o'er thee,
Who art ruthless still.

(Str. 2.)

Thee, friend, hath the Goddess gripped:
    from her hands never wrestler
    hath slipped.
Yet be strong to endure: never mourning
    shall bring our beloved returning
From the nethergloom up to the
    light.
Yea, the heroes of Gods begotten,
They fade into darkness, forgotten
  In death's chill night.
Dear was she in days ere we lost her,
Dear yet, though she lie with the
    dead.
None nobler shall Earth-mother foster
Than the wife of thy bed.

(Ant. 2.)

Not as mounds of the dead which have
    died, so account we the tomb of
    thy bride;
But O, let the worship and honour that
    we render to Gods rest upon her:
Unto her let the wayfarer pray.
As he treadeth the pathway that trend-
    eth
Aside from the highway, and bendeth
  At her shrine, he shall say:
"Her life for her lord's was given:
  With the Blest now abides she on
    high.
Hail, Queen, show us grace from thine
    heaven!"
  Even so shall they cry

But lo, Alcmena's son, as seemeth, yonder,
Admetus, to thine hearth is journeying.

Enter HERCULES, *leading a woman wholly
    veiled*

HERCULES. Unto a friend behoveth
    speech outspoken,
Admetus, not to hide within the breast

Murmurs unvoiced. I came mid thine
    affliction:
Fair claim was mine to rank amidst thy
    friends:
Thou told'st me not how lay thy wife a
    corpse;
Thou gavest me guest-welcome in thine
    home,
Making pretence of mourning for a
    stranger.
I wreathed mine head, I spilled unto the
    Gods
Drink-offerings in a stricken house, even
    thine.
I blame thee, thus mishandled, yea, I
    blame;
Yet no wise is my will to gall thy grief.
But wherefore hither turning back I
    come,
This will I tell. Take, guard for me this
    maid,
Till, leading hitherward the Thracian
    mares,
I come from slaughter of Bistonia's lord.
But if I fall—no, no! I *must* return!—
I give her then, for service of thine halls.
Prize of hard toil unto mine hands she
    came:
For certain men I found but now array-
    ing
An Athlete-strife, toil-worthy, for all
    comers,
Whence I have won and bring this vic-
    tor's meed.
Horses there were for them to take which
    won
The light foot's triumph; but for hero-
    strife,
Boxing and wrestling, oxen were the
    guerdon;
A woman made it richer. Shame it
    seemed
To hap thereon, and slip this glorious
    gain.
But, as I said, this woman be thy care;
For no thief's prize, but toil-achieved, I
    bring her.
Yea, one day thou perchance shalt say
    'twas well.

ADMETUS. Not flouting thee, nor counting among foes,
My wife's unhappy fate I hid from thee.
But this had been but grief uppiled on grief,
Hadst thou sped hence to be another's guest;
And mine own ills sufficed me to bewail.
Yon maid—I pray thee, if it may be, prince,
Bid some Thessalian ward her, who hath not
Suffered as I: Thou hast many friends in Pheræ.
Oh, waken not remembrance of my grief!
I could not, seeing her mine halls within,
Be tearless; add not hurt unto mine hurt;
Burdened enough am I by mine affliction.
Nay, in mine house where should a young maid lodge?—
For vesture and adorning speak her young:—
What, 'neath the men's roof shall her lodging be?
And how unsullied, dwelling with young men?
Not easy is it, Hercules, to curb
The young: herein do I take thought for thee.
Or shall I ope to her my dead wife's bower?
How!—cause her to usurp my lost love's bed?
Twofold reproach I dread—first, from my folk,
Lest any say that, traitor to my saviour,
I fall upon another woman's bed;
Then, from my dead wife—oh, she is reverence-worthy!—
Of her must I be heedful. Woman, thou,
Whoso thou art, know that thy body's stature
Is as Alcestis', and thy form as hers.
Ah me!—lead, for the Gods' sake, from my sight
This woman! Take not my captivity captive.
For, as I look on her, methinks I see

My wife: she stirs mine heart with turmoil: fountains
Of tears burst from mine eyes. O wretched I!
Now first I taste this grief's full bitterness.
CHORUS. In sooth thy fortune can I not commend:
Yet all Heaven's visitations must we bear.
HERCULES. O that such might I had as back to bring
To light thy wife from nethergloom abodes,
And to bestow this kindness upon thee!
ADMETUS. Fain would'st thou, well I know. But wherefore this?
It cannot be the dead to light should come.
HERCULES. O'ershoot not thou the mark; bear bravely all.
ADMETUS. Easier to exhort than suffer and be strong.
HERCULES. But what thy profit, though for aye thou moan?
ADMETUS. I too know this; yet love drives me distraught.
HERCULES. Love for the lost—ay, that draws forth the tear.
ADMETUS. She hath undone me more than words can tell.
HERCULES. A good wife hast thou lost, who shall gainsay?
ADMETUS. So that thy friend hath no more joy in life.
HERCULES. Time shall bring healing; now is thy grief young.
ADMETUS. Time—time?—O yea, if this thy Time be Death!
HERCULES. A young wife, new love-yearning, shall console thee.
ADMETUS. Hush!—what say's thou? —I could not think thereon!
HERCULES. How?—wilt not wed, but widowed keep thy couch?
ADMETUS. Lives not the woman that shall couch with me.
HERCULES. Look'st thou that this shall profit aught the dead?

ADMETUS. I needs must honour her where'er she be.

HERCULES. Good—good—yet this the world calls foolishness.

ADMETUS. So be it, so thou call me bridegroom never.

HERCULES. I praise thee, in that leal thou art to her.

ADMETUS. I?—false to her, though dead?—may I die first!

HERCULES. Receive this woman then these halls within.

ADMETUS. Nay!—I implore thee by thy father Zeus!

HERCULES. Yet shalt thou err if thou do not this thing.

ADMETUS. Yet shall mine heart be tortured, if I do it.

HERCULES. Yield thou: this grace may prove perchance a duty.

ADMETUS. O that in strife thou ne'er hadst won this maid!

HERCULES. Yet thy friend's victory is surely thine.

ADMETUS. Well said: yet let the woman hence depart.

HERCULES. Yea—if need be. First look well—need it be?

ADMETUS. Needs must—save thou wilt else be wroth with me.

HERCULES. I too know what I do, insisting thus.

ADMETUS. Have then thy will: thy pleasure is my pain.

HERCULES. Yet one day shalt thou praise me: only yield.

ADMETUS (to attendants). Lead ye her, if mine halls must needs receive.

HERCULES. Nay, to no servants' hands will I commit her.

ADMETUS. Thou lead her in then, if it seems thee good.

HERCULES. Nay, but in thine hands will I place her—thine.

ADMETUS. I will not touch her! Open stand my doors.

HERCULES. Unto thy right hand only trust I her.

ADMETUS. King, thou dost force me, sore against my will!

HERCULES. Be strong: stretch forth thine hand and touch thy guest.

ADMETUS (turning his face away). I do, as one who doth behead a Gorgon.

HERCULES. Hast her?

ADMETUS.   I have.

HERCULES.   Yea, guard her. Thou shalt call
The child of Zeus one day a noble guest.

(Raises the veil, and discloses ALCESTIS.)
Look on her, if in aught she seems to thee
Like to thy wife. Step forth from grief to bliss.

ADMETUS. What shall I say?—Gods! Marvel this unhoped for!
My wife do I behold in very sooth,
Or doth some god-sent mockery-joy distract me?

HERCULES. Not so; but this thou seest is thy wife.

ADMETUS. What if this be some phantom from the shades?

HERCULES. No ghost-upraiser hast thou ta'en for thy guest.

ADMETUS. How?—whom I buried do I see—my wife?

HERCULES. Doubt not: yet might'st thou well mistrust thy fortune.

ADMETUS. As wife, as living, may I touch, address her?

HERCULES. Speak to her: all thou didst desire thou hast.

ADMETUS. Oh dearest!—wife!—sweet face!—beloved form!
Past hope I have thee! Never I thought to see thee!

HERCULES. Thou hast: may no God of thy bliss be jealous.

ADMETUS. O scion nobly-born of Zeus most high,
Blessings on thee! The Father who begat thee
Keep thee! Thou only hast restored my fortunes.

How didst thou bring her from the shades
to light?
HERCULES. I closed in conflict with
the Lord of Spirits.
ADMETUS. Where, say'st thou, didst
thou fight this fight with Death?
HERCULES. From ambush by the
tomb mine hands ensnared him.
ADMETUS. Now wherefore speechless
standeth thus my wife?
HERCULES. 'Tis not vouchsafed thee
yet to hear her voice,
Ere to the Powers beneath the earth she
be
Unconsecrated, and the third day
come.
But lead her in, and, just man as thou
art,
Henceforth, Admetus, reverence still the
guest.
Farewell. But I must go, and work the
work
Set by the king, the son of Sthenelus.
ADMETUS. Abide with us, a sharer of
our hearth.

HERCULES. Hereafter this: now must
I hasten on.
ADMETUS. O prosper thou, and come
again in peace! (*Exit* HERCULES.)
Through all my realm I publish to my
folk
That, for these blessings, dances they
array,
And that atonement-fumes from altars
rise.
For now to happier days than those
o'erpast
Have we attained. I own me blest
indeed.
CHORUS. O the works of the Gods—in
manifold forms they reveal them:
Manifold things unhoped-for the Gods
to accomplishment bring.
And the things that we looked for, the
Gods deign not to fulfil them;
And the paths undiscerned of our eyes,
the Gods unseal them.
So fell this marvellous thing.
(*Exeunt omnes.*)
—ARTHUR S. WAY.

IV. SATIRE BY A CONSERVATIVE: ARISTOPHANES

Comedy, like tragedy, grew out of the
worship of Dionysus. At the time of
harvest festivals it was customary to indulge in revels of a very free and wanton
nature, which included phallic processions
to the accompaniment of choral songs.
These songs presented the sensuous and
licentious side of the worship of the god
of wine rather than his sorrows and trials,
and were no doubt made up at first of unconnected episodes. Later a sort of unity
was introduced by establishing a connection between the episodes, and thereafter
it was but a simple step to construct a
loose sort of plot in which a single theme
was treated from various different angles.

The comedy was as old as the tragedy,
but it was slower to receive public recognition in Athens. By the time it was

recognized, it had undergone marked
changes in subject matter, being no longer
mainly concerned with the adventures of
Dionysus, but dealing with all manner of
topics and taking the direction of lampoon
and satire on public affairs and persons.
Politics, religion, morals, literature, education, individuals—anything was appropriate. It exercised complete freedom of
speech and hesitated at nothing in its
abandoned fun-making. In technique it
borrowed from the tragedy, using' the
three actors and the chorus, and alternat-
ing between dialogue and choral. The
function of the chorus was further altered
so that it not only played its part as a
rôle of the drama, but also directly addressed the audience as a mouthpiece for
the poet. The love of the grotesque is
evidenced in the representation of the

chorus as birds, wasps, frogs, etc., instead of as humans. Indeed this element was of such importance that it often supplied the title for the play.

Aristophanes (about 448 to about 385 B.C.) was the foremost of the comic poets. His comedy acknowledges no restrictions or limitations either in its right to attack, or in its extravagance of fun and fancy, or in the extent to which the indecencies of speech and conduct are presented to the ear and eye. On the other hand, there can be no doubt of its seriousness of purpose as a corrective of what the poet deems real dangers to the life of the people. Aristophanes is a believer in frugality, thrift, and simplicity, an opponent of all forms of dishonesty and insincerity, a strong advocate of peace, a bitter enemy of the political demagogue, a keen critic of the method and aims of the new sophistry. He is essentially a conservative and a traditionalist, preaching the ways of the men of old and setting himself against all innovations. Eleven of his forty-four comedies are extant.

THE CLOUDS

There had grown up in the time of Aristophanes a new education fostered and promoted by the so-called sophists, whose methods of defending both sides of any question and whose attitude of skepticism on all matters of tradition or of moral and religious faith had brought them into ill repute among the more conservative Athenians. Aristophanes found them a fit subject for his satire. His thesis in this play, that the new education will aid one in the avoidance of one's just debts, is a particular application of the more general thesis that the new education teaches escape from all moral obligations. The *Clouds* was produced in 423 B.C.

DRAMATIS PERSONÆ

STREPSIADES.
PHEIDIPPIDES.
SERVANT TO STREPSIADES.

DISCIPLES OF SOCRATES.
SOCRATES.
CHORUS OF CLOUDS.
DICÆOLOGOS.
ADICÆOLOGOS.
PASIAS.
AMYNIAS.
WITNESSES.
CHÆREPHON.

The scene is laid in Athens.

STREPSIADES *is discovered in his chamber,* PHEIDIPPIDES *sleeping in his bed. Time, before break of day.*

STREPS. (*stretching and yawning*). Ah me, ah me! will this night never end?
Oh kingly Jove, shall there be no more day?
And yet the cock sung out long time ago;
I heard him—but my people lie and snore,
Snore in defiance, for the rascals know
It is their privilege in time of war,
Which with its other plagues brings this upon us,
That we mayn't rouse these vermin with a cudgel.
There's my young hopeful too, he sleeps it through,
Snug under five fat blankets at the least.
Would I could sleep so sound! but my poor eyes
Have no sleep in them; what with debts and duns
And stable-keepers' bills, which this fine spark
Heaps on my back, I lie awake the while:
And what cares he but to coil up his locks,
Ride, drive his horses, dream of them all night,
Whilst I, poor devil, may go hang—for now
The moon in her last quarter wanes apace,
And my usurious creditors are gaping.

What hoa! a light! bring me my tablets,
  boy!
That I may set down all, and sum them
  up,
Debts, creditors, and interest upon
  interest—
  (*Boy enters with a light and tablets.*)
Let me see where I am and what the
  total—
Twelve pounds to Pasias—Hah! to
  Pasias twelve!
Out on it, and for what? A horse
  forsooth,
Right noble by the mark—curse on such
  marks!
Would I had giv'n this eye from out this
  head,
Ere I had paid the purchase of this
  jennet!
  PHEIDIP. Shame on you, Philo!—
  Keep within your ring.
  STREPS. There 'tis! that's it! the bane
  of all my peace—
He's racing in his sleep.
  PHEIDIP. A heat—a heat!
How many turns to a heat?
  STREPS. More than enough;
You've giv'n me turns in plenty—I am
  jaded.
But to my list—What name stands next
  to Pasias?
Amynias. Three good pounds—still
  for the race—
A chariot mounted on its wheels com-
  plete.
  PHEIDIP. Dismount! unharness and
  away!
  STREPS. I thank you;
You have unharness'd me: I am dis-
  mounted,
And with a vengeance—All my goods in
  pawn,
Fines, forfeiture, and penalties in plenty.
  PHEIDIP. (*wakes*). My father! why
  so restless? who has vex'd you?
  STREPS. The sheriff vexes me; he
  breaks my rest.
  PHEIDIP. Peace, self-tormentor, let
  me sleep!

STREPS. Sleep on!
But take this with you; all these debts
  of mine
Will double on your head: a plague con-
  found
That cursed match-maker, who drew me
  in
To wed, forsooth, that precious dam of
  thine.
I liv'd at ease in the country, coarsely
  clad,
Rough, free, and full withal as oil and
  honey
And store of stock could fill me, till I
  took,
Clown as I was, this limb of the Alc-
  mæons,
This vain, extravagant, high-blooded
  dame:
Rare bed-fellows and dainty—were we
  not?
I, smelling of the wine-vat, figs and
  fleeces,
The produce of my farm, all essence she,
Saffron and harlot's kisses, paint and
  washes,
A pamper'd wanton—Idle I'll not call
  her;
She took due pains in faith to work my
  ruin,
Which made me tell her, pointing to this
  cloak,
Now threadbare on my shoulders—see,
  goodwife,
This is your work—in truth you toil too
  hard.

Boy re-enters

Boy. Master, the lamp has drunk up
  all its oil.
  STREPS. Aye, 'tis a drunken lamp; the
  more fault yours;
Whelp, you shall howl for this.
  Boy. Why? for what fault?
  STREPS. For cramming such a greedy
  wick with oil.   (*Exit* Boy.)
Well! in good time this hopeful heir was
  born;

Then I and my beloved fell to wrangling
About the naming of the brat—My wife
Would dub her colt Xanthippus or
    Charippus,
Or it might be Callipides, she car'd not
So 'twere equestrian the name—but I
Stuck for his grandfather Pheidonides;
At last when neither could prevail, the
    matter
Was compromis'd by calling him Pheidip-
    pides:
Then she began to fondle her sweet babe,
And taking him by th' hand—Lambkin,
    she cried,
When thou art some years older thou
    shalt drive,
Megacles-like, thy chariot to the city,
Rob'd in a saffron mantle—No, quoth I,
Not so, my boy, but thou shalt drive thy
    goats,
When thou art able, from the fields of
    Phelle,
Clad in a woollen jacket like thy father:
But he is deaf to all these frugal rules,
And drives me on the gallop to my ruin;
Therefore all night I call my thoughts to
    council,
And after long debate find one chance
    left,
To which if I can lead him, all is safe.
If not—but soft: 'tis time that I should
    wake him.
But how to soothe him to the task—
    (*speaking in a soft gentle tone*)
    Pheidippides!
Precious Pheidippides!
  PHEIDIP. What now, my father?
  STREPS. Kiss me, my boy! reach me
    thine hand—
  PHEIDIP. Declare,
What would you?
  STREPS. Dost thou love me, sirrah?
    speak!
  PHEIDIP. Aye, by equestrian Nep-
    tune!
  STREPS. (*angrily*). Name not him,
Name not that charioteer: he is my bane,
The source of all my sorrow—but, my
    son,

If thou dost love me, prove it by obedi-
    ence.
  PHEIDIP. In what must I obey?
  STREPS.   Reform your habits;
Quit them at once, and what I shall pre-
    scribe
That do!
  PHEIDIP. And what is it that you
    prescribe?
  STREPS. But wilt thou do't?
  PHEIDIP. Yea, by Dionysus!
  STREPS. 'Tis well: get up! come
    hither, boy! look out!
Yon little wicket and the hut hard by—
Dost see them?
  PHEIDIP. Clearly. What of that same
    hut?
  STREPS. Why that's the council-
    chamber of all wisdom:
There the choice spirits dwell, who teach
    the world
That heav'n's great concave is one
    mighty oven,
And men its burning embers; these are
    they,
Who can show pleaders how to twist a
    cause,
So you'll but pay them for it, right or
    wrong.
  PHEIDIP. And how do you call them?
  STREPS. Troth, I know not that,
But they are men, who take a world of
    pains;
Wondrous good men and able.
  PHEIDIP. Out upon 'em!
Poor rogues, I know them now; you
    mean those scabs,
Those squalid, barefoot, beggarly im-
    postors,
The mighty cacodæmons of whose sect
Are Socrates and Chærephon. Away!
  STREPS. Hush, hush! be still; don't
    vent such foolish prattle;
But if you'll take my counsel, join their
    college
And quit your riding-school.
  PHEIDIP. Not I, so help me
    Dionysus our patron! though you
    brib'd me

With all the racers that Leogaras
Breeds from his Phasian stud.

STREPS. Dear, darling lad,
Prythee be rul'd, and learn.

PHEIDIP. What shall I learn?

STREPS. They have a choice of logic;
    this for justice,
That for injustice: learn that latter art,
And all these creditors, that now beset
    me,
Shall never touch a drachma that I owe
    them.

PHEIDIP. I'll learn of no such mas-
    ters, nor be made
A scare-crow and a may-game to my
    comrades;
I have no zeal for starving.

STREPS. No, nor I
For feasting you and your fine pamper'd
    cattle
At free cost any longer—Horse and foot
To the crows I bequeath you. So be
    gone!

PHEIDIP. Well, sir, I have an uncle
    rich and noble;
Megacles will not let me be unhors'd;
To him I go; I'll trouble you no longer.
                                (*Exit.*)

STREPS. (*alone*). He has thrown me
    to the ground, but I'll not lie there;
I'll up, and, with permission of the
    gods,
Try if I cannot learn these arts myself:
But being old, sluggish, and dull of wit,
How am I sure these subtleties won't
    pose me?
Well! I'll attempt it: what avails com-
    plaint?
Why don't I knock and enter?—Hoa!
    within there!—
            (*Knocks violently at the door.*)

DISCIPLE (*half-opening the door*). Go,
    hang yourself! and give the crows a
    dinner—
What noisy fellow art thou at the door?

STREPS. Strepsiades of Cicynna, son
    of Pheidon.

DISCIPLE. Whoe'er thou art, 'fore
    Heaven, thou art a fool

Not to respect these doors; battering so
    loud,
And kicking with such vengeance, you
    have marr'd
The ripe conception of my pregnant
    brain,
And brought on a miscarriage.

STREPS. Oh! the pity!—
Pardon my ignorance: I'm country bred
And far a-field am come: I pray you
    tell me
What curious thought my luckless din has
    strangled,
Just as your brain was hatching.

DISCIPLE. These are things
We never speak of but amongst ourselves.

STREPS. Speak boldly then to me, for
    I am come
To be amongst you, and partake the
    secrets
Of your profound academy.

DISCIPLE. Enough!
I will impart, but set it down in thought
Amongst our mysteries—This is the
    question,
As it was put but now to Chærephon,
By our great master Socrates, to an-
    swer—
How many of his own lengths at one
    spring
A flea can hop—for we did see one vault
From Chærephon's black eye-brow to the
    head
Of the philosopher.

STREPS. And how did t'other
Contrive to measure this?

DISCIPLE. Most accurately:
He dipt the insect's feet in melted wax,
Which, hard'ning into sandals as it
    cool'd,
Gave him the space by rule infallible.

STREPS. Imperial Jove! what subtilty
    of thought!

DISCIPLE. But there's a deeper ques-
    tion yet behind;
What would you say to that?

STREPS. I pray, impart it.

DISCIPLE. 'Twas put to Socrates, if
    he could say,

When a gnat humm'd, whether the sound
    did issue
From mouth or tail.
    STREPS. Aye; marry, what said he?
    DISCIPLE. He said your gnat doth
    blow his trumpet backwards
From a sonorous cavity within him,
Which being filled with breath, and
    forc'd along
The narrow pipe or rectum of his body,
Doth vent itself in a loud hum behind.
    STREPS. Hah! then I see the podex of
    your gnat
Is trumpet-fashion'd—Oh! the blessings
    on him
For this discovery; well may he escape
The law's strict scrutiny, who thus de-
    velops
The anatomy of a gnat.
    DISCIPLE. Nor is this all;
Another grand experiment was blasted
By a curst cat.
    STREPS. As how, good sir; discuss!
    DISCIPLE. One night as he was gaz-
    ing at the moon,
Curious and all intent upon her motions,
A cat on the house ridge was at her
    needs,
And squirted in his face.
    STREPS. Beshrew her for it!
Yet I must laugh no less to think a cat
Should so bespatter Socrates.
    DISCIPLE. Last night
We were bilk'd of our supper.
    STREPS. Were you so?
What did your master substitute instead?
    DISCIPLE. Why to say truth, he
    sprinkled a few ashes
Upon the board, then with a little broach,
Crook'd for the nonce, pretending to
    describe
A circle, neatly filch'd away a cloak.
    STREPS. Why talk we then of Thales?
    Open to me,
Open the school, and let me see your
    master:
I am on fire to enter—Come, unbar!
    (*The door of the school is un-
    barred. The Socratic scholars*

*are seen in various grotesque
situations and positions.* STREP-
SIADES, *with signs of astonish-
ment, draws back a pace or two,
then exclaims:*)
O Hercules, defend me! who are these?
What kind of battle have we here in
    view?
    DISCIPLE. Where is the wonder?
    What do they resemble?
    STREPS. Methinks they're like our
    Spartan prisoners,
Captur'd at Pylos. What are they in
    search of?
Why are their eyes so riveted to th'
    earth?
    DISCIPLE. There their researches
    centre.
    STREPS. 'Tis for onions
They are in quest—Come, lads, give o'er
    your search;
I'll show you what you want, a noble
    plat,
All round and sound—but soft! what
    mean those gentry,
Who dip their heads so low?
    DISCIPLE. Marry, because
Their studies lead that way: They are
    now diving
To the dark realms of Tartarus and
    Night.
    STREPS. But why are all their crup-
    pers mounted up?
    DISCIPLE. To practise them in star-
    gazing, and teach them
Their proper elevations—But no more:
In, fellow-students, in: if chance the
    master come
And find us here—
    (*addressing himself to some of his
    fellow-students, who were
    crowding about the new-comer.*)
    STREPS. Nay, prythee let 'em stay,
And be of council with me in my busi-
    ness.
    DISCIPLE. Impossible; they cannot
    give the time.
    STREPS. Now for the love of Heav'n,
    what have we here?

Explain their uses to me.

          (*observing the apparatus.*)

DISCIPLE. This machine

Is for astronomy—

STREPS. And this?

DISCIPLE. For geometry.

STREPS. As how?

DISCIPLE. For measuring the earth.

STREPS.   Indeed!

What, by the lot?

DISCIPLE. No, faith, sir, by the lump;

Ev'n the whole globe at once.

STREPS. Well said, in troth.

A quaint device, and made for general use.

DISCIPLE. Look now, this line marks the circumference

Of the whole earth, d'ye see—This spot is Athens—

STREPS. Athens! go to, I see no courts are sitting;

Therefore I can't believe you.

DISCIPLE. Nay, in truth,

This very tract is Attica.

STREPS. And where,

Where is my own Cicynna?

DISCIPLE. Here it lies:

And here's Eubœa—Mark! how far it runs—

STREPS. How far it runs! Yes, Pericles has made it

Run far enough from us—Where's Lacedæmon?

DISCIPLE. Here; close to Athens.

STREPS. Ah! how much too close—

Prythee, good friends, take that bad neighbour from us.

DISCIPLE. That's not for us to do.

STREPS.   The worse luck yours!

But look! (*casting up his eyes*) who's this suspended in a basket?

          (*Socrates is discovered*)

DISCIPLE (*with solemnity*). HIMSELF. The HE.

STREPS. The HE? what HE?

DISCIPLE. Why, Socrates.

STREPS. Hah! Socrates! — (*to the scholar*) Make up to him and roar,

Bid him come down! roar lustily.

DISCIPLE. Not I:

Do it yourself; I've other things to mind.

          (*Exit.*)

STREPS. Hoa! Socrates—What hoa, my little Socrates!

SOCR. Mortal, how now! Thou insect of a day,

What would'st thou?

STREPS. I would know what thou art doing.

SOCR. I tread in air, contemplating the sun.

STREPS. Ah! then I see you're basketed so high,

That you look down upon the Gods— Good hope

You'll lower a peg on earth.

SOCR. Sublime in air,

Sublime in thought I carry my mind with me,

Its cogitations all assimilated

To the pure atmosphere, in which I float;

Lower me to earth, and my mind's subtle powers,

Seiz'd by contagious dullness, lose their spirit;

For the dry earth drinks up the generous sap,

The vegetating vigour of philosophy,

And leaves it a mere husk.

STREPS. What do you say?

Philosophy has sapt your vigour? Fie upon it.

But come, my precious fellow, come down quickly,

And teach me those fine things I'm here in quest of.

SOCR. And what fine things are they?

STREPS. A new receipt

For sending off my creditors, and foiling them

By the art logical; for you shall know

By debts, pawns, pledges, usuries, executions,

I am rackt and rent in tatters.

SOCR. Why permit it?

What strange infatuation seiz'd your senses?

STREPS. The horse-consumption, a devouring plague;
But so you'll enter me amongst your scholars,
And tutor me like them to bilk my creditors,
Name your own price, and by the Gods I swear
I'll pay you the last drachm.
SOCR. By what Gods?
Answer that first; for your Gods are not mine.
STREPS. How swear you then? As the Byzantians swear
By their base iron coin?
SOCR. Art thou ambitious
To be instructed in celestial matters,
And taught to know them clearly?
STREPS. Aye, aye, in faith,
So they be to my purpose, and celestial.
SOCR. What, if I bring you to a conference
With my own proper Goddesses, the Clouds?
STREPS. 'Tis what I wish devoutly.
SOCR.   Come, sit down;
Repose yourself upon this couch.
STREPS. 'Tis done.
SOCR. Now take this chaplet—wear it.
STREPS. Why this chaplet?
Would'st make of me another Athamas,
And sacrifice me to a cloud?
SOCR. Fear nothing;
It is a ceremony indispensable
At OUR initiations.
STREPS. What to gain?
SOCR. (*instead of the sacred meat, which was thrown on the sacrificed victim, a basket of stones is showered on the head of* STREPSIADES).
'Twill sift your faculties as fine as powder,
Bolt 'em like meal, grind 'em as light as dust;
Only be patient.
STREPS. Truly, you'll go near
To make your words good; an' you pound me thus,

You'll make me very dust and nothing else.
SOCR. (*assuming all the magical solemnity and tone of voice of an adept*). Keep silence, then, and listen to a prayer,
Which fits the gravity of age to hear—
Oh! Air, all powerful Air, which dost enfold
This pendent globe, thou vault of flaming gold.
Ye sacred Clouds, who bid the thunder roll,
Shine forth, approach, and cheer your suppliant's soul!
STREPS. Hold, keep 'em off awhile, till I am ready.
Ah! luckless me, would I had brought my bonnet,
And so escap'd a soaking.
SOCR. Come, come away!
Fly swift, ye Clouds, and give yourselves to view!
Whether on high Olympus' sacred top
Snow-crown'd ye sit, or in the azure vales
Of your own father Ocean sporting weave
Your misty dance, or dip your golden urns
In the seven mouths of Nile; whether ye dwell
On Thracian Mimas, or Mœotis' lake,
Hear me, yet hear, and thus invok'd approach!
CHORUS OF CLOUDS. (*The scene is at the remotest part of the stage. Thunder is heard. A large and shapeless Cloud is seen floating in the air; from which the following song is heard.*)
Ascend, ye watery Clouds, on high,
Daughters of Ocean, climb the sky,
And o'er the mountain's pine-capt brow
Towering your fleecy mantle throw:
Thence let us scan the wide-stretch'd scene,
Groves, lawns, and rilling streams between,
And stormy Neptune's vast expanse,
And grasp all nature at a glance.

Now the dark tempest flits away,
And lo! the glittering orb of day
Darts from his clear ethereal beam,
Come let us snatch the joyous gleam.

SOCR. Yes, ye Divinities, whom I
adore,
I hail you now propitious to my prayer.
Didst thou not hear them speak in thunder to me?

STREPS. (*kneeling, and, with various
acts of buffoonery, affecting terror
and embarrassment*).
And I too am your Cloudship's most
obedient,
And under sufferance trump against your
thunder:—
Nay (*turning to* SOCRATES), take it how
you may, my frights and fears
Have pinch'd and cholic'd my poor
bowels so,
That I can't choose but treat their holy
nostrils
With an unsavoury sacrifice.

SOCR. Forbear
These gross scurrilities, for low buffoons
And mountebanks more fitting. Hush!
be still,
List to the chorus of their heavenly
voices,
For music is the language they delight in.

CHORUS OF CLOUDS (*approaching
nearer*). Ye Clouds replete with
fruitful showers,
Here let us seek Minerva's towers,
The cradle of old Cecrops' race,
The world's chief ornament and grace;
Here mystic fanes and rites divine
And lamps in sacred splendour shine;
Here the Gods dwell in marble domes,
Feasted with costly hecatombs,
That round their votive statues blaze,
Whilst crowded temples ring with
praise;
And pompous sacrifices here
Make holidays throughout the year;
And when gay spring-time comes again,
Bromius convokes his sportive train,
And pipe and song and choral dance
Hail the soft hours as they advance.

STREPS. Now, in the name of Jove, I
pray thee tell me
Who are these ranting dames, that talk
in stilts?
Of the Amazonian cast no doubt.

SOCR. Not so,
No dames, but clouds celestial, friendly
powers
To men of sluggish parts; from these we
draw
Sense, apprehension, volubility,
Wit to confute, and cunning to ensnare.

STREPS. Aye, therefore 'twas that my
heart leapt within me
For very sympathy when first I heard
'em:
Now I could prattle shrewdly of first
causes,
And spin out metaphysic cobwebs
finely,
And dogmatise most rarely, and dispute
And paradox it with the best of you:
So, come what may, I must and will be-
hold 'em;
Show me their faces, I conjure you.

SOCR. Look.
Look towards Mount Parnes as I point—
There, there!
Now they descend the hill; I see them
plainly,
As plain as can be.

STREPS. Where, where? I prythee,
show me.

SOCR. Here! a whole troop of them
thro' woods and hollows,
A byway of their own.

STREPS. What ails my eyes,
That I can't catch a glimpse of them?

SOCR. Behold!
Here at the very entrance—

STREPS. Never trust me,
If yet I see them clearly.

SOCR. Then you must be
Sand-blind or worse.

STREPS. Nay, now by father Jove,
I cannot choose but see them—precious
creatures!
For in good faith here's plenty and to
spare.

CHORUS OF CLOUDS *enter*

SOCR. And didst thou doubt if they were goddesses?

STREPS. Not I, so help me! only I'd a notion
That they were fog, and dew, and dusky vapour.

SOCR. For shame! Why, man, these are the nursing mothers
Of all our famous sophists, fortune-tellers,
Quacks, medicine-mongers, bards bombastical,
Chorus projectors, and star interpreters,
And wonder-making cheats—the gang of idlers,
Who pay them for their feeding with good store
Of flattery and mouth-worship.

STREPS. Now I see
Whom we may thank for driving them along
At such a furious dithyrambic rate,
Sun-shadowing clouds of many-colour'd hues,
Air-rending tempests, hundred-headed Typhons;
Now rousing, rattling them about our ears,
Now gently wafting them adown the sky,
Moist, airy, bending, bursting into showers;
For all which fine descriptions these poor knaves
Dine daintily on scraps.

SOCR. And proper fare;
What better do they merit?

STREPS. Under favour,
If these be clouds (d'you mark me?) very clouds,
How came they metamorphos'd into women?
Clouds are not such as these.

SOCR. And what else are they?

STREPS. Troth, I can't rightly tell, but I should guess
Something like flakes of wool, not women, sure;
And look! these dames have noses.

SOCR. Hark you, friend,
I'll put a question to you.

STREPS. Out with it!
Be quick: let's have it.

SOCR. This it is, in short—
Hast thou ne'er seen a cloud, which thou could'st fancy
Shap'd like a centaur, leopard, wolf, or bull?

STREPS. Yea, marry, have I, and what then?

SOCR. Why then
Clouds can assume what shapes they will, believe me;
For instance; should they spy some hairy clown
Rugged and rough, and like the unlick't cub
Of Xenophantes, straight they turn to centaurs,
And kick at him for vengeance.

STREPS. Well done, Clouds!
But should they spy that peculating knave,
Simon, that public thief, how would they treat him?

SOCR. As wolves—in character most like his own.

STREPS. Aye, there it is now; when they saw Cleonymus,
That dastard runaway, they turn'd to hinds
In honour of his cowardice.

SOCR. And now,
Having seen Cleisthenes, to mock his lewdness
They change themselves to women.

STREPS. Welcome, ladies!
Imperial ladies, welcome! An' it please
Your Highnesses so far to grace a mortal,
Give me a touch of your celestial voices.

CHOR. Hail, grandsire! who at this late hour of life
Would'st go to school for cunning; and all hail,
Thou prince pontifical of quirks and quibbles,
Speak thy full mind, make known thy wants and wishes!

Thee and our worthy Prodicus excepted,
Not one of all your sophists have our ear:
Him for his wit and learning we esteem,
Thee for thy proud deportment and high
    looks,
In barefoot beggary strutting up and
    down,
Content to suffer mockery for our sake,
And carry a grave face whilst others
    laugh.

STREPS. Oh! mother earth, was ever
    voice like this,
So reverend, so portentous, so divine!

SOCR. These are your only deities, all
    else
I flout at.

STREPS. Hold! Olympian Jupiter—
Is he no god?

SOCR. What Jupiter? what god?
Prythee no more—away with him at
    once!

STREPS. Say'st thou? who gives us
    rain? answer me that.

SOCR. These give us rain; as I will
    straight demonstrate:
Come on now—When did you e'er see it
    rain
Without a cloud? If Jupiter gives rain,
Let him rain down his favours in the sun-
    shine,
Nor ask the clouds to help him.

STREPS. You have hit it,
'Tis so; heav'n help me! I did think till
    now,
When 'twas his godship's pleasure, he
    made water
Into a sieve and gave the earth a shower.
But, hark'ye me, who thunders? tell me
    that;
For then it is I tremble.

SOCR. These, these thunder,
When they are tumbled.

STREPS. How, blasphemer, how?

SOCR. When they are charg'd with
    vapours full to th' bursting,
And bandied to and fro against each
    other,
Then with the shock they burst and crack
    amain.

STREPS. And who is he that jowls
    them thus together
But Jove himself?

SOCR. Jove! 'tis not Jove that does it,
But the ætherial vortex.

STREPS. What is he?
I never heard of him; is he not Jove?
Or is Jove put aside, and Vortex crown'd
King of Olympus in his state and place?
But let me learn some more of this same
    thunder.

SOCR. Have you not learnt? I told
    you how the clouds,
Being surcharg'd with vapour, rush to-
    gether,
And, in the conflict, shake the poles with
    thunder.

STREPS. But who believes you?

SOCR. You, as I shall prove it:
Mark the Panathenæa, where you cram
Your belly full of pottage; if you shake
And stir it lustily about—what then?

STREPS. Marry, why then it gives a
    desperate crack;
It bounces like a thunderbolt, the pottage
Keeps such a coil within me—At the first,
Pappax it cries—anon with double force,
Papappax!—when at length *Papappapax*
From forth my sounding entrails thund'r-
    ing bursts.

SOCR. Think then, if so your belly
    trumpets forth,
How must the vasty vault of heaven re-
    sound,
When the clouds crack with thunder!

STREPS. Let that pass,
And tell me of the lightning, whose quick
    flash
Burns us to cinders; that, at least, great
    Jove
Keeps in reserve to launch at perjury?

SOCR. Dunce, dotard! were you born
    before the flood
To talk of perjury, whilst Simon breathes,
Theorus and Cleonymus, whilst they,
Thrice-perjur'd villains, brave the light-
    ning's stroke,
And gaze the heav'ns unscorcht? Would
    these escape?

Why, man, Jove's random fires strike his own fane,
Strike Sunium's guiltless top, strike the dumb oak,
Who never yet broke faith or falsely swore.

STREPS. It may be so, good sooth! You talk this well:
But I would fain be taught the natural cause
Of these appearances.

SOCR. Mark when the winds,
In their free courses check'd, are pent and purs'd
As 'twere within a bladder; stretching then
And struggling for expansion, they burst forth
With cracks so fierce as sets the air on fire.

STREPS. The devil they do! why now the murder's out:
So was I serv'd with a damn'd paunch, I broil'd
On Jove's day last, just such a scurvy trick;
Because, forsooth, not dreaming of your thunder,
I never thought to give the rascal vent,
Bounce! goes the bag, and covers me all over
With filth and ordure till my eyes struck fire.

CHOR. The envy of all Athens shalt thou be,
Happy old man, who from our lips dost suck
Into thy ears true wisdom, so thou art
But wise to learn, and studious to retain
What thou hast learnt; patient to bear the blows
And buffets of hard fortune; to persist,
Doing or suffering; firmly to abide
Hunger and cold, not craving where to dine,
To drink, to sport and trifle time away;
But holding that for best, which best becomes

A man who means to carry all things through
Neatly, expertly, perfect at all points
With head, hands, tongue, to force his way to fortune.

STREPS. Be confident; I give myself for one
Of a tough heart, watchful as care can make me,
A frugal, pinching fellow, that can sup
Upon a sprig of savory and to bed;
I am your man for this, hard as an anvil.

SOCR. 'Tis well, so you will ratify your faith
In these our deities—Chaos and Clouds
And Speech—to these and only these adhere.

STREPS. If from this hour henceforth I ever waste
A single thought on any other gods,
Or give them sacrifice, libation, incense,
Nay, even common courtesy, renounce me.

CHOR. Speak your wish boldly then, so shall you prosper
As you obey and worship us, and study
The wholesome art of thriving.

STREPS. Gracious ladies,
I ask no mighty favour, simply this—
Let me but distance every tongue in Greece,
And run 'em out of sight a hundred lengths.

CHOR. Is that all? there we are your friends to serve you;
We will endow thee with such powers of speech,
As henceforth not a demagogue in Athens
Shall spout such popular harangues as thou shalt.

STREPS. A fig for powers of spouting! give me powers
Of nonsuiting my creditors.

CHOR. A trifle—
Granted as soon as ask'd; only be bold,
And show yourself obedient to your teachers.

STREPS. With your help so I will, being undone,

Stript of my pelf by these high-blooded
  cattle,
And a fine dame, the torment of my life.
Now let them work their wicked will
  upon me;
They're welcome to my carcass; let 'em
  claw it,
Starve it with thirst and hunger, fry it,
  freeze it,
Nay, flay the very skin off; 'tis their
  own;
So that I may but fob my creditors,
Let the world talk; I care not though it
  call me
A bold-faced, loud-tongued, overbearing
  bully;
A shameless, vile, prevaricating cheat;
A tricking, quibbling, double-dealing
  knave;
A prating, pettyfogging limb o' th' law;
A sly old fox, a perjurer, a hang-dog,
A raggamuffin made of shreds and
  patches,
The leavings of a dunghill—Let 'em rail,
Yea, marry, let 'em turn my guts to
  fiddle-strings,
May my bread be my poison! if I care.
  CHOR. This fellow hath a prompt and
    daring spirit—
Come hither, sir; do you perceive and feel
What great and glorious fame you shall
  acquire
By this our schooling of you?
  STREPS. What, I pray you!
  CHOR. What but to live the envy of
    mankind
Under our patronage?
  STREPS. When shall I see
Those halcyon days?
  CHOR. Then shall your doors be
    throng'd
With clients waiting for your coming
  forth,
All eager to consult you, pressing all
To catch a word from you, with ab-
  stracts, briefs,
And cases ready-drawn for your opinion.
But come, begin and lecture this old
  fellow;

Sift him, that we may see what meal he's
  made of.
  SOCR. Hark ye, let's hear what prin-
    ciples you hold,
That these being known, I may apply
  such tools
As tally with your stuff.
  STREPS. Tools! by the gods;
Are you about to spring a mine upon
  me?
  SOCR. Not so, but simply in the way
    of practice
To try your memory.
  STREPS. Oh! as for that,
My memory is of two sorts, long and
  short:
With them who owe me aught, it never
  fails;
My creditors indeed complain of it,
As mainly apt to leak and lose its
  reck'ning.
  SOCR. But let us hear if nature hath
    endow'd you
With any grace of speaking.
  STREPS. None of speaking.
But a most apt propensity to cheating.
  SOCR. If this be all, how can you
    hope to learn?
  STREPS. Fear me not, never break
    your head for that.
  SOCR. Well then be quick, and when I
    speak of things
Mysterious and profound, see that you
  make
No boggling, but—
  STREPS. I understand your mean-
    ing;
You'd have me bolt philosophy by mouth-
  fuls,
Just like a hungry cur.
  SOCR. Oh! brutal, gross
And barbarous ignorance! I must sus-
  pect,
Old as thou art, thou must be taught
  with stripes:
Tell me now, when thou art beaten, what
  dost feel?
  STREPS. The blows of him that beats
    me I do feel;

But having breath'd awhile I lay my
  action
And cite my witnesses; anon more
  cool,
I bring my cause into the court, and sue
For damages.
  Socr. Strip off your cloak! prepare.
  Streps. Prepare for what? what crime
  have I committed?
  Socr. None; but the rule and custom
  is with us,
That all shall enter naked.
  Streps. And why naked?
I come with no search-warrant; fear me
  not;
I'll carry nought away with me.
  Socr. No matter;
Conform yourself, and strip.
  Streps. And if I do,
Tell me for my encouragement to which
Of all your scholars will you liken me.
  Socr. You shall be call'd a second
  Chærephon.
  Streps. Ah! Chærephon is but an-
  other name
For a dead corpse—excuse me.
  Socr. No more words:
Pluck up your courage; answer not, but
  follow:
Haste and be perfected.
  Streps. Give me my dole
Of honey-cake in hand, and pass me
  on;
Ne'er trust me if I do not quake and
  tremble
As if the cavern of Trophonius yawn'd,
And I were stepping in.
  Socr. What ails you? enter!
Why do you halt and loiter at the
  door?
    (Socrates and Strepsiades enter
      the mansion of the former.)
  Chor. Go, brave adventurer, pro-
  ceed!
May fortune crown the gallant deed;
Tho' far advanc'd in life's last stage,
Spurning the infirmities of age,
Thou canst to youthful labours rise,
And boldly struggle to be wise.

Ye, who are here spectators of our scene,
Give me your patience to a few plain
  words,
And by my patron Bacchus, whose I am,
I swear they shall be true ones—Gentle
  friends,
So may I prosper in your fair esteem,
As I declare in truth that I was mov'd
To tender you my former comedy,
As deeming it the best of all my works,
And you its judges worthy of that work,
Which I had wrought with my best care
  and pains:
But fools were found to thrust me from
  the stage,
And you, whose better wisdom should
  have sav'd me
From that most vile cabal, permitted it;
For which I needs must chide, yet not so
  sharply
As to break off from such approv'd good
  friends:
No, you have been my patrons from all
  time,
Ev'n to my first-born issue: when I
  dropt
My bantling at your door to hide the
  shame
Of one, who call'd herself a maiden muse,
You charitably took the foundling in,
And gave it worthy training. Now, be-
  hold,
This sister comedy, Electra-like,
Comes on the search if she perchance
  may find
Some recognition of a brother lost,
Though but a relic of his well-known hair.
Seemly and modest she appears before
  you;
Not like our stage buffoons in shaggy
  hide
To set a mob a roaring; she will vent
No foolish jests at baldness, will not
  dance
Th' indecent cordax; we have no old man
Arm'd with a staff to practise manual
  jokes
On the by-standers' ribs, and keep the
  ring

For them who dance the chorus: you
   shall see
No howling furies burst upon the stage
Waving their torches; other weapons
Than the muse gives us we shall not
   employ,
Nor let *ah me, ah me!* sigh in your ears.
Yet not of this I boast, nor that I scorn
To cater for your palates out of scraps
At second or third hand, but fresh and
   fair
And still original, as one, who knows,
When he has done a good deed, where
   to stop;
And, having levell'd Cleon to the ground,
Not to insult his carcass, like to those
Who, having once run down Hyperbolus,
Poor devil! mouth and mangle without
   mercy
Him and his mother too; foremost of
   these
Was Eupolis, who pilfer'd from my muse,
And pass'd it for his own with a new
   name,
Guilty the more for having dash'd his
   theft
With the obscene device of an old hag
Dancing the drunken cordax in her cups,
Like her Phrynichus feign'd to be de-
   vour'd
By the sea-monster—Shame upon such
   scenes!
Hermippus next *Hyperbolis'd* amain,
And now the whole pack open in full cry,
Holding the game in chase, which I had
   rous'd.
If there be any here, who laugh with
   these,
Let such not smile with me; but if this
   night
Ye crown these scenes with merited ap-
   plause,
Posterity shall justify your taste.

SEMICHOR. Great Jove, supreme of
   Gods, and heav'n's high king,
First I invoke; next him the Trident's
   lord,
Whose mighty stroke smites the wild
   waves asunder,

And makes the firm earth tremble; thee
   from whom
We draw our being, all-inspiring Air,
Parent of nature; and thee, radiant Sun,
Thron'd in thy flaming chariot, I invoke,
Dear to the gods and by the world ador'd.

CHORUS OF CLOUDS. Most grave and
   sapient judges, hear the charge,
Which we shall now prefer, of slights ill
   brook'd
By us your wrong'd appellants: for whilst
   we
The patronesses of your state, the Clouds,
Of all the powers celestial serve you most,
You graceless mortals serve us not at
   all;
Nor smoke, nor sacrifice ascends from
   you,
But blank ingratitude and cold neglect.
If some rash enterprise you set on foot,
Some brainless project, straight with rain
   or thunder,
Sure warnings, we apprise you of your
   folly:
When late you made that offspring of a
   tanner,
That Paphlagonian odious to the gods,
The general of your armies, mark how
   fierce
We scowl'd upon you, and indignant
   roll'd
Our thunders intermixt with flashing
   fires;
The Moon forsook her course, and the
   vext Sun
Quench'd his bright torch, disdaining to
   behold
Cleon your chief, yet chief that Cleon
   was,
(For it should seem a proverb with your
   people,
That measures badly taken best suc-
   ceed):
But if you'll learn of us the ready mode
To cancel your past errors, and ensure
Fame and good-fortune for the public
   weal,
You have nought else to do, but stop the
   swallow

Of that wide-gaping cormorant, that thief
Convicted and avow'd, with a neat noose
Drawn tight and fitted to his scurvy throat.

  SEMICHOR. Thou too, Apollo, of thy native isle,
Upon the Cinthian mount high thron'd, the king,
Hear and be present! thou, Ephesian goddess,
Whose golden shrine the Lydian damsels serve
With rich and costly worship; thou, Minerva,
Arm'd with the dreadful ægis, virgin queen,
And patroness of Athens; thou, who hold'st
Divided empire on Parnassus' heights,
Lead hither thy gay train of revellers,
Convivial god, and thus invok'd approach!

  CHOR. As we were hither journeying, in midway
We crost upon the Moon, who for a while
Held us in converse, and with courteous greeting
To this assembly charg'd us—This premis'd,
The tenor of our next instruction points
To anger and complaint for ill returns
On your part to good offices on her's.
First for the loan of her bright silver lamp
So long held out to you, by which you've sav'd
Your torch and lacquey for this many a night.
More she could name, if benefits avail'd;
But you have lost all reck'ning of your feasts,
And turn'd your calendar quite topsy-turvy;
So that the deities, who find themselves
Bilk'd of their dues, and supperless for lack
Of their accustom'd sacrifices, rail

At her, poor Moon, and vent their hungry spite,
As she were in the fault; whilst you, forsooth,
Maliciously select our gala days,
When feasting would be welcome, for your suits
And criminal indictments; but when we
Keep fast and put on mourning for the loss
Of Memnon or Sarpedon, sons of Heaven,
Then, then you mock us with the savoury odour
Of smoking dainties, which we may not taste:
Therefore it is, that when this year ye sent
Your deputy Amphictyon to the diet,
(Hyperbolus forsooth) in just revenge
We tore away his crown, and drove him back
To warn you how you slight the Moon again.

  SOCRATES (*coming out of the house in violent indignation*), STREPSIADES, CHORUS

  SOCR. O vivifying breath, æthereal air,
And thou profoundest chaos, witness for me
If ever wretch were seen so gross and dull,
So stupid and perplext as this old clown,
Whose shallow intellect can entertain
No image nor impression of a thought;
But ere you've told it, it is lost and gone!
'Tis time however he should now come forth
In the broad day—What hoa! Strepsiades—
Take up your pallet; bring yourself and it
Into the light.

  STREPS. Yes, if the bugs would let me.

SOCR. Quick, quick, I say; set down your load and listen!

STREPS. Lo! here am I.

SOCR.   Come, tell me what it is
That you would learn besides what I have
    taught you;
Is it of measure, verse, or modulation?

STREPS. Of measure by all means, for
    I was fobb'd
Of two days' dole i' th' measure of my
    meal
By a damn'd knavish huckster.

SOCR. Pish! who talks
Of meal? I ask which metre you prefer,
Tetrameter or trimeter.

STREPS. I answer—
Give me a pint pot.

SOCR. Yes, but that's no answer.

STREPS. No answer! stake your
    money, and I'll wager
That your tetrameter is half my pint pot.

SOCR. Go to the gallows, clodpate,
    with your pint pot!
Will nothing stick to you? But come,
    perhaps
We may try further and fare better with
    you—
Suppose I spoke to you of modulation;
Will you be taught of that?

STREPS. Tell me first,
Will I be profited? will I be paid
The meal that I was chous'd of? tell me
    that.

SOCR. You will be profited by being
    taught
To bear your part at table in some sort
After a decent fashion; you will learn
Which verse is most commensurate and
    fit
To the arm'd chorus in the dance of war,
And which with most harmonious cadence
    guides
The dactyl in his course poetical.

STREPS. The dactyl, quotha! Sure I
    know that well.

SOCR. As how? discuss.

STREPS. Here, at my fingers' end;
This is my dactyl, and has been my
    dactyl

Since I could count my fingers.

SOCR. Oh! the dolt.

STREPS. I wish to be no wiser in
    these matters.

SOCR. What then?

STREPS. Why then, teach me no other
    art
But the fine art of cozening.

SOCR. Granted; still
There is some previous matter, as for in-
    stance
The genders male and female—Can you
    name them?

STREPS. I were a fool else—These are
    masculine:
Ram, bull, goat, dog, and pullet.

SOCR. There you're out:
Pullet is male and female.

STREPS. Tell me how?

SOCR. Cock and hen pullet—So they
    should be nam'd.

STREPS. And so they should, by the
    æthereal air!
You've hit it; for which rare discovery,
Take all the meal this cardopus con-
    tains.

SOCR. Why there again you sin
    against the genders.
To call your bolting-tub a cardopus,
Making that masculine which should be
    fem'nine.

STREPS. How do I make my bolting-
    tub a male?

SOCR. Did you not call it cardopus?
    As well
You might have call'd Cleonymus a man;
He and your bolting-tub alike belong
To t'other sex, believe me.

STREPS. Well, my trough
Shall be a cardopa and he Cleonyma;
Will that content you?

SOCR. Yes, and while you live
Learn to distinguish sex in proper names.

STREPS. I do; the female I am perfect
    in.

SOCR. Give me the proof.

STREPS. Lysilla, she's a female;
Philinna, and Demetria, and Cleitagora.

SOCR. Now name your males.

STREPS. A thousand—as for instance,
Philoxenus, Melesias, and Amynias.

SOCR. Call you these masculine, egregious dunce?

STREPS. Are they not such with you?

SOCR. No; put the case,
You and Amynias meet—how will you
greet him?

STREPS. Why, thus for instance—
Hip! holla! Amynia!

SOCR. There, there! you make a
wench of him at once.

STREPS. And fit it is for one who
shuns the field;
A coward ought not to be call'd a
man;
Why teach me what is known to all the
world?

SOCR. Aye, why indeed?—but come,
repose yourself.

STREPS. Why so?

SOCR. For meditation's sake: lie
down.

STREPS. Not on this pallet I beseech
you, sir;
But if I must lie down, let me repose
On the bare earth and meditate.

SOCR. Away!
There's nothing but this bed will cherish
thought.

STREPS. It cherishes, alas! a host of
bugs,
That show no mercy on me.

SOCR. Come, begin,
Cudgel your brains and turn yourself
about;
Now ruminate awhile, and if you start
A thought that puzzles you, try t'other
side,
And turn to something else, but not to
sleep;
Suffer not sleep to close your eyes one
moment.

STREPS. (after a considerable pause).
Ah! woe is me; ah, woeful, well-a-
day!

SOCR. What ails you? why this moaning?

STREPS. I am lost;
I've rous'd the natives from their hiding
holes;
A colony of bugs in ambuscade
Have fall'n upon me: belly, back, and
ribs,
No part is free: I feed a commonwealth.

SOCR. Take not your sufferings too
much to heart,

STREPS. How can I choose—a wretch
made up of wants!
Here am I penniless and spiritless,
Without a skin, Heav'n knows, without a
shoe;
And to complete my miseries here I lie,
Like a starv'd sentinel upon his post,
At watch and ward, till I am shrunk to
nothing.
(A pause of some duration.)

SOCR. How now; how fare you?
Have you sprung a thought?

STREPS. Yes, yes, so help me Neptune!

SOCR. Hah! what is it?

STREPS. Why I am thinking if these
cursed vermin
Will leave one fragment of my carcass
free.

SOCR. A plague confound you!

STREPS. Spare yourself that prayer;
I'm plagued already to your heart's content.

SOCR. Prythee don't be so tender of
your skin;
Tuck yourself up and buff it like a man:
Keep your skull under cover, and depend
on't
'Twill make your brain bring forth some
precious project
For furthering your good-fortune at the
expense
Of little else but honesty and justice.

STREPS. Ah! would to Heav'n some
friendly soul would help me
To a fine project how to cheat the bugs
With a sleek lambskin.
(A long pause.)

SOCR. Whereabouts, I trow,
Sits the wind now? What ails you? are
you dozing?

STREPS. Not I, by Heaven!

SOCR.   Can you start nothing yet?
STREPS. Nothing, so help me.
SOCR.   Will your head breed no
   project,
Tho' nurs'd so daintily?
STREPS. What should it breed?
Tell me, sweet Socrates; give me some
   hint.
SOCR. Say first what 'tis you wish.
STREPS. A thousand times,
Ten thousand times I've said it o'er and
   o'er—
My creditors, my creditors—'Tis them
I would fain bilk.
SOCR. Go to! get under cover,
Keep your head warm, and rarefy your
   wits
Till they shall sprout into some fine con-
   ceit,
Some scheme of happy promise: sift it
   well,
Divide, abstract, compound, and when
   'tis ready,
Out with it boldly.
STREPS. Miserable me!
Would I were out!
SOCR. Lie still, and if you strike
Upon a thought that baffles you, break
   off
From that entanglement and try another.
So shall your wits be fresh to start again.
STREPS. (*not attending to what Socrates
   is saying*). Hah! my dear boy!
My precious Socrates!
SOCR. What would'st thou, gaffer?
STREPS. I have sprung a thought,
A plot upon my creditors.
SOCR. Discuss!
STREPS. Answer me this—Suppose
   that I should hire
A witch, who some fair night shall raise
   a spell,
Whereby I'll snap the moon from out her
   sphere
And bag her.
SOCR. What to do!
STREPS. To hold her fast,
And never let her run her courses more;
So shall I 'scape my creditors.

SOCR. How so?
STREPS. Because the calculations of
   their usury
Are made from month to month.
SOCR. A gallant scheme;
And yet methinks I could suggest a
   hint
As practicable and no less ingenious—
Suppose you are arrested for a debt,
We'll say five talents, how will you con-
   trive
To cancel at a stroke both debt and writ?
STREPS. Gramercy! I can't tell you
   how off hand;
It needs some cogitation.
SOCR. Were you apt,
Such cogitations would not be to seek;
They would be present at your fingers'
   ends,
Buzzing alive, like chafers in a string,
Ready to slip and fly.
STREPS. I've hit the nail
That does the deed, and so you will con-
   fess.
SOCR. Out with it!
STREPS. Good chance but you have
   noted
A pretty toy, a trinket in the shops,
Which being rightly held produceth fire
From things combustible—
SOCR. A burning glass,
Vulgarly call'd—
STREPS. You are right; 'tis so.
SOCR.   Proceed!
STREPS. Put the case now your
   whoreson bailiff comes,
Shows me his writ—I, standing thus, d'ye
   mark me,
In the sun's stream, measuring my dis-
   tance, guide
My focus to a point upon his writ,
And off it goes in fumo!
SOCR. By the Graces!
'Tis wittingly devis'd.
STREPS. The very thought
Of his five talents cancel'd at a stroke
Makes my heart dance for joy.
SOCR. But now again—
STREPS. What next?

SOCR. Suppose yourself at bar, sur-
pris'd
Into a suit, no witnesses at hand,
The judge prepar'd to pass decree against
you—
How will you parry that?
    STREPS. As quick as thought—
    SOCR. But how?
    STREPS. Incontinently hang myself,
And baulk the suitor—
    SOCR. Come, you do but jest.
    STREPS. Serious, by all the gods! A
man that's dead
Is out of the law's reach.
    SOCR. I've done with you—
Instruction's lost upon you; your vile
jests
Put me beyond all patience.
    STREPS. Nay, but tell me
What is it, my good fellow, that offends
thee?
    SOCR. Your execrable lack of memory.
Why how now; what was the first rule I
taught you?
    STREPS. Say'st thou the first? the very
first—what was it?
Why, let me see; 'twas something, was it
not?
About the meal—Out on it! I have lost
it.
    SOCR. Oh thou incorrigible, old doat-
ing blockhead,
Can hanging be too bad for thee?
    STREPS. Why there now,
Was ever man so us'd? If I can't make
My tongue keep pace with your's, teach
it the quirks
And quibbles of your sophistry at once,
I may go hang—I am a fool forsooth—
Where shall I turn? Oh gracious Clouds,
befriend me,
Give me your counsel.
    CHOR. This it is, old man—
If that your son at home is apt and docile,
Depute him in your stead, and send him
hither.
    STREPS. My son is well endow'd with
nature's gifts,
But obstinately bent against instruction.

CHOR. And do you suffer it?
    STREPS. What can I do?
He's a fine full-grown youth, a dashing
fellow,
And by the mother's side of noble blood:
I'll feel my way with him—but if he
kicks,
Befall what may, nothing shall hinder
me
But I will kick him headlong out of doors,
And let him graze ev'n where he will for
me—
Wait only my return; I'll soon dispatch.
                                    (Exit.
    CHOR. Highly favour'd shalt thou be,
With gifts and graces kept in store
For those who our divinities adore,
And to no other altars bend the knee:
And well we know th' obedience shown
By this old clown deriv'd alone
From lessons taught by thee.
Wherefore to swell thy lawful gains,
Thou soon shalt skin this silly cur,
Whom thou hast put in such a stir,
And take his plunder for thy pains:
For mark how often dupes like him de-
vise
Projects that only serve t' enrich the
wise.

STREPSIADES (coming out of his house to
his Son, who stands at the door)
Out of my house! I call the Clouds to
witness
You shall not set a foot within my
doors.
Go to your Lord Megacles! Get you
hence,
And gnaw his posts for hunger.
    PHEIDIP. Ah, poor man!
I see how it is with you. You are mad,
Stark mad, by Jupiter!
    STREPS. You swear by Jupiter!
Why then, I swear by Jove there's no
such god—
Now who is mad but you?
    PHEIDIP. Why do you turn
Such solemn truths to ridicule?
    STREPS. I laugh

To hear a child prate of such old men's
    fables;
But list to what I'll tell you, learn of me,
And from a child you shall become a
    man—
But keep the secret close, do you mark
    me, close;
Beware of babbling.

    PHEIDIP. Heyday! what is coming?
    STREPS. You swore but now by
        Jupiter—
    PHEIDIP. I did.
    STREPS. Mark now what 'tis to have
        a friend like me—
I tell you at a word there is no Jupiter.
    PHEIDIP. How then?
    STREPS. He's off; I tell it you for
        truth;
He's out of place, and Vortex reigns in-
    stead.
    PHEIDIP. Vortex indeed! What freak
        has caught you now?
    STREPS. No freak, 'tis fact.
    PHEIDIP. Who tells you this?
    STREPS. E'en Socrates the Melian,
And Chærephon, the flea philosopher.
    PHEIDIP. And are you so far gone in
        dotage, sir,
As to be dup'd by men like them, fellows
Whose bile has overflowed them?
    STREPS. Keep a good tongue;
Take heed you slander not such worthy
    men,
So wise withal and learned—men so pure
And cleanly in their morals, that no
    razor
Ever profan'd their beards; their un-
    wash'd hides
Ne'er dabbled in a bath, nor wafted scent
Of od'rous unguent as they pass'd along.
But you, a prodigal fine spark, make
    waste
And havoc of my means, as I were dead
And out of thought—but come, turn in
    and learn.
    PHEIDIP. What can I learn or profit
        from such teachers?
    STREPS. Thou canst learn everything
        that turns to profit;

But first and foremost thou canst learn
    to know
Thyself how totally unlearn'd thou art;
How mere a blockhead, and how dull of
    brain—
But wait awhile with patience—
            (*Enters the house hastily.*
    PHEIDIP. Woe is me!
How shall I deal with this old crazy
    father?
What course pursue with one, whose
    reason wanders
Out of all course? Shall I take out the
    statute,
And cite him for a lunatic; or wait
Till nature and his phrenzy, with the
    help
Of the undertaker, shall provide a cure?
        (STREPSIADES *returns, with a cock*
        in one hand and a hen in the
        other.)
    STREPS. Now we shall see! Lo! what
        have I got here?
    PHEIDIP. A chicken—
    STREPS.   Well and this?
    PHEIDIP.   A chicken also.
    STREPS. Are they the same then?
        Have a care, good boy,
How you expose yourself, and for the
    future
Describe them cock and hen-chick
    severally.
    PHEIDIP. Ridiculous! Is this the
        grand discovery
You have just borrow'd from these sons
    o' th' dunghill?
    STREPS. This, and a thousand others
        —but being old
And lax of memory, I lose it all
As fast as it comes in.
    PHEIDIP. Yes, and methinks
By the same token you have lost your
    cloak.
    STREPS. No, I've not lost it; I have
        laid it out
Upon the arts and sciences.
    PHEIDIP. Your shoes—
They're vanish'd too. How have you
    laid them out?

STREPS. Upon the commonwealth—
     Like Pericles
I'm a barefooted patriot—Now no more;
Do as thou wilt, so thou wilt but conform
And humour me this once, as in times
     past
I humour'd thee, and in thy playful age
Brought thee a penny go-cart from the
     fair,
Purchas'd with what my legal labours
     earn'd,
The fee for my attendance.
          (*Going towards the house of
          Socrates.*)
     PHEIDIP. You'll repent,
My life upon 't; you will repent of this.
          (*Following reluctantly.*)
     STREPS. No matter, so you'll humour
     me—What, hoa!
Why Socrates, I say, come forth, behold,
Here is my son!
I've brought him, tho' in faith
Sorely against the grain.

SOCRATES *enters*

     SOCR. Aye, he's a novice,
And knows not where the panniers hang
     as yet.
     PHEIDIP. I would you'd hang yourself
     there in their stead.
     STREPS. Oh monstrous impudence!
     this to your master!
     SOCR. Mark how the idiot quibbles
     upon *hanging*.
Driv'ling and making mouths—Can he
     be taught
The loopholes of the law; whence to
     escape,
How to evade, and when to press a
     suit;—
Or tune his lips to that soft rhetoric,
Which steals upon the ear, and melts to
     pity
The heart of the stern judge?
     STREPS. Come, never doubt him;
He is a lad of parts, and from a child
Took wondrously to dabbling in the
     mud,

Whereof he'd build you up a house so
     natural
As would amaze you, trace you out a
     ship,
Make you a little cart out of the sole
Of an old shoe mayhap, and from the
     rind
Of a pomegranate cut you out a frog,
You'd swear it was alive. Now what do
     you think?
Hath he not wit enough to comprehend
Each rule both right and wrong? Or if
     not both,
The latter way at least—There he'll be
     perfect.
     SOCR. Let him prepare: His lecturers
     are ready.
     STREPS. I will retire—When next we
     meet, remember
I look to find him able to contend
'Gainst right and reason, and outwit
     them both.   (*Exit.*

DICÆOLOGOS *and* ADICÆOLOGOS *enter*

     DICÆOL. Come forth; turn out, thou
     bold audacious man,
And face this company.
     ADICÆOL. Most willingly:
I do desire no better: take your ground
Before this audience, I am sure to
     triumph.
     DICÆOL. And who are you that
     vapour in this fashion?
     ADICÆOL. Fashion itself—the very
     style of the times.
     DICÆOL. Aye, of the modern times,
     and them and you
I set at naught.
     ADICÆOL. I shall bring down your
     pride.
     DICÆOL. By what most witty
     weapon?
     ADICÆOL. By the gift
Of a most apt invention.
     DICÆOL. Then I see
You have your fools to back you.
     ADICÆOL. No,—the wise
Are those I deal with.

DICÆOL. I shall spoil your market.

ADICÆOL. As how, good sooth?

DICÆOL. By speaking such plain truths
As may appeal to justice.

ADICÆOL. What is justice?
There's no such thing—I traverse your appeal.

DICÆOL. How! No such thing as justice?

ADICÆOL. No; where is it?

DICÆOL. With the immortal gods.

ADICÆOL. If it be there,
How chanc'd it Jupiter himself escap'd
For his unnatural deeds to his own father?

DICÆOL. For shame, irreverent wretch, thus do you talk?
I sicken at impiety so gross,
My stomach kicks against it.

ADICÆOL. You are craz'd;
Your wits, old gentleman, are off the hinges.

DICÆOL. You are a vile blasphemer and buffoon.

ADICÆOL. Go on! you pelt me—but it is with roses.

DICÆOL. A scoffer!

ADICÆOL. Every word your malice vents
Weaves a fresh wreath of triumph for my brows.

DICÆOL. A parricide!

ADICÆOL. Proceed, and spare me not—
You shower down gold upon me.

DICÆOL. Lead, not gold,
Had been your retribution in times past.

ADICÆOL. Aye, but times present cover me with glory.

DICÆOL. You are too wicked.

ADICÆOL. You are much too weak.

DICÆOL. Thank your own self, if our Athenian fathers
Coop up their sons at home, and fear to trust them
Within your schools, conscious that nothing else
But vice and folly can be learnt of you.

ADICÆOL. Methinks, friend, your's is but a ragged trade.

DICÆOL. And your's, oh shame! a thriving one, tho' late,
A perfect Telephus, you tramp'd the street
With beggar's wallet cramm'd with hungry scraps,
Choice gather'd from—Pandeletus' larder.

ADICÆOL. Oh! what rare wisdom you remind me of!

DICÆOL. Oh, what rank folly their's, who rule this city,
And let it nourish such a pest as you,
To sap the morals of the rising age.

ADICÆOL. You'll not inspire your pupil with these notions,
Old hoary-headed time!

DICÆOL. I will inspire him,
If he has grace, to shun the malady
Of your eternal clack.

ADICÆOL. Turn to me, youth!
And let him rail at leisure,

DICÆOL. Keep your distance,
And lay your hands upon him at your peril.

CHOR. (interposing). Come, no more wrangling.—Let us hear you both;
You of the former time produce your rules
Of ancient discipline—of modern, you—
That so, both weigh'd, the candidate may judge
Who offers fairest, and make choice between you.

DICÆOL. I close with the proposal.

ADICÆOL. 'Tis agreed.

CHOR. But which of you shall open?

ADICÆOL. That shall he:
I yield him up that point; and in reply,
My words, like arrows levelled at a butt,
Shall pierce him through and through; then, if he rallies,
If he comes on again with a rejoinder,
I'll launch a swarm of syllogisms at him,
That, like a nest of hornets, shall belabour him,
Till they have left him not an eye to see with.

CHOR. Now, sirs, exert your utmost care,
And gravely for the charge prepare;
The well-rang'd hoard of thought explore,
Where sage experience keeps her store;
All the resources of the mind
Employment in this cause will find,—
And he, who gives the best display
Of argument, shall win the day:
Wisdom this hour at issue stands,
And gives her fate into your hands;
Your's is a question that divides
And draws out friends on different sides:
Therefore on you, who, with such zealous praise,
Applaud the discipline of former days,
On you I call! now is your time to show
You merit no less praise than you bestow.

DICÆOL. Thus summon'd, I prepare myself to speak
Of manners primitive, and that good time,
Which I have seen, when discipline prevail'd,
And modesty was sanctioned by the laws.
No babbling then was suffer'd in our schools;—
The scholar's test was silence. The whole group
In orderly procession sallied forth
Right onwards, without straggling, to attend
Their teacher in harmonics; though the snow
Fell on them thick as meal, the hardy brood
Breasted the storm uncloak'd: their harps were strung
Not to ignoble strains, for they were taught
A loftier key, whether to chant the name
Of Pallas, terrible amidst the blaze
Of cities overthrown, or wide and far
To spread, as custom was, the echoing peal.
There let no low buffoon intrude his tricks,

Let no capricious quavering on a note,
No running of divisions high and low
Break the pure stream of harmony; no Phrynis
Practising wanton warblings out of place—
Woe to his back that so was found offending!
Hard stripes and heavy would reform his taste.
Decent and chaste their postures in the school
Of their gymnastic exercises; none
Expos'd an attitude that might provoke
Irregular desire; their lips ne'er mov'd
In love-inspiring whispers, and their walks
From eyes obscene were sacred and secure.
Hot herbs, the old man's diet, were proscrib'd;
No radish, anise, parsley, deck'd their board;
No rioting, no revelling was there
At feast or frolic, no unseemly touch
Or signal, that inspires the hint impure.
ADICÆOL. Why these are maxims obsolete and stale;
Worm-eaten rules, coeval with the hymns
Of old Ceceydas and Buphonian feasts.
DICÆOL. Yet so were train'd the heroes, that imbru'd
The field of Marathon with hostile blood;
This discipline it was that braced their nerves
And fitted them for conquest. You, forsooth,
At great Minerva's festival produce
Your martial dancers, not as they were wont,
But smother'd underneath the tawdry load
Of cumbrous armour, till I sweat to see them
Dangling their shields in such unseemly sort
As mars the sacred measure of the dance.

Be wise, therefore, young man, and turn
  to me.
Turn to the better guide, so shall you
  learn
To scorn the noisy forum, shun the bath,
And turn with blushes from the scene
  impure:
Then conscious innocence shall make you
  bold
To spurn the injurious, but to reverend
  age,
Meek and submissive, rising from your
  seat,
To pay the homage due, nor shall you
  ever
Or wring the parent's soul, or stain your
  own.
In purity of manners you shall live
A bright example; vain shall be the lures
Of the stage-wanton floating in the
  dance,
Vain all her arts to snare you in her arms,
And strip you of your virtue and good
  name.
No petulant reply shall you oppose
To fatherly commands, nor taunting vent
Irreverent mockery on his hoary head,
Crying—"Behold Iäpetus himself!"
Poor thanks for all his fond parental care.
  ADICÆOL. Aye, my brave youth, do,
  follow these fine rules,
And learn by them to be as mere a swine,
Driveller, and dolt, as any of the sons
Of our Hippocrates;—I swear by Bac-
  chus,
Folly and foul contempt shall be your
  doom.
  DICÆOL. Not so, but fair and fresh in
  youthful bloom
Amongst our young athletics you shall
  shine;
Not in the forum loit'ring time away
In gossip prattle, like our gang of idlers,
Nor yet in some vexatious paltry suit
Wrangling and quibbling in our petty
  courts.
But in the solemn academic grove,
Crown'd with the modest reed, fit con-
  verse hold

With your collegiate equals; there serene,
Calm as the scene around you, under-
  neath
The fragrant foliage where the ilex
  spreads,
Where the deciduous poplar strews her
  leaves,
Where the tall elm-tree and wide-stretch-
  ing plane
Sigh to the fanning breeze, you shall
  inhale
Sweet odours wafted in the breath of
  spring.
This is the regimen that will insure
A healthful body and a vigorous mind,
A countenance serene, expanded chest,
Heroic stature and a temperate tongue;
But take these modern masters, and be-
  hold
These blessings all revers'd; a pallid
  cheek,
Shrunk shoulders, chest contracted, sap-
  less limbs,
A tongue that never rests, and mind de-
  bas'd,
By their vile sophistry perversely taught
To call good evil, evil good, and be
That thing, which nature spurns at, that
  disease,
A mere Antimachus, the sink of vice.
  CHOR. Oh sage instructor, how sub-
  lime
These maxims of the former time!
How sweet this unpolluted stream
Of eloquence, how pure the theme!
Thrice happy they, whose lot was cast
Amongst the generation past,
When virtuous morals were display'd
And these grave institutes obey'd.
Now you, that vaunt yourself so high,
Prepare; we wait for your reply,
And recollect, or ere you start,
You take in hand no easy part;
Well hath he spoke, and reasons good
By better only are withstood;
Sharpen your wits then, or you'll meet
Contempt as certain as defeat.
  ADICÆOL. Doubt not I'm ready, full
  up to the throat

And well nigh chok'd with plethory of
    words,
Impatient to discharge them. I do know
The mighty masters of the modern school
Term me the Lower Logic, so distin-
    guish'd
From the old practice of the upper time,
By him personified; which name of
    honour
I gain'd as the projector of that method,
Which can confute and puzzle all the
    courts
Of law and justice—an invention worth
Thousands to them who practise it,
    whereas
It nonsuits all opponents.—Let that pass.
Now take a sample of it in the ease,
With which I'll baffle this old vaunting
    pedant
With his warm baths, that he forsooth
    forbids.
Harkye, old man, discuss, if so it please
    you,
Your excellent good reason for this rule,
That interdicts warm bathing.
    Dicæol. Simply this—
I hold it a relaxer, rendering men
Effeminate and feeble.
    Adicæol. Hold awhile—
I have you on the hook. Answer me
    this—
Of all the heroes Jupiter has father'd,
Which is for strength, for courage, and
    a course
Of labours most renown'd?
    Dicæol. I know of none
Superior in those qualities to Hercules.
    Adicæol. And who e'er heard Hercu-
    lean baths were cold?
Yet Hercules himself you own was strong.
    Dicæol. Aye, this is in the very style
    of the times;
These are the dialectics now in fashion
With our young sophists, who frequent
    the baths
Whilst the palæstra starves.
    Adicæol. I grant you this;
It is the style of the times, by you con-
    demn'd,

By me approv'd, and not without good
    cause;
For how but thus doth ancient Nestor
    talk?
Can Homer err? Were all his wise men
    fools?
They are my witnesses.—Now for this
    tongue,
This member out of use by his decree,
Not so by mine.—His scholar must be
    silent
And chaste withal—damping prescrip-
    tions both—
For what good fortune ever did betide
The mute and modest? Instance me a
    case.
    Dicæol. Many—Chaste Peleus so
    obtained his sword.
    Adicæol. His sword! and what did
    Peleus gain by that?
Battle and blows this modest Peleus
    gain'd;
Whilst mean Hyperbolus, whose wretched
    craft
Was lamp-making, by craft of viler sort
Garbel'd his thousands, solid coin, not
    swords.
    Dicæol. But continence befriended
    Peleus so,
As won the goddess Thetis to his bed.
    Adicæol. And drove her out of it—
    for he was cold,
Languid and listless: she was brisk and
    stirring,
And sought the sport elsewhere. Now
    are you answered?
Good sooth you're in your dotage. Mark,
    young sir,
These are the fruits of continence: you
    see
What pleasure you must forfeit to pre-
    serve it—
All the delights that woman can bestow;
No am'rous sports to catch the fair one's
    smile,
No luscious dainties shall you then par-
    take,
No gay convivial revels, where the glass
With peals of laughter circulates around;

These you must sacrifice, and without
    these
What is your life?—So much for your
    delights.—
Now let us see how stands your score
    with nature—
You're in some scrape we'll say—intrigue
    —adultery—
You're caught, convicted, crush'd—for
    what can save you?
You have no powers of speech—but
    arm'd by me,
You're up to all occasions: Nothing fear;
Ev'n give your genius scope; laugh, frolic,
    sport,
And flout at shame; for should the
    wittol spouse
Detect you in the fact, you shall so pose
    him
In his appeal, that nothing shall stick to
    you;
For Jove shall take the blame from off
    your shoulders,
Being himself a cuckold-making god,
And you a poor frail mortal—Why should
    you
Be wiser, stronger, purer than a god?
    DICÆOL. But what if this your scholar
    should incur
Th' adulterer's correction,—pill'd and
    sanded,
And garnish'd with a radish in his crup-
    per,
The scoff of all beholders—What fine
    quirk
Will clear him at that pinch, but he must
    pass
For a most perfect Ganymede?
    ADICÆOL. What then?
Where is the harm?
    DICÆOL. Can greater harm befall
    him?
    ADICÆOL. What will you say if here
    I can confute you?
    DICÆOL. Nothing—my silence shall
    confess your triumph.
    ADICÆOL. Come on then—answer me
    to what I ask.
Our advocates—what are they?

    DICÆOL. Catamites.
    ADICÆOL. Our tragic poets—what are
    they?
    DICÆOL. The same.
    ADICÆOL. Good, very good!—our
    demagogues—
    DICÆOL. No better.
    ADICÆOL. See there! discern you not
    that you are foil'd?
Cast your eyes round this company!—
    DICÆOL. I do.
    ADICÆOL. And what do you discover?
    DICÆOL. Numerous birds
Of the same filthy feather, so Heaven
    help me!
This man I mark; and this, and this fine
    fop
With his curl'd locks.—To all these I can
    swear.
    ADICÆOL. What say you then?
    DICÆOL. I say I am confuted—
Here, wagtails, catch my cloak—I'll be
    amongst you.
    SOCR. (to STREPSIADES, just returned).
Now, friend, what say you? who shall
    school your son?
    STREPS. School him and scourge him,
    take him to yourself.
And mind you whet him to an edge on
    both sides,
This for slight skirmish, that for stronger
    work.
    SOCR. Doubt not, we'll finish him to
    your content
A perfect sophist.
    PHEIDIP. Perfect skin and bone—
That I can well believe.
    SOCR. No more—Away!
        (STREPSIADES retires.)
    PHEIDIP. Trust me you've made a rod
    for your own back.
    (Follows SOCRATES into the house.)

CHORUS address the SPECTATORS.

Now to our candid judges we shall tell
What recompense they may expect from
    us,
If they indeed are studious to deserve it:

First, on your new-sown grounds in
    kindly showers,
Postponing other calls, we will descend.
The bearing branches of your vines shall
    sprout,
Nor scorch'd with summer heats nor
    chill'd with rain.
This to our friends who serve us,—but
    to him,
Who dares to slight us, let that mortal
    hear,
And tremble at the vengeance which
    awaits him:
Nor wine nor oil shall that man's farm
    produce;
For when his olive trees shall yield their
    fruit,
And his ripe vineyard tempts the
    gath'rer's hand,
We'll batter him to ruin, lay him bare;
And if we catch him with his roof untiled,
Heav'ns! how we'll drench him with a
    pelting storm
Of hail and rain incessant! above all,
Let him beware upon the wedding
    night;
When he brings home his own or kins-
    man's bride,
Let him look to't! Then we'll come down
    in torrents,
That he shall rather take his chance in
    Egypt,
Than stand the vengeful soaking we will
    give him.

STREPSIADES (*with a sack of meal on
    his shoulder, and talking to himself*)
    Lo! here's the fifth day gone—the
    fourth—the third—
The second too—day of all days to me
Most hateful and accurs'd—the dreadful
    eve,
Ushering the new moon, that lets in the
    tide
Of happy creditors, all sworn against me,
To rack and ruin me beyond redemption.
I, like a courteous debtor, who would
    fain
Soften their flinty bosoms, thus accost
    them—

"Ah, my good sir, this payment comes
    upon me
At a bad time, excuse me—That bill's
    due,
But you'll extend your grace—This you
    will cancel,
And totally acquit me."—By no means;
All with one voice cry out, they will be
    paid,
And I must be be-knav'd into the bargain,
And threaten'd with a writ to mend the
    matter—
Well, let it come!—They may ev'n do
    their worst;
I care not, so my son hath learnt the trick
Of this new rhetoric, as will appear
When I have beat this door—(*knocks at
    the door*)—Boy, boy! come forth!

SOCRATES *comes forth*

SOCR. Hail to Strepsiades!
STREPS. Thrice hail to Socrates!
But first I pray you (*setting down the
    meal against the door*) take this dole
    of meal,
In token of the reverence I bear you;
And now, so please you, tell me of my
    son,
Your late novitiate. Comes he on apace?
SOCR. He apprehends acutely.
STREPS. Oh brave news!
Oh the transcendent excellence of fraud!
SOCR. Yes, you may set your creditors
    at naught—
STREPS. And their avouchers too?—
SOCR. Had they a thousand.
STREPS. (*singing and dancing*). Then
    I'll sing out my song, and sing
    aloud,
And it shall be—Woe, woe to all your
    gang,
Ye money-jobbing caitiffs, usurers,
    sharks!
Hence with your registers, your cents-
    per-cent;
I fear you not; ye cannot hook me now.
Oh! such a son have I in training for
    you,

Arm'd with a two-edg'd tongue that cuts
    o' both sides.
The stay, support, and pillar of my house,
The scourge of my tormentors, the re-
    deemer
Of a most wretched father—Call him
    forth,
Call him, I say, and let my eyes feast
    on him—
What hoa! My son, my boy—Your
    father calls;
Come forth and show yourself.
                (*To them* PHEIDIP.)
    SOCR. Behold him present!
    STREPS. My dear—my darling—
    SOCR.   Lo! you have your darling.
    STREPS. Joy, joy, my son! all joy—
for now you wear
A face of a right character and cast.
A wrangling, quibbling, contradicting
    face;
Now you have got it neatly on the
    tongue—
The very quirk o' th' time—"What's
    that you say?
What is it?"—Shifting from yourself the
    wrong
To him that suffers it—an arch conceit
To make a transfer of iniquity,
When it has serv'd your turn—Yes, you
    will pass;
You've the right Attic stamp upon your
    forehead.
Now let me see a sample of your service,
Forsooth to say you owe me a good
    turn.
    PHEIDIP. What vexes you, my father?
    STREPS.   What! the moon,
This day both new and old.
    PHEIDIP. Both in one day?
Ridiculous!
    STREPS. No matter—'Tis the day
Will bring my creditors upon my back
All in a swarm together.
    PHEIDIP. Let them swarm!
We'll smother 'em if they dare so to
    miscall
One day as two days.
    STREPS. What should hinder them?

    PHEIDIP. What, do you ask? Can
    the same woman be
Both young and old at once?
    STREPS. They speak by law:
The statute bears them out.
    PHEIDIP. But they misconstrue
The spirit of the statute.
    STREPS. What's that?
    PHEIDIP. Time-honour'd Solon was
    the people's friend—
    STREPS. This makes not to the case
    of new or old.
    PHEIDIP. And he appointed two days
    for the process,
The old and new days—for citation that,
This for discharge—
    STREPS. Why did he name two days?
    PHEIDIP. Why, but that one might
    warn men of their debts,
The other serve them to escape the
    payment;
Else were they laid by th' heels, as sure
    as fate,
On the new moon ensuing.
    STREPS. Wherefore then
Upon the former day do they commence
Their doles of first fruits at the
    Prytaneum,
And not at the new moon?
    PHEIDIP. Because, forsooth,
They're hungry feeders, and make haste
    to thrust
Their greedy fingers in the public dish.
    STREPS. Hence then, ye witless credi-
    tors, begone!
We are the wise ones, we are the true
    sort;
Ye are but blocks, mob, cattle, empty
    casks—
    Therefore with ecstasy I'll raise
    My jocund voice in fortune's praise,
    And oh, rare son!—Oh happy me!
    The burden of my song shall be;
    For hark! each passing neighbour
      cries—
    All hail, Strepsiades the wise!
    Across the forum as I walk,
    I and my son the public talk,
    All striving which shall have to boast

He prais'd me first, or praised me
    most—
And now, my son, my welcome guest,
Enter my house and grace my feast.
                  (*Exeunt.*

PASIAS, *and a Witness*

PASIAS. Should this man be permitted
    to go on
At such a desperate rate? It must not
  be.
Better for him to have brok'n up at once
Than to be thus beset. Therefore it is
That I am forc'd upon this hostile course,
Empowering you to summon this my
  debtor
For the recovery of my own—good sooth,
I will not put my country to the blush,
But I must rouse Strepsiades—

STREPSIADES *re-enters*

STREPS. Who's this?
PASIAS. The old and new day call
    upon you, sir.
STREPS. (*to the spectators*). Bear
    witness that this man has nam'd two
    days—
And for what debt do you assail me
  thus?
PASIAS. For twelve good pounds that
    you took up at interest
To pay for your son's racer.
STREPS. I a racer?
Do you not hear him? Can you not all
  witness
How mortally and from my soul I hate
All the whole racing calendar?
PASIAS. What then?
You took the gods to witness you would
  pay me.
STREPS. I grant you, in my folly I
    did swear,
But then my son had not attain'd the art
Of the new logic unconfutable.
PASIAS. And have you now the face
    to stand it out
Against all evidence?

STREPS. Assuredly—
Else how am I the better for my school-
  ing?
PASIAS. And dare you, knowing it to
    be a falsehood,
Take the great gods to witness to your
  oath,
When I shall put it to you?
STREPS. What great gods?
PASIAS. (*starting at the question*).
    Mercurius, Neptune, Jupiter him-
    self—
STREPS. Yes, and stake down three-
    farthings as a handsel
That I will take the oath, so help me
  Jove!
PASIAS. Insolent wretch, you'll perish
    in your folly!
STREPS. Oh! that this madman was
    well scrubb'd with salt
To save his brains from addling!
PASIAS. Out upon't!
Do you make game of me?
STREPS. —I warrant me
He'll take at least six gallons for a
  dressing.
PASIAS. So may great Jove and all
    the gods deal with me
As I will handle you for this buffoon-
  ery!
STREPS. I thank you for your gods—
    They're pleasant fellows—
And for your Jupiter, the learn'd and
  wise
Hold him a very silly thing to swear
  by.
PASIAS. 'Tis well, rash man, 'tis well!
    The time will come
When you shall wish these vaunting
  words unsaid:
But will you pay the debt or will you
  not?
Say, and dismiss me.
STREPS. Set your mind at rest;
You shall have satisfaction in a twink-
  ling—   (*Steps aside.*)
PASIAS. What think you of this
    chap?
WITNESS. That he will pay you.

STREPSIADES *returns*

STREPS. Where is this dun of mine?
Come hither, friend,
How do you call this thing?
PASIAS. A kneading-trough,
Or, as we say, a cardopus—
STREPS. Go to!
Dost think I'll pay my money to a block-
head,
That calls this kneading-trough a *cardo-
pus?*
I tell you, man, it is a *cardopa*—
Go, go, you will not get a doit from me,
You and your *cardopus.*
PASIAS. Will you not pay me?
STREPS. Assure yourself I will not—
Hence, begone!
Will you not beat your march, and quit
my doors?
PASIAS. I'm gone, but take this with
you, if I live
I'll sue you in the Prytaneum before
night.
STREPS. You'll lose your suit, and
your twelve pounds besides.
I'm sorry for your loss, but who can
help it?
You may ev'n thank your cardopus for
that. (*Exeunt* PASIAS *and* WITNESS.)

AMYNIAS *enters, followed by a Witness*

AMYNIAS. Ah me, ah me!
STREPS. Who's that with his—
Ah me?
Whom has *Carcinus* sent amongst us
now—
Which of his doleful deities?—
AMYNIAS. Alas!
Would you know who I am? Know then
I am
A wretch made up of woes—
STREPS. A woeful wretch—
Granted! pass on.
AMYNIAS. Oh inauspicious chance!
Oh ye hard-hearted, chariot-breaking
fates!
Oh! Pallas my destroyer, what a crash

Is this that you have giv'n me!
STREPS. Hah! what ails you?
Of what can you accuse Tlepolemus?
AMYNIAS. Mock not my miseries, but
bid your son
Repay what he has borrow'd.
STREPS. Take me with you—
What should my son repay?
AMYNIAS. The sum I lent him.
STREPS. Is that it? Then your case
is desperate;
Truly you're out of luck.
AMYNIAS. I'm out of everything—
I overthrew my chariot—By the gods
That's being *out,* I take it, with a
vengeance.
STREPS. Say rather you are kick'd by
an ass—a trifle!
AMYNIAS. But, sir, my lawful money
is no trifle;
I shall not choose to be kick'd out of
that.
STREPS. I'll tell you what you are—
Out of your wits.
AMYNIAS. How so?
STREPS. Because your brain seems
wondrous leaky.
AMYNIAS. Look to't! By Mercury,
I'll clap you up,
If you don't pay me.
STREPS. Hark'ye, one short ques-
tion—
When Jove rains on us does he rain fresh
water,
Or only vapours that the sun exhales?
AMYNIAS. I care not what he rains;
I trouble not my cap with such con-
ceits.
STREPS. And do you think a man, that
has no art
To argue upon these rare points, will
argue me
Out of my money?
AMYNIAS. Let your debt go on,
And pay me up the interest.
STREPS. What is that?
What kind of thing is that same interest?
AMYNIAS. A thing it is that grows
from day to day,

And month to month, swelling as time
rolls on
To a round sum of money.
STREPS. Well defin'd!
One question more—What think you of
the sea?
Is it no fuller now than heretofore?
AMYNIAS. No, by the Gods; not
fuller, but as full:
That is my judgment of it.
STREPS. Oh thou miser!
That so would'st stint the ocean, and yet
cram
Thy swelling coffers till they overflow—
Fetch me a whip, that I may lash him
hence:
Take to your heels—begone!
AMYNIAS. I will convoke
My witnesses against you.
STREPS. Start! set off!—
Away! you jennet, you!
AMYNIAS. (to the spectators). Is not
this outrage?
STREPS. (smacking his whip). Will
you not bolt? will you not buckle
kindly
Into your geers, or must I mount and
goad you
Under the crupper, till you kick and
wince
For very madness? Oho! Are you off?
A welcome riddance—All the devils drive
You and your cursed chariot hence to-
gether!
(STREPSIADES goes into his house.)
CHORUS. Mark here how rarely it suc-
ceeds
To build our trust on guilty deeds:
Mark how this old cajoling elf,
Who sets a trap to catch himself,
Falsely believes he has found the way
To hold his creditors at bay.
Too late he'll curse the Sophists'
school,
That taught his son to cheat by rule,
And train'd the modest lips of youth
In the vile art of torturing truth;
A modern logic, much in use,
Invented for the law's abuse;

A subtle knack of spying flaws
To cast in doubt the clearest cause,
Whereby, in honesty's despite,
The wrong side triumphs o'er the
right—
Alas! short triumph he must have,
Who glories that his son's a knave:
Ah foolish sire, the time will come
You'll wish that son of your's were
dumb.

STREPSIADES rushes out of the house, in
great confusion, followed by his son.

STREPS. Hoa there! What hoa! for
pity's sake some help!
Friends, kinsmen, countrymen! turn out
and help!
Oh! my poor head, my cheeks are bruis'd
to jelly—
Help by all means!—Why, thou un-
gracious cub,
Thy father would'st thou beat?
PHEIDIP. Assuredly.
STREPS. There, there! he owns that
he would beat his father.
PHEIDIP. I own it, good my father!
STREPS. Parricide!
Impious assassin! Sacrilegious wretch!
PHEIDIP. All, all, and more—You
cannot please me better;
I glory in these attributes. Go on!
STREPS. Monster of turpitude!
PHEIDIP. Crown me with roses!
STREPS. Wretch, will you strike your
parent?
PHEIDIP. Piously,
And will maintain the right, by which I
do it.
STREPS. Oh shameless villain! can
there be a right
Against all nature so to treat a father?
PHEIDIP. That I shall soon make
clear to your conviction.
STREPS. You, you convince me?
PHEIDIP. With the greatest ease:
And I can work the proof two several
ways;
Therefore make choice between them.

STREPS. What do you mean?

PHEIDIP. I mean to say we argue up or down—

Take which you like. It comes to the same end.

STREPS. Aye, and a precious end you've brought it to,

If all my care of you must end in this,

That I have put you in the way to beat me,

(Which is a thing unnatural and profane)

And after justify it.

PHEIDIP. That I'll do.

By process clear and categorical,

That you shall fairly own yourself a convert

To a most wholesome cudgelling.

STREPS. Come on!

Give me your arguments—but spare your blows.

CHORUS. How to restrain this headstrong son of your's

Behoves you now, old man, to find the means,

For sure he could not be thus confident

Without some cause; something there needs must be,

Some strong possession of himself within,

That buoys him up to this high pitch of daring,

This bold assumption; which that we may know,

Give us distinctively the whole detail

From first to last whence this contention sprang;

So shall we hear, and hearing judge betwixt you.

STREPS. So please you then I will the cause unfold

Of this base treatment to your patient ears,

And thus it stands—When we had supp'd together,

As you all know, in friendly sort, I bade him

Take up his lute and give me the good song

Of old Simonides,—"the ram was shorn;"—

But he directly scouted my request—

It was a fashion out of date forsooth—

He would not sit twanging the lute, not he;

'Twas not for him to cackle o'er his wine,

As if he were some wench working the hand-mill—

'Twas vulgar and unseemly—

PHEIDIP. Grossly so;

And was it not high time that I should beat you,

Who had no better manners than to set

Your guests a chirping like a grasshopper?

STREPS. These were his very words, and more than these;

For by and by he told me that Simonides

Was a most paltry poet. This you'll own

Was a tough morsel, yet I gulp'd it down,

And pass'd it off with bidding him recite

Some passage out of Æschylus, withal

Tendering a myrtle wreath, as custom is,

To grace the recitation—He forsooth,

Flouting my tender, instantly replied—

"I hold your Æschylus, of all our poets,

First of the spouters, incoherent, harsh,

Precipitous and turgid."—Oh my friends,

Was not this more than flesh and blood should bear?

Yet, yet I smother'd rage within my heart,

And calmly said—"Call something else to mind

More to your taste and from some modern bard,

So it be good withal and worth the hearing—"

Whereat, would you believe it? he began

Repeating from Euripides—Great Jove,

Guard my chaste ears from such another dose!

A perilous long-winded tale of incest

'Twixt son and daughter of the same sad mother.

Sick to the soul I spurn'd at such declaiming,

Adding, as well I might, all that my scorn

Of such vile trash could add! till, to be short,

Words begat words, and blows too as it
  prov'd,
For leaping from his seat he sprung upon
  me,
Struck, buffeted, and bang'd me out of
  measure,
Throttled me, pounded me well nigh to
  dust—
  PHEIDIP. And what less does that
    heretic deserve,
Who will not praise Euripides, the first
In wisdom of all poets?
  STREPS. He the first!
How my tongue itches!—but the rogue
  is ready;
He'll beat me if I answer
  PHEIDIP. And with reason.
  STREPS. What reason, graceless cub,
    will bear you out
For beating me, who in your baby age
Caressed you, dandled you upon my knee,
Watch'd every motion, humour'd all your
  wants?
Then if you lisp'd a syllable I caught it—
Bryn cried the bantling—strait I gave
  you drink:
Mamman it mew'd—and that forsooth
  was bread:
Nay, I perform'd the nurse's dirtiest task,
And held you out before me at your
  needs;
And now in my necessity you show'd
No mercy to the pressing calls of nature,
But having pummel'd me till my poor
  bowels
Could hold no longer, kept me fast im-
  prison'd
To struggle with occasion as I could.
  CHOR. Now every young man's heart
    beats an alarm,
Anxious to hear his advocate's appeal;
Which if he can establish, the same right
By him asserted will on all devolve,
And beating then will be so much in
  vogue
That old men's skins will be reduc'd to
  cobwebs—
Now you, that hold up this new paradox,
Look well how you defend it, for it asks

No trivial reasons to enforce persuasion.
  PHEIDIP. Now gratefully the mind
    receives new lights,
Emerging from the shades of prejudice,
And casting old establishments aside!
Time was but now, when every thought
  of mine
Was centred in the stable; then I had not
Three words upon my tongue without a
  stumble;
But now, since I've been put into the way
Of knowing better things, and the fine art
Of subtle disputation, I am bold
To meet this question, and convince my
  hearers
How right it is to punish this old sinner.
  STREPS. Mount, mount your chariot!
    Oh, that I could see you
Seated again behind your favourite
  horses,
Tho' 'twere with four in hand, so that
  you kept
From driving me at such a pelting rate.
  PHEIDIP. Now then I ask you, gath-
    ering up my thread
Where it was broken off, if you, my
  father,
When I was but a stripling, spar'd my
  back?
  STREPS. No, for I studied all things
    for your good,
And therefore I corrected you.
  PHEIDIP. Agreed.
I also am like studious of your good,
And therefore I most lovingly correct
  you;
If beating be a proof of love, you have it
Plenteous in measure, for by what
  exemption
Is your most sacred carcass freed from
  stripes
And mine made subject to them? Am
  not I
Free-born as you? Say, if the son's in
  tears,
Should not the father weep?
  STREPS. By what one rule
Of equity?
  PHEIDIP. What equity were that

If none but children are to be chastis'd?

And grant they were, the proverb's in your teeth,

Which says old age is but a second childhood.

Again, if tears are seen to follow blows,

Ought not old men to expiate faults with tears

Rather than children, who have more to plead

In favour of their failings?

STREPS. Where's the law

That warrants this proceeding? There's none such.

PHEIDIP. And what was your lawmaker but a man,

Mortal as you and I are? And tho' time

Has sanctified his statutes, may not I

Take up the cause of youth, as he of age,

And publish a new ordinance for leave

By the right-filial to correct our fathers,

Remitting and consigning to oblivion

All *ex post facto* beating? Look at instinct—

Inquire of nature how the brute creation

Kick at their parents, which in nothing differ

From lordly man, except that they compile

No laws, and hold their rights without a statute.

STREPS. If you are thus for pecking at your father

Like a young fighting-cock, why don't you peck

Your dinner from the dunghill, and at night

Roost on a perch?

PHEIDIP. The cases do not tally,

Nor does my master Socrates prescribe

Rules so absurd.

STREPS. Cease then from beating me;

Else you preclude yourself.

PHEIDIP. As how preclude?

STREPS. Because the right I have of beating you

Will be your right in time over your son,

When you shall have one.

PHEIDIP. But if I have none,

All my sad hours are lost, and you die laughing.

STREPS. There's no denying that.— How say you, sirs?

Methinks there is good matter in his plea;

And as for us old sinners, truth to say,

If we deserve a beating we must bear it.

PHEIDIP. Hear me—there's more to come—

STREPS. Then I am lost,

For I can bear no more.

PHEIDIP. Oh fear it not,

Rather believe what I have now to tell you

Will cause you to make light of what is past,

'Twill bring such comfort to you.

STREPS. Let me have it:

If it be comfort, give it me.

PHEIDIP. Then know,

Henceforth I am resolv'd to beat my mother

As I have beaten you.

STREPS. How say you? How?

Why this were to out-do all you have done.

PHEIDIP. But what if I have not a proof *in petto,*

To show the moral uses of this beating?

STREPS. Show me a proof that you have hang'd yourself,

And with your tutor Socrates beside you

Gone to the devil together in a string;

Those moral uses I will thank you for—

Oh inauspicious goddesses, O Clouds!

In you confiding, all these woes fall on me.

CHOR. Evil events from evil causes spring,

And what you suffer flows from what you've done.

STREPS. Why was I not forewarn'd? You saw me old,

And practis'd on my weak simplicity.

CHOR. 'Tis not for us to warn a wilful sinner;

We stay him not, but let him run his course,

Till by misfortunes rous'd, his conscience
  wakes,
And prompts him to appease th' offended
  gods.
  STREPS. I feel my sorrows, but I own
  them just:
Yes, ye reforming Clouds, I'm duly
  punish'd
For my intended fraud.—And now, my
  son,
Join hands with me and let us forth
  together
To wreak our vengeance on those base
  deceivers,
That Chærephon and Socrates the chief,
Who have cajol'd us both.
  PHEIDIP. Grace forbid
I should lift up my hand against my
  masters!
  STREPS. Nay, nay, but rather dread
  avenging Jove,
God of your ancestors and him revere.
  PHEIDIP. You're mad, methinks, to
  talk to me of Jove—
Is there a god so call'd?
  STREPS. There is! there is!
  PHEIDIP. There is no Jupiter, I tell
  you so;
Vortex has whirl'd him from his throne,
  and reigns
By right of conquest in the Thunderer's
  place.
  STREPS. 'Tis false, no Vortex reigns
  but in my brain.
  PHEIDIP. Laugh at your own dull
  joke and be a fool! (*Exit.*)
  STREPS. (*striking his breast*). Insuf-
  ferable blockhead that I was;
What ail'd me thus to court this Socrates,
Ev'n to the exclusion of the immortal
  gods?
O Mercury, forgive me; be not angry,
Dear tutelary god, but spare me still,
And cast a pitying eye upon my follies,
For I have been intemperate of tongue,
And dearly rue it—Oh my better genius,
Inspire me with thy counsel how to
  act,
Whether by legal process to assail them,

Or by such apter means as thou may'st
  dictate.
I have it! Well hast thou inspir'd the
  thought;
Hence with the lazy law; thou art not
  for it.
With fire and faggot I will fall upon
  them,
And send their school *in fumo* to the
  Clouds
Hoa, Xanthias (*calling to one of his
  slaves*), hoa! bring forth without
  delay
Your ladder and your mattock, mount the
  roof,
Break up the rafters, whelm the house
  upon them,
And bury the whole hive beneath the
  ruins.
  (XANTHIAS *mounts the roof and
  begins working with his mat-
  tock.*)
Haste! if you love me, haste! Oh, for a
  torch,
A blazing torch new lighted, to set fire
To the infernal edifice.—I warrant me
I'll soon unhouse the rascals, that now
  carry
Their heads so high, and roll them in
  the dust.
  (*One of the scholars comes out.*)
  FIRST DISCIPLE. Woe! mischief!
  misery!
  STREPS. (*mounts the roof and fixes a
  torch to the joists*).
        Torch, play your part:
And we shall muster up a conflagration.
  FIRST DISCIPLE. What are you doing,
  fellow?
  STREPS. Chopping logic;
Arguing a knotty point with your house-
  beams.
  SECOND DISCIPLE. Oh horror! Who
  has set our house on fire?
  STREPS. The very man whose cloak
  you nabb'd so neatly.
  SECOND DISCIPLE. Undone and
  ruin'd—!
  STREPS. Heartily I wish it—

And mean you should so be if this same mattock
Does not deceive my hopes, and I escape
With a whole neck.

Socrates comes forth

Socr. Hoa there! What man is that?
You there upon the roof—what are you doing?
Streps. *Treading on air—contemplating the sun—*
Socr. Ah me! I'm suffocated, smother'd, lost—

Chærephon appears

Chærephon. Wretch that I am, I'm melted, scorch'd, consum'd—
Streps. Blasphemers, why did you insult the gods?
Dash, drive, demolish them! Their crimes are many,
But their contemptuous treatment of the Gods,
Their impious blasphemies, exceed them all.
Chor. Break up!—The Chorus have fulfill'd their part.
    —Richard Cumberland.

The Good Wine of Peace

[From the *Acharnians*]

Aristophanes opposed the policy of war with Sparta, deeming it useless and an undertaking involving only loss to the state. The *Acharnians* was produced in 425 B.C.

Dicæopolis. But there's Amphitheus coming back from Sparta.
Welcome Amphitheus!
Amphitheus. I'm not welcome yet.
There are the Acharnians pursuing me!
Dic. How so?
Amph. I was coming here to bring the treaties,
But a parcel of old Acharnians smelt me out,

Case-hardened, old, inveterate, hard-handed
Veterans of Marathon, hearts of oak and iron,
Slingers and smiters. They bawled out and bellowed:
"You dog, you villain! now the vines are ruined,
You're come with treaties, are you?" Then they stopped,
Huddling up handfuls of great slinging stones
In the lappets of their cloaks, and I ran off,
And they came driving after me pell-mell,
Roaring and shouting.
Dic.   Aye, why let them roar!
You've brought the treaties?
Amph.   Aye, three samples of 'em;
This here is a five years' growth, taste it and try.
Dic. Don't like it!
Amph.   Eh?
Dic.   Don't like it; it won't do;
There's an uncommon ugly twang of pitch,
A touch of naval armament about it.
Amph. Well, here's a ten years' growth, may suit you better.
Dic. No, neither of them. There's a sort of sourness
Here in this last, a taste of acid embassies,
And vapid allies turning to vinegar.
Amph. But here's a truce of thirty years entire,
Warranted sound.
Dic. O Bacchus and the Bacchanals!
This is your sort! here's nectar and ambrosia!
Here's nothing about providing three days' rations;
It says, "Do what you please, go where you will."
I chuse it, and adopt it, and embrace it,
For sacrifice and for my private drinking.
In spite of all the Acharnians, I'm determined

To remove out of the reach of wars and
    mischief,
And keep the feast of Bacchus in my
    farm.
    AMPH. And I'll run off to escape from
    those Acharnians.
              —J. H. FRERE.

THE OUTBREAK OF WAR

[From the *Acharnians*]

This passage reveals the extent to which
comedy could go in ridiculing public policies even in a time of war.

DICÆOPOLIS. Be not surprised, most
    excellent spectators,
If I that am a beggar, have presumed
To claim an audience upon public mat-
    ters,
Even in a comedy; for comedy
Is conversant in all the rules of justice,
And can distinguish between right and
    wrong.
    The words I speak are bold, but just
    and true.
Cleon, at least, cannot accuse me now,
That I defame the city before strangers.
For this is the Lenæan festival,
And here we meet, all by ourselves alone;
No deputies are arrived as yet with
    tribute,
No strangers or allies; but here are we
A chosen sample, clean as sifted corn,
With our own denizens as a kind of
    chaff.
    First, I detest the Spartans most ex-
    tremely;
And wish that Neptune, the Tænarian
    deity,
Would bury them in their houses with
    his earthquakes.
For I've had losses—losses, let me tell
    ye,
Like other people; vines cut down and
    injured.
But, among friends (for only friends are
    here),

Why should we blame the Spartans for
    all this?
For people of ours, some people of our
    own,
Some people from amongst us here, I
    mean;
But not the people (pray remember
    that);
I never said the people—but a pack
Of paltry people, mere pretended citizens,
Base counterfeits, went laying informa-
    tions,
And making a confiscation of the jerkins
Imported here from Megara; pigs more-
    over,
Pumpkins, and pecks of salt, and ropes
    of onions,
Were voted to be merchandise from
    Megara,
Denounced, and seized, and sold upon
    the spot.
    Well, these might pass, as petty local
    matters.
But now, behold, some doughty drunken
    youths
Kidnap, and carry away from Megara,
The courtesan Simætha. Those of
    Megara,
In hot retaliation, seize a brace
Of equal strumpets, hurried force per-
    force
From Dame Aspasia's house of recrea-
    tion.
So this was the beginning of the war,
All over Greece, owing to these three
    strumpets.
For Pericles, like an Olympian Jove,
With all his thunder and his thunder-
    bolts,
Began to storm and lighten dreadfully,
Alarming all the neighbourhood of
    Greece;
And made decrees, drawn up like drink-
    ing songs,
In which it was enacted and concluded,
That the Megarians should remain ex-
    cluded
From every place where commerce was
    transacted,

With all their ware—like "old care"—in
the ballad:
And this decree, by land and sea, was
valid.
 Then the Megarians, being all half
starved,
Desired the Spartans, to desire of us,
Just to repeal those laws; the laws I
mentioned,
Occasioned by the stealing of those
strumpets.
And so they begged and prayed us sev-
eral times;
And we refused; and so they went to war.
You'll say, "They should not." Why,
what should they have done?
Just make it your own case; suppose the
Spartans
Had manned a boat, and landed on your
islands,
And stolen a pug puppy from Seriphos;
Would you then have remained at home
inglorious?
Not so, by no means; at the first report,
You would have launched at once three
hundred gallies,
And filled the city with the noise of
troops;
And crews of ships, crowding and clam-
ouring
About the muster-masters and pay-
masters;
With measuring corn out at the magazine,
And all the porch choked with the multi-
tude;
With figures of Minerva, newly furbished,
Painted and gilt, parading in the streets;
With wineskins, kegs, and firkins, leeks
and onions;
With garlic crammed in pouches, nets,
and pokes;
With garlands, singing girls, and bloody
noses.
Our arsenal would have sounded and
resounded
With bangs and thwacks of driving bolts
and nails;
With shaping oars, and holes to put the
oars in;

With hacking, hammering, clattering and
boring;
Words of command, whistles and pipes
and fifes.
                              —J. H. FRERE.

A LEADING STATESMAN

[From the *Knights*]

Aristophanes had little sympathy with
a democratic form of government which
made it possible for an untrained man of
the people to rule over the destinies of the
state. The *Knights* was produced in
424 B.C.

DEMOSTHENES. O happy man! celes-
tial sausage-seller!
Friend, guardian and protector of us all!
Come forward; save your friends, and
save the country.
SAUSAGE-SELLER. Do you call me?
DEM. Yes, we called to you, to an-
nounce
The high and happy destiny that awaits
you.
NICIAS. Come, now you should set
him free from incumbrance
Of his table and basket; and explain to
him
The tenor and the purport of the Oracle,
While I go back to watch the Paphlago-
nian.   (*Exit* NICIAS.)
DEM. (*to the* SAUSAGE-SELLER *gravely*)
Set these poor wares aside; and now—
bow down
To the ground; and adore the powers of
earth and heaven.
S. S. Heigh-day! Why, what do you
mean?
DEM.   O happy man!
Unconscious of your glorious destiny,
Now mean and unregarded; but to-
morrow,
The mightiest of the mighty, Lord of
Athens.
S. S. Come, master, what's the use of
making game?

Why can't ye let me wash the guts and
    tripe,
And sell my sausages in peace and quiet?
    DEM. O simple mortal, cast those
      thoughts aside!
Bid guts and tripe farewell! Look there!
    Behold (*pointing to the audience*)
The mighty assembled multitude before
    ye!
    S. S. (*with a grumble of indiffer-
      ence*) I see 'em.
    DEM. You shall be their lord and
      master,
The sovereign and the ruler of them all,
Of the assemblies and tribunals, fleets
    and armies;
You shall trample down the Senate under
    foot,
Confound and crush the generals and
    commanders,
Arrest, imprison, and confine in irons,
And feast . . . in the council house.
    S. S. What, I?
    DEM. Yes, you yourself: there's more
      to come.
Mount here; and from the trestles of
    your stall
Survey the subject islands circling round.
    S. S. I see 'em.
    DEM. And all their ports and mer-
      chant vessels?
    S. S. Yes, all.
    DEM. Then an't you a fortunate
      happy man?
An't you content? Come then for a
    further prospect—
Turn your right eye to Caria, and your
    left
To Carthage!—and contemplate both
    together.
    S. S. Will it do me good, d'ye think,
      to learn to squint?
    DEM. Not so; but everything you see
      before you
Must be disposed of at your high dis-
    cretion,
By sale or otherwise; for the Oracle
Predestines you to sovereign power and
    greatness.

    S. S. Are there any means of making
      a great man
Of a sausage-selling fellow such as I?
    DEM. The very means you have,
      must make ye so,
Low breeding, vulgar birth, and impu-
    dence,
These, these must make ye, what you're
    meant to be.
    S. S. I can't imagine that I'm good
      for much.
    DEM. Alas! But why do ye say so?
      What's the meaning
Of these misgivings? I discern within
    ye
A promise and an inward consciousness
Of greatness. Tell me truly: are ye
    allied
To the families of gentry?
    S. S.   Naugh, not I;
I'm come from a common ordinary kin-
    dred
Of the lower order.
    DEM.   What a happiness!
What a footing will it give ye! What a
    groundwork
For confidence and favour at your outset!
    S. S. But bless ye! only consider my
      education!
I can but barely read—in a kind of a
    way.
    DEM. That makes against ye—the
      only thing against ye—
The being able to read, in any way:
For now; no lead nor influence is allowed
To liberal arts or learned education,
But to the brutal, base, and under-bred.
Embrace then and hold fast the promises
Which the oracles of the gods announce
    to you.
    S. S. But what does the oracle say?
    DEM.   Why thus it says,
In a figurative language, but withal
Most singularly intelligible and distinct,
Neatly expressed i' faith, concisely and
    tersely.
"Moreover, when the eagle in his pride,
With crooked talons and a leathern
    hide,

Shall seize the black and blood-devouring
    snake;
Then shall the woeful tanpits quail and
    quake;
And mighty Jove shall give command and
    place,
To mortals of the sausage-selling race;
Unless they choose, continuing as before,
To sell their sausages for evermore."
    S. S.   But how does this concern me?
        Explain it, will ye?
    DEM.   The leathern eagle is the
        Paphlagonian.
    S. S.   What are his talons?
    DEM.   That explains itself—
Talons for peculation and rapacity.
    S. S.   But what's the snake?
    DEM.   The snake is clear and obvious:
The snake is long and black, like a black-
    pudding;
The snake is filled with blood, like a
    black-pudding;
Our oracle foretells then, that the snake
Shall baffle and overpower the leathern
    eagle.
    S. S.   These oracles, hit my fancy!
        Notwithstanding—
I'm partly doubtful, how I could con-
    trive—
To manage an administration alto-
    gether—
    DEM.   The easiest thing in nature!—
        nothing easier!
Stick to your present practice: follow it
    up
In your new calling. Mangle, mince and
    mash,
Confound and hack, and jumble things
    together!
And interlard your rhetoric with lumps
Of mawkish sweet, and greasy flattery.
Be fulsome, coarse, and bloody! For the
    rest,
All qualities combine, all circumstances,
To entitle and equip you for command;
A filthy voice, a villainous countenance,
A vulgar birth, and parentage, and breed-
    ing.
Nothing is wanting, absolutely nothing.

And the oracles and responses of the
    gods,
And prophecies, all conspire in your
    behalf.
Place then this chaplet on your brows!—
    and worship
The anarchic powers; and rouse your
    spirits up.
                 —J. H. FRERE.

DEMUS REFORMED

[From the *Knights*]

The character Demus represents the
Athenian people. His reformation signi-
fies a harking back to the traditions of
the good old times so precious to the heart
of the conservative poet. The concluding
lines of the passage are a typical attack,
with all the freedom that characterized
the satire of the stage, on Cleon, the foremost statesman of the day.

AGORACRITUS (*the Sausage-seller*).
Peace be amongst you! Silent! Peace!
Close the courts; let pleadings cease!
All your customary joys,
Juries, accusers, strife and noise!
Be merry, I say! Let the theatre ring
With a shout of applause for the news
    that I bring.
    CHORUS. O thou the protector and
        hope of the state,
Of the isles and allies of the city, relate
What happy event, do you call us to
    greet
With bonfire and sacrifice filling the
    street.
    AG. Old Demus within has moulted
        his skin;
I've cooked him, and stewed him, to
    render him stronger,
Many years younger, and shabby no
    longer.
    CHORUS. Oh, what a change! How
        sudden and strange!
But where is he now?
    AG.   On the citadel's brow,

In the lofty old town of immortal renown,
With the noble Ionian violet crown.
  CHORUS. What was his vesture, his
    figure and gesture?
How did you leave him, and how does he
  look?
  AG. Joyous and bold, as when feast-
    ing of old,
When his battles were ended, triumphant
  and splendid,
With Miltiades sitting carousing at rest,
Or good Aristides his favourite guest.
You shall see him here straight; for the
  citadel gate
Is unbarred; and the hinges—you hear
  how they grate!
    (*The scene changes to a view of
    the Propylæum.*)
Give a shout for the sight of the rocky
  old height!
And the worthy old wight, that inhabits
  within!
  CHORUS. Thou glorious hill! pre-
    eminent still
For splendour of empire and honour and
  worth!
Exhibit him here, for the Greeks to
  revere;
Their patron and master the monarch of
  earth!
  AG. There, see him, behold! with the
    jewels of gold
Entwined in his hair, in the fashion of
  old;
Not dreaming of verdicts or dirty de-
  crees;
But lordly, majestic, attired at his ease,
Perfuming all Greece with an odour of
  peace.
  CHORUS. We salute you, and greet
    you, and bid you rejoice;
With unanimous heart, with unanimous
  voice,
Our Sovereign Lord, in glory restored,
Returning amongst us in royal array,
Worthy the trophies of Marathon's day!
  DEMUS. My dearest Agoracritus,
    come here—
I'm so obliged to you for your cookery!

I feel an altered man, you've quite trans-
  formed me.
  AG. What! I? That's nothing; if
    you did but know
The state you were in before, you'd
  worship me.
  DEM. What was I doing? How did
    I behave?
Do tell me—inform against me—Let me
  know.
  AG. Why first, then: if an orator in
    the assembly
Began with saying, Demus, I'm your
  friend,
You used to chuckle, and smirk, and hold
  your head up.
  DEM. No sure!
  AG. So he gained his end, and bilked
    and choused ye.
  DEM. But did not I perceive it? Was
    not I told?
  AG. By Jove, and you wore those ears
    of yours continually
Wide open or close shut, like an um-
  brella.
  DEM. Is it possible? Was I indeed
    so mere a driveller
In my old age, so superannuated?
  AG. Moreover, if a couple of orators
Were pleading in your presence; one
  proposing
To equip a fleet, his rival arguing
To get the same supplies distributed
To the jurymen, the patron of the
  juries
Carried the day. But why do you hang
  your head so?
What makes you shuffle about? Can't
  ye stand still?
  DEM. I feel ashamed of myself and
    all my follies.
  AG. (*his tone is that of a considerate,
    indulgent preceptor to a young man
    who has been misbehaving.*) 'Twas
    not your fault—don't think of it.
    Your advisers
Were most to blame. But for the future
  —tell me,
If any rascally villainous orator

Should address a jury with such words
  as these:
"Remember, if you acquit the prisoner
Your daily food and substance are at
  stake,"
How would you treat such a pleader?
  Answer me.
  DEM. I should toss him headlong
  into the public pit,
With a halter round his gullet, and
  Hyperbolus
Tied fast to the end of it.
  AG.   That's a noble answer!
Wise and judicious, just and glorious!
Now tell me, in other respects, how do
  you mean
To manage your affairs?
  DEM.   Why first of all
I'll have the arrears of seamen's wages
  paid
To a penny, the instant they return to
  port.
  AG. There's many a worn out rump
  will bless ye and thank ye.
  DEM. Moreover, no man that has
  been enrolled
Upon the list for military service
Shall have his name erased for fear or
  favour.
  AG. That gives a bang to Cleonymus's
  buckler.
  DEM. I'll not permit those fellows
  without beards
To harangue in our assembly; boys or
  men.
  AG. Then what's to become of
  Cleisthenes and Strato?
Where must they speak?
          I mean those kind of youths,
The little puny would-be politicians
Sitting conversing in perfumers' shops,
Lisping and prating in this kind of
  way:
"Phæax is sharp—He made a good come
  off,
And saved his life in a famous knowing
  style.
I reckon him a first rate; quite capital
For energy and compression; so collected,

And such a choice of language! Then
  to see him
Battling against a mob—it's quite delightful!
He's never cowed! He bothers 'em com-
  pletely!"
  AG. It's your own fault, in part
  you've helped to spoil 'em;
But what do you mean to do with them
  for the future?
  DEM. I shall send them into the
  country, all the pack of 'em,
To learn to hunt, and leave off making
  laws.
  AG. Then I present you here with a
  folding chair,
And a stout lad to carry it after you.
  DEM. Ah, that reminds one of the
  good old times.
  AG. But what will you say, if I give
  you a glorious peace,
A lusty strapping truce of thirty years?
Come forward here, my lass, and show
  yourself.
  DEM. By Jove, what a face and fig-
  ure! I should like
To ratify and conclude incontinently.
Where did you find her?
  AG.   Oh, the Paphlagonian,
Of course, had huddled her out of sight,
  within there.
But now you've got her, take her back
  with you
Into the country.
  DEM.   But the Paphlagonian,
What shall we do to punish him? What
  d'ye think?
  AG. Oh, no great matter. He shall
  have my trade;
With an exclusive sausage-selling patent,
To traffic openly at the city gates,
And garble his wares with dogs' and
  asses' flesh;
With a privilege, moreover, to get drunk,
And bully among the strumpets of the
  suburbs,
And the ragamuffin waiters at the baths.
  DEM. That's well imagined, it pre-
  cisely suits him;

His natural bent, it seems, his proper element
To squabble with poor trulls and low rapscallions.
As for yourself, I give you an invitation
To dine with me in the hall. You'll fill the seat
Which that unhappy villain filled before.
Take this new robe! Wear it and follow me.
  And you, the rest of you, conduct that fellow
To his future home and place of occupation,
The gate of the city; where the allies and foreigners,
That he maltreated, may be sure to find him.

               —J. H. FRERE.

RULE BY JURY

[From the *Wasps*]

Neither statesmen nor policies nor courts escape the shafts of Aristophanes' wit. The *Wasps* was produced in 422 B.C.

PHILOCLEON. At your word off I go, and at starting I'll show, convincing the stiffest opinion;
That regalia and throne, sceptre, kingdom and crown, are but dirt to judicial dominion.
First in pleasure and glee, who abound more than we; who with luxury nearer are wedded?
Then for panic and frights, the world through none excites, what your dicast does, e'en tho' gray-headed.
Soon as ever I creep from my bed and break sleep, through the courts runs a warning sensation;
There the mighty—the sly—men of four cubits high, wait my coming in hot trepidation.
First a hand, soft as wool—t'other day, it was full from the public exchequer and treasure,—

Fast upon me is laid; and my knees captive made, supplications pour in without measure.—
"Father,—neighbour and friend—help and mercy extend,—mayhap when in office and station,
Or when serving the mess, you took care to express in private a small compensation."
Knave and hangdog! my care from a swing in the air sav'd his heels on a former occasion,
Or the rogue, and be curst! had not known—
BDELYCLEON (*writing on his tablets*). Item first: *suit . . . petition . . .* and *warm supplication.*
PHIL. Loaded large thus with prayer, in the court I take chair, from my brow wrath and choler clean clearing;
As for promises made out of doors of my aid,—with the four winds of heaven they're veering.
There a thousand tones drop, all attun'd to one stop,—*mercy—pardon—release—liberation;*
Of the whole race of men, like a dicast who then receives compliment, court, adoration?
His pawns and his pledges one defendant alleges; and his griefs and his ills while detailing,
The items are thrown with such skill, that my own in the balance to nothing are failing.
With mythical tales this my fancy regales, t'other dips into Æsop and fable;
While a third slily throws out his quips and bons-mots my passion and wrath to disable.
Turn I still a deaf ear? better suitors are near:—led by hand and in court quick appearing,
The accus'd to his aid calls his imps,—boy and maid;—I bend gracious and deign them a hearing.
With bent heads . . . in tones sweet . . .

pretty lambkins! they bleat: the father submissively falling,
Does me suit as a God, for he knows, at my nod, his accounts pass without overhauling.
(*mimics*) "If the tones of a lamb soothe your ear, sure I am, that this boy's, my lord, will not prove hateful;
If beauty more warms,—sir, this girl hath her charms, and sure she would not be ungrateful."
Downward straight goes my ire, like the tones of a lyre, when the pins and the pegs are unscrewing:—
(*turning to his son*) Speak, explain, what dost say; call you this rule and sway, when the rich to your scoffs are thus suing?
  BDEL.   For our tablets more food— (*writes*) *is uncivil and rude, at the wealthy makes scoff and derision;*
But all Greece to your sway bows submissive you say; what profits gains this supervision?
  PHIL.   Great and many are won: and in primis, for one ask your learned and critical juries,
What is felt when a boy, timid, shrinking, and coy, stands display'd *naturalibus puris!*—
Comes some actor divine, the first man in his line, 'fore our presence?—acquittal's denied him:—
Till we've made him rehearse, and in smooth flowing verse, such parts as have most proved and tried him.
Say the play-house first flute gains a cause and a suit;—a melody sweet and befitting
We exact for his fee, in his muzzle which he blows deftly as court we are quitting.
Some father is gone,—dead,—defunct— well anon! leaves a girl, good;—an heiress, much better;—
The *old put* would confer a bed-fellow on her, and his will leaves him drawn to the letter.
Lords of locks, seals and keys, straight

the parchments we seize, while a codicil neatly appended
Cheats the wary and wise; and the girl's made a prize to some youngster, who's better befriended.
And the deed boldly done, further mark me, there's none dare report or inquiry request on't;
While another thus doing, there'd be forthwith ensuing Board, Commission, Report, and the rest on't.
  BDEL.   All the rest is quite right— done as gentlemen might—and I offer my best gratulation:
But to cancel a deed—where an heiress . . . take heed, 'tis a dangerous and base speculation.
  PHIL.   Crowded house, warm debate, mark some pris'ner of state:— doubts ensue,—hesitation,—adjournment:
To prevent further stir Lords and Commons refer the case to judicial discernment.
Then some pleader stands forth, and that scoundrel, whose worth show his synonyms, "fawner"—"shield-dropper"—
And their note is the same, "While *I* live," both exclaim, "the Commons have no interloper."
But the vote most he wins there, his speech who begins, "Sirs, I move with profoundest submission,
After one single turn, that the courts all adjourn, nor labour a second decision."
Even he whose voice stills thunder, hammers and mills, Cleon, dares not devour, jeer nor scoff us,
But with fly-flap in hand, taking humbly his stand, beats and brushes the vermin clean off us.
I your father might sue, graceless youngster, to you—in the warmth of paternal emotion;
Yet your duty I stake ne'er the impress would take of so earnest and warm a devotion.

Nay Theorus beside, (and his pride's
    lowest tide would dispute with
    Euphemius precedence,)
Sponge in hand blacks my shoes—you
    may doubt an you choose, 'tis a fact
    indeed almost past credence.

BDEL.   Talk and spare not for speech
    —end at last you will reach: and
    the proverb hold good, I opine, sir,

In spite of ablution, scent and perfume,
pollution show'd still that the sow
was a swine, sir.

—T. MITCHELL.

WHEN WOMEN GUIDE THE STATE

[From the *Lysistrata*]

The poet offers the proposition that the
way to avoid wars is to turn over the
control of the state to the women. The
Lysistrata was produced in 411 B.C.

MAGISTRATE.   Foremost and first I
    would wish to inquire of them what
    is this silly disturbance about?
Why have ye ventured to seize the
    Acropolis, locking the gates and
    barring us out?
LYSISTRATA.   Keeping the silver se-
    curely in custody, lest for its sake ye
    continue the war.
MAG.   What, is the war for the sake
    of the silver, then?
LYS.   Yes; and all other disputes that
    there are.
Why is Peisander for ever embroiling us,
    why do the rest of our officers feel
Always a pleasure in strife and disturb-
    ances? Simply to gain an occasion
    to steal.
Act as they please for the future, the
    treasury never a penny shall yield
    them, I vow.
MAG.   How, may I ask, will you
    hinder their getting it?
LYS.   We will ourselves be the Treas-
    urers now.

MAG.   You, woman, you be the treas-
    urers?
LYS.   Certainly. Ah, you esteem us
    unable, perchance;
Are we not skilled in domestic economy,
    do we not manage the household
    finance?
MAG.   O, that is different.
LYS.   Why is it different?
MAG.   This is required for the fight-
    ing, my dear.
LYS.   Well, but the fighting itself
    isn't requisite.
MAG.   Only, without it, we're ruined,
    I fear.
LYS.   We will deliver you.
MAG.   You will deliver us!
LYS.   Truly we will.
MAG.   What a capital notion!
LYS.   Whether you like it or not,
    we'll deliver you.
MAG.   Impudent hussy!
LYS.   You seem in commotion.
Nevertheless we will do as we promise
    you.
MAG.   That were a terrible shame, by
    Demeter.
LYS.   Friend, we must save you.
MAG.   But how if I wish it not?
LYS.   That will but make our resolve
    the completer.
MAG.   Fools! what on earth can
    possess you to meddle with matters
    of war, and matters of peace?
LYS.   Well, I will tell you the reason.
MAG.   And speedily, else you will
    rue it.
LYS.   Then listen, and cease
Clutching and clenching your fingers so
    angrily; keep yourself peaceable.
MAG.   Hanged if I can;
Such is the rage that I feel at your im-
    pudence.
STRATYLLIS.   Then it is you that will
    rue it, my man.
MAG.   Croak you own fate, you ill-
    omened antiquity.
(*To* LYSISTRATA) You be the spokes-
    woman, lady.

Lys. I will.
Think of our old moderation and gentle-
    ness, think how we bore with your
    pranks, and were still,
All through the days of your former
    pugnacity, all through the war that
    is over and spent:
Not that (be sure) we approved of your
    policy; never our griefs you allowed
    us to vent.
Well we perceived your mistakes and
    mismanagement. Often at home on
    our housekeeping cares,
Often we heard of some foolish proposal
    you made for conducting the public
    affairs.
Then would we question you mildly and
    pleasantly. Inwardly grieving, but
    outwardly gay;
Husband, how goes it abroad? we would
    ask of him; *what have ye done in
    Assembly to-day?*
*What would ye write on the side of the
    Treaty stone?* Husband says
    angrily, *What's that to you?*
You, hold your tongue! And I held it
    accordingly.
Strat. That is a thing that I NEVER
    would do!
Mag. Ma'am, if you hadn't, you'd
    soon have repented it.
Lys. Therefore I held it, and spake
    not a word.
Soon of another tremendous absurdity,
    wilder and worse than the former
    we heard.
Husband, I say, with a tender solicitude,
    *Why have ye passed such a foolish
    decree?*
Viciously, moodily, glaring askance at me,
    Stick to your spinning, my mistress,
    says he,
*Else you will speedily find it the worse
    for you,* WAR IS THE CARE AND
    THE BUSINESS OF MEN!
Mag. Zeus! 'twas a worthy reply,
    and an excellent!
Lys. What! you unfortunate, shall
    we not then,

Then, when we see you perplexed and
    incompetent, shall we not tender
    advice to the State?
So when aloud in the streets and the
    thoroughfares sadly we heard you
    bewailing of late,
*Is there a man to defend and deliver us?
    No,* says another, *there's none in
    the land;*
Then by the women assembled in con-
    ference jointly a great Revolution
    was planned,
Hellas to save from her grief and per-
    plexity. Where is the use of a
    longer delay?
Shift for the future our parts and our
    characters; you, as the women, in
    silence obey;
We, as the men, will harangue and pro-
    vide for you; then shall the State
    be triumphant again.
Then shall we do what is best for the
    citizens.
Mag. Women to do what is best for
    the men!
That were a shameful reproach and un-
    bearable!
Lys. Silence, old gentleman.
Mag. Silence for YOU?
Stop for a wench with a wimple enfold-
    ing her? No, by the Powers, may
    I DIE if I do!
Lys. Do not, my pretty one, do not,
    I pray,
Suffer my wimple to stand in the way.
Here, take it, and wear it, and gracefully
    tie it,
Enfolding it over your head, and be
    quiet.
Now to your task.
Calonice. Here is an excellent spin-
    dle to pull.
Myrrhina. Here is a basket for
    carding the wool.
Lys. Now to your task.
Haricots chawing up, petticoats drawing
    up,
Off to your carding, your combing, your
    trimming, WAR IS THE CARE

AND THE BUSINESS OF WOMEN.

(*During the foregoing lines the women have been arraying the Magistrate in the garb and with the apparatus of a spinning-woman.*)

WOMAN CHORUS. Up, up, and leave the pitchers there, and on, resolved and eager,
Our own allotted part to bear in this illustrious leaguer.
I will dance with resolute, tireless feet all day;
My limbs shall never grow faint, my strength give way;
I will march all lengths with the noble hearts and the true,
For theirs is the ready wit and the patriot hand,
And womanly grace, and courage to dare and do,
And Love of our own bright land.
Children of stiff and intractable grand-mothers, heirs of the stinging vira-goes that bore you,
On, with an eager, unyielding tenacity, wind in your sails, and the haven before you.

LYS. Only let Love, the entrancing, the fanciful, only let Queen Aphro-dite to-day
Breathe on our persons a charm and a tenderness, lend us their own irre-sistible sway,
Drawing the men to admire us and long for us; then shall the war everlast-ingly cease,
Then shall the people revere us and honour us, givers of Joy, and givers of Peace.

MAG. Tell us the mode and the means of your doing it.

LYS. First we will stop the disorderly crew,
Soldiers in arms promenading and marketing.

STRAT. Yea, by divine Aphrodite, 'tis true.

LYS. Now in the market you see them like Corybants, jangling about with their armour of mail.
Fiercely they stalk in the midst of the crockery, sternly parade by the cab-bage and kail.

MAG. Right, for a soldier should always be soldierly!

LYS. Troth, 'tis a mighty ridiculous jest,
Watching them haggle for shrimps in the market-place, grimly accoutred with shield and with crest.

STRAT. Lately I witnessed a captain of cavalry, proudly the while on his charger he sat,
Witnessed him, soldierly, buying an omelet, stowing it all in his cavalry hat.
Comes, like a Tereus, a Thracian irregu-lar, shaking his dart and his target to boot;
Off runs a shop-girl, appalled at the sight of him, down he sits soldierly, gobbles her fruit.

MAG. You, I presume, could adroitly and gingerly settle this intricate, tangled concern:
You in a trice could relieve our per-plexities.

LYS. Certainly.

MAG. How? permit me to learn.

LYS. Just as a woman, with nimble dexterity, thus with her hands disen-tangles a skein,
Hither and thither her spindles unravel it, drawing it out, and pulling it plain.
So would this weary Hellenic entangle-ment soon be resolved by our womanly care,
So would our embassies neatly unravel it, drawing it here and pulling it there.

MAG. Wonderful, marvellous feats, not a doubt of it, you with your skeins and your spindles can show;
Fools! do you really expect to unravel a terrible war like a bundle of tow?

LYS. Ah, if you only could manage

your politics just in the way that we
deal with the fleece!

MAG. Tell us the recipe.

LYS. First, in the washing-tub plunge
it, and scour it, and cleanse it from
grease,

Purging away all the filth and the
nastiness; then on the table expand
it and lay,

Beating out all that is worthless and
mischievous, picking the burrs and
the thistles away.

Next, for the clubs, the cabals, and the
coteries, banding unrighteously,
office to win,

Treat them as clots in the wool, and
dissever them, lopping the heads
that are forming therein.

Then you should card it, and comb it,
and mingle it, all in one basket of
love and of unity,

Citizens, visitors, strangers, and so-
journers, all the entire, undivided
community.

Know you a fellow in debt to the
Treasury? Mingle him merrily in
with the rest.

Also remember the cities, our colonies,
outlying states in the east and the
west,

Scattered about to a distance surrounding
us, these are our shreds and our
fragments of wool;

These to one mighty political aggregate
tenderly, carefully, gather and pull,

Twining them all in one thread of good
fellowship; thence a magnificent
bobbin to spin,

Weaving a garment of comfort and
dignity, worthily wrapping the
People therein.

MAG. Heard any ever the like of their
impudence, these who have nothing
to do with the war,

Preaching of bobbins, and beatings, and
washing-tubs?

LYS. Nothing to do with it, wretch
that you are!

We are the people who feel it the keen-

liest, doubly on us the affliction is
cast;

Where are the sons that we sent to your
battle-fields?

MAG. Silence! a truce to the ills that
are past.

LYS. Then in the glory and grace of
our womanhood, all in the May and
the morning of life,

Lo, we are sitting forlorn and disconsolate, what has a soldier to do with a
wife?

We might endure it, but ah! for the
younger ones, still in their maiden
apartments they stay,

Waiting the husband that never approaches them, watching the years
that are gliding away.

MAG. Men, I suppose, have their
youth everlastingly.

LYS. Nay, but that isn't the same
with a man:

Grey though he be when he comes from
the battle-field, still if he wishes to
marry, he can.

Brief is the spring and the flower of our
womanhood, once let it slip, and it
comes not again;

Sit as we may with our spells and our
auguries, never a husband will marry
us then.

—B. B. ROGERS.

ÆSCHYLUS PREFERRED

[From the *Frogs*]

The *Frogs* (411 B.C.) reveals Aristophanes' extraordinary ability in literary
criticism. It was no doubt inevitable that
the traditionalist should clash with the
innovator Euripides. But the play does
more than merely oppose innovation; it
uncovers, through the comic method of
satire, fundamental principles in the sphere
both of poetic language and of the representation of character, and shows a rare
quality of interpretation as brought to
bear upon the work of the tragic poets.

In the following passage, the god Bacchus, patron of dramatic art, distressed at
the decline of tragedy since the death of
Euripides, determines to visit Hades to secure the release of one of the tragic poets.
While crossing the river in Charon's boat,
he is greeted by the Chorus of Frogs.

CHORUS. Brekeke-kesh, koash, koash,
Shall the Choral Quiristers of the Marsh
Be censured and rejected as hoarse and
    harsh;
  And their Chromatic essays
  Deprived of praise?
No, let us raise afresh
Our obstreperous Brekeke-kesh;
The customary croak and cry
  Of the creatures
  At the theatres,
In their yearly revelry.
Brekeke-kesh, koash, koash.
  BACCHUS (*rowing in great misery*)
    How I'm maul'd,
    How I'm gall'd;
Worn and mangled to a mash.
There they go! "Koash, koash!"—
  FROGS. Brekeke-kesh, koash, koash.
  BACCHUS. Oh, beshrew,
    All your crew;
You don't consider how I smart.
  FROGS. Now for a sample of the Art!
Brekeke-kesh, koash, koash.
  BACCHUS. I wish you hang'd with all
    my heart.
Have you nothing else to say?
"Brekeke-kesh, koash" all day!
  FROGS. We've a right,
    We've a right;
And we croak at ye for spite.
  We've a right,
  We've a right;
  Day and night,
  Day and night;
  Night and day,
  Still to croak and croak away.
Phœbus and every grace
Admire and approve of the croaking race;
And the egregious guttural notes
That are gargled and warbled in their
    lyrical throats.

In reproof
Of your scorn
Mighty Pan
Nods his horn;
Beating time
To the rhyme
With his hoof,
With his hoof.
Persisting in our plan,
We proceed as we began,
Breke-kesh, Breke-kesh,
Koash, koash.
  BACCHUS. Oh, the Frogs, consume
    and rot 'em.
I've a blister on my bottom.
Hold your tongues, you tuneful creatures.
  FROGS. Cease with your profane en-
    treaties
All in vain for ever striving:
  Silence is against our natures.
With the vernal heat reviving,
  Our aquatic crew repair
From their periodic sleep,
In the dark and chilly deep,
To the cheerful upper air;
Then we frolic here and there
All amidst the meadows fair;
Shady plants of asphodel,
Are the lodges where we dwell;
Chaunting in the leafy bowers
All the livelong summer hours,
Till the sudden gusty showers
Send us headlong, helter skelter,
To the pool to seek for shelter;
Meagre, eager, leaping, lunging,
From the sedgy wharfage plunging
To the tranquil depth below,
There we muster all a-row;
Where, secure from toil and trouble,
With a tuneful hubble-bubble,
Our symphonious accents flow.
Brekeke-kesh, koash, koash.
  BACCHUS. I forbid you to proceed.
  FROGS. That would be severe indeed;
Arbitrary, bold, and rash—
Brekeke-kesh, koash, koash.
  BACCHUS. I command you to desist—
Oh, my back, there! oh, my wrist!
What a twist!

What a sprain

FROGS. Once again—
We renew the tuneful strain.
Brekeke-kesh, koash, koash.
    BACCHUS. I disdain—(Hang the pain!)
All your nonsense, noise, and trash.
Oh, my blister! Oh, my sprain!
    FROGS. Brekeke-kesh, koash, koash.
Friends and Frogs, we must display
All our powers of voice today;
Suffer not this stranger here,
With fastidious foreign ear,
To confound us and abash.
Brekeke-kesh, koash, koash.
    BACCHUS. Well, my spirit is not broke,
If it's only for the joke,
I'll outdo you with a croak.
Here it goes—(*very loud*) "Koash, koash."
    FROGS. Now for a glorious croaking crash,
(*Still louder*) Brekeke-kesh, koash, koash.
    BACCHUS (*splashing with his oar*). I'll disperse you with a splash.
    FROGS. Brekeke-kesh, koash, koash.
    BACCHUS. I'll subdue
Your rebellious, noisy crew—
Have amongst you there, slap-dash.
    (*Strikes at them*)
    FROGS. Brekeke-kesh, koash, koash.
We defy your oar and you.
    CHARON. Hold! We're ashore just—shift your oar. Get out.
Now pay your fare.
    BACCHUS. There,—there it is—the twopence.

Arrived in Hades, Bacchus acts as judge in a poetic contest between Æschylus and Euripides. At the conclusion of the contest he decides in favor of Æschylus.

BACCHUS. Come, no more songs!
    ÆSCHYLUS. I've had enough of 'em;
For my part, I shall bring him to the balance,
As a true test of our poetic merit,
To prove the weight of our respective verses.
    BAC. Well then, so be it—if it must be so,
That I'm to stand here like a cheesemonger
Retailing poetry with a pair of scales.
    (*A huge pair of scales are here discovered on the stage.*)
    CHORUS. Curious eager wits pursue
Strange devices quaint and new,
Like the scene you witness here,
Unaccountable and queer;
I myself, if merely told it,
If I did not here behold it,
Should have deem'd it utter folly,
Craziness and nonsense wholly.
    BAC. Move up; stand close to the balance!
    EURIPIDES.   Here are we—
    BAC. Take hold now, and each of you repeat a verse,
And don't leave go before I call to you!
    EUR. We're ready.
    BAC. Now, then, each repeat a verse.
    EUR. "I wish that Argo with her woven wings."
    ÆS. "O streams of Sperchius, and ye pastured plains."
    BAC. Let go!—See now—this scale outweighs that other
Very considerably—
    EUR.   How did it happen?
    BAC. He slipped a river in, like the wool-jobbers,
To moisten his metre—but your line was light,
A thing with wings—ready to fly away.
    EUR. Let him try once again then, and take hold.
    BAC. Take hold once more.
    EUR.   We're ready.
    BAC.   Now repeat.
    EUR. "Speech is the temple and the altar of persuasion."
    ÆS. "Death is a god that loves no sacrifice."
    BAC. Let go!—See there again! This scale sinks down;

No wonder that it should, with Death
  put into it,
The heaviest of all calamities.

EUR. But I put in persuasion finely
  express'd
In the best terms.

BAC.   Perhaps so; but persuasion
Is soft and light and silly—Think of
  something
That's heavy and huge, to outweigh him,
  something solid.

EUR. Let's see—Where have I got it?
  Something solid?

BAC. "Achilles has thrown twice—
  Twice a deuce ace!"
Come now, one trial more; this is the
  last.

EUR. "He grasped a mighty mace of
  massy weight."

ÆS. "Cars upon cars, and corpses
  heaped pell mell."

BAC. He has nick'd you again—

EUR. Why so? What has he done?

BAC. He has heap'd ye up cars and
  corpses, such a load
As twenty Egyptian labourers could not
  carry—

ÆS. Come, no more single lines—let
  him bring all,
His wife, his children, his Cephisophon,
His boors and everything, himself to
  boot—
I'll counterpoise them with a couple of
  lines.

BAC. Well, they're both friends of
  mine—I shan't decide
To get myself ill-will from either
  party;
One of them seems extraordinary clever,
And the other suits my taste particularly.

PLUTO. Won't you decide then, and
  conclude the business?

BAC. Suppose then I decide; what
  then?

PLUTO.   Then take him
Away with you, whichever you prefer,
As a present for your pains in coming
  down here.

BAC. Heaven bless ye—Well—let's
  see now—Can't ye advise me?
This is the case—I'm come in search of a
  poet—

PLUTO. With what design?

BAC.   With this design; to see
The City again restored to peace and
  wealth,
Exhibiting tragedies in a proper style.
—Therefore whichever gives the best
  advice
On public matters I shall take him with
  me.
—First then of Alcibiades, what think
  ye?
The City is in hard labor with the ques-
  tion.

EUR. What are her sentiments towards
  him?

BAC.   What?
"She loves and she detests and longs to
  have him."
But tell me, both of you, your own
  opinions.

EUR. (EURIPIDES and ÆSCHYLUS speak
  each in his own tragical style). I
  hate the man, that in his country's
  service
Is slow, but ready and quick to work her
  harm;
Unserviceable except to serve himself.

BAC. Well said, by Jove!—Now you
  —Give us a sentence.

ÆS. 'Tis rash and idle policy to foster
A lion's whelp within the city walls,
But when he's rear'd and grown you must
  indulge him.

BAC. By Jove then I'm quite puzzled;
  one of them
Has answered clearly, and the other
  sensibly:
But give us both of ye one more
  opinion;
—What means are left of safety for the
  state?

EUR. To tack Cinesias like a pair of
  wings
To Cleocritus' shoulders, and dispatch
  them

From a precipice to sail across the seas.

BAC. It seems a joke; but there's some sense in it.

EUR. Then being both equipp'd with little cruets

They might co-operate in a naval action,
By sprinkling vinegar in the enemies' eyes.

—But I can tell you and will.

BAC.   Speak, and explain then—

EUR. If we mistrust where present trust is placed,

Trusting in what was heretofore mistrusted—

BAC. How! What? I'm at a loss—
Speak it again

Not quite so learnedly—more plainly and simply.

EUR. If we withdraw the confidence we placed

In these our present statesmen, and transfer it

To those whom we mistrusted heretofore,

This seems I think our fairest chance for safety:

If with our present counsellors we fail,

Then with their opposites we might succeed.

BAC. That's capitally said, my Palamedes!

My politician! was it all your own?
Your own invention?

EUR.   All except the cruets;

That was a notion of Cephisophon's.

BAC. (to ÆSCHYLUS). Now you— what say you?

ÆS.   Inform me about the city—

What kind of persons has she placed in office?

Does she promote the worthiest?

BAC.   No, not she,
She can't abide 'em.

ÆS.   Rogues then she prefers?

BAC. Not altogether, she makes use of 'em

Perforce as it were.

ÆS.   Then who can hope to save

A state so wayward and perverse, that finds

No sort of habit fitted for her wear?

Drugget or superfine, nothing will suit her!

BAC. Do think a little how she can be saved.

ÆS. Not here; when I return there, I shall speak.

BAC. No, do pray send some good advice before you.

ÆS. When they regard their lands as enemy's ground,

Their enemy's possessions as their own,
Their seamen and their fleet their only safeguard,

Their sole resource hardship and poverty,
And resolute endurance in distress—

BAC. That's well,—but juries eat up everything,

And we shall lose our supper if we stay.

PLUTO. Decide then—

BAC.   You'll decide for your own selves,

I'll make my choice according to my fancy.

EUR. Remember, then, your oath to your poor friend;

And, as you swore and promised, rescue me.

BAC. "It was my tongue that swore" —I fix on Æschylus.

EUR. O wretch! what have you done?

BAC.   Me? done? What should I?

Voted for Æschylus to be sure—Why not?

EUR. And after such a villainous act, you dare

To view me face to face—Art not ashamed?

BAC. Why shame, in point of fact, is nothing real:

Shame is the apprehension of a vision
Reflected from the surface of opinion—
—The opinion of the public—they must judge.

EUR. O cruel!—Will you abandon me to death?

BAC. Why perhaps death is life, and
    life is death,
And victuals and drink an illusion of the
    senses;

For what is Death but an eternal sleep?
And does not Life consist in sleeping and
    eating?
                —J. H. FRERE.

V. IDEALS OF FREEDOM AND UNION

Public speech was always practised in Greece, but came to its perfection in a democratic society in which the mass of citizens directly decided questions of state policy, great and small. Any citizen might harangue his fellows; but to influence their action persuasive speech was essential, and many gave their attention to it. In a time when professional agencies for the distribution of news were quite unknown, leading officials of a city often addressed the people simply to inform them of conditions. At Athens, too, every man engaged in a law-suit had to appear and plead for himself. This regulation not only fostered proficiency in public speaking among the rank and file, but finally brought into being a class of orators who devoted their talents to composing law-court speeches to order for a fee. In other words they were professional speech-writers. They were in great demand in a city like Athens in which litigation was frequently indulged in. The speeches of Lysias show to what perfection this branch of the art of oratory was developed.

In literature as early as the Homeric poems there is abundant evidence of the importance of public speech. In historic times Solon, Themistocles, and Pericles undoubtedly owed their commanding position in part to their oratorical ability. But only from a later period have genuine speeches come down to us. And it was only in a later period, the last quarter of the fifth century B.C., that oratory was technically developed as a branch of literature.

Two influences, that of the sophists, and that of the rhetoricians, both originally from outside of Athens, carried on the development. The sophists were professional teachers of all subjects which would train the youth for public life, oratory included. They promoted discussion of any and all possible questions and argumentation, though often more specious than convincing. Rhetoricians, at first under influences from the Greeks of Sicily, studied the theory and the practice of oratory. They analyzed speech-making, wrote practical treatises, and taught. These professional influences with the still greater influence of conditions of society carried the art in Athens to heights never again reached in ancient times.

Public speakers must of course deal with the situation of the moment. Idealistic they may be, and often are; but they can not afford to be too theoretical; they must be practical to some degree for they have before them an audience to convince. Political ideals, programs for peace and union, as presented in extant speeches, must be thought to be of a kind that would appeal to the ordinary citizen. In reading orations then one may get very close to the ideas of the average man in the Athenian democracy.

AGAINST ERATOSTHENES

LYSIAS

Lysias was born at Athens, though his parents were Syracusans, about 440 B.C., and lived there most of his life. His death took place about 380 B.C.

Lysias spent his talents for oratory almost exclusively in writing speeches for others to use. He made a decided advance in oratorical prose in the direction of simplicity and clearness, bringing it closer to everyday speech and making it a more natural tool for the average man.

Eratosthenes was one of the thirty tyrants by whom the brother of Lysias had been put to death. After their overthrow in 403 B.C., Lysias returned from exile and was granted citizenship. As citizen he delivered this speech of attack both against the individual Eratosthenes and against the whole despotic form of government which was represented in his person.

It is an easy matter, O Athenians! to begin this accusation; but to end it without doing injustice to the cause, will be attended with no small difficulty. For the crimes of Eratosthenes are not only too atrocious to describe, but too many to enumerate. No exaggeration can exceed, and within the time assigned for this discourse it is impossible fully to represent them.

This trial, too, is attended with another singularity. In other causes, it is usual to ask the accusers, "What is your resentment against the defendants?" But here you must ask the defendants, "What was your resentment against your country? What malice did you bear your fellow-citizens? Why did you rage with unbridled fury against the state itself?"

I say not this, Athenians! as if I had no private misfortunes to lament, no personal injuries to revenge. But a good citizen feels the calamities of his country as sensibly as his own. Both there is good reason to resent, and with both I am justly affected.

Nor is it a small source of uneasiness that a man, who never before pled in his own or in any other cause, should be obliged to undertake an accusation upon which so much depends. I have felt uncommon anxiety on this account, especially as not only my interests, but those of my brother, are at stake; and both are unfortunately committed to my artless inexperience. But I shall make you acquainted, Athenians! with the merits of this cause in the shortest and simplest manner.

My father Cephalus was engaged to settle in this country, by the persuasion of Pericles, and he continued in it thirty years, without ever appearing before you either as plaintiff or defendant. His behaviour was so moderate and inoffensive, that it prevented him from doing injuries, and protected him against them. But there are times in which no man, how much soever he may be entitled to tranquillity, can expect to enjoy it. Such was the fatal period, when the Thirty assumed the direction of your affairs. Governed as they were, by the most abandoned principles, and actuated by the malignant spirit of calumny and revenge, they endeavoured to conceal the flagitious designs which they meditated against their country, under the appearance of promoting the public good. "The city must be purged from turbulent and corrupt men, that the contagion of their bad example being removed, other citizens may return to their duty, and public happiness be restored." This was their pretence, but you shall hear how far their conduct corresponded with it. Having first mentioned their behaviour towards myself, I shall afterwards describe what they committed against you.

Theognis and Piso, two of the thirty tyrants, gave information to their associates, that many strangers established at Athens were disaffected towards the present government. This calumny was evidently contrived, in order to afford a plausible excuse for plundering the strangers; to which measure, the colleagues of Theognis and Piso were not only disposed by avarice, but prompted by fear. Money was become necessary for their safety, as their government, founded on usurpation, and tyrannically administered, could by no means be supported. The life of man, therefore, they regarded as a matter of little moment; the amassing of wealth was the only object of their ambition. For this purpose, ten strangers were at once devoted to destruction. Among these, indeed, were two poor men; for thus the tyrants hope to persuade you, that the remaining eight had also been condemned, not from a desire of rifling their effects, but of maintaining the public interest; as if this had ever been the object of their concern!

Having thus concerted their designs, they proceeded to carry them into execution. I was seized exercising the rites of hospitality, and, my guests having been rudely dismissed, was delivered over to Piso. While his accomplices went into the workhouse to take a list of my slaves, I asked him, "If money could save my life?" "Yes, a considerable sum." "I will give you a talent of silver." "I am satisfied." I knew, Athenians! that he neither feared Gods nor men, yet in my present desperate condition, it was some small consolation even to depend on his brittle faith. After he had vowed destruction on himself and his children if he performed not his promise, I went to open my coffer in order to pay him the talent; but he, observing the contents, called one of his attendants, and ordered him to seize them. When his servant had taken not only what was agreed on between us, but three talents of silver, a hundred daricks, three hundred cyzeceni, and four cups of silver, I begged of Piso, that he would allow me a small pittance to defray the expense of my journey; but he desired me to be thankful if I saved my life. As we were going out, we were met by Melobius and Mnesitheides, who had returned from the workhouse. They enquired where we were going; Piso answered, "To my brother's house, that it likewise might be examined." They desired him to go on, but commanded me to follow them to Damasippus's house; upon which Piso whispered me to be silent and to fear nothing, for that he also would be there. When we arrived, we found Theognis placed as a guard upon several of my unfortunate companions.

Here I remained among his prisoners, and those who conducted me retired. In this unhappy condition, I thought it advisable to neglect no means of providing for my escape. Calling therefore Damasippus, I explained to him my situation; that I had been guilty of no crime, but was persecuted for my riches, and entreated him by our past friendship, to exert his influence in my behalf. He assured me of his favourable intentions, and of his resolution to intercede with Theognis, whom he supposed to be so avaricious that he would do any thing for money. Whilst they conversed, I being acquainted with the house, which had two entrances, thought proper to attempt getting out unnoticed. If I escaped, it was well; if I did not, Theognis might still be soothed by money; and should a bribe fail, my ruin, whether in staying, or attempting to escape, was inevitable.

Influenced by these motives, while they guarded only the entrance from the court, I escaped by another passage, through three doors, which all happened to be open. Flying to the country-house of Archimaus, a ship-master, I sent him to the city to get intelligence of my brother. Upon his return, he informed me, that Eratosthenes had dragged him from the road, and carried him to prison. At this mournful news, I sailed in the night to Megara. And in the meantime the Thirty issued their command, that Polemarchus should drink hemlock, without even alleging the smallest reason why he should suffer death; so far was he from being allowed a fair trial for his vindication. Having thus perished in prison, though we had no less than three houses belonging to us, they publicly exposed his body in a hired cottage, from which it was brought to be buried. Even his garments, in which he was well provided, were not used at his funeral; but of our friends, one supplied a cloak, another a pillow for his head, and each whatever happened to be nearest at hand. So shameful was their behaviour to him, though they had acquired seven hundred shields, the manufacture of our slaves, much gold, silver, and brass, with all sorts of furniture, and such a quantity of women's dress and ornaments, as they could never have expected to possess; and to crown all, a hundred and twenty slaves, of whom, giving the worst to the public, they kept the most dexterous and skilful for their private use. Such was the meanness of their avarice, that even the gold ear-rings of Polemarchus's wife Melobius plucked from her ears: the most insignificant trinket was not spared; they plundered us for our wealth, as if they had been executing the decrees of justice against us for some enormous offence. But did we deserve such treatment; we who liberally distributed our fortune for the public interest, and often lavished it for the public amusement; we who, always behaving in moderation, never gave the least cause of resentment; we who ransomed many of your citizens from the enemy, and though foreigners, showed more attachment to the country in which we lived, than such citizens as Eratosthenes to their native land? By them many Athenians were driven from their native country, and obliged to take refuge among the enemy; many, after being put to death upon unjust accusations, were impiously suffered to lie unburied; those who deserved the highest honours, they disgraced and insulted; and not satisfied with wrecking their vengeance on the present generation, they cut off your future hopes by preventing the marriages of your children. What audacity is it then for such men to approach you with their defence; to plead innocence, to solicit protection, which, would to God! they deserved? For had their conduct been capable of excuse, my sorrows might admit of consolation, and I should not at present lament the public calamities and my own.

My brother, guiltless of any injury public or private, fell a sacrifice to the cruel avarice of Eratosthenes. And let him now appear, that I may interrogate him; for though with a view to his safety, it would be impious even to name him to another, I shall feel no horror at speaking to himself in order to promote his destruction. Step up then, and answer the questions which I shall put to you. "Did you carry off Polemarchus, or not?" "I executed by fear what was commanded me by the magistrates." "Were you of the council, when our affair was examined?" "I was." "Did you concur with those who proposed to put us to death, or were you of a contrary opinion?" "I was of a contrary opinion." "Did you advise that we should die?" "I advised that you should not die." "Believing that we deserved death, or that we should have suffered unjustly?" "That you should have suffered unjustly." Thus, O most impudent, most insufferable of men, you voted for saving us, but laid hold on us that we might die! When our lives depended on your cabal, you opposed the opinion of those who sought our death; but when the life of Polemarchus depended on yourself alone, you imprisoned and murdered him! And now, dare you expect favour for what you advised without effect, rather than dread punishment for what you actually committed?

But it is unreasonable, Athenians! to believe, that he ever gave any such advice; for, is it possible, that had he opposed our death, he should have been appointed our executioner? Would his colleagues have chosen to try his fidelity by this delicate act of obedience? Surely they might have found a fitter instrument to execute their orders, than the man who disapproved of them, and who had openly declared his opinion. But on the supposition that this really was the case, it would still be of no avail to him. It is an excuse indeed for the rest of the citizens, who, in those turbulent times, were sometimes compelled to acts of violence and injustice, that their conduct was not voluntary, but in compliance with the orders of the Thirty, whom it was death to disobey: But the Thirty can never defend their own crimes by charging them on one another. Had there been any authority in the state to which their own was subordinate, and which commanded them to put the citizens to death, then indeed they might plead necessity, and perhaps be deemed worthy of pardon; but being themselves sovereign and supreme, they must likewise be themselves answerable for their behaviour. For how could you ever punish their crimes, if you admit as an excuse for the Thirty, that they obeyed the orders of the Thirty?

But Eratosthenes even exceeded these orders. For though commanded to search for Polemarchus in his house, a command highly criminal and oppressive! he pursued him flying for safety into the road, and thence dragged him to prison. If those deserve mercy, who, in order to secure themselves, violate the rights of others, is there no pity for the innocent?

"But Eratosthenes would have endangered his own safety, had he not come to my brother's house, or if, finding him there, he had denied his having seen him." Be it so. As the matter actually happened, however, there was no danger. His defence was ready, either that he did not observe him on the road, or did not know him; for in neither case was it in the power of his colleagues, either by witnesses or cross-examining, to convict him. And had you, Eratosthenes! felt anything of that humanity to which you pretend, you would rather have given warning to an innocent man pursued to death, than co-operated with his insolent oppressors. But your conduct affords sufficient proof, that, far from being dissatisfied with your commission, you delighted in executing it. The decision of the judges, therefore, will be founded on the actions which you performed, and not on the words which you pretend to have said; they will consider your actions as a proof that those words, of which you can bring no evidence, were not really spoken by you: for it is easy for the Thirty, to whose meetings we had not access, against whose violence, even in our own houses, we were not secure, to extol the humanity of their speeches, while their actions were directed against our property and our lives. But admitting that you opposed the sentiments of your colleagues, pray what would have been your conduct had you agreed with them; since, even as it was, you put Polemarchus to death? Had he been your brother or father, would you have saved him? For it would be necessary, Athenians! either to prove, that he did not carry off Polemarchus, or that he acted justly in doing so; but as he has given up both these points, you can no longer have any difficulty in your decision.

By this cause the attention of mankind has been excited: the citizens and strangers now present are big with expectation; and the fate of Eratosthenes alone must discover your sentiments of the whole cabal. Now is the time to teach your citizens, that their crimes will either meet with immediate punishment, or, though this should for a short time be deferred, and their ambition be crowned with success by the acquisition of sovereign power, that justice will still pursue and overtake them, deprive them of their usurped pre-eminence, and confound them with the meanest criminals. Now is the time to justify before strangers the expulsion of your tyrants; for if they perceive, that, after getting them into your power, you still allow them to escape unpunished, they will have reason to deem their own activity in promoting your deliverance equally officious and vain.

And how inconsistent will it appear,

that you who punished with death the commanders in the sea-engagement, because they were unable to draw up dead bodies from the bottom of a tempestuous sea, saying, that it was necessary to sacrifice the living to the virtues of the dead, should neglect to chastise those men, who, when in a private station, exerted their utmost endeavours to render us unfortunate at sea, and when vested with supreme authority, sported with the lives of your citizens? Ought not your resentment to be kindled against them and their children?—Surely I have already said enough upon this indictment; for, when a criminal is proved deserving of death, the ultimate point to which mankind can push their revenge, it is to no purpose to accumulate new charges against him. We need not, therefore, burden the libel of the Thirty with many articles; for the punishment would not be adequate, were they twice to suffer death for the least of their crimes.

Nor can they plead that defence which is so often employed with success; they can relate no services which can counterbalance their demerit; and if they admit, which of necessity they must, the truth of what has been asserted against them, they can boast of no gallant action, to blunt the edge of your resentment. They cannot elude the accusation, by shewing, like many others of your citizens, their laurels gained in the field, the ships taken from your enemies, the cities joined to your alliance. Let them speak. —When did you kill as many of our enemies abroad, as you murdered of our citizens at home? When did you seize as many of their ships, as you betrayed of ours? What city did you deliver, comparable to Athens, which you enslaved? What bulwark did you ever destroy equal to that of your country? When you confessed that you had demolished the Pireum, not to gratify the Lacedæmonians, but to render your own tyranny more firm and stable!

I have often wondered that such men as Eratosthenes should dare to defend crimes no less palpable than heinous. None surely could be capable of this audacity, but men of the most abandoned characters, and who had already shewn many previous instances of villany and baseness. This was not, therefore, the first time he had trampled on our laws, and opposed the spirit of our government. When the tyranny of the four hundred was established in the army at Samos, Eratosthenes abandoned the ship which he commanded in the Hellespont, and came hither with Hierocles and others (their names are too well known to be mentioned), with a design to oppose the friends of liberty, then struggling to preserve the democratical government. That this is the truth, the witnesses shall prove. (*The witnesses are examined*.)

After that fatal sea-fight, which, though the republic still continued for a short time to subsist, may be regarded as the aera of our misfortunes, there were five men appointed by the cabal, under pretence of acting the part of censors, and of summoning and preserving order among the tribes, but in reality to be the chiefs of the party, and to undermine the true interest of the state. Of this number were Eratosthenes and Critias, who, by their accomplices, gained a complete ascendant over the tribes, and prevailed on them to pass what laws, and to appoint what magistrates, they themselves thought proper. Thus was the state at once a prey to enemies both foreign and domestic: For the cabal well knew, that they could never build their influence on any other foundation, but the ruin of their country. Hence their enmity to the state; hence their contrivance to render your own decrees destructive of the public good, and to reduce your affairs into so deplorable a situation, that the necessity of struggling against the calamities which they occasioned, might prevent you from opposing that tyranny which they intended to establish. That Eratosthenes was one of these censors, I can prove; not by the testimony of his colleagues (this indeed is not in my power), but of those who were the instruments of his oppression. These, had they behaved wisely, would ere now have given information against him who employed them in so mean a service; disregarding engagements, by whatever oaths confirmed, which had been entered into with a public enemy, and sacrificing every scruple of conscience to the interest of their country. Let the witnesses be called and examined.—You hear then, that their testimony is entirely agreeable to what I have related.

But last of all, when he became a member of the supreme council, he was guilty of innumerable outrages, without ever having even a share in one good action. Had he been a worthy citizen, he would neither have usurped an authority unwarranted by law, and contrary to the principles of our constitution, nor given ear to those false accusations which were brought before the senate; but he would have asserted with the freedom and boldness of an honest man, that Batrachus and Æschylides did not declare the truth, but bore testimony to libels, maliciously contrived by the Thirty, for the destruction of their fellow-citizens. For in that unhappy conjuncture, such as were silent deserved as much blame as those who told falsehoods: Both were equally injurious to the state; for, because these were silent, the cabal alone spoke and acted, than which there could not possibly be a greater calamity. It is in vain then, for any one to pretend to have wished well to his country, who did not on this occasion, both by his speeches and actions, give a proof of his good-will.

Eratosthenes, however, may still insist, that, being afraid of incurring the resentment of his colleagues, he was compelled to an involuntary silence. This defence, were it founded in truth, would certainly be of great weight: But if it appears that he had no occasion to dread the resentment of his associates, and that his influence among them was so great, that he could oppose them all without danger to himself, it must be evident, that he concurred in every design which he did not openly approve. For, why did he not display the same courage in your behalf, which he exerted in the defence of Theramenes, the cause of your misfortunes—if it did not proceed from this, that, considering the state as his enemy, he naturally regarded as his friends, those who had been most active in subverting it? This I can evidently demonstrate, as well as that all those dissensions which took place among the Thirty, instead of proceeding from any praise-worthy or public cause, were only so many contests of private ambition, to decide who should have the greatest share in the government, or rather in the oppression, of their country. For had their disputes arisen about the common good, or on account of the injuries which had been offered to the citizens; when could the honest party have a fairer opportunity of discovering the integrity of their intentions, and of taking vengeance on the public enemies, than after Thrasybulus had got possession of Phyle? But instead of co-operating with this deliverer of his country, Eratosthenes departed with his partners in power, to Salamis and Eleusis, after throwing into confinement three hundred of the citizens, all of whom were condemned to death by one decree. . . .

But enough of Theramenes. The time is now come, when, insensible to pity and tenderness, you must be armed with just severity against Eratosthenes and his associates. What avails it to have conquered them in the field, if you be overcome by them in your councils? Do not shew them more favour for what they boast they will perform, than resentment for what they have already committed;

nor, after being at so much pains to become master of their persons, allow them to escape without suffering that punishment which you once fought to inflict, but prove yourselves worthy of that fortune, which has given you power over your enemies. The contest is very unequal between Eratosthenes and you: Formerly, he was both judge and accuser, but we, even while we accuse, must at the same time make our defence. Those who were innocent, he put to death without trial; to them who are guilty, we allow the benefit of law, even though no adequate punishment can ever be inflicted. For should we sacrifice them and their children, would this compensate for the murder of your fathers, your sons, and your brothers? Should we deprive them of their property, could this indemnify the individuals whom they have beggared, or the state which they have plundered? Though they cannot suffer a punishment adequate to their demerit, they ought not surely on this account to escape. Yet how matchless is the effrontery of Eratosthenes, who, being now judged by the very persons whom he formerly injured, still ventures to make his defence before the witnesses of his crimes? What can shew more evidently the contempt in which he holds you, or the confidence which he reposes in others? This you ought not to neglect, but hold it for certain, that without accomplices he would never have committed such outrages against you, or at present would he venture to defend them. And what can be the motive of those accomplices, but to remove their apprehensions on account of what they have already done, and henceforward to acquire the power of acting with impunity? But I wonder, whether they will attempt to save him by their own merit with the citizens, (whom, would to God! they had been as ready to protect, as he was to annoy) or whether, resting their sole defence on the character of the defendant, they will endeavour,

by rhetoric and chicane, to varnish the most flagrant breaches of every law human and divine? Yet these artful speakers never displayed their eloquence in defending the cause of the innocent, or in delivering you from oppression. As to the witnesses who now appear with the view to save him, but by whose testimony he must stand condemned, what can be their opinion of your understanding, if they expect that you will now deliberately pardon those who, after murdering your relations, would not permit you to bury them? Those who, should they be now saved by your simplicity, would again overwhelm you in the common ruin of your country; while your friends, whom they put to death, cannot again perish in your defence. It is indeed very remarkable, that though there were so few to undertake your cause, in itself so just, and though none durst shew their regard for such as were destroyed by the Thirty without exposing themselves to the like calamity, there should now be so many patrons ready to protect your destroyers, and to defend their proceedings.

It is still urged, in favour of Eratosthenes, that of all the Thirty he was the least culpable, and therefore deserves pardon. But surely of all the other Greeks, he was the most culpable, and therefore deserves punishment. By passing a just decree, you will shew your displeasure and indignation; by acquitting him, you become accomplices of his crimes, and cannot even make use of his defence, That you were compelled by the Thirty; for at present no man can compel you to vote in opposition to your sentiments. Do not then accuse yourselves by absolving him: Your decree cannot remain secret; it must be known to your country.

I shall conclude, with laying before you the miseries to which you were reduced, that you may see the necessity of taking punishment on the authors of them. And first, you who remained in the city, consider the severity of their government; you were reduced into such a situation as to be obliged to carry on a war, in which, if you were conquered, you partook indeed of the same liberty with the conquerors; but if you proved victorious, you remained under the slavery of your magistrates. Consider, that while they enriched their private families, they beggared you by a civil war, from which you had no advantages to expect, as you could participate with them only in their disgrace. This was the uncommon method by which they secured your fidelity, (than which, what could be more contemptuous?) not by sharing with you their riches or their power, but by exposing you to that detestation, in which they were held by all real lovers of their country. Take vengeance then for yourselves whom they thus insulted, and for your countrymen whom they banished. You were formerly enslaved by traitors to their country, you now deliberate, and fight, and govern, in concert with its deliverers. Avail yourselves of this happy revolution; shew that you are worthy of that liberty, which, notwithstanding all their guards, has been restored; avenge the enemies of the state, and secure its future tranquillity.

To such as remained in Athens, I might still with propriety say a great deal more; but this shall be sufficient. As to you of the Pireum, you will remember, that though you never lost your arms in the battles which you fought, or in the lands which you traversed, yet you suffered by these men what your foreign enemies could never accomplish; and at home, in time of peace, were disarmed by your fellow-citizens. By them, you were banished from the country left you by your fathers. Their rage, knowing no abatement, pursued you abroad, and drove you from one territory to another. Recall the same resentment which you then felt. Remember the cruel indignities which you suffered; how you were dragged from the tribunal and the altars; how no place, however sacred, could shelter you against their violence! while others, torn from their wives, their children, their parents, after putting a period to their miserable lives, were deprived of funeral rites. For these tyrants imagined their government to be so firmly established, that even the vengeance of the Gods was unable to shake it.

But you who escaped immediate death, who fled, you knew not whither, no asylum affording you protection; every where taking refuge, yet every where abandoned; who, leaving your children among strangers or enemies, and destitute of all the necessaries of life, made your way to the Pireum, where, overcoming all opposition, you showed the triumph of virtue over numbers and force, regained the city for yourselves, and freedom for your countrymen,—What must have been your situation had you proved unfortunate in the engagement? Again compelled to fly, no temples, no altars, could have saved you. The children who accompanied you, would have been reduced into the vilest servitude; those whom you left behind, deprived of all help, would at a mean price have been sold to your enemies. But why should I mention what might have happened, not being able to relate what was actually done? For it is impossible for one man, or in the course of one trial, to enumerate the means which were employed to undermine the power of this state; the arsenals which were demolished, the temples sold or profaned, the citizens banished or murdered, and whose dead bodies were impiously left uninterred. Those citizens now watch your decree, uncertain whether you will prove accomplices in their death, or avengers of their murder. You have heard, you have seen, you have suffered, and in consequence pass your decree.

—J. GILLIES.

THE PRIMACY OF ATHENS [1]

ISOCRATES

[From the *Panegyricus*]

Isocrates, who was born at Athens in 436 and died in 338 B.C., was most successful as a teacher of rhetoric and political theory. Most of his writings, of which twenty-one speeches and nine letters are extant, are devoted mainly to questions of politics, with the central theme running through them of the necessity of Greek unity to meet threatening attacks from without. His dream as a rhetorician was to establish oratory on a philosophical basis and to work out its principles as an art in such a way as to win for it recognition like that accorded poetry.

He perfected a flowery, periodic style, and introduced rhythms into prose, particularly at the close of periods. The simple style of Lysias gave way to an effort for display, which to a modern reader often must seem overdone. Doubtless its success depended on proper delivery. It was largely imitated by Greek, and later Roman, orators, and through Cicero's works has had an influence on literary prose in modern times. Isocrates' principal works are the *Areopagiticus* in which he would restore to the Areopagus its ancient powers, and the *Panegyricus*.

Isocrates claimed leadership for Athens in the new and unified nation he was struggling for not merely because of what she had achieved politically, but also and chiefly because of her intellectual and cultural supremacy. He developed this idea in the *Panegyricus* delivered in 380 B.C.

In the first place, then, the first need of our nature was supplied by the agency of our state; for even though the story is a mythical one, yet it is fit to be told even at the present day. When Demeter came into the country in her wandering, after the rape of Persephone, and was

---

[1] From *The Greek and Latin Classics*. Reprinted by permission of Parke, Austin & Lipscomb, publishers.

kindly disposed to our forefathers on account of the services they rendered her, which can be told to none but the initiated, she bestowed two gifts which surpass all others: the fruits of the earth, which have saved us from the life of wild beasts, and the mystic rite, the partakers in which have brighter hopes concerning the end of life and the eternity beyond,— under these circumstances Athens showed such love for men, as well as for the gods, that, when she became mistress of these great blessings, she did not grudge them to the rest of the world, but shared her advantages with all. Now as to the festival, we to this day celebrate it every year; and as to the fruits of the earth, Athens has once for all taught the uses to which they can be put, the operations which they require, and the benefits which arise from them. Indeed no one will venture to disbelieve this statement, after I have made a few additional remarks. For in the first place, the very considerations which would lead a man to despise the story on account of its antiquity, would give him probable reason to suppose that the events had actually happened; for that many have told the story of these events, and all have heard it, should make us regard it, though not recent, yet as worthy of belief. In the second place, we can not only take refuge in the fact that we have received the tradition and rumour from a distant period, but we can also produce greater proofs than this of these things. For most of the cities of Hellas, as a memorial of our services, send to us each year firstfruits of their corn, and those that omit to do so have often been commanded by the Pythia to pay the due proportion of their produce and perform their ancestral duties to our state. Yet can anything have stronger claims on our belief than that which is the subject of divine ordinance and of wide spread approval in Hellas, where ancient story bears common witness to present deeds, and modern events agree with the legends of men of old? Besides this, if we leave all this out of consideration and take a survey from the beginning, we shall find that those who first appeared upon the earth did not at once find life in its present condition, but little by little procured for themselves its advantages. Whom then should we think most likely either to receive it as a gift from the gods or to win it by their own efforts? Surely those who are admitted to have been the first to exist, and are at once most highly gifted for the pursuits of life and most piously disposed towards the gods. Now what high honour ought to accrue to those who have produced such great blessings, it were a superfluous task to point out; for no one could find a reward commensurate with what has been achieved.

So much then concerning the greatest of our good works, first accomplished and most universal in its effects. But, in the same period, Athens, seeing the barbarians occupying the greater part of the country, and the Hellenes confined in a small space and driven by scarcity of land into intestine conspiracies and civil wars, and perishing, either from want of daily necessities or in war, was not content to leave things so, but sent forth leaders into the states who took those most in need of subsistence, made themselves their generals and conquered the barbarians in war, founded many states on both continents, colonized all the islands, and saved both those who followed them and those who stayed behind; for to the latter they left the home country sufficient for their needs, and the former they provided with more territory than they already possessed; for they acquired all the surrounding districts of which we are now in occupation. In this way too they afforded great facilities to those who in later times wished to send out colonists and to imitate our state; for it was not necessary for them to run risk in acquiring new territory, but they could go and

live on land which we had marked out. Now who can show a leadership more ancestral than one which arose before most Hellenic cities were founded, or more beneficial than one which drove the barbarians from their homes, and led on the Hellenes to such prosperity?

Yet, after aiding in the accomplishment of the most pressing duties, Athens did not neglect the rest, but deemed it the first step only in a career of beneficence to find food for those in want, a step which is incumbent upon a people who aim at good government generally, and thinking that life which was limited to mere subsistence was not enough to make men desire to live, she devoted such close attention to the other interests of man, that of all the benefits which men enjoy, not derived from the gods but which we owe to our fellow-men, none have arisen without the aid of Athens, and most of them have been brought about by her agency. For finding the Hellenes living in lawlessness and dwelling in a scattered fashion, oppressed by tyrannies or being destroyed by anarchy, she also released them from these evils, either by becoming mistress of them or by making herself an example; for she was the first to lay down laws and establish a constitution. This is clear from the fact that, when men in the earliest times introduced indictments for homicide, and determined to settle their mutual disputes by argument and not by violence, they followed our laws in the mode of trial which they adopted.

Nay more, the arts also, whether useful for the necessities of life or contrived for pleasure, were by her either invented or put to proof and offered to the rest of the world for their use. In other respects, moreover, she ordered her administration in such a spirit of welcome to strangers and of friendliness to all, as to suit both those who were in want of money and those who desired to enjoy the wealth they possessed, and not to fail in serving either the prosperous, or those who were unfortunate in their own states, but so that each of these classes finds with us a delightful sojourn or a safe refuge. And further, since the territory possessed by the several states was not in every case self-sufficing, but was defective in some products and bore more than was sufficient of others, and much embarrassment arose where to dispose of the latter, and from whence to import the former, she provided a remedy for these troubles also; for she established the Piræus as a market in the centre of Hellas, of such superlative excellence that articles, which it is difficult for the several states to supply to each other one by one, can all be easily procured from Athens.

Now those who established the great festivals, are justly praised for handing down to us a custom which leads us to make treaties with one another, to reconcile the enmities that exist among us, and to assemble in one place; besides that, in making common prayers and sacrifices we are reminded of the original bond of kinship between us, and are more kindly disposed towards each other for the future, we renew old friendships and make new ones, and neither for ordinary men or for those of distinguished qualities is the time idly spent, but by the concourse of Hellenes opportunity arises for the latter to display their natural excellencies, and for the former to be spectators of their mutual contests, and neither spend their time dissatisfied, but each has whereof to be proud, the spectators when they see the competitors toiling on their behalf, and the competitors when they think that everyone has come to look at them. Great then as are the benefits we derive from the assemblies, in these respects, too, our state is not left behind. For indeed she can show many most beautiful spectacles, some passing all bounds in expenditure, others of high artistic repute, and some excellent in both

these respects; then, the multitude of strangers who visit us is also so great, that if there is any advantage in mutual intercourse, that also has been compassed by her. In addition to this, you can find with us the truest friendships and the most varied acquaintanceships; and, moreover, see contests not merely of speed and strength, but also of oratory and mind, and in all other productions of art, and for these the greatest prizes. For in addition to those which the state herself offers, she also helps to persuade others to bestow the like; for those recognized by us receive such credit as to be universally approved. Apart from this, whereas the other festivals are assembled at long intervals and soon dispersed, our state, on the contrary, is for those who visit her one long festival without ceasing.

Practical philosophy, moreover, which helped to discover and establish all these institutions, which at once educated us for action and softened our mutual intercourse, which distinguished calamities due to ignorance from those which spring from necessity, and taught us to avoid the former and nobly endure the latter, was introduced by Athens; she also paid honour to eloquence, which all men desire, and begrudge to those who are skilled in it: for she was aware that this is the only distinguishing characteristic which we of all creatures possess, and that by this we have won our position of superiority to all the rest of them; she saw that in other spheres of action men's fortunes are so capricious that often in them the wise fail and the foolish succeed, and that the proper and skilful use of language is beyond the reach of men of poor capacity, but is the function of a soul of sound wisdom, and that those who are considered clever or stupid differ from each other mainly in this respect; she saw, besides, that men who have received a liberal education from the very first are not to be known by courage, or wealth, or such-like advantages, but are most clearly recognised by their speech, and that this is the surest token which is manifested of the education of each one of us, and that those who make good use of language are not only influential in their own states, but also held in honour among other people. So far has Athens left the rest of mankind behind in thought and expression that her pupils have become the teachers of the world, and she has made the name of Hellas distinctive no longer of race but of intellect, and the title of Hellene a badge of education rather than of common descent.

But that I may not seem to be lingering over details of my subject when I proposed to treat of the whole, nor to be eulogizing Athens on these grounds from inability to praise her for her achievements in war, I will say no more to those who take pride in what I have mentioned; but I think that our forefathers deserve to be honoured as much for the dangers they incurred as for the rest of their services. Neither small nor few nor obscure were the struggles they endured, but many and terrible and great, some for their own country, others for the general liberty; for during the whole time they did not cease to open their state to all, and were the champions of those among the Hellenes who from time to time were the victims of oppression. For that very reason some accuse us of a foolish policy, in that we have been accustomed to support the weaker, as if such arguments did not rather justify our admirers. For it was not in ignorance of the superiority of great alliances in regard to security that we took these counsels concerning them, but, while knowing much more accurately than other men the results of such a course, we nevertheless preferred to help the weak even against our interest rather than for profit's sake to join in the oppressions of the strong. . . .

Now I ought, I think, to speak also of the achievements of Athens against the barbarians, especially as the leadership of Hellas against them was the original subject of my speech. Now if I were to enumerate all the perils we went through I should be telling too long a tale; but in dealing with the greatest of them I will try to adopt the same method of narration that I followed just now. For the races best fitted for rule and the possessors of the widest imperial power are the Scythians, the Thracians, and the Persians, and it happens that all these have had hostile designs against us, and that our state has fought decisively against all of them. Now what arguments will be left for my opponents, if I can prove that, if any of the Hellenes were unable to get justice, it was to Athens that they directed their petitions, and that, when barbarians wished to enslave Hellas, Athens was the first object of their attacks? . . .

Now honourable indeed are these deeds, and befitting those who dispute for the leadership; but akin to those which I have mentioned, and such as were to be expected from the descendants of men so great, were the achievements of those who made war against Darius and Xerxes. For although that was the greatest war ever set on foot, and never had so many perilous struggles taken place at one and the same time—against enemies who fancied themselves irresistible on account of their numbers, and allies who considered their valour unsurpassable—our ancestors conquered both, in the way that was suitable in each case, and proving superior in the face of every danger, earned as an immediate reward the meed of valour, and not long afterwards obtained the dominion of the sea, at the gift of the rest of the Hellenes, and without dispute from those who now seek to rob us of it.

Now let no one think me ignorant that the Lacedæmonians, too, in those critical times deserved credit for many good services to Hellas; but on this account I have even more reason to praise our state, in that, in conflict with such great competitors, she proved so far superior to them. But I wish to speak a little more at length about these two states, and not to skim over the subject too quickly, that it may be to us a memorial, both of the valour of our ancestors and of the hatred of the barbarians. And yet I am not unaware that it is difficult for one who comes latest to the task to speak of a subject long ago occupied by previous speakers, and on which those citizens best able to speak have often spoken on the occasion of public funerals; for it follows that the chief part must have been already used up, and only a few unimportant points omitted. Nevertheless, starting from what still remains to be said, since it is convenient for my purpose, I must not shrink from making mention concerning them.

Now I think that the greatest services have been rendered and the greatest praises deserved by those who exposed their persons in the forefront of danger for the sake of Hellas; yet it is not fair either to forget those who lived before this war and held power in these two states respectively. For they it was who trained beforehand those coming after them, inclined the multitude to virtue, and created formidable antagonists for the barbarians. For they did not despise the public interests, nor enjoy the resources of the state as their own, while neglecting her interests as no concern of theirs; but they were as solicitous for the common welfare as for their own domestic happiness, and at the same time properly stood aloof from matters which did not affect them. They did not estimate happiness by the standard of money, but they thought that the surest and best wealth was possessed by the man who pursued such conduct as would enable him to gain the best reputation for himself and leave behind the greatest fame for his children. They did not emulate one another's shameless audacity, nor cultivate effrontery in their own persons, but deemed it more terrible to be ill-spoken of by their fellow-citizens than to die nobly for the state, and were more ashamed of public errors than they are now of their own personal faults. The reason of this was that they took care that their laws should be exact and good, those concerned with the relations of every-day life even more than those that had to do with private contracts. For they knew that good men and true will have no need of many written documents, but, whether on public or private matters, will easily come to an agreement by the aid of a few recognised principles. Such was their public spirit, that the object of their political parties was to dispute, not which should destroy the other and rule over the rest, but which should be first in doing some service to the state; and they organized their clubs, not for their private interests, but for the benefit of the people. They pursued the same method in their dealings with other states, treating the Hellenes with deference and not with insolence, considering that their rule over them should be that of a general, not of a despot, and desiring to be addressed as leaders rather than masters, and to be entitled saviours and not reviled as destroyers; they won over states by kindness instead of overthrowing them by force; they made their word more trustworthy than their oath is now, and thought it their duty to abide by treaties as by the decrees of necessity; not proud of their power so much as ambitious to live in self-restraint, they thought it right to have the same feelings towards their inferiors as they expected their superiors to have towards them, and they considered their own cities as merely private towns, while they looked upon Hellas as their common fatherland. Possessed of such ideas, and educating the younger generation in such manners, they brought to light such valiant men in those who fought against the barbarians from Asia, that no one, either poet or sophist, has ever yet been able to speak in a manner worthy of their achievements. And I can readily excuse them; for it is as hard to praise those who have surpassed the virtues of other men as those who have never done anything good; for whereas the latter have no deeds to support them, the former have no language befitting them. For what language could be commensurate with the deeds of men who were so far superior to those who made the expedition against Troy, that, while they spent ten years against one city, those men in a short time defeated the whole might of Asia, and not only saved their own countries but also liberated the whole of Hellas? And what deeds or toils or dangers would they have shrunk from attempting in order to win living reputations, when they were so readily willing to lose their lives for the sake of a posthumous fame? And I even think that the war must have been contrived by one of the gods in admiration of their valour, that men of such quality should not remain in obscurity nor end their lives ingloriously, but should be thought worthy of the same rewards as those children of the gods who are called demigods; for even their bodies the gods rendered up to the inflexible laws of nature, but made immortal the memory of their valour.

Now, continuous as was the jealousy between our ancestors and the Lacedæmonians, yet in those times they exercised their rivalry for the highest objects, considering themselves to be not enemies but competitors, and not courting the barbarian with a view to the servitude of Hellas, but having one aim in the common safety, their only rivalry being which of them should achieve it. Now the first proof they gave of their high qualities was on the occasion of the expedition sent by Darius: for when the enemy landed in Attica our ancestors on their part did not wait for their allies; but, treating the

public peril as if it were their own, they went with their own forces alone to meet a foe who had despised the whole of Hellas, prepared with their small numbers to encounter many myriads, as if other men's lives and not their own were at stake; and the Lacedæmonians no sooner heard of the war in Attica than, neglecting everything else, they came to help us, making as much haste as if their own country were being laid waste. A proof of their rapidity and emulation is that our ancestors are said on one and the same day to have heard of the landing of the barbarians, marched out to protect the borders of their territory, fought a victorious engagement and set up a trophy over their enemies, while the Lacedæmonians in three days and as many nights traversed twelve hundred stadia in marching order. So strenuously did they hasten, the one to share in the dangers, and the others to fight before reinforcements should arrive. The next occasion was that of the subsequent expedition, which Xerxes led in person, leaving his royal residence and making bold to become a general, and collecting all Asia together; in the description of whose fall the highest flights of eloquence have fallen short of the reality. He reached such a pitch of arrogance that, deeming it a small task to subdue Hellas, and wishing to leave such a memorial behind him as human nature cannot attain to, he did not cease till he had devised and forced to completion the feat which is in everyone's mouth, of sailing with his army across the mainland and marching on foot through the sea, by bridging the Hellespont, and cutting a canal through Athos.

It was one, then, of such lofty pride and such great achievements, master of so many men, that they went to encounter, dividing the risk between them,—the Lacedæmonians to Thermopylæ against his land forces, choosing a thousand of their number and taking a few of their allies with them, intending in the narrow pass to bar their further advance, and our ancestors to Artemisium, having manned sixty triremes against the whole fleet of the enemy. And they took heart to do these things, not so much from contempt of their enemies as in rivalry with each other, the Lacedæmonians envying our state the battle of Marathon and seeking to do the like, and fearing lest twice in succession Athens should bring deliverance to the Hellenes, while our people on their part wished above all to preserve their existing fame, and to make it clear to all that their former victory too was due to valour and not to luck, and in the next place also to encourage the Hellenes to undertake a sea-fight, by proving to them that in naval ventures just as in those by land it is the prowess of the common people that prevails. But though they displayed equal daring, their fortunes were not alike; the Lacedæmonians were destroyed—their spirits were victorious—their bodies only fainted and failed (for indeed it would be a sin to say that they were defeated; for no one of them deigned to flee); our ancestors on their part defeated the advanced squadron, but when they heard that the enemy were masters of the pass, they sailed back home, arranged affairs in the city, and directed the remainder of their efforts so well, that, many and glorious as were their previous achievements, they excelled yet more in the closing scenes of their perils. For . . . though they might have not merely escaped the dangers besetting them, but have received special distinctions, which the Great King offered them in the belief that, if he added the fleet of our state to his forces, he would immediately conquer Peloponnesus as well,—they would hear nothing of his gifts, nor did they in anger against the Hellenes for their betrayal gladly hasten to make terms with the barbarians, but for their part they made ready to fight for freedom, and forgave the others for preferring slavery. For they considered that, though the humble states were right in seeking safety by every means, those which claimed to be at the head of Hellas could not possibly try to escape their peril. . . .

Now when an expedition against the barbarians is being proposed, who ought to have the leadership? Surely they who in the former war won the greatest fame, having often borne the brunt on their own shoulders, and in united contests having gained the prize of valour. Surely they who abandoned their own country for the general deliverance, and who not only in olden times founded the most of the Hellenic states, but also in later days rescued them from the greatest disasters. Should we not be most hardly treated, if, after having endured the largest share of troubles, we should be thought worthy of a lesser share of honours, and, after having in those days occupied the foremost post, should now be compelled to follow the lead of others?

—J. H. FREESE.

ATHENS, AWAKE!

DEMOSTHENES

[Third Olynthiac]

Demosthenes was born in 384 B.C., lived most of his life in Athens, and killed himself by poison in 322 to escape being captured by the Macedonians.

Demosthenes was the leading Athenian statesman in the period of the rise of Macedon to world power. He foresaw and vigorously opposed the designs of Philip, proclaiming in ringing speeches, which are named *The Philippics,* the new dangers confronting Greece, and passionately advocating a policy of nationalism to ward them off. His orations show clearly the contrast that exists between speeches framed for the practical uses of promoting policies and those of a man like Isocrates, which are the result of rhetorical theory and intended as works of art.

Building on a technique that had been perfected by generations of orators before him, avoiding the extreme simplicity of Lysias and the artificiality of Isocrates, adding a splendid vocabulary and a rhythmic melody, giving emphasis to all these qualities by a burning patriotism and a tremendous vigor of delivery, he won for himself the reputation of the greatest of Greek orators. About forty of his orations are extant.

The Olynthiac orations were prompted by an appeal from the people of Olynthus in 349 B.C. for aid in resisting the move of Philip against them. The Athenians themselves were not in immediate danger, but Demosthenes saw in the attack on Olynthus an indication of what was to come at a later time.

Not the same ideas, men of Athens, are presented to me, when I look at our condition, and when at the speeches which are delivered. The speeches, I find, are about punishing Philip; but our condition is come to this, that we must mind we are not first damaged ourselves. Therefore, it seems to me, these orators commit the simple error of not laying before you the true subject of debate. That once we might safely have held our own and punished Philip too, I know well enough; both have been possible in my own time, not very long ago. But now, I am persuaded, it is sufficient in the first instance to effect the preservation of our allies. When this has been secured, one may look out for revenge on Philip; but before we lay the foundation right, I deem it idle to talk about the end.

The present crisis, O Athenians, requires, if any ever did, much thought and counsel. Not that I am puzzled, what advice to give in the matter; I am only doubtful, in what way, Athenians, to address you thereupon. For I have been taught both by hearsay and experience, that most of your advantages have

escaped you, from unwillingness to do your duty, not from ignorance. I request you, if I speak my mind, to be patient, and consider only, whether I speak the truth, and with a view to future amendment. You see to what wretched plight we are reduced by some men haranguing for popularity.

I think it necessary, however, first to recall to your memory a few past events. You remember, Athenians, when news came three or four years ago, that Philip was in Thrace besieging Heræum. It was then the fifth month, and after much discussion and tumult in the assembly you resolved to launch forty galleys, that every citizen under forty-five should embark, and a tax be raised of sixty talents. That year passed; the first, second, third month arrived; in that month, reluctantly, after the mysteries, you dispatched Charidemus with ten empty ships and five talents of money; for as Philip was reported to be sick or dead (both rumors came), you thought there was no longer any occasion for succors, and discontinued the armament. But that was the very occasion; if we had then sent our succors quickly, as we resolved, Philip would not have been saved to trouble us now.

Those events can not be altered. But here is the crisis of another war, the cause why I mentioned the past, that you may not repeat your error. How shall we deal with it, men of Athens? If you lend not the utmost possible aid, see how you will have manœuvred every thing for Philip's benefit. There were the Olynthians, possessed of some power; and matters stood thus: Philip distrusted them and they Philip. We negotiated for peace with them; this hampered (as it were) and annoyed Philip, that a great city, reconciled to us, should be watching opportunities against him. We thought it necessary by all means to make that people his enemies; and lo, what erewhile you clamored for, has somehow or other been accomplished. Then what remains, Athenians, but to assist them vigorously and promptly? I know not. For besides the disgrace that would fall upon us, if we sacrificed any of our interests, I am alarmed for the consequences, seeing how the Thebans are affected toward us, the Phocian treasury exhausted, nothing to prevent Philip, when he has subdued what lies before him, from turning to matters here. Whoever postpones until then the performance of his duty, wishes to see the peril at hand, when he may hear of it elsewhere, and to seek auxiliaries for himself, when he may be auxiliary to others; for that this will be the issue, if we throw away our present advantage, we all know pretty well.

But, it may be said, we have resolved that succors are necessary, and we will send them; tell us only how. Marvel not then, Athenians, if I say something to astonish the multitude. Appoint law-revisers: at their session enact no statutes, for you have enough, but repeal those which are at present injurious; I mean, just plainly, the laws concerning our theatrical fund; and some concerning the troops, whereof the former divide the military fund among stayers-at-home for theatrical amusement, the latter indemnify deserters, and so dishearten men well inclined to the service. When you have repealed these, and made the road to good counsel safe, then find a man to propose what you all know to be desirable. But before doing so, look not for one who will advise good measures and be destroyed by you for his pains. Such a person you will not find, especially as the only result would be, for the adviser and mover to suffer wrongfully, and, without forwarding matters, to render good counsel still more dangerous in the future. Besides, Athenians, you should require the same men to repeal these laws, who have introduced them. It is unjust, that their authors should enjoy a popularity which has injured the commonwealth, while the adviser of salutary measures suffers by a displeasure that may lead to general improvement. Till this is set right, Athenians, look not that anyone should be so powerful with you as to transgress these laws with impunity, or so senseless as to plunge into ruin right before him.

Another thing, too, you should observe, Athenians, that a decree is worth nothing, without a readiness on your part to do what you determine. Could decrees of themselves compel you to perform your duty, or execute what they prescribe, neither would you with many decrees have accomplished little or nothing, nor would Philip have insulted you so long. Had it depended on decrees, he would have been chastised long ago. But the course of things is otherwise. Action, posterior in order of time to speaking and voting, is in efficacy prior and superior. This requisite you want; the others you possess. There are among you, Athenians, men competent to advise what is needful, and you are exceedingly quick at understanding it; ay, and you will be able now to perform it, if you act rightly. For what time or season would you have better than the present? When will you do your duty, if not now? Has not the man got possession of all our strongholds? And if he become master of this country, shall we not incur foul disgrace? Are not they, to whom we promised sure protection in case of war, at this moment in hostilities? Is he not an enemy, holding our possessions—a barbarian—anything you like to call him? But, O heavens! after permitting, almost helping him to accomplish these things, shall we inquire who were to blame for them? I know we shall not take the blame to ourselves. For so in battles, no runaway accuses himself, but his general, his neighbor, any one rather; though, sure enough, the defeat is owing to all the runaways; for each one who accuses the rest might have stood his ground, and had each done so they would have conquered. Now then, does any man not give the best advice? Let another rise and give it, but not censure the last speaker. Does a second give better advice? Follow it, and success attend you! Perhaps it is not pleasant: but that is not the speaker's fault, unless he omits some needful prayer. To pray is simple enough, Athenians, collecting all that one desires in a short petition: but to decide, when measures are the subject of consideration, is not quite so easy; for we must choose the profitable rather than the pleasant, where both are not compatible.

But if any one can let alone our theatrical fund, and suggest other supplies for the military, is he not cleverer? it may be asked. I grant it, if this were possible: but I wonder if any man ever was or will be able, after wasting his means in useless expenses, to find means for useful. The wishes of men are indeed a great help to such arguments, and therefore the easiest thing in the world is self-deceit; for every man believes what he wishes, though the reality is often different. See then, Athenians, what the realities allow, and you will be able to serve and have pay. It becomes not a wise or magnanimous people, to neglect military operations for want of money, and bear disgraces like these; or, while you snatch up arms to march against Corinthians and Megarians, to let Philip enslave Greek cities for lack of provisions for your troops.

I have not spoken for the idle purpose of giving offense: I am not so foolish or perverse, as to provoke your displeasure without intending your good: but I think an upright citizen should prefer the advancement of the commonweal to the gratification of his audience. And I hear, as perhaps you do, that the speakers in our ancestors' time, whom all that address you praise, but not exactly imitate, were politicians after this form and fashion;—Aristides, Nicias, my namesake, Pericles. But since these orators have appeared, who ask, What is your pleasure? what shall I move? how can I oblige you? the public welfare is complimented away for a moment's popularity, and these are the results; the orators thrive, you are disgraced. Mark, O Athenians, what a summary contrast may be drawn between the doings in our olden time and in yours. It is a tale brief and familiar to all; for the examples by which you may still be happy are found not abroad, men of Athens, but at home. Our forefathers, whom the speakers humored not nor caressed, as these men caress you, for five-and-forty years took the leadership of the Greeks by general consent, and brought above ten thousand talents into the citadel; and the king of this country was submissive to them, as a barbarian should be to Greeks; and many glorious trophies they erected for victories won by their own fighting on land and sea, and they are the sole people in the world who have bequeathed a renown superior to envy. Such were their merits in the affairs of Greece: see what they were at home, both as citizens and as men. Their public works are edifices and ornaments of such beauty and grandeur in temples and consecrated furniture, that posterity have no power to surpass them. In private they were so modest and attached to the principle of our constitution, that whoever knows the style of house which Aristides had, or Miltiades, and the illustrious of that day, perceives it to be no grander than those of the neighbors. Their politics were not for money-making; each felt it his duty to exalt the commonwealth. By a conduct honorable towards the Greeks, pious to the gods, brotherlike among themselves, they justly attained a high prosperity.

So fared matters with them under the statesmen I have mentioned. How fare they with you under the worthies of our time? Is there any likeness or resemblance? I pass over other topics, on which I could expatiate; but observe: in this utter absence of competitors (Lacedæmonians depressed, Thebans employed, none of the rest capable of disputing the supremacy with us), when we might hold our own securely and arbitrate the claims of others we have been deprived of our rightful territory, and spent above fifteen hundred talents to no purpose; the allies, whom we gained in war, these persons have lost in peace, and we have trained up against ourselves an enemy thus formidable. Or let any one come forward and tell me, by whose contrivance but ours Philip has grown strong. Well, sir, this looks bad, but things at home are better. What proof can be adduced? The parapets that are whitewashed? The roads that are repaired? fountains, and fooleries? Look at the men of whose statesmanship these are the fruits. They have risen from beggary to opulence, and from obscurity to honor; some have made their private houses more splendid than the public buildings; and in proportion as the state has declined, their fortunes have been exalted.

What has produced these results? How is it that all went prosperously then, and now goes wrong? Because anciently the people, having the courage to be soldiers, controlled the statesmen, and disposed of all emoluments; any of the rest was happy to receive from the people his share of honor, office, or advantage. Now, contrariwise, the statesmen dispose of emoluments; through them every thing is done; you the people, enervated, stripped of treasure and allies, are become as underlings and hangers-on, happy if these persons dole you out showmoney or send you paltry beeves; and, the unmanliest part of all, you are grateful for receiving your own. They, cooping you in the city, lead you to your pleasures, and make you tame and submissive to their hands. It is impossible, I say, to have a high and noble spirit, while you are engaged in petty and mean employments: whatever be the pursuits of men, their characters must be similar. By Ceres, I should not wonder, if I, for mentioning these things, suffered more from your resentment than the men who have brought them to pass. For even liberty of speech you allow not on all subjects; I marvel indeed you have allowed it here.

Would you but even now, renouncing these practices, perform military service and act worthily of yourselves; would you employ these domestic superfluities as a means to gain advantage abroad; perhaps, Athenians, perhaps you might gain some solid and important advantage, and be rid of these perquisites, which are like the diet ordered by physicians for the sick. As that neither imparts strength, nor suffers the patient to die, so your allowances are not enough to be of substantial benefit, nor yet permit you to reject them and turn to something else. Thus do they increase the general apathy. What? I shall be asked: mean you stipendiary service? Yes, and forthwith the same arrangement for all, Athenians, that each, taking his dividend from the public, may be what the state requires. Is peace to be had? You are better at home, under no compulsion to act dishonorably from indigence. Is there such an emergency as the present? Better to be a soldier, as you ought, in your country's cause, maintained by those very allowances. Is any one of you beyond the military age? What he now irregularly takes without doing service, let him take by just regulation, superintending and transacting needful business. Thus, without derogating from or adding to our political system, only removing some irregularity, I bring it into order, establishing a uniform rule for receiving money, for serving in war, for sitting on juries, for doing what each according to his age can do, and what occasion requires. I never advise we should give to idlers the wages of the diligent, or sit at leisure, passive and helpless, to hear that such a one's mercenaries are victorious; as we now do. Not that I blame any one who does you a service: I only call upon you, Athenians, to perform on your own account those duties for which you honor strangers, and not to surrender that post of dignity which, won through many glorious dangers, your ancestors have bequeathed.

I have said nearly all that I think necessary. I trust you will adopt that course which is best for the country and yourselves.

—C. R. KENNEDY.

GREECE AGAINST PHILIP

DEMOSTHENES

[Third Philippic]

The third *Philippic,* delivered in 341 B.C., contains the definite statement of Demosthenes' plan for a federation of Greek states. The orator succeeded in rousing the Athenians and certain of their near neighbors for the time being to the necessity for action, but in the face of actual defeat in the field he was unable to hold them together for any length of time.

Many speeches, men of Athens, are made in almost every assembly about the hostilities of Philip, hostilities which ever since the treaty of peace he has been committting as well against you as against the rest of the Greeks; and all (I am sure) are ready to avow, though they forbear to do so, that our counsels and our measures should be directed to his humiliation and chastisement: nevertheless, so low have our affairs been brought by inattention and negligence, I fear it is a harsh truth to say, that if

all the orators had sought to suggest, and you to pass resolutions for the utter ruining of the commonwealth, we could not methinks be worse off than we are. A variety of circumstances may have brought us to this state; our affairs have not declined from one or two causes only: but, if you rightly examine, you will find it chiefly owing to the orators, who study to please you rather than advise for the best. Some of whom, Athenians, seeking to maintain the basis of their power and repute, have no forethought for the future, and therefore think you also ought to have none; others, accusing and calumniating practical statesmen, labor only to make Athens punish Athens, and in such occupations to engage her, that Philip may have liberty to say and do what he pleases. Politics of this kind are common here, but are the causes of your failures and embarrassment. I beg, Athenians, that you will not resent my plain speaking of the truth. Only consider. You hold liberty of speech in other matters to be the general right of all residents of Athens, insomuch that you allow a measure of it even to foreigners and slaves, and many servants may be seen among you speaking their thoughts more freely than citizens in some other states; and yet you have altogether banished it from your councils. The result has been, that in the assembly you give yourself airs and are flattered at hearing nothing but compliments, in your measures and proceedings you are brought to the utmost peril. If such be your disposition now, I must be silent: if you will listen to good advice without flattery, I am ready to speak. For though our affairs are in a deplorable condition, though many sacrifices have been made, still, if you will choose to perform your duty, it is possible to repair it all. A paradox, and yet a truth, am I about to state. That which is the most lamentable in the past is best for the future. How is this?

Because you performed no part of your duty, great or small, and therefore you fared ill: had you done all that became you, and your situation were the same, there would be no hope of amendment. Philip has indeed prevailed over your sloth and negligence, but not over your country: you have not been worsted; you have not even bestirred yourselves.

If now we were all agreed that Philip is at war with Athens and infringing the peace, nothing would a speaker need to urge and advise but the safest and easiest way of resisting him. But since, at the very time when Philip is capturing cities and retaining divers of our dominions and assailing all people, there are men so unreasonable as to listen to repeated declarations in the assembly, that some of us are kindling war, one must be cautious and set this matter right: for whoever moves or advises a measure of defence, is in danger of being accused afterward as the author of the war.

I will first then examine and determine this point, whether it be in our power to deliberate on peace or war. If the country may be at peace, if it depends on us (to begin with this), I say we ought to maintain peace, and I call upon the affirmant to move a resolution to take some measure, and not to palter with us. But if another, having arms in his hand and a large force around him, amuses you with the name of peace, while he carries on the operations of war, what is left but to defend yourselves? You may profess to be at peace, if you like, as he does; I quarrel not with that. But if any man supposes this to be a peace, which will enable Philip to master all else and attack you last, he is a madman, or he talks of a peace observed toward him by you, not toward you by him. This it is that Philip purchases by all his expenditure, the privilege of assailing you without being assailed in turn.

If we really wait until he avows that he is at war with us, we are the simplest of mortals, for he would not declare that, though he marched even against Attica and Piræus, at least if we may judge from his conduct to others. For example, to the Olynthians he declared, when he was forty furlongs from their city, that there was no alternative, but either they must quit Olynthus or he Macedonia; though before that time, whenever he was accused of such an intent, he took it ill and sent ambassadors to justify himself. Again, he marched towards the Phocians as if they were allies, and there were Phocian envoys who accompanied his march, and many among you contended that his advance would not benefit the Thebans. And he came into Thessaly of late as a friend and ally, yet he has taken possession of Pheræ; and lastly he told those wretched people of Oreus, that he had sent his soldiers out of good-will to visit them, as he heard they were in trouble and dissension, and it was the part of allies and true friends to lend assistance on such occasions. People who would never have harmed him, though they might have adopted measures of defence, he chose to deceive rather than warn them of his attack; and think ye he would declare war against you before he began it, and that while you are willing to be deceived? Impossible. He would be the silliest of mankind, if, while you the injured parties make no complaint against him, but are accusing your own countrymen, he should terminate your intestine strife and jealousies, warn you to turn against him, and remove the pretexts of his hirelings for asserting, to amuse you, that he makes no war upon Athens. O heavens! would any rational being judge by words rather than by actions, who is at peace with him and who at war? Surely none. Well then; Philip immediately after the peace, before Diopithes was in command or the settlers in the Chersonese had been sent out, took Serrium and Doriscus, and expelled from Serrium and the Sacred

Mount the troops whom your general had stationed there. What do you call such conduct? He had sworn the peace. Don't say—what does it signify? how is the state concerned?—Whether it be a trifling matter, or of no concernment to you, is a different question: religion and justice have the same obligation, be the subject of the offense great or small. Tell me now; when he sends mercenaries into Chersonesus, which the king and all the Greeks have acknowledged to be yours, when he avows himself an auxiliary and writes us word so, what are such proceedings? He says he is not at war; I can not however admit such conduct to be an observance of the peace; far otherwise: I say, by his attempt on Megara, by his setting up despotism in Euboea, by his present advance into Thrace, by his intrigues in Peloponnesus, by the whole course of operations with his army, he has been breaking the peace and making war upon you; unless indeed you will say, that those who establish batteries are not at war, until they apply them to the walls. But that you will not say: for whoever contrives and prepares the means of my conquest, is at war with me, before he darts or draws the bow. What, if any thing should happen, is the risk you run? The alienation of the Hellespont, the subjugation of Megara and Euboea to your enemy, the siding of the Peloponnesians with him. Then can I allow, that one who sets such an engine at work against Athens is at peace with her? Quite the contrary. From the day he destroyed the Phocians I date his commencement of hostilities. Defend yourselves instantly, and I say you will be wise: delay it, and you may wish in vain to do so hereafter. So much do I dissent from your other counselors, men of Athens, that I deem any discussion about Chersonesus or Byzantium out of place. Succor them—I advise that —watch that no harm befalls them, send all necessary supplies to your troops in

that quarter; but let your deliberations be for the safety of all Greece, as being in the utmost peril. I must tell you why I am so alarmed at the state of our affairs: that, if my reasonings are correct, you may share them, and make some provision at least for yourselves, however disinclined to do so for others: but if, in your judgment, I talk nonsense and absurdity, you may treat me as crazed, and not listen to me, either now or in the future.

That Philip from a mean and humble origin has grown mighty, that the Greeks are jealous and quarreling among themselves, that it was far more wonderful for him to rise from that insignificance, than it would be now, after so many acquisitions, to conquer what is left; these and similar matters, which I might dwell upon, I pass over. But I observe that all people, beginning with you, have conceded to him a right, which in former times has been the subject of contest in every Grecian war. And what is this? The right of doing what he pleases, openly fleecing and pillaging the Greeks, one after another, attacking and enslaving their cities. You were at the head of the Greeks for seventy-three years, the Lacedæmonians for twenty-nine; and the Thebans had some power in these latter times after the battle of Leuctra. Yet neither you, my countrymen, nor Thebans nor Lacedæmonians, were ever licensed by the Greeks to act as you pleased; far otherwise. When you, or rather the Athenians of that time, appeared to be dealing harshly with certain people, all the rest, even such as had no complaint against Athens, thought proper to side with the injured parties in a war against her. So, when the Lacedæmonians became masters and succeeded to your empire, on their attempting to encroach and make oppressive innovations, a general war was declared against them, even by such as had no cause of complaint. But wherefore mention other people? We ourselves and the Lacedæmonians, although at the outset we could not allege any natural injuries, thought proper to make war for the injustice that we saw done to our neighbors. Yet all the faults committed by the Spartans in those thirty years, and by our ancestors in the seventy, are less, men of Athens, than the wrongs which, in thirteen incomplete years that Philip has been uppermost, he has inflicted on the Greeks: nay they are scarcely a fraction of these, as may easily be shown in a few words. Olynthus and Methone and Apollonia, and thirty-two cities on the borders of Thrace, I pass over; all which he has so cruelly destroyed, that a visitor could scarcely tell if they were ever inhabited: and of the Phocians, so considerable a people exterminated, I say nothing. But what is the condition of Thessaly? Has he not taken away her constitutions and her cities, and established tetrarchies, to parcel her out, not only by cities, but also by provinces, for subjection? Are not the Eubœan states governed now by despots, and that in an island near to Thebes and Athens? Does he not expressly write in his epistles, "I am at peace with those who are willing to obey me?" Nor does he write so and not act accordingly. He is gone to the Hellespont; he marched formerly against Ambracia; Elis, such an important city in Peloponnesus, he possesses; he plotted lately to get Megara; neither Hellenic nor Barbaric land contains the man's ambition. And we the Greek community, seeing and hearing this, instead of sending embassies to one another about it and expressing indignation, are in such a miserable state, so intrenched in our miserable towns, that to this day we can not combine, or form any association for succor and alliance; we look unconcernedly on the man's growing power, each resolving (methinks) to enjoy the interval that another is destroyed in, not caring or striving for the salvation

of Greece: for none can be ignorant, that Philip, like some course or attack of fever or other disease, is coming even on those that yet seem very far removed. And you must be sensible, that whatever wrong the Greeks sustained from Lacedæmonians or from us, was at least inflicted by genuine people of Greece; and it might be felt in the same manner as if a lawful son, born to a large fortune, committed some fault or error in the management of it; on that ground one would consider him open to censure and reproach, yet it could not be said that he was an alien, and not heir to the property which he so dealt with. But if a slave or a spurious child wasted and spoiled what he had no interest in— Heavens! how much more heinous and hateful would all have pronounced it! And yet in regard to Philip and his conduct they feel not this, although he is not only no Greek and noway akin to Greeks, but not even a Barbarian of a place honorable to mention; in fact, a vile fellow of Macedon, from which a respectable slave could not be purchased formerly.

What is wanting to make his insolence complete? Besides his destruction of Grecian cities, does he not hold the Pythian games, the common festival of Greece, and, if he comes not himself, send his vassals to preside? Is he not master of Thermopylæ and the passes into Greece, and, holds he not those places by garrisons and mercenaries? Has he not thrust aside Thessalians, ourselves, Dorians, the whole Amphictyonic body, and got preaudience of the oracle, to which even the Greeks do not all pretend? Does he not write to the Thessalians, what form of government to adopt? send mercenaries to Porthmus, to expel the Eretrian commonalty; others to Oreus, to set up Philistides as ruler? Yet the Greeks endure to see all this; methinks they view it as they would a hailstorm, each praying that it may not fall on himself, none trying to prevent it. And not only are the outrages which he does to Greece submitted to, but even the private wrongs of every people; nothing can go beyond this! Has he not wronged the Corinthians by attacking Ambracia and Leucas? the Achaians, by swearing to give Naupactus to the Ætolians? from the Thebans taken Echinus? Is he not marching against the Byzantines his allies? From us—I omit the rest—but keeps he not Cardia, the greatest city of the Chersonese? Still under these indignities we are all slack and disheartened, and look toward our neighbors, distrusting one another, instead of the common enemy. And how think ye a man, who behaves so insolently to all, how will he act, when he gets each separately under his control?

But what has caused this mischief? There must be some cause, some good reason, why the Greeks were so eager for liberty then, and now are eager for servitude. There was something, men of Athens, something in the hearts of the multitude then, which there is not now, which overcame the wealth of Persia, and maintained the freedom of Greece, and quailed not under any battle by land or sea; the loss whereof has ruined all, and thrown the affairs of Greece into confusion. What was this? Nothing subtle or clever: simply that whoever took money from the aspirants for power or the corruptors of Greece were universally detested: it was dreadful to be convicted of bribery; the severest punishment was inflicted on the guilty, and there was no intercession or pardon. The favorable moments for enterprise, which fortune frequently offers to the careless against the vigilant, to them that will do nothing against those that discharge all their duty, could not be bought from orators or generals; no more could mutual concord, nor distrust of tyrants and barbarians, nor anything of the kind. But now all such principles have been sold as in open market, and those imported in exchange, by which Greece is ruined and diseased. What are they? Envy where a man gets a bribe; laughter if he confesses it; mercy to the convicted; hatred of those that denounce the crime: all the usual attendants upon corruption. For as to ships and men and revenues and abundance of other materials, all that may be reckoned as constituting national strength—assuredly the Greeks of our day are more fully and perfectly supplied with such advantages than the Greeks of the olden time. But they are all rendered useless, unavailable, unprofitable, by the agency of these traffickers.

That such is the present state of things, you must see, without requiring my testimony: that it was different in former times, I will demonstrate, not by speaking my own words, but by showing an inscription of your ancestors, which they graved on a brazen column and deposited in the citadel, not for their own benefit (they were right-minded enough without such records) but for a memorial and example to instruct you, how seriously such conduct should be taken up. What says the inscription then? It says: "Let Arthmius, son of Pythonax the Zelite, be declared an outlaw, and an enemy of the Athenian people and their allies, him and his family." Then the cause is written why this was done: because he brought Median gold into Peloponnesus. That is the inscription. By the gods! only consider and reflect among yourselves, what must have been the spirit, what the dignity of those Athenians who acted so! One Arthmius a Zelite, subject of the king (for Zelea is in Asia), because in his master's service he brought gold into Peloponnesus, not to Athens, they proclaimed an enemy of the Athenians and their allies, him and his family, and outlawed. That is, not the outlawry commonly spoken of: for what would a Zelite care, to be excluded from Athenian franchises? It means not that; but in the statutes of homicide it is written, in cases where prosecution for murder is not allowed, but killing is sanctioned, "and let him die an outlaw," says the legislator: by which he means, that whoever kills such a person shall be unpolluted. Therefore they considered that the preservation of all Greece was their own concern: (but for such an opinion, they would not have cared, whether people in Peloponnesus were bought and corrupted): and whomsoever they discovered taking bribes, they chastised and punished so severely as to record their names in brass. The natural result was, that Greece was formidable to the Barbarian, not the Barbarian to Greece. 'Tis not so now: since neither in this nor in other respects are your sentiments the same. But what are they? You know yourselves: why am I to upbraid you with every thing? The Greeks in general are alike and no better than you. Therefore I say, our present affairs demand earnest attention and wholesome counsel. Shall I say what? Do you bid me, and won't you be angry?

[Here is read the public document which Demosthenes produces, after which he resumes his address.]

There is a foolish saying of persons who wish to make us easy, that Philip is not yet as powerful as the Lacedæmonians were formerly, who ruled everywhere by land and sea, and had the king for their ally, and nothing withstood them; yet Athens resisted even that nation, and was not destroyed. I myself believe, that, while every thing has received great improvement, and the present bears no resemblance to the past, nothing has been so changed and improved as the practice of war. For anciently, as I am informed, the Lacedæmonians and all Grecian people would for four or five months, during the season only, invade and ravage the land of their enemies with heavy-armed and national troops, and return home again: and their ideas were so old-fashioned, or rather national, they never purchased an advantage from any; theirs was a legitimate and open warfare. But now you doubtless perceive, that the majority of disasters have been effected by treason; nothing is done in fair field or combat. You hear of Philip marching where he pleases, not because he commands troops of the line, but because he has attached to him a host of skirmishers, cavalry, archers, mercenaries, and the like. When with these he falls upon a people in civil dissension, and none (for mistrust) will march out to defend the country, he applies engines and besieges them. I need not mention, that he makes no difference between winter and summer, that he has no stated season of repose. You, knowing these things, reflecting on them, must not let the war approach your territories, nor get your necks broken, relying on the simplicity of the old war with the Lacedæmonians, but take the longest time beforehand for defensive measures and preparations, see that he stirs not from home, avoid any decisive engagement. For a war, if we choose, men of Athens, to pursue a right course, we have many natural advantages; such as the position of his kingdom, which we may extensively plunder and ravage, and a thousand more; but for a battle he is better trained than we are.

Nor is it enough to adopt these resolutions and oppose him by warlike measures: you must on calculation and on principle abhor his advocates here, remembering that it is impossible to overcome your enemies abroad, until you have chastised those who are his ministers within the city. Which, by Jupiter and all the gods, you can not and will not do! You have arrived at such a pitch of folly or madness or—I know not what to call it: I am tempted often to think, that some evil genius is driving you to ruin—for the sake of scandal or envy or jest or any other cause, you command hirelings to speak, (some of whom would not deny themselves to be hirelings), and laugh when they abuse people. And this, bad as it is, is not the worst: you have allowed these persons more liberty for their political conduct than your faithful counselors: and see what evils are caused by listening to such men with indulgence. I will mention facts that you will all remember.

In Olynthus some of the statesmen were in Philip's interest, doing everything for him; some were on the honest side, aiming to preserve their fellow-citizens from slavery. Which party now destroyed their country? or which betrayed the cavalry, by whose betrayal Olynthus fell? The creatures of Philip; they that, while the city stood, slandered and calumniated the honest counselors so effectually, that the Olynthian people were induced to banish Apollonides.

Nor is it there only, and nowhere else, that such practice has been ruinous. In Eretria, when, after riddance of Plutarch and his mercenaries, the people got possession of their city and of Porthmus, some were for bringing the government over to you, others to Philip. His partisans were generally, rather exclusively, attended to by the wretched and unfortunate Eretrians, who at length were persuaded to expel their faithful advisers. Philip, their ally and friend, sent Hipponicus and a thousand mercenaries, demolished the walls of Porthmus, and established three rulers, Hipparchus, Automedon, Clitarchus. Since that he has driven them out of the country, twice attempting their deliverance: once he sent the troops with Eurylochus, afterward those of Parmenio.

What need of many words? In Oreus Philip's agents were Philistides, Menippus, Socrates, Thoas, and Agapæus, who now hold the government: that was quite notorious: one Euphræus, a man that formerly dwelt here among you, was laboring for freedom and independence. How this man was in other respects insulted and trampled on by the people of Oreus, were long to tell: but a year before the capture, discovering what Philistides and his accomplices were about, he laid an information against them for treason. A multitude then combining, having Philip for their paymaster, and acting under his direction, take Euphræus off to prison as a disturber of the public peace. Seeing which, the people of Oreus, instead of assisting the one and beating the others to death, with them were not angry, but said his punishment was just, and rejoiced at it. So the conspirators, having full liberty of action, laid their schemes and took their measures for the surrender of the city; if any of the people observed it, they were silent and intimidated, remembering the treatment of Euphræus; and so wretched was their condition, that on the approach of such a calamity none dared to utter a word, until the enemy drew up before the walls: then some were for defence, others for betrayal. Since the city was thus basely and wickedly taken, the traitors have held despotic rule; people who formerly rescued them, and were ready for any maltreatment of Euphræus, they have either banished or put to death; Euphræus killed himself, proving by deed, that he had resisted Philip honestly and purely for the good of his countrymen.

What can be the reason—perhaps you wonder—why the Olynthians and Eretrians and Orites were more indulgent to Philip's advocates than to their own? The same which operates with you. They who advise for the best can not always gratify their audience, though they would; for the safety of the state must be attended to: their opponents by the very counsel which is agreeable advance Philip's interest. One party required contribution;

the other said there was no necessity: one were for war and mistrust; the other for peace, until they were ensnared. And so on for everything else (not to dwell on particulars); the one made speeches to please for the moment, and gave no annoyance; the other offered salutary counsel that was offensive. Many rights did the people surrender at last, not from any such motive of indulgence or ignorance, but submitting in the belief that all was lost. Which, by Jupiter and Apollo, I fear will be your case, when on calculation you see that nothing can be done. I pray, men of Athens, it may never come to this! Better die a thousand deaths than render homage to Philip, or sacrifice any of your faithful counselors. A fine recompense have the people of Areus got, for trusting themselves to Philip's friends and spurning Euphræus! Finely are the Eretrian commons rewarded, for having driven away your embassadors and yielded to Clitarchus! Yes; they are slaves, exposed to the lash and the torture. Finally he spared the Olynthians, who appointed Lasthenes to command their horse, and expelled Apollonides! It is folly and cowardice to cherish such hopes, and, while you take evil counsel and shirk every duty, and even listen to those who plead for your enemies, to think you inhabit a city of such magnitude, that you can not suffer any serious misfortune. Yea, and it is disgraceful to exclaim on any occurrence, when it is too late, "Who would have expected it? However—this or that should have been done, the other left undone." Many things could the Olynthians mention now, which, if foreseen at the time, would have prevented their destruction. Many could the Orites mention, many the Phocians, and each of the ruined states. But what would it avail them? As long as the vessel is safe, whether it be great or small, the mariner, the pilot, every man in turn should exert himself, and prevent its being overturned either by accident or design: but when the sea hath rolled over it, their efforts are vain. And we, likewise, O Athenians, while we are safe, with a magnificent city, plentiful resources, lofty reputation—what must we do? Many of you, I dare say, have been longing to ask. Well then, I will tell you; I will move a resolution: pass it, if you please.

First, let us prepare for our own defence; provide ourselves, I mean, with ships, money, and troops—for surely, though all other people consented to be slaves, we at least ought to struggle for freedom. When we have completed our own preparations and made them apparent to the Greeks, then let us invite the rest, and send our embassadors every where with the intelligence, to Peloponnesus, to Rhodes, to Chios, to the king, I say (for it concerns his interest, not to let Philip make universal conquest); that, if you prevail, you may have partners of your dangers and expenses, in case of necessity, or at all events that you may delay the operations. For, since the war is against an individual, not against the collected power of a state, even this may be useful; as were the embassies last year to Peloponnesus, and the remonstrances with which I and Polyeuctus, that excellent man, and Hegesippus, and Clitomachus, and Lycurgus, and the other envoys went around, and arrested Philip's progress, so that he neither attacked Ambracia nor started for Peloponnesus. I say not, however, that you should invite the rest without adopting measures to protect yourselves; it would be folly, while you sacrifice your own interest, to profess a regard for that of strangers, or to alarm others about the future, while for the present you are unconcerned. I advise not this: I bid you send supplies to the troops in Chersonesus, and do what else they require; prepare yourselves and make every effort first, then summon, gather,

instruct the rest of the Greeks. That is
the duty of a state possessing a dignity
such as yours. If you imagine that
Chalcidians or Megarians will save
Greece, while you run away from the
contest, you imagine wrong. Well for
any of those people, if they are safe
themselves. This work belongs to you:
this privilege your ancestors bequeathed
to you, the prize of many perilous exer-
tions. But if every one will sit seeking
his pleasure, and studying to be idle
himself, never will he find others to do
his work, and more than this, I fear we
shall be under the necessity of doing all
that we like not at one time. Were
proxies to be had, our inactivity would
have found them long ago; but they are
not.

Such are the measures which I advise,
which I propose: adopt them, and even
yet, I believe, our prosperity may be
re-established. If any man has better
advice to offer, let him communicate it
openly. Whatever you determine, I pray
to all the gods for a happy result.
—C. R. KENNEDY.

THE OATH OF THE ALLIED GREEKS

The cities of Greece, which had banded
together to beat back the Persian invasion
of Xerxes, supposedly took the following
oath at the beginning of the campaign
which culminated in the decisive victory
at Platæa in 479 B.C. It may be that the
form of it, found in the historian Diodo-
rus and elsewhere, is actually of a later
date; but in any case it expresses ideas
held by Greeks not later than the fourth
century B.C.

I will not regard life as of more value
than freedom, nor will I desert my leaders whether they be living or dead. All
of the Allies dying in battle will I fitly
bury. And, after defeating the Barbarians in the war, of the cities which
fought for Greece I will let none be laid
waste; but of those which took the side
of the Barbarians I will exact a tenth.
And of the sacred places burned and cast
down by the Barbarians I will rebuild
none at all; but I will let them be a
memorial of the ungodliness of the Barbarians for men of after time.
—G. A. HARRER.

THE EPHEBIC OATH

On reaching the age of manhood and
being formally entered as citizens on the
rolls of the city, the young men of Athens,
who were termed Epheboi, took an oath
as a part of the ceremony of induction
into the regular term of military training
and service. The wording here followed
has been preserved only in the late Greek
writers Stobæus and Pollux, but it was in
use at least as early as the fourth century B.C.

I will not disgrace the sacred arms, nor
will I desert my comrade in the ranks.
I, alone or with many others, will defend
the sacred and holy places. My fatherland I will transmit in no worse state but
greater and better than I found it. I
will obey those in authority, and I will
observe wholeheartedly the laws now in
force and whatever others the people
may pass. And if anyone seeks to annul
the laws or refuses to obey them, I will
not heed him; but, alone or with many
others, I will defend them. And I will
honor the religion of my fathers. Be the
witnesses of these things the gods
Aglauros, Enyalios, Zeus, Thallo, Auxo,
and Hegemone.
—G. A. HARRER.

VI. SPECULATIONS OF THE PHILOSOPHERS

The early Greek philosophers had been interested primarily in the natural world about them, but in the fifth century the theme shifted from nature to man. Formerly verse had been the vehicle for philosophical speculation, but now prose became the medium. As a form of literature it was probably derived from the work of the rhetoricians and sophists. Socrates, often classed as a sophist himself, discussed ethical principles with his disciples by means of question and answer, and, though he wrote nothing, he may be regarded as the originator of the philosophical form. For it was his pupils Xenophon and Plato who established the dialogue as the method of such expression.

The same influences of individual freedom peculiar to the period which led to the general participation of all men in public affairs, which allowed the widest field for freedom of thought and of speech, and which awakened curiosity in all manner of subjects, fostered also searching inquiries into the education of the citizen for his career and into the training of character for his political and moral responsibilities. Consequently, ethics, religion, intellectual training, government, the constitution of society, and man's relation to his natural environment, were subjected to examination and analysis. Through the idealism and poetic gifts of Plato such themes were lifted out of the sphere of the merely scholarly into that of pure literature; and through the critical and analytical powers of Aristotle the bounds of man's knowledge were immeasurably extended.

THE PRIMITIVE STATE [1]

PLATO

[From *The Republic*, Book II]

Plato, the Prince of Philosophers, was born in Athens in 427 B.C. of rich and

[1] Reprinted by arrangement with the Oxford University Press, publishers.

aristocratic family. He was a devoted disciple of Socrates, and on the latter's death in 399 B.C. withdrew from Athens for a time. Upon his return he formed a school in a grove sacred to Academus, whence our word "academy." He visited the court of the tyrants of Syracuse more than once, possibly with the expectation of realizing through them his ideal of government. He died in Athens in 347 B.C.

His writings are in the form of dialogues, in which the chief speaker is usually Socrates. The works which have come down to us under his name include forty-two dialogues, thirteen letters, and a collection of definitions. Of these not more than thirty of the dialogues have been universally accepted as genuine. Plato's central doctrine is that of the reality of the world of ideas, which exist absolutely and independently, and which represent the perfection to which we refer all things in our judgments of the true, the good, and the beautiful. Reason is supreme and achieves knowledge only by passing through the process of dialectic from appearance to reality, or from the images of ideas to the ideas themselves. Plato's chief application of his theory is to be found in the *Republic* and the *Laws,* in which he constructs the ideal state—a state which is to be governed by those who have been trained to perfect wisdom by the method of dialectic, and which is to be preserved by the laws derived from the world of absolute ideas.

States owe their origin, their development, their political career to man's economic needs. Wars are the result of economic necessity. In its early stages the society of the state is wholly a matter of division of labor in the production of commodities; but as it grows more complex, the division of labor must be extended to other spheres than production. The final stage demands three groups of citizens—those who direct the state, those who protect it, and those who produce.

A State, I said, arises, as I conceive, out of the needs of mankind; no one is self-sufficing, but all of us have many wants. Can any other origin of a State be imagined?

There can be no other.

Then, as we have many wants, and many persons are needed to supply them, one takes a helper for one purpose and another for another; and when these partners and helpers are gathered together in one habitation the body of inhabitants is called a State.

True, he said.

And they exchange with one another, and one gives, and another receives, under the idea that the exchange will be for their good.

Very true.

Then, I said, let us begin and create in idea a State; and yet the true creator is necessity, who is the mother of our invention.

Of course, he replied.

Now the first and greatest of necessities is food, which is the condition of life and existence.

Certainly.

The second is a dwelling, and the third clothing and the like.

True.

And now let us see how our city will be able to supply this great demand: We may suppose that one man is a husbandman, another a builder, some one else a weaver—shall we add to them a shoemaker, or perhaps some other purveyor to our bodily wants?

Quite right.

The barest notion of a State must include four or five men.

Clearly.

And how will they proceed? Will each bring the result of his labours into a common stock?—the individual husbandman, for example, producing for four, and labouring four times as long and as much as he need in the provision of food with which he supplies others as well as himself; or will he have nothing to do with others and not be at the trouble of producing for them, but provide for himself alone a fourth of the food in a fourth of the time, and in the remaining three fourths of his time be employed in making a house or a coat or a pair of shoes, having no partnership with others, but supplying himself all his own wants?

Adeimantus thought that he should aim at producing food only and not at producing everything.

Probably, I replied, that would be the better way; and when I hear you say this, I am myself reminded that we are not all alike; there are diversities of natures among us which are adapted to different occupations.

Very true.

And will you have a work better done when the workman has many occupations, or when he has only one?

When he has only one.

Further, there can be no doubt that a work is spoilt when not done at the right time?

No doubt.

For business is not disposed to wait until the doer of the business is at leisure; but the doer must follow up what he is doing, and make the business his first object.

He must.

And if so, we must infer that all things are produced more plentifully and easily and of a better quality when one man does one thing which is natural to him and does it at the right time, and leaves other things.

Undoubtedly.

Then more than four citizens will be required: for the husbandman will not make his own plough or mattock, or other implements of agriculture, if they are to be good for anything. Neither will the builder make his tools—and he too needs many; and in like manner the weaver and shoemaker.

True.

Then carpenters, and smiths, and many other artisans, will be sharers in our little State, which is already beginning to grow?

True.

Yet even if we add neatherds, shepherds, and other herdsmen, in order that our husbandmen may have oxen to plough with, and builders as well as husbandmen may have draught cattle, and curriers and weavers fleeces and hides,—still our State will not be very large.

That is true; yet neither will it be a very small State which contains all these.

Then, again, there is the situation of the city—to find a place where nothing need to be imported is wellnigh impossible.

Impossible.

Then there must be another class of citizens who will bring the required supply from another city?

There must.

But if the trader goes empty-handed, having nothing which they require who would supply his need, he will come back empty-handed.

That is certain.

And therefore what they produce at home must be not only enough for themselves, but such both in quantity and quality as to accommodate those from whom their wants are supplied.

Very true.

Then more husbandmen and more artisans will be required?

They will.

Not to mention the importers and exporters, who are called merchants?

Yes.

Then we shall want merchants?

We shall.

And if merchandise is to be carried over the sea, skilful sailors will also be needed, and in considerable numbers?

Yes, in considerable numbers.

Then, again, within the city, how will they exchange their productions? To secure such an exchange was, as you will remember, one of our principal objects when we formed them into a society and constituted a State.

Clearly they will buy and sell.

Then they will need a market-place, and a money-token for purposes of exchange.

Certainly.

Suppose now that a husbandman, or an artisan, brings some production to market, and he comes at a time when there is no one to exchange with him,—is he to leave his calling and sit idle in the market-place?

Not at all; he will find people there who, seeing the want, undertake the office of salesmen. In well-ordered states they are commonly those who are the weakest in bodily strength, and therefore, of little use for any other purpose; their duty is to be in the market, and to give money in exchange for goods to those who desire to sell and to take money from those who desire to buy.

This want, then, creates a class of retail-traders in our State. Is not "retailer" the term which is applied to those who sit in the market-place engaged in buying and selling, while those who wander from one city to another are called merchants?

Yes, he said.

And there is another class of servants, who are intellectually hardly on the level of companionship; still they have plenty of bodily strength for labour, which accordingly they sell, and are called, if I do not mistake, hirelings, hire being the name which is given to the price of their labour.

True.

Then hirelings will help to make up our population?

Yes.

And now, Adeimantus, is our State matured and perfected?

I think so.

Where, then, is justice, and where is injustice, and in what part of the State did they spring up?

Probably in the dealings of these citizens with one another. I cannot imagine that they are more likely to be found anywhere else.

I dare say that you are right in your suggestion, I said; we had better think the matter out, and not shrink from the enquiry.

Let us then consider, first of all, what will be their way of life, now that we have thus established them. Will they not produce corn, and wine, and clothes, and shoes, and build houses for themselves? And when they are housed, they will work, in summer, commonly, stripped and barefoot, but in winter substantially clothed and shod. They will feed on barley-meal and flour of wheat, baking and kneading them, making noble cakes and loaves; these they will serve up on a mat of reeds or on clean leaves, themselves reclining the while upon beds strewn with yew or myrtle. And they and their children will feast, drinking of the wine which they have made, wearing garlands on their heads, and hymning the praises of the gods, in happy converse with one another. And they will take care that their families do not exceed their means; having an eye to poverty or war.

But, said Glaucon, interposing, you have not given them a relish to their meal.

True, I replied, I had forgotten; of course they must have a relish—salt, and olives, and cheese, and they will boil roots and herbs such as country people prepare; for a dessert we shall give them figs, and peas, and beans; and they will roast myrtle-berries and acorns at the fire, drinking in moderation. And with such a diet they may be expected to live in peace and health to a good old age, and bequeath a similar life to their children after them.

Yes, Socrates, he said, and if you were providing for a city of pigs, how else would you feed the beasts?

But what would you have, Glaucon? I replied.

Why, he said, you should give them the ordinary conveniences of life. People who are to be comfortable are accustomed to lie on sofas, and dine off tables, and they should have sauces and sweets in the modern style.

Yes, I said, now I understand: the question which you would have me consider is, not only how a State, but how a luxurious State is created; and possibly there is no harm in this, for in such a State we shall be more likely to see how justice and injustice originate. In my opinion the true and healthy constitution of the State is the one which I have described. But if you wish also to see a State at fever-heat, I have no objection. For I suspect that many will not be satisfied with the simpler way of life. They will be for adding sofas, and tables, and other furniture; also dainties, and perfumes, and incense, and courtesans, and cakes, all these not of one sort only, but in every variety; we must go beyond the necessaries of which I was at first speaking, such as house, and clothes, and shoes: the arts of the painter and the embroiderer will have to be set in motion, and gold and ivory and all sorts of materials must be procured.

True, he said.

Then we must enlarge our borders; for the original healthy State is no longer sufficient. Now will the city have to fill and swell with a multitude of callings which are not required by any natural want; such as the whole tribe of hunters and actors, of whom one large class have to do with forms and colours; another will be the votaries of music—poets and their attendant train of rhapsodists, players, dancers, contractors; also makers of divers kinds of articles, including women's dresses. And we shall want more servants. Will not tutors be also in request, and nurses wet and dry, tire-women and barbers, as well as confectioners and cooks; and swineherds, too, who were not needed and therefore had no place in the former edition of our State, but are needed now? They must not be forgotten: and there will be animals of many other kinds, if people eat them.

Certainly.

And living in this way we shall have much greater need of physicians than before?

Much greater.

And the country which was enough to support the original inhabitants will be too small now, and not enough?

Quite true.

Then a slice of our neighbour's land will be wanted by us for pasture and tillage, and they will want a slice of ours, if, like ourselves, they exceed the limit of necessity, and give themselves up to the unlimited accumulation of wealth?

That, Socrates, will be inevitable.

And so we shall go to war, Glaucon. Shall we not?

Most certainly, he replied.

Then, without determining as yet whether war does good or harm, thus much we may affirm, that now we have discovered war to be derived from causes which are also the causes of almost all the evils in States, private as well as public.

Undoubtedly.

And our State must once more enlarge; and this time the enlargement will be nothing short of a whole army, which will have to go out and fight with the invaders for all that we have, as well as for the things and persons whom we were describing above.

Why? he said: are they not capable of defending themselves?

No, I said; not if we were right in the principle which was acknowledged by all of us when we were framing the State: the principle, as you will remember, was that one man cannot practise many arts with success.

Very true, he said.

But is not war an art?

Certainly.

And an art requiring as much attention as shoemaking?

Quite true.

And the shoemaker is not allowed by us to be a husbandman, or a weaver, or a builder—in order that we might have our shoes well made; but to him and to every other worker was assigned one work for which he was by nature fitted, and at that he was to continue working all his life long and at no other; he was not to let opportunities slip, and then he would become a good workman. Now nothing can be more important than that the work of a soldier should be well done. But is war an art so easily acquired that a man may be a warrior who is also a husbandman, or shoemaker, or other artisan; although no one in the world would be a good dice or draught player who merely took up the game as a recreation, and had not from his earliest years devoted himself to this and nothing else? No tools will make a man a skilled workman, or master of defence, nor be of any use to him who has not learned how to handle them, and has never bestowed any attention upon them. How then will he who takes up a shield or other implement of war become a good fighter all in a day, whether with heavy-armed or any other kind of troops?

Yes, he said, the tools which would teach men their own use would be beyond price.

And the higher the duties of the guardian, I said, the more time, and skill, and art, and application will be needed by him?

No doubt, he replied.

Will he not also require natural aptitude for his calling?

Certainly.

Then it will be our duty to select, if we can, natures which are fitted for the task of guarding the city?

It will.

And the selection will be no easy matter, I said; but we must be brave and do our best.

We must.

Is not the noble youth very like a well-bred dog in respect of guarding and watching?

What do you mean?

I mean that both of them ought to be quick to see, and swift to overtake the enemy when they see him; and strong too, if, when they have caught him, they have to fight with him.

All these qualities, he replied, will certainly be required by them.

Well, and your guardian must be brave if he is to fight well?

Certainly.

And is he likely to be brave who has no spirit, whether horse or dog or any other kind of animal? Have you never observed how invincible and unconquerable is spirit and how the presence of it makes the soul of any creature to be absolutely fearless and indomitable?

I have.

Then now we have a clear notion of the bodily qualities which are required in the guardian.

True.

And also the mental ones; his soul is to be full of spirit?

Yes.

But are not these spirited natures apt to be savage with one another, and with everybody else?

A difficulty by no means easy to overcome, he replied.

Whereas, I said, they ought to be dangerous to their enemies, and gentle to their friends; if not, they will destroy themselves without waiting for their enemies to destroy them.

True, he said.

What is to be done then? I said: how shall we find a gentle nature which has also a great spirit, for the one is the contradiction of the other?

True.

He will not be a good guardian who is wanting in either of these two qualities; and yet the combination of them appears to be impossible; and hence we must infer that to be a good guardian is impossible.

I am afraid that what you say is true, he replied.

Here feeling perplexed I began to think over what had preceded.—My friend, I said, no wonder that we are in a perplexity; for we have lost sight of the image which we had before us.

What do you mean? he said.

I mean to say that there do exist natures gifted with those opposite qualities.

And where do you find them?

Many animals, I replied, furnish examples of them; our friend the dog is a very good one: you know that well-bred dogs are perfectly gentle to their familiars and acquaintances, and the reverse to strangers.

Yes, I know.

Then there is nothing impossible or out of the order of nature in our finding a guardian who has a similar combination of qualities?

Certainly not.

Would not he who is fitted to be a guardian, besides the spirited nature, need to have the qualities of a philosopher?

I do not apprehend your meaning.

The trait of which I am speaking, I replied, may be also seen in the dog, and is remarkable in the animal.

What trait?

Why, a dog, whenever he sees a stranger, is angry; when an acquaintance, he welcomes him, although the one has never done him any harm, nor the other any good. Did this never strike you as curious?

The matter never struck me before; but I quite recognise the truth of your remark.

And surely this instinct of the dog is very charming:—your dog is a true philosopher.

Why?

Why, because he distinguishes the face of a friend and of an enemy only by the criterion of knowing and not knowing. And must not an animal be a lover of learning who determines what he likes and dislikes by the test of knowledge and ignorance?

Most assuredly.

And is not the love of learning the love of wisdom, which is philosophy?

They are the same, he replied.

And may we not say confidently of man also, that he who is likely to be gentle to his friends and acquaintances, must by nature be a lover of wisdom and knowledge?

That we may safely affirm.

Then he who is to be a really good and noble guardian of the State will require to unite in himself philosophy and spirit and swiftness and strength?

Undoubtedly.

—BENJAMIN JOWETT.

EDUCATION FOR CITIZENSHIP [1]

PLATO

[From *The Republic*, Book II]

Plato protests against the almost universal practice of using Homer and Hesiod as textbooks for religious and moral instruction. The ethical standards to be demanded of a poet are summarized in the two principles that God is the source of good only, and that God is in-

[1] Reprinted by arrangement with the Oxford University Press, publishers.

variably true. Indeed, Plato would banish poetry almost altogether from his ideal state, not only because of its false religious and moral teachings, but also because he regards the fictions of poets as no more than imitations of reality and therefore harmful.

Come then, and let us pass a leisure hour in story-telling, and our story shall be the education of our heroes.

By all means.

And what shall be their education? Can we find a better than the traditional sort?—and this has two divisions, gymnastic for the body, and music for the soul.

True.

Shall we begin education with music, and go on to gymnastic afterwards?

By all means.

And when you speak of music, do you include literature or not?

I do.

And literature may be either true or false?

Yes.

And the young should be trained in both kinds, and we begin with the false?

I do not understand your meaning, he said.

You know, I said, that we begin by telling children stories which, though not wholly destitute of truth, are in the main fictitious; and these stories are told them when they are not of an age to learn gymnastics.

Very true.

That was my meaning when I said that we must teach music before gymnastics.

Quite right, he said.

You know also that the beginning is the most important part of any work, especially in the case of a young and tender thing; for that is the time at which the character is being formed and the desired impression is more readily taken.

Quite true.

And shall we just carelessly allow children to hear any casual tales which may be devised by casual persons, and to receive into their minds ideas for the most part the very opposite of those which we should wish them to have when they are grown up?

We cannot.

Then the first thing will be to establish a censorship of the writers of fiction, and let the censors receive any tale of fiction which is good, and reject the bad; and we will desire mothers and nurses to tell their children the authorised ones only. Let them fashion the mind with such tales, even more fondly than they mould the body with their hands; but most of those which are now in use must be discarded.

Of what tales are you speaking? he said.

You may find a model of the lesser in the greater, I said; for they are necessarily of the same type, and there is the same spirit in both of them.

Very likely, he replied; but I do not as yet know what you would term the greater.

Those, I said, which are narrated by Homer and Hesiod, and the rest of the poets, who have ever been the great story-tellers of mankind.

But which stories do you mean, he said; and what fault do you find with them?

A fault which is most serious, I said; the fault of telling a lie, and, what is more, a bad lie.

But when is this fault committed?

Whenever an erroneous representation is made of the nature of gods and heroes, —as when a painter paints a portrait not having the shadow of a likeness to the original.

Yes, he said, that sort of thing is certainly very blameable; but what are the stories which you mean?

First of all, I said, there was that greatest of all lies in high places, which the poet told about Uranus, and which was a bad lie too,—I mean what Hesiod says that Uranus did, and how Cronus retaliated on him. The doings of Cronus, and the sufferings which in turn his son inflicted upon him, even if they were true, ought certainly not to be lightly told to young and thoughtless persons; if possible, they had better be buried in silence. But if there is an absolute necessity for their mention, a chosen few might hear them in a mystery, and they should sacrifice not a common pig, but some huge and unprocurable victim; and then the number of the hearers will be very few indeed.

Why, yes, said he, those stories are extremely objectionable.

Yes, Adeimantus, they are stories not to be repeated in our State; the young man should not be told that in committing the worst of crimes he is far from doing anything outrageous; and that even if he chastises his father when he does wrong, in whatever manner, he will only be following the example of the first and greatest among the gods.

I entirely agree with you, he said; in my opinion those stories are quite unfit to be repeated.

Neither, if we mean our future guardians to regard the habit of quarrelling among themselves as of all things the basest, should any word be said to them of the wars in heaven, and of the plots and fightings of the gods against one another, for they are not true. No, we shall never mention the battles of the giants, or let them be embroidered on garments; and we shall be silent about the innumerable other quarrels of gods and heroes with their friends and relatives. If they would only believe us we would tell them that quarrelling is unholy, and that never up to this time has there been any quarrel between citizens; this is what old men and old women should begin by telling children; and when they grow up, the poets also should be told to compose for them in a similar spirit. But the narrative of Hephæstus binding Here his mother, or how on another occasion Zeus sent him flying for taking her part when she was being beaten, and all the battles of the gods in Homer—these tales must not be admitted into our State, whether they are supposed to have an allegorical meaning or not. For a young person cannot judge what is allegorical and what is literal; anything that he receives into his mind at that age is likely to become indelible and unalterable; and therefore it is most important that the tales which the young first hear should be models of virtuous thoughts.

There you are right, he replied; but if any one asks where are such models to be found and of what tales are you speaking—how shall we answer him?

I said to him, You and I, Adeimantus, at this moment are not poets, but founders of a State: now the founders of a State ought to know the general forms in which poets should cast their tales, and the limits which must be observed by them, but to make the tales is not their business.

Very true, he said; but what are these forms of theology which you mean?

Something of this kind, I replied:— God is always to be represented as he truly is, whatever be the sort of poetry, epic, lyric, or tragic, in which the representation is given.

Right.

And is he not truly good? and must he not be represented as such?

Certainly.

And no good thing is hurtful?

No, indeed.

And that which is not hurtful hurts not?

Certainly not.

And that which hurts not does no evil?

No.

And can that which does no evil be a cause of evil?

Impossible.

And the good is advantageous?

Yes.

And therefore the cause of well-being?

Yes.

It follows therefore that the good is not the cause of all things, but of the good only.

Assuredly.

Then God, if he be good, is not the author of all things, as the many assert, but he is the cause of a few things only, and not of most things that occur to men. For few are the goods of human life, and many are the evils, and the good is to be attributed to God alone; of the evils the causes are to be sought elsewhere, and not in him.

That appears to me to be most true, he said. . . .

But shall our superintendence go no further, and are the poets only to be required by us to express the image of the good in their works, on pain, if they do anything else, of expulsion from our State? Or is the same control to be extended to other artists, and are they also to be prohibited from exhibiting the opposite forms of vice and intemperance and meanness and indecency in sculpture and building and the other creative arts; and is he who cannot conform to this rule of ours to be prevented from practising his art in our State, lest the taste of our citizens be corrupted by him? We would not have our guardians grow up amid images of moral deformity, as in some noxious pasture, and there browse and feed upon many a baneful herb and flower day by day, little by little, until they silently gather a festering mass of corruption in their own soul. Let our artists rather be those who are gifted to discern the true nature of the beautiful and graceful; then will our youth dwell in a land of health, amid fair sights and sounds, and receive the good in everything; and beauty, the effluence of fair works, shall flow into the eye and ear, like a health-giving breeze from a purer region, and insensibly draw the soul from earliest years into likeness and sympathy with the beauty of reason.

There can be no nobler training than that, he replied.

And therefore, I said, Glaucon, musical training is a more potent instrument than any other, because rhythm and harmony find their way into the inward places of the soul, on which they mightily fasten, imparting grace, and making the soul of him who is rightly educated graceful, or of him who is ill-educated ungraceful; and also because he who has received this true education of the inner being will most shrewdly perceive omissions or faults in art and nature, and with a true taste, while he praises and rejoices over and receives into his soul the good, and becomes noble and good, he will justly blame and hate the bad, now in the days of his youth, even before he is able to know the reason why; and when reason comes he will recognise and salute the friend with whom his education has made him long familiar.

Yes, he said, I quite agree with you in thinking that our youth should be trained in music and on the grounds which you mention.

Just as in learning to read, I said, we were satisfied when we knew the letters of the alphabet, which are very few, in all their recurring sizes and combinations; not slighting them as unimportant whether they occupy a space large or small, but everywhere eager to make them out; and not thinking ourselves perfect in the art of reading until we recognise them wherever they are found:

True—

Or, as we recognise the reflection of letters in the water, or in a mirror, only when we know the letters themselves; the same art and study giving us the knowledge of both:

Exactly—

Even so, as I maintain, neither we nor our guardians, whom we have to educate, can ever become musical until we and they know the essential forms of temperance, courage, liberality, magnificence, and their kindred, as well as the contrary forms, in all their combinations, and can recognise them and their images wherever they are found, not slighting them either in small things or in great, but believing them all to be within the sphere of one art and study.

Most assuredly.

And when a beautiful soul harmonizes with a beautiful form, and the two are cast in one mould, that will be the fairest of sights to him who has an eye to see it?

The fairest indeed.

And the fairest is also the loveliest?

That may be assumed.

And the man who has the spirit of harmony will be most in love with the loveliest; but he will not love him who is of an inharmonious soul?

That is true, he replied, if the deficiency be in his soul; but if there be any merely bodily defect in another he will be patient of it, and will love all the same. . . .

After music comes gymnastic, in which our youth are next to be trained.

Certainly.

Gymnastic as well as music should begin in early years; the training in it should be careful and should continue through life. Now my belief is,—and this is a matter upon which I should like to have your opinion in confirmation of my own, but my belief is,—not that the good body by any bodily excellence improves the soul, but, on the contrary, that the good soul, by her own excellence, improves the body as far as this may be possible. What do you say?

Yes, I agree.

Then, to the mind when adequately trained, we shall be right in handing over the more particular care of the body; and in order to avoid prolixity we will now only give the general outlines of the subject.

Very good.

That they must abstain from intoxication has been already remarked by us; for of all persons a guardian should be the last to get drunk and not know where in the world he is.

Yes, he said; that a guardian should require another guardian to take care of him is ridiculous indeed.

But next, what shall we say of their food; for the men are in training for the greatest contest of all—are they not?

Yes, he said.

And will the habit of body of our ordinary athletes be suited to them?

Why not?

I am afraid, I said, that a habit of body such as they have is but a sleepy sort of thing, and rather perilous to health. Do you not observe that these athletes sleep away their lives, and are liable to most dangerous illnesses if they depart, in ever so slight a degree, from their customary regimen?

I do.

Then, I said, a finer sort of training will be required for our warrior athletes, who are to be like wakeful dogs, and to see and hear with the utmost keenness; amid the many changes of water and also of food, of summer heat and winter cold, which they will have to endure when on a campaign, they must not be liable to break down in health.

That is my view.

The really excellent gymnastic is twin sister of that simple music which we were just now describing.

How so?

Why, I conceive that there is a gymnastic which, like our music, is simple and good; and especially the military gymnastic.

What do you mean?

My meaning may be learned from Homer; he, you know, feeds his heroes at their feasts, when they are campaigning, on soldiers' fare; they have no fish, although they are on the shores of the Hellespont, and they are not allowed boiled meats but only roast, which is the food most convenient for soldiers, requiring only that they should light a fire, and not involving the trouble of carrying about pots and pans.

True.

And I can hardly be mistaken in saying that sweet sauces are nowhere mentioned in Homer. In proscribing them, however, he is not singular; all professional athletes are well aware that a man who is to be in good condition should take nothing of the kind.

Yes, he said; and knowing this, they are quite right in not taking them.

Then you would not approve of Syracusan dinners, and the refinements of Sicilian cookery?

I think not.

Nor, if a man is to be in good condition, would you allow him to have a Corinthian girl as his fair friend?

Certainly not.

Neither would you approve of the delicacies, as they are thought, of Athenian confectionery?

Certainly not.

All such feeding and living may be rightly compared by us to melody and song composed in the panharmonic style, and in all the rhythms.

Exactly.

There complexity engendered licence, and here disease; whereas simplicity in music was the parent of temperance in the soul; and simplicity in gymnastic of health in the body.

Most true, he said.

But when intemperance and diseases multiply in a State, halls of justice and medicine are always being opened; and the arts of the doctor and the lawyer give themselves airs, finding how keen is the interest which not only the slaves but the freemen of a city take about them.

Of course.

And yet what greater proof can there be of a bad and disgraceful state of education than this, that not only artisans and the meaner sort of people need the skill of first-rate physicians and judges, but also those who would profess to have had a liberal education? Is it not disgraceful, and a great sign of the want of good-breeding, that a man should have to go abroad for his law and physic because he has none of his own at home, and must therefore surrender himself into the hands of other men whom he makes lords and judges over him?

Of all things, he said, the most disgraceful.

—BENJAMIN JOWETT.

PHILOSOPHERS AS KINGS [1]

PLATO

[From *The Republic,* Books V and VI]

Plato conceives the philosopher to be that man who has passed beyond the stage of mistaking appearances for reality, who has discovered not only that the true, the good, and the beautiful may exist, but has actually beheld them as absolute ideas, and who is therefore incapable of prejudice, error, deception, injustice. He is aware that the ideal state he proposes is impracticable, but he maintains that an approximation is possible if the control be entrusted to such philosophers.

I think, I said, that there might be a reform of the State if only one change were made, which is not a slight or easy though still a possible one.

What is it? he said.

Now then, I said, I go to meet that which I liken to the greatest of the waves; yet shall the word be spoken, even though the wave break and drown me in laughter and dishonour; and do you mark my words.

[1] Reprinted by arrangement with the Oxford University Press, publishers.

Proceed.

I said: *Until philosophers are kings, or the kings and princes of this world have the spirit and power of philosophy, and political greatness and wisdom meet in one, and those commoner natures who pursue either to the exclusion of the other are compelled to stand aside, cities will never have rest from their evils,—no, nor the human race, as I believe,—and then only will this our State have a possibility of life and behold the light of day.* Such was the thought, my dear Glaucon, which I would fain have uttered if it had not seemed too extravagant; for to be convinced that in no other State can there be happiness private or public is indeed a hard thing.

Socrates, what do you mean? I would have you consider that the word which you have uttered is one at which numerous persons, and very respectable persons too, in a figure pulling off their coats all in a moment, and seizing any weapon that comes to hand, will run at you might and main, before you know where you are, intending to do heaven knows what; and if you don't prepare an answer, and put yourself in motion, you will be "pared by their fine wits," and no mistake.

You got me into the scrape, I said.

And I was quite right; however, I will do all I can to get you out of it; but I can only give you good-will and good advice, and, perhaps, I may be able to fit answers to your questions better than another—that is all. And now, having such an auxiliary, you must do your best to show the unbelievers that you are right.

I ought to try, I said, since you offer me such invaluable assistance. And I think that, if there is to be a chance of our escaping, we must explain to them whom we mean when we say that philosophers are to rule in the State; then we shall be able to defend ourselves: There will be discovered to be some natures who ought to study philosophy and to be leaders in the States; and others who are not born to be philosophers, and are meant to be followers rather than leaders.

Then now for a definition, he said.

Follow me, I said, and I hope that I may in some way or other be able to give you a satisfactory explanation.

Proceed.

I dare say that you remember, and therefore I need not remind you, that a lover, if he is worthy of the name, ought to show his love, not to some one part of that which he loves, but to the whole.

I really do not understand, and therefore beg of you to assist my memory.

Another person, I said, might fairly reply as you do; but a man of pleasure like yourself ought to know that all who are in the flower of youth do somehow or other raise a pang or emotion in a lover's breast, and are thought by him to be worthy of his affectionate regards. Is not this a way which you have with the fair: one has a snub nose, and you praise his charming face; the hook-nose of another has, you say, a royal look; while he who is neither snub nor hooked has the grace of regularity: the dark visage is manly, the fair are children of the gods; and as to the sweet "honey pale," as they are called, what is the very name but the invention of a lover who talks in diminutives, and is not averse to paleness if appearing on the cheek of youth? In a word, there is no excuse which you will not make, and nothing which you will not say, in order not to lose a single flower that blooms in the spring-time of youth.

If you make me an authority in matters of love, for the sake of the argument, I assent.

And what do you say of lovers of wine? Do you not see them doing the same? they are glad of any pretext of drinking any wine.

Very good.

And the same is true of ambitious men; if they cannot command an army, they are willing to command a file; and if they cannot be honoured by really great and important persons, they are glad to be honoured by lesser and meaner people,—but honour of some kind they must have.

Exactly.

Once more let me ask: Does he who desires any class of goods, desire the whole class or a part only?

The whole.

And may we not say of the philosopher that he is a lover, not of a part of wisdom only, but of the whole?

Yes, of the whole.

And he who dislikes learning, especially in youth, when he has no power of judging what is good and what is not, such an one we maintain not to be a philosopher or a lover of knowledge, just as he who refuses his food is not hungry, and may be said to have a bad appetite and not a good one?

Very true, he said.

Whereas he who has a taste for every sort of knowledge and who is curious to learn and is never satisfied, may be justly termed a philosopher? Am I not right?

Glaucon said: If curiosity makes a philosopher, you will find many a strange being will have a title to the name. All the lovers of sights have a delight in learning, and must therefore be included. Musical amateurs, too, are a folk strangely out of place among philosophers, for they are the last persons in the world who would come to anything like a philosphical discussion, if they could help, while they run about at the Dionysiac festivals as if they had let out their ears to hear every chorus; whether the performance is in town or country— that makes no difference—they are there. Now are we to maintain that all these and any who have similar tastes, as well as the professors of quite minor arts, are philosophers?

Certainly not, I replied; they are only an imitation.

He said: Who then are the true philosophers?

Those, I said, who are lovers of the vision of truth. . . .

And what is the next question he asked.

Surely, I said, the one which follows next in order. Inasmuch as philosophers only are able to grasp the eternal and unchangeable, and those who wander in the region of the many and variable are not philosophers, I must ask you which of the two classes should be the rulers of our State?

And how can we rightly answer that question?

Whichever of the two are best able to guard the laws and institutions of our State—let them be our guardians.

Very good.

Neither, I said, can there be any question that the guardian who is to keep anything should have eyes rather than no eyes?

There can be no question of that.

And are not those who are verily and indeed wanting in the knowledge of the true being of each thing, and who have in their souls no clear pattern, and are unable as with a painter's eye to look at the absolute truth and to that original to repair, and having perfect vision of the other world to order the laws about beauty, goodness, justice in this, if not already ordered, and to guard and preserve the order of them—are not such persons, I ask, simply blind?

Truly, he replied, they are much in that condition.

And shall they be our guardians when there are others who, besides being their equals in experience and falling short of them in no particular of virtue, also know the very truth of each thing?

There can be no reason, he said, for rejecting those who have this greatest of all great qualities; they must always have the first place unless they fail in some other respect.

Suppose then, I said, that we determine how far they can unite this and the other excellences.

By all means.

In the first place, as we began by observing, the nature of the philosopher has to be ascertained. We must come to an understanding about him, and, when we have done so, then, if I am not mistaken, we shall also acknowledge that such an union of qualities is possible, and that those in whom they are united, and those only, should be rulers in the State.

What do you mean?

Let us suppose that philosophical minds always love knowledge of a sort which shows them the eternal nature not varying from generation and corruption.

Agreed.

And further, I said, let us agree that they are lovers of all true being; there is no part whether greater or less, or more or less honourable, which they are willing to renounce; as we said before of the lover and the man of ambition.

True.

And if they are to be what we were describing, is there not another quality which they should also possess?

What quality?

Truthfulness: they will never intentionally receive into their mind falsehood, which is their detestation, and they will love the truth.

Yes, that may be safely affirmed of them.

"May be," my friend, I replied, is not the word; say rather, "must be affirmed": for he whose nature is amorous of anything cannot help loving all that belongs or is akin to the object of his affections.

Right, he said.

And is there anything more akin to wisdom than truth?

How can there be?

Can the same nature be a lover of wisdom and a lover of falsehood?

Never.

The true lover of learning then must

from his earliest youth, as far as in him lies, desire all truth?

Assuredly.

But then again, as we know by experience, he whose desires are strong in one direction will have them weaker in others; they will be like a stream which has been drawn off into another channel.

True.

He whose desires are drawn towards knowledge in every form will be absorbed in the pleasures of the soul, and will hardly feel bodily pleasure—I mean, if he be a true philosopher and not a sham one.

That is most certain.

Such an one is sure to be temperate and the reverse of covetous; for the motives which make another man desirous of having and spending, have no place in his character.

Very true.

Another criterion of the philosophical nature has also to be considered.

What is that?

There should be no secret corner of illiberality; nothing can be more antagonistic than meanness to a soul which is ever longing after the whole of things both divine and human.

Most true, he replied.

Then how can he who has magnificence of mind and is the spectator of all time and all existence, think much of human life?

He cannot.

Or can such an one account death fearful?

No indeed.

Then the cowardly and mean nature has no part in true philosophy?

Certainly not.

Or again: can he who is harmoniously constituted, who is not covetous or mean, or a boaster, or a coward—can he, I say, ever be unjust or hard in his dealings?

Impossible.

Then you will soon observe whether a man is just and gentle, or rude and unsociable; these are the signs which distinguish even in youth the philosophical nature from the unphilosophical.

True.

There is another point which should be remarked.

What point?

Whether he has or has not a pleasure in learning; for no one will love that which gives him pain, and in which after much toil he makes little progress.

Certainly not.

And again, if he is forgetful and retains nothing of what he learns, will he not be an empty vessel?

That is certain.

Labouring in vain, he must end in hating himself and his fruitless occupation?

Yes.

Then a soul which forgets cannot be ranked among genuine philosophic natures; we must insist that the philosopher have a good memory?

Certainly.

And once more, the inharmonious and unseemly nature can only tend to disproportion?

Undoubtedly.

And do you consider truth to be akin to proportion or to disproportion?

To proportion.

Then, besides other qualities, we must try to find a well-proportioned and gracious mind, which will move spontaneously towards the true being of everything.

Certainly.

Well, and do not all these qualities, which we have been enumerating, go together, and are they not, in a manner, necessary to a soul, which is to have a full and perfect participation of being?

They are absolutely necessary, he replied.

And must not that be a blameless study which he only can pursue who has the gift of a good memory, and is quick to learn,—noble, gracious, the friend of truth, justice, courage, temperance, who are his kindred?

The god of jealousy himself, he said, could find no fault with such a study.

And to men like him, I said, when perfected by years and education, and to those only you will entrust the State. . . .

They will begin by taking the State and the manners of men, from which, as from a tablet, they will rub out the picture, and leave a clean surface. This is no easy task. But whether easy or not, herein will lie the difference between them and every other legislator,—they will have nothing to do with either individual or State, and will inscribe no laws, until they have either found, or themselves made, a clean surface.

They will be very right, he said.

Having effected this, they will proceed to trace an outline of the constitution?

No doubt.

And when they are filling in the work, as I conceive, they will often turn their eyes upwards and downwards: I mean that they will first look at absolute justice and beauty and temperance, and again at the human copy; and will mingle and temper the various elements of life into the image of a man; and this they will conceive according to that other image, which, when existing among men, Homer calls the form and likeness of God.

Very true, he said.

And one feature they will erase, and another they will put in, until they have made the ways of men, as far as possible, agreeable to the ways of God.

Indeed, he said, in no way could they make a fairer picture.

And now, I said, are we beginning to persuade those whom you described as rushing at us with might and main, that the painter of constitutions is such an one as we were praising; at whom they were

so very indignant because to his hands we committed the State; and are they growing a little calmer at what they have just heard?

Much calmer, if there is any sense in them.

Why, where can they still find any ground for objection? Will they doubt that the philosopher is a lover of truth and being?

They would not be so unreasonable.

Or that his nature, being such as we have delineated, is akin to the highest good?

Neither can they doubt this.

But again, will they tell us that such a nature, placed under favourable circumstances, will not be perfectly good and wise if any ever was? Or will they prefer those whom we have rejected?

Surely not.

Then will they still be angry at our saying, that, until philosophers bear rule, States and individuals will have no rest from evil, nor will this our imaginary State ever be realized?

I think that they will be less angry.

Shall we assume that they are not only less angry but quite gentle, and that they have been converted and for very shame, if for no other reason, cannot refuse to come to terms?

By all means, he said.

Then let us suppose that the reconciliation has been effected. Will any one deny the other point, that there may be sons of kings or princes who are by nature philosophers?

Surely no man, he said.

And when they have come into being will any one say that they must of necessity be destroyed; that they can hardly be saved is not denied even by us; but that in the whole course of ages no single one of them can escape—who will venture to affirm this?

Who indeed!

But, said I, one is enough; let there be one man who has a city obedient to his will, and he might bring into existence the ideal polity about which the world is so incredulous.

Yes, one is enough.

The ruler may impose the laws and institutions which we have been describing, and the citizens may possibly be willing to obey them?

Certainly.

And that others should approve of what we approve is no miracle or impossibility?

I think not.

But we have sufficiently shown, in what has preceded, that all this, if only possible, is assuredly for the best.

We have.

And now we say not only that our laws, if they could be enacted, would be for the best, but also that the enactment of them, though difficult, is not impossible.

Very good.

And so with pain and toil we have reached the end of one subject but more remains to be discussed.

—BENJAMIN JOWETT.

THE IMAGE OF THE CAVE [1]

PLATO

[From *The Republic*, Book VII]

The use of the myth for purposes of illustration is characteristic of Plato. It is the poet in him which, not satisfied with argument only, calls to his aid the powers of the imagination and of the emotions. The image of the cave is an allegory of the process by which we proceed from ignorance to knowledge. The several stages of the process correspond to the several stages in education, from the fictions of poetry to reality as understood by philosophers.

And now, I said, let me show in a figure how far our nature is enlightened

[1] Reprinted by arrangement with the Oxford University Press, publishers.

or unenlightened:—Behold! human beings living in an underground den, which has a mouth open towards the light and reaching all along the den; here they have been from their childhood, and have their legs and necks chained so that they cannot move, and can only see before them, being prevented by the chains from turning round their heads. Above and behind them a fire is blazing at a distance, and between the fire and the prisoners there is a raised way; and you will see, if you look, a low wall built along the way, like the screen which marionette players have in front of them, over which they show the puppets.

I see.

And do you see, I said, men passing along the wall carrying all sorts of vessels, and statues and figures of animals made of wood and stone and various materials, which appear over the wall? Some of them are talking, others silent.

You have shown me a strange image, and they are strange prisoners.

Like ourselves, I replied; and they see only their own shadows, or the shadows of one another, which the fire throws on the opposite wall of the cave?

True, he said; how could they see anything but the shadows if they were never allowed to move their heads?

And of the objects which are being carried in like manner they would see only the shadows?

Yes, he said.

And if they were able to converse with one another, would they not suppose that they were naming what was actually before them?

Very true.

And suppose further that the prison had an echo which came from the other side, would they not be sure to fancy when one of the passersby spoke that the voice which they heard came from the passing shadow?

No question, he replied.

To them, I said, the truth would be literally nothing but the shadows of the images.

That is certain.

And now look again, and see what will naturally follow if the prisoners are released and disabused of their error. At first, when any of them is liberated and compelled suddenly to stand up and turn his neck round and walk and look towards the light, he will suffer sharp pains; the glare will distress him, and he will be unable to see the realities of which in his former state he had seen the shadows; and then conceive some one saying to him, that what he saw before was an illusion, but that now, when he is approaching nearer to being and his eye is turned towards more real existence, he has a clearer vision,—what will be his reply? And you may further imagine that his instructor is pointing to the objects as they pass and requiring him to name them,—will he not be perplexed? Will he not fancy that the shadows which he formerly saw are truer than the objects which are now shown to him?

Far truer.

And if he is compelled to look straight at the light, will he now have a pain in his eyes which will make him turn away to take refuge in the objects of vision which he can see, and which he will conceive to be in reality clearer than the things which are now being shown to him?

True, he said.

And suppose once more, that he is reluctantly dragged up a steep and rugged ascent, and held fast until he is forced into the presence of the sun himself, is he not likely to be pained and irritated? When he approaches the light his eyes will be dazzled, and he will not be able to see anything at all of what are now called realities.

Not all in a moment, he said.

He will require to grow accustomed to the sight of the upper world. And first he will see the shadows best, next the reflections of men and other objects in the water, and then the objects themselves; then he will gaze upon the light of the moon and the stars by night better than the sun or the light of the sun by day?

Certainly.

Last of all he will be able to see the sun, and not mere reflections of him in the water, but he will see him in his own proper place, and not in another; and he will contemplate him as he is.

Certainly.

He will then proceed to argue that this is he who gives the seasons and the years, and is the guardian of all that is in the visible world, and in a certain way the cause of all things which he and his fellows have been accustomed to behold?

Clearly, he said, he would first see the sun and then reason about him.

And when he remembered his old habitation, and the wisdom of the den and his fellow prisoners, do you not suppose that he would felicitate himself on the change, and pity them?

Certainly he would.

And if they were in the habit of conferring honours among themselves on those who were quickest to observe the passing shadows and to remark which of them went before, and which followed after, and which were together; and who were therefore best able to draw conclusions as to the future, do you think that he would care for such honours and glories, or envy the possessors of them? Would he not say with Homer, "Better to be the poor servant of a poor master," and to endure anything, rather than think as they do and live after their manner?

Yes, he said, I think that he would rather suffer anything than entertain these false notions and live in this miserable manner.

Imagine once more, I said, such an one coming suddenly out of the sun to be replaced in his old situation; would he not be certain to have his eyes full of darkness?

To be sure, he said.

And if there were a contest, and he had to compete in measuring the shadows with the prisoners who had never moved out of the den, while his sight was still weak, and before his eyes had become steady (and the time which would be needed to acquire this new habit of sight might be very considerable), would he not be ridiculous? Men would say of him that up he went and down he came without his eyes: and that it was better not even to think of ascending; and if any one tried to loose another and lead him up to the light, let them only catch the offender, and they would put him to death.

No question, he said.

This entire allegory, I said, you may now append, dear Glaucon, to the previous argument; the prison-house is the world of sight, the light of the fire is the sun, and you will not misapprehend me if you interpret the journey upwards to be the ascent of the soul into the intellectual world according to my poor belief, which, at your desire, I have expressed—whether rightly or wrongly God knows. But, whether true or false, my opinion is that in the world of knowledge the idea of good appears last of all, and is seen only with an effort; and, when seen, is also inferred to be the universal author of all things beautiful and right, parent of light and of the lord of light in this visible world, and the immediate source of reason and truth in the intellectual; and that this is the power upon which he who would act rationally either in public or private life must have his eye fixed.

I agree, he said, as far as I am able to understand you.

Moreover, I said, you must not wonder that those who attain to this beatific vision are unwilling to descend to human affairs; for their souls are ever hastening into the upper world where they desire to dwell; which desire of theirs is very natural, if our allegory may be trusted.

Yes, very natural.

And is there anything surprising in one who passes from divine contemplations to the evil state of man, misbehaving himself in a ridiculous manner; if, while his eyes are blinking and before he has become accustomed to the surrounding darkness, he is compelled to fight in courts of law, or in other places, about the images or the shadows of images of justice, and is endeavouring to meet the conceptions of those who have never yet seen absolute •justice?

Anything but surprising, he said.

Any one who has common sense will remember that the bewilderments of the eyes are of two kinds, and arise from two causes, either from coming out of the light or from going into the light, which is true of the mind's eye, quite as much as of the bodily eye; and he who remembers this when he sees any one whose vision is perplexed and weak, will not be too ready to laugh; he will first ask whether that soul of man has come out of the brighter life, and is unable to see because unaccustomed to the dark, or having turned from darkness to the day is dazzled by excess of light. And he will count the one happy in his condition and state of being, and he will pity the other; or, if he have a mind to laugh at the soul which comes from below into the light, there will be more reason in this than in the laugh which greets him who returns from above out of the light into the den.

That, he said, is a very just distinction.

But then, if I am right, certain professors of education must be wrong when they say that they can put a knowledge into the soul which was not there before, like sight into blind eyes.

They undoubtedly say this, he replied.

Whereas, our argument shows that the power and capacity of learning exists in the soul already; and that just as the eye was unable to turn from darkness to light without the whole body, so too the instrument of knowledge can only by the movement of the whole soul be turned from the world of becoming into that of being, and learn by degrees to endure the sight of being, and of the brightest and best of being, or in other words, of the good.

Very true.

And must there not be some art which will effect conversion in the easiest and quickest manner; not implanting the faculty of sight, for that exists already, but has been turned in the wrong direction, and is looking away from the truth?

Yes, he said, such an art may be presumed.

And whereas the other so-called virtues of the soul seem to be akin to bodily qualities, for even when they are not originally innate they can be implanted later by habit and exercise, the virtue more than anything else contains a divine element which always remains, and by this conversion is rendered useful and profitable; or, on the other hand, hurtful and useless. Did you never observe the narrow intelligence flashing from the keen eye of a clever rogue—how eager he is, how clearly his paltry soul sees the way to his end; he is the reverse of blind, but his keen eye-sight is forced into the service of evil, and he is mischievous in proportion to his cleverness?

Very true, he said.

But what if there had been a circumcision of such natures in the days of their youth; and they had been severed from those sensual pleasures, such as eating and drinking, which, like leaden weights, were attached to them at their birth, and which drag them down and turn the

vision of their souls upon the things that are below—if, I say, they had been released from these impediments and turned in the opposite direction, the very same faculty in them would have seen the truth as keenly as they see what their eyes are turned to now.

Very likely.

Yes, I said: and there is another thing which is likely, or rather a necessary inference from what has preceded, that neither the uneducated and uninformed of the truth, nor those who never make an end of their education, will be able ministers of State; not the former, because they have no single aim of duty which is the rule of all their actions, private as well as public; nor the latter, because they will not act at all except upon compulsion, fancying that they are already dwelling apart in the islands of the blest.

Very true, he replied.

Then, I said, the business of us who are the founders of the State will be to compel the best minds to attain that knowledge which we have already shown to be the greatest of all—they must continue to ascend until they arrive at the good; but when they have ascended and seen enough we must not allow them to do as they do now.

What do you mean?

I mean that they remain in the upper world: but this must not be allowed; they must be made to descend again among the prisoners in the den, and partake of their labours and honours, whether they are worth having or not.

But is not this unjust? he said; ought we to give them a worse life, when they might have a better?

You have again forgotten, my friend, I said, the intention of the legislator, who did not aim at making any one class in the State happy above the rest; the happiness was to be in the whole State, and he held the citizens together by persuasion and necessity, making them benefactors of the State, and therefore benefactors of one another; to this end he created them, not to please themselves, but to be his instruments in binding up the State.

True, he said, I had forgotten.

Observe, Glaucon, that there will be no injustice in compelling our philosophers to have a care and providence of others; we shall explain to them that in other States, men of their class are not obliged to share in the toils of politics; and this is reasonable, for they grow up at their own sweet will, and the government would rather not have them. Being self-taught, they cannot be expected to show any gratitude for a culture which they have never received. But we have brought you into the world to be rulers of the hive, kings of yourselves and of the other citizens, and have educated you far better and more perfectly than they have been educated, and you are better able to share in the double duty. Wherefore each of you, when his turn comes, must go down to the general underground abode, and get the habit of seeing in the dark. When you have acquired the habit, you will see ten thousand times better than the inhabitants of the den, and you will know what the several images are, and what they represent, because you have seen the beautiful and just and good in their truth. And thus our State, which is also yours, will be a reality, and not a dream only, and will be administered in a spirit unlike that of other States, in which men fight with one another about shadows only and are distracted in the struggle for power, which in their eyes is a great good. Whereas the truth is that the State in which the rulers are most reluctant to govern is always the best and most quietly governed, and the State in which they are most eager, the worst.

—BENJAMIN JOWETT.

DEMOCRACY [1]

PLATO

[From *The Republic,* Book VIII]

To Plato democracy means not a free banding together of individuals for the common good, but a pulling apart of individuals for the attainment by each of his own particular ends.

Next comes democracy; of this the origin and nature have still to be considered by us; and then we will enquire into the ways of the democratic man, and bring him up for judgment.

That, he said, is our method.

Well, I said, and how does the change from oligarchy into democracy arise? Is it not on this wise?—The good at which a State aims is to become as rich as possible, a desire which is insatiable?

What then?

The rulers, being aware that their power rests upon their wealth, refuse to curtail by law the extravagance of the spendthrift youth because they gain by their ruin; they take interest from them and buy up their estates and thus increase their own wealth and importance?

To be sure.

There can be no doubt that the love of wealth and the spirit of moderation cannot exist together in citizens of the same State to any considerable extent; one or the other will be disregarded.

That is tolerably clear.

And in oligarchical States, from the general spread of carelessness and extravagance, men of good family have often been reduced to beggary?

Yes, often.

And still they remain in the city; there they are, ready to sting and fully armed, and some of them owe money, some have forfeited their citizenship; a third class are in both predicaments: and they hate

[1] Reprinted by arrangement with the Oxford University Press, publishers.

and conspire against those who have got their property, and against everybody else, and are eager for revolution.

That is true.

On the other hand, the men of business, stooping as they walk, and pretending not even to see those whom they have already ruined, insert their sting—that is, their money—into some one else who is not on his guard against them, and recover the parent sum many times over multiplied into a family of children: and so they make drone and pauper to abound in the State.

Yes, he said, there are plenty of them —that is certain.

The evil blazes up like a fire; and they will not extinguish it, either by restricting a man's use of his own property, or by another remedy:

What other?

One which is the next best, and has the advantage of compelling the citizens to look to their characters:—Let there be a general rule that every one shall enter into voluntary contracts at his own risk, and there will be less of this scandalous money-making, and the evils of which we were speaking will be greatly lessened in the State.

Yes, they will be greatly lessened.

At present the governors, induced by the motives which I have named, treat their subjects badly; while they and their adherents, especially the young men of the governing class, are habituated to lead a life of luxury and idleness both of body and mind; they do nothing, and are incapable of resisting either pleasure or pain.

Very true.

They themselves care only for making money, and are as indifferent as the pauper to the cultivation of virtue.

Yes, quite as indifferent.

Such is the state of affairs which prevails among them. And often rulers and their subjects may come in one another's way, whether on a journey or on some other occasion of meeting, on a pilgrimage or a march, as fellow-soldiers or fellow-sailors; aye and they may observe the behaviour of each other in the very moment of danger—for where danger is, there is no fear that the poor will be despised by the rich—and very likely the wiry sunburnt poor man may be placed in battle at the side of a wealthy one who has never spoilt his complexion and has plenty of superfluous flesh—when he sees such an one puffing and at his wits'-end, how can he avoid drawing the conclusion that men like him are only rich because no one has the courage to despoil them? And when they meet in private will not people be saying to one another "Our warriors are not good for much?"

Yes, he said, I am quite aware that this is their way of talking.

And, as in a body which is diseased the addition of a touch from without may bring on illness, and sometimes even when there is no external provocation a commotion may arise within—in the same way wherever there is weakness in the State there is also likely to be illness, of which the occasion may be very slight, the one party introducing from without their oligarchical, the other their democratical allies, and then the State falls sick, and is at war with herself; and may be at times distracted, even when there is no external cause.

Yes, surely.

And then democracy comes into being after the poor have conquered their opponents, slaughtering some and banishing some, while to the remainder they give an equal share of freedom and power; and this is the form of government in which the magistrates are commonly elected by lot.

Yes, he said, that is the nature of democracy, whether the revolution has been effected by arms, or whether fear has caused the opposite party to withdraw.

And now what is their manner of life, and what sort of a government have they? for as the government is, such will be the man.

Clearly, he said.

In the first place, are they not free; and is not the city full of freedom and frankness—a man may say and do what he likes?

'Tis said so, he replied.

And where freedom is, the individual is clearly able to order for himself his own life as he pleases?

Clearly.

Then in this kind of State there will be the greatest variety of human natures?

There will.

This, then, seems likely to be the fairest of States, being like an embroidered robe which is spangled with every sort of flower. And just as women and children think a variety of colours to be of all things most charming, so there are many men to whom this State, which is spangled with the manners and characters of mankind, will appear to be the fairest of States.

Yes.

Yes, my good Sir, and there will be no better in which to look for a government.

Why?

Because of the liberty which reigns there—they have a complete assortment of constitutions; and he who has a mind to establish a State, as we have been doing, must go to a democracy as he would to a bazaar at which they sell them, and pick out the one that suits him; then, when he has made his choice, he may found his State.

He will be sure to have patterns enough.

And there being no necessity, I said, for you to govern in this State, even if you have the capacity, or to be governed, unless you like, or to go to war when the rest go to war, or to be at peace when others are at peace, unless you are so disposed—there being no necessity also, because some law forbids you to hold office or be a dicast, that you should not hold office or be a dicast, if you have a fancy—is not this a way of life which for the moment is supremely delightful?

For the moment, yes.

And is not their humanity to the condemned in some cases quite charming? Have you not observed how, in a democracy, many persons, although they have been sentenced to death or exile, just stay where they are and walk about the world—the gentleman parades like a hero, and nobody sees or cares?

Yes, he replied, many and many a one.

See too, I said, the forgiving spirit of democracy, and the "don't care" about trifles, and the disregard which she shows of all the fine principles which we solemnly laid down at the foundation of the city—as when we said that, except in the case of some rarely gifted nature, there never will be a good man who has not from his childhood been used to play amid things of beauty and make of them a joy and a study—how grandly does she trample all these fine notions of ours under her feet, never giving a thought to the pursuits which make a statesman, and promoting to honour any one who professes to be the people's friend.

Yes, she is of a noble spirit.

These and other kindred characteristics are proper to democracy, which is a charming form of government, full of variety and disorder, and dispensing a sort of equality to equals and unequals alike.

We know her well.

Consider now, I said, what manner of man the individual is, or rather consider, as in the case of the State, how he comes into being.

Very good, he said.

Is not this the way—he is the son of the miserly and oligarchical father who has trained him in his own habits?

Exactly.

And, like his father, he keeps under by force the pleasures which are of the spending and not of the getting sort, being those which are called unnecessary?

Obviously.

Would you like, for the sake of clearness, to distinguish which are the necessary and which are the unnecessary pleasures?

I should.

Are not necessary pleasures those of which we cannot get rid, and of which the satisfaction is a benefit to us? And they are rightly called so, because we are framed by nature to desire both what is beneficial and what is necessary, and cannot help it.

True.

We are not wrong therefore in calling them necessary?

We are not.

And the desires of which a man may get rid, if he takes pains from his youth upwards—of which the presence, moreover, does no good, and in some cases the reverse of good—shall we not be right in saying that all these are unnecessary?

Yes, certainly.

Suppose we select an example of either kind, in order that we may have a general notion of them?

Very good.

Will not the desire of eating, that is, of simple food and condiments, in so far as they are required for health and strength, be of the necessary class?

That is what I should suppose.

The pleasure of eating is necessary in two ways: it does us good and it is essential to the continuance of life?

Yes.

But the condiments are only necessary in so far as they are good for health?

Certainly.

And the desire which goes beyond this, of more delicate food, or other luxuries, which might generally be got rid of, if controlled and trained in youth, and is hurtful to the body, and hurtful to the soul in the pursuit of wisdom and virtue, may be rightly called unnecessary?

Very true.

May we not say that these desires spend, and that the others make money because they conduce to production?

Certainly.

And of the pleasures of love, and all other pleasures, the same holds good?

True.

And the drone of whom we spoke was he who was surfeited in pleasures and desires of this sort, and was the slave of the unnecessary desires, whereas he who was subject to the necessary only was miserly and oligarchical?

Very true.

Again, let us see how the democratical man grows out of the oligarchical: the following, as I suspect, is commonly the process.

What is the process?

When a young man who has been brought up as we were just now describing, in a vulgar and miserly way, has tasted drones' honey and has come to associate with fierce and crafty natures who are able to provide for him all sorts of refinements and varieties of pleasure—then, as you may imagine, the change will begin of the oligarchical principle within him into the democratical?

Inevitably.

And as in the city like was helping like, and the change was effected by an alliance from without assisting one division of the citizens, so too the young man is changed by a class of desires coming from without to assist the desires within him, that which is akin and alike again helping that which is akin and alike?

Certainly.

And if there be any ally which aids the oligarchical principle within him, whether the influence of a father or of kindred, advising or rebuking him, then there arises in his soul a faction and an opposite faction, and he goes to war with himself.

It must be so.

And there are times when the democratical principle gives way to the oligarchical, and some of his desires die, and others are banished; a spirit of reverence enters into the young man's soul and order is restored.

Yes, he said, that sometimes happens.

And then, again, after the old desires have been driven out, fresh ones spring up, which are akin to them, and because he their father does not know how to educate them, wax fierce and numerous.

Yes, he said, that is apt to be the way.

They draw him to his old associates, and holding secret intercourse with them, breed and multiply in him.

Very true.

At length they seize upon the citadel of the young man's soul, which they perceive to be void of all accomplishments and fair pursuits and true words, which make their abode in the minds of men who are dear to the gods, and are their best guardians and sentinels.

None better.

False and boastful conceits and phrases mount upwards and take their place.

They are certain to do so.

And so the young man returns into the country of the lotus-eaters, and takes up his dwelling there in the face of all men; and if any help be sent by his friends to the oligarchical part of him, the aforesaid vain conceits shut the gate of the king's fastness; and they will neither allow the embassy itself to enter, nor if private advisers offer the fatherly counsel of the aged will they listen to them or receive them. There is a battle and they gain the day, and then modesty, which they call silliness, is ignominiously thrust into exile by them, and temperance, which they nickname unmanliness, is trampled in the mire and cast forth; they persuade men that moderation and orderly expenditure are vulgarity and meanness, and so, by the help of a rabble of evil appetites, they drive them beyond the border.

Yes, with a will.

And when they have emptied and swept clean the soul of him who is now in their power and who is being initiated by them in great mysteries, the next thing is to bring back to their house insolence and anarchy and waste and impudence in bright array having garlands on their heads, and a great company with them, hymning their praises and calling them by sweet names; insolence they term breeding, and anarchy liberty, and waste magnificence, and impudence courage. And so the young man passes out of his original nature, which was trained in the school of necessity, into the freedom and libertinism of useless and unnecessary pleasures.

Yes, he said, the change in him is visible enough.

After this he lives on, spending his money and labour and time on unnecessary pleasures quite as much as on necessary ones; but if he be fortunate, and is not too much disordered in his wits, when years have elapsed, and the heyday of passion is over—supposing that he then re-admits into the city some part of the exiled virtues, and does not wholly give himself up to their successors—in that case he balances his pleasures and lives in a sort of equilibrium, putting the government of himself into the hands of the one which comes first and wins the turn; and when he has had enough of that, then into the hands of another; he despises none of them but encourages all of them equally.

Very true, he said.

Neither does he receive or let pass into the fortress any true word of advice; if any one says to him that some pleasures are the satisfactions of good and noble desires, and others of evil desires, and that he ought to use and honour some and chastise and master the others—whenever this is repeated to him he shakes his head and says that they are all alike, and that one is as good as another.

Yes, he said; that is the way with him.

Yes, I said, he lives from day to day indulging the appetite of the hour; and sometimes he is lapped in drink and strains of the flute; then he becomes a water-drinker, and tries to get thin; then he takes a turn at gymnastics; sometimes idling and neglecting everything, then once more living the life of a philosopher; often he is busy with politics, and starts to his feet and says and does whatever comes into his head; and, if he is emulous of any one who is a warrior, off he is in that direction, or of men of business, once more in that. His life has neither law nor order; and this distracted existence he terms joy and bliss and freedom; and so he goes on.

Yes, he replied, he is all liberty and equality.

Yes, I said; his life is motley and manifold and an epitome of the lives of many;—he answers to the State which we described as fair and spangled. And many a man and many a woman will take him for their pattern, and many a constitution and many an example of manners is contained in him.

Just so.

Let him then be set over against democracy; he may truly be called the democratic man.

—BENJAMIN JOWETT.

THE VISION OF ER [1]

PLATO

[From *The Republic*, Book X]

The vision of Er is an allegory suggested by thoughts on the immortality of the soul. Into the picture of the other world are introduced generalizations on the parts chance, virtue, and knowledge play in man's life.

[1] Reprinted by arrangement with the Oxford University Press, publishers.

Well, I said, I will tell you a tale; not one of the tales which Odysseus tells to the hero Alcinous, yet this too is a tale of a hero, Er the son of Armenius, a Pamphylian by birth. He was slain in battle, and ten days afterwards, when the bodies of the dead were taken up already in a state of corruption, his body was found unaffected by decay, and carried away home to be buried. And on the twelfth day, as he was lying on the funeral pile, he returned to life and told them what he had seen in the other world. He said that when his soul left the body he went on a journey with a great company, and that they came to a mysterious place at which there were two openings in the earth; they were near together, and over against them were two other openings in the heaven above. In the intermediate space there were judges seated, who commanded the just, after they had given judgment on them and had bound their sentences in front of them, to ascend by the heavenly way on the right hand; and in like manner the unjust were bidden by them to descend by the lower way on the left hand; these also bore the symbols of their deeds, but fastened on their backs. He drew near, and they told him that he was to be the messenger who would carry the report of the other world to men, and they bade him hear and see all that was to be heard and seen in that place. Then he beheld and saw on one side the souls departing at either opening of heaven and earth when sentences had been given on them; and at the two other openings other souls, some ascending out of the earth dusty and worn with travel, some descending out of heaven clean and bright. And arriving ever and anon they seemed to have come from a long journey, and they went forth with gladness into the meadow, where they encamped as at a festival: and those who knew one another embraced and conversed, the souls which came from earth curiously enquiring about the things above, and the souls which came from heaven about the things beneath. And they told one another what had happened by the way, those from below weeping and sorrowing at the remembrance of the things which they had endured and seen in their journey beneath the earth (now the journey lasted a thousand years), while those from above were describing heavenly delights and visions of inconceivable beauty. The story, Glaucon, would take too long to tell; but the sum was this:—He said that for every wrong which they had done to any one they suffered tenfold; or once in a hundred years—such being reckoned to be the length of man's life, and the penalty being thus paid ten times in a thousand years. If, for example, there were any who had been the cause of many deaths, or had betrayed or enslaved cities or armies, or been guilty of any other evil behaviour, for each and all of their offences they received punishment ten times over, and the rewards of beneficence and justice and holiness were in the same proportion. I need hardly repeat what he said concerning young children dying almost as soon as they were born. Of piety and impiety to gods and parents, and of murders, there were retributions other and greater far which he described. He mentioned that he was present when one of the spirits asked another, "Where is Ardiæus the Great?" (Now this Ardiæus lived a thousand years before the time of Er: he had been the tyrant of some city of Pamphylia, and had murdered his aged father and his elder brother, and was said to have committed many other abominable crimes). The answer of the other spirit was: "He comes not hither and will never come. And this," said he, "was one of the dreadful sights which we ourselves witnessed. We were at the mouth of the cavern, and, having completed all our experiences, were about to reascend, when of a sudden Ardiæus

appeared and several others, most of whom were tyrants; and there were also besides the tyrants private individuals who had been great criminals: they were just, as they fancied, about to return into the upper world, but the mouth, instead of admitting them, gave a roar whenever any of these incurable sinners or some one who had not been sufficiently punished tried to ascend; and then wild men of fiery aspect, who were standing by and heard the sound, seized and carried them off; and Ardiæus and others they bound head and foot and hand, and threw them down and flayed them with scourges, and dragged them along the road at the side, carding them on thorns like wool, and declaring to the passers-by what were their crimes, and that they were being taken away to be cast into hell." And of all the many terrors which they had endured, he said that there was none like the terror which each of them felt at that moment, lest they should hear the voice; and when there was silence, one by one they ascended with exceeding joy. These, said Er, were the penalties and retributions, and there were blessings as great.

Now when the spirits which were in the meadow had tarried seven days, on the eighth they were obliged to proceed on their journey, and, on the fourth day after, he said that they came to a place where they could see from above a line of light, straight as a column, extending right through the whole heaven and through the earth, in colour resembling the rainbow, only brighter and purer; another day's journey brought them to the place, and there, in the midst of the light, they saw the ends of the chains of heaven let down from above: for this light is the belt of heaven, and holds together the circle of the universe, like the undergirders of a trireme. From these ends is extended the spindle of Necessity, on which all the revolutions turn. The shaft and hook of this spindle are made of steel, and the whorl is made partly of steel and also partly of other materials. Now the whorl is in the form like the whorl used on earth; and the description of it implied that there is one large hollow whorl which is quite scooped out, and into this is fitted another lesser one, and another, and another, and four others, making eight in all, like vessels which fit into one another; the whorls show their edges on the upper side, and on their lower side altogether form one continuous whorl. This is pierced by the spindle, which is driven home through the centre of the eighth. The first and outermost whorl has the rim broadest, and the seven inner whorls are narrower, in the following proportions—the sixth is next to the first in size, the fourth next to the sixth; then comes the eighth; the seventh is fifth, the fifth is sixth, the third is seventh, last and eighth comes the second. The largest (or fixed stars) is spangled, and the seventh (or sun) is brightest; the eighth (or moon) coloured by the reflected light of the seventh; the second and fifth (Saturn and Mercury) are in colour like one another, and yellower than the preceding; the third (Venus) has the whitest light: the fourth (Mars) is reddish; the sixth (Jupiter) is in whiteness second. Now the whole spindle has the same motion; but, as the whole revolves in one direction, the seven inner circles move slowly in the other, and of these the swiftest is the eighth; next in swiftness are the seventh, sixth, and fifth, which move together; third in swiftness appeared to move according to the law of this reversed motion the fourth; the third appeared fourth and the second fifth. The spindle turns on the knees of Necessity; and on the upper surface of each circle is a siren, who goes round with them, hymning a single tone or note. The eight together form one harmony; and round about, at equal intervals, there is another band, three in number, each sitting upon her throne: these are the Fates, daughters of Necessity, who are clothed in white robes and have chaplets upon their heads, Lachesis and Clotho and Atropos, who accompany with their voices the harmony of the sirens —Lachesis singing of the past, Clotho of the present, Atropos of the future; Clotho from time to time assisting with a touch of her right hand the revolution of the outer circle of the whorl or spindle, and Atropos with her left hand touching and guiding the inner one, and Lachesis laying hold of either in turn, first with one hand and then with the other.

When Er and the spirits arrived, their duty was to go at once to Lachesis; but first of all there came a prophet who arranged them in order; then he took from the knees of Lachesis lots and samples of lives, and having mounted a high pulpit, spoke as follows: "Hear the word of Lachesis, the daughter of Necessity. Mortal souls, behold a new cycle of life and mortality. Your genius will not be allotted to you, but you will choose your genius; and let him who draws the first lot have the first choice, and the life which he chooses shall be his destiny. Virtue is free, and as a man honours or dishonours her he will have more or less of her; the responsibility is with the chooser—God is justified." When the Interpreter had thus spoken he scattered lots indifferently among them all, and each of them took up the lot which fell near him, all but Er himself (he was not allowed), and each as he took his lot perceived the number which he had obtained. Then the Interpreter placed on the ground before them the samples of lives; and there were many more lives than the souls present, and they were of all sorts. There were lives of every animal and of man in every condition. And there were tyrannies among them, some lasting out the tyrant's life, others which broke off in the middle and came to an end in poverty and exile and beg-

gary; and there were lives of famous
men, some who were famous for their
form and beauty as well as for their
strength and success in games, or, again,
for their birth and the qualities of their
ancestors; and some who were the reverse
of famous for the opposite qualities. And
of women likewise; there was not, however, any definite character in them, because the soul, when choosing a new life,
must of necessity become different. And
there was every other quality, and they
all mingled with one another, and also
with elements of wealth and poverty, and
disease and health; and there were mean
states also. And here, my dear Glaucon,
is the supreme peril of our human state;
and therefore the utmost care should be
taken. Let each one of us leave every
other kind of knowledge and seek and
follow one thing only, if peradventure
he may be able to learn and may find
some one who will make him able to learn
and discern between good and evil, and
so to choose always and everywhere the
better life as he has opportunity. He
should consider the bearing of all these
things which have been mentioned
severally and collectively upon virtue;
he should know what the effect of beauty
is when combined with poverty or wealth
in a particular soul, and what are the
good and evil consequences of noble and
humble birth, of private and public station, of strength and weakness, of cleverness and dullness, and of all the natural
and acquired gifts of the soul, and the
operation of them when conjoined; he
will then look at the nature of the soul,
and from the consideration of all these
qualities he will be able to determine
which is the better and which is the
worse; and so he will choose, giving the
name of evil to the life which will make
his soul more unjust, and good to the
life which will make his soul more just;
all else he will disregard. For we have
seen and know that this is the best choice
both in life and after death. A man must

take with him into the world below an
adamantine faith in truth and right, that
there too he may be undazzled by the
desire of wealth or the other allurements
of evil, lest, coming upon tyrannies and
similar villanies, he do irremediable
wrongs to others and suffer yet worse
himself; but let him know how to choose
the mean and avoid the extremes on
either side, as far as possible, not
only in this life but in all that which
is to come. For this is the way of happiness.

And according to the report of the messenger from the other world this was what
the prophet said at the time: "Even for
the last comer, if he chooses wisely and
will live diligently, there is appointed a
happy and not undesirable existence.
Let not him who chooses first be careless,
and let not the last despair." And when
he had spoken, he who had the first
choice came forward and in a moment
chose the greatest tyranny; his mind
having been darkened by folly and sen-
suality, he had not thought out the whole
matter before he chose, and did not at
first sight perceive that he was fated,
among other evils, to devour his own children. But when he had time to reflect,
and saw what was in the lot, he began
to beat his breast and lament over his
choice, forgetting the proclamation of the
prophet; for, instead of throwing the
blame of his misfortune on himself, he
accused chance and the gods, and everything rather than himself. Now he was
one of those who came from heaven, and
in a former life had dwelt in a well-
ordered State, but his virtue was a matter
of habit only, and he had no philosophy.
And it was true of others who were
similarly overtaken, that the greater
number of them came from heaven and
therefore they had never been schooled
by trial, whereas the pilgrims who came
frcm earth having themselves suffered
and seen others suffer were not in a hurry
to choose. And owing to this inexperi-

ence of theirs, and also because the lot was a chance, many of the souls exchanged a good destiny for an evil or an evil for a good. For if a man had always on his arrival in this world dedicated himself from the first to sound philosophy, and had been moderately fortunate in the number of the lot, he might, as the messenger reported, be happy here, and also his journey to another life and return to this, instead of being rough and underground, would be smooth and heavenly. Most curious, he said, was the spectacle—sad and laughable and strange; for the choice of the souls was in most cases based on their experience of a previous life. There he saw the soul which had once been Orpheus choosing the life of a swan out of enmity to the race of women, hating to be born of a woman because they had been his murderers; he beheld also the soul of Thamyras choosing the life of a nightingale; birds, on the other hand, like the swan and other musicians, wanting to be men. The soul which obtained the twentieth lot chose the life of a lion, and this was the soul of Ajax the son of Telamon, who would not be a man, remembering the injustice which was done to him in the judgment about the arms. The next was Agamemnon, who took the life of an eagle, because, like Ajax, he hated human nature by reason of his sufferings. About the middle came the lot of Atalanta; she, seeing the great fame of an athlete, was unable to resist the temptation: and after her there followed the soul of Epeus the son of Panopeus passing into the nature of a woman cunning in the arts; and far away among the last who chose, the soul of the jester Thersites was putting on the form of a monkey. There came also the soul of Odysseus having yet to make a choice, and his lot happened to be the last of them all. Now the recollection of former toils had disenchanted him of ambition, and he went about for a con-

siderable time in search of the life of a private man who had no cares; he had some difficulty in finding this, which was lying about and had been neglected by everybody else; and when he saw it, he said that he would have done the same had his lot been first instead of last, and that he was delighted to have it. And not only did men pass into animals, but I must also mention that there were animals tame and wild who changed into one another and into corresponding human natures—the good into the gentle and the evil into the savage, in all sorts of combinations.

All the souls had now chosen their lives, and they went in the order of their choice to Lachesis, who sent with them the genius whom they had severally chosen, to be the guardian of their lives and the fulfiller of the choice: this genius led the souls first to Clotho, and drew them within the revolution of the spindle impelled by her hand, thus ratifying the destiny of each; and then, when they were fastened to this, carried them to Atropos, who spun the threads and made them irreversible, whence without turning round they passed beneath the throne of Necessity; and when they had all passed, they marched on in a scorching heat to the plain of Forgetfulness, which was a barren waste destitute of trees and verdure; and then towards evening they encamped by the river of Unmindfulness, whose water no vessel can hold; of this they were all obliged to drink a certain quantity, and those who were not saved by wisdom drank more than was necessary; and each one as he drank forgot all things. Now after they had gone to rest, about the middle of the night there was a thunderstorm and earthquake, and then in an instant they were driven upwards in all manner of ways to their birth, like stars shooting. He himself was hindered from drinking the water. But in what manner or by what means he returned to the body he could not say;

only, in the morning, awaking suddenly, he found himself lying on the pyre.

And thus, Glaucon, the tale has been saved and has not perished, and will save us if we are obedient to the word spoken; and we shall pass safely over the river of Forgetfulness and our soul will not be defiled. Wherefore my counsel is, that we hold fast ever to the heavenly way and follow after justice and virtue always, considering that the soul is immortal and able to endure every sort of good and every sort of evil. Thus shall we live dear to one another and to the gods, both while remaining here and when, like conquerors in the games who go round to gather gifts, we receive our reward. And it shall be well with us both in this life and in the pilgrimage of a thousand years which we have been describing.

—BENJAMIN JOWETT.

THE SALVATION OF GOVERNMENT [1]

PLATO

[From *The Laws,* Book XII]

Plato became more and more convinced that his ideal state as set forth in the *Republic,* though satisfying in theory, could not be put into actual practice. Later he came back to the problem from a new angle with the purpose of so modifying his theory as to make it workable. Practical laws are necessary to regulate life, and laws can be devised and enforced only if entrusted to a council of wise men.

CLEINIAS. And now what, according to you, is to be the salvation of our government and of our laws, and how is it to be effected?

ATHENIAN. Were we not saying that there must be in our city a council which was to be of this sort: Ten of the oldest guardians of the law, and all those who

[1] Reprinted by arrangement with the Oxford University Press, publishers.

have obtained prizes of virtue, were to meet, and the council was also to include those who had visited foreign countries in the hope of hearing something that might be of use in the preservation of the laws, and who, having come safely home, and having been tested in these same matters, had proved themselves worthy to take part in the meeting;—each of the members was to select some young man of not less than thirty years of age, he himself judging in the first instance whether the young man is worthy by nature and education, and then introducing him to the others, and if he seem to them also to be worthy he was to be adopted by them; but if not, they are forbidden to elect him, and still more is he forbidden to accept their nomination. The meeting of the council was to be held early in the morning, when everybody was at leisure from all other business, whether public or private—something of that sort was said by us before.

CLE. True.

ATH. Then now returning to the council, I would say further,—that this institution, having all the required conditions, might save us all, and be the anchor of the state, if let down into the sea.

CLE. How so?

ATH. Now is the time for me to speak the truth in all earnestness.

CLE. Well said, and I hope that you will fulfil your intention.

ATH. Know, Cleinias, that every work has a saviour, as of the animal the soul and the head are the chief saviour.

CLE. Once more, what do you mean?

ATH. The well-being of those two is obviously the preservation of every living thing?

CLE. How is that?

ATH. The soul, besides other things, contains mind, and the head, besides other things, contains sight and hearing; and the mind, mingling with the noblest senses, and becoming one with them, may be truly called the salvation of all things.

CLE. Yes, quite so.

ATH. Yes, indeed; but with what is that intellect concerned which, mingling with the senses, is the salvation of ships in storms as well as in fair weather? In the ship, is it not the mind which pilots; and the sailors uniting their perceptions with the piloting mind, preserve themselves and the ship?

CLE. Very true.

ATH. We do not want many illustrations about such matters:—What aim would the general of an army, or what aim would a physician propose to himself, if he were seeking to attain salvation?

CLE. Very good.

ATH. Does not the general aim at victory and superiority in war, and do not the physician and his minister aim at producing health in the body?

CLE. Certainly.

ATH. And a physician who is ignorant about the body, that is to say, who knows not that which we just now called health, or a general who knows not victory, or any others who are ignorant of the particulars of the arts which we mentioned, cannot be said to have understanding about any of these matters?

CLE. Impossible.

ATH. And what would you say of the state, if a person proves to be ignorant of the aim to which the statesman should look? Ought he to be called a ruler at all; and further, will he ever be able to preserve that of which he does not even know the aim?

CLE. Impossible.

ATH. And therefore, if our settlement of the country is to be perfect, we ought to have some institution, which, as I was saying, will tell what is the aim of the state, and will inform us how we are to attain this, and what law or what man will advise us with that view. Any state which has no such institution is likely to be devoid of mind and sense, and in all her actions will proceed by mere chance.

CLE. Very true.

ATH. In which, then, of the parts or institutions of the state is any such guardian power to be found? Can we say?

CLE. I am not quite certain, Stranger; but I have a suspicion that you are referring to the assembly which you just now said was to meet at night.

ATH. You have answered rightly, Cleinias; and we must assume, as the argument implies, that this council possesses all virtue; and the beginning of virtue is not to make mistakes by guessing many things, but to look at one thing, and on this to fix all our aims.

CLE. Quite true.

ATH. Then now we shall see why there is nothing wonderful in states going astray—the reason is that their legislators have such different aims; nor is there anything wonderful in some laying down as their rule of justice, that certain individuals should bear rule in the state, whether they be good or bad, and others that the citizens should be rich, not caring whether they are the slaves of other men or not. The tendency of others, again, is towards freedom, and some legislate with a view to both at once; they want to be at the same time free and the lords of other states; but the wisest men, as they deem themselves to be, look to all these and similar aims, and there is no one of them which they exclusively honour, and to which they would have all things look.

CLE. Then, Stranger, our old assertion will hold, for we were saying that laws generally should look to one thing only; and this, as we admitted, was rightly said to be virtue.

ATH. Yes.

CLE. And we said that virtue was of four kinds?

ATH. Quite true.

CLE. And that mind was the leader of all four, and that to her the three other virtues and all other things ought to have regard?

ATH. You follow me capitally, Cleinias, and I would ask you to follow me to the end, for we have told you to what the mind of the pilot, the mind of the general and of the physician ought respectively to look; and now we may turn to mind political, of whom, as of a human creature, we will ask a question: O wonderful being, and to what are you looking? The Physician is able to tell his single aim in life, but you, the superior, as you declare yourself to be, of all intelligent beings, when you are asked are not able to tell. Can you, Megillus, and you, Cleinias, say distinctly what is the aim of mind political, in return for the many explanations of things which I have given you?

CLE. We cannot, Stranger.

ATH. Well, but ought we not to desire to see it, and to see in what it is found?

CLE. For example, in what?

ATH. For example, we were saying that there are four kinds of virtue, and as there are four of them, each of them must be one.

CLE. Certainly.

ATH. And further, all four of them we call one; for we say that courage is a virtue, and that prudence is a virtue, and the same of two others, as if they were in reality not many but one.

CLE. Quite so.

ATH. There is no difficulty in seeing in what way the two differ from one another, and have received two names, and so of the rest. But there is more difficulty in explaining why we call these two and the rest of them by the single name of virtue.

CLE. How do you mean?

ATH. I have no difficulty in explaining what I mean. Let us distribute the subject into questions and answers.

CLE. Once more, what do you mean?

ATH. Do you ask me what is that one thing which I call virtue, and then again

speak of as two, one part being courage and the other wisdom? I will tell you how that occurs: One of them has to do with fear; in this the beasts also participate, and quite young children,—I mean courage; for a courageous temper is a gift of nature and not of reason. But without reason there never has been, or is, or will be a wise and understanding soul; hence the difference.

CLE. That is true.

ATH. I have now told you in what way the two are different, and do you in return tell me in what way they are one and the same. Suppose that I ask you in what way the four are one, and when you have answered me, you will have a right to ask of me in return in what way they are four; and then let us proceed to enquire whether in the case of things which have a name and also a definition to them, true knowledge consists in knowing the name only and not the definition? Can he who is good for anything be ignorant about great and glorious truths without discredit?

CLE. I suppose not.

ATH. And is there anything greater to the legislator and the guardian of the law, and to him who thinks that he excels all other men in virtue, and has the rewards of virtue, than these very qualities of which we are now speaking, —courage, temperance, wisdom, justice?

CLE. How can there be anything greater?

ATH. And ought not the interpreters, the teachers, the lawgivers, the guardians of others to excel all other men, and perfectly to show him who desires to learn and know, or whose evil actions require to be punished and reproved, what is the nature of virtue and vice—shall the teacher be some poet who may find his way into the city, or some chance instructor of youth who professes to be better than he who has won the palm in every virtue? And can we wonder that when the guardians are not adequate in speech or action, and have no adequate knowledge of virtue, the city being unguarded should experience the common fate of cities in our day?

CLE. Wonder! no.

ATH. Well, then, as I was saying just now, what are we to do? How can we provide our guardians with a more than common virtue in speech or action, or in what way can our city be truly likened to the head and senses of rational beings because possessing such a guardian power?

CLE. What, Stranger, is the drift of your comparisons?

ATH. Do we not see that the city is the trunk, and are not the younger guardians, who are chosen for their natural gifts, placed in the head of the state, having their souls all full of eyes, with which they look about the whole city? They keep watch and hand over their perceptions to the memory, and inform the elders of all that happens in the city; and those whom we compared to the mind, because they have many wise thoughts—that is to say, the old men—take counsel, and making use of the younger men as their ministers, and advising with them,—in this way both together truly preserve the whole state:— Shall this be the order of our state, or shall we have some other order? Shall we say that they are all alike the owners of the state, and not merely individuals among them who have had the most careful training and education?

CLE. That, my good sir, is impossible.

ATH. Then we ought to proceed to some more exact training than that which has preceded.

CLE. Certainly.

ATH. And must not that of which we are in need be the one to which we were just now alluding?

CLE. Very true.

ATH. Did we not say that the workman or guardian, if he be perfect in every respect, ought not only to be able to see the many aims, but he should press onward to the one, which he should know, and knowing, order all things with a view to that?

CLE. True.

ATH. And can any one have a more exact way of considering or contemplating anything, than the being able to look at one idea gathered from many different things?

CLE. Perhaps not.

ATH. Not "perhaps not," but "certainly not," my good sir, is the right answer. There never has been a truer method than this discovered by any man.

CLE. I bow to your authority, Stranger; let us proceed in the way which you propose.

ATH. Then, as would appear, we must compel the guardians of our divine state to perceive, in the first place, what that principle is which is the same in all the four—the same, as we affirm, in courage and in temperance, and in justice and in prudence, and which, being one, we call, as we ought, by the single name of virtue. To this, my friends, we will, if you please, hold fast, and not let go until we have sufficiently explained what that is to which we are to look, whether to be regarded as one or as a whole, or as both, or in whatever way. Are we likely ever to be in a virtuous condition if we cannot tell whether virtue is many, or four, or one. Certainly, if you will take our advice, we shall in some way contrive that this principle has a place amongst us; but if you have made up your mind that we should let the matter alone, we will.

CLE. We must not, Stranger, by the God of strangers I swear that we must not; for in our opinion you speak most truly, but we should like to know how you will accomplish your purpose.

ATH. Wait a little before you ask; and let us, first of all, be quite agreed with one another that the purpose has to be accomplished.

CLE. Certainly, if that is possible.

ATH. Well, and about the good and the honourable, are we to take the same view—that each of them are many, but that our guardians are to regard them as in some sense one?

CLE. We must consider in what sense.

ATH. And are we to consider only, and to be unable to say what we think?

CLE. Certainly not; that would be the state of a slave.

ATH. And may not the same be said of all good men—that the true guardians of the laws ought to know their truth, and to be able to interpret them in words, and carry them out in action, judging of what is and of what is not well, according to nature?

CLE. Certainly.

ATH. Is not the knowledge of the Gods one of the noblest sorts of knowledge;—to know that they are and know how great is their power, as far as in man lies? We do indeed excuse the majority of mankind, who only follow the voice of the laws, but refuse to admit as guardians any who do not labour to obtain every possible evidence that there is respecting the Gods; they are forbidden and not allowed to choose as a guardian of the law, or to place in the select order of virtue, him who is not an inspired man, and has not laboured at these things.

CLE. It is certainly just, as you say, that he who is indolent about such matters or incapable should be rejected, and that things honourable should be put away from him.

ATH. Are we assured that there are two things which lead men to believe in the Gods, as we have already stated?

CLE. What are they?

ATH. One is the argument about the soul, which has been already mentioned—that it is the eldest and most divine of all things, to which motion attaining generation gives perpetual existence; the other was an argument from the order of motion of the heavens, and of all things under the dominion of the mind which ordered the universe. If a man look upon the world not lightly or foolishly, there was never any one so godless who did not experience an effect opposite to that which he may imagine. For they think that those who handle these matters by the help of astronomy, and the accompanying arts of demonstration, may become godless; because they see, as far as they can see, things happening by necessity, and not by an intelligent will accomplishing good.

CLE. But what is the fact?

ATH. Just the opposite of the opinion which once prevailed among men, that the sun and stars are without soul. Even in those days men wondered about them, and that which is now ascertained was then conjectured by some who had a more exact knowledge of them—that if they had been things without soul, and had no mind, they could never have moved according to such exact calculations; and even at that time some ventured to hazard the conjecture that the mind was the orderer of the universe. But these same persons again mistaking the nature of the soul, which they conceived to be younger and not older than the body, once more overturned the world, or rather, I should say, themselves, for what they saw before their eyes in heaven, all appeared to be full of stones, and earth, and many other lifeless bodies, and to these they assigned the various causes of all things. Such studies gave rise to much atheism and perplexity, and the poets took occasion to be abusive,—comparing the philosophers to she-dogs uttering vain howlings, and saying other nonsense of the same sort. But now, as I said, the case is reversed.

CLE. How is that?

ATH. No man can be a true worshipper of the Gods who does not know these two principles—that the soul is the eldest of all things which are born, and is immortal and rules over all bodies;

moreover, as I have now said several times, he who has not contemplated the mind of nature which is said to exist in the stars, and gone through the previous training, and seen the connection of them with music, and harmonized them all with laws and institutions, is not able to give a reason of such things as have a reason. And he who is unable to acquire this in addition to the ordinary virtues of a citizen, can hardly be a good ruler of a whole state; but he should be the subordinate of other rulers. Wherefore, Cleinias and Megillus, let us consider whether we may not add to all the other laws which we have discussed this further one,—that the nocturnal assembly of the magistrates, which has also been associated with us in our whole scheme of education, shall be a guard set according to law for the salvation of the state.
—BENJAMIN JOWETT.

LOVE [1]

PLATO

[From *The Symposium*]

Through the mouth of Socrates Plato teaches that love is a universal principle manifesting itself in all nature, from the lowest plants and animals to the philosopher. In its lower forms it is physical and material; in its highest form it passes from the physical and material to the mystical contemplation of the good and the beautiful in whatever shape embodied.

In the magnificent oration which you have uttered, I think that you were right, my dear Agathon, when you said that you would begin with the nature of love and afterwards speak of his works—that is a way of beginning which I very much approve. And as you have spoken thus eloquently of the nature of love, may I

[1] Reprinted by arrangement with the Oxford University Press, publishers.

ask you further, Whether love is the love of something or of nothing? And here I must explain myself: I do not want you to say that love is the love of a father or the love of a mother—that would be ridiculous; but to answer as you would, if I asked is a father a father of something? to which you would find no difficulty in replying, of a son or daughter: and that would be right.

Very true, said Agathon.

And you would say the same of a mother?

He assented.

Yet let me ask you one more question in order to illustrate my meaning. Is not a brother to be regarded essentially as a brother of something?

Certainly, he replied.

That is, of a brother or sister?

Yes, he said.

And now, said Socrates, I will ask about love:—Is love of something or of nothing?

Of something, surely, he replied.

Keep in mind what this is, and tell me what I want to know—whether love desires that of which love is.

Yes, surely.

And does he possess, or does he not possess, that which he loves and desires?

Probably not, I should say.

Nay, replied Socrates, I would have you consider whether "necessarily" is not rather the word. The inference that he who desires something is in want of something, and that he who desires nothing is in want of nothing, is in my judgment, Agathon, absolutely and necessarily true. What do you think?

I agree with you, said Agathon.

Very good. And would he who is great desire to be great, or he who is strong desire to be strong?

That would be inconsistent with our previous admissions.

True. For he who is anything cannot want to be that which he is?

Very true.

And yet, added Socrates, if a man being strong desired to be strong, or being swift desired to be swift, or being healthy desired to be healthy, in that case he might be thought to desire a quality which he already has. I give the example in order that we may avoid misconception. For the possessors of these qualities, Agathon, must be supposed to have their respective advantages at the time, whether they choose or not; and who can desire that which he has? Therefore, when a person says, I am well and wish to be well, or I am rich and wish to be rich, and I desire to have simply what I have—to him we shall reply: "You, my friend, having wealth and health and strength, want to have the continuance of them; for at this moment, whether you choose or not, you have them. And when you say, I desire that which I have and nothing else, is not your meaning that you want to have what you now have in the future?" He must agree with us—must he not?

He must, said Agathon.

Then said Socrates, this is equivalent, not to desiring what he has or possesses already, but to desiring that what he has may be preserved to him in the future?

Very true, he said.

Then he and every one who desires, desires that which he has not already, and which is future and not present, and which he has not, and is not, and of which he is in want;—these are the sort of things which love and desire seek?

Very true, he said.

Then now, said Socrates, let us recapitulate the argument. First, is not love of something, and of something too which is wanting to a man?

Yes, he replied.

Remember further what you said in your speech, or if you do not remember I will remind you: you said that the love of the beautiful set in order the empire of the gods, for that of deformed things there is no love—did you not say something like that?

Yes, said Agathon.

Yes, my friend, and the remark was a just one. And if this is true, love is the love of beauty and not of deformity?

He assented.

And the admission has been already made that love is of that which a man wants and has not?

True, he said.

Then love wants and has not beauty?

Certainly, he replied.

Then would you call that beautiful which wants and does not possess beauty?

Certainly not.

Then would you still say that love is beautiful?

Agathon replied: I fear that I did not understand what I was saying.

Yet you made a fair speech, Agathon, replied Socrates; but once more:—Is not the good also the beautiful?

Yes.

Then in wanting the beautiful, love wants also the good?

I cannot refute you, Socrates, said Agathon. And let us suppose that what you say is true.

Say rather, dear Agathon, that you cannot refute the truth; for Socrates is easily refuted.

And now I will take my leave of you, and rehearse the tale of love which I heard from Diotima of Mantinea, a woman wise in this and many other kinds of knowledge, who in the days of old, when the Athenians offered sacrifice before the coming of the plague, delayed the disease ten years. She was my instructress in the art of love, and I shall repeat to you what she said to me, beginning with the admissions made by Agathon, which are nearly if not quite the same which I made to the wise woman when she questioned me: I think that this will be the easiest way, and I shall take both parts myself as well as I can. Like Agathon, she spoke first of the being and nature of love, and then of his works. And I said to her in nearly the same words which he used to me, that love was a mighty god, and likewise fair; and she proved to me as I proved to him that, by my own showing, love was neither fair nor good. "What do you mean, Diotima," I said, "is love then evil and foul?" "Hush," she cried; "is that to be deemed foul which is not fair?" "Certainly," I said. "And is that which is not wise, ignorant? do you not see that there is a mean between wisdom and ignorance?" "And what may that be?" I said. "Right opinion," she replied; "which, as you know, being incapable of giving a reason, is not knowledge (for how can knowledge be devoid of reason? nor again, ignorance, for neither can ignorance attain the truth), but is clearly something which is a mean between ignorance and wisdom." "Quite true," I replied. "Do not then insist," she said, "that what is not fair is of necessity foul, or what is not good evil; or infer that because love is not fair and good, he is therefore foul and evil; for he is in a mean between them." "Well," I said, "love is surely admitted by all to be a great god." "By those who know or by those who do not know?" "By all." "And how, Socrates," she said with a smile, "can love be acknowledged to be a great god by those who say that he is not a god at all?" "And who are they?" I said. "You and I are two of them," she replied. "How can that be?" I said. "That is very intelligible," she replied; "for you yourself would acknowledge that the gods are happy and fair—of course you would—would you dare to say that any god was not?" "Certainly not," I replied. "And you mean by the happy, those who are the possessors of things good and fair?" "Yes." "And you admitted that Love, because he was in want, desires those good and fair things of which he is in want?" "Yes, I admitted that." "But how can he be a god who has no share in the good or the fair?"

"That is not to be supposed." "Then you see that you also deny the divinity of Love."

"What then is love?" I asked; "Is he mortal?" "No." "What then?" "As in the former instance, he is neither mortal nor immortal, but in a mean between the two." "What is he then, Diotima?" "He is a great spirit, and like all spirits he is intermediate between the divine and the mortal." "And what," I said, "is his power?" "He interprets," she replied, "between gods and men, conveying to the gods the prayers and sacrifices of men, and to men the commands and replies of the gods; he is the mediator who spans the chasm which divides them, and in him all is bound together, and through him the arts of the prophet and the priest, their sacrifices and mysteries and charms, and all prophecy and incantation find their way. For God mingles not with man; but through Love all the intercourse and speech of God with man, whether awake or asleep, is carried on. The wisdom which understands this is spiritual; all other wisdom, such as that of arts and handicrafts, is mean and vulgar. Now these spirits of intermediate power are many and diverse, and one of them is Love." "And who," I said, "was his father, and who his mother?" "The tale," she said, "will take time; nevertheless I will tell you. On the birthday of Aphrodite there was a feast of the gods, at which the god Poros or Plenty, who is the son of Metis or Discretion, was one of the guests. When the feast was over, Penia or Poverty, as the manner is on such occasions, came about the doors to beg. Now Plenty, who was the worse for nectar (there was no wine in those days), went into the garden of Zeus and fell into a heavy sleep; and Poverty considering her own circumstances, plotted to have a child by him, and accordingly she lay down at his side and conceived Love, who partly because he is naturally a lover of the beautiful, and because

Aphrodite herself is beautiful, and also because he was born on her birthday, is her follower and attendant. And as his parentage is, so also are his fortunes. In the first place he is always poor, and anything but tender and fair, as the many imagine him; and he is hard-featured and squalid, and has no shoes, nor a house to dwell in; on the bare earth exposed he lies under the open heaven, in the streets, or at the doors of houses, taking his rest; and like his mother he is always in distress. Like his father too, whom he also partly resembles, he is always plotting against the fair and good; he is bold, enterprising, strong, a hunter of men, always weaving some intrigue or other, keen in the pursuit of wisdom, and never wanting resources; a philosopher at all times, terrible as an enchanter, sorcerer, sophist; for as he is neither mortal nor immortal, he is alive and flourishing at one moment when he is in plenty, and dead at another moment, and again live by reason of his father's nature. But that which is always flowing in is always flowing out, and so he is never in want and never in wealth; and further, he is in a mean between ignorance and knowledge. The truth of the matter is as follows: No god is a philosopher or seeker after wisdom, for he is wise already; nor does any man who is wise seek after wisdom. Neither do the ignorant seek after wisdom. For herein is the evil of ignorance, that he who is neither good nor wise is nevertheless satisfied: he has no desire for that of which he feels no want." "But who then, Diotima," I said, "are the lovers of wisdom, if they are neither the wise nor the foolish?" "A child may answer that question," she replied; "they are those who, like love, are in a mean between the two. For wisdom is a most beautiful thing, and love is of the beautiful; and therefore love is also a philosopher or lover of wisdom, and being a lover of wisdom is in a mean between the wise and the ignorant. And this again

is a quality which Love inherits from his parents; for his father is wealthy and wise, and his mother is poor and foolish. Such, my dear Socrates, is the nature of the spirit Love. The error in your conception of him was very natural, and as I imagine from what you say, has arisen out of a confusion of love and the beloved, which made you think that love was all beautiful. For the beloved is the truly beautiful, and delicate, and perfect, and blessed; but the principle of love is of another nature, and is such as I have described."

I said: "O thou stranger woman, thou sayest well, and now, assuming love to be such as you say, what is the use of him to us men?" "That, Socrates," she replied, "I will proceed to unfold: of his nature and birth I have already spoken; and you acknowledge that love is of the beautiful. But some one will say: Of the beautiful in what, Socrates and Diotima?—or rather let me put the question more clearly, and ask: When a man loves the beautiful, what does he desire?" I answered her "That the beautiful may be his." "Still," she said, "the answer suggests a further question: What is given by the possession of beauty?" "To what you have asked," I replied, "I have no answer ready." "Then," she said, "let me put the word 'good' in the place of the beautiful, and repeat the question once more: He who loves the good loves; what does he love?" "The possession of the good," I said. "And what does he gain who possesses the good?" "Happiness," I replied; "there is no difficulty in answering that." "Yes," she said, "the happy are made happy by the acquisition of good things. Nor is there any need to ask why a man desires happiness; the answer is already final." "You are right," I said. "And is this wish and this desire common to all? and do all men always desire their own good, or only some men?—what say you?" "All men," I replied; "the desire is common to all."

"Why, then," she rejoined, "are not all men, Socrates, said to love, but only some of them? whereas you say that all men are always loving the same things." "I myself wonder," I said, "why that is." "There is nothing to wonder at," she replied; "the reason is that one part of love is separated off and receives the name of the whole, but the other parts have other names." "Give an illustration," I said. She answered me as follows: "There is poetry, which, as you know, is complex and manifold. All creation or passage of non-being into being is poetry or making, and the processes of all art are creative; and the masters of arts are all poets or makers." "Very true." "Still," she said, "you know that they are not called poets, but have other names; the specific term, poetry, is confined to that portion of the art which is separated off from the rest of poetry, and is concerned with music and metre; and this is what is called poetry, and they who possess this kind of poetry are called poets." "Very true," I said. "And the same holds of love. For you may say generally that all desire of good and happiness is only the great and subtle power of love; but those who turn towards him by any other path, whether the path of money-making or gymnastics or philosophy, are not called lovers—the name of the genius is reserved for those whose affection takes one form only—they alone are said to love, or to be lovers." "I dare say," I replied, "that you are right." "Yes," she added, "and you hear people say that lovers are seeking for their other half; but I say that they are seeking neither for the half of themselves, nor for the whole, unless the half or the whole be also a good. And they will cut off their own hands and feet and cast them away, if they are evil; for they love not what is their own, but what is another's, unless indeed by the words 'good' and 'their own' and 'bad' and 'another's' they mean the same thing. For

there is nothing which men love but the good. Do you think that there is?" "Certainly, I should say, that there is nothing." "Then," she said, "the conclusion of the whole matter is, that men love the good." "Yes," I said. "To which may be added that they love the possession of the good?" "Yes, that may be added." "And not only the possession, but the everlasting possession of the good?" "That may be added too." "Then love," she said, "may be described generally as the love of the everlasting possession of the good?" "That is most true."

"Then if this be the nature of love, can you tell me further," she said, "what is the manner of the pursuit? What are they doing who show all this eagerness and heat which is called love? Answer me." "Nay, Diotima," I replied, "if I had known, I should not have wondered at your wisdom, neither should I have come to you to learn about this very matter." "Well," she said, "I will teach you;—love is only birth in beauty, whether of body or soul." "The oracle requires an explanation," I said; "I do not understand you." "I will make my meaning clearer," she replied. "I mean to say, that all men are bringing to the birth in their bodies and in their souls. There is a certain age at which human nature is desirous of procreation—procreation which must be in beauty and not in deformity; and this procreation is the union of man and woman, and is a divine thing; for conception and generation are an immortal principle in the mortal creature, and in the inharmonious they can never be. But the deformed is always inharmonious with the divine, and the beautiful harmonious. Beauty, then, is the destiny or goddess of parturition who presides at birth, and therefore when approaching beauty the conceiving power is propitious, and diffuse, and benign, and begets and bears fruit: at the sight of ugliness it frowns and contracts in pain, and is averted and morose, and shrinks up, and not without a pang refrains from conception. And this is the reason why, when the hour of conception arrives, and the teeming nature is full, there is such a flutter and ecstacy about beauty whose approach is the alleviation of the pain of travail. For love, Socrates, is not, as you imagine, the love of the beautiful only." "What then?" "The love of generation and of birth in beauty." "Yes," I said. "Yes, indeed," she replied. "But why of generation?" I said. "Because to the mortal, generation is a sort of eternity and immortality," she replied; "and if, as has been already admitted, love is of the everlasting possession of the good, all men will necessarily desire immortality together with good. Wherefore love is of immortality."

All this she taught me at various times when she spoke of love. And I remember that she once said to me, "What is the cause, Socrates, of love, and the attendant desire? See you not how all animals, birds as well as beasts, in their desire of procreation, are in agony when they take the infection of love, which begins with the desire of union; whereto is added the care of offspring, on behalf of whom the weakest are ready to battle against the strongest even to the uttermost, and to die for them, and will let themselves be tormented with hunger or suffer anything in order to maintain their offspring. Man may be supposed to act thus from reason; but why should animals have these passionate feelings? Can you tell me why?" Again I replied, that I did not know. She said to me: "And do you expect ever to become a master in the art of love, if you do not know this?" "But that, Diotima, is the reason why I came to you; as I have told you already, I am aware that I want a teacher, and I wish that you would explain to me the cause of this and of the other mysteries of love." "Marvel not," she said, "if you believe that love is of

the immortal, as we have already several times acknowledged; for here again, and on the same principle too, the mortal nature is seeking as far as is possible to be everlasting and immortal: and this is only to be attained by generation, because generation always leaves behind a new existence in place of the old. Nay even in the life of the same individual there is succession and not absolute unity; a man is called the same, and yet in the short interval which elapses between youth and age, and in which every animal is said to have life and identity, he is undergoing a perpetual process of loss and reparation —hair, flesh, bones, blood, and the whole body are always changing. Which is true not only of the body, but also of the soul, whose habits, tempers, opinions, desires, pleasures, pains, fears, never remain the same in any one of us but are always coming and going; and equally true of knowledge, which is still more surprising —for not only do the sciences in general come and go, so that in respect of them we are never the same; but each of them individually experiences a like change. For what is implied in the word 'recollection,' but the departure of knowledge, which is ever being forgotten and is renewed and preserved by recollection, and appears to be the same although in reality new, according to that law of succession by which all mortal things are preserved, not absolutely the same, but by substitution, the old worn-out mortality leaving another new and similar existence behind—unlike the divine, which is always the same and not another? And in this way, Socrates, the mortal body, or mortal anything, partakes of immortality; but the immortal in another way. Marvel not then at the love which all men have of their offspring; for that universal love and interest is for the sake of immortality."

I was astonished at her words, and said: "Is this really true, O thou wise Diotima?" And she answered with all the authority of a sophist: "Of that, Socrates, you may be assured;—think only of the ambition of men, and you will wonder at the senselessness of their ways, unless you consider how they are stirred by the love of an immortality of fame. They are ready to run risks greater far than they would have run for their children, and to spend money and undergo any sort of toil, and even to die for the sake of leaving behind them a name which shall be eternal. Do you imagine that Alcestis would have died to save Admetus, or Achilles to avenge Patroclus, or your own Codrus in order to preserve the kingdom for his sons, if they had not imagined that the memory of their virtues, which is still retained among us, would be immortal? Nay," she said, "I am persuaded that all men do all things, and the better they are the more they do them, in hope of the glorious fame of immortal virtue; for they desire the immortal.

"They whose bodies only are creative, betake themselves to women and beget children—this is the character of their love; their offspring, as they hope, will preserve their memory and give them the blessedness and immortality which they desire in the future. But creative souls —for there certainly are men who are more creative in their souls than in their bodies—conceive that which is proper for the soul to conceive or retain. And what are these conceptions?—wisdom and virtue in general. But such creators are poets and all artists who are deserving of the name inventor. But the greatest and fairest sort of wisdom by far is that which is concerned with the ordering of states and families, and which is called temperance and justice. And he who in youth has the seed of these implanted in him and is himself inspired, when he comes to maturity desires to beget and generate. He wanders about seeking beauty that he may beget offspring—for in deformity he will beget nothing—and

naturally embraces the beautiful rather than the deformed body; above all when he finds a fair and noble and well-nurtured soul, he embraces the two in one person, and to such an one he is full of speech about virtue and the nature and pursuits of a good man; and he tries to educate him; and at the touch of the beautiful which is ever present to his memory, even when absent, he brings forth that which he had conceived long before, and in company with him tends that which he brings forth; and they are married by a far nearer tie and have a closer friendship than those who beget mortal children, for the children who are their common offspring are fairer and more immortal. Who, when he thinks of Homer and Hesiod and other great poets, would not rather have their children than ordinary human ones? Who would not emulate them in the creation of children such as theirs, which have preserved their memory and given them everlasting glory? Or who would not have such children as Lycurgus left behind him to be the saviours, not only of Lacedæmon, but of Hellas, as one may say? There is Solon, too, who is the revered father of Athenian laws; and many others there are in many other places, both among Hellenes and barbarians. All of them have given to the world many noble works, and have been the parents of virtue of every kind, and many temples have been raised in their honour for the sake of their children; which were never raised in honour of any one, for the sake of his mortal children.

"These are the lesser mysteries of love, into which even you, Socrates, may enter; to the greater and more hidden ones which are the crown of these, and to which, if you pursue them in a right spirit, they will lead, I know not whether you will be able to attain. But I will do my utmost to inform you, and do you follow if you can. For he who would proceed aright in this matter should begin in youth to visit beautiful forms; and first, if he be guided by his instructor aright, to love one such form only—out of that he should create fair thoughts; and soon he will of himself perceive that the beauty of one form is akin to the beauty of another; and then if beauty of form in general is his pursuit, how foolish would he be not to recognize that the beauty in every form is one and the same! And when he perceives this he will abate his violent love of the one, which he will despise and deem a small thing, and will become a lover of all beautiful forms; in the next stage he will consider that the beauty of the mind is more honourable than the beauty of the outward form. So that if a virtuous soul have but a little comeliness, he will be content to love and tend him, and will search out and bring to the birth thoughts which may improve the young, until he is compelled to contemplate and see the beauty of institutions and laws, and to understand that the beauty of them all is of one family, and that personal beauty is a trifle; and after laws and institutions he will go on to the sciences, that he may see their beauty, being not like a servant in love with the beauty of one youth or man or institution, himself a slave mean and narrow-minded, but drawing towards and contemplating the vast sea of beauty, he will create many fair and noble thoughts in boundless love of wisdom; until on that shore he grows and waxes strong, and at last the vision is revealed to him of a single science, which is the science of beauty everywhere. To this I will proceed; please to give me your very best attention.

"He who has been instructed thus far in the things of love, and who has learned to see the beautiful in due order and succession, when he comes toward the end will suddenly perceive a nature of wondrous beauty (and this, Socrates, is the final cause of all our former toils)—a nature which in the first place is everlasting, not growing and decaying, or waxing and waning; in the next place not fair in one point of view and foul in another, or at one time or in one relation or at one place fair, at another time or in another relation or at another place foul, as if fair to some and foul to others, or in the likeness of a face or hands or any other part of the bodily frame, or in any form of speech or knowledge, or existing in any other being; as for example, in an animal, or in heaven, or in earth, or in any other place, but beauty only, absolute, separate, simple, and everlasting, which without diminution and without increase, or any change, is imparted to the ever-growing and perishing beauties of all other things. He who under the influence of true love rising upward from these begins to see that beauty, is not far from the end. And the true order of going or being led by another to the things of love, is to use the beauties of earth as steps along which he mounts upwards for the sake of that other beauty, going from one to two, and from two to all fair forms, and from fair forms to fair practices, and from fair practices to fair notions, until from fair notions he arrives at the notion of absolute beauty, and at last knows what the essence of beauty is. This, my dear Socrates," said the stranger of Mantinea, "is that life above all others which man should live, in the contemplation of beauty absolute; a beauty which if you once beheld, you would see not to be after the measure of gold, and garments, and fair boys and youths, whose presence now entrances you; and you and many a one would be content to live seeing only and conversing with them without meat or drink, if that were possible—you only want to be with them and to look at them. But what if man had eyes to see the true beauty— the divine beauty, I mean, pure and clear and unalloyed, not clogged with the pollutions of mortality, and all the colours and vanities of human life—thither looking, and holding converse with the true beauty divine and simple? Do you not see that in that communion only, beholding beauty with the eye of the mind, he will be enabled to bring forth, not images of beauty, but realities (for he has hold not of an image but of a reality), and bringing forth and nourishing true virtue to become the friend of God and be immortal, if mortal man may. Would that be an ignoble life?"

Such, Phædrus—and I speak not only to you, but to all of you—were the words of Diotima; and I am persuaded of their truth. And being persuaded of them, I try to persuade others, that in the attainment of this end human nature will not easily find a better helper than love. And therefore, also, I say that every man ought to honour him as I myself honour him, and walk in his ways, and exhort others to do the same, and praise the power and spirit of love according to the measure of my ability now and ever.

The words which I have spoken, you, Phædrus, may call an encomium of love, or anything else which you please.

—BENJAMIN JOWETT.

WHAT IS HOLINESS? [1]

PLATO

[The *Euthyphro*]

In this dialogue Plato is not so much interested in arriving at an answer to the question of what holiness is, as in pointing out how easy it is to fall into error through hasty and careless thinking. It is a lesson in dialectic.

EUTHYPHRO. Why have you left the Lyceum, Socrates? and what are you doing in the porch of the King Archon? Surely you cannot be engaged in an action before the king, as I am.

[1] Reprinted by arrangement with the Oxford University Press, publishers.

SOCRATES. Not in an action, Euthyphro; impeachment is the word which the Athenians use.

EUTH. What! I suppose that some one has been prosecuting you, for I cannot believe that you are the prosecutor of another.

Soc. Certainly not.

EUTH. Then some one else has been prosecuting you?

Soc. Yes.

EUTH. And who is he?

Soc. A young man who is little known, Euthyphro; and I hardly know him: his name is Meletus, and he is of the deme of Pitthis. Perhaps you may remember his appearance; he has a beak, and long straight hair, and a beard which is ill grown.

EUTH. No, I do not remember him, Socrates. But what is the charge which he brings against you?

Soc. What is the charge? Well, a very serious charge, which shows a good deal of character in the young man, and for which he is certainly not to be despised. He says he knows how the youth are corrupted and who are their corruptors. I fancy that he must be a wise man, and seeing that I am anything but a wise man, he has found me out, and is going to accuse me of corrupting his young friends. And of this our mother the state is to be the judge. Of all our political men he is the only one who seems to me to begin in the right way, with the cultivation of virtue in youth; like a good husbandman, he makes the young shoots his first care, and clears away us who are the destroyers of them. That is the first step; he will afterwards attend to the elder branches; and if he goes on as he has begun, he will be a very great public benefactor.

EUTH. I hope that he may; but I rather fear, Socrates, that the reverse will turn out to be the truth. My opinion is that in attacking you he is simply aiming a blow at the state in a sacred place. But in what way does he say that you corrupt the young?

Soc. He brings a wonderful accusation against me, which at first hearing excites surprise: he says that I am a poet or maker of gods, and that I make new gods and deny the existence of old ones; this is the ground of his indictment.

Euth. I understand, Socrates; he means to attack you about the familiar sign, which occasionally, as you say, comes to you. He thinks that you are a neologian, and he is going to have you up before the court for this. He knows that such a charge is readily received by the world. I can tell you that, for even when I myself speak in the assembly about divine things, and foretell the future to them, they laugh at me as a madman; and yet every word that I say is true. But they are jealous of all of us. I suppose that we must be brave and not mind them.

Soc. Their laughter, friend Euthyphro, is not a matter of much consequence. For a man may be thought wise; but the Athenians, I suspect, do not trouble themselves about him until he begins to impart his wisdom to others; and then for some reason or other, perhaps, as you say, from jealousy, they are angry.

Euth. I am never likely to try their temper in this way.

Soc. I dare say not, for you are select in your acquaintance, and seldom impart your wisdom. But I have a benevolent habit of pouring out myself to everybody, and would even pay for a listener, and I am afraid that the Athenians know this; and therefore, as I was saying, if the Athenians would only laugh at me as you say that they laugh at you, the time might pass gaily enough in the court; but perhaps they may be in earnest, and then what the end will be you soothsayers only can predict.

Euth. I dare say that the affair will end in nothing, Socrates, and that you will win your cause; and I think that I shall win mine.

Soc. And now what is your suit, Euthyphro? are you the pursuer or the defendant?

Euth. I am the pursuer.

Soc. Of whom?

Euth. You will think me mad when I tell you.

Soc. Why, has the fugitive wings?

Euth. Nay, he is not very volatile at his time of life.

Soc. Who is he?

Euth. My father.

Soc. Your father! my good man?

Euth. Yes.

Soc. And of what is he accused?

Euth. Of murder, Socrates.

Soc. By the powers, Euthyphro! how little does the common herd know of the nature of right and truth. A man must be an extraordinary man, and have made great strides in wisdom, before he could have seen his way to this.

Euth. Indeed, Socrates, he must have made great strides.

Soc. I suppose that the man whom your father murdered was one of your relatives; if he had been a stranger you would never have thought of prosecuting him.

Euth. I am amused, Socrates, at your making a distinction between one who is a relation and one who is not a relation; for surely the pollution is the same in either case, if you knowingly associate with the murderer when you ought to clear yourself and him by proceeding against him. The real question is whether the murdered man has been justly slain. If justly, then your duty is to let the matter alone; but if unjustly, then even if the murderer is under the same roof with you and eats at the same table, proceed against him. Now the man who is dead was a poor dependent of mine who worked for us as a field labourer at our farm in Naxos, and one day in a fit of drunken passion he got into a quarrel with one of our domestic servants and slew him. My father bound him head and foot and threw him into a ditch, and then sent to Athens to ask of a diviner what he should do with him. Meantime he had no care or thought of him, being under the impression that he was a murderer; and that even if he did die there would be no great harm. And this was just what happened. For such was the effect of cold and hunger and chains upon him, that before the messenger returned from the diviner, he was dead. And my father and family are angry with me for taking the part of the murderer and prosecuting my father. They say that he did not kill him, and that if he did, the dead man was but a murderer, and I ought not to take any notice, for that a son is impious who prosecutes a father. Which shows, Socrates, how little they know of the opinions of the gods about piety and impiety.

Soc. Good heavens, Euthyphro! and have you such a precise knowledge of piety and impiety, and of divine things in general, that, supposing the circumstances to be as you state, you are not afraid that you too may be doing an impious thing in bringing an action against your father?

Euth. The best of Euthyphro, and that which distinguishes him, Socrates, from other men, is his exact knowledge of all these matters. What should I be good for without that?

Soc. Rare friend! I think that I cannot do better than be your disciple. Then before the trial with Meletus comes on I shall challenge him, and say that I have always had a great interest in religious questions, and now, as he charges me with rash imaginations and innovations in religion, I have become your disciple. You, Meletus, as I shall say to him, acknowledge Euthyphro to be a great theologian, and sound in his opinions; and if you approve of him you ought to approve of me, and not have me in to court; but if you disapprove, you should begin by indicting him who is my

teacher, and who is the real corruptor, not of the young, but of the old; that is to say, of myself whom he instructs, and of his old father whom he admonishes and chastises. And if Meletus refuses to listen to me, but will go on, and will not shift the indictment from me to you, I cannot do better than to repeat this challenge in the court.

Euth. Yes, Socrates; and if he attempts to indict me I am mistaken if I do not find a flaw in him; the court shall have a great deal more to say to him than to me.

Soc. And I, my dear friend, knowing this, am desirous of becoming your disciple. For I observe that no one appears to notice you—not even this Meletus; but his sharp eyes have found me out at once, and he has indicted me for impiety. And therefore, I adjure you to tell me the nature of piety and impiety, which you said that you knew so well, and of murder, and the rest of them. What are they? Is not piety in every action always the same? and impiety again, is not that always the opposite of piety, and also the same with itself, having, as impiety, one notion which includes whatever is impious?

Euth. To be sure, Socrates.

Soc. And what is piety, and what is impiety?

Euth. Piety is doing as I am doing; that is to say, prosecuting any one who is guilty of murder, sacrilege, or of any similar crime—whether he be your father or your mother, or whoever he may be, that makes no difference—and not prosecuting them is impiety. And please to consider, Socrates, what a notable proof I will give you of the truth of what I am saying, which I have already given to others:—of the principle, I mean, that the impious, whoever he may be, ought not to go unpunished. For do not men regard Zeus as the best and most righteous of the gods?—and yet they admit that he bound his father (Cronos) because he wickedly devoured his sons, and that he too had punished his own father (Uranus) for a similar reason, in a nameless manner. And yet when I proceed against my father, they are angry with me. So inconsistent are they in their way of talking when the gods are concerned, and when I am concerned.

Soc. May not this be the reason, Euthyphro, why I am charged with impiety—that I cannot away with these stories about the gods? and therefore I suppose that people think me wrong. But, as you who are well informed about them approve of them, I cannot do better than assent to your superior wisdom. For what else can I say, confessing as I do, that I know nothing about them? I wish that you would tell me whether you really believe that they are true.

EUTH. Yes, Socrates; and things more wonderful still, of which the world is in ignorance.

Soc. And do you really believe that the gods fought with one another, and had dire quarrels, battles, and the like, as the poets say, and as you may see represented in the works of great artists? The temples are full of them; and notably the robe of Athene, which is carried up to the Acropolis at the great Panathenæa, is embroidered with them. Are all these tales of the gods true, Euthyphro?

EUTH. Yes, Socrates; and, as I was saying, I can tell you, if you would like to hear them, many other things about the gods which would quite amaze you.

Soc. I dare say; and you shall tell me them at some other time when I have leisure. But just at present I would rather hear from you a more precise answer, which you have not as yet given, my friend, to the question, What is "piety"? In reply, you only say that piety is, Doing as you do, charging your father with murder.

EUTH. And that is true, Socrates.

Soc. I dare say, Euthyphro, but there are many other pious acts.

EUTH. There are.

Soc. Remember that I did not ask you to give me two or three examples of piety, but to explain the general idea which makes all pious things to be pious. Do you not recollect that there was one idea which made the impious impious, and the pious pious?

EUTH. I remember.

Soc. Tell me what you mean, and then I shall have a standard to which I may look, and by which I may measure the nature of actions, whether yours or any one's else, and say that this action is pious, and that impious.

EUTH. I will tell you, if you like.

Soc. I should very much like.

EUTH. Piety, then, is that which is dear to the gods, and impiety is that which is not dear to them.

Soc. Very good, Euthyphro; you have now given me the sort of answer which I wanted. But whether what you say is true or not I cannot as yet tell, although I make no doubt that you will prove the truth of your words.

EUTH. Of course.

Soc. Come, then, and let us examine what we are saying. That thing or person which is dear to the gods is pious, and that thing or person which is hateful to the gods is impious. Was not that said?

EUTH. Yes, that was said.

Soc. And that seems to have been very well said too.

EUTH. Yes, Socrates, I think so; it was certainly said.

Soc. And further, Euthyphro, the gods were admitted to have enmities and hatreds and differences—that was also said?

EUTH. Yes, that was said.

Soc. And what sort of difference creates enmity and anger? Suppose for example that you and I, my good friend, differ about a number; do differences of this sort make us enemies and set us at variance with one another? Do we not go at once to calculation, and end them by a sum?

EUTH. True.

Soc. Or suppose that we differ about magnitudes, do we not quickly put an end to that difference by measuring?

EUTH. That is true.

Soc. And we end a controversy about heavy and light by resorting to a weighing-machine?

EUTH. To be sure.

Soc. But what differences are those which, because they cannot be thus decided, make us angry and set us at enmity with one another? I dare say the answer does not occur to you at the moment, and therefore I will suggest that this happens when the matters of difference are the just and unjust, good and evil, honourable and dishonourable. Are not these the points about which, when differing, and unable satisfactorily to decide our differences, you and I and all men quarrel, when we do quarrel?

EUTH. Yes, Socrates, that is the nature of the differences about which we quarrel.

Soc. And the quarrels of the gods, noble Euthyphro, when they occur, are of like nature?

EUTH. They are.

Soc. They have differences of opinion, as you say, about good and evil, just and unjust, honourable and dishonourable: there would have been no quarrels among them, if there had been no such differences—would there now?

EUTH. You are quite right.

Soc. Does not every man love that which he deems noble and just and good, and hate the opposite of them?

EUTH. Very true.

Soc. But, as you say, people regard the same things, some as just and others as unjust; about which they dispute; and so there arise wars and fightings among them.

EUTH. Yes, that is true.

Soc. Then the same things, as appears, are hated by the gods and loved by the gods, and are both hateful and dear to them?

EUTH. True.

Soc. And upon this view the same things, Euthyphro, will be pious and also impious?

EUTH. That, I suppose, is true.

Soc. Then, my friend, I remark with surprise that you have not answered what I asked. For I certainly did not ask you to tell me that which is both pious and impious: and now what is loved by the gods appears also to be hated by them. And therefore, Euthyphro, in thus chastising your father you may very likely be doing what is agreeable to Zeus but disagreeable to Cronos or Uranus, and what is acceptable to Hephæstus but unacceptable to Here, and there may be other gods who have similar differences of opinion.

EUTH. But I believe, Socrates, that all the gods would be agreed as to the propriety of punishing a murderer: there would be no difference of opinion about that.

Soc. Well, but speaking of men, Euthyphro, did you ever hear any one arguing that a murderer or any sort of evil-doer ought to be let off?

EUTH. I should say rather that these are the questions which they are always arguing, especially in courts of law: they commit all sorts of crimes, and there is nothing which they will not do or say to escape punishment.

Soc. But do they admit their guilt, Euthyphro, and yet say that they ought not to be punished?

EUTH. No; they do not.

Soc. Then there are some things which they do not venture to say and do: for they do not venture to argue that the guilty are not to be punished, but they deny their guilt, do they not?

EUTH. Yes.

Soc. Then they do not argue that the

evil-doer should not be punished, but they argue about the fact of who the evil-doer is, and what he did and when?

EUTH. True.

SOC. And the gods are in the same case, if as you assert they quarrel about just and unjust, and some of them say that there is injustice done among them, and others of them deny this. For surely neither God nor man will ever venture to say that the doer of evil is not to be punished?

EUTH. That is true, Socrates, in the main.

SOC. But they join issue about particulars; and this applies not only to men but to the gods, who, if they dispute at all, dispute about some act which is called in question, and which some affirm to be just, others to be unjust. Is not that true?

EUTH. Quite true.

SOC. Well then, my dear friend Euthyphro, do tell me, for my better instruction and information, what proof have you that in the opinion of all the gods a servant who is guilty of murder, and is put in chains by the master of the dead man, and dies because he is put in chains before his corrector can learn from the interpreters what he ought to do with him, dies unjustly; and that on behalf of such an one a son ought to proceed against his father and accuse him of murder. How would you show that all the gods absolutely agree in approving of his act? Prove to me that, and I will applaud your wisdom as long as you live.

EUTH. That would not be an easy task, although I could make the matter very clear indeed to you.

SOC. I understand; you mean to say that I am not so quick of apprehension as the judges: for to them you will be sure to prove that the act is unjust, and hateful to the gods.

EUTH. Yes indeed, Socrates; at least if they will listen to me.

SOC. But they will be sure to listen if they find that you are a good speaker. There was a notion that came into my mind while you were speaking; I said to myself: "Well, and what if Euthyphro does prove to me that all the gods regarded the death of the serf as unjust, how do I know anything more of the nature of piety and impiety? for granting that this action may be hateful to the gods, still these distinctions have no bearing on the definition of piety and impiety, for that which is hateful to the gods has been shown to be also pleasing and dear to them." And therefore, Euthyphro, I do not ask you to prove this; I will suppose, if you like, that all the gods condemn and abominate such an action. But I will amend the definition so far as to say that what all the gods hate is impious, and what they love pious or holy; and what some of them love and others hate is both or neither. Shall this be our definition of piety and impiety?

EUTH. Why not, Socrates?

SOC. Why not! certainly, as far as I am concerned, Euthyphro, there is no reason why not. But whether this admission will greatly assist you in the task of instructing me as you promised, is a matter for you to consider.

EUTH. Yes, I should say that what all the gods love is pious and holy, and the opposite which they all hate, impious.

SOC. Ought we to enquire into the truth of this, Euthyphro, or simply to accept the mere statement on our own authority and that of others? What do you say?

EUTH. We should enquire; and I believe that the statement will stand the test of enquiry.

SOC. That, my good friend, we shall know better in a little while. The point which I should first wish to understand is whether the pious or holy is beloved by the gods because it is holy, or holy because it is beloved of the gods.

EUTH. I do not understand your meaning, Socrates.

Soc. I will endeavour to explain: we speak of carrying and we speak of being carried, of leading and being led, seeing and being seen. And here is a difference, the nature of which you understand.

Euth. I think that I understand.

Soc. And is not that which is beloved distinct from that which loves?

Euth. Certainly.

Soc. Well; and now tell me, is that which is carried in this state of carrying because it is carried, or for some other reason?

Euth. No; that is the reason.

Soc. And the same is true of that which is led and of that which is seen?

Euth. True.

Soc. And a thing is not seen because it is visible, but conversely, visible because it is seen; nor is a thing led because it is in the state of being led, or carried because it is in the state of being carried, but the converse of this. And now I think, Euthyphro, that my meaning will be intelligible; and my meaning is, that any state of action or passion implies previous action or passion. It does not become because it is becoming, but it is in a state of becoming because it becomes; neither does it suffer because it is in a state of suffering, but it is in a state of suffering because it suffers. Do you admit that?

Euth. Yes.

Soc. Is not that which is loved in some state either of becoming or suffering?

Euth. Yes.

Soc. And the same holds as in the previous instances; the state of being loved follows the act of being loved, and not the act the state.

Euth. Certainly.

Soc. And what do you say of piety, Euthyphro: is not piety, according to your definition, loved by all the gods?

Euth. Yes.

Soc. Because it is pious or holy, or for some other reason?

Euth. No, that is the reason.

Soc. It is loved because it is holy, not holy because it is loved?

Euth. Yes.

Soc. And that which is in a state to be loved by the gods, and is dear to them, is in a state to be loved of them because it is loved of them?

Euth. Certainly.

Soc. Then that which is loved of God, Euthyphro, is not holy, nor is that which is holy loved of God, as you affirm; but they are two different things.

Euth. How do you mean, Socrates?

Soc. I mean to say that the holy has been acknowledged by us to be loved of God because it is holy, not to be holy because it is loved.

Euth. Yes.

Soc. But that which is dear to the gods is dear to them because it is loved by them, not loved by them because it is dear to them.

Euth. True.

Soc. But, friend Euthyphro, if that which is holy is the same as that which is dear to God, and that which is holy is loved as being holy, then that which is dear to God would have been loved as being dear to God; but if that which is dear to God is dear to him because loved by him, then that which is holy would have been holy because loved by him. But now you see that the reverse is the case, and that they are quite different from one another. For one is of a kind to be loved because it is loved, and the other is loved because it is of a kind to be loved. Thus you appear to me, Euthyphro, when I ask you what is the essence of holiness, to offer an attribute only, and not the essence—the attribute of being loved by all the gods. But you still refuse to explain to me the nature of holiness. And therefore, if you please, I will ask you not to hide your treasure, but to tell me once more what holiness or piety really is, whether dear to the gods or not (for that is a matter about which we will not quarrel). And what is impiety?

EUTH. I really do not know, Socrates, how to say what I mean. For somehow or other our arguments, on whatever ground we rest them, seem to turn round and walk away.

SOC. Your words, Euthyphro, are like the handiwork of my ancestor Dædalus; and if I were the sayer or propounder of them, you might say that this comes of my being his relation; and that this is the reason why my arguments walk away and will not remain fixed where they are placed. But now, since these notions are your own, you must find some other gibe, for they certainly, as you yourself allow, show an inclination to be on the move.

EUTH. Nay, Socrates, I shall still say that you are the Dædalus who sets arguments in motion; not I, certainly, but you make them move or go round, for they would never have stirred, as far as I am concerned.

SOC. Then I must be a greater than Dædalus; for whereas he only made his own inventions to move, I move those of other people as well. And the beauty of it is, that I would rather not. For I would give the wisdom of Dædalus, and the wealth of Tantalus, to be able to detain them and keep them fixed. But enough of this. As I perceive that you are indolent, I will myself endeavour to show you how you might instruct me in the nature of piety; and I hope that you will not grudge your labour. Tell me, then,—Is not that which is pious necessarily just?

EUTH. Yes.

SOC. And is, then, all which is just pious? or, is that which is pious all just, but that which is just, only in part and not all, pious?

EUTH. I do not understand you, Socrates.

SOC. And yet I know that you are as much wiser than I am, as you are

younger. But, as I was saying, revered friend, the abundance of your wisdom makes you indolent. Please to exert yourself, for there is no real difficulty in understanding me. What I mean I may explain by an illustration of what I do not mean. The poet (Stasinus) sings—

"Of Zeus, the author and creator of all these things,
You will not tell: for where there is fear there is also reverence."

And I disagree with this poet. Shall I tell you in what I disagree?

EUTH. By all means.

SOC. I should not say that where there is fear there is also reverence; for I am sure that many persons fear poverty and disease, and the like evils, but I do not perceive that they reverence the objects of their fear.

EUTH. Very true.

SOC. But where reverence is, there is fear; for he who has a feeling of reverence and shame about the commission of any action, fears and is afraid of an ill reputation.

EUTH. No doubt.

SOC. Then we are wrong in saying that where there is fear there is also reverence; and we should say, where there is reverence there is also fear. But there is not always reverence where there is fear; for fear is a more extended notion, and reverence is a part of fear, just as the odd is a part of number, and number is a more extended notion than the odd. I suppose that you follow me now?

EUTH. Quite well.

SOC. That was the sort of question which I meant to raise when asking whether the just is the pious, or the pious the just; and whether there may not be justice where there is not always piety; for justice is the more extended notion of which piety is only a part. Do you agree in that?

EUTH. Yes; that, I think, is correct.

Soc. Then, now, if piety is a part of justice, I suppose that we should enquire what part? If you had pursued the enquiry in the previous cases; for instance, if you asked me what is an even number, and what part of number the even is, I should have had no difficulty in replying, a number which represents a figure having two equal sides. Do you agree?

EUTH. Yes.

Soc. In like manner, I want you to tell me what part of justice is piety or holiness, that I may be able to tell Meletus not to do me injustice, or indict me for impiety, as I am now adequately instructed by you in the nature of piety or holiness, and their opposites.

EUTH. Piety or holiness, Socrates, appears to me to be that part of justice which attends to the gods, as there is the other part of justice which attends to men.

Soc. That is good, Euthyphro; yet still there is a little point about which I should like to have further information, what is the meaning of "attention"? For attention can hardly be used in the same sense when applied to the gods as when applied to other things. For instance, horses are said to require attention, and not every person is able to attend to them, but only a person skilled in horsemanship. Is not that true?

EUTH. Quite true.

Soc. I should suppose that the art of horsemanship is the art of attending to horses?

EUTH. Yes.

Soc. Nor is every one qualified to attend to dogs, but only the huntsman?

EUTH. Yes.

Soc. As the art of the oxherd is the art of attending to oxen?

EUTH. Very true.

Soc. And as holiness or piety is the art of attending to the gods?—that would be your meaning, Euthyphro?

EUTH. Yes.

Soc. And is not attention always designed for the good or benefit of that to which the attention is given? As in the case of horses, you may observe that when attended to by the horseman's art they are benefited and improved, are they not?

EUTH. Certainly, not for their hurt.

Soc. But for their good?

EUTH. Of course.

Soc. And does piety or holiness, which has been defined as the art of attending to the gods, benefit or improve them? Would you say that when you do a holy act you make any of the gods better?

EUTH. No, no; that is certainly not my meaning.

Soc. Indeed, Euthyphro, I did not suppose that this was your meaning; far otherwise. And I asked you the nature of the attention, because I thought that you could not mean this.

EUTH. You do me justice, Socrates; for that is not my meaning.

Soc. Good: but I must still ask what is this attention to the gods which is called piety?

EUTH. It is such, Socrates, as servants show to their masters.

Soc. I understand—a sort of ministration to the gods.

EUTH. Exactly.

Soc. Medicine is also a sort of ministration or service, tending to the attainment of some object—would you not say health?

EUTH. Yes.

Soc. Again, there is an art which ministers to the ship-builder with a view to the attainment of some result?

EUTH. Yes, Socrates, with a view to the building of a ship.

Soc. As there is an art which ministers to the house-builder with a view to the building of a house?

EUTH. Yes.

Soc. And now tell me, my good

friend, about the art which ministers to the gods: what work does that help to accomplish? For you must surely know if, as you say, you are of all men living the one who is best instructed in religion.

EUTH. And that is true, Socrates.

Soc. Tell me then, oh tell me—what is that fair work which the gods do by the help of us as their ministers?

EUTH. Many and fair, Socrates, are the works which they do.

Soc. Why, my friend, and so are those of a general. But the chief of them is easily told. Would you not say that victory in war is the chief of them?

EUTH. Certainly.

Soc. Many and fair, too, are the works of the husbandman, if I am not mistaken; but his chief work is the production of food from the earth?

EUTH. Exactly.

Soc. And of the many and fair things which the gods do, which is the chief and principal one?

EUTH. I have told you already, Socrates, that to learn all these things accurately will be very tiresome. Let me simply say that piety is learning how to please the gods in word and deed, by prayers and sacrifices. That is piety, which is the salvation of families and states, just as the impious, which is unpleasing to the gods, is their ruin and destruction.

Soc. I think that you could have answered in much fewer words the chief question which I asked, Euthyphro, if you had chosen. But I see plainly that you are not disposed to instruct me: else why, when we reached the point, did you turn aside? Had you only answered me I should have learned of you by this time the nature of piety. Now, as the asker of a question is necessarily dependent on the answerer, whither he leads I must follow; and can only ask again, what is the pious, and what is piety? Do you mean that they are a sort of science of praying and sacrificing?

EUTH. Yes, I do.

Soc. And sacrificing is giving to the gods, and prayer is asking of the gods?

EUTH. Yes, Socrates.

Soc. Upon this view, then, piety is a science of asking and giving?

EUTH. You understand me capitally, Socrates.

Soc. Yes, my friend; the reason is that I am a votary of your science, and give my mind to it, and therefore nothing which you say will be thrown away upon me. Please then to tell me, what is the nature of this service to the gods? Do you mean that we prefer requests and give gifts to them?

EUTH. Yes. I do.

SOCRATES. Is not the right way of asking to ask of them what we want?

EUTH. Certainly.

Soc. And the right way of giving is to give to them in turn what they want of us. There would be no meaning in an art which gives to any one that which he does not want.

EUTH. Very true, Socrates.

Soc. Then piety, Euthyphro, is an art which gods and men have of doing business with one another?

EUTH. That is an expression which you may use, if you like.

Soc. But I have no particular liking for anything but the truth. I wish, however, that you would tell me what benefit accrues to the gods from our gifts. There is no doubt about what they give to us; for there is no good thing which they do not give; but how we can give any good thing to them in return is far from being equally clear. If they give everything and we give nothing, that must be an affair of business in which we have very greatly the advantage of them.

EUTH. And do you imagine, Socrates, that any benefit accrues to the gods from what they receive of us?

Soc. But if not, Euthyphro, what sort of gifts do we confer upon the gods?

EUTH. What should we confer upon

them, but tributes of honour; and, as I was just now saying, what is grateful to them?

Soc. Piety, then, is grateful to the gods, but not beneficial or dear to them?

Euth. I should say that nothing could be dearer.

Soc. Then once more the question is repeated that piety is dear to the gods?

Euth. Certainly.

Soc. And when you say this, can you wonder at your words not standing firm, but walking away? Will you accuse me of being the Dædalus who makes them walk away, not perceiving that there is another and far greater artist than Dædalus who makes them go round in a circle, and that is yourself; for the argument, as you will perceive, comes round to the same point. I think that you must remember our saying that the holy or pious was not the same as that which is loved of the gods. Do you remember that?

Euth. I do.

Soc. And are you not saying that what is loved of the gods is holy, but this is the same as what is dear to them —do you see that?

Euth. True.

Soc. Then either we were wrong in our former assertion; or, if we were right then, we are wrong now.

Euth. I suppose that is the case.

Soc. Then we must begin again and ask, What is piety? That is an enquiry which I shall never be weary of pursuing as far as in me lies; and I entreat you not to scorn me, but to apply your mind to the utmost, and tell me the truth. For, if any man knows, you are he; and therefore I shall detain you, like Proteus, until you tell. For if you had not certainly known the nature of piety and impiety, I am confident that you would never, on behalf of a serf, have charged your aged father with murder. You would not have run such a risk of doing wrong in the sight of the gods, and you would

have had too much respect for the opinions of men. I am sure, therefore, that you know the nature of piety and impiety. Speak out then, my dear Euthyphro, and do not hide your knowledge.

Euth. Another time, Socrates; for I am in a hurry, and must go now.

Soc. Alas! my companion, and will you leave me in despair? I was hoping that you would instruct me in the nature of piety and impiety, so that I might have cleared myself of Meletus and his indictment. Then I might have proved to him that I had been converted by Euthyphro, and had done with rash innovations and speculations, in which I had indulged through ignorance, and was about to lead a better life.

—BENJAMIN JOWETT.

LEARNING IS RECOLLECTING [1]

PLATO

[From the *Meno*]

This passage is an illustration used in the course of a discussion on the question whether virtue is a thing that can be taught. Plato maintains that certain matters of knowledge are divine gifts; our difficulty is not one of learning, but one of thinking clearly.

SOCRATES. I told you, Meno, that you were a rogue, and now you ask whether I can teach you, when I am saying that there is no teaching, but only recollection; and thus you imagine that you will involve me in a contradiction.

MENO. Indeed, Socrates, I protest that I had no such intention. I only asked the question from habit; but if you can prove to me that what you say is true, I wish that you would.

Soc. That is no easy matter, but I will try to please you to the utmost of

[1] Reprinted by arrangement with the Oxford University Press, publishers.

my power. Suppose that you call one of your numerous attendants, that I may demonstrate on him.

MEN. Certainly. Come hither, boy.

SOC. He is Greek, and speaks Greek, does he not?

MEN. Yes; he was born in the house.

SOC. Attend now to the questions that I ask him, and observe whether he learns of me or only remembers.

MEN. I will.

SOC. Tell me, boy, do you know that a figure like this is a square?

BOY. I do.

SOC. And do you know that a square figure has these four lines equal?

BOY. Certainly.

SOC. And these lines which I have drawn through the middle of the square are also equal?

BOY. Yes.

SOC. A square may be of any size?

BOY. Certainly.

SOC. And if one side of the figure be of two feet, and the other side be of two feet, how much will the whole be? Let me explain: if in one direction the space was of two feet, and in the other direction of one foot, the whole would be of two feet taken once?

BOY. Yes.

SOC. But since this side is also of two feet, there are twice two feet?

BOY. There are.

SOC. Then the square is of twice two feet?

BOY. Yes.

SOC. And how many are twice two feet? count and tell me.

BOY. Four, Socrates.

SOC. And might there not be another square twice as large as this, and having like this the lines equal?

BOY. Yes.

SOC. And of how many feet will that be?

BOY. Of eight feet.

SOC. And now try and tell me the length of the line which forms the side of that double square: this is two feet—what will that be?

BOY. Clearly, Socrates, that will be double.

SOC. Do you observe, Meno, that I am not teaching the boy anything, but only asking him questions; and now he fancies that he knows how long a line is necessary in order to produce a figure of eight square feet; does he not?

MEN. Yes.

SOC. And does he really know?

MEN. Certainly not.

SOC. He only guesses that (because the square is double), the line is double.

MEN. True.

SOC. Observe him while he recalls the steps in regular order. (*To the* BOY.) Tell me, boy, do you assert that a double space comes from a double line? Remember that I am not speaking of an oblong, but of a square, and of a square twice the size of this one—that is to say of eight feet; and I want to know whether you still say that a double square comes from a double line?

BOY. Yes.

SOC. But does not this line become doubled if we add another such line here?

BOY. Certainly.

SOC. And four such lines will make a space containing eight feet?

BOY. Yes.

SOC. Let us describe such a figure: is not that what you would say is the figure of eight feet?

BOY. Yes.

SOC. And are there not these four divisions in the figure, each of which is equal to the figure of four feet?

BOY. True.

SOC. And is not that four times four?

BOY. Certainly.

SOC. And four times is not double?

BOY. No, indeed.

SOC. But how much?

BOY. Four times as much.

SOC. Therefore the double line, boy,

has formed a space, not twice, but four times as much.

Boy. True.

Soc. And four times four are sixteen—are they not?

Boy. Yes.

Soc. What line would give you a space of eight feet, as this gives one of sixteen feet;—do you see?

Boy. Yes.

Soc. And the space of four feet is made from this half line?

Boy. Yes.

Soc. Good; and is not a space of eight feet twice the size of this, and half the size of the other?

Boy. Certainly.

Soc. Such a space, then, will be made out of a line greater than this one, and less than that one?

Boy. Yes; that is what I think.

Soc. Very good; I like to hear you say what you think. And now tell me, is not this line of two feet and that of four?

Boy. Yes.

Soc. Then the line which forms the side of eight feet ought to be more than this line of two feet, and less than the other of four feet?

Boy. It ought.

Soc. Try and see if you can tell me how much it will be.

Boy. Three feet.

Soc. Then if we add a half to this line of two, that will be the line of three. Here are two and there is one; and on the other side, here are two and also there is one: and that makes the figure of which you speak?

Boy. Yes.

Soc. But if there are three feet this way and three feet that way, the whole space will be three times three feet?

Boy. That is evident.

Soc. And how much are three times three feet?

Boy. Nine.

Soc. And how much is the double of four?

Boy. Eight.

Soc. Then the figure of eight is not made out of a line of three?

Boy. No.

Soc. But from what line?—tell me exactly; and if you would rather not reckon, try and show me the line.

Boy. Indeed, Socrates, I do not know.

Soc. Do you see, Meno, what advances he has made in his power of recollection? He did not know at first, and he does not know now, what is the side of a figure of eight feet: but then he thought that he knew, and answered confidently as if he knew, and had no difficulty; now he has a difficulty, and neither knows nor fancies that he knows.

Men. True.

Soc. Is he not better off in knowing his ignorance?

Men. I think that he is.

Soc. If we have made him doubt, and given him the "torpedo's shock," have we done him any harm?

Men. I think not.

Soc. We have certainly, as would seem, assisted him in some degree to the discovery of the truth; and now he will wish to remedy his ignorance, but then he would have been ready to tell all the world that the double space should have a double side.

Men. True.

Soc. But do you suppose that he would ever have enquired into or learned what he fancied that he knew and did not know, until he had fallen into perplexity under the idea that he did not know, and had desired to know?

Men. I think not, Socrates.

Soc. Then he was the better for the torpedo's touch?

Men. I think that he was.

Soc. Mark now the farther development. I shall only ask him, and not teach him, and he shall share the enquiry with me: and do you watch and see if you find me telling or explaining anything to him, instead of eliciting his opinion. Tell me, boy, is not this a square of four feet which I have drawn?

Boy. Yes.

Soc. And now I add another square equal to the former one?

Boy. Yes.

Soc. And a third, which is equal to either of them?

Boy. Yes.

Soc. Suppose that we fill up the vacant corner.

Boy. Very good.

Soc. Here, then, there are four equal spaces?

Boy. Yes.

Soc. And how many times larger is this space than this other?

Boy. Four times.

Soc. But it ought to have been twice only, as you will remember.

Boy. True.

Soc. And does not this line, reaching from corner to corner, bisect each of these spaces?

Boy. Yes.

Soc. And are there not here four equal lines which contain this space?

Boy. There are.

Soc. Look and see how much this space is.

Boy. I do not understand.

Soc. Has not each interior line cut off half of the four spaces?

Boy. Yes.

Soc. And how many such spaces are there in this division?

Boy. Four.

Soc. And how many in this?

Boy. Two.

Soc. And four is how many times two?

Boy. Twice.

Soc. And this space is of how many feet?

Boy. Of eight feet.

Soc. And from what line do you get this figure?

Boy. From this.

Soc. That is, from the line which extends from corner to corner?

Boy. Yes.

Soc. And that is the line which the learned call the diagonal. And if this is the proper name, then you, Meno's slave, are prepared to affirm that the double space is the square of the diagonal?

Boy. Certainly, Socrates.

Soc. What do you say of him, Meno? Were not all these answers given out of his own head?

Men. Yes, they were all his own.

Soc. And yet, as we were just now saying, he did not know?

Men. True.

Soc. But still he had those notions in him—did he not?

Men. Yes.

Soc. Then he who does not know has yet true notions of that which he does not know?

Men. He has.

Soc. And at present these notions have just been stirred up in him, as in a dream; but if he were frequently asked the same questions, in different forms, he would know as well as any one at last?

Men. I dare say.

Soc. Without any one teaching him he will recover his knowledge for himself, if he is only asked questions?

Men. Yes.

Soc. And this spontaneous recovery in him is recollection?

Men. True.

Soc. And this knowledge which he now has must he not either have acquired or always possessed?

Men. Yes.

Soc. But if he always possessed this knowledge he would always have known; or if he has acquired the knowledge he could not have acquired it in this life, unless he has been taught geometry; for he may be made to do the same with all geometry and every other branch of knowledge. Now, has any one ever taught him? You must know that, if, as you say, he was born and bred in your house.

MEN. And I am certain that no one ever did teach him.

Soc. And yet has he not the knowledge?

MEN. That, Socrates, is most certain.

Soc. But if he did not acquire the knowledge in this life, then clearly he must have had and learned it at some other time?

MEN. That is evident.

Soc. And that must have been the time when he was not a man?

MEN. Yes.

Soc. And if there have been always true thoughts in him, both at the time when he was and was not a man, which only need to be awakened into knowledge by putting questions to him, his soul must have always possessed this knowledge, for he always either was or was not a man?

MEN. That is clear.

Soc. And if the truth of all things always existed in the soul, then the soul is immortal. Wherefore be of good cheer, and try to recollect what you do not know, or rather do not remember.

MEN. I feel, somehow, that I like what you are saying.

Soc. And I, Meno, like what I am saying. Some things I have said of which I am not altogether confident. But that we shall be better and braver and less helpless if we think that we ought to enquire, than we should have been if we indulged in the idle fancy that there was no knowing and no use in searching after what we do not know; —that is a theme upon which I am ready to fight, in word and deed, to the utmost of my power.

—BENJAMIN JOWETT.

THE DEFENSE OF SOCRATES [1]

PLATO

[From *The Apology*]

The Teachings of Socrates are known to us only through the writings of others, especially of his pupils Xenophon and Plato. Socrates was regarded by many of his contemporaries, like Aristophanes, as a mere sophist, and was charged with corrupting the youth by spreading dangerous moral and religious doctrines. Brought to trial, he spoke in his own defense, half seriously, half mockingly, more concerned about the situation of his judges than about his own. Whether Plato reports the speech just as it was spoken, or writes it himself after the manner of the historians, in either case there can be little doubt that it is a true account of the point of view of Socrates on the question involved.

How you, O Athenians, have been affected by my accusers, I cannot tell; but I know that they almost made me forget myself—so persuasively did they speak; and yet they have hardly uttered a word of truth. But many as their falsehoods were, there was one of them which quite amazed me;—I mean when they told you that you should be upon your guard and not allow yourselves to be deceived by the force of my eloquence. To use such language, when they were sure to be detected as soon as I opened my lips and displayed my deficiency, did certainly appear to me most shameless— unless by the force of eloquence they mean the force of truth; for if this is their meaning, I admit that I am eloquent. But in how different a way from theirs! Well, as I was saying, they have hardly uttered a word, or not more than a word, of truth; but you shall hear from me the whole truth: not, however, delivered after their manner in a set oration duly ornamented with words and

[1] Reprinted by arrangement with the Oxford University Press, publishers.

phrases. No, by heaven! but I shall use the words and arguments which occur to me at the moment; for I am certain that I am right in this; and that at my time of life I ought not to be appearing before you, O men of Athens, in the character of a juvenile orator—let no one expect it of me. And I must beg of you to grant me a favour:—If you hear me using the same words in my defense which I have been in the habit of using, and which most of you may have heard in the agora, and at the tables of the money-changers, or anywhere else, I would ask you not to be surprised, and not to interrupt me on this account. For I am more than seventy years of age, and appearing now for the first time in a court of law, I am quite a stranger to the language which is used here; and therefore I would have you regard me as if I were really a stranger, whom you would excuse if he spoke in his native tongue, and after the fashion of his country:—Am I making an unfair request of you? Never mind the manner, which may or may not be good; but think only of the justice of my case, and give heed to that: let the judge decide justly and the speaker speak truly.

And first, I have to reply to the older charges and to my first accusers, and then I will go on to the later ones. For of old I have had many accusers, who have accused me falsely to you during many years; and I am more afraid of them than of Anytus and his associates, who are dangerous, too, in their own way. But far more dangerous are the others, who began when you were children, and took possession of your minds with their falsehoods, telling of one Socrates, a wise man, who speculated about the heaven above, and searched into the earth beneath, and made the worse appear the better cause. The disseminators of this tale are the accusers whom I dread; for their hearers are apt to fancy that such enquirers do not believe in the existence of the gods. And they are many, and their charges against me are of ancient date, and they made them in days when you were impressible—in childhood, or perhaps in youth—and the cause when heard went by default, for there was none to answer. And hardest of all, their names I do not know and cannot tell; unless in the chance case of a comic poet. But the main body of these slanderers who from envy and malice have wrought upon you —and there are some of them who are convinced themselves, and impart their convictions to others—all this class of men are most difficult to deal with; for I cannot have them up here, and examine them, and therefore I must simply fight with shadows in my own defense, and examine when there is no one who answers. I will ask you then to assume with me, as I was saying, that my opponents are of two kinds; one recent, the other ancient: and I hope that you will see the propriety of my answering the latter first, for these accusations you heard long before the others, and much oftener.

Well, then, I must make my defense, and endeavour to clear away in a short time, a slander which has lasted a long time; and I hope that I may succeed, and that my words may find favour with you, if this be well for you and me. But I know that to accomplish this is not easy—I quite see the nature of the task. Let the event be as God wills: in obedience to the law I make my defense.

I will begin at the beginning, and ask what the accusation is which has given rise to this slander of me, and which has encouraged Meletus to proceed against me. Well, what do the slanderers say? They shall be my prosecutors, and I will sum up their words in an affidavit: "Socrates is an evil-doer, and a curious person, who searches into things under the earth and in heaven, and he makes the worse appear the better cause; and he teaches the aforesaid doctrines to others." Such is the accusation, and is just what you have yourselves seen in the comedy of Aristophanes, who has introduced a man whom he calls Socrates, going about and saying that he can walk in the air, and talking a deal of nonsense concerning matters of which I do not pretend to know either much or little— not that I mean to speak disparagingly of any one who is a student of natural philosophy. I should be very sorry if Meletus could lay that to my charge. But the simple truth is, O Athenians, that I have nothing to do with physical speculations. Very many of these here present are witnesses to the truth of this, and to them I appeal. Speak then, you who have heard me, and tell your neighbours whether any of you have ever known me hold forth in few words or in many upon such matters. . . . You hear their answer. And from what they say of this part of the charge you will be able to judge of the truth of the rest.

As little foundation is there for the report that I am a teacher, and take money; that is no more true than the other. Although, if a man were really able to instruct mankind, to take money for giving instruction would, in my opinion, be honourable. There is Gorgias of Leontium, and Prodicus of Ceos, and Hippias of Elis, who go the round of the cities, and are able to persuade young men to leave their own citizens, by whom they might be taught for nothing, and come to them, whom they not only pay, but are thankful if they may be allowed to pay them. There is at this time a Parian philosopher residing in Athens, of whom I have heard; and I came to hear of him in this way:—I met a man who has spent a world of money on the Sophists, Callias, the son of Hipponicus, and knowing that he had sons, I asked him: "Callias," I said, "if your two sons were foals or calves, there would be no difficulty in finding some one to put over them; we

should hire a trainer of horses, or a farmer probably, who would improve and perfect them in their own proper virtue and excellence; but as they are human beings, whom are you thinking of placing over them? Is there any one who understands human and political virtue? You must have thought about the matter, for you have sons; is there any one?" "There is," he said. "Who is he?" said I, "and of what country? and what does he charge?" "Evenus the Parian," he replied; "he is the man, and his charge is five minæ." Happy is Evenus, I said to myself, if he really has this wisdom, and teaches at such a modest charge. Had I the same I should have been very proud and satisfied; but the truth is that I have no knowledge of the kind.

I dare say, Athenians, that some one among you will reply, "Yes, Socrates, but what is the origin of these accusations which are brought against you; there must have been something strange which you have been doing? All this rumour and talk about you would never have arisen if you had been like other men: tell us, then, what is the cause of them, for we should be sorry to judge hastily of you." Now I regard this as a fair challenge, and I will endeavour to explain to you the origin of this name of "wise," and of my evil fame. Please to attend then. And although some of you may think that I am joking, I declare that I will tell you the entire truth. Men of Athens, this reputation of mine has come of a certain sort of wisdom which I possess. If you ask me what kind of wisdom, I reply, such wisdom as is attainable by man, for to that extent I am inclined to believe that I am wise; whereas the persons of whom I was speaking have a superhuman wisdom, which I may fail to describe, because I have it not myself; and he who says that I have, speaks falsely, and is taking away my character. And here, O men of Athens, I must beg you not to interrupt me, even if I seem to say something extravagant. For the word which I will speak is not mine. I will refer you to a witness who is worthy of credit, and will tell you about my wisdom—whether I have any, and of what sort—and that witness shall be the God of Delphi. You must have known Chærephon; he was early a friend of mine, and also a friend of yours, for he shared in the exile of the people, and returned with you. Well, Chærephon, as you know, was very impetuous in all his doings, and he went to Delphi and boldly asked the oracle to tell him whether —as I was saying, I must beg you not to interrupt—he asked the oracle to tell him whether there was any one wiser than I was, and the Pythian prophetess answered, that there was no man wiser. Chærephon is dead himself; but his brother, who is in court, will confirm the truth of what I am saying.

Why do I mention this? Because I am going to explain to you why I have such an evil name. When I heard the answer, I said to myself, What can the god mean? and what is the interpretation of this riddle? for I know that I have no wisdom, small or great. What then can he mean when he says that I am the wisest of men? And yet he is a god, and cannot lie; that would be against his nature. After long consideration, I at last thought of a method of trying the question. I reflected that if I could only find a man wiser than myself, then I might go to the god with a refutation in my hand. I should say to him, "Here is a man who is wiser than I am; but you said that I was the wisest." Accordingly I went to one who had the reputation of wisdom, and observed him —his name I need not mention; he was a politician whom I selected for examination—and the result was as follows: When I began to talk with him, I could not help thinking that he was not really wise, although he was thought wise by many, and wiser still by himself; and

thereupon I tried to explain to him that he thought himself wise, but was not really wise; and the consequence was that he hated me, and his enmity was shared by several who were present and heard me. So I left him, saying to myself, as I went away: Well, although I do not suppose that either of us knows anything really beautiful and good, I am better off than he is,—for he knows nothing, and thinks that he knows; I neither know nor think that I know. In this latter particular, then, I seem to have slightly the advantage of him. Then I went to another who had still higher philosophical pretensions, and my conclusion was exactly the same. I made another enemy of him, and of many others besides him.

Then I went to one man after another, being not unconscious of the enmity which I provoked, and I lamented and feared this: but necessity was laid upon me,—the word of God, I thought, ought to be considered first. And I said to myself, Go I must to all who appear to know, and find out the meaning of the oracle. And I swear to you, Athenians. by the dog I swear!—for I must tell you the truth—the result of my mission was just this: I found that the men most in repute were all but the most foolish; and that some inferior were really wiser and better. I will tell you the tale of my wanderings and of the "Herculean" labours, as I may call them, which I endured only to find at last the oracle irrefutable. When I left the politicians, I went to the poets; tragic, dithyrambic, and all sorts. And there, I said to myself, you will be instantly detected; now you will find out that you are more ignorant than they are. Accordingly, I took them some of the most elaborate passages in their own writings, and asked what was the meaning of them—thinking that they would teach me something. Will you believe me? I am almost ashamed to confess the truth, but I must say that there is hardly a person present who would not have talked better about their poetry than they did themselves. Then I knew without going further that not by wisdom do poets write poetry, but by a sort of genius and inspiration; they are like diviners or soothsayers who also say many fine things, but do not understand the meaning of them. And the poets appeared to me to be much in the same case; and I further observed that upon the strength of their poetry they believed themselves to be the wisest of men in other things in which they were not wise. So I departed, conceiving myself to be superior to them for the same reason that I was superior to the politicians.

At last I went to the artisans, for I was conscious that I knew nothing at all, as I may say, and I was sure that they knew many fine things; and here I was not mistaken, for they did know many things of which I was ignorant, and in this they certainly were wiser than I was. But I observed that even the good artisans fell into the same error as the poets;—because they were good workmen they thought that they also knew all sorts of high matters, and this defect in them overshadowed their wisdom— therefore I asked myself on behalf of the oracle, whether I would like to be as I was, neither having their knowledge nor their ignorance, or like them in both; and I made answer to myself and the oracle that I was better off as I was.

This investigation has led to my having many enemies of the worst and most dangerous kind, and has given occasion also to many calumnies. And I am called wise, for my hearers always imagine that I myself possess the wisdom which I find wanting in others: but the truth is, O men of Athens, that God only is wise; and in his answer he means to say that the wisdom of men is little or nothing; he is not speaking of Socrates, he is only using my name by way of illustration, as if he said, He, O men, is

the wisest, who, like Socrates, knows that his wisdom is in truth worth nothing. And so I go my way, obedient to the god, and make inquisition into this wisdom of any one, whether citizen or stranger, who appears to be wise; and if he is not wise, then in vindication of the oracle I show him that he is not wise; and my occupation quite absorbs me, and I have no time to give either to any public matter of interest or to any concern of my own, but I am in utter poverty by reason of my devotion to the god.

There is another thing:—young men of the richer classes, who have not much to do, come about me of their own accord; they like to hear the pretenders examined, and they often imitate me, and proceed to examine others; there are plenty of persons, as they soon enough discover, who think that they know something, but really know little or nothing; and then those who are examined by them instead of being angry with themselves are angry with me: This confounded Socrates, they say; this villainous misleader of youth!—and then if somebody asks them, Why, what evil does he practise or teach? they do not know, and cannot tell; but in order that they may not appear to be at a loss, they repeat the ready-made charges which are made against all philosophers about teaching things up in the clouds and under the earth, and having no gods, and making the worse appear the better cause; for they do not like to confess that their pretence of knowledge has been detected—which is the truth; and as they are numerous and ambitious and energetic, and are drawn up in battle array and have persuasive tongues, they have filled your ears with their loud and inveterate calumnies. And this is the reason why my three accusers, Meletus and Anytus and Lycon, have set upon me; Meletus, who has a quarrel with me on behalf of the poets; Anytus, on behalf of the craftsmen; Lycon, on behalf of the rhetoricians: and as I said at the beginning, I cannot expect to get rid of such a mass of calumny all in a moment. And this, O men of Athens, is the truth and the whole truth; I have concealed nothing, I have dissembled nothing. And yet, I know that my plainness of speech makes them hate me, and what is their hatred but a proof that I am speaking the truth?—this is the occasion and reason of their slander of me, as you will find out either in this or in any future enquiry.

I have said enough in my defense against the first class of my accusers; I turn to the second class who are headed by Meletus, that good and patriotic man, as he calls himself. And now I will try to defend myself against them: these new accusers must also have their affidavit read. What do they say? Something of this sort:—That Socrates is a doer of evil, and a corrupter of the youth; he does not believe in the gods of the state, and has other new divinities of his own. That is the sort of charge; and now let us examine the particular counts. He says that I am a doer of evil, who corrupt the youth; but I say, O men of Athens, that Meletus is a doer of evil, and the evil is that he mixes up jest and earnest, and is too ready at bringing other men to trial from a pretended zeal and interest about matters about which he never really had the smallest interest. And the truth of this I will endeavour to prove.

Come hither, Meletus, and let me ask a question of you. You think a great deal about the improvement of youth?

Yes, I do.

Tell the judges, then, who is their improver; for you must know, as you have taken the pains to discover their corruptor, and are citing and accusing me before them. Speak, then, and tell the judges who their improver is. Observe, Meletus, that you are silent, and have nothing to say. But is not this rather disgraceful, and a very considerable proof of what I was saying, that you have no interest in the matter? Speak up, friend, and tell us who their improver is.

The laws.

But that, my good sir, is not my meaning. I want to know who the person is, who, in the first place, knows the laws.

The judges, Socrates, who are present in court.

What, do you mean to say, Meletus, that they are able to instruct and improve youth?

Certainly they are.

What, all of them, or some only and not others?

All of them.

By the goddess Here, that is good news! There are plenty of improvers, then. And what do you say of the audience,—do they improve them?

Yes, they do.

And the senators?

Yes, the senators improve them.

But perhaps the members of the assembly corrupt them?—or do they too improve them?

They improve them.

Then every Athenian improves and elevates them; all with the exception of myself; and I alone am their corruptor? Is that what you affirm?

That is what I stoutly affirm.

I am very unfortunate if you are right. But suppose I ask you a question: Would you say that the same holds true in the case of horses? Does one man do them harm and all the world good? Is not the exact opposite of this true? One man is able to do them good, or at least not many;—the trainer of horses, that is to say, does them good, and others who have to do with them rather injure them? Is not that true, Meletus, of horses, or any other animals? Yes, unmistakably; whether you and Anytus say yes or no. Happy indeed would be the condition of youth if they had one corruptor only, and all the rest of the world were their improvers. And you, Meletus, have sufficiently shown that you never had a thought about the young: your carelessness is seen in your not caring about the matter spoken of in your own indictment.

And now, Meletus, I must ask you another question: Which is better, to live among bad citizens, or among good ones? Answer, friend, I say; for that is a question which may be easily answered. Do not the good do their neighbours good, and the bad do them evil?

Certainly.

And is there any one who would rather be injured than benefited by those who live with him? Answer, my good friend, the law requires you to answer—does any one like to be injured?

Certainly not.

And when you accuse me of corrupting and deteriorating the youth, do you allege that I corrupt them intentionally or unintentionally?

Intentionally, I say.

But you have just admitted that the good do their neighbours good, and the evil do them evil. Now, is that a truth which your superior wisdom has recognized thus early in life, and am I, at my age, in such darkness and ignorance as not to know that if a man with whom I have to live is corrupted by me, I am very likely to be harmed by him; and yet I corrupt him, and intentionally, too —that is what you are saying, and that you will never persuade me or any other human being. But either I do not corrupt them, or I corrupt them unintentionally; and so on either view of the case you lie. If my offence is unintentional, the law has no cognizance of unintentional offences: you ought to have taken me privately, and warned and admonished me; for if I had been better advised, I should have left off doing what I only did unintentionally—no doubt I should; whereas you hated to converse

with me or teach me, but you indicted me in this court, which is a place not of instruction, but of punishment.

I have shown, Athenians, as I was saying, that Meletus has no care at all, great or small, about the matter. But still I should like to know, Meletus, in what I am affirmed to corrupt the young. I suppose you mean, as I infer from your indictment, that I teach them not to acknowledge the gods which the state acknowledges, but some other new divinities or spiritual agencies in their stead. These are the lessons which corrupt the youth, as you say.

Yes, that I say emphatically.

Then, by the gods, Meletus, of whom we are speaking, tell me and the court, in somewhat plainer terms, what you mean? for I do not as yet understand whether you affirm that I teach others to acknowledge some gods, and therefore do believe in gods, and am not an entire atheist—this you do not lay to my charge,—but only that they are not the same gods which the city recognizes— the charge is that they are different gods. Or, do you mean to say that I am an atheist simply, and a teacher of atheism?

I mean the latter—that you are a complete atheist.

That is an extraordinary statement, Meletus. Why do you say that? Do you mean that I do not believe in the godhead or the sun or moon, which is the common creed of all men?

I assure you, judges, that he does not believe in them; for he says that the sun is stone, and the moon earth.

Friend Meletus, you think that you are accusing Anaxagoras: and you have but a bad opinion of the judges, if you fancy them ignorant to such a degree as not to know that these doctrines are found in the books of Anaxagoras the Clazomenian, who is full of them. And these are the doctrines which the youth are said to learn of Socrates, when there are not unfrequently exhibitions of them at the theatre (price of admission one drachma at the most); and they might cheaply purchase them, and laugh at Socrates if he pretends to father such remarkable views. And so, Meletus, you really think that I do not believe in any god?

I swear by Zeus that you believe absolutely in none at all.

You are a liar, Meletus, not believed even by yourself. For I cannot help thinking, O men of Athens, that Meletus is reckless and impudent, and that he has written this indictment in a spirit of mere wantonness and youthful bravado. He has not compounded a riddle, thinking to try me? He said to himself:—I shall see whether the wise Socrates will discover my pleasant contradiction, or whether I shall be able to deceive him and the rest of them. For he certainly does appear to me to contradict himself in the indictment as much as if he said that Socrates is guilty of not believing in the gods, and yet of believing in them —but this surely is a piece of fun.

I should like you, O men of Athens, to join me in examining what I conceive to be his inconsistency; and do you, Meletus, answer. And I must remind the audience that they are not to interrupt me if I speak in my accustomed manner. Did ever man, Meletus, believe in the existence of human things, and not of human beings? . . . I wish, men of Athens, that he would answer, and not be always trying to get up an interruption. Did ever any man believe in horsemanship and not in horses? or in flute-playing, and not in flute-players? No, my friend; I will answer to you and to the court, as you refuse to answer for yourself. There is no man who ever did. But now please to answer the next question: Can a man believe in spiritual and divine agencies, and not in spirit or demigods?

He cannot.

I am glad that I have extracted that answer, by the assistance of the court; nevertheless you swear in the indictment that I teach and believe in divine or spiritual agencies (new or old, no matter for that); at any rate, I believe in, spiritual agencies, as you say and swear in the affidavit; but if I believe in divine beings, I must believe in spirits or demigods;—is not that true? Yes, that is true, for I may assume that your silence gives assent to that. Now what are spirits or demigods? are they not either gods or the sons of gods? Is that true?

Yes, that is true.

But this is just the ingenious riddle of which I was speaking: the demigods or spirits are gods, and you say first that I do not believe in gods, and then again that I do believe in gods; that is, if I believe in demigods. For if the demigods are the illegitimate sons of gods, whether by the nymphs or by any other mothers, as is thought, that, as all men will allow, necessarily implies the existence of their parents. You might as well affirm the existence of mules, and deny that of horses and asses. Such nonsense, Meletus, could only have been intended by you as a trial of me. You have put this into the indictment because you had nothing real of which to accuse me. But no one who has a particle of understanding will ever be convinced by you that the same men can believe in divine and superhuman things, and yet not believe that there are gods and demigods and heroes.

I have said enough in answer to the charge of Meletus: any elaborate defense is unnecessary; but as I was saying before, I certainly have many enemies, and this is what will be my destruction if I am destroyed; of that I am certain;— not Meletus, nor Anytus, but the envy and detraction of the world, which has been the death of many good men, and will probably be the death of many more; there is no danger of my being the last of them.

Some one will say: And are you not ashamed, Socrates, of a course of life which is likely to bring you to an untimely end? To him I may fairly answer: There you are mistaken: a man who is good for anything ought not to calculate the chance of living or dying; he ought only to consider whether in doing anything he is doing right or wrong—acting the part of a good man or of a bad. Whereas, according to your view, the heroes who fell at Troy were not good for much, and the son of Thetis above all, who altogether despised danger in comparison with disgrace; and when his goddess mother said to him, in his eagerness to slay Hector, that if he avenged his companion Patroclus, and slew Hector, he would die himself— "Fate," as she said, "waits upon you next after Hector;" he, hearing this, utterly despised danger and death, and instead of fearing them, feared rather to live in dishonour, and not to avenge his friend. "Let me die next," he replies, "and be avenged of my enemy, rather than abide here by the beaked ships, a scorn and a burden of the earth." Had Achilles any thought of death and danger? For wherever a man's place is, whether the place which he has chosen or that in which he has been placed by a commander, there he ought to remain in the hour of danger; he should not think of death or of anything but disgrace. And this, O men of Athens, is a true saying.

Strange, indeed, would be my conduct, O men of Athens, if I who, when I was ordered by the generals whom you chose to command me at Potidæa and Amphipolis, and Delium, remained where they placed me, like any other man, facing death; if I say, now, when, as I conceive and imagine, God orders me to fulfil the philosopher's mission of searching into myself and other men, I were to desert my post through fear of death, or any other fear; that would indeed be strange,

and I might justly be arraigned in court for denying the existence of the gods, if I disobeyed the oracle because I was afraid of death: then I should be fancying that I was wise when I was not wise. For the fear of death is indeed the pretence of wisdom, and not real wisdom, being a pretended knowledge of the unknown; and no one knows whether death, which men in their fear apprehend to be the greatest evil, may not be the greatest good. Is there not here conceit of knowledge, which is a disgraceful sort of ignorance? And this is the point in which, as I think, I differ from others, and in which I might perhaps fancy myself wiser than men in general,—that whereas I know but little of the world below, I do not suppose that I know: but I do know that injustice and disobedience to a better, whether God or man, is evil and dishonourable, and I will never fear or avoid a possible good rather than a certain evil. And therefore if you let me go now, and reject the counsels of Anytus, who said that if I were not put to death I ought not to have been prosecuted, and that if I escape now, your sons will all be utterly ruined by listening to my words—if you say to me, Socrates, this time we will not mind Anytus, and will let you off, but upon one condition, that you are not to enquire and speculate in this way any more, and that if you are caught doing this again you shall die;—if this was the condition on which you let me go, I should reply: Men of Athens, I honour and love you; but I shall obey God rather than you, and while I have life and strength I shall never cease from the practice and teaching of philosophy, exhorting any one whom I meet after my manner, and convincing him, saying: O my friend, why do you, who are a citizen of the great and mighty and wise city of Athens, care so much about laying up the greatest amount of money and honour and reputation, and so little about wisdom and truth and the greatest improvement of the soul, which you never regard or heed at all? Are you not ashamed of this? And if the person with whom I am arguing, says: Yes, but I do care; I do not depart or let him go at once; I interrogate and examine and cross-examine him, and if I think that he has no virtue, but only says that he has, I reproach him with undervaluing the greater, and overvaluing the less. And I say the same to every one whom I meet, young and old, citizen and alien, but especially to the citizens, inasmuch as they are my brethren. For know that this is the command of God; and I believe that to this day no greater good has ever happened in the state than my service to the God. For I do nothing but go about persuading you all, old and young alike, not to take thought for your persons or your properties, but first and chiefly to care about the greatest improvement of the soul. I tell you that virtue is not given by money, but that from virtue come money and every other good of man, public as well as private. This is my teaching, and if this is the doctrine which corrupts the youth, my influence is ruinous indeed. But if any one says that this is not my teaching, he is speaking an untruth. Wherefore, O men of Athens, I say to you, do as Anytus bids or not as Anytus bids, and either acquit me or not; but whatever you do, understand that I shall never alter my ways, not even if I have to die many times.

Men of Athens, do not interrupt, but hear me; there was an agreement between us that you should hear me out. And I think that what I am going to say will do you good: for I have something more to say, at which you may be inclined to cry out; but I beg that you will not. I would have you know, that if you kill such an one as I am, you will injure yourselves more than you will injure me. Nothing will injure me, not Meletus nor yet Anytus—they cannot, for a bad man is not permitted to injure a better than himself. I do not deny that he may, perhaps, kill him, or drive him into exile, or deprive him of civil rights; and he may imagine, and others may imagine, that he is doing him a great injury: but in that I do not agree with him; for the evil of doing as Anytus is doing—of unjustly taking away another man's life—is greater far. And now, Athenians, I am not going to argue for my own sake, as you may think, but for yours, that you may not sin against the God, or lightly reject his boon by condemning me. For if you kill me you will not easily find another like me, who, if I may use such a ludicrous figure of speech, am a sort of gadfly, given to the state by the God; and the state is like a great and noble steed who is tardy in his motions owing to his very size, and requires to be stirred into life. I am that gadfly which God has given the state, and all day long and in all places am always fastening upon you, arousing and persuading and reproaching you. And as you will not easily find another like me, I would advise you to spare me. I dare say that you may feel irritated at being suddenly awakened when you are caught napping; and you may think that if you were to strike me dead as Anytus advises, which you easily might, then you would sleep on for the remainder of your lives, unless God in his care of you gave you another gadfly. And that I am given to you by God is proved by this:— that if I had been like other men, I should not have neglected all my own concerns or patiently seen the neglect of them during all these years, and have been doing yours, coming to you individually like a father or elder brother, exhorting you to regard virtue; such conduct, I say, would be unlike human nature. And had I gained anything, or if my exhortations had been paid, there would have been some sense in that; but now, as you will perceive, not even the impudence of my accusers dares to say that I have ever exacted or sought pay of any one; of that they have no witness. And I have a witness of the truth of what I say; my poverty is a sufficient witness.

Some one may wonder why I go about in private giving advice and busying myself with the concerns of others, but do not venture to come forward in public and advise the state. I will tell you why. You have often heard me speak in times past of an oracle or sign which comes to me, and is the divinity which Meletus ridicules in the indictment. This sign I have had ever since I was a child. The sign is a voice which comes to me and always forbids me to do something which I am going to do, but never commands me to do anything, and this is what stands in the way of my being a politician. And rightly, as I think. For I am certain, O men of Athens, that if I had engaged in politics, I should have perished long ago, and done no good either to you or to myself. And do not be offended at my telling you the truth: for the truth is, that no man who goes to war with you or any other multitude, honestly struggling against the commission of unrighteousness and wrong in the state, will save his life; he who will really fight for the right, if he would live even for a little while, must have a private station and not a public one.

I can give you as proofs of what I say, not words only, but deeds, which you value far more. Let me tell you a passage of my own life which will prove to you that I should never have yielded to injustice from any fear of death, and that when I refused to yield I must have died. I will tell you a tale of the courts, not very interesting perhaps, but nevertheless true. The only office of state which I ever held, O men of Athens, was that of senator: the tribe Antiochis, which is my tribe, had the presidency of the trial of the generals who had not

taken up the bodies of the slain after the battle of Arginusæ; and you proposed to try them in a body, which was illegal, as you all thought afterwards; but at the time I was the only one of the Prytanes who was opposed to the illegality, and I gave my vote against you; and when the orators threatened to impeach you and arrest me, and have me taken away, and you called and shouted, I made up my mind that I would run the risk, having law and justice with me, rather than take part in your injustice because I feared imprisonment and death. This happened in the days of the democracy. But when the oligarchy of the Thirty was in power, they sent for me and four others into the rotunda, and bade us bring Leon the Salaminian from Salamis, as they wanted to execute him. That was a specimen of the sort of commands which they were always giving with the view of implicating as many as possible in their crimes; and then I showed, not in word but in deed, that, if I may be allowed to use such an expression, I cared not a straw for death, and that my sole fear was the fear of doing an unrighteous or unholy thing. For the strong arm of that oppressive power did not frighten me into doing wrong; and when we came out of the rotunda the other four went to Salamis and fetched Leon, but I went quietly home. For which I might have lost my life, had not the power of the Thirty shortly afterwards come to an end. And many will witness to my words.

Now do you really imagine that I could have survived all these years, if I had led a public life, supposing that like a good man I had always supported the right and had made justice, as I ought, the first thing? No indeed, men of Athens, neither I nor any other. But I have been always the same in all my actions, public as well as private, and never have I yielded any base compliance to those who are slanderously termed my disciples, or to any other. For the truth is that I have no regular disciples: but if any one likes to come and hear me while I am pursuing my mission, whether he be young or old, he may freely come. Nor do I converse with those who pay only, and not with those who do not pay; but any one, whether he be rich or poor, may ask and answer me and listen to my words; and whether he turns out to be a bad man or a good one, that cannot be justly laid to my charge, as I never taught or professed to teach him anything. And if any one says that he has ever learned or heard anything from me in private which all the world has not heard, I should like you to know that he is speaking an untruth.

But I shall be asked, Why do people delight in continually conversing with you? I have told you already, Athenians, the whole truth about this: they like to hear the cross-examination of the pretenders to wisdom; there is amusement in it. To converse with others is a duty which the God has imposed upon me, as I am assured by oracles, visions, and in every way in which the will of divine power was ever signified to any one. This is true, O Athenians; or, if not true, would be soon refuted. For if I am really corrupting the youth, and have corrupted some of them already, those of them who have grown up and have become sensible that I gave them bad advice in the days of their youth should come forward as accusers, and take their revenge; and if they do not like to come themselves, some of their relatives, fathers, brothers, or other kinsmen, should say what evil their families suffered at my hands. Now is their time. Many of them I see in the court. There is Crito, who is of the same age and of the same deme with myself, and there is Critobulus his son, whom I also see. Then again there is Lysanias of Sphettus, who is the father of Æschines —he is present; and also there is Anti-phon of Cephisus, who is the father of Epigenes; and there are the brothers of several who have associated with me. There is Nicostratus the son of Theosdotides, and the brother of Theodotus (now Theodotus himself is dead, and therefore he, at any rate, will not seek to stop him); and there is Paralus the son of Demodocus, who had a brother Theages; and Adeimantus the son of Ariston, whose brother Plato is present; and Æantodorus, who is the brother of Apollodorus, whom I also see. I might mention a great many others, any of whom Meletus should have produced as witnesses in the course of his speech; and let him still produce them, if he has forgotten—I will make way for him. And let him say, if he has any testimony of the sort which he can produce. Nay, Athenians, the very opposite is the truth. For all these are ready to witness on behalf of the corruptor, of the destroyer of their kindred, as Meletus and Anytus call me; not the corrupted youth only— there might have been a motive for that —but their uncorrupted elder relatives. Why should they too support me with their testimony? Why, indeed, except for the sake of truth and justice, and because they know that I am speaking the truth, and that Meletus is lying.

Well, Athenians, this and the like of this is nearly all the defense which I have to offer. Yet a word more. Perhaps there may be some one who is offended at me, when he calls to mind how he himself on a similar, or even a less serious occasion, had prayed and entreated the judges with many tears, and how he produced his children in court, which was a moving spectacle, together with a host of relations and friends; whereas I, who am probably in danger of my life, will do none of these things. The contrast may occur to his mind, and he may be set against me, and vote in anger because he is displeased at me on this account. Now if there be such a person among you, which I am far from affirming, I may fairly reply to him: My friend, I am a man, and like other men, a creature of flesh and blood, and not "of wood or stone," as Homer says; and I have a family, yes, and sons, O Athenians, three in number, one of whom is growing up, and the two others are still young; and yet I will not bring any of them hither in order to petition you for an acquittal. And why not? Not from any self-will or disregard of you. Whether I am or am not afraid of death is another question, of which I will not now speak. But my reason simply is, that I feel such conduct to be discreditable to myself, and to you, and to the whole state. One who has reached my years, and who has a name for wisdom, whether deserved or not, ought not to demean himself. At any rate, the world has decided that Socrates is in some way superior to other men. And if those among you who are said to be superior in wisdom and courage, and any other virtue, demean themselves in this way, how shameful is their conduct! I have seen men of reputation, when they have been condemned, behaving in the strangest manner: they seemed to fancy that they were going to suffer something dreadful if they died, and that they could be immortal if you only allowed them to live; and I think that they were a dishonour to the state, and that any stranger coming in would have said of them that the most eminent men of Athens, to whom the Athenians themselves give honour and command, are no better than women. And I say that these things ought not to be done by those of us who are of reputation; and if they are done, you ought not to permit them; you ought rather to show that you are more inclined to condemn, not the man who is quiet, but the man who gets up a doleful scene, and makes the city ridiculous.

But, setting aside the question of dishonour, there seems to be something unjust in petitioning a judge, and thus procuring an acquittal instead of informing and convincing him. For his duty is, not to make a present of justice, but to give judgment; and he has sworn that he will judge according to the laws, and not according to his own good pleasure; and we ought not to encourage you, or you allow yourselves to be encouraged, in this habit of perjury—there can be no piety in that. Do not then require me to do what I consider dishonourable and impious and wrong, especially now, when I am being tried for impiety on the indictment of Meletus. For if, O men of Athens, by force of persuasion and entreaty, I could overpower your oaths, then I should be teaching you to believe that there are no gods, and convict myself, in my own defense, of not believing in them. But that is not the case; for I do believe that there are gods; and in a far higher sense than that in which any of my accusers believe in them. And to you and to God I commit my cause, to be determined by you as is best for you and me. . . .

Not much time will be gained, O Athenians, in return for the evil name which you will get from the detractors of the city, who will say that you killed Socrates, a wise man; for they will call me wise, even although I am not wise, when they want to reproach you. If you had waited a little while, your desire would have been fulfilled in the course of nature. For I am far advanced in years, as you may perceive, and not far from death. I am speaking now only to those of you who have condemned me to death. And I have another thing to say to them: You think that I was convicted because I had no words of the sort which would have procured my acquittal—I mean, if I had thought fit to leave nothing undone or unsaid. Not so; the deficiency which led to my conviction was not of words—certainly not. But I had not the boldness or impudence or inclination to address you as you would have liked me to address you, weeping and wailing and lamenting, and saying and doing many things which you have been accustomed to hear from others, and which, as I maintain, are unworthy of me. I thought at the time that I ought not to do anything common or mean when in danger: nor do I now repent of the manner of my defense, and I would rather die having spoken after my manner, than speak in your manner and live. For neither in war nor yet at law ought I or any man to use every way of escaping death. Often in battle there can be no doubt that if a man will throw away his arms, and fall on his knees before his pursuers, he may escape death; and in other dangers there are other ways of escaping death, if a man is willing to say and do anything. The difficulty, my friends, is not in avoiding death, but in avoiding unrighteousness; for that runs faster than death. I am old and move slowly, and the slower runner has overtaken me, and my accusers are keen and quick, and the faster runner, who is unrighteousness, has overtaken them. And now I depart hence condemned by you to suffer the penalty of death, and they too go their ways condemned by the truth to suffer the penalty of villainy and wrong; and I must abide by my award— let them abide by theirs. I suppose that these things may be regarded as fated,— and I think that they are well.

And now, O men who have condemned me, I would fain prophesy to you; for I am about to die, and that is the hour in which men are gifted with prophetic power. And I prophesy to you who are my murderers, that immediately after my death punishment far heavier than you have afflicted on me will surely await you. Me you have killed because you wanted to escape the accuser, and not to give an account of your lives. But that will not be as you suppose: far otherwise. For I say that there will be more accusers than there are now; accusers whom hitherto I have restrained: and as they are younger they will be more inconsiderate with you, and you will be more offended at them. If you think that by killing men you can prevent some one from censuring your evil lives, you are mistaken; that is not a way of escape which is either possible or honourable; the easiest and the noblest way is not to be disabling others, but to be improving yourselves. This is the prophecy which I utter before my departure to the judges who have condemned me.

Friends, who would have acquitted me, I would like also to talk with you about this thing which has happened, while the magistrates are busy, and before I go to the place at which I must die. Stay then awhile, for we may as well talk with one another while there is time. You are my friends, and I should like to show you the meaning of this event which has happened to me. O my judges—for you I may truly call judges—I should like to tell you of a wonderful circumstance. Hitherto the familiar oracle within me has constantly been in the habit of opposing me even about trifles, if I was going to make a slip or error in any matter; and now as you see there has come upon me that which may be thought, and is generally believed to be, the last and worst evil. But the oracle made no sign of opposition, either as I was leaving my house and going out in the morning, or when I was going up into this court, or while I was speaking, at anything which I was going to say; and yet I have often been stopped in the middle of a speech, but now in nothing I either said or did touching this matter has the oracle opposed me. What do I take to be the explanation of this? I will tell you. I regard this as a great proof that what has happened to me is a good, and that those of us who think that death is an evil are in error. For the customary sign would surely have opposed me had I been going to evil and not to good.

Let us reflect in another way, and we shall see that there is great reason to hope that death is a good; for one of two things—either death is a state of nothingness and utter unconsciousness, or, as men say, there is a change and migration of the soul from this world to another. Now if you suppose that there is no consciousness, but a sleep like the sleep of him who is undisturbed even by the sight of dreams, death will be an unspeakable gain. For if a person were to select the night in which his sleep was undisturbed even by dreams, and were to compare with this the other days and nights of his life, and then were to tell us how many days and nights he had passed in the course of his life better and more pleasantly than this one, I think that any man, I will not say a private man, but even the great king will not find many such days or nights, when compared with the others. Now if death is like this, I say that to die is gain; for eternity is then only a single night. But if death is the journey to another place, and there, as men say, all the dead are, what good, O my friends and judges, can be greater than this? If indeed when the pilgrim arrives in the world below, he is delivered from the professors of justice in this world, and finds the true judges who are said to give judgment there, Minos and Rhadamanthus and Æacus and Triptolemus, and other sons of God who were righteous in their own life, that pilgrimage will be worth making. What would not a man give if he might converse with Orpheus and Musæus and Hesiod and Homer? Nay, if this be true, let me die again and again. I myself, too, shall have a wonderful interest in there meeting and conversing with Palamedes, and Ajax the son of Telamon, and other heroes of old, who have suffered death through an unjust judgment; and there will be no small pleasure, as I think,

in comparing my own sufferings with theirs. Above all, I shall then be able to continue my search into true and false knowledge; as in this world, so also in that; and I shall find out who is wise, and who pretends to be wise, and is not. What would not a man give, O judges, to be able to examine the leader of the great Trojan expedition; or Odysseus or Sisyphus, or numberless others, men and women too! What infinite delight would there be in conversing with them and asking them questions! In another world they do not put a man to death for asking questions; assuredly not. For besides being happier in that world than in this, they will be immortal, if what is said is true.

Wherefore, O judges, be of good cheer about death, and know of a certainty, that no evil can happen to a good man, either in life or after death. He and his are not neglected by the gods; nor has my own approaching end happened by mere chance. But I see clearly that to die and be released was better for me; and therefore the oracle gave no sign. For which reason, also, I am not angry with my condemners, or with my accusers; they have done me no harm, although they did not mean to do me any good; and for this I may gently blame them.

Still I have a favour to ask of them. When my sons are grown up, I would ask you, O my friends, to punish them; and I would have you trouble them, as I have troubled you, if they seem to care about riches, or anything, more than about virtue; or if they pretend to be something when they are really nothing, —then reprove them, as I have reproved you, for not caring about that for which they ought to care, and thinking that they are something when they are really nothing. And if you do this, I and my sons will have received justice at your hands.

The hour of departure has arrived, and

we go our ways—I to die, and you to live. Which is better God only knows.

—BENJAMIN JOWETT.

THE DEATH OF SOCRATES [1]

PLATO

[From the *Phædo*]

The conduct and the last words of Socrates in his prison before he took the poison are represented as reported by one of his favorite disciples, Phædo. Plato uses the opportunity afforded by this tribute of love to set forth his ideas on the immortality of the soul. The argument for immortality grows out of the theory that "learning is recollecting." This, in turn, leads to the hypothesis that the soul existed before the birth of the body, and therefore must continue to exist after the death of the body. The whole thought is bound up with the notion of the absolute and independent existence of ideas.

When he had done speaking, Crito said: And have you any command for us, Socrates—anything to say about your children, or any other matter in which we can serve you?

Nothing particular, he said: only, as I have always told you, I would have you look to yourselves; that is a service which you may always be doing to me and mine as well as to yourselves. And you need not make professions; for if you take no thought for yourselves, and walk not according to the precepts which I have given you, not now for the first time, the warmth of your professions will be of no avail.

We will do our best, said Crito. But in what way would you have us bury you?

In any way that you like; only you must get hold of me, and take care that

---

[1] Reprinted by arrangement with the Oxford University Press, publishers.

I do not walk away from you. Then he turned to us, and added with a smile:— I cannot make Crito believe that I am the same Socrates who have been talking and conducting the argument; he fancies that I am the other Socrates whom he will soon see, a dead body—and he asks, How shall he bury me? And though I have spoken many words in the endeavour to show that when I have drunk the poison I shall leave you and go to the joys of the blessed,—these words of mine, with which I comforted you and myself, have had, as I perceive, no effect upon Crito. And therefore I want you to be surety for me now, as he was surety for me at the trial: but let the promise be of another sort; for he was my surety to the judges that I would remain, and you must be my surety to him that I shall not remain, but go away and depart; and then he will suffer less at my death, and not be grieved when he sees my body being burned or buried. I would not have him sorrow at my hard lot, or say at the burial, Thus we lay our Socrates, or, Thus we follow him to the grave or bury him; for false words are not only evil in themselves, but they infect the soul with evil. Be of good cheer then, my dear Crito, and say that you are burying my body only, and do with that as is usual, and as you think best.

When he had spoken these words, he arose and told us to wait while he went into the bath-chamber with Crito; and we waited, talking and thinking of the subject of discourse, and also of the greatness of our sorrow; he was like a father of whom we were being bereaved, and we were about to pass the rest of our lives as orphans. When he had taken the bath his children were brought to him —(he had two young sons and an elder one); and the women of his family also came, and he talked to them and gave them a few directions in the presence of Crito; and he then dismissed them and returned to us.

Now the hour of sunset was near, for a good deal of time had passed while he was within. When he came out, he sat down with us again after his bath, but not much was said. Soon the jailer, who was the servant of the eleven, entered and stood by him, saying:—To you, Socrates, whom I know to be the noblest and gentlest and best of all who ever came to this place, I will not impute the angry feelings of other men, who rage and swear at me, when, in obedience to the authorities, I bid them drink the poison—indeed, I am sure that you will not be angry with me; for others, as you are aware, and not I, are the guilty cause. And so fare you well, and try to bear lightly what must needs be; you know my errand. Then bursting into tears he turned and went out.

Socrates looked at him and said: I return your good wishes, and will do as you bid. Then turning to us, he said, How charming the man is: since I have been in prison he has always been coming to see me, and at times he would talk to me, and was as good as could be, and now see how generously he sorrows for me. But we must do as he says, Crito; let the cup be brought, if the poison is prepared: if not, let the attendant prepare some.

Yet, said Crito, the sun is still upon the hill-tops, and I know that many a one has taken the draught late, and after the announcement has been made to him, he has eaten and drunk, and enjoyed the society of his beloved; do not hasten then, there is still time.

Socrates said: Yes, Crito, and they of whom you speak are right in doing thus, for they think that they will gain by the delay; but I am right in not doing thus, for I do not think that I should gain anything by drinking the poison a little later; I should be sparing and saving a life which is already gone, and could only despise myself for this. Please then to do as I say, and not to refuse me.

Crito made a sign to the servant, who was standing by; and he went out, and having been absent for some time, returned with the jailer carrying the cup of poison. Socrates said: You, my good friend, who are experienced in these matters, shall give me directions how I am to proceed. The man answered: You have only to walk about until your legs are heavy, and then to lie down, and the poison will act. At the same time he handed the cup to Socrates, who in the easiest and gentlest manner, without the least fear or change of colour or feature, looking at the man with all his eyes, Echecrates, as his manner was, took the cup and said: What do you say about making a libation out of this cup to any god? May I, or not? The man answered: We only prepare, Socrates, just so much as we deem enough. I understand, he said: but I may and must ask the gods to prosper my journey from this to that other world—even so—and so be it according to my prayer. Then holding the cup to his lips, quite readily and cheerfully he drank off the poison. And hitherto most of us had been able to control our sorrow; but now when we saw him drinking, and saw too that he had finished the draught, we could no longer forbear, and in spite of myself my own tears were flowing fast; so that I covered my face and wept over myself, for certainly I was not weeping over him, but at the thought of my own calamity at having lost such a friend. Nor was I the first, for Crito, when he found himself unable to restrain his tears, had got up and moved away, and I followed; and at that moment, Apollodorus, who had been weeping all the time, broke out in a loud and passionate cry which made cowards of us all. Socrates alone retained his calmness: What is this strange outcry? he said. I sent away the women mainly in order that they might not offend in this way, for I have heard that a man should die in peace. Be quiet then, and have patience. When we heard that, we were ashamed, and refrained our tears; and he walked about until, as he said, his legs began to fail, and then he lay on his back, according to the directions, and the man who gave him the poison now and then looked at his feet and legs; and after a while he pressed his foot hard, and asked him if he could feel; and he said, No; and then his leg, and so upwards and upwards, and showed us that he was cold and stiff. And he felt them himself, and said: When the poison reaches the heart, that will be the end. He was beginning to grow cold about the groin, when he uncovered his face, for he had covered himself up, and said (they were his last words)—he said: Crito, I owe a cock to Asclepius; will you remember to pay the debt? The debt shall be paid, said Crito; is there anything else? There was no answer to this question; but in a minute or two a movement was heard, and the attendants uncovered him; his eyes were set, and Crito closed his eyes and mouth.

Such was the end, Echecrates, of our friend, whom I may truly call the wisest, and justest, and best of all the men whom I have ever known.

—BENJAMIN JOWETT.

POETICS [1]

ARISTOTLE

Aristotle (384 to 322 B.C.), of Stageira in Macedonia, pupil of Plato and tutor of Alexander the Great, was the author of a large number of dialogues and treatises, of which only a small proportion are still in existence. He was the founder of the school of the Lyceum, which, from his practice of delivering his lectures while promenading, received also the name Peripatetic. He maintained that the essence of things was not to be found in the

[1] Reprinted by permission of Macmillan & Co., London, publishers.

absolute ideas of Plato, but in the nature of things themselves; that not a method of dialectic, which is based upon opinion and presupposes a theory of perfection, can ascertain the nature of things, but a method of observation, classification and analysis. He thus laid the foundations for modern science. He applied his principles not only to what we now call the natural sciences, but also to politics, ethics, and the liberal arts.

Aristotle's treatment of poetry differs essentially from that of Plato on the one hand and from that of Horace on the other. Plato questions its moral value because it deals in fictions of the imagination, and criticises it because it consists merely of imitation. Aristotle admits that it is but imitation, but maintains that it is life which it imitates, that imitation is a fact of life and therefore reality itself, and that imitation purifies us morally by holding up to view an objective picture of ourselves. Horace seeks to formulate the rules of poetic composition; Aristotle seeks to discover the principles which are essential to the art and out of which rules may grow.

I propose to treat of poetry in itself and of its various kinds, noting the essential quality of each; to inquire into the structure of the plot as requisite to a good poem; into the number and nature of the parts of which a poem is composed; and similarly into whatever else falls within the same inquiry. Following, then, the order of nature, let us begin with the principles which come first.

Epic poetry and Tragedy, Comedy also and Dithyrambic poetry, and the music of the flute and of the lyre in most of their forms, are all in their general conception modes of imitation. They differ, however, from one another in three respects,—the medium, the objects, the manner or mode of imitation, being in each case distinct.

For as there are persons who, by conscious art or mere habit, imitate and represent various objects through the medium of colour and form, or again by the voice; so in the arts above mentioned, taken as a whole, the imitation is produced by rhythm, language, or "harmony," either singly or combined.

Thus in the music of the flute and of the lyre, "harmony" and rhythm alone are employed; also in other arts, such as that of the shepherd's pipe, which are essentially similar to these. In dancing, rhythm alone is used without "harmony"; for even dancing imitates character, and action, by rhythmical movement.

There is another art which imitates by means of language alone, and that either in prose or verse—which verse, again, may either combine different metres or consist of but one kind—but this has hitherto been without a name. For there is no common term we could apply to the mimes of Sophron and Xenarchus and the Socratic dialogues on the one hand; and, on the other, to poetic imitations in iambic, elegiac, or any similar metre. People do, indeed, add the word "maker" or "poet" to the name of the metre, and speak of elegiac poets, or epic (that is, hexameter) poets, as if it were not the imitation that makes the poet, but the verse that entitles them all indiscriminately to the name. Even when a treatise on medicine or natural science is brought out in verse, the name of poet is by custom given to the author; and yet Homer and Empedocles have nothing in common but the metre, so that it would be right to call the one poet, the other physicist rather than poet. On the same principle, even if a writer in his poetic imitation were to combine all metres, as Chæremon did in his Centaur, which is a medley composed of metres of all kinds, we should bring him too under the general term poet. So much then for these distinctions.

There are, again, some arts which employ all the means above mentioned,—namely, rhythm, tune, and metre. Such

are Dithyrambic and Nomic poetry, and also Tragedy and Comedy; but between them the difference is, that in the first two cases these means are all employed in combination, in the latter, now one means is employed, now another.

Such, then, are the differences of the arts with respect to the medium of imitation.

Since the objects of imitation are men in action, and these men must be either of a higher or a lower type (for moral character mainly answers to these divisions, goodness and badness being the distinguishing marks of moral differences), it follows that we must represent men either as better than in real life, or as worse, or as they are. It is the same in painting. Polygnotus depicted men as nobler than they are, Pauson as less noble, Dionysius drew them true to life.

Now it is evident that each of the modes of imitation above mentioned will exhibit these differences, and become a distinct kind in imitating objects that are thus distinct. Such diversities may be found even in dancing, flute-playing, and lyre-playing. So again in language, whether prose or verse unaccompanied by music. Homer, for example, makes men better than they are; Hegemon the Thasian, the inventor of parodies, and Nicochares, the author of the Deiliad, worse than they are. The same thing holds good of Dithyrambs and Nomes; here too one may portray different types, as Timotheus and Philoxenus differed in representing their Cyclopes. The same distinction marks off Tragedy from Comedy; for Comedy aims at representing men as worse, Tragedy as better than in actual life.

There is still a third difference—the manner in which each of these objects may be imitated. For the medium being the same, the poet may imitate by narration—in which case he can either take another personality as Homer does, or speak in his own person, unchanged—or he may present all his characters as living and moving before us.

These, then, as we said at the beginning, are the three differences which distinguish artistic imitation,—the medium, the objects, and the manner. So that from one point of view, Sophocles is an imitator of the same kind as Homer—for both imitate higher types of character; from another point of view, of the same kind as Aristophanes—for both imitate persons acting and doing. Hence, some say, the name of "drama" is given to such poems, as representing action. For the same reason the Dorians claim the invention both of Tragedy and Comedy. The claim to Comedy is put forward by the Megarians,—not only by those of Greece proper, who allege that it originated under their democracy, but also by the Megarians of Sicily, for the poet Epicharmus, who is much earlier than Chionides and Magnes, belonged to that country. Tragedy too is claimed by certain Dorians of the Peloponnese. In each case they appeal to the evidence of language. The outlying villages, they say, are by them called κῶμαι, by the Athenians δῆμοι and they assume that Comedians were so named not from κωμάζειν, "to revel," but because they wandered from village to village (κατὰ κώμας), being excluded contemptuously from the city. They add also that the Dorian word for "doing" is δρᾶν, and the Athenian, πράττειν.

This may suffice as to the number and nature of the various modes of imitation.

Poetry in general seems to have sprung from two causes, each of them lying deep in our nature. First, the instinct of imitation is implanted in man from childhood, one difference between man and other animals being that he is the most imitative of living creatures, and through imitation learns his earliest lessons; and no less universal is the pleasure felt in things imitated. We have evidence of this in the facts of experience. Objects which in themselves we view with pain, we delight to contemplate when reproduced with minute fidelity: such as the forms of the most ignoble animals and of dead bodies. The cause of this again is, that to learn gives the liveliest pleasure, not only to philosophers but to men in general; whose capacity, however, of learning is more limited. Thus the reason why men enjoy seeing a likeness is, that in contemplating it they find themselves learning or inferring, and saying perhaps, "Ah, that is he." For if you happen not to have seen the original, the pleasure will be due not to the imitation as such, but to the execution, the colouring, or some such other cause.

Imitation, then, is one instinct of our nature. Next, there is the instinct for "harmony" and rhythm, metres being manifestly sections of rhythm. Persons, therefore, starting with this natural gift developed by degrees their special aptitudes, till their rude improvisations gave birth to Poetry.

Poetry now diverged in two directions, according to the individual character of the writers. The graver spirits imitated noble actions, and the actions of good men. The more trivial sort imitated the actions of meaner persons, at first composing satires, as the former did hymns to the gods and the praises of famous men. A poem of the satirical kind cannot indeed be put down to any author earlier than Homer; though many such writers probably there were. But from Homer onward, instances can be cited,—his own Margites, for example, and other similar compositions. The appropriate metre was also here introduced; hence the measure is still called the iambic or lampooning measure, being that in which people lampooned one another. Thus the older poets were distinguished as writers of heroic or of lampooning verse.

As, in the serious style, Homer is pre-eminent among poets, for he alone combined dramatic form with excellence of imitation, so he too first laid down the main lines of Comedy, by dramatising the ludicrous instead of writing personal satire. His Margites bears the same relation to Comedy that the Iliad and Odyssey do to Tragedy. But when Tragedy and Comedy came to light, the two classes of poets still followed their natural bent: the lampooners became writers of Comedy, and the Epic poets were succeeded by Tragedians, since the drama was a larger and higher form of art.

Whether Tragedy has as yet perfected its proper types or not; and whether it is to be judged in itself, or in relation also to the audience,—this raises another question. Be that as it may, Tragedy—as also Comedy—was at first mere improvisation. The one originated with the authors of the Dithyramb, the other with those of the phallic songs, which are still in use in many of our cities. Tragedy advanced by slow degrees; each new element that showed itself was in turn developed. Having passed through many changes, it found its natural form, and there it stopped.

Æschylus first introduced a second actor; he diminished the importance of the Chorus, and assigned the leading part to the dialogue. Sophocles raised the number of actors to three, and added scene-painting. Moreover, it was not till late that the short plot was discarded for one of greater compass, and the grotesque diction of the earlier satyric form for the stately manner of Tragedy. The iambic measure then replaced the trochaic tetrameter, which was originally employed when the poetry was of the satyric order, and had greater affinities with dancing. Once dialogue had come in, Nature herself discovered the appropriate measure. For the iambic is, of all measures, the most colloquial: we see it in the fact that conversational speech runs into iambic lines more frequently than into any other kind of verse; rarely

into hexameters, and only when we drop the colloquial intonation. The additions to the number of "episodes" or acts, and the other accessories of which tradition tells, must be taken as already described; for to discuss them in detail would, doubtless, be a large undertaking.

Comedy is, as we have said, an imitation of characters of a lower type,—not, however, in the full sense of the word bad, the ludicrous being merely a subdivision of the ugly. It consists in some defect or ugliness which is not painful or destructive. To take an obvious example, the comic mask is ugly and distorted, but does not imply pain.

The successive changes through which Tragedy passed, and the authors of these changes, are well known, whereas Comedy has had no history, because it was not at first treated seriously. It was late before the Archon granted a comic chorus to a poet; the performers were till then voluntary. Comedy had already taken definite shape when comic poets, distinctively so called, are heard of. Who furnished it with masks, or prologues, or increased the number of actors,—these and other similar details remain unknown. As for the plot, it came originally from Sicily; but of Athenian writers Crates was the first who, abandoning the "iambic" or lampooning form, generalised his themes and plots.

Epic Poetry agrees with Tragedy in so far as it is an imitation in verse of characters of a higher type. They differ, in that Epic poetry admits but one kind of metre, and is narrative in form. They differ, again, in their length: for Tragedy endeavours, as far as possible, to confine itself to a single revolution of the sun, or but slightly to exceed this limit; whereas the Epic action has no limits of time. This, then, is a second point of difference; though at first the same freedom was admitted in Tragedy as in Epic poetry.

Of their constituent parts some are common to both, some peculiar to

Tragedy: whoever, therefore, knows what is good or bad Tragedy, knows also about Epic poetry. All the elements of an Epic poem are found in Tragedy, but the elements of a Tragedy are not all found in the Epic poem.

Of the poetry which imitates in hexameter verse, and of Comedy, we will speak hereafter. Let us now discuss Tragedy, resuming its formal definition, as resulting from what has been already said.

Tragedy, then, is an imitation of an action that is serious, complete, and of a certain magnitude; in language embelished with each kind of artistic ornament, the several kinds being found in separate parts of the play; in the form of action, not of narrative; through pity and fear effecting the proper purgation of these emotions. By "language embellished," I mean language into which rhythm, "harmony," and song enter. By "the several kinds in separate parts," I mean, that some parts are rendered through the medium of verse alone, others again with the aid of song.

Now as tragic imitation implies persons acting, it necessarily follows, in the first place, that Spectacular equipment will be a part of Tragedy. Next, Song and Diction, for these are the medium of imitation. By "Diction" I mean the mere metrical arrangement of the words: as for "Song," it is a term whose sense every one understands.

Again, Tragedy is the imitation of an action; and an action implies personal agents, who necessarily possess certain distinctive qualities both of character and thought; for it is by these that we qualify actions themselves, and these—thought and character—are the two natural causes from which actions spring, and on actions again all success or failure depends. Hence, the Plot is the imitation of the action:—for by plot I here mean the arrangement of the incidents. By Character I mean that in virtue of which we ascribe certain qualities to the agents. Thought is required wherever a statement is proved, or, it may be, a general truth is enunciated. Every Tragedy, therefore, must have six parts, which parts determine its quality—namely, Plot, Character, Diction, Thought, Spectacle, Song. Two of the parts constitute the medium of imitation, one the manner, and three the objects of imitation. And these complete the list. These elements have been employed, we may say, by the poets to a man; in fact, every play contains Spectacular elements as well as Character, Plot, Diction, Song, and Thought.

But most important of all is the structure of the incidents. For Tragedy is an imitation, not of men, but of an action and of life, and life consists in action, and its end is a mode of action, not a quality. Now character determines men's qualities, but it is by their actions that they are happy or the reverse. Dramatic action, therefore, is not with a view to the representation of character: character comes in as subsidiary to the actions. Hence the incidents and the plot are the end of a tragedy; and the end is the chief thing of all. Again, without action there cannot be a tragedy; there may be without character. The tragedies of most of our modern poets fail in the rendering of character; and of poets in general this is often true. It is the same in painting; and here lies the difference between Zeuxis and Polygnotus. Polygnotus delineates character well: the style of Zeuxis is devoid of ethical quality. Again, if you string together a set of speeches expressive of character, and well finished in point of diction and thought, you will not produce the essential tragic effect nearly so well as with a play which, however deficient in these respects, yet has a plot and artistically constructed incidents. Besides which, the most powerful elements of emotional interest in Tragedy —Peripeteia or Reversal of the Situation, and Recognition scenes—are parts of the plot. A further proof is, that novices in the art attain to finish of diction and precision of portraiture before they can construct the plot. It is the same with almost all the early poets.

The Plot, then, is the first principle, and, as it were, the soul of a tragedy: Character holds the second place. A similar fact is seen in painting. The most beautiful colours, laid on confusedly, will not give as much pleasure as the chalk outline of a portrait. Thus Tragedy is the imitation of an action, and of the agents mainly with a view to the action.

Third in order is Thought,—that is, the faculty of saying what is possible and pertinent in given circumstances. In the case of oratory, this is the function of the political art and of the art of rhetoric: and so indeed the older poets make their characters speak the language of civic life; the poets of our time, the language of the rhetoricians. Character is that which reveals moral purpose, showing what kinds of things a man chooses or avoids. Speeches, therefore, which do not make this manifest, or in which the speaker does not choose or avoid anything whatever, are not expressive of character. Thought, on the other hand, is found where something is proved to be or not to be, or a general maxim is enunciated.

Fourth among the elements enumerated comes Diction; by which I mean, as has been already said, the expression of the meaning in words; and its essence is the same both in verse and prose.

Of the remaining elements Song holds the chief place among the embellishments. The Spectacle has, indeed, an emotional attraction of its own, but, of all the parts, it is the least artistic, and connected least with the art of poetry. For the power of Tragedy, we may be sure, is felt even apart from representation and actors. Besides, the production of spectacular effects depends more on the art of the stage machinist than on that of the poet.

These principles being established, let us now discuss the proper structure of the Plot, since this is the first and most important thing in Tragedy.

Now, according to our definition, Tragedy is an imitation of an action that is complete, and whole, and of a certain magnitude; for there may be a whole that is wanting in magnitude. A whole is that which has a beginning, a middle, and an end. A beginning is that which does not itself follow anything by causal necessity, but after which something naturally is or comes to be. An end, on the contrary, is that which itself naturally follows some other thing, either by necessity, or as a rule, but has nothing following it. A middle is that which follows something as some other thing follows it. A well constructed plot, therefore, must neither begin nor end at haphazard, but conform to these principles.

Again, a beautiful object, whether it be a living organism or any whole composed of parts, must not only have an orderly arrangement of parts, but must also be of a certain magnitude; for beauty depends on magnitude and order. Hence a very small animal organism cannot be beautiful; for the view of it is confused, the object being seen in an almost imperceptible moment of time. Nor, again, can one of vast size be beautiful; for as the eye cannot take it all in at once, the unity and sense of the whole is lost for the spectator; as for instance if there were one a thousand miles long. As, therefore, in the case of animate bodies and organisms a certain magnitude is necessary, and a magnitude which may be easily embraced in one view; so in the plot, a certain length is necessary, and a length which can be easily embraced by the memory. The limit of length in relation to dramatic competition and sensuous presentment, is no part of artistic theory. For had it been the rule for a hundred tragedies to compete together, the performance would have been regulated by the water-clock,—as indeed we are told was formerly done. But the limit as fixed by the nature of the drama itself is this:—the greater the length, the more beautiful will the piece be by reason of its size, provided that the whole be perspicuous. And to define the matter roughly, we may say that the proper magnitude is comprised within such limits, that the sequence of events, according to the law of probability or necessity, will admit of a change from bad fortune to good, or from good fortune to bad.

Unity of plot does not, as some persons think, consist in the unity of the hero. For infinitely various are the incidents in one man's life which cannot be reduced to unity; and so, too, there are many actions of one man out of which we cannot make one action. Hence the error, as it appears, of all poets who have composed a Heracleid, a Theseid, or other poems of the kind. They imagine that as Heracles was one man, the story of Heracles must also be a unity. But Homer, as in all else he is of surpassing merit, here too—whether from art or natural genius—seems to have happily discerned the truth. In composing the Odyssey he did not include all the adventures of Odysseus—such as his wound on Parnassus, or his feigned madness at the mustering of the host—incidents between which there was no necessary or probable connexion: but he made the Odyssey, and likewise the Iliad, to centre round an action that in our sense of the word is one. As therefore, in the other imitative arts, the imitation is one when the object imitated is one, so the plot, being an imitation of an action, must imitate one action and that a whole, the structural union of the parts being such that, if any one of them is displaced or removed, the whole will be disjointed and disturbed. For a thing whose presence or absence makes no visible difference, is not an organic part of the whole.

It is, moreover, evident from what has been said, that it is not the function of the poet to relate what has happened, but what may happen,—what is possible according to the law of probability or necessity. The poet and the historian differ not by writing in verse or prose. The work of Herodotus might be put into verse, and it would still be a species of history, with metre no less than without it. The true difference is that one relates what has happened, the other what may happen. Poetry, therefore, is a more philosophical and a higher thing than history: for poetry tends to express the universal, history the particular. By the universal I mean how a person of a certain type will on occasion speak or act, according to the law of probability or necessity; and it is this universality at which poetry aims in the names she attaches to the personages. The particular is—for example—what Alcibiades did or suffered. In Comedy this is already apparent: for here the poet first constructs the plots on the lines of probability, and then inserts characteristic names;—unlike the lampooners who write about particular individuals. But tragedians still keep to real names, the reason being that what is possible is credible: what has not happened we do not at once feel sure to be possible: but what has happened is manifestly possible: otherwise it would not have happened. Still there are even some tragedies in which there are only one or two well known names, the rest being fictitious. In others, none are well known,—as in Agathon's Antheus, where incidents and names alike are fictitious, and yet they give none the less pleasure. We must not, therefore, at all costs keep to the received legends, which are the usual subjects of Tragedy. Indeed, it would be absurd to attempt it; for even subjects that are known are known only to a few, and yet give pleasure to all. It clearly follows that the poet or "maker" should be the maker of plots rather than of verses; since he is a poet because he imitates, and what he imitates are actions. And even if he chances to take an historical subject, he is none the less a poet; for there is no reason why some events that have actually happened should not conform to the law of the probable and possible, and in virtue of that quality in them he is their poet or maker.

Of all plots and actions the epeisodic are the worst. I call a plot "epeisodic" in which the episodes or acts succeed one another without probable or necessary sequence. Bad poets compose such pieces by their own fault, good poets, to please the players; for, as they write show pieces for competition, they stretch the plot beyond its capacity, and are often forced to break the natural continuity.

But again, Tragedy is an imitation not only of a complete action, but of events inspiring fear or pity. Such an effect is best produced when the events come on us by surprise; and the effect is heightened when, at the same time, they follow as cause and effect. The tragic wonder will then be greater than if they happened of themselves or by accident; for even coincidences are most striking when they have an air of design. We may instance the statue of Mitys at Argos, which fell upon his murderer while he was a spectator at a festival, and killed him. Such events seem not to be due to mere chance. Plots, therefore, constructed on these principles are necessarily the best.

Plots are either Simple or Complex, for the actions in real life, of which the plots are an imitation, obviously show a similar distinction. An action which is one and continuous in the sense above defined, I call Simple, when the change of fortune takes place without Reversal of the Situation and without Recognition.

A Complex action is one in which the change is accompanied by such Reversal, or by Recognition, or by both. These last should arise from the internal structure of the plot, so that what follows should be the necessary or probable result of the preceding action. It makes all the difference whether any given event is a case of *propter hoc* or *post hoc*.

Reversal of the Situation is a change by which the action veers round to its opposite, subject always to our rule of probability or necessity. Thus in the Œdipus, the messenger comes to cheer Œdipus and free him from his alarms about his mother, but by revealing who he is, he produces the opposite effect. Again in the Lynceus, Lynceus is being led away to his death, and Danaus goes with him, meaning to slay him; but the outcome of the preceding incidents is that Danaus is killed and Lynceus saved.

Recognition, as the name indicates, is a change from ignorance to knowledge, producing love or hate between the persons destined by the poet for good or bad fortune. The best form of recognition is coincident with a Reversal of the Situation, as in the Œdipus. There are indeed other forms. Even inanimate things of the most trivial kind may in a sense be objects of recognition. Again, we may recognise or discover whether a person has done a thing or not. But the recognition which is most intimately connected with the plot and action is, as we have said, the recognition of persons. This recognition, combined with Reversal, will produce either pity or fear; and actions producing these effects are those which, by our definition, Tragedy represents. Moreover, it is upon such situations that the issues of good or bad fortune will depend. Recognition, then, being between persons, it may happen that one person only is recognised by the other—when the latter is already known —or it may be necessary that the recognition should be on both sides. Thus Iphigenia is revealed to Orestes by the sending of the letter; but another act of recognition is required to make Orestes known to Iphigenia.

Two parts, then, of the plot—Reversal of Situation and Recognition—turn upon surprises. A third part is the Scene of Suffering. The Scene of Suffering is a destructive or painful action, such as death on the stage, bodily agony, wounds and the like.

(The parts of Tragedy which must be treated as elements of the whole have been already mentioned. We now come to the quantitative parts—the separate parts into which Tragedy is divided—namely, Prologue, Episode, Exode, Choric song; this last being divided into Parode and Stasimon. These are common to all plays: peculiar to some are the songs of actors from the stage and the Commoi.

The Prologue is that entire part of a tragedy which precedes the Parode of the Chorus. The Episode is that entire part of a tragedy which is between complete choric songs. The Exode is that entire part of a tragedy which has no choric song after it. Of the Choric part the Parode is the first undivided utterance of the Chorus: the Stasimon is a Choric ode without anapaests or trochaic tetrameters: the Commos is a joint lamentation of Chorus and actors. The parts of Tragedy which must be treated as elements of the whole have been already mentioned. The quantitative parts—the separate parts into which it is divided—are here enumerated.)

As the sequel to what has already been said, we must proceed to consider what the poet should aim at, and what he should avoid, in constructing his plots; and by what means the specific effect of Tragedy will be produced.

A perfect tragedy should, as we have seen, be arranged not on the simple but on the complex plan. It should, moreover, imitate actions which excite pity or fear, this being the distinctive mark of tragic imitation. It follows plainly, in the first place, that the change of fortune

presented must not be the spectacle of a virtuous man brought from prosperity to adversity: for this moves neither pity nor fear; it merely shocks us. Nor, again, that of a bad man passing from adversity to prosperity: for nothing can be more alien to the spirit of Tragedy; it possesses no single tragic quality; it neither satisfies the moral sense nor calls forth pity or fear. Nor, again, should the downfall of the utter villain be exhibited. A plot of this kind would, doubtless, satisfy the moral sense, but it would inspire neither pity nor fear; for pity is aroused by unmerited misfortune, fear by the misfortune of a man like ourselves. Such an event, therefore, will be neither pitiful nor terrible. There remains, then, the character between these two extremes,—that of a man who is not eminently good and just, yet whose misfortune is brought about not by vice or depravity, but by some error or frailty. He must be one who is highly renowned and prosperous,—a personage like Œdipus, Thyestes, or other illustrious men of such families.

A well constructed plot should, therefore, be single in its issue, rather than double as some maintain. The change of fortune should be not from bad to good, but, reversely, from good to bad. It should come about as the result not of vice, but of some great error or frailty, in a character such as we have described, or better rather than worse. The practice of the stage bears out our view. At first the poets recounted any legend that came in their way. Now, the best tragedies are founded on the stories of a few houses,—on the fortunes of Alcmæon, Œdipus, Meleager, Thyestes, Telephus, and those others who have done or suffered something terrible. A tragedy, then, to be perfect according to the rules of art should be of this construction. Hence they are in error who censure Euripides just because he follows this principle in his plays, many of which end unhappily.

It is, as we have said, the right ending. The best proof is that on the stage and in dramatic competition, such plays, if well worked out, are the most tragic in effect; and Euripides, faulty though he may be in the general management of his subject, yet is felt to be the most tragic of the poets.

In the second rank comes the kind of tragedy which some place first. Like the Odyssey, it has a double thread of plot, and also an opposite catastrophe for the good and for the bad. It is accounted the best because of the weakness of the spectators; for the poet is guided in what he writes by the wishes of his audience. The pleasure, however, thence derived is not the true tragic pleasure. It is proper rather to Comedy, where those who, in the piece, are the deadliest enemies—like Orestes and Ægisthus—quit the stage as friends at the close, and no one slays or is slain.

Fear and pity may be aroused by spectacular means; but they may also result from the inner structure of the piece, which is the better way, and indicates a superior poet. For the plot ought to be so constructed that, even without the aid of the eye, he who hears the tale told will thrill with horror and melt to pity at what takes place. This is the impression we should receive from hearing the story of the Œdipus. But to produce this effect by the mere spectacle is a less artistic method, and dependent on extraneous aids. Those who employ spectacular means to create a sense not of the terrible but only of the monstrous, are strangers to the purpose of Tragedy; for we must not demand of Tragedy any and every kind of pleasure, but only that which is proper to it. And since the pleasure which the poet should afford is that which comes from pity and fear through imitation, it is evident that this quality must be impressed upon the incidents.

Let us then determine what are the circumstances which strike us as terrible or pitiful.

Actions capable of this effect must happen between persons who are either friends or enemies or indifferent to one another. If an enemy kills an enemy, there is nothing to excite pity either in the act or the intention,—except so far as the suffering in itself is pitiful. So again with indifferent persons. But when the tragic incident occurs between those who are near or dear to one another—if, for example, a brother kills, or intends to kill, a brother, a son his father, a mother her son, a son his mother, or any other deed of the kind is done—these are the situations to be looked for by the poet. He may not indeed destroy the framework of the received legends—the fact, for instance, that Clytemnestra was slain by Orestes and Eriphyle by Alcmæon—but he ought to show invention of his own, and skilfully handle the traditional material. Let us explain more clearly what is meant by skilful handling.

The action may be done consciously and with knowledge of the persons, in the manner of the older poets. It is thus too that Euripides makes Medea slay her children. Or, again, the deed of horror may be done, but done in ignorance, and the tie of kinship or friendship discovered afterwards. The Œdipus of Sophocles is an example. Here, indeed, the incident is outside the drama proper; but cases occur where it falls within the action of the play: one may cite the Alcmæon of Astydamas, or Telegonus in the Wounded Odysseus. Again, there is a third case,—to be about to act with knowledge of the persons and then not to act. The fourth case is when some one is about to do an irreparable deed through ignorance, and makes the discovery before it is done. These are the only possible ways. For the deed must either be done or not done,—and that wittingly or unwittingly. But of all these ways, to be about to act knowing the persons, and then not to act, is the worst. It is shocking without being tragic, for no disaster follows. It is, therefore, never, or very rarely, found in poetry. One instance, however, is in the Antigone, where Hæmon threatens to kill Creon. The next and better way is that the deed shall be perpetrated. Still better, that it should be perpetrated in ignorance, and the discovery made afterwards. There is then nothing to shock us, while the discovery produces a startling effect. The last case is the best, as when in the Cresphontes Merope is about to slay her son, but recognising who he is, spares his life. So in the Iphigenia, the sister recognises the brother just in time. Again in the Helle, the son recognises the mother when on the point of giving her up. This, then, is why a few families only, as has been already observed, furnish the subjects of tragedy. It was not art, but happy chance, that led the poets in search of subjects to impress the tragic quality upon their plots. They are compelled, therefore, to have recourse to those houses whose history contains moving incidents like these.

Enough has now been said concerning the structure of the incidents, and the right kind of plot.

In respect of character there are four things to be aimed at. First, and most important, it must be good. Now any speech or action that manifests moral purpose of any kind will be expressive of character: the character will be good if the purpose is good. This rule is relative to each class. Even a woman may be good, and also a slave; though the woman may be said to be an inferior being, and the slave quite worthless. The second thing to aim at is propriety. There is a type of manly valour; but valour in a woman, or unscrupulous cleverness, is inappropriate. Thirdly, the character must be true to life: for this is a distinct thing from goodness and propriety, as here described. The fourth point is consistency:

for though the subject of the imitation, who suggested the type, be inconsistent, still he must be consistently inconsistent. As an example of motiveless degradation of character, we have Menelaus in the Orestes: of character indecorous and inappropriate, the lament of Odysseus in the Scylla, and the speech of Melanippe: of inconsistency, the Iphigenia at Aulis,— for Iphigenia the suppliant in no way resembles her later self.

As in the structure of the plot, so too in the portraiture of character, the poet should always aim either at the necessary or the probable. Thus a person of a given character should speak or act in a given way, by the rule either of necessity or of probability; just as this event should follow that by necessary or probable sequence. It is therefore evident that the unravelling of the plot, no less than the complication, must arise out of the plot itself, it must not be brought about by the *Deus ex Machina*—as in the Medea, or in the Return of the Greeks in the Iliad. The *Deus ex Machina* should be employed only for events external to the drama,—for antecedent or subsequent events, which lie beyond the range of human knowledge, and which require to be reported or foretold; for to the gods we ascribe the power of seeing all things. Within the action there must be nothing irrational. If the irrational cannot be excluded, it should be outside the scope of the tragedy. Such is the irrational element in the Œdipus of Sophocles.

Again, since Tragedy is an imitation of persons who are above the common level, the example of good portrait-painters should be followed. They, while reproducing the distinctive form of the original, make a likeness which is true to life and yet more beautiful. So too the poet, in representing men who are irascible or indolent, or have other defects of character, should preserve the type and yet ennoble it. In this way Achilles is portrayed by Agathon and Homer.

These then are rules the poet should observe. Nor should he neglect those appeals to the senses, which, though not among the essentials, are the concomitants of poetry; for here too there is much room for error. But of this enough has been said in our published treatises.

What Recognition is has been already explained. We will now enumerate its kinds.

First, the least artistic form, which, from poverty of wit, is most commonly employed—recognition by signs. Of these some are congenital,—such as "the spear which the earth-born race bear on their bodies," or the stars introduced by Carcinus in his Thyestes. Others are acquired after birth; and of these some are bodily marks, as scars; some external tokens, as necklaces, or the little ark in the Tyro by which the discovery is effected. Even these admit of more or less skilful treatment. Thus in the recognition of Odysseus by his scar, the discovery is made in one way by the nurse, in another by the swineherds. The use of tokens for the express purpose of proof —and, indeed, any formal proof with or without tokens—is a less artistic mode of recognition. A better kind is that which comes about by a turn of incident, as in the Bath Scene in the Odyssey.

Next come the recognitions invented at will by the poet, and on that account wanting in art. For example, Orestes in the Iphigenia reveals the fact that he is Orestes. She, indeed, makes herself known by the letter; but he, by speaking himself, and saying what the poet, not what the plot requires. This, therefore, is nearly allied to the fault above mentioned:—for Orestes might as well have brought tokens with him. Another similar instance is the "voice of the shuttle" in the Tereus of Sophocles.

The third kind depends on memory when the sight of some object awakens a feeling: as in the Cyprians of Dicæogenes, where the hero breaks into tears on see-ing the picture; or again in the "Lay of Alcinous," where Odysseus, hearing the minstrel play the lyre, recalls the past and weeps; and hence the recognition.

The fourth kind is by process of reasoning. Thus in the Choephori:—"Some one resembling me has come: no one resembles me but Orestes: therefore Orestes has come." Such too is the discovery made by Iphigenia in the play of Polyidus the Sophist. It was a natural reflexion for Orestes to make, "So I too must die at the altar like my sister." So, again, in the Tydeus of Theodectes, the father says, "I came to find my son, and I lose my own life." So too in the Phineidæ: the women, on seeing the place, inferred their fate:—"Here we are doomed to die, for here we were cast forth." Again, there is a composite kind of recognition involving false inference on the part of one of the characters, as in the Odysseus Disguised as a Messenger. A said that no one else was able to bend the bow; . . . hence B (the disguised Odysseus) imagined that A would recognise the bow which, in fact, he had not seen; and to bring about a recognition by this means —the expectation that A would recognise the bow—is false inference.

But, of all recognitions, the best is that which arises from the incidents themselves, where the startling discovery is made by natural means. Such is that in the Œdipus of Sophocles, and in the Iphigenia; for it was natural that Iphigenia should wish to despatch a letter. These recognitions alone dispense with the artificial aid of tokens or amulets. Next come the recognitions by process of reasoning.

In constructing the plot and working it out with the proper diction, the poet should place the scene, as far as possible, before his eyes. In this way, seeing everything with the utmost vividness, as if he were a spectator of the action, he will discover what is in keeping with it, and be most unlikely to overlook inconsistencies. The need of such a rule is shown by the fault found in Carcinus. Amphiaraus was on his way from the temple. This fact escaped the observation of one who did not see the situation. On the stage, however, the piece failed, the audience being offended at the oversight.

Again, the poet should work out his play, to the best of his power, with appropriate gestures; for those who feel emotion are most convincing through natural sympathy with the characters they represent; and one who is agitated storms, one who is angry rages, with the most life-like reality. Hence poetry implies either a happy gift of nature or a strain of madness. In the one case a man can take the mould of any character; in the other, he is lifted out of his proper self.

As for the story, whether the poet takes it ready made or constructs it for himself, he should first sketch its general outline, and then fill in the episodes and amplify in detail. A general plan may be illustrated by the Iphigenia. A young girl is sacrificed; she disappears mysteriously from the eyes of those who sacrificed her; she is transported to another country, where the custom is to offer up all strangers to the goddess. To this ministry she is appointed. Some time later her own brother chances to arrive. The fact that the oracle for some reason ordered him to go there, is outside the general plan of the play. The purpose, again, of his coming is outside the action proper. However, he comes, he is seized, and, when on the point of being sacrificed, reveals who he is. The mode of recognition may be either that of Euripides or of Polyidus, in whose play he exclaims very naturally:—"so it was not my sister only, but I too, who was doomed to be sacrificed"; and by that remark he is saved.

After this, the names being once given, it remains to fill in the episodes. We must see that they are relevant to the action. In the case of Orestes, for example, there is the madness which led to his capture, and his deliverance by means of the purificatory rite. In the drama, the episodes are short, but it is these that give extension to Epic poetry. Thus the story of the Odyssey can be stated briefly. A certain man is absent from home many years; he is jealously watched by Poseidon, and left desolate. Meanwhile his home is in a wretched plight—suitors are wasting his substance and plotting against his son. At length, tempest-tost, he himself arrives; he makes certain persons acquainted with him; he attacks the suitors with his own hand, and is himself preserved while he destroys them. This is the essence of the plot; the rest is episode.

Every tragedy falls into two parts,— Complication and Unravelling or Dénouement. Incidents extraneous to the action are frequently combined with a portion of the action proper, to form the Complication; the rest is the Unravelling. By the Complication I mean all that extends from the beginning of the action to the part which marks the turning-point to good or bad fortune. The Unravelling is that which extends from the beginning of the change to the end. Thus, in the Lynceus of Theodectes, the Complication consists of the incidents presupposed in the drama, the seizure of the child, and then again. . . . The Unravelling extends from the accusation of murder to the end.

There are four kinds of Tragedy, the Complex, depending entirely on Reversal of the Situation and Recognition; the Pathetic (where the motive is passion), —such as the tragedies on Ajax and Ixion; the Ethical (where the motives are ethical),—such as the Phthiotides and the Peleus. The fourth kind is the Simple. We here exclude the purely spectacular elements, exemplified by the Phorcides, the Prometheus, and scenes laid in Hades. The poet should endeavour, if possible, to combine all poetic elements; or failing that, the greatest number and those the most important; the more so, in face of the cavilling criticism of the day. For whereas there have hitherto been good poets, each in his own branch, the critics now expect one man to surpass all others in their several lines of excellence.

In speaking of a tragedy as the same or different, the best test to take is the plot. Identity exists where the Complication and Unravelling are the same. Many poets tie the knot well, but unravel it ill. Both arts, however, should always be mastered.

Again, the poet should remember what has been often said, and not make an Epic structure into a Tragedy—by an Epic structure I mean one with a multiplicity of plots—as if, for instance, you were to make a tragedy out of the entire story of the Iliad. In the Epic poem, owing to its length, each part assumes its proper magnitude. In the drama the result is far from answering to the poet's expectation. The proof is that the poets who have dramatised the whole story of the Fall of Troy, instead of selecting portions, like Euripides; or who have taken the whole tale of Niobe, and not a part of her story, like Æschylus, either fail utterly or meet with poor success on the stage. Even Agathon has been known to fail from this one defect. In his Reversals of the Situation, however, he shows a marvellous skill in the effort to hit the popular taste,—to produce a tragic effect that satisfies the moral sense. This effect is produced when the clever rogue, like Sisyphus, is outwitted, or the brave villain defeated. Such an event is probable in Agathon's sense of the word: "it is probable," he says, "that many things should happen contrary to probability."

The Chorus too should be regarded as one of the actors; it should be an integral part of the whole, and share in the action, in the manner not of Euripides, but of Sophocles. As for the later poets, their choral songs pertain as little to the subject of the piece as to that of any other tragedy. They are, therefore, sung as mere interludes,—a practice first begun by Agathon. Yet what difference is there between introducing such choral interludes, and transferring a speech, or even a whole act, from one play to another? . . .

As to that poetic imitation which is narrative in form and employs a single metre, the plot manifestly ought, as in a tragedy, to be constructed on dramatic principles. It should have for its subject a single action, whole and complete, with a beginning, a middle, and an end. It will thus resemble a living organism in all its unity, and produce a pleasure proper to it. It will differ in structure from historical compositions, which of necessity present not a single action, but a single period, and all that happened within that period to one person or to many, little connected together as the events may be. For as the sea-fight at Salamis and the battle with the Carthaginians in Sicily took place at the same time, but did not tend to any one result, so in the sequence of events, one thing sometimes follows another, and yet no single result is thereby produced. Such is the practice, we may say, of most poets. Here again, then, as has been already observed, the transcendent excellence of Homer is manifest. He never attempts to make the whole war of Troy the subject of his poem, though that war had a beginning and an end. It would have been too vast a theme, and not easily embraced in a single view. If, again, he had kept it within moderate limits, it must have been over-complicated by the variety of the incidents. As it is, he detaches a single portion, and admits as episodes many events from the general story of the war —such as the Catalogue of the ships and others—thus diversifying the poem. All other poets take a single hero, a single period, or an action single indeed, but with a multiplicity of parts. Thus did the author of the Cypria and of the Little Iliad. For this reason the Iliad and the Odyssey each furnish the subject of one tragedy, or, at most, of two; while the Cypria supplies materials for many, and the Little Iliad for eight—the Award of the Arms, the Philoctetes, the Neoptolemus, the Eurypylus, the Mendicant Odysseus, the Laconian Women, the Fall of Ilium, the Departure of the Fleet.

Again, Epic poetry must have as many kinds as Tragedy: it must be simple, or complex, or "ethical," or "pathetic." The parts also, with the exception of song and spectacle, are the same; for it requires Reversals of the Situation, Recognition, and Scenes of Suffering. Moreover, the thoughts and the diction must be artistic. In all these respects Homer is our earliest and sufficient model. Indeed each of his poems has a twofold character. The Iliad is at once simple and "pathetic," and the Odyssey complex (for Recognition scenes run though it), and at the same time "ethical." Moreover, in diction and thought they are supreme.

Epic poetry differs from Tragedy in the scale on which it is constructed, and in its metre. As regards scale or length, we have already laid down an adequate limit:—the beginning and the end must be capable of being brought within a single view. This condition will be satisfied by poems on a smaller scale than the old epics, and answering in length to the group of tragedies presented at a single sitting.

Epic poetry has, however, a great—a special—capacity for enlarging its dimensions, and we can see the reason. In Tragedy we cannot imitate several lines of actions carried on at one and the same time; we must confine ourselves to the action on the stage and the part taken by the players. But in Epic poetry, owing to the narrative form, many events simultaneously transacted can be presented; and these, if relevant to the subject, add mass and dignity to the poem. The Epic has here an advantage, and one that conduces to grandeur of effect, to diverting the mind of the hearer, and relieving the story with varying episodes. For sameness of incident soon produces satiety, and makes tragedies fail on the stage.

As for the metre, the heroic measure has proved its fitness by the test of experience. If a narrative poem in any other metre or in many metres were now composed, it would be found incongruous. For of all measures the heroic is the stateliest and the most massive; and, hence it most readily admits rare words and metaphors, which is another point in which the narrative form of imitation stands alone. On the other hand, the iambic and the trochaic tetrameter are stirring measures, the latter being akin to dancing, the former expressive of action. Still more absurd would it be to mix together different metres, as was done by Chæremon. Hence no one has ever composed a poem on a great scale in any other than heroic verse. Nature herself, as we have said, teaches the choice of the proper measure.

Homer, admirable in all respects, has the special merit of being the only poet who rightly appreciates the part he should take himself. The poet should speak as little as possible in his own person, for it is not this that makes him an imitator. Other poets appear themselves upon the scene throughout, and imitate but little and rarely. Homer, after a few prefatory words, at once brings in a man or woman, or other personage; none of them wanting in characteristic qualities, but each with a character of his own.

The element of the wonderful is required in Tragedy. The irrational, on which the wonderful depends for its chief effect, has wider scope in Epic poetry, because there the person acting is not seen. Thus, the pursuit of Hector would be ludicrous if placed upon the stage—the Greeks standing still and not joining in the pursuit, and Achilles waving them back. But in the Epic poem the absurdity passes unnoticed. Now the wonderful is pleasing: as may be inferred from the fact that every one tells a story with some addition of his own, knowing that his hearers like it. It is Homer who has chiefly taught other poets the art of telling lies skilfully. The secret of it lies in a fallacy. For, assuming that if one thing is or becomes, a second is or becomes, men imagine that, if the second is, the first likewise is or becomes. But this is a false inference. Hence, where the first thing is untrue, it is quite unnecessary, provided the second be true, to add that the first is or has become. For the mind, knowing the second to be true, falsely infers the truth of the first. There is an example of this in the Bath Scene of the Odyssey.

Accordingly, the poet should prefer probable impossibilities to improbable possibilities. The tragic plot must not be composed of irrational parts. Everything irrational should, if possible, be excluded; or, at all events, it should lie outside the action of the play (as, in the Œdipus, the hero's ignorance as to the manner of Laius' death); not within the drama,—as, in the Electra, the messenger's account of the Pythian games; or, as in the Mysians, the man who has come from Tegea to Mysia and is still speechless. The plea that otherwise the plot would have been ruined, is ridiculous; such a plot should not in the first instance be constructed. But once the irrational has been introduced and an air of likelihood imparted to it, we must accept it in spite of the absurdity. Take even the irrational incidents in the Odyssey, where Odysseus is left upon the shore of Ithaca. How intolerable even these might have

been would be apparent if an inferior poet were to treat the subject. As it is, the absurdity is veiled by the poetic charm with which the poet invests it.

The diction should be elaborated in the pauses of the action, where there is no expression of character or thought. For, conversely, character and thought are merely obscured by a diction that is over brilliant. . . .

The question may be raised whether the Epic or Tragic mode of imitation is the higher. If the more refined art is the higher, and the more refined in every case is that which appeals to the better sort of audience, the art which imitates anything and everything is manifestly most unrefined. The audience is supposed to be too dull to comprehend unless something of their own is thrown in by the performers, who therefore indulge in restless movements. Bad flute-players twist and twirl, if they have to represent "the quoit-throw," or hustle the coryphæus when they perform the "Scylla." Tragedy, it is said, has this same effect. We may compare the opinion that the older actors entertained of their successors. Mynniscus used to call Callippides "ape" on account of the extravagance of his action, and the same view was held of Pindarus. Tragic art, then, as a whole, stands to Epic in the same relation as the younger to the elder actors. So we are told that Epic poetry is addressed to a cultivated audience, who do not need gesture; Tragedy, to an inferior public. Being then unrefined, it is evidently the lower of the two.

Now, in the first place, this censure attaches not to the poetic but to the histrionic art; for gesticulation may be equally overdone in epic recitation, as by Sosistratus, or in lyrical competition, as by Mnasitheus the Opuntian. Next, all action is not to be condemned—any more than all dancing—but only that of bad performers. Such was the fault found in

Callippides, as also in others of our own day, who are censured for representing degraded women. Again, Tragedy like Epic poetry produces its effect even without action; it reveals its power by mere reading. If, then, in all other respects it is superior, this fault, we say, is not inherent in it.

And superior it is, because it has all the epic elements—it may even use the epic metre—with the music and spectacular effects as important accessories; and these produce the most vivid of pleasures. Further, it has vividness of impression in reading as well as in representation. Moreover, the art attains its end within narrower limits; for the concentrated effect is more pleasurable than one which is spread over a long time and so diluted. What, for example, would be the effect of the Œdipus of Sophocles, if it were cast into a form as long as the Iliad? Once more, the Epic imitation has less unity; as is shown by this, that any Epic poem will furnish subjects for several tragedies. Thus if the story adopted by the poet has a strict unity, it must either be concisely told and appear truncated; or, if it conform to the Epic canon of length, it must seem weak and watery. Such length implies some loss of unity, if, I mean, the poem is constructed out of several actions, like the Iliad and the Odyssey, which have many such parts, each with a certain magnitude of its own. Yet these poems are as perfect as possible in structure; each is, in the highest degree attainable, an imitation of a single action.

If, then, Tragedy is superior to Epic poetry in all these respects, and, moreover, fulfils its specific function better as an art—for each art ought to produce, not any chance pleasure, but the pleasure proper to it, as already stated—it plainly follows that Tragedy is the higher art, as attaining its end more perfectly.

Thus much may suffice concerning Tragic and Epic poetry in general; their several kinds and parts, with the number of each and their differences; the causes that make a poem good or bad; the objections of the critics and the answers to these objections.

—S. H. BUTCHER.

SUMMUM BONUM

ARISTOTLE

[From the *Ethics*, Book I]

Whatever the *summum bonum* may be, Aristotle argues that it must be something attainable in order to be of value to man, not some ideal incapable of realization.

And now, resuming the statement with which we commenced, since all knowledge and moral choice grasps at good of some kind or another, what good is that which we say πολιτική aims at? or, in other words, what is the highest of all the goods which are the objects of action?

So far as name goes, there is a pretty general agreement: for Happiness both the multitude and the refined few call it, and "living well" and "doing well" they conceive to be the same with "being happy;" but about the Nature of this Happiness, men dispute, and the multitude do not in their account of it agree with the wise. For some say it is some one of those things which are palpable and apparent, as pleasure or wealth or honour; in fact, some one thing, some another; nay, oftentimes the same man gives a different account of it; for when ill, he calls it health; when poor, wealth: and conscious of their own ignorance, men admire those who talk grandly and above their comprehension. Some again hold it to be something by itself, other than and beside these many good things, which is in fact to all these the cause of their being good.

Now to sift all the opinions would be perhaps rather a fruitless task; so it shall suffice to sift those which are most generally current, or are thought to have some reason in them.

And here we must not forget the difference between reasoning from principles, and reasoning to principles: for with good cause did Plato too doubt about this, and inquire whether the right road is from principles or to principles, just as in the racecourse from the judges to the further end, or *vice versâ*.

Of course, we must begin with what is known; but then this is of two kinds, what we *do* know, and what we *may* know: perhaps then as individuals we must begin with what we *do* know. Hence the necessity that he should have been well trained in habits, who is to study, with any tolerable chance of profit, the principles of nobleness and justice and moral philosophy generally. For a principle is a matter of fact, and if the fact is sufficiently clear to a man there will be no reason in addition of the reason for the fact. And he that has been thus trained either has principles already, or can receive them easily: as for him who neither has nor can receive them, let him hear his sentence from Hesiod:

"He is best of all who of himself conceiveth all things;
Good again is he too who can adopt a good suggestion;
But whoso neither of himself conceiveth nor hearing from another
Layeth it to heart;—he is a useless man."

But to return from this digression.

Now of the Chief Good (*i.e.* of Happiness) men seem to form their notions from the different modes of life, as we might naturally expect: the many and most low conceive it to be pleasure, and hence they are content with the life of sensual enjoyment. For there are three lines of life which stand out prominently to view: that just mentioned, and the life in society, and, thirdly, the life of contemplation.

Now the many are plainly quite slavish, choosing a life like that of brute animals: yet they obtain some consideration, because many of the great share the tastes of Sardanapalus. The refined and active again conceive it to be honour: yet it is plainly too superficial for the object of our search, because it is thought to rest with those who pay rather than with him who receives it, whereas the Chief Good we feel instinctively must be something which is our own, and not easily to be taken from us.

And besides, men seem to pursue honour, that they may believe themselves to be good: for instance, they seek to be honoured by the wise, and by those among whom they are known, and for virtue: clearly then, in the opinion at least of these men, virtue is higher than honour. In truth, one would be much more inclined to think this to be the end of the life in society; yet this itself is plainly not sufficiently final: for it is conceived possible, that a man possessed of virtue might sleep or be inactive all through his life, or, as a third case, suffer the greatest evils and misfortunes: and the man who should live thus no one would call happy, except for mere disputation's sake.

And for these let this much suffice, for they have been treated of at sufficient length in my Encyclia.

A third line of life is that of contemplation, concerning which we shall make our examination in the sequel.

As for the life of money-making, it is one of constraint, and wealth manifestly is not the good we are seeking, because it is for use, that is, for the sake of something further: and hence one would rather conceive the forementioned ends to be the right ones, for men rest content with them for their own sakes. Yet, clearly, they are not the objects of our search either, though many words have been wasted on them. So much then for these.

Again, the notion of one Universal Good (the same, that is, in all things), it is better perhaps we should examine, and discuss the meaning of it, though such an inquiry is unpleasant, because they are friends of ours who have introduced these εἴδη. Still perhaps it may appear better, nay to be our duty where the safety of truth is concerned, to upset if need be even our own theories, specially as we are lovers of wisdom: for since both are dear to us, we are bound to prefer the truth. Now they who invented this doctrine of εἴδη did not apply it to those things in which they spoke of priority and posteriority, and so they never made any ἰδέα of numbers; but good is predicated in the categories of Substance, Quality, and Relation; now that which exists of itself, *i.e.* Substance, is prior in the nature of things to that which is relative, because this latter is an offshoot, as it were, and result of that which is; on their own principle then there cannot be a common ἰδέα in the case of these.

In the next place, since good is predicated in as many ways as there are modes of existence (for it is predicated in the category of Substance, as God, Intellect —and in that of Quality, as the Virtues— and in that of Quantity, as the Mean— and in that of Relation, as the Useful— and in that of time, as Opportunity—and in that of Place, as Abode; and other such like things), it manifestly cannot be something common and universal and one in all: else it would not have been predicated in all the categories, but in one only.

Thirdly, since those things which range under one ἰδέα are also under the cognisance of one science, there would have been, on their theory, only one science taking cognisance of all goods collectively: but in fact there are many even for those which range under one category: for instance, of Opportunity or Seasonableness (which I have before mentioned as being in the category of Time), the science is, in war, generalship; in disease, medical science, and of the Mean (which I quoted before as being in the category of Quantity), in food, the medical science; and in labour or exercise, the gymnastic science. A person might fairly doubt also what in the world they mean by very-this that or the other, since, as they would themselves allow, the account of the humanity is one and the same in the very-Man, and in any individual Man: for so far as the individual and the very-Man are both Man, they will not differ at all: and if so, then very-good and any particular good will not differ, in so far as both are good. Nor will it do to say, that the eternity of the very-good makes it to be more good; for what has lasted white ever so long, is no whiter than what lasts but for a day.

No. The Pythagoreans do seem to give a more credible account of the matter, who place "One" among the goods in their double list of goods and bads: which philosophers, in fact, Speusippus seems to have followed.

But of these matters let us speak at some other time. Now there is plainly a loophole to object to what has been advanced, on the plea that the theory I have attacked is not by its advocates applied to all goods: but those goods only are spoken of as being under one ἰδέα, which are pursued, and with which men rest content simply for their own sakes: whereas those things which have a tendency to produce or preserve them in any way, or to hinder their contraries, are called good because of these other goods, and after another fashion. It is manifest then that the goods may be so called in two senses, the one class for their own sakes, the other because of these.

Very well then, let us separate the independent goods from the instrumental, and see whether they are spoken of under one ἰδέα. But the question next arises, what kind of goods are we to call independent? All such as are pursued even when separated from other goods, as, for instance, being wise, seeing, and certain pleasures and honours (for these, though we do pursue them with some further end in view, one would still place among the independent goods)? or does it come in fact to this, that we can call nothing independent good except the ἰδέα, and so the concrete of it will be nought?

If, on the other hand, these are independent goods, then we shall require that the account of the goodness be the same clearly in all, just as that of the whiteness is in snow and white lead. But how stands the fact? Why of honour and wisdom and pleasure the accounts are distinct and different in so far as they are good. The Chief Good then is not something common, and after one ἰδέα.

But then, how does the name come to be common (for it is not seemingly a case of fortuitous equivocation)? Are different individual things called good by virtue of being from one source, or all conducing to one end, or rather by way of analogy, for that intellect is to the soul as sight is to the body, and so on? However, perhaps we ought to leave these questions now, for an accurate investigation of them is more properly the business of a different philosophy. And likewise respecting the ἰδέα: for even if there is some one good predicated in common of all things that are good, or separable and capable of existing independently, manifestly it cannot be the object of human action or attainable by Man; but we are in search now of something that is so.

It may readily occur to any one, that it would be better to attain a knowledge of it with a view to such concrete goods as are attainable and practical, because, with this as a kind of model in our hands, we shall the better know what things are

good for us individually, and when we know them, we shall attain them.

Some plausibility, it is true, this argument possesses, but it is contradicted by the facts of the Arts and Sciences; for all these, though aiming at some good, and seeking that which is deficient, yet pretermit the knowledge of it: now it is not exactly probable that all artisans without exception should be ignorant of so great a help as this would be, and not even look after it; neither is it easy to see wherein a weaver or a carpenter will be profited in respect of his craft by knowing the very-good, or how a man will be the more apt to effect cures or to command an army for having seen the ἰδέα itself. For manifestly it is not health after this general and abstract fashion which is the subject of the physician's investigation, but the health of Man, or rather perhaps of this or that man; for he has to heal individuals.— Thus much on these points.

And now let us revert to the Good of which we are in search: what can it be? for manifestly it is different in different actions and arts: for it is different in the healing art and in the art military, and similarly in the rest. What then is the Chief Good in each? Is it not "that for the sake of which the other things are done?" and this in the healing art is health, and in the art military victory, and in that of house-building a house, and in any other thing something else; in short, in every action and moral choice the End, because in all cases men do everything else with a view to this. So that if there is some one End of all things which are and may be done, this must be the Good proposed by doing, or if more than one, then these.

Thus our discussion after some traversing about has come to the same point which we reached before. And this we must try yet more to clear up.

Now since the ends are plainly many, and of these we choose some with a view to others (wealth, for instance, musical instruments, and, in general, all instruments), it is clear that all are not final: but the Chief Good is manifestly something final; and so, if there is some one only which is final, this must be the object of our search: but if several, then the most final of them will be it.

Now that which is an object of pursuit in itself we call more final than that which is so with a view to something else; that again which is never an object of choice with a view to something else, than those which are so both in themselves and with a view to this ulterior object: and so by the term "absolutely final," we denote that which is an object of choice always in itself, and never with a view to any other.

And of this nature Happiness is thought to be, for this we choose always for its own sake, and never with a view to anything further: whereas honour, pleasure, intellect, in fact every excellence we choose for their own sakes, it is true (because we would choose each of these even if no result were to follow), but we choose them also with a view to happiness, conceiving that through their instrumentality we shall be happy: but no man chooses happiness with a view to them, nor in fact with a view to any other thing whatsoever.

The same result is seen to follow also from the notion of self-sufficiency, a quality thought to belong to the final good. Now by sufficient for Self, we mean not for a single individual living a solitary life, but for his parents also and children and wife, and in general, friends and countrymen; for man is by nature adapted to a social existence. But of these, of course, some limit must be fixed: for if one extends it to parents and descendants and friends' friends, there is no end to it. This point, however, must be left for future investigation: for the present we define that to be self-sufficient "which taken alone makes life choice-worthy, and to be in want of nothing;" now of such kind we think Happiness to be: and further, to be most choice-worthy of all things; not being reckoned with any other thing, for if it were so reckoned, it is plain we must then allow it, with the addition of ever so small a good, to be more choice-worthy than it was before: because what is put to it becomes an addition of so much more good, and of goods the greater is ever the more choice-worthy.

So then Happiness is manifestly something final and self-sufficient, being the end of all things which are and may be done.

But, it may be, to call Happiness the Chief Good is a mere truism, and what is wanted is some clearer account of its real nature. Now this object may be easily attained, when we have discovered what is the work of man; for as in the case of flute-player, statuary, or artisan of any kind, or, more generally, all who have any work or course of action, their Chief Good and Excellence is thought to reside in their work, so it would seem to be with man, if there is any work belonging to him.

Are we then to suppose, that while carpenter and cobbler have certain works and courses of action, Man as Man has none, but is left by Nature without a work? or would not one rather hold, that as eye, hand, and foot, and generally each of his members, has manifestly some special work; so too the whole Man, as distinct from all these, has some work of his own?

What can this be? not mere life, because that plainly is shared with him even by vegetables, and we want what is peculiar to him. We must separate off then the life of mere nourishment and growth, and next will come the life of sensation: but this again manifestly is common to horse, oxen, and every animal. There remains then a kind of life of the Rational Nature apt to act: and of this

Nature there are two parts denominated Rational, the one as being obedient to Reason, the other as having and exerting it. Again, as this life is also spoken of in two ways, we must take that which is in the way of actual working, because this is thought to be most properly entitled to the name. If then the work of Man is a working of the soul in accordance with reason, or at least not independently of reason, and we say that the work of any given subject, and of that subject good of its kind, are the same in kind (as, for instance, of a harp-player and a good harp-player, and so on in every case, adding to the work eminence in the way of excellence; I mean, the work of a harp-player is to play the harp, and of a good harp-player to play it well); if, I say, this is so, and we assume the work of Man to be life of a certain kind, that is to say a working of the soul, and actions with reason, and of a good man to do these things well and nobly, and in fact everything is finished off well in the way of the excellence which peculiarly belongs to it: if all this is so, then the Good of Man comes to be "a working of the soul in the way of Excellence, or, if Excellence admits of degrees, in the way of the best and most perfect Excellence."

And we must add, in a complete life; for as it is not one swallow or one fine day that makes a spring, so it is not one day or a short time that makes a man blessed and happy.

Let this then be taken for a rough sketch of the Chief Good: since it is probably the right way to give first the outline, and fill it in afterwards. And it would seem that any man may improve and connect what is good in the sketch, and that time is a good discoverer and co-operator in such matters: it is thus in fact that all improvements in the various arts have been brought about, for any man may fill up a deficiency.

You must remember also what has been already stated, and not seek for exactness in all matters alike, but in each according to the subject-matter, and so far as properly belongs to the system. The carpenter and geometrician, for instance, inquire into the right line in different fashion: the former so far as he wants it for his work, the latter inquires into its nature and properties, because he is concerned with the truth.

So then should one do in other matters, but the incidental matters may not exceed the direct ones.

And again, you must not demand the reason either in all things alike, because in some it is sufficient that the fact has been well demonstrated, which is the case with first principles; and the fact is the first step, *i.e.* the starting-point or principle.

And of these first principles some are obtained by induction, some by perception, some by a course of habituation, others in other different ways. And we must try to trace up each in their own nature, and take pains to secure their being well defined, because they have great influence on what follows: it is thought, I mean, that the starting-point or principle is more than half the whole matter, and that many of the points of inquiry come simultaneously into view thereby.

We must now inquire concerning Happiness, not only from our conclusion and the data on which our reasoning proceeds, but likewise from what is commonly said about it: because with what is true all things which really are are in harmony, but with that which is false the true very soon jars.

Now there is a common division of goods into three classes; one being called external, the other two those of the soul and body respectively, and those belonging to the soul we call most properly and specially good. Well, in our definition we assume that the actions and workings of the soul constitute Happiness, and these belong of course to the soul. And so our account is a good one, at least according to this opinion, which is of ancient date, and accepted by those who profess philosophy. Rightly too are certain actions and workings said to be the end, for thus it is brought into the number of the goods of the soul instead of the external. Agreeing also with our definition is the common notion, that the happy man lives well and does well, for it has been stated by us to be pretty much a kind of living well and doing well.

But further, the points required in Happiness are found in combination in our account of it.

For some think it is virtue, others practical wisdom, others a kind of scientific philosophy; others that it is these, or else some one of them, in combination with pleasure, or at least not independently of it; while others again take in external prosperity.

Of these opinions, some rest on the authority of numbers or antiquity, others on that of few, and those men of note: and it is not likely that either of these classes should be wrong in all points, but be right at least in some one, or even in most.

Now with those who assert it to be Virtue (Excellence), or some kind of Virtue, our account agrees: for working in the way of Excellence surely belongs to Excellence.

And there is perhaps no unimportant difference between conceiving of the Chief Good as in possession or as in use, in other words, as a mere state or as a working. For the state or habit may possibly exist in a subject without effecting any good, as, for instance, in him who is asleep, or in any other way inactive; but the working cannot so, for it will of necessity act, and act well. And as at the Olympic games it is not the finest and strongest men who are crowned, but they who enter the lists, for out of these the prize-men are selected; so too in life, of the honourable and the good, it is they who act who rightly win the prizes.

Their life too is in itself pleasant: for the feeling of pleasure is a mental sensation, and that is to each pleasant of which he is said to be fond: a horse, for instance, to him who is fond of horses, and a sight to him who is fond of sights: and so in like manner just acts to him who is fond of justice, and more generally the things in accordance with virtue to him who is fond of virtue. Now in the case of the multitude of men the things which they individually esteem pleasant clash, because they are not such by nature, whereas to the lovers of nobleness those things which are pleasant are such by nature: but the actions in accordance with virtue are of this kind, so that they are pleasant both to the individuals and also in themselves.

So then their life has no need of pleasure as a kind of additional appendage, but involves pleasure in itself. For, besides what I have just mentioned, a man is not a good man at all who feels no pleasure in noble actions, just as no one would call that man just who does not feel pleasure in acting justly, or liberal who does not in liberal actions, and similarly in the case of the other virtues which might be enumerated: and if this be so, then the actions in accordance with virtue must be in themselves pleasurable. Then again they are certainly good and noble, and each of these in the highest degree; if we are to take as right the judgment of the good man, for he judges as we have said.

Thus then Happiness is most excellent, most noble, and most pleasant, and these attributes are not separated as in the well-known Delian inscription—

"Most noble is that which is most just, but
    best is health;
And naturally most pleasant is the obtaining one's desires."

For all these co-exist in the best acts of working: and we say that Happiness is these, or one, that is, the best of them.

Still it is quite plain that it does require the addition of external goods, as we have said: because without appliances it is impossible, or at all events not easy, to do noble actions: for friends, money, and political influence are in a manner instruments whereby many things are done: some things there are again a deficiency in which mars blessedness; good birth, for instance, or fine offspring, or even personal beauty: for he is not at all capable of Happiness who is very ugly, or is ill-born, or solitary and childless; and still less perhaps supposing him to have very bad children or friends, or to have lost good ones by death. As we have said already, the addition of prosperity of this kind does seem necessary to complete the idea of Happiness; hence some rank good fortune, and others virtue, with Happiness.

And hence too a question is raised, whether it is a thing that can be learned, or acquired by habituation or discipline of some other kind, or whether it comes in the way of divine dispensation, or even in the way of chance.

Now to be sure, if anything else is a gift of the Gods to men, it is probable that Happiness is a gift of theirs too, and specially because of all human goods it is the highest. But this, it may be, is a question belonging more properly to an investigation different from ours: and it is quite clear, that on the supposition of its not being sent from the Gods direct, but coming to us by reason of virtue and learning of a certain kind, or discipline, it is yet one of the most Godlike things; because the prize and End of virtue is manifestly somewhat most excellent, nay divine and blessed.

It will also on this supposition be widely participated, for it may through learning and diligence of a certain kind exist in all who have not been maimed of virtue.

And if it is better we should be happy thus than as a result of chance, this is in itself an argument that the case is so; because those things which are in the way of nature, and in like manner of art, and of every cause, and specially the best cause, are by nature in the best way possible: to leave then to chance what is greatest and most noble would be very much out of harmony with all these facts.

The question may be determined also by a reference to our definition of Happiness, that it is a working of the soul in the way of excellence or virtue of a certain kind: and of the other goods, some we must have to begin with, and those which are co-operative and useful are given by nature as instruments.

These considerations will harmonise also with what we said at the commencement: for we assumed the End of πολιτική to be most excellent: now this bestows most care on making the members of a community of a certain character; good that is and apt to do what is honourable.

With good reason then neither ox nor horse nor any other brute animal do we call happy, for none of them can partake in such working: and for this same reason a child is not happy either, because by reason of his tender age he cannot yet perform such actions: if the term is applied it is by way of anticipation.

For to constitute Happiness, there must be, as we have said, complete virtue and a complete life: for many changes and chances of all kinds arise during a life, and he who is most prosperous may become involved in great misfortunes in his old age, as in the heroic poems the tale is told of Priam: but the man who has experienced such fortune and died in wretchedness, no man calls happy.

Are we then to call no man happy while he lives, and, as Solon would have us, look to the end? And again, if we are to maintain this position, is a man then happy when he is dead? or is not this a complete absurdity, specially in us who say Happiness is a working of a certain kind?

If on the other hand we do not assert that the dead man is happy, and Solon does not mean this, but only that one would then be safe in pronouncing a man happy, as being thenceforward out of the reach of evils and misfortunes, this too admits of some dispute, since it is thought that the dead has somewhat both of good and evil (if, as we must allow, a man may have when alive but not aware of the circumstances), as honour and dishonour, and good and bad fortune of children and descendants generally.

Nor is this view again without its difficulties: for, after a man has lived in blessedness to old age and died accordingly, many changes may befall him in right of his descendants; some of them may be good and obtain positions in life accordant to their merits, others again quite the contrary: it is plain too that the descendants may at different intervals or grades stand in all manner of relations to the ancestors. Absurd indeed would be the position that even the dead man is to change about with them and become at one time happy and at another miserable. Absurd however it is on the other hand that the affairs of the descendants should in no degree and during no time affect the ancestors.

But we must revert to the point first raised, since the present question will be easily determined from that.

If then we are to look to the end and then pronounce the man blessed, not as being so but as having been so at some previous time, surely it is absurd that when he *is* happy the truth is not to be asserted of him, because we are unwilling to pronounce the living happy by reason of their liability to changes, and because, whereas we have conceived of happiness as something stable and no way easily changeable, the fact is that good and bad fortune are constantly circling about the same people: for it is quite plain, that if we are to depend upon the fortunes of men, we shall often have to call the same man happy, and a little while after miserable, thus representing our happy man

"Chameleon-like, and based on rottenness."

Is not this the solution? that to make our sentence dependent on the changes of fortune, is no way right: for not in them stands the well, or the ill, but though human life needs these as accessories (which we have allowed already), the workings in the way of virtue are what determine Happiness, and the contrary the contrary.

And, by the way, the question which has been here discussed, testifies incidentally to the truth of our account of Happiness. For to nothing does a stability of human results attach so much as it does to the workings in the way of virtue, since these are held to be more abiding even than the sciences: and of these last again the most precious are the most abiding, because the blessed live in them most and most continuously, which seems to be the reason why they are not forgotten. So then this stability which is sought will be in the happy man, and he will be such through life, since always, or most of all, he will be doing and contemplating the things which are in the way of virtue: and the various chances of life he will bear most nobly, and at all times and in all ways harmoniously, since he is the truly good man, or in the terms of our proverb "a faultless cube."

And whereas the incidents of chance are many, and differ in greatness and smallness, the small pieces of good or ill fortune evidently do not affect the balance of life, but the great and numerous, if happening for good, will make life more blessed (for it is their nature to contribute to ornament, and the using of them comes to be noble and excellent), but if for ill, they bruise as it were and maim the blessedness: for they bring in positive pain, and hinder many acts of working. But still, even in these, nobleness shines through when a man bears contentedly many and great mischances not from insensibility to pain but because he is noble and high-spirited.

And if, as we have said, the acts of working are what determine the character of life, no one of the blessed can ever become wretched, because he will never do those things which are hateful and mean. For the man who is truly good and sensible bears all fortunes, we presume, becomingly, and always does what is noblest under the circumstances, just as a good general employs to the best advantage the force he has with him; or a good shoemaker makes the handsomest shoe he can out of the leather which has been given him; and all other good artisans likewise. And if this be so, wretched never can the happy man come to be: I do not mean to say he will be blessed should he fall into fortunes like those of Priam.

Nor, in truth, is he shifting and easily changeable, for on the one hand from his happiness he will not be shaken easily nor by ordinary mischances, but if at all, by those which are great and numerous; and, on the other, after such mischances he cannot regain his happiness in a little time; but, if at all, in a long and complete period, during which he has made himself master of great and noble things. Why then should we not call happy the man who works in the way of perfect virtue, and is furnished with external goods sufficient for acting his part in the drama of life: and this during no ordinary period but such as constitutes a complete life as we have been describing it.

Or we must add, that not only is he to live so, but his death must be in keeping with such life, since the future is dark to us, and Happiness we assume to be in every way an end and complete. And, if this be so, we shall call them among the living blessed who have and will have the things specified, but blessed *as Men*.

On these points then let it suffice to have defined thus much.

—D. P. CHASE.

THE DOCTRINE OF THE MEAN

ARISTOTLE

[From the *Ethics,* Book II]

Happiness is virtue, and virtue is a mean between extremes. There are three phases of every moral act—excess, defect, and the mean between excess and defect. It is impossible that virtue be either excess or defect, too much or too little. The golden mean is not, however, the absolute middle between the extremes, but varies in relation to persons and circumstances.

Now what the genus of Virtue is has been said; but we must not merely speak of it thus, that it is a state, but say also what kind of a state it is.

We must observe then that all excellence makes that whereof it is the excellence both to be itself in a good state and to perform its work well. The excellence of the eye, for instance, makes both the eye good and its work also: for by the excellence of the eye we see well. So too the excellence of the horse makes the horse good, and good in speed, and in carrying his rider, and standing up against the enemy. If then this is universally the case, the excellence of Man, *i.e.* Virtue, must be a state whereby Man comes to be good and whereby he will perform well his proper work. Now how this shall be it is true we have said already, but still perhaps it may throw light on the subject to see what is its characteristic nature.

In all quantity then, whether continuous or discrete, one may take the greater part, the less, or the exactly equal, and these either with reference to the thing itself, or relatively to us: and the exactly equal is a mean between excess and defect. Now by the mean of the thing, *i.e.* absolute mean, I denote that which is equidistant from either extreme (which of course is one and the same to all), and by the mean relatively to ourselves, that which is neither too much nor too little for the particular individual. This of course is not one nor the same to all: for instance, suppose ten is too much and two too little, people take six for the absolute mean; because it exceeds the smaller sum by exactly as much as it is itself exceeded by the larger, and this mean is according to arithmetical proportion.

But the mean relatively to ourselves must not be so found; for it does not follow, supposing ten minæ is too large a quantity to eat and two too small, that the trainer will order his man six; because for the person who is to take it this also may be too much or too little: for Milo it would be too little, but for a man just commencing his athletic exercises too much: similarly too of the exercises themselves, as running or wrestling.

So then it seems every one possessed of skill avoids excess and defect, but seeks for and chooses the mean, not the absolute but the relative.

Now if all skill thus accomplishes well its work by keeping its eye on the mean, and bringing the works to this point (whence it is common enough to say of such works as are in a good state, "one cannot add to or take ought from them," under the notion of excess or defect destroying goodness but the mean state

preserving it), and good artisans, as we say, work with their eye on this, and excellence, like nature, is more exact and better than any art in the world, it must have an aptitude to aim at the mean.

It is moral excellence, *i.e.* Virtue, of course which I mean, because this it is which is concerned with feelings and actions, and in these there can be excess and defect and the mean: it is possible, for instance, to feel the emotions of fear, confidence, lust, anger, compassion, and pleasure and pain generally, too much or too little, and in either case wrongly; but to feel them when we ought, on what occasions, towards whom, why, and as, we should do, is the mean, or in other words the best state, and this is the property of Virtue.

In like manner too with respect to the actions, there may be excess and defect and the mean. Now Virtue is concerned with feelings and actions, in which excess is wrong and the defect is blamed but the mean is praised and goes right; and both these circumstances belong to Virtue. Virtue then is in a sense a mean state, since it certainly has an aptitude for aiming at the mean.

Again, one may go wrong in many different ways (because, as the Pythagoreans expressed it, evil is of the class of the infinite, good of the finite), but right only in one; and so the former is easy, the latter difficult; easy to miss the mark, but hard to hit it: and for these reasons, therefore, both the excess and defect belong to Vice, and the mean state to Virtue; for, as the poet has it,

"Men may be bad in many ways,
    But good in one alone."

Virtue then is "a state apt to exercise deliberate choice, being in the relative mean, determined by reason, and as the man of practical wisdom would determine."

It is a middle state between two faulty

ones, in the way of excess on one side and of defect on the other: and it is so moreover, because the faulty states on one side fall short of, and those on the other exceed, what is right, both in the case of the feelings and the actions; but Virtue finds, and when found adopts, the mean.

And so, viewing it in respect of its essence and definition, Virtue is a mean state; but in reference to the chief good and excellence it is the highest state possible.

But it must not be supposed that every action or every feeling is capable of sub-sisting in this mean state, because some there are which are so named as imme-diately to convey the notion of badness, as malevolence, shamelessness, envy; or, to instance in actions, adultery, theft, homicide; for all these and such like are blamed because they are in them-selves bad, not the having too much or too little of them.

In these then you never can go right, but must always be wrong: nor in such does the right or wrong depend on the selection of a proper person, time, or manner (take adultery for instance), but simply doing any one soever of those things is being wrong.

You might as well require that there should be determined a mean state, and excess and defect in respect of acting unjustly, being cowardly, or giving up all control of the passions: for at this rate there will be of excess and defect a mean state; of excess, excess; and of defect, defect.

But just as of perfected self-mastery and courage there is no excess and de-fect, because the mean is in one point of view the highest possible state, so neither of those faulty states can you have a mean state, excess, or defect, but howso-ever done they are wrong: you cannot, in short, have of excess and defect a mean state, nor of a mean state excess and defect.

It is not enough, however, to state this in general terms, we must also apply it to particular instances, because in treat-ises on moral conduct general statements have an air of vagueness, but those which go into detail one of greater reality: for the actions after all must be in detail, and the general statements, to be worth anything, must hold good here.

We must take these details then from the Table.

I. In respect of fears or confidence or boldness:

The Mean state is courage: men may exceed, of course, either in absence of fear or in positive confidence: the former has no name (which is a common case), the latter is called rash: again, the man who has too much fear and too little confidence is called a coward.

II. In respect of pleasures and pains (but not all, and perhaps fewer pains than pleasures):

The Mean state here is perfected Self-Mastery, the defect total absence of Self-control. As for defect in respect of pleasure, there are really no people who are chargeable with it, so, of course, there is really no name for such charac-ters, but, as they are conceivable, we will give them one and call them insensible.

III. In respect of giving and taking wealth (a):

The Mean state is Liberality, the ex-cess Prodigality, the defect Stinginess: here each of the extremes involves really an excess and defect contrary to each other: I mean the prodigal gives out too much and takes in too little, while the stingy man takes in too much and gives out too little. (It must be understood that we are now giving merely an outline and summary, intentionally: and we will, in a later part of the treatise, draw out the distinctions with greater exactness.)

IV. In respect of wealth (b):

There are other dispositions besides these just mentioned; a mean state called Munificence (for the munificent man differs from the liberal, the former having necessarily to do with great wealth, the latter with but small); the excess called by the names either of Want of taste or Vulgar Profusion, and the defect Paltriness (these also differ from the extremes connected with liberality, and the manner of their difference shall also be spoken of later).

V. In respect of honour and dishonour (*a*):

The Mean state Greatness of Soul, the excess which may be called Braggadocia, and the defect Littleness of Soul.

VI. In respect of honour and dishonour (*b*):

Now there is a state bearing the same relation to Greatness of Soul as we said just now Liberality does to Munificence, with the difference that is of being about a small amount of the same thing: this state having reference to small honour, as Greatness of Soul to great honour; a man may, of course, grasp at honour either more than he should or less; now he that exceeds in his grasping at it is called ambitious, he that falls short unambitious, he that is just as he should be has no proper name: nor in fact have the states, except that the disposition of the ambitious man is called ambition. For this reason those who are in either extreme lay claim to the mean as a debateable land, and we call the virtuous character sometimes by the name ambitious, sometimes by that of unambitious, and we commend sometimes the one and sometimes the other. Why we do it shall be said in the subsequent part of the treatise; but now we will go on with the rest of the virtues after the plan we have laid down.

VII. In respect of anger.

Here too there is excess, defect, and a mean state; but since they may be said to have really no proper names, as we call the virtuous character Meek, we will call the mean state Meekness, and of the extremes, let the man who is ex-

cessive be denominated Passionate, and the faulty state Passionateness, and him who is deficient Angerless, and the defect Angerlessness.

There are also three other mean states, having some mutual resemblance, but still with differences; they are alike in that they all have for their object-matter intercourse of words and deeds, and they differ in that one has respect to truth herein, the other two to what is pleasant; and this in two ways, the one in relaxation and amusement, the other in all things which occur in daily life. We must say a word or two about these also, that we may the better see that in all matters the mean is praiseworthy, while the extremes are neither right nor worthy of praise but of blame.

Now of these, it is true, the majority have really no proper names, but still we must try, as in the other cases, to coin some for them for the sake of clearness and intelligibleness.

I. In respect of truth:

The man who is in the mean state we will call Truthful, and his state Truthfulness, and as to the disguise of truth, if it be on the side of exaggeration, Braggadocia, and him that has it a Braggadocio; if on that of diminution, Reserve and Reserved shall be the terms.

II. In respect of what is pleasant in the way of relaxation or amusement:

The mean state shall be called Easy-pleasantry, and the character accordingly a man of Easy-pleasantry; the excess Buffoonery, and the man a Buffoon; the man deficient herein a Clown, and his state Clownishness.

III. In respect of what is pleasant in daily life:

He that is as he should be may be called Friendly, and his mean state Friendliness: he that exceeds, if it be without any interested motive, somewhat too Complaisant, if with such motive, a Flatterer: he that is deficient and in all instances unpleasant, Quarrelsome and Cross.

There are mean states likewise in feelings and matters concerning them. Shamefacedness, for instance, is no virtue, still a man is praised for being shamefaced: for in these too the one is denominated the man in the mean state, the other in the excess; the Dumbfoundered, for instance, who is overwhelmed with shame on all and any occasions: the man who is in the defect, *i.e.* who has no shame at all in his composition, is called Shameless: but the right character Shamefaced.

Indignation against successful vice, again, is a state in the mean between Envy and Malevolence: they all three have respect to pleasure and pain produced by what happens to one's neighbour: for the man who has this right feeling is annoyed at undeserved success of others, while the envious man goes beyond him and is annoyed at all success of others, and the malevolent falls so far short of feeling annoyance that he even rejoices (at misfortune of others).

But for the discussion of these also there will be another opportunity, as of Justice too, because the term is used in more senses than one. So after this we will go accurately into each and say how they are mean states: and in like manner also with respect to the Intellectual Excellences.

Now as there are three states in each case, two faulty either in the way of excess or defect, and one right, which is the mean state, of course all are in a way opposed to one another; the extremes, for instance, not only to the mean but also to one another, and the mean to the extremes: just as the half is greater if compared with the less portion, and less if compared with the greater, so the mean states, compared with the defects, exceed, whether in feelings or actions, and *vice versâ*. The brave man, for instance, shows as rash when compared with the coward, and cowardly when compared with the rash; similarly too the man of perfected self-mastery, viewed in comparison with the man destitute of all perception, shows like a man of no self-control, but in comparison with the man who really has no self-control, he looks like one destitute of all perception: and the liberal man compared with the stingy seems prodigal, and by the side of the prodigal, stingy.

And so the extreme characters push away, so to speak, towards each other the man in the mean state; the brave man is called a rash man by the coward, and a coward by the rash man, and in the other cases accordingly. And there being this mutual opposition, the contrariety between the extremes is greater than between either and the mean, because they are further from one another than from the mean, just as the greater or less portion differ more from each other than either from the exact half.

Again, in some cases an extreme will bear a resemblance to the mean; rashness, for instance, to courage, and prodigality to liberality; but between the extremes there is the greatest dissimilarity. Now things which are furthest from one another are defined to be contrary, and so the further off the more contrary they will be.

Further: of the extremes in some cases the excess, and in others the defect, is most opposed to the mean: to courage, for instance, not rashness which is the excess, but cowardice which is the defect; whereas to perfected self-mastery not insensibility which is the defect but absence of all self-control which is the excess.

And for this there are two reasons to be given; one from the nature of the thing itself, because from the one extreme being nearer and more like the mean, we do not put this against it, but the other; as, for instance, since rashness is thought to be nearer to courage than cowardice is, and to resemble it more, we put cowardice against courage rather than rashness, because those things which are further from the mean are thought to be more contrary to it. This then is one reason arising from the thing itself; there is another arising from our own constitution and make: for in each man's own case those things give the impression of being more contrary to the mean to which we individually have a natural bias. Thus we have a natural bias towards pleasures, for which reason we are much more inclined to the rejection of all self-control, than to self-discipline.

These things then to which the bias is, we call more contrary, and so total want of self-control (the excess) is more contrary than the defect is to perfected self-mastery.

Now that Moral Virtue is a mean state, and how it is so, and that it lies between two faulty states, one in the way of excess and another in the way of defect, and that it is so because it has an aptitude to aim at the mean both in feelings and actions, all this has been set forth fully and sufficiently.

And so it is hard to be good: for surely hard it is in each instance to find the mean, just as to find the mean point or centre of a circle is not what any man can do, but only he who knows how: just so to be angry, to give money, and be expensive, is what any man can do, and easy: but to do these to the right person, in due proportion, at the right time, with a right object, and in the right manner, this is not as before what any man can do, nor is it easy; and for this cause goodness is rare, and praiseworthy, and noble.

Therefore he who aims at the mean should make it his first care to keep away from that extreme which is more contrary than the other to the mean; just as Calypso in Homer advises Ulysses,

"Clear of this smoke and surge thy barque
    direct;"

because of the two extremes the one is always more, and the other less, erroneous; and, therefore, since to hit exactly on the mean is difficult, one must take the least of the evils as the safest plan; and this a man will be doing, if he follows this method.

We ought also to take into consideration our own natural bias; which varies in each man's case, and will be ascertained from the pleasure and pain arising in us. Furthermore, we should force ourselves off in the contrary direction, because we shall find ourselves in the mean after we have removed ourselves from the wrong side, exactly as men do in straightening bent timber.

But in all cases we must guard most carefully against what is pleasant, and pleasure itself, because we are not impartial judges of it.

We ought to feel in fact towards pleasure as did the old counsellors towards Helen, and in all cases pronounce a similar sentence; for so by sending it away from us, we shall err the less.

Well, to speak very briefly, these are the precautions by adopting which we shall be best able to attain the mean.

Still, perhaps, after all it is a matter of difficulty, and specially in the particular instances: it is not easy, for instance, to determine exactly in what manner, with what persons, for what causes, and for what length of time, one ought to feel anger: for we ourselves sometimes praise those who are defective in this feeling, and we call them meek; at another, we term the hot-tempered manly and spirited.

Then, again, he who makes a small deflection from what is right, be it on the side of too much or too little, is not blamed, only he who makes a considerable one; for he cannot escape observation. But to what point or degree a man must err in order to incur blame, it is not easy to determine exactly in words: nor in fact any of those points which are matters of perception by the Moral Sense: such questions are matters of detail, and the decision of them rests with the Moral Sense.

At all events thus much is plain, that the mean state is in all things praiseworthy, and that practically we must deflect sometimes towards excess sometimes towards defect, because this will be the easiest method of hitting on the mean, that is, on what is right.

—D. P. CHASE.

THE NATURE OF DEMOCRACY [1]

ARISTOTLE

[From the *Politics,* Book VI]

The government of Athens in the time of Plato and Aristotle was the nearest approach to a pure democracy which has been recorded in history. But it had fallen on evil days, in which its weaknesses were emphasized and its merits obscured. The philosophers, examining it as they found it, condemned it as an unworkable form, and set about formulating principles for reconstructing the state. Aristotle's method included an examination of the several forms of government known to him, for the purpose of discovering the underlying principles of each. Such modifications of democracy as representative government were unknown to him, although the plan he suggested bears a slight resemblance to such a scheme.

First of all let us speak of democracy, which will also bring to light the opposite form of government commonly called oligarchy. For the purposes of this enquiry we need to ascertain all the elements and characteristics of democracy, since from the combinations of these the

varieties of democratic government arise. There are several of these differing from each other, and the difference is due to two causes. One has been already mentioned,—differences of population; for the popular element may consist of husbandmen, or of mechanics, or of labourers, and if the first of these be added to the second, or the third to the two others, not only does the democracy become better or worse, but its very nature is changed. A second cause remains to be mentioned: the various properties and characteristics of democracy, when variously combined make a difference. For one democracy will have less and another will have more, and another will have all of these characteristics. There is an advantage in knowing them all, whether a man wishes to establish some new form of democracy, or only to remodel an existing one. Founders of states try to bring together all the elements which accord with the ideas of the several constitutions; but this is a mistake of theirs, as I have already remarked when speaking of the destruction and preservation of states. We will now set forth the principles, characteristics, and aims of such states.

The basis of a democratic state is liberty; which, according to the common opinion of men, can only be enjoyed in such a state;—this they affirm to be the great end of every democracy. One principle of liberty is for all to rule and be ruled in turn, and indeed democratic justice is the application of numerical not proportionate equality; whence it follows that the majority must be supreme, and that whatever the majority approve must be the end and the just. Every citizen, it is said, must have equality, and therefore in a democracy the poor have more power than the rich, because there are more of them, and the will of the majority is supreme. This, then, is one note of liberty which all democrats affirm to be the principle of

[1] Reprinted by arrangement with the Oxford University Press, publishers.

their state. Another is that a man should live as he likes. This, they say, is the privilege of a free man, and, on the other hand, not to live as a man likes is the mark of a slave. This is the second characteristic of democracy, whence has arisen the claim of men to be ruled by none, if possible, or, if this is impossible, to rule and be ruled in turns; and so it coincides with the freedom based upon equality.

Such being our foundation and such the nature of democracy, its characteristics are as follows:—the election of officers by all out of all; and that all should rule over each, and each in his turn over all; that the appointment to all offices, or to all but those which require experience and skill, should be made by lot; that no property qualification should be required for offices, or only a very low one; that no one should hold the same office twice, or not often, except in the case of military offices; that the tenure of all offices, or of as many as possible, should be brief; that all men should sit in judgment, or that judges selected out of all should judge in all matters, or in most, or in the greatest and most important,—such as the scrutiny of accounts, the constitution and private contracts; that the assembly should be supreme over all causes, or at any rate over the most important, and the magistrates over none or only over a very few. Of all institutions, a council is the most democratic when there is not the means of paying all the citizens, but when they are paid even this is robbed of its power; for the people then draw all cases to themselves, as I said in the previous discussion. The next characteristic of democracy is payment for services; assembly law-courts, magistrates, everybody receives pay, when it is to be had; or when it is not to be had for all, then it is given to the law-courts and to the stated assemblies, to the council and to the magistrates, or at least to any of them who are compelled to have their meals together. And whereas

oligarchy is characterised by birth, wealth, and education, the notes of democracy appear to be the opposite of these, —low birth, poverty, mean employment. Another note is that no magistracy is perpetual, but if any such have survived some ancient change in the constitution it should be stripped of its power, and the holders should be elected by lot and no longer by vote. These are points common to all democracies; but democracy and demos in their truest form are based upon the recognized principle of democratic justice, that all should count equally; for equality implies that the rich should have no more share in the government than the poor, and should not be the only rulers, but that all should rule equally according to their numbers. And in this way men think that they will secure equality and freedom in their state.

Next comes the question, how is this equality to be obtained? Is the qualification to be so distributed that five hundred rich shall be equal to a thousand poor? and shall we give the thousand a power equal to that of the five hundred? or, if this is not to be the mode, ought we, still retaining the same ratio, to take equal numbers from each and give them the control of the elections and of the courts?—Which, according to the democratical notion, is the juster form of the constitution,—this or one based on numbers only? Democrats say that justice is that to which the majority agree, oligarchs that to which the wealthier class; in their opinion the decision should be given according to the amount of property. In both principles there is some inequality and injustice. For if justice is the will of the few, any one person who has more wealth than all the rest of his class put together, ought, upon the oligarchical principle, to have the sole power—but this would be tyranny; or if justice is the will of the majority, as I was before saying, they will unjustly confiscate the property of the wealthy minority. To find a principle of equality in which they both agree we must enquire into their respective ideas of justice.

Now they agree in saying that whatever is decided by the majority of the citizens is to be deemed law. Granted: —but not without some reserve; since there are two classes out of which a state is composed,—the poor and the rich,— that is to be deemed law, on which both or the greater part of both agree; and if they disagree, that which is approved by the greater number, and by those who have the higher qualification. For example, suppose that there are ten rich and twenty poor, and some measure is approved by six of the rich and disapproved by fifteen of the poor, and the remaining four of the rich join with the party of the poor, and the remaining five of the poor with that of the rich; in such a case the will of those whose qualifications, when both sides are added up, are the greatest, should prevail. If they turn out to be equal, there is no greater difficulty than at present, when, if the assembly or the courts are divided, recourse is had to the lot, or to some similar expedient. But, although it may be difficult in theory to know what is just and equal, the practical difficulty of inducing those to forbear who can, if they like, encroach, is far greater, for the weaker are always asking for equality and justice, but the stronger care for none of these things.

Of the four kinds of democracy, as was said in the previous discussion, the best is that which comes first in order; it is also the oldest of them all. I am speaking of them according to the natural classification of their inhabitants. For the best material of democracy is an agricultural population; there is no difficulty in forming a democracy where the mass of the people live by agriculture or tending of cattle. Being poor, they have no leisure, and therefore do not often attend the assembly, and not having the necessaries of life they are always at work, and do not covet the property of others. Indeed, they find their employment pleasanter than the cares of government or office where no great gains can be made out of them, for the many are more desirous of gain than of honour. A proof is that even the ancient tyrannies were patiently endured by them, as they still endure oligarchies, if they are allowed to work and are not deprived of their property; for some of them grow quickly rich and the others are well enough off. Moreover they have the power of electing the magistrates and calling them to account; their ambition, if they have any, is thus satisfied; and in some democracies, although they do not all share in the appointment of officers, except through representatives elected in turn out of the whole people, as at Mantinea;—yet, if they have the power of deliberating, the many are contented. Even this form of government may be regarded as a democracy, and was such at Mantinea. Hence it is both expedient and customary in such a democracy that all should elect to offices, and conduct scrutinies, and sit in the law-courts, but that the great offices should be filled up by election and from persons having a qualification; the greater requiring a greater qualification, or, if there be no offices for which a qualification is required, then those who are marked out by special ability should be appointed. Under such a form of government the citizens are sure to be governed well, (for the offices will always be held by the best persons; the people are willing enough to elect them and are not jealous of the good). The good and the notables will then be satisfied, for they will not be governed by men who are their inferiors, and the persons elected will rule justly, because others will call them to account. Every man should be responsible to others, nor should any one be allowed to do just as he pleases; for where absolute freedom is allowed there is nothing to restrain the evil which is inherent in every man. But the principle of responsibility secures that which is the greatest good in states; the right persons rule and are prevented from doing wrong, and the people have their due. It is evident that this is the best kind of democracy, and why? because the people are drawn from a certain class. The ancient laws of many states which aimed at making the people husbandmen are excellent. They provided either that no one should possess more than a certain quantity of land, or that, if he did, the land should not be within a certain distance from the town or the acropolis. Formerly in many states there was law forbidding any one to sell his original allotment of land. There is a similar law attributed to Oxylus, which is to the effect that there should be a certain portion of every man's property on which he could not borrow money. A useful corrective to the evil of which I am speaking would be the law of the Aphytæans, who, although they are numerous, and do not possess much land, are all of them husbandmen. For their properties are reckoned in the census, not entire, but only in such small portions that even the poor may have more than the amount required.

Next best to an agricultural, and in many respects similar, are a pastoral people, who live by their flocks; they are the best trained of any for war, robust in body and able to camp out. The people of whom other democracies consist are far inferior to them, for their life is inferior; there is no room for moral excellence in any of their employments, whether they be mechanics or traders or labourers. Besides, people of this class can readily come to the assembly, because they are continually moving about in the city and in the agora; whereas husbandmen are scattered over the country and do not meet, or equally feel the want of assembling together. Where the territory extends to a distance from the city, there is no difficulty in making an excellent democracy or constitutional government; for the people are compelled to settle in the country, and even if there is a town population the assembly ought not to meet when the country people cannot come. We have thus explained how the first and best form of democracy should be constituted; it is clear that the other or inferior sorts will deviate in a regular order, and the population which is excluded will at each stage be of a lower kind.

The last form of democracy, that in which all share alike, is one which cannot be borne by all states, and will not last long unless well regulated by laws and customs. The more general causes which tend to destroy this or other kinds of government have now been pretty fully considered. In order to constitute such a democracy and strengthen the people, the leaders have been in the habit of including as many as they can, and making citizens not only of those who are legitimate, but even of the illegitimate, and of those who have only one parent a citizen, whether father or mother; for nothing of this sort comes amiss to such a democracy. This is the way in which demagogues proceed. Whereas the right thing would be to make no more additions when the number of the commonalty exceeds that of the notables or of the middle class,—beyond this not to go. When in excess of this point the state becomes disorderly, and the notables grow excited and impatient of the democracy, as in the insurrection at Cyrene; for no notice is taken of a little evil, but when it increases it strikes the eye. Measures like those which Cleisthenes passed when he wanted to increase the power of the democracy at Athens, or such as were taken by the founders of popular government at Cyrene, are useful in the extreme form of democracy. Fresh tribes and brotherhoods should be established; the private rights of families should be restricted and converted into public ones; in short, every contrivance should be adopted which will mingle the citizens with one another and get rid of old connections. Again, the measures which are taken by tyrants appear all of them to be democratic; such, for instance, as the license permitted to slaves (which may be to a certain extent advantageous) and also that of women and children, and the allowing everybody to live as he likes. Such a government will have many supporters, for most persons would rather live in a disorderly than in a sober manner.

The mere establishment of a democracy is not the only or principal business of a legislator, or of those who wish to create such a state, for any state, however badly constituted, may last one, two, or three days; a far greater difficulty is the preservation of it. The legislator should therefore endeavour to have a firm foundation according to the principles already laid down concerning the preservation and destruction of states; he should guard against the destructive elements, and should make laws, whether written or unwritten, which will contain all the preservatives of states. He must not think the truly democratical or oligarchical measure to be that which will give the greatest amount of democracy or oligarchy, but that which will make them last longest. The demagogues of our own day often get property confiscated in the law-courts in order to please the people. But those who have the welfare of the state at heart should counteract them, and make a law that the property of the condemned which goes into the treasury should not be public but sacred. Thus offenders will be as much afraid, for they will be punished all the same, and the people, having nothing to gain, will not be so ready to condemn the accused. Care should also be taken that state trials are as few as possible, and heavy penalties should be inflicted on those who bring groundless accusations; for it is the practice to indict, not members of the popular party, but the notables, although the citizens ought to be all equally attached to the state, or at any rate should not regard their rulers as enemies.

Now, since in the last and worst form of democracy the citizens are very numerous, and can hardly be made to assemble unless they are paid, and to pay them when there are no revenues presses hardly upon the notables (for the money must be obtained by a property-tax and confiscations and corrupt practices of the courts, things which have before now overthrown many democracies); where, I say, there are no revenues, the government should hold few assemblies, and the law-courts should consist of many persons, but sit for a few days only. This system has two advantages: first, the rich do not fear the expense, even although they are unpaid themselves when the poor are paid; and secondly, causes are better tried, for wealthy persons, although they do not like to be long absent from their own affairs, do not mind going for a few days to the law-courts. Where there are revenues the demagogues should not be allowed after their manner to distribute the surplus; the poor are always receiving and always wanting more and more, for such help is like water poured into a leaky cask. Yet the true friend of the people should see that they be not too poor, for extreme poverty lowers the character of the democracy; measures also should be taken which will give them lasting prosperity; and as this is equally the interest of all classes, the proceeds of the public revenues should be accumulated and distributed among them, if possible, in such quantities as may enable them to purchase a little farm, or, at any rate, make a beginning in trade and husbandry. And if this benevolence cannot be extended to all, money should be distributed in turn according to tribes or other divisions, and in the meantime the rich should pay the fee for the attendance of the poor at the necessary assemblies; and should in turn be excused from useless public services. By administering the state in this spirit the Carthaginians retain the affections of the people; their policy is from time to time to send some of them into their dependent towns, where they grow rich. It is also worthy of a generous and sensible nobility to divide the poor amongst them, and give them the means of going to work. The example of the people of Tarentum is also well deserving of imitation, for, by sharing the use of their own property with the poor, they gain their good will. Moreover, they divide all their offices into two classes, one-half of them being elected by vote, the other by lot; the latter that the people may participate in them, and the former, that the state may be better administered. A like result may be gained by dividing the same offices, so as to have two classes of magistrates, one chosen by vote, the other by lot.

—BENJAMIN JOWETT.

COSMOPOLITAN SOCIETY

FOURTH AND THIRD CENTURIES B. C.

AFTER the conquests of Alexander the Great the literary center shifted from Athens to Alexandria in Egypt, and the literature of the period (late fourth and third centuries) is known as Alexandrian or Hellenistic. It differs in many respects from the classical literature of the Athenian supremacy.

The most marked change that came over the Greek world was the change from the small restricted community life, with its more or less narrow interests, to the national life of extended monarchies; from the individual responsibilities of democratic government to the relegation of such responsibilities to the care of a life-long ruler and his ministers. The world seemed suddenly to have become vastly extended; travel became more common, so that the Greeks of one locality began to make acquaintance with those of another, and even to mingle more freely with barbarians. As a natural result, interests ceased to be centered on the city-state, but broadened out into a cosmopolitan view of society. The release from the cares of public life turned thought more and more upon the individual and upon his private and domestic life. The natural world about him also commanded more of his attention.

In Alexandria particularly, the successors of Alexander, ambitious to build a brilliant intellectual center, summoned from all parts of the Greek world the scholars and poets, and made accessible to them through the great library of Alexandria all the available literature of the past. Here developed rapidly a new spirit of inquiry and of skepticism, which issued on the one hand in a ripened literary criticism and on the other in learned experiments at innovations and new inventions.

The productions of the time marked an advance in many respects—in knowledge, critical understanding, broader interest, analysis of the individual man—but it carried with it also the defects of pedantry and artificiality. There was a conscious straining for effect, an overloading of detail, an intricacy of weaving together the material treated, which missed the simplicity and restraint of the earlier period. The skepticism often discarded the old without being able to replace it with something better.

On the formal side, it was the age of personal epigram and elegy, in which the love experience of the writer received a new emphasis. The massive epic of Homer gave place to the short epic, the comedy of public satire to the comedy of private life, the broad speculations of philosophers to the construction of ethical systems and fanciful Utopias, and the discovery of scientific principles to applied science. The rise of the pastoral, which more than any other form strikes the ancient note of spontaneity, belongs also to this age.

I. COMEDY OF MANNERS

The Macedonian conquest of most of the known world had its effect on Athens as on the whole of Greece. Decline in political power turned the thoughts of people more and more away from public affairs to the problems of private and domestic life. The outspoken political satire of Aristophanes perforce gave way before the threat of a foreign power, and in its place was gradually developed a comedy which indulged in mild satire on character and situation as manifested in the complexities of everyday experience. But the purpose of this comedy was a broader one than that of mere satire. It would mirror private life, presenting the sad, the serious, the fun and frolic, love and its troubles. This dramatic development is perhaps best described as a comedy of manners.

The plots, as known from Greek originals and Roman adaptations, are usually developed within a rather narrow range of events and characters. A young man is in love with a girl to whom his father objects either because of her doubtful character or her poverty. By the help of various accomplices the father is deceived for a time. A recognition scene, which identifies the girl, often clears up matters to everyone's satisfaction. Chance events usually play a part in the denouement, though they are worked in naturally enough. Almost never is use made of divine intervention which is so common in tragedy.

Familiar elements in the plays are love affairs, marriages, abductions, abandoned infants, deception of fathers, schemes to get money from them, birth-tokens by which persons are identified. Familiar characters, which appear in so many plays that they may be termed stock characters, are father, son, physician, slave, parasite, cook, soldier, nurse, slave-dealer, wife, girl. Curiously enough women, though they play always important rôles in the story, are often used very little on the stage and in some plays do not appear at all. The explanation of this lies in the fact that Greek women led secluded lives, appearing seldom in public, and the playwright is representing actuality. The characters need by no means always show the same characteristics. A capable playwright might individualize his stock character *father,* for example, in every play he produced. Of such elements an endless variety of stories could be constructed.

In this new comedy the technique of tragedy as perfected by Euripides was found to be better adapted to the new subject matter than that of the old comedy. A prologue, typical of Euripides, was used, not however placed always at the beginning of a play, but after a scene or two of interesting dialogue had won the favor of the audience. A chorus was inherited from an earlier day; but it was altogether a non-essential to the plot, appearing quite incidentally. The stage setting, which did not vary throughout the play, presented to the spectators a street, regularly understood to be in Athens, which led, on the spectators' left, to the harbor, and, on the right, to the center of the city. Two or three houses, perhaps with alleyways between, opened on this street. The action took place in the street in front of the houses. This is the type of play which particularly influenced the Roman and, through the Roman, the modern drama.

THE ARBITRATION [1]

MENANDER

[From the *Arbitrants*]

Menander (342 to 291 B.C.), of Athens, is the chief representative of the New Comedy. His work has been known to the modern world by the discovery of large parts of several of his comedies on papyrus in Egypt some years ago. Before that time he was known merely in brief quotations and through imitations of his work by Roman dramatists. He mirrored

[1] From The Loeb Classical Library, reprinted by permission.

the private life of the Athens of his time faithfully, and on a high level of artistic excellence. For his ability in depicting character and for spirited dialogue he is justly famous.

None of the newly-discovered plays of Menander is complete. To give the setting of the long fragment of the *Arbitrants* here printed, the plot as reconstructed may be briefly outlined. Pamphila, the daughter of Smicrines, was violated by Charisius. Later they were married, neither recognizing the other. A child is born which Pamphila's old nurse, Sophrona, exposes, with the ring of the unknown father as birth-token. Charisius learns of this child's birth and gives himself up to revelling to drown his disappointment in his wife, who, he thinks, has been untrue to him. Smicrines comes to discuss the situation. He is made arbitrator by the poor people who have found and are caring for the child. And it is at this point that the passage selected for quotation here begins. The irony of the scene in which Smicrines is made to decide a matter concerning the welfare of his own grandchild, who is of course unknown to him, is obvious. Later Smicrines tries to induce his daughter to leave her unworthy husband; but she will not, feeling her own fault. At last the real truth is discovered by husband and wife, the child is restored to them, and all's well that ends well.

SCENE:—SYRISCUS, DAVUS (*the wife of* SYRISCUS *carries the baby*), (*later*) SMICRINES.

Syriscus and Davus are at an impasse in their dispute about certain trinkets found by Davus along with a baby left exposed, which Syriscus had later adopted. Davus had held back all reference to these birth-tokens, wishing to retain them without the baby. Syriscus has accidentally discovered his treachery.

SYRISCUS. You'd shun what's fair.
DAVUS. And you, unchancy, blackmail me.

SYRISCUS. You had no right to what's not yours.
DAVUS.   Let's leave the case
To some third person.
SYRISCUS. I agree.
DAVUS.   Let's arbitrate.
SYRISCUS. Who shall it be?
DAVUS. For my part anyone will do.
(*aside*) It serves me right for why did I go shares with you?

Enter SMICRINES

SYRISCUS (*indicating* SMICRINES). Will you take him as judge?
DAVUS. Luck help me, yes!
SYRISCUS (*to* SMICRINES). Good sir,
Now, by the gods, could you give us a moment's time?
SMICRINES. Give you? And wherefore?
SYRISCUS. We've a question in dispute.
SMICRINES. What's that to me, pray?
SYRISCUS. Some impartial judge for this
We're seeking now, and so, if nothing hinders you,
Adjust our quarrel.
SMICRINES. Rascals marked for misery!
In goatskins dressed, do you debate and prate of law?
SYRISCUS. But none the less—the matter's short and easily
Decided—grant the favour, father. By the gods,
Do not despise us, for at all times it behooves
That justice gain the upper hand, yes, everywhere,
And every one that comes along should look to this
And make it his concern. It is the common lot
We all must share.
DAVUS (*aside*). I've grappled no mean orator,

Why did I give him part in this?
  SMICRINES. Will you abide
By my decision? Say.
  SYRISCUS and DAVUS (*together*). Of
    course.
  SMICRINES. I'll hear. For what's
To hinder? (*To* DAVUS) You! you
    close-mouthed fellow there! Speak
    first.
  DAVUS. I'll start a little further back,
    not simply tell
His part, that I may make the matter
    plain to you.
Within this bushy thicket here, hard by
    this place
My flock I was a-herding, now, perhaps,
    good sir,
Some thirty days gone by, and I was all
    alone,
When I came on a little infant child ex-
    posed
With necklace and with some such other
    ornaments.
  SYRISCUS (*interrupting*). About just
    these our quarrel!
  DAVUS. He won't let me speak!
  SMICRINES (*to* SYRISCUS). If you put
    in your chatter, with this stick of
    mine
I'll fetch you one.
  DAVUS. And serve him right.
  SMICRINES (*to* DAVUS). Speak on.
  DAVUS. I will.
I took him up and with him went off to
    my house.
I had in mind to rear him—'twas my
    notion then—
But over night came counsel, as it does
    to all,
And with myself I reasoned: "What have
    I to do
With rearing children and the trouble?
    Where shall I
Find so much money? Why take on
    anxieties?"
Thus minded was I. Back unto my flock
    again
At daybreak. Came this fellow—he's a
    charcoal man—

Unto this selfsame place to saw out tree-
    stumps there.
Now he had had acquaintance with me
    heretofore,
And so we fell to talking. Noticing my
    gloom
Says he, "Why's Davus anxious?"
    "Now why not?" says I,
"For I'm a meddler." And I tell him
    of the facts;
How I had found, how owned the child.
    And straightway then,
Ere I could tell him everything, he
    begged and begged;
"So, Davus, blessed be your lot!" at
    every word
Exclaiming. Then: "Give me the baby!
    So, good luck
Be yours! So, be you free! For I've a
    wife," says he,
"And she gave birth unto a baby and it
    died"—
(Meaning this woman here that holds the
    baby now) —
  SMICRINES (*to* SYRISCUS). You
    begged?
  DAVUS (*to* SYRISCUS, *who at first fails
    to answer*). Syriscus!
  SYRISCUS. Yes, I did.
  DAVUS. The live-long day
He pestered me, and when he urged, en-
    treated me,
I promised him; I gave the child, and off
    he went
Calling down countless blessings, seized
    my hands and kissed
And kissed them.
  SMICRINES (*to* SYRISCUS). You did
    this?
  SYRISCUS. I did.
  DAVUS. Well, off he went.
Just now he meets me with his wife, and
    suddenly
Lays claim to all the things then with
    the child exposed—
(Now these were small and worthless,
    merely nothing)—claims
That he should have them; says he's
    treated scurvily

Because I will not give them, claim them for myself.
But I declare he'd better feel some gratitude
For what he did get for his begging. If I fail
To give him all, no need to bring me to account.
Even if walking with me he had found these things,
And 'twere a "Share-all Windfall," he had taken this,
I that. But when I made the find alone, do you, (*to* SYRISCUS)
Although you were not by, do you, I say, expect
To have it all yourself, and not one thing for me?
In fine, I gave you of my own with all good will:
If this still pleases you, then keep it even now,
But if it doesn't suit and if you've changed your mind,
Why then return it. Don't commit nor suffer wrong.
But 'twere not fair that you get all, by my consent
In part, and, partly, forcing me. I've said my say.
  SYRISCUS. Has said his say?
  SMICRINES. You're deaf? He's said his say.
  SYRISCUS. All right,
Then I come after. All alone this fellow found
The baby. Yes, and all of this he's telling now
He tells correctly, father, and it happened so.
I do not contradict. I did entreat and beg
And I received it from him. Yes, he tells the truth.
A certain shepherd, fellow labourer of his,
With whom he had been talking, then brought word to me
That with the baby he had found some ornaments.

To claim these things, see, father, he is here himself!
Give me the baby, wife.
    (*Takes the child from his wife's arms.*)
        Now, Davus, here from you
He's asking back the necklace and birth-tokens too,
For he declares that these were placed upon himself
For his adorning, not for eking out your keep.
I too join in, and ask for them, as guardian—
On giving him you made me that.
(*To* SMICRINES) And now, good sir,
Me thinks 'tis yours to settle whether it be right
These golden trinkets and whatever else there be,
As given by his mother, whosoe'er she was,
Be put by for the baby till he come of age,
Or this footpad who stripped him is to have these things,
That others own, provided that he found them first!
"Why didn't I," you'll say, "when first I took the child,
Demand them then of you?" It was not then as yet
Within my power to speak thus in the child's behalf,
And even now I'm here demanding no one thing
That's mine, mine only. "Windfall! Share-all!" None of that!
No "finding" when 'tis question of a person wronged.
That is not "finding," nay, but outright filching that!
And look at this too, father. Maybe this boy here
Was born above our station. Reared 'mongst working-folk
He will despise our doings, his own level seek

And venture on some action suiting noble
   birth:
Will go a-lion-hunting; carry arms; or run
A race at games. You've seen the actors
   act, I know,
And all of this you understand. Those
   heroes once,
Pelias, Neleus, by an aged man were
   found,
A goatherd in his goatskin dressed as I
   am now,
And, when he noticed they were better
   born than he,
He tells the matter, how he found, how
   took them up,
He gave them back their wallet, with
   birth-tokens filled.
And thus they found out clearly all their
   history,
And they, the one-time goatherds, afterwards were kings.
But had a Davus found those things and
   sold them off,
That he might profit by twelve drachmas
   for himself,
Through all the coming ages they had
   been unknown
Who were such great ones and of such a
   pedigree.
And so it is not fitting, father, that I
   here
Should rear his body and that Davus
   seize meanwhile
His life's hope for the future, make it
   disappear.
A youth about to wed his sister once was
   stopped
By just such tokens. One a mother
   found and saved,
And one a brother. Since, O father, all
   men's lives
Are liable to dangers, we must watch,
   look out,
With forethought far ahead for what is
   possible.
"Well, if you are not suited, give him
   back," says he.
This is his stronghold in the matter, as he
   thinks.

But that's not just. If you must give up
   what is his,
Then in addition do you claim to have
   the child
That more securely you may play the
   rogue again
If some of his belongings Fortune has
   preserved?
I've said my say. (*To* SMICRINES) Give
   verdict as you hold is just.
SMICRINES. Well, this decision's easy:
   "All that was exposed
Together with the child goes with him,"
   I decide.
DAVUS. All right. But now, the
   child?
SMICRINES. By Zeus, I won't decide
He's yours who wrong him, but he's his
   who came to aid,
This man's, who stood against you, you
   who'd injure him.
SYRISCUS. Now yours be many bless-
   ings!
DAVUS. Nay, a verdict rank!
By Zeus the saviour! I, the sole dis-
   coverer,
Am stripped of all and he who did not
   find receives!
Am I to hand these over?
SMICRINES. Yes.
DAVUS.   A verdict rank—
Else may no blessing ever light on me!
SYRISCUS. Here, quick!
DAVUS. Good Heracles, how I am
   treated!
SYRISCUS. Loose your sack
And show us, for it's there you carry
   them—
       (*To* SMICRINES, *about to leave*)
                              Nay, stop,
I beg, a little, till he gives them up.
DAVUS (*aside*). Why did
I let him judge our case?
SMICRINES. Come, give, you quarry-
   slave!
DAVUS (*handing over the tokens*).
   What shameful treatment!
SMICRINES (*to* SYRISCUS). Have you
   all?

SYRISCUS. I think so, yes.

SMICRINES. You have, unless he swallowed something down while I
Gave verdict of conviction.

SYRISCUS. Hardly that, I think.
(*To* SMICRINES, *who turns to leave*)
Nay, then, good sir, may Luck attend you. Such as you
I'd sooner have the judges all.
(*Exit* SMICRINES *to City.*

DAVUS. But how unjust,
O Heracles! This verdict, was it not too rank?

SYRISCUS. You were a rascal, rascal you!

DAVUS. Look out yourself,
Yes, you now, that you keep these trinkets safe for him.
Aye, mark you well, I'll ever have an eye on you.
(*Exit* DAVUS *towards Mt. Parnes.*

SYRISCUS (*calling after him*). Go hang! Go gang your gait! But you, my wife, take these
And carry them in here to our young master's house.
For meanwhile here we will await Chærestratus
And in the morning we'll start off to work again
When we have made our payment. Stop. Let's count them first.
Count over, one by one. Have you a basket there?
Well, loose your dress and drop them in.

(*While* SYRISCUS *examines the tokens and his wife holds out the fold of her dress*, ONESIMUS *comes out of the house of* CHÆRESTRATUS.)

SCENE. SYRISCUS, ONESIMUS

ONESIMUS (*to himself*). A slower cook
Nobody ever saw. Why, this time yesterday
Long since they had their wine.

SYRISCUS (*talks to his wife of the trinkets without noticing* ONESIMUS). Now this one seems to be
A sort of rooster and a tough one too! Here, take.
And here is something set with stones. This one's an axe.

ONESIMUS (*becoming aware of* SYRISCUS *and his occupation*). What's this?

SYRISCUS (*still failing to notice* ONESIMUS). This one's a gilded ring without; inside
It's iron. On the seal is carved—a bull? —or goat?
I can't tell which, and one Cleostratus is he
Who made it—so the letters say.

ONESIMUS (*interrupting*). I say, show me!

SYRISCUS (*startled into handing him the ring*). Well there! But who are you?

ONESIMUS. The very one!

SYRISCUS.   Who is?

ONESIMUS. The ring.

SYRISCUS. What ring d'ye mean? I don't know what you mean.

ONESIMUS. Charisius's ring, my master's ring!

SYRISCUS. You're cracked!

ONESIMUS. The one he lost.

SYRISCUS. Put down that ring, you wretched man!

ONESIMUS. Our ring? "Put down" for you? Where did you get it from?

SYRISCUS. Apollo and ye gods! What awful nuisance this,
To bring off safe an orphan baby's property!
The first to come forthwith has plunder in his eyes.
Put down that ring, I say.

ONESIMUS. You'd jest with me, you would?
It's master's ring, by your Apollo and the gods!

SYRISCUS. I'd have my throat cut sooner than give it at all

To him, I vow. That's settled. I will
have the law
On each and all by turns. The boy's they
are, not mine.
> (*Returns to enumerating the
> tokens.*)

This one's a collar. Take it, you (*to his
wife*).
A chiton's fold
Of purple, this. Go, take them in.
> (*His wife with the child and
> tokens, except the ring, goes in.*)

(*To* ONESIMUS) Now tell me, you.
What's this you're saying to me?
ONESIMUS. I? This ring is his,
Charisius's. Once, when drunk, or so
he said,
He lost it.
SYRISCUS. I'm Chærestratus's tenant
slave.
So either save it carefully or give to me
That I may keep and safe deliver.
ONESIMUS. I prefer
Myself as guard.
SYRISCUS. To me that matters not one
whit,
For both of us are stopping, as it seems,
in here,
In the same lodging-place.
ONESIMUS. Just now it's no good
time,
Perhaps, when guests are coming in, to
tell him this
Our story, but to-morrow.
SYRISCUS. I will wait till then.
To-morrow, in a word, I'm ready to sub-
mit
This case to anyone you like.
> (*Exit* ONESIMUS *into the house of*
> CHÆRESTRATUS.

Now this time, too,
I've come off not so badly, but it seems
as though
A man must give up all besides and practise law.
By this means, nowadays, is everything
kept straight.
> (*Exit* SYRISCUS *into the house.
> Re-enter the group of revellers.*

> *They give an exhibition and re-
> tire into the house of* CHÆRES-
> TRATUS.)
> CHORUS.

ACT III

Enter ONESIMUS *from the house of*
CHÆRESTRATUS

SCENE. ONESIMUS *alone.*

ONESIMUS. I've started, now five
times and more, to go and show
This ring to master. I go up to him and
then,
When I'm already close and by his very
side
I'm always shirking it. And now I'm
sorry for
My former tattling. For quite constantly
he says:
"May Zeus bring wretched ruin on the
wretched man
Who told me that!" If he should make
up with his wife
As like as not he'd seize and make away
with me
Because I told the tale and know of it.
'Twas well
I kept from stirring up some other mess
with this,
For even here and now the mischief's
fairly big.
> (ABROTONON *rushes out of the
> house remonstrating with one
> and another of the revellers who
> try to detain her.*)

SCENE. ONESIMUS, ABROTONON.

ABROTONON. Let go of me! Please,
sir! Don't give me trouble, please!
(*To herself*)
I made myself, it seems, poor me, a
laughing-stock
And I knew it not. I looked for love,
instead of that
The fellow hates me with a superhuman
hate;

Even his banquet couch no more he lets
me share;
Poor wretch! I lie apart.
ONESIMUS (*to himself, not seeing*
ABROTONON). What! Give it back
to him
From whom but now I had it? No!
Nonsensical!
ABROTONON (*to herself*). Poor man,
why does he waste his money, such a
pile?
So far at least as he's concerned, poor
wretch! I might
Be basket-bearer for the goddess—yes, I
might,
For here am I left virgin, as the saying
goes,
The third day now.
ONESIMUS (*to himself*). How, by the
gods? How could I, pray?
(*Enter* SYRISCUS *through one of
the side-entrances.* ABROTONON
*stands aside until his depar-
ture.*)

SCENE. ONESIMUS, ABROTONON,
SYRISCUS

SYRISCUS. Where is the man I'm hunt-
ing everywhere?
(*Sees* ONESIMUS *in the vestibule
about to enter the house.*)
You sir
In there! Give back, good sir, that ring,
or once for all
Go show it him whom you've in mind.
Let's have it out.
I must be off.
ONESIMUS. The matter stands, my
man, like this.
The ring here is my master's,—I am cer-
tain sure—
Charisius's, but to him I hesitate
To show it, for 'twere much the same as
to declare
Him father of the child with whom the
ring was found.
SYRISCUS. Why so, you fool?
ONESIMUS. 'Twas at the Tauropolia,

The all-night women's festival, he lost it
once.
'Twould seem that it's a question of a
maiden wronged,
That she gave birth to and of course ex-
posed this child.
If someone now could find her and pro-
duce this ring,
He'd make clear demonstration. But, as
matters stand,
'Twould merely mean suspicion and con-
fusion too.
SYRISCUS. See you to that yourself.
But if you make this stir,
Wishing that I take back the ring and
give to you
A little something, that is folly. For
with me
There's no "divide."
ONESIMUS. Nor do I wish it.
SYRISCUS. Well, all right.
When I've run here and yonder—for I'm
off to town—
I'll come again to know of this, what
we're to do.
(*Exit* SYRISCUS *towards Athens.*
ABROTONON *comes up to* ONESI-
MUS.)
ABROTONON. Was it this charcoal-
man, Onesimus, who found
The baby boy the woman's nursing now
indoors?
ONESIMUS. Yes, so he says.
ABROTONON. O what a dainty child,
poor thing!
ONESIMUS. And this ring here was on
him. 'Tis my master's ring.
ABROTONON. Fie, luckless, fie! If,
then, it's your young master's child
For certain, will you see it brought up
like a slave?
You ought to die. 'Twould serve you
right!
ONESIMUS. 'Tis as I say,
Its mother no one knows.
ABROTONON. He lost the ring, you
say,
During the feast of Tauropolia?
ONESIMUS. Yes he

Was in his cups—at least, the slave at-
tending him
Informed me so.
    ABROTONON. Of course! And then
      alone he came
Upon the women as they made a night
  of it.
I know, for once just such a thing as this
  occurred
When I was by.
    ONESIMUS. When you were by?
    ABROTONON. Why yes, last year
At Tauropolia. For maids I thrummed
  the lute
And I myself played with them. Then—
  that is—not yet
Had I had knowledge of man's way and
  what it is—
That's true as true, by Aphrodite!
    ONESIMUS. But the girl?
Who was she? Can you tell me that?
    ABROTONON. I could inquire.
She was the women's friend, the women
  whom I served.
    ONESIMUS. And who's her father?
    Heard you that?
    ABROTONON. Nay, I know naught
Except I'd know her if I once caught
  sight of her.
A handsome girl, ye gods! and she's a
  wealthy one,
They say.
    ONESIMUS. It may be she's the
  one.
    ABROTONON. I do not know.
But thus it was: while with us there she
  wandered off
And of a sudden then she comes back on
  a run
Alone, and bathed in tears, and tearing
  at her hair.
Her silken Tarentine so very beautiful—
Ye gods, diaphanous!—was ruined
  utterly,
For it was all in tatters.
    ONESIMUS. Did she have this ring?
    ABROTONON. Perhaps she had it but
  she did not let me see—
For I'll not try to cheat you.

    ONESIMUS. Well, what now am I
To do about it?
    ABROTONON. Look you here! If you
  have sense
And will obey me, you will make this
  matter clear
And tell your master. If the baby's
  mother be
A free-born girl, what need to keep him in
  the dark
About the circumstances?
    ONESIMUS. Well, Abrotonon,
First thing of all now let's discover who
  she is.
And so, with this in view, I want you
  to—
    ABROTONON (interrupting). Nay, stop!
I could not do it till I clearly know the
  one
Who wronged her. This I fear—to let
  out anything
At random to those women whom I tell
  you of.
Who knows but that some boon-com-
  panion present then
Got it as a pledge from him and lost it
  afterwards
When playing dice? He gave it as se-
  curity,
Perhaps, to back some contribution. Or,
  perchance,
Agreeing on some wager, may have been
  involved
And so have given it. When men are in
  their cups
No end of things like that are apt to come
  about.
But till I know who wronged her I'll not
  search for her
Nor even tell a word of this.
    ONESIMUS. That's not half bad.
But what is one to do?
    ABROTONON. Look you, Onesimus!
Will you, I ask you, fall in with this
  scheme of mine?
As my affair I'll treat the matter—as my
  own.
This ring here I will take and then go
  in to him.

ONESIMUS. Say what you mean—
  though I begin to understand.
ABROTONON. He'll notice that I have
  it. Where I got it from
He'll ask. I'll say: "At Tauropolia,
  when I
Was virgin still." And everything that
  then befell
That other pretty girl I'll make my own,
  for I myself
Know pretty much the whole.
ONESIMUS. That beats the universe!
ABROTONON. Now, if he did it, straight
  into the trap he'll fall
And, just now being drunk, he'll be the
  first to speak,
And fluently, of all details; but I'll agree
And back up all he says; no single slip
  I'll make
By speaking first.
ONESIMUS. Delightful! Good! By
  Helios!
ABROTONON. And I'll be coy in talk,
  and, lest I make a slip,
Will work in hackney'd things like:
  "What a man you were!
How vehement and shameless!"
ONESIMUS. Good!
ABROTONON. "How rough you were,
And threw me down! And what a dress
  I spoiled, poor me!"
I'll say. But first, within the house,
  I'll take the child
And weep and kiss it; where she got it
  from, I'll ask
The one who has it.
ONESIMUS. Heracles!
ABROTONON. To cap it all
I'll say: "So here you have a baby born
  to you!"
And I will show the foundling.
ONESIMUS. O Abrotonon,
A master-stroke of malice and of roguery!
ABROTONON. If this shall be estab-
  lished and he's shown to be
Its father, at our leisure then we'll seek
  the girl.
ONESIMUS. That other point you're
  holding back: you'll be set free.

For, thinking you the mother of his
  child, of course
He'll buy your freedom instantly.
ABROTONON. I wish he might,
But I don't know.
ONESIMUS. Ah, don't you though?
  At any rate,
Abrotonon, are no thanks due to me for
  this?
ABROTONON. By the Twain Goddesses,
  of course. All this my luck
At least I'll give you credit for.
ONESIMUS. Then here's a point:
What if on purpose you stop looking for
  the girl,
Ignore the matter, and go back on me?
ABROTONON. You fool!
Why should I? Daft on babies am I,
  do you think?
May I but merely get my liberty! O
  gods,
May I get that as a wage for this!
ONESIMUS. God grant you may.
ABROTONON. Is it a bargain then?
ONESIMUS. A bargain, certainly.
For if you play your tricks on me, I'll
  fight you then;
I'll have the vantage ground. But, as
  things stand, let's see
If this now turns out well.
ABROTONON. All right, then you agree?
ONESIMUS. Of course.
ABROTONON. The ring, then, hand it
  over—do. Be quick.
ONESIMUS (giving the ring). Well,
  take it then.
ABROTONON (taking the ring). Per-
  suasion, dear, as my ally
Stand by me, make to prosper everything
  I say!
  (Exit ABROTONON into the house
  of CHÆRESTRATUS.)

SCENE. ONESIMUS alone

ONESIMUS. She knows her way about,
  that woman! When she saw
She had no chance in love for winning
  liberty,

But wanders blind, she takes the other
road. While I,
A sniffling, senseless dolt, with no such
forethought blest,
Shall be a slave forever. But from her,
perhaps,
I'll get some gain if she succeeds. That's
only fair!—
What groundless reckonings—misguided
me—to hope
To get back thanks from woman! Only
heaven send
I don't get mischief new! Now Mistress's affairs
Are ticklish—on the brink. For if the
girl is found
To be of free-born father and turns out
to be
This baby's mother, her he'll take, his
wife divorce.
Right well I know: "Desert a sinking
ship!" And yet
Here too methinks I've dodged, and
neatly too, all charge

Of this mess being stirred by me. Good-
bye, I say,
To playing meddler in affairs of other
folks.
And if again you catch me putting in my
oar
Or chattering, I'll give you leave and
liberty
To cut my—molars out!
(*Sees* SMICRINES *approaching from the
city.*)
                I say! Whom have we here
Approaching? It is Smicrines come back
from town.
He's all wrought up again. From some-
one he has learned
The truth perhaps. I think I'll make off
quick and shun
All complication, for I ought to find out
first
About Abrotonon and how she's coming
on.
(*Exit* ONESIMUS *into the house of*
CHÆRESTRATUS.)
                            —F. G. ALLINSON.

II. TYPES OF CHARACTER

THE FLATTERER [1]

THEOPHRASTUS

Theophrastus of Lesbos was born about
372 and died about 287 B.C. He was the
most distinguished of the successors of
Aristotle to the headship of the Lyceum
at Athens and the most brilliant continua-
tor of the Aristotelian system of philosophy. Of the many works he produced
only two books on botanical subjects and
the *Characters* survive in complete form.
The latter is a collection of brief descriptions of types of persons who embody this
or that moral defect, a study of the ap-

[1] Reprinted by permission of Macmillan &
Co., London, publishers.

pearance faults of character assume in
the individual. The style is condensed,
plain, realistic.

Flattery may be considered as a mode
of companionship degrading but profitable to him who flatters.

The Flatterer is a person who will say
as he walks with another, 'Do you observe how people are looking at you?
This happens to no man in Athens but
you. A compliment was paid to you
yesterday in the Porch. More than
thirty persons were sitting there; the
question was started, Who is our foremost man? Everyone mentioned you
first, and ended by coming back to your

name.' With these and the like words, he will remove a morsel of wool from his patron's coat; or, if a speck of chaff has been laid on the other's hair by the wind, he will pick it off; adding with a laugh, 'Do you see? Because I have not met you for two days, you have had your beard full of white hairs; although no one has darker hair for his years than you.' Then he will request the company to be silent while the great man is speaking, and will praise him, too, in his hearing, and mark his approbation at a pause with 'True'; or he will laugh at a frigid joke, and stuff his cloak into his mouth as if he could not repress his amusement. He will request those whom he meets to stand still until 'His Honour' has passed. He will buy apples and pears, and bring them in and give to the children in the father's presence; adding, with kisses, 'Chicks of a good father.' Also, when he assists at the purchase of slippers, he will declare that the foot is more shapely than the shoe. If his patron is approaching a friend, he will run forward and say, 'He is coming to you'; and then, turning back, 'I have announced you.' He is just the person, too, who can run errands to the women's market without drawing breath. He is the first of the guests to praise the wine; and to say, as he reclines next the host, 'How delicate is your fare!' and (taking up something from the table) 'Now this—how excellent it is!' He will ask his friend if he is cold, and if he would like to put on something more; and, before the words are spoken, will wrap him up. Moreover he will lean towards his ear and whisper with him; or he will glance at him as he talks to the rest of the company. He will take the cushions from the slave in the theatre, and spread them on the seat with his own hands. He will say that his patron's house is well built, that his land is well planted, and that his portrait is like.

—R. C. JEBB.

THE GARRULOUS MAN [1]

THEOPHRASTUS

Garrulity is the discoursing of much and ill-considered talk.

The Garrulous man is one who will sit down beside a person whom he does not know, and first pronounce a panegyric on his wife; then relate his dream of last night; then go through in detail what he has had for dinner. Then, warming to the work, he will remark that the men of the present day are greatly inferior to the ancients; and how cheap wheat has become in the market; and what a number of foreigners are in town; and that the sea is navigable after the Dionysia; and that, if Zeus would send more rain, the crops would be better; and that he will work his land next year; and how hard it is to live; and that Damippus set up a very large torch at the Mysteries; and 'How many columns has the Odeum?' and that yesterday he was unwell; and 'What is the day of the month?' and that the Mysteries are in Bœdromion, the Apaturia in Pyanepsion, the rural Dionysia in Poseidon. Nor, if he is tolerated, will he ever desist.

—R. C. JEBB.

THE DISTRUSTFUL MAN [1]

THEOPHRASTUS

Distrustfulness is a presumption that all men are unjust.

The distrustful man is one who, having sent his slave to the market, will send another to ascertain what price he gave. He will carry his money himself, and sit down every two-hundred yards to count it. He will ask his wife in bed if she has locked the wardrobe, and if the cupboard has been sealed, and the bolt

[1] Reprinted by permission of Macmillan & Co., London, publishers.

put upon the hall-door; and, if the reply is 'Yes,' not the less will he forsake the blankets, and light the lamp and run about shirtless and shoeless to inspect all these matters, and barely thus find sleep. He will demand his interest from his creditors in the presence of witnesses, to prevent the possibility of their repudiating the debt. He is apt also to send his cloak to be cleaned, not to the best workman, but wherever he finds sterling security for the fuller. When anyone comes to ask the loan of cups, he will, if possible, refuse; but, if perchance it is an intimate friend or a relation, he will almost assay the cups in the fire, and weigh them, and do everything but take security, before he lends them. Also he will order his slave, when he attends him, to walk in front and not behind, as a precaution against his running away in the street. To persons who have bought something of him and say, 'How much is it? Enter it in your books, for I am too busy to send the money yet,'—he will reply: 'Do not trouble yourself; if you are not at leisure, I will accompany you.'

—R. C. JEBB.

THE WOMEN SACRIFICING TO ASKLEPIOS [1]

HERONDAS

[Mime IV]

Herondas of Syracuse was born about 300 and died about 240 B.C. He is known as a writer of mimes. The mime of the Alexandrian period was a short dramatic composition portraying in satiric vein the people of the middle classes. It had no plot worthy of the name, but consisted of a natural, somewhat realistic, conversation on the common interests and pursuits of the types described. A few examples of it by Herondas were found some years ago on papyrus in Egypt.

[1] Reprinted by permission of Nicholas L. Brown, publisher.

PHILE. Hail, Sovereign Paion, who governest Trikka and who livest in lovely Kos and Epidauros! Hail to Koronis, who gave thee birth, and to Apollo! also to her whom, with thy right hand, thou touchest, Hygieia! and to ye whose venerable altars are here: Panakea, Epione and Iaso, Hail also! and to ye who laid waste the houses and walls of Laomedon; the healer of savage ills, Podalirios and Machaon, Hail! and to all the gods who dwell at thy hearth, and the goddesses, Father Paion! Accept propitiously what is good in my sacrifice of this cock, herald of domestic walls. We can offer little from our house: far less than we would; for we would have brought an ox or a fatted sow instead of a cock, as an offering for the healing of our ills which thou didst remove, O King, laying upon us thy gentle hands!

To the right, Kokkale; place the tablet on the right hand of Hygieia.

Ah, dear Kynno; what lovely statues. Who wrought this stone and who set it up here?

KYNNO. The sons of Praxiteles; don't you see those letters on the base? And it was Euthies, the son of Praxon, who had it set there. May Paion be kind to them and to Euthies for their lovely work. See, Phile, that child looking up to the apple; wouldn't you say she would faint if she didn't get it?

PHILE. And that old man, Kynno. And, by the Fates, how that little boy is strangling the fox-goose! If it were not plainly stone before us, you might believe him about to speak.

KYNNO. Yes, sometimes men give life even to stones.

PHILE. And this one of Battale, Kynno! would you not say it was walking, this statue of the daughter of Myttis? Anyone who had never seen Battale, seeing this image, would know her at once.

KYNNO. Follow me, Phile, and I will

show you something more beautiful than you have ever seen.

Kydilla, go and call the Neocoros.—Don't you hear me talking to you? To you, standing around with your mouth open! Yes! what does she care what I am saying? Planted there, staring at me wider-eyed than a crab! Go, I tell you, call the Neocoros, glutton! No sacrifice, nor profane work either, would ever make you worth while; you stand around forever, like a stone. I swear, Kydilla, before this god, you inflame me even when I want to stay calm. I swear, believe me, the day will come when you will be scratching a shaven head.

PHILE. No use of all that to stir her up, Kynno; she is a slave, and slaves have dull ears.

KYNNO. But the day has come and the crowd is pressing.

You—remain here; the door has opened and I see the sanctuary.

PHILE. Do you see, Kynno? What works! Wouldn't you say that a new Athene had graven all these beautiful things?—Hail to thee, Mistress!—and that naked boy: if I scratched him, wouldn't it leave a mark, Kynno? for he has flesh on him that quivers with life on the panel. And these silver tongs: if Myellos saw them, or Pataikiskos, the son of Lamprion, wouldn't their eyes pop out, believing them really of silver? And that ox with the man leading him and another with them; and that man with the hook-nose, and the one with the snub-nose: aren't they the living day! If it wer'n't so unwomanly, I would have cried out for fear of that ox injuring me; one of his eyes, Kynno, glares at me so!

KYNNO. Yes, Phile, the hands of the Ephesian Apelles were truthful in everything they did, and one could not say: "That man saw some things while other things were hidden." Whatever it occurred to him to touch, even the gods, he succeeded with. A man who has seen him or his works, without being properly

amazed, ought to be hung up and beaten like clothes in a fuller's shop.

THE NEOCOROS. Your sacrifice, women, has been well accomplished and with favorable presages. No one has evoked Paion more efficaciously than you have. Io! Io! Paion! Be favorable to these women for their good offerings and, if they have husbands, to them also and to their near kindred.

PHILE. Yes, let it be so, Great One, and may we come again in good health, bringing greater offerings, with our husbands and our children.

Koddale, cut the bird up carefully and remember to give the thigh to the Neocoros and place the honey-cake and the cakes moistened with oil, in the dragon's grotto, with words of good augury. The rest we will take home and eat. And don't forget to bring some of the sacred bread. But we must give plentifully for, at the sacrifices, the sacred bread is more plentiful when the offering is adequate.
—M. S. BUCK.

THE COBBLER [1]

HERONDAS

[Mime VII]

METRO. Kerdo, I have brought these young people to you, to see what workmanship of yours you have worth showing them.

KERDO. You have done right, Metro; I will please you.

Why don't you bring up the big bench for these ladies, Drimylos! Hey! I call, but you sleep on.

Pistos, rap this fellow's snout until he disgorges that sleep. We should have a thorn collar on him.

Well, slave? Get your legs out of the way, at once! at least, if you don't want

[1] Reprinted by permission of Nicholas L. Brown, publisher.

them shackled up to teach you where they belong.

Is this the way you polish, white-arse? Then I must fret myself to do your cleaning for you!

Be seated, Metro.

Pistos, open the top closet; not that one—the top one! The best works of Kerdo, quickly: lift them down.

My dear Metro, what goods you have come to see!

Step lively: open that drawer of sandals.

Look first at this, Metro; this sole, is it not adjusted like the most perfect of soles? Look, you also, women, at the heel-piece; see how it is held down and how well it is joined to the straps; yet, no part is better than another: all are perfect. And the color!—may the Goddess give you every joy of life!—you could find nothing to equal it. The color! neither saffron nor wax glow like this! Three minæ, for the leather, went to Kandas from Kerdo, who made these. And this other color! it was no cheaper. I swear, by all that is sacred and venerable, women, in truth held and maintained, with no more falsehood than a pair of scales—and, if not, may Kerdo know life and pleasure no more!—this almost drove me bankrupt! For enormous gains no longer satisfy the leather-sellers. They do the least of the work, but our works of art depend on them and the cobbler suffers the most terrible misery and distress, night and day. I am glued to my stool even at night, worn out with work, sleepless until the noises of the dawn. And I have not told all: I support thirteen workmen, women, because my own children will not work. Even if Zeus begged them in tears, they would only chant: "What do you bring? What do you bring?" They sit around in comfort somewhere else, warming their legs, like little birds. But, as the saying goes, it is not talk, but money, which pays the bills. If this pair does not please you, Metro, you can see more and still more, until you are sure that Kerdo has not been talking nonsense.

Pistos, bring all those shoes from the shelves.

You must go back satisfied to your houses, women. Here are novelties of every sort: of Sykione and Ambrakia, laced slippers, hemp sandals, Ionian sandals, night slippers, high heels, Argian sandals, red ones:—name the ones you like best. (How dogs—and women—devour the substance of the cobbler!)

A WOMAN. And how much do you ask for that pair you have been parading so well? But do not thunder too loud and frighten us away!

KERDO. Value them yourself, and fix their price, if you like; one who leaves it to you will not deceive you. If you wish, woman, a good cobbler's work, you will set a price—yes, by these gray temples where the fox has made his lair—which will provide bread for those who handle the tools. (O Hermes! if nothing comes into our net now, I don't know when our sauce-pan will get another chance as good!)

WOMAN. Why grumble instead of fixing the price openly, without shifting?

KERDO. Woman, they are worth a mina,—whether you look up or down. Even if Athene herself bought, I would not take a bit less.

WOMAN. Small wonder, Kerdo, that your shop is full of handsome goods! Take care of them! hold them tight! On the twentieth of Toureon, Hekate celebrates the marriage of Artakama; they should need sandals; perhaps, wretch, they will call on you with a fortune or two. But sew up your purse, so the weasels will not scatter your minæ.

KERDO. If Hekate came, with less than a mina, she would take nothing away, nor Artakama either! Think that over, if you like!

WOMAN. And has good fortune, Kerdo, never allowed you to touch the dainty feet which inspire the Desires and the Loves? But you are scabby and a disagreeable wretch to demand of us, I dare say, double the price, for which you certainly would give them to her. How much for this other pair? Give us an answer worthy of yourself.

KERDO. Every day, by the gods, Eueteris, the flute-player, comes in here to get those for five staters; but I detest her and I ask her four darics because she insulted my wife with her evil talk. But if you have need of them, buy them; I will give them to you for three darics, those, or these others, as you choose. This is because of Metro and for the sake of her lips and yours. Ah! She could carry me away with the wings of Hermes and, even if I were a stone, shoot with me into the heavens. For you have, not a tongue, but rather a sieve of voluptuousness. Ah! that one dwells close to the gods for whom, night and day, you open your lips!

Give me your foot; slip it in the shoe. Good. There is nothing to be added or cut off. All is beautifully adjusted to beauty. You might say that Athene herself made these.

You, give me your old foot also. Your shoe fits like an old hoof; you must have been stepped on by an ox. But you— if I had cut with my knife, from your naked foot, by the hearth of Kerdo, the work would not be truer than this is.

And you: You will give me seven darics, you who stand sneering by the door, prouder than a mare!

Women, if you have need again of anything else, of sandals, or of whatever you are accustomed to take home with you, send a little slave to me.

And you, Metro, come again in eight days, in any case, to get the red slippers. (A smart man must take care of the fur which keeps him warm!)

—M. S. BUCK.

III. POETRY OF THE SCHOLAR

The poets of the Alexandrian period were for the most part the critical scholars of the time, and their product was a combination, not always happy, of learning and imagination. New inventions like the mime and the pastoral make their appearance, but these are rather exceptions to the fashion in poetry than the rule. Forms invented before, such as the elegy, the epigram, the hymn, the epic, the drama, continue to be employed, but modifications in their application are introduced, due not only to the changed conditions of life, but also to the progress of learning and literary criticism. The long narrative is replaced by the short one, though the conventions of the former are carried over into the latter. Simple straightforward narration becomes involved in digression and frequent allusion. Even poetry of personal emotion, like the

elegy, is overloaded with matter that is sometimes but vaguely suggested or lugged in by main force, for no other reason, one feels, than that it is part of the learned equipment of the poet. The gods of the old-time faith are no longer creatures of simple adoration, but are the characters of a fanciful fairyland and are of value mainly as they afford material for fiction.

But not all the poetry is pedantic or drawn from books rather than from life. Indeed, the greater part of that which has come down to us—no doubt owing its survival to the very fact—is a direct expression of the life of the times and possesses merit and charm of a high order. The epigram, not confined now to the poem of an occasion, but spread over all the range of personal emotion, reveals nothing of the pedantry, though it does have the note of artificiality. The pastoral and the mime, lifting for the first time the every-day life of common people to the dignity of a proper subject matter for literature, comes straight from the soil and ranks with the best poetry of the Greek genius. The comedy of manners (see above, p. 528), representing dramatically the intrigues and sorrows and joys of the average home of a Greek city, became the model for most of the comedy of later Europe.

HYMN TO ZEUS

CLEANTHES

Cleanthes (about 331 to about 233 B.C.) was the successor of Zeno, the founder of Stoicism. He was a prolific writer, but of all his works only the *Hymn to Zeus* survives. It is an interesting combination of the new thought and of the traditional religious phraseology.

Most glorious of the Immortals, many
    named, Almighty for ever,
Zeus, ruler of Nature, that governest all
    things with law,
Hail! for lawful it is that all mortals
    should address Thee.
For we are Thy offspring, taking the
    image only of Thy voice, as many
    mortal things as live and move upon
    the earth.
Therefore, will I hymn Thee, and sing
    Thy might for ever.
For Thee doth all this universe that
    circles round the earth obey, moving
    whithersoever Thou leadest, and is
    gladly swayed by Thee,
Such a minister hast Thou in Thine in-
    vincible hands;—the two-edged,
    blazing, imperishable thunderbolt.
For under its stroke all Nature shudder-
    eth, and by it Thou guidest aright
    the Universal Reason, that roams
    through all things, mingling itself
    with the greater and the lesser lights,
    till it have grown so great, and
    become supreme king over all.

Nor is aught done on the earth without
    Thee, O God, nor in the divine
    sphere of the heavens, nor in the
    sea,
Save the works that evil men do in their
    folly—
Yea, but Thou knowest even to find a
    place for superfluous things, and to
    order that which is disorderly, and
    things not dear to men are dear to
    Thee.
Thus dost Thou harmonise into One all
    good and evil things, that there
    should be one everlasting Reason of
    them all.
And this the evil among mortal men
    avoid and heed not; wretched, ever
    desiring to possess the good, yet
    they nor see nor hear the Uni-
    versal Law of God, which obeying
    with all their heart, their life would
    be well.
But they rush graceless each to his own
    aim,
Some cherishing lust for fame, the nurse
    of evil strife,
Some bent on monstrous gain,
Some turned to folly and the sweet works
    of the flesh,
Hastening, indeed, to bring the very con-
    trary of these things to pass.
But Thou, O Zeus, the All-giver, Dweller
    in the darkness of cloud, Lord of
    thunder, save Thou men from their
    unhappy folly,
Which do Thou, O Father, scatter from
    their souls; and give them to dis-
    cover the wisdom, in whose assur-
    ance Thou governest all things with
    justice;
So that being honoured, they may pay
    Thee honour,
Hymning Thy works continually, as it
    becomes a mortal man.
Since there can be no greater glory for
    men or Gods than this,
Duly to praise for ever the Universal
    Law.

—T. W. ROLLESTON.

Hymn to Apollo

CALLIMACHUS

Callimachus (about 300 to about 240 B.C.) won fame as an erudite scholar and as a poet. As librarian of the famous library at Alexandria, he produced valuable works in literary history and in criticism; as poet he wrote hymns to the gods, epigrams, short epics, and elegies. He was typical of a period which drew its inspiration from books rather than from life, and which addressed itself in the language of learning to the cultured few instead of to the whole people. His hymns, a few epigrams, and fragments of other pieces are extant.

What force, what sudden impulse, thus can make
The laurel-branch, and all the temple shake!
Depart, ye souls profane; hence, hence! O fly
Far from this holy place! Apollo's nigh;
He knocks with gentle foot; the Delian palm
Submissive bends, and breathes a sweeter balm:
Soft swans, high hovering, catch th' auspicious sign,
Wave their white wings, and pour their notes divine.
Ye bolts, fly back; ye brazen doors, expand,
Leap from your hinges, Phœbus is at hand.
  Begin, young men, begin the sacred song,
Wake all your lyres, and to the dances throng,
Remembering still, the Power is seen by none
Except the just and innocent alone;
Prepare your minds, and wash the spots away,
That hinder men to view th' all-piercing ray,
Lest ye provoke his favouring beams to bend

On happier climes, and happier skies ascend:
And lo! the Power, just opening on the sight,
Diffuses bliss, and shines with heavenly light.
Nor should the youthful choir with silent feet,
Or harps unstrung, approaching Phœbus meet,
If soon they wish to mount the nuptial bed,
To deck with sweet perfumes the hoary head,
On old foundations lofty walls to build,
Or raise new cities in some distant field.
  Ye listening crowds, in awful silence hear
Apollo's praises, and the song revere;
Even raging seas subside, when poets sing
The bow, the harp of the Lycorean king:
Nor Thetis, wretched mother, dares deplore
Her lov'd, her lost Achilles, now no more!
But thrill'd with awe, she checks her grief and pain,
When Io Pæan sounds along the main.
The weeping rock, once Niobe, suspends
Its tears a while, and mute attention lends;
No more she seems a monument of woe,
Nor female sighs through Phrygian marble flow.
Sound Io! Io! such the dreadful end
Of impious mortals, that with gods contend;
Who dares high heaven's immortal powers engage,
Against our king a rebel war would wage,
And who rebels against our sovereign's sway
Would brave the bright far-shooting god of day.
But rich rewards await the grateful choir
That still to Phœbus tune the living lyre;
From him all honour springs, and high above

He sits in power, at the right hand of
    Jove.
Beyond the day, beyond the night
    prolong
The sacred theme, to charm the god of
    song.
Let all resound his praise; behold how
    bright
Apollo shines in robes of golden light;
Gold are his quiver, harp, and Lyctian
    bow,
And his fair feet with golden sandals
    glow.
All-bright in gold appears the Power
    divine,
And boundless wealth adorns his Delphic
    shrine.
Immortal youth and heavenly beauty
    crown
His cheeks, unshaded by the softest
    down,
But his fair tresses drop ambrosial dews,
Distil soft oils, and healing balm diffuse:
And on what favour'd city these shall
    fall,
Life, health, and safety guard the sacred
    wall.
    To great Apollo various arts belong,
The skill of archers and the powers of
    song;
By him the sure events of lots are given,
By him the prophet speaks the will of
    heaven,
And wise physicians, taught by him,
    delay
The stroke of fate, and turn disease
    away.
    But we to Nomius, heavenly shepherd,
    cry,
Since he, for young Admetus, left the
    sky;
When burning with desire, he deign'd to
    feed
A mortal's coursers on Amphrysus' mead.
His herds increas'd, and overspread the
    ground,
Kids leapt, and sportive lambkins frisk'd
    around,
Where'er Apollo bent his favouring eyes,

The flocks with milk abounded, grew in
    size,
And pregnant ewes, that brought one
    lamb before,
Now dropt a double offspring on the
    shore.
Ere towns are built, or new foundations
    laid,
We still invoke the great Apollo's aid,
And oracles explore; for with delight
He views new cities rising on the sight;
And Phœbus' self the deep foundations
    lays.
The god, but four years old, in former
    days,
First rais'd a structure on th' Ortygian
    ground
Close by the lake that ever circles round;
When young Diana, skill'd in hunting,
    laid
Unnumber'd goats, on Cynthus' moun-
    tain, dead:
The careful goddess brought their heads
    away,
And gave them to the glorious god of
    day;
He broke the horns, and rais'd with artful
    toil
A wondrous altar from the sylvan spoil,
Plac'd rows on rows, in order still dis-
    pos'd,
Which he with circling walls of horn
    enclos'd;
And from this model, just in every part,
Apollo taught mankind the builder's art.
    Besides Apollo show'd my native place
To Battus, and the fam'd Theræan race,
A crow propitious sent, that flew before,
And led the wanderers to the Libyan
    shore.
Apollo, marking from unclouded skies,
Beheld Cyrene's lofty towers arise,
And faithful swore, that Egypt's king
    should gain
The new-built city and the fertile plain.
    To tuneful Phœbus, sacred god of song,
In various nations, various names belong;
Some Bœdromius, Clarius some implore,
But nam'd Carneus on my native shore.

Thee, great Carneus! Sparta first pos-
sess'd,
Next Thera's isle was with thy presence
bless'd;
You cross'd the swelling main from
Thera's bowers,
And then resided in Cyrene's towers.
The sixth from Œdipus convey'd the god
From Lacedæmon o'er the watery road
To Thera's isle; but brought from
Thera's strand
By blameless Battus to Asbystis' land.
He rais'd a temple to record thy praise,
Appointed annual feasts, on solemn days,
In fair Cyrene; sacred hymns resound,
And slaughter'd bulls lie bleeding on the
ground.
Io! Carnean Phœbus! all must pay
Their vows to thee, and on thine altars
lay
Green herbs and painted flowers, when
genial spring
Diffuses sweetness from Favonius' wing;
But when stern winter his dark power
displays
With yellow crocus feed the rising blaze:
So flames unceasing deck thy hallow'd
shrine,
And breathe sweet odours to thy power
divine.
With transport Phœbus views the war-
like dance,
When fierce Bellona's sons in arms
advance,
And, with brown Libyan virgins, tread
the ground,
When annual the Carnean feast comes
round;
Nor yet Alcides' sons had Cyrene seen,
Her crystal fountain and extended green;
But through Azilis' woods the wanderers
stray'd,
And hid their heads within the dusky
shade,
When Phœbus standing on the horned
hill
Beheld the forest and the murmuring rill,
And show'd the warriors to his lovely
bride,

Cyrene fair attending at his side,
Who kill'd the lion on Myrtusa's rocks,
That tore the god Eurypylus's flocks.
Apollo saw not from the realms above
A city more deserving of his love;
No rising town, no mighty state obtain'd
Such gifts from Phœbus as Cyrene
gain'd,
In dear remembrance of the ravish'd
dame,
That crown'd his love, and gave the city's
name.
Nor were her sons ungrateful, but
bestow'd
Superior honours on their guardian god.
Now Io! Io Pæan! rings around
As first from Delphi rose the sacred
sound,
When Phœbus swift descending deign'd
to show
His heavenly skill to draw the golden
bow.
For when no mortal weapons could repel
Enormous Python horrible and fell,
From his bright bow incessant arrows
flew,
And, as he rose, the hissing serpent
slew.
Whilst Io! Io Pæan! numbers cry,
Haste launch thy darts, for surely from
the sky
Thou cam'st the great preserver of man-
kind,
As thy fair mother at thy birth design'd.
An equal foe, pale Envy, late drew
near,
And thus suggested in Apollo's ear:
I hate the bard who pours not forth his
song
In swelling numbers, loud, sublime, and
strong;
No lofty lay should in low murmurs
glide,
But wild as waves, and sounding as the
tide.
Fierce with his foot indignant Phœbus
spurn'd
Th' invidious monster, and in wrath
return'd:

Wide rolls Euphrates' wave, but soil'd
  with mud,
And dust and slime pollute the swelling
  flood:
For Ceres still the fair Melissæ bring
The purest water from the smallest
  spring,
That softly murmuring creeps along the
  plain,
And falls with gentle cadence to the
  main.
  Propitious Phœbus thus thy power
    extend,
And soon shall Envy to the shades de-
  scend.

          —H. W. TYTLER.

EPIGRAMS: CALLIMACHUS

ON THE DEATH OF A FRIEND

I hear, O friend, the fatal news
  Of Heraclitus' death.
A sudden tear my cheek bedews,
  And sighs suppress my breath.

For I must often call to mind,
  How from the crowd we run;
And how, to jesting still inclin'd,
  We sported in the sun.

Alas! he's gone, and part we must,
  And repartee's no more;
But, though my friend be sunk in dust,
  His muse shall ever soar.

The dart of death shall never fly
  To stop her waving wings;
Like Philomel she mounts on high,
  And still like her, she sings.

          —H. W. TYTLER.

THE NAUTILUS

A sacred shell, Zephyritis divine,
Fair Selenæa offers at thy shrine,
And thus thy Nautilus is doubly bless'd,
Since given by her, and still by thee
  possess'd.

Of late small tackling from my body
  grew;
Thin sails I spread, when winds propi-
  tious blew,
But when the seas were calm, to gain the
  shores
I stretch'd my little feet, like labouring
  oars,
And, from my busy limbs and painted
  pride,
Was call'd a Polyp as I stemm'd the tide;
Till driven by winds, on Coan rocks I
  shone,
And now recline before Arsinoe's throne.
Depriv'd of life, no more in seas I
  rest,
Or draw young Halcyons from the watery
  nest;
But be this boon to Clinias's daughter
  given,
A virtuous maid and favourite of high
  heaven;
The precious boon let Selenæa gain,
When she from Smyrna ploughs the
  foaming main.

          —H. W. TYTLER.

IMMORTAL

Beneath this tomb, in sacred sleep,
  The virtuous Saon lies;
Ye passengers, forbear to weep,
  A good man never dies.

          —H. W. TYTLER.

CRETHIS THE WITTY

The Samian virgins us'd often to play
With Crethis the witty, the pleasant, and
  gay,
But now, when they seek her, she cannot
  be found;
Their sportive companion sleeps here
  under ground,
Discharging the debt which to nature we
  owe;
For all must descend to the regions
  below.

          —H. W. TYTLER.

AN EMPTY TOMB

Had never vessel cross'd the main,
Our present grief had been in vain;
But we for Sopolis must weep,
Now plunged beneath the whelming
    deep;
The surges toss his breathless frame;
An empty tomb preserves his name.
—H. W. TYTLER.

BROTHER AND SISTER

This morning we beheld with streaming
    eyes
The flames from Melanippus' body rise;
At eve fair Basile resign'd her breath,
Disdaining to survive a brother's death;
With frantic hands she gave the deadly
    blow
That sent her soul to gloomy shades
    below.
Two mighty ills the wretched sire must
    mourn,
And weep around a son and daughter's
    urn;
Old Aristippus sunk in grief appears,
And old Cyrene melts in briny tears.
—H. W. TYTLER.

THE CHASE

The huntsman o'er the hills pursues
The timid hare, and keenly views
The tracks of hinds amid the snow,
Nor heeds the wintry winds that blow.
But should a stranger mildly say,
Accept the game I kill'd to-day,—
The proffer'd gift he quickly scorns,
And to th' uncertain chase returns:
Such is my love; I never prize
An easy fair, but her who flies.
—H. W. TYTLER.

THE RETIRED WARRIOR

Mencœtas, tir'd with war's alarms,
Gave to the gods his shining arms,
And said, this quiver and this bow
On thee, Serapis, I bestow;

This empty quiver; for my darts
Are all infix'd in hostile hearts.
—H. W. TYTLER.

MEDEA AND JASON

APOLLONIUS

[From the *Argonautica*, Book III]

Apollonius Rhodius (third century
B.C.), an Alexandrian and a pupil of
Callimachus, removed from his native city
to Rhodes as the result of a difference that
arose with his master over literary matters. He seems to have been a reactionary
in theory, opposing the new poetry that
was given vogue by the Alexandrian
scholars, and harking back to the heroic
epic as the most suitable form of poetic
expression. His epic *Argonautica* is
extant.

Although a reactionary, Apollonius is
nevertheless a true child of his times.
While he writes epic according to ancient
formula, he puts into it the same sort of
sentiment and the same quality of learning
as characterize the poetry he objected to.
Love had become the all-absorbing theme
of poetry; his romantic treatment of the
love of Medea and Jason is the earliest
extant instance of such interpretation of
its rôle in life.

Meanwhile the maid her secret thoughts
    enjoy'd,
And one dear object all her soul em-
    ploy'd:
Her train's gay sports no pleasure can
    restore,
Vain was the dance, and music charm'd
    no more;
She hates each object, every face offends,
In every wish her soul to Jason sends;
With sharpen'd eyes the distant lawn
    explores,
To find the hero whom her soul adores;
At every whisper of the passing air,
She starts, she turns, and hopes her
    Jason there:

Again she fondly looks, nor looks in vain,
He comes, her Jason shines along the plain.
As when, emerging from the watery way,
Refulgent Sirius lifts his golden ray,
He shines terrific! for his burning breath
Taints the red air with fevers, plagues, and death;
Such to the nymph approaching Jason shows,
Bright author of unutterable woes;
Before her eyes a swimming darkness spread,
Her flush'd cheeks glow'd, her very heart was dead:
No more her knees their wonted office knew,
Fix'd, without motion, as to earth they grew.
Her train recedes—the meeting lovers gaze
In silent wonder, and in still amaze.
As two fair cedars on the mountain's brow,
Pride of the groves! with roots adjoining grow;
Erect and motionless the stately trees
Short time remain, while sleeps each fanning breeze,
Till from th' Æolian caves a blast unbound
Bends their proud tops, and bids their boughs resound:
Thus gazing they; till by the breath of love,
Strongly at last inspir'd, they speak, they move;
With smiles the love-sick virgin he survey'd,
And fondly thus address'd the blooming maid:
"Dismiss, my fair, my love, thy virgin fear;
'Tis Jason speaks, no enemy is here!
Dread not in me a haughty heart to find,
In Greece I bore no proud inhuman mind.
Whom would'st thou fly? stay, lovely virgin, stay!

Speak every thought! far hence be fears away!
Scorn to deceive! we tread on hallow'd ground.
By the stern power who guards this sacred place,
By the fam'd authors of thy royal race;
By Jove, to whom the stranger's cause belongs,
To whom the suppliant, and who feels their wrongs;
O guard me, save me, in the needful hour!
Without thy aid thy Jason is no more.
To thee a suppliant, in distress I bend,
To thee a stranger, one who wants a friend!
Then, when between us seas and mountains rise,
Medea's name shall sound in distant skies;
All Greece to thee shall owe her heroes' fates,
And bless Medea thro' her hundred states.
The mother and the wife, who now in vain
Roll their sad eyes fast-streaming o'er the main,
Shall stay their tears: the mother, and the wife,
Shall bless thee for a son's or husband's life!
Fair Ariadne, sprung from Minos' bed,
Sav'd valiant Theseus, and with Theseus fled,
Forsook her father, and her native plain,
And stemm'd the tumults of the surging main;
Yet the stern sire relented, and forgave
The maid, whose only crime it was to save;
Ev'n the just gods forgave: and now on high
A star she shines, and beautifies the sky:
What blessings then shall righteous Heaven decree
For all our heroes sav'd, and sav'd by thee?

Heaven gave thee not to kill, so soft an air;
And cruelty sure never look'd so fair!"
   He ceas'd, but left so charming on her ear
His voice, that listening still she seem'd to hear;
Her eyes to earth she bends with modest grace,
And Heaven in smiles is open'd on her face.
A look she steals; but rosy blushes spread
O'er her fair cheek, and then she hangs her head.
A thousand words at once to speak she tries;
In vain—but speaks a thousand with her eyes;
Trembling the shining casket she expands,
Then gives the magic virtue to his hands;
And had the power been granted to convey
Her heart—had given her very heart away.
For Jason beam'd in beauty's charms so bright,
The maid admiring languish'd with delight.
Thus, when the rising Sun appears in view,
On the fair rose dissolves the radiant dew.
Now on the ground both cast their bashful eyes,
Both view each other now with wild surprise.
The rosy smiles now dimpling on her cheeks,
The fair at length in faltering accents speaks:
   "Observant thou to my advice attend,
And hear what succour I propose to lend.
Soon as my sire Æetes shall bestow
The dragon's teeth in Mars's field to sow,
The foll'wing night in equal shares divide;
Bathe well thy limbs in some perennial tide;
Then all retir'd, thyself in black array,

Dig the round foss, and there a victim slay,
A female lamb; the carcase place entire
Above the foss, then light the sacred pyre,
And Perseus' daughter, Hecate, appease
With honey, sweetest labour of the bees;
This done, retreat, nor, while the relics burn,
Let howling dogs provoke thee to return,
Nor human footsteps; lest thou render vain
The charm, and with dishonour join thy train.
Next morn, the whole enchantment to fulfil,
This magic unguent on thy limbs distil:
Then thou with ease wilt strong and graceful move,
Not like a mortal, but the gods above.
Forget not with this unguent to besmear
Thy sword, thy buckler, and tremendous spear:
No giant's falchions then can harm thy frame,
Nor the fell rage of bulls expiring flame.
One day, nor longer, wilt thou keep the field;
Nor thou to perils, nor to labour yield.
But mark my words: when thou, with ceaseless toil,
Hast yok'd the bulls and plough'd the stubborn soil;
And seest upspringing on the teeth-sown land
Of giant foes a formidable band,
Hurl slily 'midst their ranks a rough hard stone,
And they, like dogs contending for a bone,
Will slay each other: thou with speed renew
The glowing fight, and conquest will ensue.
Thus shalt thou bear from Æa's realms to Greece,
If such thy fix'd resolve, the golden fleece."

This said, her eyes were fix'd upon the ground,
And her fair cheeks with streaming sorrows drown'd;
Desponding anguish seiz'd her gentle mind,
Lest he should leave her comfortless behind.
Imbolden'd thus, him by the hand she press'd,
And in the language of her soul address'd:
"If safely hence thou sail'st, O, think of me!
As I for ever shall remember thee!
And freely tell me, to relieve my pain,
Where lies thy home beyond the boundless main?
Say, is Orchomenos thy native soil?
Or dwell'st thou nearer on the Ææan isle?
Let me that far-fam'd virgin's name inquire,
Who boasts the same high lineage with my sire."
She said; her tears his soft compassion won,
And thus the chief, by love inspir'd, begun:
"While on my fancy bright ideas play,
Thy image never from my soul shall stray,
If safe I sail, preserv'd by thee, to Greece,
Nor heavier labours interrupt my peace.
But if the distant country where I dwell
Thy will demands, my ready tongue shall tell.
A land there is which lofty hills surround,
For fertile pastures and rich herds renown'd,
Where from Prometheus good Deucalion came,
His royal heir, Hæmonia is the name.
Deucalion here the first foundations laid
Of towns, built fanes, and men by empire sway'd;
There my Iolcos stands, and many more
Fair ample cities, that adorn the shore.

What time, as rumour'd by the voice of fame,
Æolian Minyas to that country came,
He built, close bordering on the Theban ground,
Orchomenos, a city far renown'd.
But why your wonder should I vainly raise?
My birth-place tell, and Ariadne's praise?
For this the virgin's name you now inquire,
A lovely maid, and Minos is her sire.
Oh! may, like hers, your sire propitious prove,
Who honour'd Theseus with his daughter's love!"
Complacent thus, he sooth'd her sorrowing soul;
Yet anxious cares within her bosom roll.
"Perchance in Greece," the pensive maid rejoin'd,
"Oaths are rever'd, and solemn compacts bind.
But Minos greatly differs from my sire,
Nor I to Ariadne's charms aspire.
Then mention hospitality no more;
But, safe conducted to thy native shore,
Grant this, 'tis all I ask, Oh! think of me,
As I for ever shall remember thee,
In my great sire, the Colchian king's despite:
But if thy pride my ardent passion slight,
Fame, or some bird the hateful news will bring;
Then will I chase thee on the tempest's wing,
Brand thy false heart, thy curs'd familiar be,
And prove thou ow'st thy life, thy all to me."
Medea thus, and tears abundant shed;
And mildly thus the son of Æson said:
"In vain, dear nymph, thy missive bird shall soar
Thro' air sublime, in vain the tempest roar.
But if towards Greece thou deign'st thy course to bear,

Immortal honours shall attend thee there;
There husbands, brothers, sons, so long
    deplor'd,
Safe to their native land by thee re-
    stor'd,
Shall as a goddess reverence thy name,
And pay thee rites which only gods can
    claim.
But would'st thou grace my bed with
    bridal state,
Our love can only be dissolv'd by fate."
    His words with raptures all her soul
    subdue;
Yet gloomy objects rise before her view,
Ordain'd, ere long, Thessalia's realms to
    see;
For such was Juno' absolute decree,
That soon to Greece the Colchian maid
    should go,
To Pelias, source of unremitting woe.
    Meanwhile apart her anxious hand-
    maids stay,
In silence waiting till the close of day:
Such pleasing transports in her bosom
    roll,

His form, his words so captivate her soul,
On feather'd feet the hours unheeded fled,
Which warn'd her home: "Hence" (cau-
    tious Jason said)
"Hence let us hasten unperceiv'd away,
And here enraptur'd pass some future
    day."
    Thus the blest hours in converse sweet
    they spent,
And both unwilling from the temple
    went;
He to his comrades bordering on the
    main,
The fair Medea to her virgin train.
Her train approach'd, but stood un-
    notic'd by;
Her soul sublime expatiates in the sky.
Her rapid car she mounts; this hand
    sustains
The polish'd thong, and that the flowing
    reins.
Fleet o'er the plain the nimble mules con-
    vey'd
To Æa's walls the love-transported maid.
    —FRANCIS FAWKES.

IV. SHEPHERD SONGS

One of the oldest pursuits of men is that of the shepherd, yet it waited for Theocritus to discover it as a theme for poetry. Greek literature before him is full of allusion to it, but nowhere is the life of those who tend the sheep pictured as anything more than a life of toil and lowly labor. Its beauty and romance, the thoughts and emotions of the shepherd, his crude songs and pipings, his rural merry-makings, needed only the imaginative insight and love and the quickening art of a great poet to raise them to a permanent place in literature. Underlying the description of the life is a philosophy of nature which meditates upon the seasonal death and birth of the year and ponders the homely wisdom and superstition of those whose lives are spent in the observation of the natural world.

THE DEATH OF DAPHNIS

THEOCRITUS

[Idyll I]

Theocritus, born about 315 B.C. in Sicily, received the best training of the day under Philetas of Cos and at Alexandria, where he was an intimate of the chief men of letters. He seems to have spent his time partly in Alexandria and partly in his native country. His inspiration was the soil and the common man, whether rural or urban. He chose as his main theme the pastoral scenes and pursuits of Sicily, and sang the loves of the shepherds. His *Idylls* conform to the general literary rule of the period that a poem must be a miniature presenting a small picture of some one phase of life or expressing a single emotion.

The classical pastoral often takes the form followed here. First, the poet pictures the setting—a gathering of shepherds in some shady spot to escape the heat of noonday; then comes a challenge to song, with the announcement of the subject and the conditions imposed; the song which follows may be either a solo sung for the amusement of the group, or a contest in song before an umpire for some article of value to shepherds set up as a prize.

THYRSIS

Sweet are the whispers of yon pine that makes
Low music o'er the spring, and, Goatherd, sweet
Thy piping; second thou to Pan alone.
Is his the horned ram? then thine the goat.
Is his the goat? to thee shall fall the kid;
And toothsome is the flesh of unmilked kids.

GOATHERD

Shepherd, thy lay is as the noise of streams
Falling and falling aye from yon tall crag.
If for their meed the Muses claim the ewe,
Be thine the stall-fed lamb; or if they choose
The lamb, take thou the scarce less-valued ewe.

THYRSIS

Pray, by the Nymphs, pray, Goatherd, seat thee here
Against this hill-slope in the tamarisk shade,
And pipe me somewhat, while I guard thy goats.

GOATHERD

I durst not, Shepherd, O I durst not pipe
At noontide; fearing Pan, who at that hour
Rests from the toils of hunting. Harsh is he;
Wrath at his nostrils aye sits sentinel.
But, Thyrsis, thou canst sing of Daphnis' woes;
High is thy name for woodland minstrelsy:
Then rest we in the shadow of the elm
Fronting Priapus and the Fountain-nymphs.
There, where the oaks are and the Shepherd's seat,
Sing as thou sang'st erewhile, when matched with him
Of Libya, Chromis; and I'll give thee, first,
To milk, ay thrice, a goat—she suckles twins,
Yet ne'ertheless can fill two milkpails full;—
Next, a deep drinking-cup, with sweet wax scoured,
Two-handled, newly-carven, smacking yet
O' the chisel. Ivy reaches up and climbs
About its lip, gilt here and there with sprays
Of woodbine, that enwreathed about it flaunts
Her saffron fruitage. Framed therein appears
A damsel ('tis a miracle of art)
In robe and snood: and suitors at her side
With locks fair-flowing, on her right and left,
Battle with words, that fail to reach her heart.
She, laughing, glances now on this, flings now
Her chance regards on that: they, all for love
Wearied and eye-swoln, find their labour lost.
Carven elsewhere an ancient fisher stands

On the rough rocks: thereto the old man
　　with pains
Drags his great casting-net, as one that
　　toils
Full stoutly: every fibre of his frame
Seems fishing; so about the gray-beard's
　　neck
(In might a youngster yet) the sinews
　　swell.
Hard by the wave-beat sire a vineyard
　　bends
Beneath its graceful load of burnished
　　grapes;
A boy sits on the rude fence watching
　　them.
Near him two foxes: down the rows of
　　grapes
One ranging steals the ripest; one assails
With wiles the poor lad's scrip, to leave
　　him soon
Stranded and supperless. He plaits
　　meanwhile
With ears of corn a right fine cricket-
　　trap,
And fits it on a rush: for vines, for scrip,
Little he cares, enamoured of his toy.
　　The cup is hung all round with lissom
　　briar,
Triumph of Æolian art, a wondrous sight.
It was a ferryman's of Calydon:
A goat it cost me, and a great white
　　cheese.
Ne'er yet my lips came near it, virgin still
It stands. And welcome to such boon art
　　thou,
If for my sake thou'lt sing that lay of
　　lays.
I jest not: lad, sing: no songs thou'lt own
In the dim land where all things are for-
　　got.

Thyrsis

*Begin, sweet Maids, begin the wood-
　　land song.*
The voice of Thyrsis. Ætna's Thyrsis I.
Where were ye, Nymphs, oh where, while
　　Daphnis pined?
In fair Peneus' or in Pindus' glens?

For great Anapus' stream was not your
　　haunt,
Nor Ætna's cliff, nor Acis' sacred rill.
　　*Begin, sweet Maids, begin the wood-
　　land song.*
O'er him the wolves, the jackals howled
　　o'er him;
The lion in the oak-copse mourned his
　　death.
　　*Begin, sweet Maids, begin the wood-
　　land song.*
The kine and oxen stood around his feet,
The heifers and the calves wailed all for
　　him.
　　*Begin, sweet Maids, begin the wood-
　　land song.*
First from the mountain Hermes came,
　　and said,
"Daphnis, who frets thee? Lad, whom
　　lov'st thou so?"
　　*Begin, sweet Maids, begin the wood-
　　land song.*
Came herdsmen, shepherds came, and
　　goatherds came;
All asked what ailed the lad. Priapus
　　came
And said, "Why pine, poor Daphnis?
　　while the maid
Foots it round every pool and every
　　grove,
　　(*Begin, sweet Maids, begin the wood-
　　land song*)
"O lack-love and perverse, in quest of
　　thee;
Herdsman in name, but goatherd rightlier
　　called.
With eyes that yearn the goatherd marks
　　his kids
Run riot, for he fain would frisk as
　　they:
　　(*Begin, sweet Maids, begin the wood-
　　land song*):
"With eyes that yearn dost thou too mark
　　the laugh
Of maidens, for thou may'st not share
　　their glee."
Still naught the herdsman said: he
　　drained alone
His bitter portion, till the fatal end.

Begin, sweet Maids, begin the woodland song.

Came Aphrodite, smiles on her sweet face,
False smiles, for heavy was her heart, and spake:
"So, Daphnis, thou must try a fall with Love!
But stalwart Love hath won the fall of thee."

Begin, sweet Maids, begin the woodland song.

Then "Ruthless Aphrodite," Daphnis said,
"Accursed Aphrodite, foe to man!
Say'st thou mine hour is come, my sun hath set?
Dead as alive, shall Daphnis work Love woe."

Begin, sweet Maids, begin the woodland song.

"Fly to Mount Ida, where the swain (men say)
And Aphrodite—to Anchises fly:
There are oak-forests; here but galingale,
And bees that make a music round the hives.

Begin, sweet Maids, begin the woodland song.

"Adonis owed his bloom to tending flocks
And smiting hares, and bringing wild beasts down.

Begin, sweet Maids, begin the woodland song.

"Face once more Diomed: tell him 'I have slain
The herdsman Daphnis! now I challenge thee.'

Begin, sweet Maids, begin the woodland song.

"Farewell, wolf, jackal, mountain-prisoned bear!
Ye'll see no more by grove or glade or glen
Your herdsman Daphnis! Arethuse, farewell,
And the bright streams that pour down Thymbris' side.

Begin, sweet Maids, begin the woodland song.

"I am that Daphnis, who lead here my kine,
Bring here to drink my oxen and my calves.

Begin, sweet Maids, begin the woodland song.

"Pan, Pan, oh whether great Lyceum's crags
Thou haunt'st to-day, or mightier Mænalus,
Come to the Sicel isle! Abandon now
Rhium and Helice, and the mountain-cairn
(That e'en gods cherish) of Lycaon's son!

Forget, sweet Maids, forget your woodland song.

"Come, king of song, o'er this my pipe, compact
With wax and honey-breathing, arch thy lip:
For surely I am torn from life by Love.

Forget, sweet Maids, forget your woodland song.

"From thicket now and thorn let violets spring,
Now let white lilies drape the juniper,
And pines grow figs, and nature all go wrong:
For Daphnis dies. Let deer pursue the hounds,
And mountain-owls outsing the nightingale.

Forget, sweet Maids, forget your woodland song."

So spake he, and he never spoke again.
Fain Aphrodite would have raised his head;
But all his thread was spun. So down the stream
Went Daphnis: closed the waters o'er a head
Dear to the Nine, of nymphs not unbeloved.

Now give me goat and cup; that I may milk

The one, and pour the other to the Muse.
Fare ye well, Muses, o'er and o'er fare-
    well!
I'll sing strains lovelier yet in days to be.

GOATHERD.

Thyrsis, let honey and the honeycomb
Fill thy sweet mouth, and figs of Ægilus:
For ne'er cicala trilled so sweet a song.
Here is the cup: mark, friend, how sweet
    it smells:
The Hours, thou'lt say, have washed it
    in their well.
Hither, Cissætha! Thou, go milk her!
    Kids,
Be steady, or your pranks will rouse the
    ram.
                                —C. S. CALVERLEY.

THE INCANTATION

THEOCRITUS

[*Idyll* II]

Love, and usually unrequited love, is
the most frequent theme of the song.
Superstition is of course characteristic of
shepherd life, which is pictured with a
certain degree of realism—such rusticity
and vulgarity as are necessary to create
the illusion desired.

Where are the bay-leaves, Thestylis, and
    the charms?
Fetch all; with fiery wool the caldron
    crown;
Let glamour win me back my false lord's
    heart!
Twelve days the wretch hath not come
    nigh to me,
Nor made enquiry if I die or live,
Nor clamoured (oh unkindness!) at my
    door.
Sure his swift fancy wanders other-
    where,
The slave of Aphrodite and of Love.
I'm off to Timagetus' wrestling-school

At dawn, that I may see him and de-
    nounce
His doings; but I'll charm him now with
    charms.
So shine out fair, O moon! To thee I
    sing
My soft low song: to thee and Hecate
The dweller in the shades, at whose ap-
    proach
E'en the dogs quake, as on she moves
    through blood
And darkness and the barrows of the
    slain.
All hail, dread Hecate: companion me
Unto the end, and work me witcheries
Potent as Circe or Medea wrought,
Or Perimede of the golden hair!
    *Turn, magic wheel, draw homeward
        him I love.*
First we ignite the grain. Nay, pile it on:
Where are thy wits flown, timorous
    Thestylis?
Shall I be flouted, I, by such as thou?
Pile, and still say, "This pile is of his
    bones."
    *Turn, magic wheel, draw homeward
        him I love.*
Delphis racks me: I burn him in these
    bays.
As, flame-enkindled, they lift up their
    voice,
Blaze once, and not a trace is left be-
    hind:
So waste his flesh to powder in yon
    fire!
    *Turn, magic wheel, draw homeward
        him I love.*
E'en as I melt, not uninspired, the wax,
May Mindian Delphis melt this hour with
    love:
And, swiftly as this brazen wheel whirls
    round,
May Aphrodite whirl him to my door.
    *Turn, magic wheel, draw homeward
        him I love.*
Next burn the husks. Hell's adamantine
    floor
And aught that else stands firm can
    Artemis move.

Thestylis, the hounds bay up and down
the town:
The goddess stands i' the crossroads:
sound the gongs.
*Turn, magic wheel, draw homeward
him I love.*
Hushed are the voices of the winds and
seas;
But O not hushed the voice of my de-
spair.
He burns my being up, who left me here
No wife, no maiden, in my misery.
*Turn, magic wheel, draw homeward
him I love.*
Thrice I pour out; speak thrice, sweet
mistress, thus:
"What face soe'er hangs o'er him be for-
got
Clean as, in Dia, Theseus (legends say)
Forgat his Ariadne's locks of love."
*Turn, magic wheel, draw homeward
him I love.*
The coltsfoot grows in Arcady, the
weed
That drives the mountain-colts and swift
mares wild.
Like them may Delphis rave: so, maniac-
wise,
Race from his burnished brethren home
to me.
*Turn, magic wheel, draw homeward
him I love.*
He lost this tassel from his robe; which
I
Shred thus, and cast it on the raging
flames.
Ah baleful Love! why, like the marsh-
born leech,
Cling to my flesh, and drain my dark
veins dry?
*Turn, magic wheel, draw homeward
him I love.*
From a crushed eft tomorrow he shall
drink
Death! But now, Thestylis, take these
herbs and smear
That threshold o'er, whereto at heart I
cling
Still, still—albeit he thinks scorn of me—

And spit, and say, " 'Tis Delphis' bones
I smear."
*Turn, magic wheel, draw homeward
him I love.*
Now all alone, I'll weep a love whence
sprung,
When born? Who wrought my sorrow?
Anaxo came,
Her basket in her hand, to Artemis' grove.
Bound for the festival, troops of forest
beasts
Stood round, and in the midst a lioness.
*Bethink thee, mistress Moon, whence
came my love.*
Theucharidas' slave, my Thracian nurse
now dead
Then my near neighbor, prayed me and
implored
To see the pageant: I, the poor doomed
thing,
Went with her, trailing a fine silken train,
And gathering round me Clearista's robe.
*Bethink thee, mistress Moon, whence
came my love.*
Now, the mid-highway reached by
Lycon's farm,
Delphis and Eudamippus passed me by.
With beards as lustrous as the wood-
bine's gold
And breasts more sheeny than myself, O
Moon,
Fresh from the wrestler's glorious toil
they came.
*Bethink thee, mistress Moon, whence
came my love.*
I saw, I raved, smit (weakling) to my
heart.
My beauty withered, and I cared no more
For all the pomp; and how I gained my
home
I know not: some strange fever wasted
me.
Ten nights and days I lay upon my bed.
*Bethink thee, mistress Moon, whence
came my love.*
And wan became my flesh, as 't had been
dyed,
And all my hair streamed off, and there
was left

But bones and skin. Whose threshold
crossed I not,
Or missed what grandam's hut who dealt
in charms?
For no light thing was this, and time
sped on.
  *Bethink thee, mistress Moon, whence
  came my love.*
At last I spake the truth to that my
maid:
"Seek, an thou canst, some cure for my
sore pain.
Alas, I am all the Mindian's! But be-
gone,
And watch by Timagetus' wrestling-
school:
There doth he haunt, there soothly take
his rest.
  *Bethink thee, mistress Moon, whence
  came my love.*
"Find him alone: nod softly: say, 'she
waits';
And bring him." So I spake: she went
her way,
And brought the lustrous-limbed one to
my roof.
And I, the instant I beheld him step
Lightfooted o'er the threshold of my
door,
  (*Bethink thee, mistress Moon, whence
  came my love,*)
Became all cold like snow, and from my
brow
Brake the damp dewdrops: utterance I
had none,
Not e'en such utterance as a babe may
make
That babbles to its mother in its dreams;
But all my fair frame stiffened into wax.
  *Bethink thee, mistress Moon, whence
  came my love.*
He bent his pitiless eyes on me; looked
down,
And sate him on my couch, and sitting,
said:
"Thou hast gained on me, Simætha, (e'en
as I
Gained once on young Philinus in the
race),

Bidding me hither ere I came unasked.
  *Bethink thee, mistress Moon, whence
  came my love.*
"For I had come, by Eros I had come,
This night, with comrades twain or may-
be more,
The fruitage of the Wine-god in my
robe,
And, wound about my brow with ribands
red,
The silver leaves so dear to Heracles.
  *Bethink thee, mistress Moon, whence
  came my love.*
"Had ye said 'Enter,' well; for 'mid my
peers
High is my name for goodliness and
speed:
I had kissed that sweet mouth once and
gone my way.
But had the door been barred, and I
thrust out,
With brand and axe would we have
stormed ye then.
  *Bethink thee, mistress Moon, whence
  came my love.*
"Now be my thanks recorded, first to
Love,
Next to thee, maiden, who didst pluck me
out,
A half-burned helpless creature, from the
flames,
And badst me hither. It is Love that
lights
A fire more fierce than his of Lipara;
  *Bethink thee, mistress Moon, whence
  came my love.*
"Scares, mischief-mad, the maiden from
her bower,
The bride from her warm couch." He
spake: and I,
A willing listener, sat, my hand in his,
Among the cushions, and his cheek
touched mine,
Each hotter than its wont, and we dis-
coursed
In soft low language. Need I prate to
thee,
Sweet Moon, of all we said and all we
did?

Till yesterday he found no fault with
me,
Nor I with him. But lo, to-day there
came
Philista's mother—hers who flutes to
me—
With her Melampo's; just when up the
sky
Gallop the mares that chariot rose-limbed
Dawn:
And divers tales she brought me, with
the rest
How Delphis loved, she knew not rightly
whom:
But this she knew; that of the rich wine
aye
He poured "to Love"; and at the last had
fled,
To line, she deemed, the fair one's hall
with flowers.
Such was my visitor's tale, and it was
true:
For thrice, nay four times, daily he would
stroll
Hither, leave here full oft his Dorian
flask:
Now—'tis a fortnight since I saw his
face.
Doth he then treasure something sweet
elsewhere?
Am I forgot? I'll charm him now with
charms.
But let him try me more, and by the
Fates
He'll soon be knocking at the gates of
hell.
Spells of such power are in this chest of
mine,
Learned, lady, from mine host in Pales-
tine.

Lady, farewell: turn ocean-ward thy
steeds:
As I have purposed, so shall I fulfil.
Farewell, thou bright-faced Moon! Ye
stars, farewell,
That wait upon the car of noiseless
Night.
—C. S. Calverley.

The Herdsmen

THEOCRITUS

[Idyll IV]

Here the song is subordinated to a
realistic dialogue of rustic banter and
gossip, presenting in brief compass the
people and their interests after the manner of the mime.

BATTUS. Who owns these cattle,
Corydon? Philondas? Prythee say.
CORYDON. No, Ægon: and he gave
them me to tend while he's away.
BATTUS. Dost milk them in the gloam-
ing, when none is nigh to see?
CORYDON. The old man brings the
calves to suck, and keeps an eye on
me.
BATTUS. And to what region then
hath flown the cattle's rightful lord?
CORYDON. Hast thou not heard? With
Milo he vanished Elisward.
BATTUS. How! was the wrestler's oil
e'er yet so much as seen by him?
CORYDON. Men say he rivals Heracles
in lustiness of limb.
BATTUS. I'm Polydeuces' match (or
so my mother says) and more.
CORYDON. —So off he started; with
a spade, and of these ewes a score.
BATTUS. This Milo will be teaching
wolves how they should raven next.
CORYDON. —And by these bellowings
his kine proclaim how sore they're
vexed.
BATTUS. Poor kine! they've found
their master a sorry knave indeed.
CORYDON. They're poor enough, I
grant you: they have not heart to
feed.
BATTUS. Look at that heifer! sure
there's naught, save bare bones, left
of her.
Pray, does she browse on dewdrops, as
does the grasshopper?
CORYDON. Not she, by heaven! She
pastures now by Æsarus' glades,

And handfuls fair I pluck her there of
    young and green grass blades;
Now bounds about Latymnus, that
    gathering-place of shades.
    BATTUS. That bull again, the red one,
    my word but he is lean!
I wish the Sybarite burghers aye may
    offer to the queen
Of heaven as pitiful a beast: those
    burghers are so mean!
    CORYDON. Yet to the Salt Lake's edges
    I drive him, I can swear;
Up Physcus, up Neæthus' side—he lacks
    not victual there,
With dittany and endive and foxglove for
    his fare.
    BATTUS. Well, well! I pity Ægon.
    His cattle, go they must
To rack and ruin, all because vain-glory
    was his lust.
The pipe that erst he fashioned is doubt-
    less scored with rust?
    CORYDON. Nay, by the Nymphs!
    That pipe he left to me, the self-
    same day
He made for Pisa: I am too a minstrel in
    my way:
Well the flute-part in 'Pyrrhus' and in
    'Glauca' can I play.
I sing too 'Here's to Croton' and 'Zacyn-
    thus O 'tis fair,'
And 'Eastward to Lacinium:'—the
    bruiser Milo there
His single self ate eighty loaves; there
    also did he pull
Down from its mountain dwelling, by one
    hoof grasped, a bull,
And gave it Amaryllis: the maidens
    screamed with fright;
As for the owner of the bull he only
    laughed outright.
    BATTUS. Sweet Amaryllis! thou
    alone, though dead, art unforgot.
Dearer than thou, whose light is
    quenched, my very goats are not.
Oh for the all-unkindly fate that's fallen
    to my lot!
    CORYDON. Cheer up, brave lad! to-
    morrow may ease thee of thy pain:

Aye for the living are there hopes, past
    hoping are the slain:
And now Zeus sends us sunshine, and now
    he sends us rain.
    BATTUS. I'm better. Beat those
    young ones off! E'en now their
    teeth attack
That olive's shoots, the graceless brutes!
    back, with your white face, back!
    CORYDON. Back to thy hill, Cymætha!
    Great Pan, how deaf thou art!
I shall be with thee presently, and in the
    end thou'lt smart.
I warn thee, keep thy distance. Look,
    up she creeps again!
Oh were my hare-crook in my hand, I'd
    give it to her then!
    BATTUS. For heaven's sake, Corydon,
    look here! Just now a bramble-
    spike
Ran, there, into my instep—and oh how
    deep they strike,
Those lancewood-shafts! A murrain
    light on that calf, I say!
I got it gaping after her. Canst thou
    discern it, pray?
    CORYDON. Ay, ay; and here I have it,
    safe in my finger-nails.
    BATTUS. Eh! at how slight a matter
    how tall a warrior quails!
    CORYDON. Ne'er range the hill-crest,
    Battus, all sandal-less and bare:
Because the thistle and the thorn lift aye
    their plumed heads there.
    BATTUS. —Say, Corydon, does that
    old man we wot of (tell me
    please!)
Still haunt the dark-browed little girl
    whom once he used to tease?
    CORYDON. Ay my poor boy, that doth
    he: I saw them yesterday
Down by the byre; and, trust me, loving
    enough were they.
    BATTUS. Well done, my veteran light-
    o'-love! In deeming thee mere
    man,
I wronged the sire: some Satyr he, or an
    uncouth-limbed Pan.
              —C. S. CALVERLEY.

THE HARVEST HOME

THEOCRITUS

[Idyll VII]

The shepherd lives close to nature, a lover of all wild life, extremely sensitive to the changing seasons. Though he is forever complaining about the bitterness of love, yet he lives in sunshine under the open sky and is at heart a happy man.

Once on a time did Eucritus and I
(With us Amyntas) to the riverside
Steal from the city. For Lycopeus' sons
Were that day busy with the harvest-
    home,
Antigenes and Phrasidemus, sprung
(If aught thou holdest by the good old
    names)
By Clytia from great Chalcon—him who
    erst
Planted one stalwart knee against the
    rock,
And lo, beneath his foot Burine's rill
Brake forth, and at its side poplar and
    elm
Shewed isles of pleasant shadow, greenly
    roofed
By tufted leaves. Scarce midway were
    we now,
Nor yet descried the tomb of Brasilas:
When thanks be to the Muses, there drew
    near
A wayfarer from Crete, young Lycidas.
The horned herd was his care: a glance
    might tell
So much: for every inch a herdsman he.
Slung o'er his shoulder was a ruddy hide
Torn from a he-goat, shaggy, tangle-
    haired,
That reeked of rennet yet: a broad belt
    clasped
A patched cloak round his breast, and
    for a staff
A gnarled wild-olive bough his right
    hand bore.
Soon with a quiet smile he spoke—his eye
Twinkled, and laughter sat upon his lip:

"And whither ploddest thou thy weary
    way
Beneath the noontide sun, Simichidas?
For now the lizard sleeps upon the wall,
The crested lark folds now his wandering
    wing.
Dost speed, a bidden guest, to some
    reveller's board?
Or townward to the treading of the
    grape?
For lo! recoiling from thy hurrying feet
The pavement stones ring out right
    merrily."
Then I: "Friend Lycid, all men say that
    none
Of haymakers or herdsmen is thy match
At piping: and my soul is glad thereat.
Yet, to speak sooth, I think to rival thee.
Now look, this road holds holiday to-day:
For banded brethren solemnise a feast
To richly-dight Demeter, thanking her
For her good gifts: since with no grudg-
    ing hand
Hath the boon goddess filled the wheaten
    floors.
So come: the way, the day, is thine as
    mine:
Try we our woodcraft—each may learn
    from each.
I am, as thou, a clarion-voice of song;
All hail me chief of minstrels. But I am
    not,
Heaven knows, o'er credulous: no, I
    scarce can yet
(I think) outvie Philetas, nor the bard
Of Samos, champion of Sicilian song.
They are as cicadas challenged by a frog."

I spake to gain mine ends; and laugh-
    ing light
He said: "Accept this club, as thou'rt
    indeed
A born truth-teller, shaped by heaven's
    own hand!
I hate your builders who would rear a
    a house
High as Oromedon's mountain-pinnacle:
I hate your song-birds too, whose cuckoo-
    cry

Struggles (in vain) to match the Chian
   bard.
But come, we'll sing forthwith, Simi-
   chidas,
Our woodland music: and for my part
   I—
List, comrade, if you like the simpler air
I forged among the uplands yesterday.

"Safe be my true-love convoyed o'er
   the main
To Mitylene—though the southern blast
Chase the lithe waves, while westward
   slant the Kids,
Or low above the verge Orion stand—
If from Love's furnace she will rescue me,
For Lycidas is parched with hot desire.
Let halcyons lay the sea-waves and the
   winds,
Northwind and Westwind, that in shores
   far-off
Flutters the seaweed—halcyons, of all
   birds
Whose prey is on the waters, held most
   dear
By the green Nereids: yea let all things
   smile
On her to Mitylene voyaging,
And in fair harbour may she ride at last.
I on that day, a chaplet woven of dill
Or rose or simple violet on my brow,
Will draw the wine of Pteleas from the
   cask
Stretched by the ingle. They shall roast
   me beans,
And elbow-deep in thyme and asphodel
And quaintly-curling parsley shall be
   piled
My bed of rushes, where in royal ease
I sit, and thinking of my darling, drain
With stedfast lips the liquor to the dregs.
I'll have a pair of pipers, shepherds both,
This from Acharnæ, from Lycope that;
And Tityrus shall be near me and shall
   sing
How the swain Daphnis loved the
   stranger-maid;
And how he ranged the fells, and how
   the oaks

(Such oaks as Himera's banks are green
   withal)
Sang dirges o'er him waning fast away
Like snow on Athos, or on Hæmus high,
Or Rhodope, or utmost Caucasus.
And he shall sing me how the big chest
   held
(All through the maniac malice of his
   lord)
A living goatherd: how the round-faced
   bees,
Lured from their meadow by the cedar-
   smell,
Fed him with daintiest flowers, because
   the Muse
Had made his throat a well-spring of
   sweet song.
Happy Cometas, this sweet lot was thine!
Thee the chest prisoned, for thee the
   honey-bees
Toiled, as thou slavedst out the mellow-
   ing year:
And oh hadst thou been numbered with
   the quick
In my day! I had led thy pretty goats
About the hill-side, listening to thy
   voice:
While thou hadst lain thee down 'neath
   oak or pine,
Divine Cometas, warbling pleasantly."

He spake and paused; and thereupon
   spake I.
"I too, friend Lycid, as I ranged the fells,
Have learned much lore and pleasant
   from the Nymphs,
Whose fame mayhap hath reached the
   throne of Zeus.
But this wherewith I'll grace thee ranks
   the first:
Thou listen, since the Muses like thee
   well.

"On me the young Loves sneezed: for
   hapless I
Am fain of Myrto as the goats of Spring.
But my best friend Aratus inly pines
For one who loves him not. Aristis
   saw—

(A wondrous seer is he, whose lute and lay
Shrined Apollo's self would scarce disdain)—
How love had scorched Aratus to the bone.
O Pan, who hauntest Homole's fair champaign,
Bring the soft charmer, whosoe'er it be,
Unbid to his sweet arms—so, gracious Pan,
May ne'er thy ribs and shoulderblades be lashed
With squills by young Arcadians, whensoe'er
They are scant of supper! But should this my prayer
Mislike thee, then on nettles mayest thou sleep,
Dinted and sore all over from their claws!
Then mayst thou lodge amid Edonian hills
By Hebrus, in midwinter; there subsist,
The Bear thy neighbour: and, in summer, range
With the far Æthiops 'neath the Blemmyan rocks
Where Nile is no more seen! But O ye Loves,
Whose cheeks are like pink apples, quit your homes
By Hyetis, or Byblis' pleasant rill,
Or fair Dione's rocky pedestal,
And strike that fair one with your arrows, strike
The ill-starred damsel who disdains my friend.
And lo, what is she but an o'er-ripe pear?
The girls all cry 'Her bloom is on the wane.'
We'll watch, Aratus, at that porch no more,
Nor waste shoe-leather: let the morning cock
Crow to wake others up to numb despair!
Let Molon, and none else, that ordeal brave:
While we make ease our study, and secure

Some witch, to charm all evil from our door."

I ceased. He smiling sweetly as before,
Gave me the staff, 'The Muses' parting gift,'
And leftward sloped tow'rd Pyxa. We the while,
Bent us to Phrasydeme's, Eucritus and I,
And baby-faced Amyntas: there we lay
Half-buried in a couch of fragrant reed
And fresh-cut vineleaves, who so glad as we?
A wealth of elm and poplar shook o'erhead;
Hard by, a sacred spring flowed gurgling on
From the Nymphs' grot, and in the sombre boughs
The sweet cicada chirped laboriously.
Hid in the thick thorn-bushes far away
The treefrog's note was heard; the crested lark
Sang with the goldfinch; turtles made their moan,
And o'er the fountain hung the gilded bee.
All of rich summer smacked, of autumn all:
Pears at our feet, and apples at our side
Rolled in luxuriance; branches on the ground
Sprawled, overweighed with damsons; while we brushed
From the cask's head the crust of four long years.
Say, ye who dwell upon Parnassian peaks,
Nymphs of Castalia, did old Chiron e'er
Set before Heracles a cup so brave
In Pholus' cavern—did the nectarous draughts
Cause the Anapian shepherd, in whose hand
Rocks were as pebbles, Polypheme the strong,
Featly to foot it o'er the cottage lawns:—
As, ladies, ye bid flow that day for us
All by Demeter's shrine at harvest-home?
Beside whose cornstalks may I oft again

Plant my broad fan: while she stands by
 and smiles,
Poppies and cornsheaves on each laden
 arm.

—C. S. CALVERLEY.

THE CYCLOPS

THEOCRITUS

[*Idyll* XI]

The shepherd, like the elegist, finds
relief for himself in song, and believes in
its power to win what he longs for.

Methinks all nature hath no cure for
 Love,
Plaster or unguent, Nicias, saving one;
And this is light and pleasant to a man,
Yet hard withal to compass—minstrelsy.
As well thou wottest, being thyself a
 leech,
And a prime favourite of those Sisters
 nine.
'Twas thus our Giant lived a life of ease,
Old Polyphemus, when, the down scarce
 seen
On lip and chin, he wooed the ocean
 nymph:
No curlypated rose-and-apple wooer,
But a fell madman, blind to all but love.
Oft from the green grass foldward fared
 his sheep
Unbid: while he upon the windy beach,
Singing his Galatea, sat and pined
From dawn to dusk, an ulcer at his heart:
Great Aphrodite's shaft had fixed it there.
Yet found he that one cure: he sate him
 down
On the tall cliff, and seaward looked, and
 sang:—
"White Galatea, why disdain thy love?
White as a pressed cheese, delicate as the
 lamb,
Wild as the heifer, soft as summer
 grapes!
If sweet sleep chain me, here thou walk'st
 at large;

If sweet sleep loose me, straightway thou
 art gone,
Scared like a sheep that sees the grey
 wolf near.
I loved thee, maiden, when thou cam'st
 long since,
To pluck the hyacinth-blossom on the
 fell,
Thou and my mother, piloted by me.
I saw thee, see thee still, from that day
 forth
For ever; but 'tis naught, ay naught, to
 thee.
I know, sweet maiden, why thou art so
 coy:
Shaggy and huge, a single eyebrow spans
From ear to ear my forehead, whence one
 eye
Gleams, and an o'erbroad nostril tops my
 lip.
Yet I, this monster, feed a thousand sheep
That yield me sweetest draughts at
 milking-tide:
In summer, autumn, or midwinter, still
Fails not my cheese; my milkpail aye
 o'erflows.
Then I can pipe as ne'er did Giant
 yet,
Singing our loves—ours, honey, thine and
 mine—
At the dead of night: and hinds I rear
 eleven
(Each with her fawn) and bearcubs four,
 for thee.
Oh come to me—thou shalt not rue the
 day—
And let the mad seas beat against the
 shore!
'Twere sweet to haunt my cave the live-
 long night:
Laurel and cypress tall, and ivy dun,
And vines of sumptuous fruitage, all are
 there:
And a cold spring that pine-clad Ætna
 flings
Down from the white snow's midst, a
 draught for gods!
Who would not change for this the ocean-
 waves?

"But thou mislik'st my hair? Well, oaken logs
Are here, and embers yet aglow with fire.
Burn (if thou wilt) my heart out, and mine eye,
Mine only eye wherein is my delight.
Oh why was I not born a finny thing,
To float unto thy side and kiss thy hand,
Denied thy lips—and bring thee lilies white
And crimson-petalled poppies' dainty bloom!
Nay—summer hath his flowers and autumn his;
I could not bring all these the selfsame day.
Lo, should some mariner hither oar his road,
Sweet, he shall teach me straightway how to swim,
That haply I may learn what bliss ye find
In your sea-homes. O Galatea, come
Forth from yon waves, and coming forth forget
(As I do, sitting here) to get thee home:
And feed my flocks and milk them, nothing loth,
And pour the rennet in to fix my cheese!

"The blame's my mother's; she is false to me;
Spake thee ne'er yet one sweet word for my sake,
Though day by day she sees me pine and pine.
I'll feign strange throbbings in my head and feet
To anguish her—as I am anguished now."

O Cyclops, Cylops, where are flown thy wits?
Go plait rush-baskets, lop the olive-boughs
To feed thy lambkins, 'twere the shrewder part.
Chase not the recreant, milk the willing ewe:
The world hath Galateas fairer yet.

"—Many a fair damsel bids me sport with her
The livelong night, and smiles if I give ear.
On land at least I still am somebody."

Thus did the Giant feed his love on song,
And gained more ease than may be bought with gold.
—C. S. CALVERLEY.

THE FESTIVAL OF ADONIS

THEOCRITUS

[Idyll XV]

This picture of the women of Alexandria is in sharp contrast with the pastoral scenes of Sicily. The poet's interest is in the life of the common people, whether they inhabit the metropolis or the rural districts of Sicily.

GORGO. Praxinoa in?
PRAXINOA. Yes, Gorgo dear! At last!
That you're here now's a marvel! See to a chair,
A cushion, Eunoa!
GORGO. I lack naught.
PRAXINOA. Sit down.
GORGO. Oh, what a thing is spirit! Here I am,
Praxinoa, safe at last from all that crowd
And all those chariots—every street a mass
Of boots and uniforms! And the road, my dear,
Seemed endless—you live now so far away!
PRAXINOA. This land's-end den—I cannot call it house—
My madcap hired to keep us twain apart
And stir up strife. 'Twas like him, odious pest!
GORGO. Nay call not, dear, your lord, your Deinon, names
To the babe's face. Look how he stares at you!

There, baby dear, she never meant Papa!
It understands, by'r lady! Dear Papa!
   PRAXINOA. Well, yesterday (that
    means what day you like)
'Papa' had rouge and hair-powder to buy;
He brought back salt! this oaf of six-
    foot-one!
   GORGO. Just such another is that pick-
    pocket
My Diocleides. He bought t' other day
Six fleeces at seven drachms, his last
    exploit.
What were they? scraps of worn-out
    pedlar's-bags,
Sheer trash.—But put your cloak and
    mantle on;
And we'll to Ptolemy's, the sumptuous
    king,
To see the Adonis. As I hear, the queen
Provides us something gorgeous.
   PRAXINOA.   Ay, the grand
Can do things grandly.
   GORGO.   When you've seen yourself,
What tales you'll have to tell to those
    who've not.
'Twere time we started!
   PRAXINOA.   All time's holiday
With idlers! Eunoa, pampered minx, the
    jug!
Set it down here—you cats would sleep
    all day
On cushions—Stir yourself, fetch water,
    quick!
Water's our first want. How she holds
    the jug!
Now, pour—not, cormorant, in that
    wasteful way—
You've drenched my dress, bad luck t'
    you! There, enough:
I have made such toilet as my fates
    allowed.
Now for the key of the plate-chest.
    Bring it, quick!
   GORGO. My dear, that full pelisse be-
    comes you well.
What did it stand you in straight off the
    loom?
   PRAXINOA. Don't ask me, Gorgo: two
    good pounds and more.

Then I gave all my mind to trimming it.
   GORGO. Well, 'tis a great success.
   PRAXINOA.   I think it is.
My mantle, Eunoa, and my parasol!
Arrange me nicely. Babe, you'll bide at
    home!
Horses would bite you—Boo! Yes, cry
    your fill,
But we won't have you maimed. Now
    let's be off.
You, Phrygia, take and nurse the tiny
    thing:
Call the dog in: make fast the outer
    door!

Gods! what a crowd! How, when shall
    we get past
This nuisance, these unending ant-like
    swarms?
Yet, Ptolemy, we owe thee thanks for
    much
Since heaven received thy sire! No mis-
    creant now
Creeps Thug-like up, to maul the passer-
    by.
What games men play erewhile—men
    shaped in crime,
Birds of a feather, rascals every one!
—We're done for, Gorgo darling—here
    they are,
The Royal horse! Sweet sir, don't
    trample me!
That bay—the savage!—reared up
    straight on end!
Fly, Eunoa, can't you? Doggedly she
    stands.
He'll be his rider's death! How glad I
    am
My babe's at home.
   GORGO.   Praxinoa, never mind!
See, we're before them now, and they're
    in line.
   PRAXINOA. There, I'm myself. But
    from a child I feared
Horses, and slimy snakes. But haste we
    on:
A surging multitude is close behind.
   GORGO (to OLD LADY). From the
    palace, mother?

OLD LADY. Ay, child.

GORGO.   Is it fair
Of access?

OLD LADY. Trying brought the Greeks
to Troy.

Young ladies, they must try who would
succeed.

GORGO. The crone hath said her oracle
and gone.

Women know all—how Adam married
Eve.

—Praxinoa, look what crowds are round
the door!

PRAXINOA. Fearful! Your hand,
please, Gorgo. Eunoa, you

Hold Eutychis—hold tight or you'll be
lost.

We'll enter in a body—hold us fast!

Oh dear, my muslin dress is torn in two,

Gorgo, already! Pray, good gentlemen,
(And happiness be yours) respect my
robe!

STRANGER. I could not if I would—
nathless I will.

PRAXINOA. They come in hundreds,
and they push like swine.

STRANGER. Lady, take courage: it is
all well now.

PRAXINOA. And now and ever be it
well with thee,

Sweet man, for shielding us! An honest
soul

And kindly. Oh! they're smothering
Eunoa:

Push, coward! That's right! 'All in,'
the bridegroom said

And locked the door upon himself and
bride.

GORGO. Praxinoa, look! Note well
this broidery first.

How exquisitely fine—too good for earth!

Empress Athene, what strange sempstress
wrought

Such work? What painter painted,
realized

Such pictures? Just like life they stand
or move,

Facts and not fancies! What a thing is
man!

How bright, how lifelike on his silvern
couch

Lies, with youth's bloom scarce shadowing his cheek,

That dear Adonis, lovely e'en in death!

A STRANGER. Bad luck t' you, cease
your senseless pidgeon's prate!

Their brogue is killing—every word a
drawl!

GORGO. Where did he spring from? Is
our prattle aught

To you, Sir? Order your own slaves
about:

You're ordering Syracusan ladies now!

Corinthians bred (to tell you one fact
more)

As was Bellerophon: islanders in speech,

For Dorians may talk Doric, I presume?

PRAXINOA. Persephone! none lords it
over me,

Save one! No scullion's-wage for us
from *you!*

GORGO. Hush, dear. The Argive's
daughter's going to sing

The Adonis: that accomplished vocalist

Who has no rival in *"The Sailor's
Grave."*

Observe her attitudinizing now.

SONG

Queen, who lov'st Golgi and the Sicel
hill

And Ida; Aphrodite radiant-eyed;

The stealthy-footed Hours from Acheron's
rill

Brought once again Adonis to thy
side

How changed in twelve short months!
They travel slow,

Those precious Hours: we hail their
advent still,

For blessings do they bring to all below.

O Sea-born! thou didst erst, or legend
lies,

Shed on a woman's soul thy grace benign,

And Berenice's dust immortalize.

O called by many names, at many a
shrine!

For thy sweet sake doth Berenice's child
(Herself a second Helen) deck with all
That's fair, Adonis. On his right are piled
Ripe apples fallen from the oak-tree tall;
And silver caskets at his left support
Toy-gardens, Syrian scents enshrined in gold
And alabaster, cakes of every sort
That in their ovens the pastrywomen mould,
When with white meal they mix all flowers that bloom,
Oil-cakes and honey-cakes. There stand portrayed
Each bird, each butterfly; and in the gloom
Of foliage climbing high, and downward weighed
By graceful blossoms, do the young Loves play
Like nightingales, and perch on every tree,
And flit, to try their wings, from spray to spray.
Then see the gold, the ebony! Only see
The ivory-carven eagles, bearing up
To Zeus the boy who fills his royal cup!
Soft as a dream, such tapestry gleams o'erhead
As the Milesian's self would gaze on, charmed.
But sweet Adonis hath his own sweet bed:
Next Aphrodite sleeps the roseate-armed,
A bridegroom of eighteen or nineteen years.
Kiss the smooth boyish lip—there's no sting there!
The bride hath found her own: all bliss be hers!
And him at dewy dawn we'll troop to bear
Down where the breakers hiss against the shore:

There, with dishevelled dress and unbound hair,
Bare-bosomed all, our descant wild we'll pour:
"Thou haunt'st, Adonis, earth and heaven in turn,
Alone of heroes. Agamemnon ne'er
Could compass this, nor Aias stout and stern:
Not Hector, eldest-born of her who bare
Ten sons, not Patroclus, nor safe-returned
From Ilion Pyrrhus, such distinction earned:
Nor, elder yet, the Lapithæ, the sons
Of Pelops and Deucalion; or the crown
Of Greece, Pelasgians. Gracious may'st thou be,
Adonis, now: pour new-year's blessings down!
Right welcome dost thou come, Adonis dear:
Come when thou wilt, thou'lt find a welcome here."

GORGO. 'Tis fine, Praxinoa! How I envy her
Her learning, and still more her luscious voice!
We must go home: my husband's supper-less:
And in that state, the man's just vinegar.
Don't cross his path when hungry! So farewell,
Adonis, and be housed 'mid welfare aye!
—C. S. CALVERLEY.

THE LAMENT FOR ADONIS

BION

[Idyll I]

Bion of Smyrna, of the late second century B.C., wrote idylls after the manner of Theocritus. Nothing is known of his life, and very little of his work survives.

The festival of Adonis was celebrated by the singing of two songs, a wedding-song and a dirge. This poem is an example of the latter.

I

I mourn for Adonis—Adonis is dead,
    Fair Adonis is dead and the Loves are lamenting.
Sleep, Cypris, no more on thy purple-strewed bed:
    Arise, wretch stoled in black; beat thy breast unrelenting,
And shriek to the worlds, "Fair Adonis is dead!"

II

I mourn for Adonis—the Loves are lamenting.
    He lies on the hills in his beauty and death;
    The white tusk of a boar has transpierced his white thigh.
    Cytherea grows mad at his thin gasping breath,
While the black blood drips down on the pale ivory,
    And his eyeballs lie quenched with the weight of his brows,
The rose fades from his lips, and upon them just parted
    The kiss dies the goddess consents not to lose,
Though the kiss of the Dead cannot make her glad hearted:
    He knows not who kisses him dead in the dews.

III

I mourn for Adonis—the Loves are lamenting.
    Deep, deep in the thigh is Adonis's wound,

But a deeper is Cypris's bosom presenting.
    The youth lieth dead while his dogs howl around,
And the nymphs weep aloud from the mists of the hill,
    And the poor Aphrodite, with tresses unbound,
All dishevelled, unsandaled, shrieks mournful and shrill
    Through the dusk of the groves. The thorns, tearing her feet,
Gather up the red flower of her blood which is holy,
    Each footstep she takes; and the valleys repeat
The sharp cry she utters and draw it out slowly.
    She calls on her spouse, her Assyrian, on him
Her own youth, while the dark blood spreads over his body,
    The chest taking hue from the gash in the limb,
And the bosom, once ivory, turning to ruddy.

IV

Ah, ah, Cytherea! the Loves are lamenting.
    She lost her fair spouse and so lost her fair smile:
When he lived she was fair, by the whole world's consenting,
    Whose fairness is dead with him: woe worth the while!
All the mountains above and the oaklands below
    Murmur, ah, ah, Adonis! the streams overflow
Aphrodite's deep wail; river-fountains in pity
    Weep soft in the hills, and the flowers as they blow
Redden outward with sorrow, while all hear her go
    With the song of her sadness through mountain and city.

V

Ah, ah, Cytherea! Adonis is dead,
  Fair Adonis is dead—Echo answers,
    Adonis!
Who weeps not for Cypris, when bowing
  her head
  She stares at the wound where it gapes
    and astonies?
—When, ah, ah!—she saw how the blood
  ran away
  And empurpled the thigh, and, with
    wild hands flung out,
Said with sobs: "Stay, Adonis! unhappy
  one, stay,
  Let me feel thee once more, let me ring
    thee about
With the clasp of my arms, and press kiss
  into kiss!
  Wait a little, Adonis, and kiss me
    again,
For the last time, beloved,—and but so
  much of this
  That the kiss may learn life from the
    warmth of the strain!
—Till thy breath shall exude from thy
  soul to my mouth,
  To my heart, and, the love-charm I
    once more receiving
May drink thy love in it and keep of a
  truth
  That one kiss in the place of Adonis
    the living.
Thou fliest me, mournful one, fliest me
  far,
  My Adonis, and seekest the Acheron
    portal,—
To Hell's cruel King goest down with a
  scar,
  While I weep and live on like a
    wretched immortal,
And follow no step! O Persephone, take
  him,
  My husband!—thou'rt better and
    brighter than I,
So all beauty flows down to thee: *I* can-
  not make him
  Look up at my grief; there's despair in
    my cry,

Since I wail for Adonis who died to me—
  died to me—
  Then, I fear *thee!*—Art thou dead, my
    Adored?
Passion ends like a dream in the sleep
  that's denied to me,
  Cypris is widowed, the Loves seek their
    lord
All the house through in vain. Charm of
  cestus has ceased
  With thy clasp! O too bold in the
    hunt past preventing,
Ay, mad, thou so fair, to have strife with
  a beast!"
  Thus the goddess wailed on—and the
    Loves are lamenting.

VI

I mourn for Adonis—Adonis is dead.
  Weep no more in the woods, Cytherea,
    thy lover!
So, well: make a place for his corse in
  thy bed,
  With the purples thou sleepest in,
    under and over.
He's fair though a corse—a fair corse,
  like a sleeper.
  Lay him soft in the silks he had pleas-
    ure to fold
When, beside thee at night, holy dreams
  deep and deeper
  Enclosed his young life on the couch
    made of gold.
Love him still, poor Adonis; cast on him
  together
  The crowns and the flowers: since he
    died from the place,
Why, let all die with him; let blossoms
  go wither,
  Rain myrtles and olive-buds down on
    his face.
Rain the myrrh down, let all that is best
  fall a-pining,
  Since the myrrh of his life from thy
    keeping is swept.
Pale he lay, thine Adonis, in purples re-
  clining;

The Loves raised their voices around
him and wept.
They have shorn their bright curls off to
cast on Adonis;
One treads on his bow,—on his arrows,
another,—
One breaks up a well-feathered quiver,
and one is
Bent low at a sandal, untying the
strings,
And one carries the vases of gold from
the springs,
While one washes the wound,—and behind them a brother
Fans down on the body sweet air with
his wings.

VII

Cytherea herself now the Loves are la-
menting.
Each torch at the door Hymenæus
blew out;
And, the marriage-wreath dropping its
leaves as repenting,
No more "Hymen, Hymen," is chanted
about,
But the *ai ai* instead—"Ai alas!" is be-
gun
For Adonis, and then follows "Ai
Hymenæus!"
The Graces are weeping for Cinyris'
son,
Sobbing low each to each, "His fair
eyes cannot see us!"
Their wail strikes more shrill than the
sadder Dione's.
The Fates mourn aloud for Adonis,
Adonis,
Deep chanting; he hears not a word that
they say:
He *would* hear, but Persephone has
him in keeping.
—Cease moan, Cytherea! leave pomps
for to-day,
And weep new when a new year refits
thee for weeping.
—Elizabeth Barrett Browning.

THE EPITAPH OF BION

MOSCHUS

[*Idyll* III]

Moschus (late second century B.C.) of
Syracuse was a pupil of the great Alexandrian critic Aristarchus, and was at
once a grammarian and a poet. Extant
are eight poems and a few fragments.

This poem, attributed to Moschus, is
made after the pattern of a shepherd song
mourning the death of Daphnis, or of the
dirge sung at the festival of Adonis.

Mourn, Dorian stream, departed Bion
mourn!
Pour the hoarse murmur from thy pallid
urn!
Sigh, groves and lawns! ye plants, in
sorrow wave;
Ye flowers, breathe sickly sweets o'er
Bion's grave!
Anemonies and roses, blush your grief;
Expand, pale hyacinth, thy letter'd leaf!
Thy marks of anguish more distinctly
show—
Ah! well the tuneful herdsman claims
your woe!

Begin, and in the tenderest notes com-
plain!
Sicilian Muse, begin the mournful
strain!
Ye nightingales, that sooth the shadowy
vale,
Warble to Arethusa's streams the tale
Of Bion dead. Lamenting Nature's pride,
He sunk! ah, then the Dorian music
died!

Begin, and in the tenderest notes complain!
Sicilian Muse! begin the mournful
strain!
Ye swans of Strymon, bid so sweet a note
As Bion breathed along your green banks,
float

O'er the still wave! and tell Bistonia's maids,
That Doric Orpheus charms no more the glades.

Begin, and in the tenderest notes complain!
Sicilian Muse, begin the mournful strain!
Dear to the Muse, alas! no more he sings
By yon lone oak that shades the plashy springs.
He roams a spectre through the glooms of fear,
And chants the oblivious verse to Pluto's ear.
O'er the hush'd hills his pensive heifers rove,
Refuse their pasture, and forget their love!

Begin, and in the tenderest notes complain!
Sicilian Muse, begin the mournful strain!
Thee—thee, O Bion, snatch'd from earth away,
The Satyrs wail'd, and e'en the god of day!
Pan for thy numbers heaved his sighing breast,
And sad Priapus mourn'd in sable vest.
The Naiads in despairing anguish stood,
And swell'd with briny tears their fountain-flood.
Mute Echo, as her mimic music dies,
Amidst her dreary rocks lamenting lies.
The trees resigned their fruitage at thy death,
And all the faded flowers, their scented breath,
The ewes no milk—the hives no honey gave;
But what avail'd it the rich stores to save?
What, that the bee no balmy floweret sips,
Extinct the sweeter honey of thy lips?

Begin, and in the tenderest notes complain!
Sicilian Muse, begin the mournful strain!
Not with such grief the Dolphin fill'd the seas,
Or Philomela's plaint the woodland breeze,
Or Progne's bitter woe the mountains hoar,
Or wild Alcyone the fatal shore;
Or faithful Cerylus the cave, where lies
His mate, still breathing fondness as she dies;
Or Memnon's screaming birds his orient tomb,
As now they utter, at their Bion's doom!

Begin, and in the tenderest notes complain!
Sicilian Muse, begin the mournful strain!
The lovelorn nightingales that learn'd his song,
The swallows twittering shrill, the boughs among,
Join their sad notes; the vocal groves reply—
'Sigh too, ye turtles, for your Bion sigh!'

Begin, and in the tenderest notes complain!
Sicilian Muse, begin the mournful strain!
Who now, regretted swain, thy pipe shall play;
Touch the fair stops, or trill the melting lay?
Faint from thy lips still breathe the mellow reeds;
Still on their dying sweetness Echo feeds:
To bear those melodies to Pan be mine;
Though he may fear to risk his fame with thine!

Begin, and in the tenderest notes complain!
Sicilian Muse, begin the mournful strain!
And Galatea too bewails thy fate—
Fair nymph, who oft upon the seashore sate
Sooth'd by thy songs, and fled the Cyclops' arms—
Far other strains are thine! far other charms!
Now on the sand she sits—forgets the sea—
Yet feeds thy herds, and still remembers thee!

Begin, and in the tenderest notes complain!
Sicilian Muse, begin the mournful strain!
With thee, O swain, expired the Muse's bliss—
The roseate bloom of youth, the roseate kiss!
The fluttering Cupids round thy ashes cry,
And fond—fond Venus mixes many a sigh!
She loves thee as Adonis' parting breath—
As his last kisses so endear'd by death!
Here—here, O Meles, musical in woe,
Sad for another son thy tide shall flow!
For thy first poet mourn'd thy plaintive wave;
Each murmur deepen'd at thy Homer's grave:
Another grief (melodious stream) appears!
Alas! another poet claims thy tears!
Dear to the fountains which inspire the Muse,
That drank of Helicon—this Arethuse!
That bard his harp to beauteous Helen strung!
And the dire anger of Pelides sung:
This—in his softer lay no wars display'd,
But chanted Pan all peaceful in the shade!

He framed his reeds, or milk'd his kine, or led
His herds to pasture, singing as they fed!
And oft, so dear to Venus, he caress'd
The little Cupid in his panting breast.

Begin, and in the tenderest notes complain!
Sicilian Muse, begin the mournful strain!
The cities and the towns thy death deplore—
Than her own Hesiod Ascra mourns thee more!
Not thus her Pindar Hylæ's grief bemoans—
Not Lesbos thus Alcæus' manly tones!
Not Ceos, Paros, thus regret their bards—
And Mitylene yet thy reed regards
Beyond her Sappho's lyre; and every swain
Pipes thee, O Bion, on his native plain.
The Samian's gentle notes thy memory greet—
Philetas too—and Lycidas of Crete!
Now, breathing heavy sighs, each heart despairs,
Though erst full many a jocund revel theirs.
Thee too, dear bard, Theocritus bewails,
The sweetest warbler of Sicilia's dales!
And I, who suit to sorrow's melting tone
The Ausonian verse, but mimic music own;
If e'er the charms of melody I knew,
'Tis to thy forming skill the praise is due.
Others may claim thy gold—the gold be theirs!
Ours be the Doric Muse, thy wealthier heirs.

Begin, and in the tenderest notes complain!
Sicilian Muse, begin the mournful strain!

Though fade crisp anise, and the parsley's
  green,
And vivid mallows from the garden
  scene;
The balmy breath of spring their life
  renews,
And bids them flourish in their former
  hues!
But we, the great, the valiant, and the
  wise,
When once the seal of death hath closed
  our eyes,
Lost in the hollow tomb obscure and
  deep,
Slumber, to wake no more, one long
  unbroken sleep!
Thou too, while many a scrannel reed I
  hear
Grating eternal harshness on my ear—
Thou too, thy charm of melting music
  o'er,
Shut in the silent earth, shalt rise no
  more!

Begin, and in the tenderest notes complain!
Sicilian Muse, begin the mournful
  strain!
'Twas poison gave thee to the grasp of
  death—
Ah! could not poison sweeten at thy
  breath?

Who for those lips of melody could dare
The venom'd chalice (murderous wretch)
  prepare?
Such wretches rove with vengeance at
  their heels;
While now at this drear hour my bosom
  feels
The bursting sigh! like Orpheus could
  I go,
Or wise Ulysses, to the shades below,
To Pluto's home my steps should straight
  repair,
To hear what numbers thou art chanting
  there.
But sing, as in the genial realms of light,
Some sweet bucolic to the queen of
  night:
She once amid those golden meadows
  play'd,
And sung the Dorian song in Ætna's
  shade.
Thy music shall ascend with all the
  fire—
With all the strong effect of Orpheus'
  lyre!
Fair Proserpine shall listen to thy strain,
And, pitying, send thee to thy hills again.
O that, as Orpheus' lyre reclaim'd his
  wife,
My pipe had power to bring thy shade
  to life!
                        —RICHARD POLWHELE.

V. SCIENCE AND TRAVEL

The interest in the things of the natural world reaches back to the beginning of Greek life, and early philosophers were at work even before prose was invented. But not until Aristotle developed a definite method was much progress achieved. To him we owe not only the method, but also the beginnings of accurate observation and analysis and the formulation of many of the general principles on which modern science is based. After him, the inquiry took the direction rather of applied science, and the general scientist gave place more and more to the specialist. In the Alexandrian period mathematics, astronomy, botany, and physics were in the ascendancy, and later, in the period of Roman dominion, medicine and geography. Travel was a natural accompaniment of such progress in scientific learning, and broadened the field of observation and interest in respect not only of man and his habits, but also of the ways of nature.

The selections from the scientific literature given below are purposely passages of a rather general nature, since the technical can be read with profit only by the specialist. Further, though they belong to distinctly different periods, they are grouped together here on a topical basis rather than on a time basis, since no one era can properly be called the scientific era in contrast with others. Within the group, however, the chronological arrangement has been followed.

THE METHOD OF NATURAL SCIENCE

ARISTOTLE

[From *On the Parts of Animals*]

For Aristotle, see above, p. 490.

Every systematic science, the humblest and the noblest alike, seems to admit of two distinct kinds of proficiency; one of which may be properly called scientific knowledge of the subject, while the other is a kind of educational acquaintance with it. For an educated man should be able to form a fair off-hand judgment as to the goodness or badness of the method used by a professor in his exposition. To be educated is in fact to be able to do this; and even the man of universal education we deem to be such in virtue of his having this ability. It will, however, of course, be understood that we only ascribe universal education to one who in his own individual person is thus critical in all or nearly all branches of knowledge, and not to one who has a like ability merely in some special subject. For it is possible for a man to have this competence in some one branch of knowledge without having it in all.

It is plain then that, as in other sciences, so in that which inquires into nature, there must be certain canons, by reference to which a hearer shall be able to criticize the method of a professed

exposition, quite independently of the question whether the statements made be true or false. Ought we, for instance (to give an illustration of what I mean), to begin by discussing each separate species—man, lion, ox, and the like—taking each kind in hand independently of the rest, or ought we rather to deal first with the attributes which they have in common in virtue of some common element of their nature, and proceed from this as a basis for the consideration of them separately? For genera that are quite distinct yet oftentimes present many identical phenomena, sleep, for instance, respiration, growth, decay, death, and other similar affections and conditions, which may be passed over for the present, as we are not yet prepared to treat of them with clearness and precision. Now it is plain that if we deal with each species independently of the rest, we shall frequently be obliged to repeat the same statements over and over again; for horse and dog and man present, each and all, every one of the phenomena just enumerated. A discussion therefore of the attributes of each species separately would necessarily involve frequent repetitions as to characters, themselves identical but recurring in animals specifically distinct. (Very possibly also there may be other characters which, though they present specific differences, yet come under one and the same category. For instance, flying, swimming, walking, creeping, are plainly specifically distinct, but yet are all forms of animal progression.) We must, then, have some clear understanding as to the manner in which our investigation is to be conducted; whether, I mean, we are first to deal with the common or generic characters, and afterwards to take into consideration special peculiarities; or whether we are to start straight off with the ultimate species. For as yet no definite rule has been laid down in this matter. So also there is a like uncertainty as to another point now to be mentioned. Ought the writer who deals with the works of nature to follow the plan adopted by the mathematicians in their astronomical demonstrations, and after considering the phenomena presented by animals, and their several parts, proceed subsequently to treat of the causes and the reason why; or ought he to follow some other method? And when these questions are answered, there yet remains another. The causes concerned in the generation of the works of nature are, as we see, more than one. There is the final cause and there is the motor cause. Now we must decide which of these two causes comes first, which second. Plainly, however, that cause is the first which we call the final one. For this is the Reason, and the Reason forms the starting-point, alike in the works of art and in nature. For consider how the physician or how the builder sets about his work. He starts by forming for himself a definite picture, in the one case perceptible to mind, in the other to sense, of his end—the physician of health, the builder of a house—and this he holds forward as the reason and explanation of each subsequent step that he takes, and of his acting in this or that way as the case may be. Now in the works of nature the good end and the final cause is still more dominant than in works of art such as these, nor is necessity a factor with the same significance in them all; though almost all writers, while they try to refer their origin to this cause, do so without distinguishing the various senses in which the term necessity is used. For there is absolute necessity, manifested in eternal phenomena; and there is hypothetical necessity, manifested in everything that is generated by nature as in everything that is produced by art, be it a house or what it may. For if a house or other such final object is to be realized, it is necessary that such and such material

exist; and it is necessary that first this and then that shall be produced, and first this and then that set in motion, and so on in continuous succession, until the end and final result is reached, for the sake of which each prior thing is produced and exists. As with these productions of art, so also is it with the productions of nature. The mode of necessity, however, and the mode of ratiocination are different in natural science from what they are in the theoretical sciences; of which we have spoken elsewhere. For in the latter the starting-point is that which is; in the former that which is to be. For it is that which is yet to be— health, let us say, or a man—that, owing to its being of such and such characters, necessitates the pre-existence or previous production of this and that antecedent; and not this or that antecedent which, because it exists or has been generated, makes it necessary that health or a man is in, or shall come into, existence. Nor, is it possible to trace back the series of necessary antecedents to a starting-point, of which you can say that, existing itself from eternity, it has determined their existence as its consequent. These however, again, are matters that have been dealt with in another treatise. There too it was stated in what cases absolute and hypothetical necessity exist; in what cases also the proposition expressing hypothetical necessity is simply convertible, and what cause it is that determines this convertibility.

Another matter which must not be passed over without consideration is, whether the proper subject of our exposition is that with which the ancient writers concerned themselves, namely, what is the process of formation of each animal; or whether it is not rather, what are the characters of a given creature when formed. For there is no small difference between these two views. The best course appears to be that we should follow the method already mentioned, and begin with the phenomena presented by each group of animals, and, when this is done, proceed afterwards to state the causes of those phenomena, and to deal with their evolution. For elsewhere, as for instance in house building, this is the true sequence. The plan of the house, or the house, has this and that form; and because it has this and that form, therefore is its construction carried out in this or that manner. For the process of evolution is for the sake of the thing finally evolved, and not this for the sake of the process. Empedocles, then, was in error when he said that many of the characters presented by animals were merely the results of incidental occurrences during their development; for instance, that the backbone was divided as it is into vertebræ, because it happened to be broken owing to the contorted position of the fœtus in the womb. In so saying he overlooked the fact that propagation implies a creative seed endowed with certain formative properties. Secondly, he neglected another fact, namely, that the parent animal preexists, not only in idea, but actually in time. For man is generated from man; and thus it is the possession of certain characters by the parent that determines the development of like characters in the child. The same statement holds good also for the operations of art, and even for those which are apparently spontaneous. For the same result as is produced by art may occur spontaneously. Spontaneity, for instance, may bring about the restoration of health. The products of art, however, require the preexistence of an efficient cause homogeneous with themselves, such as the statuary's art, which must necessarily precede the statue; for this cannot possibly be produced spontaneously. Art indeed consists in the conception of the result to be produced before its realization in the material. As with spontaneity so with chance; for this also produces the

same result as art, and by the same process.

The fittest mode, then, of treatment is to say, a man has such and such parts, because the conception of a man includes their presence, and because they are necessary conditions of his existence, or, if we cannot quite say this, which would be best of all, then the next thing to it, namely, that it is either quite impossible for him to exist without them, or, at any rate, that it is better for him that they should be there; and their existence involves the existence of other antecedents. This we should say, because man is an animal with such and such characters, therefore is the process of his development necessarily such as it is; and therefore is it accomplished in such and such an order, this part being formed first, that next, and so on in succession; and after a like fashion should we explain the evolution of all other works of nature.

Now that with which the ancient writers, who first philosophized about nature, busied themselves, was the material principle and the material cause. They inquired what this is, and what its character; how the universe is generated out of it, and by what motor influence, whether, for instance, by antagonism or friendship, whether by intelligence or spontaneous action, the substratum of matter being assumed to have certain inseparable properties; fire, for instance, to have a hot nature, earth a cold one; the former to be light, the latter heavy. For even the genesis of the universe is thus explained by them. After a like fashion do they deal also with the development of plants and of animals. They say, for instance, that the water contained in the body causes by its currents the formation of the stomach and the other receptacles of food or of excretion; and that the breath by its passage breaks open the outlets of the nostrils; air and water being the materials of which bodies are made; for all represent nature as composed of such or similar substances.

But if men and animals and their several parts are natural phenomena, then the natural philosopher must take into consideration not merely the ultimate substances of which they are made, but also flesh, bone, blood, and all the other homogeneous parts; not only these, but also the heterogeneous parts, such as face, hand, foot; and must examine how each of these comes to be what it is, and in virtue of what force. For to say what are the ultimate substances out of which an animal is formed, to state, for instance, that it is made of fire or earth, is no more sufficient than would be a similar account in the case of a couch or the like. For we should not be content with saying that the couch was made of bronze or wood or whatever it might be, but should try to describe its design or mode of composition in preference to the material; or, if we did deal with the material, it would at any rate be with the concretion of material and form. For a couch is such and such a form embodied in this or that matter, or such and such a matter with this or that form; so that its shape and structure must be included in our description. For the formal nature is of greater importance than the material nature.

Does, then, configuration and colour constitute the essence of the various animals and of their several parts? For if so, what Democritus says will be strictly correct. For such appears to have been his notion. At any rate he says that it is evident to every one what form it is that makes the man, seeing that he is recognizable by his shape and colour. And yet a dead body has exactly the same configuration as a living one; but for all that is not a man. So also no hand of bronze or wood or constituted in any but the appropriate way can possibly be a hand in more than name. For like a physician in a painting, or like a flute in a sculpture, in spite of its name it will be unable to do the office which that name implies. Precisely in the same way no part of a dead body, such I mean as its eye or its hand, is really an eye or a hand. To say, then, that shape and colour constitute the animal is an inadequate statement, and is much the same as if a woodcarver were to insist that the hand he had cut was really a hand. Yet the physiologists, when they give an account of the development and causes of the animal form, speak very much like such a craftsman. What, however, I would ask, are the forces by which the hand or the body was fashioned into its shape? The woodcarver will perhaps say, by the axe or the auger; the physiologist, by air and by earth. Of these two answers the artificer's is the better, but it is nevertheless insufficient. For it is not enough for him to say that by the stroke of his tool this part was formed into a concavity, that into a flat surface; but he must state the reasons why he struck his blow in such a way as to effect this, and what his final object was; namely, that the piece of wood would develop eventually into this or that shape. It is plain, then, that the teaching of the old physiologists is inadequate, and that the true method is to state what the definitive characters are that distinguish the animal as a whole; to explain what it is both in substance and in form, and to deal after the same fashion with its several organs; in fact, to proceed in exactly the same way as we should do, were we giving a complete description of a couch.

If now this something that constitutes the form of the living being be the soul, or part of the soul, or something that without the soul cannot exist; as would seem to be the case, seeing at any rate that when the soul departs, what is left is no longer a living animal, and that none of the parts remain what they were before, excepting in mere configuration, like the animals that in the fable are turned into stone; if, I say, this be so, then it will come within the province of the natural philosopher to inform himself concerning the soul, and to treat of it, either in its entirety, or, at any rate, of that part of it which constitutes the essential character of an animal; and it will be his duty to say what this soul or this part of a soul is; and to discuss the attributes that attach to this essential character, especially as nature is spoken of in two senses, and the nature of a thing is either its matter or its essence; nature as essence including both the motor cause and the final cause. Now it is in the latter of these two senses that either the whole soul or some part of it constitutes the nature of an animal; and inasmuch as it is the presence of the soul that enables matter to constitute the animal nature, much more than it is the presence of matter which so enables the soul, the inquirer into nature is bound on every ground to treat of the soul rather than of the matter. For though the wood of which they are made constitutes the couch and the tripod, it only does so because it is capable of receiving such and such a form.

What has been said suggests the question, whether it is the whole soul or only some part of it, the consideration of which comes within the province of natural science. Now if it be of the whole soul that this should treat, then there is no place for any other philosophy beside it. For as it belongs in all cases to one and the same science to deal with correlated subjects—one and the same science, for instance, deals with sensation and with the objects of sense—and as therefore the intelligent soul and the objects of intellect, being correlated, must belong to one and the same science, it follows that natural science will have to include the whole universe in its province. But perhaps it is not the whole soul, nor all its parts collectively,

that constitutes the source of motion; but there may be one part, identical with that in plants, which is the source of growth, another, namely the sensory part, which is the source of change of quality, while still another, and this not the intellectual part, is the source of locomotion. I say not the intellectual part; for other animals than man have the power of locomotion, but in none but him is there intellect. Thus then it is plain that it is not of the whole soul that we have to treat. For it is not the whole soul that constitutes the animal nature, but only some part or parts of it. Moreover, it is impossible that any abstraction can form a subject of natural science, seeing that everything that Nature makes is means to an end. For just as human creations are the products of art, so living objects are manifestly the products of an analogous cause or principle, not external but internal, derived like the hot and the cold from the environing universe. And that the heaven, if it had an origin, was evolved and is maintained by such a cause, there is therefore even more reason to believe, than that mortal animals so originated. For order and definiteness are much more plainly manifest in the celestial bodies than in our own frame; while change and chance are characteristic of the perishable things of earth. Yet there are some who, while they allow that every animal exists and was generated by nature, nevertheless hold that the heaven was constructed to be what it is by chance and spontaneity; the heaven, in which not the faintest sign of haphazard or of disorder is discernible! Again, whenever there is plainly some final end, to which a motion tends should nothing stand in the way, we always say that such final end is the aim or purpose of the motion; and from this it is evident that there must be a something or other really existing, corresponding to what we call by the name of Nature. For a given germ does not give rise to any chance living being, nor spring from any chance one; but each germ springs from a definite parent and gives rise to a definite progeny. And thus it is the germ that is the ruling influence and fabricator of the offspring. For these it is by nature, the offspring being at any rate that which in nature will spring from it. At the same time the offspring is anterior to the germ; for germ and perfected progeny are related as the development process and the result. Anterior, however, to both germ and product is the organism from which the germ was derived. For every germ implies two organisms, the parent and the progeny. For germ or seed is both the seed of the organism from which it came, of the horse, for instance, from which it was derived, and the seed of the organism that will eventually arise from it, of the mule, for example, which is developed from the seed of the horse. The same seed then is the seed both of the horse and of the mule, though in different ways as here set forth. Moreover, the seed is potentially that which will spring from it, and the relation of potentiality to actuality we know.

There are then two causes, namely, necessity and the final end. For many things are produced simply as the results of necessity. It may, however, be asked, of what mode of necessity are we speaking when we say this. For it can be of neither of those two modes which are set forth in the philosophical treatises. There is, however, the third mode, in such things at any rate as are generated. For instance, we say that food is necessary; because an animal cannot possibly do without it. This third mode is what may be called hypothetical necessity. Here is another example of it. If a piece of wood is to be split with an axe, the axe must of necessity be hard; and, if hard, must of necessity be made of bronze or iron. Now exactly in the same way the body, which like the axe is an

instrument—for both the body as a whole and its several parts individually have definite operations for which they are made—just in the same way, I say, the body, if it is to do its work, must of necessity be of such and such a character, and made of such and such materials.

It is plain then that there are two modes of causation, and that both of these must, so far as possible, be taken into account in explaining the works of nature, or that at any rate an attempt must be made to include them both; and that those who fail in this tell us in reality nothing about nature. For primary cause constitutes the nature of an animal much more than does its matter. There are indeed passages in which even Empedocles hits upon this, and following the guidance of fact, finds himself constrained to speak of the ratio as constituting the essence and real nature of things. Such, for instance, is the case when he explains what is a bone. For he does not merely describe its material, and say it is this one element, or those two or three elements, or a compound of all the elements, but states the ratio of their combination. As with a bone, so manifestly is it with the flesh and all other similar parts.

The reason why our predecessors failed in hitting upon this method of treatment was, that they were not in possession of the notion of essence, nor of any definition of substance. The first who came near it was Democritus, and he was far from adopting it as a necessary method in natural science, but was merely brought to it, spite of himself, by constraint of facts. In the time of Socrates a nearer approach was made to the method. But at this period men gave up inquiring into the works of nature, and philosophers diverted their attention to political science and to the virtues which benefit mankind.

Of the method itself the following is an example. In dealing with respiration we must show that it takes place for such or such a final object; and we must also show that this and that part of the process is necessitated by this and that other stage of it. By necessity we shall sometimes mean hypothetical necessity, the necessity, that is, that the requisite antecedents shall be there, if the final end is to be reached; and sometimes absolute necessity, such necessity as that which connects substances and their inherent properties and characters. For the alternate discharge and re-entrance of heat and the inflow of air are necessary if we are to live. Here we have at once a necessity in the former of the two senses. But the alternation of heat and refrigeration produces of necessity an alternate admission and discharge of the outer air, and this is a necessity of the second kind.

In the foregoing we have an example of the method which we must adopt, and also an example of the kind of phenomena, the causes of which we have to investigate.

—WILLIAM OGLE.

THE ESSENTIAL PARTS OF PLANTS [1]

THEOPHRASTUS

[From *Enquiry into Plants,* Book I]

Theophrastus applied the principle of classification, which is a characteristic of Aristotle's method, to the study of plant life, and so became the first systematic botanist. His analysis of the parts of plants shows the results of scientific investigation and observation. For Theophrastus, see above, p. 538.

Now the difference in regard to parts, to take a general view, are of three kinds: either one plant may possess them and another not (for instance, leaves and fruit), or in one plant they may be

[1] From The Loeb Classical Library, reprinted by permission.

unlike in appearance or size to those of another, or, thirdly, they may be differently arranged. Now the unlikeness between them is seen in form, colour, closeness of arrangement or its opposite, roughness or its opposite, and the other qualities; and again there are the various differences of flavour. The inequality is seen in excess or defect as to number or size, or, to speak generally, all the above-mentioned differences too are included under excess and defect: for the 'more' and the 'less' are the same thing as excess and defect, whereas 'differently arranged' implies a difference of position; for instance, the fruit may be above or below the leaves, and, as to position on the tree itself, the fruit may grow on the apex of it or on the side branches, and in some cases even on the trunk, as in the sycamore; while some plants again even bear their fruit underground, for instance arakhidna and the plant called in Egypt uingon; again in some plants the fruit has a stalk, in some it has none. There is a like difference in the floral organs: in some cases they actually surround the fruit, in others they are differently placed: in fact it is in regard to the fruit, the leaves, and the shoots that the question of position has to be considered.

Or again there are differences as to symmetry: in some cases the arrangement is irregular, while the branches of the silver-fir are arranged opposite one another; and in some cases the branches are at equal distances apart, and correspond in number, as where they are in three rows.

Wherefore the differences between plants must be observed in these particulars, since taken together they shew forth the general character of each plant.

But, before we attempt to speak about each, we must make a list of the parts themselves. Now the primary and most important parts, which are also common to most, are these—root, stem, branch, twig; these are the parts into which we might divide the plant, regarding them as members, corresponding to the members of animals: for each of these is distinct in character from the rest, and together they make up the whole.

The root is that by which the plant draws its nourishment, the stem that to which it is conducted. And by the 'stem' I mean that part which grows above ground and is single; for that is the part which occurs most generally both in annuals and in long-lived plants; and in the case of trees it is called the 'trunk.' By 'branches' I mean the parts which split off from the stem and are called by some 'boughs.' By 'twig' I mean the growth which springs from the branch regarded as a single whole, and especially such an annual growth.

Now these parts belong more particularly to trees. The stem however, as has been said, is more general, though not all plants possess even this, for instance, some herbaceous plants are stemless; others again have it, not permanently, but as an annual growth, including some whose roots live beyond the year. In fact your plant is a thing various and manifold, and so it is difficult to describe in general terms: in proof whereof we have the fact that we cannot here seize on any universal character which is common to all, as a mouth and a stomach are common to all animals; whereas in plants some characters are the same in all, merely in the sense that all have analogous characters, while others correspond otherwise. For not all plants have root, stem, branch, twig, leaf, flower or fruit, or again bark, core, fibres or veins; for instance, fungi and truffles; and yet these and such like characters belong to a plant's essential nature. However, as has been said, these characters belong especially to trees, and our classification of characters belongs more particularly to these; and it is right to make these the standard in treating of the others.

Trees moreover shew forth fairly well the other features also which distinguish plants; for they exhibit differences in the number or fewness of these which they possess, as to the closeness or openness of their growth, as to their being single or divided, and in other like respects. Moreover each of the characters mentioned is not 'composed of like parts'; by which I mean that though any given part of the root or trunk is composed of the same elements as the whole, yet the part so taken is not itself called 'trunk,' but 'a portion of a trunk.' The case is the same with the members of an animal's body; to wit, any part of the leg or arm is composed of the same elements as the whole, yet it does not bear the same name (as it does in the case of flesh or bone); it has no special name. Nor again have subdivisions of any of those other organic parts which are uniform special names, subdivisions of all being nameless. But the subdivisions of those parts which are compound have names, as have those of the foot, hand, and head, for instance, toe, finger, nose or eye. Such then are the largest parts of the plant. Again there are the things of which such parts are composed, namely bark, wood, and core (in the case of those plants which have it), and these are all 'composed of like parts.' Further there are the things which are even prior to these, from which they are derived— sap, fibre, veins, flesh: for these are elementary substances—unless one should prefer to call them the active principles of the elements; and they are common to all the parts of the plant. Thus the essence and entire material of plants consist in these.

Again there are other as it were annual parts, which help towards the production of the fruit, as leaf, flower, stalk, (that is, the part by which the leaf and the fruit are attached to the plant), and again tendril, 'catkin' (in those plants that have them). And in all cases there is the seed which belongs to the fruit: by 'fruit' is meant the seed or seeds, together with the seed-vessel. Besides these there are in some cases peculiar parts, such as the gall in the oak, or the tendril in the vine.

In the case of trees we may thus distinguish the annual parts, while it is plain that in annual plants all the parts are annual: for the end of their being is attained when the fruit is produced. And with those plants which bear fruit annually, those which take two years (such as celery and certain others) and those which have fruit on them for a longer time—with all these the stem will correspond to the plant's length of life: for plants develop a stem at whatever time they are about to bear seed, seeing that the stem exists for the sake of the seed.

Let this suffice for the definition of these parts: and now we must endeavour to say what each of the parts just mentioned is, giving a general and typical description.

The sap is obvious: some call it simply in all cases 'juice,' as does Menestor among others: others, in the case of some plants give it no special name, while in some they call it 'juice' and in others 'gum.' Fibre and 'veins' have no special names in relation to plants, but because of the resemblance, borrow the names of the corresponding parts of animals. It may be however that, not only these things, but the world of plants generally, exhibits also other differences as compared with animals: for, as we have said, the world of plants is manifold. However, since it is by help of the better known that we must pursue the unknown, and better known are the things which are larger and plainer to our senses, it is clear that it is right to speak of these things in the way indicated: for then in dealing with the less known things we shall be making these better known things our standard, and shall ask how far and

in what manner comparison is possible in each case. And when we have taken the parts, we must next take the differences which they exhibit, for thus will their essential nature become plain, and at the same time the general differences between one kind of plant and another.

Now the nature of the most important parts has been indicated already, that is, such parts as the root, the stem, and the rest: their functions and the reasons for which each of them exists will be set forth presently. For we must endeavour to state of what these, as well as the rest, are composed, starting from their elementary constituents.

First come moisture and warmth: for every plant, like every animal, has a certain amount of moisture and warmth which essentially belong to it: and, if these fall short, age and decay, while, if they fail altogether, death and withering ensue. Now in most plants the moisture has no special name, but in some it has such a name, as has been said: and this also holds good of animals: for it is only the moisture of those which have blood which has received a name; wherefore we distinguish animals by the presence or absence of blood, calling some 'animals with blood,' others 'bloodless.' Moisture then is one essential 'part,' and so is warmth, which is closely connected with it.

There are also other essential internal characters, which in themselves have no special name, but, because of their resemblance, have names analogous to those of the parts of animals. Thus plants have what corresponds to muscle; and this quasi-muscle is continuous, fissile, long: moreover no other growth starts from it either branching from the side or in continuation of it. Again plants have veins: these in other respects resemble the 'muscle,' but they are longer and thicker, and have side-growths and contain moisture. Then there are wood and flesh: for some plants have flesh, some wood. Wood is fissile, while flesh can be broken up in any direction, like earth and things made of earth: it is intermediate between fibre and veins, its nature being clearly seen especially in the outer covering of seed-vessels. Bark and core are properly so called, yet they too must be defined. Bark then is the outside, and is separable from the substance which it covers. Core is that which forms the middle of the wood, being third in order from the bark, and corresponding to the marrow in bones. Some call this part the 'heart,' others call it 'heartwood': some again call only the inner part of the core itself the 'heart,' while others distinguish this as the 'marrow.'

Here then we have a fairly complete list of the 'parts,' and those last named are composed of the first 'parts'; wood is made of fibre and sap, and in some cases of flesh also; for the flesh hardens and turns to wood, for instance in palms ferula and in other plants in which a turning to wood takes place, as in the roots of radishes. Core is made of moisture and flesh: bark in some cases of all three constituents, as in the oak, black poplar and pear; while the bark of the vine is made of sap and fibre, and that of the cork-oak of flesh and sap. Moreover out of these constituents are made the most important parts, those which I mentioned first, and which may be called 'members': however not all of them are made of the same constituents, nor in the same proportion, but the constituents are combined in various ways.

—ARTHUR HORT.

GEOMETRICAL METHOD [1]

ARCHIMEDES

[From the *Method*]

Archimedes was born in 287 B.C. at Syracuse, and was killed at the taking of

[1] Reprinted by permission of The Cambridge University Press, London, publishers.

that city by the Romans in 212 B.C. He was the greatest mathematician of antiquity. He made discoveries not only in the realm of pure mathematics, but in physics also. In addition he was an inventor of useful machines, such as Archimedes' screw, and of engines of war by which for long the Syracusans held back the Romans.

A great deal of his extant work is extremely technical; but the introduction to his *Method* shows plainly enough his means of attack in the discovery of new theorems. To investigate a proposition he would use mechanical means by which he would be aided in constructing later his geometrical proofs. His giving of due credit to predecessors and his expressed hope that successors will make new discoveries admirably show the spirit of the true scientist of every age.

Archimedes to Eratosthenes greeting.

I sent you on a former occasion some of the theorems discovered by me, merely writing out the enunciations and inviting you to discover the proofs, which at the moment I did not give you. . . .

The proofs then of these theorems I have written in this book and now send to you. Seeing moreover in you, as I say, an earnest student, a man of considerable eminence in philosophy, and an admirer (of mathematical inquiry), I thought fit to write out for you and explain in detail in the same book the peculiarity of a certain method by which it will be possible for you to get a start to enable you to investigate some of the problems in mathematics by means of mechanics. This procedure is, I am persuaded, no less useful even for the proof of the theorems themselves; for certain things first became clear to me by a mechanical method, although they had to be demonstrated by geometry afterwards because their investigation by the said method did not furnish an actual demonstration. But it is of course easier, when we have previously acquired, by the method, some knowledge of the questions, to supply the proof than it is to find it without any

previous knowledge. This is a reason why, in the case of the theorems the proof of which Eudoxus was the first to discover, namely that the cone is a third part of the cylinder, and the pyramid of the prism, having the same base and equal height, we should give no small share of the credit to Democritus who was the first to make the assertion with regard to the said figure though he did not prove it. I am myself in the position of having first made the discovery of the theorem now to be published (by the method indicated), and I deem it necessary to expound the method partly because I have already spoken of it and I do not want to be thought to have uttered vain words, but equally because I am persuaded that it will be of no little service to mathematics; for I apprehend that some either of my contemporaries or of my successors, will, by means of the method when once established, be able to discover other theorems in addition, which have not yet occurred to me.
—T. L. Heath.

The Earth and Its Zones [1]

STRABO

[From the *Geography*, Book II]

Strabo was born of Greek and Asiatic parentage at Amasia, Asia Minor, about 63 B.C. In the course of a long life he travelled extensively in the Roman Empire, and frequently lived at Rome. He wrote his *Geography* largely in the reign of Augustus. The book, according to his expressed intention, was written for the educated public, but even more for the practical use of Roman statesmen. It is hardly to be thought of as presenting the results of discoveries made by the author in geographical science; but it has preserved in satisfactory form much of the scientific study of the earth from the cen-

[1] From The Loeb Classical Library, reprinted by permission.

turies before Strabo's day, and, besides, a vast deal of information about countries and cities of the world as it was known at the dawn of the Christian era.

Strabo's discussion of the zones of the earth is of interest because it indicates the great extent of his knowledge of geography and astronomy on this topic, and sets forth plainly his erroneous ideas as well.

Since the taking in hand of my proposed task naturally follows the criticisms of my predecessors, let me make a second beginning by saying that the person who attempts to write an account of the countries of the earth must take many of the physical and mathematical principles as hypotheses and elaborate his whole treatise with reference to their intent and authority. For, as I have already said, no architect or engineer would be competent even to fix the site of a house or a city properly if he had no conception beforehand of "climata" and of the celestial phenomena, and of geometrical figures and magnitudes and heat and cold and other such things—much less a person who would fix positions for the whole of the inhabited world. For the mere drawing on one and the same plane surface of Iberia and India and the countries that lie between them and, in spite of its being a plane surface, the plotting of the sun's position at its settings, risings, and in meridian, as though these positions were fixed for all the people of the world—merely this exercise gives to the man who has previously conceived of the arrangement and movement of the celestial bodies and grasped the fact that the true surface of the earth is spherical but that it is depicted for the moment as a plane surface for the convenience of the eye—merely this exercise, I say, gives to that man instruction that is truly geographical but to the man not thus qualified it does not. Indeed, the case is not the same with us when we are dealing with geography as it is when we are travelling over great plains (those of Babylonia, for example) or over the sea: then all that is in front of us and behind us and on either side of us is presented to our minds as a plane surface and offers no varying aspects with reference to the celestial bodies or the movements or the positions of the sun and the other stars relatively to us; but when we are dealing with geography the like parts must never present themselves to our minds in that way. The sailor on the open sea, or the man who travels through a level country, is guided by certain popular notions (and these notions impel not only the uneducated man but the man of affairs as well to act in the self-same way), because he is unfamiliar with the heavenly bodies and ignorant of the varying aspects of things with reference to them. For he sees the sun rise, pass the meridian, and set, but how it comes about he does not consider; for, indeed, such knowledge is not useful to him with reference to the task before him, any more than it is useful for him to know whether or not his body stands parallel to that of his neighbor. But perhaps he does consider these matters, and yet holds opinions opposed to the principles of mathematics —just as the natives of any given place do; for a man's place occasions such blunders. But the geographer does not write for the native of any particular place, nor yet does he write for the man of affairs of the kind who has paid no attention to the mathematical sciences properly so-called; nor, to be sure, does he write for the harvest-hand or the ditch-digger, but for the man who can be persuaded that the earth as a whole is such as the mathematicians represent it to be, and also all that relates to such an hypothesis. And the geographer urges upon his students that they first master those principles and then consider the subsequent problems; for, he declares, he will speak only of the results which follow from those principles; and hence his students will the more unerringly make the application of his teachings if they listen as mathematicians; but he refuses to teach geography to persons not thus qualified.

Now as for the matters which he regards as fundamental principles of his science, the geographer must rely upon the geometricians who have measured the earth as a whole; and in their turn the geometricians must rely upon the astronomers; and again the astronomers upon the physicists. Physics is a kind of Arete; and by Aretai they mean those sciences that postulate nothing but depend upon themselves, and contain within themselves their own principles as well as the proofs thereof. Now what we are taught by the physicists is as follows: The universe and the heavens are sphere-shaped. The tendency of the bodies that have weight is towards the centre. And, having taken its position about this centre, the earth is spherically concentric with the heavens, and it is motionless as is also the axis through it, which axis extends also through the centre of the heavens. The heavens revolve round both the earth and its axis from east to west; and along with the heavens revolve the fixed stars, with the same rapidity as the vault of the heavens. Now the fixed stars move along parallel circles, and the best known parallel circles are the equator, the two tropics, and the arctic circles; whereas the planets and the sun and the moon move along certain oblique circles whose positions lie in the zodiac. Now the astronomers first accept these principles, either in whole or in part, and then work out the subsequent problems, namely, the movements of the heavenly bodies, their revolutions, their eclipses, their sizes, their respective distances, and a host of other things. And, in the same way, the geometricians, in measuring the earth as a whole, adhere to the doctrines of the physicists and the astronomers, and, in their turn, the geographers adhere to those of the geometricians.

Thus we must take as an hypothesis that the heavens have five zones, and that the earth also has five zones, and that the terrestrial zones have the same names as the celestial zones (I have already stated the reasons for this division into zones). The limits of the zones can be defined by circles drawn on both sides of the equator and parallel to it, namely, by two circles which enclose the torrid zone, and by two others, following upon these, which form the two temperate zones next to the torrid zone and the two frigid zones next to the temperate zones. Beneath each of the celestial circles falls the corresponding terrestrial circle which bears the same name: and, in like manner, beneath the celestial zone, the terrestrial zone. Now they call "temperate" the zones that can be inhabited; the others they call uninhabitable, the one on account of the heat, and the other two on account of the cold. They proceed in the same manner with reference to the tropic and the arctic circles (that is, in countries that admit of arctic circles): they define their limits by giving the terrestrial circles the same names as the celestial—and thus they define all the terrestrial circles that fall beneath the several celestial circles. Since the celestial equator cuts the whole heavens in two, the earth also must of necessity be cut in two by the terrestrial equator. Of the two hemispheres—I refer to the two celestial as well as the two terrestrial hemispheres—one is called "the northern hemisphere" and the other "the southern hemisphere"; so also, since the torrid zone is cut in two by the same circle, the one part of it will be the northern and the other the southern. It is clear that, of the temperate zones also, the one will be northern and the other southern, each bearing the name of the hemisphere in which it lies. That hemisphere is called "northern hemisphere" which contains that temperate zone in which, as you look from the east to the west, the pole is on your right hand and the equator on your left, or in which, as you look towards the south, the west is on your right hand and the east on your left; and that hemisphere is called "southern hemisphere," in which the opposite is true; and hence it is clear that we are in one of the two hemispheres (that is, of course, in the northern), and that it is impossible for us to be in both. "Between them are great rivers; first, Oceanus," and then the torrid zone. But neither is there an Oceanus in the centre of our whole inhabited world, cleaving the whole of it, nor, to be sure, is there a torrid spot in it; nor yet, indeed, is there a portion of it to be found whose "climata" are opposite to the "climata" which I have given for the northern temperate zone.

By accepting these principles, then, and also by making use of the sun-dial and the other helps given him by the astronomer—by means of which are found, for the several inhabited localities, both the circles that are parallel to the equator and the circles that cut the former at right angles, the latter being drawn through the poles—the geometrician can measure the inhabited portion of the earth by visiting it and the rest of the earth by his calculation of the intervals. In this way he can find the distance from the equator to the pole, which is a fourth part of the earth's largest circle; and then he has the circumference of the earth. Accordingly, just as the man who measures the earth gets his principles from the astronomer and the astronomer his from the physicist, so, too, the geographer must in the same way take his point of departure from the man who has measured the earth as a whole, having confidence in him and in those in whom he, in his turn, had confidence, and then explain, in the first instance, our inhabited world —its size, shape, and character, and its relations to the earth as a whole; for this is the peculiar task of the geographer. Then, secondly, he must discuss in a fitting manner the several parts of the inhabited world, both land and sea, noting in passing wherein the subject has been treated inadequately by those of our predecessors whom we have believed to be the best authorities on these matters.

Now let us take as hypothesis that the earth together with the sea is sphere-shaped and that the surface of the earth is one and the same with that of the high seas; for the elevations on the earth's surface would disappear from consideration, because they are small in comparison with the great size of the earth and admit of being overlooked; and so we use "sphere-shaped" for figures of this kind, not as though they were turned on a lathe, nor yet as the geometrician uses the sphere for demonstration, but as an aid to our conception of the earth—and that, too, a rather rough conception. Now let us conceive of a sphere with five zones, and let the equator be drawn as a circle upon that sphere, and let a second circle be drawn parallel thereto, bounding the frigid zone in the northern hemisphere, and let a third circle be drawn through the poles, cutting the other two circles at right angles. Then, since the northern hemisphere contains two-fourths of the earth, which are formed by the equator with the circle that passes through the poles, a quadrilateral area is cut off in each of the two fourths. The northern side of the quadrilateral is half of the parallel next to the pole; the southern side is half of the equator; and the two remaining sides are segments of the circle that runs through the poles, these segments lying opposite to each other and being equal in length. Now in one of these two quadrilaterals (it would seem to make

no difference in which one) we say that our inhabited world lies, washed on all sides by the sea and like an island; for, as I have already said above, the evidence of our senses and of reason prove this. But if anyone disbelieve the evidence of reason, it would make no difference, from the point of view of the geographer, whether we make the inhabited world an island, or merely admit what experience has taught us, namely, that it is possible to sail round the inhabited world on both sides, from the east as well as from the west, with the exception of a few intermediate stretches. And, as to these stretches, it makes no difference whether they are bounded by sea or by uninhabited land; for the geographer undertakes to describe the known parts of the inhabited world, but he leaves out of consideration the unknown parts of it— just as he does what is outside of it. And it will suffice to fill out and complete the outline of what we term "the island" by joining with a straight line the extreme points reached on the coasting-voyages made on both sides of the inhabited world.

—H. L. JONES.

THE ACROPOLIS OF ATHENS [1]

PAUSANIAS

[From the *Description of Greece*, Book I]

Pausanias, a Greek of the second century after Christ, is known simply as the author of a *Description of Greece*, which he wrote during the reigns of the Antonines. The work, though it shows little literary or critical ability on the part of its author, is extremely useful for its rather careful description of cities, buildings, statues and paintings, and their location. It is an early guide-book, a Bædeker, which has often been invaluable to modern excavators of ancient sites.

[1] From The Loeb Classical Library, reprinted by permission.

The description of the Acropolis shows its condition five hundred years and more after the completion of its most notable structures and works of art.

There is but one entry to the Acropolis. It affords no other, being precipitous throughout and having a strong wall. The gateway has a roof of white marble, and down to the present day it is unrivalled for the beauty and size of its stones. Now as to the statues of the horsemen, I cannot tell for certain whether they are the sons of Xenophon or whether they are made merely to beautify the place. On the right of the gateway is a temple of Wingless Victory. From this point the sea is visible, and here it was that, according to legend, Ægeus threw himself down to his death. For the ship that carried the young people to Crete began her voyage with black sails; but Theseus, who was sailing on an adventure against the bull of Minos, as it is called, had told his father beforehand that he would use white sails if he should sail back victorious over the bull. But the loss of Ariadne made him forget the signal. Then Ægeus, when from this eminence he saw the vessels borne by black sails, thinking that his son was dead, threw himself down to destruction. There is at Athens a sanctuary dedicated to him, and called the hero-shrine of Ægeus. On the left of the gateway is a building with pictures. Among those not effaced by time I found Diomedes taking the Athena from Troy, and Odysseus in Lemnos taking away the bow of Philoctetes. There in the pictures is Orestes killing Ægisthus, and Pylades killing the sons of Nauplius who had come to bring Ægisthus succour. And there is Polyxena about to be sacrificed near the grave of Achilles. Homer did well in passing by this barbarous act. I think too that he showed poetic insight in making Achilles capture Scyros, differing entirely from those who say that Achilles lived in Scyros with the maidens, as Polygnotus has represented in his picture. He also painted Odysseus coming upon the women washing clothes with Nausicaa at the river, just like the description in Homer. There are other pictures, including a portrait of Alcibiades, and in the picture are emblems of the victory his horses won at Nemea. There is also Perseus journeying to Seriphos, and carrying to Polydectes the head of Medusa, the legend about whom I am unwilling to relate in my description of Attica. Included among the paintings— I omit the boy carrying the water-jars and the wrestler of Timænetus—is Musæus. I have read verse in which Musæus receives from the North Wind the gift of flight, but in my opinion, Onomacritus wrote them, and there are no certainly genuine works of Musæus except a hymn to Demeter written for the Lycomidæ.

Right at the very entrance to the Acropolis are Hermes (called Hermes of the Gateway) and figures of Graces, which tradition says were sculptured by Socrates, the son of Sophroniscus, who the Pythia testified was the wisest of men, a title she refused to Anacharsis, although he desired it and came to Delphi to win it.

Among the sayings of the Greeks is one that there were seven wise men. Two of them were the despot of Lesbos and Periander the son of Cypselus. And yet Peisistratus and his son Hippias were more humane than Periander, wiser too in warfare and in statecraft, until, on account of the murder of Hipparchus, Hippias vented his passion against all and sundry, including a woman named Leæna (Lioness). What I am about to say has never before been committed to writing, but is generally credited among the Athenians. When Hipparchus died, Hippias tortured Leæna to death, because he knew she was the mistress of Aristogeiton, and therefore could not possibly, he held, be in ignorance of the plot. As a recompense, when the tyranny of the Peisistratidæ was at an end, the Athenians put up a bronze lioness in memory of the woman, which they say Callias dedicated and Calamis made.

Hard by is a bronze statue of Diitrephes shot through by arrows. Among the acts reported of this Diitrephes by the Athenians is his leading back home the Thracian mercenaries who arrived too late to take part in the expedition of Demosthenes against Syracuse. He also put into the Chalcidic Euripus, where the Bœotians had an inland town Mycalessus, marched up to this town from the coast and took it. Of the inhabitants the Thracians put to the sword not only the combatants but also the women and children. I have evidence to bring. All the Bœotian towns which the Thebans sacked were inhabited in my time, as the people escaped just before the capture; so if the foreigners had not exterminated the Mycalessians the survivors would have afterwards reoccupied the town. I was greatly surprised to see the statue of Diitrephes pierced with arrows, because the only Greeks whose custom it is to use that weapon are the Cretans. For the Opuntian Locrians, whom Homer represents as coming to Troy with bows and slings, we know were armed as heavy infantry by the time of the Persian wars. Neither indeed did the Malians continue the practice of the bow; in fact, I believe that they did not know it before the time of Philoctetes, and gave it up soon after. Near the statue of Diitrephes—I do not wish to write of the less distinguished portraits—are figures of gods; of Health, whom legend calls daughter of Asclepius, and of Athena, also surnamed Health. There is also a smallish stone, just large enough to serve as a seat to a little man. On it legend says Silenus rested when Dionysus came to the land. The oldest of the Satyrs they call Sileni. Wishing

to know better than most people who the Satyrs are I have inquired from many about this very point. Euphemus the Carian said that on a voyage to Italy he was driven out of his course by winds and was carried into the outer sea, beyond the course of seamen. He affirmed that there were many uninhabited islands, while in others lived wild men. The sailors did not wish to put in at the latter, because, having put in before, they had some experience of the inhabitants, but on this occasion they had no choice in the matter. The islands were called Satyrides by the sailors, and the inhabitants were redhaired, and had upon their flanks tails not much smaller than those of horses. As soon as they caught sight of their visitors, they ran down to the ship without uttering a cry and assaulted the women in the ship. At last the sailors in fear cast a foreign woman on to the island. Her the Satyrs outraged not only in the usual way, but also in a most shocking manner.

I remember looking at other things also on the Athenian Acropolis, a bronze boy holding the sprinkler, by Lycius son of Myron, and Myron's Perseus after beheading Medusa. There is also a sanctuary of Brauronian Artemis; the image is the work of Praxiteles, but the goddess derives her name from the parish of Brauron. The old wooden image is in Brauron, the Tauric Artemis as she is called. There is the horse called Wooden set up in bronze. That the work of Epeius was a contrivance to make a breach in the Trojan wall is known to everybody who does not attribute utter silliness to the Phrygians. But legend says of that horse that it contained the most valiant of the Greeks, and the design of the bronze figure fits in well with this story. Menestheus and Teucer are peeping out of it, and so are the sons of Theseus. Of the statues that stand after the horse, the likeness of Epicharinus who practised the race in armour was made by

Critius, while Œnobius performed a kind service for Thucydides the son of Olorus. He succeeded in getting a decree passed for the return of Thucydides to Athens, who was treacherously murdered as he was returning, and there is a monument to him not far from the Melitid gate. The stories of Hermolycus the pancratiast and Phormio the son of Asopichus I omit, as others have told them. About Phormio, however, I have a detail to add. Quite one of the best men at Athens and distinguished for the fame of his ancestors he chanced to be heavily in debt. So he withdrew to the parish Pæania and lived there until the Athenians elected him to command a naval expedition. But he refused the office on the ground that before his debts were discharged he lacked the spirit to face his troops. So the Athenians, who were absolutely determined to have Phormio as their commander, paid all his creditors.

In this place is a statue of Athena striking Marsyas the Silenus for taking up the flutes that the goddess wished to be cast away for good. Opposite these I have mentioned is represented the fight which legend says Theseus fought with the so-called Bull of Minos, whether this was a man or a beast of the nature he is said to have been in the accepted story. For even in our time women have given birth to far more extraordinary monsters than this. There is also a statue of Phrixus the son of Athamas carried ashore to the Colchians by the ram. Having sacrificed the animal to some god or other, presumably to the one called by the Orchomenians Laphystius, he has cut out the thighs in accordance with Greek custom and is watching them as they burn. Next come other statues, including one of Heracles strangling the serpents as the legend describes. There is Athena too coming up out of the head of Zeus, and also a bull dedicated by the Council of the Areopagus on some occasion or other, about which, if one cared,

one could make many conjectures. I have already stated that the Athenians are far more devoted to religion than other men. They were the first to surname Athena Ergane (Worker); they were the first to set up limbless Hermæ, and the temple of their goddess is shared by the Spirit of Good Men. Those who prefer artistic workmanship to mere antiquity may look at the following: a man wearing a helmet, by Cleœtas, whose nails the artist has made of silver, and an image of Earth beseeching Zeus to rain upon her; perhaps the Athenians themselves needed showers, or maybe all the Greeks had been plagued with a drought. There also are set up Timotheus the son of Conon and Conon himself; Procne too, who has already made up her mind about the boy, and Itys as well—a group dedicated by Alcamenes. Athena is represented displaying the olive plant, and Poseidon the wave, and there are statues of Zeus, one made by Leochares and one called Polieus (Urban), the customary mode of sacrificing to whom I will give without adding the traditional reason thereof. Upon the altar of Zeus Polieus they place barley mixed with wheat and leave it unguarded. The ox, which they keep ready prepared for sacrifice, goes to the altar and partakes of the grain. One of the priests they call the ox-slayer, who kills the ox and then, casting aside the axe here according to the ritual, runs away. The others bring the axe to trial, as though they know not the man who did the deed.

Their ritual, then, is such as I have described. As you enter the temple that they name the Parthenon, all the sculptures you see on what is called the pediment refer to the birth of Athena, those on the rear pediment represent the contest for the land between Athena and Poseidon. The statue itself is made of ivory and gold. On the middle of her helmet is placed a likeness of the Sphinx —the tale of the Sphinx I will give when

I come to my description of Bœotia—and on either side of the helmet are griffins in relief. These griffins, Aristeas of Proconnesus says in his poem, fight for the gold with the Arimaspi beyond the Issedones. The gold which the griffins guard, he says, comes out of the earth; the Arimaspi are men all born with one eye; griffins are beasts like lions, but with the beak and wings of an eagle. I will say no more about the griffins. The statue of Athena is upright, with a tunic reaching to the feet, and on her breast the head of Medusa is worked in ivory. She holds a statue of Victory about four cubits high, and in the other hand a spear; at her feet lies a shield and near the spear is a serpent. This serpent would be Erichthonius. On the pedestal is the birth of Pandora in relief. Hesiod and others have sung how this Pandora was the first woman; before Pandora was born there was as yet no womankind. The only portrait statue I remember seeing here is one of the emperor Hadrian, and at the entrance one of Iphicrates, who accomplished many remarkable achievements.

Opposite the temple is a bronze Apollo, said to be the work of Pheidias. They call it the Locust God, because once when locusts were devastating the land the god said that he would drive them from Attica. That he did drive them away they know, but they do not say how. I myself know that locusts have been destroyed three times in the past on Mount Sipylus, and not in the same way. Once a gale arose and swept them away; on another occasion violent heat came on after rain and destroyed them; the third time sudden cold caught them and they died.

Such were the fates I saw befall the locusts. On the Athenian Acropolis is a statue of Pericles, the son of Xanthippus, and one of Xanthippus himself, who fought against the Persians at the naval battle of Mycale. But that of Pericles stands apart, while near Xanthippus stands Anacreon of Teos, the first poet after Sappho of Lesbos to devote himself to love songs, and his posture is as it were that of a man singing when he is drunk. Deinomenes made the two female figures which stand near, Io, the daughter of Inachus, and Callisto, the daughter of Lycaon, of both of whom exactly the same story is told, to wit, love of Zeus, wrath of Hera, and metamorphosis, Io becoming a cow and Callisto a bear.

By the south wall are represented the legendary war with the giants, who once dwelt about Thrace and on the isthmus of Pallene, the battle between the Athenians and the Amazons, the engagement with the Persians at Marathon and the destruction of the Gauls in Mysia. Each is about two cubits, and all were dedicated by Attalus. There stands too Olympiodorus, who won fame for the greatness of his achievements, especially in the crisis when he displayed a brave confidence among men who had met with continuous reverses, and were therefore in despair of winning a single success in the days to come. . . .

Near the statue of Olympiodorus stands a bronze image of Artemis surnamed Leucophryne, dedicated by the sons of Themistocles; for the Magnesians, whose city the King had given him to rule, hold Artemis Leucophryne in honour.

But my narrative must not loiter, as my task is a general description of all Greece. Endœus was an Athenian by birth and a pupil of Dædalus, who also, when Dædalus was in exile because of the death of Calos, followed him to Crete. Made by him is a statue of Athena seated, with an inscription that Callias dedicated the image, but Endœus made it. There is also a building called the Erechtheum. Before the entrance is an altar of Zeus the Most High, on which they never sacrifice a living creature, but offer cakes, not being wont to use any wine either. Inside the entrance are altars, one to Poseidon, on which in obedience to an oracle they sacrifice also to Erechtheus, the second to the hero Butes, and the third to Hephæstus. On the walls are paintings representing members of the clan Butadæ; there is also inside—the building is double—sea-water in a cistern. This is no great marvel, for other inland regions have similar wells, in particular Aphrodisias in Caria. But this cistern is remarkable for the noise of waves it sends forth when a south wind blows. On the rock is the outline of a trident. Legend says that these appeared as evidence in support of Poseidon's claim to the land.

Both the city and the whole of the land are alike sacred to Athena; for even those who in their parishes have an established worship of other gods nevertheless hold Athena in honour. But the most holy symbol, that was so considered by all many years before the unification of the parishes, is the image of Athena which is on what is now called the Acropolis but in early days the Polis (City). A legend concerning it says that it fell from heaven; whether this is true or not I shall not discuss. A golden lamp for the goddess was made by Callimachus. Having filled the lamp with oil, they wait until the same day next year, and the oil is sufficient for the lamp during the interval, although it is alight both day and night. The wick in it is of Carpasian flax, the only kind of flax which is fire proof, and a bronze palm above the lamp reaches to the roof and draws off the smoke. The Callimachus who made the lamp, although not of the first rank of artists, was yet of unparalleled cleverness, so that he was the first to drill holes through stones, and gave himself the title of Refiner of Art, or perhaps others gave the title and he adopted it as his.

—W. H. S. JONES.

SOUL AND NATURE [1]

GALEN

[From *On the Natural Faculties*, Book I]

Galen was born at Pergamum in Asia Minor in 131 A.D. He received his training in medicine in the Greek East, then went to Rome, where he ultimately became physician to the emperor Marcus Aurelius. Later he returned to his home to spend his life in study and writing. Many of his treatises have survived. As Hippocrates represents the beginning, Galen represents the culmination of the scientific study of medicine in the ancient world. Galen gave that study the form which was handed down to future ages.

In the *Natural Faculties* Galen explains the physiological or biological powers of the living organism. His "Nature" is the biological principle on which he based his medical teaching. In dealing with a living organism he believed he had to do with a unit governed by a *Physis* or Nature.

Since feeling and voluntary motion are peculiar to animals, whilst growth and nutrition are common to plants as well, we may look on the former as effects of the soul and the latter as effects of the nature. And if there be anyone who allows a share in soul to plants as well, and separates the two kinds of soul, naming the kind in question vegetative, and the other sensory, this person is not saying anything else, although his language is somewhat unusual. We, however, for our part, are convinced that the chief merit of language is clearness, and we know that nothing detracts so much from this as do unfamiliar terms; accordingly we employ those terms which the bulk of people are accustomed to use, and we say that animals are governed at once by their soul and by their nature, and plants by their nature alone, and that growth and nutrition are the effects of nature, not of soul.

[1] From The Loeb Classical Library, reprinted by permission.

Thus we shall enquire, in the course of this treatise, from what faculties these effects themselves, as well as any other effects of nature which there may be, take their origin.

—A. J. BROCK.

TWO SECTS IN MEDICINE [1]

GALEN

[From *On the Natural Faculties,* Book I]

Galen, in support of the biological principle, pours scorn on those who would make merely physics out of physiology.

It is quite clear, therefore, that nutrition must necessarily be a process of assimilation of that which is nourishing to that which is being nourished. Some, however, say that this assimilation does not occur in reality, but is merely apparent; these are the people who think that Nature is not artistic, that she does not show forethought for the animal's welfare, and that she has absolutely no native powers whereby she alters some substances, attracts others, and discharges others.

Now, speaking generally, there have arisen the following two sects in medicine and philosophy among those who have made any definite pronouncement regarding Nature. I speak, of course, of such of them as know what they are talking about, and who realize the logical sequence of their hypotheses, and stand by them; as for those who cannot understand even this, but who simply talk any nonsense that comes to their tongues, and who do not remain definitely attached either to one sect or the other— such people are not even worth mentioning.

What, then, are these sects, and what are the logical consequences of their

[1] From The Loeb Classical Library, reprinted by permission.

hypotheses? The one class supposes that all substance which is subject to genesis and destruction is at once continuous and susceptible of alteration. The other school assumes substance to be unchangeable, unalterable, and subdivided into fine particles, which are separated from one another by empty spaces.

All people, therefore, who can appreciate the logical sequence of an hypothesis hold that, according to the second teaching, there does not exist any substance or faculty peculiar either to Nature or to Soul, but that these result from the way in which the primary corpuscles, which are unaffected by change, come together. According to the first-mentioned teaching, on the other hand, Nature is not posterior to the corpuscles, but is a long way prior to them and older than they; and therefore in their view it is Nature which puts together the bodies both of plants and animals; and this she does by virtue of certain faculties which she possesses—these being, on the one hand, attractive and assimilative of what is appropriate, and, on the other, expulsive of what is foreign. Further, she skilfully moulds everything during the stage of genesis; and she also provides for the creatures after birth, employing here other faculties again, namely, one of affection and forethought for offspring, and one of sociability and friendship for kindred. According to the other school, none of these things exist in the natures (of living things), nor is there in the soul any original innate idea, whether of agreement or difference, of separation or synthesis, of justice or injustice, of the beautiful or ugly; all such things, they say, arise in us from sensation and through sensation, and animals are steered by certain images and memories.

Some of these people have even expressly declared that the souls possess no reasoning faculty, but that we are led like cattle by the impression of our senses, and are unable to refuse or dissent from anything. In their view, obviously, courage, wisdom, temperance and self-control are all mere nonsense, we do not love either each other or our offspring, nor do the gods care anything for us. This school also despises dreams, birds, omens, and the whole of astrology, subjects with which we have dealt at greater length in another work, in which we discuss the views of Asclepiades the physician. Those who wish to do so may familiarize themselves with these arguments, and they may also consider at this point which of the two roads lying before us is the better one to take. Hippocrates took the first-mentioned. According to this teaching, substance is one and is subject to alteration; there is a consensus in the movements of air and fluid throughout the whole body; Nature acts throughout in an artistic and equitable manner, having certain faculties, by virtue of which each part of the body draws to itself the juice which is proper to it, and, having done so, attaches it to every portion of itself, and completely assimilates it; while such part of the juice as has not been mastered, and is not capable of undergoing complete alteration and being assimilated to the part which is being nourished, is got rid of by yet another (an expulsive) faculty.

—A. J. BROCK.

NATURE'S POWERS [1]

GALEN

[From *On the Natural Faculties,* Book I]

Now Hippocrates, who was the first known to us of all those who have been both physicians and philosophers inasmuch as he was the first to recognize what Nature effects, expresses his admiration of her, and is constantly singing her

[1] From The Loeb Classical Library, reprinted by permission.

praises and calling her "just." Alone, he says, she suffices for the animal in every respect, performing of her own accord and without any teaching all that is required. Being such, she has, as he supposes, certain faculties, one attractive of what is appropriate, and another eliminative of what is foreign, and she nourishes the animal, makes it grow, and expels its diseases by crisis. Therefore he says that there is in our bodies a concordance in the movements of air and fluid, and that everything is in sympathy. According to Asclepiades, however, nothing is naturally in sympathy with anything else, all substance being divided and broken up into inharmonious elements and absurd "molecules." Necessarily, then, besides making countless other statements in opposition to plain fact, he was ignorant of Nature's faculties, both that attracting what is appropriate, and that expelling what is foreign. Thus he invented some wretched nonsense to explain blood-production and anadosis, and, being utterly unable to find anything to say regarding the clearing-out of superfluities, he did not hesitate to join issue with obvious facts.

—A. J. BROCK.

HIGH STANDARDS [1]

GALEN

[From *On the Natural Faculties,* Book III]

I should not have cared to say anything further as to the origin of these (surplus substances) after Hippocrates, Plato, Aristotle, Diocles, Praxagoras, and Philotimus, nor indeed should I even have said anything about the faculties, if any of our predecessors had worked out this subject thoroughly.

While, however, the statements which the Ancients made on these points were correct, they yet omitted to defend their arguments with logical proofs; of course they never suspected that there could be sophists so shameless as to try to contradict obvious facts. More recent physicians, again, have been partly conquered by the sophistries of these fellows and have given credence to them; whilst others who attempted to argue with them appear to me to lack to a great extent the power of the Ancients. For this reason I have attempted to put together my arguments in the way in which it seems to me the Ancients, had any of them been still alive, would have done, in opposition to those who would overturn the finest doctrines of our art.

I am not, however, unaware that I shall achieve either nothing at all or else very little. For I find that a great many things which have been conclusively demonstrated by the Ancients are unintelligible to the bulk of the Moderns owing to their ignorance—nay, that, by reason of their laziness, they will not even make an attempt to comprehend them; and even if any of them have understood them, they have not given them impartial examination.

The fact is that he whose purpose is to know anything better than the multitude do must far surpass all others both as regards his nature and his early training. And when he reaches early adolescence he must become possessed with an ardent love for truth, like one inspired; neither day nor night may he cease to urge and strain himself in order to learn thoroughly all that has been said by the most illustrious of the Ancients. And when he has learnt this, then for a prolonged period he must test and prove it, observing what part of it is in agreement, and what in disagreement with obvious fact; thus he will choose this and turn away from that. To such an one my hope has been that my treatise would prove of the very greatest assistance. . . . Still, such people may be expected to be quite few in number, while, as for the others, this book will be as superfluous to them as a tale told to an ass.

—A. J. BROCK.

UNDER ROMAN SWAY

FROM SECOND CENTURY B. C. TO SECOND CENTURY A. D.

To Macedonian overlordship succeeded Roman rule which the Greeks in time recognized would be permanent. Local self-government was regularly permitted; but foreign relations were in the hands of the Romans, and even when specially favored cities, as Athens, were called free and independent, the terms were empty. The great days of Greece were over. The fact of conquest, the attitude of the conqueror, who looked upon the Greek of his day as an inferior, had their psychological effect. Then too the very advantages of Roman rule had bad effects. In the time of the Roman empire peace within the borders was insisted on, and protection from foreign invasion was guaranteed. There was no struggle, except to make a living. Greece settled down to a long period of peace, lethargy, even. Roman paternalism did its perfect work. And to state these facts is not to deny that Greece had evidently already passed the zenith of her civilization before she came under Roman sway. It should be stated, too, that the Romans did not of set purpose attempt to check independence of thought and expression in Greece. The fact is that changed conditions brought with them little incentive to mind or spirit. Still Greek culture did not die. In the arts and sciences it lived, though it did not grow. Very significant are the types of literature in which successful works were produced. Philosophy flourished by turning all its attention to the conduct of the individual, to ethics. History, and its allies, biography and geography, all the passive arts of observation and of record, were even brilliantly written. Satire, never public, but dealing with the faults and foibles of men, was never better represented than in the writings of Lucian.

It was in this period that the Romans themselves took the lead in many fields where the Greeks formerly had gained every prize. And it was in teaching their Roman conquerors that the Greeks of the later day did perhaps their most effective work, for by the glories of their past culture ultimately they led captivity captive.

I. HISTORY

THE ROMAN CONSTITUTION [1]

POLYBIUS

[From the *Histories*, Book VI]

Polybius, of Megalopolis in Greece, was born about 207 and died about 125 B.C. Polybius was well equipped by experience for the writing of history. He took an active part in the Achæan League before he was sent by the League as a hostage to Rome in 167 B.C. At Rome he was associated with the leading statesmen on terms of such intimacy that every opportunity was afforded him for studying the government and the people. After his release he entered upon extensive travels for the purpose of becoming acquainted with the places he was to describe. He was besides a close student of the various philosophical systems, and his wide reading in literature gave him powers of understanding and interpretation which warrant the description of him as one of the greatest of the Greek historians. He conceived history as concerned mainly with politics and war; as dealing with observed facts to be reported; as under the necessity of explaining cause and effect instead of being content with a mere narration of events; and as an account of the interrelation of all states rather than a treatment of each as a separate unit. The first five books of the *History* we have complete: the rest is extant only in fragments. Beginning with a sketch of early Roman history, it covered in detail a period from the war with Hannibal, 219 B.C., to the destruction of Carthage and of Corinth in 146 B.C.

Polybius, carrying forward the work begun by Aristotle of examining existing constitutions, arrives at the conclusion that the Roman has more to commend it than any other yet tried. The principle that wins his approval especially is the

[1] From The Loeb Classical Library, reprinted by permission.

interdependence of its several parts, the check system which controls while it allows the exercise of power. His sketch is to be referred to the time of the war with Hannibal just before 200 B.C.

The three kinds of government that I spoke of above all shared in the control of the Roman state. And such fairness and propriety in all respects was shown in the use of these three elements for drawing up the constitution and in its subsequent administration that it was impossible even for a native to pronounce with certainty whether the whole system was aristocratic, democratic, or monarchical. This was indeed only natural. For if one fixed one's eyes on the power of the consuls, the constitution seemed completely monarchical and royal; if on that of the senate, it seemed again to be aristocratic; and when one looked at the power of the masses, it seemed clearly to be a democracy. The parts of the state falling under the control of each element were and with a few modifications still are as follows.

The consuls, previous to leading out their legions, exercise authority in Rome over all public affairs, since all the other magistrates except the tribunes are under them and bound to obey them, and it is they who introduce embassies to the senate. Besides this it is they who consult the senate on matters of urgency, they who carry out in detail the provisions of its decrees. Again, as concerns all affairs of state administered by the people it is their duty to take these under their charge, to summon assemblies, to introduce measures, and to preside over the execution of the popular decrees. As for preparation for war and the general conduct of operations in the field, here their power is almost uncontrolled; for they are empowered to make what demands they choose on the allies, to appoint military tribunes, to levy soldiers and select those who are fittest for service. They also have the right of inflicting, when on active service, punishment on any one under their command; and they are authorized to spend any sum they decide upon from the public funds, being accompanied by a quæstor who faithfully executes their instructions. So that if one looks at this part of the administration alone, one may reasonably pronounce the constitution to be a pure monarchy or kingship. I may remark that any changes in these matters or in others of which I am about to speak that may be made in present or future times do not in any way affect the truth of the views I here state.

To pass to the senate. In the first place it has the control of the treasury, all revenue and expenditure being regulated by it. For with the exception of payments made to the consuls, the quæstors are not allowed to disburse for any particular object without a decree of the senate. And even the item of expenditure which is far heavier and more important than any other—the outlay every five years by the censors on public works, whether constructions or repairs—is under the control of the senate, which makes a grant to the censors for the purpose. Similarly crimes committed in Italy which require a public investigation, such as treason, conspiracy, poisoning, and assassination, are under the jurisdiction of the senate. Also if any private person or community in Italy is in need of arbitration or indeed claims damages or requires succour or protection, the senate attends to all such matters. It also occupies itself with the dispatch of all embassies sent to countries outside of Italy for the purpose either of settling differences, or of offering friendly advice, or indeed of imposing demands, or of receiving submission, or of declaring war; and in like manner with respect to embassies arriving in Rome it decides what reception and what answer should be given to them. All these matters are in the hands of the senate, nor have the people anything whatever to do with them. So that again to one residing in Rome during the absence of the consuls the constitution appears to be entirely aristocratic; and this is the conviction of many Greek states and many of the kings, as the senate manages all business connected with them.

After this we are naturally inclined to ask what part in the constitution is left for the people, considering that the senate controls all the particular matters I mentioned, and, what is most important, manages all matters of revenue and expenditure, and considering that the consuls again have uncontrolled authority as regards armaments and operations in the field. But nevertheless there is a part and a very important part left for the people. For it is the people which alone has the right to confer honours and inflict punishment, the only bonds by which kingdoms and states and in a word human society in general are held together. For where the distinction between these is overlooked or is observed but ill applied, no affairs can be properly administered. How indeed is this possible when good and evil men are held in equal estimation? It is by the people, then, in many cases that offences punishable by a fine are tried when the accused have held the highest office; and they are the only court which may try on capital charges. As regards the latter they have a practice which is praiseworthy and should be mentioned. Their usage allows those on trial for their lives when found guilty liberty to depart openly, thus inflicting voluntary exile on themselves, if even only one of the tribes that pronounce the verdict has not yet voted. Such exiles enjoy safety in the territories of Naples, Præneste, Tibur, and other *civitates fœderatæ*. Again, it is the people who bestow office on the deserving, the noblest reward of virtue in a state; the people have the power of approving or rejecting laws, and what is most important of all, they deliberate on the question of war and peace. Further, in the case of alliances, terms of peace, and treaties, it is the people who ratify all these or the reverse. Thus here again one might plausibly say that the people's share in the government is the greatest, and that the constitution is a democratic one.

Having stated how political power is distributed among the different parts of the state, I will now explain how each of the three parts is enabled, if they wish, to counteract or co-operate with the others. The consul, when he leaves with his army invested with the powers I mentioned, appears indeed to have absolute authority in all matters necessary for carrying out his purpose; but in fact he requires the support of the people and the senate, and is not able to bring his operations to a conclusion without them. For it is obvious that the legions require constant supplies, and without the consent of the senate, neither corn, clothing, nor pay can be provided; so that the commander's plans come to nothing, if the senate chooses to be deliberately negligent and obstructive. It also depends on the senate whether or not a general can carry out completely his conceptions and designs, since it has the right of either superseding him when his year's term of office has expired or of retaining him in command. Again, it is in its power to celebrate with pomp and to magnify the successes of a general or on the other hand to obscure and belittle them. For the processions they call triumphs, in which the generals being the actual spectacle of their achievements before the eyes of their fellow-citizens, cannot be properly organized and sometimes even cannot be held at all, unless the senate consents and provides the requisite funds. As for the people it is most in-

dispensable for the consuls to conciliate them, however far away from home they may be; for, as I said, it is the people which ratifies or annuls terms of peace and treaties, and what is most important, on laying down office the consuls are obliged to account for their actions to the people. So that in no respect is it safe for the consuls to neglect keeping in favour with both the senate and the people.

The senate again, which possesses such great power, is obliged in the first place to pay attention to the commons in public affairs and respect the wishes of the people, and it cannot carry out inquiries into the most grave and important offences against the state, punishable with death, and their correction, unless the *senatus consultum* is confirmed by the people. The same is the case in matters which directly affect the senate itself, for if anyone introduces a law meant to deprive the senate of some of its traditional authority, or to abolish the precedence and other distinctions of the senators or even to curtail them of their private fortunes, it is the people alone which has the power of passing or rejecting any such measure. And what is most important is that if a single one of the tribunes interposes, the senate is unable to decide finally about any matter, and cannot even meet and hold sittings; and here it is to be observed that the tribunes are always obliged to act as the people decree and to pay every attention to their wishes. Therefore for all these reasons the senate is afraid of the masses and must pay due attention to the popular will.

Similarly, again, the people must be submissive to the senate and respect its members both in public and in private. Through the whole of Italy a vast number of contracts, which it would not be easy to enumerate, are given out by the censors for the construction and repair of public buildings, and besides this there are many things which are farmed, such as navigable rivers, harbours, gardens, mines, lands, in fact everything that forms part of the Roman dominion. Now all these matters are undertaken by the people, and one may almost say that everyone is interested in these contracts and the work they involve. For certain people are the actual purchasers from the censors of the contracts, others are the partners of these first, others stand surety for them, others pledge their own fortunes to the state for this purpose. Now in all these matters the senate is supreme. It can grant extension of time; it can relieve the contractor if any accident occurs; and if the work proves to be absolutely impossible to carry out it can liberate him from his contract. There are in fact many ways in which the senate can either benefit or injure those who manage public property, as all these matters are referred to it. What is even more important is that the judges in most civil trials, whether public or private, are appointed from its members, where the action involves large interests. So that all citizens being at the mercy of the senate, and looking forward with alarm to the uncertainty of litigation, are very shy of obstructing or resisting its decisions. Similarly everyone is reluctant to oppose the projects of the consuls as all are generally and individually under their authority when in the field.

Such being the power that each part has of hampering the others or co-operating with them, their union is adequate to all emergencies, so that it is impossible to find a better political system than this. For whenever the menace of some common danger from abroad compels them to act in concord and support each other, so great does the strength of the state become, that nothing which is requisite can be neglected, as all are zealously competing in devising means of meeting the need of the hour, nor can any decision arrived at fail to be executed promptly, as all are co-operating both in public and in private to the accomplishment of the task they have set themselves; and consequently this peculiar form of constitution possesses an irresistible power of attaining every object upon which it is resolved. When again they are freed from external menace, and reap the harvest of good fortune and affluence which is the result of their success, and in the enjoyment of this prosperity are corrupted by flattery and idleness and wax insolent and overbearing, as indeed happens often enough, it is then especially that we see the state providing itself a remedy for the evil from which it suffers. For when one part having grown out of proportion to the others aims at supremacy and tends to become too predominant, it is evident that, as for the reasons above given none of the three is absolute, but the purpose of the one can be counterworked and thwarted by the others, none of them will excessively outgrow the others or treat them with contempt. All in fact remains *in statu quo,* on the one hand, because any aggressive impulse is sure to be checked and from the outset each estate stands in dread of being interfered with by the others.

—W. R. PATON.

ROME AND CARTHAGE [1]

POLYBIUS

[From the *Histories,* Book VI]

Polybius subscribes to the theory that world power passes, as by a natural law, from state to state. The conflict between Rome and Carthage was not a conflict between equals, but one between a state whose decay had already set in and a state which was just reaching the height of her power. The strength of a state, moreover, is not to be measured solely by its constitution or by its military prepared-

[1] From The Loeb Classical Library, reprinted by permission.

ness or by its economic well-being, but by the spiritual health of its citizenry. Polybius introduces this passage in his account of the war with Hannibal.

The constitution of Carthage seems to me to have been originally well contrived as regards its most distinctive points. For there were kings, and the house of Elders was an aristocratic force, and the people were supreme in matters proper to them, the entire frame of the state much resembling that of Rome and Sparta. But at the time when they entered on the Hannibalic War, the Carthaginian constitution had degenerated, and that of Rome was better. For as every body or state or action has its natural periods first of growth, then of prime, and finally of decay, and as everything in them is at its best when they are in their prime, it is for this reason that the difference between the two states manifested itself at this time. For by as much as the power and prosperity of Carthage had been earlier than that of Rome, by so much had Carthage already begun to decline; while Rome was exactly at her prime, as far at least as her system of government was concerned. Consequently the multitude at Carthage had already acquired the chief voice in deliberations; while at Rome the senate still retained this; and hence, as in one case the masses deliberated and in the other the most eminent men, the Roman decisions on public affairs were superior, so that although they met with complete disaster, they were finally by the wisdom of their counsels victorious over the Carthaginians in the war.

But to pass to differences of detail, such as, to begin with, the conduct of war, the Carthaginians naturally are superior at sea both in efficiency and equipment, because seamanship has long been their national craft, and they busy themselves with the sea more than any other people; but as regards military service on land the Romans are much more efficient. They indeed devote their whole energies to this matter, whereas the Carthaginians entirely neglect their infantry, though they do pay some slight attention to their cavalry. The reason of this is that the troops they employ are foreign and mercenary, whereas those of the Romans are natives of the soil and citizens. So that in this respect also we must pronounce the political system of Rome to be superior to that of Carthage, the Carthaginians continuing to depend for the maintenance of their freedom on the courage of a mercenary force but the Romans on their own valour and on the aid of their allies. Consequently even if they happen to be worsted at the outset, the Romans redeem defeat by final success, while it is the contrary with the Carthaginians. For the Romans, fighting as they are for their country and their children, never can abate their fury but continue to throw their whole hearts into the struggle until they get the better of their enemies. It follows that though the Romans are, as I said, much less skilled in naval matters, they are on the whole successful at sea owing to the gallantry of their men; for although skill in seamanship is of no small importance in naval battles, it is chiefly the courage of the marines that turns the scale in favour of victory. Now not only do Italians in general naturally excel Phœnicians and Africans in bodily strength and personal courage, but by their institutions also they do much to foster a spirit of bravery in the young men. . . .

Again, the laws and customs relating to the acquisition of wealth are better in Rome than at Carthage. At Carthage nothing which results in profit is regarded as disgraceful; at Rome nothing is considered more so than to accept bribes and seek gain from improper channels. For no less strong than their approval of money-making by respectable means is their condemnation of unscrupulous gain from forbidden sources. A proof of this is that at Carthage candidates for office practise open bribery, whereas at Rome death is the penalty for it. Therefore as the rewards offered to merit are the opposite in the two cases, it is natural that the steps taken to gain them should also be dissimilar.

But the quality in which the Roman commonwealth is most distinctly superior is in my opinion the nature of their religious convictions. It believes that it is the very thing which among other peoples is an object of reproach, I mean superstition, which maintains the cohesion of the Roman state. These matters are clothed in such pomp and introduced to such an extent into their public and private life that nothing could exceed it, a fact which will surprise many. My own opinion at least is that they have adopted this course for the sake of the common people. It is a course which perhaps would not have been necessary had it been possible to form a state composed of wise men, but as every multitude is fickle, full of lawless desires, un-

reasoned passion, and violent anger, the multitude must be held in by invisible terrors and such like pageantry. For this reason I think, not that the ancients acted rashly and at haphazard in introducing among the people notions concerning the gods and beliefs in the terrors of hell, but that the moderns are most rash and foolish in banishing such beliefs. The consequence is that among the Greeks, apart from other things, members of the government, if they are entrusted with no more than a talent, though they have ten copyists and as many seals and twice as many witnesses, cannot keep their faith; whereas among the Romans those who as magistrates and legates are dealing with large sums of money maintain correct conduct just because they have pledged their faith by oath. Whereas elsewhere it is a rare thing to find a man who keeps his hands off public money, and whose record is clean in this respect, among the Romans one rarely comes across a man who has been detected in such conduct.

—W. R. PATON.

II. BIOGRAPHY

CÆSAR

PLUTARCH

[From the *Lives*]

Plutarch was born about 50 A.D. at Chæronea in central Greece, and died about 125. After a period of study in Athens and of travels in Egypt, Asia Minor and Italy, Plutarch withdrew to the quiet of his native town to spend the rest of his life in the pursuits of a man of letters. He was an exhaustive reader, a keen observer, and possessed of an unusual gift for retaining for future use all that he saw and read. His works, which are very extensive, fall into two groups,

the *Moral Essays* and the *Lives*. He regarded himself as primarily a philosopher, and interpreted biography as an investigation in practical ethics. In presenting the salient outlines of human character, and in interweaving anecdotes, conversations, as well as the mere facts of a life, in a style which can hold the reader's interest, Plutarch has perhaps never been surpassed by any biographer.

Plutarch's *Lives* as a general rule are grouped in pairs, each of which is made up of a biography of a Greek followed by one of a Roman, and concluding with a comparison of the two characters presented. The fact that the sketch of Cæsar is paired with a sketch of Alexander would seem to indicate that Plutarch placed the main emphasis in his interpretation on Cæsar's military genius. His account has had a profound influence, greater perhaps than that of any other ancient writer, in shaping the general idea of Cæsar that found acceptance in later history and in literature, notably in Shakespeare's *Julius Cæsar*.

There being two factions in the city, one that of Sulla, which was very powerful, and the other that of Marius, which was then broken and in a very low condition, he undertook to revive this and to make it his own. And to this end, whilst he was in the height of his repute with the people for the magnificent shows he gave as ædile, he ordered images of Marius, and figures of Victory, with trophies in their hands, to be carried privately in the night and placed in the capitol. Next morning, when some saw them bright with gold and beautifully made, with inscriptions upon them, referring them to Marius's exploits over the Cimbrians, they were surprised at the boldness of him who had set them up, nor was it difficult to guess who it was. The fame of this soon spread and brought together a great concourse of people. Some cried out that it was on open attempt against the established government thus to revive those honors which had been buried by the laws and decrees of the senate; that Cæsar had done it to sound the temper of the people whom he had prepared before, and to try whether they were tame enough to bear his humor, and would quietly give way to his innovations. On the other hand, Marius's party took courage, and it was incredible how numerous they were suddenly seen to be, and what a multitude of them appeared and came shouting into the capitol. Many, when they saw Marius's likenesses, cried for joy, and Cæsar was highly extolled as the one man, in the place of all others, who was a relation worthy of Marius. Upon this the senate met, and

Catulus Lutatius, one of the most eminent Romans of that time, stood up and inveighed against Cæsar, closing his speech with the remarkable saying, that Cæsar was not now working mines, but planting batteries to overthrow the state. But when Cæsar had made an apology for himself, and satisfied the senate, his admirers were very much animated, and advised him not to depart from his own thoughts for any one, since with the people's good favor he would erelong get the better of them all, and be the first man in the commonwealth.

At this time, Metellus, the High-Priest, died, and Catulus and Isauricus, persons of the highest reputation, and who had great influence in the senate, were competitors for the office; yet Cæsar would not give way to them, but presented himself to the people as a candidate against them. The several parties seeming very equal, Catulus, who, because he had the most honor to lose, was the most apprehensive of the event, sent to Cæsar to buy him off, with offers of a great sum of money. But his answer was, that he was ready to borrow a larger sum than that, to carry on the contest. Upon the day of election, as his mother conducted him out of doors with tears, after embracing her, "My mother," he said, "to-day you will see me either High-Priest, or an exile." When the votes were taken, after a great struggle, he carried it, and excited among the senate and nobility great alarm lest he might now urge on the people to every kind of insolence. . . .

But there was no disturbance during his prætorship, only what misfortune he met with in his own domestic affairs. Publius Clodius was a patrician by descent, eminent both for his riches and eloquence, but in licentiousness of life and audacity he exceeded the most noted profligates of the day. He was in love with Pompeia, Cæsar's wife, and she had no aversion to him. But there was strict watch kept on her apartment, and Cæsar's mother, Aurelia, who was a discreet woman, being continually about her, made any interview very dangerous and difficult. The Romans have a goddess whom they call Bona, the same whom the Greeks call Gynæcea. The Phrygians, who claim a peculiar title to her, say she was the mother of Midas. The Romans profess she was one of the Dryads, and married to Faunus. The Grecians affirm that she is that mother of Bacchus whose name is not to be uttered, and, for this reason, the women who celebrate her festival, cover the tents with vine branches, and, in accordance with the fable, a consecrated serpent is placed by the goddess. It is not lawful for a man to be by, nor so much as in the house, whilst the rites are celebrated, but the women by themselves perform the sacred offices, which are said to be much the same with those used in the solemnities of Orpheus. When the festival comes, the husband, who is either consul or prætor, and with him every male creature, quits the house. The wife then taking it under her care, sets it in order, and the principal ceremonies are performed during the night, the women playing together amongst themselves as they keep watch, and music of various kinds going on.

As Pompeia was at that time celebrating this feast, Clodius, who as yet had no beard, and so thought to pass undiscovered, took upon him the dress and ornaments of a singing woman, and so came thither, having the air of a young girl. Finding the doors open, he was without any stop introduced by the maid, who was in the intrigue. She presently ran to tell Pompeia, but as she was away a long time, he grew uneasy in waiting for her, and left his post and traversed the house from one room to another, still taking care to avoid the lights, till at last Aurelia's woman met him, and invited him to play with her, as the women did among themselves. He refused to comply, and she presently pulled him for-ward, and asked him who he was, and whence he came. Clodius told her he was waiting for Pompeia's own maid, Abra, being in fact her own name also, and as he said so, betrayed himself by his voice. Upon which the woman shrieking, ran into the company where there were lights, and cried out, she had discovered a man. The women were all in a fright. Aurelia covered up the sacred things and stopped the proceedings, and having ordered the doors to be shut, went about with lights to find Clodius, who was got into the maid's room that he had come in with, and was seized there. The women knew him, and drove him out of doors, and at once, that same night, went home and told their husbands the story. In the morning, it was all about town, what an impious attempt Clodius had made, and how he ought to be punished as an offender, not only against those whom he had affronted, but also against the public and the gods. Upon which one of the tribunes impeached him for profaning the holy rites. and some of the principal senators combined together and gave evidence against him, that besides many other horrible crimes, he had been guilty of incest with his own sister, who was married to Lucullus. But the people set themselves against this combination of the nobility, and defended Clodius, which was of great service to him with the judges, who took alarm and were afraid to provoke the multitude. Cæsar at once dismissed Pompeia, but being summoned as a witness against Clodius, said he had nothing to charge him with. This looking like a paradox, the accuser asked him why he parted with his wife. Cæsar replied, "I wished my wife to be not so much as suspected." Some say that Cæsar spoke this as his real thought; others, that he did it to gratify the people, who were very earnest to save Clodius. Clodius, at any rate, escaped; most of the judges giving their opinions so written as to be illegible, that they might not be in danger from the people by condemning him, nor in disgrace with the nobility by acquitting him.

Cæsar, in the mean time, being out of his prætorship, had got the province of Spain, but was in great embarrassment with his creditors, who, as he was going off, came upon him, and were very pressing and importunate. This led him to apply himself to Crassus, who was the richest man in Rome, but wanted Cæsar's youthful vigor and heat to sustain the opposition against Pompey. Crassus took upon him to satisfy those creditors who were most uneasy to him, and would not be put off any longer, and engaged himself to the amount of eight hundred and thirty talents, upon which Cæsar was now at liberty to go to his province. In his journey, as he was crossing the Alps, and passing by a small village of the barbarians with but few inhabitants and those wretchedly poor, his companions asked the question among themselves by way of mockery, if there were any canvassing for offices there; any contention which should be uppermost, or feuds of great men one against another. To which Cæsar made answer seriously, "For my part, I had rather be the first man among these fellows, than the second man in Rome." It is said that another time, when free from business in Spain, after reading some part of the history of Alexander, he sat a great while very thoughtful, and at last burst out into tears. His friends were surprised, and asked him the reason of it. "Do you think," said he, "I have not just cause to weep, when I consider that Alexander at my age had conquered so many nations, and I have all this time done nothing that is memorable?" As soon as he came into Spain he was very active, and in a few days had got together ten new cohorts of foot in addition to the twenty which were there before. With these he marched against the Calaici and Lusitani and conquered them, and advancing as far as the ocean, subdued the tribes which never before had been subject to the Romans. Having managed his military affairs with good success, he was equally happy in the course of his civil government. He took pains to establish a good understanding amongst the several states, and no less care to heal the differences between debtors and creditors. He ordered that the creditor should receive two parts of the debtor's yearly income, and that the other part should be managed by the debtor himself, till by this method the whole debt was at last discharged. This conduct made him leave his province with a fair reputation; being rich himself, and having enriched his soldiers, and having received from them the honorable name of Imperator.

There is a law among the Romans, that whoever desires the honor of a triumph must stay without the city and expect his answer. And another, that those who stand for the consulship shall appear personally upon the place. Cæsar was come home at the very time of choosing consuls, and being in difficulty between these two opposite laws, sent to the senate to desire that since he was obliged to be absent, he might sue for the consulship by his friends. Cato, being backed by the law, at first opposed his request; afterwards perceiving that Cæsar had prevailed with a great part of the senate to comply with it, he made it his business to gain time, and went on wasting the whole day in speaking. Upon which Cæsar saw fit to let the triumph fall, and pursued the consulship. Entering the town and coming forward immediately, he had recourse to a piece of state-policy by which everybody was deceived but Cato. This was the reconciling of Crassus and Pompey, the two men who were then the most powerful in Rome. There had been a quarrel between them, which he now succeeded in making up, and by this means strengthened himself by the united power of both, and so under the cover of an action which carried all the appearance of a piece of kindness and good-nature, caused what was in effect a revolution in the government. For it was not the quarrel between Pompey and Cæsar, as most men imagine, which was the origin of the civil wars, but their union, their conspiring together at first to subvert the aristocracy, and so quarrelling afterwards between themselves. Cato, who often foretold what the consequence of this alliance would be, had then the character of a sullen, interfering man, but in the end the reputation of a wise but unsuccessful counsellor.

Thus Cæsar being doubly supported by the interests of Crassus and Pompey, was promoted to the consulship, and triumphantly proclaimed with Calpurnius Bibulus. When he entered on his office, he brought in bills which would have been preferred with better grace by the most audacious of the tribunes than by a consul, in which he proposed the plantation of colonies and division of lands, simply to please the commonalty. The best and most honorable of the senators opposed it, upon which, as he had long wished for nothing more than for such a colorable pretext, he loudly protested how much against his will it was to be driven to seek support from the people, and how the senate's insulting and harsh conduct left no other course possible for him, than to devote himself henceforth to the popular cause and interest. And so he hurried out of the senate, and presenting himself to the people, and there placing Crassus and Pompey, one on each side of him, he asked them whether they consented to the bills he had proposed. They owned their assent, upon which he desired them to assist him against those who had threatened to oppose him with their swords. They engaged they would, and Pompey added further, that he would meet their swords with a sword and buckler too. These words the nobles much resented, as neither suitable to his own dignity, nor becoming the reverence due to the senate, but resembling rather the vehemence of a boy, or the fury of a madman. But the people were pleased with it. In order to get a yet firmer hold upon Pompey, Cæsar having a daughter, Julia, who had been before contracted to Servilius Cæpio, now betrothed her to Pompey, and told Servilius he should have Pompey's daughter, who was not unengaged either, but promised to Sulla's son, Faustus. A little time after, Cæsar married Calpurnia, the daughter of Piso, and got Piso made consul for the year following. Cato exclaimed loudly against this, and protested with a great deal of warmth, that it was intolerable the government should be prostituted by marriages, and that they should advance one another to the commands of armies, provinces, and other great posts, by means of women. Bibulus, Cæsar's colleague, finding it was to no purpose to oppose his bills, but that he was in danger of being murdered in the forum, as also was Cato, confined himself to his house, and there let the remaining part of his consulship expire. Pompey, when he was married, at once filled the forum with soldiers, and gave the people his help in passing the new laws, and secured Cæsar the government of all Gaul, both on this side and the other side of the Alps, together with Illyricum, and the command of four legions for five years. Cato made some attempts against these proceedings, but was seized and led off on the way to prison by Cæsar, who expected he would appeal to the tribunes. But when he saw that Cato went along without speaking a word, and not only the nobility were indignant, but that the people, also, out of respect for Cato's virtue, were following in silence, and with dejected looks, he himself privately desired one of the tribunes to rescue Cato. As for the other senators, some few of them attended the house, the rest being disgusted, absented themselves. Hence

Considius, a very old man, took occasion one day to tell Cæsar, that the senators did not meet because they were afraid of his soldiers. Cæsar asked, "Why don't you then, out of the same fear, keep at home?" To which Considius replied, that age was his guard against fear, and that the small remains of his life were not worth much caution. But the most disgraceful thing that was done in Cæsar's consulship, was his assisting to gain the tribuneship for the same Clodius who had made the attempt upon his wife's chastity, and intruded upon the secret vigils. He was elected on purpose to effect Cicero's downfall; nor did Cæsar leave the city to join his army, till they two had overpowered Cicero, and driven him out of Italy.

Thus far have we followed Cæsar's actions before the wars of Gaul. After this, he seems to begin his course afresh, and to enter upon a new life and scene of action. And the period of those wars which he now fought, and those many expeditions in which he subdued Gaul, showed him to be a soldier and general not in the least inferior to any of the greatest and most admired commanders who had ever appeared at the head of armies. . . .

There was no danger to which he did not willingly expose himself, no labor from which he pleaded an exemption. His contempt of danger was not so much wondered at by his soldiers, because they knew how much he coveted honor. But his enduring so much hardship, which he did to all appearance beyond his natural strength, very much astonished them. For he was a spare man, had a soft and white skin, was distempered in the head, and subject to epilepsy, which, it is said, first seized him at Corduba. But he did not make the weakness of his constitution a pretext for his ease, but rather used war as the best physic against his indispositions; whilst by indefatigable journeys, coarse diet,

frequent lodging in the field, and continual laborious exercise, he struggled with his diseases, and fortified his body against all attacks. He slept generally in his chariots or litters, employing even his rest in pursuit of action. In the day he was thus carried to the forts, garrisons, and camps, one servant sitting with him, who used to write down what he dictated as he went, and a soldier attending behind with his sword drawn. He drove so rapidly, that when he first left Rome, he arrived at the river Rhone within eight days. He had been an expert rider from his childhood; for it was usual with him to sit with his hands joined together behind his back, and so to put his horse to its full speed. And in this war he disciplined himself so far as to be able to dictate letters from on horseback, and to give directions to two who took notes at the same time, or, as Oppius says, to more. And it is thought that he was the first who contrived means for communicating with friends by cipher, when either press of business, or the large extent of the city, left him no time for a personal conference about matters that required despatch. How little nice he was in his diet, may be seen in the following instance. When at the table of Valerius Leo, who entertained him at supper at Milan, a dish of asparagus was put before him, on which his host instead of oil had poured sweet ointment, Cæsar partook of it without any disgust and reprimanded his friends for finding fault with it. "For it was enough," said he, "not to eat what you did not like; but he who reflects on another man's want of breeding, shows he wants it as much himself." Another time upon the road he was driven by a storm into a poor man's cottage, where he found but one room, and that such as would afford but a mean reception to a single person, and therefore told his companions, places of honor should be given up to the greater men, and necessary accommodations to the weaker, and accordingly ordered that Oppius, who was in bad health, should lodge within, whilst he and the rest slept under a shed at the door. . . .

Cæsar had long ago resolved upon the overthrow of Pompey, as had Pompey, for that matter, upon his. For Crassus, the fear of whom had hitherto kept them in peace, having now been killed in Parthia, if the one of them wished to make himself the greatest man in Rome, he had only to overthrow the other; and if he again wished to prevent his own fall, he had nothing for it but to be beforehand with him whom he feared. Pompey had not been long under any such apprehensions, having till lately despised Cæsar, as thinking it no difficult matter to put down him whom he himself had advanced. But Cæsar had entertained this design from the beginning against his rivals, and had retired, like an expert wrestler, to prepare himself apart for the combat. Making the Gallic wars his exercise-ground, he had at once improved the strength of his soldiery, and had heightened his own glory by his great actions, so that he was looked on as one who might challenge comparison with Pompey. Nor did he let go any of those advantages which were now given him both by Pompey himself and the times, and the ill government of Rome, where all who were candidates for offices publicly gave money, and without any shame bribed the people, who having received their pay, did not contend for their benefactors with their bare suffrages, but with bows, swords, and slings. So that after having many times stained the place of election with the blood of men killed upon the spot, they left the city at last without a government at all, to be carried about like a ship without a pilot to steer her; while all who had any wisdom could only be thankful if a course of such wild and stormy disorder and madness might end no worse than in a monarchy. Some were so bold as to declare openly, that

the government was incurable but by a monarchy, and that they ought to take that remedy from the hands of the gentlest physician, meaning Pompey, who, though in words he pretended to decline it, yet in reality made his utmost efforts to be declared dictator. Cato perceiving his design, prevailed with the senate to make him sole consul, that with the offer of a more legal sort of monarchy he might be withheld from demanding the dictatorship. They over and above voted him the continuance of his provinces, for he had two, Spain and all Africa, which he governed by his lieutenants, and maintained armies under him, at the yearly charge of a thousand talents out of the public treasury.

Upon this Cæsar also sent and petitioned for the consulship, and the continuance of his provinces. Pompey at first did not stir in it, but Marcellus and Lentulus opposed it, who had always hated Cæsar, and now did everything, whether fit or unfit, which might disgrace and affront him. . . .

Yet the demands which Cæsar made had the fairest colors of equity imaginable. For he proposed to lay down his arms, and that Pompey should do the same, and both together should become private men, and each expect a reward of his services from the public. For that those who proposed to disarm him, and at the same time to confirm Pompey in all the power he held, were simply establishing the one in the tyranny which they accused the other of aiming at. When Curio made these proposals to the people in Cæsar's name, he was loudly applauded, and some threw garlands towards him, and dismissed him as they do successful wrestlers, crowned with flowers. Antony, being tribune, produced a letter sent from Cæsar on this occasion, and read it, though the consuls did what they could to oppose it. But Scipio, Pompey's father-in-law, proposed in the senate, that if Cæsar did not lay down his arms within such a time, he should be voted an enemy; and the consuls putting it to the question, whether Pompey should dismiss his soldiers, and again, whether Cæsar should disband his, very few assented to the first, but almost all to the latter. But Antony proposing again, that both should lay down their commissions, all but a very few agreed to it. Scipio was upon this very violent, and Lentulus the consul cried aloud, that they had need of arms, and not of suffrages, against a robber; so that the senators for the present adjourned, and appeared in mourning as a mark of grief for the dissension.

Afterwards there came other letters from Cæsar, which seemed yet more moderate, for he proposed to quit everything else, and only to retain Gaul within the Alps, Illyricum, and two legions, till he should stand a second time for consul. Cicero, the orator, who was lately returned from Cilicia, endeavored to reconcile differences, and softened Pompey, who was willing to comply in other things, but not to allow him the soldiers. At last Cicero used his persuasions with Cæsar's friends to accept of the provinces, and six thousand soldiers only, and so to make up the quarrel. And Pompey was inclined to give way to this, but Lentulus, the consul, would not hearken to it, but drove Antony and Curio out of the senate-house with insults, by which he afforded Cæsar the most plausible pretence that could be, and one which he could readily use to inflame the soldiers, by showing them two persons of such repute and authority, who were forced to escape in a hired carriage in the dress of slaves. For so they were glad to disguise themselves, when they fled out of Rome.

There was not about him at that time above three hundred horse, and five thousand foot; for the rest of his army, which was left behind the Alps, was to be brought after him by officers who had received orders for that purpose. But he thought the first motion towards the design which he had on foot did not require large forces at present, and that what was wanted was to make this first step suddenly, and so as to astound his enemies with the boldness of it; as it would be easier, he thought, to throw them in consternation by doing what they never anticipated, than fairly to conquer them, if he had alarmed them by his preparations. And therefore, he commanded his captains and other officers to go only with their swords in their hands, without any other arms, and make themselves masters of Ariminum, a large city of Gaul, with as little disturbance and bloodshed as possible. He committed the care of these forces to Hortensius, and himself spent the day in public as a stander-by and spectator of the gladiators, who exercised before him. A little before night he attended to his person, and then went into the hall, and conversed for some time with those he had invited to supper, till it began to grow dusk, when he rose from the table, and made his excuses to the company, begging them to stay till he came back, having already given private directions to a few immediate friends, that they should follow him, not all the same way, but some one way, some another. He himself got into one of the hired carriages, and drove at first another way, but presently towards Ariminum. When he came to the river Rubicon, which parts Gaul within the Alps from the rest of Italy, his thoughts began to work, now he was just entering upon the danger, and he wavered much in his mind, when he considered the greatness of the enterprise into which he was throwing himself. He checked his course, and ordered a halt, while he revolved with himself, and often changed his opinion one way and the other, without speaking a word. This was when his purposes fluctuated most; presently he also discussed the matter with his friends who were about him, (of which number

Asinius Pollio was one), computing how many calamities his passing that river would bring upon mankind, and what a relation of it would be transmitted to posterity. At last, in a sort of passion, casting aside calculation, and abandoning himself to what might come, and using the proverb frequently in their mouths who enter upon dangerous and bold attempts, "The die is cast," with these words he took the river. Once over, he used all expedition possible, and before it was day reached Ariminum, and took it. It is said that the night before he passed the river, he had an impious dream, that he was unnaturally familiar with his own mother.

As soon as Ariminum was taken, wide gates, so to speak, were thrown open, to let in war upon every land alike and sea, and with the limits of the province, the boundaries of the laws were transgressed. Nor would one have thought that, as at other times, the mere men and women fled from one town of Italy to another in their consternation, but that the very towns themselves left their sites, and fled for succor to each other. The city of Rome was overrun as it were with a deluge, by the conflux of people flying in from all the neighboring places. Magistrates could no longer govern, nor the eloquence of any orator quiet it; it was all but suffering shipwreck by the violence of its own tempestuous agitation. The most vehement contrary passions and impulses were at work every where. Nor did those who rejoiced at the prospect of the change altogether conceal their feelings, but when they met, as in so great a city they frequently must, with the alarmed and dejected of the other party, they provoked quarrels by their bold expressions of confidence in the event. Pompey, sufficiently disturbed of himself, was yet more perplexed by the clamors of others; some telling him that he justly suffered for having armed Cæsar against himself and the government;

others blaming him for permitting Cæsar to be insolently used by Lentulus, when he made such ample concessions, and offered such reasonable proposals towards an accommodation. Favonius bade him now stamp upon the ground; for once talking big in the senate, he desired them not to trouble themselves about making preparations for the war, for that he himself, with one stamp of his foot, would fill all Italy with soldiers. Yet still Pompey at that time had more forces than Cæsar; but he was not permitted to pursue his own thoughts, but being continually disturbed with false reports and alarms, as if the enemy was close upon him and carrying all before him, he gave way, and let himself be borne down by the general cry. He put forth an edict declaring the city to be in a state of anarchy, and left it with orders that the senate should follow him, and that no one should stay behind who did not prefer tyranny to their country and liberty. . . .

When the two armies were come into Pharsalia, and both encamped there, Pompey's thoughts ran the same way as they had done before, against fighting, and the more because of some unlucky presages, and a vision he had in a dream. But those who were about him were so confident of success, that Domitius, and Spinther, and Scipio, as if they had already conquered, quarrelled which should succeed Cæsar in the pontificate. And many sent to Rome to take houses fit to accommodate consuls and prætors, as being sure of entering upon those offices, as soon as the battle was over. The cavalry especially were obstinate for fighting, being splendidly armed and bravely mounted, and valuing themselves upon the fine horses they kept, and upon their own handsome persons; as also upon the advantage of their numbers, for they were five thousand against one thousand of Cæsar's. Nor were the numbers of the infantry less disproportionate, there being forty-five thousand of Pompey's, against twenty-two thousand of the enemy.

Cæsar collecting his soldiers together, told them that Corfinius was coming up to them with two legions, and that fifteen cohorts more under Callenus were posted at Megara and Athens; he then asked them whether they would stay till these joined them, or would hazard the battle by themselves. They all cried out to him not to wait, but on the contrary to do whatever he could to bring about an engagement as soon as possible. When he sacrificed to the gods for the lustration of his army, upon the death of the first victim, the augur told him, within three days he should come to a decisive action. Cæsar asked him whether he saw anything in the entrails, which promised a happy event. "That," said the priest, "you can best answer yourself; for the gods signify a great alteration from the present posture of affairs. If, therefore, you think yourself well off now, expect worse fortune; if unhappy, hope for better." The night before the battle, as he walked the rounds about midnight, there was a light seen in the heaven, very bright and flaming, which seemed to pass over Cæsar's camp, and fall into Pompey's. And when Cæsar's soldiers came to relieve the watch in the morning, they perceived a panic disorder among the enemies. However he did not expect to fight that day, but set about raising his camp with the intention of marching towards Scotussa.

But when the tents were now taken down, his scouts rode up to him, and told him the enemy would give him battle. With this news he was extremely pleased, and having performed his devotions to the gods, he set his army in battle array, dividing them into three bodies. Over the middlemost he placed Domitius Calvinus; Antony commanded the left wing, and he himself the right, being resolved to fight at the head of the tenth legion. But when he saw the enemy's

cavalry taking position against him, being struck with their fine appearance and their number, he gave private orders that six cohorts from the rear of the army should come round and join him, whom he posted behind the right wing, and instructed them what they should do, when the enemy's horse came to charge. On the other side, Pompey commanded the right wing, Domitius the left, and Scipio, Pompey's father-in-law, the centre. The whole weight of the cavalry was collected on the left wing, with the intent that they should outflank the right wing of the enemy, and rout that part where the general himself commanded. For they thought no phalanx of infantry could be solid enough to sustain such a shock, but that they must necessarily be broken and shattered all to pieces upon the onset of so immense a force of cavalry. When they were ready on both sides to give the signal for battle, Pompey commanded his foot who were in the front, to stand their ground, and without breaking their order, receive quietly the enemy's first attack, till they came within javelin's cast. Cæsar, in this respect, also, blames Pompey's generalship, as if he had not been aware how the first encounter, when made with an impetus and upon the run, gives weight and force to the strokes, and fires the men's spirits into a flame, which the general concurrence fans to full heat. He himself was just putting the troops into motion and advancing to the action, when he found one of his captains, a trusty and experienced soldier, encouraging his men to exert their utmost. Cæsar called him by his name, and said, "What hopes, Caius Crassinius, and what grounds for encouragement?" Crassinius stretched out his hand, and cried in a loud voice, "We shall conquer nobly, Cæsar; and I this day will deserve your praises, either alive or dead." So he said, and was the first man to run in upon the enemy, followed by the hundred and twenty soldiers about him, and breaking through the first rank, still pressed on forwards with much slaughter of the enemy, till at last he was struck back by the wound of a sword, which went in at his mouth with such force that it came out at his neck behind.

Whilst the foot was thus sharply engaged in the main battle, on the flank Pompey's horse rode up confidently, and opened their ranks very wide, that they might surround the right wing of Cæsar. But before they engaged, Cæsar's cohorts rushed out and attacked them, and did not dart their javelins at a distance, nor strike at the thighs and legs, as they usually did in close battle, but aimed at their faces. For thus Cæsar had instructed them, in hopes that young gentlemen, who had not known much of battles and wounds, but came wearing their hair long, in the flower of their age and height of their beauty, would be more apprehensive of such blows, and not care for hazarding both a danger at present and a blemish for the future. And so it proved, for they were so far from bearing the stroke of the javelins, that they could not stand the sight of them, but turned about, and covered their faces to secure them. Once in disorder, presently they turned about to fly; and so most shamefully ruined all. For those who had beat them back, at once outflanked the infantry, and falling on their rear cut them to pieces. Pompey, who commanded the other wing of the army, when he saw his cavalry thus broken and flying, was no longer himself, nor did he now remember that he was Pompey the Great, but like one whom some god had deprived of his senses, retired to his tent without speaking a word, and there sat to expect the event, till the whole army was routed, and the enemy appeared upon the works which were thrown up before the camp, where they closely engaged with his men, who were posted there to defend it. Then first he seemed to have recovered his senses, and uttering, it is said, only these

words, "What, into the camp too?" he laid aside his general's habit, and putting on such clothes as might best favor his flight, stole off. What fortune he met with afterwards, how he took shelter in Egypt, and was murdered there, we tell you in his Life.

Cæsar, when he came to view Pompey's camp, and saw some of his opponents dead upon the ground, others dying, said, with a groan, "This they would have; they brought me to this necessity. I, Caius Cæsar, after succeeding in so many wars, had been condemned, had I dismissed my army." These words, Pollio says, Cæsar spoke in Latin at that time, and that he himself wrote them in Greek; adding, that those who were killed at the taking of the camp, were most of them servants; and that not above six thousand soldiers fell. Cæsar incorporated most of the foot whom he took prisoners, with his own legions, and gave a free pardon to many of the distinguished persons, and amongst the rest, to Brutus, who afterwards killed him. He did not immediately appear after the battle was over, which put Cæsar, it is said, into great anxiety for him; nor was his pleasure less when he saw him present himself alive.

There were many prodigies that foreshadowed this victory, but the most remarkable that we are told of, was that at Tralles. In the temple of Victory stood Cæsar's statue. The ground on which it stood was naturally hard and solid, and the stone with which it was paved still harder; yet it is said that a palm tree shot itself up near the pedestal of this statue. In the city of Padua, one Caius Cornelius, who had the character of a good augur, the fellow-citizen and acquaintance of Livy, the historian, happened to be making some augural observations that very day when the battle was fought. And first, as Livy tells us, he pointed out the time of the fight, and said to those who were by him, that just then the battle was begun, and the men engaged. When he looked a second time, and observed the omens, he leaped up as if he had been inspired, and cried out, "Cæsar, you are victorious." This much surprised the standers by, but he took the garland which he had from his head, and swore he would never wear it again till the event should give authority to his art. This Livy positively states for a truth.

Cæsar, as a memorial of his victory, gave the Thessalians their freedom, and then went in pursuit of Pompey. When he was come into Asia, to gratify Theopompus, the author of the collection of fables, he enfranchised the Cnidians, and remitted one third of their tribute to all the people of the province of Asia. When he came to Alexandria, where Pompey was already murdered, he would not look upon Theodotus, who presented him with his head, but taking only his signet, shed tears. Those of Pompey's friends who had been arrested by the king of Egypt, as they were wandering in those parts, he relieved, and offered them his own friendship. In his letter to his friends at Rome, he told them that the greatest and most signal pleasure his victory had given him, was to be able continually to save the lives of fellow-citizens who had fought against him. As to the war in Egypt, some say that it was at once dangerous and dishonorable, and noways necessary, but occasioned only by his passion for Cleopatra. Others blame the ministers of the king, and especially the eunuch Pothinus, who was the chief favorite, and had lately killed Pompey, who had banished Cleopatra, and was now secretly plotting Cæsar's destruction. . . .

Thence he passed into Asia, where he heard that Domitius was beaten by Pharnaces, son of Mithridates, and had fled out of Pontus with a handful of men; and that Pharnaces pursued the victory so eagerly, that though he was already master of Bithynia and Cappadocia, he had a further design of attempting the Lesser Armenia, and was inviting all the kings and tetrarchs there to rise. Cæsar immediately marched against him with three legions, fought him near Zela, drove him out of Pontus, and totally defeated his army. When he gave Amantius, a friend of his at Rome, an account of this action, to express the promptness and rapidity of it, he used three words, "I came, saw, and conquered," which in Latin having all the same cadence, carry with them a very suitable air of brevity. . . .

His countrymen, conceding all to his fortune, and accepting the bit, in the hope that the government of a single person would give them time to breathe, after so many civil wars and calamities, made him dictator for life. This was indeed a tyranny avowed, since his power was now not only absolute, but perpetual too. Cicero made the first proposals to the senate for conferring honors upon him, which might in some sort be said not to exceed the limits of ordinary human moderation. But others, striving which should deserve most, carried them so excessively high, that they made Cæsar odious to the most indifferent and moderate sort of men, by the pretension and the extravagance of the titles which they decreed him. His enemies, too, are thought to have had some share in this, as well as his flatterers. . . .

Cæsar was born to do great things, and had a passion after honor, and the many noble exploits he had done did not now serve as an inducement to him to sit still and reap the fruit of his past labors, but were incentives and encouragements to go on, and raised in him ideas of still greater actions, and a desire of new glory, as if the present were all spent. It was in fact a sort of emulous struggle with himself, as it had been with another, how he might outdo his past actions by his future. In pursuit of these thoughts, he resolved to make war upon the Parthians, and when he had subdued them, to pass through Hyrcania; thence to march along by the Caspian Sea to Mount Caucasus, and so on about Pontus, till he came into Scythia; then to overrun all the countries bordering upon Germany, and Germany itself; and so to return through Gaul into Italy, after completing the whole circle of his intended empire, and bounding it on every side by the ocean. While preparations were making for this expedition, he proposed to dig through the isthmus on which Corinth stands; and appointed Anienus to superintend the work. He had also a design of diverting the Tiber, and carrying it by a deep channel directly from Rome to Circeii, and so into the sea near Tarracina, that there might be a safe and easy passage for all merchants who traded to Rome. Besides this, he intended to drain all the marshes by Pomentium and Setia, and gain ground enough from the water to employ many thousands of men in tillage. He proposed further to make great mounds on the shore nearest Rome, to hinder the sea from breaking in upon the land, to clear the coast of Ostia of all the hidden rocks and shoals that made it unsafe for shipping, and to form ports and harbors fit to receive the large number of vessels that would frequent them.

These things were designed without being carried into effect; but his reformation of the calendar, in order to rectify the irregularity of time, was not only projected with great scientific ingenuity, but was brought to its completion, and proved of very great use. For it was not only in ancient times that the Romans had wanted a certain rule to make the revolutions of their months fall in with the course of the year, so that their festivals and solemn days for sacrifice were removed by little and little, till at last they came to be kept at seasons quite contrary to what was at first intended, but even at this time the people had no way of computing the solar year; only the priests could say the time, and they, at their pleasure, without giving any notice, slipped in the intercalary month, which they called Mercedonius. Numa was the first who put in this month, but his expedient was but a poor one and quite inadequate to correct all the errors that arose in the returns of the annual cycles, as we have shown in his Life. Cæsar called in the best philosophers and mathematicians of his time to settle the point, and out of the systems before him, formed a new and more exact method of correcting the calendar, which the Romans use to this day, and seem to succeed better than any nation in avoiding the errors occasioned by the inequalities of the cycles. Yet even by this gave offence to those who looked with an evil eye on his position, and felt oppressed by his power. Cicero, the orator, when some one in his company chanced to say, the next morning Lyra would rise, replied, "Yes, in accordance with the edict," as if even this were a matter of compulsion. . . .

He gave fresh occasion of resentment by his affront to the tribunes. The Lupercalia were then celebrated, a feast at the first institution belonging, as some writers say, to the shepherds, and having some connection with the Arcadian Lycæa. Many young noblemen and magistrates run up and down the city with their upper garments off, striking all they meet with thongs of hide, by way of sport; and many women, even of the highest rank, place themselves in the way, and hold out their hands to the lash, as boys in a school do to the master, out of a belief that it procures an easy labor to those who are with child, and makes those conceive who are barren. Cæsar, dressed in a triumphal robe, seated himself in a golden chair at the rostra, to view this ceremony. Antony, as consul, was one of those who ran this course, and when he came into the forum, and the people made way for him, he went up and reached to Cæsar a diadem wreathed with laurel. Upon this, there was a shout, but only a slight one, made by the few who were planted there for that purpose; but when Cæsar refused it, there was universal applause. Upon the second offer, very few, and upon the second refusal, all again applauded. Cæsar finding it would not take, rose up, and ordered the crown to be carried into the capitol. Cæsar's statues were afterwards found with royal diadems on their heads. Flavius and Marullus, two tribunes of the people, went presently and pulled them off, and having apprehended those who first saluted Cæsar as king, committed them to prison. The people followed them with acclamations, and called them by the name of Brutus, because Brutus was the first who ended the succession of kings, and transferred the power which before was lodged in one man into the hands of the senate and people. Cæsar so far resented this, that he displaced Marullus and Flavius; and in urging his charges against them, at the same time ridiculed the people, by himself giving the men more than once the names of Bruti, and Cumaei.

This made the multitude turn their thoughts to Marcus Brutus, who, by his father's side, was thought to be descended from the first Brutus, and by his mother's side from the Servilii, another noble family, being besides nephew and son-in-law to Cato. But the honors and favors he had received from Cæsar, took off the edge from the desires he might himself have felt for overthrowing the new monarchy. For he had not only been pardoned himself after Pompey's defeat at Pharsalia, and had procured the same grace for many of his friends, but was one in whom Cæsar had a particular confidence. He had at that time the most honorable prætorship of the

year and was named for the consulship four years after, being preferred before Cassius, his competitor. Upon the question as to the choice, Cæsar, it is related, said that Cassius had the fairer pretensions, but that he could not pass by Brutus. Nor would he afterwards listen to some who spoke against Brutus, when the conspiracy against him was already afoot, but laying his hand on his body, said to the informers, "Brutus will wait for this skin of mine," intimating that he was worthy to bear rule on account of his virtue, but would not be base and ungrateful to gain it. Those who desired a change, and looked on him as the only, or at least the most proper, person to effect it, did not venture to speak with him; but in the night-time laid papers about his chair of state, where he used to sit and determine causes, with such sentences in them as, "You are asleep, Brutus," "You are no longer Brutus." Cassius, when he perceived his ambition a little raised upon this, was more instant than before to work him yet further, having himself a private grudge against Cæsar, for some reasons that we have mentioned in the Life of Brutus. Nor was Cæsar without suspicions of him, and said once to his friends, "What do you think Cassius is aiming at? I don't like him, he looks so pale." And when it was told him that Antony and Dolabella were in a plot against him, he said he did not fear such fat, luxurious men, but rather the pale, lean fellows, meaning Cassius and Brutus.

Fate, however, is to all appearances more unavoidable than unexpected. For many strange prodigies and apparitions are said to have been observed shortly before the event. As to the lights in the heavens, the noises heard in the night, and the wild birds which perched in the forum, these are not perhaps worth taking notice of in so great a case as this. Strabo, the philosopher, tells us that a number of men were seen, looking as if they were heated through with fire, contending with each other; that a quantity of flame issued from the hand of a soldier's servant, so that they who saw it thought he must be burnt, but that after all he had no hurt. As Cæsar was sacrificing, the victim's heart was missing, a very bad omen, because no living creature can subsist without a heart. One finds it also related by many, that a soothsayer bade him prepare for some great danger on the Ides of March. When the day was come, Cæsar, as he went to the senate, met this soothsayer, and said to him by way of raillery, "The ides of March are come:" who answered him calmly, "Yes, they are come, but they are not past." The day before the assassination, he supped with Marcus Lepidus; and as he was signing some letters, according to his custom, as he reclined at table, there arose a question what sort of death was the best. At which he immediately, before any one could speak, said, "A sudden one."

After this, as he was in bed with his wife, all the doors and windows of the house flew open together; he was startled at the noise, and the light which broke into the room, and sat up in his bed, where by the moonshine he perceived Calpurnia fast asleep, but heard her utter in her dream some indistinct words and inarticulate groans. She fancied at that time she was weeping over Cæsar, and holding him butchered in her arms. Others say this was not her dream, but that she dreamed that a pinnacle, which the senate, as Livy relates, had ordered to be raised on Cæsar's house by way of ornament and grandeur, was tumbling down, which was the occasion of her tears and ejaculations. When it was day, she begged of Cæsar, if it were possible, not to stir out, but to adjourn the senate to another time; and if he slighted her dreams, that he would be pleased to consult his fate by sacrifices, and other kinds of divination. Nor was he himself without some suspicion and fears; for he never before discovered any womanish superstition in Calpurnia, whom he now saw in such great alarm. Upon the report which the priests made to him, that they had killed several sacrifices, and still found them inauspicious, he resolved to send Antony to dismiss the senate.

In this juncture, Decimus Brutus, surnamed Albinus, one whom Cæsar had such confidence in that he made him his second heir, who nevertheless was engaged in the conspiracy with the other Brutus and Cassius, fearing lest if Cæsar should put off the senate to another day, the business might get wind, spoke scoffingly and in mockery of the diviners, and blamed Cæsar for giving the senate so fair an occasion of saying he had put a slight upon them, for that they were met upon his summons, and were ready to vote unanimously, that he should be declared king of all the provinces out of Italy, and might wear a diadem in any other place but Italy, by sea or land. If any one should be sent to tell them they might break up for the present, and meet again when Calpurnia should chance to have better dreams, what would his enemies say? Or who would with any patience hear his friends, if they should presume to defend his government as not arbitrary and tyrannical? But if he was possessed so far as to think this day unfortunate, yet it were more decent to go himself to the senate, and to adjourn it in his own person. Brutus, as he spoke these words, took Cæsar by the hand, and conducted him forth. He was not gone far from the door, when a servant of some other person's made towards him, but not being able to come up to him, on account of the crowd of those who pressed about him, he made his way into the house, and committed himself to Calpurnia, begging of her to secure him till Cæsar returned, because he had matters of great importance to communicate to him.

Artemidorus, a Cnidian, a teacher of Greek logic, and by that means so far acquainted with Brutus and his friends as to have got into the secret, brought Cæsar in a small written memorial, the heads of what he had to depose. He had observed that Cæsar, as he received any papers, presently gave them to servants who attended on him; and therefore came as near to him as he could, and said, "Read this, Cæsar, alone, and quickly, for it contains matter of great importance which nearly concerns you." Cæsar received it, and tried several times to read it, but was still hindered by the crowd of those who came to speak to him. However, he kept it in his hand by itself till he came into the senate. Some say it was another who gave Cæsar this note, and that Artemidorus could not get to him, being all along kept off by the crowd.

All these things might happen by chance. But the place which was destined for the scene of this murder, in which the senate met that day, was the same in which Pompey's statue stood, and was one of the edifices which Pompey had raised and dedicated with his theatre to the use of the public, plainly showing that there was something of a supernatural influence which guided the action, and ordered it to that particular place. Cassius, just before the act, is said to have looked towards Pompey's statue, and silently implored his assistance, though he had been inclined to the doctrines of Epicurus. But this occasion and the instant danger, carried him away out of all his reasonings, and filled him for the first time with a sort of inspiration. As for Antony, who was firm to Cæsar, and a strong man, Brutus Albinus kept him outside the house, and delayed him with a long conversation contrived on purpose. When Cæsar entered, the senate stood up to show their respect to him, and of Brutus's confederates, some came about his chair and stood behind it, others met him, pretending to add their petitions to those of Tillius Cimber, in behalf of his brother, who was in exile; and they followed him with their joint supplications till he came to his seat. When he was sat down, he refused to comply with their requests, and upon their urging further, began to reproach them severally for their importunities, when Tillius, laying hold of his robe with both his hands, pulled it down from his neck, which was the signal for the assault. Casca gave him the first cut, which was not mortal nor dangerous, as coming from one who at the beginning of such a bold action was probably very much disturbed. Cæsar immediately turned about, and laid his hand upon the dagger and kept hold of it. And both of them at the same time cried out, he that received the blow, in Latin, "Vile Casca, what does this mean?" and he that gave it, in Greek, to his brother, "Brother, help!" Upon this first onset, those who were not privy to the design were astonished, and their horror and amazement at what they saw were so great, that they durst not fly nor assist Cæsar, nor so much as speak a word. But those who came prepared for the business inclosed him on every side, with their naked daggers in their hands. Which way soever he turned, he met with blows, and saw their swords levelled at his face and eyes, and was encompassed, like a wild beast in the toils, on every side. For it had been agreed that they should each of them make a thrust at him, and flush themselves with his blood; for which reason Brutus also gave him one stab in the groin. Some say that he fought and resisted all the rest, shifting his body to avoid the blows, and calling out for help, but that when he saw Brutus's sword drawn, he covered his face with his robe and submitted, letting himself fall, whether it were by chance, or that he was pushed in that direction by his murderers, at the foot of the pedestal on which Pompey's statue stood, and which was thus wetted with his blood. So that Pompey himself seemed to have presided, as it were, over the revenge done upon his adversary, who lay here at his feet, and breathed out his soul through his multitude of wounds, for they say he received three and twenty. And the conspirators themselves were many of them wounded by each other, whilst they all levelled their blows at the same person.

When Cæsar was dispatched, Brutus stood forth to give a reason for what they had done, but the senate would not hear him, but flew out of doors in all haste, and filled the people with so much alarm and distraction, that some shut up their houses, others left their counters and shops. All ran one way or the other, some to the place to see the sad spectacle, others back again after they had seen it. Antony and Lepidus, Cæsar's most faithful friends, got off privately, and hid themselves in some friends' houses. Brutus and his followers, being yet hot from the deed, marched in a body from the senate-house to the capitol with their drawn swords, not like persons who thought of escaping, but with an air of confidence and assurance, and as they went along, called to the people to resume their liberty, and invited the company of any more distinguished people whom they met. And some of these joined the procession and went up along with them, as if they also had been of the conspiracy, and could claim a share in the honor of what had been done. As, for example, Caius Octavius and Lentulus Spinther, who suffered afterwards for their vanity, being taken off by Antony and the young Cæsar, and lost the honor they desired, as well as their lives, which it cost them, since no one believed they had any share in the action. For neither did those who punished them profess to revenge the fact, but the ill-will. The day after, Brutus with the rest came down from the capitol, and made a speech to the people, who listened without expressing either any pleasure or resentment, but showed by their silence that they pitied Cæsar, and respected Brutus. The senate passed acts of oblivion for what was past, and took measures to reconcile all parties. They ordered that Cæsar should be worshipped as a divinity, and nothing, even of the slightest consequence, should be revoked, which he had enacted during his government. At the same time they gave Brutus and his followers the command of provinces, and other considerable posts. So that all people now thought things were well settled, and brought to the happiest adjustment.

But when Cæsar's will was opened, and it was found that he had left a considerable legacy to each one of the Roman citizens, and when his body was seen carried through the market-place all mangled with wounds, the multitude could no longer contain themselves within the bounds of tranquillity and order, but heaped together a pile of benches, bars, and tables, which they placed the corpse on, and setting fire to it, burnt it on them. Then they took brands from the pile, and ran some to fire the houses of the conspirators, others up and down the city, to find out the men and tear them to pieces, but met, however, with none of them, they having taken effectual care to secure themselves.

One Cinna, a friend of Cæsar's, chanced the night before to have an odd dream. He fancied that Cæsar invited him to supper, and that upon his refusal to go with him, Cæsar took him by the hand and forced him, though he hung back. Upon hearing the report that Cæsar's body was burning in the market-place, he got up and went thither, out of respect to his memory, though his dream gave him some ill apprehensions, and though he was suffering from a fever.

One of the crowd who saw him there, asked another who it was, and having learned his name, told it to his next neighbor. It presently passed for a certainty that he was one of Cæsar's murderers, as, indeed, there was another Cinna, a conspirator, and they, taking this to be the man, immediately seized him, and tore him limb from limb upon the spot.

Brutus and Cassius, frightened at this, within a few days retired out of the city. What they afterwards did and suffered, and how they died, is written in the Life of Brutus. Cæsar died in his fifty-sixth year, not having survived Pompey above four years. That empire and power which he had pursued through the whole course of his life with so much hazard, he did at last with much difficulty compass, but reaped no other fruits from it than the empty name and invidious glory. But the great genius which attended him through his lifetime, even after his death remained as the avenger of his murder, pursuing through every sea and land all those who were concerned in it, and suffering none to escape, but reaching all who in any sort or kind were either actually engaged in the fact, or by their counsels any way promoted it.

The most remarkable of mere human coincidences was that which befell Cassius, who, when he was defeated at Philippi, killed himself with the same dagger which he had made use of against Cæsar. The most signal preternatural appearances were the great comet, which shone very bright for seven days after Cæsar's death, and then disappeared, and the dimness of the sun, whose orb continued pale and dull for the whole of that year, never showing its ordinary radiance at its rising, and giving but a weak and feeble heat. The air consequently was damp and gross, for want of stronger rays to open and rarefy it. The fruits, for that reason, never properly ripened,

and began to wither and fall off for want of heat, before they were fully formed. But above all, the phantom which appeared to Brutus showed the murder was not pleasing to the gods. The story of it is this.

Brutus being about to pass his army from Abydos to the continent on the other side, laid himself down one night, as he used to do, in his tent, and was not asleep, but thinking of his affairs, and what events he might expect. For he is related to have been the least inclined to sleep of all men who have commanded armies, and to have had the greatest natural capacity for continuing awake, and employing himself without need of rest. He thought he heard a noise at the door of his tent, and looking that way, by the light of his lamp, which was almost out, saw a terrible figure, like that of a man, but of unusual stature and severe countenance.

He was somewhat frightened at first, but seeing it neither did nor spoke anything to him, only stood silently by his bed-side, he asked who it was. The spectre answered him, "Thy evil genius, Brutus, thou shalt see me at Philippi." Brutus answered courageously, "Well, I shall see you," and immediately the appearance vanished. When the time was come, he drew up his army near Philippi against Antony and Cæsar, and in the first battle won the day, routed the enemy, and plundered Cæsar's camp. The night before the second battle, the same phantom appeared to him again, but spoke not a word. He presently understood his destiny was at hand, and exposed himself to all the danger of the battle. Yet he did not die in the fight, but seeing his men defeated, got up to the top of a rock, and there presenting his sword to his naked breast, and assisted, as they say, by a friend, who helped him to give the thrust, met his death.

—A. H. CLOUGH.

III. PHILOSOPHY

AGAINST RUNNING IN DEBT

PLUTARCH

[From the *Morals*]

The author is not so much interested in the question of the use of credit as a factor in business as he is in the moral effects of the abuse of credit for purposes of personal gratification. For Plutarch, see above, p. 604.

Plato in his Laws permits not any one to go and draw water from his neighbor's well, who has not first digged and sunk a pit in his own ground till he is come to a vein of clay, and has by his sounding experimented that the place will not yield a spring. For the clay or potter's earth, being of its own nature fatty, solid, and strong, retains the moisture it receives, and will not let it soak or pierce through. But it must be lawful for them to take water from another's ground, when there is no way or means for them to find any in their own; for the law ought to provide for men's necessity, but not for their laziness. Should there not be the like ordinance also concerning money; that none should be allowed to borrow money upon usury, nor to go and dive into other men's purses,—as it were into their wells and fountains,—before they have first searched at home and sounded every means for the obtaining it; having collected (as it were) and gathered together all the gutters and springs, to try if they can draw from them what may suffice to supply their most necessary occasions? But on the contrary, many there are who, to defray their idle expenses and to satisfy their extravagant and superfluous delights, make not use of their own, but have recourse to others, running themselves deeply into debt without any

necessity. Now this may be easily judged, if one does but consider that usurers do not ordinarily lend to those which are in distress, but only to such as desire to obtain somewhat that is superfluous and of which they stand not in need. So that the credit given by the lender is a testimony sufficiently proving that the borrower has of his own; whereas on the contrary, since he has of his own, he ought to keep himself from borrowing.

Why shouldst thou go and make thy court to a banker or a merchant? Borrow from thine own table. Thou hast tankards, dishes, and basins of silver. Make use of them for thy necessity, and when they are gone to supply thy wants, the pleasant town of Aulis or isle of Tenedos will again refurnish thy board with fair vessels of earth, far more cleanly and neat than those of silver. For they are not scented with strong and unpleasant smell of usury, which, like rust, daily more and more sullies and tarnishes the lustre of thy sumptuous magnificence. They will not be every day putting thee in mind of the Kalends and new moons, which, being of themselves the most holy and sacred days of the months, are by reason of usuries rendered the most odious and accursed. For as to those who choose rather to carry their goods to the brokers and there lay them in pawn for money taken upon usury than to sell them outright, I do not believe that Jupiter Ctesius himself can preserve them from beggary. They are ashamed forsooth to receive the full price and value of their goods; but they are not ashamed to pay use for the money they have borrowed on them. And yet the great and wise Pericles caused that costly ornament of fine gold, weighing about forty talents, with which Minerva's statue was adorned, to be made in such a manner that he could take it off and on at his pleasure; to the end (said he) that when we shall stand in need of money to support the charges of war, we may take it and make use of it, putting afterwards in its place another of no less value. Thus we ought in our affairs, as in a besieged town, never to admit or receive the hostile garrison of a usurer, nor to endure before our eyes the delivering up of our goods into perpetual servitude; but rather to cut off from our table what is neither necessary nor profitable, and in like manner from our beds, our couches, and our ordinary expenses, and so to keep ourselves free and at liberty, in hopes to restore again what we shall have retrenched, if Fortune shall hereafter smile upon us.

The Roman ladies heretofore willingly parted with their jewels and ornaments of gold, for the making a cup to be sent as an offering to the temple of Apollo Pythius in the city of Delphi. And the Carthaginian matrons did with their own hands cut the hair from their heads, to make cords for the managing of their warlike engines and instruments, in the defence of their besieged city. But we, as if we were ashamed of being able to stand on our own legs without being supported by the assistance of others, go and enslave ourselves by engagements and obligations; whereas it were much better that, restraining our ambition and confining it to what is profitable for us, we should of our useless and superfluous plate, which we should either melt or sell, build a temple of Liberty for ourselves, our wives, and our children. The Goddess Diana in the city of Ephesus gives to such debtors as can fly into her temple freedom and protection against their creditors; but the sanctuary of parsimony and moderation in expenses, into which no usurer can enter to pluck thence and carry away any debtor prisoner, is always open for the prudent, and affords them a long and large space of joyful and honorable repose. For as the

prophetess which gave oracles in the temple of the Pythian Apollo, about the time of the Persian wars, answered the Athenians, that God had for their safety given them a wall of wood, upon which, forsaking their lands, their city, their houses, and all their goods, they had recourse to their ships for the preservation of their liberty; so God gives us a table of wood, vessels of earth, and garments of coarse cloth, if we desire to live and continue in freedom.

"Aim not at gilded coaches, steeds of price,
And harness, richly wrought with quaint device;"

for how swiftly soever they may run, yet will usuries overtake them and outrun them.

Take rather the first ass thou shalt meet or the first pack-horse that shall come in thy way, and fly from that cruel and tyrannical enemy the usurer, who asks thee not earth and water, as heretofore did the barbarous king of Persia, but—which is worse—touches thy liberty, and wounds thy honor by proscriptions. If thou payest him not, he troubles thee; if thou hast wherewithal to satisfy him, he will not receive it, unless it be his pleasure. If thou sellest, he will have thy goods for nothing, or at a very moderate rate; and if thou wilt not sell, he will force thee to it; if thou suest him, he speaks to thee of an accommodation; if thou swearest to give him content, he will domineer over thee; if thou goest to his house to discourse with him, he shuts his door against thee; if thou stayest at home, he is always knocking at thy door and will never stir from thee.

Of what use to the Athenians was the decree of Solon, by which he ordained that the body should not be obliged for any public debt? For they who owe are in bondage to all bankers, and not to them alone (for then there would be no great hurt), but to their very slaves, who are proud, insolent, barbarous, and outrageous, and in a word exactly such as Plato describes the devils and fiery executioners to be, who in hell torment the souls of the wicked. For thus do these wretched usurers make the court where justice is administered a hell to the poor debtors, preying on some and gnawing them, vulture-like, to the very bones, and

"Piercing into their entrails with sharp beaks;"

and standing over others, who are, like so many Tantaluses, prohibited by them from tasting the corn and fruits of their own ground and drinking the wine of their own vintage. And as King Darius sent to the city of Athens his lieutenants Datis and Artaphernes with chains and cords, to bind the prisoners they should take; so these usurers, bringing into Greece boxes full of schedules, bills, and obligatory contracts, as so many irons and fetters for the shackling of poor criminals, go through the cities, sowing in them, as they pass, not good and profitable seed,—as did heretofore Triptolemus, when he went through all places teaching the people to sow corn,— but roots and grains of debts, that produce infinite labors and intolerable usuries, of which the end can never be found, and which, eating their way and spreading their sprouts round about, do in fine make cities bend under the burden, till they come to be suffocated. They say that hares at the same time suckle one young leveret, are ready to kindle and bring forth another, and conceive a third; but the usuries of these barbarous and wicked usurers bring forth before they conceive. For at the very delivery of their money, they immediately ask it back, taking it up at the same moment they lay it down; and they let out that again to interest which they

take for the use of what they have lent before.

It is a saying among the Messenians,

"Pylos before Pylos, and Pylos still you'll find;"

but it may be much better said against the usurers,

"Use before use, and use still more you'll find."

So that they laugh at those natural philosophers who hold that nothing can be made of nothing and of that which has no existence; but with them usury is made and engendered of that which neither is nor ever was. They think the taking to farm the customs and other public tributes, which the laws nevertheless permit, to be a shame and reproach; and yet themselves on the contrary, in opposition to all the laws in the world, make men pay tribute for what they lend upon interest; or rather, if the truth may be spoken, do in the very letting out their money to use, basely deceive their debtor. For the poor debtor, who receives less than he acknowledges in his obligation, is falsely and dishonestly cheated. And the Persians repute lying to be a sin only in the second degree, but to be in debt they repute to be in the first: forasmuch as lying frequently attends those that owe. Now there are not in the whole world any people who are oftener guilty of lying than usurers, nor that practise more unfaithfulness in their day-books, in which they set down that they have delivered such a sum of money to such a person, to whom they have not given nigh so much. And the moving cause of their lying is pure avarice, not want or poverty, but an insatiable desire of always having more, the end of which is neither pleasurable nor profitable to themselves, but ruinous and destructive to those whom they injure. For they neither cultivate the lands of which they deprive their debtors, nor inhabit the houses out of which they eject them, nor eat at the tables which they take away from them, nor wear the clothes of which they strip them. But first one is destroyed, and then a second soon follows, being drawn on and allured by the former. For the mischief spreads like wildfire, still consuming, and yet still increasing by the destruction and ruin of those that fall into it, whom it devours one after another. And the usurer who maintains this fire, blowing and kindling it to the undoing of so many people, reaps no other advantage from it but only that he now and then takes his book of accounts, and reads in it how many poor debtors he has caused to sell what they had, how many he has dispossessed of their lands and livings, whence his money came which he is always turning, winding, and increasing.

Think not that I speak this for any ill-will or enmity that I have borne against usurers;

"For never did they drive away
My horses or my kine."

But my only aim is to show those who are so ready to take up money upon use, how much shame and slavery there is in it, and how it proceeds only from extreme folly, sloth, and effeminacy of heart. For if thou hast of thy own, borrow not, since thou hast no need of it; and if thou hast nothing, borrow not, because thou wilt not have any means to pay. But let us consider the one and the other apart. The elder Cato said to a certain old man, who behaved himself ill: My friend, seeing old age has of itself so many evils, why dost thou go about to add to them the reproach and shame of wickedness? In like manner may we say to a man oppressed with poverty: Since poverty has of itself so many and so great miseries, do not heap upon them the anguishes of borrowing and being in debt. Take not from poverty the only good thing in which it is superior to riches, to wit, freedom from pensive care. Otherwise thou wilt subject thyself to the derision of the common proverb, which says,

"A goat I cannot bear away,
Therefore an ox upon me lay."

Thou canst not bear poverty, and yet thou art going to load on thyself a usurer, which is a burden even to a rich man insupportable.

But you will say perhaps, how then would you have me to live? Is this a question fit for thee to ask, who hast hands, feet, and a voice, who in brief art a man, whose property it is to love and to be loved, to do and receive a courtesy? Canst thou not teach, bring up young children, be a porter or doorkeeper, travel by sea, serve in a ship? There is in all these nothing more shameful or odious, than to be dunned with the importunate clamors of such as are always saying, Pay me, give me my money.

Rutilius, that rich Roman, coming one day to Musonius the philosopher, whispered him thus in his ear: Musonius, Jupiter the Savior, whom you philosophers profess to imitate and follow, takes not up money at interest. Musonius smiling presently answered him: Nor yet does he lend for use. For this Rutilius, who was himself an usurer, upbraided the other with borrowing upon use. Now what a foolish Stoical arrogance was this. For what need was there of bringing here Jupiter the Savior, when he might have given him the same admonition by things that were familiar and before his eyes? Swallows run not themselves into debt, ants borrow not upon interest; and yet Nature has given them neither reason, hands, nor art. But she has endued men with such abundance of understanding, that they maintain not only themselves, but also horses, dogs, partridges, hares, and jays. Why then dost thou condemn thyself, as if thou wert less able to persuade than a jay, more dumb than a partridge, and more ungenerous than a dog, in that thou couldst not oblige any man to be assistant to thee, either by serving him, charming him, guarding him, or fighting in his defence? Dost thou not see how many occasions the land, and how many the sea affords thee for thy maintenance? Hear also what Crates says:

"Here I saw Miccylus the wool to card,
Whilst his wife spun, that they by labor hard
In these hard times might 'scape the angry jaws
Of famine."

King Antigonus, when he had not for a long time seen Cleanthes the philosopher, said to him, Dost thou yet, O Cleanthes, continue to grind? Yes sir, replied Cleanthes, I still grind, and that I do to gain my living and not to depart from philosophy. How great and generous was the courage of this man, who, coming from the mill and the kneading-trough, did with the same hand which had been employed in turning the stone and moulding the dough, write of the nature of the Gods, moon, stars, and sun! And yet we think these to be servile works.

Therefore, forsooth, that we may be free, we take up money at interest, and to this purpose flatter base and servile persons, wait on them, treat them, make them presents, and pay them pensions; and this we do, not being compelled by poverty (for no usurer will lend a poor man money) but to gratify our prodigality. For if we would be content with such things as are necessary for human life, usurers would be no less rare in the world than Centaurs and Gorgons. But luxury and excess, as it produced goldsmiths, perfumers, and dyers of curious colors, so it has brought forth usurers. For we run not into debt for bread and wine, but for the purchasing of stately seats, numerous slaves, fine mules, costly banqueting halls, rich tables, and for all those foolish and superfluous expenses to which we frequently put ourselves for the exhibiting of plays to the people, or some such vain ambition, from which we frequently reap no other fruit but ingratitude. Now he that is once entangled in usury remains a debtor all his life, not unlike in this to the horse, who, having once taken the bridle into his mouth and the saddle on his back, receives one rider after another. Nor is there any means for these debtors to make their escape into those fair pastures and meadows which once they enjoyed, but they wander about, like those Dæmons mentioned by Empedocles to have been driven out of heaven by the offended Gods:

"By the sky's force they're thrust into the main,
Which to the earth soon spews them back again.
Thence to bright Titan's orb they're forced to fly,
And Titan soon remits them to the sky."

In like manner do such men fall from the hand of one usurer or banker to another, sometimes of a Corinthian, sometimes of a Patrian, sometimes of an Athenian, till, having been deceived and cheated by all, they finally find themselves dissipated and torn in pieces by usury. For as he who is fallen into the dirt must either rise up and get out of it, or else lie still in the place into which he first fell, for that by tumbling, turning, and rolling about, he does but still more bemire himself; so also those who do but change their creditor, and cause their names to be transcribed from one usurer's book to another's, do by loading and embroiling themselves with new usuries become more and more oppressed.

Now in this they properly resemble persons distempered with cholera, who cannot receive any medicine sufficient to work a perfect cure, but continually vomit up all that is given them, and so make way for the choleric humor to gather more and more. For in the same manner these men are not willing to be cleansed at once, but do with grievous anguish and sorrow pay their use at every season of the year, and no sooner have they discharged one, but another drops and stills immediately after, which causes them both aching hearts and heads; whereas they should have taken care to get wholly clear, that they might remain free and at liberty.

For I now turn my speech to those who are more wealthy, and withal more nice and effeminate, and whose discourse is commonly in this manner: How shall I remain then without servants, without fire, and without a house or place to which I may repair? Now this is the same thing as if one who is sick of a dropsy and puffed up as a barrel should say to a physician: How? Would have me become slender, lean, and empty? And why not, provided you thereby get your health? Thus it is better you should be without servants, than that you should yourself become a slave; and that you should remain without possessions, than that you should be made the possession of another. Give ear a little to the discourse of the two vultures, as it is reported in the fable. One of them was taken with so strong a fit of vomiting, that he said: I believe I shall cast up my very bowels. Now to this his companion answered: What hurt will there be in it? For thou wilt not indeed throw up thine own entrails, but those of the dead man which we devoured the other day. So he who is indebted sells not his own inheritance nor his own house, but that of the usurer who lent him the money, to whom by the law he has given the right and possession of

them. Nay, by Jupiter (will he say to me); but my father left me this estate. I believe it well, but he left thee also liberty and a good repute, of which thou oughtest to make more account and be more careful. He who begat thee made thy foot and thy hand, and nevertheless, if they happen to be mortified, thou wilt give money to the chirurgeon to cut them off. Calypso presented Ulysses with a robe breathing forth the sweet-scented odor of an immortal body, which she put on him, as a token and memorial of the love she had borne him. But when his ship was cast away and himself ready to sink to the bottom, not being able to keep above the water by reason of his wet robe, which weighed him downwards, he put it off and threw it away, and having girt his naked breast with a broad swaddling band,

"Swam, gazing on the distant shore."

And afterwards, when the danger was over and he seen to be landed, he wanted neither food nor raiment. And is it not a true tempest, when the usurer after some time comes to assault the miserable debtors with this word Pay?

"This having said, the clouds grow thick, the sea
Is troubled, and its raging waves beat high,
Whilst east, south, west winds through the welkin fly."

These winds are use, and use upon use, which roll one after another; and he that is overwhelmed by them and kept down by their weight cannot serve himself nor make his escape by swimming, but at last sinks down to the bottom, where he perishes, carrying with him his friends who were pledges and sureties for him.

Crates, the Theban philosopher, acted far otherwise; for owing nothing, and consequently not being pressed for payment by any creditor, but only tired with the cares and troubles of housekeeping and the solicitude requisite to the management of his estate, he left a patrimony of eight talents' value, and taking only his cloak and wallet, retired to philosophy and poverty. Anaxagoras also forsook his plentiful and well-stocked pastures. But what need is there of alleging these examples, seeing that the lyric poet Philoxenus, being one of those who were sent to people a new city and new land in Sicily, where there fell to his share a good house and great wealth with which he might have lived well at his ease, yet seeing that delights, pleasure, and idleness, without any exercise of good letters, reigned in those quarters, said: These goods, by all the Gods, shall not destroy me, but I will rather lose them. And immediately leaving to others the portion that was allotted himself, he again took shipping, and returned to Athens. Whereas those who are in debt bear and suffer themselves to be sued, taxed, made slaves of, and cheated with false money, feeding like Phineus certain winged harpies. For these usurers fly to them, and ravish out of their hands their very food. Neither yet have they patience to stay and expect the season; for they buy their debtors' corn before it is ready for harvest, bargain for the oil before the olives are ripe, and in like manner for their wines. I will have it, says the usurer, at such a price; and immediately he gets the writing signed; and yet the grapes are still hanging on the vine, expecting the rising of Arcturus.

—SMITH AND GOODWIN.

ON PREFERMENT

EPICTETUS

[From the *Encheiridion*]

Epictetus (about 50 to about 125), a lame Phrygian slave, withdrew from Rome to Epirus when Domitian banished the philosophers, and there became celebrated as a teacher of Stoic philosophy.

He wrote no books, but his teachings are preserved in notes taken, apparently, from day to day by his pupils and afterwards revised, probably by the historian Arrian, for publication in the form of a *Manual*. He did not concern himself with inquiry into fundamental principles, but rather with the application to life of truths which he held to be self-evident. He maintained that political freedom was unimportant in comparison with moral freedom, and that the secret of a happy life consisted solely in self-mastery.

Remember that thou art an actor in a play, of such a part as it may please the director to assign you; of a short part if he choose a short part; of a long one if he choose a long. And if he will have thee take the part of a poor man or of a cripple, or a governor, or a private person, mayest thou act the part with grace! For thine is to act well the allotted part, but to choose it is another's.

When a raven croaks you a bad omen, be not carried away by the appearance; but straightway distinguish with yourself and say, *None of these things bodes aught to myself, but either to this poor body or this wretched property of mine, or to my good repute, or to my children, or to my wife. But to me all omens are fortunate, if I choose to have it so. For whatever of these things may come to pass, it lies with me to have it serve me.*

You may be always victorious if you will never enter into any contest but where the victory depends upon yourself.

When you shall see a man honoured above others, or mighty in power, or otherwise esteemed, look to it that thou deem him not blessed, being carried away by the appearance. For if the essence of the Good be in those things that are in our own power, then neither envy nor jealousy have any place, nor thou thyself shalt not desire to be commander or prince or consul, but to be free. And to this there is one road—scorn of the things that are not in our own power.

Remember, it is not he that strikes or he that reviles that doth any man an injury, but the opinion about these things, that they are injurious. When, then, some one may provoke thee to wrath, know that it is thine own conception which hath provoked thee. Strive, therefore, at the outset not to be carried away by the appearance; for if thou once gain time and delay, thou wilt more easily master thyself.

Death and exile, and all things that appear dreadful, let these be every day before thine eyes. But Death most of all; for so thou wilt neither despise nor too greatly desire any condition of life.

If thou set thine heart upon philosophy, prepare straightway to be laughed at and mocked by many who will say, *Behold, he has suddenly come back to us a philosopher;* or *How came you by that brow of scorn?* But do thou cherish no scorn, but hold to those things that seem to thee best, as one set by God in that place. Remember, too, that if thou abide in that way, those that first mocked thee, the same shall afterwards reverence thee; but if thou yield to them, thou shalt receive double mockery.

If it shall ever happen to thee to be turned to outward things in the desire to please some person, know that thou hast lost thy way of life. Let it be enough for thee in all things to *be* a philosopher. But if thou desire also to seem one, then seem so to thyself, for this thou canst.

Let such thoughts never afflict thee as, *I shall live unhonoured, and never be anybody anywhere.* For if lack of honour be an evil, thou canst no more fall into evil through another's doings than into vice. Is it, then, of thy own doing to be made a governor, or invited to feasts? By no means. How, then, is this to be unhonoured? How shouldst thou *never be anybody anywhere,* whom it behoves to be somebody only in the things that are in thine own power,

wherein it lies with thee to be of the greatest worth?

But I shall not be able to serve my friends. How sayst thou? to serve them? They shall not have money from thee, nor shalt thou make them Roman citizens. Who, then, told thee that these were of the things that are in our power, and not alien to us? And who can give thee that which himself hath not?

Acquire, then, they say, *that we may possess.* If I can acquire, and lose not piety, and faith, and magnanimity withal, show me the way, and I will do it. But if ye will have me lose the good things I possess, that ye may compass things that are not good at all, how unjust and unthinking are ye! But which will ye rather have—money, or a faithful and pious friend? Then, rather take part with me to this end; and ask me not to do aught through which I must cast away those things.

But, he saith, *I shall not do my part in serving my country.* Again, what is this service? Thy country shall not have porticos nor baths from thee, and what then? Neither hath she shoes from the smith, nor arms from the cobbler, but it is enough if every man fulfil his own task. And if thou hast made one other pious and faithful citizen for her, art thou, then, of no service? Wherefore, neither shalt thou be useless to thy country.

What place, then, he saith, *can I hold in the State?* Whatever place thou canst, guarding still thy faith and piety. But if in wishing to serve her thou cast away these things, what wilt thou profit her then, when perfected in shamelessness and falsehood?

Is some one preferred before thee at a feast, or in salutation, or in being invited to give counsel? Then, if these things are good, it behoves thee rejoice that he hath gained them; but if evil, be not vexed that thou hast not gained them; but remember that if thou act not as other men to gain the things that are not in our own power, neither canst thou be held worthy of a like reward with them.

For how is it possible for him who will not hang about other men's doors to have a like reward with him who doth so? or him who will not flatter them with the flatterer? Thou art unjust, then, and insatiable, if thou desire to gain those things for nothing, without paying the price for which they are sold.

—T. W. ROLLESTON.

ON CONDUCT

EPICTETUS

[From the *Encheiridion*]

Ordain for thyself forthwith a certain form and type of conduct, which thou shalt maintain both alone and, when it may chance, among men.

And for the most part keep silence, or speak only what is necessary, and in few words. But when occasion may call thee to speak, then speak, but sparingly, and not about any subject at haphazard, nor about gladiators, nor horse races, nor athletes, nor things to eat and drink, which are talked of everywhere; but, above all, not about men, as blaming or praising or comparing them.

If, then, thou art able, let thy discourse draw that of the company towards what is seemly and good. But if thou find thyself apart among men of another sort, keep silence.

Laugh not much, nor at many things, nor unrestrainedly.

Refuse altogether, if thou canst, to take an oath; if thou canst not, then as the circumstances allow.

Shun banquets given by strangers and by the vulgar. But if any occasion bring thee to them, give strictest heed, lest thou fall unawares into the ways of the vulgar. For know that if any companion be corrupt, he who hath conversation with him must needs be corrupted also, even if he himself should chance to be pure.

In things that concern the body accept only so far as the bare need—as in food, drink, clothing, habitation, servants. But all that makes for glory or luxury thou must utterly proscribe.

Concerning intercourse of the sexes, it is right to be pure before marriage, to the best of thy power. But, using it, let a man have to do only with what is lawful. Yet be not grievous to those who use such pleasures, nor censorious; nor be often putting thyself forward as not using them.

If one shall bear thee word that such a one hath spoken evil of thee, then do not defend thyself against his accusations, but make answer: *He little knew my other vices, or he had not mentioned only these.*

There is no necessity to go often to the arena, but if occasion should take thee there, do not appear ardent on any man's side but thine own; that is to say, choose that only to happen which does happen, and that the conqueror may be simply he who wins; for so shalt thou not be thwarted. But from shouting and laughing at this or that, or violent gesticulation, thou must utterly abstain. And when thou art gone away, converse little on the things that have passed, so far as they make not for thine own correction. For from that it would appear that admiration of the spectacle had overcome thee.

Go not freely nor indiscriminately to recitations. But if thou go, then preserve (yet without being grievous to others) thy gravity and calmness.

When thou art about to meet anyone, especially one of those that are thought high in rank, set before thy mind what Socrates or Zeno had done in such a case. And so thou wilt not fail to deal as it behoves thee with the occasion.

When thou goest to any of those that are great in power, set before thy mind the case that thou wilt not find him at home, that thou wilt be shut out, that the doors may be slammed in thy face, that he will take no notice of thee. And if even with these things it behoves thee to go, then go, and bear all that happens; and never say to thyself—*It was not worth this.* For that is the part of the foolish, and of those that are offended at outward things.

In company, be it far from thee to dwell much and over-measure on thine own deeds and dangers. For to dwell on thine own dangers is pleasant indeed to thee, but not equally pleasant for others is it to hear of the things that have chanced to thee.

Be it far from thee to move laughter. For that habit is a slippery descent into vulgarity; and it is always enough to relax thy neighbour's respect for thee.

And it is dangerous to approach to vicious conversation. Therefore, when anything of the kind may arise, rebuke, if there is opportunity, him who approacheth thereto. But if not, then at least by silence and blushing and grave looks, let it be plain that his talk is disagreeable to thee.

—T. W. ROLLESTON.

PRACTISING AND PREACHING

EPICTETUS

[From the *Encheiridion*]

Thou shalt never proclaim thyself a philosopher, nor speak much among the vulgar of the philosophic maxims; but do the things that follow from the maxims. For example, do not discourse at a feast upon how one ought to eat, but eat as one ought. For remember that even so Socrates everywhere banished ostentation, so that men used to come to him desiring that he would recommend them to teachers of philosophy, and he brought them away and did so, so well did he bear to be overlooked.

And if among the vulgar discourse should arise concerning some maxim of thy philosophy, do thou, for the most part, keep silence, for there is great risk that thou straightway vomit up what thou hast not digested. And when someone shall say to thee, *Thou knowest naught,* and it bites thee not, then know that thou hast begun the work.

And as sheep do not bring their food to the shepherds to show how much they have eaten, but digesting inwardly their provender, bear outwardly wool and milk, even so do not thou, for the most part, display the maxims before the vulgar, but rather the works which follow from them when they are digested.

When you have adapted the body to a frugal way of living, do not flatter yourself on that, nor if you drink only water, say, on every opportunity, *I drink only water.* And if you desire at any time to inure yourself to labour and endurance, do it to yourself and not unto the world. And do not embrace the statues; but some time when you are exceedingly thirsty take a mouthful of cold water, and spit it out, and say nothing about it.

—T. W. ROLLESTON.

IV. SATIRES ON GODS AND MEN: LUCIAN

Lucian (about 125 to 192), of Samosata in Syria, was a professional rhetorician, a travelling lecturer, and a writer of scores of short dialogues and essays of a satiric nature. His satire aimed its attack mainly at false conceptions of the gods and at erroneous ideas of the essentials of a happy life. He was the creator of the satiric dialogue as a type, made noteworthy contributions to polemical literature, and may be regarded as the inventor of such prose tales of fancy as are represented in English literature by *Gulliver's Travels*. Eighty-two pieces have come down to us under his name, but the authenticity of a number of them is questioned.

HERMES

[Dialogues of the Gods, vii]

HEPHÆSTUS. Have you seen Maia's baby, Apollo? such a pretty little thing, with a smile for everybody; you can see it is going to be a treasure.

APOLLO. That baby a treasure? well, in mischief, Iapetus is young beside it.

HEPH. Why, what harm can it do, only just born?

AP. Ask Posidon; it stole his trident. Ask Ares; he was surprised to find his sword gone out of the scabbard. Not to mention myself, disarmed of bow and arrows.

HEPH. Never! that infant? he has hardly found his legs yet; he is not out of his baby-linen.

AP. Ah, you will find out, Hephæstus, if he gets within reach of you.

HEPH. He has been.

AP. Well, all your tools safe? none missing?

HEPH. Of course not.

AP. I advise you to make sure.

HEPH. Zeus, where are my pincers?

AP. Ah, you will find them among the baby-linen.

HEPH. So light-fingered? one would swear he had practised petty larceny in the womb.

AP. Ah, and you don't know what a glib young chatterbox he is; and, if he has his way, he is to be our errand-boy! Yesterday he challenged Eros—tripped up his heels somehow, and had him on his back in a twinkling; before the applause was over, he had taken the opportunity of a congratulatory hug from Aphrodite to steal her girdle; Zeus had not done laughing before—the sceptre was gone. If the thunderbolt had not been too heavy, and very hot, he would have made away with that too.

HEPH. The child has some spirit in him, by your account.

AP. Spirit, yes—and some music, moreover, young as he is.

HEPH. How can you tell that?

AP. He picked up a dead tortoise somewhere or other, and contrived an instrument with it. He fitted horns to it, with a cross-bar, stuck in pegs, inserted a bridge, and played a sweet tuneful thing that made an old harper like me quite envious. Even at night, Maia was saying, he does not stay in Heaven; he goes down poking his nose into Hades —on a thieves' errand, no doubt. Then he has a pair of wings, and he has made himself a magic wand, which he uses for marshalling souls—convoying the dead to their place.

HEPH. Ah, I gave him that for a toy.

AP. And by way of payment he stole—

HEPH. Well thought on; I must go and get them; you may be right about the baby-linen.

—H. W. FOWLER.

A QUARREL OF THE GODS

[Dialogues of the Gods, xiii]

ZEUS. Now, Asclepius and Heracles, stop that quarrelling; you might as well be men; such behaviour is very improper and out of place at the table of the Gods.

HER. Is this druggist fellow to have place above me, Zeus?

ASC. Of course I am; I am your better.

HER. Why, you numskull? because it was Zeus' bolt that cracked your skull, for your unholy doings, and now you have been allowed your immortality again out of sheer pity?

Asc. You twit me with my fiery end; you seem to have forgotten that you too were burnt to death, on Œta.

HER. Was there no difference between your life and mine, then? I am Zeus' son, and it is well known how I toiled, cleansing the earth, conquering monsters, and chastising men of violence. Whereas you are a root-grubber and a quack; I dare say you have your use for doctoring sick men, but you never did a bold deed in your life.

Asc. That comes well from you, whose burns I healed, when you came up all singed not so long ago; between the tunic and the flames, your body was half consumed. Anyhow, it would be enough to mention that I was never a slave like you, never combed wool in Lydia, masquerading in a purple shawl and being slippered by an Omphale, never killed my wife and children in a fit of the spleen.

HER. If you don't stop being rude, I shall soon show you that immortality is not much good. I will take you up and pitch you head over heels out of Heaven, and Apollo himself shall never mend your broken crown.

ZEUS. Cease, I say, and let us hear ourselves speak, or I will send you both away from table. Heracles, Asclepius died before you, and has the right to a better place.

—H. W. FOWLER.

THE POWER OF ZEUS

[*Dialogues of the Gods,* xxi]

ARES. Did you hear Zeus's threat, Hermes? most complimentary, wasn't it, and most practicable? 'If I choose,' says he, 'I could let down a cord from Heaven, and all of you might hang on it and do your very best to pull me down; it would be waste labour; you would never move me. On the other hand, if I chose to haul up, I should have you all dangling in mid air, with earth and sea into the bargain'—and so on; you heard? Well, I dare say he *is* too much for any of us individually, but I will never believe he outweighs the whole of us in a body, or that even with the makeweight of earth and sea, we should not get the better of him.

HERMES. Mind what you say, Ares; it is not safe to talk like that; we might get paid out for chattering.

AR. You don't suppose that I should say this to every one; I am not afraid of you; I know you can keep a quiet tongue. I must tell you what made me laugh most while he stormed: I remember not so long ago, when Posidon and Hera and Athene rebelled and made a plot for his capture and imprisonment, he was frightened out of his wits; well, there were only three of them, and if Thetis had not taken pity on him and called in the hundred-handed Briareus to the rescue, he would actually have been put in chains, with his thunder and his bolt beside him. When I worked out the sum, I could not help laughing.

HER. Oh, do be quiet; such things are too risky for you to say or me to listen to.

—H. W. FOWLER.

EUROPA AND THE BULL

[*Dialogues of the Sea-Gods,* xv]

WEST WIND. Such a splendid pageant I never saw on the waves, since the day I first blew. You were not there, Notus?

SOUTH WIND. Pageant, Zephyr! What pageant? and whose?

W. You missed a most ravishing

spectacle; such another chance you are not likely to have.

S. I was busy with the Red Sea; and I gave the Indian coasts a little airing too. So I don't know what you are talking about.

W. Well, you know Agenor the Sidonian?

S. Europa's father? what of him?

W. Europa it is that I am going to tell you about.

S. You need not tell me that Zeus has been in love with her this long while; that is stale news.

W. We can pass the love, then, and get on to the sequel.

Europa had come down for a frolic on the beach with her playfellows. Zeus transformed himself into a bull, and joined the game. A fine sight he was—spotless white skin, crumpled horns, and gentle eyes. He gambolled on the shore with them, bellowing most musically, till Europa took heart of grace and mounted him. No sooner had she done it than, with her on his back, Zeus made off at a run for the sea, plunged in, and began swimming; she was dreadfully frightened, but kept her seat by clinging to one of his horns with her left hand, while the right held her skirt down against the puffs of wind.

S. A lovely sight indeed, Zephyr, in every sense—Zeus swimming with his darling on his back.

W. Ay, but what followed was lovelier far.

Every wave fell; the sea donned her robe of peace to speed them on their way; we winds made holiday and joined the train, all eyes; fluttering Loves skimmed the waves, just dipping now and again a heedless toe—in their hands lighted torches, on their lips the nuptial song; up floated Nereids—few but were prodigal of naked charms—and clapped their hands, and kept pace on dolphin steeds; the Triton company, with every sea-creature that frights not the eye,

tripped it around the maid; for Poseidon on his car, with Amphitrite by him, led them in festal mood, ushering his brother through the waves. But, crowning all, a Triton pair bore Aphrodite, reclined on a shell, heaping the bride with all flowers that blow.

So went it from Phœnice even to Crete. But, when he set foot on the isle, behold, the bull was no more; 'twas Zeus that took Europa's hand and led her to the Dictæan Cave—blushing and downward-eyed; for she knew now the end of her bringing.

But we plunged this way and that, and roused the still sea anew.

S. Ah, me, what sights of bliss! and I was looking at griffins, and elephants, and blackamoors!

—H. W. FOWLER.

EARTH'S VANITIES

[Dialogues of the Dead, ii]

CRŒSUS. Pluto, we can stand this snarling Cynic no longer in our neighborhood; either you must transfer him to other quarters, or we are going to migrate.

PLUTO. Why, what harm does he do to your ghostly community?

CR. Midas here, and Sardanapalus and I, can never get in a good cry over the old days of gold and luxury and treasure, but he must be laughing at us, and calling us rude names; 'slaves' and 'garbage' he says we are. And then he sings; and that throws us out.—In short, he is a nuisance.

PL. Menippus, what's this I hear?

MENIPPUS. All perfectly true, Pluto. I detest these abject rascals! Not content with having lived the abominable lives they did, they keep on talking about it now they are dead, and harping on the good old days. I take positive pleasure in annoying them.

PL. Yes, but you mustn't. They have had terrible losses; they feel it deeply.

ME. Pluto! you are not going to lend *your* countenance to these whimpering fools?

PL. It isn't that: but I won't have you quarrelling.

ME. Well, you scum of your respective nations, let there be no misunderstanding: I am going on just the same. Wherever you are, there shall I be also; worrying, jeering, singing you down.

CR. Presumption!

ME. Not a bit of it. Yours was the presumption, when you expected men to fall down before you, when you trampled on men's liberty, and forgot there was such a thing as death. Now comes the weeping and gnashing of teeth: for all is lost!

CR. Lost! Ah God! My treasure-heaps—

MIDAS. My gold—

SARDANAPALUS. My little comforts—

ME. That's right: stick to it! You do the whining, and I'll chime in with a string of GNOTHI-SAUTONS, best of accompaniments.

—F. G. FOWLER.

SETTLING ACCOUNTS

[Dialogues of the Dead, iv]

HERMES. Ferryman, what do you say to settling up accounts? It will prevent any unpleasantness later on.

CHARON. Very good. It does save trouble to get these things straight.

HER. One anchor, to your order, five shillings.

CH. That is a lot of money.

HER. So help me Pluto, it is what I had to pay. One row-lock-strap, fourpence.

CH. Five and four; put that down.

HER. Then there was a needle, for mending the sail; tenpence.

CH. Down with it.

HER. Caulking-wax; nails, and cord for the brace. Two shillings the lot.

CH. They were worth the money.

HER. That's all; unless I have forgotten anything. When will you pay it?

CH. I can't just now, Hermes; we shall have a war or a plague presently, and then the passengers will come shoaling in, and I shall be able to make a little by jobbing the fares.

HER. So for the present I have nothing to do but sit down, and pray for the worst, as my only chance of getting paid?

CH. There is nothing else for it;—very little business doing now, as you see, owing to the peace.

HER. That is just as well, though it does keep me waiting for my money. After all, though, Charon, in old days men were men; you remember the state they used to come down in,—all blood and wounds generally. Nowadays, a man is poisoned by his slave or his wife; or gets dropsy from overfeeding; a pale, spiritless lot, nothing like the men of old. Most of them seem to meet their end in some plot that has money for its object.

CH. Ah; money is in great request.

HER. Yes; you can't blame me if I am somewhat urgent for payment.

—F. G. FOWLER.

BONES AND SKULLS

[Dialogues of the Dead, vii]

MENIPPUS. Where are all the beauties, Hermes? Show me around; I am a newcomer.

HERMES. I am busy, Menippus. But look over there to your right, and you will see Hyacinth, Narcissus, Nereus, Achilles, Tyro, Helen, Leda,—all the beauties of old.

ME. I can only see bones, and bare skulls; most of them are exactly alike.

HER. Those bones, of which you seem

to think so lightly, have been the theme of admiring poets.

ME. Well, but show me Helen; I shall never be able to make her out by myself.

HER. This skull is Helen.

ME. And for this a thousand ships carried warriors from every part of Greece; Greeks and barbarians were slain, and cities made desolate.

HER. Ah, Menippus, you never saw the living Helen; or you would have said with Homer

"Well might they suffer grievous years of toil
Who strove for such a prize."

We look at withered flowers, whose dye is gone from them, and what can we call them but unlovely things? Yet in the hour of their bloom these unlovely things were things of beauty.

ME. Strange, that the Greeks could not realize what it was for which they laboured; how short-lived, how soon to fade.

HER. I have no time for moralizing. Choose your spot, where you will, and lie down. I must go to fetch new dead.

—F. G. FOWLER.

MENIPPUS

[*Dialogues of the Dead*, xxii.]

CHARON. Your fare, you rascal.

MENIPPUS. Bawl away, Charon, if it gives you any pleasure.

CH. I brought you across: give me my fare.

ME. I can't, if I haven't got it.

CH. And who is so poor that he has not got a penny?

ME. I for one; I don't know who else.

CH. Pay: or, by Pluto, I'll strangle you.

ME. And I'll crack your skull with this stick.

CH. So you are to come all that way for nothing?

ME. Let Hermes pay for me: he put me on board.

HER. I dare say! A fine time I shall have of it, if I am to pay for the shades.

CH. I'm not going to let you off.

ME. You can haul up your ship and wait, for all I care. If I have not got the money, I can't pay you, can I?

CH. You knew you ought to bring it?

ME. I knew that: but I hadn't got it. What would you have? I ought not to have died, I suppose?

CH. So you are to have the distinction of being the only passenger that ever crossed gratis?

ME. Oh, come now: gratis! I took an oar, and I baled; and I didn't cry, which is more than can be said for any of the others.

CH. That's neither here nor there. I must have my penny; it's only right.

ME. Well, you had better take me back again to life.

CH. Yes, and get a thrashing from Æacus for my pains! I like that.

ME. Well, don't bother me.

CH. Let me see what you have got in that wallet.

ME. Beans: have some?—and a Hecate's supper.

CH. Where did you pick up this Cynic, Hermes? The noise he made on the crossing, too! laughing and jeering at all the rest, and singing, when every one else was at his lamentations.

HER. Ah, Charon, you little know your passenger! Independence, every inch of him: he cares for no one. 'Tis Menippus.

CH. Wait till I catch you—

ME. Precisely; I'll wait—till you catch me again.

—F. G. FOWLER.

A Pagan's View of the Early Christians

[From *The Death of Peregrine*]

In a satirical essay on Peregrine, a wandering philosopher, Lucian had occasion to relate the dealings of his hero with the Christians of Syria, a province which bordered on Palestine. The paragraph is particularly interesting because it represents the objective view, erroneous though it may be, of an educated Greek less than a century and a half after the founding of Christianity.

It was now that he came across the priests and scribes of the Christians, in Palestine, and picked up their queer creed. I can tell you, he pretty soon convinced them of his superiority; prophet, elder, ruler of the Synagogue— he was everything at once; expounded their books, commented on them, wrote books himself. They took him for a God, accepted his laws, and declared him their president. The Christians, you know, worship a man to this day,—the distinguished personage who introduced their novel rites, and was crucified on that account. Well, the end of it was that Proteus was arrested and thrown into prison. This was the very thing to lend an air to his favourite arts of clap-trap and wonder-working; he was now a made man. The Christians took it all very seriously: he was no sooner in prison, than they began trying every means to get him out again,—but without success. Everything else that could be done for him they most devoutly did. They thought of nothing else. Orphans and ancient widows might be seen hanging about the prison from break of day. Their officials bribed the gaolers to let them sleep inside with him. Elegant dinners were conveyed in; their sacred writings were read; and our old friend Peregrine (as he was still called in those days) became for them "the modern Socrates." In some of the Asiatic cities, too, the Christian communities put themselves to the expense of sending deputations, with offers of sympathy, assistance, and legal advice. The activity of these people, in dealing with any matter that affects their community, is something extraordinary; they spare no trouble, no expense. Peregrine, all this time, was making quite an income on the strength of his bondage; money came pouring in. You see, these misguided creatures start with the general conviction that they are immortal for all time, which explains the contempt of death and voluntary self-devotion which are so common among them; and then it was impressed on them by their original lawgiver that they are all brothers, from the moment that they are converted, and deny the gods of Greece, and worship the crucified sage, and live after his laws. All this they take quite on trust, with the result that they despise all worldly goods alike, regarding them merely as common property. Now an adroit, unscrupulous fellow, who has seen the world, has only to get among these simple souls, and his fortune is pretty soon made; he plays with them.

—F. G. Fowler.

INDEX OF AUTHORS AND TITLES